A HANDY BOOK

OF

CURIOUS INFORMATION

COMPRISING

STRANGE HAPPENINGS IN THE LIFE OF MEN
AND ANIMALS, ODD STATISTICS, EXTRAORDI-
NARY PHENOMENA AND OUT OF THE WAY
FACTS CONCERNING THE WONDER-
LANDS OF THE EARTH

BY

WILLIAM S. WALSH

AUTHOR OF "A HANDY BOOK OF LITERARY CURIOSITIES," "CURIOSITIES OF
POPULAR CUSTOMS," ETC.

PHILADELPHIA & LONDON
J B. LIPPINCOTT COMPANY

PRINTED IN UNITED STATES OF AMERICA

INTRODUCTION

THE series of handy books which reaches its third volume with the present publication,—and which is to be continued in the future if this third volume meets with the favor that was accorded to its predecessors,*—is primarily designed as a sort of supplement to the Encyclopædias. It exploits either such subjects as are deemed beneath the dignity of more pretentious works or else such lighter aspects of familiar subjects as are similarly ignored by the Big Wigs.

For an example of the second group, take articles like BULL-FIGHTS and PLAYING CARDS. Nothing can be more trite than the subjects themselves, but the special information here supplied would be looked for in vain in authoritative books of reference.

Examples of the first group may be found on almost every page. They comprise the sort of "ana" which a host of readers are curious about. They form, in fact, the staple of the inquir: which are constantly addressed to the Correspondents' Column in our daily journal and are usually "left to our readers" and remain unanswered.

Usually but not always,—else this book, like its predecessors, would have lost a considerable part of such value as it may claim. Not to mention the London *Notes and Queries*—because all experts must take *that* for granted—there are several journals, English and American, which contain valuable departments receiving and answering queries, delving patiently into the quaint and curious lore of the past and rendering satisfactory explanations of recondite allusions, or determining mooted points in history, literature, biography, and science, or supplying lacunæ in otherwise accessible information.

To these the present compiler gratefully acknowledges his indebtedness. He would specify the New York *Sun*, and *Times*, the Philadelphia *Press*, and *Inquirer*, and the Brooklyn *Eagle* as having furnished him with much raw material that otherwise he might have overlooked. So have periodicals like *Harper's Weekly, Chambers' Journal* and *The Youth's Companion*—periodicals that freely volunteer information of this sort without any interrogative spur.

---

* "Handy-book of Literary Curiosities" and "Curiosities of Popular Customs" by W. S. Walsh, J. B. Lippincott Co., Philadelphia.

Nor is it always the raw material which has thus been laid under contribution. The scissors, it must be owned, have occasionally supplemented the pen. A small percentage of these articles are essentially a patchwork of quotations woven as deftly as possible into a new fabric.

Credit has been given where practicable. But it was not always practicable.—and more especially in the more flagrant cases—otherwise some of these papers would have been overladen with quotation marks and acknowledgments that might only too surely interfere with the reader's comfort. So a general acknowledgment must suffice where no individual reputation is detracted from,—where indeed it is only the anonymous dead that could possibly be disturbed in their coffins.

Wm. S. Walsh.

Sandy Hook, Conn.,
   July, 1913.

HANDY BOOK OF
CURIOUS INFORMATION

A 1. This notation in Lloyd's Register (see LLOYD'S) is
... to a ship in first-class condition as to hull and stores
The character A denotes new ships or ships renewed
... The stores of vessels are designated by the figures
... 1 signifying that the vessel is well and sufficiently
... (*Key to Lloyd's Register*). The term has passed into
... speech as a synonym for excellence. Thus, Dickens in
... Papers" (1847) gives this dialogue:

> " He must be a first-rater," said Sam.
> " A 1," replied Mr. Roker.

... an would be more likely to say " A number 1." *Cf.*
... in " Dred," chap. 23: " An A No. 1 cook, and no

... ures 1½, 1¾, 2, 2½, and 3 are also used with A, and
... ding scale of seaworthiness.

Abbess, Royal. Five religious foundations in Austria have
... to provide suitable homes for impoverished
... such noble families as have rendered distinguished
... the imperial family or to the state. These are situated
... Prague, Brünn, Innsbruck, and Graz. The Vienna
... was founded in 1769 by the Duchess Theresa of
... in Brünn by Emperor Leopold II in 1792, and
... Prague and Innsbruck in 1755 and 1765 respectively
... Maria Theresa, the greatest of the name. The
... are received in the Prague, Vienna, and Innsbruck
... must be able to show sixteen, those of Brünn five,
... in Graz four quarterings, respectively, on their arms.
... in Prague is the most aristocratic. Only a
... of the imperial family can be appointed its abbess. Even
... ption be specially made in favor of a lady of merely
... she has the right to the title of Royal Highness.
... is installed by a solemn court ceremonial, attended
... highest dignitaries of church and state, headed by an
... as the representative of the Emperor. The abbess
... further right of crowning the Queen of Bohemia. She
... edged to celibacy. In fact it is the usual custom for

the imperial abbesses to marry after a short term of office. Maria Theresa, a daughter of Napoleon's opponent the Archduke Charles, married Ferdinand II., King of Sicily; Maria Christine married King Alphonso XII., and became Queen Regent of Spain; Margaret Sophia married Duke Albert, heir-presumptive to the throne of Wurtemberg; Caroline Immaculata in 1894 gave her hand to Prince August Leopold of Coburg.

Absinthe, in French, means wormwood. The famous liqueur is made by steeping wormwood and other aromatic herbs in alcohol. Wormwood has been defined as the quinine of the poor. " Its bitterness is its principal merit," says a French authority. " It is a tonic, a stimulant, a frebrifuge, and a vermifuge. It is *par excellence* the herb of pale and feeble women. A slight pinch is sufficient in a litre of water."

Two kinds of absinthe, or wormwood, are used in making the liquor, the great and the small, the first, for its bitter qualities, and the last, which is gathered immature, chiefly to act in giving the delicate green color. The other plants employed in the distillation are balm, caraway, anise, and hyssop. Balm is classed medicinally as an antinervine, an important antidote in a liquor considered generally as acting too forcibly on the nervous system. The qualities of caraway and anise are familiar to every one. The last is greatly used in medicine and in many other ways for its flavor and perfume. The caraway used at Pontarlier comes from the south of France; the best anise from southwestern France and from Andalusia, in Spain. The flowers of hyssop are regarded as stimulating and expectorant.

Pontarlier is the centre of this great French industry, now more rigidly French than ever, for the neighboring countries of Belgium, Holland, and Switzerland have prohibited the manufacture, importation, or sale of the liquor. Belgium led the crusade in 1905, Switzerland followed in 1908. In Holland, where absinthe drinking has never prevailed to any considerable extent, prohibition was voted in 1910 as a preventive measure. The United States in October, 1912, forbade the importation and sale of absinthe.

Absinthe was first distilled on any large scale at Courvet, a little city of Switzerland lying across the French frontier a few miles beyond Pontarlier, France. After having passed through various hands the distillery was purchased by the ancestor of the principal establishment of Pontarlier, to which place the industry was transferred near the close of the nineteenth century, since which epoch the use of the liquor has been gradually extending.

The principal distillery of Pontarlier, which has its patent from the inventor, is an immense establishment, covering several acres, admirably appointed in every respect, kept with extraordinary neatness, and, for the convenience of transportation, connected with the railroad station, some three-quarters of a mile distant, by a track of its own.

There seems to be no doubt that absinthe as a cordial was made by the French confiseurs of the eighteenth century, but only as a flavor for other beverages. It does not appear to have become a common potation until about the beginning of the reign of Louis Philippe. The balance of evidence would seem to show that the Algerian campaign, in the days when the princes of the Orleans family were fighting so bravely in North Africa, and when the favorite song of the French troops was 'La Casquette du Père Bugeaud,' had a great deal to do with the popularization of absinthe among military men. The operations of war had to be carried out not only under a burning sun, but in all seasons, at all hours, and very often on marshy ground. Nothing is more probable than that some military surgeon, observing the ravages made by brandy on the health of the troops in such a climate as that of Algeria, prescribed as a stimulant diluted absinthe. The soldiers may have made wry faces at first at a beverage which to the uninitiated tastes very like "doctor's stuff," but with disastrous celerity they soon grew to like it and to drink it in excess. From a camp tonic dispensed to recruit exhausted strength, absinthe became the favorite pick-me-up in the Algerian cafés. It soon recrossed the Mediterranean, left its traces at Marseilles and Toulon, and with terrible quickness became domiciled in Paris.

Breakfast in France is little more than a bite of bread and a swallow of coffee. Parisian clerks and workingmen have longer noon-spells than even well-to-do folk take in New York or Chicago. All thoughts of business are put off for a good hour and a half. Master and man go off their different ways intent on meeting their friends at a restaurant. They do not fall immediately to eating, but sit at the little café tables sipping their drink. That drink is absinthe.

The practice is repeated on closing business for the night. Another absinthe is taken as an appetizer for dinner. Perhaps more than one is taken. We are assured that the dinner hour in Paris is growing later and later. Men who formerly dined at 6 or 6.30 P.M. now wait until 7 or 7.30. They wish to sit another hour before their second or third glass. It has been a long-standing complaint that the theatres are suffering from the late dining following on late drinking in the afternoon.

The Parisian article comes in two forms, pure and with gum,—*sirop de gomme,* as the French call it. In the latter article a sweet syrup is used. Two tablespoonfuls suffice for an ordinary glass, as water and sugar must be added. The glass generally used is an ordinary table goblet. The gum is poured into it,—a thickish liquid of a peculiar light-green color. Over the top of the goblet is placed a shovel-shaped spoon with perforated bottom and sides. Upon this rest several rectangular pieces of beet-sugar. A fine spray or jet of cold water is allowed gently to fall upon the sugar from a carafe especially prepared for this purpose. After the gum is poured into the glass a long slender spoon is inserted and left quiet until the water fully dissolves the sugar and falls drop by drop into the absinthe below. With this dropping comes a change in the color of the liquor. What before had been a peculiar green hue now assumes a beautiful amber slightly clouded. With a clever stirring from the spoon the beverage is ready to do its work. It is sometimes, though rarely, drunk " neat " from tiny glasses holding perhaps a teaspoonful.

Absinthe has proved the opening wedge to break up the old wine-drinking habit, said a correspondent of the New York *Sun,* writing in 1891:

Even more than Paris the south of France gives an example of this change of ways in drinking. The people of the south of France complain, with reason, that their wine no longer brings its price. Yet they set the most notorious example of neglecting it. The religion of the *apéritif* lives in more vigor in the south of France than in the capital. From the mouth of the Gironde to the Pyrenees, from the Pyrenees to the furthest shore of the Mediterranean and to the Alps, the drinkers of absinthe and vermouth are without number. And, down there, with a logic which is feminine and characteristic of the South, they cut the Gordian knot by taking their *apéritif* before and after meals, and even during meals. The innkeepers of the mountains and the plains have all adopted the same methods. It is not one glass of absinthe which they serve to their customers—it is the bottle itself. How many take two glasses, without counting the *rincette*—the final " rince " which you take free—no one can know. The number must be very high, at least in Perpignan: for in certain large cafés of that city the proprietors have been obliged in their own interest to stop the custom of passing the bottle. Instead they serve a small carafe of absinthe, out of which the client may get two fair glasses. But he is obliged to stop there or buy another portion. When I say two glasses I mean wine glasses. Before this new departure, when they gave the bottle, the proprietors were being ruined.

This exaggerated consumption of absinthe prevails equally in the mining countries of the south. In many of the districts absinthe has become the current drink. It is drunk even at the table, mixed with water. Thus absinthe has become an important factor in social life.

It is estimated that the consumption of absinthe by the French people amounts to a million gallons a year. Government and the more enlightened classes recognize the perils of this growing evil but are powerless to stop it. Unfortunately for the government, it has been from the beginning an active agent in the spread of the liqueur, deriving a revenue of $15,000,000 annually from its sale. This fact joined to the political power of the wealthy manufacturers stands in the way of prohibition. Moreover scientific authorities assert that any sudden stoppage of the supply would result in hundreds of thousands of cases of madness,—insanity of such maniacal fury as might deluge the country in blood before the army of drug victims could be placed in asylums.

Acetylene Gas. Edmund Davy, an Englishman, first made acetylene gas in 1836 from a compound produced during the manufacture of potassium tartrate and charcoal.

But the discovery of a cheap process which made the gas a commercial possibility was due to accident. In the summer of 1892 T. L. Willson, an American metallurgical investigator, had erected a smelting furnace on the bank of a stream in North Carolina. In his experiments he often had occasion to use quantities of limestone and rock-salt. Fused in the great heat of the furnace, the substances yielded a peculiar slag containing some sort of dirty-grayish matter with which Willson was unfamiliar. Week by week he dumped this slag unconcernedly into the stream, until one day the pile of slag projected above the surface of the water. The next time he dumped the red-hot slag into the stream he was surprised to see a dazzling burst of flame, which hovered above the pile and shot up into the air. Puzzled to find the reason for this phenomenon, he awaited with interest the next opportunity for dumping. It was at night, and he was amazed at the brilliant whiteness of the light. Then he placed some of the dirty-grayish material on the bank and poured water on it, but to his surprise nothing happened. When he held a match over the damp pile, however, there was an instant burst of white flame—and the discovery had been made.

Acoma, New Mexico, an Indian pueblo, is the oldest inhabited settlement in the United States. St. Augustine, known as the first permanent European settlement planted within the limits of the present United States, was founded in 1565. So early as 1539, however, we find mention of Acoma in the chronicles of Fray Marcos de Niza. Next year it was besieged by Coronado's army and captured only after a long resistance. It had evidently been built as a stronghold against the assaults of the Navajos and Apaches, who for centuries had made war upon the peaceful people. The site chosen was a great oblong rock some 400 feet above the plain. Here arose " the most wonderful aboriginal city on earth, cliff-built, cloud-swept, matchless." At the time of its conquest by the Spaniards, the inhabitants

numbered about 6000. At present the population is barely 600.
The village proper consists of three parallel rows of three-
storied adobe houses, terraced in form and some 40 feet high.
On the first story live the senior members of the family. The
daughter first married gets the second terrace. The next one
married gets the third. All other members of the family remain
with the old folk or seek quarters e'sewhere. Entrance to the
houses is effected by ladders over the roof.

The most conspicuous building in the pueblo is the ancient
adobe cathedral, which stands near the edge on the east side
of the mesa. It was built about the year 1600. It contains
a wooden image of the "Sacred Saint," whose possession is
believed to ensure good fortune and plentiful crops, so that it
is naturally coveted by other tribes. Several times it has been
captured by the Laguna Indians, and recovered only after
bloody struggles. On the patron day, in September, this
image is carried in procession from the church to the dancing
ground, where it is placed in a temporary enclosure of corn-
stalks and green branches, until sunset, two Indians mounting
guard over it with loaded rifles.

The top of the mesa is said to contain about a hundred and
fifty acres. It is only accessible by three circuitous trails, over
which, on the backs of these people, had to be brought from the
plains below every bit of material used in the construction of
the dwellings and church, besides all food, fuel, and other
articles necessary to their livelihood. One of these trails has
recently been enlarged so that material now may be brought up
in a roundabout route on the backs of burros, with which the
tribe seems plentifully supplied.

Acre. This word originally meant any field of whatever
size, being derived from the Anglo-Saxon *œger*, cognate to the
Latin *ager*, both meaning land or anything sown. In such
popular phrases as "God's acre" (q.v.), "broad acres," etc.,
it has retained its indeterminate scope. As a measure of land
it was first defined under Edward I as the amount a yoke of
oxen could plough in a day. By an act of George IV the
varying measures of the acre then current in the kingdom were
reduced to one uniform standard. The Weights and Measures
Act of 1878 now defines it as containing 4840 square yards.
Even yet the Scottish and Irish acres (respectively 6150 and
7840 square yards) differ from the English, but the latter is
current in the United States.

Advertisement, as we now know it, originated only a little
more than a couple of centuries ago, but it had its anticipations
many thousands of years ago. The ancient Jews made announce-

ments by means of public criers; the Greeks added written to oral communications of this sort; the Romans expanded the practice in many ways.

One of the first English printed advertisements was a handbill or poster got out by Caxton in 1480 and reading: " Pyes * * * of Salisbury * * * good and chepe * * * if it please any man spirituel or temporel to bye."

This was not a baker's advertisement. Caxton had printed " Pyes," or clerical rules, telling how the clergy at Salisbury dealt with the changing date of Easter; and, as the clergy could read, he was bold enough to print advertisements of his " Pyes."

For two centuries after it was introduced, printing, which should have boomed advertising, if advertising depended primarily upon printing, had little or no effect upon it. The public had to be reached by the rebus over the shop, the public criers in towns, and by boys in front of stalls calling, " What d'ye lack, master? What d'ye lack?"

Even public notices posted in cathedrals and other frequented places were seldom printed. So few copies were required for the few readers that they were cheaper hand-written.

And even the newspapers, when the civil wars in England in the seventeenth century brought them forth and they began to develop readers, had an extraordinarily small effect in developing advertising.

It is generally held that the first newspaper advertisement, in our modern sense of the word, appeared in April, 1647, in No. 13 of *Perfect Occurrences of Every Daie Journall in Parliament and other Moderate Intelligence,* and it ran as follows:

A Book applauded by the Clergy of England, called the Divine Right of Church Government, Collected by sundry eminent Ministers in the Citie of *London;* corrected and augmented in many places, with a brief Reply to certain Queries against the Ministery of *England;* is printed and published for *Joseph Hunscot* and *Charles Calvert,* and are to be sold at the Stationers' Hall and at the Golden Fleece in the Old Change.

Booksellers appear, therefore, to have been the first to take advantage of this then new medium of publicity, and they have continued to avail themselves very liberally of its benefits up to the present day.

The next oldest advertisement that has been located refers to the theft of two horses. It is contained in an early number of an English newspaper called the *Impartial Intelligencer,* published in the year 1648, and was inserted by a gentleman of Candish, in Suffolk. After this, these notifications are very few and far between for several years, until the era of the London *Gazette.*

But, although announcements in the nature of advertisements appeared in the *Gazette* almost from the first, the word itself does not occur until No. 42, April 5–9, 1666, when "An Advertisement from the Health Office in London" is addressed to the farmers of the hearth-tax. In No. 62, June 14–18, 1666, the editor inserts the following, which deserves notice as an instance of self-denial that would hard'y find a parallel to-day.

> An Advertisement—Being daily prest to the Publication of Books, Medecines and other things not properly the business of a Paper of Intelligence. this is to notifie, once for all. that we will not charge the *Gazette* with Advertisements, unless they be matter of State; but that a Paper of Advertisements will be forthwith printed apart, and recommended to the Publick by another hand.

No copy of this separate sheet has survived, and one can only conjecture what form it took. The good resolutions of the editor were soon broken. Right after the Great Fire in London we find the following in No. 94, October 8–11. 1666.

> Such as have settled in new Habitations since the late Fire and desire for the convenience of their correspondence to publish the place of their public abode. or to give notice of Goods lost or found. may repair to the Corner House in Bloomsbury on the East Side of the Great Square, before the House of the Right Honourable the Lord Treasurer, where there is care taken for the Receipt and Publication of such Advertisements.

After this date, announcements headed "Advertisements" became common, and it may be taken for granted that the word was first used in this sense by the London *Gazette.* The earliest use cited in the "New English Dictionary" is considerably later: *Luttrell's Brief Relation,* 1692.

When the public crier gave way to newspaper and periodical advertising, certain trades adopted some one organ as the best medium for advertising their special wares. The London *Morning Advertiser,* for example, became the favorite for liquor dealers, *Bell's Life* for the theatrical profession.

In the United States the first continuously printed or regular newspaper (*q.v.*) was the Boston *News Letter,* first issued April 24, 1704. This initial number contained no advertisements, though it was announced that, "notices of houses, lands. ships, vesse's, or merchandise to be sold or let. or servants run away, or goods stole or lost." would be inserted at rates ranging from twelve-pence to five shillings.

It was a Pennsylvanian who discovered the uses of hoardings

and fences and who began the new departure by painting on the wooden walls of a graveyard, "Use Jones' Bottle Ale if you would keep out of here." After the humorous inscription came the enigmatic. One man, having a certain brand of plantation bitters to sell, advertised it in all sorts of inaccessible spots under the formula S.T. 1860 X. Much discussion and argument arose over the meaning of these characters, and, when the public had reached a comfortable state of mystification, the explanation was made that they stood for "Started Trade in 1860 with Ten Dollars." (See article "Advertising, Quaint and Curious," in WALSH: *Handy-book of Literary Curiosities,* p. 17.)

Aelurophobia. This is the term which Dr. S. Weir Mitchell applies to an unreasoning horror, noted also by Shylock (Merchant of Venice, Act IV, Sc. I), for the "harmless necessary cat." The word itself was first used in this sense by the New York *Bookman.* Its etymology goes back to Herodotus. When the father of history first encountered the cat in Egypt, he called it *ailuros,* or tail waver.

The most famous of all aelurophobists—to-day, however, remembered only for this trait—was General Roberdean, who left a room because he felt that a cat was in it; he grew pale, faint, and could scarcely breathe. A kitten was then found behind a bookcase. Dr. Mitchell had an hysterical patient, a lady, who on various occasions declared that there was a cat in the room. He mentions thirty other cases in which he was certain that people could tell when a cat was near though it was neither seen nor heard. It seems to him possible that "there may be olfactory emanations distinguished by some as odors and by others felt not as odors but only in their results on nervous systems unusually and abnormally susceptible." He learned that cats cause asthma in some patients. It would even appear that some people suffer lockjaw in the presence of a cat. Temporary blindness, hysterical convulsions, and sea-sickness may be ascribed in certain instances to the same cause. "A soldier of distinction, much given to tiger shooting, is undisturbed by these great felines, but terrified by the tame cat." One of his correspondents, "Dr. S., a distinguished physician," feels "almost sea-sick" as he dictates his account of his emotions.

The result of Dr. Mitchel''s investigations appeared in *American Medicine* for July, 1905.

Discussing the matter in the London *Morning Post,* Andrew Lang says: "The smell of tiger does not frighten the hero who is afraid of cats. The question is, why is this hero, or any other person, afraid of a cat? Why does cat produce lockjaw, horripilation (as a ghost does), and other effects of terror? But, then, why does water finding in some cases produce similar effects in diviners who are not afraid of water? Dr. Weir Mitchell falls back on the inherited remainders of animal instincts of protective nature. But we are not descended from birds, or mice, or other animals that need instinctive protection from puss. A caged canary shows no sign of being mysteriously aware that a hidden cat is in the room. If we descend from big apes, are big apes afraid of cats? Here is another chance for an experiment that would be ' unco awkward ' for the cat! "

By some perverse instinct, cats, it would seem, are very fond of aelurophobes. Even strange cats, Dr. Mitchell tells us, seem to have an unusual desire to be near them, jump on their laps, and follow them.

"That is very like a cat," cried Mr. Lang. " I once had a large silver-ringed cat of unemotional temperament. But finding a lady, rather aelurophobic, in a low dress at dinner, Tippoo suddenly leaped up and alighted on her neck. He was never so friendly with non-aelurophobes." (See also CAT.)

Aeronaut, Female. The first female aeronaut was one Madame Tibe or Thible. She joined the painter Fleurant aboard a balloon called the *Gustave* which ascended at Lyons on June 4, 1784, in the presence of the royal family of France and the King of Sweden. This lady, a Lyonnaise, was the wife of a worker in wax. Hearing that Fleurant was much discouraged at repeated failures to find a male companion, she of her own volition offered to mount with him to heaven and to glory. The balloon was a Montgolfière, beneath which hung a burning chafing-dish,—" un réchaud ardent."

For some reason Madame Tibe's fame has been eclipsed by that of the Citoyenne Henri, who is usually accredited with the honor of being the pioneer female aeronaut, though her ascent took place fourteen years later.

In 1798, on the VIth day of the 10th Floréal, the famous balloonist Garnerin announced that he would have a female companion for his coming ascent. On the 7th the Bureau of Police in Paris issued an injunction (*un arrêté*) against the project. Replying to newspaper criticism, Commissioner Picquenard, of the Executive Directory, explained that the Bureau in issuing the edict was actuated by the sweet sentiments of humanity, cruelly wounded at the mere idea that a young girl should without adequate motive give herself up to an experiment whose issue she could not calculate.

"I was present," continues Director Picquenard, "when

citizen Garnerin appeared before the Central Bureau. The officials asked him first if the object of his aerial journey was the perfecting of the art of aerostation; his answer was in the negative. Asked if he had foreseen the accidents which might result merely by the pressure of the air upon organs so delicate as those of a young woman, he answered that he did not think anything of the sort would happen. Asked, in case his companion should experience pain or discomfort produced by fear or a high elevation and should lose consciousness thereupon, whether he did not think his own safety and hers would be compromised in the most perilous manner, he replied that he would be responsible for all. Surely, citizen editor, you must feel that after such responses the Central Bureau could do no otherwise than issue a philanthropic injunction, concerning which you have seen fit to make merry, perhaps without due consideration of the facts."

And citizen Picquenard wound up with the assurance that he had too much confidence in the morality and the republican principles of citizen the editor to doubt that he would change his views when the matter was brought properly before him.

Garnerin, at all events, did not change his views. He appealed to a higher tribunal, the members of the departmental administration, against the decision of the Central Bureau, and that body, after consulting with the Minister of the Interior and the Minister of Police, came to the unanimous conclusion that the Bureau was at fault, and that "there was no more scandal in seeing two people of different sexes ascend in a balloon than it is to see them jump into a carriage." Furthermore, "it is impossible to prevent a female who has reached her majority to do in this fashion all that is permitted to men, and to give in thus ascending into the air a proof at once of confidence in the experiment and of personal intrepidity."

Thereupon Garnerin inserted an advertisement in *L'Ami des Lois* for the 20th Prairial, which contained this announcement: "The young citoyenne who will accompany me is delighted to see the day approach for the journey. I shall ascend with her from the Parc de Mousseaux, some time during the next ten days." On July 8, 1798, the event actually came off, and was thus described in the *Rédacteur* three days later:

On the 22 Fructidor took place the aerostatic ascent of citizen Garnerin with the first woman who ever had the courage to trust herself in the regions of air. This event drew to the Parc de Mousseaux an immense concourse of spectators. The young and beautiful aerial nymph, accompanied by the famous Saint-Georges, who gave her his arm, made the tour of the enclosure several times amid universal applause. Lalande, the astronomer, finally offered her his hand to assist her into the car; she leaped in with the utmost intrepidity; her journey was a complete success; the travellers descended at Goussainville, four leagues away from Paris.

Next day the *Ami des Lois* came out with some personal details. It announced that the young and beautiful aeronaut was named Citoyenne Henri, and that she had been actuated by no interested· motive, although citizen Garnerin had subsequently made her a present.

The first professional female aeronaut, and the first woman to meet with a fatal accident in the pursuit of her profession, was Madame Blanchard, widow of the B anchard who made the first voyage across the English Channel (see ENGLISH CHANNEL).

Madame Blanchard was a beautiful woman, and her reckless daring made her a favorite with the Parisians. Her apparent immunity from accidents tempted her to try the same experiment that had proved fatal to her husband. In 1819 she made her last ascent from the Tivoli Gardens. On reaching a certain altitude she was to discharge fireworks attached to the car. An eye-witness thus describes what happened:

> From my window I saw her ascend. For a few moments the balloon was overwhelmed with clouds; presently it reappeared, to the horror of the spectators, one sheet of flame. There was an awful pause. Then the poor woman, enveloped and entangled in the netting of her machine, fell with an awful crash upon the slanting roof of a house in the Rue de Provence, and thence into the street, where she was taken up, a shattered corpse.

It is a little difficult to identify another female aeronaut alluded to in one of Washington Irving's letters. He was walking in company with Luttrell and Moore at the latter's suburban residence in Paris, when the conversation turned on a female aeronaut who had not been heard of since her recent ascent. Moore described her upward progress; the last seen of her, she was still ascending.

"Handed out," slipped in Luttrell, "by Enoch and Elijah."

In more modern times the first woman to receive a pilot's license from the Aero Society of France was the Baronesse de La Roche. She was also the first woman in the world who ever owned and operated an aeroplane. When she was given her first instruction by M. Chateau, the instructor for the Voisins, she made a few short jumps down the aviation field at Chalons, and then without warning started off on a long flight. She descended to the ground after flying three-quarters of a mile, and without leaving her seat rose again, this time to break the record for beginners by flying more than four miles and a half through a gusty wind without descending.

The first American woman to win a pilot's license was Miss Harriet Quimby, of New York, 1884–1902. Miss Quimby took her first lesson at the Moisant Aviation School at Hempstead Plains, Long Island, May 10, 1911. She qualified for her pilot's license by passing the required tests of the Aero Club of America (representing the federation of aero clubs of the world) on August 1 of the same year. "This does not mean, however, that I spent all this time learning to fly," she explained, in an article, "How I Won My Aviator's License," contributed to *Leslie's Illustrated Weekly* for August 24, 1911. "My lessons aggregated only 33, and actual time spent on each lesson was from 2 to 5 minutes. This is the stipulated time allotted to students at each lesson in all the leading schools of aviation in France. That my course of instruction covered as many weeks as it did was really due to adverse weather conditions."

The tests required for obtaining a pilot's license are as follows: The applicant for a license must be at least 18 years of age and must pass three tests, namely, two distance tests, consisting of covering without touching the ground a close circuit not less than 5 kilometers (3.107 miles) in length, the course to be indicated by two posts not more than 500 metres (about 1640 feet) from each other, and the aviator to change his direction at each post, so as to make an uninterrupted series of figure eights. An app'icant is required to make an altitude flight to a minimum flight of 50 metres (about 164 feet) above the starting-point. He is also required, as a further test in landing, to stop his motor not later than the time when the machine touches the ground and to stop his aeroplane at a distance of 165 feet from the point designated before the flight.

"It was 6.42 in the morning, according to the official record," added Miss Quimby, "when the first trial flight began, covering a distance estimated at about 12 miles, and the flight ended at 6.51. Was I happy when I saw the signal of Prof. Houpert indicating that I had safely gone through the first half of the test? Honestly, I was. Not because I was tired, for driving a monoplane takes little physical strength. Not because I was timid, for I had been too intent on my work for that; but because I felt that my task was half accomplished, and in my frame of mind it seemed to me that half done was all done. Approaching the point designated before my flight as the place where I should descend, I lowered my planes and made a short descent from an altitude of 75 feet, then straightened my machine and skimmed the surface of the ground, cutting off the engine just before I reached the ground, then rolled across the ground towards the canvas patch. Before I could leave my seat, my instructor, the Aero Club representatives, Captain Baldwin, and my classmates and friends were heaping their congratulations upon me.

" Waiting for a few moments for the engines to cool, I started on the second flight at 7.22, and again completed the five eights and landed at 7.31. My altitude was the third and final test. Again my faithful monoplane was put into service. The flight began at 7.45 and ended 6 minutes later, and then I was once more on earth to receive the welcome greeting of friends." Miss Quimby's fate was mournfully reminiscent of Madame Blanchard's. On July 1, 1912, she was killed by a fall from her aeroplane at Boston.

Aeroplane. This word has only recently been admitted into the dictionary. Yet so far back as 1879 a Frenchman, Victor Tatin, at the experiment station of Chalais-Meudon, applied the name "aéroplane" to a flying machine of his own invention driven by compressed air. Possibly it was from Tatin that was borrowed the corresponding English word (similar save for the accent) by Ella Merchant and Alice Ilgenfritz Jones, joint authors of "Unveiling a Parallel" (1892). The hero of this novel is a "bird-man" who soars in his "aeroplane" to Mars, where, among other wonderful things, he finds woman on terms of perfect equality with man. Fifteen years later H. G. Wells, in "When the Sleeper Wakes," gave the name "aeropile" to his imaginary airship, but the word had only a temporary vogue.

Air-brake. The earliest of George Westinghouse's inventions in the way of safety appliances for railroads. He took out his first patent in 1872. Though this brake was a clumsy affair, operated from the cab of the engine and requiring 18 seconds to transmit power from the first to the last of a train of thirty cars, it was a great advance upon the clumsy hand-brakes of the past. None of the railroads, however, would accept it. Three years later Westinghouse brought out the modern brake, which is an automatic unit in controlling the individual cars. Every locomotive is supplied with an air-compressor which fills in the engine itself, while beneath each car is a reservoir of compressed air. Each reservoir aboard a long train in rapid motion may at the same instant, by a touch from the engine-runner, actuate the brakes so as to stop the train in the shortest possible time. Westinghouse made his first application by mail to Commodore Cornelius Vanderbilt, president of the New York Central Railroad. He pointed out the superiority of his invention to the hand-brakes then in use, all of these taking ten men to handle, while his brake required only one man. He claimed that a fifty-car train running twenty miles an hour could be brought to rest in about fifty yards, as against two hundred and sixty-five yards with hand-brakes. The same train running forty miles an hour could be stopped within one hundred and ninety-five yards, as against eight hundred yards, or five-elevenths of a mile, by the old system. It is said that Vanderbilt roared with laughter over this letter. The idea of stopping a train of cars by wind appealed to him only as a joke. So he returned the missive with these words scribbled at the bottom:

"I have no time to waste on fools."

Alexander J. Cassatt, of the Pennsylvania Railroad, was next appealed to. He was younger and more progressive than his New York rival. He realized that the increase in railroad speed and in the weight of railway cars called for some improvement over the old-fashioned brakes. He summoned Westinghouse to his presence, listened to his explanations, and even advanced him money to continue his experiments. Best of all, he made a test of the new brake, which proved that Westinghouse was on the right tack. Commodore Vanderbilt, hearing of these tests, regretted his earlier haste. He wrote the inventor a courteous note appointing an interview. The note came back endorsed

"I have no time to waste on fools. GEORGE WESTINGHOUSE."

In the spring of the year 1876 an international test of safety brakes was held on the Midland Railway in England. There were ninety competitors. The Westinghouse brake easily won out. Not until ten more years of experimenting, however, did its inventor perfect it into its present form, so that it can be applied within two seconds to every car of a train of fifty. It should be borne in mind that a train of fifty cars is nearly one-third of a mile long.

Air-cushion. Ben Jonson has poetically anticipated this modern device. Sir Epicure Mammon, in "The Alchemist," enumerates, among the pleasures and comforts that are to be his when in possession of the philosopher's stone, a novel conception of his own:

> I will have my beds blown, not stuffed:
> Down is too hard.

Airship. An advertisement put forward by the European Aeronautical Society was twice printed in the *Athenæum, i.e.,* in the issues for July 25 and August 1, 1835.

FIRST AERIAL SHIP.—The Eagle, 160 feet long, 50 feet high,

40 feet wide, manned by a Crew of Seventeen, constructed for establishing Communications between the several Capitals of Europe. The First Experiment of this New System of AERIAL NAVIGATION will be made from London to Paris and back again. May be viewed from Six in the Morning till Dusk, in the Dock Yard of the Society, at the entrance of Kensington Victoria-road, facing Kensington Gardens, between the First Turnpike from Hyde Park Corner and the Avenue to Kensington Palace. Admittance every day of the Week, 1s. The Public is admitted on Sundays after Divine Service. Free Admissions the whole year Sundays and Holidays included, for Members of the Society and their Friends.

No other reference to this airship appears in any contemporary records and the whole has the appearance of a hoax. It is not explained how the ship could be intended to travel from city to city and yet be on exhibition at Kensington. The advertisement may have been suppressed after its second appearance on this account.

Alaska. This name, now applied to the whole of the territory purchased by the United States from Russia in 1867. is a corruption very far removed from the original word. When the early Russian traders first reached the island of Unaláshka, they were told by the natives that to the eastward was a great land or territory. This was called by the natives Al-ák-shak or Al-áy-ek-sa. The island now known as Unaláshka was called Na-gûn-aláyeksa, or " the land near Aláyeksa." From Aláyeksa the name became, by corruption, Aláksa, Aláshka, Aliaska, and finally Aláska, which latter is an English innovation; the Russians never used it. In all the later maps the name of the peninsula is spelled Aliáska. This spelling is preserved by Mr. Dall in the work referred to below as affording a convenient distinction between the general and specific names. In the same way Na-gun-aláyeksa became Agún-aláksa, Agún-aláshka and finally Unaláshka. In " Cook's Voyages " and in Campbell's " Pleasures of Hope " this name is spelled Onalaska, e.g., " The wolf's long howl on Onalaska's shore." The term Unalaska has no authority and is not known to either Russians or Aleuts. We have then Aláska for the territory, Aliáska for the peninsula. and Unaláshka for the island, all derived from the same root and meaning a great country or continent.—DALL, *Alaska and its Resources.*

Men now living remember well the storm of mingled derision and denunciation which was copiously directed against William H. Seward for his purchase of Alaska. He was said to have annexed an iceberg and to have squandered the nation's money upon an Arctic province, and "Seward's Folly" was destined to be an enduring epithet of contemptuous condemnation.

Yet to-day the almost incalculable wealth of that territory figures conspicuously among the nation's resources, and the development and administration of those resources form commanding issues in national politics. The few millions which Seward paid for ·Alaska are a negligible trifle when contrasted with its vast actual and potential value. Indeed, the purchase price was far more than repaid many years ago, through the · earlier and more primitive products of the territory, before later revelations which show that the purchase of Alaska is not unworthy of a place in the same category with the acquisitions of Louisiana and of California, as investments exceeding in returns the expectations of any but an inspired seer.

It was Prof. William H. Brewer (1828–1910), head of the department of agriculture at Yale College, who inoculated Seward with the idea of the Alaska purchase.

"I urged three reasons," said the professor, in an interview reported by the New York *Sun,* August 20, 1899. "We needed it, first, for its fishing rights, and, second, as a great source for ice for the Pacific coast. How laughable that reason appears now! Yet it was a scientific argument then, and the company that controls the fishing industries to-day was originally only an ice company, according to its charter. The third reason was a sentimental one, but I am inclined to think that it is being demonstrated by the events of later years. I said that the climate and scenery of Alaska were of pecuniary value. I can still see Seward smile as I told him that the people of the United States would in time want to visit Alaska for the sake of the scenery."

In the end Secretary Seward was convinced. President Johnson was not. When Johnson visited New Haven in 1866, he was beset by politicians desirous of showing him around the city. He answered that he wished to visit Yale College. A reception was arranged for him in front of the old library. After he had shaken the hands of students and professors, Brewer saw his chance and took him aside to talk Alaska to him. Johnson was won over. Next year Alaska was purchased.

There has been some dispute as to the political status of Alaska, whether it be a District or a Territory. In treaties, in presidents' messages, in Acts of Congress, and in executive and judicial records it figures as "the Territory of Alaska." Also, at times, it has been officially called the District of Alaska. But the question was authoritatively settled by the 59th Congress in the act providing for a delegate to the House of Representa-

2

tives. As finally enacted in April, 1906, it was "an act providing for the election of a delegate to the House of Representatives from the Territory of Alaska." As passed by the Senate it provided for a delegate from "the District of Alaska." It was amended in the House, and after conference the conferrees reported that in the new bill agreed upon "the words 'Territory of Alaska' are substituted instead of 'District of Alaska' in the enacting clause and elsewhere where the whole domain of Alaska is referred to."

Alligator. An animal so closely allied to the crocodile that naturalists have sometimes grouped them under a single species. There is even a singular analogy between their respective names, which are *prima facie* so dissimilar. "Alligator" is a corruption of *El legato*, or lizard, the name which the Spanish gave it when they first encountered it in South America. Having no acquaintance with the African crocodile, they saw in the novel animal only its likeness to a monster lizard. So when the Greeks came into Egypt, centuries before the discovery of America, and first saw the crocodile, they also, recognizing the resemblance, called it a lizard—κροκόδειλος—from which the English word "crocodile" is derived.

Alma Mater. This term, applied to the colleges and universities wherein men receive their scholastic training, is of Roman Catholic origin. It originated in mediæval times in the University of Bonn, Germany. Over the portal of that seat of learning still stands a statue of the mother of Christ known as the Alma Mater or beloved mother.

Almanac. The derivation of the word "almanac" is still uncertain. Many wild guesses have, indeed, been made. No lexicographic angel, however, has ventured to decide which onrushing and enthusiastic philological fool is in the right.

Among the various conjectures two of the most plausible may be noted. First, that which looks to the Arabic and derives the word, either form *al*, the, and *manah*, to count, or *al* and *men*, the months. Second, that which gives it a Teutonic origin, from the words *al*, and *monah*, the moon.

This much is certain: the thing itself is older than the word. There is preserved in the British Museum an almanac which dates back 1200 years before the birth of Christ, to the time of Rameses the Great of Egypt.

Written on papyrus, in red ink, it covers a period of six years. The entries relate to religious ceremonies, to the fates of children born on given days, and to the regulation of business enterprises in accordance with planetary influence. Such injunctions as "Do nothing at all this day," and "If thou seest anything at all this day it will be fortunate," must sound strangely familiar to modern readers of "Raphael's" or "Old Moore's Almanac." This interesting relic was found in an old tomb, and is supposed to have been buried with its Egyptian owner when he was converted into a mummy for future explorers to dig up and dissect in the interest of science and literature.

Among the Greeks and Romans, almanacs or calendars were not written for the general public, but were preserved as part of the esoteric learning of the priests, whom the people had to consult not only for the dates of the festivals, but for the proper times when various legal proceedings might be instituted. About 300 B. C., however, one Encius Flavius, secretary to Appius Claudius, stole these secrets by repeated applications to the priests and collated the information so gained. Flavius may be said to be the first almanac-publisher—in the legal sense of the verb to publish—when, as Livy relates, he exhibited the Fasti on white tablets around the Forum. From this time similar tablets containing the calendar, the festivals, astronomical phenomena, and sometimes allusions to historical events became quite common. They have been dug up in Pompeii and elsewhere.

There are also extant Christian calendars dating as far back as the fourth century, which give the names of the saints and other religious information.

One of the most famous of the calendars of the Middle Ages is that compiled by Petrus of Dacia in A. D. 1300. A MS. copy is preserved in the Savilian Library at Oxford. The symbolical Man, otherwise Man of Signs (Homo Signorum). still a common feature in almanacs, appears in this book, not it is conjectured for the first time, as it seems to have been a survival from the time of Ptolemy's "Almagesi," a collection of classic observations and problems relating to geometry and astronomy.

The first printed almanac was the "Pro Pluribus Annis," issued at Vienna in 1457, by an astronomer named Purbach. Purbach's pupil Regiomontanus brought out the first almanac of real importance. It gave the usual astronomical information not merely for one year ahead, but for the fifty-seven years 1475–1531. Regiomontanus (whose family name was not so big a word, but simply Johann Müller, or John Miller), besides being a great astronomer was a bishop.

The earliest known almanac devoted expressly to the year of issue was published by Rabelais in 1533. Thenceforth, the ephemeral and yearly character of the publication came to be definitely recognized by almanac makers.

Nostradamus set the fashion of incorporating predictions of coming events into a'manacs, a fashion that has continued to this day in all purely astrological brochures of this sort, despite intermittent efforts to suppress it by royal authority in France and elsewhere.

The *Almanach Liégeois* is a venerable remnant of seventeenth century superstition. Begun in 1625, it survived almost to the end of the nineteenth century, largely on the strength of a successful prophecy made in 1774, announcing that in April a royal favorite would play her last part. Madame Du Barry took the prediction to herself. She was frequently heard to exclaim, " I wish this villanous month of April were over." But ere it was over, Louis XV. was taken sick, early in May he died, and thus the royal mistress really played her last part.

In England only one legislative attempt to interfere with the almanac prophet is recorded. William Lilly, in his " Life," tells us how in 1650, after having yearly foretold victory to the Parliament while its power lasted, he changed his ground and predicted that the Rump stood upon a tottering foundation. For this offence he was arrested, taken before a committee of the House, and shown the words in his almanac. Forewarned, he had come forearmed. In a second edition he had had a new leaf printed, and he repudiated the first edition as a forgery.

In 1708, however, the wits of London joined informally together to abate the nuisance by attacking its foremost exponent, the astrologer almanac-maker Partridge. Dean Swift took the initiative. At the close of the year 1707 he issued a pamphlet entitled " Predictions for the year 1708, by Isaac Bickerstaff." ' The writer's professed aim was to rescue a noble art from vulgar impostors. He drew attention to the difference between the ambiguous methods of the latter and his own straightforward predictions. He apologized for the trifling character of his first bit of augury, the death of John Partridge " upon March 29th next, about 11 at night, of a raging fever."

On March 30 there appeared another pamphlet, announcing that the first of Mr. Bickerstaff's predictions had been fulfilled. Then followed a broadside " Elegy on the Death of Mr. Partridge." In vain Partridge rushed into print with a denial of his death. The wits took up the cue. Grave treatises were written to convict Partridge of futile absurdity in urging that he was still alive. The Company of Stationers, who, under the law, had the exclusive right to handle almanacs for the trade, struck his name off their rolls. Over in Portugal the inquisition, hearing of the marvellous verification of Bickerstaff's

"Predictions," ordered his pamphlet to be burned as an unmistakable emanation from the devil.

For a period Partridge was overwhelmed. Four years passed before he attempted to resume publication of his Almanac. A successor is still issued under his name.

A well-known story about Partridge runs as follows: Travelling on horseback through the English provinces he stopped for his dinner at an inn, and afterwards called for his horse, that he might reach the next town where he intended to make a visit.

"If you will take my advice, sir," said the hostler, as Mr. Partridge was about to mount his horse, "you will stay where you are for the night, as you will surely be overtaken by a heavy rain."

"Nonsense, nonsense," exclaimed the almanac-maker; there's a sixpence for you, my good fellow, and good afternoon to you."

He proceeded on his journey, and sure enough, he was well drenched in a heavy shower. He was struck by the man's prediction, and ever intent on the interests of his almanac, he immediately turned back, and was received by the hostler with a broad grin.

"Well, sir, you see I was right, after all."

"Yes, my lad, you have been so, and here's a crown for you; but I give it to you on the condition that you tell me how you knew of this rain."

"To be sure, sir," replied the man; "you see we have an almanac at our house, called Partridge's almanac, and the fellow is such a notorious liar that whenever he promises us a fine day, we always know that it will rain. Now, sir, this day is put down in our almanac as 'settled fine weather; no rain.' I looked at that before I brought your horse out, sir, and in this way I could put you on your guard."

Another famous almanac-maker was Francis Moore, at one time an assistant of Partridge's. He originally published his annual under the name of "Vox Stellarum.'" But gradually it came to be known best by its compiler's name, "Moore's Almanac,"—and later, under his successors, as "Old Moore's Almanac." It is still valued for its weather prophecies by the lower class of English farmers. It is said that the compiler used to sit at one desk firing off the monosyllables "wind, rain, hail, snow, wet, cloud, dry," etc., interchangeably, while his clerk sat at another desk attaching the dictated word to whatever day of the coming year had its line vacant. It was only necessary to be on the guard against running "snow" too far into summer, or heat too far into winter.

Once, however, the compiler escaped disaster only by an apparent miracle.

"What shall I put in for Derby Day?" asked his assistant, in the year 1867.

The query woke the weather prophet out of a comfortable after-dinner snooze.

"Oh, cold and snow!" cried the old man, in a huff.

By an extraordinary coincidence snow actually fell on June 3, 1867 (Derby Day), and the ancient faith in the weather wisdom of Old Moore received a new impetus.

A similar story is told in America. The Harpers used to print the almanacs of one Hutchins, who made them for the Southern market, to the order of a dealer in those parts, who, in giving the order, directed him to put in the predictions of rain and shine to suit the cotton-crop season, so that all who bought the almanacs might have prophecies to suit them, whether they ever came to pass or not. Hutchins made a great hit, and a great deal of money, out of a blunder that turned out better than could have been expected. He had an assistant, who was at work on the month of July, and called on Mr. Hutchins for the weather, at a moment when he was particularly engaged and was much annoyed with the demand. "Put in what you please!" he cried out; "rain, hail, thunder, snow, and done with it!"

Sure enough, by one of the strange freaks of nature, July was visited with a cold snap, and all these winter performances came off, according to the programme, and the reputation of the almanac man was made.

But to return. The ignorance, profligacy, and imposture of the almanac-makers had become so monstrous a scandal that the Society for the Diffusion of Knowledge, in 1775, undertook the publication of "The British Almanac," which was the parent of all the respectable and scholarly publications of to-day.

In France almanacs have always abounded. They are fitted to all tastes, all religions, and all superstitions. But fun is the staple of most of them. For half a score dedicated to useful purposes there are half a hundred given up to anecdotes, puns, quips, cranks, and caricatures. Old jokes are pursued through a thousand transparent changes, run a gauntlet of travesties, and at the end come out the same old jokes, only a little battered and worn by hard usage. Every event of the year is twisted and turned in every possible way to discover its humorous side. The misfortunes, the vices, and the virtues of men, all alike are food for laughter.

In fact, life itself becomes a vast field of jokes—a Potter's

Field, a Parisian Golgotha with all the skulls on the broad grin.

It was in colonial America that almanacs became most valued and of most potent influence. Good books then and there were few and expensive. The almanac, insignificant as it was in appearance, was the literary event of every year. With the exception of the family Bible it constituted the sole reading of many a colonial household. In every kitchen a nail was provided to hang up the fresh almanac on its yearly appearance. Nightly it was taken down and thumbed over until it became brown and ragged, tattered, smoked, and soiled. Its weather predictions were always gravely consulted even after their unreliability had been established. Its jokes and anecdotes formed a perpetual fund of amusement. Its sententious sayings were accepted with awe and reverence.

The first American almanac was printed by Stephen Daye at Cambridge, Mass., in 1639, under the title "An Almanac, calculated for New England, by Mr. William Pierce, Mariner." No copy is known to exist, but Governor Winthrop notes its appearance in his Diary, and the types and press upon which it was printed are now in Harvard College.

The earliest almanac in Boston was compiled by John Foster in 1676, in New York by John Clapp in 1687, in Philadelphia by Samuel Aitkin in 1685. The latter was the initial printing enterprise of the famous William Bradford. It was entitled "Kalendarium Pennsilvaniense." Copies of the first number are now so rare that the Historical Society of Pennsylvania paid $520 for the one in their possession.

A more important publication was the "Poor Richard Almanac," which Benjamin Franklin first printed in 1728, and edited as well as printed from 1732 to 1757. The name was partly suggested by its older English contemporary, "Poor Robin's Almanac," a similar medley of jest and earnest, which, starting in 1661 or 1662—some say with the poet Herrick as its editor—survived until 1820. But the Poor Richard, who was Franklin's nominal editor, was a humorous recrudescence of one Richard Saunders, "Chyrargeon,"—or surgeon,—who in the seventeenth century published an almanac entitled "Apollo Anglicanus."

By dint of unique and humorous advertising, aided by its intrinsic merits, Franklin's almanac met with immediate and continuous success. The terse proverbs and witty sayings with which it abounded, some original but many borrowed, were quoted all over the colonies for the quarter century during which Franklin compiled and reprinted it.

The chief rival of the Poor Richard Almanac was one

compiled and published at Dedham, Mass., by Nathaniel Ames, father and son, from 1726 to 1775. It attained a yearly circulation of some 60,000 copies through much the same qualities of shrewdness, good humor, and homely wit which had made Poor Richard famous.

As the revolutionary war drew near, a distinct change appeared in the tone and character of the Ames publications. They grew intensely patriotic and anti-British. Their squibs smelt of gunpowder. As, for example:

Fine weather for fighting.

Who can serve 500 masters faithfully when they are 3000 miles off?

> Stand forth the champion of your country's cause
> Nor fear the traitors aided by their laws!

Now, my brave countrymen, prepare for dire approaching civil wars.

The Ames family were the last of the great almanac-makers. The publication of almanacs was suspended by the actual outbreak of the revolution. On the re-establishment of peace, better mail facilities brought the weekly newspaper to the remotest parts of the country districts, and the almanac, which had filled so important a position, was largely supplanted as a medium of literature and popular philosophy.

China, as usual, claims to have the oldest almanac in the world. From time immemorial, so say Celestial historians, and certainly down to the present time, the astronomical board of Pekin, acting under imperial sanction, has every year drawn up a calendar which is issued by the government, and sold at every huckster stall for the sum of two cents. By imperia' edict all are forbidden, under pain of death, to publish or use any other calendar. It is a complete register of the months and days of the year according to the Chinese system, of commercial forms, official sessions, and adjournments, religious festivals, and lucky and unlucky days. Transactions suitable for every day are named. Hence the Chinese masses apply to it for positive information as to when they may, or may not, wash their persons, shave their heads, open shop, set sail, celebrate marriage, or perform any other dai'y act. .

The imperial edict puts one in mind of the somewhat parallel legal monopoly of the trade in almanacs granted to the Stationers' Company and the universities by James I. This was in 1775 abolished through the instrumentality of Thomas Carnan, a bookseller, who gained a cause over the Stationers' Company, in the Court of Common Pleas. The bill brought in by Lord North in 1799 to renew the privilege was rejected by a majority of 45.

Alum. The story runs that the manufacture of alum was introduced into Yorkshire, England, early in the seventeenth century by Sir Thomas Chaloner, who had travelled in Italy and there seen the rock-beds from which the Italians extracted alum. Riding one day in the neighborhood of Guisborough, he noticed that the foliage of the trees resembled in color that of the leaves in the alum districts abroad; and afterwards he commenced an alum-work in the hills near that town, sanctioned by a patent from Charles I. One account says that he smugg'ed over from the Papal States, concealed in casks, workmen who were acquainted with the manufacture, and was excommunicated by the Pope for this daring breach of his own monopoly. The Sansend Works were established a few years later. Subsequently certain courtiers prevailed on the king to break faith with Sir Thomas, and to give one-half of the patent to a rival, which so exasperated the knight that he became a Roundhead, and one of the most relentless foes of the king. A great monopoly of the alum-works was attempted towards the end of the eighteenth century by Sir George Colebrook, who, being an East India director, got the name of Shah Alum. His attempt failed.

Aluminium. In an address by Dr. P. T. L. Heroult at the Chemists' Club, in New York, in 1911, he predicted the coming of the aluminium age in the following words:

Aluminium is slowly wedging its way in the metal market. It looks probable that in the course of ten or fifteen years the consumption of the new metal will be equal to that of copper, and that after the golden age, the stone age, the bronze age, and the iron age we shall have the aluminium age.

Dr. Heroult, a Frenchman, and C. M. Hall, an American, are the patentees of the Hall-Heroult process for producing aluminium which has made the new metal a commercial possibility.

Looking back upon the past and contrasting it with the present, the doctor continued:

Twenty-five years ago the aluminium industry employed about 10 men; the production was 1½ tons a year, the total value of which was $30,000. Nowadays the same industry produces 50,000 tons at a value of $20,000,000 and employs from 15,000 to 20,000 men.

If we take the average consumption of copper as 900,000 tons a year at a value of 13 cents per pound, the total value of ingot metal will be $234,000,000 a year, comparing with the $20,000,000 for aluminum, say one-tenth. But 13 cents is pretty near the rock-bottom price for copper. At 20 cents per pound aluminium presents a great advantage for most uses,

Dr. Heroult told an amusing story about his first acquaintance with aluminium in large quantities. He was in a gloomy
mood at the time, he said. He and his partner had pawned
everything in sight, with other things which were not in sight.

Finally my partner had a bright idea. He brought back from
home a stick of aluminium about six inches long, which was valued
very highly in his family as a personal souvenir of Saint Claire Deville.

As we handed it to the pawnbroker, the latter said, " What is that,
bar silver?" We said, " Better than that; that is aluminium."
" Aluminium," he said, " what is that?"

He weighed it in his hand and said, " Why, is this hollow?" We
said, " No, that is aluminium and it is worth 120 francs per kilo."
After some thought he said, " Well, I will give you 2 francs for it."

On a hot summer's day 40 cents was better than nothing, and we
took the money with the firm intention of buying the stick back,
which we never did. Maybe that was one of the reasons why, later
on, I had to make good and replace it.

I remember a shop on the Grande Boulevard in Paris where there
was a display of aluminium goods, thimbles, wedding rings, brooches,
statuettes, a few coils of wire, and some quite interesting specimens
of aluminium bronze in the form of coffee-pots, sugar-bowls, etc. Every
one of those articles had on the Paris finish and sold like silver ware.

In the '90s this same shop charged the same prices, although the
cost for ingots had come as low as 25 francs per kilo.

This was a wonderful time for the aluminium makers; they were
coining money, at least on the books. Aluminium was being piled up
in the store and the stock of finished product was reckoned at the
above-named price. But this did not last long. Customers were scarce,
and finally the bankers got tired of lending money to people who piled
up stock; it became necessary to sell.

Another price was established, at 8 francs per kilo, which did not
prove successful, either. Then came the 5 marks which originated
with the Swiss company; finally it seemed to open the bung-hole of
the cask.

Now, after various vicissitudes, the price in the old country looks
pretty near settled around 20 cents per pound and will vary probably
according to the price of copper.

For several years France was the only country producing
aluminium. The number of French factories has increased in
the region of the Alps, especially in the Department of Savoie,
where there are six establishments.

The reduction plant established in 1889 at Neuhausen in
Switzerland has had a most successful existence. Starting with
an annual production of forty tons of aluminium, it turned out
no less than 2621 tons in the first nine months of 1910, valued
at more than $840,000. The company has several branches, all
operating successfully. Its stock has never yet paid less than
12 per cent.; in 1906 it paid 26 per cent. on a par value of
1000 francs ($193).

The Swiss control of the aluminium market, which had

existed for several years, passed away with the opening of the
American factories at Niagara. Neither Switzerland nor France
possesses such rich mines of oxide of aluminium and such
sources of electrical energy as the United States. Negotiations
were begun in 1910 with a view to limiting the production of
aluminium and keeping up the prices, but owing to the attitude
of American producers, the movement has had little success.

Aluminium has become indispensable in the construction
of automobiles, dirigible balloons, and aeroplanes. It is employed in paper decorations and for wrapping purposes. It has
been found of enormous advantage also in the textile industry.

Combined with silk it makes a brilliant fabric, which can
be given any desired color. Hence it is much used for ceremonial costumes and theatrical wardrobes. In addition to the
ordinary uses it is also employed in the manufacture of reticules,
scarfs, and various articles of use and ornament. Because of
the high price of copper, it has been largely used as a substitute
for that metal in the manufacture of electrical cables.

A writer in *Harper's Weekly* finds, in an episode related by
Pliny, reason to believe that aluminum was known to the
Romans and was extracted by means of a secret process. During the reign of Tiberius a worker in metals appeared at the
imperial palace. He displayed a beautiful cup made of some
white metal that shone like silver. In presenting it to Tiberius,
he purposely dropped it. The cup seemed to be hopelessly
ruined by the fall, but the artificer's hammer quickly repaired
the damage. Thus it was seen that the metal was not silver.
It presented an equally brilliant appearance, but it was more
malleable, more durable, and much lighter.

In answer to queries put by Tiberius, the artificer stated
that the mysterious metal had been extracted from an argil-
laceous earth—in all likelihood the clay known to modern
chemists as alumina. He added that the secret was confined
to himself and to Jupiter. This was an unfortunate avowal.
Tiberius, fearing that if so brilliant a metal could be obtained
from so common a substance the value of gold and silver would
depreciate to nothing, ordered the summary execution of the
discoverer and the destruction of all his workshops.

Amaranth. This flower is more familiarly known in
England and America as love-lies-bleeding, cock's-comb, and
prince's feather. It bears minute purple blossoms in compact
clusters, each cluster surrounded by a close circle of chaff leaves,
very slow to wither. The ancients looked upon it as the flower
of immortality. The phrase in the first epistle of St. Peter,
"a crown of glory that fadeth not away," is in the original,

"the amaranthine crown of glory." The purple flowers of the amaranth retain their color always, and regain their shape when wetted, and were used by the ancients for winter chaplets. Amaranth was strewn over the graves in old Greece. Homer relates that the Thessalonians wore crowns of it at the burial of Achilles. Wreaths of amaranth are still worn and are hung over doors and windows by Swiss peasants on Ascension Day. Milton speaks of

> Immortal amarant, a flower which once
> In Paradise, fast by the Tree of Life,
> Began to bloom; but soon for man's offence
> To heaven removed, where first it grew, there grows,
> And flowers aloft shading the Fount of Life.

From being the flower of immortality, amaranth became, by a natural association of ideas, the flower of death. In a poem by Longfellow it crowns the brows of Azrael, the Death Angel, while the Angel of Life wears a wreath of asphodels or daffodils, the flowers of life. Because, perhaps, death is as strong as love, amaranth is an antidote for the love-philtre.

The Swedish order of the Knights of the Amaranth was instituted in the year 1653, by Christiana, who on the occasion appeared at a *fête* in a dress covered with diamonds. At the conclusion of the ball the Queen stripped herself of the diamonds and distributed them to the company, at the same time presenting the new order of knighthood, consisting of a ribbon and medal, with an amaranth in enamel surrounded with the Italian motto, *Dolce nella memoria,* "sweet in the memory."

Amber, a hard lustrous resinous substance, now known to be a fossilized vegetable gum which originally exuded from an extinct kind of cone-bearing trees standing in prehistoric forests. Through the action of centuries it has attained its present consistency. Usually a pale yellow, it sometimes has a reddish or brownish shade. When set on fire, it burns after the fashion and with the scent of a resinous torch, showing that its parent trees were of the pine species. That it was originally liquid is proved by the fact that flies, ants, and even lizards are often found embedded within it. Evidently they had entangled themselves in the gummy substance and it had hardened around them, thousands of years ago. Hence the well-known metaphor, "a fly in amber," for any trifling or worthless object inextricably connected with persons or affairs of moment. Thus Heine likens Lessing's enemies to flies in amber, because their names have been preserved in his imperishable words.

It was by an allusion to this principle of amber that Thomas B. Reed made his reputation as a wit. "What first brought Reed to the front in this way," says Henry Cabot Lodge in the *Century*, "was a trifling incident soon after he had taken his seat in Congress. He was saying a few words on a measure before the House, when some older member, thinking to break him up, began to interrupt him with questions. Reed answered every one, till he left his tormentor nothing more to say. Then he faced the Speaker again, and drawled, 'And now, having embalmed that fly in the liquid amber of my remarks, I will proceed.'

"The newspapers of the whole country told the story next day, and Reed found himself endowed with a national reputation."

The Greeks regarded amber with superstitious reverence, owing to its mysterious origin and its equally mysterious properties. Thales, the sage of Miletus, first observed (*circa* 600 B. C.) that, when rubbed, amber becomes warm and attracts light bodies to itself as the loadstone attracts iron. This observation was the foundation of the science of electricity, ἤλεκτρον being the Greek name for amber.

Greek myth explained amber as the tears dropped by Phaeton's sisters, pityingly changed into poplar trees after Jove had hurled their brother into the Eridanus.

The Romans gave it the name of succinum or gum-stone, which might be a successful guess at its origin, but more likely was suggested by its gum-like look.

The ancients held that amber was a cure for insanity, fever, and other disorders, when taken in a drink or worn around the neck as an amulet. But it is was especially valued for purposes of adornment. Nero, among other absurdities, had given the name of amber to the hair of his empress Poppæa. From that moment amber was a third color much in request with the ladies of the Roman court. Julianus, superintendent of the gladiatorial games given by Nero, sent a knight to explore the amber-producing country. He succeeded in returning with thirteen thousand pounds of amber, including a piece weighing thirteen pounds.

The largest amber mines in the world to-day are along the Baltic, between Königsberg and Memel on the Prussian coast. Here, below a layer of sand and clay about twenty feet in depth, a stratum of bituminous wood occurs from forty to fifty feet thick and partly impregnated with amber. Rounded masses of amber also are found under the stratum in pyrites, sulphate of iron, and coarse sands. The mine is worked to the depth of one hundred feet by an open excavation in the hill-sides. When the amber in one spot is exhausted, a new excavation reveals it in another. Masses of amber are also thrown up from the sea on these coasts. After a storm when the waters are agitated, men wade into the sea and catch in nets the sea-weed borne in by the waves. This is spread upon the shore, where women and children pick off the entangled bits of amber.

The finest specimen of amber in Europe is a cup made of that material now at the Brighton Museum, England. It was found at Hove in 1870 together with weapons and utensils of stone and bronze. In the thirteenth and fourteenth centuries amber was made into knives and forks with one prong which were used by great princes and prelates. Then it was more valuable than gold. Now it is worth from $2 to $50 a pound, according to quality.

Ambergris (a French word meaning gray amber), a gray wax-like substance, believed to be the product of some disease in the sperm whale, analogous to gall-stones. It is found as a morbid secretion in the creature's intestines, and sometimes, after expulsion, floating on the surface of tropical seas. Its essential characteristic is a pungent and penetrating odor, so peculiar that art has never been able to contrive an imitation of it, though invention has been stimulated by the high price attendant on its scarcity. Inferior qualities bring eight dollars an ounce; the best, which is rarely seen, is rated at something like fifty dollars an ounce.

The largest single piece of ambergris known to whaling annals is said to have been found by Captain James Earle, of New Bedford, Mass., in the interior of a whale. It weighed 780 pounds, and was sold in chunks in various markets of the world for about $100,000.

An often quoted legend is that of the British barque *Antiope*, which, somewhere near the end of the nineteenth century, sailed from Newcastle, Australia, to San Francisco. On the voyage. in latitude twenty degrees south, a great quantity of grease was seen floating on the surface of the ocean. A calm prevailed at the time, and the sailors drew up many bucketfuls. With this grease they anointed the masts, their sea boots and oilskins. They regarded their find as ordinary grease and wasted it as such. As a matter of fact, the "grease" was ambergris, and the waste was of material worth something like $20,000.

The latter story is generally discredited by experts. It may have arisen from the fact that ambergris is often pronounced or written ambergrease, whence the idea that it is of the consistence of grease or thick oil. In reality it is solid, though light of weight, and dry to handle.

The New York *Sun* recently published an interview with

David C. Stull, who was known as the Ambergris King from the fact that he presided over the headquarters of the trade in Provincetown, Mass.

Good ambergris, he said, was worth more than twice its weight in gold. He himself had once paid $18,000 for one lump and $30,000 for one lot. The lump weighed 98 pounds. At this rate a single ton would be worth a million dollars. He told a story of a Provincetown man who some thirty years before had been out on his first trip as captain of a whaling vessel. On his way home he stopped at one of the West India islands. A native offered him five small lumps of a dirty-looking substance, asserting that it was good for something, and explaining that he had got these pieces from a dead whale which was ashore on a certain beach. He added that there was plenty more in the carcass.

Did the captain hoist all sail and get to that dead whale as fast as the winds of providence would permit? Not a bit of it. He had been sent out after sperm oil and he'd stick to his job. So he gave the native a pair of blue overalls and a jumper for the five dirty lumps and went on his way.

After making port he showed the five lumps to Mr. Stull. When the latter gave him $700 for them he almost had a fit. Still that shock was nothing to what he got a little later, for he learned that another captain had heard of the dead whale, had got what ambergris still remained in the carcass, and had sold it in New York for $30,000. It was estimated that this whale must have contained at least $50,000 worth of ambergris.

"But the whalers of to-day," concluded Mr. Stull, "are a more canny lot. In fact they have gone to the other extreme. They not only open up a captured whale the very first thing to look for ambergris, but they pick up from the flotsam of the sea all sorts of possible and impossible stuff under the fond delusion that they are taking a fortune aboard."

Ambergris has been used for centuries in the sacerdotal rites of the church, and with fragrant gums was frequently burned in the apartments of royalty. To some extent it was employed as a medicine and also as a flavoring extract. Nowadays it is utilized almost exclusively by perfumers in the preparation of fine scents.

So far nothing has been discovered which will take the place of ambergris as a base in the manufacture of perfumery. It is the best binder known. Dissolved in alcohol it holds also in solution the various oils and essences of which perfumes are composed.

The quality of a perfume depends very largely on the amount of ambergris it contains. The best French perfumers use six ounces of ambergris to a gallon. One or two manufacturers in this country use the same proportion. Others put in four ounces.

In cheaper perfumes it is cut down to two ounces, and so on until the very lowest grades are reached in which there is not a trace of ambergris. The consequence is that the mixture has no permanence whatever.

Ambergris was anciently supposed to be identical with spermaceti, the sperm of the whale, and its difference from amber, a vegetable resin, was not fully understood. So recently as 1526 John Leo says in his "Account of the Kingdom of Morocco": "Upon this shore there is great store of amber to be found, which the Portuguese and Fessian merchants buy very cheap, i.e., less than a ducat per ounce. Some say 'tis whale's dung and others of spermaceti, which being hardened by the sea is cast upon the next shore." Culpeper, in 1654, distinguishes between ambergris and spermaceti, but says nothing as to the source of either. Lemery, "Truité Universel des Drogues" (1727), was better informed.

No longer than thirty years ago was it known that ambergris is found in the head of whales. The first light thrown upon the subject in Paris was through the lectures of the late Abbé Bourdelot.

Amen Corner, in Paternoster Row, London. In 1831 Sydney Smith, newly appointed to a prebendal stall in St. Paul's Cathedral, writes, "I have just taken possession of my preferment. The house is in Amen Corner,—an awkward name on a card, and an awkward annunciation to the coachman on leaving our fashionable mansion."

To-day Amen Corner is chiefly modern, though two brick houses next to the great claret-painted wooden gates that shut in Amen Court are a survival from the past. In Amen Court there is an unbroken line of seventeenth century houses, facing the back of Stationers' Ha'l, which were built by Sir Christopher Wren. The court is the ecclesiastical residence for many of the dignitaries connected with St. Paul's. The name "Amen Corner" became famous in American politics in the last decade of the nineteenth century, because it was facetiously bestowed upon a portion of the entrance hall to the Fifth Avenue Hotel, in New York, where Thomas C. Platt, the local Republican boss, used to gather his henchmen around him.

America. The origin of this name for the two continents

of the western hemisphere is not absolutely settled, but the weight of evidence tends to these conclusions:

That it was coined from the name of an Italian explorer, a quondam companion of Columbus, Amerigo Vespucci (latinized according to mediæval custom into Americus Vespucius), who was wrongly supposed to be the original discoverer of the American mainland; that the coiner was one Martin Waldseemüller * (known to literature by his græco-latinized pseudonyme of Martinus Hylacomylus); that the word so coined first appeared in a book entitled "Cosmographiae Introductio," printed in April, 1507, at the village of St. Dié in Lorraine, and that its application was then limited to South America, editors and publishers accepting the current misconception that the West Indies discovered by Columbus were part of the mainland of Asia. Hence the little village of St. Dié, not infelicitously styled the Baptismal Font of America, has acquired an interest out of all proportion to its size. Founded about A. D. 660 by St. Deodate, ex-bishop of Nevers, its name was successively abridged to Saint Deodat, Saint Diez, Saint Diey, and finally, by an edict of Pope Leo IX to the St. Dié of modern times. About the end of the fifteenth century, Walter Lud, secretary to Rèné II, duke of Lorraine, joined some of the canons of the monastery at Saint Dié in establishing a club or society for mutual inspiration and assistance, under the title of the Gymnase Vosgien, or Academy of the Vosgès,—Saint Dié being situated in those mountains. The fame of this society attracted thither certain scholarly neighbors, notable among whom were Martin Waldseemüller, from Freiburg in Baden, and Matthias Ringmann, a native of Schlettstadt in Alsace. In 1494 the Gymnasium acquired one of those newly invented and marvellous machines, a printing-press, which in the year 1507 turned out the "Cosmographiae Introductio." Its full title may be thus translated: "An Introduction to Cosmography, together with some Principles of Geography necessary to the purpose. Also, Four Voyages of Americus Vespucius. A Description of Universal Geography, both Stereometrical and Planometrical, together with what was unknown to Ptolemy and has been recently discovered."

This book was the joint production of Waldseemüller and Ringmann, but the latter's labors seem to have been confined to translating Vespucci's Italian into Latin. Certainly Wald-

---

* "Wald-see-müller" in German means "miller of the lake in the woods." In Greek "hyle" means a forest and "mylos" a miller. Hence the compound Hylacomylus, frequently corrupted into Ilacomilus.

seemüller wrote the famous paragraph in the introduction, now imprinted on the memories of American geographers, which suggested that, as each of the three older continents (Europe, Asia, Africa) had a name, this newly discovered one also should have a name. Here is the original Latin text, and its English equivalent:

Nunc vero et hae partes sunt latius lustratae, et alia quarta pars per Americum Vesputium (ut in sequentibus audietur) inventa est, quam non video cur quis jure vetet ab Americo ·inventore, sagacis ingenio viro, Amerigen quasi Americi terram, sive Americam dicendam; cum et Europa et Asia a mulieribus sua sortita sint ·nomina.

Now verily, as these parts are more extensively explored, and another fourth part has been discovered by Americus Vesputius (as will hereafter appear), I see no reason why any one should forbid this to be named Amerige, after Americus, the discoverer, a wise and sagacious man, or as much as to say the land of Americus, or indeed America, inasmuch as both Europe and Asia have a feminine form of name from the names of women.

Let us give Lud, the ducal secretary, all the credit that is due to him also. In the same year, 1507, and probably before the appearance of the "Cosmographiae Introductio," he had published a four-leaved pamphlet, "Speculi Orbis Declaratio," condensing the narratives of Amerigo Vespucci, and also containing some Latin verses ending as follows:

Sed quid plura: situ, gentis, moresque repte
'Americi parva mole libellus habet.

But hold, enough! Of the American race,
New found, the home, the manners here you trace,
By our small book set forth in little space.

Nevertheless, it was Waldseemüller who drew and engraved the *mappo mundi,* or map of the world, affixed to the "Introductio." On this map the name of America designates a narrow strip of land then thought to be an accurate outline of the southern continent, the first attempt ever made by any cartographer to locate it under that designation.

The only plausible opponent of the Vespucci theory is Dr. Jules Marcou. He claims that the explorer was baptized Alberico (or Albericus in Latin), but that the name Americus or Americo was unknown in Italy, or indeed anywhere in the old world, before the year 1504. It comes, he insists, from a certain ridge of mountains near Costa Rica which from time immemorial have been called by the natives Amerrique. Of course it was not spelled so in a language which had no letters or spelling. This chain was supposed to be the Eldorado of the new world. Hence Amerrique became the favorite name among gold hunters seeking transatlantic and transpacific shores. Possibly Vespucius had it on the brain, talked largely about it, and having been named Alberico was nicknamed Americo. This is thrown out merely as a suggestion. What appears certain to Marcou is that he never signed the name Americo.

America, Cost of its Discovery. A Chicago antiquary has ascertained that the famous first voyage of Columbus cost only $7000 in terms of our present currency.

Isabella of Spain did not bear the whole, or even the greater part, of the expense. The two brothers, Martin and Vicente Pinzon, who respectively commanded the Pinto and the Nina, while Columbus himself managed the Santa Maria, not only supplied two of the vessels of the little fleet, but also contributed a considerable proportion of the funds necessary for its equipment and maintenance.

The account books of the Pinzons, lately discovered, show what the brothers contributed to the discovery of America, or, at least, what were certain of the more important items of expense incidental to the expedition. Columbus in his capacity of commander received the munificent sum of 1500 pesetas, or about $300 a year, while his two captains received 900 pesetas a year. The members of the crews are said to have received 50 reals a month, which would amount to about $2.50 in current cash. The cost of the food was fixed at six pesetas a month for each man, which is to say about $1.50 for the month, and four to five cents a day. The cannon of all three ships cost about 14,000 pesetas, or not very much more than it will cost to fire a single charge from one of the big cannon on the latest dreadnoughts. From August, 1492, to March, 1493, the duration of the first expedition, Columbus is said to have given to his pilots and sailors, according to these old account books, 22,000 pesetas as their pay.

The expedition appears to have cost altogether about 36,000 pesetas, or a little over $7000 in the money of to-day.

America. This famous yacht was built at New York by George Steers and launched in March, 1851. Her principal owner was J. C. Stevens, who in 1844 had founded the New York Yacht Club and become its first commodore. She was of the type known as a New York pilot-boat. Her trial races were sailed against the sloop *Maria*, also owned by Commodore Stevens. The *Maria* was known as the fastest yacht in the world, and it was thought the *America* did well in winning one race out of three. The year 1851 was notable for the opening of the first world's fair ever held, at the Crystal Palace in

London. Among the ceremonies attending the opening was a great international yacht-race at Cowes, England. The *America* was sent over to represent the nation which had built her and whose colors she bore. . She sailed across the ocean in seventeen days under cruising rig. From the moment of her arrival at Cowes she became an object of curiosity and apprehension. The fame of the New York pilot-boats, then as now swift and seaworthy vessels, was great in England. " The most singular unanimity prevailed," wrote the correspondent of the *New York Herald*, " that the ' Yankee ' (as she is most improperly styled) was able to outsail creation, with the exception, at least, of another Yankee, the *Maria*. Yet still the lurking hope, which ever filled Mr. Micawber's bosom, that ' something might turn up ' to save the honor of the old land, was lingering around many a heart, and now and then the cheerful assurance would burst forth that, even if the *America* carried off the cup this time, there would be half a score of British schooners this time twelvemonth ready and able to beat her. She was ' only a trick of build ; ' she would only win once and then be found out."

Among the crowds came majesty itself. The royal family and the court shared in the universal curiosity excited by the stranger. The royal yacht, the *Victoria and Albert,* bore its distinguished namesakes down to the Isle of Wight to gratify this curiosity.

The Regatta of the Royal Yacht Squadron was scheduled for Friday, August 22, 1851. A challenge cup made of silver was to be the guerdon of the victor. Shortly after nine o'clock the yachts were at their stations off the club-house, the *America* lying considerably astern,—a strange-looking craft enough, with her long, low b'ack hull, her breadth of beam and her thick, stiff-looking, rakish masts. Pitted against her were fourteen yachts, of which six were schooners and eight cutters. Among these were the flower of the English sporting navy, the choicest products of transatlantic shipbuilding skill. At ten o'clock the signal gun was fired from the club-house. Before the smoke had well cleared away the fleet was under way, moving steadily to the east with the tide and a gentle breeze. The only laggard was the *America,* which did not move for a second or so after the others. Steamers, short boats, and yachts of all sizes buzzed along on each side of the course and spread away for miles over the rippling sea.

If the British heart leaped with a momentary exultation over the slowness of the *America* in getting under way, it was only momentary. She soon began to creep up on her opponents, passing some of the cutters to windward. In a quarter of an hour she left them all behind, save only the *Constance, Beatrice,* and *Fairy Queen,* which were well together, and went a'ong smartly with the light breeze. In another quarter of an hour she was clear of them all. Off Sandown Bay, the wind freshening, she carried away her jib-boom, but, as she was well handled, the mishap produced no ill effect, her competitors gaining a trifle, but not approaching her. From the moment she rounded St. Catherine's Point the race was practically over.

"Pshaw, sir! catch her?" said an old sea-dog to the *Herald* correspondent, "You might as well set a bulldog to catch a hare."

When finally she reached the starting vessel at 8.35 P.M. there was no competitor in sight, but twenty minutes later the *Aurora* arrived at the stake-boat and was awarded second honors.

In the *Illustrated London Journal,* a few days later, appeared a cartoon which showed the interior of the cabin of the royal yacht. The queen was at lunch, waiting the return off the Needles of the racers. Her Majesty says:

"Signal master, are the yachts in sight?"
"Yes, may it please your Majesty."
"Which is first?"
"The *America.*"
"Which is second?"
"Ah, your Majesty, there is no second!"

The victory was received by the British public with goodnatured regret. Something of the prevailing sentiment is shown in the following verses that appeared at the time in the *London Punch:*

THE BATTLE OF THE YATCHES, OR THE VICTORY OF THE YANKEE
YACHT AMERICA.

A Pathetic Copy of Verses Made by a British Tar at Spithead.

Oh, weep ye British sailors true,
 Above or under hatches,
Here's Yankee Doodle been and come
 And beat our crackest yatches.
They started all to run a race,
 And wor well timed with watches;
But oh! they never had no chance,
 Had any of our yatches.

The Yankee she delayed at first.
 Says they, "She'll never catch us,"
And flung up their tarpaulin hats—
 The owners of the yatches!
But presently she walked along;
 "Oh dear," says they, "she'll match us."
And stuck on their tarpaulin hats,
 The owners of the yatches.

Then deep we ploughs along the sea
    The Yankee scarcely scratches;
And cracks on every stitch of sail
    Upon our staggering yatches.
But one by one she passes us
    While bitterly we watches
And utter imprecations on
    The builder of our yatches.

And now she's quite hull down ahead,
    Her sails like little patches.
For sand barges and cotters we
    May sell our boasted yatches.
We faintly hear the club-house gun—
    The silver cup she snatches,
And all the English clubs are done,
    The English clubs of yatches!

They say she didn't go by wind,
    But wheels, and springs, and satches.
And that's the way she weathered on
    Our quickest going yatches.
But them's all lies, I'm bound to say—
    Although they're told by batches—
'Twas bulk of hull and cut of sail
    That did for all our yatches.

But novelty, I hear them say,
    Fresh novelty still hatches!
The Yankee yacht the keels will lay
    Of many new club yatches.
And then we'll challenge Yankeeland,
    From Boston Bay to Natchez,
To run their crackest craft agin
    Our spick and span new yatches.

Soon after the victory an English nobleman, Lord de Blaquiere, bought the *America,* selling her subsequently to Viscount Templeton, who changed her name to *Camilla.* After being in commission for short periods, she was laid up at Cowes and Gosport until 1859, and in that year was taken to Pitcher's Yard at Northfleet on the Thames. When hauled out of the water, she was found to be so rotten that she was entirely rebuilt, Pitcher taking out the frames and substituting new frames of the same shape in English oak. Her planking was stripped and replaced with teak and elm, and she was redecked, so that a practically new vessel of the same form was turned out of the repair shops. Nothing of the old *America* survived save the golden eagle which formerly graced her stern, and this had been left behind at Gosport.

The subsequent history of the *America* must be summarized as briefly as possible. At the outbreak of the civil war she was purchased from her English owner by some one in Savannah, where she arrived late in 1861. Her purchaser's name has not been preserved in the customs records. At Savannah a gun was mounted on her and she was renamed the *Memphis*. She was no longer a racing yacht, but a blockade runner and despatch boat for the Confederacy. Lurking about the Florida keys, dodging men-of-war, and now and then slipping over to Nassau or Bermuda, she lived the life of a pirate schooner. Finally she was trapped in the St. John's River in Florida. A gunboat was sent to capture her. To prevent this her captain scuttled and sunk her. She was floated, and assigned to the government for the use of the Naval Academy, who restored to her the old name of *America*. In 1870 the United States government sold her for $5000 to General Butler, in whose family she still remains.

The late Dixon Kemp from time to time called attention to the interesting fact that the golden eagle taken off the *America's* stern might be seen on the top of the Eagle Hotel at Ryde, England, this hostelry being just opposite the entrance to Ryde Pier. Winfield Thomson, in his "History of the America's Cup," says: "She left the yard at Northfleet minus the golden eagle and scroll that had adorned her stern, and for years that patriotic emblem graced the parapet of the Eagle Hotel at Ryde, a sign of a publican."

Some time in May, 1911, the bird was reported to have flown from its perch, or, in Thomson's more mellifluous language, "that patriotic emblem no longer graced the parapet of the Eagle Hotel." A correspondent of the London *Field* learned that the eagle had been bought by Messrs. Purnell and Purnell of Ryde. "The eagle is a nice piece of decorative carving," says this authority, "and is well-proportioned and in perfect preservation. It seems to be carved from pine. It is nine feet across the wings, and is two feet nine inches high. A slight curve is observable in its structure, as the bird and scroll originally spread across the curved stern of the yacht. Messrs. Purnell have gone to considerable trouble to ascertain how the *America's* eagle came to be placed over the Eagle Hotel. It was removed from her stern before she went up to Pitcher's Yard, Northfleet, in 1859, by Camper and Nicholsons, at Gosport, and an old pensioner of Camper and Nicholsons, William Nobbs, recollects seeing the eagle in their store at Gosport, after its removal from the stern of the yacht."

In order to preserve the history of the *America's* eagle, several affidavits have been made in connection with its removal from Gosport to Ryde, which are of interest. Among others, George Gawn, a former yacht hand, testified as follows:

I remember perfectly well the international yacht race in the Solent which was won by the schooner *America* from the *Arrow* in the year 1851. As a lad I was with my father employed on Lord Templeton's yacht the *Smoke Pigs*, and in the year of the race remember quite well sailing to Gosport and there seeing the *America* on the beach with this eagle on her stern. I also remember the stir and talk that was caused when the *America* had been at Gosport and the eagle which was on her stern was brought to Ryde and fixed on the Eagle Hotel, where the same always has been and now remains. (See *New York Evening Post,* June 7, 1911.)

In 1912 the eagle came into the possession of the New York Yacht Club.

America's Cup. This trophy, which was won by the yacht *America* in 1851 (see above entry), is alternatively known as "the Queen's cup."

The latter name is sometimes deemed an error. Would-be experts have pointed out that the Royal Yacht Squadron Cup competed for in the famous race at Cowes was established by the Royal Yacht Club and not by the Queen. True enough. But these critics forget a strange bit of boorishness on the part of the English yachting authorities. After the race they refused to give the *America* the trophy she had won, presenting it instead to one of her badly beaten opponents. Queen Victoria, hearing of the unsportsmanlike proceeding, immediately presented another cup. It is this duplicate cup which is held to-day by the New York Yacht Club.

The *America's* cup is a silver pitcher, worth originally one hundred guineas. By common consent it became the property of Stevens after the victory. He presented it to the New York Yacht Club, of which he was commodore. In 1857 it was dedicated as "perpetually a challenge cup for friendly competition between foreign countries." The trophy at once assumed a new value out of all proportion to its cost. In place of being forgotten after a few years, like the ordinary challenge cups, it has become more and more famous with each recurring struggle for its possession, until to-day it is looked upon with covetous eyes by the entire foreign yachting world.

The first effort to win back the silver trophy was made on August 8, 1870, by James Ashbury's English schooner yacht *Cambria*. She contended against a fleet of American keel and centre-board schooners which started from anchorage. The centre-board *Magic* won the race, beating the English yacht by 39 minutes, 12.3 seconds.

The *America* was among the cup-defenders. The Navy Department, to which she belonged, yielding to the pressure of patriotic sentiment, had put her in racing trim and entered her for the contest. She gave a good account of herself, coming in fourth and beating the *Cambria* (which came in fifth) by 13 minutes, 47.5 seconds.

Ampulla. The legend of the ampulla brought from heaven by a white dove, and containing the oil with which the Frank king Clovis was anointed by St. Rémy at his baptism, in 496, is, as every respectable legend ought to be, considerably younger than the fact it relates to. It is mentioned for the first time by Hincmar, Archbishop of Rheims, who was born in 806 and died in 882. The ampulla was always used thereafter at the coronation of the kings of France down to Charles X, being kept at Rheims in the tomb of St. Rémy. It was a glass vial, forty-one millimetres high, with an aperture sixteen millimetres in circumference. It was filled with a kind of "gruel thick and slab," which, in the long run, had become solidified and of a reddish-brown color. When it was time to use it at the ceremony of coronation, the High Prior of St. Rémy, from whose neck the rich shrine which contained it hung by a silver chain, scooped from it a particle by means of a golden needle. and this was mingled with the chrism (a compound of oil and balm), preparatory to the anointing of the king.

The legend says that there was such relation between the vial and the life of the reigning king as caused the bulk of the ba'm it contained to diminish if his health happened to be impaired. The ampulla was destroyed in 1793 by Ruhl, a member of the convention, then appointed commissioner in the department of the Marne. But before delivering the vial to that officer, Abbé Seraine, the curé of St. Rémy, took out of it a part, which was reverently kept in a crystal vessel enclosed in a silver-gilt shrine, and was used for the last time at the coronation of Charles X, in 1825.

Andes, Christ of the. At Cambre Pass, on the mountain frontier between Chili and the Argentine Republic and nearly 13,000 feet above the level of the sea, stands a colossal statue bearing the above name. Cast in the bronze from the cannon of opposing Chileans and Argentines, it was placed on the boundary line in March, 1904, as a symbol of the perpetual peace which then and there was sworn to by the rival nations. "Sooner shall these mountains crumble to dust," says an inscription on its base, "than shall the people of Argentine and Chili break the peace to which they have pledged themselves at the feet of Christ the Redeemer." The entire monument consists of a figure of the Savior, twenty-six feet high, placed on a gigantic column surmounted by a globe, whereon the configuration of the earth is outlined. One hand holds a cross and the other is extended in blessing.

Apes in Hell, Leading. What is the origin of the ancient saying that o'd maids are doomed to lead apes in hell?

This question has never been definitely settled. Steevens explains it by saying that the "leading of apes in hell" is an act of retribution to be performed by women who have avoided the responsibilities of caring for children, *leading them* about in this life.

Malone says that this was one of the duties of the bear-ward, who carried an ape along with his bear. Beatrice says ("Much Ado About Nothing," Act ii, Sc. 1):

> Therefore I will even take sixpence in earnest
> Of the bear-ward, and lead his apes into hell.

The explanation given by Nares is that, inasmuch as the word "ape" is synonymous with the word "fool," it means that coquettes who here lead men on without the intention of marrying them will be doomed to do the same hereafter.

Douce says that homicides and adulterers were formerly compelled to lead an ape by the neck, with the tail of the ape in their mouths.

There is among the Harleian MSS. a warrant of Richard III, appointing John Brown to the office of bear-herd, which speaks of his "diligent service to the king" as the ground for granting him the privilege of wandering about the country leading bears and apes. (See also WALSH: *Handy-book of Literary Curiosities,* p. 64.)

Appendicitis. How recently this disease has come into prominence with the medical profession and the public may be realized from the fact that the word does not make its appearance in the great "New English Dictionary" published by the Oxford Press. Dr. Murray, the editor, explained this omission in a letter to *Notes and Queries:*

When the portion of the dictionary dealing with *app-* was written in 1883, we had before us a single reference, from a recent medical source, for this word. As words in *-itis* are not (in origin) English in form, but Græco-Latin, and thus do not come within the scope of an English dictionary, unless, like *bronchitis,* they happen to be in English use, I referred our quotation for *appendicitis* to a well-known distinguished medical professor . . . His answer was that *appendicitis* was a name recently given to a very obscure and rare disease; the term was purely technical or professional, and had even less claim to inclusion in an English dictionary than hundreds of other Latin or Latinized Greek terms of which the medical lexicons are full and which no one thinks of as English.

The New York *Scrapbook* for April, 1909, published a

communication that sets up an interesting claim as to the first operation for appendicitis performed in the United States or, for that matter, in any country.' It was suggested by this paragraph, which had appeared in a previous number of the *Scrapbook*.

In January, 1885, the first operation for appendicitis was performed at St. Luke's Hospital, Denver, Colorado. The patient was a young lady of Davenport, Iowa, who has the distinction of being the first person on record to have the vermiform appendix removed. It was because of this operation, which was purely experimental, and only resorted to in the last extreme, that the possibility of removing the appendix was discovered. The case is written up in all the medical books, and in the *Colorado Magazine*, which prefaces the account with a note that states that investigations show that this case antedates all others by more than two years.

The paragraph brought out the following letter:

5 SEASIDE TERRACE, LYNN, MASS., Feb. 14, 1909.

TO THE EDITOR OF THE SCRAP BOOK:

In the February number of *The Scrap Book*, under the heading of "Important First Things in America," I note one in reference to an operation for appendicitis performed in Denver in 1885.

For the first two months after the battle of Gettysburg, July to September, 1863, I had charge—acting as hospital steward—of a ward in the Seminary hospital containing twenty-four wounded men as patients. One of these was a young French-Canadian, belonging, I think, to a Michigan regiment. He had been shot through the abdomen, the ball entering just below the umbilicus and passing out to the right of the spine, but without perforating any of the intestines.

During the first three weeks, in dressing the wound, several times I found that the appendix had exuded from the abdominal wound, which I would replace and again apply compresses and bandages.

One afternoon, upon returning from a short absence, I found that the patient himself had removed the bandage, which had become loosened, and, finding the appendix again outside the wound, had taken a pair of scissors and cut it off. To say that I was frightened is putting it mildly.

As soon as I could, I found the attending surgeon and reported the case. Keeping careful watch the next few days, and seeing no ill results, the case was finally forgotten—there were so many distractions. But the wound healed, and when the hospital was closed, five or six weeks later, our patient, with the other inmates of the hospital, all on the road to complete recovery, were transferred to hospitals in Baltimore, and I to Washington.

The name of this extraordinary patient, as also the young surgeon's, I cannot now recall.

I have mentioned the incident to many surgeons since, and, to my surprise, they have invariably said that it was the first case of the kind they have ever heard of.   J. W. COLCORD.

It is evident, from the following paragraph in the *Boston Transcript*, that, in popular belief at least, the loss of an appendix may involve serious moral deterioration to the loser.

The Rev. Samuel Van Vranken Holmes, who preached at Harvard last Sunday, has furnished the clerk with documentary evidence regarding the inestimable value of appendices. In Buffalo, where he ministers to a large and influential church, he has lately been involved in a little unpleasantness with the Torreyites. It chanced that his course of addresses on the modern view of Scripture synchronized with the Torrey meetings and drew down upon him the rebuke of that mighty evangelist, whereupon his mails grew heavy with letters of protest. One of those epistles ran something like this: "Sir: I understand now why you have been led astray by the higher critics. It is less than a year, I am told, since you underwent the operation for appendicitis, and any physician will inform you that when the vermiform appendix comes out the patient suffers the total loss of his moral nature. This explains your case pretty clearly."

Apple. The commonest of all fruit and man's greatest friend in the vegetable kingdom. Having appeared on earth about the same time as its beneficiary, it has followed him in his migrations about the globe, gathering up with it a train of mystic traditions. In Greece its name (Μηλον) was applied to sheep and to all other forms of wealth; for sheep in the earlier ages were the truest representatives of property. This is indicated in the English word "pecuniary," derived from the Latin *pecunia* (money), and that in its turn from *pecus,* a flock of sheep. Theophrastus enumerates the apple among the more civilized (urbaniores) fruit. The myths that concern it meet us in every age and country. Aphrodite's apple of discord is a far-off echo from Eve's apple of sin and death, for legend, poetry, and painting are alike satisfied that it was an apple which grew on the tree of the knowledge of good and evil. Iduna in the prose Edda keeps a box of apples, whereof the gods, "when they feel the approach of age, have only to taste, and forthwith they become young again." In Grecian myth the dragon guards the sacred apples of the Hesperides, as in Hebrew scripture the serpent watches over the apple in the Garden of Eden. The golden bird seeks the golden apples of the king's garden in many a Norse story; and when the tree bears no more, Frau Bertha reveals to her favorite that it is because a mouse gnaws at the tree's root. Indeed, the kind mother-goddess is sometimes personified as an apple-tree. But oftener the apple is the tempter in Norse mythology also, and sometimes makes the nose grow so that the sacred pear alone can restore it to normal size. Azrael, the angel of death, is sometimes fabled to perform his mission by holding an apple to the nose of the dying. It is, however, the healing fruit of the Arabian tales. And in England there is a common rhyme:

> Eat an apple going to bed:
> Make the doctor beg his bread.

In many parts of Germany the apple is deemed potent against warts. In England a decayed apple is rubbed against the excrescences. In Pomerania an apple eaten on Easter morning is a preventive of fevers, and in Westphalia of jaundice. In Silesia and Thuringia an apple is scraped, from the top to cure diarrhœa, and from the bottom to cure costiveness. But in Hesse apples are avoided on New Year's day, lest they produce abscesses.

The apple has been a phallic emblem with many races. In various parts of rural England, the young people join hands and dance around apple-trees, carolling their hopes for a prolific year, much in the same fashion as if the tree were the clearly phallic maypole. The blossoming of an apple-tree in harvest betokens a marriage or sometimes the funeral of the master of the house. Horace mentions the use of apple-pips in love affairs. A lover would take a pip between the finger and thumb and shoot it upward, and if it struck the ceiling his or her wish would be fulfilled. This superstition survives in Germany, where on New Year's night it is customary to shoot an apple-seed from between the fingers with an invocation; and in the direction of its flight the sweetheart may be looked for. Apples also figure everywhere in the divinations, on Hallowe'en or All Saints' Day (see WALSH, *Curiosities of Popular Customs*, p. 507).

The custom of throwing an apple-peel over the head to determine the marital future of the thrower is ancient and widespread. The initial of the coming sweetheart may be detected in the form the rind assumes when it has fallen. If the rind break, a life of celibacy is indicated.

Within the limits of its well-marked characteristics no fruit has been brought nearer to perfection than the apple. Springing from a harsh and crabbed ancestry, it now holds its own with the most luscious grapes and peaches. It is in England and Normandy and the United States that the most notable improvement in quality has been effected. Selection is the special cause of this improvement, for in most other respects the culture of pippin fruit was carried on with great skill and success in several of the Mediterranean countries at least two thousand years ago. The trick of grafting, for instance, is mentioned by Pliny as a common practice long before his time. Pliny knew twenty-nine sorts of "apples," including under this term the quince and probably the citron family also. In England there are some four or five hundred distinct varieties which have been obtained by cherishing and even worshipping the fruit for centuries. Whatever art the Romans had in improving the quality of their fruit, no doubt they brought it with them to British shores. So well was the indigenous stock nursed and developed, whether by Roman settlers or by monks, that when St. Brieuc and his eighty companions sought refuge in Armorica from the ravaging English, one of the number planted in their new home an orchard three miles long, which preserved his name for over six centuries, and laid the foundation, as some maintain, of the Normandy cider industry. Be this as it may, the apple was a characteristic fruit of Britain; and in every age, as was to be expected, the clergy were its cultivators in chief. They grew the fruit in their gardens, prayed for it in their religious ceremonies, sheltered it with their laws, and named it when pronouncing the blessings of God upon their princes. From them the esteem and veneration would soon pass down to the common folk, ready as they always were to weave the teachings of the Church into their everyday superstitions and language. The Latin chronicles and institutes, and the early English poems, contain many references to the apple and pear; whilst it is probable that a drink was made of the fermented juice long before Wiclif and Chaucer employed the term cider, or syder, to denote a strong coarse brew of any kind.

A little apologue (pray do not scent a pun), which went the round of the American press in 1911, sums up very neatly the valuable properties of the common or garden apple:

"Do you know what you're eating?" said the doctor to the girl

"An apple, of course."

"You are eating," said the doctor, "albumen, sugar, gum, malic acid, gallic acid, fibre, water, and phosphorus."

"I hope those things are good. They sound alarming."

"Nothing could be better. You ate, I observed, rather too much meat for dinner. The malic acid of apples neutralizes the excess of chalky matter caused by too much meat, and thereby helps to keep you young. Apples are good for your complexion; their acids drive out the noxious matters which cause skin eruptions. They are good for your brain, which those same noxious matters, if retained, render sluggish. Moreover, the acids of the apple diminish the acidity of the stomach that comes with some forms of indigestion. The phosphorus, of which apples contain a larger per cent. than any other fruit or vegetable, renews the essential matter of the brain and spinal column. Oh, the ancients were not wrong when they esteemed the apple the food of the gods—the magic renewer of youth to which the gods resorted when they felt themselves growing old and feeble. I think I'll have an apple," concluded the doctor.

Apple Kings. The title of "apple king of the world" was bestowed upon Frederick Willhouse, of Kansas, who died in January, 1911, at the age of eighty-two. He owned, planted, and superintended the largest and most profitable apple orchard in the world, comprising at the time of his death 1600 acres in Leavenworth, Osage, and Miami Counties. His first crop, gathered in the fall of 1880, was 1500 bushels from 537 acres. Ten years later his orchards made their greatest yield, 79,710 bushels, aside from "culls." It required 200 cars to ship the crop to Eastern markets.

More than any other man in this country he taught and proved that apples could be grown with profit. He had faith in the American apple, but he considered that its development required study. "He knew not only all that was known about the culture of the fruit and the pests that infest orchards, but also all about the preservation, care, and marketing of his products. If some of his best cider was 'treated' by men to whom it had been sold and afterward turned out as champagne, he as a good prohibitionist in prohibitionist Kansas was not to be blamed."—*New York Sun,* January 14, 1911, editorial page.

Another pomologist who gained the title of "apple king" was E. L. Stewart, president (1911) of the Washington State Horticultural Society. "He got a yearly net return of $725 an acre from a six-acre orchard, and for five years the same orchard has paid him an annual net interest of 10 per cent. on a valuation of $4000 an acre.

"B. B. Holcomb sold $1806 worth of apples from one acre in the Wenatchee Valley, and the same year the peaches, apples, and pears from the Richey and Gilbert thirteen-acre orchard at North Yakima sold for $15,192, or $1168 an acre. From one acre of apples in the Wenatchee Valley A. V. Huff one season sold 2200 boxes which at $1.50 a box netted him $2000, and Charles B. Reed the same year got a net return from his pear orchard of $1700 an acre, while O. C. Haggart, who lives near Spokane, one year sold $360 worth of strawberries and p'ants from one-third of an acre."—*New York Sun,* July 14, 1911.

A few interesting statistics about apple-raising were given to a reporter of the Washington (D. C.) *Post* by Mr. Moore, a former governor of Washington State, in August, 1911.

"The farmers who raise apples," said Mr. Moore, "are making money, of course, but it might amaze you to know, when you pay five or eight cents for a single apple, that our home orchard man sold it for about one cent. I paid fifteen cents for my apple at breakfast this morning.

"I do not know how many people handled it before it got to the hotel, but the farmer at home got a mighty small part of the price I paid. With the small price paid to the producer of apples, it is amazing how much a small orchard will bring in. I know a school-teacher who bought ten acres of apple-trees, and out of the profits from ten acres he was enabled to buy one hundred acres. Now he has just sold that orchard for $150,000."

Apple, Mike. In Connecticut there grows a peculiar fruit called the "Mike apple." It has a fair skin and an excellent flavor. Each individual apple exhibits somewhere in its pulp a red speck, like a tinge of fresh blood. And thereby hangs a strange tale.

In the eighteenth century a farmer called Micah Rood lived upon the outlands of Norwich, Conn. He was full of youthful zeal and ambition. Suddenly his habits changed. He grew idle, restless, and intemperate. He neglected his cattle; he shunned his neighbors. Some attributed the change to witchcraft; others hinted at insanity. Next spring, when the orchards burst into blossom, a strange phenomenon was noticed in Rood's orchard. On one apple-tree the flowers had changed from white to red. August came, and the red blossoms developed into fruit. When the large yellow apples fell from the branches, each was found to contain a well-defined globule, known thereafter as "the drop of blood." Conjecture developed into suspicion and it was recalled that during the previous autumn a foreign peddler had passed through Norwich, had spent the night at Micah Rood's, and had never been seen again. Some one suggested that the young farmer had murdered him for his money and buried the body under the apple-tree. But though search was made the *corpus delicti* was never found. Micah died a mental and physical wreck in 1728.

Apple-trees. What may be the oldest of all the apple-trees in America that can be traced directly back to an English ancestry still stands in front of the chief commissary's office in Vancouver, Washington. The story engraved on a tablet in the enclosure built around this relic from the past runs as follows:

"At a lunch party in London about 1825, given in honor of some young gentlemen who were about to embark for Fort Vancouver in the employ of the Hudson's Bay Company, seeds of the fruit eaten were slyly slipped by some young ladies into the waistcoat pockets of the young men, and upon their arrival at their destination the young men in overhauling their wardrobes discovered the seeds and gave them to Bruce, the gardener at the fort."

Originally there were three trees which grew from these seeds, but the two others have disappeared.

The Vandiver apple-tree out in Missouri is believed by Westerners to be the largest in America. The St. Joseph *Observer* gives this account of how it was measured in July, 1911:

A Pleasant Hill man was out to the Amos farm northeast of town the other day and measured that famous Vandiver apple-tree, which is supposed to be the largest in the West, if not in the entire United States. The tree measured exactly thirteen feet around at a distance of two feet above the ground, which is a little better than four feet in diameter. Seventy-five or eighty years has this old monarch stood, and it is still a bearing tree.

The most famous apple-tree in American history is that which until recently survived on the battle-field of Appomattox, Va. When (April 9, 1865) General Robert E. Lee surrendered to General Ulysses S. Grant the two leaders met under an old apple-tree to discuss terms. The original tree has disappeared, but in 1911, on the anniversary of the surrender, Colonel George R. Armes, U. S. A., planted a young apple-tree on the exact spot where the great Southerner capitulated. The battle-field came into possession of Colonel Armes in 1891.

Apricot. Originally apricock,—from the Latin *proecoquus* or *praecox,* which was corrupted into the Low Greek *praikokion,* "early ripe,"—this word is derived from the same root as the adjective "precocious." In its original habitat, in Armenia, the apricot flowers very early, and hence may rightly be called precocious. The Greek word was corrupted into the Spanish *albaricoque,* and that into the French *abricot,* whence it passed newly mutilated into the English language. A freak of amateur etymology would derive "apricot" from the Latin *in aprico coctus* (cooked in April), which has at least a humorous claim upon notice.

The English Notes and Queries in 1850 published the following communication concerning a gigantic apricot tree in the garden of John Edwards Langton, Esq., of Maidenhead Berks, which the writer holds to be the largest tree of its sort in England:

It is a standard tree; and the trunk at one foot from the ground measures 4 feet 11 inches in circumference; at five feet from the ground (where the branches spring forth) the circumference is 4 feet 8 inches. It has four huge limbs, two of which measure respectively 44 and 33½ inches round. It had originally a fifth which fell a victim to a storm a few years since. The height is about 30 feet. The branches cover a space of 126 feet in circumference. It has borne *fourteen* bushels of fruit in a season; and *sixty* people have dined under its shade! The fruit is large, of a deep orange color, and delicious in flavor.

Archery in modern England differs in every way from that which prevailed when the long-bow was the favorite national weapon, and when English bowmen were the dread of Europe. Those were the days when the sheriffs looked to it that the people duly utilized their spare hours in practice with the bow and arrow, and when a man was pilloried in Cornhill for selling bad bowstrings. Bows, bowstrings, and arrows are now unknown among the yeomanry who, during the fourteenth and fifteenth centuries, supplied the archers that fought at Cressy, Poictiers, and Agincourt, and who do most of the fighting for the British realm. Strength of pull is not now, as then, the *sine qua non* of success on the battle-field. It is left to amateurs to sustain, not as a calling, but as a recreation, the reputation of English archery, and the responsibility is lightened by little sympathetic encouragement from the public. The bow, from being the favorite weapon in war and peace, has yielded in popularity to the rifle and the golf-stick. It is altogether ignored in the public schools, and when taken up by grown men is often only a last resort. Archery has lost ground. Once it was the ruling passion of Englishmen from prince to peasant, and country gentlemen carried their bows, as they now carry their guns, in search of deer and pheasant. But in these times neither prince nor peasant knows the sight of the bow. London itself is hard'y conscious that the headquarters of archery in England is in its very midst.

The prizes for archery in the olden days appear to have been various. We often hear of a complete suit of forest green, a deer, or a butt of wine. When the latter was the prize, the butt was commonly set up for a mark, and it was gained by him who cleft the bung. A round-headed arrow, called a bolt, was used for this purpose. The sign of a well-known inn in London, the Bolt in Tun, refers to this custom; and, as inns are remarkable for retaining their original signs, it is not improbable that its first owner had gained a butt of wine by his skill in archery.

Although the more robust of the old English yeomanry, with a Spanish yew bow, could give to the flight of their lighter shafts a range of twenty score, the ordinary distance at which they succeeded in wounding or killing man and horse was twelve score, or 240, yards. By the statute 33 Henry VIII, no youth having attained his full vigor was permitted, under a considerable fine, to practice at any shorter marks. Some very noticeable instances of success at this distance occur in the older chronicles. Drayton introduces a gray-haired veteran endeavoring to incite the youth of his day to join an expedition, destined for France, which resulted in victory at Agincourt, by quoting the feats of archery traditionally handed down by those who drew a good bow at Cressy.

> "And, boy," quoth he, "I've heard my grandsire say,
>   That once he did an English archer see
> Who, shooting at a French, twelve score away,
>   Quite through the body, nailed him to a tree."

Neade, a famous archer under Charles I, puts the ordinary range of the bow at from 320 to 400 yards. Carew states that the Cornish archers shot with ease 480 yards. There are accounts of the shaft being sent the distance of half a mi'e by some of the strong-armed bowmen of olden time.

None of the latter figures are historical. The longest shot authentically recorded in England is that of a secretary of the Turkish embassy, who in 1794 shot an arrow 463 yards with the wind, and 415 against it, in the presence of several members of the Toxopholite Society, who measured the distance and preserved the arrow.

The English record for recent times is that made in 1905, on the links at Le Touquet, by Sir Ralph Payne Gallwey. Shooting with a Turkish bow he covered a distance of 367 yards with his best arrow.

It is a remarkable fact, that, for at least two centuries after the invention of gunpowder and the gradual improvement in the construction of firearms coexistent with it, the bow should continue to hold its own as a valuable arm of the service. Bows were found on board that redoubtable man-of-war, the *Mary Rose*, sunk in an action with the French squadron at Spithead during the reign of Henry VIII; and one or two of those very rare specimens of old English missile weapons, found in the vessel's arm-chest by the divers employed to remove her timbers and those of the *Royal George*, are now preserved among the curiosities of the Tower and of the United Service Museum.

When Clerkenwell Church was being rebuilt (1791), contemporary archers manifested their respect for Sir William Wood, an old marshal of the Finsbury Archers, by expending a considerable sum in the re-embellishment and removal of his monument from the outside of the old to the interior of the new building; and the epitaph still survives to tell us—

> Sir William Wood lies very near this stone,
> In 's time, in archery excelled by none.
> Few were his equals, and this noble art
> Has suffered now in its most tender part;
> Long did he live the honour of the bow,
> And his great age to that alone did owe.

Queen Catherine, consort to Charles II, presented him with a large and splendid silver badge, now in possession of the Royal Toxophilites, Regent's Park. The tradition is, that the king, at a grand parade of bowmen in 1669, seeing an arrow remarkably well aimed, inquired who the archer was, and immediately knighted him.

Archery as a modern social pastime was revived in the later eighteenth century by Thomas Waring, "the father of modern archery." His doctor sometime in 1777 had recommended him to try the bow as a means of expanding a contracted chest. Sir Ashton Lever invited him to pitch his target in the gardens of Leicester House. In a very little time Mr. Waring's example was followed by others, Sir Ashton Lever himself among the number, and in 1780 a Royal Toxophilite Society was formed under the patronage of the Prince of Wales afterwards George IV. There is a well-known picture of His Royal Highness in the costume of captain-general of the Royal Kent Archers, a society which sprang into existence a little afterward. Before Mr. Waring's time there were only four archery societies, all of them in the north of England, and all organizations having an historical and antiquarian rather than a practical interest. In less than a decade after the founding of the Royal Toxophilites of Leicester House, upward of fifty associations formed after the same model sprang up in different parts of England. Early in the nineteenth century these figures were nearly doubled. Two societies should be named as presenting a connecting link between ancient and modern bowmanship,—the Royal Edinburgh Bowmen and the Richmond (Yorkshire) Archers. The former of these lay claim by royal charter to the curious privilege of acting as the body-guard of the reigning sovereign whenever he or she approaches within five miles of their metropolis. When George visited Scotland, this privilege was asked for and was granted. For more than two centuries, without the omission of a single year, the Edinburgh Bowmen have held a toxophilite competition for the silver arrow. The principle on which the managers of this meeting have gone, has been to select a part of England in which a taste for archery existed, and to choose a particular town—first, with an eye to its accommodation; secondly, with an eye to the opportunity offered to it of maturing and fostering local efforts. The society, we are also told, "helps to establish a kind of brotherhood among associations, some of whom, being in the remotest corners of the country, would scarcely otherwise be heard of out of their own respective districts." In other cases, again, where a society may be languishing and it is desirable to impart to it an impetus, the assembly of renowned bowmen and bowwomen has the effect of endowing it with fresh life and vigor.

Since the Grand Archery Meetings commenced in 1844, the highest score was made by H. A. Ford. This gentleman, who was champion of England from 1850 to 1860, marked in 1857 at Cheltenham the total of one thousand two hundred and fifty-one. Previously, in 1854, he had made one thousand and forty-five at Shrewsbury; and subsequently, in 1858, he made one thousand and seventy-six at Exeter.

A very remarkable case of the survival in modern America of the ancient English bow and arrow was discovered in 1878 by Professor Nathaniel S. Shaler, of Harvard, on the borders of Virginia and Kentucky. There, in a secluded valley, he found men hunting squirrels and rabbits with the old English short bow. These were not the contrivance of boys or of to-day, but were made and strung and the arrows fitted in the ancient manner. The men, some of them old, were admirably skilled in their use; they assured him that, like their forefathers before them, they had ever used the bow and arrows for small game, reserving the costly ammunition of the rifle for deer and bear. Thousands of these Kentucky families remain immovable in the original settled areas, and through endless intermarriage are keeping fresh not only the clan instinct with its primitive and fierce attributes, but something of the usetudes and speech of Elizabethan England, the progenitrix of the Anglo-Saxon overseas.

Argan. Among the most remarkable trees of the world is the argan, which abounds in Southern Morocco but is seldom seen elsewhere. A "forest" of argans has a curious scattered appearance, because the trees grow singly and far apart. They are very leafy, but seldom exceed twenty feet in height. The branches put out horizontally, and begin a yard above the ground. Sheep, cattle, and camels feed on the leaves, and goats will stand on their hind legs to reach them, but horses and mules refuse to touch them. The wood is very hard, and extremely useful to the natives, who make charcoal from it. The fruit, resembling a large olive, is used to feed cattle and to manufacture a valuable oil. It also furnishes the principal sustenance of many of the poorer natives.

Argand Lamp. Argand, a poor Swiss, invented a lamp with a wick fitted into a hollow cylinder up which a current of air was allowed to pass, thus giving a supply of oxygen to the interior as well as to the exterior of the circular frame.

At first Argand used the lamp without any chimney. One day he was busy in his workroom and sitting before the burning lamp. His little brother was amusing himself by placing a bottomless oil flask over different articles. Presently he placed it upon the flame of the lamp, which instantly shot up the long, circular neck of the flask with increased brilliancy. It did more, for it flashed into Argand's mind the idea of the lamp-chimney, by which his invention was perfected.

Arkansas or Arkansaw? Two pronunciations of the name

of this State are in common use—Ar-*kan*-sas and Arkan*saw*. History, philology, and even legis'ative enactment have decided in favor of the last form, and it is now universal among the inhabitants of the State. Outsiders, and especially New Englanders, usually prefer to pronounce the word as it is spelled. They forget that it is an attempt upon the part of the first French missionaries of Marquette's time to reproduce phonetically in French the name of a tribe of Indians. No Frenchman would ever pronounce the combination of letters in the manner favored by the New Englanders. The final *s* was and is silent, and the *a* has the nasal *aw,* so common in many Frenchmen's speech. As for the old comparativists, who, regardless of the inconsistency of English spelling, always inquire, "if Arkansas is Arkan*saw.* why is not Kansas, Kan*saw,*" they may be glad to learn that Kansas was *Kansaw,* and early Anglo-American travellers so pronounced it, and even attempted to spell it phonetica'ly in English, as can be seen in the report of Lieutenant Long's expedition to the Rocky Mountains, 1819–1821, where the word is spelled *Konza*—the nearest combination of English letters that can approach the true French sound.

In Arkansas, however, in the early days of statehood there was uncertainty as to the pronunciation.

From 1844 to 1848 Arkansas was represented in the United States Senate by Chester Ashley and Ambrose Sevier. Ashley, a New Englander by birth, always said Ar-kan'-sas. Sevier, a native of Tennessee and a grandson of Col. John Sevier, the hero of King's Mountain and the governor of the former State of Franklin, remained true to the Southern tradition and always spoke of his adopted State as Arkansaw'. At that time George M. Dallas, of Pennsylvania, was vice-president. Courteous gentleman as he was, Dallas always recognized this difference. In alluding to or addressing Mr. Ashley he always said "the senator from Arkan-sas," while Mr. Sevier always was "the gentleman from Ar-kan-saw."

Finally, to settle the question, the General Assembly of the State appointed a committee to investigate the subject. The committee decided upon Ar-kan-saw'. Thereupon the Assembly unanimously adopted the following concurrent resolution:

Concurrent resolution declaring the proper pronunciation of the name of the State of Arkansas.

Preamble: Whereas, Confusion of practice has arisen in the pronunciation of the name of our State, and it is deemed important that the true pronunciation should be determined for use in oral official proceedings; and

Whereas, The matter has been thoroughly investigated by the State

Historical Society and the Eclectic Society of Little Rock, which have agreed upon the correct pronunciation, as derived from history and the early usage of the American immigrants; be it therefore

Resolved, By both Houses of the General Assembly, that the only true pronunciation of the name of the State, in the opinion of this body, is that received by the French from the native Indians, and committed to writing in the French word representing the sound, and that it should be pronounced in three syllables, with the final "s" silent, the "a" in each syllable with the Italian sound, and the accent on the first and last syllables, being the pronunciation formerly, universally and now still most commonly used, and that the pronunciation with the accent on the second syllable with the sound of "a" in man and the sounding of the terminal "s" is an innovation to be discouraged. March, 1881.

The word "Arkansas" has no apparent connection with either the Comanche or Apache jargons, but it has a strong structural affinity with the language of the people who dwelt in that region prior to the Spanish conquest. Both orthography and pronunciation doubtless have been modified by the Creole element, but the similar forms and their pronunciation are sufficiently well preserved to indicate a custom which we might well consider good authority. For instance, we find Arkansas, Tensas, Aransas, and Kansas. In the first three the pronunciation is uniform; the final syllable is pronounced with silent *s* and Italian *a*, frequently broadened to *aw*. In the case of Kansas the intrusion of the Anglo-Saxon element has made short work of French vowels, and *Kansä* is now rarely heard.

· **Artichoke, Jerusalem.** The name of this esculent is one of the wonders of popular misapprehension. It is not an artichoke and it has no connection with Jerusalem. It was first cultivated in Italy (in the Farnese Garden at Rome, to be specific), and the Italians gave it the name of *Girasole articiocco*, or "sunflower artichoke." *Girare* means "to turn" and *sole* is the sun. A current superstition, supported by Ovid's poetical fable of Apollo and the nymph Clytie, declares that the turn-sole or sunflower (*q.v.*) always turns its flowers towards the sun. Science classifies the plant—under the name of *Helianthus tuberosus*—in the same family as the common sunflower (*Helianthus annuus*), which it resembles in stem, leaves, and flowers, though the latter, except in a favorable season, are inferior in size and color to those of the common sunflower.

Authorities are divided as to whether it is a native of North or South America. Alphonse de Candolle, in his "Origin of Cultivated Plants," p. 43, says it is a native of North America, and was brought to France in 1603 by Lescarbot and sold as *Topinambaux*, the present name being *Topinambour*. Littré gives *Topinambour* as the original name, being that of a people of Brazil, whence the plant was transplanted. Candolle says there is no such plant in Brazil. The word "Topinambour" is probably a French imitation of the Indian name for the plant, and is now derisively applied to gross, savage, or ignorant people.

One authority says the Jerusalem artichoke was introduced into England in 1617 by a Frenchman from Canada, where it was already known. Parkinson speaks of "Battatas de Canada, or Hierusalem Artichokes." Before this date, however, it had been brought to England from Italy or Spain as a delicacy. We read of it in Moffat's "Memoirs" as a dainty "sometimes only in the Isle of Sicily," selling for a crown apiece; and considered a fit gift for a king. In the expenditure account or Henry VIII's privy purse, is an entry of 3s 4d, paid to the servant of the Master Treasurer as a reward for bringing to the king a present of artichokes.

Lord Bacon, in his "Essay on Plantations" (1625) says: "See what esculent things will grow speedily within the year," and instances the "Artichock of Jerusalem." "Artichokks" or "Archecokks" are mentioned in Venner's "Via Recta," 1620, and very frequently in the literature of the 17th century, but rarely after the more nutritious potato superseded it in popularity. The artichoke tubers used to be called "Jerusa'em potatoes," and a soup made from them was called "Palestine Soup," thus extending their erroneous designation. Peacock says—in "Gryll Grange," ch. 1—"From this *girasole* we have made Jerusalem, and from the Jerusalem artichoke we make Palestine soup."

Artillery Company, The Ancient and Honorable. London and Boston alike boast of a civic militia troop bearing this title, the latter being the legitimate transatlantic offspring of the former.

Bear in mind that artillery in its original sense meant the cross-bow and the long-bow. It was this sort of artillery that was used, in practice on Finsbury Field, by those citizen warriors of ancient London who in August, 1537, banded themselves together as the "Fraternity" or "Guild" of St. George. Members enjoyed the privilege of wearing embroidered silk, velvet, satin, or damask gowns or jackets, of any color except purple and scarlet. They were also exempt from pena'ties for death or injury to any man interposing between them and their mark, provided only that before shooting they had uttered the word "fast."

How this fraternity gradually merged into the Artillery Company is left in some uncertainty by historians. Not till

1610 does the inquirer feel his feet on solid ground. In that year the Company's "Great Vellum Book" began to be kept, and two years later the Privy Council gave permission for a body of citizens, not exceeding in number 250, to go through a regular course of drill. Their first captain was Edward Panton, whose claims to a kind of patent right in the chieftainship of the body involved it in a long quarrel. By the time that quarrel was settled, the company, which had obtained from the Privy Council the right to increase its numbers to 500 men, had become fairly established. In 1641 the city granted it the present exercise ground in Bunhill Fields. Its original place of exercise had been the Artillery Garden in Moorfields, known also as the Teazel Ground, which, whatever its fruitfulness in thistles, could scarcely have been very savory. The soil being marshy, and the southern part requiring to be raised, "upwards of a thousand cartloads of bones from St. Paul's charnel-house were removed there, and this deposit was afterwards covered with dirt from the street."

Captain G. A. Raikes, the most recent historian of the company, boasted that it is "the only military body over which Parliament has no control." Governed under numerous royal warrants, the Crown appoints its chief. For some time the company had claimed the right of electing absolutely its own captain-general. The lord mayor and aldermen endeavored to reduce this right to a privilege of presenting two or three candidates for the office to the lord mayor and aldermen, who should choose one from among them. The Privy Council, to whom the matter was referred for decision, compromised the dispute between the corporation and the company by awarding the appointment of president to the former and of the inferior officers to the latter; but it took the opportunity to claim the nomination to the post of captain-general for the sovereign. The intention probably was to infuse a royalist element into the company; and the enrolment of the young Prince of Wales, the Count Palatine, and the Duke of York was meant as a step in that direction. But the city was not good recruiting-ground for royalism, and from April, 1644, to January, 1657, the election of members was entirely suspended. The company appears to have taken no part in the great events of which the City of London was the centre. There is ground for belief that the reason why the company does not appear as such in the civil wars is that, had it been possible for a body of London citizens to defy its surroundings, the Artillery Company might have chosen to besiege Puritan Gloucester instead of relieving it. An early historian of the company, Anthony Highmore, declares in so many words that the company, before the close of the civil war, fell into the hands of the cavaliers. Oliver Cromwell during his protectorate revived the company, and it dutifully attended his funeral with all such panoply of woe as could be represented by cypress and black baize. But it hastened to purge away its obligatory republicanism on the Restoration by electing the Duke of York as its commander-in-chief, and inviting General Monk to a solemn exercise in the presence of the lord mayor and aldermen.

The Great Plague which devastated London in 1663–1665 suspended musters and exercises, and the company had much trouble in saving their ground from being made the site of a plague pit. Attending feasts and escorting the lord mayor on his return from the annual pilgrimage to Westminster appear to have been the principal functions of what civic records describe as "the military glory of this nation." But the London artillerymen were docile and loyal. When their captain-general, the Duke of York, declared his displeasure that they should have elected as leader a person like Sir Thomas Player, who "had behaved himself so that no honest man ought to countenance him," no more is heard of Sir Thomas Player's probably Protestant leadership. The citizens generally considered the duke's presence at court a menace to the Protestant religion, and hissed and hooted him in the Poultry to the cry of "No pope!" but the Artillery Company entertained him at a splendid banquet. On James's accession, it burst into a flame of loyal devotion. It was, however, a king that the company loved, not a James or a Charles in particular. William follows James, and the London artillerymen acclaim William as their captain-general. If death robs them of a William, they are equally content with a George of Denmark. When George of Hanover succeeds to George of Denmark's wife, the Artillery Company, which had assumed the title of "Honourable" in 1685, is as clear that it had always abhorred Pretenders as at James's accession it had been clear that it had always detested the "anti-monarchical" doctrine of the right of subjects to make religion a ground for deposing a king.

The Artillery Company paraded before George I in St. James's Park, the officers in scarlet, a color then first used in the company, the fusiliers in buff, with laced hats, wigs in black bags, white stockings, and black gaiters. So delighted was His Majesty with the company's warlike appearance that he bestowed on it a gratuity of 500*l.* The money was appropriated to the building of a new armory house. Money, in fact, occupies a greater space than war in the records of the company. Though

it is not very manifest on what the money was spent, there was
a chronic deficiency of it, and perpetual appeals were made to
the members of the corporation. Stern retrenchment had to be
practised. The entertainment after a grand march was restricted to roast beef and a pint of wine for each member. On
one occasion it was ordered that no more cannon be fired for
a year; on another that "the company dismiss themselves so
seasonable as to prevent the unnecessary expense of candles."
In 1758 the company considered it could not afford the expense
of teaching its members "the Prussian Exercise." Private
liberality indeed offered to overcome this impediment to the
company's military proficiency; but conservative objections were
interposed to the disuse of "an exercise practised by His
Majesty's Footguards."

The Ancient and Honorable Artillery Company of Massachusetts was founded in 1638 on the model of the London
body. In vain Governor Winthrop, the chief opponent of the
plan, had pleaded the alarming precedent of the Prætorian
Band. Captain Keayne, a merchant tailor and a former
member of the London Artillery Company, was its first commander. He is said to have been "distinguished for his piety
and benevolence." But his piety and benevolence did not spoil
him for a tailor; the General Court of the colony fined him
200*l.*, for that he, "an eminent professor of the Gospel," and
who had "come over for conscience' sake," took more than
sixpence in the shilling profit for foreign goods. In adherence
to old customs and ceremonies the New England Company
exceeds that of old England. But neither the one nor the
other has any warlike achievements to record. It is true that
individual members of the "Honourable Company" joined the
trainbands and trampled down King Charles's undisciplined
cavaliers. In the same way the "Ancient and Honourable
Company" contributed brave men to the colonial and the
Federal armies. But as a body each a'ike, while civil war raged
in its country, tranquilly subsided, and reappeared in its bravery
only when all real need for its assistance was over.—See CAPTAIN
G. A. RAIKES, *History of the Honourable Artillery Company*
(1878) ; *Saturday Review,* September 14, 1878.

Ascot, Royal. In the early summer of 1711, Queen Anne,
driving six miles out from Windsor Castle, came upon the
common then known as Ascot Heath. She noticed its fitness
for her favorite sport of horse-racing and directed that a "round
heat" should be prepared here. On August 6, 1711, she was
present at the first meeting.

The title Royal Ascot has been given to the yearly event

from its most distinctive feature, the Royal Progress or procession of carriages from Windsor to the race-course. This dates back to 1814, after the entrance of the allies into Paris. On that occasion the crowd went wild over the announcement of the peace just concluded, and swamped the royal cortege headed by the prince regent, so that they reached Ascot in a fragmentary condition. When the prince had ascended the throne as George IV, he formally established the Royal Progress in the fashion it has ever since retained. Eight or nine carriages, each drawn by four bays, constituted the cortege. The last carriage contains the sovereign with his consort and any foreign monarch that may be visiting Windsor. A gorgeous array of huntsmen, outriders, postilions, footmen, and many well-equipped mounted equerries add a brilliant effect of varied colors. The Gold Cup which was raced for on Cup Day was instituted by George III in 1807. The first winner was Master Jockey, a three-year-old.

Ascot has been the scene of many historic episodes. Here Frederick, Prince of Wales, son of George II and father of George III, disgraced himself by flinging a bottle at the winner as it was on the homestretch. He had placed his money on another horse. Luckily the bottle fell short.

In 1832 William IV, appearing with his queen at the window of the royal stand to acknowledge the salutations of his subjects, was struck by a stone hur'ed at him by some one unknown. He escaped with only a bruise. The incident produced a great burst of loyalty from the assembled crowd.

The procession in 1834 was made especially interesting by the fact that it marked the first appearance of Princess Victoria at a race meeting. She rode in the first carriage with the king and queen and her mother the Duchess of Kent. In 1838 Victoria made her first entry into Ascot as queen and was received with wild enthusiasm.

The Cup Day of 1844 was one of the most notable in the history of the race. Nicholas I, Emperor of Russia, and the King of Saxony were among the royalties present. The race was won by an unnamed colt owned by Lord Albemarle, who paid a compliment to the Czar by christening it The Emperor. This so pleased the autocrat that he requested permission to make a yearly presentation of a piece of p'ate, value £500, to be called the Emperor's Plate and to take the place of the Gold Cup. The offer was accepted, and from 1845 to 1853 inclusive the Gold Cup was superseded. The first trophy given by the Czar was a reduced copy of Falconetti's statue of Peter the Great, raised on a three-cornered base, on whose sides were engraved views of Windsor Castle, the Winter Palace at St. Petersburg, and the Kremlin at Moscow.

In 1845 the race was again won by The Emperor, despite the fact that he started at an outside price. The stewards were placed in a quandary in 1854, for England was then at war with Russia. Though the official card announced that the winner of the race would receive "a piece of plate, value 500 sovereigns, the gift of his Majesty the Emperor of All the Russias," the prize itself had not been, and never was, received from Russia. Ever since the Gold Cup has remained the leading item in the Ascot programme.

It used to be a favorite expression that the sun always shone when the queen went among her people, but 1860 proved an exception and the Royal Progress from Windsor was made in torrential rain. As it turned out this was the last occasion on which Queen Victoria visited Ascot, for after the death of the prince consort, although by no means withdrawing her patronage, the queen did not attend another race meeting.

The lightest jockey who ever won on the British turf rode the winner of the Ascot Stakes in 1840. He was really only a small boy and scaled no more than 56 pounds. Possibly it is of this lad the story is told, that, being summoned after the race into the royal box and questioned by the queen about his weight, he stammered, "Please, ma'am, master says as how I mustn't tell anybody how much I weigh"—an answer which naturally created a great deal of amusement.

Another favorite Ascot anecdote relates to Dr. Pusey, the High-church Anglican, who had a country house near the race-course. A rather "sporty" parson, revisiting Oxford during Ascot week, inquired about the Tractarian leader, whom he had venerated when an undergraduate. He was told by the censor of Christ Church that Pusey had gone to Ascot. "You don't mean to tell me," exclaimed the clergyman, naturally astonished, "that the dear old doctor has gone racing at his time of life!" "Well, he has not exactly gone racing," replied the other, "but he certainly is 'making a book.'" The "book" that Dr. Pusey was "making" proved to be his commentary on the "Minor Prophets," which had, of course, no connection with our modern turf prophets.

Auction. Herodotus (Book i, 196) makes the earliest known historical reference to this method of disposing of property, animate or inanimate.

The Babylonians, he said, had a custom which was followed also by the Heneti, an Il'yrian people. Girls of a marriageable age ·were directed to repair annually to a designated place, where the young men likewise congregated.   Here they were sold by the public crier.   The pretty girls were put up first and were carried off by the highest bidders.   But, as poor young men could not afford a pretty girl and had to be bribed to marry an ugly one, the purchase money obtained for the beauties was distributed as a dowry among the homely ones, in due proportion to their degree of homeliness.   Thus the ugliest became the wife of him who was most easily satisfied; and thus the finest women were sold, and, from the money which they brought, small fortunes were given to the ugliest and to those who had any bodily deformity.   A father could not marry his daughter as he pleased, nor was he who bought her allowed to take her home without giving security that he would marry her.   But, after the sale, if the parties were not agreeable, the law enjoined that the purchase money should be refunded.

The most stupendous of all auctions is that described by Gibbon in his "Decline and Fall of the Roman Empire" (Vol. i, ch. V).   It was nothing less than the public sale, on March 28, A. D. 193, of the Roman Empire by the Prætorian Guards. They had murdered Pertinax, and that emperor's father-in-law, Sulpicianus, had hopes of succeeding to the bloodied throne.   He had already begun to use the only effective argument, says Gibbon, when the more prudent of the Prætorians, apprehensive that in this private contract they should not obtain a just price for so valuable a commodity, ran out upon the ramparts, and with a loud voice proclaimed that the Roman world was to be disposed of to the best bidder by public auction.

The offer reached the ears of a vain old man, a wealthy senator, Didius Julianus, who, in utter oblivion to the commotion that had been raging in the city, was indulging in the luxury of the table.   Urged by his female relations, his freedmen, and his parasites, he now hastened to the Prætorian camp, where Sulpicianus was still in treaty with the guards, and began to bid against him from the foot of the rampart.

The unworthy negotiation was transacted by faithful emissaries, who passed alternately from one candidate to the other and acquainted each of them with the offers of his rival.   Sulpicianus had already promised a donation of 5000 drachms (above £160) to each soldier, when Julian, eager for the prize, rose at once to the sum of 6250 drachms, or upwards of £200 sterling.   The gates of the camp were instantly thrown open to the purchaser, he was declared emperor, and received an oath of allegiance from the soldiers, who retained humanity enough to stipulate that he should pardon and forget the competition of Sulpicianus.

Didius enjoyed his ill-gotten dignity for only two months, March 28 to June 2.   The senate and nobles professed their loyalty, but the people made no attempt to conceal their indignation at this insult to the state, and the armies of Britain, Syria, and Illyricum broke out into open revolt. Septimius Severus, the commander of the Pannovian legions, was declared emperor and hastened to Rome. Didius, abandoned by the Prætorians, was condemned and executed by order of the senate, which at once acknowledged Severus.

The London *Illustrated News* for December 29, 1855, published a note which succinctly sums up the results of the three greatest auction sales held in London between the years 1645 and 1855.

The three most important sales of articles of *virtu* that have been disposed of by public auction in England, since the dispersion of that formed by King Charles I., and sold by order of the Commonwealth, have been those of the Duchess of Portland; of Horace Walpole, at Strawberry-hill; and Mr. Bernal, sold this year by Messrs. Christie and Manson. The Duchess of Portland's sale consisted of thirty-seven days, and brought £10,973 2s. 6d. The Strawberry-hill sale was contained in twenty-four days' sale, and brought £33,450 11s. 9d. Mr. Bernal's thirty-two days of articles of *virtu* brought £61,964 11s. 3d.: to which, if his books and prints be added (seven days), selling for £6587 2s. 6d., would make thirty-nine days, and a total of £68,551 13s. 9d. By those well acquainted with each of these sales it is affirmed that the articles at Strawberry-hill produced twice what they did at the Duches ' sale; and at the Bernal sale they produced twice what they did at the Strawberry-hill sale, and this in a year of war. It surely follows that the taste for articles relative to art and mediæval history has been progressing to a great and almost unforeseen extent.

Auction by Candle. To sell by "inch of candle" is an expression freely used by English writers of the seventeenth and early eighteenth century. In those days goods were sold, lands rented, and auctions conducted "by the candle." When the company had assembled, the auctioneer lit a small piece of candle, usually an inch or less, and bids were received so long as the candle burned. The last bid before the flame expired secured the thing offered. Sometimes a red ring was placed at a certain distance below the flame and the bidding was over immediately that ring was reached.

The custom seems to have been imported from France in the time of Charles I. It is mentioned in the records of the House of Lords as early as 1641. Milton, writing in 1652 as secretary to the Council of State, says, "The Council thinks it meet to propose the way of selling by inch of candle, as being the most probable means to procure the true value of the goods." Under date of November 6, 1660, Pepys records a keen competition at the sale of two ships, when, he says, "we have much to do to tell who did cry last."

An advertisement in the London *Gazette* of 1684 announced that "on the 15th of March next will be exposed to sale by the candle two elephants, the one male, the other female. The price and places where to be seen and sold shall be notified by printed bills on the 5th of March." Undoubtedly the first noun referred to the upset price fixed by the vendor.

Although the custom has been practically extinct since the middle of the eighteenth century, a curious survival still lingers in the west of England, where land is let in this manner. For example, in the little village of Tatworth in Somerset County, there is a six-acre lot which belongs to no one in particular; but its annual value is shared among certain property holders in the neighborhood. All entitled thus to share meet once a year at the village inn, where they style themselves a "court" and appoint a steward to conduct the letting. An inch of candle is solemnly lighted, the bidding begins, and the last bidder before the candle goes out gets the field for the ensuing year. The steward shares the rent among those entitled to receive it, and all present settle down for a convenient evening.

Auctioneers. Two men have won for themselves a permanent niche in the Auctioneer's Hall of Fame,—the English George Robins, who presided over the auction mart in Bartholomew Lane, London, close to the Bank of England, and the American Frederick Keese. Both had a vivid fancy, a luxuriant vocabulary, a personal magnetism that often lured a bidder beyond the financial limits where he had purposed to confine himself, and underneath it all a contagious humor. But while Robins effervesced, Keese sparkled. One lost himself in a riot of exuberant hyperbole; the other entrenched himself behind a battery of puns and quips and verbal conceits.

George Robins has been celebrated both in prose and verse. A quite creditable sonnet of anonymous authorship thus describes him in action:

> High in a hall, by curious listeners fill'd,
>   Sat one whose soul seem'd steeped in poësy;
> So bland his diction, it was plain he will'd
>   His hearers all should prize as high as he
> The gorgeous works of art there plac'd around.
>   The statues by the Phidian chisel wrought:
>   Endymion, whom Dian lov'd distraught;
> Dian herself, Laocöon serpent bound:
> The pictures touch'd by Titian and Vandyke
>   With rainbow pencils, in the which did vie
>   Fair form and colour for the mastery:
> Warm'd his discourse till ear ne'er heard the like.
>   "Who is that eloquent man?" I asked one near.
>   "That, sir? that's Mr. Robins, auctioneer."

In his "Portraits of Public Characters" (1841) James Grant supplies a more prosaic but equally vivid sketch. "His favorite dress is a surtout of a brownish hue, a colored waistcoat, and light cassimere small clothes. He can boast of a very high, well-developed, arched forehead; with a rather full face. His eyebrows are prominent and protruding; but his eyes are small, though quick in their motions: they have a shrewd, if not sly, expression. His complexion is as rough and ruddy as if he were the bailiff on one of those estates which he describes with such graphic effect. He has all the appearance of one who, notwithstanding the extent and importance of his business, enjoys the pleasures of life."

Great as was Robins's pen, it was his tongue and his personality that wrought the real miracles. "He could wring money from a stone," says E. V. Lucas, in "A Little Portrait Gallery," *T. P.'s Weekly,* February 3, 1907. "Again and again when every one thought they had reached the limit and finished bidding, he would extract another fifty or hundred pounds. All men whose business it is to get round men have recourse to tricks. Next to his golden tongue George's most useful ally was an arm-chair. With these he cou'd do almost as much as Orpheus with his lute. The arm-chair was placed on the rostrum, and into it George would occasionally fling himself in satisfaction or despair, and from its security he would study his audience, mark down the more pregnable faces, mature fresh campaigns, recollect and conjoin new and more potent adjectives."

It is surmised that Charles Lamb, a frank admirer of the auctioneer, had Robins in mind when he celebrated the enchanted tongue of his imaginary Captain Jackson. "He was a juggler who threw mists before your eyes—you had no time to detect his fallacies. He would say 'Hand me the *silver* sugartongs; and before you could discover it was a sing'e spoon, and that *plated,* he would disturb and captive your imagination by a misnomer of 'the urn' for a tea-kettle, or by calling a homely bench a sofa."

Though the sonneteer first quoted shows him knocking down works of art, Robins was at his best when dealing in real estate. Like Antæus his strength was renewed at contact with Mother Earth. He wrote his own advertisements, and his announcements of mansions and messuages for sale remain masterpieces of their sort. He had no half-tones. His pretended concessions were humorously veiled embellishments, as in the case of that terrestrial paradise whose only drawbacks

5

were "the litter of the rose-leaves and the noise of the nightingales" (see ADVERTISEMENT).

Has there ever been a female auctioneer? Apparently not, but she is an imminent possibility of the future. The following article in the New York *Sun* of May 10, 1912, is enlightening:

Mayor Gaynor's secretary said yesterday, in a letter to Mrs. Eli Sobel of 16 West Ninetieth street, that a woman could become a public auctioneer in this city by paying $100 for a license and putting up a bond of $2000. Friends came flocking to the millinery shop at 824 Columbus Avenue, of which she is manager, to congratulate her on being the first woman to squeeze into so ancient a profession as auctioneering. To all of them she said:

"But I'm not. I haven't taken out any license. I merely asked the mayor if it was possible. A woman who was in here the other day said the profession was closed to women and I told her I'd find out about it from Mr. Gaynor."

Mrs. Sobel admitted that some time she might want to be an auctioneer. She knows the business, because until her husband died last year she was his helper in the auction room that he had for many years at 44 Bowery. She thinks mercantile auctioneering would be a good vocation for a woman—that the presence of a woman on the block would be in itself good advertising. But just now her hands and arms are full of spring hats.

Auerbach's Cellar. A tavern in Leipsic, Germany, which disappeared in 1912. It owed its chief fame to Goethe, who here located the scene in "Faust" wherein Mephistopheles, standing upon a wine cask, takes his flight into space, to the stupefaction of the drinkers.

The old building to which the cellar belonged was built by Dr. Stromer d'Auerbach between 1530 and 1538, the worthy doctor storing there the wine which he intended for his own use. Later, as the wine was good, he conceived the idea of selling it, and in this way was established the tavern to which his name has since been attached. From the earliest years of the seventeenth century legend placed in this cellar the famous adventure of Faust and Mephistopheles. Goethe, studying at Leipsic from 1765 to 1768, frequented the cellar and there talked with his friends of art, literature, and politics and later turned the legend to account.

Automobile. Probably the first scientific hint of the wonders that were to be in the way of horseless carriages was made by Roger Bacon, who in his *Opus Magnum* declared: "One may also make carriages which without the aid of any animal will run with remarkable velocity" (see STEAM). It is probable also that the earliest motor car ever described in print was that designed and built by a Jesuit missionary in

China, to carry him on his rounds, an improvement on the wind coaches of the natives. It was driven by a jet of steam playing on a mill-wheel connected by gearing with one of its axles. (See *Notes and Queries,* Series Ten, vol. xi, p. 431.) In the first year of James I's reign in England, a patent was issued (June 10) to Hugo Upton, "for the sole making of an instrument which shall be driven by the wind for the transportation or carriage of anything by land." Had Master Upton received a hint from the kite-carriages of China? That these were known to John Milton is apparent from the lines

> The barren plains
> Of Sericana, where Chineses drive
> With sail and wind their cany waggons light.

A century later we find the London *Daily Advertiser* of March 4, 1742, announcing the arrival, from Berne in Switzerland, of a chaise that travels without horses. A certain August Pinchbeck either owned this machine or constructed another on its model, for the same paper in the following August records that "Mr. Pinchbeck's curious machine chaise that travels without horses ran from Hampstead to Tottenham Court in less than forty minutes in the sight of several hundreds of people; at which place it will continue to be shown during the time of the fair."

Later, April 13, 1742, it is described as "one of the most complete pieces of mechanism ever invented, having those good properties which will always recommend things of this sort. . . . The whole thing, though capable of carrying three persons, weighs less than two hundred weight."

From the same authority it appears that many other attempts were made in the eighteenth century to construct an automatic road carriage. The *Public Advertiser* of May 16, 1759, announces that "Mr. Ladd's patent four-wheel carriage, that goes without horses and will carry four or five persons at the rate of six miles an hour, is at Mr. Cook's Great Rooms, Spring Gardens. It is on solid mechanical principles."

Still more celebrated is the sailing chariot invented by Simon Stevin, of Bruges, Brussels. Sterne mentions it in the second volume of "Tristram Shandy" (first published in 1759), but avoided any explanation of its mechanism almost as deftly, and indeed almost in the same language, as did the *Advertiser.* "Tho' I cannot guess," says the elder Shandy, "upon what principles of philosophy he (the inventor) has achieved it,—yet certainly his machine has been constructed on very solid ones."

At the beginning of the nineteenth century George Medhurst, of London, projected a general system of transport on common roads by the aid of motors driven by air, which was to be compressed at convenient stations by windmills, water-mills, or by hand. Medhurst vainly endeavored to form a company with a capital of £50,000 to work his project. His patent specifications are interesting documents. That of 1799 relates to " a condensing wind-engine, capable of being applied to all kinds of purposes, in which steam, water, wind, or horses are employed "; that of 1800 to " a new improved method of driving carriages of all kinds, without the use of horses, by means of an improved Æolian engine, and which engine may also be applied to various other useful purposes." (See the *Antiquary,* October, 1896.)

A furious diatribe against the then management of railroads and steam-engines in the *Aldine Magazine* for December 22, 1838, contains some vague yet interesting prophecies of present-day motors and their possible development:

As a well-known engineer has pronounced them to be, the railroads are in their construction a disgrace to the age and to the country. If something be not promptly achieved in its favor, if the united aid of science and the legislature be not called forth, the whole system must speedily destroy itself even by its own impotence. Independently of this, we have not a doubt that, ere many years have passed, it will be superseded by a new, a cheaper, a more simple, more easily manageable, and yet far more powerful agent than steam. In the interim we urge the foundation of stage-coach companies—more particularly of steam-carriage companies—for turnpike roads or, what would be better, for stone tramways. Maceroni's steam carriage will go sixteen or eighteen miles an hour on a common turnpike road, a speed nearly if not quite equal to the average speed of the trains on many of the railroads.

In 1831 a committee appointed by the English Parliament decided that steam-propelled carriages weighing three tons could safely carry fourteen passengers on the ordinary roads at an average speed of ten miles an hour. The first steam-omnibus, constructed by Walter Hancock, ran from the bank at Paddington in April, 1833. It outstripped parliamentary expectation, for it carried as many as twenty-five passengers at a speed of from ten to fifteen miles an hour. Two years later the same Hancock ran what was cal'ed a steam-engine coach between Whitechapel and his house at Stratford. Colonel Macirone and Sir Charles Dance also ran nine miles an hour.

Lady Dorothy Nevill, a nonagenarian when her "Leaves " from her note-book was published in 1907, remembers experiments made in her native county of Norfolk as far back as 1842.

In that year an inventor named Parr patented a steam-carriage to run for hire between Norwich and Yarmouth. In 1843 it was experimented with on the Yarmouth road, but proved a failure. The wheels refused to revolve unless lifted up from the road, when, as an eye-witness testified, "they at once flew around with a'arming velocity."

Prints of the old steam-carriages are now scarce and rare, as they are eagerly snapped up by automobilists who make a hobby of collecting all memoranda referring to the infancy of their favorite recreation. Lady Neville remembers one of the most curious of these prints representing an accident that happened in Scotland in 1834. It was designed by an eye-witness of the catastrophe, and shows the unlucky passengers as they were being shot into the air. Many were fatally wounded. The boiler of the carriage had burst, owing to an overstrain. It was hinted, however, that the accident was really caused by the trustees of the road between Paisley and Glasgow, who, being much opposed to the new method of locomotion, purposely kept the surface of the highway in such a condition as to interfere with the progress of the coaches. The remains of the wreck are still preserved in a museum at Glasgow. The constructor was John Scott Russell, still remembered as the builder of the *Great Eastern* steamship.

This and other accidents encouraged the enemies of the horseless coach to concerted action, and it was finally put down by legislative interference. Thus a great industry was held in abeyance for half a century.

It is in fact recorded that at the end of 1833 there were as many as twenty steam-carriages completed or under way in or around London a'one. A number of companies were formed or projected to work these carriages. But what with the competition of the railways, the difficulties as to tolls, the imperfections of the roads, and indeed of the engines themselves, by the year 1840 all this interest appears to have died out, and the problem of carrying passengers by steam-power on common roads had been abandoned for the time being. Even the great George Stephenson gave it as his opinion that "steam-carriages on ordinary roads would never be effective, or at least sufficiently serviceable to supersede horse-carriages." James Watt went further. He declared they were out of the question "unless God will work a miracle in favor of these carriages."

Some premonitory g'impse not only of the automobile but also of the aeroplane may have been present to the mind of Alexander Dumas when he penned this passage in "The Brigand":

For those who are carried onward by the hand of God all the rules of motion are transposed, and, when they have reached their goal, it seems to them that they have made the journey, not on foot. not on horseback, not in a carriage, but in some fantastic machine, rolling through cities, villages, and fields like a locomotive, emitting smoke and flame. or in a balloon, sailing so rapidly through the air that plains. villages, and cities vanish like mere specks lost in space.

A rather curious entry in the diary of Lord Sutherland Gower tells of his first experience with an automobile, in Paris, in 1891.

One day that July in Paris I had my first experience of a steam-motor car. An engineer named Serpalet came to the entrance of my hotel, with a steam carriage that he has invented, which he calls a " steam phaeton." It is worked by steam and runs on three wheels. Six people can be seated in this carriage; the boiler is at the back. We went up the Champs Elysées and into the Bois at a good pace, rather surprising but not alarming the horses when passing them. The carriage can be turned with ease, and can be slowed down or stopped without difficulty; but whether this will be a gain to locomotion is doubtful; it was De Lesseps who recommended me to see this new invention.

Automobile, Father of the. This title has been claimed respectively for a Frenchman and an American. The Frenchman was Joseph Cugnot (1725–1804), to whom in 1911 a monument was raised by his admirers. at his birthplace in the commune of Void, department of the Meuse. In 1769 Cugnot constructed a steam-carriage, running upon three wheels, one in front and two at the sides, and put in motion by an engine composed of two single-acting high-pressure cylinders, the pistons of which acted alternately on the front wheel. It only travelled two miles and a quarter an hour, and would work only for 12 or 15 minutes at a time. But it was an important experiment. The French Minister of War authorized Cugnot to proceed with the construction of a new and improved machine, which was finished and ready for trial in the course of the following year. The new locomotive was composed of two parts, one being a carriage supported on two wheels, somewhat resembling a small brewer's cart. furnished with a seat for the driver; while the other contained the machinery, which was supported on a single driving-wheel four feet two inches in diameter. The engine consisted of a round copper boiler with a furnace inside provided with two small chimneys, two single-acting thirteen-inch brass cylinders communicating with the boiler by a steam-pipe, and the arrangements for communicating the motion of the pistons to the driving-wheel, together with the steering gear.

Cugnot's locomotive, in short, presented a simple and ingenious form of a high-pressure engine; and, though of rude construction, it was a highly creditable piece of work, considering the time of its appearance and the circumstances under which it was constructed.

It met with an accident at one of its trials in Paris, and was locked up in the Arsenal; but Cugnot was granted a pension of 300 livres, which, though interrupted during the French Revolution, was restored by Napoleon, the First Consul showing more enlightenment in Cugnot's case than he did in regard to Fulton (see STEAMSHIP). Cugnot's locomotive is still preserved at Paris, in the Conservatoire des Arts et Métiers, and it is, without exception, the most venerable and interesting of all machines extant connected with the early history of steam locomotion.

The American claimant is George B. Selden, of Rochester, New York, born (1846) in Clarkson, Monroe County. In 1895, after sixteen years of struggle with the Washington office, he succeeded in obtaining a patent for a machine he had invented in 1879. Says George Gray Haven in *The Scrapbook*, vol. x, —

Selden occupies a peculiar position to the automobile—he is and he isn't the father of it. He was the first man to foresee it in 1879, describe it, and patent it accurately; yet to all intents and purposes it was not America, but France, which first gave the automobile to the world.

However, even then for four years the patent was idle. In 1899 Selden sent a copy of it to the late Colonel Albert A. Pope, of Hartford, Connecticut. Colonel Pope, manufacturer of bicycles, had been making some electric vehicles, and even some gasoline machines, under the name of the Columbia and Electric Vehicle Company. The upshot was that Selden made a contract with the company, and gave it the exclusive license and right of sub-license under the patent. At last, after twenty-six long years, Selden received his first five hundred dollar check out of the thing he had spent so much of his time and money on.

With the recent history of the Selden patent people are more or less familiar, for a good deal of it has been in the courts and at various stages in the newspapers. It was not to be wondered at that many people bitterly contested Selden's claim, and that some are still doing so. For, as I said in the beginning, it is a most peculiar case. Various American and European constructors were marketing actual cars, apparently without the slightest knowledge of Selden or his patent, but along lines answering the description of his claim.

At once a large number of manufacturers recognized the Selden patent, probably on the advice of counsel, and in 1903 these manufacturers banded together and formed the Association of Licensed Automobile Manufacturers—the A. L. A. M. They have worked with Selden to sustain his patent. One of the rules they put in force was that no one was to be allowed to enter the association except those who had been engaged in the business at or prior to the date of the organization. Thus, some time later, when Selden decided to go into the business himself, building the "Selden" car, he had to acquire the rights of another company which since 1903 had given

up building cars and gone into the building of marine engines
exclusively. It may be noted that the Selden patent covers only
gasoline automobiles; motorcycles, power-boats, and air-ships do not
come under it, whatever sort of engine is used. It simply covers the
gas-engine as applied to road locomotion, either for passengers or
freight.

The most strenuous opponent of the Selden claims was Henry
Ford, who started a new company about the time the A. L. A. M. was
formed, refusing to come into the association, or, looking at it in
another way, being debarred unless he adopted the method Selden
himself did to enter under cover of his own patent. In fact, a very
large part of the business was not in the organization at that time.
In 1005 the independents formed their organization, the American
Motor Car Manufacturers' Association, to fight the patent, in connection with several foreign makers.

The case was carried to the courts with the usual delays.
Eminent counsel appeared on both sides. Coudert Brothers appeared
for the independents, and, among others, the famous patent lawyer.
Frederick P. Fish, for the Selden patent. Experts from all over the
world were called in, including the celebrated Dugald Clerk, the
English authority.

Every word of the Selden claim was subjected to the most searching examination. Finally, in 1909, after six years of litigation.
Judge Hough, of the United States Circuit Court in New York, gave
his decision for the patent. At once the majority of the independents,
rather than risk further damages, became members of the association.
covering now perhaps eighty-five per cent. of the annual output.

In the course of the suit the old cylinder of 1879 was introduced
in evidence, and later Selden had the other two cylinders bored out
and set up. Then he had a road wagon constructed as near as possible
to his original specifications, and as "a man skilled in the art" would
have done it in 1879. Some changes were made, such as from flame
to electric ignition.

The wagon, with the date on it, 1877, ran successfully on the
streets of Rochester in 1908, and later was brought to New York,
where it also ran, though not very well. Its few tests had worn it out
probably. For one thing, it needed a larger water-jacket. Of course
the opposing counsel criticized it a great deal, but, as Mr. Fish pointed
out, it was better than any of the original patents of the sewing-
machine, the incandescent light, telephone, or telegraph. None of them
worked to any degree. The important thing was the idea they embodied, not the minor defects which mechanics could overcome.

Another American claim for paternity has been put forward
by certain enthusiasts for Robert Dudgeon, who in 1856 invented
and used what he called a steam road-wagon. The original
was shown at the Crystal Palace Exhibition, and was destroyed
when that Palace burned down. A second wagon is still in the
possession of Dudgeon's heirs. The general plan is similar to
that of the original, save that the wheels (heavy cart-wheels in
the first instance) were made solid out of segments of cedar, with
iron flanges and tires. Sixty gallons of water were stored under
the seats which formed the two sides of the vehicle.

On its first trip it carried, besides Mr. Dudgeon, a number

of his workmen, one of whom survived to be interviewed by the New York *Tribune* in 1890.

" Mr. Dudgeon," he said, " built the wagon to carry him from his place of business in Columbia Street to his home, One-hundred-and-eighth Street, Harlem. He always contended that when streets were once made smooth horseless carriages would be used generally. Roads and streets for horses were considered by him unfit for wheeling, and we have discovered that he was right. But even with the bad streets, laid with rough stones and poorly graded, the steam-wagon used to make trips regularly from Harlem to the shop and back, and on Sundays it was used to take Mrs. Dudgeon to church.

" But the wagon was used only as a motor on these occasions. A carriage was coupled on behind it, and in this the women sat while the driver and the men occupied seats in the steam-wagon."

According to this authority it took two bushels of coal to run the car to One-hundred-and-eighth Street. " But it made good time," he added, " and could be guided and steered as nicely and was as easily controlled as the horseless carriages of to-day. Of course, it made considerable noise, and that was probably one reason why the city authorities, after it had been in use for about ten years, refused to allow Mr. Dudgeon to make his trips in it. With a clear road it went easily fifteen miles an hour."

The wagon remained in New York for a short time after its use on the streets had been forbidden, and then the inventor sent it to his country home at Peacock's Point, Long Island, near Glen Cove, where it is now. It made many trips on the country roads, to the edification of the rustics, but with its banishment from New York the wagon's occupation was gone, and it was at one time reduced to the level of the ordinary stationary engine. The running gear was taken off, and the mechanism which had originally been made and placed in position to propel a wagon through the streets of New York was degraded to the level of farm labor.

Aviation, Father of. This title is popularly bestowed in France upon Louis Pierre Mouillard, who died in poverty at Cairo, Egypt, in the year 1897. On February 25, 1912, there was unveiled at Heliopolis, just outside of Cairo, a monument erected to his memory by the French National Aerian League, in grateful acknowledgment of the fact that a man of their nation has enabled the French to claim as a national discovery the means whereby human aviation has become possible,—*i.e.,* tne " gauchissement," or twisting, of the tips of the wings which allows the gliding flight of the vulture and other large birds as distinct from the flight by flapping of the wings.

Beneath the bust is the word "oser," "to dare," which Mouillard placed on the title-page of his book, "The Conquest of the Air"; and a vulture with outstretched planing wings is the only purely decorative feature.

As a matter of fact, Louis Mouillard never flew, and never attempted to fly save once, as a boy, when he was caught on the edge of a cliff and soundly cuffed by an irate old beadle; but it was he who set forth in two volumes the principles of flight, which were put into practice later by the Wright brothers.

In "The Empire of the Air" (1881), Mouillard explained to a heedless world that to seek to fly by imitating the beating of a bird's wings was not feasible; that, instead of trying this impossible feat, men should imitate such birds as fly with steady wings and avail themselves of the currents of the air.

Mouillard spoke to a small audience; indeed, only one of his works appeared during his lifetime. The second, "Flight with Fixed Wings," was not published until 1911. But he had pointed the way, and ten years after his death the Wrights demonstrated that he had solved the mystery. Long ago, no doubt, he could have built an aeroplane much like those of to-day, but only a few fellow-scientists believed in him, and they could never lend him the money that might have made his dream a reality.

Mouillard's claim to the title has been contested by other nations than the French (see FLYING MACHINES).

Avocado, or **Alligator Pear.**   These are the official and the popular names of a fruit which originally came from South America.   Other names have been applied to it in English, as butter pear, vegetable marrow, midshipman's butter, palta, and aguacate; but "avocado" has received the sanction of the United States Department of Agriculture and the American Pomological Society.   It is so unlike other fruits as to suggest a class of its own, for which the generic name of salad fruit has been suggested.   Wherever it has been introduced its rich nut-like flavor has made it a favorite, and its reputation is growing year by year.

The demand for the avocado has always kept in advance of the supply.   This is evidenced by the high prices paid for it, ranging usually from 20 to 50 cents each at retail.   Although the markets are at present limited, there does not seem to be any immediate danger of overproduction.

It is not a dry-land plant, and its cultivation should not be attempted for profit on any lands which are not supplied with a generous rainfall or which cannot be brought under irrigation.

High winds are decidedly inimical to the tree. The wood is brittle and is liable to be broken by winds. The flowers also are destroyed by severe winds, and the fruit, which hangs from pendulous branches and fruit stems, is easily blown about, bruised, or broken from the tree. For this reason commercial culture should not be attempted in localities of high winds unless it is possible to provide protection by windbreaks.

One characteristic in soil is demanded—good drainage. The tree is very impatient of standing water about its roots. Soil that is underlain by an impervious layer should not be chosen for the orchard.

Aweto. This insect, one of the strangest in the world, is found in New Zealand. It is known to naturalists as the *Hipialis rivescens,* and is a sort of cross between a caterpillar and a vegetable. It is always found at the foot of a large myrtle tree, known to the Maoris as a rata. Burying itself among the roots a few inches below the ground, it there lives until it is full grown and then undergoes a marvellous transformation. The spore of a vegetable fungus (the *Sophoeria robertsii*) fastens itself to the neck of the caterpillar, just between the head and the first ring, and there grows upward to the height of from six to eight inches. In shape this stem somewhat resembles a cat-tail. It shoots up two or three inches above the ground in which the caterpillar is buried. Below the earth it grows into the aweto, filling up every possible space within the outer skin, but leaving the external form unchanged. As soon as vegetable matter has been entirely substituted for animal, both plant and caterpillar become hard and dry and perish. The whole has now a brown color and looks like a wooden caterpillar with a huge horn standing up from the back of its neck. How the caterpillar manages to propagate its species no one can tell. Usually the caterpillar becomes a chrysalis, the chrysalis changes into a moth, the moth lays eggs, and these eggs again become caterpillars, and so on without stopping. "Many reasons," says John Charles Leampfert in a contribution to *Harper's Young People,* "are given why the plant shoots up from the back of the neck of the aweto, but they have been found worthless upon further investigation. Mine is that the aweto has a slimy substance oozing out from its neck, which, while the aweto is boring at the foot of the rata tree for its only food, catches the seed of the fungus and holds it fast there till the latter begins to grow. When it has sucked all the vegetable life out of the aweto it must naturally die, for it finds no further nourishment. The aweto is often found in large numbers."

B.

Babel, Tower of. Two different piles of ruins in Babylonia are diversely credited with being remnants of that tower whose building caused the confusion of tongues (Genesis, chap. xi). The first lies on the east bank of the Euphrates River, five miles above the modern city of Hillah; the second is a conical mound known as Birs Nimrud, or Nimrod's Tower, six miles and a half southwest of the same city. Biblical scholars throw the weight of their opinions in favor of Birs Nimrud as being the site of the abortive heaven-penetrating shaft. The ruins at this point, which consist mainly of kiln-bricks, huge stones, and vitrified mortar, almost hidden from sight by sands, the accumulations of centuries, are 198 feet in height and nearly 800 yards in circumference. Sir R. K. Porter, who has given much study to the Birs Nimrud ruins, believes its vitrified appearance to be the results of numerous lightning strokes, conclusions which, taken in connection with the tradition that the tower was destroyed by fire from heaven, forms an interesting subject for thought. Porter also says that, with the exception of natural accumulation and decay, the tower is, in his estimation, almost in the condition it was left at the time of the confusion.

The actual height at which the last stone of that famous structure rested is likewise a matter of merest conjecture. Herodotus, who lived about 1700 years after the recorded date when that "great spiral way to heaven" was attempted, says that he saw at Babylon a structure consisting of eight towers raised one above another, each seventy-five feet in height, but whether this ruin was the remains of the tower of Babel it was even then impossible to ascertain. Herodotus, usually minutely exact in his writing, leaves us in ignorance as to how the upper level of each of these seventy-five foot towers was reached from the level below.

Most orientalists maintain that God did not put a stop to the work until the tower had reached a height of 10,000 fathoms, or about twelve miles. In Ceylonese tradition it is said to have been as high as 20,000 elephants, each standing one above the other. St. Jerome asserts, on the authority of persons who had examined the ruins, that it did not reach a height exceeding four miles. Other statements are still more extravagant.

Baby-show. The first baby-show in the United States (or anywhere else in the world) was held at Springfield, Ohio, on

October 14, 1854. Conceived half in jest, its projectors were surprised at the whole-hearted enthusiasm which greeted the idea. On the appointed day, a muster of "infantry in arms" (the contemporaneous newspaper jest) rallied in a tent specially prepared for them. At eleven A.M. a large circle was formed by a rope around the tent, and outside of this the uninterested adults were made to stand, which they did patiently, under the promise that the babies would soon be exhibited. Nine ladies and six gentlemen were then elected, whose duty it was to enter the tent, examine the babies, and award the premiums. The judges were about to proceed to their task when a telegraph was received, announcing that an additional lot of babies were on the train from Dayton, and would be there at twelve o'clock, and requesting a postponement of the examination until said babies arrived. The request was acceded to. A few minutes after twelve the judges entered the tent, which presented a novel, amusing, and interesting sight. The mothers and nurses, seated, had the "little darlings" all ready for inspection. One lady pointed with pride to the chubby legs of her boy; while another glowingly referred to the delicate but well-formed features of her girl. One boasted of having the largest of its age; another, of the smallest and smartest. Some of the babies seemed to feel their importance on this occasion; and, in spite of the most earnest entreaties, would be in mischief, and keep up a continued noise. Others lay quietly in their mothers' arms, watching the proceedings with apparent interest; while others insisted on hiding their innocent faces in their mothers' bosoms. One hundred and twenty-seven babies were entered for exhibition, and they came from almost everywhere. Several counties, including Hamilton of Ohio, were well represented; and there were babies from Indiana, Louisiana, Pennsylvania, and Massachusetts. Large and fat children seemed to predominate. One from Indiana, only five months old, weighed 27½ pounds, and another, four months old, weighed 20 pounds. A pair of twins, of Clark County, attracted much attention. They were very pretty and as near alike as two peas. An elderly lady was present with her seventeenth baby, only two months old. She claimed nothing extraordinary in the child she presented, but thought she was deserving of a premium. The judges were a long time in their investigations. After they retired, the mothers, with their children in their arms, walked into the Floral-hall, where they remained, while the spectators crowded past them to take a look at the babies. Though the "show" was ended, the excitement was not over. Everybody wanted to know the premium babies. The judges, not being able to consult without interruption on the ground, retired to the Anthony-house in the city. There they were followed by hundreds, anxious to learn the result. The discussion regarding the comparative merits of the different babies was not over till six o'clock in the evening, when the following prizes were awarded: First prize, a splendid service of silver plate, including a large salver, to the daughter of William Romner, of Vienna, Clark County, aged ten months. Second prize, a service of silver plate, to the son of William McDowell, of Fulton, Hamilton County, Ohio, aged thirteen months. Third prize, a plain service of silver, to the daughter of Mr. A. Canon, of Philadelphia.

Backgammon. The European variety of a group of games where the throws of dice or lots are turned to account by the moving of pieces on a board. Thus, to the excitement of chance is added the more logical element of skill. All these games are an evolution from the simpler forms of dice and lot-throwing (see DICE). Professor Edward B. Tylor surmises that when Greek writers mention dice-playing they mean some game of this class; otherwise there would be no sense in Plutarch's remark, that, in life as in dicing, one must not only get good throws, but know how to use them. That the Greeks derived the game from the East is made probable from the story which the same author tells of the Persian queen, Parysatis, mother of Artaxerxes. He describes her as terrible at dice: By "careful playing" she succeeded in winning from the king the eunuch Mesabates, who had cut off the head and hand of Cyrus, and straightway ordered that hapless individual to be flayed alive. The Persian game is to this day known as *mard* and is very similar to European backgammon. Still another oriental variety is the Hindoo patchesi, which is nearly akin to the Aztec game of patolizli, or potolli, described by the Spanish conquerors of Mexico. The Chinese have a famous backgammon game known as "The Table of Promotion of Mandarins." It is played by two or more persons on a large paper diagram upon which are printed the titles of the various officials and dignitaries of the government. Moves are made by throwing dice, and the players, whose positions on the diagram are indicated by colored sticks of wood, are advanced or set back, according to the throws.

A quaint story is told of the origin of this game. The emperor Kienlung, tradition says, was in the habit of walking at nightfall among the houses occupied by candidates who had come up to Peking for the triennial examination. Night after night he heard the sound of dice issuing from one of the houses. Finally he summoned the offender before him to explain his conduct. The latter, fearing punishment, told the monarch that he had constructed a chart on which he had written the names of all the positions in the government, and that he and his friends threw dice, traversing the board according to their throws, and were thus impressed with a knowledge of the various ranks and steps leading to political advancement.

The emperor commanded him to bring the chart next day for his inspection. That night the unfortunate young man, whose excuse was a fiction created at the moment, sat until daybreak, pencil in hand, and made a chart according to his story, which he carried to His Majesty. The august prince was much pleased with the diligence of the scholar who improved his mind even while amusing himself, and dismissed him with many compliments.

In Japan a great many games are played on boards or diagrams, the moves being made by throwing dice. All of them come under the general name of "Sugroku." The most popular is called "Travelling Sugroku." It is played upon a large sheet of paper on which are represented the various stopping places of a journey,—as, for example, the fifty-three post-stations between Tokio and Kioto.

The method of playing the classic form of backgammon may be made out from a fifth century Greek epigram, recording a game played by the emperor Zeno. The latter, it appears, got his men so blocked that, having the ill luck to throw 2, 5, 6 (three dice were used in those days, as was still the custom in the middle ages), the only moves open obliged him to leave eight blocks.

In the Roman empire the game was known as "Twelve Lines" (*Duodecim Scripta*) or "Tables" (*Tabulæ*). This was the game of which Ovid says that it had as many lines as the year has months. He advises the lover, when playing with his mistress, to curry favor with her by giving himself bad throws and playing them ill. "Among the Christian antiquities in Rome," says Professor Tylor, "is a marble slab on which a backgammon-table is cut, with a Greek cross in the middle, and a Greek inscription that Jesus Christ gives victory and help to dicers if they write His name when throwing the dice—Amen. Carelessly scratched as it is, by some stone-cutter whose faith went beyond his trictrac, it shows that the board was like ours, even to the division in the middle which makes the two groups of six points on each side." From ancient Rome, too, we inherit the habit of making the backgammon-board with a draught-board on the reverse side, at any rate the commentators so interpret Martial's epigram on the tabula lusoria:

Hic mihi bis seno numeratur tessara puncto
Calculus hic gemino discolor hoste perit.

Here twice the die is counted to the point of *size*,
Here, twixt twin foes of other hue, the draughtman dies.

It was from Rome that backgammon spread all over Europe, and we still speak of the *tables*, which is, of course, the Latin *tabulæ*. A distich of the Elizabethan period says:

Man's life is a game of *tables*, and he may
Mend his bad fortune by his wiser play.

There is no doubt it was once a very fashionable amusement. Henry VIII was playing at it with his queen, Anne Boleyn, when an account of Sir Thomas More's execution was brought to him. Looking sternly at her, he said, " Thou art the cause of this man's death"; and then he withdrew, in evident perturbation, to the solitude of his chamber.

Bagpipe. In literature and history this musical instrument is mainly associated with Scotland and the Scotch. There is reason to believe, however, that the English, through inheritance from their Roman conquerors, were the original bagpipers of Great Britain. We know that during the sixteenth century the bagpiper was a regular functionary in the establishments of English princes and nobles, while no such musician was found at the Scottish court. Nor is there any reference to instrument or musician in any of the few Highland poems that have survived from the Middle Ages. James I used to play the bagpipe; but he may have learnt it, among other accomplishments, in England. The harp, till within very recent times, has been the national instrument of Scotland. In fact, the bagpipe has never been very popular there, save in the Highlands. In 1630 the magistrates of Aberdeen issued the following suggestive order: " The magistrates discharge the common piper of all going through the town, at night or in the morning, in time coming, with his pipe; it brings an uncivill forme to be usit within sic a famous burghe, and being often found fault with, as well by sundry neighbours of the town as by strangers."

The trouble seems to be that this much bedamned and much belauded instrument belongs to no nation in particular. Its antiquity is indisputable. Chinese traditions make it the oldest instrument in the Celestial Empire. The Egyptians employed the bagpipe drone and a player of this instrument is sculptured on a Hittite slab dating back to a thousand years before Christ. A Grecian bas-relief preserved in one of the Roman museums shows a bagpiper playing a pipe exactly like that now used by Highlanders. A Roman coin of the time of Nero bears a similar device. Nero himself is said to have played on the bagpipe. Its Latin name was *utricularis tibia* and its invention was accredited to Pan, Mercury, and other classical gods. The Jews attributed it to Tubal Cain.

The bagpipe is almost universal throughout Asia, though at present it is not so much in use as in former ages. It is familiar to Chinese musicians, and is met with in Persia. During the Middle Ages it made its home in every European country. In Austria dancing to the bagpipe was a favorite diversion as early as the thirteenth century. In Germany at the same period its popularity is attested by the legend of the Pied Piper of Hamelin. It became a court instrument played by minnesingers and troubadours not only in Germany but in France and Spain. From Boccaccio we learn that in 1348 a bagpiper accompanied the fugitives who fled from plague-stricken Florence to the country. In Belgium pipers took part in religious services, and there were masques of pipers. On one occasion, at a feast of the Blessed Virgin, "many wild beasts danced round a cage containing two apes playing on bagpipes." Comic pictures of pigs, bears, and other animals playing this instrument attest its mediæval vogue in divers countries; and the esteem in which it was held is further shown in its being pictured as a component part of the celestial instrument played by angels. Raphael introduces a bagpiper in his picture of the Nativity. The instrument was supposed, also, to influence the actions of animals. In Sweden an ecclesiastic dignitary of the sixteenth century relates that the shepherds employed the bagpipe to induce their flocks to come together and feed with relish.

In France, during the seventeenth century, five different forms of the bagpipe were used, and two of these, the cornemuse and the musette, were much in vogue; in fact, the musette, which was modelled on the Irish uilleann, was the fashionable instrument in the days of Louis XIV. Ladies vied with one another as players and as owners of beautifully decorated specimens. In 1649 the Court Band included four musettes. Mersenne wrote that with a skilful player this instrument did not yield to any other. In the French army, also, the musette was used up to the opening years of the last century. In Italy, especially in the Sicilies, it is common. The Italian peasant believes that it is the best-loved music of the Virgin Mary, also that it is the instrument upon which the shepherds expressed their joy when they visited the Saviour.

The pifferari, or peasant-pipers of Italy, are especially in

evidence at the Christmas season, when they flock down to the
neighboring cities, stopping to play at every shrine on the road.

In Scotland the bagpipe may have been known before the
time of James I (the VIth of Scotland), but it first emerges
into history during the minority of that monarch, when the
unity of the clans was in a measure broken, and the sanguinary
spirit that succeeded found itself better attuned to the clamor
of the pipes than to the tenderer notes of the harp.

The bagpipe was rarely played within doors, except in the
halls of chieftains, where it is still a customary piece of state
to have the pipes playing all the time of dinner. At Balmoral,
when royalty comes there, bagpipers play during all the time
of dinner, only they are removed to the outside and perform
marching on the terrace opposite the dining-room window. At
marriage processions and funerals it was also used, as being the
instrument which could be most conveniently played while the
musician was walking along with the crowd.

Every clan had three appropriate tunes peculiar to itself.
These were "The Gathering of the Clans," or "Pibroch"; its
March; and its Lament, or "Coronach." We are all familiar
with Scott's fine version of "The MacGregor's 'Gathering,'"
beginning

> The moon's on the lake and the mist's on the brae.

The "Pibroch" became especially famous during the Seven
Years' War, when Pitt insisted that the Highlanders should be
called out in defence of the British rights in North America,
despite the fears of the loyalists who thought it might not be
safe to trust them so soon after the defeat at Culloden. Pitt
carried his point, and the Highlanders fought as fiercely for
king and country against the French in America as if France
had not been the traditional ally of the Scotch Highlanders in
the Jacobist insurrections.

In the expedition against Fort Duquesne Major Grant, of
Montgomery's Highlanders, was independently sent forth with
400 of his men and 500 provincials in reconnoissance. The
Highlanders, with the same reckless daring that had wrought
woe to their brethren at Culloden, insisted on advancing with
drums beating and the pipes "skirling" the pibroch. Thus
warned, the enemy fell upon them, and, after a desperate conflict, sent the shattered column reeling back. Only 150 Highlanders reached Loyal Henning. In the battle of Quebec a year
later, the pibroch worked to better purpose. There it rallied a
broken Highland regiment and inspired them to renew their
charge with such fury as to change a threatened defeat into
victory.

Byron's reference to the sound of the "pipes" at Waterloo is familiar:

And wild and high the Cameron's Gathering rose,
  The war-note of Lochiel, which Albyn's hills
Have heard, and heard, too, have her Saxon foes;
  • How on the noon of night that pibroch thrills
  Savage and shrill! But with the breath that fills
The mountain-pipe, so fill the mountaineers
  With the fierce native daring that instils
The stirring memory of a thousand years,
And Evan's, Donald's fame rings in each clansman's ears.

Yet the bagpipe has its enemies. The Germans call it a dudelsack, which sounds opprobrious if not actually libellous. In the year 1895, at Milwaukee, Wisconsin, some offshoots from the Vaterland had an opportunity legally to testify to their horror of the instrument. A procession of freaks belonging to a show was headed by a bagpiper, whose instrument alarmed all neighboring horses, causing so much injury to one of them that its owner brought suit for damages against the showman. Justice and jury were all of German birth. They gave the plaintiff a verdict of $125, and found that "the dudelsack is not a musical instrument," and that the horse " was scared to death by an unearthly noise made by a fiend with the aforesaid dudelsack."

Ball and **Ball Games.** Recent excavations near Cairo, Egypt, have brought to light small balls of leather and others of wood obviously used in some outdoor sport, and probably dating back to at least 2000 years before Christ. These are the oldest balls of the kind in existence. Hence Egypt may be the birthplace of the original ball game, whatever it was. We know, however, that the Greeks and Romans played ball at a remote period. We do not know the exact nature of any of these ancient games, Egyptian, Greek, or Roman.

Hand-ball, something like that we still play, is the earliest ball game that emerges from the mists of history,—in Italy under the name of *pallone,* in France under that of *jeu de paume,* in Britain under that of "fives," because the ball is struck with the hand or "bunch of fives." Hand-ball, therefore, may be considered the parent of all our modern games of ball, the ancestor of tennis, lawn tennis, cricket, and base-ball. Very gradual was the evolution to a game where something besides the naked hand was used for striking the ball. First the hand was covered with a glove to protect it. Then came the first rude form of racquet—a spoon-shaped basket strapped to the arm, much like that still used in the Basque game of *pelote.* Early in the fifteenth century this was succeeded by a *battoir* or battledore covered with parchment and with a wooden handle. So popular were these battoirs that every available bit of parchment was used up in their manufacture, even to manuscripts of the classics, as witness the familiar story of the French tutor in the sixteenth century. While playing ball he noticed that there were faint Latin characters on his racquet. Taking it home with him to decipher, he found that the parchment was evidently a portion of the missing books of Livy which scholars had mourned for ages. He at once obtained the address of the maker, but arrived there only to find that he was too late. The MS. had all been used up.

The *battoir* was soon succeeded by a racquet something like that now in use in lawn tennis. In France, the new game retained the old name of the *jeu de paume,* though that was no longer rightly descriptive; in Italy, it came to be called simply *la palla,* the ball. In England it was known as tennis, and there, as elsewhere, was the favorite game of the royal courts. In 1555, one Messer Antonio Scaino, a learned doctor of the church, published a valuable treatise, "Trattato della Palla," which did much to assimilate and coördinate the rules of the game in the different countries where it was played. Some of the terms which he makes use of have survived to our day in the more modern lawn tennis, as *due* (deuce) and *vantaggio* (vantage). With the close of the seventeenth century, the game of tennis languished and indeed it had become well-nigh extinct until within our own days when the interest excited by lawn tennis recalled attention to the more venerable game of which it was the offspring. At present tennis is played considerably in England and in America.

Balloon. The first idea of the balloon is said to have presented itself to Stephen Montgolfier, a paper maker by trade, through an accident differently narrated by two of his early biographers. One version is that Montgolfier happened to fling a paper bag into the fire. It became filled up with smoke and in that condition hung suspended for a time in the chimney. The other story represents Montgolfier as boiling water in a coffee pot over which a conical paper cover was seen to swell and rise as it became filled with vapor. Hence the idea entered his mind of a bag rendered lighter than the surrounding atmosphere by inflation which in due course reached full development in the balloon (see FLYING MACHINES).

Ballyhack, a little seaport town of Wexford County, Ireland. Its name is used humorously in such phrases as "Go to Ballyhack!" much as if it summed up all that was unpleasant or degenerate in Ireland. Possibly it is the cacophonous name that suggests something outlandish or banal. Much in the same way Oshkosh is sometimes taken as the type of provincialism in the United States.

Bamboo. There is no tree which serves so many useful purposes as the bamboo. The native of India obtains from it a part of his food, many of his household utensils, and a wood at once lighter and capable of bearing greater strains than heavier timber of the same size. Besides, in expeditions in the tropics, under the rays of a vertical sun, bamboo tanks have more than once been used as barrels, in which water has been kept fresher than could have been done in vessels of any other kind.

Upon the west coast of South America, and in the islands near Asia and Australasia, especially in the Philippines, bamboo furnishes all the material for the construction of houses, pleasant, substantial, and preferable to those of stone, which recurring earthquakes only too frequently bring down upon the heads of the tenants.

To the Filipino it is an essential for existence. It constitutes the whole or a part of every article he makes. Without it he could scarcely avoid extinction.

From foundation to roof-tree his dwelling-place is all bamboo, save for the grass thatch occasionally used in place of bamboo roofing. The posts on which it rests are large bamboo poles; the floor is of narrow bamboo slats bound together by bamboo strips; the walls are of a thin variety of bamboo split open and flattened out into boards; the doors and the windows are of bamboo, and they open and shut by means of hollow bamboos which slide upon smaller bamboos. Not a nail, not a bit of iron, enters into the work of construction. Bamboo rafters are fastened to bamboo plates with bamboo pegs and bound down with strips of pliable bamboo rope.

The very ladder which reaches to the single door of this primitive house on stilts is all bamboo. Sapling bamboo rungs are inserted into two stout bamboo poles, and the whole is bound together with bamboo strips.

Rice is frequently cooked in the hollow joint of a green bamboo over a blazing heap of bamboo twigs. Indeed the first sprouts of the young bamboo of a certain species are boiled and eaten by the poorer classes. When the Filipino needs water he fastens a hollow bamboo joint to a bamboo sweep by means of a bamboo rope and lowers it into the well which he has scooped out with bamboos. Or, if he have no well, he takes a stout bamboo about eight feet long, removes from the interior all partitions which separate each joint, leaving the one at the butt end, and thus in a few minutes is provided with a vessel that will hold several gallons of water and outwear the best pail ever manufactured. This he fills at the nearest stream, deftly balances it upon his shoulder with the open end just high enough to save the contents, and trots back to his hut with far greater ease than would the white man with a single bucketful.

His musical instruments, mainly flutes and crude violins, are made entirely of bamboo, even to the bow of the latter and its strings and pegs. So are his agricultural implements, his fish-traps and his fishing gear, and his weapons of war. When at last he dies, he is carried to his grave in a bamboo mat suspended from a bamboo pole, his grave is dug with a bamboo scoop, and a bamboo cross is his only monument. (BRADFORD K. DANIELS, in *Sunday Associated Magazines,* March 20, 1910.)

The loftiest of the bamboos is the Sammot. In the tracts where it grows to the greatest perfection it sometimes rises to the height of 100 feet, with a stem only 18 inches in diameter at the base. The wood itself is only an inch in thickness.

In one day the bamboo attains the height of several inches, and with a microscope its development can be easily watched.

A remarkable feature is the blossoming of the bamboo. With all its marvellous rapidity of growth it blooms only twice in a century, the flower appearing at the end of each 50 years. Like other grasses, the bamboo dies after having borne seed.

Colonel Yule, in his translation of Marco Polo, refers to the Hindoo who readily believed all the wonderful things told him about Europe, but could not be made to understand how it was possible for human beings to exist in a land destitute of bamboos.

The varieties of the bamboo differ in size from slender reeds to tree-like growths often reaching a height of 70 feet or more, with a stem over 15 inches thick. The stem, tapering from the base, is divided at very irregular intervals (measurable sometimes in inches and sometimes in feet) by joints whose position is marked on the exterior by nodes.

Banana. The banana shares with the apple, though less extensively, the superstition that it was the forbidden fruit of the Garden of Eden. It is one of the curiosities of the vegetable kingdom. One cannot call it either a tree, a bush, a shrub, an herb, or a vegetable, but a herbaceous plant with the status of a tree. Though it sometimes reaches the height of 30 feet there is no woody fibre in any part of its structure. The bunches of fruit growing on the dwarf banana plant are often heavier than the stalk which supports them. No other plant gives such a quantity of food to the acre. It yields 40 times more by

weight than the potato and 133 times more than wheat. No
insect will attack it. It is immune from disease of any sort.
It bears two crops every year. Hence it is obtainable ten months
out of the twelve.

The banana is ever widening its habitat. The limits of its
successful development used to be given as 30 degrees north and
31 degrees south of the equator. But Dr. S. Rung, of Bonn
University, says that its cultivation has been slowly creeping
up the warm coasts of Spain and Portugal till it has nearly
reached the 37th parallel, and Hubertus Anhagen reports that
the plant is doing well in Palestine and Syria, several degrees
north of the 30th parallel, in the latitude of Charleston and
Savannah.

There is now no doubt that the history of banana cultivation
will be much like that of many other useful plants. Hardy
varieties of apples are growing to-day in central Minnesota,
where, forty years ago, the farmers were saying that the apple-
tree would never endure the long winters. Dr. M. Zagorodsky
and other authorities in plant geography predict that, as experience is gained and the cultivation of the banana widens,
varieties of it will be developed that will withstand even considerable degrees of drought and frost and enlarge the area of
cultivation to an important extent.

In September, 1911, the New York *Globe* reported that " a
bunch of about 150 huge red bananas has just ripened in Central
Park conservatory, where two similar bunches grew to perfection
last year."

At one time the banana-tree was utilized mainly as a shade
for the coffee-shrub. To-day the fruit rivals the apple in popularity, and its cultivation has led to the multiplication of mushroom towns in Central and Southern America devoted to this
and to hardly any other business. An especially flourishing
settlement of this sort is Bocas del Toro (literally Mouth of
the Bull), in the State of Panama, 60 miles up the coast north
of Colon. Here the soil is so rich and moist that the banana
grows so prolifically that the bunches ordinarily bearing in
other countries from 100 to 175 separate bananas here reach
the maximum of 300 of " big yellows " on a single stem, which
is a big shoulder load for the burliest negro.

The fruit from Bocas is exceptionally large, and at an
average of six inches for each banana in length, the entire
amount of them landed in New York every year, if placed in
a single string, end to end, would reach considerably more than
twice around the earth.

A visit to one of the big iron steamers from Bocas del Toro

unloading a cargo composed solely of bananas is well worth the trouble. From out the hatches, fore and aft, three or four streams of yellow and green are making their way. Here there are no longshoremen's hooks nor ponderous derricks. The bunches are so delicate that they must be handled with care, so lines of men are formed from each open hatchway to the vessel's rail.

Large mattresses or cushions are utilized on which to rest the bunches when they are passed up. They are seized in turn by the deck workers, who struggle under their loads. Sometimes 200 men are thus employed on one vessel, and these can clear it of 25,000 bunches in less than four hours. No skilled labor is employed, yet, with the assistance of four or five overseers, the work is accomplished without a great deal of loss.

After the vessel is unloaded of the salable fruit, there still remains in the hold, as well as 'tween decks, a vast amount of smashed and rotten refuse of the cargo. Men wearing rubber boots shovel the stuff together and throw it out on the dock. Then the decks and ship's sides are scraped and the hold is scalded out with live steam.

The planters at Bocas del Toro get from 40 to 75 cents a bunch for the fruit. The latter price is a little above that of other ports from which bananas are shipped, for the reason that the bunches contain so much greater a percentage of fruit. The bunches that are in prime condition bring $1.50 on the New York pier, while the inferior grades are sold all the way down from this figure.

The red bananas have been superseded almost entirely by the yellow on account of the very perishable character of the former in transportation, nearly 50 per cent. being often lost. The yellow fruit is much hardier, and will stand quite a deal of cold weather.

In the days before the control of the fruit industry in New York had passed from the Italians to the Greeks, Mr. Charles A. Dana interviewed a serious-minded merchant at the curbstone corner of Nassau and Frankfort Streets as to conditions and prospects of trade. The report was a model of concise lucidity: " Maka da mon' on da peanutta ; lose it all on da dam banan '."

Banjo. A musical instrument of the guitar class, chiefly used by the negroes of the United States and their stage imitators. The name is traced through *Banjore,* a corruption of the Spanish *bandore* or *bandora,* to the Latin *pandura,* an ancient musical instrument with the strings. A negro folk story ascribes a high antiquity to the banjo.

Noah he sent out a dove to look for dry land,
An' de dove he come back wid a banjo in his hand;
He picked up de banjo an' played dis yer tune,
An' all of de animiles dey fel down in a swoon.

Be its antiquity and parentage what they may the banjo appeared among the negroes in the United States with a neck, handle, or finger board affixed to a gourd, and is said to have originally had but three strings; a fourth one subsequently appeared. The head was made of the skin of animals or snakes and was tacked to or stuck on the gourd.

It remained for "Joe" Sweeney, a once famous delineator of negro character, to add a fifth string to the banjo. Though any number of strings have since been at times essayed, the orthodox instrument of to-day still holds to Sweeney's numeration. There is some doubt as to whether it was the fifth string (known as the "melody" or "chanterelle") or the fourth (known as the "bass") that was adopted by "Joe," but more probably it was the bass, because the other strings, as tuned, give the intervals do, mi, sol, do of the octave, and the need of the addition of a lower or bass sound would naturally have occurred to one musically inclined and seeking to improve the instrument.

It was Joe Sweeney who gave notoriety to the instrument and brought it into public favor,—its very name is sometimes said to be a corruption of Band Joe,—but in a rude and simple form it was known to the negroes long before his time. "The first one I ever saw," writes "Johnny Reb," a contributor to the Richmond *Dispatch,* in March, 1895, "was made in this way: A large gourd covered with a raw sheepskin served for the drum, and the strings were of horsehair, pulled from a white horse's tail. It had only four strings. I am confident that Sweeney added the bass string. My father's carriage-driver was a banjo-player. He played two or three changeless tunes on one cord. I saw Joe Sweeney for the first time about 1842, while I was at school at Prince Edward Courthouse. He and his brother Sam were together. Joe led on the violin and Sam played the banjo. Both had good voices, especially Sam, a rich, full, baritone of great sweetness and power. Even at this distant day I can recall some of the tunes they sang—' Old Dan Tucker,' 'Do Johnnie Booker,' 'Julianna Johnson,' 'Oh, Susana,' 'The Blue-Tailed Fly,' 'Jim Crack Corn,' and 'I Don't Care.' "

"Since the days of Joe Sweeney wonderful advances have been made in banjo music, and, well as he played, he could not be compared with such players as Shakelford, or the Davis brothers of Richmond. They have gone away beyond him in variety and technical execution. In fact, the mode of playing has changed. I do not know but one man now who can give the real old Joe Sweeney touch, and that is Polk Miller. He can do it when he wants to. In my early days my banjo served me a good turn.

"When I went to Princeton College I carried my banjo with me. No one had ever seen the instrument in the town. No one had ever heard a negro song. I was the recipient of much hospitality and good cheer. I cannot say that my banjo added anything to my scholastic proficiency."

Maurice Thompson, in an article in the *Century,* ascribes the invention of the banjo to a Georgian negro, who died in his mountain home, not far from a moonshine still, and was buried there. His grave, marked by a large boulder, has become, according to Mr. Thompson, the shrine of many American writers, who have taken the trouble to chisel their names on his granite tomb.

Banking, Women and. Mr. Louis Windmuller, president of the Maiden Lane Savings Bank, in New York, is quoted as authority for the statement that, " after a trial lasting five years, we have found that women tellers—paying and receiving— are superior to men." A Miss Clare was employed as paying teller in that bank for years. "Up to the time we engaged Miss Clare," added Mr. Windmuller, "we had experienced a lot of trouble with our men employés; so we decided to employ women. There has never been a shortage since. Every night the accounts are found to balance to a cent." Miss May Bateman, who organized a woman's bank for women in London, testifies to the same effect. "It was a bold project," she told a New York *Sun* correspondent, "to launch a bank run by women for women, but the experiment has been a huge success. At the outset we had to face a very great amount of prejudice in every quarter, but that has now to a large extent been overcome. The undertaking has clearly demonstrated that women are quite competent to transact banking business.

"But I have learned that the business of a bank manager possesses far greater human interest than ever I could have imagined. One would believe that his outlook is hedged in by pounds, shillings, and pence, finance, figures, and heavy ledgers. The exact opposite is the reality of the position.

"I have come to the conclusion that there is no more human profession than that of a bank manager. Personality plays a great part in it. A bank manager who is to be successful must gain the whole-hearted trust of his clients, for his counsel is sought on many points."

It has been said that Miss Bateman's bank was the pioneer woman's bank. In a small way, however, it was anticipated by Mrs. Priscilla Wakefield, who so far back as 1799 started, in the English village of Tottenham, a rudimentary Savings Bank (see SAVINGS BANK) for the benefit of women and children. It was arranged that members should pay every month a certain sum, graded according to age, which entitled them to a pension after they had reached sixty. This, therefore, was really a deferred annuity bank, closely resembling the system of voluntary old-age pensions issued by savings banks as lately authorized by the Legislature of Massachusetts. In 1801 there was added a fund from which loans were made to those who had been members for six months, and a department for receiving savings on which 5 per cent. was paid. This Tottenham bank, in 1804, was regularly organized under the name of the " Charitable Bank."

The first savings bank to open its books to women depositors was the old Bank for Savings, formerly in Chambers Street, New York City, in 1819. Since that time women's bank accounts have grown until women represent about forty per cent. of the total depositors in the United States.

Kansas to-day is the banner state of the female financier. According to the annual report for 1910, issued by Miss Anna Speck of the bank-commissioner's office, there were in that year 549 women holding official bank positions in Kansas,—viz., 4 presidents, 15 vice-presidents, 250 assistant cashiers, and 250 tellers. If to this were added stenographers and book-keepers the list would be swollen into the thousands. Miss Speck thinks, that, " if women were at the head of all our financial institutions, there would be little need of bank supervision and there would be no bankers' colony in our penitentiaries."

Bank-note Caricatured. A famous caricature by George Cruikshank appeared in 1818, when the penalties for crime in England were excessively harsh. About three hundred offences, ranging from murder to the theft of a piece of cloth, were punishable by death. Cruikshank, passing Newgate one day when a great crowd had gathered to witness the execution of several men and women, was shocked to learn that the women were guilty only of passing £1 counterfeit notes. He went home and, moved by pity and shame, produced his caricature, which he called " a bank-restriction note, not to be imitated." A row of criminals was represented hanging by the neck from a gallows. A figure of Britannia devouring her children was surrounded by transports bearing to Australia the lesser unfortunates who had escaped death. In place of the well-known signature of

Abraham Newland was substituted that of " J. Ketch." Cruikshank's publisher, Hone, begged to be allowed to print and publish the caricature. It proved so successful that Hone realized $3500 within a few days after it was first exhibited in his windows. The crowds indeed grew so great that the mayor had to send soldiers to clear the street. The bank directors were alarmed. At a meeting hastily convened they decided to stop the issue of the one-pound notes, a measure which had a sensible effect in diminishing the hangings at Newgate.

Bank-note, A Misprinted.—Mistakes rarely evade the vigilance of Uncle Sam's inspectors in the Washington Bureau of Engraving and Printing. The most notable exception was a national bank-note which showed $50 on one side and $100 on the other. The manner of its discovery was odd. A clerk in a Western hotel, in making up his accounts one day, found a discrepancy he could not explain. He placed the pile of bills at his left hand, and as he counted each one, turned the note over and deposited it on a pile at his right.

He found that when he counted from left to right his cash balanced exactly, but when he counted it back again a shortage of $50 was shown. He consumed two hours in vain endeavor to find out what was the matter, and finally was obliged to call on the manager for assistance.

The manager himself had no better success. Again and again he counted the bills, always with the same result—one time the cash balanced and the next the shortage was developed. Finally each bill was examined separately, both obverse and reverse; whereupon the mystified men discovered the cause of their trouble. One of the bills had the design of $50 on the obverse and that of $100 on the reverse. It further appeared that the clerk had received the bill as $100.

Communication with the Treasury Department was had, and it was found that that department had a record of the bill. It was discovered in 1890 that one sheet of bank-notes printed for a national bank of Kansas City had been reversed in the press. One plate bore the obverse of a $50 bill at the top and the obverse of a $100 bill at the bottom. The other plate bore the reverse of the two notes. After each had been printed it was laid aside to dry before being run through for the obverse printing. In some way the pressman had turned one sheet upside down, with the result that two misprinted bills came forth—one with a $50 obverse and $100 reverse, the other with a $100 obverse and a $50 reverse.

The cashier of the bank was the first to become aware of the error. He found that something was wrong after he had paid out the note with the $50 face and the $100 back by coming across the one with the $100 face and the $50 back. The note held by the cashier was returned to the Treasury and destroyed, a perfect note being issued in its stead.

Bank-notes. The oldest bank-notes are the " flying money " or " covenant money " issued in China in 2697 B.C. Originally these notes were issued by the Treasury, but the attendant expense dictated their transfer to the banks under government inspection and control. The notes were printed in blue ink on paper made from the fibre of the mulberry tree. One issued in 1339 B.C. is still carefully preserved in the Asiatic Museum in St. Petersburg.

Both the British Museum and the American Bank Note Company in New York possess specimens of Chinese bank-notes issued under the Ming Dynasty in the middle of the fourteenth century, nearly fifty years before the establishment of the first European bank at Barcelona in 1401.

The *Illustrated London News* for December 7, 1844, printed the following paragraph under the heading " A Commercial Curiosity ":

A gentleman, near Aylesbury, has in his possession a Bank of England note for *sixpence*, issued in the year 1700, of which the following is an exact copy:

No. 165.

I promise to pay to T. Caddel, or bearer, on demand, the summe of sixpence.—London, 8th day of May, 1700.

For the Governor and Company of the
Bank of England.

—— 6d.
JOHN WAGE.

The sum of fifty guineas has been offered for this curiosity.

On one occasion the Bank of England had presented to it for payment a hard ball of paper.

It was a £5 note which had been given by a prominent artist to his sister for payment of a bill.

The young woman had placed it in the pocket of her dress and promptly forgot it till the same dress made its return from the laundry.

Washing, starching, and ironing had not improved the bank-note's appearance, but, when the ball of paper was carefully un-rolled, there was sufficient to see that it had been a bank-note, and the bank paid the money without hesitation.

More than once the Bank of England has paid twice for one bank-note. On one occasion they lost in this way £30,000.

It happened that one of the directors, desirous of purchasing an estate, drew from the bank a single note for the amount mentioned. This, on returning home, he placed on the mantel-piece, when, immediately on doing so, he was called from the room.

A few moments later he came into the room again, but alas! the note had mysteriously disappeared. To the director's mind there seemed little doubt that the valuable piece of paper had fallen into the fire. Robbery was out of the question, for no one had entered the room.

His colleagues at the bank, believing this story, gave him a second note on the understanding that the first, if found, should be returned.

Thirty years afterward, when the director had been dead a considerable time, a stranger presented the missing note.

Being payable to bearer, the bank could not avoid their obligation, and they had to be the losers of the sum. It was learned afterward that a builder had bought the banker's house. and in the course of the demolition had discovered the note hidden in a crevice of the chimney.

How a bank-note once saved a man's life is a most romantic story.

In the ordinary course of business many years ago a Bank of England note—now in possession of a famous collector— was paid into a Liverpool merchant's office.

On coming into the hands of the cashier he found, while examining it to discover its genuineness, that there were faint traces of red writing upon it. The note had been in circulation for years, and it was only by the dint of extraordinary pains that the partly obliterated characters were finally deciphered.

This was the message it bore: " If this note should fall into the hands of John Dean of Longhill, near Carlisle, he will learn thereby that his brother is languishing a prisoner in Algiers."

Mr. Dean was communicated with, and he appealed to the Government to endeavor to obtain his brother's release from captivity.

Interesting themselves warmly in the matter, the Prime Minister and the joint Foreign Secretaries, after the most arduous and determined inquiries, learned that the unhappy prisoner, who had traced the above sentence with a splinter dipped in his own blood, had been a slave to the Dey of Algiers for about eleven years.

Eventually, the Government succeeded in ransoming Mr. Dean from the Dey, but the poor fellow had endured so much privation and hardship while working in the galleys that he lived but a short while after his freedom.

Bank-notes of the value of thousands of pounds are annually lost or destroyed by accident. In the forty years between 1792 and 1832 there were outstanding notes of the Bank of England, presumed to have been either lost or destroyed, amounting to £1,330,000 odd, every shilling of which was clear profit to the bank. In many instances, however, it is possible to recover the amount of the note from the bank in full. Notice has to be given to the bank of the note supposed to be lost or stolen, together with a small fee and a full narrative as to how the loss occurred. The note is then "stopped"—that is, if the document should be presented for payment the person "stopping" the note is informed when and to whom it is paid. If presented (after having been "stopped") by any suspicious looking person (and not through a banker), one of the detectives always in attendance at the bank would be called to question the person as to how and when the note came into his or her possession. It is quite a mistaken idea that "stopped payment" of a bank-note has the effect supposed by very many people. It simply means that the Bank of England carefully keeps a lookout for the note which has been "stopped," and, though it cannot refuse to pay such note immediately upon its being presented, a notification would at once be made to the person who stopped it, and the bank would give all the assistance in its power to enable the loser to recover the amount.

In the case of a bank-note having been, say, burnt by mistake, if the number is known and notice sent to the Bank of England, it will pay the amount, after an interval of five years from the date of lodging notice of destruction, should no one have presented the note for payment in the mean time. The bank in such cases also insists on a guarantee being given by a banker or two householders that it shall be repaid in the event of the document turning up and being again tendered for payment. It is not at all an unusual circumstance for a mutilated note to be presented for payment, burnt, perhaps, half through, with marks of burning on the fringes. Nor is the damage always accidental. The men who indulge in the luxury of lighting their pipes with a bank-note are not always, as some may think, millionaires or recognized lunatics of society. The spoilt notes are more often than not presented by workmen or laborers, who confess, without hesitation, that they have intentionally lighted their pipes with them from mere braggadocio.

Banks, Curiosities of. The Bank of England has its own water supply. One artesian well, 400 feet deep, gives a supply of seven thousand gallons an hour. As a direct consequence of the high cost of water in London, the bank authorities in 1910 placed a contract to sink another well. This renders the bank independent of the public supply of water. One curious use to which this water is put is not generally known: the bullion department is nightly submerged in several feet of water by the action of machinery. The same machinery is so adjusted that, if a dishonest officer during the day or night should take even one from a pile of 1000 sovereigns, the whole pile would instantly sink and a pool of water would take its place.

Philip Hone, a well-known New York merchant, in a lecture delivered in 1885 before the Mercantile Library of that city, recalled the banking conditions of his boyhood, half a century previous:

"There was but one bank in the city, the Bank of New York in Pearl Street, then Hanover Square, of which Mr. William Seton was cashier and Mr. Charles Wilkes was the first teller. Those were the blessed days of specie currency; and if you will indulge me, and laugh with me instead of frowning at me, I will describe how pleasantly it worked. The few notes which were given out by the merchants and shopkeepers (and the sequel will show how few they must have been) were collected, of course, through the bank. Michael Boyle, the runner (how delightfully do his jocund laugh and pleasant countenance mix up with the recollections of my early years!), called, several days before the time, with a notice that the note would be due on such a day, and payment expected three days thereafter.

"When the day arrived, the same person called again with a canvas bag, counted the money in half-dollars, quarters, and sixpences (those abominable disturbers of the peace, bank-notes, were scarcely known in those days), carried it to the bank, and then sallied out to another debtor; and so all the notes were collected in this great commercial city, and in such a circumscribed circle did its operations revolve. Well do I remember Michael Boyle, running around from Pearl Street to Maiden Lane, Broadway, and William Street (the business limits of which district, happily for him, did not extend north of the present Fulton Street), panting under the load of a bag of silver, a sort of locomotive sub-treasurer, or the embodiment of a specie circular."

Banyan, or fig-tree of India (*Ficus Indica*), the most astounding piece of vegetation on the face of the earth. So says Lassen.

"From one single root," he continues, "it produces a vast green temple of many halls, with cool shady bowers impervious to the light, and seems created expressly and exclusively for the purpose of supplying shelterless primeval humanity with ready-made dwellings. For neither is its wood of much use, nor are its fruits eatable for man, and, if it inspires the Hindus and their neighbors with a profound veneration, it is owing to the surpassing marvel of its well-nigh preternatural growth, its indestructible duration and everlasting self-renewal; to which traits the mysterious gloom of its galleries and avenues adds not a little, yielding a most grateful retreat from the torrid summer heat. The trunk of the tree, at a moderate height from the ground, branches out into several stout limbs, which stretch from it horizontally; from these, slender shoots—the so-called ' air-roots '—grow downward until they reach the ground, where they take root, whereupon they increase in thickness and become strong supports for the mother-limb. The central trunk repeats the branching out process at a greater height, and the second circle of limbs in its turn sends down a number of air-roots, which form an outer circle of props or pillars. As the central trunk increases in height, it goes on producing tier upon tier of horizontal limbs, and these add row after row to the outer circle of pillars, not indeed with perfect regularity, but so as to form a grove of leafy halls and verdant galleries, multiplying *ad infinitum.* For this evolution is carried on a gigantic scale. The highest tier of horizontal limbs is said to grow sometimes at an elevation of two hundred feet from the ground, and the whole structure is crowned with the dome of verdure in which the central trunk finally culminates. The leaves, which grow very close together, are five inches long by three and a half broad, and their fine green color pleasantly contrasts with the small red figs, which, however, are not eaten by men."

To complete this picture of the banyan it is necessary to conceive of the animal life that abounds in its branches and the human interest supplied by the crowds which generally encompass it. Its bright scarlet twigs afford room for flights of paroquets, green pigeons, doves, and numerous other brightly-plumaged birds, whose screaming and chattering and endless flitting motion amongst the higher branches, give one the idea of a vast aviary. Squirrels are seen frisking about on every branch, chasing one another up and down the most dangerous-looking and polished stems, some of which are sixty feet in height. Active monkeys are seen sitting upon the highest branch, eating the figs and young leaves, or chasing one another from branch to branch, clearing enormous distances by the most incredible leaps; the old gray patriarchs and sober dame monkeys looking on at the gambols of the younger ones with a gravity quite edifying.

In the sunbeams that struggle through the heavy foliage may be seen swarms of bright-colored flies, insects, and mosquitoes, fluttering out their short lives, or an occasional shade-loving butter-fly peculiar to the heaviest jungle.

7

Whilst this drama is being enacted up in the branches, the road and shade beneath are swarming with troops of children at play or chasing the monkeys; village maidens in Indian file, balancing their water-pots on their heads, are seen returning from the neighboring well; heavily-laden elephants; swift riders, with their gaily caparisoned horses; and weary foot-travellers are all seen reposing under the shade of this beautiful tree; whilst in the distance herds of buffaloes or humped cattle browse on the grass that has been blanched for want of sunshine.

In all the older stems of the tree abound owls, venomous snakes, scorpions, and lizards; and near these stems no one ever dreams of reposing.

These trees grow singly and not in forests,—indeed one banyan-tree is in itself a forest, or at least a good-sized grove. Many have been accurately measured, and several have attained historical importance. Thus, the central trunk of one handsome banyan-tree near Madras was found to be 28 feet in diameter. It was surrounded by a first circle of 20 secondary trunks, each about 11 feet in diameter and from 30 to 50 feet high, and after that by almost innumerable tertiary and quaternary growths of decreasing bulk. The largest known tree, situated on an island in the Nerbudda, has over 1300 big trunks and 3000 small ones. Armies of 6000 or 7000 men have frequently been encamped in its bowers. From afar it presented the aspect of a solitary green hillock. A violent hurricane shattered it in 1783, and since then the river has been continually carrying off portions of the tree or of its domain, so that now it is reduced to a skeleton of its former glory.

Barber, Barber's Pole. The barber's is a venerable as well as a valuable art. The prophet Ezekiel refers to him: "Take thou a barber's razor, and make it pass upon thine head and upon thy beard."

He was a notable institution in ancient Athens, his shop being much frequented by statesmen, poets, and philosophers, who came thither to have their hair cut or their beards trimmed or curled and scented with costly essences, and, incidentally, to discuss the news of the day. Shaving was little known until the time of the Macedonian conquest. Plutarch explains that Philip caused his warriors to be shaved, in order that they might not be siezed by the beards in battle. Varro tells us that barbers were unknown in Rome until Ticinius Mena brought them thither from Sicily. Then they were so highly prized that the first barber of Rome had a statue erected to his memory after death.

In the early middle ages barbers flourished mightily in Europe and encroached upon the twin provinces of dentistry and surgery. A long strife, whose settlement required .the interference of kings and councils, followed between barbers and the regular surgeon-dentists. Nevertheless, until the time of the French Revolution the barber-surgeons continued to exercise the privilege of using the lancet and drawing teeth, although the regular surgeons were prohibited from "barbery or shaving."

Hence comes the modern barber's pole, the parti-colored staff which in former times reminded the public that the proprietor of the shop before which it was placed could "*breathe a vein*" as well as he could mow a beard.

The two spiral ribbons painted around the pole represent the two long fillets or bandages, one twisted around the arm before bleeding, and the other used to bind it afterward. Originally, when not in use, the pole, with a bandage wound about it, so that both might be together when needed, was hung out at the door as a sign; but later, for convenience, instead of hanging out the identical pole, another one was painted in imitation of it and given a permanent place without. The pole was also decorated with the symbols of the other branch of his profession; that which is now but a gilt knob, was originally the copper basin with a semi-circular gap in one side, which was fitted about a man's throat while his face was lathered, so as to save his clothes from being soiled.

It was one of these basins of which the invincible knight, Don Quixote, deprived a poor barber, who had put it over his head to save his new hat from the rain,—under the belief that that he was capturing the famous helmet of Mambrino.

So recently as July 17, 1797, Lord Thurlowe, in his speech for postponing the further reading of the Surgeons' Incorporation Bill, in the House of Peers, stated, "that by a statute still in force, the barbers and surgeons were each to use a pole. The barbers were to have theirs blue and white striped, with no other appendage; but the surgeons', which was the same in other respects, was likewise to have a galley-pot and a red rag, to denote the particular nature of their vocation." This description is well versified by Gay, in his fable of "A Goat without a Beard":

> His pole with pewter basins hung,
> Black rotten teeth in order strung;
> Ranged cups that in the window stood,
> Lined with red rags, to look like blood,
> Did well his threefold trade explain,
> Who shaved, drew teeth, and breathed a vein.

The barber's instruments, numerous as well as valuable, were always exposed to the idle fingering of the bystanders

waiting for a place in his chair. Hence there was fastened
conspicuously to the wall a "table of forfeits" adapted to
every offence of this kind; but this was done more in mockery
than earnest, as the rules were of a facetious nature, and, in
any case, the barber had no authority of himself to enforce the
penalties. Shakespeare speaks of—

> The strong statutes
> Stand like the forfeits in a barber's shop,
> As much in mock as mark.

Other Elizabethan dramatists afford us many curious
glimpses into the interior of a barber-shop.

Ben Johnson says, "I can compare him to nothing more
happily than a barber's virginals, for every man may play upon
him." This is an allusion to the lute, cither, and virginals,
which at one time, for the amusement of waiting customers,
formed a part of the necessary furniture of a barber-shop, now
superseded by the banjo or a newspaper. If not engaged himself in "trimming" a customer, the barber passed his time in
life-delighting music; "for you know," says Tom Brown, "that
a cither is as natural to a barber as milk to a calf or dancing
bears to a bagpipe." They had curious customers sometimes.
Vossing writes that he would always have his hair combed in a
measured and rhythmical manner, by a barber skilled in the
rules of prosody. "More than once," he says, "I have fallen
into the hands of barbers who could imitate any measure of
song in combing my hair, expressing very intelligibly, iambics,
trochees, etc."

It was only natural that any one place which afforded so
diverse a list of luxuries and necessities should have become a
favorite resort for all classes of people, the lounging place for
the idle and the fashionable and a storm centre of gossip. The
barber's reputation for garrulity dates back to classic times.
Horace could find no stranger expression for anything that was
public and notorious than "all the barbers knew it" (omnibus
et lippis notum et tonsoribus esse). Plutarch's story is well
known.

A talkative man was trimming the beard of King Archelaus.
and asked, "How shall I cut it?"

"In silence," replied the king.

Compare with these stories the following passage from
Rowley's "A Search for Money" (1609):

As we were but asking the question, steps me from over the way
(overlistening us) a news-searcher, viz., a barber; hee, hoping to
attain some discourse for his next patient, left his baner of basons
swinging in the ayre, and closely eavedrops our conference. The saucie
treble-tongued knave would insert somewhat of his knowledge (treble-

tongu'd knave I call him, and thus I'll prove it; hee has a reasonable mother tongue, his barber-surgeon's tongue, and a tongue between two of his fingers, and from thence proceeds his wit, and 'tis a snapping wit, too).

In Monkwell Street, London, not far from St. Giles Street, stands the famous Barber-Surgeons' Hall, esteemed one of the best works of Inigo Jones. Here a fine picture by Holbein commemorates the bestowal of their charter by Henry VIII. Henry, in all his bluff majesty, is surrounded by seventeen of the company, among whom appears Dr. Butts, whom Shakespeare immortalized in the play of "Henry VIII."

The "Worshipful Company of Barbers," so the guild is still named, was established in 1308. Richard le Barbour, as Master of the Barbers, was given supervision "over the whole of his trade in London." Once a month he had to go the rounds and rebuke any barbers whom he found acting disgracefully or entering on other trades less reputable than their own. The master of a city company not only had this power of supervision over the members of his trade or profession, but he successfully prevented unauthorized folk from performing the mysteries.

It is difficult to give any particular date when the different companies ceased to be connected, save in the vaguest way, with the trades whose names they bear. But there is no doubt that, until comparatively recent times, this connection was close. As late as 1799 several barbers were prosecuted and fined for exercising the trade in the city without being members of the company.

Two instances may be cited to explain the nature of the discipline they exercised, and also its severity. In 1647 we find in the minutes of the company that Mr. Heydon complained "to this Court of his apprentice here present in Court for his evill and stubborne Behavior towards him and frequent absences out of his service in Day time and in late hours at night. The said apprentice being in Court to answer to the same did rudely and most irreverently behave himselfe towards his said Master and the whole Court, in saucy language and behavior using severall Oathes protesting that he will not serve his Master whatever shall come of it. This Court did therefore cause the Haire of the said apprentice (being undecently long) to be cut shorter."

In the year 1607 the company expended eleven shillings on "a pece of blacke buckaram to make coote for correction of apprentices." This coat, familiarly called "bulbeggar," was put over the head and shoulders of the sturdy barber appointed to chastise an apprentice. This prevented the criminal from recognizing his executioner, who would otherwise have been waylaid in Monkwell Street by the apprentices in a body and soundly drubbed in return.

There seems to be some authority for the statement that the last man in London who practised the twin trade of barber-surgery was one Middleditch, who died in Great Suffolk Street in 1826.

The *Strand,* in the volume for 1909, gives the following account of a London barber then at the height of his fame:

The quick-shaving champion of England and possibly of the world, is Robert Hardie, of Shepherd's Bush. Mr. Hardie's record of shaving five men in one minute and 15 seconds stood for some years, but not long ago the champion of the razor thought he would try for new and better time, so he managed to shave six men in one minute and 29 seconds. Mr. Hardie, a little time back, issued a challenge to the world for £500, and this money can be won by anybody who will take up the cudgels at either quick or blindfold shaving, and is able to beat the existing champion's times.

Mr. Hardie can shave one man, no matter how harsh his beard, in 12 seconds, or he will allow himself to be blindfolded and then make a clean job of it in 27 seconds. Besides these times, which are accomplished by the aid of an ordinary razor, Mr. Hardie will give any man a perfectly satisfactory shave with the aid of a carving-knife in 45 seconds, and with a pen-knife in 28 seconds.

Base-ball. The national game of the United States, though American in its ramifications, has its roots in the Old World. In 1748 a game called base-ball was played by the family of Frederick, Prince of Wales. It is just possible that the resemblance between this and the American game extends beyond the name. But the point cannot be determined from any extant records.

The origin of base-ball may be traced back without difficulty to the club-ball of the fourteenth century. In Strutt's "Sports and Pastimes" (London, 1801) is a rude engraving of two men engaged in this or some analogous pastime. One is delivering a ball to the other, who stands with the deprecatory aspect so familiar in mediæval figures, ready to receive it with a rude kind of club. In this delivery of a ball and its reception with a bat, the germ both of base-ball and of cricket is readily recognized. It is curious that the attitude of these two figures is more nearly approached in base-ball than in cricket. This may be due to the fact that cricket was an independent offshoot, while base-ball is the brilliant Americanization of another off-shoot known both here and in England as " rounders."

The method of obtaining runs is much the same as in rounders. The rough humor that put a man out by hitting him with the ball as he ran from base to base has disappeared, and instead the ball is thrown to a baseman who in the earlier American game had to touch the player in order to put him out. Now in certain cases a player is forced out if the baseman catch the ball and touch the base before the runner reaches it. The American bat is a development of the stump or stick employed at rounders by English schoolboys, and may be said to come between it and the cricket bat.

Though base-ball sprang from rounders, it has in the past half-century developed into a great deal more. Ever since professional base-ball came in vogue in America, the rules have been elaborated. Each season's experience has shown weak spots in the permissible methods of play, and these have been strengthened by new rules.

The official birth of base-ball dates from September, 1845, when the Knickerbocker Club of New York was organized and promulgated a code of rules which forms the crude basis for the present highly developed game.

The first match game ever played—between rival nines, both selected from the Knickerbocker Club—took place at Hoboken, N. J., on June 19, 1846. At the end of four innings, the leading nine had made the requisite twenty-one runs and were declared winners.

Other clubs were founded in New York. Still others sprang up elsewhere. The pioneer New England club, the Olympic, was born in Boston in 1854. The Elmtree followed in 1855. The first match game of base-ball ever played in New England dates from the latter year. It was fought out on the Boston Common between these two clubs.

By 1857 base-ball had reached the West. There were some differences in the game as played in New England and in New York. It was seen that, in order to give consistency and solidity to the game, some general governing body was necessary. A tentative effort was made in New York in 1857, when a convention of players was held and rules for the season were drawn up. Not until next year, however, did the National Association of Base-ball Players come into existence. On March 9, 1859, it held its first annual meeting in Cooper Institute.

At the second annual meeting, held March 1, 1860, many important revisions of the code were effected. The diamond supplanted the square on which the game had hitherto been played; canvas bags supplanted stakes, a pitched ball took the place of the thrown ball; nine innings, and not a certain number of runs, constituted a game; three men, and not one man, put out the side; nine players constituted a side; the base runner could not be put out by a thrown ball. As to-day, the base runner could not run three feet out of the line of base; he could not score from third after two men were out, if the batter had not reached first base safely; in case of rain, at least five innings constituted a game, and the distances between bases were ninety feet.

At this time, however, a catch of a fair bound or a foul bound disposed of the batsman.

The Association then numbered sixty clubs, of which twenty-three belonged in New York City, and sixteen to Brooklyn. Boston, Albany, Detroit, Baltimore, Newark, Newburgh, Jersey City, Poughkeepsie, Washington, New Haven, and Troy were also represented.

In the convention of 1864 the "fly-game"—the modern rule that a ball must be caught on the fly and not on the bound —was finally adopted, after having been voted down at several previous conventions.

During the season of 1867 the National Club of Washington —composed of government clerks—made a famous tour, the most extensive on record up to that time. Leaving Washington on July 11, it won its first game at Columbus, Ohio, where it defeated the Capitol Club by 90 to 10. At Cincinnati it defeated Harry Wright's Red-stockings by 53 to 10. Other victories credited were at Louisville (82–21), at St. Louis (113–26), and at Chicago, where it beat the Excelsiors by 49 to 4. The only defeat it sustained was at Rockford, Ill., where the Forest City Club made 29 runs to the Nationals' 23.

Up to 1868 stringent laws had been passed against the receiving of any salaries or rewards, but professionalism gradually crept in, and in 1869 was formally recognized when the famous Cincinnati Red Stockings, frankly a salaried club, made a spectacular tour, playing clubs from Maine to California without a single defeat. They won fifty-six games, tied one, and scored a total of 2389 runs to 574.

On March 17, 1871, the first convention of delegates from representative professional clubs was held in Collier's saloon. Broadway and Thirteenth Street, New York, when the National Association was formed, and thereafter base-ball gradually reached the professional footing on which it now stands.

The year 1874 was marked by the trip of the Boston and Athletic (Philadelphia) Club to England. Arriving in Liverpool on July 27, fourteen games were played at Liverpool, Manchester, London, Sheffield, and Dublin, the Bostons winning 8 and the Athletics 6.

One of the most spectacular of recorded feats in fielding is credited to "Wee Willie" Keeler, in a match played at Baltimore, in the early nineties, between the Baltimores and the Bostons. Keeler was right fielder for the home club. Right field there and then was a terror to visiting players, and a discomfort even to the visited. It ran down a rough and weedy hill and was backed by a fence which sloped upward at an angle of 65 degrees. The two clubs were engaged in a frantic duel for the pennant. Late in the game, with runners on bases, Stahl, of the Bostons, drove to right field a long fly that looked like a certain winner for his club. Keeler, realizing that the ball would be out of reach from the field itself, leaped nimbly upon the slope of the fence, and, mounting higher and higher, reached for and caught the ball just as it was sailing over the fence. His momentum carried him further up the incline and ended by precipitating him over the other side of the fence, but he firmly held the ball aloft as he disappeared. His reappearance a moment later was greeted with what the reporters, with a nice mixture of metaphors, called "a rousing ovation."

Up to date this had been the greatest individual feat ever performed on the field. In 1895, however, Bill Lange, centre fielder for the Chicagos, established a new record in Washington. Incidentally he saved himself from fines, aggregating $200, imposed upon him by Captain Anson. Having missed a train from New York he had arrived on the ball-field only just in time to join in the game. In the first half of the eleventh inning Chicago broke a tie by scoring one run. Washington in its half had one man on first base with two out, when "Kip" Selbach, its hardest hitter, sent the ball flying over Lange's head. "Home run!" howled the Washington fans. Lange, a man weighing 225 pounds, turned his back to the ball and sprinted desperately toward the centre-field fence. Then, as the ball was going over his head, he reached and caught it, turned a somersault, crashed against the fence, broke through it, and crawled back out of the wreckage, never having let go of the ball.

The crowd stood up on the benches, stamped, howled, whistled,—went mad. Lange limped in home.

"Fines go, Cap?" he asked, briefly.

"Nope," said Anson, more briefly.

Hugh S. Fullerton, an expert authority, writing in the *American Magazine* for June, 1910, signalizes as the greatest episode in base-ball history the famous tenth inning in a game played at Columbus, Ohio, between the home team and the St. Louis. It was the last day of the season. St. Louis and Brooklyn were almost a tie for the championship, the situation being as follows:

If both teams lost or both won, St. Louis would capture the pennant for the fifth consecutive time, an unparalleled record. *A fortiore* the same result would follow if St. Louis won and Brooklyn lost. On the other hand, Brooklyn could only become champion if on that last day Brooklyn won and St. Louis lost.

In the early stages of the St. Louis-Columbus game, the victory of the Brooklyns (playing in the East) was announced. The championship, therefore, depended on the success or failure of the St. Louis club. One can imagine the excitement and suspense of the spectators at Columbus and the fans all over the country when the ninth inning left the two antagonists close-locked in a tie. St. Louis scored one run in her half of the tenth inning. More excitement, more suspense. Then came a moment of almost frantic unrest with two men out and a runner on second base. " Big Dave " Orr came to the plate for Columbus. Three balls! Two strikes! The next ball pitched must decide the greatest event of the base-ball year. It whirled from the pitcher's hand, it was met fair and square by Orr's bat, it sailed back over centre field,—the longest hit, some say, ever made,—and home came the man from second base and home came Big Dave.

That hit decided the American Association race, kept St. Louis from breaking all records as a pennant winner, and made Dave Orr's name immortal if base-ball retains its hold to eternity.

An immortality less pleasant was won on September 23, 1908, by Fred Merkle, whose failure to touch second base at a critical moment lost the pennant for New York in the League race. It was the last half of the ninth inning. The score was a tie. With two men out, with McCormick on third base and Merkle on first, Bridwell hit safely, sending in the winning run for the " Giants." Merkle, of course, should have run to second base and touched the bag. His failure to do so was noticed by Chicago's second baseman, Johnny Evers, who, recovering the ball, touched the bag and put in a claim that Merkle was out and hence that McCormick's run could not be counted. Umpire O'Day sustained the claim, and the game then closed in a tie, as it had to be called on account of darkness.

On appeal the board of directors of the National League upheld O'Day's decision. As it happened, the official end of the base-ball season on October 7 found New York and Chicago tied for the championship. The tie game of September 23 was accordingly played off on October 8, and was won by Chicago in the presence of the largest crowd ever gathered on the diamond. Thus, through an oversight of one of its best men, New York

lost the pennant for that year, and consequently lost the opportunity to line up against the Detroits, champions of the
American League, in the world's championship series for the
year 1908.

Base-ball at Night. For the first time in the history of
organized base-ball, two league teams met in a night game at
Grand Rapids, Mich., on July 8, 1909. The clubs were the
Grand Rapids and the Zanesville, of the Central League. They
fought seven innings by electric light, Grand Rapids winning
by a score of 11 to 10. According to the current newspaper
accounts, the illumination was much better for batters than for
fielders, being furnished by thirty arcs on the grand stand and
around the diamond, while ten search-lights swept the sky and
carried to the out-field. Three fly balls hit to the out-field were
caught.

The newspaper account called this the first game of base-
ball by electric light, whereas it was only the first game played
by league teams. To set them right, a correspondent wrote to
the New York *Sun:*

> The great publicity given in the last few days to the so-called first
> game of base-ball by electric light is amusing. Some thirty years ago
> the first match game ever played by electric light took place at Straw-
> berry Hill, near Nantasket Beach, Boston harbor, between nines repre-
> senting the great dry-goods firms of Jordan, Marsh & Co. and R. H.
> White & Co. The game was played under the auspices of the New
> England Weston Electric Light Company for a purse of $50. The game
> was widely advertised, but at almost the last moment the two firms
> mentioned forbade their employees taking part, so it was played *sub rosa.*
>
> For this reason it is inexpedient to mention any names of players,
> as some of them may still be employed in these establishments, although
> a number of players were recruited from the various jobbing houses in
> the dry-goods trade. After the game there was a fine supper served to
> players and officials by the electric light company, and of this the
> present writer has the most vivid remembrance, for at the much talked-
> of game he was   THE OFFICIAL SCORER.

Base-ball, Father of. In Greenwood Cemetery, Brooklyn,
there stands a tall marble slab surmounted by a huge base-ball.
On one of its sides are carved two base-ball bats crossed over a
base-ball glove. The small bronze name-plate facing the low
mound bears the simple inscription: "In Memoriam, Henry
Chadwick, Father of Base-ball. Born October, 1824. Died
April 20, 1906." This bronze tablet is in the shape of a base-
ball diamond. In the centre of the inscription are a quill and
fountain pen, in memory of the fact that Chadwick was the
sporting editor of the Brooklyn *Daily Eagle* from the early days
of the quill until the advent of the fountain pen. His signature, "Old Chalk," was much beloved by base-ball enthusiasts.

who watched daily for more than a quarter of a century for his reports and comments upon the game. The marble sphere surmounting the monument signifies more than a prosaic base-ball; it is a sphere of the globe symbolizing the world in which once lived and moved the " Father of Base-ball."

Basilisk. The basilisk, famous in ancient and mediæval folklore, was a fabulous animal, gifted with marvellous powers of destruction. It was usually represented as an eight-limbed serpent or small dragon, sometimes with wings and sometimes without, the wings being variously like those of a bat, a grasshopper, or a butterfly. Upon its head was a circle of white spots resembling a crown. It was probably from this decoration that it derived its name of *basiliscos,* or little king. The cockatrice, a species of basilisk, possessed in addition a crest or comb like a cock's. Pliny assures us the basilisk had a voice so terrible that its sound struck terror to all other serpents. The Bible (Proverbs xxiii. 32, etc.) classes it with the lion, serpent, and dragon as among the most formidable of creatures. It was said that its bite was poisonous, that its breath was suffocating, that no plant (with one exception) could live in the neighborhood of its lair, that its dead body, suspended in a temple, would prevent swallows from building their nests there, and spiders from weaving their webs. But its most remarkable attribute was its eye, with which it darted death at every creature it looked upon. So fatal was its gaze, that it would itself die on seeing its reflected image in a mirror. In the mediæval romance of " Alexander the Great " it is related that a basilisk, having constituted itself the champion of an Asian city which that hero was besieging, climbed upon the ramparts and slew no less than two hundred Macedonians upon whom it fixed its eyes.

It is true, that, according to some authorities, the eye of a basilisk lost its power in case man or animal caught sight of it first. It was even said that in that case the basilisk would die. Thus Dryden,

> Mischiefs are like the cockatrice's eye:
> If they see first, they kill; if seen, they die.

But the balance of chances was in the monster's favor. A simultaneous look was as fatal to the basilisk's victim as a prior one. Another not infrequent superstition was that women were beyond its power, and could seize it with impunity. Among animals the weasel was unaffected by the glance of its eye, and could attack it successfully, for when wounded by the basilisk's teeth it found a ready remedy in rue, the only plant the monster could not wither. But its most dangerous enemy was the cock, the sound of whose crowing would kill it. Hence travellers

were wont to take that bird with them in passing over regions
that were infested with basilisks. Still, with all allowances, the
basilisk was a sufficiently dangerous creature to make it matter
for congratulation that it was necessarily a not very common one.
For popular legend held that it was hatched by a toad from an
egg laid by an old cock—a rare fruit among even the oldest
cocks. At a time when the belief in basilisks was most extended,
there is no record of a live one ever having made its appearance,
though dead ones were occasionally sold by vendors of curiosities.

Battle Bell, known also as the Asses' Bell and the Martinella,
was a famous bell in mediæval Florence, which was tolled continually day and night from the arch of the Ponte Santa Maria
for thirty days before the beginning of hostilities. This was done
as an *ipso facto* declaration of war, and, according to the old
chroniclers, "for greatness of mind, that the enemy might have
time to look to their defenses." It was then taken down and
hung in the portable belfry of a car which accompanied the
carroccio or big car bearing the gonfalon standard. After the
battle of Monte Aperto, fought September 4, 1260, and referred
to in Dante's *Inferno,* canto X, "the standard of the banished
Florentines, with their battle bell, the Martinella was tied to
the tail of a jackass and dragged in the dirt." (Ampère, *Voyage
Danteuse.*)

Battle-ship, First American. This was the old *Texas,*
authorized August 3, 1886, by the national appropriation act
which provided besides for building the armored cruiser *Maine,*
so that these two vessels became the first armored cruising ships
constructed by the United States. The keel of the *Texas* was
laid down in 1889 and she was completed in 1892. She was a
little over 300 feet long with a partial 12-inch steel belt. She
had a displacement of 6315 tons. Compare these figures with
those of the new *Texas* which supplanted her (length 554 feet,
tonnage 27,000 tons), and you will see one reason why the pride
of the navy in the last decade of the nineteenth century was
considered in 1911 only fit to be a target for her namesake, the
pride of the navy in the second decade of the twentieth century.

Bayonet. This appendage to the firearm is said to have
derived its name from the fact that it was first made at Bayonne,
in France. The story runs that a Basque regiment was hard
pressed on a mountain ridge near Bayonne. It was suggested
that, as their ammunition was exhausted, they should fix their
long knives into the barrels of their muskets. The suggestion
was acted upon. The first bayonet charge was made, and the
victory of the Basques led to the manufacture of the weapon
at Bayonne and its adoption into the armies of Europe.

A dagger or pike was frequently affixed to the end of the musket when the soldiers had exhausted their ammunition. There is no doubt, however, that the bayonet in its present shape was first manufactured in Bayonne. The method of fastening it is also of French invention. It was first used by Marshal Catenat, in 1693, at the battle of Marsaglia, and by means of it the slaughter was immense and the rout of the allies complete. Marshal Tallard, at the battle of Spires, in 1703, and the Duc de Vendome, in 1705, at Calimata, in Italy, obtained victories by its means, and this led to its adoption by other nations. The Spaniards were uniformly defeated by the bayonet alone in all their contests with the French, at the close of the campaign in 1794. During one of the campaigns in Flanders, the British army, under William II, was thrown into consternation at seeing the French fire upon them with fixed bayonets, but they rallied, and drove the enemy off the field. Bayonets were first used by the English grenadiers in the reign of James II; and in the reign of Queen Anne two horse grenadiers rode before her carriage with bayonets fixed by two rings to the muzzle of the musket. The general introduction of this weapon superseded the use of the pike.

In 1856 Sir Charles Napier issued a pamphlet in praise of the bayonet, calling it the queen of weapons. This provoked a lengthy discussion in the columns of the London *Times*. Dr. G. T. Guthrie, an eminent army surgeon, protested that a great delusion existed in England regarding the efficacy of the bayonet: "Opposing regiments formed in line and charging with fixed bayonets never meet and struggle hand to hand and foot to foot; and this for the best possible reason, that one side turns round and runs away as soon as the other comes close enough to do mischief. The battle of Maida is usually referred to as a remarkable instance of a bayonet fight; nevertheless the sufferers, whether killed or wounded, English or French, suffered from bullets, not bayonets. Wounds from bayonets were not less rare in the Peninsular war. It may be that all those who were bayoneted were killed, yet their bodies were seldom found."

General Sir John Scott Lillie, "as an old soldier who witnessed the greater part of the battles and sieges which took place during those wars," agreed with Dr. Guthrie, saying, "I never witnessed a bayonet wound or two hostile lines come in contact, for this simple reason—that one party gave way overcome by its fear of this weapon, before it was physically vanquished. But," he continued, "this fact does not by any means tend to controvert Sir Charles Napier's reason for championing the bayonet as the queen of weapons; it tends, in my humble opinion, rather to support those reasons. When the great object in warfare is to make the enemy show his back as expeditiously as possible, the weapon that will tend the most effectually towards the accomplishment of this object ought to be regarded as the most efficient. Sharpshooters covering the front of a line may amuse themselves as the enemy approaches, but the corps that mean to make him show his back should be concealed behind the summit or brow of an undulating plain, well selected across his line of march, and wait patiently until he arrives within 50 yards of the top, then suddenly appear in line, fire a well-directed volley into his column, and charge through the smoke, and, when the atmosphere becomes clear, the backs of their foes will be discerned descending much more rapidly than they ascended, all from 'the fears of the bayonet.' Therefore, in my humble opinion, Sir Charles Napier is right in designating it 'the queen of weapons.'"

Beacon. Early in the history of navigation certain headlands and reefs became known as peculiarly dangerous to the seaman, and human ingenuity was set to work to contrive means to give notice of the proximity of the peril. In the daytime no warning was deemed necessary, but at night, and especially when no stars were visible, the most natural device was an artificial light in such a position that the seaman could not fail to be warned in time. Beacon fires were employed among all ancient nations. The beacon light was used by the Romans as a means of promoting the safety of their shipping on the great inland sea which was but a Roman lake, and on every prominent headland from the Pillars of Hercules to the mouth of the Nile, in Europe, Asia, and Africa a bonfire blazed during every night in the year. The Romans did everything in an orderly way, and, as we learn from Pliny and other writers, some of these fires were kept up at the expense of the imperial treasury, others were maintained out of provincial sources, others were kept blazing by the petty kings and potentates, the duty being made obligatory by their Roman masters.

But many localities were dangerous where neither mountain nor headland offered a suitable place for a fire, and hence artificial structures were employed from which the beacon might send forth its beneficent light. A tower was built and on a portion of the top a hearth was prepared. During the day the fire smouldered, at evening it was revived, the wood being piled on with liberality, and the man whose duty it was to watch it being punished with death if he forsook his post. Here was the origin of the light-house.

Bean. A native of Egypt and of the West Indies, this

vegetable has been cultivated in Europe from time immemorial. It is indigenous to South America. Researches made in 1883 among the ancient Peruvian sepulchres prove that the bean was cultivated by the Incas before the time of Columbus. These sepulchres date back to a period beginning with the twelfth century and ending with the fifteenth. Within them was found a great number of beans of no less than fifty species, forty-nine of them being peculiar to the Western Hemisphere.

Among the ancient Greeks the bean had a bad name. It begot insomnia and nightmare. To dream of it boded trouble. Even ghosts fled shuddering from the smell of beans. The goddess Ceres, out of her abundant kindness, refused to include it in her gifts to man. The oracles avoided it, for fear of clouding their vision. Hippocrates too condemned it because it injured the sight, and Cicero because it corrupted the blood and inflamed the passions. The Roman priests would not even name it, as a thing unholy.

Pythagoras held that certain souls after death became beans. Hence his own death was expedited. Being pursued by enemies who thirsted for his blood because they believed him a magician, he came upon a bean-field. Recognizing in the vines only fellow souls, he would not trample upon them, but waited for his pursuers to come up and slay him.

"Avoid beans, as you would matricide," is the substance of a couple of lines in the "Golden Verses" of Pythagoras. This cryptic saying (taken, apparently, in conjunction with the story of the philosopher's death) has been the source of much unnecessary discussion among critics,—unnecessary because so familiar an author as Plutarch has glossed them in so familiar a book as that "Of the Training of Children."

"Abstain from beans," quotes Plutarch, and thus proceeds to explain, "That is, keep out of public offices, for anciently the choice of the officers of state was made by beans."

By a curious perversion of ingenuity, De Quincey made Pythagoras' saying a starting-point for certain attacks upon Coleridge as a plagiarist. He tells the story himself in his "Reminiscences of the Lake Poets."

He had long been anxious to meet Coleridge. In 1805 he paid a visit to a Mr. Poole, a neighbor of the poet's, hoping through him for an introduction. At dinner Poole asked:

"Pray, my young friend, did you ever form any opinion or conjecture of others, upon that most revolting dogma of Pythagoras about beans? You know what I mean: that monstrous doctrine in which he asserts that 'a man might as well, for the wickedness of the thing, eat his own grandmother as meddle with beans.'"

"Yes," I replied, "the line is, I believe, in the Golden Verses. I remember it well."

P.: "True. Now our dear, excellent friend Coleridge, than whom God never made a creature more divinely endowed; yet, strange it is to say, sometimes steals from other people, just as you or I might do—I beg your pardon—just as a poor creature like myself might do, that sometimes have not wherewithal to make a figure from my own exchequer; and the other day, at a dinner party, this question arising about Pythagoras and his beans, Coleridge gave us an interpretation which, from his manner, I suspect not to have been original. Think, therefore, if you anywhere read a plausible solution."

"I have; and it was in a German author. This German, understand, is a poor stick of a man, not to be named on the same day with Coleridge; so that, if Coleridge should appear to have robbed him, be assured that he has done the scamp too much honour."

P.: "Well, what says the German?"

"Why, you know the use made in Greece of beans, in voting and balloting? Well, the German says, that Pythagoras speaks symbolically; meaning that electioneering, or more generally all interference with political intrigues, is fatal to a philosopher's pursuits and their appropriate serenity. Therefore, says he, follower of mine, abstain from public affairs as you would from parricide."

P.: "Well, then, Coleridge *has* done the scamp too much honour; for, by Jove! that is the very explanation he gave us!"

De Quincey himself has the grace to add that through a passage in Jeremy Taylor he was reminded that Plutarch was the original interpreter of Pythagoras. One would have thought that no question of plagiary could arise in regard to a text so amply be-commentated. Nevertheless, he adds that, in order to forestall less generous discoverers of this and other transgressions, it becomes incumbent upon him to give an extended account of all Coleridge's plagiarisms.

The modern Athens looks more favorably upon the bean than did its forerunner in the Hellenes.

Boston baked beans are known around the globe. In the city of Boston alone about thirty-two million quarts of baked beans are devoured annually, to say nothing of the pork that goes with them and the brown bread that is also served. There are factories or bakeries which handle nothing but baked beans from one year's end to the other. One of the largest of these, which supplies restaurants wholly, bakes fourteen thousand quarts of beans a week. Other bakeries also furnish brown bread, while nearly every bakeshop that makes bread, pastry, and pies also bakes beans several times a week. There are bakeries with ovens that will hold two thousand quarts each.

The New York *Tribune* is responsible for the following estimate which it put forward in the year 1908:

Taking the average height of a Bostonian as 5 feet 6 inches and the height of a beanpot as 10 inches, one can easily figure that a Bostonian in a year eats more than two and five-seventh times his own height in baked beans, and more than his own weight. There are twelve plates of beans served in restaurants from each pot of two quarts. Boston pays for baked beans in a year the price of two of Uncle Sam's modern battle-ships.

The *Tribune* adds that dwellers in New York's Little Italy and the Ghetto of the West End, take as kindly to baked beans as do the natives of New England stock. In fact, baked beans possess a charm for people of all nationalities who go to live in Boston, permanently or temporarily. Every time a convention is held there people from all parts of the country make a dash for the nearest restaurant and call for some of the baked beans of which they have heard so much. One bakery in the heart of the Italian quarter turns out one thousand quarts daily, entirely for Italian consumption.

The invention of baked beans and pork is sometimes credited to an eccentric Englishman, Daniel Day Good, familiary known as Good Day, who was a maker of pumps and blocks at Wapping Old Stairs. On the first Friday in each of a long series of Julys he assembled a party of friends under the branches of the Fairlop Oak in Hainault Forest in the county of Essex and there regaled them on bacon and beans. This oak had a history of five centuries and had attained a girth of forty-eight feet when it was blown down in February, 1820. A fair was held for many years about this tree on the day of Mr. Good's bean feast. (See WALSH, *Curiosities of Popular Customs*, pp. 419–420.)

Bears. Up to 1909 the polar bears at the London Zoo had nothing but a splash bath, the big brown bear toiled up a pole out of a pit, and the rest of the bears lived in dens. Pit and den were the old names, and they very well described the old cages. Now the polar bears have a large and deep pool to swim in, and there are enclosures of rock and water in which the other bears may walk abroad. "The change is complete. It is not less complete perhaps for the bears themselves than for the children who come to look at them. The bears of the old Zoo were rotund and sluggish creatures, sedentary in sawdust behind iron bars. The bears of the new zoo are lithe, active animals, which can bound and run and dive—new beasts, indeed, altogether. . . . Since Teddy, Nellie, and Roosevelt have taken up their residence in their new enclosure, they have not cost the Zoological Society a penny. They are accommodating animals with simple tastes in bread, beans, and nuts, and their appetites are as constant as the food supply thrown to them by visitors; they have also the convenient habit of stopping eating when they have had enough. So the old bear-pit has gone and the pole with it, and the sight of a brown bear perched on the top of a post accepting buns and oranges on the point of an umbrella remains merely a memory. The pit will not be missed, least of all by the bear which spent its days in that unlovely gloom."—*London Spectator*, May 6, 1911.

Beaver. Indian traditions in the Western States and in Canada ascribe the rescue of the world from its aqueous ages to the industry and intelligence of the beaver,—the animal which first knew how to control and turn to account the opposing elements of land and water. Originally the beavers were of gigantic size, say the legends. Not till they had completed their appointed work on the unfinished earth did the Great Spirit smooth them down to their present dimensions. These primeval monsters, with their fellow-workers, the musquash and the otter, dived and brought up the mud, and made mountains and lakes, caves and cataracts, dividing the land from the waters, while the envious spirits of evil pelted them with gigantic rocks, which still strew the plains and valleys with monstrous boulders of misshapen stone.

Small wonder the Indians believed in the intelligence and mechanical skill of the beaver as being prior and superior to that of man in the development of the New World. That a creature whose engineering structures were based, consciously or unconsciously, on principles known only to highly civilized man, should embellish them with conveniences known to half-civilized man, was a natural inference. Even when they credited the beaver with a wish to insert windows in the walls of his lodge, it was no great flight of fancy to men who had seen with their own eyes that the same animal could construct a dike a mile long, with the precise section which human experience has determined to be that best adapted to resist the forces of pent-up water.

So far as the most careful modern observation shows, there is but one claim which has been seriously made for the beaver's sagacity which is matter for doubt. It has been asserted that the animal always cuts the trees it selects, so that they may fall towards the water. There is evidence that this is not *always* the case. But trees growing near the water naturally tend to lean towards the stream, and naturally extend the heaviest growth of branches over the water, where light and space are greatest, and the greater number of those cut by the beavers would probably fall in that direction without any special provision. But the inseparable features of a beaver-colony, the dike, or "dam," and the less famous, but almost equally wonderful, "canal," suggest an estimate of brain-power or inherited instinct for mechanics which an exhaustive examination of the facts heightens rather than diminishes.

The object of the dam is to supply a temporary want,—not a permanent necessity always present to the beaver-mind. In summer, the beavers wander up the streams, finding food without difficulty. In winter, they require a permanent supply of water at a certain level, in which they can swim beneath the ice, store their supply of branches for food so as to be accessible without exposing themselves, and keep a "moat" round their lodges. Left to itself, the stream would run low in winter, when the freezing of the snow and earth stops the water-supply. Hence the necessity for the dam to maintain it at a constant level. Such a train of arguments supposes a number of "concepts" in the beaver's brain which would occur to no other animal. To carry it out efficiently would puzzle most human beings not instructed in engineering. Moreover, the work must be done with the material at hand, so that beaver-dams are found built of branches and mud, of grass, of sand, and of mud only. To get the wood to the water-side, the beaver clears paths, or "rolling-ways," cuts a water-channel to meet and assist in the transportation of the wood, and in some cases actually makes a long canal for water-carriage and safe travelling.

Thus this little rodent anticipates civilized man and makes a road to bring commodities to its city, instead of shifting to a fresh encampment as the Indian does when supplies are exhausted (see *Spectator,* January 28, 1893: Review of H. T. Martin's *Castorologia: the History and Traditions of the American Beaver.*)

Harper's *Weekly* thus gives the story of a record made by a young beaver in captivity in Regent's Park Gardens in London. Just as the town clocks were striking noon, it was placed at work upon a tree 12 feet long and 2 feet 6 inches thick. The beaver began by barking the tree a foot above the ground.

That done he attacked the wood. He worked hard, alternating his labor with dips in his bathing pond. He bathed and labored alternately until 4 o'clock in the afternoon, when he ate his supper of bread and carrots and paddled about in his pond until half-past 5 o'clock.

Ten minutes later, when only one inch of the tree's diameter remained intact, he bore upon his work and the tree fell. Before it fell the beaver ran as men run when they have fired a blast. Then as the tree lay on the ground he portioned it out mentally and again began to gnaw.

He worked at intervals all night, cut the log into three parts, rolled two of the portions into the water and reserved the other third for his permanent shelter. The work done, he took a bath.

Bede House (*i.e.*, praying house). The charitable institution for women known by this name was founded at Rising, England, in the reign of James I, by the eccentric Henry Howard, Earl of Northampton. The Howard badge is still worn by the inmates on Sundays and holidays. Nor is this the most curious detail of dress, for the old ladies are garbed in the fashions that ruled at the time of the foundation,—blue gowns, scarlet cloaks, and high peaked hats not unlike those that have survived in Wales. The rules under which admittance is obtained were drawn up by the founder.

Every applicant must prove herself to be of "an honest life and conversation, religious, grave and discreet, able to read (if such an one may be had), a single woman, her place to be void upon marriage, to be 50 years of age at least, no common beggar, scold, haunter of taverns, inns or ale houses." Once in, she must hear prayers read by the governess twice a day and be very regular in her attendance at church. Furthermore, she must never be found guilty of atheism, heresy, blasphemy, neglect of duty, or misbehavior in the performance of it, or she will be forthwith expelled.

Bee. The smallest honey-bees in the world are found in the East Indian islands and on the mainland of Hindustan, the largest are in Hindustan. The pigmy honey collectors are known to entomologists as *Apis floria.* Their honey-combs are no larger than a child's hand, and the cells are about the size of a small pinhead. Honey and wax alike are excellent. The little creatures build combs on the branches of low trees. As they do not provide for winter, they work all the year through, raising broods like themselves. The giant bees of India are as large as field crickets. These monsters of the bee world build honey-combs from 6 to 7 feet in height and 4 feet or more in width. Each weighs from 300 to 400 pounds.

Beefsteak. So far as the records go, the highest price ever paid for beefsteak was at Circle City, Alaska, a town that sprang up almost in a night during the Klondike gold excitement. The first beefsteak to reach there sold for $48 a pound. It was a ten-pound steak shipped from a point 250 miles away. When the precious bit of meat reached the camp, the miners turned out in a body to see it. It was placed on exhibition and attracted as much attention as an elephant. Everybody wanted a piece of it, and the prices offered were such as would have resulted in a mining-camp quarrel if it had not been decided to raffle the steak off for the benefit of a hospital which Bishop Rowe was trying to establish for the miners at Circle City. Bids were started at $5 a pound, and rose briskly to $35. Finally, in order to avoid complications, it was decided to sell tickets at prices from 50 cents to $2.50 for the privilege of drawing for a slice. After $480 worth of tickets had been sold, the drawing began, and, to the relief of those in charge of the sale, no trouble resulted.

Bells, Curious and Historical. The history of bells is full of romance. No one knows just how old that history is. Exodus tells of the bells of gold worn by the Jewish high priests. Bronze bells were found in the ancient palace of Nimrod. They were used in India and China long before they were known in Europe. In civilized times they have not only been associated with social and religious affairs, but also with a great many important historical events. In the year 1282, at the ringing of the Sicilian Vespers, 8000 French were slain in cold blood by John of Procida, who thought that he would thus free Sicily from Charles of Anjou. Again, on St. Bartholomew's day, 1572, bells gave the signal for the slaughter of the Huguenots.

In the middle ages it was recognized that the power that pulled the bells held the town, as it was chiefly by their assistance that soldiers could .be summoned, the people roused, and help procured.

Such importance was attached to them that it was about the bitterest humiliation to which a vanquished city could be put when its bells were melted down by a conqueror to make cannons, and a source of rejoicing when an enemy's guns were seized and recast into bells.

The honor of inventing the large kind of bells now used in churches is sometimes ascribed to Paulinus, Bishop of Nola, a city of Campania, who flourished in the fifth century of the Christian Era. Hence their name, *campana,* given them in the lower Latinity which survives in Italian and in a modified form in other languages. Unfortunately, the name *campana* for a bell antedates Paulinus.

The oldest bell in the United States, and probably in both Americas, hangs in the rectory of the small village of East Haddam, Conn., famous also as preserving Nathan Hale's school-house on an adjacent hill. The bell bears date " A. D. 803." Presumably it came from an old monastery in Spain, and may have been brought over to this country as ballast or old iron in some sailing ship. It is said to have been purchased from a New York junk-shop and presented to the rectory.

Myth, however, makes the age of this bell doubtful. Myth also hangs dubiously around a bell said to be in Chicago, preserved in a show-case somewhere, and known to some people as the Bell of the Fig-tree. It is described as of bronze, greenish brown in color, and bearing on one side the initial " F."

This is said by the New York *Sun* to be the first bell that was ever rung across the waters of the New World, from the belfry of the first church. The church was erected in the town of Isabella, founded in San Domingo by Columbus in 1495 and named after his queen. King Ferdinand himself recognized the compliment paid to his consort by presenting this bell to the church. The city was destroyed by an earthquake in 1564.

More than three hundred years later, in 1868, a shepherd wandering among the ruins found this bell among some tangled vines. A fig-tree growing near it had thrust its branches into the ruined bell-tower and so forced the bell from its place and held it in the tree.

The bell in the belfry of the Episcopal Church at Ellicott-ville, N. Y., was cast in Moscow in 1708, as one of a chime of bells in a cathedral. In the great fire at Moscow during Napoleon's invasion, in 1814, the cathedral was destroyed. Several years afterward the bell was sold with a lot of old metal which became ballast for a vessel sailing to New York. Andrew Meneeley, of Troy, discovered the bell in a scrap pile in New York years afterward. He bought it, and for a long time it was kept by him at his bell foundry as a curiosity.

In 1831 a resident of Ellicottville went to Troy to buy a bell for the newly finished Episcopal Church. He induced the foundryman to sell him the old Russian relic.

An old bell treasured at the Washington Headquarters in Newburgh has a history of interest. It is small, weighing barely twenty-five pounds, exceedingly sweet-toned, and was made, as a Latin inscription informs us, at Amsterdam, Holland, in 1716. In 1719 it was sent to America, being a present to the settlers at Newburgh.

At that time there was no church edifice there, and the bell was lent to the Lutheran Church at New York, where it hung for some time, calling the Knickerbockers to worship, ringing in their weddings, and knelling at their funerals. It remained there until 1733, when the pioneers built a church, and the bell was removed to Newburgh. It was the first one ever rung in that region.

The bell that now hangs in the steeple of the Reformed Church at Fifth Avenue and 48th Street in New York was cast in 1731 expressly for its predecessor, the old Middle Dutch Church on Nassau Street, and all in accordance with a will left by Colonel Abraham De Peyster. During the British occupation of New York, when a portion of the church was turned into a riding school for His Majesty's dragoons, the bell was **taken down.** It was not restored to its proper place until the evacuation. In 1844 the building was sold to be converted into the city post-office, and the bell was removed to the new church in Ninth Street near Broadway, in 1855 it was again moved to a church in Lafayette Place, and on the completion of the Fifth Avenue Church it found a permanent resting place.

In the steeple of the Baptist Church at Petaluma, California, there formerly hung a bell which had been cast for the famous vigilance committee at San Francisco in the historic days of 1856. At its summons the committee gathered for council and for action. It sounded the death knell of many a rascal. In 1858 the citizens of Petaluma purchased it for $550 and hung it in the Baptist steeple. During the Civil War it was rung whenever victory crowned the Union arms. Naturally it became obnoxious to Southern sympathizers. One morning it was found broken into pieces. There is every reason to believe that it had been deliberately destroyed.

Few persons perhaps have heard of the bells of the Bastille. Fewer still know that they are yet in existence. After the destruction of the prison, they found their way to the great foundry in Romilly, but the manager of the works disobeyed the orders he received and did not destroy them.

Now they are back in Paris, in a private house in the Avenue d'Eylau. On each bell is engraved: "Made by Louis Chéron for the Royal Bastille, in the year 1761." All are ornamented with the royal arms and a huge cross.

In the cathedral church of Nôtre Dame is a bell contemporaneous with Joan of Arc—"the blessed bell" which sounded the tocsin when the maid of Orleans appeared in August, 1429, and Paris was besieged by the English. This historic bell, referred to by Victor Hugo in his "Nôtre Dame de Paris," was given to the cathedral in 1400 by Jean de Montaign. It was refounded in 1686, and then rebaptized under the name of Emmanuel Louise Thérèse, in honor of Louis XIV and Marie Thérèse of Austria.

So, if this bell is not the same bell which the heroine of Domremy heard, nevertheless the same metal vibrates to-day at the great religious ceremonies of the metropolitan church. In view of later events it seems rather more than a coincidence that when all the other bells of Nôtre Dame were destroyed by the Revolutionists Joan's bell should have been spared.

The convent of St. Mark at Florence, now a museum, has preserved its old bell, given by Cosmo de' Medici. It is known as the weeping bell, because it sounded the death knell of Savonarola, mingling its tones with the groans of the crowd. The effect of the atmosphere during four centuries threatened it with ruin. It was replaced by a new bell in 1912, but the old one is preserved in the second cloister. The curator of the museum, Signor Guido Corocci, made an exhaustive examination of the old bell, on which some of the original inscriptions can still be read. The principal scheme of decoration is a frieze of children, which, in the opinion of Signor Corocci, was executed by Michelozzo after designs of Donatello.

Bell of St. Patrick, preserved with its shrine in the Royal Irish Academy at Dublin, is said to have been bequeathed to a church in Belfast by St. Patrick himself in A. D. 557. It is constructed in rude and primitive fashion from two plates of sheet iron, bent over so as to make four sides and fastened together by large-headed iron rivets. The corners are rounded by a gentle inclination of the parts which join. One of the plates constitutes the face, the crown and upper third of the back, as well as the adjacent portion of each side, being doubled over at the top and descending to meet the smaller plate, which overlaps it at the junction. Subsequently to the securing the joints by rivets, the iron frame was consolidated by the fusion of bronze into the joints and over the surface, giving to the whole a metallic solidity which very much enhanced its resonance, as well as contributed to its preservation. The handle is of iron, let in by projecting spikes to perforations on the ridge of the bell, and further secured on the outside by bronze attachments of its straps.

The shrine for the bell was made in A. D. 1095, a period when metal work had been brought to a high development in Ireland, and is a contemporary work with the Ardagh Chalice, the Cross of Cong, the Lismore Crosier, and other perfections of the Irish metal workers. This shrine is made of brass, on which the ornamented parts are fastened down with rivets. The front is adorned with silver-gilt plates and knotwork in golden filigree. The silver work is partly covered with scrolls, some in alto-relievo and some in bass-relief. It is also decorated with gems and crystals, and on the sides are animal forms elongated and twisted into interlaced scrolls.

Replicas of both bell and shrine have been placed in the Metropolitan Museum in New York City.—VINCENT F. O'REILLY, in New York *Evening Sun,* May 4, 1909.

Bells, Big. The largest bell in the world is the Tzar Kolokol, or Tzar Bell, which now stands in the middle of a square in Moscow and is used as a chapel. Cast in the year 1733, an attempt was made to hang it so that it might be rung, but it broke from its supports and fell to the ground, making a great hole, into which it sank and lay for over 100 years. In

1836 it was raised by the Emperor Nicholas. The broken side forms the doorway to the present-day chapel.

This bell weighs 440,000 pounds, or about 219 tons, is 19 feet 3 inches in height, 3 feet thick, and 22 feet 8 inches in diameter.

Moscow also contains the largest bell in Christendom that is in actual use. It weighs 128 tons. The qualifying phrase " in Christendom " is used because China claims to have at least two bells, also in actual use, which are even larger.

The larger of these hangs in the great Buddhist monastery near Canton. It is 18 feet high and 45 feet around, being cast of solid bronze. This is one of eight monster bells that were cast by command of the Emperor Yung-lo about A. D. 1400. It cost the lives of eight men, who were killed in the process of casting. On both sides it is covered with an inscription in embossed Chinese characters about half an inch in length, covering even the top piece from which it swings, the total number being 84,000.

The second bell, only 3 feet shorter than its rival at Canton, hangs in a temple of its own to the north of Pekin, almost on the way to the Great Wall of China.

According to a Chinese legend, that finds an analogue in many European traditions, this bell had to be cast over again and again, always to be found cracked when taken out of the mould. In vain the reigning Son of Heaven stormed and swore. At last the virgin daughter of Sing-Sing-Whangsho, the bell-founder, threw herself into the seething liquid while the bell was boiling and bubbling in the moulds. Needless to say that this time the bell was cast to the satisfaction of the Son of Heaven and the sons of earth alike, all save the bereaved father, whom the emperor consoled, however, by ennobling not only himself but also five generations back of his dead ancestors, as well as Alheed, the beautiful maiden and most heroic of them all.

An eighteen-foot bell in far-away Burma had less luck, and indeed rivalled the misfortune of the Tzar Kolokol of Moscow. Lieutenant-Colonel Macgregor, in *T. P.'s Weekly* for May 4, 1906, tells us that this abortive bell is to be seen on the right bank of the River Irrawaddy, a few miles above Mandalay. It was intended to be used in connection with the giant Menjon Pagoda, beside it. The bell was finished right enough, but not the pagoda, which to this day remains the largest household heap of bricks in the world. " How the bell got into its present position I cannot tell. In the efforts to suspend it, at any rate, its supports broke down, and now it rests with one lip dipping deep into the ground, while the other side leaves a gap between, through which several others and myself once crept, just twenty years ago, during the Burmese campaign—and we picnicked there."

The largest bell in England is Big Ben of Westminster (*q.v.*), which weighs 14 tons, but there is a third bell at Moscow, one at Novgorod, one at Cologne, one at Olmutz, and one at Vienna which are heavier, so that, reckoning up all the bells of the world, Big Ben comes in as only eleventh in order of size. After Big Ben the largest bells in England are Great Peter at York Minster (10 tons), Great Tom at Oxford (7 tons), Great Tom at Lincoln (5 tons), and the bell of St. Paul's (also 5 tons).

The great bell of St. Peter's at Rome is 8 tons in weight. The Kaiser-glocke in Cologne weighs 25 tons.

Bellman or **Town-crier.** The custom in London for house-keepers to keep watch within their own ward by night, for the preservation of the peace and for apprehending suspected persons, was one of great antiquity. In addition to this safeguard, Stow tells us there belonged to each ward " a bellman, who, especially in the long nights, went through the streets and lanes ringing a bell and saluting his masters and mistresses with some rhymes suitable to the festivals and seasons of the year, at the same time bidding them look to their lights." This latter custom is said to have originated in the reign of Queen Mary, January, 1556, and to have been first practised in Cordwainer Street by Alderman Draper. The duty of the bellman, alternatively known as the town-crier, appears to have been the seeing that the lanterns which the citizens were bound to provide for lighting the streets were duly hung out before the doors; and his habitual cry was, " Hang out your lanterns! " " Look to your lanterns! "

In a collection of time-honored witticisms entitled " The Pleasant Conceits of Old Hobson, the Merry Londoner " (1606), there is a jest entitled " How Maister Hobson hung out a lantern and candlelight," which has some antiquarian interest.

When the order of hanging out lanterne and candlelight first of all was brought up, the bedell of the warde where Maister Hobson dwelt, in a darke evening, crieing up and down, " Hang out your lanternes! " " Hang out your lenternes! " using no other wordes, Maister Hobson tooke an emptie lanterne, and according to the bedell's call hung it out. This flout by the Lord Mayor was taken in ill part, and for the same offence Hobson was sent to the counter; but, being released the next night following, thinking to amend his call, the bedell cryed out with a loud voice, " Hang out your lanternes and candle! " Maister Hobson hereupon hung out a lanterne and candle unlighted, as the bedell again commanded; whereupon he was sent again to the counter; but the next night, the bedell being better advised, cryed " Hang out your lanterne and candle light! " " Hang out your lanterne and candle light! " which Maister Hobson at last did, to his great commendation, which cry of lanterne and candle light is in right manner used to this day.

In ancient times the bellmen's duties were of the most varied description, and related to objects lost or found, sales by public auction or private contract, weddings, christenings, or funerals.

They proclaimed the cause of the condemnation of criminals, and all other matters of public concern, except ecclesiastical. They also cried all kinds of goods, and were sworn to tell truly and well to the best of their ability and power.

Gradually the newspaper, the street poster, the travelling wagon with its big bell and showy signs, and a thousand other means of advertising superseded the bellman.

Liverpool appears to have been the last of the large English cities to give up this functionary, its last bellman being one Francis George, who retired in March, 1890, after a public career of some sixty years.

In addition to making public proclamations, it was part of the bellman's duty on all civic occasions to walk before the Mayor of Liverpool with a portion of the regalia.

" It was Mr. George's distinction in that capacity during his long period of office to walk before fifty-three mayors," said the Liverpool *Post* in its notice of George's retirement. " In these later days, the office of bellman has become practically a sinecure. The duties which he had to discharge have become obsolete, and other means of announcement have superseded that of the bellman.

" Up to the present, however, to the bellman's house in Greek Street are taken lost and strayed children who may be found wandering about uncared for in the streets of Liverpool. During his long tenure of office Mr. George has received from police officers at the bellman's house the custody of no fewer than 130,000 stray children, whom he restored to their parents."

Latterly this was the old bellman's chief emolument, each parent paying a shilling for the recovery of the lost children. His annual salary from the corporation was only £25.

Bell-rope in Trains. In early railroad days the locomotive engineer was the master of the train. The conductor had little or no authority. In the year 1842 the Erie Railroad (then the New York and Erie) ran only between Piermont on the Hudson, its eastern terminus, whence it connected with New York by boat, and Turner's, 47 miles to the west of New York. Captain Ebenezer Ayres (1802–1880) was a pioneer conductor on the only train between the two terminal points. It was made up of freight and passenger cars. The captain resented the autocracy of the engineer. Furthermore, if he himself needed for good cause to stop the train between stations, there was no method of signalling from the rear cars to the engine. Necessity stimulated his invention. He procured stout twine sufficiently long to reach from the locomotive to the rear car. To the end of this string next the engineer he fastened a stick of wood. He then informed the engineer, a German named Abe Hammil, that if he desired to have the train stopped he would pull the string and raise the stick, and would expect the signal to be obeyed. Hammil looked upon this innovation as a direct blow at his authority. When the train left Piermont he cut the stick loose. At Turner's he told Captain Ayres that he proposed to run the train himself, without interference from any conductor. Next day the captain again rigged up his string and stick of wood.

"Abe," said he, "this thing's got to be settled one way or the other to-day. If that stick of wood is not on the end of this cord when we get to Turner's, you've got to lick me or I'll lick you."

The stick was not on the string when the train reached Turner's. Then and there the captain settled forever the question of authority on railroad trains. Hammil abdicated as autocrat of the pioneer Erie train, and the twine and stick of wood, manipulated by the conductor, controlled its management. That was the origin of the bell-rope, now one of the most important attachments of railroad trains and street cars.

Captain Ayres continued a conductor on this road under its different managers until he was superannuated and retired on a pension in the year 1880. He died a few months later, in Owego, N. Y., at the age of 78.

Bernard, St., Hospice of. This famous monastery was founded in the year 962 by Bernard de Menthon, a neighboring nobleman, for the benefit of pilgrims journeying to Rome.

For many years after it was erected it was continually being attacked by bands of robbers who infested the mountains. In those days the brave monks were compelled at times to barricade the doors of their stronghold and wait until the weather drove the besiegers away before they dared venture forth. Once it was destroyed by fire. Here Napoleon was entertained when he took his army over the Alps into Italy in the spring of 1800. One hundred and eighty of his soldiers held the pass for a year.

Tourists visiting the hospice from Western Europe naturally ascend the path on the Swiss side. The last village one passes is Bourg St. Pierre, and at the inn here the landlord will point with pride to the tiny table and cloth-covered arm-chair which were used by the great soldier as he sat at breakfast early on the morning before he set out on that memorable journey across the Alps. His army numbered thirty thousand men, and for miles they had literally to fight their way, foot by foot, waist-deep in snow. Napoleon converted the hospice into barracks, and the great room where travellers are now sheltered was turned into a huge hospital ward.

The Grand St. Bernard is one of the most desolate spots that the mind can conceive. Wild, rocky, bare, it seems too desolate for living things to inhabit. Yet here a handful of devoted men live cheerfully, giving up everything, that they may save others from perishing.

That the work is necessary to-day is owing to the fact that hundreds of poor Italians travel on foot yearly by this, the shortest route back to their own country, that they may winter in their warm native climate. Many of them lose their way, owing to the sudden and violent snow-storms which are of almost daily occurrence on the bare, bleak slopes of the Alps, and, were it not for the brave dogs sent out to rescue them, would never wake up from the deadly snow slumber into which they fall.

Among American tourists in Switzerland, there is much rivalry for securing " real " St. Bernards to take home with them. They evidently do not know that the St. Bernards are mongrels. The original St. Bernards saw the light toward the end of the 14th century. The mother was a Wallis shepherd dog, the sire a mongrel of a Great Dane and a Spanish mountain mastiff. In the winter of 1812 nearly all the dogs lost their lives in the snow. In 1816 the last St. Bernard died. But a monk of St. Martingny had a mongrel St. Bernard, and this was crossed with a Wallis sheep dog. The breeding being done in a scientific manner, the present race of St. Bernards, though mongrel like the first, is better and stronger than the old ones, it is said.

The training of the animals is a very simple matter. During the summer months some of the assistants at the monastery take the young dogs out into the valleys or hollows, where there is always snow. One man will go and lie down in the snow and bury himself in it, and then a dog is sent to look for him. The animal is taught to bark when he has found him, and also to rouse the man up if he is asleep. When the man wakes up and stands on his feet the dog leads him to the hospice, running along in front to show him the way.

About a dozen of the dogs are always kept at the hospice. A recent visitor describing what he saw there gives a **delightful** sketch of one splendid creature which he watched. The dog was coming back through the snow after a fruitless search for lost travellers. Evidently he was very tired and much cast down in mind as he ploughed his way through the snow, a good deal embarrassed by the little cask strapped to his neck.

The visitor, wading knee deep through the snow, followed the dog around to the kennels, toward which he plodded slowly and wearily. Here the other dogs crowded eagerly around him, exactly like human beings, anxious to hear the news. But he had nothing to tell, and with drooping head went and lay down heavily in a corner to pant. It was dinner time and a monk came in with the meal. The other dogs yelped with delight; they were hungry and ate heartily, but the dog who had just come in lay still and only flopped his tail once or twice against the floor.

The monk tried to tempt him to eat, but in vain. "He is disappointed because he has found nobody. He will get over it by and by," said he. Poor, grand old dog! It was not his fault that there was nobody to be saved that day. He had done his best, and now tired out and mortified by the want of success, he refused to eat.

Father Darbellay, the then provost of the Alpine hospice, whose article on "The Rescue Dogs of St. Bernard" (*Wide World Magazine,* May, 1909) is authority for much of the above, states that the animals frequently remain out on the mountains searching for lost travellers for fifteen, eighteen, and even twenty-four hours at a stretch.

"On one occasion," he writes, "we went down the pass to seek some travellers who, we knew, could not possibly find their way, as it was snowing hard, bitterly cold, and very dark. We had three dogs with us and sent them on ahead. Presently we heard one barking. I hastened in the direction of the sound, and there found the animal pawing away in the snow. I knew some one was buried there, and, pushing away the snow with our hands, we soon came across the body of a man. We gave him some wine and biscuits. Hearing another dog barking, I was hastening away, when the animal that had found the individual mentioned gripped me by the coat and pulled me over in the snow. I wondered what was the matter, and got up quickly, discovering, with the aid of a lantern, that I was on the brink of a precipice; the dog had saved me from stepping over to my death. On this particular hunt we found eight persons, including one woman and a little child. The latter was very weak and ill. One of the brethren removed his outer coat, wrapped the child in it, tied it to the back of one of the dogs, and sent it off to the hospice. We then wended our way in the same direction."

The most famous of all the Alpine St. Bernards was "Barry," who lost his life while performing his duty.

"During the ten years he was with us," said the provost, "he saved the lives of forty persons who had lost their way in the snow. On one occasion he found a child ten years old lying in the snow under the influence of the fatal slumber which precedes death. The dog warmed the child with its breath, and then roused it from sleep by licking it. This much accomplished, Barry, by lying down on his side, gave the child an obvious invitation to get upon his back and ride. The child did so, and was thus carried to the monastery. Barry was killed by some unknown person, probably in mistake. The inscription on his monument is: 'Barry the heroic. Saved the lives of forty persons, and was killed by the forty-first.'"

Bicycle. It was a Michaux who invented the cranked pedal that distinguishes the modern cycle from the hobby-horse and célérifères of the eighteenth century (see CYCLING), but whether the honor belongs to Pierre the father or Ernest the son is a matter of dispute. When Bar-le-duc, the birthplace of Pierre Michaux, raised a modern monument to the "inventors and propagators of the pedal," the names of both father and son were discreetly inscribed thereon. The two worked side by side in a little coachsmith's forge in the cité Godot-de-Mauroi, an alley swept away years ago by the street improvements of the Champs-Elysées district of Paris.

Henri Michaux, a younger brother of Ernest, tells a story that supports the paternal claims. In May, 1861, he says, one Brunel left a draisine at the forge to be repaired. Young Ernest, then still in his teens, seized the opportunity of indulging in a ride. "But it's as fatiguing as walking," he complained to his father. The latter was seized with a bright idea.

"Put a couple of foot-rests in front," he suggested, "or, better still, fix a bent handle on the axle—like a grindstone, you know."

If we are to trust to Henri (writing thirty years after the event concerning an episode that occurred in his childhood), the wooden crank with a big nail driven into it to form a pedal was the result of this chance inspiration. At all events, the first bicycle was produced in the little forge and was dubbed a velocipede. On this vehicle Ernest would take long rides near the Mabille Gardens, then the nightly resort of the jeunesse dorée of imperial France.

Neither Michaux—father or son—was keen-witted enough

to take out a patent.. Hence, as the "velocipede" began to attract attention, rival manufacturers appeared. The most successful was Pierre Lallemont, who rode a pedalled machine on the Boulevards in 1863, and who three years later (November 20, 1866) took out an American patent, which he assigned to James Carroll, of New Haven, Conn. The exclusive right to manufacture velocipedes under this patent was purchased by Calvin Witty, of New York. So early as April, 1869, the *Galaxy* predicted that Mr. Witty "will undoubtedly make a large fortune, not merely by constructing machines, but by the 'royalty' which he obtains from the sale of manufacturer's privileges in all parts of the country. As a slight indication of the extent to which the manufacture of velocipedes is carried on, it may be mentioned that Mr. Witty employs, himself, the resources of 7 large carriage makers, and keeps their establishments busy day and night. He has seventy men at work in one establishment in New York and also keeps actively employed a large number of workmen at two manufactories in Connecticut, one at Newark, N. J., one at Wilmington, Del., and a second in New York City."

The first bicycle seen in London arrived from Paris about 1868. It had two wheels of equal size connected by a backbone which bore the saddle. A Coventry manufacturer soon invented a lighter wheel, with a steel rim grooved for the tire and with spokes of thin steel wire. This wheel was stronger and lighter than its predecessor, and, with the invention of almost frictionless ball bearings, did away with much of the terrible vibration which had earned for the first bicycle its nickname of "boneshaker."

Simultaneously the size of the front wheel was increased and that of the hind wheel lessened, until the former attained a prodigious height. This speedily came to grief. The "safety," with its two wheels of equal size, reverting to the earlier type of 1868, and its greatly improved gearing, drove the high-wheeled machine out of fashion.

The introduction of the bicycle into America dates back to 1865 when Pierre Lallemont, at Ansonia, Conn., constructed his wooden bicycle, or "boneshaker," and rode on it from that town to New Haven.

By 1870 the wooden bicycle or velocipede had entirely disappeared, and there is no record of any successor until 1876, when John Keen and David Stanton brought over racing bicycles and gave exhibitions throughout the country. Some English makes of the machine were exhibited in the Centennial Exhibition at Philadelphia, but the true beginning of American

9

cycling dates from the spring of 1878. The public rose against the innovation. They ridiculed the machines as playthings and their riders as cranks. In Boston, where the first bicycle club in the country was organized, the police soon began to intercept the riders and warn them off the streets. Adverse ordinances were revived against them in other New England towns, and indeed everywhere they appeared from 1878 to 1879. Cyclers came into their own only through the untiring efforts of Mr. Isaac B. Potter, of the Brooklyn Bicycle Club, who successfully framed and passed a bill through the Legislature which legally recognized the rights and privileges of cycle riders in New York State. The immediate effect of this bill was the opening of Central Park in New York to the riders, and the ultimate result was the passing of " liberty bills " in almost all the States of the Union. These accorded to cyclists the same rights and privileges that are granted to vehicles. The League of American Wheelmen, founded in Newport, R. I., in 1880, gave increased impetus to the sport, an impetus so great that nothing it might seem would stop it. Cycling, said the *Illustrated American* of June 4, 1892, is " not a craze, like roller-skating, but an established sport, and has come to stay and grow in popularity as the years roll on. Prejudice has been swamped; narrow-mindedness and prudery have been crushed out. The machines, as now made, enable every one to ride, from the small boy to the bishop. It is true that in this country the sport began very modestly, but it has attained great proportions. The number of meets throughout the country has multiplied; the men ride more; new clubs are being organized every week; and all over the United States wheelmen are becoming more numerous and more powerful as a factor."

Nevertheless, the débâcle came in the year 1900. With the advent of the automobile the general public lost its overwhelming interest in the bicycle.

Big Ben of Westminster. The name popularly given to the bell that strikes the hour in the clock-tower of the Houses of Parliament. It was christened St. Stephen, but the sobriquet has superseded the canonical name. How this came about is thus explained: When the new Houses of Parliament were erected in 1851, Sir Benjamin Hall, as president of the board of public works, had much to do with carrying out the plans of the architects. The value of his encouragement and assistance was fully recognized by his co-workers. So, when in September, 1856, the question came up in Parliament as to the name of the great bell that was to be hung in the tower, a member shouted, "Why not call it 'Big Ben'?" This suggestion was received with mingled laughter and applause, for Sir Benjamin was an enormous man, both in height and girth, and had often been called "Big Ben." From that day on the bell, whose peal every Londoner knows, has been known only as "Big Ben."

The present Big Ben is the second of the name that has hung in the tower. Big Ben the First, designed by the maker of the clock, Edmund Beckett Denison, afterwards Lord Grimthorpe, was cast at Stockton-on-Tees in August, 1856. The mould for it took six weeks to prepare, while the metal for it was melted in two furnaces, each containing 10 tons. When turned out and trimmed, it weighed 15 tons, was 8 feet high, and 9½ feet in diameter at the mouth. When, however, it was transported to London and tested at the foot of the clock-tower, it was found that, owing to a flaw in the metal, the bell must, without doubt, sooner or later, be broken by the blows of the hammer.

Big Ben the Second, designed also by Mr. Denison, was cast on April 10, 1858, by George Mears, taken out of the mould on the 24th, and sent to Westminster on May 31, tried and passed as to tone by Dr. Turle on June 18, and raised with great difficulty to its place in October. During November Big Ben the Second was subjected to a long series of trials under hammers weighing from 4 to 7 hundredweight each, and having successfully passed these tests, it was put in its place, where, however, it had not hung long before it also cracked. The crack, which was widened by filing to prevent vibration, seemed to Earl Grey and others rather to improve the tone of the bell, which had been so profoundly doleful as to strike a chill to the hearts of his hearers. The two bells cost the nation, in round numbers about £40,000, or $200,000.

Besides Big Ben, which strikes the hours, four smaller bells are attached to the Westminster Clock to strike the quarters. The exact dimensions of the bells are—great bell, 7ft. 6 in. in height, 9 ft. diameter at the mouth; weight, 13 tons 10 cwt. 3 qrs. 15 lb. Of the quarters: 1st quarter: weight, 1 ton 1 cwt. and 23 lb.; 2d: 1 ton 5 cwt. 1 qr. 2 lb.; 3d: 1 ton 13 cwt. 2 qrs. 13 lb.; 4th: 4 tons 13 cwt. 2 qr. 13 lb. The notes of the bells are respectively—great bell, E sharp; 1st quarter, G; 2d, F: 3d, E (octave to great bell); 4th, B; and the reading of the chimes is, taking the notes as represented by the above figures —1st quarter: 1, 2, 3, 4; half-hour: 3, 1, 2, 4—3, 2, 1, 3; 3d quarter: 1, 3, 2, 4—4, 2, 1, 3—1, 2, 3, 4; hour: 3, 1, 2, 4— 3, 2, 1, 3—1, 3, 2, 4—4, 2, 1, 3, when the great bell will strike the hour. The latter is struck on ordinary occasions with a hammer, but the clapper is available for the announcement of great events.

Billiards. There is an historic anecdote about Herbert Spencer and billiards. He was playing, with a subaltern of remarkable proficiency, a game of "50 up." Spencer gave a miss in balk. His opponent made a run of fifty and out in his first inning. The philosopher, irritated beyond measure at not getting an opening, reproved the officer in solemn tones.

"Mr. ——," he said, "a certain dexterity in games of skill argues a well-balanced mind, but such dexterity as you have shown is evidence, I fear, of a misspent youth."

And indeed an authority on billiards has confessed (*Saturday Review,* December 14, 1867) his humiliation at the thought that without the devotion of a lifetime eminence cannot be attained in this apparently simple art of knocking three balls about with a stick. It is the more humiliating, he adds, when we consider that in the prosecution of this art not the slightest mental effort is required. "Neither chess nor whist can be played, even moderately well, by an arrant fool; but a billiard-table will be found in every well-conducted lunatic asylum in the kingdom." Billiards, in fact, he considers the exact antithesis to chess. "The latter brings into play one of the rarest powers of the human mind—the power, namely, of prevision, by which future results are clearly brought within the range of mental vision, and in accordance with which they are inevitably accomplished. The former requires a well-strung and well-disciplined condition of body, so that between hand and eye the most perfect sympathy may exist. Chess is a contest of brains; billiards, of steady nerves and correct eyesight. Chess is a great mental, billiards a great manual, effort. And despite all practice and all proficiency, the best billiard-players will always be ready to acknowledge that what they actually perform falls very far short of what they see and know ought to be performed." The reason, he maintains, is that a human being can by no amount of hard work convert himself into a machine, and by nothing short of machinery can the operation of billiards be brought to perfection.

It is interesting to note that another authority, writing nearly ten years later in the same periodical (January 30, 1875), holds that there is no more beautifully scientific game than billiards. "It calls all the mental faculties into play, to the full as freely as whist, with the single exception of the memory." You must be ready, he says, to shift and modify your combinations, adapting them to each fresh situation of the rapidly rolling balls. "If you hesitate unduly you are lost, for in practice 'pottering play' is found to be invariably suicidal. Yet you must always call the teachings of your former experience into council. You must look out for what you mean to leave, and must feel your adversary as if you were fencing with him. Power of profound calculation is as essential as presence of mind." Every skilled billiard-player, he continues, must have a sort of mathematical instinct. He must divine rather than study the angles of incidence and reflection. He must allow for the disturbing influence of the " side " he imparts by striking his own ball in a particular spot with a peculiar motion of the wrist and arm. He must estimate " strengths " with extreme nicety—not merely the strength of his own stroke, but the smoothness of the cloth and the elasticity of the cushions. " After a variety of impacts and consequent rebounds, he should still be able to tell pretty nearly where three balls will be left lying. Then he equally needs mere mechanical gifts; his eye should be sure and his hand steady. He is all the better for a certain reach of body that dispenses him from frequently employing the rest. His grasp of the cue should almost amount to genius—it should be free and flexible, yet firm. And the head and hand must act in a common sympathy with iron nerves. It is not given to any player to command fortune, and the most magnificent game may be foiled by balls clashing unexpectedly. But if a man is to take leading rank among masters of the art, it may be said broadly that he should be equal to any execution in any emergency."

The origin of billiards is wrapt in obscurity. It has, of course, its myths and its legends. One of the cleverest of these was invented quite recently by the Paris *Gaulois*. It claimed as its authority a letter discovered in the British Museum attributing the invention to a London pawnbroker named William Kew, who flourished at some vague period in the sixteenth century. Kew not only lent money, but he sold cloth, and for the latter purpose had a yard measure with which he used to compute the amounts. One day to distract himself he took three round balls which are the emblems of his avuncular trade, and placing them on his counter began to hit them about with the yard measure. He found it made a pretty game. He got a kind of skill in making one ball glance off the other, and his friends who saw him thus employed called the game " Bill's yard." It was soon shortened into billiard. But the yard was the instrument with which the balls were knocked about, and the difficulty arose what to call it. They called it after the name of the pawnbroker—a Kew.

Even the French might not believe this cock-and-bull story,

but that the mention of the MS. in the British Museum convinces such skeptics as are daring enough to doubt the *ipse dixit* of the Paris *Figaro*.

In actual fact billiards was not an invention of any one human being. Like all the other great games of the world, it was a gradual evolution. It probably began as an indoor adaptation of the old game of bowls which was played on a green lawn. In winter and on rainy days your sportsman was deprived of his favorite pastime. Hence undoubtedly sprang the idea of bowling indoors on an imitation green lawn. But playing with the hand at such close quarters proved too easy for genuine sport, so the cue was introduced to put skill at a premium. Out of this developed the modern game of billiards.

That England was the birthplace of the game may be taken for granted. We hear of it there so early as the reign of Elizabeth, and then as a well-established pastime. Ben Jonson has the lines

> Even nose and cheek withal
> Smooth as is a billiard-ball.

And a greater than Jonson sent Cleopatra to billiards in his play of "Antony and Cleopatra," doubtless because the skill of Mary Queen of Scots with the cue was the talk of all Britain. More than two centuries later Byron wrote—no matter of what:

> You'll never guess, I'll bet you millions and milliards,
> It all sprang from a harmless game of billiards.

The billiards of Byron's time was the old English six-ball game, which requires for a table of full size a room eighteen by thirty feet. This alone was enough to restrict the game in a country like the United States where the twenty-foot lot is the rule and the large house the exception. Brought into general use in America by Phelan and Collander, ten years before the civil war, the six-pocket game reached its zenith in 1859, when Phelan and Secreiter played at Detroit their epoch-making game of 2000 points of four-ball caroms on a 6 x 12 six-pocket table, won by the former.

In September, 1864, the carom table, now in general use, was first exhibited at a much-attended tournament in Philadelphia, in Sansom Street Hall, above Sixth. The newly organized Union League Club was just forming its habits and customs, and its new building provided a home for the game, more famous in amateur contests than any other. From 1864 to the great Centennial tournament and on to Schaeffer's early triumphs and the great runs of Sexton and Slosson, billiards was at its zenith.

Since Schaeffer won the world championship, and said with perfect truth that in six months he could master the English game, billiards has not held its old place, though it remains one of the world's great games. Tennis, golf, and squash have come in, and more active exercise is sought by men under thirty than was desired by their predecessors of the same age a generation ago. But American play and the American table still remain in the world's lead, and the play in Philadelphia is better than it ever was, as more than one amateur tournament has shown since the great display in 1904 made by Mr. Rolls, a Philadelphian.

A billiard table of present-day pattern can be built in twenty-four hours if carte blanche be given to the manufacturer, but to get the right effects he demands from one month to six. The wood, however, must have gone through a preliminary seasoning for a period of very nearly seven years. Rich, deep Spanish mahogany is used, pollard oak, ebony, and satin wood.

The handsomest table ever made in America was for Mme. Patti. It was of rosewood and amaranth woods, with hand-painted panels. It cost $3000 and is now at Craig-y-nos, her castle in Wales.

Tables are not always covered in green. Blue is sometimes used and a pure olive green. The late Prince Leopold was the first to make use of the latter color, and olive green is known to-day in the billiard world as " Prince Leopold's color."

The balls also must be well seasoned before they are used for play. Manufacturers have incubators in which to store them that they may undergo the drying process. Some incubators will hold fully 3000 balls. When they are first made they are " green." Solid ivory is the only satisfactory material; " artificial balls " (those made of composition) are much heavier and do not wear well. English makers, to give the red balls a perfect color, steep them in a decoction that is sometimes described as the " guardsman's bath." This is extracted from the old coats of " Tommy Atkins," and for billiard balls it is the finest scarlet dye known.

In billiard cues, length, weight and balance are the proper considerations. The wood proper is ash, with leather tips that are made by French peasants, and are not procurable elsewhere than in France. Each cue is or should be constructed so that it will balance in the middle when placed across the finger. For this reason, the end in the hand is usually of lighter wood, and here some ornamentation is given. Beadlike mouldings that assist the hand in its grip are preferred. The most expensive cues are ornamented with successive curving bands of colored wood inlays, and these are so perfectly joined that they are similar to enamels, the effect being that of peacock's eyes.

Billion. In Great Britain a billion is reckoned as a million millions. In the United States it is only a thousand millions. This is one of the few instances in which a thing is bigger in the old country than in the new. In France also a billion means a thousand millions, but there they waste a word, for they already have the word *milliard* to designate this number.

Reckoning the billion in their own way, British mathematicians can indulge in an orgy of numerals and statistics in order to explain to the meanest intelligence exactly what that figure means. Here is one of the simplest forms in which explanation has been put:

What is a billion? The reply is very simple: a million times a million. This is quickly written, and quicker still pronounced. But no man is able to count it. You count 160 or 170 a minute, but let us even suppose that you go as far as 200, then an hour will produce 12,000; a day, 288,000; and a year, or 365 days (for every four years you may rest from counting, during leap-year), 105,120,000. Let us suppose, now, that Adam, at the beginning of his existence, had begun to count, had continued to do so, and was counting still—he would not even now, according to the usually supposed age of our globe, have counted near enough. For, to count a billion, he would require 9512 years, 34 days, 5 hours, and 20 minutes, according to the above rule. Now, supposing we were to allow the poor counter 12 hours daily for rest, eating, and sleeping—he would need 19,024 years, 68 days, 10 hours, and 40 minutes!

Even an American, with his paltry thousand millions as a basis for computation, can make a most respectable showing. Since the birth of Christ, we are reminded, only a little more than a billion minutes have passed into history. If a railway train running at the rate of a mile a minute had been at the dawn of the Christian era started around the earth on a straight track, its object being to run a billion miles without stop, it would have been necessary for that train to circle the earth 40,000 times, and it would not have come to the end of its journey until nearly New Year's eve, 1628—16 centuries after Christ was born and eight years after the Mayflower landed at Plymouth Rock. During its frantic flight it will have seen the Saviour live and die; Rome and its marvellous grandeur will have risen, flourished, and decayed; Britain will have been discovered and vanquished by the hosts of Cæsar, and London and Paris will have been built; kings and emperors will have reigned and great wars will have been fought; throughout the middle ages, upon which history sheds but a faint candle-light, the rushing train will have sped on its seemingly interminable journey; Christopher Columbus will have been born and America discovered, and not until nearly two centuries after that great western world has been added to the map will the engine-driver have closed the throttle and brought his machine to a full stop at his destination.

The wealth of Mr. John D. Rockefeller, the richest man in the world, has sometimes been computed at a thousand million, or in American notation a billion dollars. Let us assume this to be correct, and then imagine the world's richest man sitting down to count his " pile," in supposititious silver dollars. If he had the entire sum before him and could handle it as rapidly as the ticks of a watch—about $5 to the second—it would take him, working day and night, six years and four months to finish his pleasant task. Of course if he worked on a union labor scale he would be just 19 years on the job. In order to have coined it for this pastime the mint would have had to work making dollars for 32 years without pause day or night.

A pile of a thousand million dollars stacked as coins are ordinarily stacked would reach a height of 248 miles. Set edge to edge these dollars would form a glittering ribbon stretching from New York to Salt Lake City. To coin the dollars would require the use of 31,250 tons of silver and to haul it to the mint 2083 freight cars, drawn by 104 locomotives, would be necessary, while the combined length of the trains carrying it would be more than 14 miles.

At the ordinary valuation of agricultural lands in the best farming sections of the country, a billionaire could buy a farm as large as the combined area of the States of New York, New Hampshire, and Massachusetts. If he could buy land at $1 an acre he could purchase all the territory of the United States east of Montana, Wyoming, Colorado, and New Mexico.

In the ordinary box of safety matches there are 50 sticks. If a consignment of one billion matches were ordered from the manufacturer, the boxes in which they were packed would make a pile 158 miles in height. Packed in freight cars, they would fill 12 to the roofs. To box them alone, not to take into consideration the labor of making and labeling the boxes, 1000 girls would be kept busy a month, working in eight-hour shifts.

On the entire surface of the earth there are but a comparatively few more than a billion human beings, yet science tells us that for untold ages they have been increasing with steady regularity.

And yet financiers speak glibly of a billion dollars!

Biscuit. In the year 1550 King Henri II, of France, was making a tour of the provinces with his court. Stopping at a small Languedoc village, the local master-baker was commanded to supply a cake which should be not only palatable but also of a kind not procurable in any other place.

The order gave the master-baker furiously to think, as the French idiom phrases it. For he was an ambitious man who would fain establish a reputation. Therefore he thought day and night, and the more he thought the less he succeeded in puzzling out a new recipe. He mixed flour, sugar, and milk, and then, in despair, went away, seeing that nothing new could come of this mixture, and turned into the nearest inn to drown his disgust in a pot of wine.

His little son, who was also his apprentice, remained alone in the bakehouse, and wondered what was to be done with the dough, since his father had left no instructions. And the father did not return, for he had taken rather more wine than was good for him and he had fallen asleep behind his pot. The boy, knowing that the dough would spoil unless it was baked very soon, decided at last that, whatever the consequences might be, he must act on his own responsibility and do the best he could. So he made the dough into small round cakes, and put them into a moderately hot oven. Presently he took them out again, and then it occurred to him that the cakes would look much better glazed. Therefore he put a glaze on them, and pushed them back into the oven.

He was just about to take them out again when his father came hurrying in, gave a quick glance round, and asked, " Where is the dough I prepared before I went out?" "Here it is, Father. I have made it into little cakes, and they have been baked twice" (*bis cuits*), said the lad. The father, in a fury, raged around the bakehouse, then took up one of the little cakes, put it into his mouth, and—was delighted, for the boy had invented by a mere chance a cake which the father had vainly tried to produce. The little bis-cuit became the national cake of France, and has kept its name and fame to this day.

In the Utica (N. Y.) *Globe* the following record appeared in the issue for October 28, 1911:

A unique "world's championship" is held by Will S. Gabel, of Beloit, Kan., secretary of the Mitchell County Statewide Fair Association. Mr. Gabel claims the world's short-time championship in transforming standing grain to "light" biscuits. His record is 30 minutes flat.

Mr. Gabel's record was made with the aid of his motor car, and the wheat in the process passed through all the ordinary stages—the field, header box, thrasher, mill, and bakery—all in 30 minutes.

"Some of us farmers got into a discussion as to how quickly this could be done," said Mr. Gabel. "It arose over an article in a farm journal which stated that some one had done it in just an hour. I thought I could beat that, despite the fact that my farm was a mile and a half from the mill.

"I made arrangements with the harvesters, millers, and an uptown baker. The header entered the wheat field on my farm at 3: 14 o'clock in the afternoon—this was a few weeks ago. After one minute we gathered the heads from the box and carried them to a threshing machine, which was under full steam in the same field. After another minute the wheat was threshed. About half a bushel was sacked. We placed it in the motor car and made quick time to the door of the mill, a mile and a half from my farm.

"The mill hands grabbed the sack and poured it into the feed pipe just above the rollers. In three minutes it was crushed and sifted. At 3:29 o'clock we hastened with the flour in the motor car to a bakery, three blocks away. Fourteen minutes later the baker pulled from the oven the smoking hot light biscuits, all ready to eat. It was just 3: 44 o'clock when the first bite was taken, or half an hour to the minute from the time the grain was standing in the field."

Mr. Gabel says that he has investigated carefully and is positive that he established a world's record. A Nebraska farmer has a record of 16 minutes, but he ground the wheat in a coffee grinder in the field and baked it in the field. This record is outlawed because he did not pass through the ordinary process and the product wasn't real flour.

Blackleg. The etymology of the word is uncertain. Being a slang—or, more properly a sporting—term, its origin in its metaphorical and opprobrious signification is lost in obscurity. Worcester's and Webster's dictionaries define it as a "notorious cheat and gambler," "a sharper at race-courses." Johnson (Latham's edition) quotes from Byron's "Hints from Horace":—

> Fool'd, pillaged, dunn'd, he wastes his term away,
> And, unexpell'd, perhaps retires M. A.;
> Master of Arts! as hells and clubs proclaim,
> Where scarce a blackleg bears a brighter name!

According to the same authority a "leg" in sporting language means a "person who bets on races without himself running horses,"—that is, the vast majority of race bettors. "He likes," says Thackeray in the "Book of Snobs," "to announce at Rummer's that he is going to run down to spend Saturday and Sunday in a friendly way with Hocus, the leg, at his little box near Epsom. It is also suggested that there is some connection between "leg" and "leg bail" and the verb to "levant,"—that is, to elope without paying. According to Wright, the term "blackleg" is used in Scotland to denote "a person employed to carry a message from one lover to another." Mr. Raikes and his loving public should take note. Dr. Murray connects "blackleg" with "blackneb." The latter term implied "a person charged with democratic sympathies" at the time of the French revolution, or one viewed generally as being disaffected to government. Thus, in Scott's "Antiquary" (1816) we find "Take care, Monkbarns! we shall set you down among the blacknebs by and by."

Blotting-paper. The use to which this material can be put was discovered by mere accident. One day early in the nineteenth century, ordinary paper was being made in a mill in Berkshire, England. A careless workman forgot to put in the sizing, and the whole lot went to apparent waste. Shortly afterward the angry proprietor, having sufficiently relieved his outraged feelings, sat down to write a note. He deemed some of the condemned paper would be good enough for the purpose. To his renewed annoyance, the ink spread all over the surface. Suddenly the thought flashed over his mind that this paper would do for drying ink, in lieu of the sand then universally used. Experiments proved that he was right. He disposed of his entire damaged stock under the advertised name of blotting-paper. His success led to the general use of paper of this sort. At first it was always pink in color, owing to the fact that red rags were used. Red was a fast color and difficult to bleach. Therefore it was of little value in the manufacture of writing-paper. But red (or pink, as it developed into when run through the machinery) was as satisfactory as any other color for blotting purposes. Here, then, was a method of utilizing apparently useless material. For a long time pink was the predominant color in blotting-paper. The reason why this sort of paper dries up ink is that it is a mere mass of hair-like tubes that suck up liquid by capillary attraction. Put a fine glass tube into water, and you will find that the liquid will rise in it, owing to this same principle of capillary attraction. The art of manufacturing blotting-paper has been carried so far that the product possesses extremely absorbent qualities.

The United States Senate and the British Parliament are said to be the only bodies in the world that still cling to the use of sand in lieu of blotting-paper. The Senate sand, known as black sand, comes from a mine near Pittsburgh. It costs $2 a quart, but one quart lasts two years. On the desk of every senator stands a little sand-shaker, reinforced by a package of blotting-paper, the latter costing one cent a package. "It is an amusing fact," says the *Associated Sunday Magazines* for March, 1908, "that old senators, whom one would expect to find old-fashioned, generally use modern blotters, while young senators, like Mr. Beveridge, are scrupulous in their use of sand."

Blue. This color was first assumed in England by the Covenanters, in opposition to the scarlet badge of Charles I, and was, therefore, adopted by the soldiers of Lesley and Montrose in 1639. Its adoption is a piece of religious pedantry, the precept being taken from Numbers xv, 38: "Speak unto the children of Israel, and tell them to make to themselves fringes on the borders of their garments, putting in them ribbons of blue." This color was also a party distinction in Rome, for, in the factions of the Circus of the Lower Empire, the emperor, Anastasius, secretly favored the *Greens* while Justinian openly protected the *Blues.* The latter, therefore, became the emblem of loyalty, the former of disaffection, and, for some other unknown reason, the Blues were regarded as the party of the established and orthodox Church. The imputation of heresy cast against the others served as a pretext for every act of oppression. James III granted to the city of Edinburgh a banner, still esteemed a sort of palladium and called, from its color, the Blue Blanket. The True Blue dye was invented by a Mr. Scott, in 1802.

Blue Flower, Blue Rose. The blue flower ("die blaue Blume") was the mystic symbol of the German Romantic School, representing the nameless longings, the unsated heart hunger, the dim aspirations of the poet reaching out towards the unattainable with a vague sense of kinship to the infinite and a consequent dissatisfaction at every form of merely material happiness. In "Heinrich von Ofterdingen," a symptomatic emanation from this phase of Teutonic idealism, Friedrich von Hardenberg (who wrote under the name of Novalis) makes his titular hero start on the quest for this emblematical flower. "'The blue flower,' says Heinrich, 'is what I long for. Such wild passion for a flower was never heard of; I would fancy I was mad if I did not think with such perfect clearness.' Falling into sweet slumber, he dreamed of indescribable adventures. He found himself on the margin of a spring. Dark blue rocks with many-colored veins rose at a distance; the sky was black blue, and altogether pure. But what attracted him infinitely most was a high, light-blue flower, which stood close by the spring, touching it with its broad glittering leaves. Round it stood innumerable flowers of all colors, and the sweetest perfume filled the air. He saw nothing but the *blue flower*, and gazed on it long with nameless tenderness. All at once it began to move and change; the leaves grew more resplendent, and clasped themselves round the waxing stem; the flower bent itself towards him, and the petals showed like a blue spreading ruff, in which hovered a lovely face" (Carlyle's Trans.).

Alphonse Karr, the well-known French writer, who was something of a romanticist himself, transformed the abstract blue flower into "une rose bleue," and gave it a permanent place in French literature. For many years he resided at Nice, where he combined literary labor with the enthusiastic cultivation of flowers. Many new varieties that bear his name were the result of his ingenuity and skill.

His ineffectual effort to produce a *botanical* blue rose doubtless made the expression seem to him peculiarly fitting when applied to immaterial aspirations. He introduced it into the very title of "Les Roses Noires et les Roses Bleues." "There was only a blue rose there," he says, "that is to say, a rose which one dreams of but never gathers." And again, in "La Promenade des Anglais," he writes, "Many authors have spoken of a sky-blue rose very common, as they assert, in Italy, where they themselves have seen it. To-day it is absolutely unknown, and everything points to the certainty that it never existed."

An Englishwoman borrowed Karr's phrase and made it the title of her novel "Blue Roses" (London, 1877), whose temporary vogue acclimated the unknown flower in British soil. The dedication, "To Any Reader," runs as follows: "Whoever or whatever, you may be, I am sure that you also have had some ungrasped ideal, some illusory hope, some golden dream, some will o' the wisp of the heart. I dedicate this book to-day to your blue roses and mine."

As an actual possibility, an ideal of horticultural ambition, the blue rose has haunted the dreams of hard-headed men of science. A Mr. E. G. Hill, of Richmond, Virginia, has announced his purpose of presenting the world with this phenomenon. For nearly twoscore years he has deemed it an imminent possibility. Nor does that floral wonderworker Luther Burbank say him nay.

"Some day, surely," Burbank is reported to have said. "the blue rose will be developed. In our day we are only making a beginning."

On the other hand M. De Candolle claimed that it would be impossible to produce the rose in a blue variety. Yellow and blue, he argued, are fundamental types of color in flowers. They are antagonistic and exclude each other. Cultivation may change yellow to red or white, but never to blue. And blue may become red, but never yellow. Having already a yellow rose, we must necessarily forego the blue one,—at least until such time as the Zoölogical Society has produced a phœnix.

Nevertheless, it is worth while continuing the experiment. A large standing premium has been offered by the Horticultural

Society of Paris for the first genuine blue rose that is presented to them.

Boa Constrictor. The specific name of a large tropical American serpent. Linnæus erroneously believed it to be the largest of the boa family (a distinction properly belonging to the python), and the name has taken hold of the popular fancy as that of the largest and most terrible of all serpents. It is commonly ascribed to any great crushing snake, whether a boa or a python. But the former is an exclusive denizen of the Western Hemisphere, its range being from tropical· Mexico to Brazil, while the python proper inhabits Africa and India. The boa rarely exceeds 15 feet in length; the python sometimes reaches 30 feet. The python is savage and not easily tamed; the boa, on the contrary, is of a very gentle disposition, and readily domesticates itself in the palm or reed-thatched huts of the natives, where it hunts rats during the night.

In November, 1911, England was excited by the news that two favorite boa constrictors in the Regent's Park had met with a sad accident, which at first looked like murder and cannibalism. In short, one had swallowed the other overnight.

"The two serpents," said the New York *World* in a cable dispatch, "had lived amicably together nearly a twelvemonth. They were of the same species, but one was nine feet long and the other eleven. It is not supposed that the larger one intended to eat the other, and they are still less likely to have quarrelled; snakes are, between themselves, peaceable and gentle animals. Both were usually fed with pigeons. One afternoon their keeper had placed two birds—one for each serpent—in the glazed apartment, 15 feet by 6 feet, which was the boa constrictors' dwelling.

"The bigger serpent, having quickly swallowed his own appointed meal, observed the second pigeon visibly sticking in the jaws of his messmate. He perhaps only thought of taking a playful bite out of it. The keeper had left them, and it is conjectured that, both the serpents having got their teeth fastened in the pigeon's bones, neither could withdraw. At last the larger one swallowed the other. An explanation has been found in the peculiar structure and action of the joints of the serpent's jawbones. We are told that this gorging boa constrictor, though his body is swollen to threefold bulk, having a brother reptile inside, down to within twenty-four inches of his tail, will not die of surfeit; but he will have to eat nothing more for the next four or five months."

Boomerang. This curious weapon, peculiar to the natives of Australia, is a piece of carved wood, 30 or 40 inches long, pointed at both ends, and curved almost in the form of a crescent. The mode of using it is as singular as the weapon itself. Ask a black to throw it so that it will fall at his feet, and away it will go for fully 40 yards in front of him, skimming along the ground at 3 or 4 feet from the surface, then suddenly rise in the air to the height of 40 or 60 feet, describe a curve, and finally drop at the feet of the thrower. During its course it revolves with great rapidity and with a whizzing noise. In an expert hand the boomerang is a formidable weapon, striking without revealing the presence of the projector, and shooting round a corner, if need be, like the Irishman's gun. But it is dangerous in the hands of a novice, as it may return and strike the thrower. Hence the frequent application to the boomerang of the Shakespearean words:

> 'Tis the sport to have the engineer
> Hoist with his own petard.

All this is marvellous enough; but the marvel has grown to preposterous dimensions at the hands of credulous or too imaginative travellers. It is said, for example, that an expert can throw a boomerang so that it will kill an enemy behind a tree and then hustle back to its owner, who stands ready to hurl it on a fresh mission of carnage. We are assured that a flock of cockatoos, speeding in intricate gyrations through the air to avoid a hunter, is pursued at every turn by this erratic weapon, which strikes down a dozen or more and so returns to the hand that threw it. Old wives' fables these, at which Australians laugh. The war boomerang is not made for return. It is only slightly bent; it goes hopping and bounding along the earth like a hoop, and, where it strikes, it wounds or kills, and there's an end on't. The return boomerang is used only in light hunting or in sport, and, though it might give a man a painful rap, it could not seriously injure him. It is true that a native, if he saw a flock of cockatoos or any other birds flying by him in a straight course, could cast his weapon so as to come upon their manœuvres at a given point, and perhaps knock one down; but his boomerang would drop too, having no power of flight after it has struck anything.

The boomerang is sufficiently remarkable without being looked on as a long-bow and drawn by every tourist in the colonies.

It is an uncanny instrument; its movements are so unexpected and out of reason that it seems to be alive and to take a savage delight in strange shoots and dashes, which make the tenderfoot dodge every time it turns, lest it should hit him on the head.

Another yarn, that the Australian black throws the boomerang with his back to the object he desires to hit, is a piece off the same cloth as the others. An expert thrower can cause his boomerang to shoot behind him after a short preliminary excursion in front, and come very near a given object, but if he wants to hit anything, either in hunting or war, he doesn't fool away his time with the return boomerang, but throws the heavy, nearly straight one, which goes direct to the mark without any flourishes. Such is the boomerang—a two-formed utensil, with one shape for business, the other for sport.

Boot-jack. An implement for removing shoes and especially boots, which has gone out of date since the virtual disappearance of the latter from urban life. This is how the New York *Evening Telegram* makes "an old-timer" speak of it, even so far back as 1890:

> The reign of the boot-jack has been coincident with that of the formation and advancement of our country. I can easily recall, as I presume nearly all old men can, the time when the boot-jack was supreme in every household. This faithful servant held a place of honor beside each hearth-stone. That was before the days of railroads, telegraphs, and telephones. In that earlier day the usual means of travelling was on horseback or by stage-coach. Every man wore boots, either as a gentleman of fashion, a military officer, or as a horseman. All labor was by hand; the tailor, the cobbler, the candle-maker, and all the rest had their assured places in the community. But the time was fast approaching when, with the increasing enterprise of the times, the boot-jack was to be dethroned. One invention after another, one machine after another, one discovery after another, all these combined to drive the craftsmen more and more from their former vantage ground and to prepare the boot-jack for its nameless grave. People began to patronize machine goods. At last came Goodyear's inventions, revolutionizing the boot and shoe industry. The taste of the age changed, too. Boots were found to be clumsy, stiff, uncomfortable, and heaven knows what besides. Shoes came into favor on every side. In the regeneracy of the martial spirit of our people, in the freaks of fashion, and in the revolutionary methods of boot and shoe manufacturers, the boot-jack of our daddies met its death. The reign of the boot-jack is over. Well, what of it? Nothing. Only a few of us old fogies seem to notice the change. We cling to our boots as we do to the spirit of the past. We shall in all probability die with our boots on, for the habit has now grown on us too strong to be lightly cast aside. But in the decline of the boot-jack the old-timer may note the so-called progress of his age. Do you really think we have progressed? Progressed whither? We make more noise and bustle, and we sputter around more than we did a generation ago—but what does that signify? It has been rightly said that an American knows the price of everything and the value of nothing—and in the latter class I am sure all old-timers, like myself, will place the ruthless dethronement of the familiar boot-jack of our daddies.

Boston Common. Not every one knows that there was once a "spinning school" on Boston Common. Winsor's Memorial

History of Boston records that, upon the arrival in Boston of some Irish spinners and weavers, a spinning craze took possession of the town, "and the women, young and old, high and low, rich and poor, flocked into the spinning school, which, for want of better quarters, was set up in the Common, in the open air. Here the whirr of their wheels was heard from morning to night." Thirty-five years later the Society for Encouraging Industry and Employing the Poor again used the Common as a spinning school, about three hundred young women appearing there, seated at their wheels, as a sort of example and advertisement.

Bow Bells. A chime of bells attached to the church of St. Mary-le-Bow, or Bow church, in the very heart of the ancient city of London. Hence your true cockney has ever been held to be one born within sound of Bow Bells. According to Fynes Moryson, "the Londoners, and all within the sound of Bow Bells, are in reproach called Cockneys and eaters of buttered toasts." Beaumont and Fletcher speak of "Bow Bell suckers," *i.e.,* "children born within the sound of Bow Bells." *Anthony Clod,* a countryman, addressing *Gettings,* a citizen, in Shirley's "Contention for Honour and Riches," says, "Thou liest, and I am none of thy countryman: I was born out of the sound of your pancake bell," meaning the bell rung on Shrove Tuesday, when pancakes were in request, as they still are, and the London apprentices held a riotous holiday.

"In the year 1469 (says Stow), it was ordained by a Common Council that the Bow Bells should be nightly rung at nine of the clock. Shortly after, John Donne, mercer, by his testament, dated 1472, gave to the parson and churchwardens two tenements in Hosier-lane (now Bow-lane) to the maintenance of Bow Bell, the same to be rung as aforesaid, and other things to be observed, as by the will appeareth. This Bell being usually rung somewhat late, as seemed to the young men, 'prentices, and others in Cheap, they made and set up a rhyme against the clerk as followeth:—

> Clarke of the Bow bell, with the yellow lockes,
> For thy late ringing thy head shall have knockes.

As well as the clerk's reply—

> Children of Cheape, hold you all still,
> For you shall have the Bow bell rung at your will.

William Copeland, churchwarden, either gave a new bell for this purpose, or caused the old one to be recast in 1515—Weever says the former."

The ringing of Bow Bell at nine P.M., a custom observed to the present day, is a vestige of the Norman curfew (see WALSH, *Curiosities of Popular Customs, s.v.*). Simultaneously with the ringing, lights were ordered to be exhibited in the steeple and remain there during the night, to direct the traveller towards London.

Bow church, in the words of old Stow, "for divers accidents happening there, hath been made more famous than any other parish church of the whole city or suburbs." If not originally a Roman temple, as was once believed, it was one of the earliest churches built by the Norman conquerors of England. It was at one time garrisoned and besieged; it was afterward the scene of an assassination, it was ravaged by storms. Stow did not live to see the greatest disaster of all, when church, steeple, and bells were utterly destroyed in the Great Fire of 1666. The church was rebuilt by Sir Christopher Wren. The steeple, finished in 1679, had been prepared for 12 bells, but, funds running short, only 8 were placed. In 1739 it was found necessary to repair a crack in the Great Bell at a cost of £290. In 1758 a committee of "several respectable citizens" presented a petition to the vestry, setting forth that on all public occasions the Bells of Bow are particularly employed, that *the tenor bell is the completest in Europe,* but the other seven are very much inferior, and by no means suitable to the said tenor. "Your petitioners, therefore, request that they may be allowed, at their own expense, to recast the seven smaller bells, and to add two trebles." Accordingly, the set of ten bells was completed by subscription, and was first rung June 4, 1762, the anniversary of the birth of King George III.—STOW's *Chronicles of London;* CUNNINGHAM's *Hand-book of London;* TIMBS' *Curiosities of London.*

Bowie-knife, an implement formerly much used, both in warfare and in hunting, by the frontiersmen of the Southwest States in America. It was the invention of James Bowie, one of the most notorious of these gentry. Born in Logan County, Kentucky, in 1796, his family moved to Louisiana in his boyhood. In 1811 he purchased a small plantation known as the Bayou Terrebonne, where he lived by lumbering, fishing, and hunting until he discovered a method, legal after a fashion, but not too scrupulously honest, of making a small fortune out of negroes. The United States had recently abolished the slave-trade. All Africans brought surreptitiously into the country in violation of the statutes were subject to confiscation and sale, one-half the purchase money going to the authorities, the other half to the informer. Bowie, with his brother and two other partners, bought negroes at a dollar a pound from the slave ships of the pirate Lafitte, as he hove to outside of New Orleans. Then they informed upon themselves, bid in the slaves when seized and sold, got back half the money they had paid, and found themselves free to offer their purchases where they willed. Once lawfully within the boundaries of the United States, the blacks became marketable property. The profits were enormous. Few people bid against the partners at the auctions; the slaves were consequently admitted at a nominal expense, and found ready sale in the open market at from five hundred to a thousand dollars apiece. Much of the profit was spent in riotous living in New Orleans, Louisiana, and Natchez, Mississippi.

Riotous living involved frequent tavern brawls. Bowie is said to have invented his knife while confined to his bed from the effects of a wound received in some such brawl. Being a man of much mechanical ingenuity, he whittled from a piece of white pine the model of a hunting-knife, which he sent to two brothers named Blackman, in the city of Natchez, and told them to spare no expense in making a duplicate of it in steel. This was the origin of the dreaded bowie-knife. It was made from a large saw-mill file, and had a two-edged blade, nine inches long, of a faintly curved outline, and thick enough at the back where it joined the handle to serve for sturdy hammering. Bowie had a neat spring sheath made to enclose the knife. This he wore constantly at his belt.

He found himself in constant need of the weapon. One of his fiercest neighbors at the Bayou Terrebonne was a Spaniard who repeatedly annoyed the Colonel with petty insults. At last his conduct became so unbearable that Bowie challenged him. In accepting, the hidalgo named knives as the weapons to be used, and also stipulated that the combatants were to be seated face to face astride of a trestle, the four legs of the trestle to be buried about a foot in the earth, so that it could not by any possibility be overturned. Each of the principals was permitted to use whatever kind of knife he might select. When the combatants met, Bowie's knife excited the ridicule of his adversary. The result, however, proved the superiority of the "bowie" over the long Spanish hunting knife worn by his adversary. The men took their seats on the trestle, both naked to the waist. At the signal the Spaniard drew back his arm to make a lunge. Bowie instantly thrust his knife straight forward into the other's body, and, drawing it quickly across, disembowelled him before he realized he had been struck. Bowie presented the knife used in this duel to Edwin Forrest, who always wore it when he played "Metamora."

A more memorable affair was Bowie's fight with a certain Colonel Norris Wright. After long bickerings it had been agreed that each should fetch a dozen friends with him to the levee opposite Natchez and there end the feud with pistols. The battle was to have been fought out between detachments of threes, who were to succeed one another, but the actual event developed into a general *melée* after the first shot, the combatants using knives and pistols indiscriminately. Seven had been killed, Bowie had been borne down to earth, desperately wounded, as an apparent eighth, when he managed to bury his knife in the heart of Colonel Wright, and with the death of their principal the adherents of the latter took flight.

Bowie and his knife were now notorious. Bowie himself was thought to be as good as dead, else the vengeance of Colonel Wright's friends had been swift and sure. The bowie-knife sprang into immediate popularity. Local smiths worked day and night forging and shaping them. Eventually the chief cities of the Western and Middle States furnished rivals in their manufacture.

Bowie did not die. He found it best, however, to emigrate to Texas, then (1829) still a Mexican State but already quick with revolt. Here he married the daughter of Ex-Governor Veremendi. She survived the union only two years. When Texas declared for independence, Bowie accepted a commission as colonel in the insurgent army, and closed his career, March 6, 1836, at the bloody battle of the Alamo.

Many stories are afloat which show Bowie's rough sense of justice and essential kindliness. One was contributed to the San Francisco *Chronicle* by a Methodist clergyman in 1890. He was one of the pioneer missionaries sent to Texas by the Methodist Conference. Travelling on horseback, he crossed the Mississippi below Natchez, and next day was overtaken by another horseman dressed in buckskin, armed with a rifle, pistol and knife. Entering into conversation, he found the stranger to be intelligent, pleasant, and well acquainted with the geography of the country. Neither inquired the name or business of the other. Both were aiming at the same destination, Texas. Finally they reached a new town filled with wild, desperate characters from other States.

The minister posted a notice that he would preach at the court-house the first evening of his arrival there. At the hour named he found the rude structure thronged to overflowing— with men only. He gave out a hymn. All joined in singing, and sang well. But when he announced his text and attempted to preach, one brayed in imitation of an ass, another hooted like an owl, etc. Determined not to be driven from his purpose, he attempted again to preach, but was stopped by the same species of interruption. He stood silent and still, not knowing whether to vacate the pulpit or not. Finally his travelling companion, who, unknown to him, was in the house, arose and with stentorian voice exclaimed, "Men, this man has come here to preach to you. You need preaching to, and I'll be ――― if he shan't preach to you! The next man that disturbs him shall fight me. My name is Jim Bowie."

The preacher said that after this announcement he never had a more attentive and respectful audience, so much influence had Bowie over that reckless and dangerous element.

Boycott. This word might be defined as "to taboo, to shun, to isolate;" but in fact it justifies its existence because no other term exactly fills the bill. To boycott a man or a body of men, or a thing, means to have nothing to do with him, them, or it. Thus, you boycott a manufactured article by refusing to buy it, and if possible preventing other people from buying it, and you boycott an individual (or individuals) by refusing to work for him, to sell to him, to buy from him, and even to recognize his existence.

The word arose during the agrarian troubles in Ireland in 1879–1881. Captain Charles Cunningham Boycott (1832–1897) became in 1873 agent for Lord Earne's estates in County Mayo, and himself farmed on his own account 500 acres near Loughmask. On August 1, 1879, a notice was posted on his gate threatening his life if he attempted to collect from the tenants any rents without a further reduction of the 10 per cent. abatement already granted by Lord Earne. All but three tenants, however, paid up on the 10 per cent. basis. Next year, under the influence of the land league, a 25 per cent. abatement was insisted upon. Boycott issued eleven processes and made attempts to serve them in September, 1880, but his agents were beaten back and he had to place himself under police protection. Meanwhile Charles Stuart Parnell, leader of the agitation, in a speech made at Ennis on September 19, advised tenants who could not make good their demands to resort to aggressive measures against landlords and their agents. The result was seen in the treatment of Boycott. Laborers refused to work for him; his walls were thrown down; his cattle driven hither and thither; and he and his family found it impossible to obtain provisions from the neighborhood, so that the very necessaries of life had to be brought to them from a distance by steamer. Moreover, he was hooted and spat upon in the public roads, and the delivery of letters and telegrams at his home was interfered with. At last, early in November, 1880, a body of 50 Orangemen from County Cavan (later known as Emergency Men) volunteered to gather in Boycott's crops, and were granted an escort of 900 soldiers with 2 field-pieces. By the end of the month the work had been done and Boycott left for Dublin. Hotels there refused to accommodate him, being intimidated by threatening letters, and he went on to London, and thence to the United States. On his return to Ireland in the autumn of 1881, he again experienced some rough usage, but the personal rancor against him soon quieted down, and when in 1886 he became agent for Sir H. Adair's estates in Suffolk, England, he was even accustomed to spend his holidays in Ireland. He never obtained any compensation from the government.

The word "boycott" first came into use toward the end of 1880. The *Daily News* of December 13 printed it capitalized, but it has now become incorporated into the language as a lower-case verb.

"It has always been my conviction," says a correspondent of the New York *Nation*, writing under date of April 7, 1903, that the boycott was a device of the devil, but I did not know till recently that I had Biblical authority for it: 'And he causeth . . . that no man should be able to buy or to sell, save he that hath the mark, even the name of the beast or the number of his name' (Revelation, xiii, 17, Revised Version).

J. M. H.

(See also WALSH, *Handybook of Literary Curiosities*, p. 119.)

Braintree, a post-village of Norfolk County, Massachusetts, 10 miles south of Boston. Down to 1792 Braintree included the present towns of Randolph and Quincy. John Adams, John Quincy Adams, and John Hancock were all born there before the separation.

"In the present town of Braintree," says an old issue of *Harpers' Magazine*, "resides M——, a manufacturer of heavy carriages and heavy mechanical work of all sorts, which has been shipped to all parts of the world. His extensive business relations have given him a keen insight into human nature. A few years ago, while travelling on the cars in New York, he fell in with a very affable but high-flown gentleman, who was ostensibly acquainted with everything worth knowing. After conversing awhile relative to mechanical work, the gentleman asked M—— where he was from.

"'Braintree, Massachusetts,' was the reply.

"'Braintree? Braintree?' was the rejoinder. 'It must be an unimportant place. I think I never heard of it before.'

"'Ah? astonishing,' quietly remarked M——. 'It is the

only town in the United States that ever produced two presidents.' "

Bridge of Boils. This oddly named bridge was built by Sir John Aird. It is in Peru, on the railway from Lima to Oroya, spanning a deep and precipitous chasm over 600 feet wide and resting on three gigantic piers. Many of the men employed on the work were ex-sailors, whose training enabled them to work at dizzy heights. Although the work was necessarily of a most dangerous character, there were comparatively few accidents. But an epidemic of bubonic plague broke out. So the bridge was officially christened Puente de las Verrugas, or Bridge of Boils, a name which it still retains.

Bronco. The Chicago *News* in 1911 published this interview with an old-timer who knew all about the bronco in his best days:

Twenty-five or thirty years ago broncos were as common in the western country as political reformers are now. If you walked down the main street of any prairie town you would see anywhere from a dozen to a hundred of the critters tied to the hitching-posts. Each was equipped with a big Texas saddle that covered it from the mane to the tail. These ponies were as homely as the proverbial mud fence. They were branded all over, until they looked like a lesson in geography. Many of them had their ears slit and these generally came from the Indian Territory.

The ponies used to be driven from the big ranges in large droves in charge of accomplished bronco-busters. You could buy a good crazy bronco for $10 or $15 and a man would break it for you for $5.

People see the bronco-busting contests in the travelling shows nowadays and think they are looking at a genuine sample, but it's all a base imitation. The horses used in the shows are bad citizens and could not be recommended for family use, but they are not wild horses by a whole lot. They have been handled for weeks together, have been saddled and bridled scores of times and are familiar with the presence of man. They plunge around and tear up the ground and give an entertainment that is well worth the money, but they have learned a number of tricks and seldom hurt themselves or riders.

In the good old days a wild bronco was the wildest thing in the United States. I have seen dozens of them saddled and ridden for the first time, and it was the most exciting spectacle imaginable. I used to have the most enthusiastic admiration for the men who did the work. They were perfectly cool and calm and risked their necks as indifferently as you would light a cigar. I'd a good deal rather saddle an avalanche and ride it down a mountain side than climb aboard a wild-eyed bronco. When the critter was broken so that the owner could lead or ride it home, his troubles were nicely begun. He had an earthquake in his barn, and he never felt safe anywhere near that building until time had convinced the branded horse that nobody wanted to murder it. Getting the confidence of a bronco was tedious work. The animal associated man with red-hot branding iron, and it's no wonder if it declined to consider terms of intimacy.

But when the owner had gained the affection and esteem of the branded outcast, he had a horse that was great solace to him. A bronco hasn't much capacity for sentiment and he won't go out of his way to save your life like the heroes of horse fiction, but if you treat him right he'll give you the most faithful service.

The branded beast would start out early in the morning and take a slow, easy lope and keep it up all day over all kinds of roads and where there were no roads at all. A man could go to sleep in the saddle and dream of his good old grandmother and the pies she used to make, the motion was so rhythmical. If he came to a swollen river, which would be fatal to an automobile·or any other engine, it was all in the day's work to the pony; it would slide down the bank into the water, swim across, climb the opposite bank, which usually was as steep as the side of a house, and take the old steady lope, without drawing a long breath.

Brottus, a word of uncertain origin whose use is limited almost entirely to Savannah, Georgia, and its immediate environs, and even there only to children and negroes. It means a little something over and in excess of a given quantity and partakes of the nature of a gratuity. A child or a negro who, either upon his own account or in the performance of an errand for parents or employers, makes a purchase at a store will usually ask, " What are you going to give me for brottus? " The shopkeeper seldom fails to honor this request for a small return for the customer's patronage. So he adds to the commodity purchased a little more of the same, or perhaps in the case of a child gives some article of trifling value,— as a bit of candy or a "specked" apple or orange. A request for brottus is, of course, considered beneath the dignity of adult whites.

Brougham, a light four-wheeled cab carrying two passengers and drawn by a single horse, which first appeared in London about the year 1838. The accepted tradition is that ex-Lord Chancellor Brougham grasped the idea that a refined and glorified street cab might be modified into a convenient carriage for a gentleman, and, calling on his coach-makers, whose warehouse was in South Audley Street, proposed to them that they should build this modification of the street cab. The ex-chancellor, however, did not received much encouragement from his coach-builders, who were old-fashioned trades-people, and did not approve of new-fangled inventions. So Lord Brougham—the tradition is given for what it is worth—went to some neighbors of theirs in Mount Street, Grosvenor Square, who at once accepted his idea and built the required vehicle. Their noble customer was pleased, and in his turn he did his best to influence the world of fashion, and began with his personal friends, advising them to order carriages like his new one. "This story may or may not be true," says George Augustus Sala in the London *Daily Telegraph*, but it is worth mentioning that so recently as 1858, twenty years after the introduction of the brougham, I saw the great orator and advocate descend from his carriage at the door of his mansion in Grafton Street, Piccadilly. It was not by any means a brougham; it was a wonderful, antiquated yellow chariot, with very high springs, and very much resembling a glorified post-chaise from its hue of bright yellow. Well, the poet tells us that one always returns to one's first love, and perhaps Brougham got tired of the very brougham which he is said to have invented."

Buck-board. A four-wheeled vehicle in which a long elastic board or platform is used instead of the ordinary body, springs, and gear. The name is suggestive of bucking or bouncing, and may have arisen from the irregular motion of the wagon. Nevertheless, a circumstantial story attributes name and invention to one Dr. Buck, a Pennsylvanian, and fixes the date of the invention in 1820.

For many years, we are told, Dr. Buck was the military store-keeper of Washington, D. C., having charge of all stores *en route* to army posts in the Southwest. At that time the transportation of merchandise of all sorts was exclusively by wagon. Along the rough roads of East Tennessee, especially, much difficulty was experienced from overturned wagons and other mishaps.

Dr. Buck overhauled the outfit in use. For wagon bodies he substituted long boards set directly on the axles or hung below. These were loaded in such a manner that there were no further delays from breakdowns, and in special emergencies the load could be shifted or taken off in a hurry. The new "buck-board" was imitated all over the country, and it retains a modified popularity even in automobile construction.

Buffalo. The American animal popularly so called is more scientifically a bison. Its close relation, the European bison, is the largest extant species of European wild ox. The peculiar characteristic of the American bison, now practically extinct in a wild state, is the great mass of brown or blackish-brown hair which clothes the head, neck, and forepart of the body. The species formerly roamed over a third of North America in vast numbers. They were invaluable to the Indian. Their tendons or sinews supplied strong strings for sewing and for bowstrings; their straight foreleg bones were fashioned into clubs; their horns were used for goblets or carved into spoons; their skins afforded warm clothing in winter, and were used also as horse blankets and tent coverings; and their flesh provided the Indian with his most wholesome and savory food.

Government figures show that the herds of bison in the United States in 1850 numbered about 40,000,000 heads. From

1850 to 1883 the number slain was more than 250,000,000, or 8,000,000 each year; a record which has few parallels. In 1881 the buffalo-hide hunters shipped 50,000 buffalo hides to the East. The next year the number was 200,000 and in 1883 40,000. Only 300 were reported in 1884 and after that there were none at all. In 1883 Sitting Bull and his band, with some white hunters, killed the last 10,000 of the northern herd. By 1890 the total number of stragglers remaining in the United States was estimated at about 100, and it began to look as if another year or so would witness the death of the last survivor. Steps were taken to save the bison from extinction, with such good results that, according to the figures of the American Bison Society, there were, in 1912, 2108 of them distributed among three government herds and various private ones.

This rapid extinction of one of the zoölogical wonders of the United States was not accomplished without protest. So far back as 1879 in its issue for March 26, the *Pall Mall Gazette* noted that "the buffalo has lately attracted more than usual attention in the United States, owing to the fact that he is being rapidly exterminated. Thousands of buffaloes are slain each year merely for the sake of their hides and tongues, and fears are entertained that, unless some steps are taken to put a stop to this wholesale slaughter, the animal will soon disappear altogether from the Western plains. In the mean time, experiments recently made seem to show that buffaloes are even more valuable animals than has hitherto been supposed. These experiments have been conducted by Colonel Ezrah Miller, of Mahwah, New Jersey, who take much interest in the subject. He has found that common cows can bear buffalo calves, a fact not before ascertained. He has also proved that the thoroughbred buffalo is easily domesticated and easily kept, that the cows yield milk that will compare favorably with that of the best Alderneys both in quantity and quality, and that a buffalo fattened upon such food as is given to American cattle makes excellent beef. All these facts Colonel Miller has demonstrated at his farm in Mahwah. In his opinion there is profitable business to be done by establishing buffalo ranches on the plains, where calves can be collected, domesticated, and shipped to the East."

The *Gazette* added the suggestion that Americans might do the English a good service "if they will send buffalo beef to this country. One of our chief requirements is some kind of beef, as good as ordinary American beef, but distinguishable by flavor or otherwise from that article, that our butchers may not be able to palm it off on their customers and sell it at the same high price as that charged for British beef. Perhaps American bison or buffalo beef, which is said to have a ' venison taste' about it, will serve to put an end to this nefarious practice."

The finest stuffed specimen of the American buffalo is in the Smithsonian Institution at Washington. It was killed in 1868 near Wakeeney, Kansas, by Byron Tyler. So the Kansas City *Star* informs us. It supplies these further particulars:

Tyler was a boy of 19 when he killed the animal. He was employed as a telegraph operator at Wakeeney, then known as Ogallah, and killed buffalo only as a pastime. Later he killed them as a business and shipped their carcasses to St. Louis, where they were sold at fancy prices.

"It was early one morning that I saw the big fellow while browsing across the hills," said Tyler, in telling of the hunt, in which he brought down the Smithsonian specimen. "I was carrying a .32 calibre rifle. Getting close to the big bull, I shot him just behind the right foreleg. He fell dead at the first shot."

Friends of Tyler told him the buffalo was of extraordinary size and induced him to send the hide and bones to the institute. Prof. Henry, who was prominently connected with the museum at that time, was delighted with the gift. He wrote Tyler a personal letter thanking him for the beast.

In *Chambers's Journal* for August 31, 1889, an account is quoted from "an American paper" of the manner "in which the bison has in a little more than twenty years been extirpated." The writer says that in 1866 large firms organized hunting parties, and paid $2.50 for every bison as he lay dead on the plains. The professional hunter used to hunt on horseback and as he approached the bison almost closely enough to touch it, he fired the fatal bullet. This writer claimed to have killed more than a hundred buffalo in one day, hunting so long as the horse he rode could keep up. A few years later improved rifles were invented and the slaughter was conducted in a different manner. The horse assisted only in finding the herd whereupon the huntsmen would take a position on the leeward side nearly a mile away, and pick off the animals one after the other as fast as they could reload. "The result of this wholesale slaughter is stated in a pithy manner, which, however, suggests exaggeration, the writer telling us that in one district, at the close of one particular winter, a man could travel 50 miles in jumping from one carcass to another. The skin was the part of the animal which was valued.

The largest herd of buffalo in the world is now owned by Canada, and is kept in a national reserve set apart for them near Wainwright, a city that has sprung up 125 miles east of

Edmonton on the Grand Trunk Pacific Railroad. This descriptive extract is from *The World of To-day:*

In the Wainwright National Park were placed more than five hundred buffalo, which were transported across the international boundary line by train from the Pablo ranch. The rounding up and loading on the cars of this large number of untamed animals and their young was no slight task, and after a long period of hard work more than a hundred and fifty of the most unruly had to be left behind, having stampeded every time an attempt was made to drive them toward a corral.

An especially well organized effort will be made to ship these a little later. In addition, seventy-five buffalo now confined in a park at Banff will be sent to the Wainwright reserve. The natural increase of the herd has brought up the number to nearly a thousand. In the present favorable environment it is expected that they will multiply rapidly.

Although kept within the boundaries of the reserve, the bison can hardly be said to be in confinement. Their stamping ground covers an area of 107,000 acres—105 square miles. It is twenty-five miles in an air line the longest way across. A wire fence eight feet high and seventy-three miles long encloses it.

Building, Biggest. The main building of the Buffalo World's Fair in 1902—more strictly known as the Building of Manufactures and Liberal Arts—was hailed at the time as the largest building ever erected by man. It covered 1687 x 787 feet of ground space, or 31 acres, and cost $1,750,000. Its architect was George B. Post, of New York. An enthusiastic contributor to the *Buffalo News,* who had been admitted to inspect it prior to the opening, thus records the statistics actual and comparative:

" Two of the biggest pyramids could be placed side by side within it. The next largest building in the world, St. Peter's at Rome, could be set up in it and viewed from the galleries as an exhibit. The Chicago Auditorium is one of the most notable buildings in the West, extending from Michigan Street to Wabash Avenue, but it and 19 more of the same size could be set down under the roof of the Manufactures' Building. I had the good fortune to visit this building while workmen were still engaged on the roof trusses, and they looked like spiders and flies up among the massive beams and girders. The central hall is a room of a fraction less than 11 acres, without a supporting pillar under its roof. The iron and steel in the trusses of this building would build two Brooklyn bridges. It is theoretically possible to mobilize here the largest standing army of the world, that of Russia. There are 40 carloads of glass in the roof. The lumber in the building represents 1100 acres of average Michigan pine-trees. The building will be provided with 10,000 electric lights."

Bull, Champion. Though ordinary bulls are vanquished and put to death at the close of a Spanish bull-fight, an exceptional bull in rare cases triumphs over all its persecutors and vindicates its right to survive. Such a bull was Lechuzo, who made his first appearance in the arena at San Lucar, Andalusia, in 1890. So suddenly did he clear the ring of all matadors and picadors that the spectators rose in admiration and demanded and obtained his reprieve. Again at Cordova, after he had been healed of the wounds received at San Lucar, Lechuzo drove all his enemies before him. Once more his life was spared at the demand of the spectators. So Lechuzo came to be regarded as invincible, and finally ended his days in peace at the age of ten years. Some of his admirers sought to erect a monument to his memory at San Lucar, the scene of his first triumph, but nothing came of the proposal.

Bull-dog derives his name, his fame, and his distinctive heritage of traits, mental, moral, and physical, from the fact that he is the descendant of dogs used for ages in bull-baiting. Here courage and tenacity were all-important. The dog's duty was to seize the bull by the nose and hold him. The delight of the bull was to disembowel the dog. If one dog was gored and disabled, or killed, as often happened, he was out of the contest, and another dog was set on. The prize, or bet, or whatever was at stake, was awarded to the dog that went farthest and fairest in. After the contest the owners of the dogs paid the owner of the bull a shilling apiece for his service, and the bull was taken home to have his snout dressed.

A generation or so of this kind of work taught the dog owners that, the courage of the dogs being equal, it was the low-set dog, the fellow closest to the ground, that offered the bull the smallest opportunity for tossing. Therefore, they selected the short-legged, cloddy dogs for the work. That is why the modern bull-dog is a short-legged, heavy-set animal.

It is worth noting that the bull was allowed to protect his nose by thrusting it into a hole scooped in the ground. Some wily old bulls, not having this perquisite allowed them, pawed out holes for themselves.

Another thing was found out, too. As soon as a dog sunk his teeth in the pulpy nose of the bull, the flesh of the tortured animal would swell, so that it covered the dog's nostrils, and frequently choked him off. Therefore the indefatigable dog breeders set themselves to breed the turn-up, which is so desired a feature of the modern bull-dog. It was not long before they had the dog whose breathing was unaffected by the swelling of the bull's nose, as its nostrils were well back from the line formed by the clenched teeth.

Finally, the owners of the bulls were wont to complain of the damage some of the long-teethed dogs did to the bull's features. Too frequently the bull's countenance would wear out in the course of a morning's diversion. Willing to oblige, the dog breeders began to call out the long-teethed dogs, and propagated only (1) the courageous dog, that went fairest and farthest in; (2) the low-set dog, that was extremely hard to gore; (3) the dog whose turned-up nose enabled him to breathe comfortably while the bull's flesh swelled; and (4) the dog whose teeth were so short as not to do unnecessary damage to the bull.

When bull-baiting became illegal bull-dogs found their occupation gone. Then it was that dog-fighting had its vogue, at first openly, but of recent years secretly. The dogs that had battled with the bulls were now pitted against each other. Here great courage was a requisite, as in bull-baiting, but there were also demanded long teeth, and not only an ability to withstand any punishment, but the ability to inflict it.

Bull-fight. The endurance, agility, and ferocious courage of the bull have caused him to be selected as an object of sport by many nations at many periods. Pictorial sculpture at Beni Hassan and Thebes indicate that the Egyptians pitted bull against bull nearly three thousand years before the Christian era. Strabo gives us the additional information that the bulls were carefully trained for the occasion and that the encounters took place in the avenues to the temple. They seem, however, to have been discontinued by succeeding dynasties, as no such representations exist on walls of later periods. Bull-fights which included men and beasts as combatants were common among the Thessalonians more than three hundred years before Christ. Julius Cæsar is believed to have witnessed such exhibitions in Thessaly and to have introduced them into Rome about B. C. 45. In the early Christian ages they were prohibited throughout the Latin empire, both by the emperors and the popes. Gibbon, however, describes a feast celebrated at Rome in 1332, which included a bull-fight in the Coliseum, with the Roman nobles as participants. The bull-fight was introduced into the Spanish peninsula by the Moors in the eighth century. When they were expelled in 1492, Catholic Spain adopted the Mahommedan sport. In the sixteenth century Pope Pius V vainly decreed its extinction; in the eighteenth Charles III tried persuasion and also failed. Later Charles VI succeeded by the force of an edict. Joseph Bonaparte, however, restored the bull-fight, in order to curry favor with the nation whose throne he had usurped. Ever since then the ancient sport has flourished, despite the denunciations of the more humane races who find their delight in shooting pigeons and hounding hares and foxes to death.

In its fully developed form the bull-fight, or more literally bull-feast (*Fiesta de tores*), is not an amusement in which any one may share, but a performance by highly trained professionals,—a spectacle, therefore, rather than a game. In this respect it resembles the great American sport of base-ball, which it also resembles in the glory which surrounds the chief participants. It may be a question, indeed, whether a great matador is not a more important person in Spain than a great pitcher or catcher in America. He is a popular idol; songs are made about him and dogs named after him; his exploits are painted on fans; people crowd around him when he appears on the streets or in the hotels.

Most towns of any importance in Spain have a regular Plaza de Toras. It is an open amphitheatre, sometimes very large. The ring at Madrid, for example, will hold fifteen thousand people. In small towns which can only afford one fight a year, the market-place or principal square is fitted up. A strong stockade or barrier runs around the ring. It is about six feet high, and has a ledge about two feet from the ground, for the convenience of the men who have to jump over. Inside of the barrier there is a passage rather higher than the level of the ring, then another barrier. The seats rise from this second barrier, so that even if the bull gets out of the ring he cannot get at the spectators. These seats, which are mere rough benches without a back, rise in tiers, and above them are the boxes. The whole great round is exactly divided by the sun and the shadow,—*sol y sombra,*—the sunny seats being, of course, the plebeian and cheaper ones.

A *fiesta* may be given by a town council, by a politician in search of popularity, by a charitable association to raise money for the poor, or by an impressario in the way of business. It is said that a bull-fight was once given in aid of the Society for the Prevention of Cruelty to Animals!

The ring is hired by the company or the municipal authority to which it belongs. The chief local magnate, civil or military, is appointed president. His function is to give the signal for the beginning or ending of each part of the *fiesta* and to decide all disputes. His position is about as pleasant as that of an American base-ball umpire. If his generalship does not please the people, they consider themselves entitled to howl unlimited abuse at him.

The horses and bulls are provided by the *empresa,* or

managing committee. The former are usually broken-down hacks. The latter come for the most part from Navarre, Castile, and Andalusia, and are a specially selected, specially cared-for class. All are pedigreed. At the age of one year the young bulls are separated from the heifers, branded with the owner's mark, and turned out. loose on the plains to graze with others of their own age. When a year older the young bulls are gathered together, in order that their mettle and fighting qualities may be tested. One of them is separated from the herd and chased by a man on horseback, who, by the skilful use of a blunted lance, overthrows the escaping bull, whereupon another rider comes in front of the animal with a sharper lance, to withstand the expected attack. If the bull, on regaining his feet, attacks the rider twice, he is passed as a fighting animal; but if he turns tail and runs off, he is set aside to be killed or to be used in agricultural work. And so with each animal until the whole herd of two-year-olds have been tested. Each bull that has stood the test successfully is then entered into the herd book, with a description of its appearance, and receives a name, such as Espartero, Hamenco, and the like. This process of selection goes on from year to year until the bull is five years old, when, should its mettle still prove true, it is ready for the arena, and flaming posters appear on the walls of Madrid or Seville announcing that Espartero (or whatever his name is) will on such and such a date make its first and final appearance. A good warrantable five-year-old bull for the fighting ring costs from $350 to $500. After obtaining the bulls the next step is to find the fighters. The usual way is to hire the troupe of some well-known espada, or those of two espadas.

Bundling. The mode of courtship known as bundling, or tarrying, was prevalent in certain regions of New England, especially in the Connecticut Valley. The practice existed in many parts of Europe and is said still to linger in Wales. It was no doubt brought from England by early immigrants. That it could flourish throughout the whole colonial age, alongside a system of doctrine and practice so austere as that enforced by New England divines and magistrates, is but one of many instances of the failure of law and restraining precept to work a refinement of manners. That during much more than a century after the settlement this practice found none to challenge it, on grounds of modesty and moral tendency, goes to show how powerful is the sanction of traditional custom. Even when it was attacked by Jonathan Edwards and other innovators, the attempt to abolish it was met by violent

11

opposition and no end of ridicule. Edwards seems to think that, as "among people who pretend to uphold their credit," it was peculiar to New England; and there appears to be no evidence that it was practised elsewhere in America, except in parts of Pennsylvania, where the custom is a matter of court record so late as 1845, and where it probably still lingers in out-of-the-way places among people both of English and of German extraction.

That Pennsylvanians carried the custom even out into the wild West seems evident from a letter published in the *Waverley Magazine* of Boston in 1865:

I haven't dated this letter because I don't know where I am. I am about nine miles from Julesburg at a little settlement on the South Platte River. . . . I am stopping at a little hotel about ten by thirty feet. The landlord is from Pennsylvania and seems to be doing a thriving business. It is just large enough for the bed and candle-box, set on a chair, upon which I am writing this letter. It is in one end of the building, and separated from the next room by a bedquilt, which you must crawl under to come in or go out. But it is my room, and, after the jolting I have had upon the pony, I expect to have a good night's——

Was ever a poor pilgrim in such a fix? Just as I had written "night's" above, and had "sleep" on the point of my pen, I heard a knock on the floor outside the bedquilt.

"Crawl under," said I.

Enters the landlord's daughter, a buxom young lady about seventeen years of age. She opened her rosy lips and spake as follows:

"Mister, don't take off your clothes when you go to bed."

"Why?"

"Because I am going to sleep with you to-night."

"Well, if you have no better reason than that——"

"Hush! Shut up! You told pa you would not sleep with a man."

"I had rather sleep with a wet dog."

"Well, I have given up my bed to a sick man. I have been hard at work all day, and have to work hard all day to-morrow, and I can't afford to set up all night. That bed is wide enough for us both. I shall stay on the back side, and if you don't stay on your side, you'd better, that's all."

As she said this she raised from her dress an infernal jack-knife, such as farmers used in trimming fruit-trees, and then let it fall back with a chug. I comprehended the situation in half a moment, and unto the maiden I quoted as follows:

"Miss young lady, your intentions may, or may not, be honorable. I am travelling by myself. My natural protectors are miles and miles away beyond the boundless prairie, ignorant of the perils which may beset their idol. Thus far I have not been insulted by your sex. I am a man of few words, but they are always emphatic. I will give you part of that bed, and that's all I will do. If you attempt, during the silent watches of the night, anything contrary to this firm determination, by St. Joseph, my patron saint, I will shoot you right through the mid-riff."

As I concluded, I laid a Slocum pistol upon the candle-box. A low chuckle outside the bedquilt gave evidence that *pater-familias* had heard and approved the arrangement.

My antagonist laughed, and saying, "Mister, I reckon we under-stand each other," bounced over the back side of the bed.

Bungalow. This word is an Anglo-Indian corruption of the Hindoo *bangla,* an adjective which primarily means "Ben-galèse," or "Bengal," but which turned into a noun is the name given in India to a thatched hut.

The early British residents in India, being engaged in military administrative or commercial pursuits, lived for the greater part of the year a nomadie life in tents. As they found nothing in the indigenous buildings of Bengal that was suited to their requirements, their first dwelling-houses, built out of local materials, were naturally planned on the model of the Indian service tents to which they were accustomed. It con-sisted, in other words, of a wide and lofty room, surrounded by double walls of canvas with partitions at two or more corners for bath- or store-rooms. In the beginning, to be sure, the tent may occasionally have been covered with the sun-proof thatch or bangla. The name and the thatch were all that were taken, and now the origin of the name is for-gotten even by most Indians, who accept the resonant, tri-syllabic "bungalow" as the Englishman's own name for his own peculiar house.

For the sake of precision, it should be added that, being the product of a warm climate, the Englishman's bungalow is usually built of bamboo, with interstices between the canes to admit every wind that blows, and is surrounded by a veranda.

In America both the word and the thing have suffered a sea change. The thing, adapting itself to the severe climatic conditions of the New World, is here built of almost any material except bamboo, and the name has come to be some-what loosely applied to any woodland or country cottage, of a single story and with a projecting roof, which aims to bring under its roof the charms of the out-door life.

The reason for this license is not far to seek. Of all other forms of foreign architecture we have specimens constantly before our eyes. Tourists come home from Switzerland with miniature châlets in their trunks and from Mexico with little adobe huts. Every Japanese shop window is crowded with models of houses whose tiny sliding screens and imitation thatch roofs proclaim their oriental origin. These also are eagerly snapped up by travellers and brought back with them to America.

With the Swiss châlet, therefore, the Mexican adobe hut, and the Japanese cottage we are familiar from our infancy. Not so with the Indian bungalow. The genuine thing is practically unknown to the American public. Even among architects it is an alien form. Few of us have ever visited India. Fewer still have brought back models of Hindoo architecture for general distribution.

There is only one distinctive feature which wins for the American rival of the Anglo-Indian bungalow the name coined in India. With rare exceptions it consists of a single story; it is on one floor. As such it calls for a definite type of building that exactly fills a recognized want. But note a paradox: the harder some builders plan to keep to the idea of a single floor, the more difficulty they find in achieving a real bungalow. Yet there is no mystery connected with this miniature building. Its characteristics are recognizable at a glance. We all know a bungalow when we see one.

And a bungalow, as we use the term, is distinctively American. It may have come to us originally from the far-away East. Adopted by us it has adapted itself to New World conditions. It has been modified according to the needs and tastes of our Western civilization. It has borrowed hints from the châlet of the Swiss and even from the adobe huts and the thatched villas of alien races. Many an American bungalow finds its prototype in one or another or maybe in all of the little toy houses already mentioned.

In their way the houses they represent are each as perfect and as satisfying as a Greek temple or a Gothic cathedral. They deserve the name of classic. If you adhere to their more important characteristics, you will have a model bungalow of the sort that has acclimated itself in America. No one feature or detail of any one of them may be really essential to the American bungalow.

Butterfly. Grimm, of the famous "Tales," has endeavored to prove that the name butterfly, as well as milkthief, both of which in his time were applied to what scientists call by the noisier name of lepidoptera, arose from an old superstition that elves and fairies used to disguise themselves as butterflies in order to steal milk and butter. It is more probable that the legend is the result rather than the cause,—one of the many attempts to explain an otherwise inexplicable name.

A modern etymologist suggests a simpler derivation. There is a jargon in use among high-school boys, which aims to make conversation unintelligible by transposing the first letters of the words used. Thus "high school" becomes "sky hool," and "spring day" would be transformed to "ding spray." One of the oldest examples is, "wenny ody bot a gotch?" Translated this becomes "anybody got a watch?"

Now, a butterfly is primarily a fluttering creature. Fluttering past seems to be just about its whole occupation. Nothing could be more simple than the step from "flutter by," which is highly descriptive, to "butterfly," which sounds more like a grown-up name. One of our youthful linguacides would do it in a minute.

How long ago this must have happened, or whether the words forms at that time would have made the change possible, may be left to those who wish to investigate.

The largest butterfly known is found only in British New Guinea. Specimens are worth anything from $100 upward. The male measures eight inches across the wings and the female not less than eleven inches, a wing spread exceeding that of many small birds. The story of the first discovery of this gigantic butterfly is a curious one. A naturalist saw a specimen perched on the top of a tree and, failing to capture it by any other means, finally shot it. From the fragments he decided that the species was entirely unknown to science. Forthwith he fitted out an expedition at a cost of many thousands of dollars to go in search of the insects. Two members of the party fell victims to the Papuan cannibals and another was rescued only in the nick of time. In spite of this inauspicious commencement to his enterprise, however, the naturalist persevered and ultimately succeeded in obtaining perfect specimens.

Everybody knows the great orange-red butterflies with bold black bands and white dots that come sailing along by the thousands in the autumn. But not every one knows that they migrate like the birds in the fall, flying all the way from Canada to Cuba and taking other long flights so that they get into the sunny south for the winter. They have extraordinary power on the wing and have been seen flying at sea 500 miles from land.

Vast flocks of hundreds of thousands on their way southward settle on trees and bushes like a swarm of bees, and, as they are pretty much the color of certain autumn foliage, you might easily pass their roosting place without noticing them. They rest for the night and are off in the morning as soon as their wings are dry.

Buttons have been found in ancient Egypt. Yet, so far as we know, the Egyptian dress never required buttons, all the fastenings being by bands slipped into place or by ties and loops. The button or toggle is European rather than Eastern, and south European rather than northern. Even two or three centuries ago the north European dress was all tied together, the hose and doublet being secured by points and laces. The south of Europe was obviously the home of the button invention. Thence the buttons found their way to Egypt at a very ancient date, for specimens have been found there whose materials appear to belong to the twelfth dynasty (say 2500 B. C.), while others probably come down to the eighteenth dynasty (say 1500 B. C.). It is possible that, if more examples can be produced, we may find in the history of these buttons another of the valuable clues which help to date the early history (or pre-history) of Europe by its connection with the long record of Egypt.

C.

Cab. The taxicab is the most recent evolution in the hackney carriage, or vehicle let for hire. Each of the gradual steps in this evolution is interesting. To begin with: the primitive carriages of the Middle Ages had been discountenanced as likely to make men effeminate, and had fallen into almost total desuetude when, in 1625, Captain Baily, a retired sea-captain of ingenious mind, established the hackney carriage in London. An account of this enterprise is given by one Garrard in a letter to Lord Stratford, dated April 1, 1634, and quoted in the *Pall-Mall Gazette* January 5, 1870.

"I cannot," Mr. Garrard says, "omit to mention any new thing that comes up amongst us, though never so trivial. Here is one Captain Baily: he hath been a sea captain, but now lives on the land about this city, where he tries experiments. He hath erected, according to his ability, some four hackney coaches, put his men in livery, and appointed them to stand at the Maypole, in the Strand, giving them instructions at what rates to carry men into several parts of the town, where all day they may be had. Other hackney men seeing this way, they flocked to the same place, and perform their journeys at the same rate. So that sometimes there is twenty of them together, which disperse up and down, that they and others are to be had everywhere, as watermen are to be had at the waterside. Everybody is much pleased with it, for whereas before coaches could not be had but at great rates, now a man may have one much cheaper."

The number in London was at first limited to 20, but within 30 years the authorized number was increased to 200. In the time of Charles II a proclamation was issued, stating that the excessive number of hackney carriages (then about 400) was found to be a common nuisance, "by reason of their rude and disorderly standing and passing to and fro in and about our cities and suburbs: the streets and highways being thereof pestered and much impassable, the pavement broken up, and the common passages obstructed and made dangerous: henceforth none shall stand in the street, but only within their coach-houses, stables, and yards." In 1710 the number was limited to 800, which was increased to 1000 in 1771, and to 1100 in 1802.

Meanwhile, in France the renaissance of public carriages had more than kept pace with the English. There the moving spirit was a certain Nicholas Sauvage, who, living at the sign of

St. Fiacre in the Rue St. Martin, gave the name of his dwelling to the modern French fiacre, or cab. In its origin this was a kind of hooded gig, and allowed but a single passenger, as the driver occupied one end of the only seat. Gradually it came to be known as the *cabriolet de place,* while the word *fiacre* was transferred to four-wheelers.

Not until 1820 did the cabriolet, under the abbreviated name of " cab," cross the channel into England. Fourteen years later a Birmingham manufacturer, one Hansom, patented the hansom cab, " the gondola of London," as Beaconsfield named it, Hansom's patent safety cab, as the inventor called it. This originally consisted of a square body, the two wheels, about seven and one-half feet in diameter, being the same height as the vehicle.

In 1910 there were over 10,000 hansoms and 5000 " growlers," or four-wheelers, in use in London. The latter are alternatively known as " Clarences," after the Duke of Clarence.

Cable. The first submarine electric telegraph, or cable (as we now call it with our superior verbal economy), was that which established communication between Calais and Boulogne on one side of the English Channel and Dover on the other. The London *Illustrated News* thus alludes to the experiment in its issue for August 18, 1849 :

ELECTRIC TELEGRAPH BETWEEN LONDON AND PARIS.—The French government has accorded to Mr. Jacob Brett the authorization to establish on the coast of France a submarine electric telegraph between Calais and Boulogne, which, crossing the Channel, will go to Dover on the coast of England. The treaty entered into with Mr. Brett guarantees certain advantages to the French government, and leaves us all the expense at the charge of Mr. Brett, assuring him, however, a privilege for ten years in case the experiment should succeed. The works must be terminated by the 1st of September, 1850, at the latest; but it is probable that they will be finished sooner. This first application of the submarine electric telegraph, if it should succeed, as from the long examinations which have been made there is every reason to hope, will produce on the relations between France and England results of which it is impossible at present to estimate the importance. Dover, the point at which the submarine telegraph is to join England, is united to London by a direct telegraphic line: the capitals will, therefore, be in this manner in almost instantaneous communication.

On October 4 of the same year the same paper recorded the successful completion of the enterprise and the consequent rejoicings at Calais:

On Monday a series of experiments were tried with the most satisfactory results; and as the same results were achieved on Tuesday, the great enterprise may now be regarded as actually finished and complete. On Monday morning congratulatory messages to the President of the French Republic were sent direct from England to Paris, also to the King of Prussia and the Emperor of Austria, at Berlin and Vienna, and messages were also transmitted to London from the principal cities in Europe, who were included in the Continental system of telegraphic communication. During the whole of Monday, the town of Calais presented the appearance of *a fête*, and numbers of the inhabitants crowded on the ramparts, watching with interest and wonder the various experiments which were tried with the submarine wires. In the evening an entertainment was given at the Hôtel de Ville, to those English gentlemen, promoters of the undertaking, who were on the spot and had assisted in its completion. Those were Sir James Carmichael, Mr. Crampton, C.E., Mr. Wollaston, and Mr. Tatham, of the Gutta Percha Company. M. Mayer, the Mayor of Calais, presided; and, in addition to the English guests, there were present MM. Legros Devot, representative of the people; De Hamel, Councillor of State and member of Academy of St. Petersburgh; Dupont, Vice-Consul of Russia; and M. Bonhom, British Consul; together with the principal inhabitants of Calais and the officers of the garrison. During the whole of the proceedings the utmost harmony prevailed. A portion of the electric coil is to be placed in the Museum of Calais, in juxtaposition with the balloon of the celebrated aëronaut, Blanchard, who, in 1795, made his first *supra*-marine voyage from Dover to Calais.

And thus were nullified the predictions of some of the most eminent scientists of the day. Even at that time, when a transatlantic cable was suggested as a possible evolution from the channel cable, science held back.

Consulted on the scientific side of the project, Faraday asserted that the first cables were made too small. Then he said that "the larger the wire, the more electricity would be required to charge it"; and in this quite incorrect opinion he was supported by other eminent scientists. As a result of this dictum the current was increased until the operation "electrocuted" the wire, and the cable broke down. Long afterward Lord Kelvin, by sending messages through heavy cables with incredibly weak electric currents, proved that Faraday was mistaken.

Airy submitted the project to mathematics, and arrived at the conclusion that a cable could not be submerged to the necessary depth, and that if it could, no recognizable signal could ever travel from Ireland to Nova Scotia.

The humorists, as often happens, were even duller than the scientists. Yet *Punch* succeeded in keeping his skirts clear from posthumous ridicule. The issue for October 31, 1857, has a funny article on "an apparently funny invention" which had just been patented by John de la Haye, of Manchester: "It consists in a contrivance for submerging electric cables. Apparently funny we call it, because, even if we were not so wise as we should be, and are, experience, which would have taught even ourselves wisdom, would have made us know better than to make fun of any invention without sufficiently understanding it to be quite sure that it involved something impossible or absurd. There are wiseacres yet living who ought to blush at a gas-lamp and hide their faces at the sight of a locomotive. We will not risk classification in their category, by comparing the project of Mr. de la Haye with the devices of the Laputan sages —but its seeming oddity suggests to us a question which appears not to have occurred to any one of a numerous meeting of engineers to whom, at the Town-hall, Manchester, the plan was expounded by its inventor: who, according to the *Times,* said that—

The plan he would adopt would be to encase a cable prepared like that for the Atlantic Ocean in a soluble compound (the composition of which he would not now mention), capable of floating it for a time on the surface of the water. The coating he proposed to use for this purpose he supposed would hold it on the surface of the waves while about five miles of cable were paid out from the vessel before it began to dissolve, and as it would dissolve gradually, so the cable would sink gradually to the bed of the ocean. By this means he calculated that there would always be about five miles of cable lying on the surface of the water in the wake of the vessel, and the remainder would describe an incline to within 100 or 200 feet of the bed of the ocean, so that there would be comparatively little strain, and consequently less liability of breakage. The cable would descend into the ocean almost horizontally instead of perpendicularly.

On January 26, 1850, the *Illustrated News* makes its first allusion to the project that was made possible by the success of the first submarine cable:

ELECTRIC TELEGRAPH BETWEEN THE UNITED STATES AND ENGLAND. —The projectors of an electric telegraph communication between New York and the Isle of Wight will bring their plan before Congress at its present session. They propose to lay down a substantial insulated wire of thirty-six fibres, coated one-half inch with gutta percha, and to guarantee its working with perfect integrity for ten years. They offer to complete it in twenty months from the date of contract, for a sum not to (see TELEGRAPH) exceed 3,000,000 dollars.

Cactus. What the camel is among animals, that the cactus is among plants,—the most highly specialized of desert-haunting organisms. It has been developed in, by, and for the desert. Like camels, cactuses take in their water supply whenever they can get it, and never waste any of it on the way by needless evaporation. As they form the perfect central type of desert vegetation, and are also familiar plants to every one, they may be taken as a good illustrative example of the effect that desert conditions inevitably produce upon vegetable evolution. Quaint, shapeless, succulent, jointed, the cactuses look at first sight as if they were all leaves and had no stem or trunk worth mentioning. Really they are all stem and no leaves; what look like leaves being joints of the trunk or branches, and the foliage being all dwarfed and stunted into the prickly hairs that encumber the surface. All plants of very arid soil tend to be thick, jointed, and succulent; the distinction between stem and leaves disappears; and the whole weed, accustomed to times of long drought, acquires the habit of drinking in water greedily at its rootlets after every rain, and storing it away for future use in its thick, sponge-like, and water-tight tissues. To prevent undue evaporation, the surface also is covered with a thick, shiny skin—a sort of vegetable mackintosh, which effectually checks all unnecessary transpiration. Of this desert type, then, the cactus is the furthest term. It has no flat leaves with expanded blades to wither and die in the scorching air. The thick and jointed stems do the same work,—absorb carbon from the carbonic acid of the air, and store up water in the driest of seasons. Then, to repel the attacks of herbivores, who would gladly get at the juicy morsel if they could, the foliage has been turned into sharp defensive spines and prickles. There is a gigantic cactus of the Mexican deserts which contains a great quantity of drinkable water in its soft, fleshy lobes, and sometimes relieves the thirst of travellers in those arid regions. Another water-bearer has recently been found to exist in the desert tortoise, a fine specimen of which was recently brought from the Cajon Pass, in San Bernardino County, Cal. The water is contained in a bag under the carapace, and a pint of it can be taken from a full-sized specimen. It is believed that the creature gets the water from the above-mentioned cactus, on which it feeds. The cactus and tortoise are almost the only life of those wastes, and nature has doubtless found it necessary to endow them with this water-bearing power. Foremost among the sights which astonish the tourist is that of the grotesque cactus of Arizona Territory. The plant is leafless, having a bare, fleshy stock, protected everywhere by sharp and venomous barbs. Its flowers vary from white and yellow to deep crimson or purple. These blossoms are wax-like, and call to mind Aladdin's fabled experience among the fairy plants, with their sparkling fruits of diamonds and other gems. The fruit is as varied in color as the flowers. It is egg-shaped, with a crown on the upper side, and contains a large quantity of seeds, surrounded by a nicely flavored juicy substance. The fruit varies in size according to the species, all the way up from a canary's to an ostrich's egg. The cactus is almost imperishable, and can live many months without water, although it is only seen in its perfection under a plentiful supply. So hardy is the plant that a piece from any part will take root and grow if placed in the ground, even though it has lain around for a time. It thrives equally well on a piece of bare rock in a scorching tropical sun as it would packed in ice in a northern zone. It is a veritable paradox—a natural curiosity in the vegetable kingdom.

The people of those regions of South America where the cactus thrives have found a use for that growth to the betterment and improvement of their farm buildings. In the cactus regions the farm buildings during all kinds and conditions of weather present a fine white appearance. To obtain this effect a white-wash is used made of the sliced leaves of the common cactus macerated in water for 24 hours. This produces a solution of a creamy consistence, to which lime is added and well mixed. When this whitewash is applied to any surface, whether of wood, brick, iron, or other material, a beautiful pearly white appear-ance is produced. Not only is it a better color than the ordinary whitewash made from lime, but it is lasting and will endure through the storms and frosts of many years.

The ordinary whitewash of to-day will not last longer than a single season, especially where the rainfall is heavy. It has been suggested that in those sections of western United States where the cactus is such a nuisance the plant could be utilized to good advantage.

Cakes, Gigantic. Possibly the largest cake ever made is that with which, in June, 1730, Frederick William 1, King of Prussia, regaled his army. A huge repast of roast beef and vege-tables had been washed down by mighty draughts of beer and ale, when the 30,000 guests saw their dessert approaching in a great car drawn by 8 horses. This consisted of a cake 18 yards long, 8 yards broad, and more than ½ yard thick. Among its ingredi-ents were 36 bushels of flour, 200 gallons of milk, 1 ton of butter, 1 ton of veast, and 5000 eggs. The 30,000 soldiers, already glutted, found it impossible to eat up all the cake, and the remnants were distributed among the inhabitants of neighboring towns and villages.

At the Crystal Palace revels which celebrated the end of the Exhibition year and the beginning of 1852, a monster Christmas cake was prepared by the Messrs. Stuples, London caterers. The height of the cake was 4 ft. 9 in., and the weight 3½ cwt., or nearly 400 lb. More than half a thousand eggs were used in its preparation; and some idea may be formed of the quality when we state that the fruit was in the proportion of three pounds to one pound of flour. It was baked in eight parts, no oven being large enough to contain the whole at one time.

The form was hexagonal, and composed of three stages. In the centre of each side of the lower stage were well-executed medallions of her Majesty, on alternate blue and pink grounds, encircled by wreaths of laurel; the edges of the compartments being decorated with a Grecian scrollwork border, while equestrian statues of the Duke of Wellington, the Emperor Napoleon, the Emperor of Austria, etc., stood at the angles. The next stage was ornamented in a similar classic style, but with naval heroes, admirals, etc. Upon the upper stage Nineveh bulls supported a classic vase filled with holly and evergreens, from the midst of which rose the royal standard of England; the flags of various nations being plentifully distributed about the cake.

On Wednesday (Twelfth-day), public notice having been given that the cake would be distributed, the attendance of children was greater than on any day since the commencement of the revels. Great was the anxiety shown on many a little face, immediately on receiving the Twelfth-night character, to proceed with *more than possible* speed to the spot where the cake was to be obtained in exchange for it, and numerous were the endeavors by " children of a larger growth " to induce the inflexible officials to include them with the " infantry " on this occasion only. The distribution commenced at a few minutes past two, and continued without interruption for nearly an hour and a half, the children forming a long square between barriers erected for the purpose. The process of cutting up the cake, which occupied the whole of the morning, was a source of considerable attraction, but the distribution was unquestionably the most pleasing of all the performances of the day, not only to the children, but also to the visitors, who seemed to take great interest in observing the delight of the little ones as they came in quick succession to receive their share of the long-to-be-remembered Crystal Palace Twelfth Cake.

During Christmas week of 1889, there was on view in North End Road, Fulham, an enormous cake that towered almost to the ceiling of the confectioner's shop. It was made to represent a fortress, and weighed over 4000 pounds. In its composition had been used 600 pounds of flour, 400 pounds of butter, 400 pounds of sugar, 600 pounds of icing sugar, 900 pounds of currants, 450 pounds of sultanas, 300 pounds of candied peel, 200 pounds of almonds and 5000 eggs.

Camel. The so-called " ship of the desert " was a native of Asia from the earliest known times. That it was the great commercial vehicle of the East in ancient as in modern days is evidenced by the Scriptures. When Joseph's brethren had cast him into the pit, " they lifted up their eyes and looked, and, behold, a company of Ishmaelites came from Gilead, with their camels bearing spicery and balm and myrrh, going to carry it down to Egypt." The domesticated condition of the animal at this early period is also proved by Genesis xxxii 15, which states that among the presents sent by Jacob to propitiate Esau were " thirty milch camels with their colts." In Leviticus the camel is enumerated among the forbidden animals, " because he cheweth the cud, but divideth not the hoof; he is unclean unto you" (xi, 4).

There is no satisfactory evidence that camels ever permanently existed in the wild state. Those mentioned by Disdorus and Strabo as denizens of Arabia probably owed their parentage to animals which had temporarily escaped from the control and protection of man.

Purchas mentions camels in his " Pilgrimage." He states that there are three kinds: " the first, called Hajuin, of tall stature, and able to carry a thousand pounds weight; the second less, having a double hunch, fit for carriages to ride on, called Becheti, bred only in Asia; the third sort, called Raguahill, small, able to travel (for they are unfit for burdens) above a hundred miles a day. The King of Timbuctoo can send messengers on such camels to Segelmess or Darha, nine hundred miles distant, in the space of eight days at the farthest." He adds that such enduring swiftness would be almost incredible were it not corroborated by the best authorities, who all agree in their accounts of the speed of the Heirie, or Maherry of the desert, Purchas's " Raguahill."

And indeed, though the slender and shrunken limbs of the camel, his light quarters, and his shambling gait seem little adapted to the performance of any feat of speed or strength, we know that his powers of endurance enable him to accomplish a long journey in a shorter space than even the horse, and he can bear a burden greatly disproportioned to his own weight. In Algeria the camel carries from 450 to 675 pounds; at Cairo, according to one authority, he carries 1500 pounds for a distance of three miles, and 1000 from Cairo to Suez, which is eighty-four miles; in Cabul, according to General Harlan, the burden of the Arabian camel is, upon the plains, 400 pounds; in European Turkey the one-humped camel is said to carry from 400 to 500 pounds, and Burnes estimates the load of the same animal in Bokhara at 500 pounds.

With respect to food, there is no doubt that the camel can endure three or even more days of entire privation; but long abstinence from food is seldom necessary, because, although there are tracts of desert six days' journey in width, which are absolutely destitute of vegetation, yet there are few portions of the Libyan or Arabian deserts where more or less of the shrubs on which the camel feeds do not occur at very much shorter intervals. On the ordinary routes, therefore, the camel is not fed at all, even on long journeys, but is left to snatch such food as he can during the march of the caravan, or to gather it more leisurely as he halts.

Scientists explain that the camel's hump is an immense collection of fat, stored in reticulated cells, piled up one upon another, which is concentrated food. When fodder cannot be had, a peculiar set of absorbent vessels draws upon the magazine—the hump—carrying the fat into the circulation till food from without puts a stop to draft on the back. The hump is very sensibly diminished at times—even being almost completely levelled, but that which was thus borrowed to sustain life temporarily, is immediately replaced when the stomach is set in motion again in its accustomed manner.

Oddly enough, nature has provided a very similar arrangement for the leech.

The power of the camel to abstain from water is much more severely tested than his ability to dispense with food. He is patient under thirst; but Lieutenant Burnes tells us it is a vulgar error to believe that he can live any length of time without water; he generally pines and dies on the fourth day, and with great heat will even sink sooner. His ability to do without water for so long a period even as that already mentioned is due to the lining of the second stomach, or honey-comb bag, and of a portion of the first stomach, or paunch, with great masses of cells, in which water is stored up and long retained. The store of water is well known to the Arabs, who, when sore pressed by thirst, will sometimes kill some of the camels of the caravan, and thus avoid perishing themselves.

When the camel was introduced into Africa is uncertain. The earliest reference bearing on this point is made by Julius Cæsar (*Bell. Afric.,* 68), who tells how he brought home with him from Tuba twenty-two camels. This was half a century before the Christian era. The Louvre possesses a terracotta statuette, representing a camel, which was found in Cyrenaica, and belongs to the *second* century B. C. But it is a question whether the camel was of common use in the Barbary States (Tunis, Algeria, Morocco) before the *Byzantine* period.

The first camels seen in the United States were probably those brought over by the United States storeship, *Supply,* Lieut. Porter commanding, which were landed at Indianola, Texas, on May 14, 1856. There were thirty-four in all. They came mostly from Egypt and Smyrna. A year later the *Supply* brought another cargo. In 1858 one hundred camels were landed at New Orleans by private enterprise.

The Bedouins decorate their baggage camels in the most fantastic manner. A huge pack saddle is surmounted by a still larger pannier; above this again is a sort of chair, in which the rider sits. The long strips of leather hanging down the sides are simply for decorative purposes.

"I have seen camels, when too young to go on long treks, being carried in these panniers, and they are always used for the Bedouin children," writes one traveller.

"This tribe has many quaint and curious customs. Perhaps the most curious of these is the manner in which they show their esteem for certain strangers. One evening when a young camel had been killed for the meal, I noticed the women collecting the blood in a bowl. Then, to my astonishment, they started painting my camels on the necks and flanks with the blood. Unknowingly I was the recipient of the greatest honor that can be paid a stranger. The blood dried on and remained for a long time, acting as a talisman among all the Sherarat tribe."

Can-Can. This not too decorous dance is said to have been invented by a grisette named Elise Sargent, who was known to the Paris of 1842 as Queen Pomaré, in jocose allusion to the real Aimata Pomaré who was Queen of Tahiti in that year, when the island was put under protection of the French fleet by some native chiefs. The queen protested against this act. Admiral Dupetit Thouars sought to establish the protectorate by force, but on the intervention of England his action was disavowed by Louis Philippe. Public attention in France was thus directed to Tahiti, which was painted as a sort of Savage Eldorado, and Queen Pomaré, with her princesses, clothed simply in crowns of lotus-flowers, became a favorite subject with chansonniers and vaudevillists. Elise Sargent, a dancer in the Jardin Mabille at Paris, whose grace and wit had made her famous, was hailed by the students at the Closerie des Lilas as Queen Pomaré on account of her African style of beauty and her African taste in adornment. To celebrate her coronation she invented the can-can. She also introduced the polka at the Chaumière, whence it forced its way into the salons. Pomaré became the town-talk. Dramatic authors used to send her tickets and announce in the gazettes when she had promised to avail herself of them. Balzac sketched her in one of his novelettes. Gautier left a finished portrait of her. Eugene Sue consulted her when writing his "Mysteries of Paris," and much of the information there contained in regard to the lives of Parisian courtesans was supplied by her. The events of 1848 turned the tide from her in the dancing gardens. In vain did Emile de Girardin cry "On with the dance," to the Parisians, whom he did not like to see crowding in the streets and about the National Assembly. Pomaré fell a victim to consumption and died in a hospital at the age of twenty-eight.

Cape Horn was discovered by Sir Francis Drake in 1578, unless he was anticipated, as the Spaniards claim, by their own Commodore Gasrola Jofre de Loaysa in 1515. It was first doubled in 1616 by Lemaire and Schouten.

Jacob Lemaire was a Dutch navigator and merchant, director-general of a company which in 1615 sent an expedition to find a new route to the Pacific Ocean. He discovered the strait which bears his name, doubled Cape Horn and sailed to the East.

Cards. See PLAYING CARDS.

Carnegie Library. Perhaps Mr. Andrew Carnegie himself was not aware that the idea of the libraries with which his name is associated did not originate with him, but belonged in the first place to one Houei-T'ze, a wealthy Chinese merchant of the fifth century.

This pioneer not only donated libraries throughout China and Turkestan, but furnished workmen for the jobs. He also stipulated that his portrait should be hung back of the librarian's desk. Then he installed a corps of Buddhist monks in each; thus he knew that the libraries could get along without any further financing from him. For a religious wave was at that time sweeping the nation. By singular coincidence, both library givers made their money in commerce.

The name of the great Chinese Carnegie would have been still unknown had it not been for the zeal of a band of French explorers and the aid of a friendly sand-storm which wrecked huge stone walls and disclosed the evidences of the early philanthropist's work. The expedition, under M. Pelliot, left Paris in 1906 and returned in 1911. Evidence disclosed that the first library discovered had been walled in about 1035, under fear of the menace of a hostile invasion of troops. Over 20,000 rolls of manuscripts were discovered, together with thousands of crudely bound books, paintings, statuettes, and a list of 200 libraries.

"Libraries I have given by the score," read the ancient document. "I have scattered them over all the land, that the light of learning may never be dimmed and that the grateful may do honor to memory as long as Buddha lives. Into dark places have I thrown the light and the light will be with me forever."

With regard to Mr. Carnegie's donations, more than 1300 of his library buildings are scattered over the earth and his gifts

12

to them aggregate over 40 million dollars. The first of these libraries was established in Homestead, Penna., but it outgrew the structure in which it was housed, and Mr. Carnegie built a better one for the city, when the first one reverted to the Carnegie Steel Company, which used it for an office building (see LIBRARY).

Carp. In the second act, Scene 1, of "Hamlet," we find Polonius saying to Reynaldo, " See you now; your bait of false-hood takes this carp of truth "; which would seem to imply that your carp was a gullible creature. But this fish was not regarded as an easy prey by the skilled anglers of the later seventeenth century. Master Izaak Walton says: " The carp is the queen of rivers . . . a very subtle fish . . . if you will fish for a carp you must put on a very large measure of patience. . . ."

Elsewhere, with pain, one notes unflattering reference to Cyprinus, which Vanière lauds thus: " Of all the fish that swim the watery mead, not one in cunning can the carp exceed." Buffon was so impressed with its extreme caution and wiliness that he designated it " the fresh-water fox "; as for Walton, to that which we have already quoted, there is appended the remark, " He is hard to be caught." Now, whatever may be thought of old Izaak as a naturalist, it must be admitted that as regards the deluding coarse fish he was decidedly " all there."

There is one table delicacy the German epicure must have, and that is carp, and the carp, to be eaten in perfection, must be killed immediately before cooking. Saxony is noted for its carp, and in that kingdom the problem of conveying the living fish for long distances to remote markets has assumed considerable importance. For several years past fresh-water fish have been imported in casks of water from various points to the cities, at some considerable expense. The living fish can be purchased daily in the markets of Dresden, Chemnitz, and other cities, and are naturally preferred to fish transported in ice. Living sea fish are also transported to a less extent in salt water tanks. They are to be found thus far only in a few of the larger cities. The desirability of providing cheaper means of transporting Saxon carp to distant points reached by fluvial routes has led to the introduction of ingeniously devised river craft for the purpose. They consist of scows 65 feet long and 16 feet wide. The interior is divided by partitions into thirty compartments. In the bottom and sides of a scow, as well as in the inner partitions, cracks are left open so that when floating in a river there is a continual circulation of fresh water. The city of Hamburg demands very large quantities of carp, especially in the autumn, and this economical method of bringing the living fish from the remote breeding places does much to increase the demand. These craft made the first journey down the river during the month of September.

Cat. According to the Greeks, Apollo once made a lion to frighten his hunting sister, Diana. But she threw eternal ridicule on him by caricaturing his creation in the person of a cat. An Arab story is equally plausible. When Noah entered the ark, so runs this tale, the family represented to him that their provisions were endangered by the presence of mice and other rodents. The patriarch addressed himself in prayer to Allah, who thereupon made the lion sneeze a full-grown cat from his nostrils. So the mice were kept in subjection during the entire period of the Deluge.

Now, whatever the story of the cat's creation, it is in evidence that he has been known as a domesticated animal for nearly four thousand years. Just sixteen hundred and eighty-eight years before the Christian era cats begin to appear on the Egyptian monuments.

But the cat of the Pyramids was not quite the same animal as the cat of the nineteenth century. He was called Maou, to be sure, which indicates that he spoke the same language. His statues, his medals, and his pictures show the form so familiar to us; his mummies and his mummy-cases are cat-like. It is in his habits, as depicted in the hieroglyphics, that he differs from his descendants. He had a taste for hunting in marshes and for swimming back to his master with a booty of dead ducks. Documentary evidence also points to the fact that he belonged to a larger and wilder breed than our grimalkin, a breed retaining much of the strength and the furor of a state of nature. Herodotus asserts that he was in the habit of killing his own offspring, and this for no better reason than that he wanted the exclusive attention of his wife. He was addicted, moreover, to suicide, rather due to a temporary aberration of intellect, however, than to malice prepense. When a building caught fire, the cat often lost his head and plunged straight into his own funeral pyre.

"Whenever this happens," says Herodotus, "it diffuses universal sorrow. Also, in whatever family a cat dies, every individual cuts off his eyebrows."

The cat was held sacred by the Egyptians. He was consecrated to the goddess Pasht, or Bast, or Bubastis. She usually wears the head of a cat. In her temples cats were kept as sacred animals. They were embalmed at their death and safely stored in honorable tombs. Or, if they were not attached to the temple in their lifetime, they were after death carried to sacred buildings, salted, and then buried in the holy city of Bubastis.

You remember the story of how Cambyses stormed the city

of Memphis? He assailed it not with any weapons fashioned
by human hand. He simply gathered together a lot of cats,
and used them as projectiles. Thereupon the city surrendered
without further struggle.

In Hellenic history we find no mention of cats until we reach
the time of Theocritus, one hundred and sixty years after
Herodotus. But that poet was a native of Syracuse. He had
spent many years in Egypt. He may have merely cultivated
an exotic taste.

Agathias, a writer of the age of Justinian, is the first Roman
authority on cats. He mentions Thomas only to blame him.
Thomas, it appears, had killed his tame partridge. Agathias,
a clever man, made a couple of epigrams on the subject. Straightway one of his disciples, named Damocharis, rushes to console
him with another epigram. He calls the cat one of the dogs of
Actæon; declares that, in eating the partridge of Agathias, he
had devoured Agathias himself, and charges him with thinking
of nothing but partridges while the mice dance and rejoice.
It is evident from all this hullabaloo that cats were kept in the
Eastern Empire for the destruction of mice, and that they were
far from holding the worshipful position of semi-sacerdotal Maou
in ancient Egypt.

Pliny mentions the cat. So also does Palladius. But it is
only in his quality of mice-destroyer. In a Pompeian mosaic
he is again represented as a bird-fancier. He has a quail under
his left paw and his mouth is about to open on the neck of his
victim. He is rather a more formidable animal than the modern
Pussy. A rude funeral monument of the Gallo-Roman period
exhausts the list of Roman cat-effigies. Here a young girl holds
a cat in her arms, while a cock stands at her feet. It is true
that Palliot, a heraldic author who flourished in the seventeenth century, assures us that various companies of Cæsar's
soldiers had cats emblazoned on their banners. There was a
sea-green cat for the *Ordines Augustei*, a half-cat on a red ground
for the *Felices Seniores,* and a cat with one eye and one ear for
the *Alpini*. Now Palliot goes so far as to give us an engraving
of the half-cat, a picturesque animal with his "back up," even
to the tip of the tail, but with no hinder moiety.

The Middle Ages saw a sad degeneration in the esteem
wherein cats were held. The animal which had once been worshipped as a sort of divinity was now held to be an exponent of
darkness. A black cat, especially, was the devil incarnate. Numerous legends attest the fact that, when Satan desired to
trouble the peace of the faithful, he loved to assume the form of
a black tom-cat. Cats of all colors haunted blood-stained castles

and accompanied witches on their nocturnal gambols. Nay, witches themselves, and sorcerers, often took the form in which their great master delighted. A French peasant of Billancourt was one day engaged in cooking an omelet. A black cat, sitting in the chimney, looked on with approval.

"It is done," cried the cat (evidently a skilled cook) ; "turn it over."

Now, the woman was a good Christian, so she threw the omelet straight into the cat's face. Next day one of her neighbors, long suspected of being a sorcerer, had a scar on his cheek as of a recent burn.

Sometimes the cat proved more than a match for the arch-enemy himself. A French architect, being unable to finish an audaciously planned bridge, summoned the devil to his assistance. Satan agreed to help him on condition that he should have the first soul that crossed it. The work done, the architect scared a cat over. Satan, though disappointed, advanced to seize his prey, whereupon the cat showed fight and finally drove the devil from the field.

The evil repute of the cat still clings to him. A Finisterre cat which has served nine masters in succession is believed to have the right of carrying off the soul of the ninth to hell. In Upper Brittany there are sometimes seen enormous cats engaged in holding a meeting. If any one presumes to intrude upon their presence, they surround and tease him for a time. Then a long needle is driven into his heart, and he is dismissed. Hypochondria ensues, and he slowly wastes away.

A black tom-cat, says a Russian proverb, at the end of seven years becomes a devil. A Breton farmer, who neglected to take the usual precaution of putting his tom-cat to death before it completed its seventh year, was found dead in bed one morning, with his throat terribly torn. Suspicion fell upon innocent persons, who were likely to be hanged on circumstantial evidence. Luckily, a boy observed that the cat of the house was always watching the corpse with eyes that blazed with rage. So he fastened to the dead man's arm a string, the end of which he dropped through the window into the yard. Then he told the police to watch the body secretly, while he pulled the string. They did so. When the boy gave the string a pull, the corpse's arm jerked. The cat imagined its master had revived. With one bound it sprang on to the bed and furiously tore away at the corpse's wounded neck. Whereupon it was condemned to be burned alive and the suspects were set free.

There is a popular belief that a cat's viciousness has some relation to the length of its tail; for if the end be cut off, it

cannot take part in the Witch's Sabbath.· When a Walloon
maiden chooses to dismiss a suitor with contumely, she gives him
a cat and tells him to count its hairs. It is a French belief that
a bachelor who treads on a cat's tail will find no woman willing
to marry him within the ensuing twelvemonth.

In Germany, England, and France many a religious *fête* of
the Middle Ages culminated in pitching a cat from a height
or into a bonfire. So recently as 1818 a decree was issued in
Ypres, Flanders, forbidding the throwing of a cat off a high tower
in commemoration of a Christian festival.

Fontenelle told Moncrif that he had been brought up to
believe that not a single cat could be found in town on St. John's
Eve, because that was the date when they attended the Witches'
Sabbath. Hence people threw all stray cats into the fire to
anticipate their departure.

Some people have a great antipathy to cats. Of these was
Napoleon. It is said that after his victory at Wagram, while
temporarily sojourning in the palace at Schonbrunn belonging
to the conquered Emperor of Austria, the conqueror called out
loudly for assistance. An equerry entered, and found his master
half undressed, agitated, perspiring, frantically striking out at
some object unseen. A cat had hidden behind the bed curtain,
and Napoleon, almost as scared as puss herself, was making
desperate lunges at her through the hangings (see AELURO-
PHOBIA).

In 1877 a Belgian society was formed for the improvement,
mental and moral, of the domestic cat. One of the initial efforts
was to train the cat to rival the carrier-pigeon. A cat's sense of
locality, as all catophiles know, is extraordinary. The most
astute and accomplished of human scientists would have his idea
of locality totally confused by being tied up in a meal-bag, carried twenty miles from home, and let out in a strange neighborhood in the night. Experiment proved that this was mere
child's play to the cat, not the superior cat, either, but the
every-day average cat. The invariable result was that the de-
ported animal reappeared at his own hearthstone next morning,
and calmly ignored the whole affair. This skill in travelling
through unknown regions, without chart or compass, suggested
the possibility of using cats as special messengers. In April,
thirty-seven cats residing in the city of Liége were taken in bags
20 miles into the country. They were liberated at 2 o'clock in the
afternoon. At 6.48 the same afternoon one of them reached
home. Within twenty-four hours all the rest of his companions
had been accounted for. A proposal was then made to establish

a regular system of cat communication between Liége and the surrounding villages, but the project came to nothing.

In England cats are supposed to have been known at a very early period; they are not aboriginal, but probably were first introduced by merchants from Cyprus, who traded with the Britons for furs. Nevertheless they were either difficult to naturalize or, notwithstanding their prolific nature, extremely scarce; for in the tenth century, among the laws enacted by Hoel Dda, or Howel the Good, Prince of Wales, for preserving and fixing the prices of various animals, the cat was thus introduced: " The price of a kitten before it could see was one penny, twopence until proof could be given of its having caught a mouse, after which fourpence "—a great sum in those days when the value of specie was so high. The animal was required to be perfect in its senses of seeing and hearing, to have its claws whole, to be a good mouser, and, if a female, a careful nurse. If it failed in any of these qualifications, the seller was to forfeit a fourth part of its value to the buyer. Should any one steal or kill the cat that guarded the prince's granary, the offender was to forfeit either a milch ewe, her fleece and lamb, or as much wheat as, when poured on the cat suspended by its tail with its head touching the floor, would form a heap sufficient to cover the tip of the tail.

There are many false ideas regarding the cat held by a great many persons, among others that a cat can see better at night than in the daytime, and that it is able to see in perfect darkness. As a matter of fact, the cat, like all other animals, cannot see at all in perfect darkness, though, with the assistance of its whiskers or feelers, and its surefootedness, it is able to move about with some agility. A cat can see better in the dusk than can a human being, however, because the cat's eyes are sensitive to the ultra-violet rays of the spectrum, and the pupil is capable of great expansion, thus admitting all the light there is available; but see in absolute darkness it cannot.

Another firmly-rooted idea is that cats, if given the opportunity, will suck the breath out of sleeping children. This is utterly absurd. A cat, liking a warm, clean place, will if it has a chance slip into a child's crib, and, if the crib is narrow, may happen to take up a position on top of the baby. As a good-sized cat will average 10 pounds in weight, while an average baby at one month of age will weigh only 8 pounds, and at four months only 12½ pounds, it may be readily comprehended, if we imagine a proportionate weight in warm flesh and soft fur on top of our own bodies, that it may be a serious thing—the baby may be smothered to death, as has sometimes happened.

Cat Cloister in Florence. The sacristy in the church of San Lorenzo in Florence, built by Michel Angelo in 1523-9 as a mausoleum for the Medici family, is known to all travellers. Very little known, however, is the adjacent cloister devoted almost wholly to cats. "It is a large square cloister," says Charles Warren Stoddart, in *Ave Maria* for January, 1890, " with light arches leaping from column to column all the way round, in sunshine and shadow; and with the customary campanile towering far above it, and, whenever the bell strikes the quarter-hours, flooding the air with affrighted doves—such white doves, sailing dizzily against such a vast blue sky! Between the columns of the cloister is a parapet, and beyond it a moat, four or five feet in depth, and dry save when the rain rains into it; and this moat, backed by all the columns and the parapet, surrounds a kind of island terrace, that rises out of the moat as high as the parapet, and is covered with the greenest grass and a little cluster of the darkest cypresses. So here you have an odd garden in the centre of a cloister, surrounded by a moat, quite out of reach of everybody. It seems to be a kind of enchanted spot— and so it is; for that island is the kingdom of the cats, as many as choose to colonize there; and, as is usually the case with cats, their name is legion. Cats! Fat ones and lean ones; the lazy and the lively, and the dreamy and contemplative. Cats with tails and cats without them; cats whose lives have evidently been a burden to them—and to others, and who have sought the seclusion of the cloister in which to end their days. There they are fed regularly, through the charity of some one who long ago left a legacy for their sole sake; and they are fed irregularly by any one who chooses to feed them as I chose to do, and found to my humiliation that these pampered felines look with indifferent eyes upon the bait of the worldling—the sleekest of them even seemed to pity my proffer of good-fellowship. So there they lay, the tabbies of the cloister, sunning themselves in the rich grass of spring; shading themselves under the boughs of the cypress of their native land; climbing into these boughs in some cases, and sprawling there in an attitude of such luxurious content that I feared lest some feathered innocent might fly to the velvety embraces of the cunning and slaughterous beasts, and all unwittingly seek sudden death in the most peaceful nook in Florence. . . . After all, thought I, as I turned away and left that happy family purring in concert, is there anybody or anything in the whole wide world more comfortable than a convent cat?—a cat that has nothing whatever to do but to pose for the edification of the idly curious, and to let the world go by, as it sits washing its pink-tipped face with gracefully curved paws, before resuming its favorite pastime, a sedate friendly game of puss in the cloister."

Cat Mummies. In March, 1890, a startling sale took place in Liverpool,—an auction held by Leventon and Co., consignees of 180,000 mummified bodies of cats. These remains were what might commercially be called a job lot left over from the exploitation of a cat cemetery in Beni Hassan, about 100 miles from Cairo. The discovery of this cemetery was made by a fellah, who, while employed in husbandry, fell into a pit. This pit had an opening, and he entered the opening. A subterranean chamber developed itself, followed by other subterranean chambers. All was silent, strangely silent, for a temple of even cat ghosts. In these chambers were laid away, shelf on shelf and pile on pile, small yellow bundles. There were limitless bundles stretching through the gloom of seemingly endless mortuary halls. He unwrapped one and found it to be a cat. They were all cats, embalmed, swathed, and wrapped up like mummies to protect them from the cold and microbes of later and degenerate eras. Satisfying himself of the extent of the cat mine, he told his master. The master came into conference with an Alexandrian speculator. The speculator found that the supply already exceeded the demand in the cat market, but tried Liverpool as a venture, feeling sure, no doubt, that the thrifty British merchant would find some use for them either as mechanical toys, historical relics, projectiles at election meetings, unique mantel ornaments, or fuel. The British merchant met the expectation, and promptly offered them as fertilizing material for farms. "There has been no fall in nitrate shares as yet, but who can tell the outcome? If the great desert of Sahara is in whole or part merely the yellow shroud which Time has kindly placed over a limitless cat cemetery, there is no reason why the products of Egypt, instead of the chemicals of Chili, should not woo the cotyledon from its parent bean or cause the ample turnip-top to wave magnificent above feeding herds on English soil. The discovery of this wonderful deposit, which runs over 93 per cent. of pure cat to the ton, throws a bright white light upon the home-life of that glorious people who spent their time writing letters to each other with pickaxes on the face of the earth."—*Illustrated American,* July, 1890.

The auction was a queer one. The auctioneer used a dead cat as a hammer, and knocked its gray companions down, in ton lots, with a cat's head. The consignment represented only the amount left after the Egyptian farmers had glutted themselves and their lands with the tabbies which laborers dug out by hundreds of thousands. After being brought in the steamers *Pharos* and *Thebes* to Liverpool, however, the mummies brought only £3 13s. 9d. per ton, or about one-tenth of a penny per cat.

Catalogue. The first digested list of publications in the English language was compiled, towards the close of the sixteenth century, by Andrew Maunsell, a bookseller of contemporary renown, who lived close by where the Bank of England now stands. It is a scarce and valuable work, inasmuch as it records the titles of many books now lost and the names of many authors now forgotten. The work is dedicated "To the Queene's most Sacred Majestie," to "The Reverend Diuines and Lovers of Diuine Bookes"; and to "The Worshipful, the Master, Wardens, and Assistants of the Companie of Stationers, and to all other Printers and Booksellers in general." The following is the title: "The first part of the Catalogue of English Printed Bookes: which concerneth such matters of Diuinitie as have bin either written in our owne tongue, or translated out of anie other language: and haue bin published to the glory of God, and edification of the Church of Christ in England. Gathered into alphabet, and such method as it is, by Andrew Maunsell, bookseller. *Unumquodque propter quid.* London: printed by John Windel, for Andrew Maunsell, dwelling in Lothburie, 1595." Folio, pp. 123; dedication pp. 6; with the device of a pelican and its offspring rising from the flames, round which is this legend: *Pro Lege, Rege, et Grege:* Love kepyth the Lawe, obeyeth the Kynge, and is good to the Commonwelthe."

In the same year in which this catalogue was printed, Maunsell published a second part, "which concerneth the sciences mathematicale, as arithmetick, geometrie, astronomie, astrologie, musicke, the art of warre and navigation; and also of physicke and surgerie."

Cedar. The *Pinus cedrus,* as its botanical name implies, is of the genus pine, but it differs materially from any pine indigenous to Europe or America. It is a native of Palestine, the most famous cedars beng those of Mount Lebanon. When the prophet Ezekiel would describe the Assyrian monarch as one of the most magnificent of princes, he likens him to the cedar of Lebanon: "Behold the Assyrian was a cedar in Lebanon, with fair branches and of high stature, and his top was among the thick boughs. His boughs were multiplied, and his branches became long. The fir trees were not like his boughs, nor the chestnut trees like his branches; nor any three in the garden of God like unto him in beauty." The beauty and durability of the wood indeed made it especially appropriate for the great temple at Jerusolem.

Solomon must have made serious havoc among the cedars of

Lebanon, as he employed 80,000 hewers to get out timber for the temple and his palace. He sent 10,000 at a time to prepare timber and boards. An Assyrian king set such value upon Lebanon's cedar as to transport huge beams of it to Nineveh, where it was used in the erection of the royal palace. Hiram also supplied the timber for roofing the second temple and the gigantic statue of Diana, at Ephesus, was carved from the same wood. So also, it is said, were the ships of Serostris, the Egyptian conqueror.

The Emperor Hadrian in A.D. 125 came to the rescue of the imperilled trees. High on the rocky slopes he carved his imperial anathema against all who should cut them. Nevertheless depredations went on for centuries, until the forest at the end of the nineteenth century had dwindled down to a grove of 400 trees.

To save it from complete destruction and preserve it, Rustem Pasha, governor-general of Lebanon, issued a special ordinance containing a series of stringent regulations calculated to check, if not quite put a stop to, the vandalism and carelessness of most travellers.

It is forbidden to put up tents or other kinds of shelter within the district of the trees, or to light fires or to cook any provisions in their vicinity. No one is allowed to break off a bough or even a twig from the trees. It is forbidden to bring any beasts of burden within the district. Should oxen, sheep, goats, or other pasturage cattle be found within the prescribed limits they are summarily confiscated.

But, if the cedars are few in number, these few are of royal blood. They are not the largest of trees, though some of the trunks measure over 40 feet round. Their beauty lies in the wide-spreading limbs, which often cover a circle 200 feet or 300 feet in circumference. Some are tall and symmetrical, with beautiful horizontal branches; others are gnarled and knotted, with inviting seats in the great forks, and charming beds on the thick foliage of the swinging boughs.

The wood has a sweet odor, is very hard, and seldom decays. "The vitality of the cedar," says a writer in *Scribner's Monthly*, "is remarkable. A dead tree is never seen, except where lightning or the axe has been at work. Often a great bough of one tree has grown into a neighbor, and the two are so bound together that it is impossible to say which is the parent trunk. Perhaps the unusual strength and vitality of the cedars are due to their slow growth. When a little sprout, hardly waist high, is said to be ten or fifteen or twenty years old, one cannot help asking, What must be the age of the great patriarchs of the grove? It is hard to tell exactly. By the aid of a microscope

I have counted more than 700 rings on a bough only 30 inches in diameter. Those who have studied the matter more deeply think that some of these trees must be more than 1000 years old. Indeed, there is nothing wildly improbable in the thought that perhaps the Guardian, for instance, may have been a young tree when Hiram began cutting for the temple at Jerusalem."

This tree has been introduced into England, but chiefly for ornament. Several were planted in the Royal Gardens in 1683, and in 80 years acquired a circumference of 12 feet and a height of 70 feet. The branches extend over a space of 40 feet diameter.

The white cedar, or cypress, and the red cedar, or juniper, are very different from the cedar of Lebanon; indeed they do not belong to the family of pines. Yet the latter shares some of its characteristics. As an instance of the extraordinary vitality of the red cedar in the state of Washington, the Seattle *Intelligencer* told, in 1910, of some shingles cut in a Washington mill and sent east for exhibition purposes. Those shingles were cut from a moss-covered cedar log lying on the ground, and which had growing over it another cedar tree the roots of which encircled the fallen log. The growing tree had 750 rings, which indicates, according to the accepted theory, that it was 750 years old. Yet its growth started after the tree from which the shingles were cut had fallen to the ground. Here was a cedar log, fallen and lifeless, which had lain exposed to the weather for not less than 750 years, and yet was free from rot to the extent that merchantable shingles could be sawed from it.

"Every man who has worked in the woods or in clearing land in this State," concludes the *Intelligencer,* "has seen similar instances of the ability of red cedar to resist the ravages of time. In alluvial soil along the river banks, in digging ditches, cedar logs have been found covered by four or five feet of alluvium, which were yet sound save for a few inches on the extreme outside, although, under similar conditions, almost any other wood would have decayed in a few years. Conjecture halts at any attempt to estimate the length of time which might have elapsed since those logs were growing trees."

Cent.   The first American cent was coined and circulated in 1793. Previous to this date several patterns had been struck off. These were experiments, and were not circulated. The so-called "Washington pennies," which existed previous to this date, were not issued by the government and were models or medals. The cent of 1793 was very similar in appearance to the cent of later dates. Instead of the wreath, however, it bore around the words "one cent" a chain composed of thirteen links, but this type was changed in the first year of issue. Cents were issued annually until the year 1857, except that during the year 1815 none were coined. The small nickel cents made their appearance in 1857, and the coinage of the copper cents was stopped. Some of the old cents are quite rare, and consequently are now valuable. The rarest cent is that of the series of 1799. It is said that their scarcity is due to the fact that a firm in Salem, Mass., then engaged in the slave trade, obtained a large quantity of these cents from the mint, drilled holes in them, and shipped them to Africa to exchange them for slaves. The African chiefs would string them and wear them round their necks. If this story be true eager coin collectors are more likely to find specimens of the cent in Africa than in America.

One of the most puzzling questions is, What becomes of the pennies? About 80,000,000 of them are manufactured and put into circulation every year, and, though a great many eventually come back to the treasury for redemption, the majority are never seen again. They simply disappear. Inasmuch as they are practically indestructible, it must be presumed that they are lost. They are subject to more accidents·than other coins; changing hands oftener, and being of such small value, they are carelessly treated.

It is an interesting fact that during periods of commercial depression pennies accumulate in the sub-treasuries, and when trade revives they flow out rapidly. Thus the cent is a barometer of business. When it circulates freely, prosperity reigns, and *vice versa*. Even a big storm, or a spell of very cold weather, which keeps the penny-spending population at home, is reflected in the demand for coppers.

One of the most remarkable hoaxes in history was perpetrated, about 1906, in connection with pennies. A rumor was started to the effect that in the coining of cents of 1902 a large quantity of gold had been accidentally spilled into the molten copper, on which account it was averred that the government was anxious to recall the issue as far as possible.

While this strange report was in circulation, an advertisement appeared in a newspaper, stating that a certain clothing store in the city of Washington would pay " 18 cents for 1902 pennies." As a result, within a few days practically all of the 1902 cents in the Piedmont section of North Carolina, and in half a dozen towns in South Carolina, were bought up by speculators. The current price was three cents apiece; two days later it rose to five cents, and on the following day one purchaser paid $33 for 330 of the precious coins. He claimed afterward that he sold them for 15 cents each.

For about a week the price for 1902 pennies ranged from 8 to 12 cents. But the exposure arrived when deliveries of large quantities of them were made at the dry-goods store in Washington. The firm declared that its offer was to pay 18 cents for one thousand nine hundred and two pennies—which was, of course, preposterous. But the victims of the joke had no redress, and one more financial bubble went to join the multitude that have been punctured in the past.

Chairs are of such high antiquity that their origin is lost in the twilight of fable. The Jewish rabbins tell us of one that belonged to Abraham. He fashioned it with his own hands from a tooth that fell out of the mouth of Og, a huge giant among his servants who experienced a sudden trembling before the patriarchal wrath. Abraham made this his favorite seat until his death. Yet there are not wanting other rabbins who declare that it was not a chair but a bed which was carved out of Og's tooth.

The chair represented on the earliest monuments of Oriental antiquity is without a back, the legs are tastefully carved, and the seat adorned with the heads of rams. The cushion appears to be made of some rich stuff embroidered or painted. The legs were strengthened by a cross bar, and frequently ended in the feet of a lion or the hoofs of a bull, either of gold, silver, or bronze. On the monuments of Khorsabad, in the rock tablets of Malthaiah, we find representations of chairs supported by animals, and by human figures, sometimes prisoners, like the caryatidæ of the Greeks. In this they resembled the arm-chairs of Egypt, but appear to have been more massive than they. Chairs and couches, adorned with feet of silver and other metals, were looked upon as great objects of luxury in Persia from whence they were probably introduced into Asia Minor and Greece. In the Lycian sculptures we have representations of stays or arms on either side of the seat, such as lions. This fashion, introduced into Asia Minor by the Persians, was originally borrowed from the Assyrians.

Chairs have, of course, been connected with literature. What may be called Shakespearian chairs present quite an interesting item of history. Within the kitchen of the house in which he was born, at Stratford-on-Avon, Mr. Ireland, who visited it in 1792, tells us was a small arched recess for a chair. Here often sat John Shakespeare, and here his son William passed his earliest days. "In the corner of the chimney," says Ireland, "stood an old oak chair, which had for a number of years received nearly as many adorers as the celebrated shrine of the Lady of Loretto." This relic was purchased in July, 1790, by the Princess Czar-

..oryska, who made a journey purposely to obtain intelligence relative to Shakespeare. Being told he had often sat in this chair, she placed herself in it and expressed an ardent wish to become its purchaser; but being informed that it was not to be sold at any price, she gave a handsome gratuity to old Mrs. Harte and left the place with apparent regret. About four months after, the anxiety of the princess could no longer be restrained and her secretary was despatched express, as the fit agent, to purchase this treasure at any rate. The sum of twenty guineas, or somewhat more than $100, was the price fixed on, and the secretary and chair, with a proper certificate of its authenticity, on stamped paper, set off in a chaise for London.

With all due anxiety to supply relic-hunters who visit Stratford, and who sometimes feel disappointed with the little which remains there connected with the poet, the absence of the genuine chair was not long felt. A very old chair is still in the place; and Washington Irving thus speaks of the chair he saw in 1820: " The most favorite object of curiosity, however, is Shakespeare's chair. It stands in the chimney-nook of a small, gloomy chamber, just behind what was his father' shop. Here he may many a time have sat when he was a boy, watching the slowly revolving spit with all the longings of an urchin, or of an evening listening to the crones and gossips of Stratford, dealing forth churchyard tales, and legendary anecdotes of the troublesome times of England."

In this chair it is the custom for every one who visits the house to sit; whether this is done with the hope of imbibing any of the inspiration of the bard, I am at a loss to say; I merely mention the fact; and mine host privately assured me, that though built of solid oak, such was the present zeal of devotees, that the chair had to be new-bottomed, at least once in three years. It is worthy of notice also, in the history of this extraordinary chair, that it partakes something of the volatile nature of the Santa Caso of Loretto, or the flying chair of the Arabian enchanter; for, though sold some years since to a Northern princess, it has found its way back again to the old chimney corner.

There was found, however, by Ireland, during the visit of which we have already spoken, in 1792, in a house in Stratford, a chair which, there can be little doubt, was really often occupied by the immortal bard. It was in the house of the father of Anne Hathaway, who afterward became Shakespeare's wife. Ireland purchased this chair, which he engraved in his " Picturesque Views on the Avon." He says that it was called Shakespeare's courting chair.

With a similar desire to please relic-hunters and lovers to

that which has been already shown, this chair, although long since gone, has a successor dignified by the same name, in an old settle in the passage through the house, and which has but one bit of old wood in it.

In Walmer Castle, the home of the Duke of Wellington, is the chair occupied by Pitt and another that was the favorite of the Iron Duke, also the chair in which he died.

A valuable arm-chair is in the possession of the Earl of Radnor. It originally cost forty thousand dollars, and was presented by the city of Augsburg to the Emperor Rudolph II of Germany about the year 1576. It is of steel, and took the artist about thirty years to make. The chair became the property of Count Tessin, ambassador from the court of Sweden to the English court. Gustavus Brander afterwards bought it, as an antique, for eighteen hundred guineas, and sold it to the Earl of Radnor for six hundred guineas.

The Shah of Persia owns the most valuable arm-chair in the world. He has an arm-chair of solid gold inlaid with precious stones. About the year 1900 some of the stones were stolen from one of the legs of the chair, and the Shah, full of indignation, ordered the arrest of a number of servants and held the keeper of the palace responsible for the furniture, with the intimation that if the thief was not discovered the keeper would be beheaded. The culprit being eventually found, he was forthwith beheaded and his head carried on a pole by the imperial body-guard through the streets of Teheran.

When the Pilgrim fathers left England they brought their chairs with them in the Mayflower. In Pilgrim Hall, Plymouth, there are many articles, including chairs, that belonged to the Pilgrims. In the rooms of the Massachusetts Historical Society is the chair owned by Governor Winthrop. In the school at Wittenberg. formerly the university, is still shown the chair as well as the drinking-cup and the table of Martin Luther. Barcena, the Jesuit, tells us that when Satan once appeared to him, his humility led him to invite the prince of darkness to sit in the chair, as being more worthy of it than the Jesuit himself. In the vestry of John Bunyan Church, in Bedford, is the chair in which the "glorious dreamer" sat. In the council chamber in New York is the chair which was used by the immortal Washington when he took his farewell of the American navy. Another which was wont to be filled by Dr. Benjamin Franklin, ex-president of the Philosophical Society. This chair for many years was not in the college building, but was long ago restored to its proper place in the library by Rev. John Bray, of Humphreysville, Ct.

Still another, dated 1700, belonged to the first president of Yale College, Rev. Abraham Pierson.

Chameleon. There are popular notions that the chameleon lives on air and that he constantly changes his colors, some say at his own caprice (with the object of terrorizing or astonishing the spectators) and some say in accordance with the colors of the surrounding objects. These notions—cherished by most of us from infancy, repeated in many a juvenile book on animals, and constantly utilized by the poets—are mere vulgar errors. The food of the chameleon is certainly a light diet, but not quite so unsubstantial as the air; he lives on small insects, principally flies, which he catches by darting out his tongue at them as they fly past. The tongue, which is capable of being greatly elongated and darted out with great rapidity, is covered at its point with a glutinous saliva, to which the insects adhere, and they are thus drawn into the animal's mouth. It is true the chameleon can exist without food for a very long period, and this fact, together with the almost invisible size of his actual food and the rapidity with which he catches it, has probably given rise to the error alluded to. As to his changing color, it is perfectly true that he does so, but neither of the explanations of the fact given above is the correct one. It is now pretty well established, thanks to the researches of Cuvier, that this change of color is due to the action of the lungs (which are of an extraordinary size) upon the blood, when the animal is under the influence of fear or other passions. And in this he very much resembles man, who turns white, red, bluish, yellow, or other colors, under the influence of fear, anger, or disease. It is said, also, that the chameleon is deaf. Another error. His sense of hearing is not acute, but still he hears.

Chameleon Fishes. The colors shown on many well-known colored plates of West Indian fishes published in standard works on ichthyology are, we find, not those of normal conditions, but rather those of dying, dead, and rapidly fading fishes. Experiments in the New York Aquarium have shown that such colors are merely the vestiges of the last convulsive color excitements of the specimens used. This is the explanation of the rapid changes for which the dying dolphin is celebrated. Even if painted from newly caught wild fishes, held in a portable aquarium, as some of them were, they show hiding or alarm colors only, and in every case represent merely one of several possible phases of coloration.

In fact it has been possible to show, by experiments with living fishes in the Aquarium, just which paintings and photo-

13

graphs reproduced in standard works were made from dead specimens and which were not.

It is well known that northern sea fishes habitually frequenting green or yellow seaweed acquire to some extent the general color tone of their habitat, and that trout from dark water are dark colored, while those inhabiting waters where there is sandy or gravelly bottom are light colored. Such conditions have long been appreciated at the Aquarium, where fishes kept in tanks lined with white tiles habitually wear their lighter colors, only an occasional blind fish remaining unchanged. The pale, colorless fishes of the Mammoth Cave gradually become darker when exposed to light in the Aquarium. These fishes, although with eyes that are virtually useless, are still able to distinguish light from darkness.—*Century Magazine.*

Champagne. The invention of champagne is attributed to one Dom Perignon, a Benedictine monk who was appointed cellarer to his monastery in the year 1668. In the pursuit of his new duties he fell upon the idea of " marrying " the different wines produced in the vineyards around him. He had noticed that one sort imparted fragrance and another generosity, likewise that the blackest grapes produced a white wine that kept good, instead of turning yellow and disintegrating as did the white wine made from white grapes. This white or gray wine produced from the province of Champagne became famous, and most famous of all that produced from Perignon's own district, Haut Villiers. He also discovered that a piece of cork was in every way superior as a stopper to the old-fashioned flax dipped in oil. By experiment after experiment he finally evolved an effervescent wine such as we now call champagne, which was at once hailed as pleasanter to the taste and more exhilarating to the spirits than the still wine. It was at a *souper d'anct* that the Marquis de Sillery introduced the new wine to court circles. In the midst of the festivities, we are told, a dozen blooming damsels, dressed as Bacchanals, suddenly appeared bearing flower-wreathed bottles in their hands, and great was the exultation when the corks popped and the liquor fizzed and sizzled in tall glasses made expressly for holding the new wine, to be followed by still greater exultation when the wine itself was tasted and pronounced exquisite. Thereafter sparkling wine was an indispensable adjunct to all the *petit soupers* of the period.

Charter Oak, a tree which once stood in Hartford, is memorable in the history of Connecticut as the hiding-place of the colonial charter in 1687. The motive for the hiding was to keep the charter out of the hands of Sir Edmund Andros, the newly appointed governor of all New England. According to some what doubtful tradition, Captain Joseph Wadsworth was the hero of the incident. There is reason indeed to believe that the original charter was secreted, possibly in the oak-tree of tradition, some time before Andros's arrival at Hartford, and that a duplicate figured in the historic scene in the council chamber. The oak-tree was several centuries old and had reached a diameter of seven feet when it was blown down by a storm in 1856. A monument, unveiled in 1909 by the Society of Colonial Wars of Connecticut, marks the spot where it stood, at an angle of lawn between two roads now known respectively as Charter Oak Avenue and Charter Oak Place. It is a simple granite obelisk encircled by oak-leaves and resting upon a globe which in turn rests upon four dolphins.

The inscription reads:

> Near this spot stood the
> Charter Oak,
> Memorable in the history
> of the
> Colony of Connecticut
> As the hiding-place of the Charter
> October 31, 1687.
> The tree fell
> Aug. 21, 1856.

Long before Mark Twain had become a citizen of Hartford and a sharer of its glories he made humorous capital out of the local patriotism and its chief object of self-gratulation. This passage occurred in one of his early speeches:

I went all over Hartford with a citizen whose ancestors came over with the Pilgrims in the *Quaker City*—in the *Mayflower* I should say—and he showed me all the historic relics of Hartford. He showed me a beautiful carved chair in the Senate chamber, where the bewigged and awfully homely old-time governors of the Commonwealth frown from their canvas overhead. "Made from Charter Oak," he said. I gazed upon it with inexpressible solicitude. He showed me another carved chair in the House. "Charter Oak," he said. I gazed again with interest. Then he looked at the rusty, stained, and famous old Charter, and presently I turned to move away. But he solemnly drew me back and pointed to the frame. "Charter Oak," said he. I worshipped. We went down to Wadsworth's Athenæum, and I wanted to look at the pictures; but he conveyed me silently to a corner, and pointed to a log rudely shaped somewhat like a chair, and whispered "Charter Oak." I exhibited the accustomed reverence. He showed me a walking-stick, needle-case, a dog-collar, a three-legged stool, a boot-jack, a dinner-table, a ten-pin alley, a toothpicker——

I interrupted him and said, "Never mind—we'll bunch the whole lumber-yard, and call it——"

"Charter Oak," he said.

"Well," I said, "now let us go and see some Charter Oak for a change."

I meant that for a joke; but how was he to know that, being a stranger? He took me around and showed me Charter Oak enough to build a plank-road from here to Great Salt Lake City. It is a shame to confess it, but I began to get a little weary of Charter Oak finally; and when he invited me to go home with him to tea, it filled me with a blessed sense of relief. He introduced me to his wife, and they left me alone for a moment to amuse myself with their little boy. I said, in a grave, paternal way,

"My son, what is your name?"

And he said, "Charter Oak Johnson."

This was sufficient for a sensitive nature like mine. I departed out of that mansion without another word.

Chauffeur. Early light-houses, both in Europe and America, were illumined by a primitive construction consisting of a grate, or chaffeur, placed on their summit, in which billets of wood or coal were burned. These coal lights survived in England as late as 1822, and on the Baltic Sea as recently as 1846.

The name "chauffer," by which our forefathers in England designated these grates, will doubtless recall the new much-spoken-of "chauffeur" of the modern automobile; but whereas the latter name is one which in French means "one who heats: a stoker; a fireman; hence an engine driver," the old "chauffer" is believed to have been an English corruption of the "chaufour," an apparatus wherein to burn lime ("chau-four," lime oven).

Check, Cheque. According to the *Strand Magazine* for August, 1906, the smallest check ever drawn by any government was that with which the United States for a period of five years annually rewarded Maurice Proctor, of Mineral Point, Iowa Co., Wisconsin, for his services in carrying the mails from that town to Dodgeville. It took the form of a postal warrant for one cent, duly drawn upon the Treasurer of the United States in favor of Mr. Proctor and signed by W. Allen.

The distance from Mineral Point to Dodgeville is eight miles. Proctor ran a stage line for passengers and goods between these two towns. But he wanted to see the magic legend "U. S. Mail" painted gayly on his coach, so in good faith and in due form he offered to undertake the task of transporting Uncle Sam's epistles. Some twenty competitors were eager to secure the same contract, but none could quite underbid Mr. Proctor's one-cent proposal. The post-office officials, having found Mr. Proctor financially responsible for the amount involved in the transaction, awarded him the contract. "Twice a day, fair weather or foul, good crops or bad crops, employés of Mr. Proctor carry the mails on this arrangement. It is to be wondered if, the world round, any government job is so well done for so little. This odd contract was recently renewed for a period of four years, the four cents being payable in four annual instalments. When Mr. Proctor received his first cheque from the Treasury Department he was immediately offered thirty-six dollars for the curiosity, and he sold it at this price."

A check for fifty cents issued by the Standard Oil Company as a refund on empty barrels is said to be preserved as a curiosity in the archives of that company. It is endorsed by forty business men of Middletown, New York, so that it obviously assisted in settling $20 worth of indebtedness.

One of the queerest of recorded checks was drawn by Joseph C. Palmer, a California pioneer. In the 'fifties he was a member of the banking firm of Palmer, Cook and Co. "To show his readiness to adopt original methods in an emergency," said the San Francisco *Bulletin* in an obituary article, " it is related that once a depositor called to draw a large sum of money ($28,000) from the bank. Mr. Palmer's consent was necessary, but he had been called away to attend to some duty in a lumber-yard a mile or more from the bank.

" Thither the depositor hastened and made known his wants and the necessity of having them attended to at once. Mr. Palmer could find neither pen, pencil, ink, nor paper. But without a moment's hesitation he picked up a shingle, borrowed a piece of red chalk, and with it wrote a check on the shingle in large and distinct letters for $28,000.

" This was good when presented for all the money the depositor had in bank."

Cheese. Cheese and the curdling of milk are mentioned in the book of Job. David was sent by his father, Jesse, to carry ten cheeses to the camp and to look how his brethren fared. " *Cheese of kine* " formed part of the supplies of David's army at Mahanaim during the rebellion of Absalom. Homer states that cheese formed part of the ample stores found by Ulysses in the cave of the Cyclop Polyphemus. Euripides, Theocritus, and other early poets mention cheese. Ludolphus says that excellent cheese and butter were made by the ancient Ethiopians; and Strabo states that some of the ancient Britons were so ignorant, that, though they had abundance of milk, they did not understand the art of making cheese. There is no evidence that any of these ancient nations had discovered the use of rennet in making cheese, but they seem merely to have allowed the milk to sour, and to have formed their cheese from the caseous part of the milk, after expelling the serum or whey. As David, when too young to carry arms, was able to run to the camp with ten cheese, ten loaves, and an ephah of parched corn, the cheeses must have been very small.

Of the English cheeses in his day Thomas Fuller, in " The Worthies of England," gives a quaint account: " Poor men eat cheese for hunger, rich for digestion. It seems that the ancient British had no skill in the making thereof till taught by the Romans, and now the Romans may even learn of us more exactness therein. The county of Chester doth afford the best for quantity and quality; and yet their cows are not (as in other shires) housed in the winter; so that it may seem strange, that the hardiest kine should yield the tenderest cheese. Some essayed in vain to make the like in other places, though hence they fetched both their kine and dairy maids. It seems they should have fetched their ground too (wherein surely some occult excellency in this kind), or else so good cheese will not be made. I hear not the like commendation of the butter in this county; and perchance these two commodities are like stars of a different horizon, so that the elevation of the one to eminency is the depression of the other."

English and Germans are greater consumers of cheese than Americans. Both are surpassed by the Norwegians. But the greatest of all cheese countries, alike as consumer and producer, is Switzerland, with the culminating point in Zermatt. It is even asserted that the social rank of a family in that part of the Swiss confederation is determined by the age and the quality of the cheese in its larder. There are patricians who own cheeses a century old. These are served only on solemn occasions,— christenings, weddings, or funerals.

Each pantry contains at least as many cheeses as there are living children in the family. For every birth a cheese is made and named after the newcomer, then put away until his or her wedding. On that occasion all guests eat a slice from the bride's and the bridegroom's cheese, as harbingers of good luck for both. The remainder is carefully put away to be served at the death of the eponymic owner.

In 1910 it was reported that an ancient cheese dating from 1785 had been discovered in a concealed shelter at Les Ormonts. It was as hard as a rock and had to be cut with a saw. It is reported to have tasted good.

The United States is the country of mammoth cheeses. It has been a sort of staccato custom to present monsters of this sort to the president. The precedent was set in the time of Jefferson at the beginning of the nineteenth century. Immediately that his election was assured, the inhabitants of Cheshire, Mass., assembled in a triumphant mass meeting and resolved to build a cheese that should eclipse all records. It was further resolved that Elder John Leland, the champion Jeffersonian of New England, should accompany the gift to Washington and present it to the chief magistrate as a New Year's gift.

July 20, 1801, was fixed upon for the construction of this trophy. Darius Brown at once constructed a monstrous cheese hoop 4 feet in diameter and 18 inches high, which the village blacksmiths strengthened with huge iron bands. Elder Leland announced from his pulpit that the curds were to be brought in to Elisha Brown's cider-mill, opposite the Whitford Rocks. Levy was laid upon every milk cow and mild-yielding heifer within the precincts of the town, except those owned by Federalists. Great caution was exercised to preserve the orthodoxy of the product from any leaven of Federal heresy.

When July 20 arrived, ever sort of wheeled vehicle and every beast of burden—horse, ox, ass, or mule—was pressed into service, and all good Jeffersonians hastened to the appointed rendezvous from highway, cross-road, and bridle-path. As each contributor drew up to the cider-mill, a committee received him with congratulatory greetings. The cream was passed to a committee composed of the most accomplished dairy-women of the town, who placed the curd within the great hoop.

"The last deposit having been made, the giant screw slowly descended from the ponderous beam, and, taking the monster preparation in its resistless clasp, soon copious streams of foaming whey descended to the ground. Then Elder Leland majestically arose and in solemn and eloquent words dedicated this monster cheese to their honored friend, Thomas Jefferson, President of the United States of America. A suitable hymn, lined off by the elder to the tune of Mear, was sung with great effect. The assemblage was then dismissed with a benediction and proudly returned to their homes, thoroughly alive to the fact that it had been participant in the exercises of the greatest day Cheshire had ever known as a locality, and which has never been matched in its history since."

So writes the editor of the Berkshire *Evening Eagle,* in a commemorative article that appeared in January, 1912. The same authority adds that on the eleventh day the great cheese was removed from the cider-press. It proved to be in perfect shape and condition, and was removed to the dairy-house of Darius Brown to be cured and dried.

The great cheese made its journey to Washington from Cheshire, Mass., in a wagon drawn by six horses, and bearing the label, "The greatest cheese in America for the greatest man. in America."

Jefferson, however, was exceedingly shy of accepting any gifts, and insisted on paying for the cheese, which cost him $200.

And six months later there was still some of that cheese left, notwithstanding the President's lavish hospitality.

All the original documents referring to the presentation and acceptance of the cheese are preserved by the descendants of Darius Brown in Cheshire. In responding to Elder Leland's presentation speech, Jefferson extended his warmest thanks to the people of Cheshire, saying that he looked upon this New Year's gift as a token of the fidelity of the very heart of the people of the land to the great cause of equal rights to all men.

"I shall cause," continued he, "this auspicious event to be placed upon the archives of the nation, while I shall ever esteem this occasion as one of the happiest in my history. And now, my reverend and most respected friend, I will, with the consent and in the presence of my Cabinet officers, proceed to have this monster cut, and you will take back to your Berkshire home a portion of it that your people may test its richness, flavor, and equality, and you will convey to them my heartiest thanks. Tell them never to falter in the principles which they have so nobly defended, having bravely and successfully come to the rescue of our beloved country in the time of its deepest and greatest peril. I wish them health and prosperity, and that rivers of milk may never cease to abundantly flow in to not only themselves but their posterity."

The steward of the White House then, on a signal from the President, advanced with a huge and glittering knife and carved the monster cheese in the presence of the President and Cabinet, foreign diplomats, and many distinguished men and women of ancient note. Its color was a beautiful annotto, somewhat variegated in shade owing to the mixture of so many curds, and it was the object of the greatest curiosity. Great slices were served up with bread to the President, Cabinet, diplomatic representatives in the order of their rank and station, and to others, until all had been feasted. Elder Leland was then introduced, person by person, by the President to the entire gathering. The presentation of this cheese and the attendant ceremonies became of great notoriety in the year 1802, and accounts of the event were published in the press all over the United States and in many foreign countries.

A cheese of even larger proportions was sent to President Jackson by a dairy farmer who wanted to bring the excellence of the dairy products of his neighborhood prominently into notice.

This particular cheese was over 4 feet in diameter, 2 feet thick, and weighed 1400 pounds. In order to get rid of it, it was announced that at a certain reception the President's mansion would be thrown open to the people and that they would be entertained with cheese. And that cheese vanished in two hours.

An eye-witness wrote that it was "surrounded with a dense crowd as it stood in the vestibule, who, without crackers, purveyed away 1400 pounds. The whole atmosphere of every room and throughout the city was filled with the odor. We have met it at every turn—the halls of the Capitol have been perfumed with it from the numbers who partook of it having carried away great masses in their coat pockets." There can be no doubt, however, that the astute dairy farmer was imbued with a rare genius for advertising.

It was customary for some of the friends of Martin Van Buren, who succeeded Jackson in the Presidency, to send him a monster cheese every year. This, on one occasion, he caused to be distributed to his callers at a public reception. But it proved a costly gift, for the crumbs were trodden into the carpet and ruined the upholstery of the splendid furniture of the room known as the East room.

The *Illustrated London News* January 6, 1829, records the arrival in England of what up to that time was the largest cheese ever made in the world. Here is the item:

LARGE CHEESE.—There has just been received, by the packet ship *Margaret Evans,* from the United States, an immense cheese, made from the milk of seven hundred cows; its weight is 1474 pounds; its circumference is 13 feet, thickness 18 inches: every inch thick will weigh three-quarters of a hundredweight. It was exhibited at the great fair at New York, and gained the highest premium: made by Messrs. Austin and Stone, Austinburgh, Ashtabula County, Ohio: purchased by Mr. John Craft, 20, Philpot-lane, City.

The biggest of all big cheeses, however, was that exhibited in 1911 at the National Dairy Show in Chicago. This was 5 feet high and 8 feet in diameter. It weighed 12,361 pounds, or three times more than the greatest of its predecessors. Nicholas Simon made it at Appleton, Wisconsin, with the help of the assistant dairy and food inspectors of Minnesota and Wisconsin, and more than 40 expert cheesemakers and their aides.

The greatest care had to be exercised to insure the curd being uniform, as it was furnished by 32 different cheese factories, the milk coming from 8000 thoroughbred Holstein and Guernsey cows pasturing on 1200 farms.

No building in Appleton was large enough for the manufacture and care of the cheese. Consequently it was made in the open air. To the 12,000 pounds of curd were added 330 pounds of cheese salt and 31 pounds of rennet. It took five hours to manufacture the cheese after the curd was delivered. As it was impossible to find an adequate cold storage plant in the Middle West it was necessary to build a special refrigerator 12 by 15 feet around and about it. A specially equipped flat car was provided to ship it to Chicago. Altogether, it was estimated, the services of 2000 men had been called in requisition for the production and shipment of the cheese.

An oddity in the way of cheese-industry is the cheese offered for sale by a German religious community which devotes itself to the rescue of fallen women. Under the head-line " Pious Cheese," the Frankfurter *Press* in January, 1912, quotes from a letter sent out by the head of the order. Their product is described as " pure cheese made by the pure hands of repentant women at our home in X——. Every purchaser of twenty kilos or more will be credited with a memorial mass, which we will celebrate at our chapel on the death of the purchaser. Retail customers will receive with each purchase a prayer coupon, and when five of these are sent to us by the same person they will be exchanged for a mass coupon. As it is made in our home by women of scrupulous cleanliness, our cheese is of incomparable quality, and to taste it means to buy it."

Another floating newspaper paragraph that possesses a general interest for all cheese eaters may be rescued from oblivion. " Dr. Adametz, a Swiss scholar, has been taking a census of the inhabitants of a cheese. The microscopic examination of one gramme of a fresh Emmenthaler cheese, such as is sold in England under the name of Gruyère, contained no fewer than ninety thousand so-called microbes. This prodigious encampment, after seventy days, proved to have increased to a tribe of eight hundred thousand. Another sort of cheese contained within a single gramme board and lodging for about two million microbes, while in a gramme cut from the rind of the same cheese Dr. Adametz found about five million of these inhabitants! A piece of cheese upon our tables, of a few pounds' weight, may consequently contain more microbe inhabitants than there are human inhabitants in the whole world."

Cheese was put to a strange use during one of the naval conflicts between Brazil and Uruguay in the mid-nineteenth century. Captain Coe, of the latter, fired away at his enemy, Admiral Brown, until the first lieutenant reported that all the shot was gone.

" Powder gone, eh ? " asked Coe.

" No, sir; lots of that yet."

" We had a darn'd hard cheese—a round Dutch one for dessert at dinner to-day ; do you remember it ? " said Coe.

" I ought to; I broke the carving-knife in trying to cut it, sir."

" Are there any more aboard ? "

" About two dozen. We took them from a droger."

" Will they go into the 18-pounders ? "

" By thunder, commodore, but that's the idea. I'll try 'em," cried the first luff.

And in a few minutes the fire of the old *Santa Maria* (Coe's ship), which had ceased entirely, was reopened, and Admiral Brown found more shot flying over his head. At last one of them struck his mainmast, and, as it did so, shattered and flew in every direction.

" What the devil is that which the enemy is firing? " asked Brown. But nobody could tell.

Directly another one came through a port and killed two men who were standing near him, and then, striking the opposite bulwarks, burst into flinders.

" By Jove, this is too much; this is some new-fangled bomb-shell or other; I don't like 'em at all," cried Brown; and then, as four or five more of them came slap through his sails, he gave the order to fill away, and actually backed out of the fight, receiving a parting broadside of Dutch cheeses.

Cheque. See CHECK.

Cherry. The cultivation of the cherry was begun in the East. The first garden cherries known to Europe, as well as the name by which they established themselves in popular favor, came from Cerasos, an old Greek town on the shores of the Black Sea. In Latin the Greek word *cerasos* became *cerasus,* in French *cérise,* in English *cherry.* Plutarch tells us that the Roman general Lucullus, returning from his victories over Mithridates in the distant Pontus, brought back much gold and silver, and in addition a cherry-tree from Cerasos to grace his triumph. The fruit and the tree were till then unknown in Italy. Ferrero very sensibly remarks that this humble gift to his countrymen was infinitely more precious than the gold and silver spoil of his wars. Italian cherries became famous the world over, and in the course of the next 120 years the culture of the tree had spread far and wide and reached even remote Britain.

In Nova Scotia the largest of all cherries is raised, a luscious black variety. The Bear River district on Annapolis Basin is the centre of the cherry-growing industry, and the marketing of the fruit has brought about an unusual custom. A buyer may go around early in the summer, when the trees are in bloom and bid so much for such trees as he fancies. If his offer is accepted, that tree is his for that season. No one but the birds will steal his fruit.

But if you are not a dealer in fruit and merely want enough cherries for home use, you may happen around at any time when cherries are ripe and rent a tree for an hour or two hours or a day—whatever time you like. If two or more want the same tree the owner holds an auction. The winner owns that tree for just as long as he specifies and no more. and it is up to him to pick what he can. When he is through, the tree is rented again.

Tourists find this cherry-tree gambling a pleasant diversion. Although the sport lasts all through the cherry season, one Sunday, when the fruit is ripening well, is set apart and excursions are made from near-by places. On "Cherry Sunday" the orchards are thronged, picnic parties camp out under the trees, and by nightfall not a square meal is left for a bird. Below a tree which has been rented by periods will be a group waiting for their turn, while those in the branches pick fast and furiously against time. It is all done in the best of good nature, even those who have invested in a tree to find it stripped taking the misadventure in good part.

The cherry-blossoms of Japan are famous. As amazing as anything in all the necromancy of gardening is the evolution of this blossom from the single little wild mountain flower to the wide-spread two-inch blossom.

"Beginning with the stock of the wild mountain or Yoshino cherry, the gardeners grafted the shoots of the flowering varieties close to the ground, then enlarged the petals, changed stamens to petals, and multiplied the petals. These they curled in cup-like forms beyond the possibilities of a plum-blossom, and, beside the one indentation of the traditional heart-shaped petal, cut deep notches like a sparrow's beak or made serrated edges like the petals of a pink or daisy.

"They called the latter flower the "little chrysanthemum." They curled and broadened the stamens, stood them upright like the sail of a junk, and in some cases left two pistils of pale green in the heart of the rosiest flowers as a charming color contrast."— *Century.*

New York has had many interesting and some famous trees, but never before, until the arrival, in April, 1912, of the 2500 cherry-trees presented to the city by the Emperor of Japan, has it had a gift equal to this in quantity or importance. Several of the trees were planted on Riverside Drive in the vicinity of Grant's Tomb, close to the little tree planted by Li Hung Chang. Said a New York paper of that date:

"Park Commissioner Stover is having this huge batch of trees carefully examined by experts to detect any evidence of parasites which might do injury to other park foliage, and as rapidly as those which are above suspicion are approved they will be set out along Riverside Drive and in Central Park. The cherry-blossom is the national flower of Japan, and the Japanese residents of New York have taken a keen interest in this exceptional gift of their government and are hoping that the majority of them will flourish as successfully here as they do on the boulevards of Japan."

In the planting of the first batch of the trees a patriotic tribute was paid to both countries. Three groups of thirteen each were set out near Grant's Tomb in honor of the thirteen original American commonwealths, and at the same time in recognition of the lucky number of Japan, incidentally reversing an Occidental tradition.

Cheshire Cheese, Ye Olde. The name of a famous London tavern in Wine Court, between two dark little alleys running off Fleet Street. The entrance leads into a low-ceiling room, subdivided into numerous partitions and cosey corners. To the left is the dining-room. The furniture everywhere is nicked, elbow-rubbed, and black with age. No straight line meets the eye. Everything gives the impression of sinking foundation and warping woodwork. From the centre arises a spiral step-worn flight of stairs, ascending to the kitchen and to the upper dining-room. The walls are adorned with pictures of Dr. Johnson and other celebrities, for, though Boswell never mentions its name, the Cheshire Cheese derives its chief fame from its Johnsonian traditions. Johnson's old arm-chair is still shown in the upper dining-room, but he is said to have loved the ground-floor best, a brass plate recording the fact:

> The Favorite Seat of
> Dr. Samuel Johnson.
> Born 18th September, 1709.
> Died 13th December, 1784.
> In him a noble understanding and a masterly intellect were united with grand independence of character and unfailing goodness of heart, which won the admiration of his own age and remains as recommendation to the reverence of posterity.

The date of the tavern's founding is uncertain, as the original building was destroyed in the Great Fire of London, but some of the household jokes have been handed down from the time of Ben Jonson.

For example, it was here that Jonson and John Sylvester challenged each other to a contest at capping verses. Sylvester began:

> I John Sylvester
> Have kissed your sister.

Ben Jonson quickly retorted:

> I Ben Jonson
> Have kissed your wife.

"Nay," said Sylvester, "that is not rhyme."

"But it is the truth," said Jonson.

It was here also that Herrick first read the poem he wrote on the occasion of Jonson's death.

Besides its literary celebrities, the "Cheese" preserves reverent memories of one who in a smaller field of usefulness was equally pre-eminent,—old William the waiter. He was the "only William" of London, and since his death, which threw the "Cheese" and its habitués into mourning for weeks, no person by the name of William has been employed in the tavern, as a mark of respect to the head henchman.

It is recorded of William that when the pudding, for which the "Cheese" is famous, was being served, he hobbled around the table offering further helpings.

"Any gentleman say pudden?" he cried.

"No gentleman says pudden," growled a surly customer.

"Of course, you've 'ad two 'elps already, sir," was William's retort.

Talking of "pudden," there is really only one word which the tavern's parrot can clearly articulate. On one occasion it got away and flew all over London. It was advertised, and after three days a man came to the "Cheese" and asked for the host, Charlie Moore.

"I caught a parrit," said he.

Moore described it. It was the "Cheese" parrot, undoubtedly. But the man was not convinced.

"You forgot something," said he. "Don't your parrot say a word?"

"Yes; it says 'pudden.'"

"That's your parrit, sir," said the man. "It's been on the roof the 'ole bloomin' night yellin' 'Pudden!' till you'd a-thort it was Christmus. Come 'n' take your bird away."

Chess. All sorts of hypotheses as to the origin and antiquity of this game have been put forward by many authorities, learned and unlearned, wise or otherwise. Clearing away all the smoke of controversy, these facts alone can be accepted as settled: That the game was known in Persia and in Arabia by the middle of the sixth century, and that it originated in India, where it was known as *chaturanga*, "a complete army." The Persian *catrang* and Arabic *shatrasj* are merely phonetic variations of the Sanskrit *chaturanga*.

According to Persian tradition, an Indian king presented a game of catrang to a Persian king between the years 531 and 579 A.D. In return the Persian king sent the Indian the game of nard or backgammon. This tradition was afterward utilized by Firdusi, the Persian poet, in a famous passage in his *Shanamah* (1000 A.D.), and is corroborated by Arabic authors. The latter not only report that nard was sent to India, but also state that satranj was invented in India. Their authority is later, however, than that of the Persian tradition. In the (Sanskrit) literature of India the earliest known reference to chess is found in the *Horschacavita*. This work dates from the seventh century. But both the board and the game are referred to as familiar matters. The inference is obvious, that neither was a novelty in the India of the seventh century.

Here then we have corroborative evidence from three sources, Persian, Arabic, and Sanskrit, all pointing to the same period, the middle of the sixth century, as that in which chess flourished in India. Furthermore we have the independent evidence of a Chinese writer of the tenth century, that chess was introduced into China in the sixth century, presumably from its Hindoo neighbor.

But there is every reason to believe that some primitive form of the chaturanga, or chess, existed in India long before the sixth century A.D. As early as the second century B.C. (some authorities say the fifth) references are found to a board of eight squares in distinction to the board used for backgammon and parchesi. (WASHBURN HOPKINS, New York *Nation,* June 14, 1900.)

Consequently the history of chess divides itself into three distinct periods:

The first is that of the ancient Hindoo game called chaturanga, in which the moves and powers of all the pieces employed (with the exception of the queen) were the same as they are at this day. The origin of this game is lost in the twilight of fable; but there can be no question that it was invented in India. The board consisted then, as it does now, of sixty-four squares. The game was played by four persons, each having a king, a rook, a knight, and, lastly, a bishop (then represented by a ship), together with four pawns. The two opposite players were allied against the other two, and the moves were decided by the turn of an oblong die having four faces marked with the numbers two, three, four, and five; the two and five being opposites, as were the three and four.

The second or mediæval period in the history of chess occupies one thousand years—that is, from the sixth to the sixteenth century of our era. At the commencement of this period the improvement made in the game is very decided. The board and the powers of the pieces still remain the same, but the two allied forces have each united on one side of the board, whilst the adversaries have done the same on the other. One of the allied kings then becomes a subordinate piece, called *farzin,* or *vizier*— *i.e.,* counsellor or minister,—with only half the power that he had previously possessed as an independent sovereign. At the same time the rook is transferred to the corner of the board and the bishop to the place he now occupies. Finally, the die is dismissed, and the whole game is reduced to a pure trial of mental power and intellectual skill.

The third or modern period commences with the sixteenth century. The change made here consists, first, in extending the power of the bishop, allowing him to command the whole diagonal, instead of every third square, as formerly; secondly, in transforming the vizier into the queen and giving her the enormous power of the rook and bishop combined; and, lastly, in allowing the pawns to advance one or two squares of pleasure, at the first move. To these improvements we may add that of castling the king, either according to the Italian method or that of the Anglo-French school. It is just probable that our go-ahead posterity will introduce some further modifications— such, for instance, as giving the queen the additional power of the knight. (DR. FORBES DUNCAN, *Illustrated London News,* July 8, 1854.)

Whoever was the inventor of chess had the game of war in his mind's eye. Chess is a battle, the chess-board a battle-field, the pieces are opposing armies. And the last were Asiatic armies, as may be gathered from the composition of the forces. For aught we know, chess may have been the prehistoric *kriegspiel,* or war-game, designed to give, in miniature, instruction in the then theory of war. More than any other game, it demands the military quality of instant seizure of the right moment for the right move. In whist the effect of a wrong lead may often be recovered, but in chess, against equal play, the effect of a false move is not to be undone. In the former case the penalty may be only the loss of a point, whereas in the latter, unless error answers error, the first mistake must lead to the loss of the game. Finally, in chess as in war, reading must supplement practice.

Perhaps the race of warriors is not even yet extinct who look down on book study as a means of developing military capacity. But the experience of every succeeding war proves the truth of Napoleon's dictum: "Study the campaigns of Cæsar, Hannibal, Alexander, Gustavus Adolphus, Turenne; penetrate yourself with the spirit of those great men. That is the way to become a leader and to understand war." The advice applies in every pursuit of art or science, and most especially to chess. Book study is indispensable to all players who have the ambition to become masters.

Chess, Blindfold. The practice of playing chess without seeing the board and men is of great antiquity. In very early times the inhabitants of India carried the feat to a considerable success; and, down to the period when Tamerlane the Great named one of his sons Schachrokh, in honor of chess, blindfold playing was highly valued, both as a mnemonic feat and as a pastime. Great, however, as the achievements of the ancients were in this respect, they are, if we may judge by the records that have descended to us, completely eclipsed by the performances of modern times. In the year 970 a Greek named Tchelebi acquired high renown throughout the East for his skill in playing without the board against two persons at the same time. In 1266 a Saracen called Buzecca played in Florence three games simultaneously against some of the best Italian masters; two of these games he conducted by memory alone, for the third he had the aid of the board and men. Paolo Boi, of Syracuse, has the reputation of having played three games at once, all blindfold, and early in the eighteenth century, Father Socchieri, of Pavia, played three games at once against three players without seeing any of the boards.

It remained for Philidor, the greatest genius at chess known up to his time, to play blindfolded, in England in 1783, against three of the best players then living, winning two games and drawing the third, surprising his antagonists and the throng of onlookers by keeping up a lively conversation all the while. Philidor, lively Frenchman that he was, still holds the palm as a conversationalist and player at the same time.

In the early nineteenth century Kieseritzky, a Pole, and Harrwitz, a German, performed the three-game feat without the conversation.

While these gentlemen were winning their maturer laurels, a stripling in the German principality of Lippe-Detmold was also engaged in emulating the feats of Philidor. Little Louis Paulsen (born 1833), the son of a farmer, had become the chess champion of his native village at the precocious age of seven. He had even beaten the schoolmaster, who in return told him all about the great Frenchman who had actually played a game of chess without the assistance of the board and men. Louis was eager to ascertain how many moves he could remember in the same manner, and, after a few trials in which he played the moves on both sides by himself mentally, he announced to his friends and comrades that he was ready to play them one and all blindfold. The challenge was accepted, and the unseeing champion was vic-

14

torious. Shortly afterward the struggle for a livelihood compelled Louis Paulsen to abandon the practice of chess for some years.

In 1854 he emigrated to the United States and established himself as a tobacconist in Dubuque, Iowa. He resumed the practice of chess, made some local fame, and in 1857 competed unsuccessfully for a prize at the first American chess congress in New York. Though he failed in his main object, he astonished every one by playing four games blindfold at the same time against four of the chief amateurs of the United States. Paul Morphy, the prize winner at the congress, was one of his antagonists. Finally, on May 10, 1858, at Chicago, he performed his greatest feat, playing ten games together, without seeing a chessboard, against ten strong opponents. He won nine games and tied the tenth.

"During this unexampled match," says the London *Illustrated News* (August 14, 1858), "upwards of nine hundred and twenty moves were *made,* those considered must have been as many thousands; and not only did Paulsen never make the slightest error, but often during very intricate combinations he corrected the mistakes of his open-eyed adversaries. This is perhaps the most astounding feat of memory the world has ever heard of."

Yet Paulsen assured his friends that he could play better without the board than with it, that he could almost as easily play twenty games at a time in this manner as he could play ten, and that he performed his marvellous feats with the greatest care and without experiencing headache or uneasiness of any kind.

Paulsen was on an exhibition tour in England when the *News* published this information, with his portrait. On September 18 of the same year the same paper was called upon to chronicle another astonishing achievement by another American visitor. Young Paul Morphy, on August 27, at Queen's College, Birmingham, had contested eight games without the aid of chess-board or men, against eight members of the British Chess Association. He won six games, lost one, and tied one. Again the *News* selects big adjectives to characterize the event. Paulsen's game had been "unexampled"; Morphy's "may fairly be pronounced unparalleled; because," the *News* hastens to explain, "although we have lately recorded a similar one wherein more games were played simultaneously blindfold by Mr. Paulsen, it must be remembered that in that instance the contest extended over three or four sittings, and Mr. Paulsen was enabled, if he chose, and needed the assistance, to refresh his memory by consulting the chess-board during the intervals; while the games be-

fore us were all played out at once, Mr. Morphy never quitting
the room from the first move to the last. What adds to the
wonder is the fact that he rarely paused a minute to consider
any move; and when, as was once or twice the case, a wrong one
was announced to him—such as *K's* Kt so and so, instead of
Q's Kt—he instantly corrected it, quietly observing, "The *K's* Kt
cannot go to the square indicated; you mean, of course, *Q's* Kt.
My answer is," etc.

In 1890 a blindfold exhibition game took place at the
Bohemian Chess Club in London which constituted an original
departure from the old methods. Two blindfold players—Mr. A.
Curnock and Mr. T. Laurence—carried on six games against
each other, all at the same time. They began at 6 P.M., each
player having the move in three of the contests, and sat side by
side, with their faces turned towards the blank wall; while in
another corner of the club-room the members, for their own
amusement, followed the games on six boards. Mr. Curnock.
winning the toss, called out the first move in game No. 1. Mr.
Laurence replied; then a move was called on board No. 2, and so
on. After the first move and reply had been made in all the
six games the players proceeded to the second move, beginning
again at game No. 1. This continued for five hours, the fifteenth
move being reached at each board, showing that the rate of play
was thirty-six moves per hour in each game. Play was of the
highest order, and victory fell to Mr. Laurence, who won two
games by brilliant combination. The remaining four games were
drawn for want of time to finish them.

It has been urged that the strain upon the mind of the blindfold player is greater than even the normal man can stand.

J. H. Blackburne, of London, another famous blindfold
player, with a record of twelve simultaneous games, who made
annual exhibition tours through all the principal chess centres
of England, Ireland, and Scotland, was liable to get very violent
at times.

Poor Morphy himself, on his return from his European trip
in 1859, went mad, and took a dislike to the game and its
devotees. He considered himself the greatest living lawyer. He
continually had a roll of papers with him which he fancied were
his briefs, and very often he pleaded his own case on a street
corner in New Orleans. He also imagined that he was robbed
of his father's inheritance by some relatives, and continually
threatened a lawsuit. He was perfectly harmless, and only became violent when any one talked to him of chess, or when
he met anybody he knew to be a chess player. He would then
shout very violently: "I have no time, I have no time." He

would often say that if he had not played chess he would have married a rich girl and would have been happy. Every afternoon, between 3 and 4 o'clock, he would walk up and down Canal Street in New Orleans and take off his hat when passing a lady, whether he knew her or not. There was, however, some method in his madness. When he saw a really pretty girl he followed her for hours until the girl in question went home. He would then take her address and go quietly home.

It would seem indeed that it is to the overstrain of these blindfold games which so many champions have hazarded that chess owes its evil reputation as the favorite pastime of unsound minds.

Chess Champions and Championships. The London *Saturday Review,* in its October issue, 1880, made a shrewd and pregnant suggestion. Comparing small things with great it opined that national characteristics find as significant expression in combats at chess as on theatres of war and enterprise. Recalling the international chess tournament in 1843 fought by the English Howard Staunton and the French St. Amant, the *Review* detected on the part of the Frenchman greater *finesse,* more inventiveness, more dash, combined with uncertainty of aim; on the English side, more judgment, less speculation, more determined "hard pounding" on a definite point. Refusing, however, to judge from an isolated instance, the Reviewer searched the voluminous military history of chess, to find in the performances of such Frenchmen as La Bourdonnais and Philidor more of genius and brilliancy; in those of such Germans as Anderssen (who, nevertheless, is credited with the "most brilliant game on record"), Von H. der Laza, and Jaenisch, more of science and depth; in those of Englishmen, such as Staunton, Lewis, Cochrane, more of sound practical judgment. "Every quality," he continued, "has of course its value in its proper place; and genius has sometimes stolen a march upon the slower judgment. Some twenty years back (in 1858) America sent over to Europe the youthful, but peerless, Paul Morphy. He came, he saw, he conquered. Such an exhibition of skill was never before seen, and has not been seen since. The most accomplished players in the Old World were vanquished one after another; and, if ever genius and judgment, boldness and caution were duly combined, they were so in this wonderful player. It has always been matter for regret with patriotic chess enthusiasts that the great English champion, Mr. Staunton, was unable to arrange for an encounter with the conquering American. The Eastern world has produced first-rate players, one of whom, Ghulam Kassim, of Madras, was a distinguished writer on the subject. Italy had sent forth redoubtable performers and excellent critics at a time when chess was almost unknown here. As scientific and thoroughly exhaustive critics, however, the Germans, it may well be believed, more than hold their own."

Among the players mentioned by the *Saturday Review* Philidor was the earliest of the great European masters of the game. His surname, despite its sound and its apparent derivation, was not one of those Grecized or Latinized forms of real or adopted surnames which were common in a somewhat earlier period. It is said to have been bestowed by Louis XIII. on the first of the great chess-player's family who became known to the Court and the public—Michael Danican. The latter was so successful in his musical performances before the king that Louis pronounced him to be " another Filidori," the name of a famous Italian hautboy-player who had delighted the French Court a short time before. The sobriquet thus bestowed upon Danican was retained as a second surname by his family until, in the reign of Louis XV., it attained a world-wide celebrity in the person of his great-grandson. The younger Philidor, like all his ancestors, was at first a Court musician, copyist, and composer. He learned chess in the course of his professional avocations, that game being the only recreation allowed to the royal musicians while in attendance at the chapel where the king heard mass every morning. Philidor is reported to have distinguished himself by his proficiency in the game before he had emerged from childhood; his reputation soon brought him into notice, and led to his being matched against the best players at the Café de la Regence and other places of aristocratic resort, and later in life established him in England as a professional chess-player, assisted and salaried by a number of noblemen and gentlemen who formed themselves into a club for the encouragement of the game and the support of its greatest living master. It is conceded that in such mere *tours de force* as blindfold-playing he never reached the marvellous facility displayed by Paul Morphy, Louis Paulsen, or J. H. Zukertort, and that his ideas of the science of the game were less accurate and complete than those of his successors. But this was only to be expected from the length of time during which, since his death, chess has been made a subject of intense technical and even scientific study by men of equal powers with his and higher education.

Paul Morphy (1837–1884) was a native of New Orleans. His parents were wealthy and he himself was a member of the bar. From the age of ten, when his father taught him chess, until he was nearly thirty, when he wearied even of his triumphs, he devoted himself assiduously to the game. Before he was thir-

teen he could beat anybody in New Orleans. When he was thirteen (May, 1850), he beat the famous Löwenthal, then on a visit
to America. One game was tied. The two others were won by
Morphy.

So great was his fame by the time he was 21, that, when he
arrived in New York to take part in the first congress of the
American Chess Association, opening October 5, 1857, the first
prize was universally conceded him even before the entries for
the grand tournament had been completed. Certainty became
more sure as the congress progressed, and he overthrew, either in
the grand tournament or in side play, one after another of those
men who had long been looked up to as the magnates of the
American chess world.

Flushed with these triumphs, he crossed over to England.
The first antagonist he met was Löwenthal, whom he had already
defeated in New Orleans. His manhood fulfilled the promise of
the child. He defeated Löwenthal again in the proportion of
three games to one. In England also he met and vanquished
other stars. In Paris he defeated Harrwitz, in Breslau he over-
came the still more celebrated Anderssen.

"There is something exceedingly romantic and chivalrous
about this young man's coming over to Europe and throwing
down the gauntlet to all our veterans. He is certainly a very
Admirable Crichton of chess, and, like the accomplished Scot,
he is as courteous and generous as he is brave and skilful." So
said a London journal of August 29, 1858; and piquancy and
interest are added to the passage by the fact that it was written
by Löwenthal, just after the wonderful American had beaten
him in a set match, the first played by Morphy after his arrival
in Europe.

In fact press and public, not only in England but on the
Continent, went wild over Morphy. Great banquets were given
in his honor by London and Paris clubs. His bust was crowned
with laurels at the Cercle des Echecs. Besides Löwenthal, other
great players whom he had vanquished publicly recognized his
supremacy. "He can give odds to any living player!" cried
St. Amant, the old opponent of Staunton. The tributes of
Anderssen and others were all in the same strain.

Morphy's return to America was greeted with new honors.
On May 25, 1859, a large and brilliant company, composed of the
leaders of the bar, of the pulpit, of the business world, of the
literary guild, and of society, male and female alike, assembled
for the purpose of binding a chaplet of victory on the brow of the
youthful conqueror and laying at his feet a costly and magnificent
token of admiration for his European exploits. (HENRY SEDLEY:
Chess in America, in *Harper's Magazine,* 1887.)

It was not until 1871 at Cleveland, Ohio, that the second American chess congress was held. Morphy had long ago retired and new stars had arisen. The first prize was carried off by Captain George Henry Mackenzie, born in 1837. A Scotchman by birth, and a retired officer in the British army, Mackenzie came to America in 1862, entered the Union army, and served until the close of hostilities in 1865. In the Old World he had made a reputation as a chess-player which had been confirmed and enhanced in the New.

Again, in 1880, at the fifth American chess congress, held in New York, Captain Mackenzie won the first prize. He next competed, with smaller but still distinguished success, at various international congresses in Europe. Finally, at the congress held at Frankfort, Germany, in 1887, he capped the climax of his achievements by winning the first prize and with it the title of Chess Champion of the World.

He was the first American to carry away the honor. Morphy, like Mackenzie, had been champion of America, and his extraordinary performances abroad had gained for him an unapproachable eminence. But he had never won the first prize at an international tournament, for the very sufficient reason that he had never entered one.

Chewing Gum. From 1890 to 1900 was the greatest era in the history of chewing gum in the United States. The press, the pulpit, and the medical profession were largely occupied in denouncing the habit all through that decade. Said the New York *Sun,* in the latter part of 1890, " Cynical critics point out that no fancy of the American people had become such a craze as the public indulgence in the gum-chewing habit, and that no craze has flourished so in the face of public odium. The habit, as a matter of cold fact, has reached a stage now that makes it impossible for a New Yorker to go to the theatre or church, or enter the street-cars or railway train, or walk on a fashionable promenade without meeting men and women whose jaws are working with the activity of the gum-chewing victim. And the spectacle is maintained in the face of frequent reminders that gum chewing, especially in public, is an essentially vulgar indulgence that not only shows bad breeding, but spoils a pretty countenance and detracts from the dignity of those who practise the habit. Cynics who observe it have sighed for the return of the sturdy discipline of their youth, when the schoolmaster used to spank everybody caught chewing gum in public."

Since 1900 the craze has declined, especially among the young women of the cities, but to some extent it maintains its popularity in the smaller towns and villages.

The best gum is that made from the chiclezapote tree in

Mexico. In its crude state this gum was long used by the Mexican Indians for a similar purpose. When they went out on the plains they found that it kept their throats from becoming parched if they could get no water. But it was unknown to Americans until 1870, when a lump fell into the hands of Thomas Adams, a Staten Island photographer. He was on the lookout for some quick way of making a fortune. His first idea was that the substance might be made to take the place of gutta-percha, or soft rubber, but after experiments extending over a period of two years, he was forced to give up the idea as impracticable. A lot of the useless stock was left on his hands. One day he happened to break off a bit and chewed it. He found it was pleasant to the taste. That hint was sufficient; he would manufacture the article into chewing gum. A prominent manufacturer assured him that the substance was no good for the purpose; but, nothing daunted, Adams set to work on his own account, and sold his article on a small scale to dealers. Orders began to pour in—the thing was a success. By 1890 Mr. Adams was employing two hundred and fifty hands in a factory six stories high. When he died he left each of his four sons independently rich.

Chewing gum of an inferior grade is still made from the gum of the New England spruce tree, and from paraffin, which is the residue of crude petroleum in process of refining. But the Mexican gum has nearly succeeded in driving all competitors out of the market. Physicians are not quite agreed as to the wholesomeness of the gum-chewing habit. Some have denounced it in unmeasured terms, declaring that it was the frequent source of dyspepsia, stomach trouble, mental weakness, and even insanity. Others have claimed that the habit is beneficial when practised in moderation. Gum chewing, they assert, opens the salivary glands, thus causing an abnormal production and flow of saliva. Swallowing the saliva gives material aid to the discharge of green and starchy foods. Nature created it for that purpose. Hasty eating prevents a sufficient quantity of it from assimilating with the food. People who eat in haste can repent at leisure by chewing gum.

Chicago. The history of Chicago is generally supposed to begin with the establishment of Fort Dearborn by "Mad Anthony" Wayne in 1795, but there is good reason to think that the French had placed a stockade on "the piece of land six miles square at the mouth of the Chicago River" over 100 years before. The neighboring territory was a land of desire in the time of the Grand Monarque. Three nations—France, England, and Spain —made it the stamping ground of their chicanery, and even then they were aware of the rich promise of the country around the head waters of the Mississippi. English and Spanish explorers and spies swarmed over this region; the chivalry of Versailles went into willing exile for the glory of France and "one log hut by Thunder Bay." To strengthen their position in the lake country, Fort de Miami was built as early as 1683 by French soldiers, and there is in existence an old map of 1718, which shows conclusively that it occupied the same site as the subsequent Fort Dearborn.

Though incorporated August 12, 1833, the settlement did not become a city until 1837. "But her ladyship cannot cut four years off her age by any such subterfuge," says the *Post*, "for it is perfectly clear to any unprejudiced observer that she was really born in 1833, and that in 1837 she merely emerged from long clothes."

"Chicago" is an Anglicized form of the Indian word "shegahg," originally meaning skunk, but whose uses were extended so as to make it a synonym for "strong," "pungent," "mighty." It was applied to the wild onion, to a line of Indian chiefs, to thunder, or the voice of the Great Spirit, and among other rivers to that which runs through the present city of Chicago. In this case the name was not meant as a tribute to the magnitude of the stream, but merely commemorated the tradition that one of the Shegahg chiefs had at some remote period been drowned in its waters. *Chicagou*, as the French name of the river, may be traced back at least as far as 1679. The first mention of the word is in Hennepin's account of La Salle's expedition from the lake to the Illinois River.

Chicago claims the distinction of being the mail-order centre of the universe. In 1910 one of the biggest mail-order houses broke all postal records by mailing 6,000,000 catalogues, each weighing two ounces—the whole weighing 450 tons. The sacks holding the catalogues weighed sixty-five tons. If these pamphlets had been sent on one train thirty cars would have been filled.

Professor Buck, of the philology department of the University of Chicago, has been looking into the linguistic conditions of that city. He awards to Chicago the front rank for cosmopolitanism, there being no fewer than fourteen languages, besides English, spoken there by colonies of at least 10,000 persons each. Newspapers appear regularly in ten languages, and church services may be heard in about twenty languages. Chicago is the second largest Bohemian city in the world, the third Swedish, the third Norwegian, the fourth Polish, the fifth German. In all, there are some forty foreign languages spoken by numbers ranging from half a dozen to half a million, and aggregating over a million

Chicory. Chicory is best known to laymen, when growing

wild on dry chalky soils, under the name of "wild endive." It belongs to a tribe of composite plants known scientifically as *Cichoraceæ*, which include also dandelion and garden lettuce. It shoots above the soil a tuft of leaves, and when it runs to flower, sends up a stem from one to three feet high, rigid, rough, branched, clothed with leaves and blue flowers. It has a long root like that of a carrot, which becomes enlarged by proper cultivation, and is the part used for the manufacture of a substitute for coffee. Every part of the plant is perfectly wholesome; the root when fresh is tonic, and in large doses slightly aperient. Chicory is cultivated extensively in Belgium, Holland, and Germany. It is cultivated in France for its leaves, as herbage and pasturage; in Germany and Flanders for its roots. It was first cultivated in England about 1780, by the well-known agriculturist, Arthur Young.

When chicory is to be used for coffee, the roots taken up by the grower are partly dried, and then sold to the manufacturer, by whom they are cut into slices, roasted, and ground. The ground chicory thus made is used by many of the European poor as a substitute for coffee by itself. It has not of course the true coffee flavor, but it makes a rich and wholesome vegetable infusion of a dark color, with a bitterish sweet taste, which would probably be preferred by a rude palate to the comparatively thin and weak, and at the same time not very palatable, infusion of pure coffee of the second or third quality. Nevertheless, in the middle of the nineteenth century a great clamor arose in England against what had become the too prevalent practice of adulterating coffee with chicory.

The arguments pro and con were neatly summed up by the *Illustrated London News* of July 5, 1851. "The grocers," said the *News*, "have lately adopted the practice of mixing chicory, worth 3d. or 4d. a pound, with coffee, worth four or five times that sum, and of selling the 'half-and-half' at the same price which they would charge for the coffee unmixed. They allege that the mixture is really better than pure coffee, and that the public like it. Perhaps so; and if they would only carry their kindness to the public so far as to sell coffee as coffee, and chicory as chicory, and allow the poor public to mix for themselves, there would be no harm done which could with any justice be laid upon the heads of the grocers. But the grocers persist in clutching the knavish profit on the inferior article; and when the chancellor of the exchequer is asked to lend his aid to prevent the fraud by authorizing the excise-officers to exercise the same supervision over coffee as they now do over tea, Sir Charles Wood declines to interfere. His agricultural friends have discovered that one of the best-paying crops that can be raised in this country is chicory, and they deprecate all attempts to prevent the fraud of the grocer, lest the consumption of chicory should be diminished, and the British farmer lose a growing market. Sir Charles Wood yields to the soft persuasion, although it is proved that the relative consumption of coffee has largely diminished, to the loss of the revenue. Thus one class of the natives, the chicory growers, are protected, and another class, the knavish grocers, are encouraged in knavery, in order that the foreign article—good coffee—may not find its way to the longing lips of the great bulk of the English people."

The result of the discussion which took place on the subject in the House of Commons in 1851 was characterized by the same authority as a positive disgrace to the English people. " If the public desire to drink chicory, by all means let them drink it; and we shall rejoice if their predilection for that article should put money into the pockets of the British farmer; but let it be incumbent upon the vendors to vend it as chicory, at the chicory price, and not to palm it off upon the easily-cheated multitude as coffee, at an overcharge of two or three hundred per cent. It is bad enough that such a fraud should be perpetrated; but it is still worse that a man like the chancellor of the exchequer should lend all the weight and authority of the government to support it."

Next year the subject was again taken up by Parliament, and this time resulted in the passage (August 3, 1852) of an act which forbade licensed dealers in coffee to keep and sell chicory except under its own name and in two-ounce packages, sealed and labelled with an exact description of the contents.

Chimes. The oldest peal of bells in the United States is a set of four, bearing the date 1682, which hangs in the Moorish belfry of the Spanish cathedral in St. Augustine, Florida.

Next to them in point of age come the eight bells of Christ Church in Boston, which were brought from England in 1744. The church itself was founded in 1723 with Timothy Cutler as its first rector. Each bell has an inscription. Let us copy four of the most interesting. That on the great bell reads, " This peal of eight bells is the gift of a number of generous persons in Christ Church in Boston, New England, Anno 1744 A. R." The third bell says, " We are the first ring of bells cast for the British Empire in North America. A. R. 1744." The sixth tells us, " The subscription for these bells was begun by John Hammock and Robert Temple, church wardens, 1744." The eighth concludes, " Abel Rudhall of Gloucester cast us all."

The oldest chime of bells in the Middle States is that at old

Christ Church, Philadelphia, which still fulfil their ancient function of welcoming every holiday and holy day, especially the advent of Christmas and New Year.

On February 22, 1753, the vestry of old Christ Church in Philadelphia passed a resolution to raise by lottery the necessary purchase price for a ring of bells. The scheme was evidently a success, for a little later the vestry agreed to purchase a bill of exchange for £450 to be employed in procuring a " ring of eight bells." The tenor, it was decided, should weigh 1800 pounds and the rest in proportion. The bells were cast by Lester and Peck at their foundry in Whitechapel, London. The entire weight of the peal of eight bells was 9000 pounds. When landed in Philadelphia, a committee waited upon the man who had accompanied them from London, to determine on what terms he would hang them. He refused all money compensation, asking only that the bells should be muffled at his death. The agreement was duly carried out by the church officials, not only at his death, but at that of his wife also.

During the Revolution, when the Quaker City was in danger of falling into the hands of the British, the precious bells were taken down and sunk in the Delaware by the patriots.

An old and interesting chime of bells hangs in the belfry of old St. Michael's Church in Charleston, S. C. They were eight in number, and were imported from England in 1764 at a cost of £581. On the evacuation of Charleston by the British in 1782, Major Traille, of the Royal Artillery, claimed the bells as a perquisite of war, took them back with him to England, and sold them. Sir Guy Carleton, however, who was then in New York, disapproved of the action of his subordinate and ordered the restoration of the bells. In the interim they had been resold in London to a former merchant of Charleston, one Rybenau, who generously reshipped them to Charleston in 1783. During the second year of the Civil War, Charleston being then under siege, they were removed for better security to Columbia, S. C. By one of the strange ironies of fate, this move proved disastrous, for during the occupation of Columbia by Sherman's army the bells were burned in the fire of February 17, 1865. Nevertheless, the fragments were carefully preserved, and after the war these pieces of old metal were shipped to England, where they were recast into a new peal of eight bells by the successors of the original bell-founders, Mears and Steinbank, in the original moulds which had turned them out a century previous. In February, 1867, the eight bells came back to Charleston. The entire set had crossed the Atlantic five times, and two of the bells seven times.

Chimneys—that is, chimneys with fireplace and flues—are comparatively modern. None of the Roman ruins show chimneys like ours. There is none in the restored buildings in Herculaneum and Pompeii. Roman architects complained that their decorations were smoked up. A kitchen in Rome was always sooty. Braziers were used in the living rooms. The chimney of antiquity consisted of a hole in the roof. ·The wealthy Romans used carefully dried wood, which would burn in the room without soot. The modern chimney was first used in Europe in the 14th century. The oldest certain account of a chimney places it in Venice in 1347.

The tallest and largest chimney in the world is that which was topped off in 1909 at the works of the Boston and Montana Copper and Silver Mining Co. near Great Falls, Montana. It is 506 feet in height. The foundation of the chimney consists of an annular mass, the circular inner edge of which is forty-seven feet in diameter at the bottom, and the octagonal outer boundary 103 feet across flats at the footing level, tapering to sixty-four and eighty-one feet diameters at the top of the concrete. The foundation was constructed of 1:3:5 slag concrete. The sand and stone were obtained from the smelter furnaces. In the work of construction 5200 barrels of cement, 2000 cubic yards of sand, and 4000 cubic yards of slag were used. The cost of materials and construction was in the neighborhood of $50,000.

A factory chimney in Glasgow, Scotland, holds second place with 427 feet of altitude.

The tallest chimney in New York city (353 feet high) was erected in connection with the power-house of the Metropolitan Traction Company at Ninety-sixth Street and the East River. A total of two million and a half of bricks was used in its construction. The diameter is 22 feet on the inside.

Wales has probably the longest chimney in the world. It is two miles high and has a brook running through it. The chimney is connected with the copper works at Cwmavon, near Aberavon. This is how it came to be built. About 60 years ago the copper smoke from these works was the plague of the neighboring countryside. It settled upon and destroyed the grass for 20 miles around, while the sulphur and arsenic in the fumes affected the hoofs of cattle, causing gangrene. The company tried all sorts of devices to remedy the trouble, but in vain.

Finally, Robert Brenton, who was later engineer of the Sind Railway in India, solved the problem. The copper works are at the foot of a high, steep mountain. Mr. Brenton constructed a flue or chimney running continuously from the base to about 100 feet above the summit, following the natural slope of the ground. The brick which lined it, and of which it was largely constructed, was burned close by. A small spring, rushing out near the mountain top, was turned into the chimney, and allowed to flow through almost its entire length to condense the smoke. Once a year it is swept out, and about a ton of precipitated copper obtained. Its top can be seen for between 40 and 50 miles.

Chittim-wood. When Sir Samuel Baker was exploring Cyprus, he was told by certain monks that they believed the Scriptural "chittim-wood" to be a species of pine which grows only on the mountains between the monastery of Kyker and the town of Khrysokus, a pathless and almost inaccessible region. Boughs, as specimens of the tree, were fetched by a trustworthy messenger, and were sent to Sir Joseph Hooker, Director of the Royal Gardens at Kew, who, in a brief description published by the Linnean Society, said of this newly-found tree, that it differed from the known forms of *Cedrus* in the shortness of the leaves and the smallness of the female cones. In size of cone, size, form and color of leaf, it approached the Algerian far more closely than any Taurian, Himalayan, or Lebanon cedar. Among tree cultivators it may be called the Cyprus cedar. Sir Samuel Baker wrote that he found two varieties of cypress. One he described as a tree thirty feet high, with a girth of six or seven feet, the wood cedar-colored, emitting a powerful aromatic scent, resembling that of sandal-wood. This was (in Sir Samuel's opinion) the celebrated chittim-wood. Why should Solomon have sent for cedar, which is so common in Asia Minor? The No. 2 variety of cypress is an intensely hard wood, resembling somewhat lignum vitæ.

Christmas Card. The Christmas card is the legitimate descendant of the "school pieces," or "Christmas pieces," which were popular from the beginning to the middle of the nineteenth century. These were sheets of writing paper, sometimes surrounded with those hideous and elaborate pen flourishes forming birds, scrolls, etc., so unnaturally dear to the hearts of writing masters, and sometimes headed with copperplate engravings, plain or colored.

These were used by school-boys at the approach of holidays for carefully written letters exploiting the progress they had made in composition and chirography. Charity boys were large purchasers of these pieces, says one writer, and at Christmas time used to take them round their parish to show them and at the same time solicit a trifle.

The Christmas card proper had its tentative origin in 1845. The honor of its invention is claimed for three men, all famous in other connections, the Rev. Edward Bradley (better known as

Cuthbert Bede, author of "Verdant Green"); J. C. Horsley, R. A., and the late W. C. T. Dobson, R. A. Cuthbert Bede had a card printed from his own design for circulation in 1845, and two years later his printers, a Newcastle firm, put a number of cards on the market. About the same time, in 1846, J. C. Horsley designed a card for Sir Harry Cobe of Summerly's Printing House, Old Bond Street.

The subject was a typical scene of feasting and jollity. One thousand copies were printed, and one of the few survivors sold a few years since for £50. Joseph Cundall, a London artist, also issued a card in that year. It was printed in lithography, colored by hand, and was of the usual size of a lady's card.

Not until 1862, however, did the custom obtain any foothold. Then experiments were made with cards of the size of an ordinary carte de visite, inscribed simply, "A Merry Christmas," and "A Happy New Year." After that came to be added robins and holly branches, embossed figures and landscapes. "I have the original designs before me now," wrote "Luke Limner" (John Leighton), to the London Publishers' Circular, December. 31, 1883; "they were produced by Goodall & Son. Seeing a growing want and the great sale obtained abroad, this house produced (1868) a Little Red Riding Hood, a Hermit and His Cell, and many other subjects in which snow and the robin played a part." (See also WALSH: *Curiosities of Popular Customs, s. v.*)

Chrysanthemum was known to a few enthusiasts in England as far back as 1764, when Philip Miller (1691–1771) received a specimen from Nimpu and cultivated it at the botanical garden at Chelsea. Still further back, some time indeed in the seventeenth century, a chrysanthemum from the East was grown at Danzig; but whether the climate were unfavorable or whether the white and gold splendors of the flower were not appreciated by contemporary Prussians, it is impossible to say. At any rate, there is no record of immediate descendants of the first plant. The honor of introducing the plant to Europe is claimed by France on behalf of one Pierre Blancard, a gardener who left Marseilles one evening in November, 1808, by the rumbling diligence that took the mails to Paris. He carried with him, as objects of special solicitude, two modest earthenware pots, in which, on long stems, covered with beautiful, velvety foliage, grew clusters of flowers—one yellow, clear and pure as gold, the other of color in this flower unknown in France; how, là-bas, in the pots on his knees. If a fellow-traveller chaffed him concerning his flowers, he answered not a word, and if curiosity moved another to ask questions about them, Blancard answered gravely, "They are a variety of the large family of pyrethrums," and would say no more.

No sooner had the stage-coach reached Paris than the southerner made his way to a compatriot who had the entrée at Court, and persuaded him to secure an audience with the Empress Josephine, at Malmaison. The empress, who adored flowers, received him and his two humble earthenware pots, from which sprang the radiant beauty of the flowers, and listened graciously, as with the eloquence of the South he told how he, a sailor, had been struck, in Japan and China, with the extraordinary wealth of color in this flower unknown in France; how, là-bas, in the far-off countries, their beauty shone in the hedge-rows and round the kiosks, and how the gold and the snow of the chrysanthemum spread a glory everywhere. Not without difficulty had he managed to bring home a few roots, which, being planted in his little garden down at Aubagne, in face of the blue waters of the Mediterranean and under the sun of the South, had revived, and were now in full bloom; those he carried with him, and of which he begged her Majesty's gracious acceptance, being the choicest of his collection. Thus Josephine de Beauharnais, the daughter of another South, received in her Malmaison retirement the first of the flowers which were destined to a most glorious career both in Europe and America.

Its hundred years in Europe are but a short span in the life of the flower which, six centuries before Christ, gave Confucius the subject for a rhapsody, when, describing the beauties of autumn, he drew attention to "its shining glory, its delicate petals hanging around the centre in sheaves of golden threads, and its tassels on which the light of the sun has been filtered ten thousand times." A thousand years after Confucius, Tao Ming Yang, gardener and wielder of the pen, sang of the flower in such accents of genius that the name of his native town was changed to that of Town-of-the-Chrysanthemum (Chu-Hsien, the Chu-San of to-day).

Church around the Corner, The Little. The popular name given to the Church of the Transfiguration in New York City, a low, rambling, picturesque brown structure in Twenty-ninth Street a short distance to the east of Fifth Avenue. Its famous sobriquet came about in this fashion: In 1870 the veteran actor, George Holland, died in New York. Mrs. Holland's sister wished that the funeral should be held at her own church,—a fashionable place of worship in Fifth Avenue presided over by a clergyman named Sabine.

Joseph Jefferson, as an old friend of the Holland family, called upon this fashionable rector at his fashionable church, seeking to make arrangements for the funeral. He had with him one of Holland's orphaned sons. The reverend gentleman objected to holding the services for an actor.

"There is," he said, "a little church around the corner where you may get it done."

"Then," said Mr. Jefferson, solemnly, "God bless the little church around the corner!"

Proceeding with his boy companion, now in tears, to the "little church," Jefferson met with a cordial reception from Rev. George H. Houghton, its pastor. A few days later the services over the dead actor were conducted in the presence of an audience which had doubtless been greatly augmented by the publication of the story in the daily papers. Mark Twain, then a young man, voiced the general feeling with an individual intensity, in the *Galaxy* for February, 1871, his diatribe concluding with these words: "Was it not pitiable, that spectacle? Honored and honorable old George Holland, whose theatrical ministry had for fifty years softened hard hearts, bred generosity in cold ones, kindled emotion in dead ones, uplifted base ones, broadened bigoted ones, and made many and many a stricken one glad and filled it brim full of gratitude, figuratively spit upon in his unoffending coffin by this crawling, slimy, sanctimonious, self-righteous reptile!"

The Reverend Mr. Houghton maintained his hold upon the gratitude and affection of theatrical people until his death in 1897, when he was succeeded by a like-minded son. Hundreds of actors have been borne to the grave from the Little Church around the Corner; it has been a favorite place for theatrical weddings, and has in fact been largely supported by stage folk.

In her "Old Woman's Gossip," Fanny Kemble Butler records a Paris episode not unlike that of Holland in New York. A certain Philippe, the predecessor and model of Frederic Le Maitre and a friend of Kemble, Mrs. Butler's father, was an actor, not only immensely popular for his professional merit, but greatly respected for an order of merit not always applauded by Parisians, that of a moral character and decent life. At his funeral a serious riot occurred when the Archbishop of Paris, in accordance with the received opinion and custom of the day, refused to allow his burial in consecrated ground; "the profane player's calling, in the year of grace 1823, or thereabouts, being still one which disqualified its followers for receiving the sacraments of the Roman Catholic Church, and therefore, of course, for claiming Christian burial." The general feeling of the Parisian public, however, was in this case too strong for the ancient anathema of the church. The Archbishop of Paris was obliged to give way, and the dead body of the worthy actor was laid in the sacred soil of Père la Chaise. "I believe that since that time the question has never again been debated, nor am I aware that there is

15

any one more peculiarly theatrical cemetery than another in Paris."

In a letter of Talma's to Charles Young upon the death of Fanny Kemble's uncle John, he begs to be numbered among the subscribers to the monument about to be erected to Mr. Kemble in Westminster Abbey; adding the touching remark, " Pour moi, je serai heureux si les prêtres me laissent enterrer dans un coin de mon jardin."

The moral effect of this species of class prejudice is " admirably illustrated," continues Fanny Kemble, " by an anecdote I have heard my mother tell. One evening when she had gone to the Grand Opera with M. Jouy, the wise and witty Hermite de la Chaussée d'Antin, talking with him of the career and circumstances of the young ballet women (she had herself, when very young, been a dancer on the English stage), she wound up her various questions with this : ' Et y en a-t-il qui sont filles de bonne conduite? qui sont sages?' ' Ma foi!' replied the Hermite, shrugging his shoulders, ' elles auraient grand tort; personne n'y croirait.' "

Molière, it will be remembered, was also forbidden Christian burial by Harlay, Archbishop of Paris, because he was an actor.

" What," cried Madame Molière, " they refuse the burial rites to a man who deserves an altar!"

She sent a remonstrance to the king. It is said that Louis XIV asked the archbishop how deep consecrated ground may run. The answer was, fourteen feet.

" Very good," returned Louis, " let Molière's grave be dug sixteen feet, and then it cannot be said to be buried in consecrated ground, nor need it scandalize the clergy."

Churches, Queer. The oldest church in New England stands in the village of Hingham, Mass. It is known as " The Old Ship Meeting House," and was built in 1635, a time when a strong stockade was necessary to defend the worshippers from Indian attacks. The stockade, of course, has been removed, but the church remains (1912) almost unchanged,—a square frame structure, with a pyramid roof and a belfry at the peak inclosed by a railing. There is a vestibule projecting from the front door. There are two rows of six windows in each wall, the upper ones furnishing light and air to the gallery, which extends all around. In early days the unconverted were assigned to the gallery seats, the men on one side and the women on the other, while the " professors " sat below and sexes were divided by the middle aisle. Attendance was compulsory. It cost a peck of corn to stay away from meeting or to leave the building before service was finished.

The old meeting-house has had but 10 pastors during the 276 years of its existence, which, you will notice, gives them an average pastorate of 27½ years. Six of them served 246 years. The first pastor got his salary in corn, most of which was the proceeds of fines imposed upon the congregation for not attending meeting.

The last vestige of the first church in New York disappeared in 1908 to make room for the custom-house that now stands on the Bowling Green site, replacing the former office of the Cunard steamship line. Up to that date a tablet near the entrance to the office bore this inscription:

The Site of Fort Amsterdam,
Built in 1626.
Within the fortification
was erected the first
substantial church edifice
On the Island of Manhattan.
In 1787 the fort
was demolished
and the Government house
built upon this site.

Of all the buildings within the palisades of the old Fort Amsterdam there remained a vestige of only one, the old church originally built within the centre of the Fort. The first service in it was held in 1638.

The government house was torn down in 1815 and private residences took its place. A new row of brick stores was built from the church out to Whitehall Street, and in all probability the upper story was remodelled.

But the wide arch over the main doorway and the ornamented coping of the windows, closed with a solid wall of brick to form the rear of a store, still showed where the old edifice stood.

In 1840, when the fashionable residential section had begun its gradual march uptown, the church was again transformed The wall between it and the adjoining store was removed, and from that time the site in the middle of the block was occupied by a livery stable.

A church in a Pennsylvania town is said to possess the distinction of being the work of one pair of hands. These hands carried every block of stone of which it was constructed, cut each into shape, and laid it in place. The builder was one George Taylor, who obtained the stone from Brobst Mountain. He spent six years in completing the work. The church is 60 feet long and 38 feet broad; its tower is 60 feet high.

There is a church in Santa Rosa, California, which, though not the work of one man, is as unique in its way as the church in

Pennsylvania. It was built of one tree, yet it is the largest church in that part of the country.

The miners in the Myndd Newydd coal mines in Wales have no call to shave, shine their boots, or don Sunday garb when they go to worship. They have a chapel all their own at the bottom of the shaft, so that when they descend the pit they can go to their devotions and thence to their several stations. The pillars and beams are of rough timbers and a coal trolley serves as pulpit. The miners sit on rough wooden benches and the oldest among them acts as pastor. A chapel more finished in appearance, the St. Anthony, exists in the salt mines of Wieliczka, Austria. It is a Byzantine excavation, with altar, crucifix, and life-sized saints, apparently of black marble, but really made of salt.

In the old German town of Oberstein an ancient church stands built in the great rock rising from the river. The front is of stone, but the church itself is hollowed out of the rock and penetrates far into its heart. Tradition says that in the fourteenth century the Count of Oberstein, one of the old robber barons, fell in love with a beautiful young lady, the daughter of a neighboring knight. His brother also sought the fair maiden's hand and the two suitors had a violent quarrel. The count flung his hapless brother from the top of his castle wall, high up the precipitous cliff. Repenting of his awful deed, he vowed that he would build a church where his brother's body first touched the ground. He did so, excavating the church in the rock; and tradition goes on to say a miraculous spring of clear water sprang from the crag as a token that heaven was appeased. This curious church is now the only Protestant place of worship in the town.

Circulation of Blood. A contributor to the *Atlantic Monthly* for June, 1880, drew surprised attention to the fact that Shakespeare had " anticipated " Harvey's discovery of the circulation of the blood in the following lines from " Julius Cæsar ":

> You are my true and honorable wife,
> As dear to me as are the ruddy drops
> That visit my sad heart.
> Act ii, Scene 1.

Now, in actual fact Shakespeare's conception of the circulation of the blood was that held by scientific schools long before Harvey's time (it had been taught by Hippocrates, Galen, and Paracelsus),—namely that the blood ebbs and flows between the heart and extremities of the body, not by a circuitous motion (outward by the arteries and back by the veins), but to and fro or up and down by each route independently. Thus, we find in " King John " the lines

Melancholy
Had baked thy blood and made it heavy-thick
Which else runs tickling up and down the veins.
Act iii, Scene 3.

Though most educated people are aware that Harvey was the first to announce the fact of the circulation of the blood, comparatively few know the precise nature of his discovery or realize how bitterly his right to the title of discoverer has been disputed. Harvey was born in 1578, published his great work in 1628, and died in 1657. It is unquestionably true that, read by the light of Harvey's discovery, it is easy to discern in the writings of ancient and mediæval authors what seem to be statements of the fact that the blood circulates through the body; and consequently, Plato and Hippocrates among the ancients, and Servetus, Colombo, and Cesalpino among later writers, have been credited with a perfect knowledge of all that Harvey was the first to announce in distinct terms. Science, however, clearly distinguishes between guessing and discovering; and a critical examination of the statements made by the older anatomists, which have been held to imply a knowledge of the circulation as announced by Harvey, discloses them to be nothing but vague guesses, which had so little influence on the minds of the authors themselves that they constantly make use of other expressions plainly indicating total ignorance of the facts propounded by the English physiologist.

Judging from the views expressly combated by Harvey in the introduction to his magnum opus, the "Exercise on the Motion of the Heart and Blood in Animals," it would appear as if the anatomists of the period held that respiration and the pulsation of the heart and arteries exercised in common the function of cooling and ventilating the blood, air being sucked into the arteries during their expansion, and "fuliginous vapours" expelled from them when they contracted. But not only was it thought that the arteries cooled the body generally as the lungs cooled the heart; another function of a precisely opposite character was ascribed to them. Taking their origin from the heart, or workshop for the elaboration of heat and vital spirits, they carried the spiritualized blood to all parts of the body to cherish their heat. It was further held that the arteries drew the spiritual blood from the heart after the manner of bellows, but that nevertheless the heart expanded and contracted simultaneously with the arteries; no account being taken of the physical impossibility of such a process.

Harvey's discovery was that the whole mass of the blood was propelled from the left side of the heart through the arteries, that it was carried to the right side of the heart by the veins, that the circle was completed by its being returned to the left side of the heart through the lungs, and that this circular motion was incessant. That the theory was new and startling, and that it would meet with violent opposition, its author was fully convinced. In the eighth chapter of his *Exercise* we find him expressing no doubt that the passage of the blood from the one set of vessels into the other would be admitted by his contemporaries, this fragment of his theory having been maintained by Galen in the second century of our era and by Rueldo Colombo in the sixteenth. The part of his doctrine that he fears will bring on him the enmity of mankind is that which maintains the whole mass of the blood to be in perpetual circular motion. If, however, Harvey shared the common lot of disturbers of established opinions, he is also to be regarded as singularly fortunate in having lived to see his doctrine triumphant over opposition and accepted by almost all competent judges of its truth. Not ten years after the publication of his views, Descartes gave in his adherence to them; and anatomists throughout Europe began to swear by Harvey instead of Galen. Vesling of Padua exposed the fallacy of the attacks made by Primerose of Paris; Riverius taught and defended the circulation of the blood from the chair of medicine in the University of Montpellier; and as Riolan, the professor of anatomy in the University of Paris, continued to teach the older views of function, a second chair of anatomy was instituted in the Jardin du Roi, from which Pierre Dionis instructed admiring crowds of students in accordance with the Harveian doctrine.

Cities in the World, Oldest. The honor of being the oldest of all extant cities must be given to Damascus in Syria. Other cities were built before it, but they have perished or been destroyed. Tyre and Sidon have crumbled away on the coasts of Phœnicia; Baalbec is a ruin; Palmyra is buried in the Great Syrian desert; Nineveh and Babylon have disappeared from the Tigris and the Euphrates. Damascus, which is mentioned in Genesis xiv, 15, remains what it was before the days of Abraham, a centre of trade and travel, the " Eye of the East " as Julian the Apostate called it. Its fruits and flowers are as celebrated now as they were in ancient times. From Damascus comes our damson, or blue plum; the damasco or apricot of Portugal; the damask rose, introduced into England by Henry VIII; damask, our fabric of cotton and silk; and damaskeening, the beautiful art of inlaying wood and steel with gold and silver. Here Diocletian established a great factory for arms especially famous for its keen and elastic Damascus blades, the secret of whose manufacture was lost when Tamerlane carried the artificer into Persia. It was near Damascus that Saul of Tarsus saw the light above the brightness of the sun. "The street which is called straight" wherein he prayed (Acts ix. 11) still runs through the city. Mohammed, surveying Damascus from a neighboring height, was afraid to enter, "because it was given to man to have but one Paradise, and for his part he was resolved not to have it in this world."

Among ruined cities probably the oldest in the Eastern Hemisphere is Nineveh, the ancient capital of Assyria. As it is mentioned in the Khammurabi code, it must have been known as a place of importance at least as early as B.C. 2500. It was the fall of Nineveh in B.C. 606 and the consequent distribution of the Assyrian Empire that left Babylon, its old time rival, the leading power in the East.

Whether the ruined cities of Central and Southern America can claim a higher antiquity than Babylon or Nineveh is uncertain.

Recently a claim has been put in for a former city in an Arizona table-land near Phœnix, whose ruins lying under ten feet of prairie dust were uncovered in the year 1909 by A. Lafave, a mining engineer. He claimed that they were 10,000 years old. The buildings of sandstone show great architectural skill, and in the walls were found a box of cotton bolls and a sealed jar of corn, both well preserved. The Arizona climate does not permit the growth of cotton in the present age, so Mr. Lafave assumes that sufficient time must have elapsed since the cotton which he found was grown to have wrought a complete change in the character of the country. This period he also gauges as something like 10,000 years. He is satisfied that the ruins are older than those of Nineveh or Babylon. He believes that the race which built this town was possessed of a high civilization, from the abundance of artistically wrought pottery, and that it subsequently was broken up by internal dissension and possibly degenerated into the cliff-dwelling tribes.

It has been generally conceded that St. Augustine, Fla., is the oldest white settlement in the United States, having been founded by Pedro Menendez in 1565; but there is evidence to show that the town of Tucson, in Arizona, antedates St. Augustine by at least thirteen years. In the year 1552 their Catholic Majesties Ferdinand and Isabella of Spain issued a charter to and for the pueblo of Tucson. This charter, after being mislaid for a matter of three hundred years or more, was recently discovered among the archives of the Church of San Xavier del Bac, which is situated about ten miles below the present town of Tucson.

Accompanying the charter of the pueblo of Tucson is an account, in the handwriting of Padre Marco Niza, of the founding of the pueblo. Padre Niza was a Jesuit who accompanied the expedition organized in the City of Mexico for the exploration of Arizona and New Mexico, under the charge of Coronado, the function of the worthy padre having been the Christianizing of the natives and the recording of the progress and exploits of the expedition. If his account is to be received as historical— and every presumption is in its favor—a church was founded at San Xavier del Bac and a small town begun to support and protect the church on the site of the Indian village of Tucson, the name having been preserved until the present day.

Acoma (q. v.) is the oldest extant of all aboriginal cities in the United States.

The most ancient city in New England is Agamenticus, or, as it was afterward called, Old York. It was founded or built in or about 1640, under patent from King Charles II to Ferdinando Gorges, and was named after Mount Agamenticus.

According to Indian legend the basis of this mount was formed by a hecatomb of wild-beast skins, weapons, and implements raised over the remains of a good Indian called Saint Aspenquid, who taught his fellow-men how to make baskets and pottery, bread and clothing, and how to cultivate corn. Another legend handed down from the red men asserts that the Isles of Shoals were connected with the mainland at Boar's Head. One day long ago there was a great noise and the bottom of the land fell out, the sea came in and covered the earth between the islands and the Head. It may be that at this time Mt. Agamenticus was formed.

It is suggested that the saint whom the natives honored might have been Bjorn Asbrandson, of Icelandic fame, who is reported to have left Iceland on a voyage of discovery about 998, and was seen in Vinland about 1028, by Gudleif, who was driven on these shores by an east wind, and returned to Iceland the same year. He was not much of a saint in his native land, but may have repented, as Gudleif represents him in 1028 to be "old and gray headed," adding "that the natives treated him with the greatest deference and honor." (ANDREW K. OBER, in *Portland Transcript.*)

City made to Order. It is proposed that the permanent capital of the Australian Confederation shall be a city built upon an entirely unoccupied site and planned in advance in every detail. The site which has been agreed upon is in New South Wales, and is described as being an elevated plain of about 1000 miles in area, shut in by mountain ranges on three sides. It is watered by a clean mountain stream formed from melting snows, which has a daily mean average flow of 52,000,000 gallons. The government proposes to invite world-wide competition in the planning of the city.

The Australian city has its analogue in North America. Prince Rupert, in California, the Pacific terminus of the Grand Trunk Railway, was laid out as a model city long prior to its official establishment, and was surveyed, cleared, and improved with sidewalks, sewers, parks, etc., and made entirely ready for occupancy before residence of any kind was allowed on its three square miles of water front on Prince Rupert harbor.

Another city made to order is the Indiana steel town of Gary.

City, Most Dangerous. Americans frequently complain that their great cities are too negligent of the safety of their inhabitants. New York and Chicago especially are cited as places where life and limb are continually imperilled. English people are fond of repeating the charge. Yet, if we are to trust the statistics of England's capital as compiled by its metropolitan police, London holds the record as the most dangerous city in the world. In 1891 the number of people killed by vehicles in the area controlled by the commissioners of the metropolitan police was 147. By 1901 this number had increased to 186, and in 1909 it was more than twice as large as the number for 1901— namely, 396. And the figures of the total number of people injured, not necessarily fatally, are correspondingly serious. They are: 1891, 5637; 1901, 9197; 1909, 16,536.

The following are the details of the fatalities in 1909: 17 by motor cabs, 4 hansom cabs, 3 four-wheel cabs, 26 by motor tramway cars, 3 horse tramway cars; 52 by motor omnibuses, 9 horse omnibuses; 46 by motor cars (uncovered), 16 carts, 50 vans; 21 by motor cars (covered), 2 covered carts, 31 vans, 5 broughams and private carriages; 1 by motor cycle, 12 cycles, 2 fire-engines; 3 by traction-engines, 3 ridden horses.

The share that mechanically driven vehicles had in that year's total number of accidents may be set down thus: 1238 motor cabs, 2177 motor tramway cars, 1087 motor omnibuses, 1166 motor cars (uncovered), 635 motor cars (covered), 276 motor cycles, 6 traction-engines.

City, World's Wickedest. One of the worst cities in the world is Irkutsk in Siberia. With a population of 120,000, as many as 500 murders are committed here every year, making the highest known average in Christendom. Arrests average only one in 50 murders, and only one-half the arrests are followed by convictions.

Irkutsk once thought it would have a vigilance committee

to rid the city of its criminal element. It got one with a vengeance. Ex-convicts and active thugs enrolled themselves by the
score, and after forming a compact organization volunteered
for service. The governor granted them exceptional powers.
First of all they "fixed" the police. Then began a reign of
crime almost unparalleled. Rich merchants under pretense that
they were suspects were shot in broad daylight. Next, under
cover of "house inspection" and "penal confiscation" burglary
blossomed forth on every hand. Soon no man's life or property
was safe, and it took all the powers of the government to rid
the city of its vigilants.

Clock. It is said that the first clock was invented by Pope
Sylvester II. in A.D. 996. There is no sufficient evidence for this
statement. At all events, no clock of that date has survived to
our time. There is acceptable historical evidence that in the
year 1288 a clock and a chime of bells were put up in a former
clock-tower at Westminster, that the funds were supplied out of a
fine imposed upon a chief justice who had offended the government, that the clock bore the inscription *Discite justitiam, moniti,*
and that the bells were gambled away by Henry VIII. Still
more definite and reliable is the account of how Henry Vic or
de Wyck, the Nuremberg wizard, set up a clock in the palace of
Charles V, King of France, in February, 1379. Some chroniclers
call this clock "the parent of modern time-keepers."

Time-keeping, however, was not the sole object of the early
clockmakers. Beauty as well as use was contemplated by them,
and the beauty was not alone that of harmony in design but of
ingenious complexity in detail.

A very old and very curious clock is still extant at Prague,
built probably by one of the old Nuremberg artists. It stands
near the old Hussite Church. The clock itself forms part of the
original tower, while the face or dial is exposed to the street.
The dial is six or eight feet in diameter, and has a great number
of hands—recording hours, minutes, days, months, years, and
even centuries. The dial is set in an elaborate frame-work, about
eight feet high and fifteen long, and this metal frame-work is
ornamented with many curious and quaint devices. One of these
is connected with the striking of the hours.

Longfellow, in his "Hyperion," tells us that on the belfry
of the Rauthaus in Coblentz is a huge head, with a brazen helmet
and a beard, and whenever the clock strikes, at each stroke of the
hammer this giant's head opens its great jaws and smites its teeth
together as if it would say, "Time was—Time is—Time is past!"
This figure is known in all the country round as "The man in
the Custom House," and when a friend from the country meets

a friend from Coblentz, instead of saying, " How are all the good people in Coblentz? " he says, " How is the man in the Custom House? "

There was once in the dome of the Town Hall at Heidelberg a very famous clock. It was destroyed by French soldiers in 1693. As the hammer struck each hour the figure of an old man, almost life-size, opened a door and walked out in full view of the streets below, removed his hat, bowed and returned to his niche. As he closed the door a cock flapped his wings and crowed; Father Time made some blind strokes with his scythe, while mimic soldiers dressed as French and Germans fought on a platform below. At midnight and noon the chimes played national airs, and once each 24 hours the life of man was illustrated with figures depicting the seven ages. The astronomical charts and diagrams were said to have been even more intricate and complicated than those of the Strasburg clock (*q.v.*). The French soldiers debated the matter long and earnestly before destroying such a marvel, until they saw the French soldiers in the automatical fight on the clock's platform overcome by the German troops, after which they willingly ruined both clock and hall.

But it is said that Droz, a mechanic of Geneva, produced a clock which excelled all others in its marvellous business. On it were seated a negro, a shepherd, and a dog. When the clock struck the shepherd played six tunes on his flute, the dog approached and fawned upon him. The King of Spain came to see this wonderful invention, and was delighted beyond measure.

" The gentleness of my dog," said Droz, " is his least merit. If your Majesty touch one of the apples which you see in the shepherd's basket, you will admire the animal's fidelity."

The king took an apple, upon which the dog flew at his hand, barking so loudly and so naturally that a real dog which had come into the room began to bark also. The courtiers became terrified, thinking this must be an affair of witchcraft, and, crossing themselves, hastily departed. Only one ventured to remain, and Droz requested him to ask the negro what time it was. He did so in Spanish, but received no reply. Droz remarked that the negro had not learned Spanish, and the question was repeated in French, when the negro immediately replied. This frightened the questioner quite out of his wits, and he, too, beat a hasty retreat, sure that the whole thing must be of the devil.

The famous clock of Strasburg is thrown completely into the shade by the great World Clock, or the 10,000-year time indicator. It was constructed in Germany, during many years' labor, by Christian Martin, clock-maker. The clock marks the years and leap years, and will run for a hundred centuries, when its mechanic works will have to be changed. The face of the clock is about ten feet square, and has a large number of dials and little niches where 122 little figures have their abiding place. These latter are to allegorize human life. Every minute a sorrowful looking angel hits a bell with a sledge hammer. When he has done this fifteen times another angel in a red robe strikes the first quarter. The Genius, dressed in a Louis XIV. costume, turns a dial so that the figure is shown. At the same time the figure of a child appears at a lower door. At the second quarter a youth appears, at the third a middle-aged man with spectacles and a high hat, and at the fourth a decrepit old wreck with a white wig. While all this is going on below, Death, in the shape of a Comanche Indian with wings, has been vainly endeavoring to hammer a bell in an upper niche, but an angel has headed him off in every case and protected the human family " by raising the right hand in an allegorical relation," as per programme, until the fourth quarter. Then Death gets the better of the struggle, strikes the hour, and bundles the old man off into eternity.

The twelve apostles are trotted out each hour. Above them is a figure of Christ, who blesses with both hands each apostle in passing with mathematical exactness. At morning, noon, and night a number of bell ringers ring their respective bells with vindictive energy and an old man drops upon his knees, as if some one had kicked his legs out from under him. All these and many other wonders exposing the family secrets of the Zodiac, the heathen gods, the seasons, the moon, and the globe, all run regularly. The whole structure is surmounted by a cock, which crows at 6 and 12 o'clock.

The clock at Beauvais Cathedral is composed of 92,000 separate pieces, and comprises 52 dial-plates, which give the time in the principal capitals of the world, as well as the local hour, the day of the week and the month, the rising and setting of the sun, the phases of the moon and the tides, besides a series of terrestrial and astronomical evolutions. The framework is of carved oak, 26 by $16\frac{1}{4}$ feet.

In the eighteenth century a jeweller named James Cox, of Shoe lane, London, constructed what he called a perpetual clock. He sought to obtain perpetuity by a cleverly contrived attachment which utilized the rise and fall of the barometer to supply the necessary energy.

The movement of the mercury actuated a cog wheel in such a manner that whether the mercury rose or fell the wheel always revolved in the same direction and kept the weights that supplied the movement of the clock always wound up. The barometer bulb dipped into a mercury cistern. The cistern hung attached to the extremities of two rockers, to the left end of one and the right end of the other.

The bulb was similarly attached to the other extremities of the rockers, which are thus moved every time there is a change in the amount of mercury in bulb and cistern respectively. The rockers actuated a vertical ratchet, and the teeth were so arranged that the wheel they controlled could only move in one direction, whether the ratchet ascended or descended.

The clock itself was of strong and superior workmanship, and was jewelled with diamonds at every bearing, the whole being enclosed in a glass case which, while it excluded dust, displayed the entire mechanism. The fate of Cox's clock was partly revealed in a work called " Travels in China," published in 1804 and written by John Barrow.

In this book it is stated that in the list of presents carried by " the late Dutch Ambassador " were " two grand pieces of machinery that were part of the curious museum of Cox." One of these apparently was this perpetual clock, and it was taken by the Dutch Embassy to China, where in the journey from Canton to Pekin both the instruments suffered some slight damage. Efforts were made to repair them at Pekin, but on leaving the capital it was discovered that the Chinese Prime Minister Ho-tchang-tong, had substituted two other clocks of very inferior workmanship and had reserved Cox's mechanism for himself. So far so good. But no one knows whether this clock is still in existence or, if so, where is its abiding place.

The most famous and, when it was put up, the largest and most elaborate clock in the world is the one in the British House of Parliament at London, known officially as the Westminster Clock, but popularly sharing with its chief bell the affectionate title of Big Ben. This stands practically on the site where the first English clock was erected in 1298. Here, also, Edward III erected a tower containing a clock and a great bell, upon which the hours were struck.

The present Westminster clock was placed there in 1859. Its four dials are made of iron and glass, in such a way that they can be brilliantly lighted at night. They are 180 feet from the ground, and their diameters are 22½ feet—a size which made them larger than any then extant dial (*q.v.*) save one, at the cathedral at Malines, and that one has only an hour-hand. The minute-hand of the Westminster clock jumps nearly seven inches every half-minute—this kind of action by a remontoir-train being considered better than the old way of having the wheels move all the time as they do in an ordinary clock. The train is about fifteen feet long and nearly five feet wide. The escapement is known as the "three-legged double"; and any error is corrected at the Greenwich Observatory, whither the great clock telegraphs its time twice every day. The train of wheels that carries the hands is wound up once a week; but the train that controls the striking part is wound up twice a week. The great, or hour, bell is nine feet in diameter, weighs 30,000 pounds, and can be heard at a distance of ten miles. The quarter-hour bells can be heard four or five miles, and they weigh 8000, 3700, 2800, and 2350 pounds respectively. The cost of the movement of striking-work was $20,000; of the hands and dials, $26,500; of the bells, $30,000. Among the bells is Big Ben (*q.v.*).

Clocks were first illuminated, so that the hour could be read at night, in 1826, and the first of this kind was placed in St. Bride's, London, in that year. Clocks were first synchronized by Messrs. Barraud & Lund so that they could be regulated by an electric wire from a standard clock, and in November, 1878, the same firm put into operation in London an electric circuit of 108 clocks.

The first clock regulated by a pendulum was made in 1639 by the son of Galileo. Richard Harris placed a clock of this kind in St. Paul's in 1641, and Christian Huygens made good ones previous to 1658. The first clock to strike the hour was placed in Westminster in 1368.

There are two clocks in Worsley, Lancashire, England, that never strike 1, but 13, whenever the hour after noon or midnight comes round. One is at Worsley Hall, owned by the Earl of Ellesmere. It was put there by the earl's ancestor, the Duke of Bridgewater. He had it made to strike the unlucky number so as to ensure his workmen's return on time after dinner. Many had complained that they failed to hear the clock when it struck one.

This recalls a story told of the clock at Westminster. In the reign of William and Mary a soldier was condemned by court-martial for being asleep when he should have been on duty on the terrace at Windsor. He denied the charge, solemnly declaring that he had heard the clock strike 13 and had imagined it to be a mistake for 12. The officials all scoffed at his plea. But while he was in prison awaiting execution many strangers came forward of their own accord and swore that the clock actually did strike 13 instead of 1. Thereupon the soldier was pardoned and released.

The most trustworthy clock in the world is said to be that in the basement of the observatory at Berlin, installed by Professor Foerster in 1865. It is enclosed in an air-tight glass cylinder, and has frequently run for two or three months with an average daily deviation of only fifteen one-thousandths of a second. Yet astronomers are not satisfied even with this remarkable accuracy, and their efforts are constantly directed toward securing ideal conditions for a clock, by keeping it not only in an air-tight case but also in an underground vault, where neither changes of temperature nor of barometric pressure can ever affect it.

Another very modern wonder in the way of a clock is the radium timepiece invented by the Englishman Harrison Martingale. It is claimed that, if not touched, this ingenious clock could run for thirty thousand years. On a quartz rod in an exhausted glass vessel is supported a tube containing a small quantity of radium. An electroscope is attached to the lower end of this tube. It consists of two long strips of silver. The natural action of the radium sends an electric charge into the strips and causes them to separate until they touch the sides of the vessel, where they are instantly discharged and fall together again. Every two minutes this operation is repeated automatically, so that each beat of this wonderful timekeeper is in reality two minutes long.

A Frenchman named Alphonse Duhamel constructed a timepiece twelve feet high composed entirely of bicycles or their component parts.

The framework is a huge bicycle wheel, round which are arranged twelve ordinary-sized wheels, all fitted with pneumatic tires. A rim within the large wheel bears the figures for the hours, the figures themselves being constructed of crank rods. The hands are made of steel tubing, which is used for the framework of bicycles. The minute strokes on the dial are small nickel-plated pieces. The top of the clock is an arrangement of twelve handle-bars.

The clock strikes the hours and the quarters, bicycle bells, of course, making the chimes. The pendulum is made of various parts of a bicycle frame. It is said that the clock, besides being a curiosity, is an excellent timepiece.

An oddity in clocks is the invention of a Frenchman, M. Paul Cornu. It consists of a dial mounted above a reservoir and having a sort of a seesaw mounted upon its support. The reservoir holds sufficient alcohol to last for a month, and this serves as fuel for a small flame that burns at one end. The heat from the flame causes the air to expand in the bulb of the seesaw directly above it. As a result the seesaw moves every five seconds. This movement is the sole motive power that actuates the hands.

A Bohemian, Joseph Bayer, a glass-cutter by trade, resident in the country of his birth, has employed glass as a medium for building a clock. With the exception of the spring every portion is of crystal glass. The three hands, hour, minute, and second, as well as the apparatus for striking, are all of glass. The clock is sixteen inches high.

An Italian, Sirio Tiburzi, of Fabriano, Italy, has tried his hand at a clock made solely of wicker work and poplar twigs. The dial, cord, and weights are of wicker work, the remaining parts are of both wicker work and poplar twigs. The mechanism is similar to that of a tower clock with the exception of the striking parts, with which it is not equipped. It stands eight feet high and will run twenty-seven hours with one winding.

A German shoemaker spent fifteen years of his leisure moments in constructing a clock of the grandfather shape nearly six feet high, made entirely of straw. The wheels, pointers, case, and every detail are exclusively of straw. The most remarkable fact is that it is reported to keep perfect time.

The Tsar of Russia is the possessor of a unique clock that records not merely the passing seconds, minutes, and hours, but the days, weeks, months, and years. The clock was invented and manufactured by two peasants, who presented it to the emperor as a token of their loyalty.

Clover. The trefoil leaves of the clover plant, and hence its association with the mystic number three, have made it sacred even from Pre-Christian times. Thus, in Druidic worship it was a symbol of religion, setting forth the three grades of Druids, Bards, and Neophytes. In Christian mythology its leaf is frequently held to symbolize the Trinity, and some Irish authorities hold that it is the true and original "shamrock" which St. Patrick used to illustrate how three separate objects such as leaves could yet be one. Nevertheless it is not in its trefoil form that it has been the most fruitful source of superstition. Everywhere the four-leaved clover is held to be a harbinger of good luck to the finder, partly on account of its rarity and partly perhaps of its cross-like form. An English rhyme says:

> When sitting in the grass we see
> A little four-leaved clover,
> 'Tis luck for thee and luck for me,
> Or luck for any lover.

A German proverb says of a lucky man: "Er hat ein vierblattriges Kleeblatt gefunden"—"He has found a four-leaved clover." In German-speaking countries, indeed, the superstition is most firmly rooted, and takes on the most varied forms. If the bearer or wearer of a four-leaved clover should come across witch work or any uncanny performance, he can detect and spoil it all unharmed. If a man loves a woman (or *vice versa*), and can obtain two four-leaved clovers and induce her to eat one, while he himself swallows the other, mutual love is sure to result. Nay, according to a very good gypsy authority, even a trin-patrini kas, or three-leaved clover, will have this effect. A maiden who, unbeknown to her lover, slips a piece of clover into his shoe as he starts on a journey, will secure his sure and safe return to her embrace. Moreover, it is advisable on all occasions when you make a gift to anybody, no matter what it is, to conceal it in clover leaves, since this will render the gift doubly acceptable. Also, take a four- or three-leaved clover, and, making a hollow in the end or top of your alpenstock or cane, put the leaf therein, taking care not to injure it, and close the opening carefully. Then, so long as you walk with it, you will be less weary than if it were wanting, and will enjoy luck in many ways.

It is believed in the Tyrol that any one can acquire the art of working wonders in magic if he only searches for and finds the four-leaved clover on St. John's eve. In the Passierthal the peasants believe that if a traveller should on that day fall asleep lying on his back by a certain brook, there will come flying a white dove bearing a four-leaved clover, which it will let fall on the sleeper's breast. Should he awake before the clover fades and at once put it into his mouth, he will acquire the power of becoming invisible at will. A stranger superstition, related in Wolf's *Zeitschrift für Deutsche Mythologie,* is to the effect that if, while a priest is reading the service, any one can, unknown to him, lay a four-leaved clover on his mass book, the unfortunate clergyman will not be able to utter a word; he will stand stock still and bewildered until the person who has played the trick pulls his robe. Then he can proceed. When all is over the man who regains his four leaf clover will always have luck at all kinds of gambling.

Not only is a four-leaved clover lucky, but a "clover of two," or a piece with only two leaflets on one stem, may be used as a charm to discover your future lover. The following rhyme is current in rustic England:

A clover, a clover of two,
Put it on your right shoe;
The first young man (woman) you meet, in field, street or lane,
You'll have him (her) or one of his (her) name.

Cockchafer. In France the cockchafer is treated in the same way as is the ladybird (*q.v.*) by the children of East Yorkshire. Before taking flight the cockchafer moves its wings up and down for a few seconds and inflates its body with air. French children say then that it is counting its money, and they sing to it this very old refrain:

> Hanneton, vole, vole,
> Va-t'en à l'école.

In Western France a different rhyme is in use:

> Barbot, vole, vole, vole,
> Ton père est à l'école,
> Qui m'a dit, si tu ne vole,
> Il te coupera la gorge,
> Avec un grand couteau de Saint Georges.

In the neighborhood of Berlin cockchafers are exchanged by the boys for pins. At the beginning of the season they are expensive, but when they are cheapest—that is in May—they can be bought at the rate of three for one pin. The children then sing the following couplet:

> Käfer mai, käfer mai,
> Für eine Nadel giebt es drei.
> (" Cockchafers, cockchafers, three for a pin.")

The following folk-song is in use also in the same district concerning the cockchafer:

> Maikäfer fliege,
> Dein Vater ist Kriege,
> Deine Mutter ist in Pommerland,
> Pommerland ist abgerbrannt.
> (" Cockchafer, fly away, your father's at the war, your mother's
> in Pomerania, Pomerania is burnt out.")

Cock fighting and the breeding of roosters for that purpose were known to the Greeks and Romans and may have been introduced into Britain by the latter. There it found congenial soil. William Fitzstephen in his " Description of the City of London " (1791), says that it was the annual custom on Shrove Tuesday for the boys to turn the school-rooms into cockpits, where masters and pupils congregated to enjoy the sport. Teachers even derived part of their income from the sums paid by boys for chanticleers.

A Westmoreland squire named Graham bequeathed to Wreay School, on Windermere Lake, a silver bell to be fought for every year. Three roosters on each side were pitted against each other by two rival captains. The bell was affixed to the hat of the victorious captain, who retained it for a year, only to pass it over to the next victor. And thus, year after year, the bell was handed down from captain to captain until the sport was put an end to in 1834.

Gervase Markham, writing in the reign of James I, says. " There is no pleasure more noble, delightsome, or void of cozenage and deceit, than this pleasure of cocking is." It was cultivated with a perfectly clear conscience by the first gentlemen of England. So important a place did cock-fighting take among the amusements of that age, that certain birds were as famous by name as any race-horse is to-day, and the last winner of the Derby was not a greater celebrity than were, about 1610, the two celebrated cocks, Noble and Griswold, whose names are handed down to us as those of "the two famousest cocks that ever fought." But perhaps a still wider reputation was enjoyed by a certain hen whose name was Jinks, the mother of so many brilliant fighters that she was regarded at last with a sort of superstitious awe. Extreme care was taken from the moment she laid an egg to insure the health of what might turn out to be a valuable fighter. At a month old the young birds were censed every morning with burning rosemary or pennyroyal, and then taken for a constitutional on a grass plot. Directly the comb appeared it was cut away and the scar rubbed with butter. If the chicken crowed too soon he was cast out; for a good fighter never raised his voice until late in life. When a promising bird had been selected, no pains were spared with him. He was given strange and elaborate food,—cheese-parings, chopped leeks, toast sopped in wine. In short no racer of our day is more delicately nourished and guarded by his fortunate owner.

The professional cock-masters preserved a great mystery about the dieting and lodging of a cock during the days which preceded a battle. Gervase Markham calls this "a secret never yet divulged, but kept close in the breasts of some few." Everything was believed to depend on these precautions. The tricks of the trade were jealously guarded, each different cock-master, no doubt, having different panaceas. The training exercise, however, was less secret. The bird was taken out of his pen after his morning meal, and a pair of "hots" (soft padded rolls of leather) were carefully fastened over the spurs. Another cock similarly protected was brought out, and the two birds, being set on a lawn of fine turf, were encouraged to fight and buffet one another until the prize cock showed signs of weariness. He was then taken up, deprived of his "hots," and buried in a basket of sweet straw, packed around him in such a way that he could scarcely stir,—"and so shall he stew and sweat until evening." This basket was called the "stove," and before the cock was put into it he was made to swallow a lump of chopped rosemary and pounded barley sugar mixed in butter.

Some amateurs liked to put their cock into a cock-bag, but this was not held to be so efficacious as a "stove," because the air could not pass so freely through it. All the next day the cock rested, and on the following morning the cock-master took him into a green enclosure. Then, putting him down on the turf and holding some ordinary "dunghill" rooster in his arms, the master showed it to him, ran from him, enticed him to follow, and occasionally allowed him to get a stroke at the "dunghill." When thoroughly heated with this pastime, the fighter was once more stuffed with butter of rosemary and then "stoved" in the basket of straw until the evening. This kind of training went on for six weeks, the last three days being spent in absolute rest and fasting, so that it was a fresh and hungry bird that was at length brought out and put into the pit.

None of the incidental refinements which made eighteenth century cock-fighting so cruel had occurred to the simplicity of the seventeenth. No additions were made to the armor of the birds: no metal spurs or needles were fixed to their vigorous legs. All that was done was to clear decks for fighting, to cut off the long feathers of the neck and tails, to clip the wings, to smooth and sharpen the beak and heels with a knife. It was important to leave no feathers on the crown of the head for the foe to take hold of. Then, after a final ceremony, when the cock-master had licked the head and eyes of the champion all over with his tongue, the bird was turned into the pit to try his fortune. After the battle was over, each combatant was tenderly taken up and his wounds were cleansed. He was then wrapped in flannel and put into his basket to recover, so wrapped in flannel and pressed down with straw that he could scarcely breathe, and thus left motionless for the night.

In the middle of the eighteenth century Bourne attacked cock-fighting as "a heathenish diversion, which ought certainly to be confined to barbarous nations." By that time it had grown to be a hideous performance, such as we still see it in practice in the "sporting pictures" of a hundred years ago, where the birds, provided with long steel spurs, stab one another to death in a pit, surrounded by a ring of leering old gentlemen in boots and breeches.

A famous cockpit that flourished in the early part of the nineteenth century was the Royal Cockpit situated in Tufton Street, London. It was approached through one of the vilest neighborhoods of Westminster. About the doors loafed groups of ruffians from morning until night. Within all was gloom and dirt. On two sides were galleries, in which were the respective coops of the feathered gladiators. In the centre was a raised stage, covered with matting; this, by a curious perversion of language, being called the "pit." Here the battles of the birds took place. The atmosphere was pestiferous with damp straw and sawdust mingling with the effluvia of the birds and the great unwashed; yet hither came the cream of the *beau monde,* including royalty itself. Here might be seen the unwieldly bulk of the *bon vivant* Duke of Norfolk, roaring out bets upon "the red" or "the yellow," while some costermonger, slapping him upon the back, would yell, "I'll take it." Beau Brummel and the prince regent were frequent visitors, the future sovereign entering into the row and excitement with an eagerness second to none. Until put down by act of Parliament in 1834, cock-fighting was a thoroughly aristocratic sport which few thought of decrying.

Cocoa-nut. A familiar proverb of uncertain origin and varied application runs thus: "That (or this) accounts for the milk in the cocoa-nut." Now, there is no milk in the cocoa-nut, though lexicographers all agree that there is. Even the eleventh edition of the Encyclopædia Britannica says, *s.v.,* "The fruit consists of a thick external husk or rind of a fibrous structure within which is the ordinary cocoa-nut (*sic*) of commerce. The nut has a very hard wooden shell enclosing the nucleus or kernel, the true seed, within which again is a milky liquid called cocoa-nut milk." In actual fact the liquid is not milky. It consists of about a pint of clear limpid juice, slightly acidulous, cool and refreshing—*the water of the cocoa-nut.* Nor is it called milk in the habitat of the parent palm. Wherever English is spoken in the torrid zone it is invariably known as the water of the cocoa-nut. "The real milk of the cocoa-nut, a white fluid which warrants the designation, is an artificial product. The half-ripe meat of the nut is grated and leached with fresh water; the percolated fluid is heavy and white, it contains a large amount of the vegetable fat cells, is very nutritious and is fragrant with the characteristic savor of the nut. It is used as a beverage or as a diluent of coffee and chocolate infusions; it is a valuable component in cookery, since under the influence of heat it takes on a custardy consistency. This is the real milk of the cocoanut; the proverb accounts for this milk not at all."— N. Y. *Sun,* May 26, 1912.

Cocos-Keeling Islands. A group of some twenty small islands lying about 750 miles to the southwest of the Dutch East Indies is known by the name of the Cocos or Keeling Islands, but more usually by the hyphenated compound Cocos-Keeling. They were first discovered at the beginning of the nineteenth century by William Keeling, "general for the East India adventurers." Their next visitor, six years later, was John Clunies Ross (1786–1854), a native of Wiesdale in the Shetlands, who had got into some scrape while serving before the mast on a British man-of-war, had been marooned or had deserted, and for ten years previous had been cruising around strange waters as a pirate or a privateer (accounts differ), and now with his crew determined to settle down to a quiet life in the Cocos archipelago. Their plans were disturbed by the arrival of another renegade sailor, Alexander Hare, with a force of Malay slaves and a harem of dusky beauties. A bitter struggle ensued, which ended in the defeat and ejectment of Hare. Ross had another fight with one of his own lieutenants, a sailor named Davis, who raised a revolt that was speedily quelled, and from that time on he enjoyed undisputed sway as king of the Cocos Islands. He proved to be a benevolent autocrat, ruling justly and well, and establishing a prosperous trade with the neighboring ports in Java and Sumatra. In 1837 Charles Darwin visited the island on which King Ross I had built his royal palace, studied the formation of the coral reefs there, and has given the result of his researches in his "Voyage of the Beagle," the evolutionist's first published work. Incidentally he speaks highly of the king and of his little kingdom. His son, bearing the same name, succeeded him as Ross II, on the pioneer's death in 1854, and the dynasty has since been continued by a grandson, George, who mounted the throne in 1872, and a great-grandson, Sydney, who followed in 1910. Father, son, grandson, and greatgrandson all married Malay women. Hence Ross IV is only one-quarter white.

King Ross I, fearing embarrassing attentions perhaps on the part of the British authorities whom he had offended, had caused himself to be naturalized as a Dutch subject. Ross II, however, renewed his allegiance to England, and at his solicitation Captain Fremantle, commanding the British frigate *Juno,* visited the Cocos group in 1857 and hoisted the union jack over them in the name of Queen Victoria.

Although the British government takes more interest in the group than formerly, and causes it to be visited once a year by a representative of the governor of the Straits Settlements, who usually makes the trip from Singapore on board a man-of-war and furnishes an extremely interesting report on his return, yet the British penal code has never been introduced into the islands. There is no police force and no crime, and the currency of the islands consists of bits of parchment bearing the signature of the head of the Ross family and convertible at a fixed ratio into rupees or dollars when an islander makes a rare visit to Batavia or Singapore. The Rosses, who are Presbyterians, have all married Malays, and in spite of the fact that the population of more than a thousand are nearly all Moslems, the Ross influence has been sufficiently great to cause monogamy to prevail. In fact, no one on the islands has more than one wife. (See article by Ex-Attaché in New York *Tribune,* July 24, 1910.)

The Cocos-Keeling government numbered in 1910 nearly 1000

subjects, representing almost every race in the East,—Malays, Chinese, Negroes, Hindoos, East Indians, and Papauns. They live in an enchanted region, where the rats climb trees and nibble the cocoanuts, where the giant land-crab scuttles to and fro, brandishing claws of so formidable a character that it can nip through wire netting as easily as can a man with cutting pliers, can tear up tin with ease, and break with its great pincers the wooden bars of a cage that would serve to imprison a large wild animal.

As to the rats—thereby hangs a story. Until a few years ago not a rat was seen in Cocos. But a ship was wrecked off the islands and the rats swam ashore. They increased at such a rate that they became a nuisance and caused a tremendous loss by spoiling the buds of the cocoanut, which are extremely tender.

The King of the Cocos Islands endeavored to exterminate the rodents and imported cats for that purpose. The trouble of catching the rats was apparently too much for the cats, who found a delicious shell fish on the shore which they liked much better. Feasting on these they grew fierce and wild. They are now a greater nuisance than the rats.

One of the interesting facts about Cocos Islands is that they are only eight feet above the sea level. The waters around them are infested with sharks.

Cold Storage. Macaulay has familiarized us with the fact that Francis Bacon died a victim to science in what may have been the first experiment in cold storage. At the end of March, 1626, being near Highgate on a snowy day, he left his coach to collect snow, with which he meant to stuff a fowl in order to observe the effect of cold on the preservation of its flesh. In so doing he caught a chill, and took refuge in Lord Arundel's house, where, on April 9, he died of the disease now known as bronchitis. Macaulay adds, " In the last letter that he ever wrote, with fingers which, as he said, could not steadily hold a pen, he did not omit to mention that the experiment of the snow had succeeded excellently well."

On December 11, 1663, Samuel Pepys made this entry in his diary: " Fowl killed in December, Alderman Barker said, he did buy, and, putting into the box under his sledge, did forget to take them out to eat till April next, and they then were found there, and were, through the frost, as sweet and fresh and eat as well as at first killed."

If we turn to nature, there are instances in Siberia of mammoths preserved in ice, so that their flesh is still eatable, from a period probably coeval with the first appearance of man on this globe.

As the Romans brought to their banquets the dainties of all

the known world, it seems reasonable to suppose that they had some knowledge of how to preserve them in ice. We know that they iced their drinks, a custom which was introduced into France in the seventeenth century. A passage in Boileau's Third Satire, "Le Répas Ridicule," 1664, alludes to this use of ice:

> J'approuvais tout pourtant de la mine et du geste
> Pensant qu'au moins le vin dut reparer le reste;
> Pour m'en eclaircir donc j'en demande. . . .
> Mais qui l'aurai pensé? pour comble de disgrace,
> Par le chaud qu'il faisait nous n'avions point de glace
> Point de glace, bon Dieu! dans le fort de l'été
> Au mois de Juin!

In October, 1912, the International Cold Storage Association opened a public subscription for Charles Tellier, of Paris, to whom they credited the origin of the modern science of cold storage. At that time Tellier was 84 years old. He had spent his entire fortune in the development of his numerous discoveries.

In 1875, he had a steamer, the *Frigorifique,* specially fitted up for cold storage, which was to have a temperature below the freezing point even under the equator. The steamer sailed from Rouen in 1876 on her first trip to the Rio de la Plata with some fresh meat that was perfectly preserved for three months. and she returned with a cargo of frozen meat from the Rio de la Plata.

Tellier's process was immediately applied to fishing boats off Morocco and along the French coast. Eventually an enormous trade based entirely on cold storage had grown up all over the world. But the man who invented the scheme had been almost forgotten until the Cold Storage Association interested itself in his behalf.

Communion. Some curious particulars of the celebration of the communion in eighteenth century Scotland are given in Henry Grey Graham's "Social Life in Scotland," vol. ii. He states that the elements varied in different places, sack, claret, port, and even ale being used. Short bread was occasionally substituted for bread. He quotes a still more startling assertion from the "Journals of Bishop Robert Forbes," edited by J. B. Craven, D.D. (London, 1886, p. 182).

Mr. John Maitland was attached to Lord Ogilvie's regiment in the service of Prince Charles, 1745. He administered the Holy Eucharist to Lord Strathallan on Culloden Field (where that nobleman received his death wound), it is said, with oatcake and whiskey, the requisite elements not being obtainable.

The same story without the whiskey adjunct is found in

Robert Chambers's "History of the Rebellion in Scotland," vol. ii, p. 319 (Edinburgh, 1827).

"It appears that his Lordship did not die immediately after his wound. He lived to receive the Viaticum from a Catholic priest who happened to be upon the field. The sacred morsel was hastily composed of oatmeal and water which the clergyman procured at a neighboring cottage. This clergyman went to France, became an abbé, but, revisiting his native country, gave this information to one of our informants—the Scottish bishop so often quoted."

A correspondent of *Notes and Queries,* 11, ii, 453, protests against this story as impossible in either version. "No Catholic priest would dream of using such matter for consecration." He suggests, however, "it is not impossible to believe that the oils for extreme unction and consecrated species for the Viaticum were brought to the field and kept ready to hand in a neighboring cottage, and in this way, perhaps, many of the Scottish Catholics would receive the last sacraments, but we may be sure no whiskey or oatcake would be used for them."

Cardinal Gibbons, in the "Faith of Our Forefathers," mentions a few Protestant devices. "I am credibly informed that in a certain Episcopal church in Virginia, communicants partake of the juice of the blackberry instead of the juice of the grape. And the New York *Independent* of September 21, 1876, relates the following incident: 'A late English traveller found a Baptist mission church in far-off Burmah using for the communion service Bass's pale ale instead of wine.' "—31st edition, 1887, p. 348.

Congreve Rocket. Sir William Congreve (1772–1828) is chiefly remembered to-day by his invention of the war rocket which still retains his name. His father, Lieutenant-General Sir William Congreve, was comptroller of the Royal Laboratory at Woolwich; hence the son had ample opportunities for experimenting with military material. It was in the year 1805 that he first demonstrated, before the prince regent and Pitt, the uses of his rocket, a cylindrical tube of metal containing a mixture of nitre, sulphur, and charcoal, which, being ignited at the base, propelled the tube forward. Not until 1809 was he able to make a trial of its efficacy in actual warfare at sea, Lord Cochrane using it in his attempt to burn the French fleet in the Basque Roads. Though the attempt was a failure, the value of the rocket was conceded, and its inventor was allowed to raise and organize two rocket companies, one of which served under him at the battle of Leipzig in 1813. The Congreve rockets did not do much actual damage to the enemy, but their noise and glare helped to throw the French into confusion. The Czar of Russia showed his appreciation of Congreve's services to the allied army by making him a knight of the order of St. Anne. At the passage of the Bidassoa again, the rockets caused terror by their novelty, though they did little real damage.

Corinthian Capital. Vitruvius tells of its origin in this wise: "A Corinthian virgin of marriageable age fell a victim to a violent disorder. After her interment, her nurse, collecting in a basket those articles to which she had shown a partiality when alive, carried them to her tomb, and placed a tile on the basket for the longer preservation of its contents. The basket was accidentally placed on the root of an acanthus plant, which, pressed by the weight, shot forth towards spring its stems and large foliage, and in the course of its growth reached the angles of the tile and then formed volutes at the extremities. Callimachus, happening at the time to pass by the tomb, observed the basket and the delicacy of the foliage which surrounded it. Pleased with the form and novelty of the combination, he constructed from the hint thus afforded columns of this species in the country about Corinth, and arranged its proportions, determining their proper measures by perfect rules." Vitruvius, it must be owned, is an authority not quite impeccable, but in this instance there seems no particular reason why his story should be doubted. And, at all events, if it is not true, it is gloriously invented.

Coronation. Not the oldest coronation, but the oldest of which any contemporary relic survives, was the coronation (about B.C. 600) of the Ethiopian King Aspalut. An engraved record on stone is preserved in the Cairo Museum. A cast is on exhibition in the Egyptian sculpture gallery at the British Museum. The inscription appears on a tablet of granite 5 feet 9 inches high, which was discovered at Gebel Barkal, opposite the ancient city of Napata in the Soudan. Forty-five lines of hieroglyphics tell how Aspalut was selected for the throne and how he celebrated his accession. All the "divine brethren"—the sons of the late monarch—were brought into the temple and placed before the god Amen Ra in order that he should indicate his preference. But the image made no sign. Then Aspalut, a scion of the ancient royal house of Kush, was introduced. Immediately the god touched him, he was declared to be the appointed successor, and then and there he was anointed and enthroned. To commemorate his elevation, it is added that Aspalut appointed annual feasts. Unfortunately, the last four lines referring to these celebrations are so badly damaged that little can be made out except a cheerful reference to "one hundred and forty barrels of beer"—probably a usual royal gift on these occasions.

Coronation Mantle. There are three mantles used at the coronation of a British king,—the lower one of crimson velvet, the middle one of purple velvet, and the topmost and smallest one of pure cloth of gold. The latter is officially known as "the pall." After the coronation it becomes the perquisite of the lord great chamberlain of England. Hence the sovereign generally has a new one made for him. The other robes may descend from father to son. George V made an innovation by donning the pall which George IV had worn at his coronation. It is described as a magnificent example of the handloom industry of the Spitalfields weaver, the badges being woven into the surface of the fabric instead of being applied by embroidery. On the occasion of the fourth George's coronation, the lord chamberlain was Peter Robert Burrell, who then bore the title of Lord Gwydyr and later succeeded to that of Baron Willoughby d'Eresby. At the time of the fifth George's coronation the mantle had passed into the keeping of one of his descendants, the twenty-fifth Baron d'Eresby. Instigated by his American wife, *née* Breese, the baron placed this mantle at the royal disposal. A persistent rumor, which brought some dismay to respectable British bosoms, represented that the pall had been taken for the occasion from the waxwork effigy of King George IV in his coronation robes which had long been one of the glories of Madame Tussaud's waxwork show. The mistake was not an unnatural one. That King's uniforms and official costumes, and all the coronation robes save the pall, together with other personal effects, had been sold at auction by order of his executors, at Phillips's auction rooms in Bond Street, on June 9, 1831, or just a year after his death. The coronation robes were bought in by Madame Tussaud for her famous museum of waxworks.

Counterfeit. The first counterfeit "greenback" in the United States was one imitating the $10 issue of 1862, and was circulated in the same year. The forgers were members of the notorious Johnson family whose headquarters were at Lawrence, Indiana. Nobody dreamed of forgery at that early period; greenbacks themselves were unfamiliar; and the stirring events of the war largely diverted people's minds from business matters. So the forgery escaped immediate detection.

Pete McCartney was the financial backer of the Johnsons, and after the plate had been worked the Johnsons attempted to unload McCartney. His suspicions being aroused, he stole the plate and caused it to be electrotyped. Then he returned it to its old hiding place. The electrotype was an improvement on the original, and McCartney worked off his series in Indianapolis. Over $100,000 of the spurious stuff was readily placed in circulation.

Meanwhile the Secret Service officers, led by Major Woods, had been apprised of the counterfeit, and were laying for the Johnsons and McCartney. They failed to track the latter to his rooms, where the printing was going on, but arrested him at the post office. In company with the Johnsons, who had been found at Lawrence, he was forwarded under strong escort to the military prison at Washington.

While the train was crossing the mountains, McCartney, although handcuffed and shackled at the time, managed to make his escape, and in two weeks he had returned to Indianapolis, secured possession of his electrotype, and disappeared. It cost the government many thousands of dollars before the officers again laid hands on him. Meanwhile the Johnsons succeeded in making terms. They escaped prosecution by turning up the original plate and giving the officers certain pointers with reference to other offenders. Neither the Johnsons nor the government knew until long afterward that McCartney had an electrotype and had stolen a march on his former associates.

The day on which a forged note was first presented at the Bank of England forms a memorable era in its history. For sixty-four years the establishment had circulated its paper with freedom; and during this period no attempt had been made to imitate it. To Richard William Vaughan, a Stafford linen-draper, belongs the melancholy celebrity of having led the van in this new phase of crime, in the year 1758. The records of his life do not show want, beggary, or starvation urging him, but a simple desire to seem greater than he was. By one of the artists employed, and there were several engaged on different parts of the notes, the discovery was made. The criminal had filled up to the number of twenty; and deposited them in the hands of a young lady to whom he was attached, as a proof of his wealth. There is no calculating how much longer bank-notes might have been free from imitation, had this man not shown with what ease they might be counterfeited. From this period forged notes became common.

Cow Tree or Milk Tree, a native of Venezuela, whose stem contains a milky latex. This flows out in considerable quantities when a notch is cut in the tree.

"Among the many curious phenomena which presented themselves to me in the course of my travels," says Humboldt, "I confess there were few by which my imagination was so powerfully affected as by the cow tree. On the parched side of a rock on the mountain of Venezuela, grows a tree with dry and leathery foliage, its large woody roots scarcely penetrating into the ground. For several months in the year its leaves are not moistened by a shower; its branches look as if they were dead and withered; but when the trunk is bored, a bland and nourishing milk flows from it. It is at sunrise that the vegetable fountain flows most freely. At that time the blacks and natives are seen coming from all parts, provided with large bowls to receive the milk, which grows yellow and thickens at its surface. Some empty their vessels on the spot, while others carry them to their children. One imagines he sees the family of a shepherd who is distributing the milk of his flock."

Crater Lake Park, in the Cascade Mountains, in that part of Oregon known locally as the Land of Burnt-Out Fires. It was created a national park in the year 1902. It has an area of 249 miles, and its eponymic feature, Crater Lake (the crater of an extinct volcano), is 20 miles in circumference and 2000 feet in depth. The lake and the huge cliffs that surround it present the appearance of a great ragged-rimmed basin, with an almost sheer descent of 2000 feet to the silent waters.

One of the weird features of Crater Lake is that, while it has an altitude of 6000 feet, its waters are said never to freeze, although ice forms on the adjacent Klamath lakes, which are at a considerably lower altitude. Again, while Crater Lake is always open water, ducks and other waterfowl are never seen upon its bosom during the winter. Gamy trout, however, are plentiful.

Cremation. Probably the first person in modern England who publicly commended the practice of burning the body after death and who set the example by condemning her own body to the flames was Honoretta Pratt. The daughter and eventual heiress of Sir John Brookes, of York, this lady married John Pratt, treasurer of Ireland.

Robert Pierpont, *Notes and Queries* (7th series, xii. 385), calls attention to a monument in St. George's burial ground, Hanover Square, erected to the memory of Mrs. Pratt. From the reverse side he copied this inscription:

"This worthy woman believing that the Vapours arising from graves in the church yards of populous cities must prove hurtful to the inhabitants and resolving to extend to future times as far as she was able that charity and benevolence which distinguished her through life ordered that her body should be burnt in hope that others would follow the example, a thing too hastily censured by those who did not inquire the motive."

On the obverse side a semi-obliterated inscription yielded the date, "20 September 1769." This was doubtless the date of the lady's death, for the Annual Register for 1769, under date, 26 September, p. 133, says: "Last night the will of Mrs.

Pratt, a widow lady, who died at her house in George Street, Hanover Square, was punctually fulfilled by the burning of her body to ashes in her grave in the new burying ground adjoining to Tyburn turnpike."

The cemetery has now been secularized. Writing in *Notes and Queries* for January 25, 1908, Mr. Arthur Leveson-Gower says: "The slabs of the above-mentioned monument will probably be still found lying on the ground under the wall furthest from the chapel attached to the burial ground; but the inscription is by now, in all probability, completely obliterated."

Cricket. The national game of England was in mediæval times under the ban of the law. In 1477 Edward IV forbade the playing of " cloish, ragle, half-bowle, onekeboard and handyn and handout." The latter is held to be the primitive form of cricket. " Whoever," so the statute continues, " shall permit these games to be played in their house or yard is punishable with three years' imprisonment. Those who play at any of the games are to be fined ten pounds or lie in jail two years." The main reason for this interdict was that the new recreations were interfering with the cultivation of archery (*q.v.*).

The early history of cricket is involved in some obscurity, but it is certain that some country clubs had been formed before the end of the eighteenth century. Old prints are extant showing the players in knee-breeches and stockings, holding bats with a curved projection at the bottom on the right-hand side. Evidently the method then in use was to strike the ball with the bottom of the bat,—a method probably derived from hockey. Sussex and Kent were the cradle of the game. Laborers and artisans welcomed it as eagerly as did the gentry. Games took place on the village green, and the clergyman was often seen playing with his parishioners on Sunday afternoon. This was before Sunday (*q.v.*) was misnamed the Sabbath. The game was found to adapt itself to contests between different villages and towns, and by and by counties entered the list. As soon as games occurred at a distance, it was found that men who lived by their work must be paid. This was the origin of the "player," *i.e.*, the professional.

Cricket and Women. In June, 1777, a cricket match was played at the Oaks, in Surrey, " between the Countess of Derby and some other ladies of quality and fashion." Among the spectators was Lady Derby's brother, the Duke of Hamilton, who then and there fell in love with Miss Elizabeth Burrell, " probably when she took bat in hand. Then her Diana-like air communicated an irresistible impression. She got more notches in the first and second innings than any lady in the game." So says the *Morning Post* of January 22, 1878, in an announcement of the duke's engagement to Miss Burrell.

The *Public Advertiser* of July 29, 1768, describes a cricket match which took place at Upham, in Wiltshire on Saturday, July 23, between eleven married and eleven single women, for a plum-cake and a barrel of ale, " which was won with difficulty by the latter."

A still earlier game between female teams was thus announced in the *General Advertiser* of Saturday, July 11, 1747:

" On Monday next will certainly be played in the Artillery Ground, London, the Match at Cricket so long expected between the Women of Charlton and Singleton, in Sussex, against the Women of Westdean and Chilgrove in the same County."

This game, it would seem, was a very rough one, for the same paper, in its issue for the succeeding Wednesday, states that, " on Monday last in playing the Women's Cricket Match the Company broke in, so that it was impossible for the game to be played out ; and some of them being very much frightened and others hurt, it could not be finished until this morning, when at nine o'clock they will finish the same, hoping the company will be so kind as to indulge them in not walking within the Ring, which will not only be a great Pleasure to them, but a general Satisfaction to the Whole." The result of this appeal, however, was never reported.

Cricket in the United States.   Before 1747 cricket had been exported to America from its British home.   The earliest recorded games took place in the lower part of New York City near what was afterward Fulton Market.   The *Gazette and Weekly Post Boy* gave an account of a game played there on May 1, 1751. The contestants were eleven London men and eleven New Yorkers.   The latter won, making 80 and 86 to their opponents' 43 and 37.   Boston was early in the field as a cricketing centre. A copy of the by-laws and playing rules of its first club, dated May 1, 1809, are yet in existence.   The Young America Club, of Philadelphia, has a copy of " The Laws of Cricket," taken over by Benjamin Franklin more than a century ago.   The first club which gained any permanent foothold was the Union Club, of Philadelphia, organized by a few Englishmen about 1831 or 1832.   The Philadelphia, Germantown, and Young America, three of the leading clubs of the present day, were the first native organizations.   They date their existence from 1854.   New York had an organization some years before that, but it was, and still is, largely composed of Englishmen.   On October 22 and 23, 1838, there was a match between New York and Long Island. The New York men won, and subsequently organized themselves into the St. George Cricket Club. Their grounds were at Broadway and Thirtieth Street, until the opening of Fifth Avenue cut their field. They then removed to the Red House at One-Hundred-and-Fifth Street near Second Avenue. The growth of the city subsequently compelled them to move again. Their grounds are now at St. George's, on Staten Island. They have there an excellent field, which affords a very pretty wicket, and is also used for lawn-tennis tourneys.

Outside of New York, Boston, and Philadelphia, cricket is played but little in the United States, save along the Canadian border, where base-ball is unknown. In Canada, of course, the game is played a great deal.

The first international contest between the United States and Canada took place in New York in 1853. The series continued until 1860, and after that the Civil War prevented any further contests for several years. The United States won five and lost two games of the series.

Interesting periods in the history of cricket in America are the years 1859, 1868, 1872, 1879, 1881, and 1882, when international matches were played between England and the United States. The first English eleven which visited us (1859) was composed of professionals, under the leadership of George Parr. They won with ease five games played in Montreal and Hamilton, Canada, Hoboken, Philadelphia, and Rochester.

The season of 1879 was made notable by visits of teams of the most prominent professionals and amateurs in England and Ireland. On May 7 and 8 Lord Harris's amateur eleven, while on their way home from Australia, easily defeated an eleven chosen from the clubs of New York and Philadelphia. In September and October an eleven of English professionals, led by Daft, and another of Irish amateurs, played in the United States and Canada. The Irishmen were soundly beaten by an American eleven in Philadelphia. Of the other games, each of the visiting elevens won nine, while three were drawn. Alfred Shaw took a team of English professionals through the United States in October 1881, on their way to Australia. Three of the five games were declared drawn on account of the weather. In the game played on October 7, 8, and 10, at Philadelphia, the strongest eighteen that ever took the field in America, consisting of seven professionals and eleven amateurs, were defeated by 132 runs. A second Australian team returning home from England played against eighteens of the leading New York and Philadelphia clubs in October 1882, and won easy victories. A peculiar episode in cricketing annals was the visit of eighteen American base-ball players to England in 1874. They played seven cricket games, and won six, the other being drawn on account of rain. Their excellent fielding and straight bowling astonished English cricketers, while their heavy hitting was almost equally surprising.

The records of individual players in America do not show nearly so many remarkable feats as those of English players. Centuries, or individual innings of one hundred runs or more, have been seldom scored. The first on record, and for many years the greatest, was made on October 3 and 4, 1844, in a match between the Union Club, of Philadelphia, and the St. George, of New York. The gentleman who electrified America by achieving this then astonishing feat was James Turner, of the Union Club. He succeeded in scoring 120 runs against excellent bowling. One of the bowlers whom he faced was Samuel Wright, the father of Harry and George Wright, of base-ball fame. Turner's score stood first for over a quarter of a century. It was, however, subsequently surpassed. The largest individual score ever made in America (204 runs) was that of A. Browning, of the Montreal Club, in a match with Ottawa, on July 1, 1880. George M. Newhall, one of a family famous in American cricketing annals, made the record individual score in the United States, on July 1, 1880,—180 runs, not out. On the same day the Montreal Club scored 402 for the loss of nine wickets, the largest total ever made in America. In a game between the Young America and Baltimore Clubs, the former made 357 runs for five wickets, George M. and D. S. Newhall carrying out their bats after scoring 159 runs subsequent to the fall of the last wicket.

Croatan. The name of a tribe of Indians, now extinct, once resident in Virginia. The word acquired a strange interest in colonial history. The first English colony, sent to America by Sir Walter Raleigh, under the auspices of Sir Richard Grenville, settled on Roanoke Island near Albemarle Sound in 1587. When provisions grew low, Grenville and Governor Whyte returned to England for supplies, the latter leaving behind as a pledge of his return his little granddaughter, Virginia Dare, the first English child born in America. It was agreed, that, if the colonists abandoned the island for the mainland, they should cut on a certain pine tree the Indian name of the place to which they had gone. If they left in distress, a cross was to be cut above the name. Next spring the governor returned, to find the island deserted, and the word "Croatan" carved on the pine tree, but without the cross. The mainland was searched far and near, and at last they found a tribe who bore the strange name, but who were peacable and friendly and knew nothing of the lost colonists. No trace of the latter was ever discovered. Mrs. Margaret

17

J. Preston has made this story the subject of a ballad, "The Mystery of Croatan."

Crocodile. This reptile has always exercised a weird fascination over men, with the result that the ancient Egyptians worshipped it while living and mummified it when dead, and naturalists and travellers have told and repeated all manner of anecdotes and fables concerning it.

It is probably the crocodile, and not the whale, which is referred to under the name of " leviathan " in Job, and under that of " Than " (translated " dragon ") in Ezekiel xxix, 3, 4:—

" Behold, I am against thee, Pharaoh King of Egypt,—the great dragon that lieth in the midst of his rivers, which hath said, My river is mine own, and I have made it for myself; but I will put hooks in thy jaws, and I will cause the fish of thy rivers to stick unto thy scales, and I will bring thee up out of the midst of thy rivers, and all the fish of thy rivers shall stick unto thy scales."

Here we have a clear allusion to the mode of taking the crocodile which, according to Herodotus, was practised by the early Egyptians: " When the fisherman has baited the hook with the chine of a pig, he lets it down into the middle of the river, and, holding a young live pig on the brink of the river, beats it. The crocodile, hearing the noise, goes in its direction, and, meeting with the chine, swallows it, but the men draw it to land. When it is drawn out on shore, the sportsman first of all plasters its eyes with mud, and, having done this, afterwards manages very easily."

Pliny tells us that in the land of the Tentyris it was the habit of the natives to spring on the backs of crocodiles and in that position to subdue them. Yet Charles Waterton, the eccentric English naturalist, met with a storm of ridicule when, in his " Wanderings," he claimed to have subdued a crocodile in exactly this fashion. The Indians had caught him by means of a hook in the river Essequibo and pulled him within two yards of the Englishman.

" I saw he was in a state of fear and perturbation. I instantly dropped the mast, sprang up and jumped on his back, turning half round as I vaulted, so that I gained my seat with my face in a right position. I immediately seized his forelegs, and by main force twisted them on his back, thus they served me for a bridle."

T. P. O'Connor, moreover, assures us that Sir Richard Burton once managed to muzzle a crocodile with a lasso, to jump upon his back, and snatch the fearful joy of an erratic ride upon him. On another occasion, Sir Richard and a friend of his, Lieutenant

Beresford, visiting the once sacred Crocodile Preserve near Karachi, noticed that these reptiles and certain islets of reeds happened to make an almost continuous bridge across the tank. "By George!" cried Beresford; "I believe I could cross on their backs!" and before a word could be said to dissuade him from the mad attempt he had started. He succeeded in hopping from one crocodile to another, before it had time to move or dive, and arrived at the opposite side of the tank,.to the stupefaction of the spectators.

A story that was universally accepted in the middle ages gave rise to the expression crocodile's tears.

Sir John Mandeville says, "In many places of Inde are many crocodiles—that is a manner of a long serpent. These serpents slay men and eat them weeping." Topsell also writes, "There are not many brute beasts that can weep, but such is the nature of the crocodile that, to get a man within his danger, he will sob, sigh, and weep as though he were in extremity, but suddenly he destroyeth him. Others say that the crocodile weepeth after he hath devoured a man."

Both Shakespeare and Spenser notice this fable; the former says

> The mournful crocodile
> With sorrow snares relenting passengers;

While the latter, in the "Faerie Queene," has a passage too long to quote. (See WALSH, *Handy-book of Literary Curiosities, s.v.*).

And yet this myth is not all a myth. According to Lindsay Johnson, an ophthalmic surgeon of London, crocodiles do cry. They shed copious tears, but not outwardly from the eyes. The tears run down into the throat and mouth; so, after all, the story about crocodile's tears is not without foundation, for the animal cries, not from emotion, but to lubricate its food.

Still another myth is noted and delightfully commented upon by Edward Topsell: "Some have written that the crocodile runneth away from a man if he wink with his left eye, and look steadfastly upon him with his right eye; but if this be true, it is not to be attributed to the virtue of the right eye, but only to the rareness of sight which is conspicuous to the serpent from one eye."

Crocodile Bird. There is a curious story about a bird which tends upon the crocodile. In its original simplicity it was told by Herodotus and in this form has been confirmed by modern investigators. But meanwhile it had grown to such monstrous and incredible proportions that the whole story had come to be doubted. Herodotus, after stating that all other birds and beasts avoid the crocodile, adds that he is at "peace with the trochilus, because he receives benefit from that bird. For, when the crocodile gets out of the water on land, and then opens its jaws, which it does most commonly towards the west, the trochilus enters its mouth and swallows the leeches which infest it. The crocodile is so well pleased with this service that it never hurts the trochilus."

Pliny amplified and distorted the story in a remarkable fashion. This is how it appears in Holland's translation:

"When he [the crocodile] hath filled his belly with fishes, he lieth to sleep upon the sands in the shore: and for that he is a great and greedie devourer, somewhat of the meat sticketh evermore between his teeth, in regard whereof cometh the wren, a little bird called there Trochilos, and the king of birds in Italy; and she for her victual's sake hoppeth first about his mouth, falleth to pecking or picking it with her little neb or bill, and so forward to the teeth which she cleanseth and all to make him gape. Then getteth she within his mouth, which he openeth the wider, by reason that he taketh so great delight in this her scraping and scouring of his teeth and jaws. Now, when he is lulled as it were fast asleep with this pleasure and contentment of his; the rat of India, or ichneumon, spieth his vantage, and seeing him lie thus broad gaping, whippeth into his mouth and shooteth himself down his throat as quick as an arrow, and then gnaweth his bowels, eating an hole through his belly and so killeth him."

Edward Topsell, in his great "Historie of Serpents" (London, 1608), repeats this story, enlarging and gloating over the misery of the unfortunate reptile. After the ichneumon's attack, he tells us, the crocodile "tumbleth to and fro, sighing and weeping, now in the depth of water, now on the land, never resting till strength of nature faileth. For the incessant gnawing of the ichneumon so provoketh her to seek her rest, in the unrest of every part, herbe, element, throwes, throbs, rowlings, tossings, mournings; but all in vain, for the enemy within her breatheth through her breath, and sporteth herself in the consumption of those vital parts, which waste and wear away by yielding to impracticable teeth, one after the other, till she that crept in by stealth at the mouth, like a puny thief, come out at the belly like a conqueror through a passage opened by her own labor and industry."

In the *Ibis* for May, 1893, J. M. Cook narrates a personal experience during the year 1876. He and his brother-in-law, hearing the natives speak about the curious habits of the crocodile birds, determined to watch them. "For this purpose, during the dark hours, we had a small pit dug on the western side of a large sand-bank, and about the peep of day the following morning we ensconced ourselves in the pit. We watched patiently until about noon, when two large crocodiles came out of the water on to the bank, and apparently were soon asleep. Several crocodile birds commenced flitting over them, and through our field-glasses we watched one bird, and saw it deliberately go up to a crocodile, apparently asleep, which opened its jaws. The bird hopped in and the crocodile closed its jaws. In what appeared to be a very short time, probably not more than a minute or two, the crocodile opened its jaws, and we saw the crocodile bird go down to the water's edge. As the sand-bank was, I should say, at least half a mile across, and the bird's back was turned towards us, we could not see whether it vomited in the water or drank; but in the course of a few seconds it returned to the crocodile, which opened its mouth again, and the bird again entered. The mouth was closed, and in a short time was opened again for the bird to come out, and the same operation was repeated at the river bank. We saw the same bird enter the crocodile's mouth three times, and on three occasions run to the water to either vomit or drink."

Eventually Mr. Cook shot two of the birds, which he later identified as the spur-winged plover.

To this account the editor of the *Ibis* adds a note, in which he says that "the story is universally believed on the Nile, but, so far as we know, is not confirmed by eye-witnesses since the days of Herodotus, Aristotle, and Ælian."

Here the editor is wrong. Many mediæval and modern writers have repeated the story first told by Herodotus. Giovanni Leone, an author and traveller who lived and wrote in the later fifteenth and earlier sixteenth century,—*i.e.*, at least 1300 years after Ælian,—tells it in a manner which makes it hard to believe that he was not speaking from personal observation.

Again, Paul Lucas, who wrote in 1719, distinctly says that he saw, close to his boat, some birds like "a lapwing, and near it in bigness," which went "into the crocodiles' mouths or throats, and, after they had stayed a little while, the crocodiles shut their mouths, and opened it again soon after to let them go out." He was told by the people that these birds "feed themselves on what remains between this animal's teeth by picking them; and, as they have a kind of spur or very sharp thorn in the tops of their wings, they prick the crocodile and torment him when he has shut his mouth, till he opens it again and lets them out; and thus they secure themselves from the danger they were in."

Confirmation of another part of Herodotus's story is added by Robert Curzon in "A Visit to the Monasteries of the Levant" (London, 1849). He tells how he had on one occasion stalked a large crocodile, and was on the point of firing at it, when he saw that it was attended by a bird called a ziczac, which is of the plover species, of a grayish color, and as large as a small pigeon. The bird was walking up and down close to the crocodile's nose. "Suddenly it saw me," says Curzon, "and, instead of flying away, jumped up about a foot from the ground, screaming 'Ziczac! ziczac!' and dashed itself against the crocodile's face two or three times." Thereupon the crocodile, aroused to its danger, jumped up and dashed into the water and disappeared. "The ziczac, proud apparently of having saved his friend, remained walking up and down, uttering his cry, as I thought, with an exulting voice, and standing every now and then on the tips of his toes in a conceited manner." He concludes by saying that he felt some consolation for the loss of his game in having witnessed a circumstance the truth of which has been disputed by several writers on natural history (p. 150).

Can it be that, after all, the Egyptians have been right through all these ages, and that they have more real knowledge of the habits of the birds inhabiting their own country than modern ornithologists are inclined to allow?

In the same way we find the utmost harmony existing between sheep and cattle and starlings, which perch upon their backs and relieve them of the insect larvæ deposited in their skins. So the rhinoceros bird is on terms of intimacy with the rhinoceros and hippopotamus, relieving them of insect pests and by its watchful vigilance proving a valuable sentinel. Gordon Cumming has described how his sport was spoiled by the bird, in the same way as Curzon's was spoiled by the impertinent ziczac.

Croquet, a lawn game, a modification of the old game of pall-mall (q.v.), which sprang into sudden popularity in the last half of the nineteenth century. Pall-mall, the great game under Charles II and with his obsequious courtiers, virtually died out of England with the death of that monarch, though it continued to flourish in France. About 1860, however, a game called crokis sprang up in Ireland, which conserved though it modified some of the features of the older pastime, especially that of "cracking" a ball through a hoop with a mallet. The resemblance between the mallet of pall-mall and the mallet of croquet, which is the final form of the Irish resuscitation, is too complete to be ignored. There are now a pair of mallets used in the reign of the Stuarts which, according to John Timbs, were found in 1854 in the house of one B. L. Vulliamy, Pall Mall, in a box. These contained four pairs of the mailles or mallets and one ball, such as were formerly used for playing the game of pall-mall in the Mall of St. James's Park. Each maille was 4 feet long and made of lance-wood; the head slightly curved, measuring out-wardly 5½ inches, the inner curve being 4½ inches. The ball was of box-wood 2½ inches in diameter.

Croquet itself has some resemblances to pall-mall, though played with more balls and more hoops. It is said that the game was brought to Ireland from the south of France, and was first played on Lord Lonsdale's lawn in 1852. It came to England about 1856, and soon became popular, especially as it was taken up by the aristocratic classes. The demand at last became great enough to induce a toy-maker named Jaques to manufacture croquet sets sufficiently cheap to bring it within the reach of the masses. Toward the end of 1863, Captain Mayne Reid issued a manual of croquet, containing 129 rules—most of them contradicting the more modest regulations of Jaques. A third champion jumped into the ring in the person of Routledge, the publisher, who included among his six-penny hand-books a primer of croquet with many new rulings. Con-fusion became worse confounded when innovations on the im-plements became the order of the day. One nobleman had leather buffets placed on the heads of the mallets; another altered the shape of the hoops; another the color of the balls. Still another, thinking it derogatory to his dignity to be fettered with rules, had a third set drawn up for his own especial use. This work he entrusted to a lady, who incontinently appropriated the larger part of Captain Reid's manual and then produced her treatise as the Rules of the Earl of Essex. The professional author soon instructed the amateur in the mysteries of the art of copyright, in return for which lessons the noble pupil paid the sum of £100, with costs.

Crow. In the popular mythologies of many countries the crow is said to have been originally created white and to have fallen from its albino purity through personal or vicarious tres-pass. The Mahometans say that it betrayed, by an ill-timed caw, the hiding-place of the prophet, who cursed it and it turned black. Long before Mahomet—in the most ancient, indeed, of the Vedas—the original sin of the crows is said to be that of carrying abroad the secrets of the councils of the gods, whereupon Indra "hurled them down through all the hundred stories of his heaven."

According to Roman mythology, it owes its black plumage to Æsculapius, for his mother, the nymph Coronis, had a quarrel with his father, Apollo, who so far lost his temper—probably he had the worst of the argument—as to kill the unfortunate nymph upon the spot. Apollo had the grace to mourn his rash act, and he determined that the crow should mourn, too, and so he changed its white feathers into black, and the crow was made to " put on sullen black incontinent."

In Norway there is a Hill of Bad Spirits where the souls of wicked men fly about in the likeness of crows. In Sweden a similar spot is known as the Place of Crows and Devils. Thibet possesses an Evil City of Crows. All the schoolmen agree that they are actually imps. Among pagan authors, Pliny called the crow a bird of ill-omened garrulity, whose conversation was especially ominous at the summer solstice. The appearance of a flock of crows above the heads of an army or to the left of the camps would alarm the bravest soldiers of antiquity, as it presaged coming defeat. Shakespeare's Cassius says:

> Ravens, crows, and kites
> Fly o'er our heads and downward look on us
> As we were sickly prey; these shadows seem
> A canopy most fatal, under which
> Our army lies, ready to give up the ghost.

The cawing of a crow has always been held to bode evil. Thus, Butler, in " Hudibras," asks:

> Is it not om'nous in all countries
> When crows and ravens croak upon trees?

The children of Lancashire and Yorkshire have no friendly feeling for this bird, as is evidenced by this rhyme:

> Crow, crow, get out of my sight,
> Or else I'll eat thy liver and lights.

Yet the crow is not always a messenger of evil. Much depends upon the exact number of crows that you see. A modern proverb says, " One is lucky, two is unlucky, three is health, four is wealth, five sickness, and six death." In ancient times, however, a single crow was unlucky, while a pair of them boded good. If a crow appeared at a Greek wedding, the guests would cry, " Maiden, scare away thy crow," for should it remain in sight a divorce would surely follow. *Per contra,* two crows saved Alexander the Great in Egypt, and in the year 1147 another pair brought succor to Alonzo of Spain. One perched on the prow, the other on the stern of his ship, pointed the prow of the royal barque into port. To find a dead crow was anciently considered a lucky omen, portending length of life to the finder.

Crown Inn, Oxford, directly in the road from London to Stratford. Aubrey, who lived near enough to Elizabethan days to be an authority on such matters, relates the traditionary gossip that Shakespeare "was wont to go into Warwickshire once a year, and did commonly lye at the Crowne Tavern, in Oxford, where he was exceedingly respected." The house, in

Shakespeare's time, was kept by Mr. and Mrs. D'Avenant, the supposititious father and the indubitable mother of Sir William D'Avenant, the poet. Shakespeare, however, is said to have been both his godfather and his father. " Now, Sir William would sometimes, when he was a-pleasant over a glass of wine, with his most intimate friends, say that it seemed to him that he wrote with the very spirit that Shakespeare wrote with, and was contented enough to be thought his son." Mrs. D'Avenant was a landlady of very light report; but " a very beautiful woman, and of a very good wit, and of conversation extremely agreeable; " and her husband was " a very grave and discreet citizen," who looked better after his guests than the conduct of his wife. The tradition which Aubrey preserves does not rest solely, however, on his authority. " That notion," said Pope to Spence, " of Sir William D'Avenant being more than a poetical child only of Shakespeare, was common in town; and Sir William himself seemed fond of having it taken for truth."

Dates, which upset so many traditions, are in favor of the D'Avenant legend. The future poet laureate and author of " Gondibert ' was baptized in St. Martin's Church, Oxford, on the 3d of March, 1605–6, and Shakespeare died on the 23d of April, 1616. The latter's route from London to Oxford was by way of Uxbridge (famous for a treaty to no good purpose), by Beaconsfield (the birthplace and property of Waller) on to East Wickham, Stokingchurch, Thetisford, Whatley, and Oxford. At Oxford he passed a night: he would then go on by the way of Woodstock, Enstone, and Shipstone, over the Avon, by Clopton's bridge, to his native Stratford. On his right lay Charlecote, on his left the Collegiate church of Stratford, while before him was Henley Strutt (leading to Henley in Arden), the meadows about Ingon, his mother's property, the woods of Welcombe, and the little hamlet or village of Shottery.

Cuba. This is not a Spanish word, though it sounds and looks like one. We have it on the authority of the U. S. Board on Geographic Names that it is the name by which the island was known to the Lucayan Indians who were with Columbus when he first saw it; but what the word conveyed to them does not seem to be known nowadays.

One of the villages or " cities " on the island was called by them " Cubanacan," and Columbus, still supposing himself to be on the coast of Asia, imagined from the similarity of the names that this must be a city of " Kublai Khan," the Tartar sovereign celebrated by Marco Polo.

The survival of this original name at this date is the more remarkable, as the island has been baptized and rebaptized many

times since its European discovery. Columbus first called it
Juana, in honor of Prince John, the son of Ferdinand and
Isabella. After Ferdinand's death it was called, in his memory,
Ferdinandina. Subsequently this name was changed to Santiago,
after St. James, the patron saint of Spain; and still later it was
named Ave Maria, in honor of the Virgin Mary.

Cuckoo. Is it owing to the simpler, kindlier, purer atmosphere of democracy that the American cuckoo is superior to his
kin across the sea, especially his British kin? Mr. Alexander H.
Japp, the historiographer of the foreign bird (" Our Common
Cuckoo," London, 1900), concedes the fact, but is at some pains
to discover other reasons.

To begin with, in England the males greatly outnumber the
females. Some naturalists put the proportions at twenty to one.
This saps all pretence of virtue. The domesticities count for as
much among the citizens of the air as among us poor plumeless
ephemerals.

Look at the bullfinch, for example. He is the most exem-
plary of birds, true to his wife, tender to his children, loyal
even to a human friend. Now, the bullfinch mates for life.
The cuckoo has not the decency to stick to his wife for even a
season. Nor does she exact it. She is worse than he. She
spends the spring and summer in flirting with a succession of
males, laying eggs with indecent and reckless frequency from the
middle of April to the middle of June.

A lady bullfinch, knowing that she will have to feed and
nurse her offspring, takes care that they shall not number more
than four or five.

A lady cuckoo—of course the term "lady" is here used in
merest irony—a she cuckoo, then, doesn't care. Not even will she
go to the trouble of building a nest. She simply lays an egg
under a hedge, and then flies with it in her mouth to the first
nest that comes handy. It may be a wren's nest; it may be a
hedge-sparrow's. She has no choice.

> The hedge-sparrow fed the cuckoo so long
> That it had its head bit off by its young.
>
> SHAKESPEARE.

From parentage so careless and so disreputable, what indeed
could one expect in the progeny? But the young cuckoo is interesting, even if he be wicked. As soon as he is out of his shell, the
naked, feeble, sprawling youngster proceeds to shoulder his foster-
brethren, hatched and unhatched, out of the home that is legitimately theirs. Nature, the jade, comes to his assistance. Not
only has she given the fledgling great strength of shoulder and
wing-stump, but she hollows out his back behind the shoulder,
forming a sort of shovel that handily lifts up whatever it once

succeeds in getting under. This hollow disappears when the bird is about twelve days old and has secured the nest all to itself. Is it not plain that nature arms the ingrate with full resources to exercise its instinct of self-preservation? But why has not the same agency developed among birds thus liable to be duped some counteracting instinct? Mr. Romanes has come forward with a very plausible suggestion.

The deposition of a parasitic egg is comparatively a rare event in the history of most birds, and, therefore, is unlikely to prompt the development of a special instinct to meet it.

Whatever the explanation, the fact remains that the mother acquiesces in the murder of her legitimate brood, and lavishes her affection upon the blood-stained usurper. A wren, so we are told, will frequently starve herself to overfeed her monstrous foster-child.

A still more startling accusation is sometimes brought against the female cuckoo. It is charged that she has the cunning, and eke the ability, to change the color of her own egg in mimicry of those among whom she purposes to deposit it. In fairness it must be allowed, however, that this charge has not been proved.

Not only Mr. Japp, but other ornithologists, concede that the American cuckoos are less depraved than the English. They build a rough nest, lay four or five eggs, and tend their offspring until full fledged. Nevertheless, a lurking suspicion is insinuated by the British authorities, that, whenever the American cuckoo exceeds the fifth egg in a season, she distributes the supernumeraries in her neighbor's nests, after the bad old transatlantic fashion.

Says Mr. Japp: "Evidence accumulates year by year to prove that the character of the American cuckoo, if once as good as painted, is deteriorating from the high standard ornithologists of old were found to give it. They are no longer the 'unqualifiedly well-behaved parents' of Dr. Bowdler Sharpe, nor do they 'faithfully incubate all their delicate sea-green eggs,' as Professor A. Newton has it."

Thus has the decline from the Jeffersonian simplicity of our forefathers influenced even the fowls of the air.

The reckless and erratic habits of the light-hearted rover have enveloped him in an atmosphere of romance. Even phlegmatic rustics have always appreciated him. In England in the good old days he used to be honored as the incarnate spirit of song among the Penates of every rural homestead. The cuckoo clock, with its eternal and monotonous chime, stood enshrined in the passage or at the bottom of the stairs. No sooner had he made his April appearance than all the village urchins were imitating his note, which indeed needs nothing of the vocal versatility of the mocking-bird. For, as Paganini made his reputation on a single string, so the character of the cuckoo's performance is severe simplicity. That he is the most self-satisfied of all musicians is self-evident. But the odd thing is that, as he pleases himself, so he always holds his audience spellbound. Even when he breaks into a concert of real singers, the first impulse to turn him out melts into welcome from his fellow-choristers.

Cumberland's Bowlder Stone, a notable landmark on Drummossie Moor in Scotland. This is the rock on which William Augustus—Duke of Cumberland and generalissimo of the forces of his father, George III—ate his breakfast on the morning of April 16, 1746. Here also, later in the day, the duel between tartan and scarlet, claymore and cannon, being over and the Jacobite cause in Great Britain forever ruined, the victorious duke is said to have written an order to give no quarter upon a certain playing card,—the nine of diamonds,—hence called the Curse of Scotland. (See WALSH, *Handy-book of Literary Curiosities, s.v.*). The story is not accepted by historians, but it still survives locally. It is extremely unlikely indeed that the idea of giving quarter to bare-legged caterans ever entered the head of English soldier or general. Hence there was no necessity for any precise order to slay and spare not. A characteristic medal struck in honor of the royalist victory presents the duke as a young man of twenty-five, plump, cheerful, and jaunty, mounted on horseback. Beneath him the artist has represented a ragged Highlander prostrate among his own inhospitable mountains, his claymore shattered, his buckler—inaccurately shaped, by the way—broken. Under this design is the legend

> Thus to expire be still the rebel's fate
> While endless honors on brave William wait.

For a while the soldier prince was the most popular man in England; but the trial and execution of the Jacobite lords brought about a revulsion of feeling. The London inns were crowded with prisoners, and people made parties of pleasure to hear their trial. Everywhere the Scotch cried out loudly against the duke for his severities in the Highlands. It would seem also that he exerted his influence in turning the king's mind from mercy toward Lord Kilmarnock. Popular feeling at last exploded in the jest which has labelled him forever. It was proposed in the city of London to present him with the freedom of some company, when one of the aldermen said aloud, "Then let it be the Butchers'." From that day he was dubbed by his enemies "The Butcher of Culloden."

Cycling. Strictly speaking, no one invented the bicycle or the tricycle. Each is the developed result of a long series of mechanical devices for the acceleration of human speed. Crude anticipations of both occur in the bass-reliefs of Egypt and Babylon and the frescoes of Pompeii. Sporadic inventions in the same line are recorded in the seventeenth and eighteenth centuries. It was not until the beginning of the nineteenth century that any devices of this sort came into general use. Nevertheless the more important pioneers deserve a flying notice.

In August, 1665, John Evelyn notes in his diary, that he had called at Durdans near Epsom, and found there Dr. Wilkins, Sir William Petty, and Mr. Hooke, "contriving chariots, new rigging for ships, a wheele for one to run races in, and other mechanical inventions; perhaps three such persons together were not to be found elsewhere in Europe, for parts and ingenuity." We are left to conjecture what that "wheele" may have been, yet the vague description would indicate some primitive form of bicycle.

The "célérifère" proposed by a Frenchman, M. de Sivrac, in 1690, seems to have differed little from the "velocipede" invented nearly a century later by Blanchard and Magurier and described in the *Journal de Paris* (July 27, 1779). Both were clumsy four-wheel affairs, and both were propelled by the rider, seated astride of the bar and pushing with his feet against the ground.

The draisine was a signal improvement, and appears to have been the first of all self-propelled machines on two wheels. Its invention is attributed to Baron Karl Drais von Sauerbronn (1785–1851), and it is fully described in his "Abbildung and Beschreibung seiner neu erfundenen Laufmaschine," Nuremberg, 1817. But probably the first allusion to its existence is found in a letter written by Bettina von Arnim (Goethe's Bettina) to her brother. This letter is not dated, but internal evidence shows that it was written in 1802 or 1803. In it Bettina makes a passing allusion to Herr von Drais and his experiments with a draisine, "a kind of seat with wheels, which Herr von Drais moves along with his hands and feet." It consisted of a wooden bar connecting two wheels, one in front of the other, the front wheel being so pivoted on the frame that it could be turned sideways by a handle, that in this way steered the machine. In England the draisine achieved a great though temporary vogue under various names, the most popular of which were "hobby-horse" and "dandy-horse." The nearest approach to modern nomenclature was made in such newly coined words as "bicipede" and "tricipede," which had some slight vogue about 1819. "Bicycle," it may here be interpolated, was a coinage of the year 1867.

Dandy-horses figure in the caricatures of the early nineteenth century. The dandies who rode them were laughed at as riding in their carriages and walking in the mud at the same time. The rider bestrode the bar. Grasping the steering handles and leaning well forward against the padded cushion, he propelled the machine by practically running along the ground while resting his weight on the seat and cushion. The chief difficulty, as with the modern bicycle, was found in the act of balancing. Once proficiency in this respect had been attained, the rider when going down hill could put up his feet and "coast," exactly as the bicycler now does. Going up hill was quite a different story. The machine was heavy and had to be pushed up. Small stones and gravel easily imbedded themselves into the front wheel, and then the rider was liable to go flying "over the handles," with his machine executing a somersault after him.

The essential missing link between the dandy-horse and the modern cycle was the crank action. The invention of this device is usually credited to either Pierre or Ernest Michaux or both (see BICYCLE). The Scotch, however, put forth a prior claim for a blacksmith in Dumfries named Kirkpatrick Macmillan. In the year 1840, it appears, he affixed cranks to the dandy-horse, and these cranks were in turn connected to long levers which acted upon the rear wheel. On this machine he rode from Keir, in the county of Dumfries, to Glasgow, a distance of 70 miles, and caused such a commotion in the latter city that the police arrested him as a public nuisance. Nor was he released until he had promised to abstain from all future exhibitions of the kind in Glasgow. Macmillan died in 1878, and it was not until 1893 that his fame as a pioneer was established by his countrymen.

None the less, the fact remains that the first bicycle seen in London arrived from Paris about 1868. It was introduced under the name of "velocipede," but it established itself in popular favor as a "bone-shaker" before the more dignified title of bicycle was seized upon by its admirers.

The motor cycle came in at a bad time. It was caught between the bicycle boom on one hand and the automobile boom on the other and got squeezed by both. It partakes a little of both and not a great deal of either. The principal objection to it has been that it is neither fish, flesh, nor fowl. It necessitates the care of an engine just as an automobile does, but does not give you as comfortable a seat nor a chance to take others with you. Again, it lacks the lightness which is a bicycle's chief distinction. You cannot comfortably lift it over fences or carry it up and down stairs.

D.

Dahlia. In 1784 Vincent Cervantes, director of the Botanical Garden in the city of Mexico, sent to Cavanilles, director of the Botanical Garden in Madrid, a plant hitherto unknown to botanists. It was tall, thin, with nodding little flowers, each only a yellow central disk surrounded by five or six red or orange petals. The Madrid director called it "dahlia," in honor of Dr. Dahl, a Swedish botanist recently deceased. In Germany it happened there was another flower of that name. So, when the newcomer reached there, Wildenow rechristened it "giorgina," after a Russian explorer named Georgi, a name which it retained (in Germany only) until very recent years. The dahlia was first introduced into Britain from Spain by the Marchioness of Bute in 1789.

Botanists and gardeners soon noticed the extraordinary facility with which the color of the flowers could be varied, and their interest increased when the first double dahlia was produced in 1808. Then arose a keen rivalry among German and English florists in the production of new varieties of form and color. English florists took the lead in the development of the dahlia until about 1835, after which they were hard pressed by the Germans. In 1836 one of the latter exhibited 200 varieties, mostly of his own production.

Dam. On May 10, 1904, Congress at Washington authorized the construction, at a cost of $5,000,000, of an irrigation dam at Belle Fourche, in South Dakota, which was expected to be the largest earth embankment in the world. This dike, which closes the lowest depressions in the rim of a natural basin, is 6200 feet long, 20 feet wide on top, and 115 feet high in the highest place.

The inside face of this structure, which has a slope of 2 to 1, is protected from wave and ice action by 2 feet of screened gravel, on which are placed concrete blocks, each 4 by 6 feet and 8 inches thick. The cubical contents of this dike will be 42,700,000 cubic feet, or about half of the famous pyramid of Cheops. The reservoir created by this dam will cover about 9000 acres, and will be the largest lake in the State.

Before its completion, however (so recently as June, 1911), Congress appropriated the sum of $6,000,000 for the construction of a rival in Idaho, which is to be the highest dam in the world. It is at a point in Boise River canyon called Arrow Rock. A construction camp for the maintenance of between 600 and

1000 men was established, with the expectation that the work would be finished within 6 years. The dam will impound flood waters to irrigate the 300,000 acres of land in the Payette-Boise project.

The Boise River runs wide at Arrow Rock and the formation of rock is that of sandstone. Boring tests made show that there is about 90 feet to bed-rock where the structure is to be anchored. The dam is to be constructed of concrete, into which there will be incorporated, to the extent of 25 per cent. of the total masonry, hand-placed rock in pieces weighing from 25 to 200 pounds.

While the Arrow Rock dam when completed will be the largest built by the reclamation service and will bear the distinction of being the highest in the world, its storage capacity falls below other big dams, owing to the fact that as favorable a site could not be found on the Boise River as at the other points in the United States where dams have been built by the service.

Dance. The longest dance known to authentic history is that of William Kemp, who, at the age of 17 and in the reign of Queen Elizabeth, danced from his native village to London, where he educated himself and became an actor. Perhaps he was not a good actor, for he presently reverted to the morris. He danced all the way from London to Norwich, and wrote a pamphlet about it—"Kemp's Nine Daies' Wonder, performed in a daunce from London to Norwich. Containing the pleasures, paines and kind entertainment of William Kemp, betweene London and that Citty, in his late Morrice." He seems to have encountered more pleasures than " paines." Gentle and simple, all the way, were very cordial. The gentle entertained him in their mansions by night. The simple danced with him by day. In Sudbury " there came a dusty tall fellow, a butcher by his profession, that would in a Morrice keep me company to Bury. I gave him thankes, and forward wee did set; but ere ever wee had measur'd halfe a mile of our way he gave me over in the plain field, protesting he would not hold out with me; for indeed my pace in dauncing is not ordinary. As he and I were parting, a lusty country lasse, being among the people, cal'd him faint hearted lout, saying: ' If I had begun to daunce I would have held out one myle, though it had cost my life.' At which words many laughed. ' Nay.' saith she, ' if the dauncer will lend me a leash of his belles I'le venter to treade one myle with him myself.' I lookt upon her, saw mirth in her eies, heard boldness in her words and beheld her ready to tucke up her russat petti-coate; and I fitted her with bels. which she merrily taking, gar-nisht her thicke short legs, and with a smooth brow had the tabur begin. The drum strucke, forward marcht I with my merry

Mayde Marian, who shook her stout sides, and footed it merrily to Melford, being a long myle. There parting with her (besides her skinfull of drinke), and English crowne to buy more drinke; for, good wench, she was in pittious heate; my kindness she requited with dropping a dozen good courtsies, and bidding God blesse the dauncer. I bade her adieu; and to give her her due, she had a good eare, daunst truly, and wee parted friends." Kemp, you perceive, wrote as well as he danced. One wishes he had danced less and written more.

A longer dance, but one that it were base flattery to call historical, is a dance recorded in the semifabulous chronicles of William of Malmesbury, who quotes as his authority a formal deed, " relating the particulars and attesting the truth," which was drawn up and subscribed by Bishop Peregrine, the successor of Hubert. " I, Ethelbert, a sinner, will give a true relation of what happened to me on the day before Christmas, A.D. 1012, in a certain village, where there was a church, dedicated to St. Magnus, the martyr, that all men may know the danger of disobeying the commands of a priest. Fifteen young women, and eighteen young men, of which I was one, were dancing and singing in the church-yard, when one Robert, a priest, was performing mass in the church; who sent us a civil message, entreating us to desist from our diversion, because we disturbed his devotion by our noise. But we impiously disregarded his request: upon which the holy man, inflamed with anger, prayed to God and St. Magnus, that we might continue dancing and singing a whole year without intermission. His prayers were heard. A young man, the son of a priest, named John, took his sister, who was singing with us, by the hand, and her arm dropped from her body without one drop of blood following; but, notwithstanding this disaster, she continued to dance and sing with us a whole year. During all that time we felt no inconveniency from rain, cold, heat, hunger, thirst, or weariness; and neither our shoes nor our clothes wore out. Whenever it began to rain, a magnificent house was erected over us, by the power of the Almighty. By our continual dancing we wore the earth so much, that, by degrees, we sunk into it up to the knees, and at length up to the middle. When the year was ended, Bishop Hubert came to the place, dissolved the invisible ties by which our hands had been so long united, absolved us, and reconciled us to St. Magnus. The priest's daughter, who had lost her arm, and other two of the young women, died away immediately; but all the rest fell into a profound sleep, in which they continued three days and three nights: after which they arose, and went up and down the world."

Probably the longest recorded dance of modern times is one thus noted in *Le Matin* of Paris, in October, 1911:

An extraordinary waltzing match in which eight couples competed took place at Allessandria, Piedmont, Italy.

The dancers commenced at 10 o'clock in the evening of the 25th instant and did not cease until they were compelled to do so from exhaustion.

At midday on the 26th, when there remained only two couples in the contest, the jury ordered the termination of the match, which had lasted fourteen hours; and Legaldi, who was adjudged champion, fainted immediately afterward.

Dane Holes. Curious well-like excavations, popularly supposed to date from the Danish conquest of England, are still extant in the counties of Kent and Sussex. Always about 3 feet in diameter, they are rarely less than 60 feet in depth. The means of ingress and egress must have been provided by rude ladders or hide ropes.

Among the explanations offered by archæologists is that they were places of refuge, that they were connected with some esoteric worship, that they were dug for the extraction of chalk and flint, or that originally they were used as granaries. They are found close together in groups, and are thus reminiscent of the custom among various early tribes of clustering in restricted areas.

Dark Days. In the year 358, just before the earthquake of Nicomedia, the darkness was very dense from two to three hours. Two years afterward, in all the provinces of the Roman empire, there was obscurity from early dawn to noon. The stars were visible, and its duration precludes the idea of a solar eclipse. At the return of light, the sun appeared first in a crescent form, then half its face was seen, and was gradually restored to its whole visible disk.

In 409 the stars were seen by day at Rome. About 536 the sun was obscured for fourteen months, so that very little of his light was seen. In 567 such darkness prevailed from 3 P.M. till night that nothing could be seen. In 626, half the sun's disk was obscured for eight months. In 733 he was again darkened, and people were generally terrified.

In 934 Portugal was in darkness for two months, the sun having lost its brightness. The heavens were then opened in fissures by strong flashes of lightning, when there was suddenly bright sunlight. On September 21, 1091, the sun was darkened for three hours. On February 28, 1206, for six hours complete darkness turned the day into night. In 1241, on Michaelmas day, the stars were visible at 3 P.M. In 1547, April 23–25, three days, the sun was so obscured that many stars were visible at once. Thus says Humboldt in " Cosmos."

If we come nearer to our own time, to May 19, 1790, history and tradition assert the occurrence of a remarkable day prevailing over New England, and to some extent in some other places. Darkness came on between 10 and 11 A.M., and continued until midnight, growing gradually denser and denser, even till eleven at night. Candles and lamps were lighted for the people to see to dine and to perform work about the house. These became requisite before twelve o'clock, M. In the evening, so dense was it, that farmers could scarcely, even with the aid of a lantern, grope their way to the barn to take care of the cattle. The birds retired to their roosts at 11 A.M., and the day was converted into night.

Date. Mahometan tradition asserts that, when Adam was driven from Paradise, he was allowed to take with him three things,—a myrtle because it bore the loveliest and most odorous of flowers, a wheat ear because it yielded the most nourishment, and a date because it was the most glorious fruit of the earth. This date from Paradise was, in some marvellous way, brought to the Hejaz; thence have come all the date-palms in the world, and Allah destined it to be the food for all the true believers, who shall conquer every country where the date-palm grows. The Jews and the Arabs, again, looked upon this tree as a mystical allegory of human beings, for, like them, it dies when its head (the summit) is cut off, and when a limb (branch) is once cut off it does not grow again.

Those who know can understand the mysterious language of the branches on days when there is no wind, when whispers of present and future events are communicated by the tree. Abraham of old, so the rabbis say, understood the language of the palm.

The date-palm is indeed a tree of glory and of mystery. Its fecundity, rivalled only by the banana and the bread-fruit, makes it one of the most valuable food-stuffs known to the countries where its fruit will ripen. Each tree produces from 8 to 10 bunches of fruit, and the total yield, by weight, of a palm in full bearing varies from 100 to 400 pounds a year. An acre of land under dates will feed more people than under any other known crop except plantain.

But the fruit itself by no means exhausts the economic value of the date-palm. The bark yields a fibre which is employed for ropes, matting baskets, and sacks. The leaves serve to thatch the Berber's hut and to make little cases for packing the fruit. The footstalks boil the family kettle, or yabbah, and supply fencing for the cottage garden. The timber takes a good polish for cabinet work, or, cut into lengths, supplies the ordinary post of the North African circular hut. The unripe dates can be boiled down for vinegar. The ripe fruit, besides being eaten dry, may be made into spirits or pressed fresh for an agreeable syrup. Finally, the tree can be tapped for toddy, as is done in Algeria with centenarian palms as soon as they attain their hundredth birthday. A gallon of toddy a day can be drawn off for a whole fortnight; after that, the drain is injurious.

Day. What is a day? Does it include all the twenty-four hours from midnight to midnight, or only the hours from sunrise to sunset? A confusion of terminology on this score has sometimes introduced a confusion of thought. The word day is frequently used as merely the antithesis to night. Even the law distinguishes between a *dies naturalis,* or natural day, and a *dies artificialis,* or artificial day.

Astronomers also have their various days: the absolute solar day, ranging from about half a minute under to the same amount over 24 hours at different times of the year; the mean solar day, being our common day of 24 hours; the lunar day of nearly 25 hours, and the sidereal day of about 4 seconds short of 24 hours.

To revert to the natural day. Not everywhere nor everywhen does it include twenty-four hours if you measure the day from sunrise to sunrise. As you approach either the north or the south pole, strange phenomena occur. For example: At Wanderbus, in Norway, the day lasts from May 21 to July 22 without interruption; and at Spitzbergen, the longest day contains three and a half months.

Even if you remain within the radius where the sun rises and sets punctually every twenty-four hours, nevertheless the limit of the artificial day—*i.e.,* the period of light—varies according to latitude. Thus, at Tornea, in Finland, the longest day has twenty-one hours and a half, and the shortest two and a half, of light.

At St. Petersburg and Tobolsk, the longest has nineteen and the shortest five hours.

At Stockholm and Upsala, the longest day has eighteen and a half hours. At Hamburg, Danzig, and Stettin, the longest day has seventeen hours, and the shortest seven.

At Berlin and London, the longest day has sixteen and a half hours, and the shortest about eight.

What time does the day begin? This time has been fixed arbitrarily by different people. The Jews, Chaldeans, and Babylonians began the day at sunrise, the Athenians at sunset, the

Umbri in Italy at noon, the Egyptians and Romans at midnight. The United States, England, and most of the European countries follow the Roman custom: the day commences as soon as the clock has struck midnight of the preceding day.

In our latitude, when does the longest day occur? And the shortest? Every school-boy will answer, if he remembers his text-book, June 21 and December 21, respectively. Yet the date is not absolutely and unalterably fixed. December 22, for example, was the shortest day of the year 1911. The *Evening Sun* for that date supplied a simple and lucid explanation:

"To-day is the shortest day for the northern half of the earth that the year 1911 supplies. The sun turned up at 7:17 o'clock this morning and will go off duty at 4:30 o'clock this afternoon, giving us just nine hours and thirteen minutes of its services.

"This is all because of the winter solstice. It is the time when the sun is furthest south on its annual slant over the tropic of capricorn, making its maximum declination to the axis of the earth, a figure placed by the scientists at 23.465 deg.

"This solstice usually falls on December 21, making that the shortest day. The departure from that convention this year is due to the fact that the astronomical year is longer than the calendar year. Our sphere makes one complete circuit around the sun in 365.2422 days, and this difference of a quarter of a day a year is the excuse for the appearance of February 29 every fourth year. As 1912 is a leap year the difference between astronomical and calendar time is now almost at a maximum. This disparity of about twenty-three hours makes the shortest day fall on Dec. 22 instead of Dec. 21.

"All over the world this date marks a turning point in the calendar, though in every case it is not the shortest day. South of the equator it is quite the contrary, for the people there are enjoying their longest day. At the South Pole it is high noon of the six-month day, and at the North Pole it is midnight of the 'great night.'"

Days of the Week. Friday (*q.v.*) is not the only day that has been blacklisted by superstition. Unlucky days among the Mahometan Malays of Cochin-China are the third day of the new moon, being that on which Adam was expelled from Paradise; the fifth, when the whale swallowed Jonah; the sixteenth, when Joseph was put into the well; the twenty-fourth, when Zachariah was murdered; and the twenty-fifth, when Mahomet lost his front teeth.

Some of the English superstitions connected with the various days of the week have been commemorated in English folk-lore rhymes as follows:

Sunday's child ne'er lacks in place;
Monday's child is fair in the face;
Tuesday's child is full of grace;
Wednesday's child is sour and sad;
Thursday's child is loving and glad;
Friday's child is loving and giving;
And Saturday's child shall work for its living.

Sneeze on a Monday you sneeze for danger;
Sneeze on a Tuesday you kiss a stranger;
Sneeze on a Wednesday you sneeze for a letter;
Sneeze on a Thursday for something better;
Sneeze on a Friday you sneeze to your sorrow;
Sneeze on a Saturday your sweetheart to-morrow;
Sneeze on a Sunday your safety seek,
The devil will chase you the whole of the week.

Cut your nails Monday you cut them for news;
Cut them on Tuesday a pair of new shoes;
Cut them on Wednesday, you cut them for health;
Cut them on Thursday 'twill add to your wealth;
Cut them on Friday you cut them for wo;
Cut them on Saturday a journey you'll go;
Cut them on Sunday you cut them for evil,
For all the week long you'll be ruled by the devil.

Monday for wealth,
Tuesday for health,
Wednesday the best of all,
Thursday for crosses,
Friday for losses,
Saturday no luck at all.

Born of a Monday, fair in face;
Born of a Tuesday, full of God's grace;
Born of a Wednesday, merry and glad;
Born of a Thursday, sour and sad;
Born of a Friday, godly given;
Born of a Saturday, work for your living;
Born of a Sunday, never shall want;
So there's the week, and the end on't.

Dead-letter Office. A division of the United States Post-office department under control of the first assistant postmaster-general at Washington, to which letters and packages unclaimed or undeliverable are sent from local post-offices. The articles that accumulate in this *de facto* museum of curiosities almost defy belief. Yet the dead-letter clerks are never astonished at anything. When they open a package, it is nothing unusual for them to find a horned toad, a centipede, a chameleon, a baby alligator, a stuffed gopher, a petrified frog, an opium pipe, spirit photographs, coffin plates, poker chips, or a set of false teeth.

Anent the latter, a story is current in the department. An

old man rushed up to the clerk in charge and claimed a set of false teeth locked up in a glass case.

"Why do you think they are yours?" asked the curator.

"Because I would know them anywhere," said the old man. "I bought them myself ten years ago, and used them until they were lost in the mails when I sent them to the city to be mended."

The teeth were taken out of the case; the claimant popped them into his mouth; and, lo! they fitted. A few minutes later, after subscribing to certain formalities, he walked out of the place perfectly happy.

Poisonous animals, living as well as dead, are frequently received at the office. Visitors to Arizona generally consider it the proper thing to send home a few horned toads as typical souvenirs from the regions explored. Sometimes a live Gila monster is forwarded at second-class rates. A living rattlesnake with nine rattles which went astray in the mails now reposes in a glass jar of alcohol labelled—"From Florida." "But the most alarming parcel to date," says Rene Bache in the *Associated Sunday Magazines* for December 13, 1908, "proved to contain seventeen small snakes, all squirming and wriggly; one of which, by the way, an adder spotted in yellow and black, made its escape, and crawled out from under a desk a day or two later, to the great alarm of the women clerks."

Sometimes people refuse to accept letters or parcels addressed to them. All of them find their way at last to the Dead-letter office. Of these is an ugly cloth-covered doll, a life-size "nigger" baby in looks, which represents the effort of a discarded suitor to get even with the lady in the case. On the day of her marriage with another man, he mailed the doll to her; but she would have none of it, and the letter-carrier was requested to take it away again.

Awhile ago much trouble was made by rats which ate the contents of packages stored in the Dead-letter Office. All parcels that go astray in the mails are stuck away in big pigeon-holes, a circumstance that offered a fine opportunity to the predatory rodents. They were much addicted to cutting up cotton cloth and other dress fabrics for their nests; but what they seemed to enjoy most was wedding cake (pieces of which are frequently found in lost packages), and the bran stuffing of dolls and pin-cushions. The mischief was finally done away with by the help of ferrets.

At the end of one year all the accumulated merchandise is sold at auction, the packages being opened and their contents made up into fresh parcels, for the sake of condensation. A catalogue describing the parcels by number, and giving brief account of what is in them, is printed, care being taken to avoid even the slightest misrepresentation. Thus, for example, " cheap jewelry " figures frequently in the list.

For more than fifty years this annual sale of " dead-letter " matter has been carried on by the United States government. Twelve million letters and parcels are opened, examined, and recorded each year, an average of from 40,000 to 50,000 a day. These figures do not take into consideration an average of 11,000,000 postal-cards which go astray every twelve months.

To carry out the rules of the Post-office Department regarding unclaimed articles the Dead-letter Office records the address and contents of parcels of third-class matter of apparent value, and of fourth-class matter and letters containing articles of merchandise. When such articles cannot be delivered or restored to the sender, they are filed for a period of one year from the date of recording, except such as are unaddressed, which are held not less than six months. All articles that remain unclaimed at the expiration of the time prescribed are then prepared for sale at public auction in such manner as not to destroy their identity.

Dead letters containing valuable enclosures are recorded in the Dead-letter Office, and, when they cannot be delivered to the party addressed nor to the writer, the contents are sold and a careful account is kept of the amount realized in each case, which is subject to reclamation by either the party addressed or the sender for four years from the recording. When matter containing money cannot be delivered to the person addressed or returned to the sender, it is held three months, at the end of which time the amount of money is entered upon the letter or other matter accompanying the cash, and upon the records. The money is delivered to the third assistant postmaster-general, whose receipt therefor is filed. He then deposits all such moneys in the treasury to the credit of the postal revenues. All currency found in dead letters or other matter is subject to reclamation within four years from the recording by the department.

But not all the packages received at the Dead-letter Office find their way into the annual scrap-heap. Out of the 7,000,000 letters that go astray in this way, a large proportion are returned to the sender or delivered to the addresses. Of course the sender may generally be determined by the simple process of opening the letter. But first every effort is made to correct a mistaken or decipher an illegible address. Famous for her feats as a " blind reader " is a certain woman employee. Her performances in this line are nothing short of marvellous. Once in awhile it happens that somebody mails a cryptogram for a joke, affording a problem of much difficulty. Mr. Bache instances a letter that bore in lieu of superscription the following lines:

> There is a young man in Brooklyn,
>   Far away to the sea,—
> B. O. B. Bob, we call him.
>   Oh, letter carrier, find him for me!

There were in addition only the words " St. Marks Ave." in one corner. It might have seemed a hopeless puzzle; but not so to the "blind reader," who looked up St. Marks Ave. in a Brooklyn directory, and sent a circular to every person named Robert living there. As a result, the right one applied for the letter and got it.

The British have their Dead-letter department as well as the Americans. Some of the most extraordinary perversions of addresses which have been detected by this process have been preserved by the department in a book that is shown to visitors. One would not at first sight recognize that " Santlings, Hilewite," was intended for " St. Helen's, Isle of Wight," or that " Haselfeach in no famtshere " meant " Hazelbeach, Northamptonshire." Metropolitan places come in for their share of distortion. Holborn Viaduct is consolidated into " Obanvidock," and Mile End appears as " Mailand." Either an excess of loyalty or some haziness as to the precise division of labor between the sovereign and her ministers must have prompted the person who addressed a letter " to the Sectery of Wore, Chesley Osbitile, London, Queen Victoria," while the importance of preserving a broad distinction between urban and rural districts may perhaps have animated Lord Northbrook's correspondent, who addressed his lordship as " Lordnorthbrook, Stroton House, Country." Of course there are addresses which are absolutely hopeless.

Dead Sea, an inland lake on the southeastern borders of Palestine, occupying a part of the deepest chasm on the surface of the earth, " caused," says the Encyclopædia Britannica, " after the end of the Eocene period by the earth movement which resulted in the raising of the whole region out of the sea." The earliest references to the Dead Sea or its basin are in the biblical narratives of Lot and Abraham, who call it the Salt Sea, from its most obvious peculiarity; its waters containing about 25 per cent. of salts. As the sea has no outlet, this percentage increases with the years. To the quantity of solid matter suspended in its waters the Dead Sea owes, besides its saltness, its buoyancy and its poisonous properties. The human body floats on the surface without exertion: indeed it is practically impossible for it to sink. But the saline incrustations which form on the surface of the skin are a source of much inconvenience to the bather after he emerges, for it may take a couple of days to scrape them off.

Perhaps a better idea of the density of the water of this inland sea may be realized from the following statistics: In a ton of water from the Caspian Sea there are eleven pounds of salt; in the Baltic, eighteen pounds; in the Black Sea, twenty-six pounds; in the Atlantic thirty-one pounds; in the English Channel, seventy-two pounds; in the Mediterranean, eighty-five pounds; in the Red Sea, ninety-three pounds, and in the Dead Sea, 187 pounds.

No natural feature of the world has been more maligned than the Dead Sea. There are no sea-birds there, to be sure, because there are no fish for them to prey on. Owing principally to the large proportion of chloride and bromide of magnesia, fish cannot live in its waters. The absence of sea-fowl has led to the story that no bird could fly across this sea and live. The scanty rainfall makes vegetation precarious; hence the story that no plant can live on the accursed soil. Josephus advanced the absurd theory that Sodom and Gomorrah had been submerged under the waters of the lake. But the writer of Genesis xix makes no reference to an inundation as causing the destruction of those cities. Rather he had in mind a rain of fire and brimstone from heaven.

There is no passage in the canonical books of the Bible distinctly connecting the Dead Sea with Sodom and Gomorrah, but popular tradition and irresponsible evangelical teachings have deeply impressed upon the average human mind the belief that its bed marks the spot where once stood the cities of the plains destroyed by Divine wrath. In Palestine the modern name for the sea is Bahr Lut, or Sea of Lot. A pillar of rock salt in the Jebel Usted range is to-day pointed out as Lot's wife (q.v.). Hence a number of exaggerations sprang up and gathered strength from century to century until even the conservative mind protested against them. Dr. Philip Schaff, professor in the Presbyterian Theological Seminary at New York, was a man of undoubted probity and piety. In his travels published in 1877, he told the simple truth regarding the pillar of salt, so far as its physical origin and characteristics are concerned, and left his reader to draw the natural inference as to its relation to the myth. Finally Dean Stanley, of Westminster, visiting the country and thoroughly exploring it, conceded that the physical features of the Dead Sea and its shores suggested the myths and legends, and he sums up the whole as follows: " A great mass of legends and exaggerations, partly the cause and partly the result of the old belief that the cities were buried under the Dead Sea, has been gradually removed in recent years."

Death, Clock of. The popular name for the first astronomical clock in England, made for Henry VIII in 1540, by Nicholas Cratzer, a German who came over to London by invitation of Cardinal Wolsey. It is now in Hampton Court Palace. It tells the hour, the month, the day of the month, the position of the sun, the number of days that have elapsed since the beginning of the year, the phases of the moon and its age, the hour at which it crosses the meridian, and the time of high water at London Bridge. The winding of the cumbrous mechanism occupies half an hour every week. The weights descend to a depth of over 60 feet.

The legend which has given to the clock its present name tells that when Anne of Denmark, queen of James I, died at Hampton Court, the clock, which was striking 4 at the moment, immediately stopped. Since then, the legend continues, it has always stopped at the death of any one who had been long resident within the palace.

A clock standing in the court-yard of the palace at Versailles is known as L'horloge de la Mort des Roi,—"the Clock of the King's Death." It contains no works, but consists merely of a face in the form of a sun, surrounded by rays. On the death of a king the hand was set to the moment of his demise and remained unaltered till his successor had joined him in the grave. The custom originated under Louis XIII, and continued until the revolution. It was revived on the death of Louis XVIII and the land continues to this day fixed on the precise moment of that monarch's death.

In 1889 a curious story, possibly a newspaper fake, made the rounds of the American press. It appears thus in the Philadelphia *Ledger:*

A wonderful old clock, said to have been made in England nearly 200 years ago and to have belonged to the Rev. Dr. William Tennent, a Presbyterian minister, who died in 1777, was found recently in an old farm-house near Freehold, N. J. It is related that during the time that Dr. Tennent was in his famous trance the clock, for some mysterious reason, refused to go. After his death the clock was sold to a man named Wilbur Huntley, who kept it at his home some distance southeast of Freehold, in memory of his venerable pastor. Huntley died a suicide. After his tragic end the clock became the subject of serious speculation. Its hands would never pass the hour of 1 o'clock at night. It would strike the midnight hour, but at 1, the hour when Huntley killed himself, it would utterly cease its functions. It is said that by pressing the hands forward and straining them past the hour of 1 they could be started on afresh, but as soon as 1 o'clock at night again was reached the clock would stop. It would tick merrily through the hour of 1 at noonday. It still ticks away as solemnly and regularly as when brought from the shop nearly two centuries ago, but its 1 o'clock defect has never been cured.

This story is one of a number of similar newspaper yarns that have appeared at intervals in American papers, and are interesting, at least, as showing a widespread and deeply rooted superstition.

There is another story, less marvellous but equally insistent, which has required incessant hammering before it received its death-blow. The dials of "dummy" clocks, hung up as signs, invariably mark the hour 8:18. It has been said that the custom grew up because Lincoln was shot at eighteen minutes past eight. It has been shown, however, that the custom was common even in England long before that fateful Good Friday. Jewellers and watchmakers explain that this time is the readiest to suggest itself because the hands of watch or clock spread themselves across the dial in a nearly straight line when the hour hand approximates VIII and the minute hand 18 minutes after.

The last nail in the coffin of this story was driven home by Miss Clara Laughlin in the December, 1910, number of *McClure's Magazine.* She showed that Lincoln did not arrive at Ford's Theatre before 8.30 at the earliest. "After having interviewed every discoverable survivor of the audience at Ford's theatre that fateful Good Friday night, and being told that the presidential party arrived at 8.30, at 9.00, at 9.30, and at all times between," she was indebted to Mr. George C. Maynard for a definite statement. Mr. Maynard, then of the War Telegraph Office and now of the National Museum, was in the habit of keeping his theatre programs. On the margin of the long play-bill of that night he made a note of the point in the play at which Mr. Lincoln came in, and wrote down the lines being spoken as the presidential party entered the box. *Florence Trenchard* was trying to tell a joke to *Dundreary,* who—of course —did not see it.

"'Can't you see it?' she said.

"'No, I can't see it,' he assured her.

Just then Mr. Lincoln entered the state box on the upper right-hand side of the house, and Miss Keene, catching sight of him, said, "Well, everybody can see *that!*" nodding toward the box. And the orchestra struck up "Hail to the Chief," the audience cheered, and the play was at a standstill for a minute."

Miss Laughlin adds, " In the elder Sothern's prompt-book (preserved by his son) this incident occurs late in the first act; whether it was the same in Miss Keene's version I have been unable to learn, but it probably was, and that would fix the time of Mr. Lincoln's entrance at about half-past eight or a quarter to nine."

Death Valley, probably the most arid spot in the Western Hemisphere, forms part of a depression in the southeastern part of California, 35 miles long and 8 miles broad. It extends through San Bernardino and San Diego counties and crosses the Mexican border into Lower California. At King's Springs the depression is 250 feet, and at the crossing of the Southern Pacific Railway 261 feet, below sea-level. The deepest part is probably 400 feet below. The valley received its sinister name from the fact that in 1850 a party of gold-seekers with their families made a one-day camp in the valley and less than half of them survived, the remainder being overcome by the heat and aridity. A few escaped over the Panamints to the bountiful Californian plains ; the others returned to the East. Ten years later a party of prospectors came across the camp with its wagons and chains, yokes, camp equipments and children's toys ; even the tracks made in the sand by the little ones could still be traced.

Geologists tell us that this valley offers a striking illustration of the condition of the entire world at an early geological period. Except for a little oasis of 30 acres it is a mere waste of sand, hemmed in on all sides by the Funeral and Panamint mountains, bleak, precipitous, scarred, rocky. Nothing grows in the valley except sage brush and the gnarled and thorny mesquite at rare intervals. The only animals that can live in it are the horned lizard and the rattlesnake, the gauntest of coyotes, the leanest of wild-cats, the centipede, and the tarantula.

The California mining bureau has recorded that men, with plenty of water at their command, have died there of thirst, the arid air sapping the moisture from their bodies faster than they could supply it. In summer the air is kiln-arid until it contains but one per cent. of humidity ; well-shaded thermometers soar to 135 degrees Fahrenheit. Sand storms choke and stifle every living and growing thing in their path. A dusty fog fills the air clear to the mountain tops and spreads a pall of darkness over the valley. Plumes of dust wave above the cloud masses, and slender, sinuous sand-spouts a mile high go careering down the valley in the arms of the gale.

An unvarying stream of salt and alkali water flows into the head of the valley from a spring in the Panamints, and continues-either as a stream or marsh down the centre for 60 miles until it reaches the bottom of the depression. For the most part the marsh is an impassable area of acrid salt slush, but at places a crust of salt and sand has formed, throwing up the sharpest of cones and pinnacles, divided by the narrowest of crevices. The points vary from an inch to a yard or more in height and make walking impossible. During one of the many unsuccessful attempts at utilizing the great borax deposits of the valley, the borax-makers constructed an eight-mile bridge across the marsh by levelling the crust with sledge-hammers. Beneath this bridge is an unfathomed abyss of salt slime, where many of the early pioneers found their graves, after insanity and death had put a merciful end to their agonizing torturing thirst.

There is only one man who ever spent more than a day in this valley and came out of it alive. That man is H. W. Manton, of Rhyolite, California. His dismal tale of suffering appeared in the California papers. For about a week he was lost in the heart of Death Valley. Circulating helplessly around in the trackless waste he tramped 80 miles over sands so hot that he could scarcely walk on them, though shod with heavy boots. During all that time he had no food and but one drink of water.

When he staggered up to Cub Lee's Furnace Creek ranch, more dead than alive, his tongue was swollen to such a size that his mouth could no longer contain it. His lips and eyelids were cracked open; his clothing was in tatters, and his shoes were coated with a heavy incrustation of borax and other alkalies, which had eaten great holes in the leather.

At first he could not drink. The touch of water was as fire to his parched lips and tongue. Kind-hearted ranchmen and miners forced the fluid into his mouth with a straw, with a spoon—any way to get him revived.

Derby Day. This is the second and the greatest day in the three days of horse-racing at Epsom Downs, Surrey, England, beginning on the Tuesday after Trinity Sunday. Hence Derby day always falls on Wednesday.

That racing near Epsom existed in the time of Charles I is evident from Clarendon's History of the Rebellion: " A meeting of Royalists (1648) was held on Banstead Downs under pretence of a horse-race and six hundred horses were collected and sent to Reigate."

Banstead Downs then included much of what is now called Epsom Downs. Heywood, in " The English Traveller " (1655), speaks of racing at Epsom. Under the patronage of royalty, after the Restoration, the sport again became popular. Not, however, until the reign of George III, in 1780, were the Derby stakes instituted by the earl whose name they bear. (See HORSE-RACING.) Entries for three-year old colts of either sex are fifty guineas apiece, with a forfeit of £25 if the candidate be withdrawn. Since 1890 the owner of the winner is guaranteed £5000, the owner of the second, £300, the owner of the third, £200. The breeder of the winner is guaranteed £500.

To the first Derby, May 6, 1780, there were thirty-six subscribers. The stakes, £1125, were won by Sir Charles Burbury's entry, Diomed. The richest Derby, £7350, was won by Lord Lyon in 1866. The poorest Derbies (£925 each) were in 1785, 1792, and 1802. The largest number of subscribers was 278 in 1870, when Sir Bevis won; the smallest number 29, in 1785 and again in 1786. The largest field that ever competed was 34, in 1862, when Caractacus won. The smallest was 4, in 1794, when Doedalus won.

The greatest number of Derbies ever captured by any one jockey was by Robinson, in 1817, 1824, 1825, 1827, 1828, and 1836. Four jockeys have won the Derby five times,—viz., F. Archer, J. Arnull, F. Buckle, and Chit. No jockey has ever won more than two Derbies in succession. In 1820 the Derby was run during a hurricane, and appropriately won by Sailor, a son of Scud; in 1839 and 1867 the start occurred in a snow-storm.

The Derby has twice resulted in a dead heat. In 1828 The Colonel and Cadland could not be divided, but the latter won the decider. In 1884 St. Gatien and Harvester ran a dead heat and the stakes were divided. Mr. Hammond, who owned St. Gatien, was at one time employed at 6s. a week in the stable of Capt. Machell, who owned Harvester, and little did he think that the day would ever come when he would be in a position to offer to cut up the Derby stakes with his whilom master. Diomed, the winner of the first Derby, found his way to America, as other Derby winners have done since, the price paid for him being 50 guineas. In 1900 Flying Fox won the Derby for the Duke of Westminster. He was sold to go to France, and the price paid for him was 37,500 guineas. The Turf, it will be perceived, has grown in importance, though a large amount of consideration was always bestowed upon it. Thus, Pepys, in his Diary under date 1663, records: "Having intended this day to go to Banstead Downs to see a famous race, I sent Will to get himself ready to go with me; but I hear it is put off because the Lords do sit in Parliament to-day." Years afterwards the Commons used not to sit in Parliament because the Derby was to be run. A sterner generation has altered all that. The founder of the race won it in the eighth year of its existence,

1785, with Sir Peter Teazle. It has been the great ambition of the house of Stanley to win it again. Yet no other Derby has ever fallen to any of the earls. Nor has an Earl of Derby ever won the St. Leger, though the present earl came very near doing so with his Oaks winner, Keystone II, in 1906. This ambition to win the Derby has possessed many of the most distinguished owners of horses, to whom money has been no consideration, and they have been constantly disappointed, whilst other owners who were devoid of any special veneration for the race and would rather have won another stake worth a little more, have found themselves successful.

To win the Derby was the chief object of Lord George Bentinck's life, but, though he owned some of the best race-horses of his generation, the much-coveted prize never fell to his lot. One year he entered five. Of these two died in training, the third became a roarer, the fourth a lady's hack. The fifth alone ever saw the course, but it was as a wheeler in a four-in-hand that had the privilege of hauling a coach-load of friends down to the Derby. It was Lord George who made the first motion that the House of Commons adjourn for the Derby day, that being in 1847, and until 1892 it was always done. In the latter year the motion was lost by 14 votes, but on the afternoon of the Derby day only thirty-five members were present in the House of Commons, or five less than was necessary to make a "house," so that no business was done. Driven almost mad by his repeated failures, Lord George threw up the sport which had refused to grant him his heart's desire, and disposed of his stables. Among the animals thus sold was Surplice, who in 1848 won for its purchaser the coveted honor denied to its original owner. The unhappy peer, with a heart already weakened by the excitement of the course, could not recover from the irony of Surplice's win, and a little later Lord George's lifeless body was discovered by a keeper at night lying on the edge of the park at Welbeck Abbey, and the verdict of "Death from the visitation of God" closed a grim episode in the history of the race.

Lord Beaconsfield, then Mr. Disraeli, tells us that the day after Surplice's victory, Lord George, lamenting what he had missed, moaned out in the library of the House of Commons, "You do not know what the Derby is." "Yes, I do; it's the blue ribbon of the turf," was Mr. Disraeli's reply. By this he intended to convey the idea that it is the highest turf honor, the "blue ribbon' in England being the color worn with the highest honor given by the Queen, the insignia of the Knights of the Garter. Mr. Disraeli, therefore, did not mean that the Derby was a temperance affair, as has sometimes been asserted by unconscious humorists.

The first royal victory was gained in 1788 by the Prince of Wales's Sir Thomas, a 6 to 5 on favorite. More than a century was to pass before the royal colors were borne first past the post. Persimmon in 1893 just beat Mr. Leopold de Rothschild's good horse St. Frusquin—who reversed the running soon afterwards at Newmarket, with a 3 lb. advantage of weight, however—and Persimmon's own brother, Diamond Jubilee, won by half a length from the Duke of Portland's Simon Dale in 1900. Both these horses were owned by the then Prince of Wales, afterward Edward VII.

Around the race of 1844 hovers a story which might well have sprung from the brain of that morbid but consummate genius Edgar Allan Poe. Crockford, the owner of a notorious gambling-hell, had a favorite, Ratan, poisoned on the eve of the race, and in the fury of his rage was seized with a fit of apoplexy, which proved fatal. Crockford also had a runner entered for the Oaks, and, to avoid disqualification in the event of the filly winning, his friends concocted a gruesome plot. At early morning the body of the dead owner was propped up at the window of his house, where it could be seen by the crowds visiting the course; the trick succeeded, the filly won, and its backers chuckling over their grisly ruse, drew their winnings even as the crowd were cheering the inanimate figure on their way home. The Derby of that year was won by Running Rein, a four-year-old owned by a Jew; but, fraud having been proved, Running Rein was deprived of his honors and the stakes were awarded to the second horse.

The first foreigner to win the Derby was Count La Grange in 1865, with the French horse Gladiateur. Englishmen, resenting the carrying off of the "Blue Ribbon" by a foreigner, were very bitter, publicly insulting the owner of the horse, and intimating that history had merely repeated itself, and that the Derby of '65 was only a parallel of '44.

Caractacus brought off a great surprise in the Derby of 1862, as he started at 40 to 1. Jim Goater was offered the mount, but he declined it, and steered The Sprite, owned by his brother. Caractacus was ridden by the stable lad, Parsons. Horse and boy were very fond of each other. In the race Parsons frequently spoke to his mount, stroking him, patting his neck, and encouraging him with such words as "Get along, Crackey," and "Good lad, Crackey." After Caractacus won, Mr. Snewing, the owner, went to see Parsons weigh in. To his horror the jockey failed to draw the weight. The bridle was sent for, and (Mr.

19

Snewing often said afterward), "Oh the agony I felt at that moment I would not undergo again for one thousand pounds!" This set matters right, but all was not yet over. Lord Stamford objected on the ground that only his own horse, Ensign and three others had gone the full course, the flag having fallen when a lot of the competitors were in front of the starting-post.

Admiral Rous, however, was at the head of affairs, and he was about the only man present that did not lose his head. On his lordship making the protest, Admiral Rous took his watch out of his pocket and, noting the time, said, "Twenty minutes! The objection, to hold good, should have been lodged within a quarter of an hour, according to the sixtieth rule of racing." The exciting events of the day so upset Mr. Snewing that, when he woke up in his house in Euston Square the next morning, all seemed like a dream to him. "Is it true that I have won the Derby, or have I dreamt it?" he called out to his niece. "Make haste down, uncle, and see the drawing-room hung with light-blue ribbons," she replied. Even that did not satisfy him, and he said, "Send out for a newspaper and let me see it in print." A copy of the London *Times* was brought him, and, looking over it, he said, "Now I am satisfied; I know that I have won the Derby."

In 1834, when Plenipotentiary carried off the stakes, Mr. Batson, his owner, allowed his tenants to hold their farms rent free for a year. When Mundig won for Mr. Bowes in the following year, the church bells were rung at his country-seat at Streatlam, in Durham, and the counties of York and Durham were ablaze with bonfires. When Amato won in 1838, the Stock Exchange took a holiday, Mr. Crockford, the book-maker, paying its members in the aggregate £30,000. Amato was known as "the coughing pony," and the Derby he won was the only race he ever started in. A short time before the race the betting was 100 to 1 against his chances.

The Derby of 1867 was long remembered for the reckless plunging of the Marquis of Hastings, the wildest blue-blooded gambler of the mid-Victorian era. He laid thousands of pounds against Hermit, and stood to lose over £100,000 in the event of that animal winning. Hermit's victory (at 66 to 1 against) compelled the Marquis to sell the last of his kingly heritage in his magnificent estate of Loudom in Scotland, and thus bring himself almost to beggary; at the next Derby the spendthrift nobleman was hooted as a defaulter, and before the year closed he had died broken in mind and body.

If the Marquis of Hastings was the unluckiest of all Derby-day patrons, Lord Falmouth was the luckiest. It was in 1870 that he won his first Derby. The horse was Kingcraft, trained by Matthew Dawson and ridden by Tom French. Wonderful fortune attended the efforts of the bearers of the "magpie" jacket during the Cornish earl's turf career. In fourteen years, viz., from 1870 to 1883, which was his last whole season on a large scale on the turf, Lord Falmouth, with a stud which rarely numbered twenty horses in training, carried away in public money the enormous sum of £238,198. In 1884 he sold in two days all his race-horses at Heath House, and all his brood mares, stallions, yearlings, and foals, for a total aggregate of 111,880 guineas. No such instance of long sustained and continuous good fortune can be found in the splendid annals of the English turf.

Fred Archer, the greatest of all English jockeys, was associated with most of Lord Falmouth's later triumphs. His first important success in the popular black and white was on Atlantic in the Two Thousand of 1874. It was not without considerable hesitation that his lordship gave Archer the mount, but the boy showed the nerve and resource of a veteran. Despite a handicap of three-stone dead weight, he steered his mount home as straight as a die and won by a neck. Archer won his first Derby for Lord Falmouth in 1877, Silvie being the horse.

Probably the largest gift ever handed to a jockey for winning a race was when Wells, in 1868, was presented by Sir Joseph Hawley with the Derby stakes for steering Blue Gown. They amounted to £6850. When Teddington won in 1851 Sir Joseph gave Marston a thousand pounds, and Mr. Stanley, the real owner of the horse, another thousand. Daley, the rider of Hermit in 1867, received £3000.

In the year 1881, the prize was for the first time captured by an American horse, Iroquois, ridden by Fred Archer.

> The Yankee came down with Long Fred on his back,
> And his colors were gleaming with cherry and black;
> He flashed to the front, and the British star paled
> As the field died away, and the favorite failed.
>
> Oh! A was an Archer, A 1 at this fun,
> And A was American, too.—and A won!
> And B was the Briton, who ready to melt
> A sort of a je ne sais (Iro)—quois felt,
> To see his blue riband to Yankee-land go,
> B, too, none the less, was the hearty "Bravo!"
>
> *Punch,* 1881.

Iroquois belonged to Pierre Lorillard, and had also won the St. Leger stakes.

Dials, Clock. Until the year 1912 the American clock with the largest dial was that in the tower of the Communipaw depot of the Central Railroad of New Jersey. The San Francisco *Chronicle* thus describes it: "The dial is a few inches over fourteen feet in diameter. Twelve panes of glass are used in the dial, the central one being five feet in diameter and three-eighths of an inch in thickness. The minute hand is seven feet long and weighs forty pounds, while the hour hand is five feet long and weighs twenty-eight pounds. In one hour the minute hand travels over forty-eight feet, while a day's journey is about six ordinary city blocks, or about 1152 feet. The motive power is furnished by a weight of 700 pounds hung from a three-eighths inch steel cable, and the clock will run for ten days without rewinding. At night the clock is illuminated by strong electric lights and a large reflector behind the ground-glass dial. The variation is not more than a second in a week. Such is a brief sketch of the largest one-dial clock at present running in the United States."

The article added that the largest four-dial clock in America was that in the New York Produce Exchange, each dial being 12½ feet in diameter. But it went on to show that these records would all be surpassed by a clock then in course of construction for the *Chronicle* building itself,—of course, in San Francisco. The four dials of this clock would each be 16½ feet in diameter, and consequently each surpasses by 2 feet the single dial of the Communipaw clock, and by 4 feet that of any of the dials of the New York Produce Exchange.

Dice. There was a Greek legend that dice were invented at the siege of Troy by Palamedes, a hero unmentioned by Homer. Herodotus, however (i. 94), ascribes the invention to the Lydians. Under pressure of a great famine and instigated by a desire to economize their stores, they devised dice and bowls. Every other day for eighteen years they abstained from food, devoting their entire waking hours to gaming.

The Indian epic, the Mahabharata, claims the invention for Hindustan, and likewise furnishes the earliest instance of fraudulent (i.e., "loaded" or "cogged") dice. "In those days," says the poet, "it was the custom to play at dice, and Doorjoodhen, having made a false set, challenged Judishter, the commander of the troops he was fighting, to play, which being accepted by him, he, in a short time, lost all his wealth and kingdoms. Doorjoodhen told him then that he would give him one more chance to recover the whole, but that if he again should lose he must retire with all his brothers for the space of twelve years into banishment. . . . Judishter, hoping that fortune would not always be unkind, consented to these terms, but having lost as before, he was constrained by the princes, who were umpires, to relinquish his kingdoms to Doorjoodhen, and retire into banishment from Gudrapoor, his capital city, now known by the name of Delhi."

Tacitus assures that the ancient Germans not only would hazard all their wealth, but even stake their liberty, upon the turn of the dice; and he who lost, submitted to servitude, though younger and stronger than his antagonist, and patiently permitted himself to be bound, and sold in the market. The Saxons, the Danes, and the Normans, were all of them greatly addicted to the same infatuating pastime.

Dice playing was a fashionable diversion in the reign of Henry the Eighth. Hall, speaking of this monarch, says, "The king about this season was much given to play at tennis and at the *dice,* which appetite certain crafty persons about him perceiving, brought in Frenchmen and Lombards to make wagers with him, and so he lost much money; but when he perceived their craft, he eschewed their company, and let them go."

In England cogged dice were known by the name of fulhams, or fullams, because first made at Fulham. An alternate name was gourds. Thus Pistol, in *Merry Wives of Windsor,* Act I, sc. 3, says: "Let vultures gripe thy guts for gourd and Fullam holds."

The Freemasons profess great veneration for the cubical stone, and point out that the eyes on the two faces opposite to one another always make up the number seven; the six sides of the cube represent the six working properties of nature: contraction, expansion, circulation, fire, light and sound, whilst the cube as a whole represents the seventh property in which the six are comprised, or the comprisal of all; the six working days of the week and the Sabbath of rest.

Dickens's Dutchman, the name popularly given to Charles Langheimer (1807–1884), an incorrigible petty thief, a Saxon by birth, who spent the greater part of his life in the Eastern Penitentiary, in Philadelphia. Dickens visited that institution in 1842, and in his "American Notes" he speaks of the horrors of solitary confinement there, and instances this man as one of the most affecting examples. "I never saw such a picture of forlorn affliction and distress of mind," says Dickens, "my heart bled for him, and when the tears ran down his cheeks and he took one of the visitors aside to ask, with trembling hands nervously clutching at his coat to detain him, whether there was no hope of his dismal sentence being commuted, the spectacle was really too painful to witness." The plain facts of the case, however, are that Langheimer was a consummate hypocrite who found a pleasure in feigning imaginary woes. He might have earned money at his trade as a paper-maker, but he could not resist the temptation to steal. As fast as he served out one term and was released, he returned on a fresh conviction. It was even thought that he committed thefts for the express purpose of being sent back to jail, preferring his quarters there to the cold comfort of the outside world. He took advantage of the notoriety conferred upon him by Dickens to turn an honest penny whenever he could. During his last confinement in the Penitentiary, he had a box into which visitors dropped a pittance. English tourists always asked for Langheimer's cell and rarely left without slipping a coin into his hand.

Dillagrout Soup. William the Conqueror, according to mediæval legend, had a fine sense of what was becoming at a royal table. At one of his little dinners he was so well pleased with a savory soup compounded by his cook, Tezelin, that he sent for him and asked how it was named.

" I call it dillagrout," was the reply.

" A poor name for so good a soup!" cried the king. " Nathless "—everybody said " nathless " in those days—" we bestow upon you the manor of Addington."

This manor eventually reverted to the crown. In the reign of Henry III we find it in the hands of the Bardolfs, and held on the tenure of "making pasties in the king's kitchen on the day of his coronation, or providing some one as his deputy, to make a dish called grout, and if suet (seym) was added, it was called malpigernoun." At James II's coronation the lord of the manor claimed to find a man to make a dish of grout in the royal kitchen, and prayed that the king's cook might be the man. The claim was allowed, and the claimant knighted. But what was this grout? Was it identical with Tezelin's dillagrout and the Bardolfs' malpigernoun? And was a pottage called Bardolf, of which a fourteenth-century recipe has been printed by the Society of Antiquaries, identical with these? If so, as among the ingredients were almond milk, the brawn of capons, sugar and spice, chicken parboiled and chopped, etc., it was doubtlessly a dish for a king.

Diving. The earliest reference to diving as a business rather than a sport occurs in Homer's " Iliad " (Bk. iii, lines 345, etc.)., where Patroclus rather infelicitously compares the fall of Hector's charioteer to the action of a diver diving for oysters.

Thus it would seem that the art was known about 1000 years before the Christian era. Thucydides is the first to chronicle the employment of divers for mechanical work under water. He tells how divers during the siege of Syracuse sawed down the barriers constructed under water to damage or destroy any Grecian ships that might attempt to enter the harbor. The earliest mention of any appliance for assisting divers is by Aristotle, who describes certain instruments for respiration through which they can draw air from above the water and which thus enable them to remain a long time under water. The first diving-bell, or some similar contrivance known as a colimpha, is recorded to have been used by Alexander the Great. The colimpha, we are told, had the power of keeping a man dry and at the same time of admitting the light. In Pliny and in Roger Bacon we catch baffling hints of similar contrivances. Leonardo da Vinci in a posthumous paper claimed that he had invented a diving-dress for himself; but, "in view," said he, "of the wickedness of men, I do not publish or divulge the method I have invented for remaining under water, for they would make use of it in order to commit murder at the bottom of the sea, by destroying vessels and causing them to sink, together with those on board."

The earliest pictorial representation of anything approximating to the modern diving apparatus is an engraving in Vegetius's *De Re Militari* (1511). A diver is shown wearing a tight-fitting helmet, to which is attached a long leather pipe leading to the surface. Here the open end is kept afloat by means of a bladder. It has been opined that this apparatus was suggested by the action of the elephant when swimming. The animal instinctively elevates its trunk so that the end is above the surface of the water though the head may be below it. Thus it is enabled, even when submerged, to take in fresh air at every inspiration.

All this time Nature had been giving another hint that dull man might have utilized if his wits had been sharp enough. Among spiders the diving-bell is as old as creation. In an ordinary aquarium you might notice, amid immersed portions of grass or reed, a sort of purse, closely resembling in shape and size the shell of a pigeon's egg, but pierced transversely through the middle. It is filled with air, and perfectly closed, except in its lower part, where there is an aperture just sufficient for the egress and ingress of a very small spider. A strong and semitransparent substance, resembling white gauze, forms the texture of the bell, firmly moored and anchored to the submerged plants by threads and cables, which hinder it from mounting to the surface.

Samuel Henri Berthoud (1804–1891), a French naturalist, was the first to study these natural diving-bells, and he tells nature students how to follow him in his observations.

Watch, he says, the lady coming out of her retreat. Her length is about one-eighth of an inch, her body is brown, and on the upper part of the back is drawn a dark patch, having four little dots on its centre. This spider lives under water, and yet requires air to breathe. Her Maker has taught her how to solve a problem which would have baffled the genius of Newton. She swims on her back, and her abdomen is enveloped in a bubble of air, which, reflecting the prismatic colors, looks like transparent mother-o'-pearl. She then rises to the surface of the water, and elevates above it the lower portion of her body, for amongst the arachnidæ the orifice of the organs of respiration is placed in the abdomen. Once on the surface, she breathes strongly, inhales as much air as she possibly can; then she gets beneath the water and gives out gently the liquid particles with which her lungs are gorged to excess; the long, silky, clammy threads which cover her retain in its place around her the bubble with which she is surrounded. This done, she dives with precaution, and carries into her nest—her diving-bell—a provision of air to replace what she had consumed. When once ensconced in her nest, she lies in ambush, with her cunning little head lowered, watching for any prey that may chance to pass. Woe to the tiny worm that wriggles on the stalk near her den! She darts forward, seizes him, and bears him off to her bell of impermeable gauze. While her habitation was in process of making, and until it was finished, it was naturally filled with water. But once the work was ended, it became necessary to expel the water, and replace it by atmospheric air. In order to attain this end, our spider had to make more than a hundred trips to the surface. Each bubble that she introduced into the bell, mounted towards the top by its specific levity, displacing an equal quantity of water, which was forced out through the orifice below, until at length the bell contained nothing but air. —*Fantaisies Scientifiques* (1861).

Doiley. Few shops in the London of the early eighteenth century acquired more celebrity than Doiley's warehouse. The founder was a refugee from France after the revocation of the edict of Nantes, who established a connection with the weavers of Spitalfields, then rising to eminence through the fostering care of the English government and the patronage of the English noblemen. Doiley, a man of great ingenuity, invented and introduced a number of stuffs, some entirely new and all hitherto unknown in England. Combining the different articles of silk and woollen, he spread them into so great a variety of forms and patterns that his shop became a depot of fashions. Says Addison's *Spectator*, " If Doiley had not, by his ingenious inventions, enabled us to dress our wives and daughters in cheap stuffs, we should not have had the means to carry on the war."

In another paper (No. 319) an imaginary correspondent, fond of striking bold strokes in dress, is made to say, " A few months after this I brought up the modish jacket, or the coat with close sleeves. I struck this first in a plain Doiley, but that failing I struck it a second time in blue camlet," which was also one of Doiley's stuffs.

Doll. Doubtless the earliest children of earth possessed dolls, as do the later ones. In tiny sarcophagi discovered in Egypt, there have been found, by the side of the little mummies which once were little Egyptian children, pathetically comic little imitations of themselves, placed there by loving mothers within reach of the cold little baby fingers. In Pompeii a child's skeleton was found clasping a doll to her breast.

The oldest doll, and indeed the oldest piece of sculpture that has ever been upturned from the earth, was a pumice-stone figure found (1889) in a bed of gravel 320 feet below the surface of the ground at Nampa, Idaho, between the Boise and the Snake rivers, on the Oregon Short Line Railroad. The region thereabouts is covered by extensive lava deposits of the post-tertiary or quaternary period. A Mr. M. A. Kurtz was engaged in boring an artesian well on his property in Nampa. Drilling through 60 feet of soil, he reached 15 feet of lava, then 100 feet of quicksand, and in succession 6 inches of clay, 40 feet of quicksand, 6 feet of clay, 30 feet of quicksand, 12 feet of clay, then clay balls mixed with sand, and then coarse sand. From the latter the doll was brought up by the sand-pump. Mr. Kurtz, getting hold of what he thought a petrified twig, washed it in a barrel, and found instead a well-proportioned red doll. Professor Putnam of Cambridge and Professor Haynes of Boston decided that it was a genuine antique carved from a light pumice stone. The coating of red material that enveloped it was a cement of oxide of iron which the centuries had slowly gathered around it. The Snake River rises in the mountains surrounding the Yellowstone River, where glaciers were of great extent. The sudden melting of these may have been the cause of the rapid accumulation of silt in a lake which from a few thousand or a few hundred years ago occupied the site of the village of Nampa. —*Scientific American,* January, 1890.

The greatest doll manufactory in the world is still the little German town of Sonneberg, in the Thuringian Forest. Here are made a vast number of wax and wooden babies annually sent out to all portions of the world, together with toys mostly carved out of wood from the neighboring forests. Sonneberg's toy industry dates back to the thirteenth century. It commenced with the manufacture of such common articles as wooden shingles, wooden household utensils, which the inhabitants of the mountain villages, mostly wood cutters and charcoal burners, used to produce in their leisure hours, their houses being surrounded by splendid groves of maple and beech, by fir and pine woods. Some of these poor mountaineers, as soon as the stock of their industrial labor had grown to a man's load, carried it down to the lowlands of Franconia, returning to their homes only when the last article had been disposed of or exchanged for domestic necessaries.

Such was the origin of the toy manufacture in the villages around Sonneberg. Nuremberg was then the great city for the disposal of toys, and for centuries the people of Thuringia looked upon the Nuremberg merchants as their benefactors. The Nurembergers saved them the trouble of hawking, as their forefathers had to do, their productions about the country. At last, native merchants sprang up and acquired a sufficient degree of wealth to command trade. Thus it came to pass that at the end of the seventeenth century Sonneberg, a very small place then of not more than seven hundred inhabitants, became the centre of the district of the manufacture of wooden articles and toys.

About the middle of the eighteenth century religious dissensions in the Salzburg districts induced a party of wood carvers, turners, and painters from Berchtesgaden to settle in the mountains near Sonneberg, chiefly in Judenbach, on the high-road running from South to North Germany. In skill they excelled all the native makers, and, as they were a very good-natured people, the Thuringians profited a good deal in the manufacture and painting of toys, chip-boxes, and chests of drawers.

At present 10,000 different toys are manufactured at Sonneberg. A show-room there, be it ever so large, cannot hold all. Changes in form and fashion are constantly taking place to meet a continual demand for something new.

The consequence is a constant rivalry among the makers for improving their manufacturers. Schools of drawing and modelling are established, not only in Sonneberg, but in most of the large villages round about. The learning of drawing is obligatory for both the boys and girls of the district.

The people—men, women, and children—who assist in the manufacturing of dolls and toys have a hard life of it. The little children assist after they have returned from school, and next morning stop at the factories to receive or deliver work. It is not strange, therefore, that the children of Sonneberg have a grievance against all dolls and toys in general, and an American writer who spent some time among them says:

> Those who do not sell dolls make them; those who do neither are in the cradle. Even the dogs, the goats, and the cows haul cart-loads of dressed or undressed dolls through the streets. Every one you meet has a basket on his head or a hamper on his back with just as many sham babies in it as there is room for. There is not a boy nor a girl in the whole Sonneberg Valley who does not hate and despise with all the passion in his little breast every creature in dolldom. It makes no difference whether she is a blonde or a Spanish beauty, whether

she has a hole or a music box in her chest, whether she has a set of teeth or a prisms-and-prunes expression painful in her mouth, whether she can sing or shut her eyes, dance or say her prayers, she is detested and abhorred by the authors of her creation, even to the fourth generation. The keenest enjoyment of the little Sonneberger is realized on finding a girl who has dropped from some modeller's cart, taking her by the heels and dashing her imaginary brains over the cobble-stones. —*New York Herald*, December 15, 1895.

Originally a religious institution, dolls have been "play actors" (their mission in miracle and mystery plays being still religious), fashion disseminators, and vehicles for illustrations in art and history. An amusing story is told of the time when, in the absence of fashion magazines, the "colonies" were left in sartorial darkness, just about to be illumined by the fashion dolly. A number of Catholic ladies of Georgetown purposed forming a convent of Visitation nuns, but were at a loss for the proper garb. In this dilemma a letter to a French convent soon brought back a "poupée," arrayed in proper cap, guimpe, veil, etc. At the New York Custom House Madame Poupee was thrown in durance vile, failing to "give a satisfactory account of herself." Nobody had ever seen work of art or tool of trade in this guise before. Finally, one sagacious official allowed she was only "one o' gods the Papists worshipped," and there was no duty on them, so she was honorably discharged. Doubtless she was as much a surprise to the pious ladies as to the government officials.

The doll of to-day is not only interesting as an evolution, but because of her progressive tendencies. She is stylish, coming with a ready-made wardrobe, from hose and corsets to French caps, aprons, and, if she be very young, a nursing bottle as a tribute to her orphan condition. She is luxurious, having her tailor-made gowns, accordion capes, silk blouses, kid gloves, parasols, carriage, and servants. She is gregarious, and no right-minded little girl with a properly indulgent mamma will separate Mrs. Dolly from husband and children. It is the proper fad to buy the whole family. Dolly has been relegated to the small girl, but good advice states that a miss well on in her teens may be as devoted to her doll family as was Mistress Dorothy when first Sir William Temple dawned upon her.

The talking doll is more ancient than the phonograph. By whatever mechanism worked, talking dolls of one sort or another are mentioned in old chronicles. The Edison talking doll is a gruesome thing. With a face of stoic calm she (or he) stands up and grinds out a "Twinkle, Twinkle," or the lamb and Mary episode in a way to set your teeth on edge when you once understand it. The phonographic soul within her has much to learn before her voice, at least, will soften an o'er-strict petite maman. Besides, one naturally protests against a crank—a key is bad enough.

The fin de siècle Edison doll is the very latest phase in this evolution. It is an accomplished child of science, and can repeat rhymes from Mother Goose. It was sold for $10 without a wardrobe, has a metallic body in which is placed a phonograph, and is altogether a thing of beauty and a joy so long as it keeps in order. But alas for the Edison doll! It has had to go into court for some reason or other, and the manufacture of the Edison doll family has been discontinued. The doll of to-day is so arranged anatomically that it can stand up and sit down, and can be wound up to take a stroll across the nursery floor. It is cosmopolitan, and the dolls' dressmaker is versatile. It is attired in the costumes of every nation.

Dollar (a corruption of the German *thaler*, from *thal*, a dale or valley), the name of a silver piece that was first coined in 1518, in Joachimsthal, the dale of Joachim, ten miles from Carlsbad. Here there was a mediæval Bohemian mine rich in silver. The coins kept up the reputation of the mine. Hence Joachimsthaler (eventually contracted to thaler) became a synonym for good money, and thaler (corrupted into dollar and cognate forms) became a familiar word in other tongues than German. One of its earliest appearances in English was in "Macbeth" (act i, sc. 2), where Ross tells Malcolm of slain Norsemen denied burial till their king had disbursed

> Ten thousand dollars to our general use.

Doubtless the word was well known before that date,—1606. It freely occurs in the "Travels" of the Englishman Sandys (1610), who shows that it was already current in three continents, Europe, Africa, and Asia. Sandys tells of hiring a boat in Egypt for twelve dollars; he explains how "Dutch dollars" (*sic*) circulated in Jewry and Phœnicia on a par with the Spanish pieces of eight; he found the monastery on Mount Sinai to be "receiving an annual revenue of 60,000 dollars from Christian princes."

In 1642 the colony of Massachusetts ordained that "considering the often occasions we have of trading with the Hollanders of the Dutch plantation and otherwise that the Holland ducatour shall be current at six shillings and the Rix Dollar and Royall-of-eight shall be five shillings."

Incidentally it may be explained that ducatour is early New Englander for ducat and Rix is a corruption of Reichs or imperial, the thaler being the coin of the German Empire. It was under Charles V, Emperor of Germany, King of Spain, and Lord of Spanish America, that German thalers and Spanish pieces-of-eight became the chief coin of the old world and the new, the latter flowing into New England from Southern Europe and the West Indies.

Dollar Mark. The symbol $ prefixed to the Federal currency is sometimes said to be a modification of the English £ for pounds. This is unlikely. So also is the explanation, much affected in old-time arithmetics, that it is a sort of hastily formed monogram of the initials U. S.;—thus $. Equally plausible at first sight, and equally fallacious on fuller examination, is the conjecture that it is a modification of the figure 8, designating the Spanish coin of eight reals, or "piece of eight," an equivalent of the dollar, its symbol being written 8. Other fallacies, which may be mentioned only to be dismissed, are: That the sign comes from the abbreviation used to mark the Roman money unit. The old Romans reckoned by sesterces, and to denote it used both HS and JIS, forms easily changed into our mark. That it comes from the Spanish contraction for *peso,* a dollar, indicated in Spanish accounts by combining P and S; or, from the Spanish *fuertes,* hard, used to distinguish coin from paper money.

Having cleared the ground in this fashion, there remains to be considered a theory which was argued out at some length in the *Atlantic Monthly* in an article entitled "The Story of the Two Pillars," and still remains the most satisfactory ever offered.

From very early times pillars· have been used to signify strength and sovereignty, and by the Phœnicians were connected as religious emblems with their temples. When Solomon's temple was built by Tyrian workmen, there were set up with great ceremony before its porch two pillars of brass, one called Jachin, or "He shall establish," and the other, Boaz, or, "In it is strength."

Symbolic pillars appear upon ancient Tyrian coinage as supporters of the chief device. There is a tradition that Melcanthus, the Tyrian explorer, sailing through the Straits of Gibraltar, tarried near their western extremity and planted on the site of the present Cadiz the Tyrian pillars of sovereignty. Over them he built a temple to Hercules, or, more probably, to the Phœnician god afterward identified with Hercules. As the colony grew and the temple gained wealth from votive offerings, the first rude pillars were replaced by others made of blended gold and silver, quadrangular in shape, "like anvils," and bearing mystical inscriptions. "These pillars," says Flavius Philostratus, "are the chains that bind together the earth and the sea." When Cadiz (originally Gades) increased in power and wealth, the Pillars of Hercules became her metropolitan emblem, as a horse's head was of Carthage.

The Spanish proclivities of the Emperor Charles V led him to incorporate the arms of the Holy Roman Empire with those of Spain. The pillars of Cadiz were made the supporters of the device. On the standard dollar coined in the imperial mint at Seville,—hence known as "colonnato," or in English "pillar piece,"—these pillars were entwined with a scroll. This was sometimes supposed to represent the serpents sent by Juno to destroy the infant Hercules in his cradle. In reality it was but the revival of an older custom. Though the Tyrians were not the first to coin money, they were foremost in giving it general circulation. Their coinage was the earliest currency of the world, and its device the recognized money symbol. Hence the pillar pieces of Charles V only familiarized the world anew with the symbol borne by the older pillar pieces of the Tyrians.

Our dollar mark, therefore, was first a religious emblem, then a general symbol of sovereignty, and finally, through Tyrian enterprise and Spanish domination, was accepted as a monetary token, and so came to bear its present significance.

Dominos. An Italian legend gives the following as the origin of dominos: Two monks who had been committed to a lengthy seclusion contrived to beguile the dreary hours of their confinement without breaking the rule of silence by showing each other small flat stones marked with black dots. By a preconcerted arrangement the winner would inform the other of his victory by repeating in an undertone the first line of the vesper prayer. In process of time the two monks managed to complete the set of stones and to perfect the rules of the game, so that when their term of incarceration had expired the game was generally adopted by all the inmates of the convent as a lawful pastime. It very soon spread from town to town, and became popular in Italy; and the first line of the vespers, "Dixit Dominus Domino meo," was reduced to the single word Domino, by which the game has since been known.

This is ingenious and interesting, but absolutely unscientific. Science tells us that dominos are a natural evolution from dice (*q.v.*). Put two dice faces side by side and you have a domino. Exactly when and where some great genius discovered this, even science refuses to say. Yet the Chinese, with a jocund hardihood that out-Italians the Italians, have sought to solve the unsolvable. They claim that dominos were invented in what would be the twelfth century of the Christian era by Hung Ming, a hero of popular romance, for the amusement of his soldiers and to keep them awake while on watch. It may be accepted as a fact that the game of dominos, wherever and whenever it originated, was perfected in China and thence distributed to the European world.

As there are twenty-one possible throws with two dice, so twenty-one dominos may be regarded as natural dominos. However, the Chinese have doubled up some of the numbers so as to make a full set for playing thirty-two in all. All over Eastern Asia the customary outfit of dominos is thirty-two. Our dominos, obtained by way of Europe, are only twenty-eight and are modified by the introduction of blanks. The domino game of Europe and America is the match game. It is played in China, but is an unimportant one among the many Chinese games of dominos. The Chinese domino games are all of them dice games elaborated. Dominos are also used in China, like dice, for fortune telling. That system of divination has an extensive literature of its own. The Chinese dominos all have astrological names.

The Esquimaux of far northern Alaska have dominos. In their game they use flat pieces of bone of somewhat irregular shapes. They do not hesitate to stake the last article they possess on the turn of a domino. Sometimes they put up their wives and lose them. Now and then it happens that a wife thus disposed of will sit down and win herself back for her former owner.

Learn the following formula, and you will always be able to tell the markings of any domino that, unseen by you, a friend draws at random from a pile. Tell him to multiply either of the numbers of spots by five, add seven, double the result, and finally add the second number of spot and then inform you what the sum is. You now subtract fourteen, and the remaining digits are the number of spots on his domino. Suppose he selects the domino marked 3 and 6. Following your directions, he multiplies the 3 by 5 (15), adds 7 (22), doubles (44), adds the other number (6), and tells you that the sum is 50. You now subtract 14 from the 50, leaving 36. And the two digits, 3 and 6, are the number of spots his domino is marked with.

Donkey. Glory has been pernicious to the ass. Legend says that the cross upon its back is meant as a reminder that the humble have been and will again be exalted, and that its meekness emphasizes the moral that even under the greatest honors we should still remain humble. Legend is audaciously wrong. When Jesus rode into Jerusalem on an ass, he selected the beast upon which it was then considered most honorable to ride. The donkey was of old, and indeed it still remains in many places, the steed of the rich, the high in place, and the luxurious.

" There was no humility intended or expressed in that notable procession; on the contrary, it was our Saviour's one and only assertion of personal consequence, this solitary concession to the earthly ambitions of the disciples."

So says Phil Robinson in " The Poet's Beasts " (London, 1885). The same author opines that, viewed naturally instead of traditionally, the cross-stripe on the donkey's back gives the " heavy-headed thing " a very interesting significance, for it may be the last lingering vestige of a zebrine ancestry. " All the other stripes have been thrashed off its hide. Bewildered by ill-usage, they have run together and blended into a color that, like the character of the wearer, is monotonous, dull, serious, solemn."

There was a time when the wild ass, the onager, was so courageous and so fleet of foot that the east and the south wore its hide as a robe of honor, and kings and chiefs took the wild ass for their cognizance and badge. Oriental children wore shreds of ass-skin round their necks, that they might grow up generous and brave. Thus prized, the wild ass soon came under domestication, and the undersized drudge of southern Europe, known also in the London streets, is the latest and most degraded variation of the species. " But intermediate between the proud vagabond of the desert and the costermonger's ' moke ' come many animals more worthy physically of their lineage. In Egypt the white ass still claims something of the respect, and fetches the high price, of olden days, and during the Egyptian war I remember seeing more than one of these animals figuring conspicuously in the British camp. All over Asia Minor the donkey of superior caste is the recognized ' hack ' of the well-to-do, and I have seen them not only in the Levant, but in southern Europe and in eastern Africa sumptuously caparisoned as steeds."

Silenus may have been ridiculous—

> Silenus on his ass,
> Pelted with flowers as he on did pass,
> Tipsily quaffing.

But neither Keats nor any of his classic predecessors saw anything ridiculous in the animal he bestrode. Indeed the fact that Silenus was put upon an ass only emphasized the importance of the animal in Bacchic worship, and in no way derogates from the dignity of the boon companion of the gods. Says a learned commentator upon the pageant, " The ass was in fact the Symbol of Silenus' wisdom and his prophetical powers."

This is only partly true. At many periods and in many places the ass has been proverbial for dulness and obstinacy.

Ancient Egyptians symbolized an ignorant person by the head and ears of an ass. The Romans thought it a bad omen to meet one. Mediæval Germany made the ass the symbol of St. Thomas, the incredulous apostle; the last boy to enter school on St. Thomas' day was called Thomas the Ass. And there is an unpleasant fresco in the Catacombs which represents a Christian as worshipping a crucified ass.

Door. The savage has no door to his dwelling. Even when he has ceased burrowing in the ground, like a rabbit or a wild dog, and has advanced to the dignity of a hut, a kraal, a canoe turned upside down, or other construction, in which he may dwell and howl and paint himself and eat his foe, he still lacks the final grace of a door. The early Hebrews and Egyptians, the Greeks and the Romans, had door-ways, but no doors. Mordecai sat in the gate, but Haman's door is nowhere mentioned. The great temples of Nineveh, Babylon, and Ephesus were doorless. So was the Parthenon. Go and look at its modelled counterfeit in the Metropolitan Museum of New York; through the lofty portal you see the wilderness of columns and the gigantic statue of the goddess. Skins, linen veils, tapestries and silk curtains were anciently hung across door-ways, then, as they still are in the East, to ensure privacy for the inmates. Gaza and Somnauth had gates. But the door is an invention of modern times, an offshoot of modern civilization. Wherever you find most luxury, there you will also find most doors. Every trade, every calling, every sect and creed, every division and subdivision of the body social, has its characteristic door.

"Royalty," says George Augustus Sala, writing in 1860, "rattle through the big door of Buckingham Palace, while Lieut.-Colonel Phipps modestly slips in by the side-postern, hard by the guard-house, and the grooms and scullions, the footmen and turnspits, the cooks and bottle-washers, modester still, steal round the corner into Pimlico, and are admitted by a back door opposite the Gun tavern. So the Duke of Mesopotamia's guests to ball or supper are ushered up the lofty flight of steps, and in at the great hall-door; while Molly, the housemaid's friend, creeps down the area steps, and taps at the door opposite the coal-cellar. So the theatre has its doors—box, pit, and gallery—with one private, sacred portal for the Queen Bee when she condescends to patronize the drama; a door leading into a narrow, inconvenient, little passage generally, with a flight of stairs seemingly designed for the express purpose of breaking the neck of the stage-manager, who walks in crab-like fashion before Majesty, backward, in an absurd court-suit, and holding two lighted tapers in battered old stage candlesticks, hot drops of wax from which fall in a bounteous shower upon his black silk smalls. Just contrast this multitude of doors with the simple arrangements of the Roman amphitheatres. Apertures there were in plenty to allow the audience departure, but they were common to all; and the patrician and his client, the plebeian and the freedman, struggled out of the Coliseum by the same vomitories. There was but one special door in the whole circus; and that was one entrance through which was envied by nobody, for it was of iron, and barred, and on the inside thereof was a den where the lions that ate the gladiators lay."—*Household Words*, No. 282.

Numberless are the superstitions and the consequent observances that have crystallized around doors and door-ways. Special importance has always been attached to the act of entering a dwelling. For are you not penetrating into the sacred hearth, the centre of a home? Mottoes more or less descriptive of the character of the occupants were inscribed over door-ways in Greece and Rome,—they may be seen in unveiled Pompeii,—and are still familiar in many parts of Europe.

Magic doors are abundant in folk-lore. The forbidden door of Bluebeard's story is only one of a host of such doors leading to rooms or caves of mystery in the legendary tales of all lands. Enchanted doors opening in the sides of hills and mountains are another familiar feature of legend. In short the magic doors of fairy tale and romance are of infinite variety like the

> Charm'd magic casements, opening on the foam
> Of perilous seas, in faery lands forlorn.

In England and in Scotland a still prevalent custom is that of opening doors, and sometimes windows, whenever a death occurs in the family. This is to give free egress to the departing spirit or free entrance to the angel of death.

> Open lock, end strife;
> Come death, and pass life.

So says Meg Merrilies in "Guy Mannering" when she unbars the door and lifts the latch of the Kairn of Dernclough after the smuggler has died there.

In Sussex, and possibly in other counties of England, it used to be customary to keep the front door of a house, through which the corpse was carried, wide open until the close of the burial service. Failure to do this might result in a second death. Mrs. Latham, author of a work on "The Old-World Lore of Sussex," tells of a funeral that took place about the middle of the nineteenth century from St. Mary's Almshouse in Chichester. "As soon as the body had been carried out," she says, "the niece of the deceased locked the door of the apartment, and had hardly done so when she heard the inmates of the almshouses thumping and rattling it to force it open. On finding all their efforts useless one of them exclaimed. 'Hang that good-for-nothing woman! Her locking this door before the old girl is buried will bring death among us pretty soon again.' "

As a contrast to all this melancholy superstition, it is refreshing to remember that at Christmas time the open door is associated not with departure but with welcome. It is lucky then to be the first to open the door of the house and to bid Father Christmas welcome. Contrast of a different kind may be found in the custom of the closed door in Holland—in many Dutch villages and towns the chief door of a house is never opened except on the occasion of a funeral or a marriage—and of the ancient " porte di mortuccio " of Italy. The latter, the doors of the dead, may still be seen in many of the houses at Perugia, by the side of the principal door of the house. A modern traveller describes them as " tall, narrow, and pointed at the top, just wide enough for a coffin to pass through." These " porte di mortuccio " are now mostly disused and blocked up, and their existence is therefore often overlooked by the careless passer-by. These narrow doorways were originally made for the exclusive passage of the dead, the ancient belief being that where death had once passed out death could the more easily pass in." This grimmer side of the open-door idea never seems to have occurred to British folks.

Door-knockers. With the simplification that labor-saving inventions have introduced as civilization passed out of its heterogeneous beginnings, the picturesque accessories of the earlier door are gradually disappearing. Gone, or almost gone, are the door-knocker of the past; the brass plate underneath; the bells which flanked it for servants and visitors; the latch, surviving verbally in the now unmeaning word latch-key; the bolts at top and bottom, and even the iron chain that enabled one to peer outdoors without actually opening.

The old-fashioned bell and the door-knocker have been superseded by the electric button. With the tearing down of old buildings and the equipping of new ones with all the modern improvements, the knocker's day was numbered. In London or Paris, and eke in New York or other American cities, such houses as still cling to the old fashion have, for the most part, plain metal rings in lieu of the clasped hands, the queer faces, and the other grotesque objects that were made to resound at the will of postman, tradesman, or visitor.

But the knocker still survives in the literature that was contemporary with it. Every reader of Dickens remembers the knocker which actually existed in Craven Street. London, until comparatively recent times.

It represented a man's head with an iron ring emerging from behind the ears and hanging below the chin. At the opening of the "Christmas Carol" Scrooge, having put the key in the lock of the door, sees in the knocker, without its undergoing any intermediate process of change, not a knocker, but Marley's face with a dim light about it, "like a bad lobster in a dark cellar." Again, after Scrooge had undergone his mental and moral trans- formation, he said of it, "I shall love it as long as I live. I scarcely ever looked at it before. What an honest expression it has in its face! It's a wonderful knocker." This honest face has disappeared from Craven Street for all time, and lovers of Dickens will search in vain for it on the door of No. 8.

Mrs. Gamp's knocker, which Mr. Pecksniff sounded vigor- ously, but which was so constructed as to wake the street with ease and even spread alarms of fire in Holborn without making the smallest impression on the premises to which it was addressed, is also gone. Mrs. Gamp lived in Kingsgate Street over a barber and bird fancier, next door but one to the famous mutton-pie shop and directly opposite the original cats' meat warehouse. All these places have vanished, for Kingsgate Street was one of the narrow lanes sacrificed to make the Kingsway, the widest, finest road London possesses.

Then there was the Nicklebys' knocker on the lodging-house on the Strand, where double knocks were not allowed for second- floor tenants, and the Kenwigs' knocker, which Mr. K. proudly muffled with a new white kid glove when his sixth offspring arrived. In all these districts changes so great have been made that there is hardly any Dickens-land now left in London.

Door-plates. These are following the door-knocker into desuetude and oblivion. In the early half of the nineteenth century, and even later, every man of prominence had his name graven upon a plate and that plate affixed to his front door, so that all might know who dwelt within. The daily task of the negro houseman was to rub the door-plate until it shone. It took the place of the Lares and Penates of the Romans, and was attended to just as carefully as were the ancient household gods.

"Everything is changed now," moaned a former dealer in door-plates and door-knockers, talking to a *Sun* reporter in 1880 ; "I suppose the reason is that people don't have homes as they used to. They simply live in houses and apartments and move around so much that a door-plate couldn't possibly endure the peripatetic existence A collection of brass door-plates screwed to the portal of a big apartment building would, I confess, look rather odd."

Dover's Powder. Thomas Dover, physician and buccaneer, was the first to compound and prescribe the famous powder which bears his name. Dover (1660-1742), who studied medicine under the great Sydenham, appears to have been engaged in practice at Bristol in the latter days of the English buccaneers, of whom Sir John Hawkins was the most famous, when in 1708 he was induced to become the promoter of an expedition of adventure, not to say pillage, to the South Seas. There were two ships in this expedition. Dampier was the pilot, and Dover, on account of his large financial interest in the undertaking, was made third in command, with the title of Captain Dover, under Captain Woodes Rogers. He proved himself well worthy of the title before he returned to Bristol. In a successful attack on the city of Guayaquil, Captain Dover led the assault; and the prizes of the expedition were so numerous and so rich that his ships brought home plunder of the value of one hundred and seventy thousand pounds sterling.

The finding of Alexander Selkirk on Juan Fernandez Island was the most interesting of all his experiences. This occurred February 2, 1707.

Duck. It is a curious fact that this fowl is not mentioned anywhere in the Old Testament (unless there be an allusion to it in 1 Kings, iv, 23, under the name of " fatted fowl "), yet recent excavations in Gezer unearthed a skilfully modelled clay duck, of a period certainly earlier than the Old Testament records. In popular usage the word covers both genders, although technically it is restricted to the female, the male being called a drake. New uses for ducks as destroyers of various insect pests have from time to time appeared in American papers. Here is an especially startling item:

Joseph Junette, who farms one of the Job ranches on the bluffs, near Alton, Ill., says he will quit farming and educate ducks to eat potato bugs. "A dollar a day a duck " will be his motto. Just now Mr. Junette is enjoying an income of $15 a day from fifteen ducks, which he has trained to clear potato patches of the little spotted pests. He shut up the ducks in a pen and fed them on potato bugs exclusively, after starving them until they were glad to get the bug diet.

Junette tried them first on his own potato patch, which comprised several acres. The ducks went through the patch like a neighborhood scandal. After this Junette shut up his brigade so they would not acquire a taste for other diet and would be hungry and able to earn their wages the next time out.

The ducks are in great demand on the farms in Junette's neighborhood. Farmers are glad to pay $1.50 an hour for the services of the brigade. Junette has in sight an income of $90 a week from the fifteen ducks already educated and thus employed.—*New Orleans Times-Democrat.*

Dynamo. The popular name (abbreviated from "dynamo-electric machine") given to a machine for converting mechanical into electrical energy.

The first dynamo ever constructed was that made by Michael Faraday in 1831. This "prince of experimenters" discovered that when a disc or flat plate of copper was made to rotate between the poles of a powerful magnet, currents were produced in the plate from the centre outward. By touching the revolving plate with one end of a wire whose other end was brought in contact with the rim, he found that a current of electricity passed along the wire and could be made to indicate its existence by deflecting the needle of a galvanometer, decomposing a chemical solution, or by any of the well-known effects produced by electricity in motion. Faraday saw the importance of this discovery and the great uses in the way of practical application to which it might be put, but he did not himself stay to develop it. He left that to others, and with it the wealth which might thus be acquired, and himself went on to investigate other obscure and little known phenomena connected with physics and electricity, regarding this as his proper work. When, many years afterward, he came to see the first application of this discovery of his to the production of the illumination of the North Foreland Lighthouse, he said, after looking at the large magneto-electric machines there, "I gave it to you an infant; you have made it a giant."

E.

Eagle, The War. This bird, best known as Old Abe, was captured early in 1861 on the Flambeau River in Wisconsin, by a Chippewa Indian named Chief Sky. A white man purchased him for a bushel of corn, and in his turn sold him to one Mills, who presented him to Company C of the 8th Wisconsin just as the newly recruited lads were about to start for the front. It was they who named him after the man in the White House They carried him alongside the colors on a perch at the end of a staff. Hence the 8th Wisconsin soon came to be known as the Eagle Regiment.

Beginning with Farmington, Miss., Old Abe and his followers went through thirty-six battles. He was wounded before Corinth and again at Vicksburg. It is said that at Corinth the Confederates made special efforts to kill Old Abe, at the direction of General Price. " I would rather have him than a whole brigade," Price is said to have remarked, such was the eagle's value in encouraging the troops.

We are told that whenever the gray coats showed up Abe would utter the shrill eagle's cry, by way of giving the alarm. He stayed with his command until it was mustered out in 1864. In September of that year Lewis, the Wisconsin war Governor, formally accepted him on behalf of the State. Old Abe was exhibited at the Chicago Sanitary Fair that winter, and his history, published in a pamphlet, brought $16,000 for the sick soldiers.

It is pleasant to record that he lived long and happily afterward. He was much in demand at conventions and veterans' reunions. He died in March, 1881, as a result of breathing smoke at the fire of the Madison capital. Leonard W. Volk, the sculptor, used him as the model for several eagles on his war monuments.

Earthquake Plant. A popular name given to the abrus, a plant that grows wild in Cuba and certain parts of India and is characterized by a strange sensitiveness to weather conditions. Baron Nowack, an Austrian, was the first scientist to investigate the claims made for it, by the natives of tropical regions, as a herald of earthquakes. He decides that it was a veritable vegetable barometer, forecasting storms, cyclones, and especially seismic disturbances such as earthquakes and volcanic eruptions.

King Edward VII, it is said, once asked Baron Nowack to foretell the state of the weather on a stated evening in the future. With the help of the abrus the Baron worked out the problem. He predicted that the night in question would witness a violent thunderstorm. The prediction, it is added, came true. Thereupon a royal invitation was issued for him to come to London and cultivate his seismological vegetable on an elaborate scale.

The abrus changes its color on the approach of a period of fissure in the crust of the earth. This change of color seems to coincide with the appearance of spots of a certain magnitude upon the surface of the sun. Observation of the plant must accordingly be conducted simultaneously with studies of the sun. It is not yet determined what is the connection between the two phenomena, but Baron Nowack is of opinion that sun spots and earthquakes are dependent phenomena, because the effect of both upon the plant seems identical. If the abrus begins to change color and if coincidentally there be a spot of any magnitude upon the sun, the appearance of a fissure in the surface of the earth may be expected.

Echo. In classic mythology Echo was a nymph—daughter of Earth and Air—who loved Narcissus, and at his death pined away until nothing remained of her but a voice, which inherited her immortality and wandered about the world repeating every sound that reached it.

One of the most extraordinary echoes in the world is to be heard by the side of a small lake in Bavaria. On one hand rises a perpendicular cliff several thousand feet high, while on the other side is a dense forest. If a pistol is fired on the lake, the woods send back a faint echo that gradually dies away, but presently it is heard from the cliff, continually increasing in power, till it bursts over one's head like a deafening peal of thunder.

Addison, in his "Journey to Italy," tells of a very similar echo that inhabits the old Simonetta palace about two miles out from Milan. It forms three sides of a quadrangle. Mr. Addison declared that upon firing a pistol, he heard the sound returned fifty-six times, though the air was then foggy, and consequently not proper for making an experiment to advantage. At first the repetitions were very quick, but the intervals were greater in proportion as the sound decayed. This astonishing echo was probably never designed by the architect, but it is occasioned by two parallel walls of a considerable length, between which the sound is reverberated from one to the other till the undulation is quite spent. Some persons assert that the sound of one musical instrument in this place resembles a great number of instruments playing in concert.

A more recent traveller, Mr. Samuel L. Clemens, in his "Innocents Abroad," describes another notable Italian echo which repeated and re-repeated a girl's laughing cry:

"Ha!————ha!——ha!——ha!—ha!—ha! ha! h-a-a-a-a-a!" and finally went off into a rollicking convulsion of the jolliest laughter that could be imagined   It was so joyful—so long continued—so perfectly cordial and hearty, that everybody was forced to join in. There was no resisting it.

Then the girl took a gun and fired it. We stood ready to count the astonishing clatter of reverberations. We could not say one, two, three fast enough, but we could dot our note-books with our pencil points almost rapidly enough to take down a sort of short-hand report of the result. I could not keep up, but I did as well as I could.

I set down fifty-two distinct repetitions, and then the echo got the advantage of me. The doctor set down sixty-four, and thenceforth the echo moved too fast for him also. After the separate concussions could no longer be noted, the reverberations dwindled to a wild, long-sustained clatter of sounds such as a watchman's rattle produces.

In the Roman Campagna, at the sepulchre of Metella, the wife of Sulla, the echo repeats five times, and in five distinct keys; it will also repeat an hexameter line, or any sentence which can be spoken in two and a half seconds.

Still another famous Italian echo is in the Cathedral at Pisa, long celebrated for its leaning tower. Sing two notes and there is no reverberation; sing three and they are at once taken up by the walls of the edifice, swelled, prolonged, and varied, till they seem as a divine harmony from some majestic organ.

There is a cavern in Finland in which, if you test your lungs to the top of their capacity, there will answer you such horrible roarings, moanings, and mutterings that you will be glad to rush out in absolute terror.

An echo that repeats seventeen times is to be found between Bingen and Coblentz, on the banks of the river Naha. A peculiarity of this echo is that, although the speaker's voice may be almost inaudible, the volume of sound apparently increases in the echo.

In the chapel of the Abercorn family at Paisley, the shutting of the door produces an echo that sounds like the roll of thunder, and a note of music is caught up and repeated time after time. Margery, the daughter of Bruce and wife of William Wallace, lies buried in this chapel.

The echo of the "Eagle's Nest," at Killarney, is said to repeat a bugle note at least one hundred times, and the effect of firing a cannon is to give the impression of thunders of artillery that gradually die in the distance.

In the park at Woodstock, Oxfordshire, England, there is said to be an echo that in the day-time will repeat seventeen syllables, and at night twenty syllables. But this echo, even at its best, is still one behind the echo on the north side of Shipley church, in Sussex, which clearly repeats twenty-one syllables.

Among other noted echoes is that heard from the suspension bridge across the Menai Strait, in Wales. The sound of a blow from a hammer on one of the main piers of the structure is returned in succession from each of the cross-beams that support the roadway and from the opposite pier at the distance of five hundred and seventy-six feet, in addition to which the sound is many times repeated between the water and the roadway at the rate of twenty-eight times in five seconds.

Eddystone Light-house. The Eddystone Rocks are about 9 miles distant from the Ram Head on the coast of Cornwall. The small surface space presented by the largest of the rocks and its exposed situation made the erection of a light-house unusually dangerous. The first structure was a wooden one designed by Winstanley and begun in 1696. It was soon found that the sea rose to a greater height than had been expected, so great, indeed, that the lantern, 60 feet above the rock, was often buried under water. Thereupon Winstanley raised the height to 120 feet,—too high for its strength to bear. In November, 1703, such injury had been received that Winstanley went there in person to superintend the repairs. On the 26th of that month, a violent storm carried away the whole edifice, with Winstanley and his men, not a soul of whom escaped.

One catastrophe led to another. The *Winchelsea* man-of-war was wrecked, with great loss of life, on the Eddystone Rocks. Not until July, 1706, however, was a new light-house begun, under direction of John Rudyerd, of London. The tower, 92 feet high, was all of timber.

The edifice was finished, and the new light first shown on the 28th of July, 1708. It continued to be regularly exhibited during forty-seven years, when it accidentally took fire, and, being formed of such combustible materials, the whole fabric was destroyed A.D. 1755.

As it was quite evident that a "light" was absolutely necessary at this spot, and—strange to relate—as the "authorities" had now really learned some wisdom by experience, preparations were immediately made for the erection of another light-house. On the 5th of April, 1756, Smeaton first landed on the rock, and prepared for the erection of a light-house of stone. He arranged for the foundation by cutting the surface of the rock into regular horizontal benches, and into these the foundation stones were to be carefully dovetailed or notched. The first stone was laid in 1757.

Edelweiss. A funeral oration by Ralph Waldo Emerson over the body of his friend Thoreau concluded with these words:
" There is a flower known to botanists, one of the same genus with our summer plant called ' Life Everlasting,' a *Gnaphalium* which grows on the most inaccessible cliffs of the Tyrolese mountains, where the chamois dare hardly venture, and which the hunter, tempted by its beauty and by his love (for it is immensely valued by the Swiss maidens), climbs the cliffs to gather, and is sometimes found dead at the foot, with the flower in his hand. It is called by the botanists *Gnaphalium leontopodium,* but by the Swiss *Edelweisse,* which signifies *Noble Purity.* Thoreau seemed to me living in the hope to gather this plant, which belonged to him of right."

The Danes were the first to cultivate the flower, imported for the purpose from Switzerland, with any measure of success. In 1911, however, French horticulturists established a thriving business at Fontenay and Chatillon, just outside the gates of Paris. All through the Alpine tourist season, they shipped large orders to the different Swiss resorts, for it was found to flourish more freely under cultivation than ever it did on the snowy heights of the Alps. Thus the French exotic growth either comes back to the place of its origin or goes to England. But though most of the edelweiss on the market comes from Paris, you might ask for it in any of the Paris florists' shops without finding a single blossom. Whimsically enough, there is no charm about it unless you have been to the Alps to get it.

Thus another illusion must be added to the souvenirs provided for tourists in summer haunts at home or abroad, none of which apparently are produced in the place where they are purchased. See also WALSH: *Handybook of Literary Curiosities,* 268.

Eden Hall, Luck of. Eden Hall is the ancient seat of the celebrated border clan of Musgrave, near Penrith, Cumberland, England. The Luck, a painted cup or goblet of very thin glass, is a cherished heirloom whose advent into the family is explained by ancient legend. The family butler, so the legend runs, went one night to the well of St. Cuthbert, on the grounds of Eden Hall, to draw some of its famous water. He found the goblet on the margin of the well. Around it a group of fairies danced in the moonlight. He seized it, a struggle ensued and he carried it off, the fairies singing as he went

> If e'er this cup do break or fall,
> Farewell the luck of Eden Hall.

It is said that the wild Duke of Wharton once barely escaped shattering the Luck. He dropped it after drinking from it, but a butler deftly caught it in a napkin.

To-day it is safely kept in a leather case, much resembling the narrow stem and graceful labial expression of the morning glory. The goblet itself is shaped like a very tall tumbler, widening at the top, with a double rim of glass and two rings a little distance from each other at the base. The cup is ornamented with an interlacing pattern, very much like that seen in the ivory carvings and metal chasing of the eleventh and twelfth centuries; the glass is of colored enamel, chiefly blue and yellow, and very neatly executed. It is most probably Byzantine, and dates about the twelfth century.

Doubtless some pilgrim Musgrave, perhaps a Crusader, brought the precious vessel home in safety and, admiring its rare beauty, it is not surprising that such mystical power was assigned to it.

Uhland has a ballad on The Luck of Eden Hall, familiar to all English-speaking people through Longfellow's translation.

There are many tales of different lands in which a cup or other vessel figures as a fairy gift. An Icelander married a fairy, who, desiring Christian baptism for their child, deposited the infant for that purpose at the churchyard gate with a golden goblet as an offering (Einar Gudmund's Collection). In Zealand a Troll caught stealing beer leaves his copper kettle behind him, which is treasured by the family. A Troll-maid who marries a mortal brings as her dowry a multitude of copper vessels. The dracæ or water-spirits inveigle women and children to their subaqueous dwellings by floating cups. Fairy caldrons appear in many legends.

According to a tradition of the seventeenth century, an ancestor of the noble house of Duffus was one day walking in a field near his house, when he heard a noise like a whirlwind and voices crying, "Horse and Hattock" (words used by the fairies in moving from one place to another), and he was immediately caught up and carried through the air to the French king's cellar at Paris; having drunk heartily, he fell asleep, and was found the next day with a silver cup in his hand. The king, having questioned him as to his name, residence, and mysterious journey, allowed him to go and to keep the silver cup, which is still preserved in the family under the name of the "Fairy Cup."—*American Notes and Queries*, March 30, 1880.

Eel. This fish, the *anguilla* of the ichthyologist, has been a source of myth and marvel from the earliest days. Aristotle called eels "the solitary race that have neither seed nor offspring." Pliny, accepting this error, sought an explanation in the fact that they rubbed themselves against the rocks after they were weary of life, and that a new breed issued from the detritus. Naturalists of lesser fame imagined that, like Virgil's bees, eels issued from the carcasses of animals. Greek poets, whose habit it was to attribute to Jupiter all offspring that could not otherwise be accounted for, held him and a white-armed goddess named Anguilla accountable for these slimy reptiles. Arches-tratus, in his description of an Attic feast, makes Anguilla boast of her Jovian progeny. In Egypt the eel was worshipped as a god.

So recently as the seventeenth century, Jan Baptista Van Helmont (1577–1664) believed that the eel came from Maydew and might be obtained by the following process: "Cut up two turfs covered with May dew, and lay one upon the other, the grassy sides inward, and thus expose them to the heat of the sun; in a few hours there will spring from them an infinite quantity of eels." Others of his contemporaries opined that they pro-ceeded from the skins of old eels, or from those of snakes, while even to this day the belief is prevalent in some parts of the world that eels are not born from other eels, but from other fishes, and even from animals which do not belong at all in the class of fishes.

On the coast of Germany a fish related to the cod, *Zoarces viviparus*, which brings its young living into the world, owes to this circumstances its name "Allmuter," or "eel mother," and similar names are found on the coast of Scandinavia. It is an ancient and still prevalent belief that eels pair with water snakes. In Sardinia the fishermen say that the so-called water beetle, Dyticus roselii, is the progenitor of eels, and they therefore call this insect "mother of eels."

It was not until 1873 that the problem was scientifically solved by Syrski at Trieste. He discovered the males among the smaller specimens, all the larger being females. L. Jacoby, a later observer, found no males exceeding 19 inches in length, while the female frequently reaches a length of 39 inches or more.

In ancient Rome the murænas, or sea eels, were thought to have a regular language—"low and sweet, and with an intima-tion so fascinating that few could resist its influence." It is added that the Emperor Augustus possessed, or feigned to possess, the ability to understand this language.

Eels were known to the old pharmacopœia. Hippocrates forbade their use as food in tabes and diseased spleen. Galen prescribed them as medicine in nephritic complaints, where the gluten might be thought to concrete gravel into stone. Pliny asserted that their use as food impaired the singing voice. The monks of Salerno complained "that to live on eels is a sure recipe for spoiling the voice."

Donne has it: "If you would make some notorious drunkard to loath and abhore his beastly vice, and forever after to hate the drinking of wine, put an eel alive into some wyde-mouthed bottle with a cover, having in it such a quantity of wine as may suffice of itself to suffocate and strangle the eel: which done, take out the dead eele and let the partie whome you would have reclaymed, not knowing hereof, drink of that wine only as much as he listeth."

In an old work, "The Anglers," in eight dialogues in verse, we find the following:

> An eel?—thy fat is sanative for blows.
> Its virtuous drops th' obstructed ear unclose.

There is a prevalent, but erroneous, belief that thunder has the effect of rousing eels from their mud, and many fishermen expect to make big catches during thunderstorms.

But away with fables! The truth about the eel is more marvellous than any imputed fiction. Like the Pacific salmon, the female spawns only once (in salt or brackish water) and then dies. The male also survives only a short period after giving the first evidence of sexual maturity. The eel is able to pass from pond to pond or river to river, owing to the fact that each gill is enclosed in a kind of pouch or bag, within which the fish can retain water for the purpose of moistening the gills during its overland journey. It is a connecting link between fishes and reptiles in that it is fitted with both lungs and gills, the only animal so endowed.

The eel has still other claims to be regarded as one of the strangest creatures in the whole animal world. As it often lives under stones, and in mud and sand, its eyes must be protected in some way, so nature has provided it with an arrangement which may be likened to a pair of spectacles. Some people are said to carry their heart in their pocket, but the eel, in addition to having a heart located in the proper place and performing the usual functions of that useful organ, also has one in its tail, called a lymphatic heart, the pulsations of which may be seen under a microscope. The animal can easily be killed by striking it on the tail.—JOHN N. COBB, *N. Y. Tribune*, December 12, 1909.

Eggs. The *Saturday Review*, in one of those famous "middle" essays which delighted mid-Victorian Englishmen, fell foul of (no pun is intended, despite the pun-provoking associations) the ridiculous fuss and fury exhibited by the common or barnyard fowl in laying its eggs.

"Why she should be so clamorous," urged the essayist, "is inconceivable, unless it be to annoy other hens who are less oviparous; for indeed if there are hens who never lay, their bitter consciousness of incompetency must be considerably aggravated by the clatter and cackle of the hens who do. It is singular, if hens dislike the process, that Providence should have seen fit to condemn them to it as a piece of almost daily discipline and probation. If they do not dislike it, why attract so much attention to an unimportant operation?"

But is the operation unimportant? Not, certainly, if you judge it by its result. The egg of any bird is a mystery of mysteries, a succession of bags bagged up, a series of envelopes enveloped in one another, bags and envelopes jointless and seamless. The apple in the dumpling, the fly in the amber, the full-rigged glass ship in the bottle, is simplicity itself compared to an egg, where there are eight or nine or ten of these sacks in sacks ensacked. "As full of meat as an egg" is an obvious platitude. "As full of mystery as an egg" is no paradox. The shape of eggs offers as much diversity as their size and weight. A few, like those of the owl and the tortoise, are spherical or nearly so; a few more, like the grebe's or the cormorant's, are elliptical, with symmetrical ends; the great majority, like the domestic hen's, are ovoid, or blunter at one end than the other. The hen's egg is always laid blunt end foremost.

Whatever the form of the egg, however, the yolk is always spherical. This is due to the fact that it is enclosed in a fluid, the albumen, or "white," which makes the pressure constant on every portion of the yolk's surface.

A flock of 100 hens produce in eggs' shells about 137 pounds of chalk annually; yet not a pound of the substance, or perhaps not even an ounce, exists around the farm house within the circuit of their feeding grounds. The materials of their manufacture are found in the food consumed and in the sand, pebble stones, brick dust, bits of bone, etc., which hens and other birds are continually picking from the earth. The instinct is keen for these apparently innutritious and refractory substances, and they are devoured with as eager a relish as the cereal grains or insects. If hens are confined to barns or outbuildings, it is obvious that the egg-producing machinery cannot be kept long in action unless the materials for the shell are supplied in ample abundance.

Most people are aware of the power of egg-shells to resist external pressure on the ends, but not many would credit the results of tests recently made. Eight ordinary hen's eggs were submitted to pressure applied externally all over the surface of the shell, and the breaking pressures varied between 400 pounds and 675 pounds per square inch. With the stresses applied internally to twelve eggs, these gave way at pressures varying between

32 pounds and 65 pounds per square inch. The pressure required to crush the eggs varied between 40 pounds and 75 pounds. The average thickness of the shells was 13-1000 inch.

The ostrich, of all extant birds, lays the largest egg in actual dimensions. Relatively to its size, however, the kiwi, a strange wingless New Zealand species, is the champion, with an egg not less than five inches long, although the extreme length of the bird itself is only twenty-seven inches. The smallest birds' eggs are those of the minuter species of humming birds. Nevertheless, the cuckoo lays the relatively smallest egg. Though the jackdaw and the cuckoo are of the same size, the former's egg is five or six times larger than the latter's. The fact that the cuckoo (*q.v.*) is accustomed to deposit its eggs in the nests of birds usually much smaller than itself doubtless accounts for this phenomenon.

An ostrich egg would shrink into insignificance beside that laid by the now extinct epyornis, which measured 9 x 13 inches. An epyornis egg is not beautiful, but it is rare, which is not surprising, since the bird ceased laying thousands, or perhaps hundreds of thousands, of years ago. Hence the market price of a good specimen is about one thousand dollars. The habitat of the epyornis was Madagascar, where many of its eggs have been exhumed from the drifting sands of the southern portion of the island. This bird is supposed to have given rise to the fable of the roc in the "Arabian Nights."

The eggs of the great auk are even more valuable than those of the epyornis. It is true that in 1879 two were sold in Edinburgh for four dollars apiece, but a few years later the pair sold for two thousand four hundred dollars. The specimen in the Natural Museum at Washington was purchased in 1851 for one hundred dollars. It is impossible to say what it would bring nowadays. We only know that the maximum sum so far reached for a good specimen was close to $1500. This was paid by a collector in North London. The favorite haunts of the great auk were Labrador and the southwest coast of Iceland. Audubon adds that it was not uncommon in what is now Newfoundland and about Nahant, Massachusetts. The eggs were about 5 inches long and 2 or 3 inches wide. They weighed about a couple of pounds. Just sixty-eight specimens are known to be in existence. Each has its history. In the Natural History Museum at Newcastle, England, which possesses one of the finest of all collections relating to sea-birds, the curator keeps in a locked drawer what appears at first sight to be a large number of great auks' eggs. But only one is a real specimen, the rest are chalk or plaster models of other existing treasures. So good

eglantine." In the list of the fairest flowers with which the brothers of Imogene propose to sweeten her sad grave, Shakespeare makes especial mention of the eglantine:

> Thou shalt not lack
> The flower that's like thy face, pale primrose, nor
> The azur'd harebell, like thy veins, no, nor
> The leaf of eglantine, whom, not to slander,
> Out-sweeten'd not thy breath.
>
> *Cymbeline*, Act IV, Scene 2.

Leigh Hunt has—

> Wild rose, sweetbrier, eglantine,
> All these pretty names are mine,
> And scent in every leaf is mine,
> And a leaf for all is mine,
> And the scent—oh, that's divine!
> Happy, sweet and pungent, fine,
> Pure as dew and pick'd as wine.

But if we wish to hear golden words attached to the poet's flower, it is to Keats we must turn. We find that in the " Ode to the Nightingale," it is called " the pastoral eglantine," and in " Endymion," " the dew-sweet eglantine." Note also the lines:

> Rain-scented eglantine
> Gave temperate sweets to that well-wooing sun.

In " Isabella," that storehouse of jewelled words and phrases, Keats says:

> Come down, we pray thee, ere the hot sun count
> His dewy rosary on the eglantine.

In 1496 the Amsterdam Chamber of the Eglantine was founded, taking for its motto the words " Blossoming in Love." Nearly a century afterward two of the literary guilds of Antwerp established branches at Amsterdam, bearing the titles of the Fig-tree and the White Lavender Bloom. Henceforth the Eglantine Chamber was known as the Old Chamber.

Electoral College of the United States. Never perhaps in all history has ingenious calculation been so utterly baffled as in the case of the machinery established by the Constitution for the choosing of president and vice-president. The electoral college was intended by the founders to work in a very different manner from that to which it has been wrested by their successors. Alexander Hamilton's paper on the election of the president (*Federalist*, No. 68) explains the object that they had in mind, and demonstrates that none of them, including himself, had the slightest notion of how the system would work in its practical application. " The mode of appointment of the chief magistrates of the United States," he remarks, " is almost the only part of the system which has escaped without severe censure, or which has received the slightest mark of approbation from its opponents." This unanimity of praise he holds to be amply justified. " I hesitate not to affirm," thus he continues, " that, if the manner of it be not perfect, it is at least excellent. It unites in an eminent degree all the advantages, the union of which was to be wished for." The notion of Hamilton was that, without having a direct popular election, " the sense of the people should," in his words, " operate in the choice of the person to whom so important a trust was to be confided." The election was not to be made by the federal legislature; he hardly discusses that possibility, which would indeed have been quite inconsistent with the whole theory of the presidential office. The executive and the legislature were to be independent bodies. The election was to be a popular one; that is, it was to express the general feeling of the people at the time; but it was not to be made by direct popular election. Hamilton feared that the direct popular election of the chief magistrate might give rise to tumult and disorder. He thought that such tumult and disorder would be less likely to happen in the choice of several intermediate electors than in the actual choice of the president himself. On the other hand, he wishes to hinder " cabal, intrigue, and corruption." These, he thinks, might happen in the case of any " pre-existing bodies of men "—a phrase which of course takes in both the federal legislature and the legislatures of the several States. He holds that such bodies would be more open to corrupt influences, from foreign powers or otherwise, than a body of men chosen specially for the purpose, whom, he says, there would not be time to corrupt. He thinks it also important to shut out all persons who might be supposed to have any special devotion to the president for the time being, among whom he counts senators, representatives, and all persons holding any office of profit or trust under the United States. All of these are actually shut out by the Constitution. His belief was that the people would make a discreet choice of electors, and that the electors would make a discreet choice of a president.

In all this there is a great deal of wisdom, granting the one point which Hamilton and everybody else at the time seem to have taken so completely for granted as not to discuss the possibility of anything else,—that the electors really would elect. If they had not expected that the intermediate body would exercise a discretion of their own, the founders of the Constitution would certainly not have invented such an intermediate body. Their notion was that the electors would freely discuss and deliberate, and that each man would vote for the candidate whom he personally believed to be best fitted for the place. Hamilton conceived a state of things in which the electors would represent the general feeling of the people at the time; in which a majority of them would express the general wishes of the majority of the people, but in which they would go to the work of election altogether unfettered by instructions as to particular persons. Nor was the expectation at all an unreasonable one. It was what might be fairly expected to happen in any community which was not yet broadly divided into two strongly marked political parties. The case is the same as that of intermediate election for any other purpose, say for parliamentary representatives. Where there are no sharp political differences, where the questions are likely to be less as to ends than as to the adaptation of means to ends, it is quite intelligible that election by chosen electors may give a better representative body than direct popular election. But as soon as sharply marked and organized political parties arise, it is no use asking whether the intermediate election will or will not provide a better representative body, for the intermediate election will come to be a mere form) The only question asked of the intermediate electors, the only instructions given to them, will be for whom they will vote at the final election. In the present condition of England or of the United States such a process would be an empty and cumbrous form. In Norway we can well understand that it may be otherwise.

So it has been with the American presidency. The founders of the Constitution believed that the people would elect men whom they could trust, men who represented their general political wishes, and would leave it to them freely to choose a president. As it has happened, the provision of the Constitution of which Hamilton could say that it was the one which was most generally approved is the one which has most utterly broken down. The election of electors has become a mere form. The electors exercise no discretion; they simply vote for the man of their party, the man for whom they are chosen to vote.

The rule that the choice of the electors settles the choice of the president is so thoroughly taken for granted that popular language has adapted itself to what is the practical aspect of the case. We hear that Tilden or Hayes has carried such a State. That means that that State has elected electors who must, unless they break their faith to their party, vote for Tilden or for Hayes. Yet, as far as the law goes, these electors may vote according to their personal discretion, for Tilden or Hayes or any one else that they choose. But the possibility of their doing so is not taken into consideration. It is assumed that the popular vote, the vote for the electors, decides the vote for the president whom those electors are to choose. In popular speech the election of electors is often spoken of as the election of the president. And so it practically is, with one important qualification. It is always possible—and it has sometimes happened—that a president may be chosen who has not the popular vote in his favor. This is no more than may always happen in any representative body. The majority who carry a measure may have been chosen by small majorities in their several constituencies, while the minority who vainly oppose it may have been chosen by large majorities, and may really represent a majority of the people. Let representation be ever so closely apportioned to population, let there be universal suffrage and equal electoral districts, still there is always the chance that the minority may in this way get the upper hand.—*Saturday Review*, December 9, 1876.

Electric Light.   The earliest notice of an electric light appeared in the *Journal of the Society of Arts*, vol. i, p. 323.

" On Friday last [*i.e.,* May 18, 1853] one of the Citizen Steamers started from Chelsea for Gravesend at 9 P.M., carrying an electric light with a parabolic reflector on each paddle-box, returning to town at 3 A.M.   The lamps brilliantly illuminated both banks of the river, shedding a flood of light on the objects and edifices in the way, including Chelsea College, the Houses of Parliament, St. Paul's, and Greenwich Hospital. The effect, as seen from the bridges, is said to have been remarkably striking and beautiful.   The shipping in the pool, below London Bridge, was as conspicuously seen as in the light of day—a most important fact in relation to the subject of safety to life at sea, and the national question of a perfect system of light-houses on the British coast."   See LIGHTING, ELECTRIC.

Elephant.   The popular notion about elephants is derived from the courts and camps of the East.   They are rightly enough believed to play a prominent part in reviews, durbars, and other solemn pageants in which Oriental magnificence is seen side by side with Western symmetry and order.   Most people are aware that most of the tigers annually slain in India are shot by sportsmen securely seated in a howdah on the back of an elephant.   So far so good.   Some people may need to be reminded that these useful beasts are employed for many domestic purposes, and are often maintained all over India by native gentlemen who never faced a tiger or handled a gun.   English gentlemen engaged in commercial or agricultural pursuits in the interior of the country find such an animal to be well worth his keep in many ways. It brings in the collections of rent from an out-station to head-quarters.   It takes important letters or supplies right across country.   It will carry half-a-dozen servants, with bed, baggage, and cooking apparatus, to any place where these adjuncts or necessaries cannot readily be obtained. It enables the native agents of a factory to travel about with security against accidents or robbery. Where roads have not been constructed, or are impassable for vehicles during the rainy season, the elephant is equal to any emergency. To swim rivers, to skirt or wade through swamps, to step cleverly over fences, to fray a path through reeds, to break down forest trees firmly connected by long trailing creepers, is a comparatively easy task to this sagacious, powerful, and obedient servant. It is true that three or four miles an hour is the average rate of progress, and that it is hardly fair to exact of an animal more than fifteen or twenty miles of march in the day.

The cost of an elephant's keep, in food and attendance, is very considerable. Not every kind of leaf is palatable to him; whole tracts of country covered with forest trees are absolutely useless for the feeding of elephants. He must have a mahout to give him his daily bath and rub him down afterward. He must be protected from tropic rains in a high-roofed barn. Moreover, an elephant may, under bad management, become as fertile a source of quarrel as rabbits or hares. Some have a vicious habit of getting rid of their fastenings, and making nightly expeditions into fields of rice or sugar-cane. A mahout, with the recklessness or nonchalance of Asiatic menials, will take his elephant right through a field of rice, wheat, or pulse to save a circuit of a few hundred yards, or he will permit it to pluck the finest fruits of the orchard, or, as he passes through a village, will slyly connive at a push or a shove that annihilates a line of storehouses, or huts made of wattles, mud, and thatch, Incensed land-owners, defrauded of their rents or defied by their tenants, have often been known quietly to send a *posse* of servants on an elephant into the garden or field of their adversary, and to trust to subsequent chicanery and corruption to meet and counteract the tale of a plundered homestead and a ravaged crop.

Wild stories have been told about the longevity of the elephant. Pliny set its maximum age at 300 years; Aristotle declared for 200 years. Philostratus was content with no such modest figures. He asserted that an elephant belonging to King Porus not only lived long enough to become a great favorite with that monarch, but actually survived its royal master for four solid centuries! In actual fact the average age of an elephant is about 100 years.

Wild elephants were caught and trained at an early period. Arrian (*circa* 104 A.D.) gives an account of the capturing of elephants in India which does not differ much from modern methods.

The history of the Maccabees informs us, that in the army of Antiochus, " to every elephant they appointed a thousand men, armed with coats of mail, and five hundred horsemen of the best; these were ready on every occasion; wherever the beast was, and whithersoever he went, they went also; and, upon the elephants were strong towers of wood, filled with armed men, besides the Indian that ruled them." The elephant was domesticated by the Carthaginians, who employed it in their wars with Rome. No African race has since succeeded in reclaiming this highly intelligent and naturally docile animal, a fact which is often cited in proof of the general inferiority of the negro race. Although Cæsar does not allude to the fact in his " Commentaries," it is generally believed that he brought elephants with him to Britain, and that they contributed to his conquest of the island. An old writer tells us that Cæsar, having attempted unsuccessfully to cross the Thames, fenced a large elephant which he had with him with a coat-of-mail, built a large turret on it, and putting up bowmen and slingers, ordered them to pass first into the stream. The Britons, terrified at sight of this unknown and monstrous animal, fled in the wildest confusion.

In the year 802 an elephant was sent to Charlemagne by Haroun-al-Raschid, Caliph of the Saracens. In 1255 Louis IX, of France, presented an elephant to his English contemporary Henry III, which he had probably procured from some of the African chiefs during his invasion of Palestine by way of Egypt. This elephant was kept in the Tower of London; and Henry III, in a precept to the sheriff of London, says, " we command you, that, of the farm of our city, ye cause without delay, to be built at our Tower of London, one house of forty feet long, and twenty feet deep, for our elephant." Matthew Paris, *Historia Anglorum*, says this was the first elephant ever seen in England. Pope Leo X was presented with an elephant by Emanuel of Portugal; and we read about the same period of another at the court of the Queen of Bohemia.

During the middle ages little was known about these animals except through the inaccurate representation of them upon medals. So recently as 1673 Sir Thomas Browne, in his " Vulgar and Common Errors," notices the prevalent opinion that the elephant has no joints and never lies down.

Shakespeare endorses the vulgar error, when he makes Ulysses say, " Troilus and Cressida," act ii, sc. 3:

> The elephant hath joints, but none for courtesy; his legs are legs for necessity, not for flexure.

In the earliest carved example of the elephant in the Cathedral at Exeter the hocks are turned the wrong way.

The following advertisement appeared in the *Flying Post,*
London, on November 29, 1701:

This is to give notice that there is lately arrived a large elephant,
the biggest that ever was in Europe, and performs varieties of exercise for Diversion and Laughter, viz.: Exercises the Musket, flourishes the Colours, very nimble and swift in several Postures; He also
bears two persons upon his Trunck, two upon his ears and ten upon
his Back; with several varieties. It is to be seen at the White Horse
Inn in Fleet Street from 10 in the morning till 6 at Night.

Evidently Lester Wallack was wrong when, in his " Memories
of Fifty Years," he declared that the first elephant ever exhibited alive in England came over in Elliston's day. But undoubtedly this was the first elephant that ever went mad on English
soil and had to be killed. The event created much excitement and
was naturally in everybody's mind. Wallack tells us that
Elliston, in his gouty old age, used to go to Drury Lane theatre
every night, particularly if one of his own famous parts were
being acted by the elder Wallack. " Being wheeled down to the
prompter's place in an invalid chair, he would sit and watch all
that was going on. In the mad scene in *The Belle's Stratagem,*
Doricourt, who is feigning madness, has a little extravagant business and, at a certain exit, utters some wildly absurd nonsense,
such as ' Bring me a pigeon pie of snakes.' On the night in
question, when the town talks of nothing but the dead elephant,
my father, on his exit after the mad scene, shouted, ' Bring me
a pickled elephant,' to the delight of the easily pleased house, but
to the disgust of the sensitive Elliston, who, shaking his gouty
fist at him, cried:
" Damn it, you lucky rascal. They never pickled an elephant
for me in the days I played Doricourt!"
The first elephant exhibited in America is announced, in an
advertisement printed in the Philadelphia *Aurora,* July 28, 1796,
as having just arrived " from New York in this city, on his way
to Charleston. He possesses the Adroitness of the Beaver, the
Intelligence of the Ape, and the Fidelity of the Dog. He is the
largest among Quadrupeds, the earth trembles under his feet;
he has the power of tearing up the largest trees and yet is
tractable to those who use him well. . . . This Elephant
now offered for public Exhibition is about three years, near six
feet high. He is of the largest species, growing to the height of
sixteen feet. . . . He was purchased in New York for Ten
Thousand Dollars."
Grown people were charged half a dollar and children a
quarter to see this great sight.
In his " Land of the White Elephant " (New York, 1874),

Frank Vincent gives an interesting account of the elephants employed in the immense timber-yards at Maulmain.

The power, sagacity, and docility displayed by these trained animals are wonderful. They are chiefly employed in drawing, stacking, and shifting the huge teak logs, some of them weighing as much as two tons, which are cut in the forests upon the banks of the Salween, and floated down the river to timber-yards. A log that forty coolies can scarcely move, the elephant will quietly lift upon his tusks, and holding it there with his proboscis, will carry it to whatever part of the yard he may be directed by his driver. He will also, using trunk, feet, and tusks, pile the huge timbers with the utmost precision. It is surprising to see the sagacious animal select and pick out particular timbers from the centre of a large heap at the driver's command. The elephants are directed by spoken orders, pressure of the driver's feet, and the goad. It usually requires a year and a half to train an elephant thoroughly for the lumber business. Sometimes an animal will break his tusks 'rom being forced by an ignorant or brutal driver to carry an excessive load, but generally he knows his own strength, and refuses to lift more than his tusks will bear. Should these break off close to the head, the elephant would die; if only cracked, they are bound with iron, and rendered as serviceable as before.

These of course are only ordinary elephants. Even in Siam white elephants are very scarce. One might say indeed that they do not exist even there, for at its whitest the elephant is merely light-colored or spotted. Probably the lightest albino ever seen in Siam was one brought over to Bangkok in 1880 by a European circus. But the rains fell and the paint came off and there was much public indignation. The elephant died a few days later; "the judgment of Buddha," said the Siamese whose duty it was to supply him with food.

Sometimes in the rutting season a tame elephant goes temporarily mad, and is transformed from a serviceable drudge into a demon of inventive malice and deliberate revenge. An elephant has been known, when in this state, to take up a commanding position on a high road and near a village, and to deal death and destruction round him for a week together. Old women and children caught and pounded to a jelly; corpses whirled round in mockery by the trunk of the infuriated animal; several houses unroofed or thrown down; portly native gentlemen flying out of their palanquins; communication stopped, and the whole neighborhood in a panic—this has not unfrequently been the tenor of the police reports for days, until a spherical bullet from the practised hand of a sporting magistrate or indigo-planter gives the destroyer his quietus.

There are only two or three places where a shot is effective. Either the charge of the animal must be awaited, and the aim must be taken at the hollow just above the trunk. or, if the sportsman has not coolness enough for this venture, a side shot through the eye will do equally well. It is well known that the English Major Rogers killed some twelve hundred wild elephants in the jungles of Ceylon, and rarely failed in despatching his victim at one shot. But then he had thoroughly studied the habits of the animal, whether single or in herds, was a first-rate shot, and had the assistance of a native so cool and daring as to be able to walk up to a herd and pull the tail of an unsuspecting beast, which, in consequence, looked round and presented a favorable shot to the experienced sportsman.

Elevated Railroad, familiarly known in New York and other American cities as the L.

A very close approximation to the modern elevated road was conceived of in France by J. Telle and described in a pamphlet which he issued about the beginning of 1855. The Paris *Illustration* for April 26, 1856, made this idea the subject of illustration and accompanying explanation. It quotes from Telle's pamphlet the purposes of the invention, among which are: The clearing of the streets of Paris or any other large city, the lowering of transportation fares, the saving of time, and the establishment of closer civic relations.

"The means of execution," continued M. Telle, "are as simple as the end in view: they consist in creating a net-work of railways or even a single line in the interior of great centres of trade. This net-work or line will in no way interfere with the use of sidewalks and driveways already established on the surface of the ground. It will run sometimes above and sometimes below street level. In the former case it will be elevated at a height of one story upon arches in the form of a viaduct. Whenever our railway is crossed by streets, quays, boulevards, canals, rivers, or railroads, it will ever be placed above or below the soil in such fashion that it can never interfere with traffic or pedestrianism. If it be above the soil, there will be established at the point of meeting a bridge constructed of arches, or other supports, so that our railway is never halted in its progress. If necessary, a second story may be superimposed, and the upper one can be devoted to freight alone, the lower one to passengers. The structures put up to the right or left of the elevated railway, which we shall call *maisons ferrées* (iron houses) may be sold, or rented, or retained as circumstances may determine."

It may be added, with a semblance at least of truth, that the elevated road originated in the Himalayas. At Kulu there is an aerial railroad centuries old which is in annual use at a great religious festival celebrated there.

From a cliff overhanging a precipitous gorge 700 feet wide and more than 100 feet deep a rope is stretched. The other end is fastened to a strong stake on the opposite side of the ravine. The rope is nearly 2500 feet long. When stretched taut the upper end is several hundred feet higher than the lower. Down the terrible incline slides the worshipper or performer, technically the jheri; the precaution having first been taken to wet the rope so it will not catch fire by friction. The jheri sits astride on a kind of rough wooden saddle fitted with holes through which the rope is threaded. Bags of sand are attached to his legs to enable him to maintain an upright position during his headlong descent, and also to increase the momentum. The lower end of the rope is wound round with rugs and carpets, in order to check the descent at landing, and prevent the jheri from dashing his brains out against the pole to which the rope is fastened. The first few hundred yards of the descent are accomplished with lightning speed, as is indicated by the stream of smoke that follows in the jheri's wake. The incline then diminishes and the pace becomes slower and slower, so that by the time he reaches the goal he is able to stop himself without danger. A successful flight is thought to assure a prosperous agricultural season.

New York was the pioneer city in establishing the elevated metropolitan railway as we know it to-day. The first line was constructed by Charles T. Harvey on Greenwich street and first operated in 1867. The first stretch of road was built from Battery Place up to the old School 29. The first car ran over it July 2, 1867. The structure was extended to Cortland Street in 1868 and to 29th Street, via 9th Avenue, in 1869. The road had a single track. The motive power was a cable. The experiment was unpopular—passengers disliked the dizzy height —and it failed in 1870.

On December 1, 1875, the Gilbert Road, called after its projector, Dr. Rufus H. Gilbert, was definitely authorized. In September, 1877, the Court of Appeals ended the weary course of litigation by declaring its charter constitutional. It was opened to traffic from Rector street to Central Park along Sixth avenue, but it had then passed from the Gilbert incorporators and was known as the Metropolitan Elevated Road. Dr. Gilbert's first plan was to erect a pneumatic tube suspended from lofty arches, the same principle as had been employed in the Beach underground road, of which a sample section under Broadway from Warren street nearly to Murray street had been opened to inspection on April 26, 1870. Dr. Gilbert's idea was that cars blown through this high tube would be noiseless and out of-sight, thus overcoming the difficulties which interfered with the first Greenwich street elevated. When the pneumatic tube was found impracticable Dr. Gilbert returned with a new plan, to retain the lower half of the tube and to operate a steam road in this trough, for a part of the objection was that property owners were not willing to concede to elevated passengers the privilege of inspection of second story domesticity. In the final stage the Gilbert road became no more than a steam operated elevated. Elevated roads were assigned to Ninth, Sixth, Third, and Second avenues, and allotted evenly to Dr. Gilbert's company and the New York Elevated, which was then the corporation owning the Greenwich street line.

In its issue for August 31, 1889, *Chambers' Journal* had this item from America, annotated by its own editor: An engineer of Chicago has proposed a system of elevated railways for that city, the lines to be at a height of 120 feet above the pavement, so as to clear the roofs of the largest houses. This plan is put forward chiefly on account of its non-obstruction of the light, and also because its noise will not be so troublesome as that of a railway at a lower elevation. The passengers would be raised to the aerial stations by means of lifts.

"This plan," says Wiseacres, editorially, "is never likely to be carried out, if for nothing else than that it would quite destroy the architectural features of a city. It is far better to keep metropolitan lines below ground and out of sight as much as possible; and, although the unhealthiness of a vitiated atmosphere may be pleaded, every one knows that fresh air can be secured in the tunnels if only the directors of the railroad will go to the necessary expense."

Elevator or Lift. The word "lift" is universal in England for what in America is best known as an "elevator." The earliest mention of any device of this sort is found in Vitruvius, who describes a hoisting machine, invented by Archimedes (*circa* B.C. 236), which was worked by ropes coiled upon a winding drum by a capstan and levers. Another hoisting machine mentioned by the same authority was made to rotate by men walking inside the capstan. A primitive elevator of this sort is still extant in the convent of St. Catherine on Mount Sinai. This is worked by a capstan, and is used to lift either passengers or freight from the ground floor to the second story.

About the close of the seventeenth century a Parisian inventor named Villayer constructed a lifting apparatus for a single person. He called it a flying chair. It was simply a chair attached to a rope which was passed over a pulley—or something which did duty for one—and had a weight at its other end to counterbalance the chair and the occupant. It continued in fashion until a mishap occurred to the king's daughter at Versailles. The machinery failed to work when she was half way up, and there she stuck for three good hours before she could be rescued by her servants, who had to break away the wall to release her. " Flying chairs " were not much used at court afterward. This story is told in Dangeau's Journal of the Court of Louis XIV, published posthumously in 1720.

Some years later M. Thronier, who dabbled in mechanics in his leisure time, made a similar chair, which he worked from the balcony outside his window. He thus escaped the danger of being shut up in a shaft as the king's daughter had been. M. Thornier kept his arrangement secret and had many a laugh at the expense of his friends who came to visit him. When they left him he would make some excuse for not going down stairs with them, but when they reached the courtyard they were amazed to find him standing there awaiting them. To their questions he would return jesting replies, and then seat himself in his chair and go up so quickly that they were unable to discover how he did it. Nemesis overtook him. One day, instead of surprising his friends agreeably he did so disagreeably, for the machinery broke and he came greatly to grief. He used the staircase after his recovery.

Steam hoists for the lifting of freight came in with the beginning of the nineteenth century.

The father of the modern platform elevator was Henry Waterman, of New York, who in 1850 constructed one for the firm of Hecker Brothers, flour merchants. It was operated by means of a lever within the framework of the platform. Almost simultaneously George H. Fox and Co., of Boston, started into the business, and introduced successive improvements. The worm gear of 1850 was supplanted by a wire rope in 1852. Cyrus W. Baldwin, of Brooklyn, began the experiments which led to the perfecting of the hydraulic elevator some time in the mid-fifties.

Accidents were frequent with all the early elevators. A notable one occurred at the store of Emmons, Danforth and Scuddor in State Street, Boston. An elevator platform built by Albert Betteley, of the firm of William Adams & Co., fell from a great height into the cellar beneath the hoistway. It was laden with seven boxes of sugar. Mr. Betteley, hastily summoned to the scene, was surprised to find the sugar intact in the unbroken boxes. Reasoning from effect to cause, he divined that, as the cellar was almost air-tight, the platform in its rapid descent had compressed the air beneath so as to form an " air-cushion," which had broken the fall. On this hint he acted, and a few months later took out a patent for an air-cushion, now universally used in connection with dumb-waiters and to a great extent in connection with passenger elevators.

The first passenger elevator worked by steam was invented

by Otis Tufts, of Boston. His so-called vertical screw railway was patented August 9, 1859. It was notable also as being the first elevator with a closed car. Before the end of the year Tufts put up one in the Fifth Avenue Hotel in New York. A few months later he put up another in the Continental Hotel in Philadelphia. These, however, were the only screw passenger elevators ever made. The expense ($25,000) was found to be prohibitive, especially as the machine was slow and cumbrous.

So recently as January 25, 1908, John G. Adams wrote to *Notes and Queries*, 10th Series, IX. 67 : " While recently stopping at the Fifth Avenue Hotel in New York I noticed in one of the passenger elevators a tablet upon which was recorded the following :

" In this space was erected and operated in 1859 Taft's vertical screw railway, the first passenger elevator ever built."

In 1875 the Fifth Avenue screw elevator gave place to a more roomy and more modern rope elevator. This had been patented by the same Mr. Tufts in 1861, when he found the screw elevator was not the thing. His improvement on the old rope elevator consisted in providing a number of ropes, each of which would sustain five times the weight of the car. The strain on these ropes was equally distributed by a system of levers. Mr. Tufts put up his first rope elevator in the American House, Hanover Street, Boston, in 1868, the storm and stress of the civil war period having interfered with the earlier adoption of his invention. This was substantially the passenger elevator as we know it to-day. It is usually worked by steam, but not infrequently by water pressure from a city main, or by tanks in the top of the building. A steam passenger elevator (engine, hoistway, and all) costs from $5000 to $7000. A passenger hydraulic elevator can be put in for about $2500, and one for freight for about $1600.

In 1878 Colonel A. C. Ellithorpe, of Chicago, patented various improvements on Betteley's air-cushion. One of the first tests of the new apparatus was made at the Parker House in Boston in the year 1880. Eight persons walked into the car. The ropes were cut. With a rush and roar that was heard a block away, the elevator fell, breaking the glass windows on the way and badly shaking up the eight passengers. No one was seriously injured, however. It was ascertained that the air reservoir at the bottom had not been excavated deeply enough, and no provision had been made for the partial escape of the air by means of valve or wire grating. The mishap taught the inventor caution and enabled him to perfect his machine. The next trial, which happened in the same year at the Chicago Exposition, was entirely successful. The car weighed 2800 pounds and carried a score of passengers. When the ropes were cut, it fell noiselessly 109 feet. The passengers walked out smiling, amid the cheers of the spectators. In other experiments baskets of eggs taken into the car and glasses of water held by the passengers landed with their contents unbroken or unspilled. It was found that the car stopped rather suddenly but very gently when it reached the air-cushion and then settled slowly to the bottom of the well. (See "The Vertical Railway" in *Harper's Magazine*, vol. lxv, page 889.

The *Builder* for September 10, 1859, thus condensed a recent article in the New York *Herald*, which had celebrated the opening of the Fifth Avenue Hotel:

This gigantic establishment, which is six stories high exclusive of basement, covers an acre of ground, and contains 500 rooms for guests. The accommodation is in every respect perfect, but perhaps the most powerful feature in the hotel is that it will contain a vertical railway, that is, a carriage will move from the top to the bottom of the building and from bottom to top. It will be forced up by the application of steam power, and the descent will be regulated by the resistance of hydraulic power, so as to guard against accidents. The car will be attached to a shaft which, being turned by steam, will cause the car to proceed upward by means of a screw, or on the principle of the inclined plane. The car stops at each floor, and passengers are landed, and others taken in. In the same way, in making the descent, it stops at each floor. It is stated that there will be contrivances at each of these landings to prevent accidents. Behind the vertical railway is a baggage elevator, moved by the same power. The object of this is obviously to save the necessity of taking trunks up and down the stairs—a great convenience. Near the vertical railway there is a capacious staircase for those who prefer using their legs.

English Channel. Jean Pierre Blanchard, a French aeronaut residing in England, was the first balloonist to dare the crossing of the Channel, and he succeeded in the attempt. He took with him Dr. Jefferies, an American who had graduated from Harvard College in 1763 and was practising medicine in England. The pair had previously made a number of aerial ascents together. At one o'clock on January 7, 1785, they took their seats in a balloon, ascended from Dover Cliffs, and sailed in the direction of Calais. Blanchard was in command. They carried with them only thirty pounds of sand ballast, which proved too little for so long a voyage. To their surprise, the air appeared to grow lighter as they advanced over the water, so that they sank too freely. At about mid-channel they were compelled to discharge all their ballast in order to maintain their level. But the balloon still descended. To obtain momentary relief they ejected a parcel of books. When three-fourths of the distance across the channel, they sighted the French coast. The balloon was now contracting and sinking rapidly. They threw out of the car everything available,—anchors, cordage, provisions. Finally they cast off part of their clothing, fastened themselves to the cords suspended from the balloon-ring, and prepared to cut away the car. But presently, approaching the coast near Calais, they began to rise; then ascended rapidly, soaring in a magnificent arch above the high grounds. When above the forest of Guines, they descended gradually, seized the branches of a tree to arrest their flight, and at three o'clock were safely and happily landed. This thrilling two-hour voyage made a great sensation. Blanchard was honored by a special summons to the court of Louis XVI, who made him a present of 12,000 livres and settled upon him a yearly pension of 1200 livres. The car of the balloon is preserved at Calais.

It should be remembered that at this time there were two kinds of balloon in use, the Montgolfier or hot-air balloon and the balloon filled with hydrogen gas. Blanchard's had been of the latter kind. Pilatre de Rozier, friend of Montgolfier and first man who had ever gone up in a balloon (see FLYING MACHINES), determined to essay a cross-channel voyage, starting from the French side, in a balloon of his own construction which combined both the hot-air and the gas principles. He called this the Charles-Montgolfière. A friend named Romaine agreed to accompany him. Thousands of spectators watched the ascent of this extraordinary composite balloon from Boulogne on June 15, 1785. For a quarter hour all went well. Then it was seen that the smaller globe had caught on fire, and a few moments later the whole apparatus was aflame at an altitude of 3000 feet. Presently it fell, a charred and shapeless mass, upon the sea-shore. Both of the men were killed.

They were the first martyrs in the cause of the new science. A monument close to Boulogne marks the scene of the disaster, whose memory is further perpetuated in the names and signs of the cafés and inns of the neighborhood.

A rival claim has been put forward for an Italian named Grimaldi, as an anticipator of Blanchard, but the claim rests on very doubtful foundation. A book named " La Storia del Anno MDCCLI " (" History of the Year 1751 ") is said to have been printed in Amsterdam for a Venetian librarian. This book has an account of Grimaldi's invention, " riding which he flew from Calais to London making seven leagues an hour." The only allusion to this book is found in an authentic work entitled " Memorie degli Architetti Antichi e Moderni " (" Memoirs of Ancient and Modern Architects "), published in

Parma, 1781. The author never saw the book in question and is somewhat doubtful of his áuthority, but he says tentatively:

" He (Grimaldi) only once put himself to the risk of crossing the sea, and that was from Calais to Dover, and the same morning he arrived thence in London. He has lately made a trip from the London Park as far as Windsor Lodge and back, the whole in less than two hours." (See FLYING MACHINES, on pages 351–354.

Engraving is classed among modern inventions, and it is usually held that the familiar engraving of St. Christopher bearing Christ upon his back is the earliest known specimen of the art. This dates from the year 1423. The only existing impression was found pasted on the inside of a cover of a manuscript in the library of a Suabian convent. A somewhat dubious story, current in 1850, says that an accident carried this date five years backward. " A few weeks ago," says the *Illustrated London News* in June, 1850, " some person at Malines, who was about to burn an old chest which contained a quantity of mouldy papers, perceived, pasted on the inside of the lid, a print which was become very obscure from dirt and age. A person, however, was present, who had a knowledge of prints, and who carefully took off the fragments; and, having united them again, found clearly marked the date of 1418. This rare specimen, which belongs to the Flemish school, has been purchased for the Royal Library at Brussels, at the price of 500 francs." The subject of the print is not stated.

It must be added that the Romans knew of some process whereby they inserted the likeness of a writer in his book, which at least served the purpose of engraving. Martial, Seneca, and Cicero allude to it. Pliny makes a clearer statement, but, unfortunately, he does not seem to have understood the process. " By some means or other," says he, " Marcus Varro introduced the portraits of seven hundred individuals in his numerous books, as he could not bear the idea that all trace of their features should be lost." These illustrations were reproduced somehow, for " not only did Varro confer immortality "—upon the author's features—" but also he transmitted them to all parts of the earth, so that anywhere it might be possible to see them." Pliny calls this a " most blessed invention, and if it were not engraving, what could it have been? The learned have been inquiring and debating for three hundred years, but they will never agree. Any day, however, Herculaneum may yield some old papyrus which will decide the question.

A pretty mediæval romance, but one which has little authority to support it, appears in a book by Papillon, a French wood-engraver and an authority on his art. According to this, the first engraved blocks were cut by a pair of twins, Alexander Alberic Cunio and his sister Isabella.

The maiden Isabella is described as being surpassingly beautiful, talented, and accomplished; at thirteen she understood Latin and geometry, wrote excellent verse, played upon several instruments, and had begun to design and paint with delicacy and taste; while her brother, the chivalric Alberic, was of quite ravishing beauty, and one of the most charming youths in fourteenth-century Italy. At fourteen he commanded a squadron of horse in the wars, and displayed extraordinary valor. After distinguishing himself by defeating two hundred of the foe, he returned to his amiable sister, and in conjunction with her designed and executed eight wonderful wood-blocks illustrating the progress of Alexander. On the completion of this remarkable series he once more ventured on the field of battle, being accompanied by the passionate lover of his beautiful sister. This brave action, however, proved fatal, for he was killed, and his friend dangerously wounded while defending him in the midst of the enemy. This so affected the twin sister that she resolved never to marry, and pining away in the approved style of mediæval romance, died at the interesting age of twenty. This is a pretty and effective story. The only fault about it is that it isn't true. The author of it had an exuberant imagination, and latter-day authorities ascribe it to that peculiarity rather than to sober history. At all events, there has always been a squabble about it between various writers on the art of wood-engraving, though the general opinion is, as nobody has ever seen the engravings ascribed to this romantic pair, that the whole story is a myth of the Middle Ages.

John Foster established the first printing-press in Boston, and as his first book issued in April, 1675, Increase Mather's sermon, "The Wicked Man's Portion." He is famous, also, among print-collectors, as the first American engraver. Although a self-taught artist, he left behind him several prints which are very creditable in execution. He was an engraver in fact before he set up as a printer on his own account. The earliest extant example of his work is a portrait of that remarkable New England divine Richard Mather, which was intended apparently as a frontispiece for a life of Mather written by his son, the more remarkable Increase Mather, and published (1670) from Samuel Green's press in Cambridge, Mass.

Only one copy of the book containing this frontispiece is now known to be in existence. Six years later Foster made the first map engraved in America, entitled, "A Map of New England, being the first that was ever here cut, and done by the best pattern that could be had, which being in some places defective, it made the others less exact; yet doth it sufficiently show the scituation of the Countrey, and conveniently well the distance of places."

This quaintly named map, now of extraordinary value in its first "state" (or earliest impression), was originally published in Boston in 1677 in William Hubbard's "Narrative of the Troubles with the Indians in New England, from the first planting thereof in the year 1607, to this present year 1677." This book, printed by Foster, is seldom found with the first issue of the map. A perfect copy is valued at about $650. In this first issue of the map the White Mountains are called by Foster "The White Hills." This was altered by some blunder into "Wine Hills" in the London reprint.

Envelopes. The invention of the envelope in England is usually attributed to S. K. Brewer, a bookseller and stationer of Brighton. The story runs that about 1830 he had for sale some small sheets of paper whereon it was difficult to write the address. Accordingly he devised small envelopes and had metal plates made for cutting them to the desired shape and size. They caught the fancy of the Brighton ladies, and his orders so multiplied that he finally had them made for him by Dobbs & Co., London. This was the beginning of the trade.

There is no doubt, however, that envelopes were in use before the time of the worthy Brighton bookseller. So far as is known, the idea of post-paid envelopes originated early in the reign of Louis XIV of France, with M. de Valfyer. In 1653 he gained the royal approval for the establishment of a private post, and placed boxes at the corners of streets for the reception of letters enclosed in envelopes that were sold at offices established for the purpose. Valfyer had also sold artificial *formes de billet,* or notes applicable to ordinary business communications, with blanks to be filled up by pen with such special matter as the writer desired. One such *billet* has, by a fortunate misapplication, been preserved to our time. Pélisson, the friend of Mme. de Sévigné (and of whom she said that "he abused the masculine privilege of being ugly"), was tickled by this skeleton form of correspondence, and filled up the blanks of such a *forme* with a letter to Mdlle. de Scudery, addressing her, according to the pedantic fashion of the time, as "Sappho," and signing himself "Pisandre." This billet is still extant, and is probably the oldest existing example of a prepaid envelope.

In the English State-paper Office is a letter addressed to the Right Hon. Sir William Trumbull, Secretary of State, by Sir

James Ogilvie, and dated May 16, 1696. It is now attached to an envelope 4¼ x 3 inches in size, cut nearly the same as our modern ones. The next known example is an autograph letter (in an envelope) of Louis XIV to his son by Madame de Montespan, the Comte de Toulouse, admiral of the fleet at the siege of Barcelona. Dated Versailles, April 29, 1706, it is written, sealed, and addressed by the royal hand. Le Sage in his "Gil Blas" (Book 4, chap. 5), published 1715, in describing the epistolary correspondence of Aurora de Gusman, makes one of his characters say that after taking two billets, "Elle les cacheta tous deux, y mit une *enveloppe,* et me donna le paquet." In the British Museum there is an envelope, exactly like those now in use, with an ornamental border, bearing date 1760, from Mme. Pompadour to the Duchesse d'Aiguillon, also a letter from Frederick of Prussia addressed to an English general in his service, dated at Potsdam, 1766, which is folded in an envelope of coarse German paper similar in form to modern ones, except that it opens at the end, like those used by lawyers for deeds, instead of at the top.

An early allusion to envelopes in English literature is to be found in Swift's "Advice to Grub Street Verse-Writers," 1726, wherein he playfully twits Pope for his small economies which betimes led him to write his verses on bits of paper left blank or written on only one side. He tells them to have their verses printed with *wide margins,* and then,—

> Send them to paper-sparing Pope,
>   And when he sits to write,
> No letter with an envelope,
>   Could give him more delight.

It has, however, been conjectured that this did not refer to anything resembling our modern envelope, which could have been of little use to Pope, but to a half-sheet of paper used as a cover. Be that as it may, an old family in Yorkshire preserves an envelope exactly like the square modern pattern, sent from Geneva, in 1750. In the *Gentleman's Magazine,* May, 1811, is a copy of a letter from Father O'Leary, of which it is said "the envelope being lost, the exact address cannot be ascertained"; and Charles Lamb writes to Bernard Barton, March 20, 1826,— "When I write to a great man at the Court-End he opens with surprise a naked note such as Whitechapel people interchange, with no sweet degrees of envelope. I never enclosed one bit of paper in another, nor understood the rationale of it. Once only I sealed with a borrowed seal, to set Walter Scott a wondering, signed with the imperial quartered arms of England, which my friend Field bears in compliment to his descent in the female line from Oliver Cromwell. It must have set his antiquarian curiosity upon watering."

Not until Sir Rowland Hill secured the establishment of the penny post on January 10, 1840 (see Post-office) did envelopes become popular in England. Before then double postage was charged for one piece of paper enclosed within another, no matter how thin each might be and how light the letter. So long as this rule was enforced, only franked letters were enveloped, though at a still earlier day an envelope was used as a mark of respect, especially when writing to a superior.

On May 6, after the penny post had been established, the use of envelopes became general. Stamped and adhesive envelopes were issued by the post-office. Edward Hill, a brother of Rowland, in partnership with Warren de la Rue, was the inventor of the first envelope machine. This was patented March 17, 1845.

Exchange, Royal. The idea of the Royal Exchange in London originated with Sir Richard Gresham (1485?–1549), and was carried into execution by his son Sir Thomas Gresham, the great merchant prince of the sixteenth century.

In 1537 Sir Richard's business had taken him to Antwerp. Here he noted what a great accommodation the Bourse was to the merchants who frequented it, and he wrote a letter to Thomas Cromwell suggesting that a similar building should be put up in Lombard Street. As nothing came of the proposal, he wrote again next year, offering to share in the cost, which he estimated at £2000. If the Lord Privy Seal would induce Alderman Sir George Monoux to part with certain property at cost price, he engaged to raise £1000 toward the building. The king addressed Monoux on the subject, an arbitration was suggested and accepted, and then for some unknown reason the matter was dropped.

In 1561 Thomas Gresham, the son, received from Richard Clough, his factor in Antwerp, a letter expressing his astonishment that London should have gone so long without a bourse:

" Considering what a city London is," he wrote, " and that in so many years the same found not the means to make a burse, but merchants must be contented to stand and walk in the rain, more like pedlars than merchants. In this country and in all other, there is no kind of people that have occasion to meet but ye have a place for that purpose; indeed and if your business were done (here) and that I might have the leisure to go about it, and that I would be a means to Mr. Secretary to have his favor therein, I would not doubt but to make so fair a burse in London as the great burse is in Antwerp, without soliciting of any man more than he shall be well disposed to give."

Gresham remembered the attempt made by his father in 1538 and its failure. He resolved to take the matter up again and appealed to the court of aldermen. One of them sounded him as to what he himself would be willing to contribute to the enterprise. This was in 1563, two years after the receipt of Clough's letter. Gresham took time to consider. In 1565 he sent in the offer. He would himself erect a "comely burse" if the city would provide a suitable site. The site was found on the north side of Cornhill. On June 27, 1566, Sir Thomas laid the foundation stone. Every one of the aldermen laid his stone or brick, with a piece of gold for the workmen. The plan of the building at Antwerp was closely followed. The design, the architect (Henryke), and most of the material came from Flanders, much to the disgust of English masons and bricklayers. On January 23, 1571, Queen Elizabeth visited it in state for the formal opening, but she refused to accept the proposed name of the Bourse, and ordered by a herald and trumpet that henceforth the building should be called the "Royal Exchange and no otherwise."

Gresham's Exchange was totally destroyed in the Great Fire of 1666, was speedily rebuilt, and was again burned in 1838. The present building by Tite was opened in 1844.

Express. The American express business had a singular beginning. In January, 1839, William Frederick Harnden (1812–1845) came down to New York for a short rest. As ticket-master in the office of the Boston and Worcester Railroad, he had been worn out by sixteen hours of daily toil. Though at that time there were only 2818 miles of railroad in the United States (all built within the previous ten years), the officials were cruelly overworked. There was no express company in existence. One day a bright thought struck Harnden.

"Do you know," he said to his friend James W. Hale, "I think that I could make a living running errands for people between New York and Boston?"

Hale chimed in with the idea. He himself was employed in the Hudson News-room, at No. 1 Wall Street, New York. One of his duties was to fetch papers down to the Boston boat on its tri-weekly trips. Besides the papers he carried consignments of money or parcels from persons who could not get down to the boats themselves. All these he would turn over to any reliable passenger who was willing to deliver them.

On the stage lines the drivers or the passengers were the parcel deliverers. No one ever thought of asking money for his services.

"Go ahead," advised Hale. "You ought to make money. I'll get you a lot of customers here in New York."

Harnden bought a couple of extra-large carpet-bags, and announced that he was in the business of carrying parcels between New York and Boston or intermediate points, at low prices. His first announcement appeared in a Boston paper dated February 23, 1839. His offices were at No. 1 Wall Street, New York, with his friend Hale, and at No. 9 Court Street, Boston. The "express" was for some time easily carried by Harnden in his two valises, but he soon succeeded in obtaining the confidence of the business public. In a few months he was employing two messengers, one of them being Hale and the other a brother, Adolphus Harnden. The latter lost his life in the burning of the steamer *Lexington* in Long Island Sound January 13, 1840.

In 1840 the business was extended by a branch line to Philadelphia, and in the same year an international express was founded by Harnden in partnership with D. Brigham, Jr. In the same year Alvin Adams established another express line, also between Boston and New Nork. Other rivals followed. In 1854 many of these companies amalgamated. Thus under its extant name of Adams Express Company the services started by Harnden and Adams were consolidated.

Eyes, Artificial. The first mention in print of any maker of artificial eyes appears to be an advertisement in St. James's *Evening Post,* June 11, 1734. Notice is therein given that a Thomas Gamble, who lived at "The Black Raven," a seed shop over against Water Lane, was "the only Operator in Artificial Eyes and the only survivor of the famous Mr. James Smith deceased," who apparently had left the secret to Gamble.

"All Gentlemen, Ladies and others," continues the advertisement, "may be furnished with all sorts of Artificial Eyes, exactly like the natural; they having the Motion, Bigness and Color exact to the truly natural: He hath made them for several Persons so nicely that they have worn them many years . . . his artificial Eyes have been sent for to most parts of Europe by Persons of the best Quality, and whereas he hath received advice out of this Country that several persons would use them, but then are told that the Remaining Part of their Ball must be taken out first: This is to satisfy them to the contrary, for if they have any Ball left, they may wear it without any trouble at all." (See also *Pearson's Magazine* for February, 1897.)

F.

Fan. The fundamental idea of the fan, if we are to credit Chinese legend, was hit upon centuries ago at a certain Feast of Lanterns (see LANTERNS), by one Kansi, beautiful daughter of an eminent mandarin. This young woman found herself so hot that, in violation of all etiquette, she took off her mask, and then was fain to hide her blushes and eke to cool her face by the operation we now call fanning. Kansi's young companions saw and approved; "instantly," says the narrator, "ten thousand hands agitated ten thousand masks." Other writers are content with the simpler and less specific explanation that the fan originated in the necessity felt in all hot countries for keeping off flies from the sacred offerings in the temple, from the hands and faces of the officiating priests, and from the profaner persons of the population in general.

In India and China the original model of the fan is said to have been the wing of a bird. Certainly an admirable fan can be made from two birds' wings, joined by a strip of wood. The fan of the high priests of Isis was in the form of a half-circle, made of feathers of different lengths. Such, too, were the fans carried in triumphal processions, which among the Egyptians served also as military standards in time of war. The Sibyls are said to have been in the habit of fanning themselves as they delivered their oracles—the fan being evidently not regarded in those days as in any way connected with frivolity; and even now, not alone in the East, but in Europe, the fan plays an important part in certain religious ceremonies. The Pope is on certain occasions of grand ceremony followed by two fan-bearers; and in the Greek Church it is a part of the ordination of deacons to arm the newly received ecclesiastic with a fan, that he may protect the officiating priest from flies during the celebration of the mass.

The earliest reference to fans on the part of a classical author occurs in Euripides's tragedy of "Helena," where one of the characters, a eunuch, relates how, according to the Phrygian custom, he has fanned the hair, face, and bosom of the beautiful heroine. The fans carried by the Roman ladies were not, like the most ancient Chinese fans, made in one piece, whether of paper, gauze, or silk, but were composed of little tablets of perfumed wood. The ladies of high fashion were followed when they went out walking by fan-bearers or *flabelliferæ;* and guests of both sexes were fanned at dinner by slaves charged with that particular duty.

The fans of the Middle Ages were in good society worn from the girdle by chains of gold, and were usually made of feathers,—those of the peacock, ostrich, parrot, and pheasant being the favorites. Sold in large numbers on the markets in Turkey and Morocco, they came direct to Venice, whence they were distributed all over Italy. For many years after its first introduction into Italy the fan was considered a symbol of levity, and the woman who carried one was regarded much as a woman who waltzed was looked upon at the beginning of the present century. Catherine de Medicis is said to have introduced the fan (*circa* 1560) into France, where it was quickly adopted, not only by women but by effeminate men. Ten years later fans reached Elizabethan England, either from France or from Italy, though probably from the former.

Fans may be divided into two classes: those consisting of one web of paper or silk and those which are made up of several thin strips of wood or other material. The former are held to be the best for fanning, the latter for shuffling, or for the manœuvre known in the days of the "Spectator" as "flirting" the fan. In countries where the use of the fan is thoroughly understood, this convenient appendage to a lady's dress is much employed in signalling. The practice in question is the subject of one of Calderon's comedies, which has been imitated, under the title of "Le Mouchoir, les Gants, et l'Éventail," by a modern French author, whose work was in due time adapted to the English stage, where, if we mistake not, it became known as "Love's Telegraph."

A French author declares that there are a hundred different ways of using the fan. Of these, however, he only mentions one: which consists in so holding this weapon and shield of coquetry that its bearer may receive a love-letter unobserved. That the fan may serve to hide blushes, facilitate whispering, and so on, need scarcely be pointed out. Those who desire full information on this subject cannot do better than study Gosson's "Pleasant Quippes for Upstart Gentlewomen," published in 1596, soon after the introduction of the fan into England, and full of remarks on its use and abuse.

China and Japan still remain preëminently the countries of the fan. There the fan is still carried not only for use in every-day life, but also as an article of military equipment. The massive bronze fan which until recently was carried by a Japanese mail-clad warrior quite sufficed to knock down an adversary; and it was frequently used in lieu of a sword for replying in summary fashion to real or fancied insult. On one memorable occasion, in 1828, the Dey of Algiers used a fan in this manner, under pretext of having been provoked by the resident French consul. That blow was dearly paid for. The dey having refused to apologize, his dominions were invaded, and the French, after occupying Algiers and the surrounding districts, "provisionally" (so they assured the English government) and merely with a view to an honorable peace, established themselves permanently in the dey's capital, and gradually took possession of what is now called Algeria.

The oldest historical fan in existence, preserved in the Cathedral of Monza, near Milan, formerly belonged to Theodolinda, Queen of the Lombards in the sixth century. Another of her possessions, in the same church, is the famous Iron Crown.

Farm. The largest farm in the world was said in 1912 to be that owned by Don Luis Terrazas in Chihuahua, Mexico. According to the *Scrapbook*, it included 8,000,000 acres of fertile land and measures 150 x 200 miles. On its mountains and through its valleys roam over 1,000,000 cattle, 700,000 sheep, and 100,000 horses, requiring the services of 2000 horsemen, herdsmen, shepherds, and huntsmen.

Each year at least 150,000 head of cattle and 100,000 sheep are slaughtered, dressed, and packed, this ranch being the only one in the world which maintains its own slaughtering and packing plant. And this means a very considerable additional profit to its august and fortunate owner.

"On the gigantic estate are 5 reservoirs, which cost $500,-000, and 300 wells, which cost over another $500,000. Don Luis Terrazas is a scientific farmer, and raises every kind of grain in his great fields. His homestead is declared to be the finest farm-house in existence in any country. It is capable of accommodating 500 guests at a time, and was erected at an expense of $2,000,000. It is a veritable country palace, and the gardens are more carefully laid out and the stables are more costly than those of any emperor. On the homestead alone are employed over 100 male servants."

The title of largest individual farmer in the United States was in the same year claimed by the New York *Tribune* for David Rankin, a member of the Missouri delegation to the Republican National Convention, which renominated President Taft. "He was the oldest delegate in the convention, having passed his eighty-third year. His farm in Atchison County, Mo., comprises 25,000 acres, 18,000 acres being given to the cultivation of corn and the other 7,000 to pasturage. Last year his corn crop reached over 1,000,000 bushels. He has 10,000 cattle and 25,000 hogs. ' I made my first start,' said Mr. Rankin, ' with just $100. . I began buying and driving cattle to market on a small scale sixty-one years ago. That was from Burlington, Iowa, and Chicago was my destination. I sold those cattle at a spot less than two blocks from where the Coliseum now stands.' "

Fastnet Rock Light-house. The most costly light-house in the world is that erected in 1900–12 on the Fastnet Rock, a small pinnacle on the S. E. corner of the coast of Ireland. It is the first light seen by the great liners on their passage to England, and the last landmark they pass on their way to New York.

The new tower cost $420,000 to build. It displaced the structure erected on the rock in 1840. The old tower measured, with its lantern, ninety-one feet in height. It stood well up on the rock, but it soon was discovered that it was not strong enough to stand the strain put upon it. In very stormy weather the waves dashed right over the lantern, although the latter was 173 feet above the level of the sea. On one occasion a full cup of coffee standing on the table in the top room was thrown to the floor when a heavy wave thundered against the rock. Later it was discovered that the structure was being undermined gradually. Costly strengthening works had to be put in periodically to prevent a collapse of the tower.

In the year 1900, a British light-house builder, William Douglass, was asked by the Irish Commissioners to prepare plans and erect a new tower of stone on dreaded Fastnet. Mr. Douglass surprised his brother engineers by selecting as a site the ledge of a chasm that had been eaten away by the waves on the extreme western edge of the rock at the point where the fullest fury of the waves was experienced. He argued like this: "If I build my tower on this ledge, the base will receive the heaviest seas before they rise to their full height, and if the base is composed of solid masonry and arranged in steps, this would be an excellent buffer to break up the·strength of the waves."

Even to land on the Fastnet Rock is an exciting experience. It is seldom that one can step direct from a boat on to the rock, and the builders reached their work by means of a rope lowered from a long boom to the boat. Catching hold of this rope just above their heads and placing their feet through a kind of stirrup, they were swung through the air on to terra firma.

While the foundations were being secured, a special steamer

was used, whose duty it was to transport the building material to the scene of operations. This steamer cost $50,000. She carried all the granite blocks of which the new tower is composed. The stone was obtained from quarries in Cornwall. The new tower is 147 feet in height, with a graceful elliptical curve on its circular face from the base to the lantern gallery. At the foundation it is 52 feet in diameter, and is perfectly solid for a height of 48 feet. It took more than a year to lay the first twenty courses, the tower consisting of 89 courses. In all, 2074 stones, weighing from 1½ to 3 tons apiece and representing a total weight of 4633 tons, were used. The base of the structure is made solid by a marvellous system of dovetailing, by which one stone is grafted into its fellows above as well as into those on each side of it. This makes the light-house one solid mass, and if it were possible to lift the whole structure up and place it on a slant, it would not fall to pieces.—*New York Press*, January 14, 1912.

February 30. At Ottley, in England, postal cards can be bought for a penny apiece, which contain the following:

A CURIOUS GRAVESTONE

The following appears on a gravestone in the churchyard of the picturesque village of Fewston, in the Washburn Valley near Otley, Yorkshire:

> To the memory of Joseph Ridsdale of Bluberhouse
> Who died Febuary 29, 1823, aged 79 years
> Also Elizabeth his wife March 18 1813
> aged 59 years.
> And William their son, died Febuary the 30th
> 1802 aged 23 years.

It will be seen that the letter "r" is omitted from February in each case, that it is impossible to have February 29 1823 or February 30, 1802, as the former is not a leap-year and the latter is quite out of the question; and that the order of the dates when death occurred is reversed.

See *Notes and Queries,* 10th series, i. 233, and viii. 330, for this and other instances.

First and Last Inn in England. A hostelry bearing this singular name is situated in the parish of Sennen, Cornwall, about three-quarters of a mile from the Land's End. The name is justified by the position of the inn. As the traveller nears it from inland, he may read upon one face of the sign-board "The Last Inn in England"; and, upon the opposite face of the sign-board, as he approaches the house from the Land's End, "The First Inn in England." It is, altogether, a traveller's "wonderment"; but though the house is small, the landlady will assure him that he can be provided with a dinner of "fish, flesh, and fowl," in the course of an hour. Sennen lies about nine miles south of Penzance, over rather a wild country; and at three miles distance from Sennen is the famed Logan or Logging Stone (see WALSH, *Curiosities of Popular Customs,* p. 626).

The Land's End, in Cornwall, consists of a promontory covered with greensward, whose granite cliffs present, to the ever-stormy sea that dashes against that coast, a precipitous rampart. The descent from the high road, distant about a quarter of a mile from the sea, to the very brink of the cliffs, is by a steep smooth lawn. In 1840 a horseman was run away with on this spot. Horse and rider were seen rushing down the green declivity with ungovernable speed, and the immediate destruction of both seemed inevitable; but, upon the very ledge of the precipice, the horseman had the luck or dexterity to let himself drop on the turf, thus saving his life. "The horse leapt into the sea, and the impress left on the sod by his hinder feet, about a yard from the brink of the precipice, has been preserved to this day in commemoration of the event." So says *Dolman's Magazine* for January, 1847.

Floating Church. The pioneer of these singular edifices was launched at Bordentown, New Jersey, in 1847. It was designed and built by a New Yorker, Clement L. Dennington, on behalf of the Churchman's Missionary Association, for the seamen of the port of Philadelphia, and was towed down to that city and permanently moored to the wharf at the foot of Market Street.

"The building," says a contemporary report, "is firmly fastened on a substantial deck 38 feet by 90, with guards extending 8 feet outside around it, and resting on two boats of 80 tons each, placed ten feet apart, and strongly connected together. The church will seat 500 persons, and is to have a fine-toned organ and bell. The top of the spire is 70 feet from the deck; and the edifice is 32 feet wide by 85 feet long, including the vestry."

Seats were free and every effort was made to attract seamen and boatmen to the services.

By the published documents of the association, "the following gentlemen compose the Board of Managers, by whose efforts the edifice has been erected, assisted by benevolent individuals of that city, who feel an interest in the religious benefit of the class for whom it is intended: Right Rev. Bishop Potter, D.D., James C. Booth, William C. Kent, John M. Collum, Isaac Welsh, George Colhoun, G. B. Mitchell, Edward L. Clark, T..R. Wucherer, Joseph R. Massey, Joseph E. Hover, William G. Allen, James M. Aertsen, George S. Twells. The chaplain in charge of the church is the Rev. Mr. Trapier, formerly a lieutenant in the navy, and now an ordained minister in the Episcopal Church."

Floating Islands. One of the geographical mysteries of the State of Michigan is an island that every summer comes to the surface of Lake Orion, and every winter goes back again to the depths whence it arose.

Its periods of appearance and disappearance are nearly regular. It comes to the surface along about the middle of August, and goes down again about February 15. All efforts to control its appearance or its disappearance have uniformly failed.

On one occasion a number of farmers and teamsters decided to put the island out of the floating business. They hauled many loads of stone and deposited them on it during the early part of the winter, believing that when it went down in February it would go down for good, weighted as it was with stones. But the following August saw it bob up again from below—minus its load of stones.

At another time an effort was made to keep it on the surface and it was chained to the surrounding country with heavy log chains. When its time for departure came it departed—and the log chains departed with it. The log chains were never recovered.

The island is composed of soft mud and rushes, and there are some skeptical souls who attribute its formation and appearance and disappearance to the gathering of vegetation in one spot by the currents of the lake and its subsequent decay.

Henry's Lake in the Rocky Mountains, in a depression or gap called Targee's Pass, possesses another famous floating island.

"Henry's Lake is of oval shape and has an area of forty square miles. It is entirely surrounded by what seems to be solid land, and one really concludes that it has no outlet. On the west side lies a level meadow, which floats on the water, and the hidden outlet is beyond it. Near the rim of the basin, which at no distant day must have been the pebbly beach of the lake, is a shallow pool, out from which flows a creek, the source of the north fork of Snake River.

"A species of the blue-joint grass of luxuriant growth floats upon the water and sends out a mass of large hollow white roots, which form a mat so thick and firm that a horse can walk with safety over the natural pontoon. The decayed vegetation adds to the thickness of the mat and forms a mould in which weeds, willows and small trees take root and grow. Back from the new border the new land is firm, and supports pine and aspen trees of small growth.

"An island of the same turfy formation floats about the lake. The floating body of land is circular and measures 300 feet in diameter. A willow thicket thrives in the centre, interspersed with small aspens and dwarf pines. The little trees catch the breeze and are the sails that carry the island on its orbit. One evening it was within a stone's throw of our camp. Next morning it was five miles away."—*Virginia City, Nev., Chronicle.*

Flower, Largest. The largest flower in the world is said to be the *Rafflesia Arnoldi,* or Arnold's rafflesia.

It was discovered in March, 1818, on the island of Sumatra, by Dr. Joseph Arnold (1728–1818), a noted English botanist. This floral monster is a parasite on the roots of a species of wild vine. As it possesses no leaves, it may be said to consist of flower alone. The centre, containing stamens and pistil, is a foot wide. Each petal is a foot long, and ¼ inch thick in the thinnest part, increasing to ¾ inch at the thickest part.

The entire flower measures about a yard across and weighs about 15 pounds. Its ground tint is flesh-colored or yellow, with heavy mottlings of a dull purple.

In christening his flower Dr. Arnold linked his own name with that of Sir Stamford Raffles, British governor of Sumatra, by whom he was employed as a naturalist.

Flying Machines. Mr. Edison, in 1890, put on record his opinion that humanity should be ashamed that it had left unsolved the problem of aerial navigation when Nature had already solved it with birds. With the study of bird flight, indeed, aviation (*avis,* a bird) really began. It may be more than a coincidence that the first flying machine recorded in credible history was a wooden dove invented in the fourth century B. C., by Archytas of Tarentum. According to Aulus Gellius (A. D. 117–180) this was "so contrived as by a certain mechanical art and power to fly, so nicely was it balanced by weights and put in motion by hidden and enclosed air."

Various guesses have been made as to the nature of this hidden and enclosed air. Mediæval philosophers hinted vaguely at the possibility of some ethereal substance so light that it would sustain in air a vessel containing it. Elaborating on this hint Friar Roger Bacon (1214–1294) dimly forecast the modern balloon. He suggests that a large hollow globe made of very thin metal and filled with ethereal air or liquid fire would float on air like a ship on water. Bacon went even further. In the following passage he predicted the aeroplane or heavier-than-air machine:

"There may be made some flying instrument, so that a man

sitting in the middle of the instrument and turning some mechanism may put in motion some artificial wings which may beat the air like a bird flying."

Giotto, in his famous campanile in Florence, introduced a bass-relief of a flying man, and Leonardo da Vinci made three sketches showing his own ideas on the subject. Jean Baptiste Dante is credited with having made the first successful soaring flight at Perugia in the fifteenth century. Three centuries later (in 1742) the Marquis de Bacqueville is said to have repeated the feat by flying over the Seine in Paris. Details are lacking, but from the evidence available it would seem that both Dante and De Bacqueville used some sort of aeroplane glider.

The balloon idea reappeared after 1766, when Henry Cavendish discovered that hydrogen was many times lighter than air. Dr. Black, an Edinburgh chemist, suggested the use of hydrogen for balloons, an idea shortly after put into practical use by Tiberius Cavallo in the form of small soap bubbles filled with that gas.

It was left to the Montgolfier brothers and to the physicist Dr. Charles to devise the man-carrying balloon.

Etienne and Pierre Montgolfier, sons of a paper maker in Annonay, France, began their experiments in 1782. Their first public success was achieved in their native village, January 5, 1783. A linen globe of 105 feet circumference, inflated over a fire fed with bundles of chopped straw, rapidly rose when liberated to the height of more than a mile. At the end of ten minutes it descended, a mile and a half away. The feasibility of the hot-air balloon was thus, for the first time, demonstrated.

The first hydrogen balloon was designed by the brothers Robert, of Paris, under the superintendence of Professor J. A. C. Charles. On February 27, 1783, it rose from the Champs de Mars, 3000 feet. Franklin was present at the ascension. " Very fine! " said one of the spectators. " But what's the use of it?" " What's the use of a baby?" retorted Franklin.

On September 19, 1783, the Montgolfiers repeated at Paris the experiment made at Annonay, and were again successful. This time they suspended from their balloon a cage containing a sheep, a cock, and a duck. These—the pioneer aerial travellers—returned safely to earth.

The first human beings to go up in a free balloon were the Pilatre de Rozier, on October 15, 1783, in a captive balloon, *i.e.*, a balloon attached to the ground by ropes.

The first human beings to go up in a free balloon were the same Rozier and the Marquis d'Arlandes, November 21, 1783.

For the first women air travellers see AERONAUTS, FEMALE.

The first person in Great Britain to navigate the air was James Tytler (1747(?)–1805), who earned the nickname of Balloon Tytler from his experiments in this field. He constructed a fire balloon after the pattern of the Paris Montgolfiers of 1783, with which, on August 27, 1784, he made an ascent at Comely Gardens, Edinburgh, to a height of 350 feet (*Gentleman's Magazine*, 1784, ii, 709, 711).

A far greater sensation was created next year in England by the first aeronaut who essayed a flight from that soil. He was no Englishman, however, but an Italian, Vincent Lunardi (1759–1806), secretary to Prince Caramanico, the Neapolitan ambassador to the Court of St. James. About 2 P.M., on September 15, 1784, Lunardi went up in a balloon from the grounds of the Royal Artillery Company in London. His companions were a dog, a cat, and a pigeon; he passed over London in a northerly direction, and first descended in a cornfield on South Mimms Common, where he parted with his cat. He then rose again and finally landed in a meadow at Stondon, four miles from Ware, at 4.20 P.M.

More than a quarter century later, in 1815, a monument was erected to mark the latter spot. It bears the following inscription:

Let Posterity Know and Knowing be Astonished That On the 15th Day of September 1784 Vincent Lunardi of Lucca in Tuscany The 1st Aerial Traveller in Britain Mounting From the Artillery Ground in London And Traversing the Regions of the Air For Two Hours And Fifteen Minutes In this spot Revisited the Earth On this Rude Monument For Ages be Recorded That Wonderous Enterprise Successfully Atchieved By power of Chemistry And the Fortitude of Man That Improvement in Science Which The Great Author of all Knowledge Patronizing by His Providence The Invention of Mankind Hath Graciously Permitted To Their Benefit And To His Own Eternal Glory.

The first ascension in the United States is said to have occurred in Philadelphia, where, on December 28, 1783, a carpenter named Wilcox was lifted to a considerable height by several small gas-filled balloons. Confirmation of this exploit is lacking. At all events the credit is generally given to François Blanchard, a Frenchman, who had already (1785) won international fame as the first balloonist to cross the English Channel (*q.v.*). On January 9, 1793, at 10 A.M., he rose from Philadelphia, under the patronage and in the presence of George Washington.

Blanchard was the pioneer in the search for dirigible balloons. In 1784 he had invented a boat-like car with aerial oars. Advance was slow until 1884, when Captain Renard and Captain Krebs produced a man-carrying dirigible which actually

23

returned to the starting-point against a wind. The propelling power was a 220-pound electric motor which developed nine horsepower. Then came the famous dirigibles of Santos Dumont and others.

These are probably the last efforts in that line. More and more fully it now came to be recognized that progress lay in abandoning the balloon idea and seeking the mimicry of birds. This was the plan advocated by Mouillard, whom the French accordingly styled the Father of Aviation (see AVIATION, FATHER OF). The ascription was warmly denied by the Wright brothers, who granted that Mouillard was a careful student and an able interpreter of the flight of birds, but ridiculed him as a mere child in experimentation. The Wrights put forward Otto Lilienthal and Samuel P. Langley as the real fathers of aviation.

It is the Wright brothers themselves who deserve that title, by dint of actual performance. They scored their first success as far back as December 17, 1903, with a flight of 300 yards in 59 seconds. Nearly two years later (October 5, 1905) the first great flight in the world's history is claimed, about 25 miles in 38 minutes 3 seconds. Public evidence was lacking in both cases. At last, finding a financial backer, Wilbur Wright brought his aeroplane to Europe and continued his experiments, first at Issy, Paris, then at Le Mans, when he inaugurated a new phase in the world's travel. His flights grew longer and loftier, and more daring. Meanwhile, he was studying every minute detail—shape, size, weight, area of the plane, the exact manipulation required to produce certain results—and the outcome was the great flight on October 10, 1908, when he was in the air 1 hour 9 minutes 45 2-5 seconds, covering over 70 kilometres, the first time in the world a man had remained in the air in a machine heavier than that element for an hour.

When Louis Blériot, on July 15, 1909, flew across the English Channel from Baraque to Dover, the feat was considered the acme of daring. It has since been many times repeated. The first woman to cross the Channel alone and driving her own aeroplane, was Miss Harriet Quimby (see AERONAUTS, FEMALE), who, on April 16, 1912, flew from Dover to Hardelot. She had been preceded by Miss Mary Davis, who had been only a passenger, however, on an aeroplane flown by Gustav Hamel, from Hendon, near Dover, to Gris Nez, in France, on April 2, 1912.

Foot-ball. There used to be an impression among the learned that the ball game played by Nausicaa and her maidens (HOMER, *Odyssey*) was a sort of foot-ball. Modern scholars know that this is an error. It was a mere dancing game in which a ball was tossed. Nevertheless, the Greeks did indulge in an out-door sport—called by them "harpaston"—which bore a close resemblance to the Rugby foot-ball of to-day. It was developed from three earlier games, of which the names alone have come down to us.

The Romans, having a more primitive game of their own which they called "follis," eagerly adopted the Greek improvement. The first revision of foot-ball rules on record is that ordered by the Emperor Augustus in 28 B. C. Augustus, unlike the modern folliphobiast (the word is expressly coined for this occasion only), complained that the game then played was too mild to serve in the training of Roman warriors. A mighty contest arose among the athletes of the Eternal City over the new rules and the old, just as centuries later there was to be great agitation over Rugby and Association rules.

The new Roman game survived well on into the Middle Ages under the name of "Calcio." It has been revived in Italy in recent years.

A rough form of foot-ball is found scattered nearly all over the primitive world. The Eskimo know it in the Arctic regions and the South Sea islanders in the tropics. Cortez recorded a game of this sort among the Aztecs. The Celts claim that foot-ball was once a rite of their sun-worshipping ancestors. The old Teutons played the game with the skulls of their enemies.

The first mention of foot-ball in English literature is found in William Fitz Stephen's "History of London" (1175). Chester, however, has a legend, that, during the Danish invasion of England in 982, the citizens of that town captured a Dane and, after beheading him, kicked his head about the streets for sport. This proved so attractive that it was repeated whenever the head of an enemy could be secured. Finally there was substituted for the occasional head a perennial "balle of leather, called a foot-balle, of the value of four shillings," which the shoemakers of Chester were bound by their charter to deliver on Shrove Tuesday to the drapers. From a cross at the Rode tree it was kicked to the common hall of the city or *vice versa*. The game often degenerated into a rough and tumble scrimmage, and the ball itself might be left perdu for half an hour at a time, while the players chased one another through alleys and lanes and even into the houses of respectable citizens. Sconces were cracked, bones were broken, lives lost. The custom spread to other places. Frequently one town would challenge another, the ball would be placed midway between the rivals, and each side strove to drive it into the enemy's stronghold. In due course foot-ball reached London and set the city agog at stated intervals. Philip Stubbes, in his "Anatomie of Abuses" (1583), denounced the game quite in the manner of a modern college president.

"As concerning foote-balle," he says, "I protest unto you it may rather be called a friendlie kind of fight than a play or recreation, a bloody and murthering practice than a felowy sport or pastime. For dooth not every one lie in wait for his adversary, seeking to overthrow him and picke him on the nose, though it be on hard stones, or ditch or dale, or valley or hill, so he has him down, and he that can serve the most of this fashion is counted the only felow, and who but he. So that by this means their necks are broken, sometimes their backs, sometimes their arms, sometimes their noses gush out with blood, sometimes their eyes start out, and sometimes hurt in one place and sometimes in another; for they have the sleights to mix one between two, to dash him against the heart with their elbows, to butt him under the short ribs with their griped fists, and with their knees to catch him on the hip and picke him on his neck, with a hundred such murthering devices."

At Rugby foot-ball gradually developed from a game of individual strength, pace, and courage into a game of pace, artfulness, and skilful combination. It was at Rugby in 1823 that "running with the ball" was invented by a town boy named William Webb Ellis (*Saturday Review*, November 5, 1892). The innovation was eagerly adopted by the young men and became a feature of Rugby foot-ball and eventually of foot-ball everywhere.

The first reference to foot-ball in the New World is found in Spellman's "Relation of Virginia" (1609). It existed as a simple campus sport, with rules, regulations, or regular contests in the older American colleges as early as 1800. Until so recently as 1878 an unlimited use of hands, fists, and feet was permitted in getting and keeping control of the ball. Accidents were frequent. Protests arose.

On July 2, 1860, foot-ball was proscribed at Harvard. An elaborate funeral ceremony was planned and carried out by the sophomore class. A coffin was provided for an effigy labelled "Football Fightum." The mourners, disguised in black robes and masks and carrying pumpkin lanterns of gruesome aspect, followed the coffin in solemn midnight procession. Arriving at the appointed place in the campus, the coilin was lowered into a freshly dug grave. The sextons filled it in. At the head was planted a black board, whereon was printed in white letters the following:

Hic jacet
FOOTBALL FIGHTUM
Obiit July 2, 1860
Æt. LX. years
Resurgat.

Resurgat ("It will rise again") was better prophecy perhaps than the funeral cortege had dared to hope. Again and again Football Fightum rose from its grave at Harvard until in the fall of 1876 it re-established itself as a permanent and all-important feature of undergraduate athletics. Meanwhile it had flourished apace at other colleges, being played chiefly between the Freshman and the Sophomore classes.

The first intercollegiate game, between Princeton and Rutgers, took place at New Brunswick on November 6, 1869. Twenty-five men fought on each side. Rutgers won: 6 to 4. The return game was a triumph for Princeton: 8 to 0. From 1869 to 1878 Princeton played 24 games, winning 20, losing 3, and tying 1.

In January, 1895, the annual report of President Charles W. Eliot, of Harvard University, was largely devoted to a denunciation of collegiate and especially of intercollegiate football. "The game of foot-ball," said President Eliot, "grows worse and worse as regards foul and violent play, and the number and gravity of the injuries which the players suffer. It has become perfectly clear that the game as now played is unfit for college use. The rules of the game are at present such as to cause inevitably a large number of broken bones, sprains, and wrenches, even during trial or practice games played legitimately; and they also permit those who play with reckless violence or with shrewd violations of the rules to gain thereby great advantages. What is called the development of the game has steadily increased its risks, until they have become unjustifiable. Naturally the public is losing faith in the sincerity of the professed desire of coaches, captains, and promoters to reform it."

Foot-ball, despite President Eliot's warning, retained its advocates, grown only more vehement in fact by opposition. Noisiest among the president's critics was one of the most promising among the younger politicians. His name was Theodore Roosevelt. At a dinner of the Washington Harvard Club held in Washington on February 7, he first gave public utterance to his opinions. This is how the Washington correspondent of the Boston *Advertiser* reported the occasion and the speech:

Theodore Roosevelt came loaded for bear and the particular bruin that he was after was prexy. These were his sentiments, as they came spitting out from between his lips, with bull-dog vigor:

" I came here to-night filled with that spirit of an individual's right to express his own opinion which is the inalienable privilege of every Harvard man, and I want to say that I agree with a great many Harvard men in emphatically disagreeing with President Eliot in his remarks upon foot-ball in his recent report. I believe in athletics and I believe in foot-ball. We don't want to abolish foot-ball—at least not till we beat Yale. [Great applause.]

" And I want to say right here that I decline to subscribe to the doctrine of the sacredness of the human arm or leg. What matters a few broken bones to the glories of foot-ball as an intercollegiate sport? It is all nonsense to say that foot-ball is a game that benefits only a few. Look at the youngsters on every vacant lot in Washington during the fall season playing at foot-ball! Does anybody suppose that there would be these activities if it were not for the great heroes on the great teams whom these boys read about and look up to and glorify?

" Is there a boy in college that would not gladly risk a broken bone for the honor and glory of being on one of the great teams? [Cries of " No! " " No! "] Now, when I was in college I was not much of an athlete, being deterred from taking part in sports because of trouble with my eyes; but it fell to my lot afterward to go through some rather rough experiences in the West, and I have ridden to hounds on Long Island, and broken three or four bones in the sport. Now I do not mind that, and I am a middle-aged father of a family, too, with three growing boys.

" I say I am the father of three boys. I do not know whether they are going to make athletes in college or not; but I will say right here that if I thought any one of them would weigh a possible broken bone against the glory of being chosen to play on Harvard's foot-ball eleven I would disinherit him! "

As a climax this was a corker. It almost dazed the alumni present, who, however, recovered in an instant and shouted their plaudits in wild enthusiasm, one fellow exclaiming: " That's the stuff, Teddy! "

The change of rules since 1894, abolishing " the flying wedge " and other forms of mass-play subject to abuse, was expected to result in less rough playing and fewer casualties in the 1895 season. The expectation was not realized. The Yale-Harvard game at Springfield, November 24, was generally described as exceeding in brutality any game of previous years. The newspaper accounts were filled with graphic descriptions of the " slugging " which resulted in " a frightful laceration of the eye for Butterworth," " a broken leg for Brewer," " a broken collar-bone for Wrightington," " a broken nose for Hallowell," and " concussion of the brain for Murphy." Six men were taken off the field disabled, and two more ordered off for " slugging." Most of the injured were Harvard men, and the blame was generally charged upon Yale for precipitating violence. In the game on Thanksgiving Day between Harvard and the University of Pennsylvania, played in Philadelphia, five of the Harvard players were injured so badly as to be taken off the field. In each game Harvard was defeated.

The protests from press and public swelled to a mighty volume. The New Haven *Palladium* denounced the Yale-Harvard game as "worse than a prize-fight." It went further. "Saturday's game," it cried, "was undoubtedly the worst exhibition of recklessness and brutality that has been publicly made since the days of the Roman gladiators." The New York *Post* stigmatized it as "not only brutal but brutalizing." It pointed out that there were actually seven casualities among twenty-two men who began the game. This is nearly 33 per cent. of the combatants, a larger proportion than among the Federals at Cold Harbor—the bloodiest battle of modern times—and much larger than at Waterloo or at Gravelotte. What has American culture and civilization to say to this mode of training our youth?"

Football and Women. Until early in the nineteenth century it was a very ancient custom practised at Inverness, Scotland, for the spinsters to meet the matrons in an annual game of football. All the available women took part, and the men surrounded the players and urged on their sisters, wives, and sweethearts in their struggle, directing their efforts by word of mouth, and encouraging the exhausted to struggle on and secure the much-coveted prize. The honors of these unusual combats, strange to say, rested more often with the married than the single, for the men selected their wives from those who showed most prowess and endurance on the football field. Hence all the better players were mated, and frequently more than a match for the less tough and skilful maidens.

Foot-ball, the Father of Modern. On the wall of the athletic field at Rugby School, Rugby, England, a stone tablet preserves the name of the lad who originated that form of foot-ball which is now universally known as the Rugby game. The inscription reads:

"This stone commemorates the exploit of William Webb Ellis, who, with a fine disregard for the rules of foot-ball as played in his time, first took the ball in his arms and ran with it, thus originating the distinctive feature of the Rugby game. A. D. 1823."

Apart from the interest attaching to the Rugby game as a clean, healthful sport, there is the further interest that from it was developed the great American college game.

As the tablet at Rugby testifies, carrying the ball was

prohibited by the rules of the game until Ellis made his startling reformation. The game so instituted is much more complex than the association, or "socker" game, which still competes with the Rugby game for the favor of English youth.

There are fifteen players on each side; ten of these are called "forwards," two "half-backs," one "three-quarter back," and two "backs." The ball being kicked off from the middle of the field, the object of each side is to score a goal; this may be done either by touching the ball down behind the opponent's goal line and then making a "try," or place-kick, or by a direct drop-kick over the bar on the rebound of the ball from the ground. The bar is ten feet clear of the ground, and is supported by two posts, eleven feet or more in length, which are placed eighteen and one-half feet apart. There are many intricacies in the Rugby game, necessitating sixty rules to cover all possible points.

This is the sport from which enthusiastic young America has developed the national game of foot-ball, with its mass plays, flying-wedge formations, and other subtleties.

Footmen, Running. Lady Dorothy Nevill, in her "Reminiscences" (1908), tells of a curious old tavern sign in Charles Street, London,—"The Running Footman." She regretfully adds that she fears it is but a modern reproduction of an ancient original. Be that as it may, it is at present unique, and it recalls the old days when noblemen were preceded by runners, whose especial duty lay in clearing the way. The legend beneath the footman, clad in green coat and knee-breeches, states, "I am the only Running Footman," which is true enough, for there exists no other sign of this kind.

In the eighteenth century these men were frequently matched to run against horses and carriages. One of the last recorded contests was in 1770 between a famous running footman and the Duke of Marlborough, the latter wagering that in his phaeton and four he would beat the footman in a race from Windsor to London. His Grace won by a very small margin. The poor footman, worn out by his exertions and much chagrined by his defeat, died, it was said, of over-fatigue.

In the north of England the running footman was not quite extinct till well into the middle of the nineteenth century. So recently as 1851, on the opening of an assize court there, the sheriff and judges were preceded by two running footmen. About the same date the carriage of the High Sheriff of Northumberland, on its way to meet the judges of assize, was attended by two pages on foot, holding on to the door handles of the carriage and running beside it. These running footmen were dressed in a short livery jacket and white trousers, and wore a jockey cap.

Running footmen were wont to sustain their energies by a mixture of sherry and eggs, a small supply of the wine being frequently carried in the silver ball topping their canes. They could do seven miles an hour without difficulty, and more if put to their mettle.

Lady Dorothy believes that the Duke of Queensberry—"Old Q.," the star of Piccadilly—was the last nobleman who retained running footmen. These he himself was in the habit of engaging after having made them give an exhibition of their speed. Any one wishing to serve "Old Q." in the capacity of running footman had to run a sort of trial up Piccadilly, whilst his future master sat on the balcony of his house carefully watching the performance. On one occasion, a particularly likely-looking candidate having presented himself, orders were given that he should exhibit his running powers in the Duke's livery. The man ran well, and "Old Q.," delighted, shouted out to him from his balcony, "You will do very well for me." "And your livery will do very well for me," replied the man, and straightway made off at top speed and was never heard of again.

Forget-me-not. There is a great deal of indefiniteness, not only as to the origin, but as to the application of this name. In Germany the bright blue flower of the veronica or speedwell is the *vergiss-mein-nicht,* but in England and elsewhere the *myosotis* is held to be the true forget-me-not. German legend is full of explanations of the origin of the pretty name. In one a knight dashes into a lake to pluck the flowers growing on the further bank. On his return his strength is exhausted. Feeling that he cannot regain the shore, though very near it, he throws the flowers at his lady-love's feet, and, crying "forget me not," disappears beneath the waves. This, of course, is mere myth.

Foundling Hospital. Captain Thomas Coram, the originator of the Foundling Asylum in London, was an amiable eccentric. A tough old sea-dog born in 1668 and living till 1751, he passed the intervening period in throwing out and agitating a variety of schemes which at least were of no use to himself. He ended his days in an almshouse, making the appropriate *apologia* that, as he had never wasted his substance in self-indulgence, he was not ashamed to confess poverty in his old age. At one time he resided in Taunton, Mass., where he distinguished himself by presenting fifty-nine acres of land to the township, on consideration that it should be used for the purposes of the Church of England if ever that

church came to be established in America. Returning to
England, he was shocked by the number of children whom
he saw exposed in the streets of London. On October 17,
1739, after seventeen years' agitation, he succeeded in obtaining
a charter for a foundling asylum, which, in 1741, was opened
in Hatton Garden. Fourteen years later the present edifice
was built.

The institution was expressly established for the reception,
maintenance, and education of exposed and deserted young
children. At first these were admitted by lot, but the method
proved unsatisfactory, and in 1756 Parliament, by way of
remedying the all too patent evils, threw wide open the door
to worse evils by declaring that the hospital ought to be enabled
to support and educate all the children that should be offered.
And now the carriage of children to London became a regular
trade. One man, coming up with five children in baskets, got
drunk on the way and lay asleep all night on a common. Next
morning three of the children were dead. Fifteen thousand
children were received in three years. Only 4400 lived to be
apprenticed. The total expense incurred during this interval
is put at half a million pounds. Of more remote evils it is
unnecessary to speak. This monstrous abuse had to stop, and
the hospital was eventually put upon a more satisfactory basis.
Until 1801, however, it was the practice, on payment of £100,
to receive children without exacting any clue to their parentage,
—a plan open to very obvious abuses, which was abolished in
that year.

One of the minor difficulties, which still persists though in
a minimized form, is that of naming the foundlings. In
former times " persons of quality and distinction " used occasionally to act as sponsors and honored the children with their
names. This practice has been abandoned, because the children, when they grew up, used to claim relationship on the
strength of it. " Eminent deceased personages " were then
selected, and the children were christened Wickliffe, Huss,
Shakespeare, Bacon, Oliver Cromwell, Michael Angelo, William
Hogarth, Isaac Walton, and by similar names, until, at length,
when their numbers increased faster than the invention of the
governors, they were even called " after the creeping things
and beasts of the earth." The duty of preparing a suitable
list is now very sensibly left to the treasurer of the institution.

Among the curiosities of the London Foundling Hospital
is its connection with art and artists. Speaking figuratively
the Royal Academy (q.v.) of London may be called its most
illustrious foundling.

And this is the manner of it: William Hogarth was one of its first governors, and he induced many of his brother artists to co-operate with him in ornamenting the hospital with their own works. A committee took to dining here annually on the 5th of November, and at these gatherings the pictures were received, examined, and discussed. The dinner became so popular that so early as 1757 there were 154 persons present. This was an anticipation of the Royal Academy dinner. In 1760 the next step toward the foundation of the Academy was taken. The interest excited in the pictures formally presented at the hospital suggested to all the artists of London that they should hold a general exhibition of their works in some more public place.

This was initiated on April 31, 1760, under the name of "the annual exhibition of United artists," and its success led to the formation of the Royal Academy in 1768.

Hogarth's interest in the Foundling Hospital was exhibited in many curiously characteristic ways. He invented an extraordinary coat of arms, including "a young child lying naked and exposed, extending its right hand proper; a lamb argent, holding in its mouth a sprig of thyme proper, supported on the dexter side by a terminal figure of a woman full of nipples proper; Britannia holding in her right hand a cap argent"; and various other inventions of eighteenth century heraldry. Another marvellous device of Hogarth's was the heading for a power of attorney, which is something between an orthodox allegory and the picture of Gin Lane. It contains Captain Coram with the charter under his arm, an idealized beadle, an exposed child in a gutter, boys with mathematical instruments, and little girls going in pairs to church.

The hospital's gallery still boasts the possession of Hogarth's full-length portrait of Captain Coram, *à propos* of which the artist asserted himself to be as good a portrait-painter as Vandyke; and with a picture of "Moses before Pharaoh's Daughter," which he doubtless considered equal to Raffaelle. He also gave it a certain number of tickets in a lottery for another picture, the "March to Finchley." The hospital, luckily, had the winning ticket, and is still in possession of the picture.

· Every one who has been in Florence, Italy, remembers *Lo Spedale degli Innocenti* in the "great square of the Santissima," with medallions of half-swaddled children in Luca della Robbia ware adorning the spaces between the arches of the loggia. Up the steps of that loggia came one night a poor, a very poor man. His wife had just presented him with a child, whom, in the depths of their poverty, they were unable to bring up; so, according to the custom of his fellow-towns-people in such circumstances, he was about to make it over to the tender mercies of the Foundling Hospital. He passed the poor little infant through the small square aperture left for that purpose in the grated window, rang the bell, and turned away. At that moment a man who was waiting near came up hastily, popped in a second child, and fled. The governors of the hospital cannot be called strict in their laws, yet even they feel that a man must draw a line somewhere, and they draw it at twins. Twins are what they cannot and will not put up with. The officials therefore hastened after our poor friend, overwhelmed him with reproaches for having attempted to palm off twins upon them, refused to pay the smallest heed to his assurances to the contrary, and insisted upon his taking away both the children. Imagine the horror of the poor man returning to his poor home thus burdened, and the dismay of his wife on being called upon to support *two* infants when *one* was beyond her means! Out of this dire misfortune, however, better days were to dawn for them. The second child was the offspring of wealthy parents, who only wished its birth to be concealed for a short time; and who had not only secreted among its clothing a sum of money sufficient at once to improve the circumstances of its involuntary foster-parents, but had accompanied it (as is not infrequently done) by marks whereby they should be enabled to trace and eventually to claim their child; and, as the story runs, they so effectually patronized the poor couple, who for a while had taken good care of the little stranger thus unexpectedly left upon their hands, as to place them above the reach of poverty for the rest of their days.

Fountain Pen. The fountain pen is not an invention of recent years. In Samuel Taylor's "Universal System of Short-hand Writing." published in 1786, we find proof of the fountain pen's great age.

"I have nothing more to add," wrote Samuel Taylor, "for the use or instruction of the practitioner, except a few words concerning the kind of pen proper to be used for writing short-hand. For expeditious writing some use what are called fountain pens, into which your ink is put, which gradually flows. when writing, from thence into a smaller pen cut short to fit the smaller end of this instrument, but it is a hard matter to meet with a good one of this kind."

This undoubtedly is the pen described and illustrated *s.v.* in Hutton's *Mathematical Dictionary* published in 1795. Hutton's definition begins, "Fountain pen is a pen contrived to contain a quantity of ink and let it flow very gently, so as to supply the writer a long time without the necessity of taking fresh ink." The accompanying illustration shows that the instrument in a crude fashion anticipated the main features of the modern fountain pen.

Frankincense. The twelfth chapter of Pliny's "Natural History" is devoted to spice trees and those yielding incense. Arabia he styled Felix (Happy) because it was the only country that produced frankincense. Nevertheless, he added, "Unworthy country as it is for that surname, in that it thinketh itself beholden to the gods above, whereas indeed it has greater cause to thank the infernal spirits beneath. For what hath made Arabia blessed, rich, and happy but the superfluous expense that men be at in funerals: employing those sweet odors to burn the bodies of the dead which they knew by good right were due unto the gods." He notes that only certain families were allowed to gather frankincense, the members whereof were compelled to follow strict observances on the days when they approached the sacred trees. They must not have looked upon the dead and must have been freshly purified in body. The first and favorite season occurs in the dog-days of summer: "They cut the trees where they see the bark to be fullest of liquor and thinnest. They make a gash or slit only to give more liberty; but nothing do they pare or cut clean away. There gushes out a fat foam or froth. This soon congeals and grows to be hard, and where the place will give them leave they receive it in a quilt or mat made of date-tree twigs, plaited and wound, wickerwise, one within another. For elsewhere the floor all about is paved smooth and rammed down hard. The former is the better way to gather the purer and cleaner frankincense; but that which falleth upon the bare ground proves the weightier. That which remains behind and sticks to the tree is patted and scraped off with knives, or such like iron tools; and therefore no marvel if it be full of shavings of the bark." We are told that the whole forest is partitioned up among divers men, none of whom would encroach upon his neighbor nor wrong him, "so just and true they be in Arabia. But believe me, at Alexandria, where frankincense is tried, refined, and made for sale, men cannot look carefully enough to their shops and workhouses, or they will be robbed. The workman that is employed about it is all naked, save that he hath a pair of trousers or breeches, to cover his shame, and those are sewed up and sealed too, for fear of thrusting into them. Blindfolded he is sure enough, that he may not see the way to and from, and hath a thick coif or mask about his head, for doubt that he should bestow any in

mouth or ears. And when these workmen be set forth again, they
be stripped stark naked as ere they were born, and sent away.
Whereby we may see that the rigor of justice cannot strike
so great fear into our thieves here, and make us so secure to
keep our own, as, among the Sabeans, the bare reverence of
religion of those woods."

The contrast drawn here between the relative honesty of
the true believer and the pagan is curious enough!

Franklin, State of. An American State occupying what
is now East Tennessee, which was founded in 1785 and disappeared from the map of the United States in 1788. At that
early period the boundary of North Carolina extended in-
definitely westward, including all of what is now Tennessee
in its sweep, and, by the treaty of Fort Stanwix in 1768, all
this western territory had been opened up to settlement. The
settlers on the Watauga River, framing a code of laws signed
by every adult male, became a body politic known as the
Watauga Association. Their numbers and their spirit of independence were both increased by immigrants driven from
North Carolina by the tyranny of the royal governor Tryon.

After the Revolution a convention held at Jonesboro' on
August 23, 1784, supplemented by another on December 14,
formed a separate State government, variously called Franklin
and Franklan in its official documents. John Sevier was
unanimously chosen governor. The legislature sat at Jonesboro' in 1785. But North Carolina reasserted her jurisdiction, and civil war seemed imminent. Fortunately, the
North Carolina party in Tennessee overthrew the Franklin
party at the polls in May, 1788, and all the original territory
peacefully reverted to the parent State. The North Carolina
legislature passed an act of oblivion and admitted John Sevier
as a member of its own Senate. In 1789 North Carolina
ceded the region to the United States, and in 1790 the Territory
of Tennessee was organized. Tennessee became a State in 1796.

A curious race of people, who called themselves Malungeons,
were among the original Franklanders. They were supposed
to be of Moorish descent. They affiliated neither with whites
nor blacks, were never classed with Indians or negroes, and
claimed to be Portuguese. They lived to themselves exclusively
in the mountain fastnesses of East Tennessee, where their
descendants became moonshiners. They were never slaves,
and enjoyed all the rights of citizenship until the State Constitution of 1834 deprived them of their vote. This was, of
course, restored in reconstruction times. Such is the mystery
which surrounds the origin both of race and name that to-day
a Malungeon is the Tennessean bugaboo for frightening chil-

dren withal. "As tricky as a Malungeon" is a proverbal expression among Tennesseans. It has been suggested that for etymological purposes "Malungo," an African word incorporated into the Portuguese language, and signifying "comrade, mate, companion," is sufficiently indicative of the united and exclusive mode of existence peculiar to the Malungeons.

Freemason, Female. Current traditions affirm that one woman, and one only, was ever initiated into the mysteries of freemasonry. The traditions are not unanimous as to the name and station of this female Mason, but the larger number agree that it was an Irish lady, the Honorable Elizabeth St. Leger. She was a daughter of Lord Doneraile and a cousin to Gen. Anthony St. Leger, who instituted the famous St. Leger races and the Doncaster Stakes.

The generally received story of her connection with the Masonic body is contained in a rare tract published in Cork in 1811. A few copies were subsequently (1869) struck off for members of the St. Leger family. Slightly condensed the story runs as follows:

Lord Doneraile occasionally opened lodge at Doneraile House in County Cork. Previous to the initiation there of a gentleman into the first degrees of Masonry, Miss Elizabeth, then in her teens, happened to be in a chamber adjoining the temporary lodge-room. The wall between was undergoing repairs, so that the young lady—her curiosity excited by the sound of voices and knowledge that mysteries were being enacted across the partition—found little difficulty in picking a brick out with her scissors. Through the orifice so made she witnessed the first two degrees. Curiosity appeased, her next impulse was fear. There was no mode of escape except through the very room where the concluding part of the second degree was still being solemnized. As the room was a very large one and the celebrants were all gathered at the far end of it, she summoned up resolution enough to attempt an escape through the nearer end. With light but trembling step she glided along unobserved, laid her hand on the knob of the door, and, gently opening it, was confronted, to her dismay, by a grim and surly *tyler* with his long sword unsheathed. A shriek that pierced through the apartment alarmed the members of the lodge, who all rushed to the door.

There they found Miss St. Leger, trembling and in tears. After the first outburst of surprise and anger, general regret was expressed for the fate which the young girl had brought down upon herself. Death, all agreed, was the only possible issue.

"Oh, no, gentlemen," said Lord Doneraile, "I am not

going to lose my only daughter! You must find some other way out of it."

"There can be only one other way," replied the spokesman, "but she is not a man; if she were she might be sworn in a Freemason."

"Then," said Lord Doneraile, "she must be sworn in without being a man."

The alternative was accepted; the young lady was sworn in then and there, and proved as loyal to her oath as the best man among them.

Miss St. Leger eventually married Richard Alworth, Esq., of Newmarket. It is added, that, whenever a benefit was given at the theatres in Dublin or Cork for the Masonic Freemason Orphan Asylum, she walked at the head of the Freemasons, with her apron and other insignia of Freemasonry, and sat in the front row of the stage box. The house was always crowded on those occasions. She died in 1775, at the advanced age of eighty. Her portrait formerly hung on the wall of almost every lodge-room in Ireland.

There was another "only female Freemason" who hailed from Canterbury. Her exploits are pictured in a famous old engraving accompanied by an explanatory poem, entitled "The Freemasons Surprised, or the Secret Discovered: A True Tale from a Masons' Lodge in Canterbury."

The engraving shows the interior of a large tavern, where a meeting of Freemasons is in progress. On the table are three candlesticks, one of them overthrown and broken, a bowl of punch, glasses, pipes, and tobacco. The ceiling has been burst through by the weight of a young woman in the loft overhead, whose legs in stockings and shoes are exposed to her hips, and appear struggling in the air above the heads of the astounded, laughing, or terrified Freemasons.

The opening lines of the verses contain the gist of the matter:

> The chambermaid, Moll, a girl very fat,
> Lay hid in the garret as sly as a cat,
> To find out the secrets of Masons below,—
> Which no one can tell and themselves do not know.
> Moll happened to slip and the ceiling broke through
> And hung in the posture you have in your view,
> And frightened the Masons, tho' doing no evil,
> Who stoutly cried out, "The Devil! The Devil!
> With phiz white as apron the Masons ran down
> And called up the parson, his clerk, and the town
> To lay the poor devil thus pendant above.

So far so good. But, whatever may be true about **modern**

times, it seems to be a fact, established by certain ancient manuscripts quoted by Rev. A. F. A. Woodford in his edition of Kenning's "Masonic Cyclopedia," that in the early ages of English Freemasonry there were "dame" Masons as well as "Master" Masons. The Masonic "apprentice" is charged, for example, in one manuscript, that he shall not steal nor pick away his "master's" or "dame's" goods, and, in another manuscript, that he shall not disclose his "master's" or "dame's" counsel or secrets,—whence Mr. Woodford infers that at one time the widows of Masons were permitted to carry on work under the guild, and in that case the apprentice would serve out his time.

Furthermore, both in Germany and in France, there once existed several systems of what historians call "androgynous" and stigmatize as "spurious" Freemasonry. The female Freemasons of Germany belong to the order known as Mopses.

A French book published in Amsterdam in 1745, and entitled "The Order of Freemasons Betrayed, Or The Order of the Mopses Revealed," professes to tell all about them.

The author says that, when Pope Clement XII excommunicated the Freemasons, a new order was formed in Germany, under the patronage of the government and of certain great personages, with signs and pass-words and all the paraphernalia of Masonry. They adopted the dog, a symbol of fidelity, as their emblem and called themselves Mopses or Pug-Dogs. As a further means of concealment, they admitted women into their order. Over each of their lodges they set a grand master and a grand mistress, each ruling alternately for six months, who were addressed as Grand Mopses. On the admission of a candidate a brass collar and chain were attached to the neck, by which he or she was led blindfold, and immediately all the initiated began to bark and howl like dogs.

The Mopses, however, were an ephemeral folk, and nothing has been seen of them for full two hundred years. But in France Maçonnerie d'Adoption, "another mixed development of the craft," flourished for a considerable part of the eighteenth and was revived in the early years of the nineteenth century. Between about 1730 and 1760 the polite nation boasted of many androgynous orders of Freemasonry.

Later, or for some score of years before the outbreak of the Revolution, secret societies were the rage with all classes, even with the great ladies of the French court. Under the patronage of the Cardinal de Rohan, Cagliostro established his system of Egyptian Masonry, installed himself as grand cophte, and opened lodges for sisters as well as brethren at

Strasburg, Lyons, and Paris. Another order, the Loge du Contrat Social, received the particular protection of the Princesse de Lamballe, who as grande maitresse was in the habit of conferring the four degrees of "appentie," "compagnonne," "maitresse," and "parfaite maitresse."

Under date of February 26, 1781, Queen Marie Antoinette writes to her sister Marie Christine to say that Freemasonry is thought little of in France, as it is so public:

"These latter days the Princesse de Lamballe has been appointed grand-mistress in a loge. She has told me all the pretty things that are said to her. There is no harm in that. . . . Everybody goes there, what is said is generally known; where then is the danger?"

The new sisterhood passed away with the new régime, and, although it was partly revived under Napoleon I, and again under the Bourbons, it gradually came to an end and does not now exist.

In America something of the same kind seems to have been set on foot in the middle of the nineteenth century. An adoptive rite—the term "adoptive" here, as in France, being somehow the Masonic equivalent for female—was instituted in 1855. This consisted of five degrees,—"Jephtha's daughter, or the daughter's degree," "Ruth, or the widow's degree," "Martha, or the sister's degree," and "Electa, or the Christian martyr's degree," the whole "assemblage" being called the "Eastern Star."

These extravagancies, however, were not real Freemasonry and soon died a natural death. So by a roundabout journey we get back to our original proposition, that there was only one (genuine) female Freemason.

The Newcastle *Courant* of January 4, 1770, contained this advertisement:

This is to acquaint the public that on Monday the first instant, being the Lodge (or Monthly Meeting) Night of the Free and Accepted Masons of the 22nd Regiment, held at the Crown near Newgate (Newcastle), Mrs. Bell, the landlady of the house, broke open a door (with a poker) that had not been open for some time past; by which means she got into an adjacent room, made two holes through the wall, and, by that stratagem, discovered the secrets of Freemasonry; and she, knowing herself to be the first woman in the world that ever found out the secret is willing to make it known to all her sex. So any lady who is desirous of learning the secrets of Freemasonry, by applying to that well-learned woman (Mrs. Bell that lived fifteen years in and about Newgate) may be instructed in the secrets of Masonry.

Fresh-air Fund. The originator of the movement was Rev. Willard Parsons. In *Scribner's Magazine*, vol. 9, page

515, Mr. Parsons told, in a modest and simple way, "The Story of the Fresh-air Fund." In the summer of 1877, when pastor of a small church in Sherman, Penna., he went down to New York and gathered a little company of the poorest and neediest children he could find. "They were taken out among my people, who were waiting to receive them as their guests for a fortnight during the midsummer heat. Others took the place of the first company; and at the end of the season the good people had entertained sixty poor city children for a fortnight each; and that, too, without any compensation save the consciousness of having done a simple Christ-like act of charity to one in need." This novel experiment met with gratifying success.

After the first season it was an easy matter to induce the New York *Evening Post* to take up the enterprise and raise the necessary fund to carry on and enlarge it, which it did for four years. In the spring of 1882 the enterprise was transferred from the *Post* to the New York *Tribune*.

"Every sort of entertainment has been given to swell the fund, from children selling pin-wheels and wild flowers by the wayside, netting, perhaps, a few coppers, to the more pretentious fair and festival, netting its hundreds of dollars; from the boys' circus in the barn to the finished entertainments in public halls. Children have pulled weeds in the garden and boys gone without their Fourth of July fire-crackers; the small savings-bank of the dead child has often been sent to bring life and happiness to the poor sick one; in fact, from Maine to California, from Canada to Florida, from South America, from the Old World, and even from Africa, have come voluntary contributions to carry on this most humane work among the poor of our overcrowded city."

Nor was it difficult to find temporary homes for the children. Mr. Parsons found success here not through circulars or letters, but through personal appeals. Among his own parishioners a practical interest was aroused when he showed them something of the conditions of the poor in city tenements, and the simple plan of relief was most heartily accepted. Similar results were achieved in other rural neighborhoods by similar methods. First a call was made on the various clergymen, on the editor of the local paper, and a few of the leading citizens. Interest being thus enlisted, a local committee was appointed. On the zeal and earnestness of this committee depended in great measure the success or failure of the enterprise.

It was no easy matter, Mr. Parsons confesses, to select

the children for these trips. In the summer nearly 200 workers among the poor aided in selecting and preparing the children for the country. These workers were from the church missions, bible missions, hospitals, dispensaries, industrial schools, day nurseries, model tenement houses, and kindred organizations. As soon as the local committee had reported what number they could receive, their list was apportioned among people who had children to send. Before the season was over, all had opportunities to send their most needy ones.

The children selected manifest all degrees of ignorance of the country—from those who imagine they know all about it, having played under the trees in a city square, to the boy who was shown a large herd of Alderneys by his farmer-host, and, after intently watching them chew the cud, asked, "Say, mister, do you have to buy gum for all them cows to chew?"

"Those who apply for a chance to send their children to the country are instructed that they must be poor and needy, without any infectious disease, clean, and free from vermin. A physician then inspects each child. Each day the Board of Health furnished a list of the houses where there was any contagious disease; which was of immense help. With that list before him, it was easy for the examiner to stop any child who came from an infected house. The majority were refused on account of their hopeless condition as to vermin. It is a herculean task to get the average tenement-house child in a suitable condition to be received into country families."

One of the most gratifying results of this fresh-air enterprise is the readiness with which the idea has been taken up by others, till to-day there are vacation societies for about every class of the poor. Many of the city churches now have a fresh-air fund provided for the indigent sick. Societies and hospitals have their country summer houses; missions their cottages by the sea. Working girls' vacation societies secure a fortnight in the country for girls of that class who need the change. Other societies provide the same boon for mothers with or without young children. King's Daughters open houses for a few weeks or for the season and obtain a quota of inmates from the city.

Conspicuous among the enterprises is that started by the New York comic paper Life, which took hold of a deserted hamlet containing a score of well-shaded cottages, and turned it into a populous village with accommodations for three hundred visitors at a time.

Mr. Parsons tells a number of stories showing what permanent influences for good have entered into the lives of little slum children merely through this temporary outing in wholesome country surroundings. Two instances will suffice. One of these refers to a little fellow sent from one of the wretched homes that drink has caused. The boy had never before known kind treatment. The pure, simple, and wholesome life, with the abundant food of the hillside farm, stirred his nature to depths and called out all his latent energies. " A few months ago, while in a bank, a well-dressed fellow immediately behind me in the line, reached out his hand, saying:

" ' I suppose you don't know me; but I am Henry C——.'

" ' Why,' said I, ' you must be the boy that Mrs. Y—— spanked and fitted out with a complete suit of homespun, with the jacket sleeves of a different color ! '

" ' Yes, I am the identical boy. I can't tell whether it was due to the spanking or to the Joseph-like coat, but that two weeks changed my whole life. I went to work when I came back, and have been with the same firm ever since. See here.' said he, and he opened his bank-book, showing several thousand dollars he was about to deposit for the firm, ' don't that look as though the firm had confidence in me? I literally came up out of the very lowest slums, and my present prosperous condition is due to the interest that family in the country has always taken in me since my visit with them in 1878.'

" A few days since I was stopped on Broadway by a well-dressed and prosperous-looking young man.

" ' I am one of your fresh-air boys—I am John ——.' I readily recalled the boy. In 1878 he was one of a party taken to central New York. It had been a hot and very dusty ride, and at the end of the journey this Five Points boy looked so thoroughly disreputable that the person who was to take him utterly refused to accept such a dirty and ill-looking boy. The tears of the lad, when he found that no one wanted him, flowed in streams down his dirty face, while the two tear-washed streaks, the red and white and black spots about his eyes and mouth, gave him a most unpromising look. Before I reached the hotel with the sobbing and ' left-over ' boy, a man came out of a small butcher-shop, and so heartily and kindly invited the boy to stay with him that the tears ceased instantly. A thorough bath and a new suit made a wonderful transformation. The family took a great interest in and became strongly attached to him. The change from the wretched Cherry Street tenement, with its drunken and often brutal parents, to the clean and cheerful family of the butcher, where he was kindly treated, made a strong impression. The family kept track of the boy by corresponding with him, and have claimed a visit from him every year since. He is now married, lives in a comfortable flat, and has a good position as a commercial traveller."

Frog. In an interesting little treatise Mr. St. George Mivart exalts the common frog as one of the most wonderful of animals. Beginning existence (as a tadpole) with the organization of a fish, it undergoes a remarkable metamorphosis and becomes an air-breathing quadruped, capable of easy and rapid movement over the ground. The structure of man himself is hardly more complex than that of the frog, which presents relationships of analogy or affinity to very different animals, such as fishes, serpents, tortoises, and crocodiles, as well as to the human system. So much for the modern naturalist. The greatest of his ancient predecessors, Pliny himself, attributes not only natural but supernatural attributes to the little monster. He tells us, in Holland's version, that, "if a man take out the tongue of a frog alive so that no other part thereof stick thereto, and, after he hath let the frog go againe into the water, apply the said tongue unto the left pap of a woman whiles she is asleepe, in the very place where the heart beateth, shee shall answer truly and directly in her sleepe to any interrogatione or question that is put to her."

"But," continues Pliny, "the magicians tell more wonders than so of the frogs, which, if they be true, certes froggs were more commodious and profitable to a commonwealth than all the positive written laws that we have; for they would make us beleeve, that if the husband take a frogg, and spit him, as it were, upon a reed—" with other processes—conjugal infidelity is henceforward a thing no longer to be feared.

Other marvels are also performed by frogs, if Pliny's authorities are to be credited; but these will suffice. Enough that in the Middle Ages frogs still remained all that Pliny had painted them, and had gathered fresh beauties from mediæval superstition. The witches' cauldron would have lacked some of its most stimulative ingredients if the component parts of frogs were absent from it; and " Syr Cranion," as the frog was called, held a high place in the esteem of those deluded or deluding dames. Call to mind the incantations which Shakespeare puts into the mouth of his weird sisters.

The most estimable of all frogs is the *Rana esculenta,* or edible green frog, which for centuries has been known to epicures in France and Italy. It was in the latter country that the preparation of frogs for food led to one of the most remarkable discoveries of the eighteenth century, when the invalid wife of Galvani had some frog soup made for herself as a restorative (see GALVANISM). Such soup was well known before Signora Galvani's day. In one of the Ayscough MSS. in the British Museum (a treatise " On the Prolongation of Life," of the time of Elizabeth or James the First), frog-broth is thus described by a quaint old gentleman who marshalled his recipes in the shape of letters addressed to various friends:

"Frog broath . . . give mee leave to present you wh. a super-numerarie dish of frog-broath: you will either receive it and taste of it as a raritie, or as an antidote, for the ancients held it of soveraine force to help thosse whom venemous creatures had stung. Ælius and Paulus commend their broath with salt and oile in such poisonous bitings. I have knowne some that have drunke it, and eaten the flesh of them boiled and fried, troubled afterwards with such vehement vomiting that they suspected themselves poisoned. In Fraunce I once, by chance, eate them fried, but thought they had bein another meate, otherwise I had not bin so hastie. But it might bee that thosse were frogs from standing-pooles and marshes: palustres ranas venendas creddit Ælius. But bee they of what sort you will, I think penurie made some use them, and luxurie others, whose fat feeding and wanton stomacks crave unnatural things, mushrups, snailes, &c. For my parte, I would interdict them altogethere, especiallie seeing for gaine the seller mixes any kind of them, rubetas et mutas ranas, wh. without doubt are poison, and some have observed that mosse frogs, which when they are flead of a white colour, are more hurtful. Over fondnesse makes us take aniething, al mixtures of herbes in sallets. And as I have heard, some Italian merchants at Antwerp, to have more varietie than others in them, unwittingly mixed the seeds of aconite, and al that eate that sallet died."

To explain the word " Rubetas " in the foregoing letter, you must go back again to Pliny, who says, " The venomous frogs and todes called Rubetæ, live both on land and also in water." But, in truth, the esculent frog, whether served in broth, stewed with a sauce velouté, or fried in batter, is a very dainty dish. Benson Hill, who wrote a capital "Diary of Good-living," commended frogs highly. "With due reverence," he observes, "for the noble sirloin, I cannot but think that the hind-legs of some half-dozen good-sized frogs, taken out of a fine crystal pool, fried with an abundance of cream and parsley, well crisped, would make a convert of the most bigoted John Bull, provided you did not tell him the name of the dish until he had accustomed himself to its flavor."

Samuel Breck, the diarist of the Revolutionary period, informs us that in America of that date all the stories told about the frog-eating Frenchman were believed, even by persons of education.

When the first French squadron arrived at Boston, where Mr. Breck's early years were passed, the whole town, most of whom had never seen a Frenchman, went to the wharves " to catch a peep at the gaunt, half-starved soup-maigre crews." To their astonishment, they saw portly officers and stout, vigorous sailors. Could these hearty-looking people belong to the lantern-jawed, spindle-shanked race of *mounseers?*

As to the frog-eating, however, there was no doubt; but the manner of it was not quite understood, as will be seen. A Mr. Nathaniel Tracy, who lived in a beautiful villa at Cambridge, gave a dinner to the French admiral and his officers. There was a tureen of soup at each end of the table. Mr. Tracy sent a plate from his tureen to his next neighbor, the French consul, who, putting his spoon into the plate, fished out a large frog. Not knowing at first what it was, he held it up by one of its hind legs, and looking at it cried out, "*Ah, mon Dieu, une grenouille!*" It was passed from hand to hand, amid a roar of laughter. By this time several plates had been sent round, and in each was found a full-grown frog! The uproar was universal. "What's the matter?" asked the host (who seems not to have understood French), seeing frogs held up by the hind leg all round the table; "why don't they eat them? If they knew the confounded trouble I had to catch them, in order to treat them to a dish of their own country, they would find that with me, at least, it was no joking matter." The poor man had politely caused all the swamps in Cambridge to be searched in order to furnish his guests with what he believed to be in France a standing national dish. "Thus," says Mr. Breck, "was poor Tracy deceived by vulgar prejudice and common report."

Fur. The oldest of all New York's local industries is the fur trade. In 1615 a Dutch syndicate colonized a few families there, chiefly for the purpose of preparing for shipment to Holland the furs received in barter from the Indians. For more than a quarter century beavers' skins to be used in making bi-sexual head gear had been growing scarcer and more expensive.

By 1610 the great fur markets of Germany, France, Holland and England were paying for beaver, bear, fox, wolf, and other skins nearly thrice the prices that had ruled twenty years before. Forest fires, wars, failures of crops that caused the extermination of fur-bearing animals for food, and other causes destroyed many sources of fur supplies in Europe.

This stimulated the fur merchants of Europe to adventure to North America. England and Holland were the most active because of the large ownership of fur merchants of those nations in shipping. In 1615 Holland chartered the New Netherlands Trading Company, which in 1621 was succeeded by the Dutch West India Company. In 1624 this corporation, which possessed a monopoly in fur trading in as large a zone as it could trade in profitably, sent to the island of Manhattan thirty families, of whom most of the men were fur dressers; a part of this colony was at once sent to what is now Albany, then commonly called Beaverwyck.

The corporation soon built up a large and very profitable business, mainly in beaver, bear, mink, and fox skins. In 1664, when the English took New Amsterdam, the Dutch fur traders had thirty-nine fur-trading stations within 300 miles of Manhattan Island.

Exports of furs from here to the world's greatest fur market,

Leipsic, began in 1625 and have gone on ever since, except when wars have interrupted communications. To-day 65 per cent. of the fur trade of this nation is done on Manhattan Island. New York has become within a few years far and away the world's largest converter of furs into wearing apparel.

Most of this manufacturing is done on about two square miles of Manhattan Island. The industry gives direct and indirect employment to about 15,000 men and women, and the annual trade in finished products is nearly $35,000,000.

The foundations of the fortunes of the Astors and of many other old families of this city were made in the fur trade. The first John Jacob Astor learned the fur business from an old Quaker next to the Quaker meeting-house in what is now Liberty place. In 1809 John Jacob Astor completed his plan for active competition in buying furs against the Hudson's Bay Company. He opened a chain of fur-buying posts from the Great Lakes to the Pacific coast, and opened a ship-repairing and provisioning station in the Sandwich Islands for his fur-trading ships plying between the Pacific coast and the fur-markets of the coasts of China.

John Jacob Astor's son, William Backhouse Astor, in his day the best-informed man in the American fur trade, perfected in 1827 the Astor system of fur trading in all markets and at all sources for peltry trading with Indian and white hunters and trappers, and formed the American Fur Company, which was the first American holding corporation. When the first John Jacob Astor retired from business with a fortune estimated at $25,000,000 he said that most of it was made in the fur trade, chiefly from profits in selling to the world's greatest fur market, Leipsic.—New York *Sun*, October, 1911.

G.

Galvanism. When, in the year 1780, in Bologna, Italy, the wife of Professor Louis Galvani fell ill, and in her sickness conceived a longing for frog-soup, her husband little suspected that this circumstance would be instrumental in rendering his name immortal. The frogs were slain and skinned and made ready for the stewing pot, when the invalid lady happened to touch the leg of one of them with a knife which had become impregnated with magnetic power from a neighboring electrical machine. To her surprise the leg of the frog, on being thus brought in contact with the electric force, began to move with a convulsive action as if the life were still in it, becoming passive again on the withdrawal of the instrument. Of course the good lady—herself a physician's daughter, and probably possessed of some smattering at least of medical knowledge—communicated what she had observed to her husband; and he, after making a multiplicity of experiments, contrived to wring from nature the secret of that strange phenomenon which we now call galvanism.

Game Law, First. The first game law ever enacted for the protection of birds is in Deuteronomy xxii, 6: "If a bird's nest chance to be before thee in the way in any tree, or on the ground, whether they be young ones or eggs, and the dam sitting upon the young, or upon the eggs, thou shalt not take the dam with the young, 'But thou shall in any wise let the dam go, and take the young to thee.'"

While this command was primarily intended for the protection of doves and pigeons, the clause "on the ground" covers sparrows, larks, quail and other low builders which the Israelites captured for food or for caged pets.

Gates and **Gate-posts.** One does not expect to find much romance associated with gate-ways, but it none the less exists. One English gate-way with a curious history is situated at Brislington, a suburb of Bristol. A striking structure of stone, it causes many people to wonder how it came there, but it is, as a rule, useless to make inquiries on that point. The fact is that the gate was a part of Bristol Castle. When that ancient building was demolished, the gate was given to a Brislington gentleman, who re-erected it at the entrance to his stables. These offices, together with the dwelling to which they were attached, have now disappeared, but the gateway still remains, and gives access to a market garden. The statues which occupied the niches, however, are gone, though there is some doubt whether these were ever removed to Brislington. Another "transplanted" gate-way has a still more romantic history. This is the classic arch, flanked by Tuscan columns, at the entrance to Dyrham Park, South Mimms, in Hertfordshire. It looks as if it had grown, so to speak, on the spot, and yet it was a triumphal arch erected in London in 1660 in celebration of the restoration of Charles II. Under it the monarch probably passed when he made his way amid the acclamations of a great multitude to Whitehall. When the arch was removed to South Mimms is not known, but it has certainly been there for centuries, a mute witness that there may be romance in gate-ways.

Every gate-post has a gruesome association with the cruel past. Posts placed outside a house, be they wood or stone, are invariably supplied with a ball at the head, and the probability is that few know its meaning. This ball is nothing less than the survival of the barbaric practices of our forefathers, who hung over their gates the heads of their enemies killed in combat. All London's public bridges and gates were also adorned with the heads of criminals, and rather than let the custom die the moderns have substituted balls of stone or wood for human heads.

Giants. "There were giants in the earth in those days" (Genesis, vi, 4) is a text which led to many astonishing mathematical divagations. According to the ingenious calculations of M. Henrion, a French academician who was heard from in 1718, Adam was 123 feet 9 inches in height and Eve 118 feet 9 inches. Their children and their children's children exhibited a sad falling off. Noah, for example, was only 27 feet; Abraham 20 feet; Moses 13 feet in height. On Monsieur Henrion's authority we are glad to learn that a process, apparently designed to whittle away the human race to vanishing point, was suddenly and permanently arrested at the beginning of the Christian era. Henrion's figures were quite eclipsed by those of Arabic and Rabbinical legend. The latter asserts that Adam was at first created so tall that his head reached the heavens, terrifying the angelic denizens so badly that God reduced him to a thousand or (some say) to a hundred feet. It would seem that the latter estimate was too low, for we are told that after he was driven out of paradise he waded through an ocean that separated this world from Eden.

The Scriptures speak of the Rephaim and their allied tribes, the Anakim, the Emim, and the Zuzim, as giants; the sons of Anak in especial being "men of great stature," before whom the children of Israel were "as grasshoppers." The height of Og, king of Bashan, one of the last representatives of the race of Rephaim, is roughly indicated by the fact that his bedstead at Rabbath measured 9 x 4 cubits. (Deuteronomy, iii, 11). Estimating the cubit at eighteen inches, the bedstead must have been 13½ feet long. King Og, however, may not impossibly have been impelled by vanity to use a bedstead not in proportion to his actual size, but in proportion to his fancied importance. It is curious to observe that the words in Deuteronomy translated "bedstead of iron" are also susceptible of the rendering, "sarcophagus of black basalt;" but this does not militate against the probability of our supposition.

Again Arabic legend is content with no such puny proportions. King Og, on this authority, was so tall that like Adam he could reach the heavens and he survived the deluge by wading. The only discomfort that he suffered during the flood was an enforced Lenten diet, his sole food consisting of whales which he roasted on the disk of the Sun.

Goliath, according to the old Testament, was six cubits and a span in height. Again accepting the cubit at 18 inches, his height would be 9½ feet.

Classic myth had its Titans and Cyclops. Classical literature and even classical natural history abounded in monsters. Plato and Pliny both tell of the body of a giant (presumed by the finders to be Orion) which was found in a mountain in Crete and measured 46 cubits, or 69 feet. Plutarch gravely tells us that Sertorius opened a grave to examine the body of Antæus which was buried therein, and finding it sixty cubits " he was infinitely astonished." And no wonder. The body of a man ninety feet high might well have raised astonishment to the infinite degree. Trallianus, who lived in the sixth century, asks us to believe, that, when the Athenians dug up the body of Macrosyris, they found it was 100 cubits high. It was reserved for Boccaccio, in the fourteenth century, to raise Trallianus just one hundred per cent.—" or more." A corpse dug up " in our day " at Drepanum, in Sicily, had been reduced to fragments in the process, but " it was calculated by those who know the entire man from measuring the least bone, that he must have been of the height of 200 cubits or more."

In deciding upon the claims of the authentic giants of antiquity, it must be borne in mind that the ancients were prone to magnify the size of their kings and heroes. To be considered a giant in strength and size was the aim of every warrior. We are told of Alexander that, on one of his Asian expeditions, he ordered a huge suit of armor to be made, out of all proportion to his own figure, which was really under the medium height, in order to fool posterity into the idea that he was of giant mould. Charlemagne and his paladins have been represented as of great stature. Eginhard describes the great emperor as "seven of his own feet" in height, from which we may infer either that he had a disproportionately small foot or that he was a very tall man. His nephew Roland, the hero of Roncesvalles, was reported to be even taller. As it happens, we have some direct evidence on this point. Hakewill, quoting Camerarius, says: "Francis I, King of France, who reigned about a hundred years since, being desirous to know the truth of those things which were commonly spread touching the strength and stature of Rouland, nephew to Charlemagne, caused his sepulchre to bee opened, wherein his bones and bow were found rotten, but his armour sound, though covered with rust, which the king, commanding to be scoured off, and putting it upon his owne body, found it so fit for him as thereby it appeared that Rouland exceeded him little in bignesse and stature of body, though himselfe were not excessive tall or big." We have similar evidence in relation to the body of William the Conqueror, which was reported to have been dug up, four hundred years after burial, and found to be eight feet in length. Stowe tells us that, when the English took Cannes, in 1562, some soldiers broke into the monument in search of booty, and found nothing remarkable about the bones.

How much poetry remains if we credit the Arthurian legend that the blameless king was "fifteen foot longe" in the prime of his life, while Guinevere was twelve feet long? We cannot somehow wax poetic over the sorrows of a man of fifteen feet, however blameless he may have been, nor over the loves of a lady of twelve feet, however moving her tale. Enormous size is no disqualification for human emotion or conduct; but somehow, by some association of ideas, to be amazing in any outside and visible effect of body conveys an idea of moods and passions of amazing sort within. Once more, however, appearances are deceitful.

During the seventeenth century the Empress of Austria gathered together at Vienna all the giants and dwarfs to be found in the German Empire. They were all housed in one building, and there were some apprehensions that the dwarfs would be terrified at the sight of the giants. Instead of this, however, the dwarfs teased, insulted, and even robbed the giants, just as Jack and Hop-o'-my-Thumb do in the children's story-books, until the monsters were forced to pray for protection from their lively little enemies.

"Often," says Fuller, "the cockloft is empty in those whom Nature has built many stories high" (a sentiment which may be found also in Bacon's "Apothegms"); but he believes as little apparently in dwarfs as in giants, for, in his essay "Of Natural Fools," he says, "their heads sometimes so little that there is no room for wit, sometimes so long that there is no wit for so much room."

One need not discredit the Roman tradition that the Emperor Maximinus was 8½ feet high, for this height comes within the limit of recorded fact. Quetelet mentions as the tallest man known to history a certain Scotchman, 8 feet 3 inches high, who was secured by Frederick the Great for his regiment of gigantic guards. This height, however, was exceeded by Charles Byrne, or O'Brien, the first professional giant,—*i.e.*, the first to exhibit himself for hire. He was the wonder of London in the latter eighteenth century, and died in 1783 at the age of twenty-three. His skeleton is preserved in the Museum of the Royal College of Surgeons in London, and gives assurance that his reputed height of 8 feet 4 inches was no exaggeration.

A second Irish giant who also took the name of O'Brien placed his own height at 8 feet 3½ inches, though his barber, who wrote an account of him in the *Mirror* for 1826, asserted that he really measured 4 inches more. From this source we learn that he used to sleep on two beds joined together, as any ordinary couch would have been useless to him. He was courageous, possessed the warm temperament of an Irishman, and was endowed with more than average intelligence for a bricklayer. The superior barber continues:

"Mr. O'Brien enjoyed his early pipe, and the lamps of the town (Northampton) afforded him an easy method of lighting it. When at the door of Mr. Dent, in Bridge Street, he withdrew the cap to the lamp, whiffed his tobacco into flame, and stalked away as if no uncommon event had taken place."

On one occasion he kissed a young lady who was leaning out of the upper window of a house to look at him as he walked along the street. And at another time, travelling in the carriage made specially to accommodate his unusual proportions, he was stopped by a highwayman. The giant thrust out his head and as much of his body as possible, to see what was the matter, whereupon the highwayman was so panic-stricken that he clapped spurs to his horse and fled.

The celebrity of these two Irishmen appears to have produced quite a crop of Irish giants, who all dubbed themselves by the name of O'Brien. A correspondent of *Notes and Queries* says he once saw one made:

"A tall, lathy, overgrown, beardless lad was called into a booth, on Ham Common, and, in ten minutes after, consenting to hire himself to the showman for the day, he was transformed into a whiskered giant at least a foot taller and twenty stone heavier than before; so that actually his very mother and sisters, who paid to see the 'Irish Giant,' did not recognize him."

Of American professional giants the most famous was Captain Martin Van Buren Bates, of Kentucky, who had an English wife almost as famous as himself. The captain's height was officially given as 7 feet 11½ inches, and his weight as 496 pounds. He wore a 26 collar and a No. 15 boot. His wife, whom he met on a trip to England in 1871, had already won fame as Miss Anna Swan. She was exactly the same height as her husband and weighed just 96 pounds less. It may interest lady readers to know that sixty-five yards of goods were required to make this lady's wedding gown.

A reporter who visited the giant couple at their residence in Selville, Ohio, in 1889, gave a vivid picture of the domicile of these mammoth people: "It is a difficult matter," he said, "to convey an adequate idea of the proportions of such a dwelling as the one occupied by the Ohio giants. A door that is six feet six inches high is a large opening in the side of a house,—that is, a dwelling-house, not a church. But the doors in the domicile of the Bates giants are ten feet high, and the knobs are nearly as high as the reporter's head. The house was built by Captain Bates in 1876 and is elegantly furnished.

"The couch upon which the big couple sleep was made especially for them, and is a curiosity to look at. It is extensive enough to give the great big people room to stretch in, and it looks as big as an ordinary-sized floor. It is really ten feet long, wide in proportion, and about twice as high as a common bed. The magnificent dressing case is also a huge affair, with a glass upon it nearly as big as the side of a house.

"In the sitting-room is a piano of ordinary size itself, but it is mounted on blocks two feet high, so that the instrument is always up in the air, out of the reach of the common folks. There are two rocking-chairs in this room that are so big that the reporter had to climb into one of them the same as an infant would clamber into a high chair."

Giraffe. In Europe the giraffe was first heard of in 1787, when it was described by a Frenchman named Levaillant, who had journeyed into the land of the Hottentots and Kaffirs. Levaillant's accounts of the long-necked animal were received with general incredulity, and it was not until some living specimens arrived in France that Frenchmen succumbed to the evidence of their senses. Then for a period the giraffe formed the popular and scientific sensation in Paris.

In 1834 the London Zoölogical Society commissioned one Thibaud to proceed to Kordofan for the express purpose of obtaining animals of this species. In April, 1835, a female and three males were captured in Dongola, and successfully transported by M. Thibaud and the Arabs in his employ from Wadi Alfa to Cairo, Alexandria, and Malta, in which latter place they passed the winter of 1835–36. In the May following, they were established in the Zoölogical Garden in Regent's Park, London. In 1839 a fawn was born. A second born in 1841 was presented in 1844 to the Zoölogical Gardens in Dublin. Four others followed.

Sir Frederick Leveson-Gower, in "Leaves from a Diary" (p. 9), tells us that an incident which made a great impression on his childish mind, when living on the island of Malta, was the arrival there of these four giraffes. He is misinformed when he adds that "they were the first that had ever been seen in the West," though undoubtedly they were the first ever landed on English soil. "They were taken to England," he adds, "and were for some years at the Zoölogical Gardens. One, however, died shortly afterwards and the Gardens possessed only the three survivors. In connection with the recent announcement of the birth of a giraffe at the Zoölogical Gardens, it was stated that 'most of the zoölogical gardens in Europe have been supplied with giraffes in the descendants of an original four which reached the London Zoölogical Gardens from Kordofan in 1835.'"

The giraffe is the most costly exhibit in a menagerie, because it is the most difficult to catch. The long-legged and long-necked animal, keen of eye and nose and ear, can see, smell, and hear a hunter miles away. Traps and pitfalls cannot be employed against him. His delicate legs would be crushed in any trap strong enough to hold him; neck as well as legs would be in danger if he tumbled into a pitfall. There is but one way, and that a long and tedious one, to capture him alive. Giraffes must be surrounded and chased until they bring up weary and helpless in a bamboo enclosure. This means a careful drive over many miles, lasting many days, for if they reached the pen in their first rush of terror they would dash in headlong and destroy themselves. Even after capture the giraffe is difficult to manage. The nearest seaport is at least five hundred miles away. It is well nigh impossible to drive him over the wilderness. Men have tried the experiment, but the risk of accident is too great. The best method is to pen the giraffe in a bamboo cage open at the top, so that head and shoulders stick out. Then the cage is lashed to great bamboo poles from twenty to thirty feet long, and as many natives as are necessary lift the ends to their shoulders and give the queer beast a free ride to the ocean.

The problem of transportation does not cease with the journey to the seaport. The shipping of the giraffe and the voyage are fraught with peril. The giraffe's legs break very easily; if he slips the fragile underpinnings double under him and snap. In transferring the animal from shore to ship his long, helpless neck may become tangled in the tackle or strike a spar, mast, or shroud, in which case good-by to the giraffe.

Good-Friday. Perhaps no Christian festival has so many names as Good Friday. Our Anglo-Saxon and Danish forefathers called it " Long Friday," in allusion to the length of the day's services and fasting; in France it is "Holy Friday"; in Germany either " Still Freitag" ("Quiet Friday") or " Charfreitag," in allusion perhaps to the exhibition of the crucifix for adoration after being veiled all through Lent. In the Greek Church it has been known at various times as " The Pascha of the Cross," " The Preparation," " The Redemption," and " The Day of the Cross," and to these names the Latins have added " The Day of the Lord's Passion," " The Sixth Holy Day of the Pascha," and many others. " Good Friday" seems to be peculiar to the English language.

Good-Friday is not a day suggestive of mirth, yet it has given birth to one little witticism that lawyers sometimes refer to facetiously on Holy-Thursday. It was of the Protestant judge in Ireland who on the latter day directed the crier, in the usual way, to " adjourn court until to-morrow morning." " What!" exclaimed a lawyer, " adjourn until *to-morrow!* Why, your Honor, to-morrow will be Good-Friday, and the only judge ever known to hold court on that day was Pontius Pilate!" Of course a further adjournment was ordered. This anecdote elicited the statement from a gentleman of prominence on the bench that judicial records furnish no instance of a criminal having been either sentenced or executed on Good-Friday, although Friday itself was a favorite day for hangings. See WALSH, *Curiosities of Popular Customs,* p. 479.

Goose and **Goose-liver Pie** (*Paté de foie gras*). If a list of the benefactors of man were to be compiled, the goose would occupy a high place. There is barely a part of the bird but serves some purpose useful to man. Since ages immemorial the goose has fed him with its flesh and bedded him on its down. The fat is not only the best substitute for butter, but also an

25

excellent preventive against soreness from chafing, a most practical application for tender feet, an approved cure for chapped
hands. The elegant swans' skins which the city of Poitiers,
more especially, sends forth into the fashionable world are really
but the tanned skins of geese. And is there not that special
part of it which—ere, in this iron age of ours, the late Mr.
Gillott's steel invention had supplanted it—Lord Byron could
so justly and felicitously apostrophize as—

> My gray goose-quill:
> Slave of my thoughts, obedient to my will;
> Torn from thy parent bird to form the pen,
> That mighty instrument of little men!

The goose is a representative mythological and historic bird.
But for the cackling of the Capitoline geese, it is doubtful
whether Rome would ever have grown into her imperial purple
and papal scarlet. The goose is the special bird of the archangel Michael and the bishop Martin, on whose festivals,
Michaelmas and Martinmas respectively, it forms the indispensable standby dish of the pious in most parts of Europe.
In British lands it runs a race with roast beef for the chief
place on the table on Christmas-day. It is also intimately connected with the history of the reformation of Germany. John
Huss of Hussinec wore the goose displayed in his family arms,
"huss" being Bohemian for "goose." In allusion to this he
was called the Bohemian goose, whilst his more successful successor, Luther, received the name of the Saxon swan. "They
have roasted the Bohemian goose, but they'll have to keep their
hands off the Saxon swan!" was a common saying among the
Protestants in Luther's time.

The breeding and fattening of this useful bird has from
times immemorial formed an important rural and suburban industry in most parts of Europe, the chief object of the fattening
process being the production of solid flesh and fat. But in
certain parts of the Alsatian provinces which Germany wrested
from France, more especially in Toulouse and most of all in
Strasburg, the object is to produce morbid enlargement and
fatty degeneration of the liver of the bird to be turned into
goose-liver pie, or paté de foie gras.

Strasburg claims the invention of this dish. A certain
Mathieu, cook of Cardinal Rohan, prince-bishop of Strasburg,
passed for a long time as the inventor. The honor is actually
due, however, to Marshal de Saxe's cook, Close. When the
marshal, who had been the king's lieutenant in Alsace for several
years, left Strasburg, Close, declining to enter the service of his
successor, Marshall de Stainville, established himself as a pastry-

cook in Strasburg. He married Mathieu's widow, and started the goose-liver tureen business in a small shop in the Meisengasse, where the business is still conducted.

The fattening of geese for the tureen is now carried on in Strasburg very extensively. It is chiefly in the hands of women. It is almost entirely confined to the winter season. The fatteners or "crammers" buy their birds late in autumn, either lean or half-fattened. Young, well-formed geese are selected generally. Some crammers, however, will also take older birds. In some establishments the geese are fed first, for several weeks, with broad beans, and only during the last eight or ten days with maize; but most of the Strasburg geese-crammers prefer feeding their birds with maize from the beginning.

When the geese are about nine months old, they are transferred to a cellar, half underground, where wide and sloping stone tables are arranged one above the other on tiers, as far as the eye can see. Each goose is laid gently but firmly on a stone so that its tail projects beyond the ledge, and its legs, body, and wings are tied down tight with plaited whipcord. The legs and wings are well spread out to paralyze vigorous action, and they can move only the neck. Naturally they struggle with all their ineffective might, until, after days of vain endeavor, they succumb to a dull resignation broken only by an occasional low cry. Hundreds of geese lie thus inert, strapped each to its stone, and gasping hysterical nothings to one another.

Every two hours, six times a day, the birds are crammed with a thick paste made of buckwheat, chestnut flour, and stewed maize. Expert crammers simply push the food down with the middle finger. The less skilful generally use a funnel and a smooth wooden stick to expedite the descent of the food.

The most difficult task is to determine the right moment for death, which may be at any time from a fortnight to four weeks. Hitherto the work has been done by peasant girls. Now a pensive gentleman—a connoisseur in the obesity of geese —breaks upon the scene, climbs upon the topmost tier of all, and proceeds to examine the birds that may be "ripe." He has an eye as judicious as that of a gardener inspecting melons; and his is the responsible task of pronouncing what birds would die a natural death within twenty-four hours if not despatched beforehand. If a goose dies a natural death, he is good for nothing. He must be unstrapped and executed at the precise psychological moment when Nature is growing tired of supporting him, and the knack of detecting that moment can only come of long experience.

The "ripe" birds have stomachs of the size of pumpkins

and reveal, when opened, livers weighing from one to two and
in exceptional cases even three pounds. For twenty-four hours
the carcass is kept hanging in a cool and airy place, after which
the liver is carefully removed, so that no scratch or other blemish
may be found upon it. A fine liver must be of a nice light
salmon or cream color.

The livers are neatly wrapped in a wet muslin or fine linen
cloth, to be taken to the pastry-cook, who pays for them according to size and quality. The pastry-cook seasons and spices the
raw liver, after which he places it in the tureen along with
truffles and other ingredients. The dearest tureens generally
contain only one large liver, while the less expensive contain
two or several smaller livers. When the contents of the tureen
have been duly baked, a layer of fresh hog's lard is poured over
the mass, to keep it from contact with the air.

Grape-fruit, a dessert fruit of the genus *Citrus*, so called
because it grows in clusters not unlike a mammoth bunch of
grapes. It is a native of the East India islands, and about the
year 1890 was introduced into Florida by one Captain Shaddock.
But for a considerable period the crop proved unsalable. The
American public pronounced it pleasing to the eye but not to
the taste. The first two car-loads shipped from Lakeland to
Chicago and purchased from the grower, as a speculation, at
50 cents a box, not only failed to return the original investment,
but cost the speculator $225 in freight. Now the number of
grape-fruit consumed annually in the United States exceeds
4,000,000 boxes (at $3.50 a box), and that means approximately
half a billion grapes. *Leslie's Weekly* in April, 1910, claimed
for its former proprietor, Mrs. Frank Leslie, the honor of redeeming the grape-fruit from ostracism. In about 1895 she
was on a visit to Henry Plant, the builder of the East Coast
Railway in Florida. "James E. Ingraham was then, as now,
the vice-president of the road, and it was in his car that Mrs.
Leslie and her party travelled. On reaching the home of Mr.
Plant, the travellers were first introduced to the delights of the
refreshing citric fruit, which hung in clusters on the trees,
bending the branches down almost to the ground. Thousands
of bushels lay on the ground under the trees from which they
had fallen. There was no market for them. Only a few of the
native Floridians liked them, so the fruit that could not be
eaten by Mr. Plant's immediate friends was left where it fell.

"Nearly every plantation in lower Florida had numbers
of the grape-fruit trees, and under each one was the same display of golden-yellow balls which had fallen from the branches.
Passing one of these plantations, Mrs. Leslie asked the planter
what he would take for his crop. 'Why, madam, there is no

market for it. Nobody wants grape-fruit. Help yourself.' The party helped itself, and grape-fruit was thenceforth a regular part of the daily menu. So much did Mrs. Leslie appreciate the fruit that she decided to introduce it to her friends up North. She carried home several boxes, and later Mr. Ingraham sent her forty barrels, which she distributed among her friends, with instructions how to prepare them for the table. Encouraged by the unanimous praise which issued from all recipients of the fruit, Mr. Ingraham had a famous New York physician make an analysis of it and to certify to its remarkable qualities as a tonic, especially in the spring. As a result of this combined effort of Mr. Ingraham and Mrs. Leslie, a demand for grape-fruit grew rapidly."

Grasshopper. "I was born under the sign of the Grasshopper," says Thomas Hood somewhere. The allusion is to the gilt figure of a gigantic grasshopper which surmounts the spire of the Royal Exchange in London and acts by way of a vane. The grasshopper formed the crest to the coat-of-arms of Sir Thomas Gresham, the prosperous London merchant who founded the Exchange. The current legend is that Gresham had been born in great poverty, and that his mother, unable to support a child, had left him to perish alone in a large field near her hovel. It happened that an older boy, coming along the field, was attracted by the chirp of a grasshopper to the spot where the baby lay. He took it to his own home, and it was adopted into his family. In the heyday of his prosperity, when selecting a coat-of-arms to consort with his dignity as a baronet, Gresham took the grasshopper as his crest.

The story has not a leg to stand on. As will be seen by reference to the article EXCHANGE, Sir Thomas was the legitimate oldest son of Richard Gresham, an eminent London merchant. The crest had been in the family for some generations.

A writer in the London *Oracle* in 1808, who dates his letter from Tom's Coffee House, July 24, tells how, on the preceding Sunday, he had made one of a group of spectators who watched the installation of the grasshopper on the newly finished Exchange. "You well know," says Civis, "that nothing of consequence can be transacted in the city without certain conjectures as to the profit and loss. Policies were soon opened whether the grasshopper would attain the place of destination. The bulls prognosticated its rise; the bears anticipated its fall; whilst the omniummongers awaited the event in anxious suspense. In the meantime the glittering insect was carefully inclosed in a frame, where it looked as splendid and as dignified as Bajazet in his cage. The word 'aloft!' was given, and up mounted the grasshopper, like the adventurous aeronaut

Garnerin. The ascent was slow and solemn, and the suspended cargo had almost reached the point proposed, when, as Dr. Johnson finely observes—'What are the hopes of man?'—the rope broke, and down came the grasshopper and its tenement in complicated ruin! The effects of such a tremendous crash in the city are easier imagined than described. . . . Yet amid this scene of distress the natural waggery of the citizens burst forth: one observed that a tumble so near the alley was nothing extraordinary; another hinted that a rope was but a frail tenure; a third remarked that the firm of Grasshopper and Co. was line-ally connected with the Bank of Air; whilst a fourth, who is supposed to be conversant with the secrets of futurity, drew a deduction from the aspiring hops of a certain *soi-disant* Emperor, and from the accident to his prototype, and certain rumors on the Spanish Walk predicted the downfall of Bonaparte!"

Great Tom, the name familiarly given to the chief bell of St. Paul's Cathedral, in London, more reverently known as the Great Bell, which was finished and hung (1716) in the southern clock-tower, above the two bells which strike the quarters. It cannot be raised and rung, but is hung on gudgeons, or axles, on which it moves when struck by the hammer of the clock. It is tolled only at the deaths and funerals of any of the royal family, the Bishop of London, the Dean of the Cathedral, and, should he die in his mayoralty, the Lord Mayor. The bell weighs 11,474 pounds; its diameter is 9 feet; the hammer lies on the outside brim of the bell, has a large head, weighs 145 pounds, is drawn by a wire at the back part of the clockwork, and falls again by its own weight upon the bell; the clapper weighs 180 pounds. This hammer is also used to toll the bell in case of a demise or funeral; but the sound is not then so loud as when the hour is struck, in consequence of the heavy clock-work not being attached when the bell is tolled, and causing the hammer to strike with greater force than by manual strength.

A persistent popular delusion claims that this bell is the same (only recast) as that which from the reign of Edward I hung in the belfry in front of Westminster Hall, and which was first known as Edward of Westminster and then as Great Tom. True enough, the old Westminster bell was sold by William III to St. Paul's Church, and was recast by Wightman, but it proved too faulty for use. Whereupon Sir Christopher Wren, the architect of St. Paul's, employed Richard Phelps "to make a bell proper for the clock, all of new metal; and the agreement was so ordered, that this new bell should be delivered and approved before he was paid anything for it; and that he should accept the bell cast by Wightman, in part payment towards the new one, so far and at so much as the weight produced, at the price of old bell-metal; and Wightman's bell was likewise to remain at the church till the new bell was approved. And there were all other due and necessary cautions made in the agreement with Mr. Phelps, as may be seen by it, at the office of the works, at St. Paul's. This new bell, then, after trial, being found good, and approved of, Wightman's faulty bell was delivered to Mr. Phelps for the balance of his account."—WREN: *Answer to the Tract "Frauds and Abuses at St. Paul's."*

Greenwich, a parliamentary borough of London, England, situated on the River Thames, is locally memorable as the site of Greenwich Naval Hospital, but gathers to itself an international importance from the fact that it contains the most famous observatory in the world.

Greenwich is first heard of in the reign of Ethelred, when it was (1011–1014) a station of the Danish fleet. It was a royal residence from the thirteenth to the seventeenth centuries, and was the birthplace of Henry VIII, Queen Mary, and Queen Elizabeth. The observatory, established in 1675, crowns a hill 180 feet high in Greenwich Park, a favorite holiday resort of Londoners. Its latitude is 51° 28' 38" N.; its longitude, of course, is marked 0° 0' 0" (*i.e.*, no degrees, no minutes, no seconds), as being the arbitrary point from which longitude is generally reckoned by the civilized world. (See INTERNATIONAL DATE LINE).

Probably no hill in the world has had so strangely varied a history or played so important a part in the affairs of men as that at Greenwich. The granite line across the footpath on its summit is the meridian from which the longitude on every British map and chart is calculated. To a great extent foreign geographers and cartographers follow in their lead. All England sets its time by the mean-solar clock. There is a large galvano-magnetic clock fixed on the outside wall of the observatory and divided into twenty-four hours. There are still many who believe this clock is kept going by the sun. They do not know that the fixed stars are the real time-keepers from which Britishers check their daily progress.

"To this galvano-magnetic clock in the wall," said the London *Graphic* in 1910, "comes every Monday a woman who makes $2500 a year out of the queerest occupation in England. She sells the time to London watchmakers. Her name is Miss Belleville of Maidenhead. Eighty years ago the then astronomer royal suggested to her father that if he took the corrected time of a certified chronometer every week he could no doubt find numerous clients. So he bought a famous watch made for the

Duke of Essex, one of the sons of George III, and soon worked up a business with it. When he died his widow sold the time till she reached the age of 81, and then she handed the business over to her daughter. When Miss Belleville visits Greenwich at the beginning of every week her chronometer is corrected and she is given an official certificate. From that her fifty customers correct their watches and clocks."

Grog, Grogram, Grosgrain. These three words have a curious interconnection. Grogram is an English corruption of the French *gros grain,* a name formerly applied to a heavy stuff of silk and wool with a rough surface, but now mainly limited to heavy silks, and in this sense still a well-known word in commercial circles. In its turn "grogram" has been corrupted into "grog," the sailors' name for a mixture of rum and water. The facts are as follows:

Edward Vernon, of the old Staffordshire house of that name, was put by his father, secretary of state to William and Mary, into the British navy. After distinguishing himself under Sir George Rooke and Sir Charles Wager, both in the West Indies and the Mediterranean, and rising to the rank of rear-admiral, he was suddenly appointed vice-admiral of the blue while a member of Parliament for Penryn, and selected to command the great expedition which was sent out in 1739 to break up the power of Spain in the Caribbean and the Gulf of Mexico. He attacked Porto-Bello on the 20th of November in that year, and, after a furious two days' engagement, took the place with all its treasure and munitions of war and two Spanish line-of-battle ships. A number of American colonial troops served under him. Hence the great victory made him as popular in the American colonies as in England. The seat on the Potomac, afterwards owned and occupied by Washington, was named Mount Vernon in his honor. Later he quarrelled with the government and was struck from the lists of the navy, nominally for too great severity towards his men, though really because of his too small respect for the lords of the admiralty. In the British navy he was gratefully remembered as the chief who first ordered rum and water to be regularly served out to the crews of his squadron. He began this practice on board of the *Burford,* his flagship at the capture of Porto-Bello, and, as he had acquired the nickname of "Old Grog" from his habit of walking the quarter-deck in a "grogram" cloak, this endearing epithet was transferred by Jack Tar to the new beverage.

Guinea. Though the last guinea ever issued from the English mint bears the date of 1813 and the coin itself has entirely disappeared from circulation, Englishmen still continue to talk about guineas, and to reckon in guineas, and to read about guineas in fiction and in poetry,—as, for instance, in the famous Tennysonian quotation—

And the jingling of the guinea helps the hurt that honor feels.

Grouts and maundies were revived for a brief period in the Victorian era, yet mankind, including the poets, has forgotten all about these. Why then do they still cling to the guinea? Possibly because the word itself is a catchy one, so that dealers have found readier customers for their goods at " one guinea " than at " one pound one." Whatever the reason, the name still survives and is used as an equivalent for one pound one, especially in the honorariums demanded by lawyers and physicians.

In 1663 the Royal Mint was authorized to coin gold pieces of the value of twenty shillings, " in the name and for the use of the Company of Royal Adventurers of England trading with Africa." These pieces were to bear the figure of a little white elephant, and $44\frac{1}{2}$ of them were to contain 1 pound troy of " our Crowne gold." Almost as soon as they were issued, they received the popular name of guineas, because they were made of gold imported from the Guinea coast of West Africa and were intended for use in the Guinea trade. The name was extended to later coins of the same intrinsic value. The guinea was subsidiary to silver coin, but that metal, which remained the sole standard until 1816, was in such an unsatisfactory state that by 1695 the guinea had gradually risen to the value of 30 shillings.

The rehabilitation of the silver coinage in the time of William III brought down the value of the guinea to 21s. 6d. in 1698. Here it stood until December, 1717, when it was fixed once for all at 21s. The coinage of the guinea having been suspended in 1813, a new coin, the sovereign or pound, was in 1817 issued to take its place. The value of the sovereign is 20 shillings.

The elephant stamped on the guinea was an allusion to the arms of the Royal Adventurers. Later a castle accompanied the elephant, in honor of Sir Robert Holmes, who, August 8, 1666, captured, in Schilling Bay, Holland, 160 Dutch merchantmen containing bullion and gold dust from Cape Coast Castle in Guinea. Dryden celebrates the exploit in " Annus Mirabilis " (1666), where he thus introduces its hero:

> Holmes, the Achates of the general's fight
> Who first bewitched our eyes with Guinea gold,
> As once old Cato in the Romans' sight
> The tempting fruits of Afric did unfold.
> —Stanza clxxiii.

H.

Hangman's Stone. Numerous large boulders in England and North America have received this name, in consequence of a legend which attaches much the same story to each. There were two fields in the parish of Foremark, Derbyshire, called the great and the little Hangman's Stone, from the boulders which they contained. The former was five or six feet high, with an indentation running across the top. This peculiar mark was explained by tradition. Once upon a time a thief, having stolen a sheep, placed his booty on the top of the stone while he rested, but it slipped off, and strangled the man with the rope which tied the sheep to his back, the indentation being made by the friction of the rope passing back and forth in the struggles of the dying man to extricate himself. (See WALSH, *Curiosities of Popular Customs,* p. 512.

Hay. How and when men first learned to make hay will probably never be known. For haymaking is a "process," and the product is not simply sun-dried grass, but grass which has been partly fermented, and is as much the work of men's hands as flour or cider. Probably its discovery was due to accident. The London *Spectator,* June 22, 1892, indulged the ingenious surmise that man may have learnt it from the *pikas,* the "calling-hares" of the steppes, which cut and stack hay for the winter. That idea would fit in nicely with the theory that Central Asia was the "home of the Aryan race," if we were still allowed to believe it, and haymaking is certainly an art mainly practised in cold countries, for winter forage. No meadows in the world, the *Spectator* continues, are so good as those in England, or so old. Yet from the early Anglo-Saxon times, old meadow has been distinguished from "pastures," and has always been scarce. Two-thirds of what is now established meadow-land still shows the marks of ridge and furrow; and from the great time required to make a meadow—ten years at least on the best land, a hundred on the worst—men have always been reluctant to break up old pasture. The ancient meadows, with their great trees, and close, rich turf, are the sole portion of the earth's surface which modern agriculture respects and leaves in peace. Old customs cling even to the tenure of these sacred spots of earth. "Joint holdings" exist in meadow-land long after they have disappeared in connection with the cultivated portions. The Thames Valley is still full of such joint tenancies. In the

Stour Valley, with Essex on the one side and Suffolk on the other, are numbers of " common meadows," in which several men own portions, and which they must jointly agree to mow or " feed," as the case may be, each year. At Bampton, in Oxfordshire, the sections of the " common meadow " are annually redistributed by lot among sixteen owners. But the old meadows only supply a part, though probably the most valuable part, of the yearly crop of hay. The change from arable to grass, which has marked the last twenty years of English farming, has covered what were once cornfields with " sown grasses " or " leys."

The *Spectator* complains that half the beauty of the " haysel " has been lost since the mowing-machine was invented, and the other " time-saving appliances " of modern farming. " For the most picturesque sight in the cycle of rural toil was to watch the mowers. But the steady rushing of the steel through the falling grass, the rhythmic movement of the mowers, as they advanced *en échelon,* right foot foremost, down the meadow, and the ring of the whetstones on the scythes, have almost given place to the rattling machine."

Hell-for-Certain. The name of a creek in the Kentucky Mountains. John Fox, Jr., once wrote a story about the creek, the mountains, and the moonshiners there, which he published under the name of " Hell-fer-Sartain." He had never visited the spot then, but a few years later he repaired the omission.

" There was a church on Hell-fer-Sartain," writes Mr. Fox in *Scribner's,* " and I had heard there was a Sunday-school known officially as the Hell-fer-Sartain Sunday-school, and moreover that a philanthropical lady had offered to give this school a library provided she should be permitted to design the book-plates. Moreover, I had heard of the preacher of Hell-fer Sartain, and he fitted the niche in which imagination would place him. About him I had heard these words:

" ' He's a good man an' there ain't a word agin' him '—the speaker paused—' leastwise not for a long time. 'Bout fifteen year ago he got in a fuss with a fat feller, an' he an' a friend o' his'n waited for him in the lorrel an' shot him, but they didn't kill him. They're good friends now. The preacher paid the feller not to prosecute him, an' atter the thing was over he tol' as how bein' nervous he put a bullet between his teeth when he saw the fat feller comin', an' he was so blame nervous that he bit the bullet in two.'

" ' And he kept on preaching? ' I asked.

" ' Oh, yes; folks have never held that up agin him.'

Mr. Fox, nothing daunted, found his way first to Devil's **Jump Branch** and then along that tributary to the parent-stream. At the point of junction, "I halted in the road and looked back at those massive, moss-grown, rhododendron-tufted boulders—that branch anyhow was well named—and I couldn't help thinking what a perilous leap at that point the old boy would have into his domains. As I rode down I was politely told the name of the creek by a man and by a woman, each without a smile and each correcting my pronunciation to Hell-fer-Certain—for the present generation of mountaineers is losing its dialect fast."

Hoosier. A nickname for a citizen of Indiana. Its first appearance in literature is somewhat notable, as marking the entrance of Indiana upon the stage of letters. This event took place January 1, 1833, in a poem by John Finley, entitled "The Hoosier's Nest," and published as "the address of the carrier of the Indianapolis *Journal.*" A few lines will be sufficient to show the character of the poem:

> Blest Indiana! In whose soil
> Men seek the sure rewards of toil,
> And honest poverty and worth
> Find here the best retreat on earth,
> While hosts of preachers, doctors, lawyers,
> All independent as wood sawyers.
> With men of every hue and fashion.
> Flock to this rising "Hoosher" nation.
> Men who can legislate or plough,
> Wage politics or milk a cow—
> So plastic are their various parts,
> Within the circle of their arts,
> With equal tact the "Hoosher" loons
> Hunt offices or hunt raccoons,
> A captain, colonel, or a 'squire,
> Who would ascend a little higher,
> Must court the people, honest souls,
> He bows, caresses, and cajoles,
> Till they conceive he has more merit
> Than nature willed he should inherit,
> And, running counter to his nature,
> He runs into the Legislature,
> Where if he pass for wise and mute,
> Or chance to steer the proper chute,
> In half a dozen years or more
> He's qualified for Congress' floor.

The word sprang into general use at once, and before the year was over the newspapers were discussing the origin of the term —so closely was the spirit of learning linked with that of poesy in that early time. Among the theories suggested is one advanced by James Whitcomb Riley, according to whom the earlier settlers were so pugnacious that they even bit off the ears of their opponents. Any one, therefore, seeing an ear lying upon a

are mounted; so that a horse marine is not the *rara avis* that the joke would imply.

To these facts the London *Globe* adds a few others. It reminds us that the royal marines are in good company. They by no means have the monopoly of the sobriquet. For many years the Seventeenth Lancers were known as the "horse marines," two troops of that distinguished cavalry regiment having been employed as acting marines on board the frigate *Hermione* during some severe fighting on the West Indian station in 1795. And, logically, if the term is considered applicable, even in affectionate jocularity, to the royal marines, the distinction should equally be shared by the Queen's (Royal West Surrey) and the Devonshire regiments, both of which served in the fleet in Lord Howe's victory of June 1, 1794, by the 2d Battalion of the Welsh Regiment, which distinguished itself at St. Vincent, in 1797, and bears the distinction on its colors, and also by half the line regiments in the service, for they at one time or another in their career have been either marine corps, sea service foot, or employed, like the marines, as soldiers embarked for service afloat. There is a significant portrait in existence of a typical horse marine of this school in the coffee-room of the United Service Club, in Pall Mall, London. It depicts at full length Admiral of the Fleet the Right Hon. Sir George Cockburn, G. C. B., in the naval uniform of a rear admiral, in cavalry Hessian boots and spurs, the latter in virtue of the honorary office of major-general of marines, which he held at the time.

It is interesting to find that the "horse marine" joke was anticipated in France, which never had any organized corps of marines on shipboard. Molière's "Les Précieuses Ridicules" was acted in 1659. In scene 12 the Vicomte de Jodelet explains to Mademoiselle Madelon and Mademoiselle Cathos that he and the Marquis de Mascarille are old friends.

"Our acquaintance began in the army," he says, "and the first time that we saw each other he was commanding a regiment of cavalry on the galleys of Malta."

"True enough," responds the marquis, entering into the full spirit of the joke, "nevertheless, you were in the service ahead of me, and I remember that I was still only a petty officer when you commanded two thousand horse."

It has been suggested that the chief instrument of Jodelet's horse marines must have been "la trompette marine," which is also mentioned by Molière, in Le Bourgeois Gentilhomme. "There was a musical instrument of that name in the seventeenth century, a sort of large violoncello with one string, which

Gasc, in his French dictionary, explains as " an obsolete one-stringed musical instrument," and again as " a term of derision."

After all, is it possible that horse marine refers to the hawser or *hawse*, as sailors generally mispronounce it?

" Marines to the hawse, bluejackets aloft! " would not sound strange to the nautical ear. It is suggested that when marines first manned the hawse it would not entail any great energy of wit to play upon the word and give these fine fellows a name which seems to puzzle the learned in these days. Others recall the sea horse, and the horse-fish or hippocampus, that odd little fish with a head like that of a horse. Then there are the horse marines, or marine horse, the fabulous animals constituting Neptune's team.

Horticultural Societies. The Royal Horticultural Society of England claims to be the oldest association of this sort, and can justify its claim. This is all the more remarkable because England was not the pioneer in gardening. The science was already well advanced in Holland, Belgium, France, and parts of Germany when it was recognized by only a few Englishmen who had gained all their knowledge on the Continent. Simon Hartlib, in his *Discours of Husbandrie used in Brabant and Flanders* (1650), declares that old men in Surrey still recollected the advent of the first " gardeners " there, and the intense prejudice awakened among the land-owners who believed that spade-work injured the soil. Speaking of the cultivation of vegetables, he complains that it was still hardly known in the north and west, " where a little of it might have saved the lives of many poor people who starved in the last few years. The English," he continues, " imported even plants that grow wild in the hedge-rows because they would not take the trouble to gather them."

Evidently there is some exaggeration here, for a Company of Gardeners was extant in Hartlib's time, and had indeed been chartered so far back as 1606 for the purpose of putting a stop to frauds practised by gardeners in the city. Here a mystery confronts us. The word " city " was then used only in its restricted sense. " What sort of frauds did the ingenuity of English gardeners contrive at the very beginning of the seventeenth century? " asks Mr. Frederick Boyle (*Cornhill Magazine*, June, 1909). " Is it possible that the term included green-grocers and herbalists? "

Hour-glass, a device for measuring intervals of time, consisting usually of two pear-shaped bulbs of glass arranged somewhat in the form of a figure 8. The origin of these timepieces

goes back to an unknown antiquity. In a Greek bass-relief at
the Mattei Palace in Rome representing the marriage of
Thetis and Peleus, Morpheus holds an hour-glass in his hand.
This shows at least that such implements were known to ancient
Greece. We are further informed that the Athenians carried
hour-glasses much as the moderns carry watches. They appear
to have followed in the direct course of evolution from the
clepsydra, or water-clock (*q.v.*). The latter had obvious defects. The water must always be of the same temperature in
order to flow with the same facility, it was wasted by evaporation, it must be supplied at regular intervals. Hence the search
for some more reliable agent and its discovery in ordinary sand.

Sand, when very fine and dry, flows through an orifice with
regular speed whether the quantity be great or small, whereas
water descends more swiftly the greater the weight of it above
the orifice. Moreover, the flow of sand cannot be made more
rapid by any amount of pressure. A piston or plunger pressed
down forcibly on the sand in the tube will not increase or
diminish the flow. The pressure is not obliterated; it does some
work, but that work is exerted against the sides of the tube and
will rupture it unless it be made of strong material. This
singular property of sand becomes of high value in mining and
quarrying. When a hole is bored in a hard rock, partly filled
with gun-powder, and exploded by means of a fuse or an electric
wire, the products of combustion are blown out of the hole and
scarcely any useful effect is produced in blasting the rock. When
a plug of wood is driven in after the powder, this also is blown
out, and the blast is nearly as ineffective as before. But when
the charge is plugged with sand, this refuses to be driven out;
the force of the explosion expends itself laterally and the rock
is riven into fragments.

Hour-glasses were formerly used in churches to regulate the
length of sermons. This was especially the case after the Reformation, when long sermons came into fashion. Earlier
Catholic divines contented themselves with a homily varying
from 10 to 30 minutes in length; but their successors of the
protesting bodies, conceiving it their duty to assert and maintain theses relating to doctrine and discipline, made their
sermons argumentative and sometimes spun on the argument
to inordinate length. The hour-glass literally corresponded
with its name, for it ran for an hour before the sand had all
passed through, and the preacher claimed his full sixty minutes.
Sometimes, however, he was provided with a half-hour glass
for a thirty-minute-sermon.

About the middle of the seventeenth century, when Puritan

sermons occasionally reached the inordinate length of two hours, the hour-glass limit came to be applied. Many pulpits were furnished with iron stands for its reception. An example still exists at Compton Bassett Church, Wilts, with a fleur-de-lis handle for turning the glass when the sand has run out. Another, at Hurst in Berkshire, has a fanciful wrought-iron frame, with foliages of oak and ivy and an inscription, " As this glass runneth, so man's life passeth."

Many old stories relating to pulpit hour-glasses have just a dash of impish humor. One preacher had exhausted his sand-glass, turned it, and gone through three-fourths of another running; the congregation had nearly all retired; and the clerk, tired out, audibly asked his reverend superior to lock up the church and put the key under the door when the sermon was done, as himself and the remaining auditors had all made up their minds to leave.

Hugh Peters, satirized in " Hudibras," after preaching an hour, turned his hour-glass and said, " I know you are good fellows; so let's have another glass." Daniel Burgess, an eloquent Nonconformist divine in the early part of the last century, let his hour-glass run out while preaching vehemently against the sin of drunkenness; he reversed it, and exclaimed, " Brethren, I have somewhat more to say on the nature and consequences of drunkenness, so let's have the other glass, and then "—which was a regular toper's phrase. A rector of Bibury used to preach two hours with two turns of the glass; after the giving out of the text, the squire of the parish withdrew, smoked his pipe, and returned to the blessing.

Pretty and graceful lines have often been suggested by these time-measures. In the excellent song,

> Five times by the taper's light
> The hour-glass we have turn'd to-night,

we are left to guess as we like at the actual hour in the evening to which the watchers had arrived; probably five hours after sunset or dusk. One poet finds a moral exemplar in the hour-glass:

> Steady as truth, on either end
> Its hourly task performing well.

Sidney spoke of " Next morning—known to be morning better by the hour-glass than by the day's clearness." Under an hour-glass in a grotto near the water, these lines were written:

> This babbling stream not uninstructive flows,
>   Nor idly loiters to its destined main;
> Each flower it feeds, that on its margin grows,
>   Now bids thee blush whose days are spent in vain.

Nor void of moral, though unheeded glides
    Time's current stealing on with silent haste;
For lo! each falling sand his folly chides
    Who lets one precious moment run to waste.

Bloomfield's lines, " The Widow to her Hour-glass," typify the trickling of the sand very cleverly:

I've often watched thy streamy sand
    And seen the growing mountain rise,
And often found life's hopes to stand
    On props as weak in wisdom's eyes,
        Its conic crown
        Still sliding down,
Again heap'd up, then down again,
The sand above more hollow grew,
Like days and years still filtering through
And mingling joy and pain.

After what we have said touching the hour-glass, little need be added concerning other varieties in which the sand runs through in a much shorter space of time. The egg-glass, egg-boiler, or egg-timer has its orifice and its quota of sand regulated to a flow in about three minutes; and any other number of minutes might be selected to fit the idiosyncrasies of any particular egg or egg-eater. The half-minute glass, used on shipboard, assists in determining the velocity with which the ship is moving. The log-line is divided by knots, at intervals equal to a hundred and twentieth part of a nautical mile; and there are a hundred and twenty half minutes in an hour. When the line is thrown overboard, the mariner counts how many of the knots pass through his hand while the sand of the half-minute glass is running; and in this way so many knots an hour denote the ship's speed in miles.

I.

Ice-cream. To "Dolly" Madison, wife of the President of the United States, is sometimes given the credit for inventing ice-cream. It is further asserted that it was another woman, Nancy Johnson, wife of a young naval officer, who invented the ice-cream freezer. Truth, however, must not be sacrificed to gallantry. Ice-cream was introduced to the English aristocracy of the late eighteenth century by a London confectioner named Gunton, who may or may not have been its inventor. It is quite possible, of course, that among the many mistresses of the White House Dolly Madison may have been the first to serve ice-cream at the presidential receptions, and thus have popularized in this country a delicacy that had been known for at least half a century in England.

Impressionist. A painter (or by extension a writer) who endeavors to express the general impression produced by a scene or object without elaboration of detail. The first example of its use in England detected by the "New English Dictionary" is in the London *Evening Standard* of February 1, 1881: "To create this misty sentiment is the aim of the modern impressionist."

Degas, Manet, Claude Monet, and other artists were refused admission by the Salon on account of their disregard and absolute independence of the established art canons of the day. Napoleon III invited them to exhibit in the Salon des Refusés. One of the paintings by Claude Monet was entitled "Une Impression." This name was applied to the entire collection. An alternative origin makes the term arise from a phrase in the Preface to Manet's catalogue of his pictures exhibited in 1867 during the Exposition Universelle, from which he was excluded. "It is the effect," he wrote, "of sincerity to give to a painter's works a character that makes them resemble a protest, whereas the painter has only thought of rendering his impression."

Inchcape or **Bell Rock**, a dangerous reef on the coast of Scotland, where so many ships were lost that the Abbot of Aberbrothok caused a float to be fixed upon the rock, with a large bell attached to it, so arranged that the swinging motion of the waves should cause it continuously to toll, and most loudly in rough weather. Southey's ballad, "Sir Ralph the Rover," is founded on this story. Later shipwrecks, amongst others that of the *York*, seventy-four guns, which was lost with all her crew, prompted the setting up of a beacon here. In 1806 Parliament approved of a bill for a light-house. In August, 1807, Robert Stevenson landed here with a band of men. Work was begun by preparing the rock for the erection of a temporary pyramid, on which a barrack house was to be placed for the reception of the workmen. As the rock was dry for only a few hours at spring-tides, the men had to retreat to a vessel moored off it, while these operations were being carried on. After many accidents and the narrow escape of the engineer with thirty-one workmen from being overwhelmed by a rising tide when the attending vessel had broken adrift, the light-house was completed in 1810.

"The Bell Rock tower is 100 feet in height, 42 feet in diameter at the base, and 15 at the top. The door is 30 feet from the base, and the ascent is by a massive bronze ladder. The light is a revolving red and white light; and is produced by the revolution of a frame containing 16 argand lamps, placed in the foci of paraboloidal mirrors, arranged on a quadrangular frame, whose alternate faces have shades of red glass placed before the reflectors, so that a red and white light is shown successively. The machinery which causes the revolution of the frame containing the lamps is also applied to tolling two large bells, in order to give warning to the mariner of his approach to the rock in foggy weather."—*Household Words*, 1855.

Index Expurgatorius. There is a story that a certain Protestant author announced to a dignitary of the Catholic Church in Rome that he was at work on a catalogue of all the great books of the world. "A work of supererogation," exclaimed his Eminence; "we already have such a book in Rome and we call it the *Index Expurgatorius.*" The story is probably the invention of some heretical enemy. It is a verifiable fact, however, that no less learned and distinguished a Roman scholar than Lord Acton spoke quite as lightly of the Index. You have only to turn to the article with which he closed his *Home and Foreign Review,* after it had been indirectly censured in a Brief of Pius IX, to find him asserting that "one of the great instruments for preventing historical scrutiny has long been the Index of prohibited books, which was accordingly directed, not against falsehood only, but particularly against certain departments of truth." Lord Acton adds that it had been used "to keep the knowledge of ecclesiastical history from the faithful, and to give currency to a fabulous and fictitious picture of the progress and action of the Church;" but that this scheme could only have succeeded, even partially and for a time, in an age when every party virtually had its own prohibitive Index to brand inconvenient truths, and none cared for knowledge which could not be made available for argument.

There have been four principal editions of the Roman Index, the first of which was issued under Paul IV in 1559; the second, often called the "Tridentine Index," because prepared by a commission appointed at the Council of Trent, was published under Pius V in 1564; the third was prepared and printed in 1590, under direction of Sixtus V, but never formally published, owing to his death in that year, and its suppression by his successors; the fourth, based largely on that of Sixtus, was published in 1596 by Clement VIII. Of this last there have been some forty editions since, with occasional changes, the principal of which are those of Alexander VII in 1664, and Benedict XIV in 1758. But in the few years preceding the issue of the first Roman Index by Paul IV several local "catalogues" of prohibited books had been put forth, as *e.g.*, by the Sorbonne, by the University of Louvain, at Venice, at Milan, and in England under Henry VIII. It may be observed that by the second rule of the Roman Index all writings by heretical (*i.e.*, Protestant) authors on religious subjects are *ipso facto* forbidden; but many Protestant works not professedly on religious subjects and many works by Roman Catholic authors have from time to time been placed on the Index.

In a general way it may be said that during the sixteenth century the main object of the Index was to combat the Protestant Reformation, and in the subsequent period, which may be illustrated by the edition of Benedict XIV, to suppress heterodox or suspected teaching within the pale of the Church. The earlier editions include most of the books censured during the middle ages before the invention of printing had prompted the establishment of any regular Index. For it must be remembered that this method of suppressing views held to be dangerous is not only not of papal but not even of Christian origin. Diocletian made it a special object to burn the Hebrew Scriptures, and Julian sought to attain the same end by withholding from Christians the means of instruction which might enable them to propagate their belief. The early councils of the Church condemned hererodox books, after which the emperor destroyed them. Pope Leo I himself burnt heretical books, but it is curious that the first instance of a general council ordering books to be burnt is that of the Third Council of Constantinople in 681, which ordered the Monothelite Letters of Pope Honorius to be burnt.

It is true also that in 1542 a bull of Paul III organized the

Roman Inquisition, as a tribunal independent of the bishops for the suppression of heresy and heretical literature, which was vigorously enforced by himself and his successors. But the first Italian list of prohibited books which can be called an Index was issued in 1545 by the Senate of Lucca, under the influence of the Roman Inquisition. It was not till fifteen years later that Paul IV published in 1559, during the second suspension of the sittings of the Council of Trent, the first papal Index, in a bull which opens with the startling announcement that "many of the regular clergy, who thought they could combat the Lutheran and other heretics of the day by studying their works, have so devoted themselves to this study as to have fallen themselves into the errors of the heretics." And accordingly all previous permissions to read their works were cancelled, except in the case of the inquisitors general and cardinals expressly authorized by the Pope.

Meanwhile "heresy" had retorted in kind. The Protestant censorship of the sixteenth century chiefly differs from the Roman Index in this respect, that from the want of any uniform organization it could not formally denounce the possession or perusal of forbidden books as a mortal sin, or visit it with excommunication. But—through the instrumentality of universities, theological faculties, consistories, or censors especially appointed for the purpose—the civil power in Germany, Switzerland, and Holland forbade the reading of unorthodox and especially of "Romish" books. In England convocation censured heretical publications and the Star Chamber suppressed them, while under Elizabeth no printing-presses were allowed except in London, Oxford, and Cambridge, and no "popish books" could be imported from the Continent without the permission of the Council.

To return to the first papal Index. It is arranged alphabetically and adopts a threefold classification (followed in all later editions) of works avowedly heretical, which are absolutely and *ipso facto* forbidden; works shown by experience to be dangerous, whether for their heterodoxy or on other grounds, —as, *e.g.*, books on astrology and the like; and, lastly, anonymous works, mostly by heretics, containing mischievous doctrines. This Index, as being the first of the kind which had appeared, naturally attracted very general notice throughout Europe, and in many quarters, on account of its contents, excited great surprise. It was remarked, as Spondanus says, that, unlike previous edicts on the subject, it prohibited works not dealing with religious questions at all, works by Catholic writers, and works condemned simply because the printer himself was suspected.

The books ordered to be given up to the inquisitors were generally burnt, though this is not expressly enjoined, but even in Rome it was found impossible to carry out the decree in all its strictness.

India, First Englishman in. In the *Manchester Guardian* for January 20, 1910, the then Roman Catholic Bishop of Salford claimed that Father Thomas Stephens, an English Jesuit and a native of Wiltshire who landed in India in 1579, was the first English resident of the latter country. Father Stephens was a friend of Richard Campion the Jesuit, who was martyred for his faith under Queen Elizabeth, and a convert to Catholicism. In 1575 he was received as a novice by the Society of Jesus, in Rome, and four years later was sent to India as a missionary. He died and was buried there probably at Gua in 1619. An accomplished Scholar, well acquainted with the Hindoo language and literature, he wrote a poem in the vernacular versifying the story of the Gospels. See *Notes and Queries,* 10, ix. 208.

Indian Corn, or Maize. A gift of the New World to the Old,—probably originated in Mexico. Now it is grown all over the world, and the average annual crop is about four billion bushels. The United States furnishes about two-thirds of that total.

Every year some new use is found for corn. In the old days there were only two ways to dispose of it—to feed it to cattle, and, in the shape of cornmeal, to some people. The meal had to be used for local consumption, because when made, as it then was, from the whole kernel, it soon became rancid.

To-day it is used directly for food in the form of corn-bread, hominy, and other dishes. Indirectly it is the food for the entire meat-eating world. But it has a thousand uses outside of its food value.

From the germ, which is separated from the kernel in the milling process, the oil is extracted by chemical and mechanical processes and constitutes a product which is coming into use in the manufacture of paint.

The vulcanized oil is used extensively in surfacing linoleum and oilcloth and is applied to a number of other purposes. After the oil is extracted there is left a valuable residuum known as corn oil cake, which is sold here and abroad and is used in the fattening of sheep and other animals. Nearly fifty million pounds of this material are annually shipped to Great Britain and Germany, and there used by farmers, who find it cheaper than materials of a similar nature which they can grow at home.

A corn product which is coming into extensive use is glucose, made from starch, water, and sulphuric acid. Confectioners use large quantities of glucose, which is a colorless, sweetish sirup useful as food when properly taken. Nearly two hundred million pounds of glucose are sent out of this country each year to all parts of the world.

From corn-starch also comes dextrin of several kinds, used extensively in the making of glue, paste, and mucilage. When one licks a postage-stamp one gets a taste of dextrin, flavored often with some harmless preservative.

One other use of corn may be mentioned as in all probability having an important bearing on future industrial pursuits. Denatured alcohol is already extensively manufactured from corn, both at home and abroad. Despite the advancing price of the grain, it is still one of the most economical sources of a product which under different legal restrictions from those now in existence may become important as a source of heat, light, and power in homes, especially farm-homes.

Experiments conducted here and abroad demonstrated that bulkheads constructed of corn-stalks were nearly impervious to water when a shot passed through them. Some of the largest ships are now protected with a belt of corn-pith cellulose, made largely from corn grown in the Ohio Valley. The same material, or modified forms of it, is used in the manufacture of high explosives, such as gun-cotton and smokeless powder.

Pyroxylin varnish, another material made from cellulose, is a very useful product manufactured in connection with the other products just mentioned.

From time to time the attention of the country has been directed toward the vanishing supply of wood for the manufacture of paper or paper pulp. Various attempts have been made to manufacture paper from other materials, and a good many years ago, samples of fine paper were produced from cornstalks. The processes as followed were, however, not economical, so that the work was abandoned. More recently new light has been thrown on the subject through improved methods and processes.

Like the grain, the stalks contain a number of products which can be separated under proper chemical, physical, and mechanical processes. It has been demonstrated that a form of low-grade molasses can be taken from corn-stalks without in any way detracting from their value for the manufacture of paper.

Experimental work at the agricultural colleges and stations having shown the value of the cob as a stock food, large quantities of ground grain and cobs are used for feeding. The cob is also ground and mixed with various highly concentrated feeds, such as cotton-seed meal, and sold for stock food. Large quantities of cobs furthermore are utilized in certain parts of the Mississippi Valley in the manufacture of corn-cob pipes.

Indian Summer. When the Pilgrim Fathers landed in New England, they naturally knew little of the climatic conditions of their new home. With October came the first flurries of snow. The frost nipped the woods and the chill of the air foretold the coming of winter. "We will now have winter," it is further related that one of the band remarked, and no doubt the worthy Bradford, Endicott, and Winthrop nodded their heads in approval. Continuing, history tells us that the friendly Indians pointed to the skies and to the west and told the fathers that summer would come again before the winter. They were right. In the last days of October it grew warm again. The air was filled with slanting sunshine. The world seemed wrapped in an atmosphere of sleepy warmth. The fathers looked forward and remarked, " Lo, the Indians' summer." This may or may not have been the origin of the term. It is an expression, however, that is applied to a short season of pleasant weather, which commonly occurs in the latter part of October or the early part of November.

India-rubber. During the years 1830–1836 there was an India-rubber mania in the United States which almost equalled the subsequent gold fever and the petroleum craze. The crude gum was imported into the country; companies for its manufacture into shoes were organized. But their product was wholly unsatisfactory. The shoes that were made easily enough in winter were softened and destroyed by the heat of summer. Charles Goodyear (1800–1860) had been for a period a prosperous merchant in Philadelphia. But the panic of 1834 swept him into bankruptcy. Then he remembered that some years previous he had devised an improved valve for a crude India-rubber life-preserver which he had purchased. He now sought this out and carried it to the New York office of the Roxbury (Mass.) Rubber Company. There he was informed that, while the device was a good one, the material itself was proving itself worthless. Unless some new method of treating India-rubber could be found, the industry was threatened with extinction. On this hint Goodyear determined to act. His family was ever in want, he himself was frequently in prison for debt; but every dollar that he could get hold of was spent in his investigations. Luckily the raw material at that time cost only four or five cents a pound.

During the winter of 1835 he tried a compound of India-rubber and alcohol, which he made into a pair of boots. Summer came and turned his boots into a sticky, foul-smelling, semi-liquid mass, which he buried hastily in his garden. The first gleam of hope came a little later, when he found that, by boiling a compound of India-rubber and magnesia in quick-lime and water, an article was obtained which apparently answered all requirements. He obtained a patent and for a brief period seemed to be on the road to wealth. Then it was discovered that a drop of any weak acid—apple-juice, for example, or vinegar and water—destroyed the effects of the lime and made the rubber sticky. In 1836 he found in nitric acid a curing process superior to anything yet achieved. A partner with capital was found, and a store on Broadway was opened; but the panic of 1837 swept away the partner's capital, and once more Goodyear found himself face to face with ruin. He persistently refused to give up his experiments. His friends decided that he was insane and even talked of putting him into an asylum. One of them thus described him to a stranger:

"If you see a man with an India-rubber coat on, India-rubber shoes, and an India-rubber cap, and in his pocket an India-rubber purse with nothing in it, you will know that it is Goodyear."

The Roxbury company at last agreed to make goods according to his patent specifications. The United States Government ordered 150 mail-bags of the new material. When finished they looked nice and shiny. A few weeks of heat reduced them to a slimy mass.

Not till 1839 did the right process come to him, almost by accident. He had been treating the rubber with sulphur when he dropped the mixture on the stove. The effect produced by the heat was such that he instantly saw the right method. All he needed was to apply a certain degree of heat to a mixture of rubber and sulphur, and he would have an article that warmth would not melt and cold would not turn into a hard, brittle mass.

There was plenty of backing for him after that, and eastern Massachusetts and Rhode Island profited by the invention that cost him so many years of his time and so much suffering to discover.

Inn, Tavern. No remains of any pre-Roman tavern exists in England, nor any reference thereto in English literature. Yet, since the Romans had inns, one may safely conjecture that they established them during their stay in Britain (A.D. 43–296). Some antiquarians surmise that official posting houses were dotted along the main-road, some twenty miles apart, but that with the coming of the Angles and the Saxons and the disorder they brought in their train, these were rudely swept away, and England was innless for some considerable time. Doubtless the monasteries took their place. Any traveller was hospitably received there. If he could pay, so much the better; if not, he was cheerily welcomed in the name of charity. As the centuries sped on, travel became more general, and the monasteries had to subsidize certain houses which became inns, many with chapels of their own. · Here pilgrims on their way to the local shrines returned thanks to the saint under whose tutelage they had started.

The title of the oldest inn now extant in England is claimed for "The Fountain," in Canterbury, where stayed the wife of Earl Godwin when she went to meet her husband on his return from Denmark in 1029. This is a respectable antiquity indeed! It is also claimed for "The Fountain" that Archbishop Lanfranc stayed there during the rebuilding of his palace in 1070. The story, also, goes that the four knights who murdered Thomas à Becket made the house their meeting-place. It has its place, too, in later history, in that it was a scene of gayety and activity in the September of 1299, when the marriage of Edward I to Margaret of France was solemnized at Canterbury Cathedral. Next, perhaps, comes the "Ostrich," at Colnbrook, which, as it now stands, claims an existence of seven hundred years. "The George and Dragon," at Speedhurst, in Kent, is assigned to the reign of the third Henry, and "The Running Horses" at Leatherhead was referred to revilingly by Shelton in the time of Henry VIII.

The highest inn in England is "The Tan Inn," perched at the summit of the Pennines, at an altitude of 1727 feet. Then comes the Derbyshire "Cat and Fiddle." There used to be a sign on "The Traveller's Rest," at the summit of the exquisite Kirkstone Pass, stating that it was "the highest inhabited house in England"; but it falls short of "The Tan Inn" by 250 feet. However, the Traveller's Rest, though it takes only fifth place in height among English inns in Cloud-land, certainly can claim to be the best known, for very few folk, be they pedestrians, sleepy hucksters, cyclists, or motorists, ever think of passing a spot which was established as a land-mark in literature by the poetry of the Lake School.

The sign of the Saracen's Head seems to have been as common in the streets of old London as that of the Red Lion or the King's Arms afterward became. Selden, in his "Table Talk," gives an uncivil reason for it; he says, "When our countrymen came home from fighting with the Saracens, and were beaten by them, they pictured them with large, big, terrible faces (as you still see the sign of the Saracen's Head is), when, in truth, they were like other men. But this they did to save their own credit." The number of Saracens' Heads gradually diminished, however, and by the middle of the eighteenth century only two hostelries under this hideous significance remained worthy of notice, both of them being distinguished for the ideal representation of the Saracenic countenance.

> At the Saracen's Head Tom poured in ale and wine,
> Until his face did represent the sign,

says Osborne, in 1701; and an obnoxious sergeant of the compter is described in 1617, in Fenner's "Counter's Commonwealth," as having "a phisnomy much resembling the Saracen's Head without Newgate, and a mouth as wide vaulted as that without Bishopsgate," perhaps referring to another sign of the Bull and Mouth, a corruption of Boulogne Mouth or Harbor, which had been a sign in the time of Henry VIII, after the taking of Boulogne in 1544.

The two Saracens' Heads were the one "without Newgate" in the steep ascent of what has since been called Snow Hill, and the other between Leadenhall Street and Aldgate. Both these taverns have long been buried beneath London improvements, and Snow Hill itself has almost entirely disappeared.

London once boasted two Devil Taverns as well as two Saracens' Heads. One of them was famous as the place where Wanley and Neve started the Society of Antiquaries, the other was still more famous for its association with Ben Jonson and his friends. This, the original Devil's Tavern, stood nearly opposite St. Dunstan's church. The sign represented that sainted smith tweaking the devil by the nose, the appellation of "Devil" being a vulgar abbreviation of the full title, "St. Dunstan's and the Devil." Next to the Mermaid it was the favorite resort of the Elizabethan wits, and had the advantage of maintaining its reputation until it was pulled down in 1788 to give way to Child's banking house.

Here Ben Jonson held his celebrated club in the great room known as the Apollo. For the meetings of this club he composed the Leges Convivales, or Convivial Rules, one of which commanded that no insipid verses should be read there "Insipida poemata null recitantur"), an indirect commendation of his own lucubrations which manifested his sturdy faith in himself. According to one account, these rules were "engraven in marble" and placed over the chimney, but the *Tatler* describes them as "in gold letters." Either the original or a copy of them was preserved in the banking house (gold letters upon panelling), together with the bust of Apollo which adorned the club-room.

In the Devil Ben Jonson's word was law. Pope alludes to this supremacy in the lines

> A Scot will fight for Christ's Kirk o' the Green;
> And each true Briton is to Ben so civil,
> He swears the Muses met him at the Devil.

After Jonson the reputation of the ancient place was sustained, sometimes but indifferently, by his followers. Killigrew laid the scene of the "Parson's Wedding" there, and Shadwell in his "Bury Fair," 1680, says, in the character of Old-wit, "I myself, simple as I stand here, was a wit in the last age. I was created Ben Jonson's son in the Apollo."

In the early eighteenth century the Apollo seems to have become a sort of public hall, where great ladies auctioned off their jewels and poet laureates rehearsed their court codes. Says an epigram of the period

> When laureates make odes, do you ask of what sort?
> Do you ask if they're good or are evil?
> You may judge—from the Devil they came to the court,
> And go from the court to the Devil.

One of the last, if not the last public reading which took place at the Devil was that of Kenrick, who delivered his Shakespeare lectures there in 1774; and probably the last literary convivial supper held in the old place was on the occasion when Dr. Johnson proposed to the club in Ivy Lane to celebrate the birth of Mrs. Lennox's first literary child there. It was an elegant entertainment for the celebration of an authoress's first published book, for the doctor had directed that a magnificent hot apple-pie should make a part of it, and this he stuck with bay leaves, because Mrs. Lennox had written verses, and beside that he had prepared a crown of laurel with which to encircle her brows after some ceremonies of his own invention, intended to represent an invocation of the Muses. The guests were Mrs. Lennox and her husband, and about eighteen friends and members of the club.

Sir John Hawkins writes the account of the affair. "The night passed, as must be imagined, in pleasant conversation and harmless mirth, intermingled at different periods with the refreshments of coffee and tea. About five Johnson's face shone with meridian splendor, though his drink had been only lemonade; but the far greater part of us had deserted the colors of Bacchus, and were with difficulty rallied to partake of a second refreshment of coffee, which was scarcely ended when the day began to dawn. This phenomenon began to put us in mind of our reckoning; but the waiters were all so overcome with sleep that it was two hours before we could get a bill, and it was not till near eight that the creaking of the street door gave the signal for departure." It is a pleasant reminiscence with which to close the history of the old place —a pleasant reminiscence, and perhaps its last, for in 1788 it was obliterated from the spot where it had been so long famous.

Less famous perhaps, but more notorious, was the Rose Tavern which stood in Russell Street, Covent Garden, next door to old Drury Lane, and was demolished in 1776 when Garrick enlarged the theatre. The sign of the Rose was enclosed in an oval medallion on the new front.

So long as it existed the tavern was the resort not only of the wits and of the players connected with the theatres, but of the wild roysterers who went there to drink and sallied forth to commit all sorts of nocturnal depredations. These titled bullies and distinguished ruffians organized themselves into companies bearing different names, the Mohocks seeming to be the more general title. Sometimes rival societies were formed, such as the Scowrers, who preferred to band themselves together for the purpose of checking the Mohocks. These gentlemen are immortalized by Shadwell in his play of " The Scowrers," and the Rose Tavern is made the scene of their exploits; speaking of which one of the characters says: " Puh, this is nothing; why I knew the Hectors and before them the Muns and the Tityre Tu's: they were brave fellows indeed. In those days a man could not go from the Rose Tavern to the Piazza once but he must venture his life twice."

Gay, in his " Trivia," asks:

> Who has not heard the Scowrer's midnight fame?
> Who has not trembled at the Mohock's name?
> Was there a watchman took his hourly rounds
> Safe from their blows, or new-invented wounds?
> I pass their desperate deeds and mischief done,
> Where from Snow-hill black steepy torrents run;
> How matrons, hooped within the hogshead's womb,
> Are tumbled furious thence; the rolling tomb,
> O'er the stones thunder'd, bounds from side to side,
> So Regulus, to save his country, died.

The mention of Gay brings us back to the Rose and to the better part of the society that met in its rooms; not,

however, without a glance at the awful tragedy which had its
rise there on the 14th of November, 1712, when the infamous ·
Lord Mohun met the Duke of Hamilton and the terms of that
bloody duel were arranged between the seconds.   Who has
forgotten the admirable account of it in Thackeray's "Esmond,"
and who could hope to add anything to that pathetic story?
The Rose was doubtless a comfortable as well as a celebrated
resort, in spite of its evil connections, for it continued to
attract the wits of the "Augustan" period.   Swift, in his
verses on his own death, says—

> Suppose me dead, and then suppose
> A club assembled at the Rose,
> Where, from discourse of this and that,
> I grow the subject of their chat.

It is significant that the nomenclature of the thirteenth
century manor is preserved in every detail of the modern inn.
The hosteller remains as the ostler who now confines his attention to four-footed visitors; the chamberlain has changed his
sex (though only since the days of Sir Roger de Coverley)
and has become the chambermaid.   In most old manor-house
provisions, wine and ale were served from a special department close to the porch and called the "bower," from Norse
bür, meaning "buttery."   Frequenters of a modern inn resort
for the same purpose to the "bar."   Lastly the presiding
genius in every hotel or tavern, no matter how humble, is
invariably referred to as "the landlord."   The very word "inn,"
like the French "hotel," anciently implied the town residence
of a nobleman.   The Inns of Court were nearly all of them
houses of the nobility converted for the purpose of lodging
the law students there.

But the English preferentially know their inns by a more
democratic name—a name which carries the mind back many
generations before there were any manorial lords, to the tribal
chief, and even beyond the tribal chief to the common dwelling
of our Aryan forefathers.   They generally refer to it as the
public house,—the one secular place of resort where all may
forget their social differences.

Maskell and Gregory, joint authors of "Old Country Inns
of England" (London, 1911), assure us that no extant English .
inn has a history of more than 800 years and that very few
hostelries can trace their independent existence to a period
earlier than the fourteenth century.   They have their friendly
gibe, of course, as the Fighting Cocks in St. Albans, said to be
the oldest inhabited house in England, whose sign-board until
a few years ago modestly chronicled the fact that it had been

"Rebuilt after the Flood." They speak a little more seriously about the "Fountain" at Canterbury, which was commended by the German ambassador when he lodged there in 1299 on the occasion of the marriage of King Edward I. But evidently they are not quite sure of their historical footing until they reach such comparatively modern houses as the Saracen's Head at Newark, whose title-deeds refer back to 1341; the Seven Stars of Manchester, proved by local antiquaries to have existed before the year 1356; and the Crown Inn at Rochester, built by the same Symond Potin who in 1316 founded St. Catharine's Hospital for Poor Pilgrims in the same town.

International Date Line. There is an old problem which may be restated as follows: Suppose a man could keep pace with the sun above him and, journeying ever westward, could make the complete tour of the world in twenty-four hours. He starts, we will say, at noon on Monday. Of course it is Tuesday noon when he gets back to his starting-point. Now, all along his journey he asks the civilized people he meets what time it is. At first the uniform answer will be "Monday noon." But somewhere or other the answer must begin to be "Tuesday noon." Where will the answer shift from "Monday noon" to "Tuesday noon?"

Obviously there must be some place on the earth's surface, some parallel of longitude, which is generally accepted by civilized races as conventionally marking the beginning of the day. And in fact most civilized nations have accepted the line drawn by English astronomers at exactly their antipodes,— viz., the 180th meridian of longitude reckoned either east or west from Greenwich observatory. There is a grand-total of 360 degrees, one-half of which equals 180. That meridian is known, therefore, as the international date line.

But the line is not drawn with absolute accuracy. Being arbitrary, it can, of course, be arbitrarily changed to suit the convenience of the inhabitants in its neighborhood. For example, it is less confusing to have the line occur in the sea than on land, and wherever possible a shift from earth to water has been made. Navigators can grasp the matter more easily than landsmen.

Starting from the North Pole then, the date line follows the 180th meridian until it approaches the Siberian coast. There it bends to the east and passes through Bering Strait, thence in a southwesterly direction between the Aleutian Islands and Asia. It reaches its furthest westerly deflection (about 116 degrees east longitude) just below the Philippine Islands. Next it curves back to the 180th meridian and follows it to the equator. Again, it bends eastward, passing between numerous groups of islands, leaving the Samoan group on the east and the Tongas on the west. Sweeping almost to the 165th meridian, it then curves back gradually to the 180th and follows it to the South Pole.

It is on reaching this line that ships change their reckoning from Monday (we will say) to Tuesday if they are sailing eastward. In other words they drop one day. If they are sailing westward, however, they repeat one day.

A curious discussion in the English *Notes and Queries,* VIIth Series, turns upon possible legal tangles which depend upon relative differences in time. T. Adolphus Trollope, the novelist, started the ball rolling by citing an imaginary case in which a married man made what he supposed was a bigamous marriage at Naples at 11 A.M. Subsequently it turned out that his wife had died at 10.30 A.M. Now, at 10.30 A.M. London time, it was 11.23 A.M. in Naples, and Mr. Trollope desired to know whether the second marriage was legal and valid or bigamous and null. The general consensus of opinion was against the validity of the marriage. One of the correspondents cited what he stated was an actual case. A certain ship or its cargo, he said, was insured for (say) £10,000 up to 12 P.M. of (say) October 31, 1870. From that hour reinsurance was effected with another firm of underwriters for double the original amount. The ship was wrecked in the South Pacific on the very night on which the first insurance expired, and the second came in force. The cargo was lost, and only one or two of the officers and a few of the hands escaped. They reported that the ship was lost at twenty minutes after 12, Liverpool time, but of course some time before 12 at the place where the wreck occurred. The action, needless to state, was for the recovery of the larger sum.

Jules Verne, in "Round the World in Eighty Days," has a striking situation at the very climax of the story. It appears that the hero, Phileas Fogg, has lost his bet, for he really reaches England after circumnavigating the globe on the eighty-first day after starting, according to the reckoning kept on board ship. In other words, he had seen the sun rise eighty-one times, though each day was a little less than twenty-four hours long, so that the grand total of $81 \times \frac{x}{x}$ was equal to the grand total of $80 \times 24 = 1920$. He had been 1920 hours on his journey but they had divided themselves up into 81 instead of 80 days.

This is a confusing subject, and many efforts have been
27

made to explain away what is in fact a totally unnecessary confusion.

Owing to this apparent paradox, it is quite possible for a sailor to encounter three Thursdays in a week. Exempla gratia: Let a vessel sail east around the world and arrive Thursday according to the reckoning aboard. On the day following let the crew land; they will find it Thursday ashore. And again on the next day they board a vessel that has just arrived from a cruise around the world, sailed in a westerly direction; they will find it is Thursday aboard that ship.

The *American Notes and Queries* for March 15, 1890, gives the following extract from the journal of a traveller on his way from China to San Francisco:

We ran a northeasterly course at first, going as high as 47 degrees 58 minutes north, in which latitude we crossed the 180th degree of longitude on July 9, and consequently had two Fridays and 8 days in the week. This fairly puzzled one of our party, who came down to breakfast in a bewildered state of mind, asking whether to-day was yesterday or to-morrow, and declaring that he had certainly gone to bed on Friday night, and yet had got up again on Friday morning! For my part I must say that it looked very strange to see in my diary, " Friday, 9th July, No. 1," " Do. do., No. 2."

Inventions. Some of the largest fortunes have been made from very simple little things as novelties. It is said the toy, "Dancing Jim Crow," yielded its inventor an annual income of $75,000; that another toy by John Giltin enriched him to the extent of $100,000 a year during its popularity; that Dr. Plimpton, inventor of the roller skate, made $1,000,000 from his patent; that the man who first placed the rubber tip on lead pencils made $100,000 a year; that Harvey Kennedy for his shoe lace made $2,500,000; that the ordinary umbrella benefited six people as much as $10,000,000; that the Howard patent for boiling sugar in vacuo produced millions; that Sir Josiah Mason, inventor of steel pens, made an enormous fortune which, on his death, he left to English charities; that the patentee of the pen for shading in different colors made a yearly income of $200,000; that the inventor of the simple metallic heel plate sold 143,000,000 plates a year and realized $1,500,000 as royalty; that the inventor of the modern baby carriage (a woman) enriched herself to the extent of $50,000 a year; that a woman in Port Elizabeth, South Africa, invented the Mary Anderson curling iron and derived a yearly royalty of $40,000.

Inventions Anticipated. H. G. Wells's "Anticipations," a look ahead into the future, attempts to predict what will be the condition of posterity in the way of moral, mental, and mechanical progress: "But what is the use of vaticinations of this sort?" some Gradgrind may growl. "They have never been fulfilled in the past; why should we expect that Mr. Wells has any greater gift of prophecy than tutti quanti."

Gradgrind, if he ventures to say anything of this sort, will write himself down, or speak himself down, a worse—well— donkey than Dogberry.

It is astonishing to find how many of Mr. Wells's predecessors have hit the bull's eye of fact in what seemed to their contemporaries like speculative shafts aimed at the air.

And yet, after all, where is the wonder?

The poet is essentially a prophet. He is the preacher of order and harmony. Order and harmony will be the last results of human effort. What we call the ideal is not a misapprehension of the past, but a forecast of the future. The Golden Age lies before us, not behind.

When we speak of the good old days and the wisdom of antiquity we are usually wrong, unless we right that wrong by forcing the meaning awry from the intent of the speaker. The old days will be good, antiquity will be wise—when they arrive. But they lie before us: we have not reached them. The world, as yet, is only in its semi-savage childhood, only recently has it emerged from the helpless stupidity of the embryo. When it is older, when it has travelled further away from the chaotic past, it will be wiser and better.

Though the poet has a habit of lauding the *tempus actum,* he is really lauding not the actual past, but (unbeknown perhaps to himself) an ideal past, which may represent the actuality of the future. Posterity will read a new interpretation into his verses, suggested by the light of what, to posterity, will be the present.

All this may seem a mere play of fancy; it is the rigid truth.

Great men of the imaginative temperament build better than they know. The world looks back and sees what they were striving for, what they were aiming at, though they themselves knew it not, or only dimly recognized it. And this not only in the realm of imagination and morals, but also in that of plain hard fact. Some of the greatest discoveries of modern science, some of its most pregnant inventions, have been shadowed by poets and romancers of long ago.

They themselves did not fathom their own meaning. They could not have interpreted into plain prose their own oracles. But the meaning is there; the oracle is there. We of this older and wiser day can compass the meaning, can explain the oracle.

The law of gravitation was announced by Newton in the year 1685. Had it not been foreseen by Shakespeare in 1609? At all events, in "Troilus and Cressida," he put these lines into the mouth of Cressida:

> But the strong base and building of my love
> Is as the very centre of the earth
> Drawing all things to it.
>
> Act iv, Sc. 2.

Twelve years earlier he had made Romeo say:

> Turn back, dull earth, and find thy centre out.
> *Romeo and Juliet*, Act ii, Sc. 1.

Inasmuch as Romeo is thinking of his attraction toward Juliet, this looks like an allusion to the law of gravitation.

A more marvellous anticipation is contained in these lines, which seem at least to indicate that Shakespeare knew (what was not known even to botanists until two centuries later) that plants have sex:

> Pale primroses
> That die unmarried, ere they can behold
> Bright Phœbus in his strength, a malady
> Most incident to males.
> *The Winter's Tale*, Act IV, Sc. 3.

Sir William Harvey, in 1628, announced his discovery of the circulation (*q.v.*) of the blood, and the all-important part played by the heart in this function. About the year 1603, Shakespeare had made Brutus say to Portia:

> You are my true and honorable wife,
> As dear to me as are the ruddy drops
> That visit my sad heart.

Shakespeare's great contemporary, Marlowe, expressly anticipates the Suez Canal in the second part of "Tamburlaine the Great," Act V, Sc. 3:

> And here, not far from Alexandria,
> Whereat the Tyrrhene and the Red Sea meet,
> Being distant less than full a hundred leagues,
> I meant to cut a channel to them both,
> That men might quickly sail to India.

Another contemporary, Ben Jonson, anticipated the modern air-cushion (*q.v.*). In another play he credits the Dutch with an invention that foreshadows the Holland submarine boat:

> It is an automa, runs under water,
> With a snug nose, and has a nimble tail
> Made like an auger, with which tail she wriggles
> Between the costs of a ship, and sinks it straight.

In France Cyrano du Bergerac, whom Molière himself plundered of ideas, manifested much scientific prescience. The airship in which the hero of his "Voyage to the Moon" (1650) made his trips to that sphere was a pretty close foreshadowing of Montgolfier's balloon, and elsewhere in the same book he anticipates the phonograph (*q.v.*).

As will be seen from the very title of Chapter XIII—"Of the Little Animals that make up our Life, and likewise cause our Diseases"—Cyrano had a prescientific foreknowledge of bacilli and of the germ theory of disease. Chapter XVI is titularly of equal luminosity, "Of Miracles: and of the Curing by the Imagination." Here the faith cure is anticipated as well as the real explanation of its success. Cyrano believes that it is enough "for the recovery of one's health, eagerly to wish for it, and to imagine himself cured," and he puts this dilemma to the Lunarians who believed that the cures were wrought by a miracle: If a patient pray for health, he must either die, continue sick, or recover. "Had he died, then would it have been said kind Heaven hath put an end to his Pains; Nay, and that according to his Prayers, he was now cured of all Diseases, praised be the Lord: Had his Sickness continued, one would have said, he wanted Faith; but because he is cured, it's a Miracle forsooth. Is it not far more likely, that his Fancy, being excited by violent Desires, hath done its Duty and wrought the Cure? For grant he hath escaped, what then? must it needs be a Miracle?"

Both Cyrano and Swift write about storing sun-heat purged of light, or sunlight purged of heat (Swift evidently with his tongue in his cheek), and these dreams or jests may yet be realized in sober earnest from such phosphorescent substances as uranium, pollonium, and radium. Swift also makes his Gulliver watch men freezing air, a feat that was accomplished in the Royal Institution Library in 1894 and now is one of the commonplaces of science.

Indeed Gulliver's powers of prediction are positively uncanny. For example: In 1877 Professor Hall, of the National Observatory at Washington, D. C., announced his discovery that Mars had two moons hitherto unknown to astronomers. He described them as being each about the size of a 40-acre lot. Revolving round the planet like two pretty little golden shuttles, one of these presents the phenomenon of travelling almost three times as fast as Mars itself.

Now, it is an astonishing fact that Swift in "Gulliver" (1726), as well as Voltaire in "Micromegas," allude to these moons, thus by a full century anticipating that very science of astronomy against which their sarcasms were levelled.

Voltaire's allusion is very brief. Micromegas, an inhabitant of Sirius, is represented as swinging around the solar system:

"He travelled about one hundred millions of leagues after leaving Jupiter. Coasting by Mars, he saw two moons circling about the planet, which have hitherto escaped the observation of astronomers on the earth."

Swift is more circumstantial. And the wonder is that he is so nearly correct in his details. Here are his words (he is speaking of the Laputans, an imaginary race of pseudo-astronomers):

"They have likewise discovered two lesser stars or satellites which revolve about Mars, whereof the innermost is distant from the planet exactly three of its diameters, and the outermost five of its diameters; the former revolves in the space of ten hours, and the latter in twenty-one and a half hours."

Now mark. Mars's two moons do in fact consist of an inner and an outer one. The diameter of Mars is a little over 4000 miles. Gulliver estimates the distance of the inner moon from the planet at three times the diameter of the latter, which would be 12,000 miles. It is actually 10,000 miles. Gulliver's estimate for the distance of the outer moon is 20,000 miles. It is really 15,000 miles. He sets down the time of revolution for the inner moon as $7\frac{1}{2}$ hours; for the outer at $20\frac{1}{2}$. As a matter of fact the former is 10 hours, the latter 30.

Pretty good for a guess at moons that had never been seen by scientists.

One of the most remarkably explicit prophecies that ever obtained fulfilment was made by Erasmus Darwin, grandfather of the evolutionist, in the following lines from "The Loves of the Plants:"

> Soon shall thy arm, unconquered steam, afar
> Drag the slow barge or drive the rapid car;
> Or on wide waving wings, expanded, bear
> The flying chariot through the field of air.

The steamboat, the automobile, and the aeroplane are here predicted as coming wonders. The steamboat arrived in 1807, the automobile in 1890, the aeroplane in 1911. Now it must be borne in mind that "The Loves of the Plants" was published in 1789.

In his ninth "Bridgewater Treatise" Babbage insisted on the permanence of all spoken words. The pulsations of the air, he says, once set in motion, continue in ever widening waves to the very end of the universe:

"Every atom impressed with good and with ill retains at once the motions which philosophers and sages have imparted to it, mixed and combined in ten thousand ways with all that is worthless and base. The atmosphere we breathe is the ever-living witness of the sentiments we have uttered . . . and (in another state of being) the offender may hear, still vibrating in his ear, the very words uttered, perhaps thousands of centuries before, which at once caused and registered his own condemnation."

This was a novel and striking idea to Babbage's contemporaries. Many informed him that it almost made them afraid to speak, from the dread that the sounds were to last and perchance come back to them in the hereafter.

Imagine, therefore, his surprise when his friend, Henry Reed, of Philadelphia, pointed out to him that his theory had been anticipated, as far back as the fifteenth century, in the works of no less a man than Chaucer. Here is a passage in the latter's "House of Fame." Note the extraordinary parallelism to Babbage. Note also how the old poet uses a favorite similitude with the popularizer of science to-day, that of sound-waves compared to the waves of water set in motion by a stone thrown into a stream:

> Sound is naught but air that's broken
> And every speech that is spoken,
> Whe'er loud or low, foul or fair,
> In his substance is but air.
> .   .   .   .   Take heed now
> By experience, for if that thou
> Throw in a water now a stone
> Well wotst then it will make anon
> A little rounded as a circle,
> Par venture, as broad as a coréicle,
> And right anon thou shat see well
> That circle cause another wheel,
> And that the third, and so forth, brother,
> Every circle causing other,
> Much broader than himselfen was,—
> Right so of air, my live brother,
> Ever each air another stirreth
> More and more and speech upbeareth
> Till it be at the House of Fame.

Leonardo da Vinci was one of the most astonishingly fecund of men. It is only recently, through the publication of mere selections from his posthumous manuscripts, that the world has been able to realize how many inventions he anticipated, and how many truths, divined by him but not revealed to the world, had to be subsequently rediscovered by others.

One volume, the so-called Codice Atlantico, preserved at

Milan, has been most closely studied. From it we see that Leonardo was a pioneer both in method and in actual discovery. He founded himself on observation and experiment. He divined the circulation of the blood. He anticipated Copernicus in propounding the theory of the earth's movement; long before Kepler and Galileo he demonstrated that the faint light we see on a new moon is reflected from the earth. He declared that "motion was the cause of all life." He forestalled Lamarck's classification of vertebrate and invertebrate. He takes his place, in virtue of his researches into rocks and fossils, with the masters of modern science who have proclaimed the continuity of geological causes. In botany, in physics, in mechanics, he made discoveries of equal originality. In applying his scientific knowledge, he forestalled many modern inventions. He had glimpses even of the telephone. He is entitled to a distinguished place among the forerunners of Watt. He was the first inventor of screw propulsion. He made paddle-wheels. He attacked the problem of aerial navigation. He invented swimming-belts. He anticipated by many years the invention of the camera obscura. He was great alike as a civil and a military engineer. He watered the Lombard plain by the invention of sluices; he was one of the first to recommend the use of mines for the destruction of forts, and he anticipated the inventions of our time in suggesting breech-loading guns and mitrailleuses.

Jules Verne invented nothing himself, but he stimulated invention in others. "When I was ten years old," says Simon Lake, "I read Jules Verne's 'Twenty Thousand Leagues under the Sea.'" When Mr. Lake was forty years old the result of this reading was made known to the world in the submarine boat *Argonaut*.

The phrase "Around the World in Eighty Days" is a mere commonplace to-day. Two ladies did better than Phileas Fogg so far back as 1890,—"Nellie Bly" and Miss Elizabeth Bisland. A trip to the moon such as Verne conceived has not yet been realized, to be sure, nor all the features of his story "Five Weeks in a Balloon;" but flying has reached a stage considered equally impossible when these romances were written, and more romances are daily being constructed revolving on aerial accomplishments still to come.

Two books of comparatively recent date have contained a large number of prophecies already realized; they are Bulwer-Lytton's "The Coming Race" and Edward Bellamy's "Looking Backward." The former prophesied the household of the future as being operated entirely by mechanism or mechanical appliances, life to be practically servantless; such present domestic institutions as the vacuum cleaner, the pneumatic chambermaid, the fireless cooker, the various electrical household devices such as washing-machines, irons, refrigerators, cooking utensils, sewing-machines, and carpet-sweepers are active realizations. Much of this has come true.

In many kitchens work is done almost entirely by electrical power, cooking is carried out on electric heaters and in electric ovens, automatic time attachments indicating when each dish is ready. Polishers, cleaners, and dishwashers are driven by small motors. In household laundries washing-machines, and wringing-machines, each driven by a small motor, do the family washing within an hour, all with a minimum need of servants.

A near accomplishment of a whimsical fancy, also from Lytton's book, that of turning on the music from a universal supply house, is the tel-harmonium, the ingenious device for switching on music.

In "Looking Backward" Bellamy describes the ideal shop of the future—there being no officious clerks, but all purchases being made, all packages tied up, all change counted and values estimated by mechanical aids. Adding-machines which can work faster and more accurately than man are now with us. Weighing and counting machines by which any commodity can be counted without the use of tabulated figures save, it is calculated, from 40 to 90 per cent. of time and labor over all old methods.

In a later book, "Equality," Mr. Bellamy pursued the same line of fancy on a larger scale.

Hitherto we have been confining ourselves to modern literature. To realize still more clearly that there is nothing new under the sun, you need only take up any popular work on modern inventions and bring to bear upon it a moderate acquaintance with ancient literature. If, as may happen, your reading has been among the curiosities, corners, and byways of ancient literature, the means of verifying the adage will be proportionately abundant. Thus it is patent to a tolerable number of well-informed persons that a sort of prediction of the discovery of the mariner's compass and of the continent of America—if not, indirectly, of steam navigation—is to be found in the *Medea* of Seneca, vv. 375, etc. :—

> Venient annis sæcula seris
> Quibus Oceanus vincula rerum
> Laxet, et ingens pateat tellus,
> Tethysque novos detegat orbes,
> Nec sit terris ultima Thule.

Irish Giant.   The success of the Cardiff Giant fraud in the United States prompted a similar experiment in Great Britain. There it was less successful, and the exhibit in the case, a stone image said to be the fossilized remains of Fin Macoul (the greatest of all Irish giants) still remains in the possession of the London and Northwestern Railway Company at Liverpool.

In the early seventies of the nineteenth century two show-men, named Dyer and Kershaw, exhibited this pretended fossil in Manchester, Liverpool, and other English cities, claiming for it that it had been dug up near the Giants' Causeway in Ireland.   They subsequently went to law over the owner-ship and the case was thrown into chancery, the railroad com-pany being enjoined at the same time from moving the " giant." Dyer and Kershaw have since passed away, but the case is still in chancery and the " giant " remains in the possession of the railway, with charges of nearly $1000 against it for storage.

The " giant " is a figure in stone, 12 feet 2 inches long and weighing three tons.   Some years ago a man claiming to know the history of the " giant " said that the figure had been carved out of rock at Carrickfergus, Ireland, and was seized on by the showmen as a means of making money by exhibiting it as the remains of the celebrated Fin Macoul.   Fin keeps silent and the true story may never be known.

Irish Jaunting Car.   The first jaunting car in Ireland was established in 1815 by a Milanese, Carlo Bianconi, who settled in Dublin and drove every day to Caher and back, charging two pence a mile; from this small beginning, in 1837 he had established sixty-seven conveyances, drawn by nine hundred horses.

The extension of modern manufacturing towns and cities demanded still greater conveniences, which were supplied at first by the omnibus lines, which up to 1860 were the chief means of urban and interurban transportation.   To these suc-ceeded the street railroad, traversed by cars drawn by one or more horses, and these in turn became wholly inadequate to meet the demand of the suburban districts.

The cable car, drawn by underground cable, was the next innovation; but this, about 1880 to 1890, was supplanted by the electric trolley lines; and these again were supplemented in many cities by elevated and subway lines, in which the cars were propelled by electricity supplied by a third rail. This latter device has already been applied to extended lines of railroads, and it is not unlikely that the present century will witness the electrification of most of the railroad lines in thickly settled countries.

Iron Ships. It was the fight between the *Merrimac* and the *Monitor,* March 9, 1862, which finally convinced the world of the superiority of iron for the construction of the man-of-war. Thereafter wooden ships were doomed. But neither the Southern nor the Northern iron-clad was an absolute pioneer. Iron ships had been known to the merchant marine for nearly half a century, despite their repudiation by a famous naval constructor of the early 1800's,—"Don't talk to me of iron ships; they are contrary to nature."

The first iron ship has more reputed birthplaces than Homer. Both the Clyde and the Mersey claim preëminence in this respect. But there is record of an iron boat, intended apparently for passenger service, which was built and launched on the river Fo·s in Yorkshire in 1777. We know that by 1787 iron was beginning to be used for the shell plating of lighters in the canal service. In 1816 Sir E. J. Robinson, of Edinburgh, designed an iron vessel which was not launched until three years later, and in the interim (1818) the iron lighter *Vulcan* appeared on the Monkland canal near Glasgow. Owing to this accidental priority, the *Vulcan* is often referred to as the first iron ship.

The first large screw steamer built of iron was the *Great Britain,* which inadvertently added a fresh proof of the value of that metal in ship-building and contributed a signal refutation of one of the leading arguments against it,—viz., that, if an iron ship grounded and was exposed to bumping on a shore, the bottom would be easily perforated. In 1846 the *Great Britain* ran ashore in Dundrum Bay, Ireland, and settled on two detached rocks. Though she remained aground for 11 months, she was finally got off and repaired and afterward did good service.

Ivory-carving. The oldest extant art (extant still, though sadly decadent) is the art of carving ivory. It would almost seem as if the beauty of the material had excited the faculty of carving it into beautiful forms. The earliest remains in Western Europe yield fragments of bone incised with pictures by some prehistoric Landseer. The graves of Egyptian kings so old that all modern chronology has to be rearranged to include them contain ornaments of ivory. There are some in the British Museum dating from the "time of Moses," and a box at the Louvre bears the name of Hatasou, a queen of Egypt who must have lived many centuries earlier. The Pyramid builders were ivory-carvers. The Ninevites both imported carvings from Egypt and made them for themselves. Six centuries before Christ the Cypselidæ sent to Olympia an offering which consisted of a coffer of cedar inlaid with gold and ivory. The cryselephantine statues of the time of Phidias have been made famous for us by ancient writers, though nothing of them has come down to us. Though such sculptures of the Roman time before Constantine are extremely scarce, they do exist, and from the fourth century of the Christian era we have a complete succession of works—a fact which sets ivory-carving alone among the arts. The consular tablet gave way to the religious triptych. The triptych was in its turn supplanted by the heathen imagery of a more advanced Christian age, but until our own day the art has survived. It is perhaps, as an art, at a lower ebb now than at any previous period since the third century, but signs are not wanting of a disposition to revive it, and meanwhile more mechanical skill in cutting is being attained.

It is a puzzling fact that no elephant's tusk of to-day and no tusk surviving from the past would afford pieces large enough for the plaques and diptychs of the middle ages. The leaves of one diptych at Paris measure each fifteen inches in length, and nearly six in width, while a single tablet in the British Museum is sixteen inches and a quarter long, and five inches and a half broad. Yet the largest of the tusks at the South Kensington Museum is only sixteen inches and a half in circumference, and a pair exhibited in 1851 did not exceed twenty-two inches in circumference at the base. It has been conjectured that the ancient carvers were able to bend the pieces of ivory or to flatten them, but all efforts made in modern times to recapture the secret have failed.

The largest and finest example of carving in bone is the retable of Poissy in the Louvre, containing, as it does, about seventy separate plaques and being no less than seven feet six inches in width. It was made for the brother of Charles V of France, and a smaller example of the same kind of work is in the Hôtel Cluny. If this reredos is the largest, a "pietà" at the British Museum is the smallest, and perhaps the most beautiful, of the religious ivories remaining. It is less than three inches in height, and consists of two groups so arranged that one, representing the Agony in the Garden, is formed without distortion on the back of the other and more important face.

J.

Jacqueminot Rose. This was named in honor of Viscount Jean François Jacqueminot (1787–1852), an illustrious soldier under the first Napoleon who especially distinguished himself by his bravery at Waterloo. The Bourbons put him on half pay. In 1827 he was elected a deputy from his native town of Nancy. He advocated a reform of the royal body-guard and the dismissal of the Swiss Guards. With Pajol he directed the expedition of Rambouillet which resulted in the abdication and flight of Charles X. The Orleans dynasty whom he had assisted to the vacant throne found in him a loyal partisan, and Louis Philippe rewarded him with many offices, including the command of the National Guards in Paris. Nevertheless, on the outbreak of the Revolution of 1848, he showed extraordinary indecision, and lost his command, which was given first to Bugeaud and then to Lamoriciere, whereupon he retired to private life.

Jade. An inconspicuous stone which to a superficial glance seems little superior to serpentine. Jade and jadeite, moreover, the latter a cousin to the first, occur in pretty large masses in those countries where they are most admired. Outside of Asia and Oceanica few, if any, specimens of true jade have been discovered. Reported finds in America and Europe have usually turned out valueless. Hardness is one of its characteristics. It will scratch glass and quartz. But diamonds and other stones are even harder. Toughness is its peculiar quality. To work it needs patience of a kind that is scarce known out of China. Is it any marvel that the inhabitants of China have carried the working of jade to its highest development and inoculated the world with the mild madness of jade worship?

The world was early prepared for that worship. A predilection for jade and tough minerals akin to it is noted among the imperishable articles left by peoples who lived when Europe was not the Europe we know. Columbus and his successors found a jade-like stone held in great honor among the Indians of South and Central America. In ancient European tombs of the period of the smoothed-stone implements, axes and hatchets of jade or jadeite point to a veneration for the material that cannot be explained on the theory of its beauty alone, or on that of its toughness. It is probable that its color attracted men at first, but it is also plain that early man saw in jade something specially good, or he would not have taken so much trouble to find and to carve it. As always he reasoned by analogy from the mineral to something else.

Jade undoubtedly shared with certain other minerals, certain roots, certain animals, the reverence that was accorded to night, the earth, and the under world. It belonged to the country whither the sun retires at dusk, from which it returns at dawn. The jade color is seen in the sky just above the set sun and just before sunrise. It also recalls the season when shrubs and grass renew their color and make the earth green. It holds the color of vegetation and of the deep sea-water. These are its cosmical or celestial analogies. Connected in the mind of primitive men with spirits that may be good or bad, as they choose, it became a favorite for talismans and amulets such as are found in the old graves of North America, carved of shell or a jadelike mineral, either for wearing on the breast or for piercing the cartilage of the nose, or the lower lip, or the lobe of the ear. Amulets of Amazon stone, a kind of jade, have been found in Egypt.

But jade was also very early associated with the inner person. Very early, in China at any rate, the idea existed that a cup made of jade gave health to him who drank from it, and, naturally, would counteract poison. Indeed, the faintest drop of poison was supposed to cause the liquid in which it lay hidden to foam up when brought in contact with jade. Emperors, princes, governors, and others who were exposed to the underhand attacks of rivals, fathers of families who through their own cruelty or the wickedness of others were in danger of the poison death, would of course give high prices for cups of jade. It was in China and is to-day pre-eminently the lucky stone, so that a sceptre carved out of jade is one of the gifts that the Emperor of China is apt to make to a man whom he wishes to honor.

Sword handles and belt clasps, ear-rings and rings for the fingers, bangles for the wrists and ankles, ornaments for the hair of women, pipe-stems, and mouth-pieces, screens to place before the paper so that spies should not read, paper-weights, figures of all sorts, knickknacks, bottles for medicine, plates cups, vases, sceptres—the list of objects wrought by the Chinese in this tough material would never end. To honor jade still more the precious stones were used as decorations and skilfully inlaid; rims and legs of gold were fitted to thin cups of jade, which ring when struck like a piece of metal. Sometimes large and elaborate pieces of furniture have been carved from a single block of this hard material. A German collector, Alfred Schwab of Biel, has a rack for hats and coats made from a single stone. The sides and back are pierced to form fantastic figures, tigers, rams, and other animals; eagle's heads jut forward as pegs for hats.

It may be imagined that a material so much sought for and so costly would not long remain without attempts to imitate it. And certainly the Chinese have gone so far in the fabrication of a glass exactly like jade—if it may be called glass—that experts are often at fault in regard to small pieces in which there is little or no carving.

But all this does not explain why jade has held its own so well in competition with other stones to which curative or prophylactic qualities were ascribed. The clue is probably to be found in America. The Spaniards appear to have received from the Indians the belief that the green Amazon stone resembling jade was good for the kidneys, but for that matter they might have found the same idea at home. The word "jade" is from the Spanish *piedra de ijada,* an allusion to such curative powers, meaning stone of the stomach, or colic stone. "Sympathetic magic" is the term used by Mr. J. G. Frazer in "The Golden Bough" for this order of superstitious analogies between living things and inanimate. A green stone was hung against the stomach, if we may believe Galen, as a remedy for cramps. Thus, when the stone became specialized as a remedy for troubles of the bowels, it began a career which is not ended yet, passing from article of medicine to fetich and lucky stone, thence to preventive poisoning, then to articles of luxury, and at last to its present position of artistic eminence, where American and European collectors dispute fine pieces just as they do canvases of Rembrant and figurines from Greece and Asia Minor, namely, for their beauty and artistic worth.

Japanese in America, First. The first Japanese who came to America is said to have been Manjiro Nakahama, a boy of 14 years, who was picked up by an American sailing vessel in the North Pacific. The boy, with some companions, had sailed out for deep-sea fishing, and was driven from home by a storm. He and his comrades suffered much, until they landed on a desert island. The boy's companions were left in Hawaii, after the party was rescued by American sailors, but Nakahama came to this country, and was sent to a New England school. He later did good service for the American government, by acting as interpreter for Commodore Perry in the negotiations with Japan.

Jockeys, Female. In England matches have occasionally been run between a lady and a gentleman rider. In 1907 a notable episode occurred at Epsom. A gentleman of local note as a rider and the wife of a veterinary surgeon rode a mile race on the flat for £100 a side. The lady used a six-year old gray mare 16 hands high. The gentleman's horse, a gray gelding, 14 hands high, had already won in Ireland and in Melton Mowbray. Moreover, the weights were slightly in his favor. Hence he was the favorite at 2 to 1. To the general surprise, the gray mare took the lead from the first, made all the running, and won easily by eight lengths.

The most famous, however, of all lady riders was Mrs. Thornton, who took a prominent part in some sensational races at the beginning of the nineteenth century. The first took place August 25, 1804, on the Knavesmire at York. It was a match between Captain Thornton's Zingarillo and Mr. Flint's Thornville over a four-mile course. The stake was £1000. Thirty thousand spectators collected and the Yorkshire constabulary had to be called out to maintain order and keep the course clear. Mrs. Thornton appeared at the starting-post in a sensational costume. Her tight-fitting dress was of imitation leopard-skin. Her sleeves and her cap were blue. The betting, 6 to 4, was in her favor. But, though she led for the first three miles, Mr. Flint pushed to the front and won easily. The victory was unpopular and there were loud cries of fraud. Presently it was averred that Flint had used every device known to the unscrupulous jockey. Captain Thornton refused to pay the stakes. Mr. Flint posted him as a defaulter, and, meeting him next year at the York races, struck him across the shoulders with a horsewhip. He was arrested and fined for assault.

Meanwhile Mrs. Thornton had determined to redeem her defeat. Her next match was with Mr. Bromhead for 4 hogsheads of Burgundy, with 2000 guineas forfeit, the lady herself staking 600 guineas. Mr. Bromhead failed to appear and paid the forfeit, the lady cantering over the course alone. Her third race was with the famous Frank Buckle for 500 guineas a side. Buckle's mount was on Mr. Bromford's Allegro, the lady's on a mare named Louisa. Again she startled the crowd by her costume,—purple cap and waistcoat, long nankeen skirts, purple shoes, and embroidered stockings. Every inch of the five miles was hotly contested, and the race was in doubt up to the very last, when Mrs. Thornton just managed to reach home by half a neck.

The village of Liberty, New York, still remembers the exploits of Mrs. Ada Evans Dean in 1906. She had entered her horse Moorish Dance for a couple of races at a meeting there. At the last moment her jockey wired her that he could not take the mount. She jumped into a train, and, arriving just before the first race, she with some difficulty persuaded the judges to let her ride her own horse. "Amid the shouts of the gathered thousands," we are told, "she raced round the track in the van of ten stalwart rivals." Flushed with her success, she ran again, this time in the last race, and won again by the skin of her horse's teeth. Never before, she assured the gaping reporters, had she taken part in a horse-race.

In 1908 a Miss Mary Money, who claimed to have won twenty-eight races and fourteen silver cups in various American towns, crossed the Atlantic with the expectation of obtaining a riding license from the French Jockey Club.

Joliet. On April 22, 1895, the city council of Joliet, Ill., passed "An Ordinance Declaring the Proper Pronunciation of the Word Joliet." In the preamble it is stated that great confusion has arisen over the word, to the annoyance of the citizens; that its etymology has been carefully investigated, and that its only correct pronunciation has been determined by the etymological investigators at Joliet. Then we have the first section of the ordinance:

SECTION 1. That the only official, correct, and proper pronunciation and spelling of the name of this city shall be Jo-li–et; the accent on the first syllable, with the " o " in such first syllable pronounced in its long sound. as in the words " so," " no," and " foe." and that any other pronunciation be disowned and discouraged as interfering with the desired uniformity in respect to the proper pronunciation of the name of our city.

The second section of the ordinance provides that the school officers of the place must enforce such rules as shall secure the prescribed pronunciation of Joliet at school.

Etymologically this pronunciation has not a leg to stand on. The city is named after Louis Jolliet, a seventeenth century French Canadian explorer of the Mississippi. "We are sure," said the New York *Sun* of May 2, 1895, "that M. Jolliet would never have known his own name if it had been spoken by any one in the way in which the council of the city of Joliet has prescribed that it shall be spoken. The true sound and the original spelling of Jolliet's name have both been lost in Joliet; and the people there might as well stick to the thing they have got. We guess they'll stick to it anyhow."

Jumping Bean and **Jumping Cocoon.** Visitors to the Southwestern States and Mexico have often watched the queer motions of "jumping beans," the seed-vessels of a plant, each of which contains the pupa of an insect whose spasmodic movements cause the bean to hop and roll about.

The bean, which looks much like a kernel of coffee and is about the same size, comes from the States of Vera Cruz, Sonora and Guerrero, and is generally secured in April. With ordinary care the worm will live for months. The bean should be kept warm and not be handled if the worm is to show its activity. The Mexicans know these beans as " brincones," which means " jumpers." In some sections they are used in games of chance, such as placing them in circles and seeing which man's bean will hop from the centre to the outer ring first. Sometimes large sums are staked on this most uncertain result.

In the shops the beans can be had for a few cents, sometimes as low as one cent and sometimes as high as five cents, according to the size and the activity manifested. Great numbers of them are mailed to curiosity collectors in all parts of the world, and may not infrequently be seen in shop windows in New York and other Eastern cities.

Even more remarkable are the " jumping cocoons " found in South Africa. The cocoon is formed by the mother insect, and is very hard. The pupa, when ready to emerge, must cut its way out. The front of its head has a sharp, chisel-like edge, and by driving this against the inside of the shell it gradually makes a hole. The violent motions of the pupa within cause the cocoon to leap so that one has been seen to spring out of a small glass tumbler.

John O'Groat, or **Johnny Groat,** the reputed builder of John O'Groat's house, the ruins of which are still pointed out at Duncan's Bay Head, on the northernmost point of the mainland of Scotland. Tradition is not entirely agreed as to the personality of John O'Groat. One legend states that he was a poor man, who used to ferry passengers over to the island of Stroma for a groat. But the most popular story makes him the descendant of a Hollander, De Groot, who, in the reign of James IV, settled in the vicinity, and it goes on to tell how John and his seven cousins would yearly meet to celebrate the memory of their ancestor, and have a yearly quarrel over the question of precedence, until finally John invented a method of settling the difficulty. He built an eight-sided house of one room, with eight windows and eight doors, and an octagon table in the centre of the room, so that all might enter simultaneously. each at his own door, and there might be no head of the table.

K.

Kaiser-glocke, or Emperor's Bell, which was hung in the Cathedral at Cologne in the year 1875, is the fourth largest bell in Europe, being outclassed only by three bells at Moscow (see BELLS, BIG). All the other bells of Cologne Cathedral put together do not equal this monster. Its dimensions are: 12 feet in height, 11 feet in diameter, 33 feet in circumference; its weight is 25 tons, and its clapper weighs 16 cwt. The furnace wherein the French guns of which the bell is made were cooked consumed ten tons of coal, and burned furiously for twelve hours, melting down and artistically stewing no less than twenty-two captured cannon, some of which were field-pieces of the Louis XIV period, taken from the French Royal forces during their campaign in the Palatinate. When the fluid metal resulting from this grand brew of artillery was "turned on" into the mouth of the casting, it flowed freely and incessantly for twenty-nine minutes ere the "form" was full to the brim, and took three weeks to cool.

Kangaroo. When Captain Cook discovered Australia he saw some of the natives on the shore with a dead animal of some sort in their possession. Sending sailors in a little boat to buy it of them he found it was something quite new, so he sent the sailors back to inquire its name. The sailors, not being able to make the natives understand them, received the answer, "I don't know," or, in the Australian language, "Kan-ga-roo." The sailors supposed this was the name of the animal, and so reported it. Thus the name of the curious animal is the "I-don't-know," which is almost equal to the name given to one of the monstrosities in Barnum's Museum, the "What-is-it?" The New English Dictionary holds that this story is of recent origin and lacks confirmation.

Key of Death. The tradition concerning this key runs as follows: About 1600 a stranger named Tebaldo established himself as a merchant in Venice. He sought the hand of a young lady in marriage, but she, being already engaged, refused him. Enraged, he manufactured for himself a formidable weapon. This was a large key. The handle turned easily and disclosed a spring which, being pressed, sent out from the other end of the key a needle so fine that it entered the flesh and buried itself there without leaving any external trace.

Armed with this weapon Tebaldo waited at the church **door** for the maiden as she passed in to her marriage. Then, unperceived, he sent the slender needle into the breast of the bridegroom, who, seized with a sharp pain from an unknown cause, fainted, was carried home, and soon died, his strange illness, baffling the skill of physicians. Again Tebaldo demanded the maiden's hand, and again he was refused. In a few days both her parents died in a like mysterious manner. Suspicion was excited. On examination of the bodies the small steel instrument was found in the flesh. There was universal terror; no one felt that his own life was secure. The young lady went into a convent during her mourning, and, after a few months, Tebaldo begged to see and speak with her, hoping now to bend her to his will. She, with an instinctive horror of this man, who had from the first been displeasing to her, returned a decisive negative; whereupon Tebaldo contrived to wound her through the grate. On returning to her room she felt a pain in her breast, and discovered a single drop of blood. Surgeons were hastily summoned. Taught by the past, they cut into the wounded part, extracted the needle, and saved her life. Tebaldo was suspected, his house was searched, the key discovered, and he perished on the gallows.

There is a tradition that Duke Francis of Padua had a poisoned key of a similar character, which unlocked his private library. When he desired to rid himself of an obnoxious member of his household or suite, he would send him to bring a certain volume from his bookcase. As the key was turned in the lock, out shot a poisoned needle, stabbed the hand of the holder, and instantly shot back again. Examination of the hand revealed only a small, dark-blue spot, but in a few moments the person grew strangely giddy, and would be found on the floor, apparently in a fit. In twenty-four hours he would be dead, apparently of apoplexy.

In Edgar Saltus's remarkable story, "The Truth about Tristrem Varick," the hero uses a somewhat similar instrument to rid himself of the man who has wronged him.

Key West. The name of this island has no reference to position, for "west" is simply a corruption of the Spanish *hueso*, bone. "Key" (written *Cayo* by the Spaniards) is the corruption of an American Indian word signifying an islet, sandbank, or rock in the sea. It is applied to numerous rocky islands of the West Indies, and generally with reference to some more considerable body of land in the neighborhood. Thus, we have the Florida Keys and the Keys of New Providence, Eleuthera, and Abaco, the three latter being islands in the Bahama group.

The Spanish discoverers of Key West, a small coral island which constitutes the southernmost point of land in the United States, gave it the name of *Cayo Hueso,* from the quantities of long-unburied human bones which they found strewn over the coast, and which were believed to have lain there ever since about the year 1700, when many inter-tribal battles were fought by the Indians then occupying the numerous islands included in the Florida Keys.

For many years the island was but the haunt of smugglers and pirates, but it is now one of the most thriving and important of our naval stations. Key West, or Thompson's Island, as it is sometimes called, was settled in 1822, and the city was named Port Rodgers, or Allentown. Its broad streets are picturesquely surrounded by tropical shrub plants of the most gorgeous description.

From its situation near a dangerous reef, in waters greatly frequented by shipping, its principal occupation is "wrecking," —that is, saving goods and rendering assistance to vessels that have failed to clear the Florida reefs. The salvage company employs 50 vessels, manned chiefly by Conchs, or natives of the Bahama Islands.

The remarkable chain of rocky islets called the Florida Keys begins at the Cape, and extends nearly 200· miles in a southwesterly direction, ending in a cluster of sand-heaped rocks, known as the Tortugas, from the vast numbers of turtles with which they are frequented. Key West has been described as being "to Cuba what Gibraltar is to Ceuta; to the Gulf of Mexico, what Gibraltar is to the Mediterranean."

Keyne, Well of St. This well, situate about three miles from the town of Liskeard and within a short distance of the parish church of St. Keyne, is the most celebrated spring in Cornwall. The only things at all striking in the locality are five large trees (two oak, two ash, and one elm), growing as if from one root, immediately above the well. The chief attraction of the well lies in the supposed magic quality of its water. This has always made it a favorite place of resort with all lovers of the marvellous, who flock to drink the limpid stream, hoping thereby to obtain that power it is supposed capable of conferring. Robert Southey thus describes its virtues in a humorous poem entitled the " Well of St. Keyne: "

> If the husband of this gifted well
>   Shall drink before his wife,
> A happy man thenceforth is he,
>   For he shall be master for life.
>
> But if the wife should drink of it first,
>   God help the husband then.

The Rev. Whittaker says, that "not one husband in Cornwall has been known for a century past to take advantage of
the quality, and to secure his sovereignty for ever; the advantage is generously resigned up to our wives, and the
daughters of St. Keyne reign in every family."

Khaki. Accident led to the invention of the olive-colored
cloth known by this name and used mainly for soldiers' uniform.
British troops in India formerly wore a cotton cloth of greenish
brown. It always faded when washed with soap. A business
man from England, discussing this defect with some British
officers, casually remarked that a fortune awaited the manufacturer who might discover a process for making a cotton
drill that would not fade. One of the officers, a young man,
took the hint. He hired a skilful dyer and the two began a
systematic search for an olive dye for cotton cloth that would
not yield to soap or soda. Years were spent in vain experiments. One day they happened upon a bit of dyed cloth, lying
amid hundreds of similar scraps, that retained its color under
the severest tests. The puzzling part of it all was that this
scrap had been derived from a piece of cloth that had been
subject to the same processes. For a long time the experi
menters tried to solve the riddle. The one bit of cloth of
khaki mentioned was the only piece that kept its color against
all attacks.

Finally by the merest chance they hit upon the secret. The
dye in which this scrap had been dipped had remained for a
time in a metal dish of a peculiar kind. This metal, in connection with the chemicals of the dye, had furnished the very
thing needed. They made the experiment with other pieces, the
dye held, and their fortunes were made.

Kindergarten. Frederick Wilhelm August Froebel (1782–
1852) was born in a small village in Thuringia, Germany. His
childhood was sad and solitary. His father was a poverty-
stricken clergyman, whose second wife, "a real stepmother,"
alternately neglected or abused the child. Probably the home
was not free from conjugial discord, for, when one of his elder
brothers came home on a vacation, little Friedrich, thawed out
of his reserve by fraternal solicitude, naïvely inquired why God
had not made all people men or all women, so that there should
be no quarrelling. His brother, undertaking to solve the problem, explained to him the processes of vegetation, the com-
pensating nature of imperfections in male and female flowers
and how the harmonies of beauty and use were born out of
the clash of opposites. This, he says, was to him the beginning of all satisfactory thought, and ever after Nature as

seen in vegetation was his normal school. Another fruitful object lesson was unconsciously furnished to him by workmen employed in repairing the old village church. His principal amusement was to watch them from the window of the rectory and, by utilizing such pieces of furniture as he was able to move, to imitate them in their labor. It was the recollection of this unsatisfied building instinct which suggested to him, in later years, that children ought to be provided with materials for building among their playthings. But he was thirty-two years old before he devoted himself to his life-work, the previous years having gone to university study at Jena, teaching science in the Weiss Museum of Mineralogy at Berlin, and three years' service as a volunteer in the German army, 1813–1816. Having spent two years with Pestalozzi at Yverdon, he began the application of his own system, which grew out of that of the Swiss educator, to the training of his nephews and nieces. It was fourteen years before another school was started. His own finally failed for lack of support. His teaching rested on this fundamental principle, that the starting-point of all we see, know, or are conscious of, is *action,* and therefore that human development must begin in action. Life, action, and knowledge were to him the three notes of one harmonious chord; book study even subservient to the discipline of the mental and physical power through observation and active work. The authorities of the country met his efforts at first with indifference, then with opposition, and in 1851 the government at Berlin, without assigning any reason, forbade any kindergarten to be established within the Prussian dominions. This check in reality was his death-blow, and the next year was his last.

When a friend was lamenting over the slow advance of his method, he replied, "If, three hundred years after my death, it shall be completely established, I shall rejoice in heaven."

Fifteen years after his death, however, the prospects did not seem very bright. Froebel's own country had rejected him altogether. Prussia had excluded him by ministerial edict. In Prussia, however, the able daughter of an able mother— the Empress Frederick William—had educated her own children on his plan in their country and headed a society to introduce the system into her native England.

France still waited for the fall of the empire to see the introduction, without credit, of the methods of Froebel in her *écoles maternelles,* or "mother schools." Austria-Hungary, under the dawning liberty born of disaster, was beginning to introduce kindergartens, a work in which Hungary has made especial progress. Italy had already (1868 and 1871) seen the first kindergartens opened, which, after twenty years of united freedom, were to furnish the instructors to graft the new system on the public schools of the kingdom. Finland, that little enclave of home rule which lies in the despotism of Russia like the few limpid drops locked in the unyielding crystal, was to introduce it a dozen years later. England, which was reorganizing its school system by the education act of 1870, paid no heed to the new method; and nearly twenty years later, a teacher or two appointed by the London school-board, slight recognition elsewhere, and a vigorous but somewhat ineffectual propaganda showed all the progress made. In London, in Manchester, in Dublin, excellent institutions exist, but "as regards influencing public opinion scarcely anything had been done," even in 1889. TALCOTT WILLIAMS, *The Kindergarten Movement, Century.*

Switzerland had been the first country in the world to adopt Froebel's method. This was largely due to the fact that it was then the only republic in Europe. The kindergarten, as Mr. Williams says, is especially adapted to training childhood in a democratic state; because it recognizes the voluntary activity of the individual as the best means of education, and social contact as its best medium. Froebel himself refused to educate a duke's son alone. "He sought for his own nephews and nieces the companionship which the common school brings, and which is to-day too often shunned to the mutual loss of rich and poor."

It was Froebel's own opinion that the spirit of American nationality was "the only one in the world with which his method was in complete harmony and to which its legitimate institutions would present no barriers." Not long before his death he had said, "If they will not recognize and support my cause in my native country, I will go to America, where a new life is freely unfolding itself and a new education of man will find a footing." The success of his disciples who have established kindergartens in our cities makes this desire a prophecy. Among these disciples women played a distinguished part. Miss Elizabeth Palmer Peabody led in the vigorous polemic. In her wake there appeared women of social and personal eminence who put theory into practice by organizing free kindergartens. It was Miss Susan E. Blow, daughter of a man prominent in affairs and politics, who opened the first school in St. Louis in 1873. Under the influence of Dr. William T. Harris, this school was early incorporated in the public school system. In Boston it was Mrs. Quincy A. Shaw, wife of the fortunate possessor of the largest collection of Millets in the world, who opened the school first in 1868. So early as 1877 the city took over 14 schools and 800 pupils after the most careful inquiry and experiment yet given the kindergarten in our educational history. In Philadelphia Miss Anna Hallowell, a school-teacher, led the way in 1879. In San Francisco the leader was Mrs. Sarah B. Cooper, teacher of a Bible-class, backed by the wives of new-made millionaires and ably seconded by a young woman, Mrs. Kate Douglas Wiggin, who in 1889 repeated in New York the labors for this reform which she had begun in San Francisco ten years before.

Kings, Curious. The great Bismarck could barely tolerate the little kings and grand dukes with whom he had to deal in wielding the German Empire. To his Boswell, Dr. Busch, he ever spoke of them with the utmost contempt, and he seems to have disposed of them with scant courtesy when they got in his way or worried him.

"They are like flies," he said: "there is no getting rid of them. But Weimar is the worst of the lot. He said to me to-day, 'Please tell me where did you disappear to so quickly yesterday? I should have been glad to put some further questions to you.' I replied, 'That was exactly it, your Royal Highness. I had business to do, and could not enter into a lengthy conversation.' He fancies that the whole world has been created merely for his sake, for his amusement, the improvement of his education, and the satisfaction of his curiosity, which is insatiable, and he has absolutely no tact. Somebody observed that, as a rule, he does not think of what he says, but rather repeats phrases that he has learned by rote. Mittracht told another story about this august personage: Someone was introduced to him. 'Ah! Very pleased indeed. I have heard so much to your credit. Let me see, what was it I heard?'"

His Majesty of Weimar, however, and the other kinglets or dukelets of Germany, had a legitimate claim to their titles in that they had inherited the right divine to govern wrong. There have been other so-called kings who were not born in the purple, but have assumed the title without the dignity or have had it thrust upon them, thus adding materially to the gayety of nations. The early part of the nineteenth century saw a number of these burlesque royalties. First in order of time, probably, was a French adventurer, Baron de Thierry, who at the head of 100 followers recruited in Sydney, Australia, proclaimed himself King of New Zealand. He had not sufficient funds to maintain a monarchy. His subjects deserted and his reign collapsed. In the year 1840, when New Zealand had just begun to whet the cupidity of Christendom, a race was run from Sydney between a British and a French man-of-war. The former won by a few hours, and so secured New Zealand for the British crown.

Two famous adventurers followed on the heels of Thierry. David de Mayrena founded the Malay kingdom of Sedan in the Philippines, but was soon after assassinated by his so-called subjects. A happier yet not altogether a happy fate was reserved for his contemporary, a certain Antoine-Orélie de Tounens, a lawyer at Periqueux, who obtained such influence over a South American tribe that he blossomed forth as Antoine-Orélie I, King of Araucania. This country lies just south of Chili, and boasts of being the only portion of the New World that has never been conquered by the white man. Antoine's subjects, also, rose in rebellion when they wearied of the king whom they had originally welcomed, and His Majesty had to flee back to France, where he died (1880) in comparative poverty, though not without bequeathing his crown to his secretary. That gentleman, Gustav Achille Laviarde, assumed the title of Achille I, but was content to rule his kingdom from the height of his rooms in the Place des Trone, Paris, and do a little dealing in Araucanian decorations with French " gogos " and parvenues. He would exhibit with much pride the will of the first king of Araucania. This document, written in cryptographical characters, was translated by a sworn translator on January 1, 1880; authenticated by the minister of the interior, and registered by the minister of foreign affairs. It was stamped with the seal of royalty, and appointed Achille Laviarde heir to the throne, to the exclusion of all members of the Tounens family. The acceptance of M. Achille Laviarde was joined to this document.

Even at the present day, in many a group of the East or West Indies or other far-away archipelago, one may hear of a white man, German, American, English, or what not, who has made himself the potentate of some little island practically unknown to the world at large. Unless the possession is decidedly important the government which happens to have that particular section of the world under its wing says nothing and all goes serenely along. There are likewise several rulers in this section of the world whose fathers or grandfathers were the original white kings and who succeeded to their thrones and a share of native blood. The Ross dynasty of the Cocos Islands (q.v.) is conspicuous.

The heirs of William Webster, " King of Waiou," have made themselves famous in international litigation by their claim against New Zealand for territory worth two million and a half dollars. Webster was an American. He had been a ship's carpenter on a whaler, but had deserted to cast his lot in with a small band of settlers scattered here and there in Auckland, amid the villagers of its cannibal lords.

The great Coromandel chief known to the white men as Hooknose became the friend of the deserting whaler, and he married the daughter of the chief. His busy mind not content with mere proprietorship of the vast areas of native domains he had acquired of which he claimed possession, he established trading stations all over the Gulf and Firth of Thames. Through these he reaped a large profit at the time of the influx of immigration to New South Wales, by buying shiploads of maize, potatoes, and other food from the natives and sending them across to Australia. His head-quarters were at the native village of Herskine, where the Maoris lived in large native "whares," and where he kept a boarding house for the benefit of the numerous adventurous spirits who came and went and with whom money or kind was frequently plentiful.

It was then that, from the influence and power he possessed, Webster became known as the "King of Waiou."

In 1849 he returned to the United States to join the California goldseekers, and he then disappeared from view, but his memory still lives through his litigant heirs.

Another famous deserter—from a whaling ship also, though in this case from an English one—was Patrick Watkins, a red-headed Irishman, who rose to be King of the Galapagos Islands lying off the coast of Ecuador in South America. Charles Island was the scene of his landing. The exact spot is known to this day as Pat's Passage. King Patrick he called himself, and for several years he ruled the islands and made slaves of some sailormen who landed there. He is said to have been responsible for the first sea post-office established there, that being the way devised by one sea captain to warn others of the presence on the islands of King Patrick.

He turned up later in Payta, Peru, where he sought to make a Peruvian girl his queen. He actually got her consent to accompany him back to his island kingdom, but Pat was caught one day hiding upon a vessel and seized by the authorities. He died in jail, and thus the reign of the King of the Galapagos came to an untimely end.

Commodore David Porter, father of Admiral Porter, visited the islands in his ship, the *Essex*, during the war of 1812 and brought back the story of King Patrick. Porter made the islands his head-quarters while he raided British whaling ships during the war. The ships were accustomed to put in there for water and fresh vegetables and fell an easy prey to the Americans.

David Glasgow Farragut was a midshipman on the *Essex*, and he kept a journal of the cruise. In telling of one of the expeditions he wrote in 1813:

"We then separated, our ship going to Charles Island to examine the post-office—a letter-box nailed to a tree, in which whalers and other visitors deposited records of their movements. Found nothing new but some fresh tracks of men."

A man who visited the island in 1884 described this sea post-office as consisting then of a candle-box nailed to a tree, and said that it looked old enough to be the same box found by Farragut.

In the early '90s the British warship *Amphion* visited the Galapagos and erected a new post-office to commemorate her visit. The crew of the warship put a new box on top of a post on the beach above high water and cut the name of their ship in it. Since then it has been the custom of callers at the post-office to inscribe their names on the post as a sort of postmark.

In the later years of the nineteenth century young Archibald C. Everett was a New York stock-broker and a man about town. The stock market went back on him: he deserted civilization, and finally wound up in Arorai, one of the Gilbert Islands. In all the glory of a white flannel suit he burst upon King Rovaka, who held the suzerainty under a British protectorate. He pleased and was pleased. Briefly he married the king's daughter and succeeded to his throne. The New York *Sun* of May 18, 1911, thus summed up his tale of felicity as ingenuously confided to a reporter when King Everett last visited New York:

Two hundred odd wives; he isn't concerned enough to count them.
Perfect domestic harmony the year round, rain or shine.
A population which thinks it an honor to increase his harem.
Lobster and chicken, as in the old Broadway days.
Much time to think things over.
Plenty of cocoanut milk, wine, and palm cider, quite as effective as any of the bruts.
Kings for friends.
The right to live among gentle cannibals without fear of being used for fuel.
He has never refused to marry any one since he's been king.
He has often married a dozen or so in one month, to accommodate ambitious parents.
He is rich as riches go in the Gilbert Isles.
Is he happy? Well, he came back and told all these things with a smile on his face.

In the year 1910 there came to the little town of Albion, in Illinois, the story of how one of its former citizens had died the king of a Fiji island, after a prosperous reign of twenty-five years. His name was Edward Thompson. He had wooed and won and then been jilted by a belle of his own town. In despair he had fled to San Francisco and sailed for the South Seas. On the island of Naikeva, in the Fijis, he met his fate. Her name was the Princess Lakanita. She was the daughter of the native king by a Spanish half-breed. She fell in love with the white man with the blue eyes. He did not yield to her entreaties that he should stay. But, knowing that revolution was in the air, he promised to return in case her life was ever imperilled. So he sailed away to other islands. Probably he had almost forgotten his promise when one day, as he lay smoking on the deck of the schooner, a canoe came alongside and a native of Naikeva called up and asked if the "white man with the blue eyes" was still with them. When he found Thompson he implored him to come back and save the princess and her father from death.

That night the schooner set out for Naikeva, and they arrived there just in time to fight. The old king and his enemy were both killed in the battle, but Thompson and his men at the head of the royal forces completely routed the revolutionists. Thompson, however, was hurt, and on his recovery was taken with one of the fevers that play havoc with the health of the islanders. The princess nursed him back to health and begged him to stay with her. By this time he was very much in love with the dusky queen and decided, since he was at war with American women and their insincerity, that he would stay. And so the traders sailed away and left him happy with his brown-skinned love.

Of all Yankee rulers in savage parts the longest and most peaceful reign was enjoyed by David O'Keefe, the King of Yap. David, to be sure, was an American only by adoption, for he was born in Tipperary. He emigrated to Savannah, Georgia, married there, became the father of a girl baby, and in 1871 sailed away for China. His ship was wrecked on the coast of Yap. He escaped, and within a few years was king of the country, through a sort of progressive assimilation. He was never formally voted into power. He simply acquired all the property of the tribal chiefs, assumed the regal title, and designed a royal ensign emblazoned with the letters O'K. Above this floated the Stars and Stripes. Then he built himself a castle on Terang, one of the three islands of the Yap group. Every six months he sent his wife a share in his profits and a promise to return home soon.

That promise he was fated never to keep. One day his Majesty was surprised by the approach of a triumphal procession escorting a bride whom the chiefs had selected for him. In vain he protested. Such, at least, was the story he sent home. The dusky lady was forced upon him. She became his consort under the name of Queen Dollyboy. She bore him seven children.

In May, 1901, after a thirty years' absence, Mrs. O'Keefe in Savannah received a letter from King David enclosing $2000 and announcing that he would return before the year was out. It is known that with two of his sons he sailed for Hong Kong on one of his own schooners, the *Santa Cruz*. Nothing more is known. Ship and king and princes disappeared forever. Mrs. O'Keefe and her daughter, now a married woman with a child, despatched a lawyer to Yap. He landed there in the spring of 1903. The missing king had left an estate valued at a million dollars. He had also left a will which ignored the genuine Mrs. O'Keefe, but made the daughter a legatee to a not inconsiderable amount and divided the bulk of his property between Queen Dollyboy and her children.

Kipling wrote a story, " The Man Who Would be King." America can boast of a man who wouldn't be king. He is Lieutenant Charles S. Ripley, of the United States Navy. Since early colonial days the Ripleys have dwelt along the rock-bound coast of Maine as sailors and fishermen. Early in the nine-teenth century one of the family had set sail for the Orient around Cape Horn and never returned. Late in the same century Charles S. Ripley, a great-grandnephew of the missing man, was in the Samoan archipelago aboard the U. S. Ship *Vandalia*. It was during the triangular imbroglio that almost precipitated war between Germany, Great Britain, and the United States. Old King Malietoa looked upon the Americans as his friends. He took a special interest in Lieutenant Ripley, plied him with questions, and told him in turn of a New England Ripley who had been shipwrecked on the Samoan coast nearly a century previous, had married a Samoan princess, and had become one of the ancestors of the reigning dynasty,— of Malietoa himself. Of course the lieutenant speedily identified this adventurer as his long-lost great-uncle. Malietoa, rejoicing in his newly found kinsman, insisted on riveting the relation-ship by adopting young Ripley as his son. The latter reluctantly consented, but as a mere matter of form. Malietoa died, and his successor, Matoofa, speedily followed him. It became the duty of an international commission to find a new king. After exhaustive investigation of the royal archives, they reported that Malietoa's adopted son, Lieutenant Ripley, then on the retired list of the United States Navy and an unaspiring citizen of the State of Colorado, was the only person whose title to the crown was clear. He was requested to enter into his kingdom, but declined. Why? Because the maiden whom he later married found nothing alluring in the prospect of reigning with him in the palace of the kings of Samoa.

John Davis Murray graduated in 1891 as a mechanical engineer from Purdue University, in Lafayette, Indiana. He went out to the Christmas Islands, a group of three dots in the Pacific Ocean about 250 miles southwest of Java, as a member of the Phosphate Mining and Shipping Company, an English syndicate which owns the islands. The deposits of phosphate are among the most valuable in the world. The mines are worked by natives almost entirely, and, because of their traditions and their inability to recognize anything short of absolute authority, Murray was formally invested with the title of King of the Christmas Islands, with all the solemnity necessary to impress the simple minds of the natives. He administered the laws, held court, decided disputes between the workmen, and held absolute authority over them, and his decrees were carried out with promptness and vigor.

In the autumn of 1910, King John was in London, where he fell in love with a maiden and married her. But, as she refused to share his throne on a savage island, he abdicated and settled in England.

Another royalty who abdicated under similar romantic circumstances was Carlos I, King of the Ilocanos in the heart of the Philippine Islands. He was born plain Carl Haffke, of peasant parents, in Germany. He was first heard of as a messenger-boy on the force of the Western Union Telegraph in Omaha. Then he enlisted in the navy, and was on Admiral Dewey's flagship at the battle of Manila Bay. He became a court stenographer in the Philippines. In this capacity he was enabled to give good advice to a party of Ilocano chiefs who had been involved in the toils of the law. The cholera broke out in the tribe, the king and all his family were carried off, and the chiefs besought Haffke to accept the vacant throne. More than one hundred thousand of the people, the chief assured him, were ready and willing to hail him as their king. Haffke dictated his own terms. First he exacted a dollar a head from every man, woman, and child in the tribe, with which sum he agreed to purchase farming machinery and to teach them agriculture. Next he asked for his own use one-twentieth of the profits of the enterprise, and lastly he demanded all necessary servants and appurtenances for the palace. These terms were accepted, and a formal document was drawn up in both Spanish and English and signed by all parties to the contract. After reigning over the Ilocanos for a year, Haffke, in a homesick mood, decided to make a trip to Nebraska and visit the girl he had left behind him there. Many of the tribe followed him to Lingayen and made him promise to come back to his people and bring them a white "Queen." But the girl refused to go to the Philippines, and for her sake Haffke resigned his "kingly" office and settled down to the practice of law in Nebraska.

A serio-comic melodrama was that presented by the concluding episode in the life of Baron James A. Harden-Hickey. This adventurous Franco-American had already piqued the curiosity of the Old World by meteoric apparitions as editor of a satirical Parisian journal, *Triboulet*, as a Catholic converted to Buddhism, and as the author of "Euthanasia," a cheerful little book on the art if not the duty of committing suicide. In 1893 he electrified the New World by announcing himself King of Trinidad.

"The principality of Trinidad," as he himself was careful to explain, was not the Trinidad of asphalt fame, situated near the mouth of the Orinoco, but a small rocky island, 5 miles in length and 2 or 3 in breadth, 700 miles from the coast of Brazil, between Bahia and Rio de Janeiro. It was absolutely uninhabited when Harden-Hickey came upon it in 1888. Finding guano there, he projected a great plant for its exploitation, including costly wharves and capacious warehouses. He lured to Trinidad a colony of 40 Americans. Finally, in September, 1893, he formally took possession of his island and proclaimed himself prince sovereign under the name of James I. He adopted a flag for his principality, printed postage-stamps and paper money, and even established an order of knighthood. Then, in the spring of 1895, a British cruiser called at his stronghold and formally took possession. Brazil in her own behalf protested against the action of England, for Brazil, newly awakened to the existence of Trinidad, claimed it for her own. Britain explained that her occupation was only temporary for the purpose of installing a cable station. Her warship eventually did abandon the island to Brazil. Meantime James I was ignored on all sides. He sent an ambassador with a futile protest to Washington, and on the failure of this diplomat—an ex-wine merchant raised to the name and dignity of "Comte de la Boissiere, grand chancellor and secretary for foreign affairs of the Principality of Trinidad"—His Majesty passed out of history until his death was recorded in 1909.

Knickerbocker. This name is no invention of Washington Irving's, though he bestowed it upon a fictitious chronicler, Diedrich Knickerbocker, to whom he attributed the comic " History of New York " (1809). In his prefatory " Account of the Author," Irving puts into the mouth of Seth Handaside, the real landlord of the Independent Columbian Hotel, this description of his imaginary boarder:

" As my wife, by some of those odd ways in which women find out everything, learnt that he was of very great connections, being related to the Knickerbockers of Schaghticoke, and cousin-german to the congressman of that name, she did not like to treat him uncivilly." And in his " Author's Apology," dated Sunnyside, 1848, which appears in editions of that and later dates, Irving says: " When I find after a lapse of nearly forty years this haphazard production of my youth still cherished among them—when I find its very name become a ' household word ' and used to give the home stamp to everything recommended for popular acceptance, such as Knickerbocker societies, Knickerbocker insurance companies, Knickerbocker steamboats, Knickerbocker omnibuses, Knickerbocker bread, and Knickerbocker ice—and when I find New Yorkers of Dutch descent priding themselves upon being ' genuine Knickerbockers '—I please myself with the persuasion that I have struck the right chord."

" Knickerbocker," in fact, is an old Holland name, originally spelled " Knickerbacker," and derived from *knikker,* meaning a marble such as boys play with, and *bakker,* meaning a baker. The meaning of the full name is " marble baker." The name first appears in this State in the records of Albany. On February 28, 1707, the city of Albany purchased from the Indians 500 acres of land at Schaghticoke on the east side of the Hudson River near Albany, and on October 13, 1709, Johannes Knickerbacker, a miller of Albany, leased thirty morgen of the Schaghticoke land. He was the oldest of seven children of Herman Jansen Knickerbacker, of Albany, who, it is said, was the first of that name to come to America. There were Knickerbackers in New York city in 1764, and presumably much earlier. We have the record that on August 3, 1764, an execution issued against Capt. Harman Knickerbacker of New York as security of Thomas Cregier at the suit of Frederick Kortz was returned " nulla bona."

The records of the Revolution show several Knickerbackers among the American soldiers. Among them may be mentioned Col. John Knickerbacker, of the Fourteenth Regiment of Albany County Militia (born 1723; died 1802), and Ensign

29

Philip Knickerbacker, of Col. Livingston's Regiment of Militia (born 1745). The congressman referred to by Irving was Herman Knickerbocker, who was born in Albany, N. Y., July 27, 1782; received a liberal education; studied law, and began practising at Albany. He moved to Schaghticoke and became known as the Prince of Schaghticoke on account of his liberality. He was elected to the Eleventh United States Congress (March 4, 1809, to March 4, 1811) as a Federalist; served in the State Legislature in 1816 and died at Williamsburg, N. Y. (now New York City), January 30, 1855. Irving visited Congressman Knickerbocker in Washington in February, 1811, and in a letter dated February 7 refers to him as *my cousin Knickerbocker.*

Kremlin, Cross of the. This cross, reputed to be of solid gold, used to surmount the church of Ivan Veliky which dominates the Kremlin. Napoleon I had it pulled down, intending to place it over the Dome des Invalides in Paris, as a revenge upon the Russians for firing Moscow. The revenge was all the sweeter because the cross was popularly believed to have a legendary connection with the greatness of Russia. With enormous difficulty the cross, measuring sixteen feet, was brought down. According to the Comte de Ségur, it had to be abandoned on the march to Smolensk, and was sunk with a quantity of other impedimenta in Lake Semlevo. The lake having been drained in 1911, a careful search brought to light innumerable remains of dead horses, harness, carts, uniforms, and other relics, but no trace of the cross.

The *Novoe Vremya* argues that it never left Moscow and was probably buried under the wreckage of the Kremlin caused by the blowing up of its buildings at Napoleon's command. The real gold cross remained undetected on one of the churches which escaped destruction.

L.

Labor Unions. These are not of quite such recent origin as many people suppose. "I am credibly informed," wrote Mandeville, the author of "The Fable of the Bees," in his "Essay on Charity and Charity Schools" (1714–1728), "that a parcel of footmen are arrived to that height of insolence as to have entered into a society together and made laws by which they oblige themselves not to serve for less than such a sum, nor carry burdens or any bundle or parcel above a certain weight, not exceeding two or three pounds, with other regulations directly opposite to the interest of those they serve, and altogether destructive to the use they were designed for. If any of them be turned away for strictly adhering to the orders of this honorable corporation, he is taken care of till another service is provided for him; but there is no money wanting at any time to commence and maintain a lawsuit against any master that shall pretend to strike or offer any other injury to his gentleman footman, contrary to the statutes of their society. If this be true, as I believe it is, and they are suffered to go on in consulting and providing for their own ease and conveniency any further, we may expect quickly to see the French comedy ' Le Maitre le Valet ' acted in good earnest in most families; while, if not redressed in a little time, and these footmen increase their company to the number it is possible they may, as well as assemble when they please with impunity, it will be in their power to make a tragedy of it whenever they have a mind to it."

Lady-bird. The most popular of all insect folk rhymes is probably one which concerns that species of coleoptera, or beetle, which is known to science as the *Coccinella* and to English and American children as the lady-bird. There are many variants, but the most usual form is this:

> Lady-bird! Lady-bird! fly away home,
> Your house is on fire and your children alone!

Sometimes the last words of the second line are " your children all warm " and another couplet is added, as follows:

> Except little Nan, who sits in her pan
> Weaving gold laces as fast as she can.

While this is being sung the insect is usually placed on the tip of the index-finger of the left hand, and, if the charm works the insect flies away; if it fails to do this, it is either blown off or

flicked away with the finger.   This is not the only rhyme concerning the lady-bird, however.   In some parts of Norfolk the
following is sung:

> Bishop, Bishop Barnabee,
> Tell me when your wedding be.
> If . it be to-morrow day,
> Take your wings and fly away.

In Scotland the lady-bird is called the " Lady Lanners," and the
following rhyme using that name is said to be peculiar to the
county of Lanark:

> Lady, Lady Lanners,
> Lady, Lady Lanners,
> Tak' up yer clowk about your head,
>   An' flee awa' to Flanners.
> Flee owre firth, an' flee owre fell,
> Flee owre pule an' rinnan well,
> Flee owre muir an' flee owre mead,
> Flee owre livan, flee owre dead,
> Flee owre corn, an' flee owre lea,
> Flee owre river, flee owre sea,
> Flee ye east, or flee ye west,
> Flee till him that lo'es me best.

Alternate names for the lady-bird in England are lady-bug,
lady-fly, and lady-cow.   In France it is known as *vache à Dieu*
and *bête de la Vierge,* as though it were a creature especially
favored by providential care.

In Russia it is " the little cow of God," and the children say:

> Little cow of God,
> Fly to the sky;
> God will give you bread.

In some parts of Germany the lady-bug is said to be sacred
to the goddess Holda, or " the Lady Holda," as she is called.
There is a legend of a peasant maiden who was fond of lady-
bugs, and who was taken to Holda's realm in a carriage drawn
by the insects, to be protected during an approaching war, and
who, at its close, was sent home with an outfit of fine linen.   The
German peasantry believe that the lady-bird's home is in heaven,
or in the sun, and call it little sun, little bird of the sun, sun-
calf, moon-calf, sun-chick, God's calf, little house of God, Mary-
bird, lady-hen, and lady-cow.   German children tell it, in rhyme,
to " fly skyward," or to " mount the throne and bring back fair
weather."   They say that if one kills a lady-cow the sun will hide
its face next day.   They also tell it to flee because its house is
on fire, and in one part of Germany they say that the angels cry
because the house of the lady-cow burns.

In Swedish popular belief, the coming harvest is foretold

by the number of spots upon its wing-cases; if there are more than seven, corn will be dear.

In Piedmont the lady-bug is " the chicken of St. Michael," and the child rhyme is:

> Chicken of St. Michael,
> Put on your wings and fly to heaven.

In Tuscany it is called lucia, probably from St. Lucia:

> Lucia, lucia, put out your wings and fly away,

say the children, who also call it "little dove," and sometimes " St. Nicholas." When a child loses a tooth, he buries it in a hole, and invokes the insect:

> St. Nicholas, St. Nicholas,
> Make me find bone and coin.

Laetare Medal. A decoration annually given by the University of Notre Dame to some lay member of the Church in the United States for specially distinguished service in art, literature, science, or philanthropy.

The announcement of the award of the Laetare Medal is always made from the pulpit of the university church by the president on the fourth Sunday of Lent. The medal takes its name from the word beginning the Introit of the Mass on that day, " Laetare." Although the award is made then and the recipient named, the actual giving does not take place until some time later. The occasion of the formal presentation of the medal always brings together noted dignitaries of the Church in America, and other men and women eminent in all lines of work.

The custom of giving the medal originated at the University of Notre Dame in 1883. At a meeting of professors attention was called by discussion to the lack of honors for the thousands of Catholic men and women of the laity who work earnestly by upright lives and by distinguished service for advancing education, morality, and human welfare, and religion. The suggestion was made that the university should single out some man or woman every year for honor and confer some tangible evidence of appreciation. And so the idea of the medal took form. It is modelled on the ancient observance followed by the Pope of sending the Golden Rose as a mark of special honor to sovereigns and other notable persons.

The gift of the Laetare Medal is confined to lay members of the Catholic Church in the United States. It is a large disk of pure gold beautifully enamelled and chased, and bears some appropriate design in relief, which varies from year to year, and which is suited to the profession or line of work in which the recipient has earned distinction. Around the border surrounding the design appears in Latin the motto, "Truth is mighty and shall prevail." A handsome address beautifully painted in water-color on silk accompanies the medal. The address is of high artistic value and is always the work of some noted artist.

The long list of recipients form a distinguished honor roll of the laity of the Catholic Church in the United States. The medal was first conferred on John Gilmary Shea, the historian, in 1883. Eliza Ann Starr, art critic, was the first female to receive it.

Lamb, Scythian. This is a singular vegetable production of which many fabulous stories have been told by Sir John Mandeville (Travels, chap. xxvi) and others. It was said to be part animal, part vegetable, and to have the power of devouring all other plants in its vicinity. In reality it is merely the prostrate stem of a woolly fern (*Cibotium Barometz*) turned upside down. Erasmus Darwin alludes to the plant and its attendant legends in the "Botanical Garden" (1791), Bk i, 1. 279.

In "Travels into Muscovy and Persia" (1636), by the ambassador from the Duke of Holstein, reference is made to a gourd that closely resembles a lamb "in all its members," and is so called by the natives of Samara, in Russia, where it grows wild. "It changes places in growing, as far as the stalk will reach, and wherever it turns the grass withers, which the Muscovites call feeding. They further say that when it ripens the stalk withers, and the outward rind is covered with a kind of hair, which they use instead of fur. They shewed us some of these skins, which were covered with a soft frizzled wool, not unlike that of a lamb newly weaned, and swore that they came from that fruit." The authors add that Scaliger speaks of them, saying that they grow until the grass fails them, when they die for want of nourishment. He also says that the wolf is the only animal that feeds upon the gourd, and that it is used as a bait to catch him, which statement the ambassadors affirm agrees with what the Muscovites told them.

Lantern. The Chinese and the Japanese excel in the manufacture of lanterns, and many strange customs and superstitions cling around their use.

It is usual in Chinese towns to hang outside each building a lantern bearing in large characters the occupant's name. If a boy is born in the house, an extra lantern decorated with the character "Prosperity" tells the tale. If a death occurs, a white lantern, with fluttering strips of paper, on which are written the name, age, and virtues of the deceased, is placed just over the door. White lanterns are also carried, even at midday, by those who follow the corpse to the grave.

When a man marries, his bachelor friends give him a pair of lanterns, the bride receiving a similar present from her sisters or cousins. And in the wedding procession figure numbers of bright-red lanterns, matching in color the trunks and trays holding trousseau and wedding presents which precede the elaborate sedan chair containing the lady.

In most large towns, during the first month of the year, "lantern markets" are held, which in picturesque effect often surpass any of the regular festivals. The narrow streets of Canton, for instance, festooned from side to side with an almost infinite variety of brightly colored lanterns, become a sort of fairyland. Fishes, beasts, birds, insects, fruits, and flowers mingle in oddest confusion, while at intervals are hung the popular "tsao-ma-tangs." These curious lanterns have figures of men, women, animals, etc., pasted on wire frames, placed one within another. When lit, the current of air caused by the flame turns their frames, and horses gallop, men run, armies march, ships sail, etc. The market contains lanterns of all sizes, and of values ranging from a thousand dollars to a few "cash" (the tenth of a cent) each. It is always crowded with customers, for not only must people prepare themselves for festivals, births, deaths, or marriages, but, as houses and shops are lit by lanterns, and as all who go abroad at night carry them, the consumption is enormous. They who have had sons born during the last year, and others who hope for that blessing before the present one expires, buy largely, and after carefully attaching their names and addresses hang the purchases as votive offerings in temples near their homes. Wax figures of men dressed in silken robes are also sold. These are placed before the ancestral altars, and are collectively known as "Sam Sing," respectively as "Fok" or Happiness, "Lok" or Rank, and "Sow" or Longevity.

Another fine display of lanterns can be seen at Canton in the spring, when on several successive evenings fishermen assemble and march through the streets. Each one carries a pole with a dangling lantern in fish form, while the middle of the procession is always occupied by a dragon forty or fifty feet long. Its head, tail, and joints are supported on poles held by men whom the body conceals; as they walk, this huge monster, representing the ruler of the deep, moves along in an undulating and life-like manner. The pageant is a "chin-chin" to the water-gods, arranged to persuade them to avert disastrous storms and send the fishermen good luck.

The next lantern festival propitiates the " Fang Shui," or " Spirits of the Air." If displeased, they may prevent the crops from ripening, and, to ward off that disaster, all house-holders, during the second week of the sixth month, display at least one lantern. These are fastened to the highest peak of the roof, or else to long poles planted for the purpose. As most people take pride in exhibiting numbers of lights, this " Feast of Lanterns," as it is called, has on dark evenings a very brilliant effect. None fail to observe it, as the " Fang Shui " are by far the most important Chinese deities. To honor them, pagodas are erected. A house whose location they do not approve will bring bad luck to all who live there.

A somewhat vexatious law in China compels every doctor, after. dark, to hang up in front of his house as many lighted lamps as he has sent patients into the next world. One evening a European, who was staying in Pekin on business, set out in search of a doctor for his wife, who had been suddenly taken ill. He called at the houses of a good many, but was deterred by the large number of lamps exhibited before each. At length, after tramping about for several hours, he came to the house of a doctor where only three lamps shed a melancholy light over the entrance. Our happy European dashed into the house of this excellent man, wakened him, and took him off to his lodgings.

" I presume you are the best practitioner in this city ? " he said to his companion, as they went along.

" What makes you think so ? "

" Because you have only three lanterns hung over your door, while your colleagues have dozens displayed on their house-fronts."

" Ah! is that the reason ? " calmly replied the pigtailed Celestial. " The fact is, I only lately set up in practice, and have had but three patients."

In Japan no house is complete without a varied supply of chochin, or paper lanterns. No coolie is so poor but he must own at least one, for there is a law compelling all foot passengers to carry a lighted lantern after nightfall. This is made of crinkled white bast paper, with little or no ornamentation save the Chinese characters which spell the family name.

A paper lantern burns outside most houses and shops at night ; dozens of them are hung closely together along the sloping eaves of private dwellings ; the houseboats and sampans that glide along the bay or river are profusely hung with colored lanterns that shed forth a delightful, rosy glow, which enhances the charms of geisha or musme, and adds to the brilliancy of the festive night.

Numbers of great balloon-like lanterns illuminate the space

in front of the theatres: yadoyas (inns) and tea-houses are equally well marked by the brilliant illumination, which i maintained all night.

The wooden lanterns hung beside the doors of the dwellings in certain streets of Kioto tell the passer-by that they are the homes of geishas (dancing girls). The surface of plain lanterns is used for advertising purposes, and "he who runs may read" that within are various commodities for sale.

Some of the street lamps are made wholly of wood, the post and lantern being carved and quite ornamental, and guiltless of paint. Over these is often built a roof of fancy shingles, and sometimes a larger, rougher one is placed over the first to protect it from the weather. Fine fretwork is made use of for the panels and slides, the designs being mostly trees, flowers, birds, and fishes, but always artistic, for even the common people thoroughly appreciate the beautiful in art or nature.

At the midsummer feast of lanterns, when the souls of the dead are supposed to come back to earth and revisit their old haunts, hundreds of paper lanterns are used for decorating the graves on the hillside and the streets of the town. Each little straw boat, in which the spirits take their departure, is brilliantly lighted with paper lanterns, as it is launched forth on its journey to the spirit-land.

At the matsuris and processionals of the temples, several of which occur every year, not only are the temples themselves and the dwelling-houses decorated with chochin, but the entire length of the streets is lined with them.

Every jinrikisha coolie must carry a lantern, fastened to the shaft of his vehicle, and he is compelled by law to keep it lighted at night. For this purpose the Yumikari-chochin has of late years come into general use. It is a curious and interesting sight to see a string of rickshas—the law compels them to run single file—moving along the streets, with their bobbing lights, and no one can say he has really seen the world until he has gone slumming in a ricksha at night in a Japanese city; it gives one a new experience, and a wild, weird sensation obtainable nowhere else.

All the paper lanterns in Japan—unlike those of China—are collapsible, being held in place, when open, by a spring or chain. The framework is made of thin strips of bamboo; this is covered with crinkled bast paper which is very strong and durable. These fragile creations last the Japanese a long time, so deliberate are they in their movements, and so careful. They are oiled or varnished, to make them waterproof, and the decorations are put on after the frame is covered.

From Odwara come the handsomest lanterns in Japan. In

elder and more ceremonious days the daimio, or nobleman, made use of an Odawara-chochin to light his way when he went in state to pay his annual visit to the shogun, or travelled from one province to another. The Odawara-chochin is considerably decorated; in addition to the owner's "mon," something after the order of a crest, which is always painted on one side, it is mounted with a decorative brass band at the top and bottom. The footmen and coolies had each their own special lanterns, which were carried on their shoulders; but this particular one was hung inside the kago or norimono in which the daimio, according to his rank, travelled. During the day each lantern was put into a net or bag, and tied behind one of the portmanteaus.

"Although gas and electricity light every Japanese city," Miss Scidmore tells us that " the manufacture of paper lanterns increases apace, for now all the quarters of the globe demand them. Constructing the flimsy frames is a sleight-of-hand process, and with the same deftness the old lantern-makers dash on designs, characters, and body-colors, with a bold brush. But one must live in Japan to appreciate the softened light of lanterns, and in the lavish and general nightly use of them learn all the fairylike and splendid effects to be obtained with a bit of paper, some wisps of bamboo, and a little vegetable wax poured around a paper wick."

In some parts of Germany and Switzerland there still survives a custom which was once well-nigh universal in those countries. This was the use of lanterns of different varieties and sizes by which, at night, the rank of the party could be easily distinguished.

The lanterns were carried by the servants who were sent to escort their mistresses home from places of amusement, and they made the square in front of the Royal Opera House, where most of the entertainments were then given, quite picturesque, with their lights bobbing up and down in every direction.

The differences between some of these lanterns were slight, but they had to be strictly observed, or trouble arose. The order of rank, as set forth in the "rank list," was something from which they could never swerve. Some had lanterns of tin, some of brass; some had wax lights, and others tallow; even the number of lights was prescribed for each separate class or rank.

Lantern for the Dead (French *lanterne des morts*). A curious feature found in many church-yards from the twelfth to the fourteenth century, especially in France. It consists of a hollow stone erection, sometimes 20 or 30 feet high, surmounted by a lantern and presenting a general resemblance to a small light-house. The lantern seems to have been lighted only on certain feasts or vigils, and in particular on All-Souls' Day (Halloween). Lecointre, in his "Archelogue de Poitiers," suggests that erections of this sort were put up in order to protect the living from the fear of ghosts and to safeguard them from the terror of the night that walketh in the darkness, as the Psalmist calls it. Violet le Duc agrees with Lecointre that such was the idea attached to the *lanterne des morts* in the twelfth century, but opines that these columns belong by tradition to the usages or superstitions of a very remote antiquity. "We cannot but regret," he says, "that we have no lanterns of the dead, prior to the twelfth century, remaining. We cannot doubt of their existence, since they are mentioned several times, amongst other instances in the battle waged between Clovis and Alaric, but we do not know the form of these first Christian monuments."

Law Courts among Birds. It is a noteworthy yet a seldom noted fact that many kinds of birds hold court for the trial and punishment of their delinquent fellows.

Crow trials are the most frequent. An entire community of sable vindicators of the law may meet together on a hill or in a field. The accused is stationed in the middle. The accusers pour out their tales. The charges are not made individually, nor is the evidence given by separate witnesses, but by a general clamor collectively raised. At the end of the proceedings the prisoner at the bar is either acquitted, when he flies away amicably with judge and jury, or he is found guilty, in which case the whole tribe fall upon him with beak and claw until he is dead.

Rooks have the same custom. The Rev. J. Edmund Cox, an English clergyman and ornithologist, describes a rook trial he once witnessed. Riding along a quiet road in the neighborhood of Norwich, he was startled by a great cawing from an adjoining rookery. He tied his horse to a gate and cautiously crawled for a hundred feet or so to a gap in the hedge of a meadow. Here he obtained a good view of the proceedings.

Surrounded by some forty or fifty noisy and indignant rooks stood the culprit in the dock. Perky and jaunty at first, he gradually lost his bravado and at last subsided into an excellent imitation of the famous jackdaw of Rheims after he had been cursed by the cardinal with bell, book, and candle. Evidently the jury brought in a verdict of guilty, for, in a grand finale, the circle of rooks suddenly closed in upon the accused and pecked him to death. Judgment executed, the whole assembly burst into vociferous screaming and dispersed, some seeking the adjacent rookery, but the greater number flying away across the fields.

During the early spring it is not unusual for young and inexperienced sparrows to pilfer twigs and straws from the nest which their elders are building. If the theft be detected a passerine posse will visit the offender's nest and summarily scatter it to the four winds, after giving him a sound thrashing.

Far severer is the justice that is meted out to dishonest sparrows in Europe by their frequent neighbors the martins. A tragic story is told in Garret's "Marvels of Instinct," on the authority of one Father Bougeant: A sparrow had appropriated to his own use a nest which a martin had just built. The rightful owner summoned his friends to the rescue. Several hundred strong, the martins flew to the attack. Like Brer Terrapin the usurper lay low, and, presenting his large beak at the opening of the nest, severely pecked such of the too daring besiegers as ventured within his reach. After a quarter of an hour the martins withdrew from the contest, leaving the sparrow to premature self-congratulation upon his superior strategic skill. Alas, Nemesis was only too surely on his track! The martins speedily returned, each bearing some of the tempered earth whereof they make their nests. With one accord they fell upon the nest and, plastering the opening all over with the soft earth, enclosed the thief in his stolen property, much in the same way as the hero of Poe's "Amontillado" was shut up in the wine cellar. Then, as in Poe's story, he was left to his fate.

The Grand Rapids *Herald* in 1910 reported a successful lynching that had taken place on a farm near Mariette, Mich. Two farmers sitting in a barn noticed a sparrow entering a swallow's nest which clung to the side of a beam. A moment later he started to pitch out the young birds. Three swallows, attracted by their outcry, speedily pounced upon the intruder. After confining him to the nest for a few minutes they threw him out. He dropped about a foot, there was a jerk, and Mr. Sparrow was seen hanging as nicely as though an expert executioner had been in charge,—a horse-hair being wound several times around his neck. After a few ineffectual struggles he kicked his last. Of course you may rationalize this apparent miracle by assuming that the horse-hair was accidentally wound around the bird's neck during the struggle with his antagonists.

Even in human law circumstantial evidence has led to the conviction of many an innocent man. Small wonder then that innocent birds have been done to death unjustly by a feathered judge and jury. Bishop Stanley tells us that a French surgeon at Smyrna, being unable to procure a stork because of the Turkish veneration for these birds, stole the eggs from a stork's nest and left hen's eggs in their place. The female stork in all innocence hatched out the chickens. The male immediately deserted the partner of his joys and sorrows. Three or four days later he returned, in company with many other storks, who forming a circle placed the unhappy female in the middle and began to adjudicate the case. The bringing forth even unintentionally of young chickens instead of young storks is evidently a heinous crime in the stork code, for at the close of the trial they all fell upon the prisoner at the bar and straightway killed her.

The stork's wife, like Cæsar's, must be above suspicion!

More remarkable still is a story that comes from Berlin. Two storks had built their nests upon a chimney. The owner of the house, finding an egg in the nest, substituted a goose's egg in its place. The female stork hatched it, to the stormy indignation of her companion. After circling three or four times around the nest he flew away. For some days the bereaved consort fed the young goose. On the morning of the fourth day the human inmates of the house were disturbed by a loud clamoring. This was found to proceed from nearly four hundred birds gathered together in a compact body and apparently listening to the harangue of a solitary stork standing some twenty yards away. When one orator retired, another took his place and addressed the court. In this fashion the proceedings continued until about eleven in the forenoon. Finally the whole court rose simultaneously in the air, emitting dismal ululations. All this time the female stork had sat trembling in the nest. Nor was her fear unwarranted, for suddenly the whole company of storks launched themselves upon her. At their head was a particularly irate male, presumably the injured spouse, who struck her violently three or four times, knocked her out of the nest, and then killed her. He next turned his attention to the unhappy gosling, which he likewise immolated. Then the nest was destroyed, and the storks flew away,—no doubt perfectly satisfied in their own minds that the law had been vindicated and that justice had been done.

Rev. George Gogerley is the author of an interesting volume of reminiscences, entitled "The Pioneers, a Record of the Bengal Missions," which appeared nearly three-quarters of a century ago. He describes some of the curious habits of the flamingo, a bird of odd shape and brilliant plumage, very common in the marshy lands of Bengal. "My friend Mr. Lacroix," he continues, "when once sailing in his boat up the Hooghley, went on shore. His attention was shortly directed to a large gathering of these peculiar-looking birds in a field some little distance off. Knowing their timid character, he approached as near as he could without being observed or exciting. alarm, and, hiding himself behind a tree, noted all their proceedings. After a great deal of noisy clamor, they formed themselves into a circle, in the centre of which one of their number was left standing alone. Again there was a considerable amount of screeching bird oratory, when suddenly all the birds flew on the unhappy solitary one and literally tore him to pieces."

Bosworth Smith, a more acute observer and a more reliable reporter than any yet quoted, has his stories too about birds. When the nest of a too self-assertive rook, he says, is built in a tree in advance of the colony and without its formal leave, the rooks assemble on the disputed tree and discuss the matter, like so many sanitary inspectors, in all its bearings, and end by "certificating" or "condemning" it.

Sometimes the verdict appears to be "Not guilty, but don't do it again," for it does not follow, even if the young are safely reared in the tree licensed for one year, that it will be occupied again in another. Something, perhaps, may have happened in the interim which makes the jury determine that it is unfit for rook occupation. Sometimes a solitary position far from the rookery is assigned as a punishment to an obstinate marauder who has committed the unpardonable fault of being found out once too often.

"Social ostracism for the breeding season," Mr. Smith concludes, "must be a severe penalty to a bird so eminently sociable as the rook; but, like ostracism at Athens, it seems to be carefully divested of all painful consequences afterwards; for, as soon as the young are flown, the culprit is allowed to return to the community with all his old rights and privileges unimpaired. Unlike Draco of Athens, whose laws were said to be written not in ink but in blood, and who recognized but one penalty for all offences,—death,—rooks recognize degrees in guilt, and reserve the extreme penalty of the law for the more heinous."

Lawn-Tennis. A modern application of the ancient game of tennis (*q.v.*), played with racket and balls on a court traversed by a net, but without enclosing walls. Historically it dates from 1874, when Major Wingfield took out a patent for a game called "sphairistike," described in the specifications "a new and improved portable court for playing the ancient game of tennis." Wingfield's court narrowed at the net, so that its outlines were those of an hour-glass. The present rectangular shape was substituted in 1877. Within a year after its birth sphairistike had been rebaptized lawn-tennis and had begun its career of triumph. Simultaneously it crossed the Atlantic, Dr. James Dwight and the brothers F. R. and R. D. Sears being mainly instrumental in making it known in the United States.

In 1877 the first championship game was played in England and resulted in a victory for Spencer Gore. He anticipated the tactics afterward brought to perfection by the Renshaws, which aimed at forcing the adversary back to the base-line and killing his return with a volley from a position near the net. A memorable performance in the history of the game was the championship competition in 1886, when William Renshaw beat H. F. Lawford a love set in 9½ minutes. The longest rest in first-class lawn-tennis was recorded in 1880, when 81 strokes were played between Lawford and E. Lubbock.

R. D. Sears won the first American championship in 1881, and retained it for six successive years, until in 1887 ill health forced him out of the competition and the title went to H. W. Slocum.

The first English lady champion was Miss M. Watson (1884), the first American, Miss E. C. Roosevelt (1890).

Lawyer, First Female. Common sense and common law allow anybody to plead his own cause in a law-court. Indeed the lawyer or attorney is an after-thought of civilization. He has grown into a necessity because the average citizen is ignorant of the law and of its methods and would be at a hopeless disadvantage against any one better instructed. Hence the indispensable attorney (" one appointed "). When Valerius Maximus (Book viii, ch. 8, example 2) tells us of a female pleader in Rome, one Afrania, our surprise is tempered on discovery that she pleaded only her own causes. Being of a litigious disposition, she was perpetually involving herself in lawsuits. She would never employ an advocate, but always appeared in person and managed her own cases. This confident behavior made her unpleasantly notorious, so that women of her clamorous turn were usually stigmatized with her name. Valerius Maximus sums up her character in a noxious term which will not bear reprinting. The *Recreative Magazine,* in vol. iii, page 283 (London, 1822), cites the analogous English case of Mary Tucker, who " pleaded her own cause in a case of libel, and got acquitted thereby," but gives no further particulars. The same authority adds that England once had a female constable. " On the 21st of April, 1788, the Court of King's Bench determined that a woman was competent to serve the offices of commissioner of the sewers and overseer of the poor. Mr. Justice Ashhurst observed that the statute of Elizabeth mentioned substantial house-keepers without distinction of sex." The Review also mentions a parish where a woman was chosen constable, and refers the reader to Dodsley, 1788.

Among the clay tablets of ancient Babylonia preserved in the British Museum is one, as old as B.C. 550, which contains the records of a legal case instituted by " a woman of Borsippa " against her brother-in-law, " a man of Babylon," to regain possession of property bequeathed by her husband. The evidence showed that the husband had bought the property with the money obtained as her dowry. After a few years, having no children of their own, they adopted a son. Shortly afterward the husband mortgaged the estate. Later he died, and his brother attempted to claim the mortgaged property.

The widow took the matter before the court at Borsippa ; which referred it to the Higher Court at Babylon. Here the case was duly heard, and the judges rendered a decision to the effect that, as the property had been the husband's, the widow could have it upon paying off the mortgage, and that the brother had no claim. Eventually the estate would be the property of the adopted son. It is expressly stated, as though a matter of some interest, that the woman pleaded her own case in the High Court of Babylon without assistance.

But even before the admission of women to the bar in the United States one woman at least had been allowed, though somewhat unwillingly, to plead her own cause in a temporary emergency. This was Myra Clark Gaines, who eventually won a lawsuit against the city of New Orleans for a property representing many million dollars. While the suit was in its preliminary stages before the Louisiana State judges, she was in the habit of attending court with her husband, General Edmond P. Gaines, the latter dressed in full uniform and wearing his sword. On one occasion, at New Orleans, her counsel for some reason threw up their briefs, whereupon the general intimated that, as a legal man himself, he might claim the right to represent his wife. Virginian law, however, was his forte, and in the court of a civil law State he felt rather at sea, so he begged that his wife might be heard on her own behalf. The judge consented, and the general, "with that grand dignity for which he is so distinguished," led forward Mrs. Gaines, who addressed the jury at length, and read a number of documents. The judge after a time raised the frivolous technical objection that the documents were not in evidence. The lady had too high a spirit to submit to such tyrannical dictation, and the judge again interfered, and, as she still persisted, appealed to her husband " to control his wife in Court." Whereupon, so we are told by the authoress of "Court Circles of the Republic" (1871), "the stately old general rose to his full altitude of six feet three, and, assuming the position of a commander of grenadiers and gracefully touching the belt of his sword, responded, ' May it please your honor, for everything that lady shall say or do I hold myself personally responsible in every manner and form known to the laws of my country or the laws of honor.' " This reply, and the significant gestures by which it was accompanied, led the judge to exclaim that " the court would not be overawed by the military authorities," and then proceed to overawe the gallant general by a threat " to reduce to an exception of recusation " something which had been said.

Mrs. Carrie Burnham Kilgore (1836–1908) was the first woman admitted to practise in Pennsylvania. She was born in Craftsbury, Vermont. When only 15 years old she was a teacher in the Vermont schools, and three years later she was teaching Greek and higher mathematics in the high school at Madison, Wis. Later she was preceptress of Evansville Seminary, in that State. In 1864 Mrs. Kilgore was graduated with the degree of doctor of medicine from the New York Hygieo-Therapeutic Medical College. A year later she came to Philadelphia and began reading Blackstone. When she registered in 1870 as a law student, the innovation excited the ridicule of the press, bar, and bench. A woman as a lawyer became a matter for comment even in European periodicals.

Mrs. Kilgore was denied admission to the law school of the University of Pennsylvania in 1871, but ten years later was admitted, and in 1883 was graduated with the degree of bachelor of laws. In 1873 she argued before the State Supreme Court her right to the elective franchise, and the chief justice pronounced her address " an able and exhaustive argument." In 1881 she appeared before the joint session of the legislature in support of the bill for women's admission to the legal profession. In 1884 she was admitted to the Delaware County courts and to one Philadelphia Common Pleas Court, and two years later she was admitted to the Supreme Court by act of assembly, and also to the federal courts. She was admitted to the United States Supreme Court in 1890, being the fourth member of her sex to win such admittance.

The first woman admitted to the bar in Europe was Mlle. Chauvin, in Paris. She was born at Jargeau, in the Loiret, and was left an orphan at an early age. At school she was an infant prodigy. In 1884 she took her bachelorship of letters, in 1885 her bachelorship of science, became a licentiate of philosophy 1890, and a doctor of laws in 1892. Her original intention had been to qualify for a post as teacher, but her academic success led her to think of higher triumphs, and she became an ardent exponent of the rights of women. The thesis which won her her doctorship of laws dealt with "Professions Accessible to Women," and was a powerful plea for the admission of women to all the "carrières" without distinction. After teaching law for five years in a "lycée" for young ladies, she determined to go to the bar. Her application was strongly contested, but it was found by the judges that the law was on her side, and she was duly sworn in toward the end of 1897. Since then she has been gradually building up a very considerable practice, but her appearances in the courts are few and far between.

Lead-pencil. The first lead-pencil was made in England in the Elizabethan era, but, as a matter of fact, it was not a *lead*-pencil at all, but a graphite pencil, such as we write with to-day. Graphite was originally called plumbago (from the Latin *plumbum,* "lead") or black lead, but, since the mineral contains no lead, the names are singularly inappropriate. The first person who used the name "graphite" (Greek "grapho," "I write") was A. G. Werner in 1789.

In the early days of lead-pencil making the graphite was sawed into thin sheets and cut into strips smaller and smaller until they were of a size to be covered with light wooden slips, and thus serve as pencils.

The first pencils created much excitement. The graphite mines of England were considered of inestimable value and were protected by law. But there was great waste—first, in digging, for many of the pieces were too small for cutting, and again in the manner of cutting the graphite, which was so crude that half the material was lost.

In 1795, Conte, a Frenchman, conceived the idea of using pulverized graphite and binding clay. This discovery resulted in pencils of varying hardness, according to the amount of binding clay added, each pencil being of exactly the same hardness throughout its length.

Soon after this discovery improvements followed in mixing, rolling, and sharpening the graphite composition, which was cut into lengths, placed in a warm oven to harden, and finally incased in wood, as seen to-day.

It was not until 1860 that so-called lead-pencils were manufactured in the United States. Once started, however, the growth of the industry was rapid, and now it is estimated that there are more than four million dollars invested in it. To-day American lead-pencils are sold all over the world.

Leap-year Birthdays. If a man happen to be born on

February 29th,—in Leap-year, of course,—may he celebrate his birthday only on the quaternary return of the day? The law says no, although here Blackstone is at fault. The author of the "Commentaries," without noting any exception, says explicitly that a man child attains his majority "on the day preceding the twenty-first anniversary of the person's birth." Now, in 1910 Gilbert Tangye became the father of a son on February 29th. A London barrister set himself to looking up law and precedent on this subject of leap-year birthdays. His first appeal to Blackstone disheartened him. But Mr. Tangye delved deeper, and in the statutes of King Henry III. he found a law that appeared to make it clear sailing for the youngster. This statute, De Anno et Die Bissextili, was made at Westminster in 1236. Here is King Henry's proclamation of it:

The King unto his Justices of the Bench, greeting.

Know ye.................to take away from henceforth all doubt and ambiguity that might arise hereupon, the day increasing in the Leap Year shall be accounted for one year, so that because of that day none shall be impleaded, but it shall be taken and reckoned of the same month wherein it groweth, and that day, and the day next going before, shall be accounted for one day, and therefore we do commend you, that from henceforth you do cause this to be published afore you and observed.
Witness Myself
at Westminster.

While this language is rather ambiguous, Mr. Tangye insisted it was plain to him as a lawyer that it means that his son's birthdays will occur legally on February 28 in three years out of every four. His opinion was considered important enough to run the rounds of the British press and to be cabled over to America.

Letter. The first woman letter writer on record was Queen Jezebel, the wife of Ahab, and it is not surprising to find that she used her pen for purposes of deception. The story is told in 1 Kings, xxi, 5–10. When Ahab was mourning because he could not obtain Naboth's vineyard by fair means, Jezebel conceived of foul ones: "So she wrote letters in Ahab's name and sealed them with his seal, and sent the letters unto the elders and to the nobles that were in his city and that dwelt with Naboth." They suggested a plot which resulted in the death of Naboth by stoning. An earlier letter mentioned in the Bible was written by a man and was equally detestable. When we remember the contents and the purpose of David's letter to Joab, how it did for Uriah what Jezebel did for Naboth and from a dirtier motive, we could have wished of this too that it had never been preserved (II Samuel xi, 14).

It is pleasant to recall that the earliest letter from an Englishwoman whereof any copy exists is that harmless bit of flattery sent from Matilda, Queen of Henry I, to Archbishop Anselm. She styles him her "worthily reverenced lord," and herself "the lowest of the handmaidens of his Holiness," epithets which may owe their origin to some clerical secretary. Anne Boleyn's last cry of love and anguish to her lord is worth a ream of the letters of earlier date written at second hand.

The posthumous publication of letters by celebrities arose about the middle of the eighteenth century, and soon grew to be so common that Dr. Arbuthnot declared that the anticipation added a new terror to death. In 1781 Dr. Johnson writes, "It has become so much the fashion to publish letters that I put as little into mine as I can." Nevertheless, when Boswell subsequently asked him if it would be proper to publish any of his letters after death, Johnson contented himself by remarking, "Nay, sir, when I am dead you may do as you will with mine."

One of the most venerable of English peers was once told that several of his letters were catalogued for sale in a London auction room. "It is a matter of indifference to me," said the noble lord; "from the day I became a public man I never wrote a line worth the reading by any one except the person to whom my letter was addressed."

On the other hand it must be noted that many great people have looked upon this matter with very opposite emotions. In some there has been no little affectation, in others a remarkable candor. Pope addressed his letters to his friends, but he carefully and elaborately wrote and rewrote them for posterity, and he was not sorry to see some of them get into print (he rather helping them to that end than obstructing them), that he might have a foretaste of the enjoyment which was more especially intended for after ages. Every line in Walpole's letters reads as if it were as much intended for *us* of any year to come, as for the friend to whom the letter was directed; but this diminishes neither Walpole's credit nor our appreciation. Pepys never intended his "Diary" to be perused by any mortal eye but his own. The Rev. Mr. Smith, however, deciphered the short-hand, and the best social history of Pepys's time fell into the hands of a delighted and grateful public. Evelyn wrote *his* "Diary" for his own satisfaction, indifferent as Dr. Johnson about his letters, whether it were published or not after his death. Evelyn's descendants were ignorant of its value, and it is to a stranger we owe those sketches of contemporary men and things which now enrich our literature. Pepys, Evelyn, Walpole,—diaries and letters; of how many exquisite stories we should have known nothing but for those three individuals! It matters little whether they intended we should enjoy that knowledge or not; sufficient for us that we *do*. And let us note, in passing, another letter-writer,—Lady Mary Wortley Montagu. Her letters are not quite so popular, so much read, or so well known, perhaps, as they used to be; they may have had their day, but the writer was well assured they would at least have *that*. "Keep my letters," she once wrote to a friend; "they will be as good as Madame de Sévigné's forty years hence."

In dealing with old letters as much caution is necessary as in dealing with old pictures. Forged letters are as thick as leaves in Vallambrosa. Half a century ago the London *Athenæum* notes the prevalence of these counterfeits. "One man," it says, "forges for the pure love of sport, and throws his forged papers into a collection, to be found a hundred years later, merely to perplex the pundits. Another forges to sustain a crotchet or a principle. But the most industrious and the most facile are those who forge for profit. Every one familiar with old papers is aware that the publication of historical documents—letters, plays, poems, maps, charts, and cylinders—has now ceased to be a learned profession, and has become a manufacture. As the "Old Bailey" had its tribes of rascals ready to witness against anybody and anything for money, so literature has its race of outcasts ready to furnish any document that may be wanted, from a Wardour-street pedigree, derived from scrolls in a Cheshire muniment room, up to a copy of Homer from a monastery at the summit of Mount Athos.

Furthermore it is no paradox to say that there are "authentic" letters which are no more authentic in their contents than if they had been forged. That is to say, they intentionally misrepresented the feelings of the writers. Fun, profit, or mystification was at the bottom of it. Sterne, writing to Garrick in April, 1762, reveals an amusing conspiracy that he had planned. "Crebillon," he says, "has made a convention with me which, if he be not too lazy, will be no bad persiflage. As soon as I get to Toulouse, he has agreed to write me an expostulatory letter upon the indecorums of Tristram Shandy, which is to be answered by recriminations upon the coarseness of his own works. These are to be printed together—Crebillon against Sterne, Sterne against Crebillon. The copy is to be sold and the money equally divided. This is good Swiss policy!"

Nothing came of this design, but it illustrates how a letter may be authentic yet not be genuine.

There seems to have been, at one time, a regular manufactory for the production of letters by Shelley, Keats, and Byron. The

market was swamped by these cleverly-forged documents.   In the
year 1862, Robert Browning, the poet, edited a volume of letters
by Shelley, and critics said that they would prove useful to all
future biographers of that wayward genius. These letters turned
out to be forgeries.   One epistle was found to be a "crib" from
an article by Sir Francis Palgrave, in the *Quarterly Review.* Another was slightly altered from a paper in a literary annual.
When research was made, the discovery ensued that the supposed original had been purchased by Mr. Moxon, the publisher,
at an auction.   The auctioneer had had them consigned to him
by a bookseller in Pall Mall, and the bookseller had bought them
from two unknown women, who looked as much like ladies as
the letters looked like genuine productions. If Mr. Moxon had
not sent a copy of the volume to Mr. Tennyson, a long time
might have elapsed before the fraud could have been discovered.
But Mr. Palgrave, on a visit to the laureate, happened to open
the book, and his eye fell on a letter from Shelley to Godwin,
written from Florence. Mr. Palgrave recognized in it a portion
of an article on Florence, in the *Quarterly,* written by his father,
Sir Francis. Mr. Moxon called in all the copies of this volume
of pseudo-epistles, and suppressed the publication altogether.
A curious result has followed. The volume is worthless, but it is
rare; and simply on account of its rarity is prized by collectors.
(See LOVE-LETTER.)

Letter-box. Apparently this useful adjunct to the postal-
delivery system originated in Paris as a part of the first penny
post established in any country. In 1650 a system had been
organized whereby letters posted in Paris could be conveyed to
any part of the city at a cost of a sou apiece, their collection and
distribution being expedited by means of boxes—to all intents
and purposes similar to our modern letter-boxes—placed in and
about the capital. But the citizens of Paris did not take kindly
to the postal novelty, which was destined to share the same
fate as the six-sous omnibus, a contemporary invention, attributed to no meaner person than Pascal. Furetière, in his " Roman
Bourgeois," explains how the letter-box experiment came to fail:
" Certain boxes," he says, " were at that time newly affixed to
all the street corners to hold letters sent *from* Paris *to* Paris.
But these things were ordained under such unlucky stars that
the letters never reached their destination; and when the boxes
were opened nothing was found but mice, that some mischievous
wags had dropped therein."

Not until the spring of 1850 was the letter-box revived in
Paris, and it was then a copy of a Belgian innovation. The
first specimen was erected in the Rue de la Paix. It is thus

described (with an illustration) by the *Illustrated London News* of March 9, 1850: "It consists of a bronze columnar design, raised upon a granite socle; the opening for the receipt of letters being in the upper portion of the column and having a projection to keep out the rain; a door for the removal of letters being provided towards the base." London followed the example of Paris early in 1885. Cast-iron letter-boxes were erected by the authorities of St. Martin's Le-Grand, the first one being at the corner of Fleet Street and Farringdon Street. It was much less ornamental than the Paris pillar.

"Our Letter-box," says the *Illustrated London News* of January, 1885, "is a stove-like design, reminding one of the latest of the London conduits. An outer panel of the box bears this inscription:—

LETTER BOX

For Stamped and Unpaid Letters only.

Newspapers posted here will not be forwarded.

Letters containing Money or Valuable Articles should be Registered at a Post-office.

THE NEAREST POST-OFFICE IS AT 101, FLEET-STREET.

General Post Letters

For the Morning Mails, are collected here, 5 a.m.; for the Evening Mails, 5.30 p.m.

Letters bearing an Additional Penny Stamp may be Posted for the Evening Mails, 6 p.m.

Then followed, as in the American letter-boxes, a schedule of hours of collection and delivery.

Letter Press. John Evelyn in his "Diary" under date November 27, 1655, notes that Samuel Hartlip "told me of an ink that would give a dozen copies, moist sheets of papers being pressed upon it, and remain perfect."

Knowledge of the invention must have died out entirely, for at the date of Watt's patent (1780), there was no suggestion that the process was in use or was even known. This patent was for the process, not merely for the press.

Letter Written in America, First. Dr. Diego Alvarez, Chanca, a native of Seville, physician in ordinary to their Spanish Majesties Ferdinand and Isabella, accompanied Columbus on his second voyage of discovery to America as the physician of his fleet. Toward the end of January, 1494, he wrote a letter to the municipal council (Cabildo) of Seville, narrating all he had seen and heard up to date. This letter, the first description of the New World ever penned, left the port of Isabella, in the island of Hispaniola or San Domingo, on February 2d, in care of Don Antonio de Torres, commander of the twelve vessels sent back by Columbus to Spain with the news of the discoveries, and arrived there April 8, 1494. Everything Dr. Chanca says in his letter, therefore, regarding those just-discovered islands of the New World, he learned in the short space of time between November 3, 1493, when he saw the first island (Dominica), and the last week of January, 1494—that is, in less than three months.

The original manuscript is preserved in the Seville Library. It was first translated into English in 1847 by R. H. Major, of the British Museum, for the Hakluyt Society in London. This is said to be inaccurate, owing to the translator's imperfect acquaintance with the nuances of the Andalusian dialect used by the Spanish author. · A more recent translation, by Dr. A. M. Fernandez de Ybarra, is officially filed in the archives of the Smithsonian Institution at Washington.

Lia Fail, or Stone of Destiny. The coronation stone of the·Irish kings set up on the Hill of Tara when that was the royal centre of Ireland.

Other names given it were the Tanist Stone, or Stone of the Heir-Apparent; Innisphail, or Stone of Fortune; and a local or popular name of Bod Fhearghais. It was also called the "roaring stone," from its supposed miraculous property of sounding when the rightful king was placed upon it, and remaining mute under a pretender; and it was believed to carry with it the destiny of Ireland, giving the sovereignty of whatever land in which it was established to one of Irish blood. A long legendary history of wonderful wanderings connects it on one side with Jacob's pillar at Bethel, and on the other with the ancient Scottish Coronation Stone of Scone, now in the Coronation Chair at Westminster Abbey.

The identity of the Lia Fail with the Stone of Scone has been accepted as veritable fact by many unimaginative books of reference, even by the reliable "Lippincott's Gazetteer." Dean Stanley, in his "History of Westminster Abbey," shows a lurking leaning toward the romantic history, as if it were half against his will that he accepted the testimony of sober-minded antiquarians and geologists.

The traditional story is too long for repetition here. A writer in *The Spectator* (the article is copied into *The Living Age* in July, 1884) shows how little historic basis there is for even the latter part of the legend,—the transfer from Tara to Scone,—and how much to disprove it, declaring it to be impossible that the Irish royal stone ever left Tara at all. He quotes Mr. Petrie, a searching investigator of 1839, as saying that the Lia Fail was originally placed on the side of the "Hill of Hostages," and there remained "till some time after 1798, when it was removed to its present position in the Rath, called the ' Farradh,' to mark the graves of the rebels slain at Tara in the insurrection of that year." Stanley says, "One of the green mounds within that venerable precinct [Tara] is called the Coronation Chair, and a rude pillar" over the rebel graves " is by some thought to be the original Lia Fail."

Quite as convincing is the evidence of the geologists, Professors Ramsay and Geikie, as to the witness borne by the stone (of Scone) itself. They pronounce it to be of red sandstone precisely similar to that found in the neighborhood of Scone and of Dunstaffnage Castle. Professor Ramsay says, " It can never have been derived from any of the rocks of Tara, which are of the Carboniferous era, or from those of Iona, where no red sandstone exists; and it is equally impossible it should have belonged to the limestone rocks around Bethel or the nummulitic strata of Egypt."

Mr. Skene authoritatively sums up the discussion thus:

" It was the custom of Celtic tribes to inaugurate their kings on a sacred stone supposed to symbolize the monarchy. The Irish kings were inaugurated on the Lia Fail, which never was anywhere but at Tara, the *sedes principalis* of Ireland; and the kings of Scotland, first of the Pictish monarchy and afterwards of the Scottish kingdom which succeeded it, were inaugurated on this stone, which never was anywhere but at Scone, the *sedes principalis* both of the Pictish and Scottish kingdoms." (See CORONATION STONE in WALSH, *Curiosities of Popular Customs,* p. 281.

Liberty Bell. This, the most famous bell in America, now stands in the entrance or vestibule of the old Philadelphia State-house, on Chestnut Street between Fifth and Sixth Streets. It is scarcely necessary to add that this building enshrines the famous Independence Hall, wherein " the Representatives of the United States of America in General Congress assembled," on July 4, 1776, adopted that Declaration which severed our ties with the motherland. (See WALSH, *Curiosities of Popular Customs,* pp. 589–590.)

In the year 1751 this bell was ordered from Robert Charles, a London bell-founder. The specifications were that it should weigh 2000 pounds and cost £100,000 sterling, that it should be made by the best workmen, that it should be examined carefully before being shipped, and should contain around it, in well-shaped letters, the inscription:

" By order of the Province of Pennsylvania for the State House in Philada. MDCCLII."

Beneath this inscription should be placed a quotation from Leviticus, xxv, 10:

" Proclaim liberty throughout the land unto all the inhabitants thereof."

The full text in Leviticus reads, " And ye shall hallow the fiftieth year, and proclaim liberty," etc. Possibly in selecting the text the good Quakers had in mind the arrival of William Penn and their forefathers more than fifty years before.

In August, 1752, the bell arrived. Though apparently in good order, it was cracked by a stroke of the clapper while being tested, and was recast in Philadelphia by Isaac Norris. Even then the bell proved defective. The original had been considered too high in tone, the result of an inadequate supply of copper. Too much copper had been added when it was recast, and its tone was consequently too low. This second failure provoked many witticisms. Norris undertook once more to cast the bell. He succeeded in pleasing the experts, and the bell was hung in the steeple in June, 1753.

On noon of Monday, July 8th, 1776,—not the 4th, as generally believed,—the bell fulfilled the prophecy of its motto and rang out the tidings that the Declaration of Independence had been ratified by the thirteen States.

On July 8, 1783, while being tolled for the funeral of Chief Justice Marshall, the bell was again cracked. Ineffectual efforts were made to restore its tone by enlarging the crack and clipping its edges. It was removed from the tower to a lower story and a new bell was hoisted in its place. Later the Liberty Bell was placed in Independence Hall, and still later it was shipped to its present position in the entrance hall. Its last trip among the many that it has made to various expositions was to the World's Fair in St. Louis.

Library.   Of all the apartments in the house of a man who adds to brains and breeding the wherewithal for gratifying his gentle tastes, none can yield him more exquisite delight than his library—and none is a more intimate portion of his best self.

Have we not all felt, and reciprocated, the joy with which Xavier de Maistre takes us by the hand and leads us from book-shelf to book-shelf in his memorable " Journey Around my Room?"

Sweet, indeed, to the bibliomaniac, are the moments whiled away in sorting and dipping into his books! The dinner hour may strike; Madame Bibliomaniac may be kept waiting. He dines upon prose and sips poetry instead of port. His work is too full of delight ever to be finished. Like Penelope's web it is done to-day to be undone to-morrow. A new edition, a new author, picked up by some divine accident at an auction or from a book-stall, deranges the whole order. Each volume, ere it takes its place, opens at some rare or curious passage, and, by a kind of instinct which is the bibliomaniac's secret, his eye falls at once upon every rich and suggestive bit.

The whole pedigree of books rises up before the reader's mind. How far back can the origin and growth of books be carried? Does not Mader, that thrice-learned, that incalculably ingenious, that immortally ingenuous German, begin his history with a chapter "Of Antediluvian Writers and Librarians?" Had not Thebes the great library of the "King of Kings,"—old Osymandyas,—a library rightly called "The Treasury of Remedies for the Soul"?

Did not Pisistratus found the first library of Athens, to be carried away by Xerxes into Persia, and to be brought back, long after, by Seleucus Nicator?

How many great men of Greece were made prouder and more famous by their wealth of books! There were Polycrates of Samos, Euclid of Athens, the poet Euripides, and, above all, Aristotle, whose choice collection passed from Theophrastus to Ptolemy Philadelphus and was transported to Rome during the dictatorship of Sulla.

We know that numerous libraries flourished in republican and imperial Rome, and that in the time of Constantine they had reached the respectable number of twenty-nine. Yet, strange omission! hardly anything survives in the way of contemporary enumeration of the volumes in either Greek or Roman libraries, or of such details in the description of their contents as might be expected from observant scholars. However minute and precise the Roman and Grecian bibliophiles might be in their accounts of foreign libraries or the great libraries of the past, they furnish no data as to the libraries which they were in the habit of visiting. Thus, Aulus Gellius, in his *Noctes Attici*, speaks of meeting friends in the Tiberian library, of making researches in the library of Trajan, and of finding a book, "after a long hunt," in the Library of Peace. But he does not say a word as to the number of volumes, as to the class or character of the books, as to the order of their arrangement, or as to the conditions whereby they were made accessible to the public, either in these or in any other contemporary Roman libraries. Yet Aulus Gellius is responsible for the extravagant statement that the Ptolemæan Library at Alexandria contained 700,000 volumes—an estimate which the calmer Eusebius reduces to 100,000.

Two exceptions only may be noted in the case of Roman

libraries, and both these are private. The collection of Tyrannion, a contemporary of Cicero, is rated on the questionable say-so of Suidas at 60,000 volumes, and that which Serenus Sammonicus, preceptor of the younger Gordian, bequeathed to his imperial pupil is more authoritatively estimated at 30,000 volumes. In these meagre details dwells all our real knowledge as to the contents of the libraries of the great classical periods.

Of one thing we may be certain, however—the first public library in the history of the world was established in Rome during the reign of Augustus. It was speedily followed by others. These, it would appear, were used as meeting-places and reading-rooms for learned and unlearned alike. That books might occasionally be borrowed from a library is indicated by still another passage in Aulus Gellius, though the library in question was at Tivoli and not at Rome. He and his friends, dining one warm summer at a plutocrat's villa near Tibur, were drinking melted snow, despite the protest of one of the party, who said that Aristotle had declared the practice unwholesome. "Thereupon he fetched a treatise by Aristotle out of the library of Tibur, which was then very conveniently accommodated in the Temple of Hercules," etc. Scholars have bewailed the loss of the Alexandrian Library already alluded to. It was founded at Alexandria by Ptolemy Soter, B.C. 290. As has been said, the number of volumes has been variously estimated as from 100,000 to 700,000. Two centuries and a half after its foundation (in B.C. 47), that portion which was preserved in the Bruchion building was accidentally consumed by fire by the auxiliary soldiers under Julius Cæsar. Nevertheless, the Alexandrian Library maintained its bulk by new accessions until the capture of the city by the Saracens in A.D. 640, when it was barbarously destroyed by order of the calif Omar.

The philosopher Philoponus, by his zealous effort to save his precious storehouse, precipitated its ruin. He solicited Amron, the Mohammedan chief, to give him the books of philosophy.

Amron declined acting until he could obtain permission from the calif, and accordingly stated Philoponus' request to his master. The reply has passed into history: "If these writings of the Greeks agree with the Koran, or Book of God, they are useless, and need not be preserved; if they disagree, they are pernicious, and ought to be destroyed."

Accordingly the manuscripts were sent to heat the 4000 public baths and six months were barely sufficient for the consumption of the precious fuel. This is the account of Abulfaragius, a Syrian writer, and it is not contradicted by Egyptian writers. Gibbon discredits the story, chiefly on the ground of "the six months clause," as he considered that the collection could not have grown to more than 700,000 volumes, which would give less than 200 volumes to a bushel. On the other hand, if the manuscripts had been dispersed it is singular that none of them afterwards appeared in any of the great libraries. At all events, the Alexandria library ceased at the date of Omar.

From glimpses afforded by the classics, and the oldest of illustrated manuscripts still actually extant or transmitted by tradition through the dark ages, it is safe to say that the main features of the early Roman libraries were reproduced, as late as the year 1587, for preservation to the present day in the famous library of the Vatican.

Dating from about the third century of the Christian era quite another form of library was developed in the monasteries. Beginning with a few manuscripts kept on shelves or in chests in the cloisters, these miniature collections of service-books, theological commentaries, and stray copies of the ancient classics, by gradual accretions through the centuries, at last overflowed the cloisters and were assigned to separate rooms and later to suites of rooms. The mediæval universities adopted the form thus evolved in the monasteries and developed them into types still familiar in the college libraries of to-day.

The current edition of the "Encyclopædia Britannica" states that Humphrey Cheetham's library at Manchester (established in 1653) was "the first free library in England." A contributor to *Notes and Queries,* however, sets up a prior claim for a library still extant in Bristol which was founded by Robert Redwood in the year 1615 and was rebuilt in 1740.

That was the germ of the public library of to-day.

Startling is the revolution in the old and the modern methods of lending books.

The old monastic library issued only one volume annually to each monk entitled to use its books. In the year 1471, when Louis XI wished to borrow a book from the Medical Faculty of Paris, he was required to deposit plate in pledge and to get one of his nobles to join him in a guarantee for the safe return of the book. Nay, so recently as 1790, in these United States of America, the rules of the Harvard College Library allowed the librarian to admit students into the room, but not more than three at a time.

To-day in Paris there is not one among the priceless treasures of the National Library that is not at the command of the humblest applicant of good reputation. In London, with the reorganization of the British Museum, the conditions of access were made so easy that, despite the lavish provisions of space in the reading-room, it became necessary, in the interests of the higher classes of readers, to fix the limit of age that might exclude " the rush of young men from University and King's colleges to the presses that contain the Latin dictionaries and Greek Lexicons and Bohn's cribs."

And if the character of the libraries has changed, how much more so the characteristics of librarians!

The librarian of the older days was a being who devoted himself to the simple accumulation of books. What he had got together with so much pains he naturally wished to retain. Like the miser, however, who loses sight of the real meaning of money in the mere pleasure of hoarding, the librarian forgot that it was more necessary books should be read than that they should be kept. He hated to see them used too much, because usage wore them out. He liked short hours and hard conditions. He closed his library in summer for cleaning and repairs. He was never so happy as when all the books were on the shelves. In due course of evolution he was succeeded by another and a broader type. This librarian rejoiced most when his shelves were empty. He loved to see the books used, even if they were occasionally abused. He loved to grant his patrons easy access to the book-shelves, even if a thief sometimes passed himself off as a reader. He invented all sorts of schemes to facilitate the finding of books; he stood ready to direct, advise, and encourage readers in their researches.

Library Curios. There are at least five libraries in the world which contain over one million volumes. These, in the order of their magnitude, are the Bibliotheque Nationale of Paris (which claims 3,000,000), the British Museum, the Imperial Library at St. Petersburg, the Congressional Library at Washington, and the New York Public Library (Astor-Tilden-Lenox foundations).

Of these the British Museum is the most interesting to men of British birth or British descent. The origin of that gigantic institution is curious enough. In the year 1753 Sir Hans Sloane offered to the nation his natural history collection, coins, manuscripts, and printed books for $100,000, about one-fourth of their estimated value. At the same time Parliament was reminded that the manuscripts collected by Robert Harley, Earl of Oxford, were still purchasable for $50,000, and furthermore that no proper building had yet been provided for those collected by Sir Robert Cotton, and handed over to the nation in 1700 by his descendant, Sir John Cotton.

The government declared itself unable to find money for these purposes, but, as a compromise, passed a bill authorizing a lottery, with 100,000 $15 tickets, for prizes amounting to a total of $1,000,000, the balance of $500,000, after deducting expenses, to be handed to Sir Hans Sloane's trustees to purchase the Sloane and Harleian collections, acquire a building, and invest whatever was left to produce an income. The 100,000 tickets were all sold, and thus the British Museum came into existence.

The oldest library in the United States is the Philadelphia Library, formerly situated at Fifth and Library Streets, but now at Juniper and Locust Streets, with a branch (the Ridgway) at Broad and Christian Streets. It was founded in 1731, the fourth year of George II's reign, by fifty young men, artisans and gentlemen of that town. Joining themselves into a literary association, which they called the Junto, they subscribed one hundred pounds for the purchase of books, and further agreed to pay each ten shillings annually during fifty years for the same purpose. The library was well sponsored, being Benjamin Franklin's "first project of a public nature." Franklin says:

At the time I established myself in Philadelphia there was not a good bookstore in any of the colonies southward of Boston. In New York and Philadelphia, the printers were indeed stationers; they sold only paper, etc., almanacs, ballads, and a few common school-books. Those who loved reading were obliged to send for their books from England; the members of the Junto [his club] had each a few. We had hired a room to hold our club in. I proposed that we should each of us bring our books to that room, where they would not only be ready to consult in our conferences, but become a common benefit, each of us being at liberty to borrow such as he wished to read at home. . . This was accordingly done, and for some time contented us. . . Yet some inconveniences occurring, each took his books home again. And now I set on foot my first project of a public nature, that for a subscription library. The institution soon manifested its ability, was imitated in other towns and in other provinces. . . Reading became fashionable, and our people, having no amusements to divert their attention from study, became better acquainted with books, and in a few years were observed by strangers to be better instructed and more intelligent than people of the same rank in other countries.

The books were at first kept in the house of Robert Grace, whom Franklin characterizes as "a young gentleman of some fortune, generous, lively, and witty, a lover of punning and of his friends." Afterward they were allotted a room in the State-house; and, in 1742, a charter was obtained from the proprietaries. In 1790, having in the interval absorbed several other associations and sustained a removal to Carpenter's Hall, where its apartment had been used as a hospital for wounded American soldiers, the library was at last housed in a building especially erected for it at Fifth and Library Streets, where it remained until within the last few years.

It brought only about eight thousand volumes into its new quarters, for it had languished somewhat during the Revolution and the war of words which attended our political birth. But it had received no injury.

Library, Five-foot. Literature by weight or by measure has always suggested humorous possibilities to the jokesmiths who batten on human ignorance. Anecdote No. 1510 in K. Arvine's "Cyclopædia of Anecdotes" (Boston, 1851) runs as follows:

> LITERATURE BY MEASURE.—A steward wrote to a bookseller in London, for some books to fit up his master's library, in the following terms: "In the first place I want six feet of theology, the same quantity of metaphysics, and near a yard of old civil law, in folio."

Du Maurier has a caricature in *Punch* which illustrates a dialogue that is exactly in point:

> SIR G. M. GOES IN FOR CULTURE.—"Look 'ere, Clarke. 'Appy thought! I'll make this little room the libery, you know; 'ave a lot o' books. Mind you order me some."
>
> "Yes, Sir Gorgius. What sort of books shall I order?"
>
> "Well, let me see—suppose we say a couple o' 'undred yards of 'em. Hay? That's about the size of it, I think!"

In one respect Sir Georgius approximated to the truth. Two hundred yards of books would more than suffice to contain all that is valuable as wit or as wisdom in what the past has bequeathed to us.

Coventry Patmore worked for twenty years as an assistant librarian in the British Museum. He could never, he used to say, resist the temptation to look into and taste the flavor of every book that passed through his hands; and it is interesting to note that the net result of these tests was that at the end of his long term of service he reached the depressing conclusion that, of the forty miles of shelves in the Museum, forty feet would contain all the real literature of the world. How much of the forty miles of shelving was, in Patmore's opinion, devoted to conserving real rubbish we are left to conjecture.

Charles William Eliot made a more radical estimate. Shortly after resigning from the presidency of Harvard College, he startled the scholastic world by declaring that a five-foot shelf is large enough to hold all the books required for a liberal education. Later being pressed for more details, he furnished a partial list of the books. "It is my belief," he said, "that the faithful and considerate reading of these books, with such rereadings and memorizings as individual taste may prescribe, will give any man the essentials of a liberal education, even if he can devote to them but fifteen minutes a day." The selections as far as have been made follow. It is necessary to explain that several titles are supposed to be bound into one volume: " Autobiography of Benjamin Franklin"; "Journal of John Woolman"; "Fruits of Solitude," by William Penn; Bacon's " Essays" and "New Atlantis"; Milton's "Areopagitica" and "Tractate on Education"; Sir Thomas Browne's "Religio Medici"; Plato's "Apology," "Phædo," and "Crito"; "Golden Sayings" of Epictetus; "Meditations of Marcus Aurelius"; Emerson's "Essays"; Emerson's "English Traits"; complete poems of Milton; Jonson's "Volpone"; Beaumont and Fletcher's "The Maid's Tragedy": Webster's "Duchess of Malfy"; Middleton's "The Changeling"; Dryden's "All for Love"; Shelley's "Cenci"; Browning's "Blot on the 'Scutcheon"; Tennyson's "Becket"; Goethe's "Faust'; Marlowe's "Dr. Faustus"; Adam Smith's "Wealth of Nations"; "Letters of Cicero and Pliny"; Bunyan's "Pilgrim's Progress"; Burns's "Tam O'Shanter"; Walton's "Complete Angler" and "Lives of Donne and Herbert"; "Autobiography of St. Augustine"; Plutarch's "Lives"; Dryden's "Æneid"; "Canterbury Tales"; " Imitation of Christ," by Thomas à Kempis; Dante's "Divine Comedy"; Darwin's "Origin of Species"; "Arabian Nights."

Library, Free. In this age of freely flowing fountains of knowledge, it ought to interest readers to be told that the first free library in England was established at All Hallows' Church in Bristol by the fraternity of Calendars. The church itself dates from the reign of Henry I; the Calendars were founded before the Conquest. Leland describes the "original" of the "Calendaries, otherwise the Gild or Fraternite of Brightstowe," as running backward to a "time oute of mynde." They were a body of priests and seculars whose office it was to register events both national and local, and to instruct the youth of the town; to which duties was added the not more easy task of converting Jews to Christianity, in which they were as successful as the more feverish and expensive modern society, being ascertained to have made at least one convert. The library was in the northwest aisle of the church, where four stout Norman piers thatsupported it are still extant. Here the prior gave open lectures on the contents of the books to all comers.

The free public library system such as we now know it dates back, in both England and America, no further than the middle of the nineteenth century. Yet a very full suggestion of the possibilities which have since been realized in the public library system was made so far back as 1817, in a pamphlet published at Ballston Spa, N. Y. The full title reads: "The Intellectual Torch; developing an original, economical and expeditious plan

31

for the universal dissemination of knowledge and virtue; by means of free public libraries. . . . Second edition, revised by the author." The first edition seems to be unknown, but there is reason to believe that it was the pamphlet entitled "The Intellectual Flambeau, demonstrating that rational happiness and virtue exist with the dissemination of philosophy, science and intelligence," Washington, 1816.

The author of this pamphlet was Dr. Jesse Torrey, Jr., who seems to have been born about 1787 and to have spent his early years in Lebanon, N. Y. It is a little singular that his name is to be found in no biographical dictionary of easy access. He might have remained utterly unknown but for the efforts of Prof. Frederick J. Taggart, of Stanford University, California, who published the result of his personal researches in the New York *Nation* for September 22, 1898.

From this article the facts here presented have been gleaned. Torrey has this to say of himself:

At the age of seventeen years, convinced of the inestimable benefits of reading useful books, I anxiously desired that they might, if possible, be extended to the great mass of the human family; and endeavored to discover some effective plan for this purpose. Indigence, which in most nations involves the majority, appeared to present the greatest obstacle. Hence the suggestion occurred that governments, or associations of individuals, might promote the object by establishing, in various districts, *free circulating libraries*, to be equally accessible to all classes and sexes without discrimination.

Professor Taggart points out that Torrey, who was thirty years old at the time he published his "second edition," used the same arguments for the establishment of free public libraries as those which were employed by the parliamentary advocates of the Ewart Act in 1850 and in the report of the trustees of the Boston Public Library in 1852. Thus, he anticipates the now familiar contention that the cost of libraries would be repaid through the decrease in crime that must follow their establishment. In his prefatory address "To the People of the United States," the author, speaking of himself in the third person, tells us that—

he has long cherished a decided confidence that if the community would appropriate as much wealth to the instruction of the rising generation as is now devoted to the punishment of crimes, the desired object would be attained, and human misery averted, to a much greater extent. The plan here proposed, for the general diffusion of knowledge through the medium of free libraries, has been submitted to the consideration of several of the most eminent statesmen and philanthropists in the United States, and received their unanimous and cordial approbation.

In the body of the pamphlet his principal argument is one

on which the Boston Public Library trustees laid special emphasis. He says:

> But the education of youth should not cease with the expiration of their attendance on public schools. The chasm between this period and that of their *corporeal* maturity contains many stumbling blocks and dangerous snares. The art of reading, without books to read, is to the mind, as is a set of good teeth to the body, without food to masticate; they will alike suffer the evils of disease, decay, and eventual ruin.
>
> Intellectual cultivation is the basis of virtue and happiness. As mental improvement advances, vice and crimes recede.

Turning to consider the means by which he proposed to effect the establishment and maintenance of these institutions, it is apparent that Torrey realized the necessity of legislative aid, and in this shows an advance over such of his own contemporaries as believed that men appreciated only those things for which it was necessary to pay.

> If our constitution does not now authorize measures which are likely to produce the greatest possible benefit to the country and security to its liberties, it ought *without delay* to be so amended that it should.
>
> Let American legislators, both national and sectional, perform their duty to their country, and its posterity, and to mankind, by listening to the wise counsels of many conspicuous living sages, and pursue without hesitation the inestimable *"parting advice"* of George Washington, Benjamin Rush, Samuel Adams, and other departed friends and patrons of man, and establish public schools, and judiciously selected free public circulating libraries, in every part of the republic. And as all men are vitally interested in the universal dissemination of knowledge and virtue, let all classes combine their influence and means, in aiding the cause of human happiness.

One of Torrey's suggestions for the raising of the necessary funds for his project is " by a liberal system of duties on ARDENT SPIRITS, for the universal establishment of free LANCASTERIAN SCHOOLS AND FREE PUBLIC LIBRARIES." He continues:

> For this purpose, as well as to discourage intemperance, we earnestly recommend that a duty of fifty cents per gallon be imposed upon all spirituous liquors manufactured within the United States;—and one dollar per gallon upon all wines and spirituous liquors which shall be imported:—the monies accruing from the duties on domestic liquors, to be appropriated to the establishment of free Lancastrian and common schools, and free circulating libraries, in the respective districts in which the taxes shall be levied and collected:—and the duties on imported liquors to be applied to the same purpose, in such manner and place as the wisdom of Congress shall suggest.

Life-boat. It is a curious circumstance that the first life-boat should have been invented by a landsman who had always lived away from the sea and had had no personal experience of the perils against which he was anxious to provide a safeguard. This was Lionel Lukin, a native of Dunmow, and afterward a coach-builder in Long Acre, London. The buoyancy of his boat was secured by a projecting gunwale of cork which was added to its upper frame, and a hollow, water-tight compartment at the bottom of the boat.

Lukin first exhibited a model of what he called his "unim-mergible boat" about the year 1784. George IV, then Prince of Wales, encouraged him by offering to pay the cost of all his experiments. The design was patented in 1785, but the only boat fitted out on Lukin's principle was a Bamborough coble, which was reported to have saved several lives. Lukin died at Hythe, in Kent, in 1834. The following inscription on his tombstone is still legible:

This Lionel Lukin
was the first who built a life-boat, and was the original Inventor of that principle of safety by which many lives and much property have been preserved from shipwreck, and he obtained for it the King's Patent in the year 1785.

Despite royal patronage, Lukin's life-boat attracted little attention. Four years after the issuing of his patent, the *Adventure* was wrecked at the mouth of the Tyne, in the presence of thousands of people, who saw the crew drop off one by one from the rigging, and yet were unable to afford them any assistance for lack of a boat that could live on so rough a sea. This distressing spectacle moved the people of South Shields to offer premiums for the best model of a life-boat. Out of numerous designs two were selected, William Wouldhave's and H. Greathead's. The committee would appear to have combined the two plans of Wouldhave and Greathead, and given the result to the latter to build. At all events, Greathead built the life-boat which was launched at South Shields in 1790. This boat differed from Lukin's in the substitution of cork for the side air-chambers, but its special point of originality was a curved instead of a straight keel. This important improvement is what won for Greathead the title of father of the life-boat. Like all its rivals, however, this boat lacked one great essential: it had no means of freeing itself from water or of self-righting if upset. It performed no important service until 1791, when it saved the crew of a brig at the entrance of the Tyne. Between then and 1797 it saved several other crews. Notwithstanding this, no other life-boat was built until 1798, when the then Duke of Northumberland ordered one to be built at his own expense by Greathead, and also endowed it.

Before the end of 1803 the inventor had built thirty-one of his boats. In 1802, after 200 lives had been saved at the mouth of the Tyne alone, Greathead applied to Parliament for a reward, and received £1200. His original life-boat was lost, in 1821, upon the rocks at the mouth of the Tyne. All hands were saved. A boat which he built in 1802 is still in existence at Redcar in Yorkshire. After doing excellent service for over seventy years it was placed on the retired list and transferred to the shed where it now reposes.

William Wouldhave's partisans have not allowed his claims to go unnoted. His tombstone in the church of St. Hilda in South Shields bears the model of a life-boat and the following quaint inscription:

Sacred to the Memory of
WILLIAM WOULDHAVE,
who died Sept. 28th, 1821,
Aged 70 years.
Clerk of this Church
and Inventor of that invaluable blessing to mankind,
the Lifeboat.

Heaven genius scientifik gave,
Surpassing vulgar boast; yet he from soil
So rich, no golden harvest reaped; no wreathe
Of laurel gleaned, nor but the sailor's heart,
Nor that ingrate, A palm unfading this
Till shipwrecks cease, or lifeboats cease to save.

The idea of Wouldhave's form of boat was suggested to him, it is said, by the following circumstance: Having been asked to assist a woman to put a skeel of water on her head, Mr. Wouldhave noticed that she had a piece of a broken wooden dish lying in the water, which floated with the points upwards, and turning it over several times he found that it always righted itself. This observation suggested to him the construction of his model, but he does not seem to have done more than construct the boat which was long known at Shields by the name of Wouldhave's cork boat.

The father of the life-boat in America was Joseph Francis, born in Boston, March 12, 1801, died in Washington, May 10, 1893. In 1890 Congress voted him a medal of pure gold, said to be the largest and finest ever given by this government to any individual. It was presented to him with appropriate ceremonies at the White House by President Harrison, and is now on exhibition at the National Museum in Washington. As large as a teaplate and two-thirds of an inch thick, its value is placed at $6000. There is also shown in the same museum Francis's original life-car, which saved 201 lives from the wreck of the *Ayrshire* in 1847, and at which people laughed when it was first made.

"You can scarcely imagine," said the then nonagenarian inventor to a reporter on the St. Louis *Globe-Democrat* in April, 1892, "how strong was the popular prejudice against life-boats when they were first introduced. When I conceived the idea of making them out of corrugated iron, people derided the notion, regarding it as a mad freak, inasmuch as every one knew that iron would sink. Commanders of passenger vessels felt insulted by applications to furnish them with life-boats, conceiving them to imply that their ships were not seaworthy or that their own skill in navigation was impugned."

Lightning and its usual accompaniment of thunder were reckoned among the unsolvable mysteries of nature until Benjamin Franklin, 1749, showed, by a happy and bold experiment, the identity of the lightning-flash with electricity. (See LIGHTNING-ROD.) Lightning is simply an electric spark, very often more than a mile long, which passes either between two clouds or between a cloud and the earth. The sound of the thunder which follows varies with the conditions of the lightning. As the flash passes, the air through which it travels becomes heated. There is expansion and compression, and then a sudden rush of air into the partial vacuum thus produced. If the flash be straight and short, the thunder will be heard as a sharp clap; if it be long and not straight, successive peals will be heard one after another, accompanied by a rattle, and, shortly afterward, by a roll, the rolling sound being the echoes from the clouds. The storm is ushered in by phenomena which the observant eye cannot mistake. Warm weather, then sultriness, accompanied by a feeling of depression, which people explain by the familiar expression, "thunder in the air"—these are the preludes to something unusual which is about to happen. The conditions may last for days.

On the horizon a cloud of a peculiar shape may be seen banking itself up like a huge puff of steam. The thunder-cloud is a dense black, and forms overhead. If you watch it, you can see it growing like an army preparing for battle. All clouds are usually charged more or less with electricity. The smallest particle of water which composes the cloud has its own charge. Some particles may have what is known as a positive charge, others a negative. This is supposed to account for the peculiar motions of a cloud bent on business. It heaves itself up as if some unseen power were tearing it asunder by means of attraction and repulsion. The consequence is that parts of clouds break away, charged with more electricity than they can carry. The charge becomes cramped for room, a state of tension ensues, and then the charge leaps across the intervening air-gap from cloud to cloud, or from cloud to earth, in the shape of a lightning-flash.

This is the dangerous time. In its path to earth lightning knows of no obstacle. The duration of the flash seldom lasts more than one-hundred-thousandth part of a second, but in this inconceivable space of time it can do untold damage. Given a perfect conductor, the flash will pass harmlessly to earth; but if the conductor be imperfect, like the mason-work of a chimney-stock or a church-spire, the masonry is shattered as if it were built of cardboard. Sometimes there are heat-effects, as when bell-wires in a house are fused. Other effects of lightning are produced on compass-needles. The magnetism of these necessary instruments to the sailor may be altered or destroyed, and an unknown error in the pointing of the compass may have the most dire results. A ship, struck by lightning, has been known to turn about and make for home, under the impression that it was on its outward course.

Fire-balls rank among the most whimsical of all electrical phenomena. They are not always quite spherical, though this is their normal shape. Usually their contours are clearly defined, yet they are sometimes encircled by a kind of luminous vapor, such as we often see encircling the moon. In size they vary from that of an orange to that of a millstone. One remarkable thing about them is the slowness with which they move, which sometimes enables their course to be watched for several minutes. In October, 1898, a fireball made its appearance in a room in Marseilles and advanced toward a young girl seated at a table. Her feet were hanging down without touching the floor. The luminous globe moved along the floor in the girl's direction, began to rise when quite near her, then circled around her several times in spiral fashion, and finally darted up the chimney, and, on emerging into the open air, gave out upon the roof an appalling crash which shook the entire house.

It was a case of coming in like a lamb and going out like a lion.

A similar occurrence is recorded as having been observed in Paris on July 5, 1852, in a tailor's room. In this case the fire-ball, having escaped up the chimney, produced a tremendous explosion on reaching the summit, which sent the chimney top flying and scattered it in bits all over the neighborhood court-yard and surrounding roofs.

Two remarkable phenomena of this sort are identified with St. Martin of Tours. The story is quaintly recorded in "La Gloire des Confesseurs," a work written by Gregory, the twentieth Bishop of Tours.

On the dedication day of an oratory constructed by Gregory

in one of the outer buildings of the episcopal palace the procession which transferred the relics of St. Martin to the oratory was dazzled and blinded by a brilliant globe of fire that suddenly appeared in their path. Priests, deacons, choristers, and laymen were seized with terror and prostrated themselves, face downward, upon the ground. Then Gregory remembered the legend that on the occasion of the death of St. Martin a globe of fire had been seen to leave the saint's head and ascend heavenward. Gregory decided that he was now in presence of a second miracle, vouchsafed as evidence alike of Martin's sanctity and of the genuineness of his relics. This globe of fire did no damage of any sort. "Discurrebat autem per totam, cellulam, tanquam fulgur, globus igneus."

Lightning often produces wounds of greater or less severity. It perforates the bones and causes injuries similar to those inflicted by firearms. What is more remarkable, it may kill without leaving the slightest mark or abrasion. This fact was known to the ancients. A passage from Plutarch is famous: "Lightning struck them dead without leaving any mark on them, nor any wound or burn—their souls fled from their bodies in fright like a bird which escapes from its cage."

Lightning may cause total or partial paralysis, the loss of speech or sight, temporary or permanent. Among its more harmless pranks is that of shaving off a man's hair and beard, or even depilating the entire body. Generally the victim may consider himself lucky if he leaves a handful of hair as a ransom to the lightning and escapes with a fright.

A case is cited where a young girl of twenty had her hair shaved off as clean as if done by a razor, yet she felt not the slightest shock and was for some minutes unconscious of her loss.

One of the strangest tricks to which lightning is addicted is that of undressing its victims. It displays much more skill and cleverness in such diversions than is to be found in animals or even in many human beings.

Here is one of the most curious instances on record, as narrated by Moraud:

"A woman in man's costume. A storm suddenly comes on. A flash of lightning strikes her, carries off and destroys her clothes and boots. She is left stark naked, and she has to be wrapped up in a cloth and taken thus to the neighboring village."

In certain cases lightning makes a fantastic choice of its victims. It kills one and spares another; it injures a third; it benefits a fourth. It seems to be governed by all sorts of eccentric tastes and peculiarities.

Thus, in April, 1901, lightning struck a stable in the Duchy of Posen and killed ten out of twenty cows housed within. Beginning with the cow nearest the door it spared the second, killed the third and so on. All the uneven numbers were killed, the others were not even scorched. The shepherd who was in the stable at the time rose unhurt. The stable itself escaped, although it was full of straw.

Here is a still more extraordinary story. It would seem that lightning can distinguish between colors and has its preferences. At Lapleau in Corrèze it declared itself in favor of black. One day lightning fell on a grange full of hay and straw and covered with thatch, without setting it on fire. Then it went to the sheepfold, killed seven black sheep and left the white uninjured.

Is it then best to wear long white garments during a storm? M. Flammarion replies that lightning is too uncertain to be depended upon.

An entertaining chapter gives stories of photo-electric pictures made by lightning upon animate and inanimate objects. M. Flammarion attributes them to flashes of a special character, which he terms " Ceraunic rays," from " keraunos," lightning.

A curious story is told of Dr. Derendinger, a Viennese physician. Returning home by rail in the summer of 1865 his purse was stolen on the way.

This purse was made of tortoise shell. On one side was a steel plate marked with the doctor's monogram—two D's intertwined.

Some time after the doctor was called to attend a stranger who had been found lying insensible under a tree. He had been struck by lightning. The first thing he noticed on examining the man's body was that on his thigh there was a reproduction, as though by photography, of his own monogram. His astonishment may be imagined. He succeeded in reviving the stranger, who was taken to a hospital. The doctor told the attendants that a search through the clothes of the patient would probably reveal a tortoise-shell purse. So, indeed, it did. The victim of lightning was the thief. The electric fluid had been attracted by the steel plate and had imprinted the monogram on the body.

Near the village of Combe-Hay, in England, there was a wood composed largely of oaks and nut trees. In the middle of it was a field, about fifty yards long, in which six sheep were struck dead by lightning. When skinned there was discovered on them, on the inside of the skin, a facsimile of part of the adjacent landscape.

This record was communicated by James Shaw to the Meteorological Society of London at its session of March, 1857. Here are his own words:—

"I may add that the small field and its surrounding wood were familiar to me and my schoolmates, and that when the skins were shown to us we at once identified the local scenery so wonderfully represented."

Lightning-rod. No anecdote in American history, save perhaps the incident of Washington and the cherry-tree, is better known than that of Franklin and the kite, whereby the Philadelphia sage is said to have proved his theory of the identity of lightning with electricity. Both stories have been told by that reverend liar M. L. Weems in his respective lives of the two revolutionary worthies. But, whereas Mr. Weems invented the first, he only elaborated the other into the form now generally accepted in school-books. His version appears in chapter xxxv of "The Life of Benjamin Franklin; with many Choice Anecdotes and Admirable Sayings of this Great Man, never before published by any of his Biographers." Philadelphia: Published by Uriah Hunt, 1829. Weems begins by explaining that Franklin " foreseeing what a blessing it would be to mankind to disarm the lightnings of their power to harm," did not, " in the pitiful spirit of modern inventors, cautiously conceal the dawnings of a discovery that promised so much glory to his name. On the contrary, and with a philanthropy that throws eternal loveliness over his character, he published his ideas, inviting all the philosophers to make experiments on this important subject, and even pointed the way—*i.e.*, by insulated bars of iron raised to considerable heights in the air." Nevertheless, it appears that Providence, "pleased with such disinterested virtue," determined to reserve to Franklin, even against his will, the honor of confirming the truth of his own great theory. He went about the matter in that spirit of simplicity which characterized all his actions.

" To a common kite, made of silk rather than paper, because of the rain, he fixed a slender iron point. The string which he chose for his kite was of silk, because of the fondness of lightning for silk; and for the same reason at the lower end of the string he tied a key. With this simple preparation, he went out on the commons back of Philadelphia, as a thundergust was coming on, and raised his kite towards the clouds. The lightning soon found out his metallic rod, as it soared aloft on the wings of the kite, and greeted its polished point with a cordial kiss. With joy he beheld the loose fibres of his string raised by the fond salute of the celestial visitant.

" He hastened to clap his knuckle to the key, and behold! a small spark! Having repeated a second, and a third time, he charged a phial with this strange visitor from the clouds, and found that it exploded gunpowder, set spirits of wine on fire, and performed in all respects as the electric fluid."

It is generally held that the spot where this experiment took place was in the neighborhood of what is now Fourth and Race Streets, though Washington Square, at Sixth and Walnut, also claims the honor. In an engraving which illustrates the story in an early edition of Weems, Franklin is accompanied by his son, represented as a boy of eight or ten, whereas in fact William Temple Franklin was at that period in his twenty-second year.

To come down to historical fact, the whole matter of Franklin's researches into the electrical phenomena of nature, and the manner whereby one of their by-products was the invention of the lightning-rod may be summed up as follows:

In the year 1747 Franklin first turned his attention to this study. One of his London correspondents, Peter Collinson, had presented to the Philadelphia Library a glass tube of the kind then used for producing electricity by rubbing with silk or skin. Franklin was fascinated. "For my own part," he says in a letter to Collinson, dated March 28, 1747, "I never was before engaged in any study that so totally engrossed my attention and my time . . . for what with making experiments when I can be alone, and repeating them to my friends and acquaintance, who, from the novelty of the thing, come continually in crowds to see them, I have during some months past, had little leisure for anything else." Among the crowds came three men who were actuated by something more than idle curiosity,—Ebenezer Kinnersley, Thomas Hopkinson, and Philip Syng. They collaborated with him, and Franklin reported the results of all their labors, as well as his own, to Peter Collinson by letter. Within six months Hopkinson had observed the power of points to throw off "electrical fire," as he called it; Syng had invented an electrical machine, consisting of a sphere revolved on an axis with a handle, which was better fitted than tube-rubbing for throwing off the electrical spark; and Franklin had discovered and described what is now known as positive and negative electricity. Then followed Franklin's attempts to identify lightning with the electric spark produced by mechanical means. Collinson duly laid all Franklin's letters before the Royal Society of London. Franklin was laughed at, but Collinson refused to join in the laughter. He induced Edward Cave, printer and the editor of the *Gentleman's Magazine,* to issue an abstract entitled "New Experiments and Observations in Electricity made at Philadelphia in America" (1751). One copy passed over to France, and was warmly welcomed by Count de Buffon, then the greatest name in contemporary science. At his request, it was translated into French, and its enormous vogue prompted succeeding translations into German, Latin, and Italian.

Louis XV insisted that every experiment described in the pamphlet should be repeated in his presence. Abbé Nollet, who taught the royal children natural philosophy, was sceptical at first, even insisting that no such person as Benjamin Franklin had ever existed, but had simply been invented by his own enemies to tease him, for was not he himself engaged on researches into the nature of electricity?

Up to this time the lightning-rod and its uses in warding off the thunderbolt from buildings and living creatures had not been practically tested. It existed only as a very definite conception in Franklin's mind. He had outlined the idea in a letter to Collinson dated July 29, 1750, stating his belief that lightning could be attracted by points as was the machine-made electricity, and suggesting that a man stand in a sort of sentry-box on the top of some high tower or steeple and with a pointed rod draw electricity from passing thunder-clouds. He lamented that the experiment could not be tried in Philadelphia, because there was no eminence there high enough for the purpose, little dreaming that the electric current would be as active in a valley as on the top of the Alps.

This suggestion was seized upon by Buffon, D'Alibard, and Du Lor. Each hastened to test it and each succeeded. But they did not use steeples; they erected lofty iron rods. D'Alibard bore off the first honors. On a hill at Morly, May 10, 1752, he raised a rod ninety-nine feet high, " a thunderbolt having passed over the place where the bar stood, those who were appointed to observe it drew near and attracted from it sparks of fire, the same kind of commotion as in the common electrical experiment."

Ere Franklin heard of this transatlantic verification of his theory, he could write them that the same experiment had succeeded in Philadelphia though made in a different and an easier manner. Discarding the idea of a steeple, he had not even undertaken to erect a lofty iron rod. He had simply discovered that a kite would answer all purposes. He thus describes the kite and the process of utilizing it:

Make a small cross of two light strips of cedar, the arms so long as to reach to the four corners of a large thin silk handkerchief when extended; tie the corners of the handkerchief to the extremities of the cross, so you have the body of a kite, which, being properly accommodated with a tail, loop, and string, will rise in the air, like those made of paper; but this being made of silk is easier to bear the wet and wind of a thunder-gust without tearing. To the top of the upright stick of the cross is to be fixed a very sharp pointed wire, rising a foot or more above the wood. To the end of the twine, next the hand, is to be tied a silk ribbon, and where the silk and twine join, a key may be fastened. The kite is to be raised when a thunder-gust appears to be coming on, and the person who holds the string must stand within a door or window, or under some cover, so that the silk ribbon may not be wet; and care must be taken that the twine does not touch the frame of the door or window. As soon as any of the thunder-clouds come over the kite, the pointed wire will draw the electric fire from them, and the kite with all the twine will be electrified, and the loose filaments of the twine will stand out every way and be attracted by an approaching finger. And when the rain has wetted the kite and twine, so that it can conduct the electric fire freely, you will find it stream out plentifully from the key on the approach of your knuckle. At this key the phial may be charged: and from electric fire thus obtained, spirits may be kindled, and all the electric experiments be performed which are usually done by the help of a rubbed glass globe or tube, and thereby the sameness of the electric matter with that of lightning completely demonstrated.

Franklin never wrote out the kite story, though he told it to Priestley and to others in conversation, whence it found its way to the public, and he did not deny it when it appeared in print. In his Autobiography he makes this passing allusion both to the first French experiment and to his own: "I will not swell this narrative with an account of that capital experiment, nor of the infinite pleasure I received in the success of a similar one I made soon after with a kite at Philadelphia, as both are to be found in the histories of electricity." This paragraph was written in 1784.

Agassiz opines that every important invention or discovery must undergo three stages of opposition. Its enemies urge—

First. It isn't true.

Second. It is impious.

Third. It isn't new.

This process was exemplified in the case of the lightning-rod. As soon as it had established itself as a truth, it was assailed as an insult to Providence. Later it was attacked as a plagiarism.

John Adams reports one wiseacre who as late as 1758 began to prate upon the presumption of philosophy in erecting iron rods to draw the lightning from the clouds. "He railed and foamed against the presumption that erected them, in language taken partly from Scripture and partly from the disputes of tavern philosophy, in as wild and mad a manner as King Lear raves against his daughters' disobedience and ingratitude. . . . He talked of presuming upon God, as Peter attempted to walk upon the water; attempting to control the artillery of heaven—an execution that mortal man can't stay."

The Rev. Thomas Prince, reasoning on a religio-scientific basis, attributed to the multiplication of lightning-rods the earthquake shock of 1755, expounding his theory from the pulpit in this wise:

The more points of iron are erected round the earth to draw

the electrical substance out of the air, the more the Earth must needs be charged with it. And therefore it seems worthy of consideration, whether any part of the earth being full of this terrible substance may not be more exposed to more shocking earthquakes. In Boston are more erected than anywhere else in New England, and Boston seems to be more dreadfully shaken. Oh, there is no getting out of the mighty hand of God! If we think to avoid it in the air, we cannot in the earth. Yea, it may grow more fatal."

So late as 1770 it was maintained that, as lightning " is one of the means of punishing the sins of mankind and of warning them from the commission of sin, it is impious to prevent its full execution."

George III, having good cause to dislike Franklin's political opinions, sought to discredit his scientific ones by ordering the substitution of blunt for pointed ends on Kew Palace. Seeking from Sir John Pringle a commendation of the change, he was told in uncourtierly words that " the laws of nature are not changeable at royal pleasure." Whereupon Sir John received an intimation that a president of the Royal Society entertaining such an opinion ought to resign, and he resigned accordingly, and to the end of his life was pursued by the royal displeasure. Franklin, all unwitting of the disasters that had been heaped upon his friend, cheerily wrote that the king's action is " a matter of small importance to me," adding, " if I had a wish about it, it would be that he had rejected them altogether as ineffectual. For it is only since he thought himself and family safe from the thunder of heaven that he dared to use his own thunder in destroying his innocent subjects."

The court sided with the king, the wits with the philosopher:

> While you, great George, for safety hunt
> And sharp conductors change for blunt,
>   The nation's out of joint.
> Franklin a wiser course pursues,
> And all your thunder fearless views
>   By keeping to the point.

The world was now ripe for the third stage in the anti-lightning-rod crusade.

Very soon after Franklin's invention was announced, a French professor cited some ancient Roman and Tuscan instructions how to call down (*elicere*) lightning, and he pointed out that the Romans had a regular rite for Jupiter Elicius. The further fact was recalled that on the top of the highest tower of the Castle of Dunio on the Adriatic a long rod of iron, set up from time immemorial, served to predict the coming of equinoc-

tial storm.s. A soldier was always stationed beside it when the
sea threatened a tempest. From time to time he put the point of
his long javelin close to the rod. Whenever a spark passed between the two pieces of iron, he rang a bell to warn the fishermen. The Celtic nations also were in the habit of sticking their
swords in the earth with the point upward, near springs, on
the approach of a thunder-storm, as a protection against lightning. The Persian king Artaxerxes had some knowledge of the
power of iron to attract lightning. Again, Josephus Flavius,
in describing the great temple of Herod in Jerusalem, states that
the roof was studded with an army of golden points, and that a
similar arrangement was found on the earlier temples of Solomon
and Zerubbabel. It is stated that none of these temples, in spite
of their location upon an altitude, was ever struck by the lightning. Coming down to the Middle Ages, an edict of Charlemagne mentions that the peasants were in the habit of setting
up long pointed poles in the ground on the approach of a storm,
and in a sermon of St. Bernardinus of Siena, it is related how
sailors would bind a sword with its point directed upward to
the mast of their vessel on the approach of a storm.

Apparently a good prima facie case could be made against
Franklin. Dr. Hennig, however puts down all instances of this
kind to pure superstition. The idea was to frighten away the
storm demons by means of the upwardly-directed swords. Among
uncivilized peoples it is a common custom to threaten approaching storms by the din of arms, and the ancient Gauls and
Romans would shoot arrows into the gathering storm clouds
to ward off the hostile powers of the weather.

As regards the golden points upon the temple at Jerusalem
and other places, Josephus himself tells us that the purpose of
these points was to keep off the birds.   .

An unavailing attempt also has been made to unearth a pre-
cursor of Franklin in Prokop Divis (1696-1765), who really
was a contemporary working along the same lines, though the
American outstripped him by a couple of years. Divis was a
Catholic priest, a native of Zamberk, Bohemia, who in his latter
days, as pastor of Prendice in Southern Moravia, devoted his
leisure to physical experiments, and independently worked out
the propositions that lightning was but an electric spark and
that metallic points would attract and discharge electricity more
speedily than anything else. Emperor Francis Stephen invited
him to Vienna in 1750 to repeat his experiments before the
imperial court.

In 1753 Professor Reichman, of St. Petersburg, while observing a storm from a hut, was killed by lightning that descended

an insulated iron bar specially erected for purposes of study. Divis showed that an iron bar of this sort was unsafe and dangerous, and explained how in case of a storm a stroke of lightning could be averted by a conductor, an idea that had been gradually maturing in his mind. The proposition was derided by the Berlin Academy of Science, which does not seem yet to have heard of Franklin's recent experiments, unknown also to the Bohemian priest. Nevertheless, Divis constructed a long rod which on June 15, 1754, he erected at Prendice. A storm came rushing on from the north. "Shafts of lightning were seen darting from the clouds and flying towards the conductor. In a few minutes a white cloud enveloped the machine. The storm soon passed away without doing any damage." So runs a contemporary account. In 1756 Divis was compelled to remove his machine by the superstitious clamor of the neighboring farmers, and it was taken to Bruck, where it still remains.

Lion. Frances Power Cobbe was one of the earliest of the lion's detractors. She calls the King of Beasts " a great carnivorous impostor," challenges its claim to majesty, and asks proof of its supposed magnanimity and generosity " beyond the blandness of its Harold Skimpole countenance and the disdainful manner in which it throws back its mane, as if it were quite incapable of the pettiness (of which it is, nevertheless, frequently guilty) of picking up and eating a humble black beetle." It is true also that the lion is sometimes excelled in size and generally in ferocity by the tiger, in elegance of the form by the leopard and jaguar, and in beauty of coloring by most of the great cats. Yet it would be useless, even if it were advisable, to try to depose the lion from the throne on which universal consent has established him.

It would be useless, because the magnificent presence and kingly voice of the lion would always suffice to rethrone it as often as it was dethroned. It would be unadvisable because no other beast could be crowned in its stead.

Yet, despite its awesome voice and presence, the lion is not really courageous. The ancients, recognizing this, put a lion's head upon their statues of Fear. It avoids attacking any formidable antagonist. It dreads man and all his works. It skulks in secluded places where it can lie hidden and pounce upon passing prey. If it misses its aim, it sulks, but rarely pursues. Worst of all, it is a humbug. Livingstone tells us that when it is scared it trots away slowly until it thinks it is out of sight and then bounds off like a greyhound.

King James I, according to Howe's Chronicles, often sought

to divert his friends with lion fights in the Tower, but as often failed, owing to the unwillingness of the captives.

> There were divers other lions put into that place one after another, but they showed no more sport nor valor than the first; and every one of them, so soon as they espied the trap-doors open, ran hastily into their dens. Lastly there were put forth together the two young lusty lions which were bred in the yard, and were now grown great. These at first began to march proudly towards the bear, which the bear perceiving came hastily out of a corner to meet them; but both lion and lioness skipped up and down and fearfully fled from the bear, and so these, like the former lions, not willing to endure any fight, sought the next way into their den.

Did Shakespeare hint at this trait in the king of beasts in the play scene in " Midsummer Night's Dream "?

> *Snug.* Have you the lion's part written? Pray you, if it be, give it me, for I am slow of study.
> *Quince.* You may do it extempore, for it is nothing but roaring.

Lions and tigers have often been put together to fight, but the lion has invariably declined the combat. They have accidentally got into each other's cages, and the tiger has killed the lion. As regards their comparative courage in the presence of man, all the evidence is in favor of the tiger. Yet the poets nearly always insist on having it the other way. From Spenser to Allan Ramsay, they claim that the lion defeated the tiger in single combat when the prize was the sovereignty of the animal world. Hearken to John Wilson:

> The shaggy lion rushes to the place,
> With roar tremendous seizes on his prey.
> Exasperate see! The tiger springs away,
> Stops short, and maddens at the monarch's growl;
> And through his eyes darts all his furious soul.
> Half willed yet half afraid to dare a bound,
> He eyes his loss, and roars and tears the ground.

Lloyd's. Some confusion has arisen from the fact that there are two establishments in London, both identified (though in different ways) with the shipping interests, that are known to their respective clientèles as Lloyd's. The first and most ancient is Lloyd's Subscription Rooms in the eastern part of the Royal Exchange; the other is Lloyd's Register of British and Foreign Shipping at 71 Fenchurch Street.

The first is an association of underwriters for the collection and distribution of maritime and shipping intelligence. It had its origin in the later seventeenth century in the meeting of merchants for business and gossip in a coffee-house kept by Edward Lloyd in Tower Street, London. The earliest mention of these meetings occurs in the London *Gazette* for February 18, 1668; but they are there spoken of as no new thing. Their growing importance induced Lloyd, in 1692, to remove his coffee-house to Lombard Street. Soon afterward he began the issue of *Lloyd's News,* devoted to mercantile and maritime information, which was eventually succeeded by the daily *Lloyd's List,* still extant as the second oldest newspaper in London. In 1774 the association moved to the Royal Exchange, in 1811 it was reorganized, and in 1871 incorporated. Its agents are to be found in every large seaport of the world.

"Lloyd's Register," which is entirely distinct from *Lloyd's List* or its publishers, is an annual volume issued by an association of ship-owners, merchants, and underwriters. This was established with the object of securing an accurate classification of the sea-worthiness of mercantile vessels. The earliest copy extant is dated 1764–5–6. Here we find already adopted the familiar classification of ships in groups, designated by the vowels A, E, I, O, and U (see A 1).

Loaf, a Monster. One of the exhibits of the Louisiana Purchase Exposition, held at St. Louis in 1904, was a loaf of bread weighing 100 pounds. The baker who sent it in, Andrew Newberg, of Austin, Texas, claimed that it was the largest loaf in the world. The claim was never contested. But in 1911 Mr. Newberg broke his own record by contributing a still larger loaf to a barbecue in Moulton, Texas, where it was cut and distributed to a large crowd. Here is a contemporary record: "This gigantic mass of the staff of life weighed 140 pounds and was two feet high, three feet wide, and twelve feet long. After the ingredients were mixed the baking process consumed over an hour, a special oven being used for the purpose. Mr. Newberg accompanied the bread to its destination to see that it was safely carried."

London Stone. This famous stone, for long ages the most noted landmark of the ancient city, is now (reduced to a fragment of about a cubic foot) built into a niche in the outside wall of the church of St. Swithin and St. Mary Bothaw in Cannon Street, being visible through a circular opening covered by an iron grating or grille. The fragment thus preserved constitutes a portion of the stone pillar that stood in Cannon Street, on what was, before the great fire of 1666, the highest ground in London. After this catastrophe, which broke out near the stone, the ground was graded and its level changed. Even before the fire the original stone was much worn away, and it was then cased over by a new stone having an aperture at the top through which the venerable relic could be seen. Its site, according to some authorities, marked the middle of the ancient Watling Street. "On the south side of this high street" (Canwick Street), says Stow, "neere unto the chauncell, is pitched upright a great stone called 'London Stone,' fixed in the ground very deep, fastened with bars of iron and otherwise so stronglie set, that if cartes do runn against it through negligence, the wheeles be broken and the stone itself unshaken. The cause why this stone was there set, the very time when, or other memory hereof, is there none; but that the same hath long continued there, is manifest, namely since, or rather before the time of the conquest." Camden considers the stone to have been the great central milliarium or mile-stone of London under the Romans (similár to that in the forum of Rome), from which all British high-roads radiated and all distances were measured.

But it is possible that the Romans simply made use of a monument they already found standing.

When Sir Christopher Wren changed the grade of the streets after the fire, he found the foundations so extensive that he was convinced the stone must have been once enclosed in or formed part of, some large building. Tradition asserts that the stone was the altar of the Temple of Diana on which the ancient British kings took the oath on their accession, being only kings presumptive till they had laid their hands on this stone. This seems borne out by the fact that Jack Cade, when he entered London in 1450, struck his staff on London Stone and exclaimed: " Now is Mortimer lord of the city . . . and now, henceforward, it shall be treason for any that calls me other than Lord Mortimer."

The stone was regarded as a sort of palladium of the city, having, according to a more remote legend, been brought hither from Troy by Brutus, and with his own hand laid as the foundation of London. An ancient saw ran:

> Tra maen Prydain
> Tra lled Llyndain.

(Meaning: " So long as the stone of Brutus is safe, so long will London flourish.")

Here proclamations and announcements of importance were wont to be made. In " Pasquil and Marforius " is the command: " Set up this bill on London Stone. Let it be done solemnly with drum and trumpet." And again: " If it pleases them these dark winter nights to stick uppe their papers upon London Stone."

Lone Tree, an immense cottonwood, 4 feet thick and very tall, which stood in Nebraska, almost in the centre of the continent, half way between New York and San Francisco,—or, to be exact, within one mile of that centre. Under its branches rested thousands of the Argonauts of '49 *en route* to the Eldorado of the Pacific coast. In fact, it was the best-known camping ground along the old California trail. From 1849, when the gold seekers rushed across the great plains, down to the completion of the Union Pacific Railroad, the cottonwood stood out boldly as a guidepost to the wagon trains trekking westward. Being one of the few trees between the Missouri and the Rockies, it soon became the best-known landmark on the trail. After the railroad was completed and there was no further use for the old tree, it incontinently rotted away and died.

In 1910 a monument was erected to the tree on the spot it had occupied, haply, for centuries, by survivors of the Nebraska pioneers and by other men who held it in kindly memory. It was made from Vermont marble and was chiselled in the East. It represents the trunk of a giant cottonwood and bears this inscription:

"On this spot stood the original Lone Tree on the old California trail."

Lot's Wife. In the Library of Congress, at Washington, there is a specimen of rock salt, taken from a pillar of salt, near the Dead Sea (*q.v.*), known locally as Lot's wife. This was given to the Library by Mr. Edward P. Montague, Editor of a book entitled, "A Narrative of the late Expedition to the Dead Sea, from a Diary of one of the Party" (Philadelphia, 1849). Under date of April 26, 1848, the Diary tells how the party explored the Dead Sea in a row-boat, and were especially impressed by an immense column rounded and turret-shaped, facing towards the southeast.

"This we are told by our Arabs is the Pillar of Salt in which Lot's wife was encased at the overthrow of Sodom. With some difficulty we landed here, and our esteemed commander and Dr. Anderson obtained specimens from it, and Mr. Dale took a sketch of it. Our boat's crew landed also, and their curiosity was gratified by their gathering specimens, some from its summit, and others from its base. It was measured, and found to be sixty feet in height, and forty feet in circumference. We cannot suppose that Lot's wife was a person so large that her dimensions equalled those of this column. Many think the statue of Lot's wife was equal to the pillar of salt which the Bible speaks of. Let that pillar be where it may, and whatever its size, they will not probably credit that that is the pillar. Their preconceived notions having much to do with the matter, they would have everybody think that she was at once transformed into a column of fine grained beautifully *white* salt, about five feet or a few inches more in height, and in circumference that of a common sized person of the nineteenth century. Be that as it may, no two minds have, perhaps, formed exactly the same opinion on this matter who have not visited this spot. But here we are, around this immense column, and we find that it is really of solid rock salt—one mass of crystallization. It is in the vicinity which is pointed out in the Bible in relation to the matter in question, and it appears to be the only one of its kind here. My own opinion of the matter is, that Lot's wife having lingered behind, in disobedience to the expressed commands of God—given in order to insure her safety—that while so lingering she became overwhelmed in the descending fluid, and formed the model or foundation of this extraordinary column."

Lotteries were known to the ancients. Did not the Roman soldiers cast lots for the raiment of our Saviour at the very foot of the cross? They were following a long-established custom. Lotteries were features of the Roman saturnalia and of the banquets of the aristocracy under the empire. Some of the emperors adopted lotteries on a grand scale. Nero's prizes were sometimes a house, and at others a slave. Heliogabalus introduced the element of absurdity; one prize would be perhaps a golden vase, and the next six flies.

At various times in the history of the modern world lotteries have been employed as a source of revenue by the governments. They have always proved a sure and ready means for replenishing a depleted treasury. But they have always resulted in the impoverishment and demoralization of the people. Particularly disastrous were their effects upon the poor. Between 1816 and 1828, lotteries yielded an annual income of 14,000,000 francs to the French government. In May, 1836, they were suppressed. Next January it was found that 525,000 francs more were on deposit in the savings-banks of Paris alone than in the corresponding month of the preceding year. Parliamentary lotteries existed in England from 1709 till 1826. Their harmful influence began to attract attention in 1819. It took seven years of agitation to secure their suppression,—so powerful were the interests that backed them.

Lotteries appeared in the United States very early in its history. They were legacies from the colonial period and from the mother-land herself. In the year 1612 " his gracious Majesty, King James I, in special favor for the plantation of the English colonies in Virginia, granted a lottery to be held at the west end of St. Paul's; whereof one Thomas Sharplys, a tailor of London, had the chief prize, which was 4000 crowns in fair plate." Still another drawing for the same laudable purpose was organized in 1619.

Harvard College owed its early prosperity to the same source. In 1772 the General Court of Massachusetts granted that college the right of holding a lottery to improve the condition of its treasury. In 1794, in answer to a petition from the corporation, and again in 1806, the grant was repeated. On the last occasion $29,000 was raised. Other colleges, as well as hospitals and churches, owed their origin to the same means.

Roads, bridges, and other public works were constructed. The attendant evils were too insidious to be noticed at once. Finally cumulative disaster wrought its own remedy. The first movement for the suppression of lotteries began in Pennsylvania in 1833, and extended so rapidly to other States that by 1875 no fewer than 26 States had passed laws for abolishing them and making the advertisement of them or of foreign lotteries a penal offence.

Louisiana was the last State to hold out against the reform. Before the civil war, indeed, a general law forbidding lotteries existed on the statute books. During the " carpet-bag " régime in 1868, this law was superseded by an act granting a charter to the Louisiana State Lottery for a term of 25 years, at an annual license fee of $10,000.

Stowe, a good authority on contemporary matters, says that the first English lottery took place in 1569, by order of Queen Elizabeth, beginning January 11th and continuing day and night till May 6, a period of 115 days, probably the longest on record. It was drawn at the west door of St. Paul's Cathedral, a temporary building being erected there for the purpose. The profits were applied toward the repairs of the harbors and fortifications. The capital prize was of the value of £5000. Of this amount £3000 was paid in cash, £700 in plate and jewelry, and the rest, according to an authority, in " good tapestry, meet for hangings, and other covertures, and certain sorts of good linen cloth." The various prizes, apart from the money, were placed on view " at the house of Mr. Dericke, the queen's goldsmith, in Cheapside," and attached to the original proclamation, which is still in the possession of the Society of Antiquaries, was a sheet of wood cuts representing the various pieces of gold and silver plate. The price of the tickets was 10 shillings each and their total number 400,000. They were subdivided into halves and quarters, and these still further " for convenience of the poorer classes."

So popular did the scheme become that it eventually was merged into a patent monopoly, the rights being leased out to various speculators, whose individual profits were, of course, enormous. The most popular lottery at this time, and one which maintained its existence until the end of the eighteenth century, was known as "The Royal Oak Lottery," because it was originally established after the Restoration, for the relief of "loyal and indigent officers" who had suffered during the Revolution and whom it was not convenient to recompense by drafts upon the exchequer. Eventually this lapsed into a mere public gaming company under royal license, paying the crown £4000 a year for its privileges.

The dearth of public funds was the moving cause of the first lottery for public purposes. This was in 1694, when money was wanted for that siege of Namur in which Captain Shandy and Corporal Trim afterwards distinguished themselves; but the lottery was in fact a loan with prizes thrown in as a bonus; for, while the tickets were ten pounds each, the very blanks were entitled to twenty shillings a year for sixteen years.

During madding times of the South Sea bubble, the drawings of most of the accredited lotteries took place at the Guildhall. On such occasions the old civic building was the scene of the greatest excitement. So great was the excitement that poor medical practitioners would attend the meetings, with lancets all ready for bleeding people who might be overpowered by emotion on hearing the fate of the tickets they held.

At the drawing, cards or pieces of paper, inscribed with as many numbers as there were tickets, were placed in a hollow wheel. These were drawn out, one by one, usually by a boy from the Bluecoat School, the number it bore being announced to the audience; from a second and similar wheel another Bluecoat boy would then draw out a paper on which was inscribed either the fateful word "blank" or the amount of a certain prize.

Clergymen as well as laymen, in the Old World as in the New, did not scruple to avail themselves of the opportunities offered by a lottery, and piously thanked the Almighty when luck favored them. So good and holy a man as the Reverend Samuel Seabury, father of the first Protestant Episcopal bishop in the United States, made the following entry in his diary under date of June, 1768. "The ticket No. 5866, by the blessing of God, in the Light-house and Public Lottery of New York, appointed by law, Anno Domini 1768, drew in my favor £500, of which I received £425, which the deduction of fifteen per cent. makes £500, for which I now record to my posterity my thanks and praise to Almighty God, the Giver of all good gifts. Amen!"

In *Chambers's Journal* for January 27, 1866, a former Bluecoat boy tells this among other stories of his own early experiences in lotteries: "Even pious folks were bitten by the spirit of gambling, and I remember a lady of great respectability and benevolence, whose husband had made her the present of a lottery ticket, actually causing prayers to be offered up in a church in Holborn for her good luck. It is to be hoped that when the clergyman read out from his pulpit, 'The petitions of this congregations are desired for the success of a person engaged in a new undertaking,'—which was the form of words used—that he did not know what they were to pray for."

The year 1714 is notable for the greatest lottery ever held in England and probably in the world. The total amount of money subscribed amounted to £1,500,000, a truly prodigious sum when it is considered how much greater the relative value of money was in those days than to-day. In 1736 a special act of Parlia-

ment was passed, authorizing a public lottery for the purpose of
providing funds for the building of a bridge over the River
Thames at Westminster. To this end 125,000 tickets, of the
face value of £5 each, were quickly disposed of. Encouraged
by its success, Parliament sanctioned other lotteries in succession,
until the bridge was finally completed and paid for. By another
act, passed in 1753, the sum of £300,000 was raised by similar
means and expended upon the primary purchases of collections,
from which the British Museum was ultimately formed.

But the most sensational of all lotteries was a private adventure which offered a thousand pounds for a penny. Two hundred
thousand tickets at a penny apiece were disposed of within two
days. The drawing took place at Dorset Gardens Theatre, Salisbury Square, on October 19, 1698. The winner, according to a
story circulated by the promoters of the lottery, was a poor boy,
who owed his good fortune to his charity. A poor old woman
in Branford had solicited alms from him, and he gave her all he
had, a slice of bread and butter. At their next meeting she
presented him with a penny, telling him to keep it till a chance
offered. The boy invested it in a lottery ticket and won the
capital prize. One thousand pounds for a penny is proportionately the largest winning known in all lottery history. There
were not wanting sceptics, however, who declared that they had
heard the story before and that the whole affair was a swindle.

The largest actual prize ever won in an English lottery was
the famous Pigot diamond, provided you accept its preliminary
valuation, £40,000. This was the capital prize in a lottery in
January, 1801, and became the property of a young man, who,
however, sold it for a comparatively low price. Later it was
disposed of to the Pasha of Egypt for £30,000.

No formal estimate of value could be put upon the Leverian
Museum, a magnificent collection of natural history and other
curiosities formed by Sir Arthur Lever, which was disposed of in
this manner in 1784, the winner being a Mr. Parkinson. Nor
could any mere sum of money express the actual value of
Boydell's Shakespeare Gallery of pictures by Reynolds, North-
coke, West, and other celebrated painters which was lotteried
in 1784.

Capital prizes of £20,000 not unfrequently headed the list
at some of the great lottery drawings. The first person to win a
prize of this amount in its entirety was James Calvert in 1780.
He was the owner of a large vinegar factory, still standing in
the City Road, London. Strangely enough, in a succeeding
lottery he won another prize of £5000. Yet he lived to see all of
his immense fortune squandered in futile striving after a repe-

tition of his exceptional good luck, and died in 1799 in the direst poverty.

In 1809 Christopher Bartholomew died in a mean garret in Windmill Street. At one time he had been sole owner of two celebrated and valuable hostelries, the White Conduit House and the Angel Inn at Islington, and had also inherited a large fortune in money from his parents. Not content with this degree of wealth, he became imbued with the mania for lottery gambling, being known to expend and lose as much as £1000 on tickets in a single day. He was ultimately forced to subsist on the charity of his old-time friends. By some freak of chance it was at this period he made his first winning, the thirty-second share of a £20,000 prize. With the money he was persuaded to purchase a small annuity; but, the old fever coming over him once more, he lost even that in lottery speculation and died a simple pauper.

An anti-lottery pamphlet put forward in the later eighteenth century summarized other examples of the havoc caused by the lottery craze. A Kentish squire lost his six hundred a year in five months; a nobleman's steward gambled away his own estate and part of his master's; a West India widow lost the cargo of two ships; an honest lady at St. James sold her plate to continue her play, and lost the last remnants of her fortune. A silkman from Ludgate, a young draper from Cornhill, a country parson, and a host of others accuse the Royal Oak of their ruin. So "Squire Lottery" is indicted and condemned to death.

The Squire Lottery of history, however, survived this and many other hard knocks for a half century longer. On October 18, 1826, the last state lottery was drawn in England, and almost immediately afterward an act of Parliament came into force rendering all such forms of gambling unconstitutional and illegal.

There were not a few who regretted the death of Squire Lottery. Among the mourners was Charles Lamb. He whimsically protested that the abolition of the lottery limited the area of hopes and expectations, which, however baseless they might be, had abundant value of their own in cheering the dead level of humdrum existence. "The true mental epicure," he wrote, "always purchased his ticket early and postponed inquiry as to its fate to the last possible moment, during the whole of which intervening period he had an imaginary twenty thousand pounds locked up in his desk, and was not this well worth all the money?" And he sympathetically describes the happiness of a gentleman who by the mistake of a lottery office enjoyed for ten minutes the sensation of possessing £20,000.

The journals of Charles Young supply a ghastly story told by Theodore Hook in the actor-clergyman's presence. Hook was travelling by stage from London to Sudbury. Inside the coach he had but one companion, a brown-faced, melancholy-looking man, with an expression of great querulousness, quite in character with the tone of his conversation, which was one of ceaseless complaining. "Sir," said he, "you may have known unfortunate men, possibly, in your day—you may, for aught I know, be an unfortunate man yourself—but I do not believe there is such another unfortunate man as I am in the whole world. No man ever had more brilliant prospects than I have had in my time, and every one of them, on the very eve of fulfilment, has been blighted. 'Twas but the other day that I thought I would buy a ticket in the lottery. I did so, stupid ass that I was, and took a sixteenth. Sir, I had no sooner bought it than I repented of my folly, and, feeling convinced that it would be a blank, I got rid of it to a friend, who I knew would thank me for the favor, and at the same time save me from another disappointment. By Jove! sir, would you believe it?—I know you won't; but it is true—it turned up thirty thousand pounds."

"Heaven and earth!" said Hook, "it is incredible. If it had happened to me, I should certainly have cut my throat."

"Well," said he, "of course you would, and so did I;" and, baring his neck, he exposed to Hook's horror-stricken gaze a freshly-healed cicatrix from ear to ear.

Hook himself dabbled in the lottery and had his superstition concerning lucky numbers. Once in his later years, when he was completely ruined and deeply in debt, he applied to his friend Shackell for money to purchase a ticket of a certain number in a Hamburg lottery. Hook's story ran that while he was seated at his fireside late the night before, looking steadily into the grate while pondering over his own unfortunate affairs, and the chance of bettering them by gaining some big lottery prize, he had seen the number to which he referred distinctly indicated in the live embers of the fire, and felt confident it was a good omen. Shackell humored Hook's whim, purchased the ticket, and to his no very great surprise it drew a blank. Next year Hook repeated the request, and in regard to the very same number, asserting that he had again seen the figures more than once, and more distinctly than ever, and that he was convinced luck would this time be in his favor. Shackell, however, refused to be persuaded, and afterward learned from Hook that he had found a clue to the mystery. It seems that the fire grate had certain raised figures at its back, forming the manufacturer's number, and that when the fire had burned itself low and the back of the grate was still red-hot, these figures were readily discernible through the embers; hence Hook's superstitious fancy that he had alighted upon a winning number in the Hamburg lottery.

An English newspaper in 1867 told a sad story of M. Brandimarte Saletti, secretary of the Municipal Council of Florence. He had asked his head clerk to purchase four lottery tickets for him, the numbers of which he knew were not as yet sold, at 25 francs each, and accordingly handed him a hundred-franc note. The clerk, a most trustworthy person, carefully folded the note and placed it in his waistcoat pocket. Meeting a friend on his way home, however, he utterly forgot the commission, till next morning, as he passed the lottery office, it recurred to him. It was too late; the numbers his employer had desired him to purchase had been bought up, and the list closed. On reaching his office he found M. Saletti absorbed in business, and he determined to delay the confession of his lapsus of memory till after the drawing. He therefore dived into his own particular office, and said nothing. M. Saletti, however, an inveterate lottery player, was on the alert, and at the exact hour rushed to the nearest office, where the pleasant spectacle greeted him of the four numbers he had selected having won no less than 1,800,000 francs. Wild with delight, M. Saletti rushed home to tell the glad news, and the frantic excitement of the family can be conceived. On his way back to the Hotel de Ville he met the syndic of Florence, M. Terezzi, whose congratulations were most hearty; then Count Cambray-Digny, the finance minister, who did his best to calm him, and laughingly said, "Only think of its being you who thus help to empty the treasury." Once in his own office, he rang. More dead than alive, appeared his head clerk. "Give me quickly the receipt," asked M. Saletti. "Here, sir, are the hundred francs." "What hundred francs?" "Do what you will with me, sir; send me to the gallows or to the guillotine; but I forgot to buy the tickets!"

In Italy, and especially in Naples, lottery speculation still runs riot under governmental sanction. Every Saturday a drawing is made. On Friday evenings, when the last numbers may be played, the stations of the Banco Lotto are filled with people: poor folk playing 4 cents, which is the lowest received, housewives playing 10 cents or a lira, footmen placing 10 and 20 lire for their mistresses. A slip is given, marked with the numbers you have chosen, and then, once a week, a child from the foundling asylum draws the numbers from the bag, in the presence of a regularly constituted committee, who see that the drawing is fair. When a popular number is drawn, there are cheers, as when, after the great Messina earthquake, the number

28 came out. That was the date of the disaster, and the number had been played by thousands. The government lost more heavily that week than for years previous.

Everybody plays dates when anything unusual occurs. Books are published which supply factitious numbers for even domestic happenings. Animate and inanimate things are tagged with numerals. An American long resident in Naples told a newspaper correspondent of his experiences.

"When people came to call, they talked of numbers," said this authority. "For instance, one day a dog ran into the drawing-room of one of our acquaintances, upset a valuable vase, and threw the master of the house almost into an apoplectic fit with rage. His daughter played the numbers for 'dog,' 'vase' and 'anger.' She won some money, and told us about it gleefully. She explained further, that if one runs into a very blonde or very dark person in turning a corner, you play 'meeting' and 'dark' or 'fair,' as the case may be. When a letter is lost you play 'letter' and 'loss.' There were numbers for every adventure that can befall us here below.

"We laughed, but before long my wife began to dream numbers, and, just as a joke, we played them. We won at first. After that we were in for Banco Lotto. We made fun of it, but when the numbers were posted on Saturday mornings we were apt to stroll around to see what they were.

"Just before we left we had an experience which pretty thoroughly disgusted us with the game. We had a fire in a back room and the cook's clothes were burned. The house was in confusion, though there is precious little danger from fire in the great stone Italian houses. Everybody, from the prince who lived on the 'grand floor' and had his own marble stairway, to the porter who dwelt in an underground cave, played the numbers that week.

"We chose 'fire,' 'fright,' and 'clothes' for our symbols; but, would you believe it?—'smoke,' 'confusion,' and 'underwear' came out. It was a low trick for fate to play on us, and I don't care after that if they do suppress Banco Lotto. It's too much for the Anglo-Saxon brain."

William W. Story, in his "Roba di Roma," supplies other instances, that concern the papal lottery in his day. He tells of a poor shopkeeper hard driven by his creditors who went to his priest, an uomo apostolico, and prayed him earnestly to give him three numbers to play in the lottery. "But how under heaven," says the innocent priest, "has it ever got into your head that I can know the five numbers which are to issue in the lottery?" "Eh, padre mio! what will it cost you? Just look at me and my wretched family; if we do not pay our rent on Saturday, out we go into the street. Pray content me this once." " My son, I will give you a rule for always being content: Avoid Sin, think often on Death, and behave so as to deserve Paradise— and so——"

"Enough, enough, my father; that's enough.   Thanks, thanks. God will reward you."   So he rushes home, takes down the " Book of Fate," calls wife and children, and they decide in consultation what numbers are the three that correspond with the words sin, death, and paradise. The three numbers are drawn, but the poor priest's life becomes a burden. For the story gets wind, and all the country-side is after him for numbers. He protests the drawing was all chance. Every word he spoke turned into numbers, and off ran his hearers to play them.

In Austria-Hungary the lottery flourishes as vigorously as it does in Italy. " Playing in the various lotteries is so general," writes in 1911 a Vienna correspondent to a paper in Hamburg, " that the people who do not buy a ' chance ' or a fraction of one for every drawing are exceptions. When a man makes his calculations for the year's expenditures, a certain amount is charged to the lottery account, with the same belief as to the necessity for the investment as though it were rent, coal, or church dues. In addition to the individual playing, many men and women are members of lottery associations, to which they contribute a certain sum annually, for which they participate with the other members in the various drawings. Sometimes, when people of moderate means have gambled for years without seeing any return for their investment, they stop. But there are thousands who have not yet made the first step who are recalled to the ranks by items such as this, which appeared last week in a Vienna paper: ' The first prize in the Hungarian class lottery, valued at 600,000 marks, was won by a lottery association in Warsaw. The association has twenty-four members, all poor.' "

Matrimonial projects have injected their element of comedy into the history of lotteries. Men and women alike have availed themselves of this means to raffle themselves off for a dowry that should be shared with the winning partner in the connubial speculation. Two instances, one of a man, the other of a woman, may be quoted from different periods and widely separated communities.   In 1810 the Louisiana *Gazette* published the following advertisement:

A young man of good figure and disposition, unable, though desirous, to procure a wife without the preliminary trouble of amassing a fortune, proposes the following expedient to obtain the object of his wishes: He offers himself as the prize of a Lottery to all Widows and Virgins under 32; the number of tickets to be 600, at 50 dollars each; but one number is to be drawn from the wheel, the fortunate proprietor of which is to be entitled to himself and the 30,000 dollars.

In 1872 *Once a Week* contained the following note from abroad:

A young lady in Calcutta, Dona Pepa de Vergas by name, offers her heart and hand, and, what is more, her dowry, as the prize of a lottery, for the sum of a lac of rupees, on the following conditions: "1. Twenty-two thousand tickets at five rupees each. 2. The takers of tickets are simply to send in their names, the amount of their subscription to be collected when the sum mentioned has been subscribed for. 3. The lottery to take place at a date to be hereafter announced at the Town Hall, Calcutta, and to be drawn and conducted by Miss de Vergas. 4. The owner of the winning number will have the option of the following choices: (a.) To marry Miss de Vergas, and share with her—on the principle of community of goods—her fortune of one lac of rupees. (b.) Or, in the case of refusing the marriage, the sum of 50,000 rupees will be paid to him, Miss de Vergas retaining for herself 50,000 rupees. 5. Miss de Vergas reserves to herself the right of refusing to marry the owner of the winning number, should he prove to be a person she would not care to espouse. In that case the winner will be paid the sum of 50,000 rupees. A young lady of birth, of noble family, well educated—she speaks Spanish, French, and a little English —clever, and a brilliant beauty; to all these qualifications add a fortune of 100,000 rupees."

History fails to record the results of either of these experiments.

Lotus. The name has been applied to various plants. The lotus of the Greeks was probably the *Zizyphus Lotus,* a common plant in southern Europe. Its fruit contains a mealy substance that is used for bread making and also for distilling a fermented drink. Anciently this fruit was much eaten by the poorer classes, hence *lotophagi,* or "lotus-eaters." It has been suggested, however, that the Libyan tribe called by this name in Homer's "Odyssey" (Book iv, 603) ate really a kind of clover —the poa of Strabo. Victor Bérard identifies the land of the Homeric opium eaters with the modern Jerba.

When Odysseus reached the Lotophagi country, many of his sailors lost all desire to continue their journey home after tasting of the lotus. Both Greeks and Romans used the expression "to eat the lotus" to denote forgetfulness. So in modern days Lord Randolph Churchill denounced a distinguished viceroy of India as "lulled to languor by the land of the lotus." The lotus of India, however, is usually identified with the *Nelumbium speciosum,* a species of water-lily which has a place in the mythology of the Hindus and is the principal motif in their decorative designs.

Love Letter, First. Since the year 1911 there have been dug up from the ruins of Babylon numerous clay tablets that were used for epistolary purposes nearly 2,000 years before the Christian era. Their cuneiform inscriptions have been laboriously deciphered. They show how little life and human nature have changed while the world has been growing old. There is the complaint of a man that the food at his boarding place is not good; he longs for the food he used to have at home. There is the plea of a mother that her wayward son return and be forgiven. And, most familiar of all, there is a letter evidently written by a young man who has gone to Babylon to make his fortune, and who wants his sweetheart to join him there and become his wife. Here in full is the oldest extant love-letter:

> To Bibeya from Gimil Marduk: May Shamash and Marduk grant thee, for my sake, to live forever. I write this to inquire after thy health. Let me know how it goes with thee. I am now settled in Babylon, but I am in great anxiety because I have not seen thee. Send news when thou wilt come, that I may rejoice at it. Come in the month of Arakhsamna (November-December). Mayest thou, for my sake, live forever.

Lutine or Bad News Bell. Whenever news is received at Lloyd's Insurance offices in London (see LLOYD's) that a ship is overdue, or when definite news comes of the loss of a ship, a bell known as the " Bad News Bell " is rung by the " caller." At its tolling all transactions are suspended until the news it heralds is read.

The bell used for this purpose has a history of its own. It belonged to the British frigate *Lutine,* which sank off the Dutch coast in 1799 with a cargo of ore and specie valued at $6,000,000.

Many attempts, some partially successful, have been made to recover the golden cargo of the *Lutine.* About $500,000 of the sum has been raised, the bulk of it in 1800. It was in one of these attempts that the bell was found. In 1911 the wreck was again located, and search for the treasure was once more begun.

M.

Macadam (*adj.*), **Macadamize** (*v.a.*). John Loudon Macadam (1756–1836) was an old Scottish gentleman, who, living in Ayrshire, a neighborhood of detestable roads, hit upon the happy idea that if you cover a road with a quantity of small stones you will keep it dry and prevent ruts. He further economically resolved that the necessary process of gradual comminution should be carried out, not by the constructors of the road, but by the carriage-wheels of those that used it. People laughed at the foible of the old Scotchman, but before he died he was making ten thousand pounds a year by his superintendence of the various mail trusts on his system.

Coachmen were, of course, very slow to believe the railways could improve upon the macadamized road. They were very angry with the unreasonable public. "They will want," said an honest coachman, "to leave London at nine o'clock and get to Oxford at five minutes before nine." A railway historian remarks: "The honest coachman little thought that he was a prophet. We do not yet travel at that imaginary rate, but our electric messages do." *

Macadam's roads, as constructed and repaired under his own superintendence, were formed entirely of angular pieces of stone not above six ounces in weight and of such a size as to pass freely through a ring 2½ inches in diameter. In January, 1879, however, the *Pall Mall Gazette* complained that "modern contractors, instead of adhering to this method, cover the roads with large jagged stones, rendering them unfit for traffic; and, owing to the supineness of the vestries, are allowed to 'macadamize' to their hearts' content in this fashion, without any reference to the safety, comfort, and convenience of the public." It surmised that "if Mr. Macadam could return to this mortal life he would be shocked to find how great atrocities are committed in his name. and there can be little doubt that he would repudiate with indignation the term 'macadamized' as applied to the roads subjected to the process known by this designation."

Macaroni (from an Italian dialect word *maccare*, "to bruise" or "to crush." A more amusing etymology is given at

---

* Personal Recollections of English Engineers, and of the Introduction of the Railway System into the United Kingdom. By a Civil Engineer, author of the "Trinity of Italy." Hodder and Stoughton.

some length in WALSH, *Handy-book of Literary Curiosities, s.v.*).
This is a generic name for many varieties and forms of edible
paste that originated in Italy and are still mainly manufactured
there, though in America important factories have been established to turn out the most popular forms,—vermicelli, noodles,
and spaghetti. Serious history usually looks upon macaroni as
indigenous to Italy, but does not wholly repudiate the traditions
that they were introduced there by the early Greek colonists or
that the Japanese and the Chinese were acquainted with the dish
in pre-Italian times. It has only kindly tolerance, however, for a
popular Italian legend which professes to account for macaroni.
In the year 1220, so this legend runs, and under the reign of
King Frederick of Suabia, there flourished a great magician
named Chico. He lost his fortune, and, by consequence, his
friends, and so determined to devote the rest of his hermit and
spartan life to inventing a dish that should prove of lasting value
to humanity. Just as he was perfecting this invention, a certain
Jovanella, wife of a scullion in the royal kitchen, peered through
his window and discovered his secret. She informed King
Frederick that an angel had revealed to her in a dream how to
concoct a dish that was marvellously palatable and wholesome.
The king believed her, and she prepared it for him by combining
meat, cheese, tomatoes, and garlic with tubes made from flour,
eggs, and salt. So pleased was Frederick with the result that he
gave her 100 pieces of gold and called the tubes macaroni, from
macarus, meaning " divine."

So, for a while, Jovanella flourished and made money by
selling her handiwork to the nobles and merchant princes of the
neighborhood.

But the time came when Chico, satisfied that he had at last
perfected his invention, sallied out to inform the world of what
he had to give it. He had not gone far before he detected the
familiar odor of macaroni issuing from a tureen, and by pursuing his inquiries he learned how he had been betrayed by
Jovanella. In despair he committed suicide. One version of
the story says that Jovanella confessed the truth on her death
bed, and thus the memory of Chico was vindicated and the
credit for his discovery returned to him.

Mace (an old French word corrupted in France to *masse,*
but retaining its ancient spelling in England) was originally a
weapon of offence made of iron and steel and capable of breaking
through the stoutest armor. At public functions maces were
borne by sergeants at arms of the royal body-guards for the protection of the king's person, but eventually they degenerated into
mere ceremonial paraphernalia.

33

The ancient use of the mace introduces us to a remarkable instance of ecclesiastical casuistry. The clergy was forbidden to shed blood, and, as thus the sword was inhibited, this might have been thought sufficient to keep them from the battle-field. But not so; they adopted the mace; though they could not cut a man's throat, yet might they break his head. So Bishop Otho, half-brother of William, fought alongside of the Conqueror at the bitter battle of Hastings with great effect, the brothers being, as you may say, " a pair of nut-crackers."

The oldest piece of civic regalia in the world is a crystal mace belonging to the London mayoralty and exhibited in public only at the induction of the Lord Mayor on November 8th and at the coronation of the sovereign.

It dates from Saxon times, as the workmanship of its crystal and gold shaft with jewelled head declares. From the time before the Normans this mace, which is barely eighteen inches long, has symbolized sovereignty over the city when the Lord Mayor was still known as the portreeve, and London was an independent state.

The Royal Society in London treasures among its insignia a mace that was presented to it by Charles II in 1663. A more ancient origin was long accredited to it, for it was believed to be the identical " bauble " which Oliver Cromwell ordered to be removed from the House of Commons when he uttered the remarkable words " Take away that fool's bauble." This error, however, was detected and exposed by Charles Richard Weld, the librarian of the society.

He showed that Cromwell's " bauble " was a mace that had been made expressly for the Commonwealth Parliament a few weeks after the execution of Charles the First, and was quite different in form from the royal mace, being nearly destitute of ornament. This mace was used in the House of Commons till within a month of the Restoration, when a new mace was ordered to be made, to be like that formerly used in the time of Charles the First. The mace in the possession of the Royal Society has, not only a large crown and cross, but also the royal arms and the letters " C. R.," four times repeated, which makes it evident that it is not identical with the Commonwealth mace.

Not satisfied with this evidence, Mr. Weld instituted a rigid search among the archives in the Lord Chamberlain's office for the warrant which, he supposed, might be in existence for the making of a mace for the society; and was so fortunate as to find, in the book of warrants for the year 1663, a warrant under the head of " Jewel House," ordering " one guilt mace of 150 oz. to be prepared and delivered to Lord Viscount Brouncker, President of the Royal Society of London, for improving of natural knowledge by experiments, being a guift from his Majestie to the said Society." The discovery of this document, dated 1663 (the year in which the Royal Society received the mace from Charles II), entirely destroyed the long-entertained belief of the identity of the "bauble" mace and that in the possession of the Royal Society.

The latter is of silver, about 4 feet in length, and very massive. It bears the following inscription:

Ex Munificentiâ
Augustissimi Monarchæ
CAROLI II.,
Dei Gra. Mag. Brit. Fran., et Hib., Regis &c.
Societatis Regalis ad Scientiam Naturalem promuenda institutæ
Fundatoris et Patroni,
An. Dni. 1663.

As to the mace made for the House of Commons in 1649, it is still retained by that body. The designer was Thomas Maundy. It is substantially as it came out of Maundy's hands, save that the original head with the non-regal symbols was replaced by one with regal symbols at the Restoration.

There are two maces in the House of Lords, the earliest dating from the reign of William III.

The oldest mace in the United States, a silver staff made in England in 1753, is preserved in the State House at Norfolk, Virginia. Another, of similar workmanship and dating from 1756, is in South Carolina.

In the American Congress the mace is the symbol of the office of sergeant-at-arms, being borne aloft by that officer when he is called upon to enforce order on the floor. In appearance it is not unlike the Roman fasces,—consisting as it does of thirteen ebony rods, representing the original States, bound together transversely with silver bands. Each rod is tipped with a silver spear-head, and the whole is surmounted by a globe, with an eagle perching on it, globe and eagle being both of solid silver.

The mace was adopted in 1789. The original was destroyed by the British at the burning of the Capitol, August 24, 1814, and for a quarter century after that, cross sticks of wood were used. Not till 1842 was the present mace made. It has been in constant use ever since. Though handled comparatively little, the outlines of the map of the world on the silver globe are now almost entirely effaced.

While the House is in session the mace is kept in an upright position on a marble pedestal on the right of the speaker. It is not taken down during a recess; but when the House is in committee of the whole it is removed. As soon as the speaker resumes his seat it is put up again. When not in the House it is kept in the office of the sergeant-at-arms, always well guarded by a member of the Capitol police force. In fact, the mace is never without an attending guard day or night. Even when it has to be taken from the Capitol to be repaired, as has happened on several occasions, a policeman accompanies it and watches over it.

Whenever a member on the floor refuses to take his seat or obey the speaker's commands, the sergeant-at-arms can be ordered by the speaker to take down the mace, bear it to the floor of the House, and hold it over the unruly member. That member is then in contempt, and he cannot again resume his duties and privileges as a member of the House except by a vote of his colleagues. It is not often that a speaker has had to resort to such drastic measures; the members, as a rule, respect his authority.

There is only one instance in the last quarter century when the mace was put to its intended use. That was when Jerry Simpson ("Sockless Jerry") of Kansas was trying to make it hot for Speaker Reed and refused to subside. The mace did the work, and order was restored.

Madstone. The first madstones in the United States came from Chicago. Thus, the famous Parker madstone was brought here about the year 1804 by a Dr. Parker, who sold it to a Mr. Milam of Winona, Mississippi. It is described as about half the size of a hen's egg, an irregular rounded cube of whitish-gray color, marked with small radiated discs like rough coral, but with nothing like the weight or solidity of coral. Under the microscope the stone shows a great number of minute pores. It is broken into five pieces which are bound together with wire.

In the early seventies the stone achieved an international reputation. The *Pall Mall Gazette*, of London, in January, 1874, celebrated it in this fashion: " Eleven hundred applications of the stone have been made to mad-dog and snake wounds, without a single failure to cure. Two hundred and fifty applications have been made by Mr. Benjamin Milam, to whom the stone was bequeathed by his late father. The latest cure the stone has effected is that of a Dr. Hudgins, of whose case there is a long report in the *Winona Advance*. Dr. Hudgins was bitten on the 20th of May last by a mad dog while attempting to destroy it, and received a slight wound in the left wrist. He was some months later seized by hydrophobia, and, the case appearing hopeless, Mr. Milam was telegraphed for on the 11th ult., and shortly afterwards appeared with the 'madstone.' The wound had cicatrized, but the skin was pared off by Drs. Holman and Trotter, and the stone bound on. After an hour the bandage was removed and the stone firmly adhered, so that considerable pressure was needed to disengage it. The application was made at 8 P.M. and the stone dropped off at 4 A.M. It was immersed in hot water for an hour, dried, and again applied. Three applications were made, and Dr. Hudgins is now perfectly well, and not only free from any symptoms of hydrophobia, but also from the terrible fear and anxiety which before oppressed him."

The Pointer madstone was as famous in the South as the Parker madstone was in the Southwest. It claimed an almost equal antiquity, having been brought over from China by " Tom " Pointer of Halifax, Virginia, about 1815. Later it was broken, but large fragments remain in the hands of Pointer's descendants. In 1889 one of those descendants, D. Pointer, of Memphis, Tenn., thus described his fragment in the Memphis *Commercial Appeal:*

The stone we have is quite ordinary in appearance. It is black and might be mistaken for a chunk of coal. One side is smooth, but the other, the porous side, that is applied to the bite, is rough. When the stone is used it is laid on the spot where the bite has scratched the skin. If poison has been deposited there, the madstone will stick and absorb the poisonous substance.

I recollect on one occasion, when a member of our household had been bitten, the doctor gave up the patient and said he could not live till morning. The bite was on the arm and the swelling was immense. The patient could not open his eyes. There was no doubt about this being a case of the rabies. The doctor having given up the case and declared that death would ensue before morning, I asked him if I could not try the efficacy of the madstone. He had no objection, stating that it could do no good, but, to appease my insistence, he said it could do no harm. So I applied the stone. It adhered. Presently it had absorbed all that it could contain of the poisonous substance and fell off. By that time the sufferer had been benefited sufficiently to be able to open his eyes. I placed the stone in a bucket of lukewarm water, the usual way of treating it, and the poison at once exuded and rose to the top of the water, forming a green scum. When the stone had emptied itself it was again applied to the sore, and before it had filled up again it fell off, all the poison having been absorbed. The patient recovered, though the doctor, a disbeliever in the madstone, had given him less than twelve hours to live.

There are many people in this city in Mississippi who can vouch for the efficacy of this stone. I remember a cure before the war in which Phelan Lucas, who now lives at Holly Springs, was deeply interested. Mr. Lucas had a valuable negro bitten by a rattlesnake while working in the field. The bite was in the thumb. The negro came in from the field with his hand and arm fearfully swollen and suffering great pain. There was apparently no chance for him to live long. Mr. Lucas said afterward that anybody could have bought that negro for ten dollars then. But the madstone was got from my father's, and the negro was cured.

Persons who have seen so many and such positive cures as I have cannot doubt the efficacy of the madstone.

Magic Lantern. An instrument for projecting on a white wall or screen magnified representations of transparent pictures painted or photographed on glass. The invention is usually attributed to Athanasius Kircher, who is said to have described it in the first edition (1646) of his "Ars Magna Lucis et Ombræ." De Chales, in "Cursus Mathematicæ" (1674), says that in 1665 "a learned Dane" exhibited at Lyons a contrivance under the name of *Lanterna magica,* evidently identical with the modern instrument. The "New English Dictionary" quotes the earliest English reference from Phillips' Dictionary, which, under the title "Magic Lanthorn," describes it as "a certain small optical Macheen that shows by a gloomy light upon a white wall, spectres and monsters so hideous that he who knows not the secret believes it to be performed by Magic Art." The N. E. D. adds that the first magic lanterns in England were made by Philip Carpenter, *circa* 1808. But the instrument was familiar long before this on the continent. Smollett, in "Count Fathom" (1784), alludes to the travelling Savoyards who stroll about Europe amusing ignorant people with the effects of a magic lanthorn. Only of recent years has the instrument been improved and its use extended so as to become a valuable aid to the scientist and the instructor. By its means finely executed photographs on glass can be shown, greatly magnified to large audiences, thus saving the trouble and expense of preparing large diagrams. It can also be used in the form of a microscope to exhibit on a screen the forms and movements of minute living organisms, or to show to an audience delicate physical and chemical experiments which otherwise could be seen only by a few at a time.

Mahogany. A dark-colored wood largely used for household furniture, the product of a species of cedar indigenous to Central America and the West Indies.

It is a beautiful tree, tall and shapely, with the lowest branches at least sixty feet from the ground. At the bottom is a huge swelling, after the manner of the cypress, and the tree is to be cut above that, six or eight feet from the roots.

In Mexico, Honduras, and Central America the contractor gives $5 for a single tree. This is cheap enough. But the expense of getting it out makes mahogany an expensive lumber. It stands deep in the forest in the midst of an almost impenetrable jungle. There are no groves of them—the trees are scattered, perhaps not more than two to an acre. There may be no water-course at hand on which the logs can be floated to the port. The tree has to be located by the "hunter," whose business it is to roam through the forest in search of mahogany trees and to blaze a way to them, so that they may be found again. Then the workmen must cut their laborious way to the tree, using for the purpose the deadly machete.

The first work to be done is to build a platform around the trunk, so that the cutters can stand upon it and wield their axes. At last the great monarch of the tropical forest comes crashing down through the thick growth around it.

The workmen trim it up, cut it into lengths, and manage to get it hauled and rolled to the nearest creek, there to lie until the floods of the rainy season lift it and carry it down stream and on to the ocean port. The logs are then piled on the beach to wait for a vessel, and on its arrival they are rolled back into the water and rafted and pulled out to the ship's side. Here the derricks are put to work and the logs are lifted over one by one, lowered with much difficulty into the hold, and when enough logs have come aboard the vessel is ready.

For many years "old mahogany" has been almost a synonym for sumptuousness in the home or in business and public edifices. It is less honored in its native land. Most of the trees are so far away from the coast and from any present means of transportation they are almost worthless to the owner. Hence in the lands across the Gulf one finds railroad ties made of mahogany. In the state of Chiapas, in Mexico, a bridge spanning the Rio Michol, 150 feet long by 15 feet wide, is built entirely of solid mahogany. The bridge is used both by teams and by foot passengers and though roughly constructed is very substantial. None of the massive timbers were sawn, as there is not a sawmill in the region, but all were hewn out with the axe from the logs. On a New York valuation at least $200,000 worth of material was used in the construction of this rude country bridge.—*Harper's Weekly.*

A curious book called the "Anecdote Library" (London, 1819) is authority for the statement that the first use to which mahogany was applied in England was to make a box for holding candles. Dr. Gibbons, an eminent physician in the latter end of the seventeenth century, had a brother, a West India captain, who brought over some planks of this wood as ballast. As the doctor was then building himself a house in King Street, Covent-garden, his brother thought they might be of service to him. But, the carpenters finding the wood too hard for their tools, they were laid aside for a time as useless. Soon after, Mrs. Gibbons wanting a candle-box, the doctor called on his cabinet-maker (Wollaston, of Long-Acre) to make him one of some wood that lay in his garden. Wollaston also complained that it was too hard. The doctor said he must get stronger tools,

The candle-box was made and approved; insomuch, that the doctor then insisted on having a bureau made of the same wood, which was accordingly done, and the fine color, polish, etc., were so pleasing, that he invited all his friends to come and see it. Among them was the Duchess of Buckingham. Her Grace begged some of the same wood of Dr. Gibbons, and employed Wollaston to make her a bureau also; on which the fame of mahogany and Mr. Wollaston was much raised, and things of this sort became general.

One of the largest logs of mahogany recorded in print was one which was sold by auction at Birkenhead Dock on March 28, 1850. The *Illustrated London News* of April 6 following gives a picture of this monster and describes it as follows:

The tree that this log was manufactured from grew in the Mosquito territory of Honduras. The length of the trunk, clear of branch, was 72 feet; its circumference, where it was cut (twelve feet above the ground), was 30 feet; and the entire tree turned out 17,000 feet of sound wood: say, three logs 20 feet long each from the trunk, and some very large logs from the branches. It was cut on the works of Messrs. Carmichael and Co.; and two of the logs were shipped on board their vessel the *Atlantic;* the large one, together with the log cut off the end of it, which measures 20 feet long, 4 feet 11 inches deep, 3 feet 8 inches thick, containing 4326 feet. The logs were landed at the Morpeth Dock, Birkenhead, February 1st. The weight of both is 16 tons 13 cwt. The other piece is nearly as large, having the curl attached.

For the monster log there was great competition; and eventually it sold at 1s. 10½d. per foot, the purchase-money amounting to £316 17s. 6d.

The *Illustrated London News* concludes its article as follows:

The best qualities of mahogany, such as the finest Spanish, bring a very high price. Some years since, Messrs. Broadwood, the pianoforte manufacturers, gave the large sum of £3000 for three logs of mahogany! These logs, the produce of a *single tree*, were each about 15 feet long and 38 inches square; they were cut into veneers of eight to an inch. The wood was particularly beautiful, capable of receiving the highest polish; and, when polished, reflecting the light in the most varied manner, like the surface of a crystal; and, from the wavy form of the pores, offering a different figure in whatever direction it was viewed. Dealers in mahogany generally introduce an auger before buying a lot; but they are seldom able to decide with much precision as to the quality of the wood, so that there is a good deal of lottery in the trade. The logs for which Messrs. Broadwood gave so high a price were brought to this country with a full knowledge of their superior worth.

Mail-coaches. An antiquary of Notts, England, William Streton, quotes an inscription on " a very neat tablet " on the north wall of Stapleford Church, Notts:

"To the Memory of Thomas Gray, who died July 9, 1802, aged 73 years. His public spirit and skill in the improvement of roads made him a blessing to the neighborhood in which he lived, but the great facility of conveyance by the Mail Coaches being first projected, plan'd and put in practice by him, made him a blessing to the kingdom at large."—*N. and Q.*, Tenth Series, iii, 236.

Man in Armor. This name was sometimes applied to the Champion of England, but more specifically indicated his imitator, a horseman clad in complete steel (or polished brass) who for centuries was a figure in the Lord Mayor's processions. A strange apparition even in that pageant of curious figures, that gathering of ambiguous functionaries, he was out of place, somehow, jostled by the modern hussar on the one hand, and the still more modern police constable on the other; and he was the subject of some derision, which yet boasted an affectionate and admiring leaven on the part of the populace. A few years after Queen Victoria had dispensed with the services of the Champion of England at her coronation, his understudy, as theatrical folk might call him, disappeared from the mayor's pageant. "When his place knew him no more, he was certainly missed. It was felt by many that a better institution might better have been spared. His abolition was the severest blow yet dealt to civic authority. He was, in his way, a grand creature." *All the Year Round*, November 9, 1872.

Mandrake, a plant nearly allied to the belladonna, which is found in North Africa, part of Southern Europe, and Asia Minor. Like the belladonna it has poisonous properties, only more narcotic in their nature, and for this reason small bits of the root were often administered before a surgical operation. Plato and Demosthenes both speak of it as a soporific, and in the East an indolent person is still described as one who has eaten mandrake. Hence Shakespeare makes Cleopatra say:

> Give me to drink mandragora,
> That I might sleep out this great gap of time
> My Antony is away.

Shakespeare also alludes to the superstition that the mandrake makes insane those who eat it. In "Macbeth" (Act i, Scene 3) Banquo, after the meeting with the weird sisters, asks, in wondering fear—

> Were such things here as we do speak about,
> Or have we eaten on the insane root
> That takes the reason prisoner?

But the most uncanny and most wide-spread of all the superstitions connected with the mandrake originate in its root. Because this is forked and flesh-colored and bears a curious resemblance to the human form, human characteristics were attributed to the plant. The ancient Greeks sometimes called it *anthropomorphon,* and the Romans *semihomo.* Mediæval folk-lore held it to be a living creature, "engendered under the earth, of the seed of some dead person put to death for murder" (THOMAS NEWTON: *Herbæ of the Bible*), or "growing up beneath the gallows from which a thief is suspended" (GRIMM: *German Mythology*). Hence in Germany it was popularly called *Galgemannlein.*

The superstition that the mandrake dripped human blood when pulled from the ground, and emitted loud shrieks which killed or made insane those that heard it, is very ancient and very wide-spread. Its first appearance in literature is in Homer's "Iliad."

Josephus (viii, 6, §3) records that it was the custom in a certain Jewish village to pull up the roots by means of a dog, which was killed by the shriek thereupon emitted. Shakespeare has a reference to this belief as extant in his own day:

> And shrieks like mandrakes torn out of the earth,
> That living mortals, hearing them, run mad.
> *Romeo and Juliet,* Act iv, Sc. 3.

And Grimm tells us that he who desires to possess a mandrake must "stop his ears with wax so that he may not hear the deathly yells which the plant utters as it is being dragged from the earth. Then, before sunrise on a Friday, he must go out with a dog 'all black,' make three crosses around the mandrake with the point of a sword, loosen the soil about the root, being careful that the wind is to his back, tie the root to the dog's tail, and, going to a safe distance, offer the beast a piece of bread. The dog will then run at the bread, drag out the mandrake root, and fall dead, killed by the horrible yell of the plant."

After the dog is buried on the spot with religious honors and secret sacred rites, the root is to be taken up, "washed with wine, wrapped in silk, laid in a casket, bathed every Friday, and clothed in a little, new white smock every new moon.

"If thus considerately treated it acts as a familiar spirit, and every piece of coin laid by it at night doubles before morning."

Mediæval wonder-mongers saw their opportunity in the human aspect of the root. They added their cunning art, carved heads with human features upon it, even cultivated the hair on it, and then declared that it came thus from the earth. These images so prepared went by the names of *Erdman* ("earth-man"), *Mannikin,* and *Alraun.* Matthiolus tells us that in his day Italian ladies had been known to pay as much as twenty-five and thirty ducats in gold, or half-sovereigns, for one of them. About the time of Henry VIII they began to be exported to England, where they met with a ready sale. So late as 1810 these images were to be seen in the seaport towns of France, and were credited with the power of exciting the passion of love. This power is a very ancient attribute of the mandrake. In Genesis, xxx, 14–16, is the account of how Leah used them to attract Jacob.

A remarkable letter is preserved by Mr. Moncure D. Conway in *Harper's Magazine,* vol. 65, p. 892. It was written in 1675 by a burgess of Leipsic to his brother at Riga, and shows exactly the popular notions regarding the mandrake at that time. The writer, hearing that his brother had endured divers great sorrows, sends him an erdmann as a mascot to bring future good fortune. He explains that he had purchased it for sixty-four thalers, and continues:

> When thou hast the Erdmann in thy house, let it rest three days without approaching it, then place it in warm water. With the water afterward sprinkle the animals and sills of the house, going over all, and soon it shall go better with thee, and thou shalt come to thy own, if thou serve the Erdmanniken right. Bathe it four times every year, and as often wrap it in silk cloths, and lay it among thy best things, and thou need do no more. The bath in which it has been bathed is especially good. If a woman is in child-pain and can not bear, if she drink a spoonful she will be delivered with joy and thankfulness. And when thou goest to law put Erdmann under thy right arm, and thou shalt succeed, whether right or wrong. Now, dear brother, this Erdmanniken I send with all love and faith to thee for a happy New Year. Let it be kept, and it may do the same for thy children's children. God keep thee!—HANS N.

It is certainly remarkable that in 1675 so much as sixty-four thalers could be obtained for one of these little figures; but it is probable that the dealing in them had become very secret, on account of the danger one incurred of being suspected as a witch if the root was found upon him or her. In 1630 three women were executed in Hamburg on this account.

Frequently the erdmann was put into a glass bottle and carried about on the person. Marvellous tales were told of the powers for good and for evil possessed by this bottle-imp. It could fill its owner's pockets with gold, and could perform many other services. But woe to the unfortunate wight who died with one upon his person! He became the property of the devil. Nor was it an easy task to get rid of it,—for unless one could sell it for a little less than he paid, it would remain upon his hands. He might throw it into the water or into the fire; it would always turn up in his room. In Lower Wurtemberg there is a spot said to be haunted by the ghost of a merchant who had vainly endeavored to rid himself of his erdmann. This diabolical phase of the superstition was not unknown in France and England. Joan of Arc was suspected of carrying one of these imps in her pocket. The question was even put to her point-blank at her trial. But she answered that she knew not what a mandrake was. In 1603 one Margaret Bouchey was hanged at Romorantin, near Orleans, on the charge of keeping a living mandrake fiend which was stated to be in the form of a female ape.

In England it is still believed that the mandrake is watched over by Satan, and that, if it be pulled up at certain holy times and with certain invocations, the evil one will appear to do the bidding of the bold mortal. There also, as well as in various parts of southern Germany and Austria, the mandrake is a potent love-charm and is associated with fertility in woman. This is the superstition which finds literary form in Macchiavelli's comedy "La Mandragola," and which no doubt gathers strength from the allusion in Genesis. In some districts of Bohemia the roots are gathered on Good Friday, dried and pulverized, and given to the cows to increase their store of milk. In various Alpine regions mandrake is used as a charm against nightmare, toothache, and cramp, and also against the attacks of robbers. In many parts of Europe it is supposed to indicate the place of buried treasures and to have the power of extracting money from the most unwilling. The Icelandic form of the last superstition is especially quaint. The practitioner must steal a coin from a poor widow during the performance of mass on either Christmas, Easter, or Whitsuntide. This coin, placed under the herb, will draw to itself from the pockets of the bystanders all coins of a similar denomination.

Manhattan. The most plausible guess at the origin of the name of the island which originally determined the limits of New York city was made by Rev. A. S. Anthony, a Delaware Indian from Ontario, and endorsed by Dr. Daniel D. G. Brinton in the *Journal of American Folklore* (vol. i, p. 30). Mr. Anthony derived the word from *Manahahtank,* "the place where they gather the wood to make bows." *Manhtaht* in the Manhattan dialect meant bows and arrows. This tribe was closely related to their neighbors, the Mohicans, and the latter in their turn to the Delawares. Consequently the Anthony-Brinton etymology has good philological reasons behind it. Moreover, it is confirmed by the Rev. John Heckwelder, whose manuscript account of the early history of Manhattan is preserved in the archives of the New York Historical Society. This authority incidentally mentions that the Mohicans gave the name *Manahahtank* to the island, from the wood that grew there and was used by them for their arrows. Nevertheless, Heckwelder holds that the similarly sounding word *Manhattan* means "a drunken bout," and refers to the occasion when the innocent natives first tasted fire-water and experienced its effects.

This occurred in 1524, when the Florentine navigator, John Verrazano, landed where the lower extremity of New York city now lies, and produced the spirituous liquors which he had carried on his voyage. Tradition says that, delighted with this novel species of jovial entertainment, the Indians gave their settlement the name of *Manna-ha-ta,* "place of drunkenness," or, in Irving's free translation, "the Island of Jolly Topers," " a name which," he says, " it continues to merit to the present day." This account is supplemented by a grave historian, who suggests that the intoxication on this occasion was probably confined to the crew of the visiting vessel.

Nearly a hundred years later Hudson rediscovered the island, and the political career of the State of New York was begun when, in 1526, Peter Minuit, the newly appointed Governor of New Netherland, arrived at New 'Amsterdam, and bought of the Manhattans their beautiful island for the value of sixty guilders (about $24 of our money), and paid for it in cheap trinkets, hatchets, knives, etc., an event in history as important and as creditable to the honesty of the purchasers as was the treaty of William Penn, which poets and painters never weary of celebrating.

It is scarcely worth while to dwell upon the many facetious and fanciful derivations of Manhattan, which wits have ascribed to its being the island of *manna,* flowing with milk and honey; or to the custom among the squaws of wearing men's hats, whence arose the appellation Man-hat-on! The latter etymology is Diedrich Knickerbocker's, who has, indeed, as he somewhere admits, indulged too freely in the bold, excessive manner of his favorite, Herodotus.

It may be of interest to add that the Iroquois name for New York, according to Cuoq (Lexicon Iroquois, p. 11) was "*Kanonno,* jonc dans l'eau, pays de joncs," from *ononna* ("rush") and *o* ("in the water"). The exact signification of this Iroquois word as applied to New York is not apparent. At p. 164, Cuoq states that in the Tsonnontouan (Seneca) dialect the word signifies "mine," and asks if there were, in the time of the Dutch, any *mines* in the vicinity of Manhattan or New York. In the Mohawk dialect *Kanonno* means "laths in the water," or "walnut-tree dipping into the water." It is in the Cayuga dialect that the word means "rushes in the water."

Mantis (known also as the "leaf" or "praying insect"), one of the greatest oddities of the insect world. For hours together it will remain in an attitude as of saintly contemplation, its forelegs or "arms" raised and joined as in prayer. Let a fly or other unwary insect approach, and out darts an arm, and the victim is straightway caught and devoured. The mantis, in short, has to depend upon craft to capture its daily food.

The ancient Greeks endowed it with supernatural powers. The modern Hottentots in Nubia pay it superstitious reverence. Any man on whom it alights is *ipso facto* sanctified and looked upon as a favorite of heaven. Woe to the Hottentot who destroys a mantis! He will lose his skill in hunting and become an outcast. The Mahomedans hold that the mantis ever turns its face in silent prayer toward Mecca. In the south of Europe its sanctified attitude has earned it similar respect.

The Chinese are no whit awed by the mantis. They utilize one peculiarity of the females, which is a desire to fly at one another at the slightest provocation and fight to the death. These are kept in bamboo cages and matched like fighting cocks. When let out into the open, the fight begins. Their powerful forelegs are able to strike tremendous blows, the result often being that the weaker of the two has one or more of its limbs severed by one successful stroke of the enemy, or even its body may be cut through.

The male mantis has a hard task on hand when wooing his mate. She is both larger and stronger than he, and should his advances not prove favorable he rarely has the opportunity of retreating; for while she will not accept him as her lover, she takes care that he does not become the husband of another of her species by killing him as a final act of refusal and then dining off his remains.

Marathon Race. Herodotus (vi, 105) tells the story of Phidippides, or Pheidippides, a courier who was dispatched from Athens to Sparta to solicit aid against the invading army of Persia commanded by Darius. He accomplished a very creditable "cross-country run," arriving in Sparta on the second day after leaving Athens. On his return, he told how the great god Pan had accosted him in an Arcadian dell on Mount Parthenium, and bade him inquire of the Athenians why they neglected his worship, seeing that he had always been their friend and assuring them he would remain so. This pledge was fulfilled by the "Panic" fright which fell upon the Persians on the plain of Marathon (August 12, B.C. 490) and turned the tide of battle in favor of the Greeks. Thereupon the Athenians dedicated a temple to Pan and honored him with annual sacrifices and a torch race.

Robert Browning's poem "Pheidippides" gives a variant

legend. Immediately on the winning of the victory, the courier takes back the tale from Marathon to Athens, and drops dead as he pants out the words, "Rejoice! We win!" (Xairere nikomen!)

Is this an invention of Browning's? Herodotus is silent on this score, and indeed, according to him, no martyr messenger was needed; the whole army returned the same day to Athens. Browning declares that the common Attic salutation *xairere* dates from this use of it by Pheidippides. This is untrue and even absurd. Even school-boy knows that the Homeric heroes hail one another with the bidding "Rejoice!"

Marines, the technical term applied to sea soldiers,—that is, to troops designed for maritime warfare and quartered on shipboard. They are essentially unknown to any but the British and the American navy, and in the latter remain only as a memory. Though marines and marine artillery are mentioned among the armed forces of some other nations, they have little in common with British and American marines.

The origin of the British marine force was an order in council (1664) directing "1200 Land souldgers to be forthwith rayzed to be distributed in his majesty's fleet prepared for sea-service." This body was named the "Admiral's Regiment," and was the germ which by a constant process of evolution during a period of nearly two centuries and a half produced not merely the marine force, but the royal navy, organized, disciplined, and trained as it is to-day.

The American marine corps (abolished by President Roosevelt) was the oldest branch of the naval service; indeed it antedated the actual formation of the navy on being authorized November 10, 1775, by the Continental Congress. Two battalions of American marines were then organized for duty afloat when required. They were the fighting men of the old frigates. In the days when two frigates were lashed together, the marines with their pikes bore the brunt of the fighting and composed the boarding parties. The bluejackets in those days sailed the vessels and only aided in fighting. The marine corps had the distinction of being the first to plant the American flag over a foreign port, which was done at Derne, Tripoli, in 1803. For this conspicuous service the word "Tripoli" was inscribed on its colors. See HORSE MARINE.

Matches, Friction, or Lucifer. There are two English claimants for the honor of having invented the friction match substantially as we know it to-day. The pretensions of John Walker, a chemist of Stockton-upon-Tees, are supported by so high an authority as Michael Faraday. Some time in the year

1829 Walker, experimenting with chlorate of potash in his laboratory, found it could instantly be set on fire by friction. He had dipped a small stick into the chlorate and stood scratching it in an aimless fashion across a piece of sand-paper. Suddenly it flamed up and commenced to burn the stick. As he held it up in astonishment and as the thin white flame consumed the stick, the chemist's brain evolved the friction match.

Walker, however, like most students, was a man of no commercial sagacity. After he had made a few boxes of splints · saturated with chlorate of potash and other combustible chemicals and presented them to his friends, he let the matter drop. Fortunately, some of these splints fell into the hands of Faraday. Seeing at a glance the intrinsic worth of the invention, he hastened to make it public.

The other claimant is Isaac Holden, also an English chemist, residing in London. In his evidence, given before the English patent committee in October, 1871, he testified that the idea had come to him in young manhood. At that time he was delivering lectures on chemistry to a large academy. He had to rise at four in the morning to pursue his preliminary studies, and experienced the gravest inconvenience from his tedious efforts to obtain a light from flint and steel. "Of course I knew, as other chemists did, the explosive material that was necessary to produce instantaneous light; but it was very difficult to obtain a light on wood by that explosive material, and the idea occurred to me to put under the explosive material *sulphur*. I did that, and published it in my next lecture, and showed it. There was a young man in the room whose father was a chemist in London, and he immediately wrote to his father about it, and shortly afterwards lucifer matches were issued to the world." (*Pall Mall Gazette*, November, 1871.)

These pioneer lucifer matches had to be supplemented by a piece of sand-paper, or emery, through which they were drawn in order to ignite them. Twopence was the price of the small square box containing fifty matches and the bit of paper. These matches were known as "congreves," after Sir William Congreve, inventor of the Congreve rocket. Possibly it was the rocket and not the man that suggested the new use of an old name.

The safety match dates from about 1856. The principle is the division of the combustible elements, some being placed in the box and some on the match-tip.

As Mr. Holden testified, chemists had long known that there were explosive materials which would produce instantaneous light. Phosphorus was discovered in 1669, and so early as 1680 Godfrey Hanckwitz introduced the practice of rubbing it between folds of brown paper till it took fire. Later came the idea of making it ignite a stick, one end of which had been dipped in sulphur. So-called "chemical" matches appeared in the early nineteenth century. They were sold in little cases, called phosphorus boxes, containing a few matches, at first as high as fifteen shillings a box. They were small pieces of wood dipped first in sulphur and then in a composition of chlorate of potash, flowers of sulphur, colophony, gum or sugar, and cinnabar for coloring. Accompanying them in the box was a phial containing sulphuric acid. The match being dipped into the acid was instantly ignited by the chemical action induced between the acid and the chlorate of potash. The other ingredients were added merely on account of their combustible qualities.

It was these "chemical matches" undoubtedly which Dr. Saugrain, a Parisian who had emigrated to St. Louis, made for Lewis and Clark when they were getting ready for their famous expedition across the western territory.

"With intense interest," says a historian, "Captain Lewis stood by while the chemist physician dipped sulphur-tipped splints of wood into phosphorus, and lo! his little matches glowed like Lucifer's own. 'You can make the tips yourself,' he said. 'I will seal the phosphorus in these small tin boxes for safety.'" This occurred in St. Louis in the year 1803, at the time when Lewis and Clark outfitted for their immortal exploration.—Eva E. Dye: *The Conquest of the West,* pp. 158–159.

On the expedition's return, when passing the Multnomah near where Portland, Ore., now is, Clark entered an Indian house to buy wapato. "Not, not!" said the inmates. With sullen looks they shook their heads. No gift of his could buy the precious wapato. Deliberately then the Captain took out one of Dr. Saugrain's phosphorus matches and tossed it into the fire. Instantly it spit and flamed. "Me-sah-chie! Me-sah-chie!" the Indians shrieked, and piled the cherished wapato at his feet. The screaming children fled behind the beds and hid behind the men. An old man began to speak with great vehemence, imploring his god for protection. The match burned out and quiet was restored. Clark paid for the wapato, smoked, and went on.

The historian may be at fault here. Most probably Captain Lewis, instead of throwing the match into the fire, used it to draw flames out of a bottle. This might well have surprised the Indians into acknowledging him as "big medicine." An analogous story is told about friction matches, when the serviceable sort were first put on the market. In those days grain crops were harvested with the sickle. A young man from New York went out to a field where a lot of Irish harvesters were at work, and taking out a cigar proceeded to use a match to light it. Drawing the match over the sole of his boot, it took fire, when the entire band of reapers threw down their sickles in terror and fled, exclaiming, "Och, an' did ye see the divvel draw the fire out of his fut!"

While the price of matches was so high, it is not surprising that the tinder-box with its flint and steel remained in vogue among the great mass of the people. The use of flint and steel in striking a light survives only among primitive peoples and possibly in remote corners of Europe. Every boy, however, knows that he can call forth at pleasure a brilliant shower of fiery sparks from a dry pavement of coarse sandstone or rough asphalt, provided that his shoes are well shod with iron or steel. He has frequently seen such showers emitted when a powerful horse sets his shoulders to the work of drawing a too heavy load over slippery granite or paving-stones.

In all these instances, as well as in a thousand more where the process is slower, the scientist explains the result as due to friction or rubbing together. Rub any two hard substances—or, indeed, any solid substances—together, and there will always be heat. If the operation is continued with sufficient energy, the heat will increase in intensity until it is visible in the form of "fire." It is this which is displayed when the flint is struck against the steel, or against another piece of flint. To put it briefly, the mechanical energy exerted in producing the friction is transformed into heat, which actually becomes so intense as to set fire to the minute particles of iron or steel that are separated from the mass by the violence of the action. Of course there must be oxygen gas present, otherwise no sparks of light will be emitted at the moment of exerting the friction. If flint and steel be struck against each other in a vacuum, there is no light produced, but the particles of steel thrown off, if afterward examined by a microscope, show distinct signs of having been in a molten state. But in order to get a permanent light from the evanescent shower of sparks, it is necessary that the incandescent particles of steel should be allowed to come into contact with easily ignited material, which will burn slowly,— such a substance, for example, as the tinder produced by the imperfect combustion of linen or cotton rags, or, better still, the substance called amadou, or German tinder, which is a peculiar preparation of several species of fungi (mushroom order) belonging to the genus *Polyporus*. This smouldering tinder may then be touched with a sulphur-tipped wooden splint, which at once bursts into flame.

Now, these are exactly the principles that were turned to account in the old-fashioned tinder-box.

First let us inquire about the tinder which gave its name to the box. Do you know how it was made? You took an old cotton stocking arrived at that time of life when darning was no longer possible. You tied it up and you burned it over the box, so that the black ashes all dropped together in a heap, which you were careful not to disturb. That made the best tinder, but if your stockings were new and good you used old rags. The tinder was put into a large round tin box, big enough for a pie dish. Then a piece of jagged steel, which might have been the remains of an old horseshoe, had to be purchased. The flint, struck edgewise on the steel, sent sparks into the tinder, which smouldered and prepared itself for the matches,—thin strips of wood, diamond-pointed at the ends and dipped in brimstone.

Sir Walter Besant has picturesquely explained the discomforts which attended the use of the tinder-box. He imagines a young father waked up some night in the latter part of the eighteenth century: "John," says his wife, "I wish you would light the candle. I must warm baby's pap." John says never a word, but he obeys. It is a bitterly cold night. He throws a coat over his shoulder and gropes about for the tinder-box. First he falls over a chair and barks his shins, then he bangs his head against a chest of drawers. At length he finds the tinder-box and sits down to light his candle. The baby is now in the active state that follows the first whimper of discontent. John puts the farthing rush on the floor and takes the tinder-box between his knees. It is difficult always to hit the steel with the flint in the dark. Mostly you hit your knuckles, your nails, or your joints. At last a spark falls upon the tinder. By this time the baby is bawling. John nurses the spark; he blows it; he shakes it; he watches it spread; then he puts the brimstone match to it. This is a strip of wood five inches long and one inch broad, tipped with sulphur. The sulphur melts, catches fire, and at last the candle is lit. One parent gets back into bed bleeding at the knuckles, bruised on the shin, chilled through and through, certain of a bad cold for the morrow, and conscious of a sinful temper for the time being; the other parent then arises, and in due course of time—just before the baby goes off into an apoplexy of bawling—the pap is warmed and administered.

The first United States patent for a friction match was issued to A. Phillips, October 24, 1836. He describes his invention as consisting in the substitution of chalk for sulphur.

Maternity. A story is extant of a certain rabbi who, finding that his serious eloquence could not keep his flock awake, roused them from their slumbers by shouting, " Once there was a Jewess who had six hundred thousand children."

Up started the congregation, all attention. A demand for the woman's name followed.

" Jochebed," continued the preacher. " Was not her son Moses equal to six hundred thousand who came from Egypt?"

This was a joke, and a pretty poor one at that. But there is still extant a memorial tablet—put up in all seriousness and accepted seriously by many people even to the present day— which preserves the record of a parturitive phenomenon that is hardly more credible. You may find the first English record in a book published in 1638 and entitled " The Valley of Varietie; or Discourse Fitting for the Times, containing very Learned Passages out of Antiquitie, Philosophy and History," by Henry Peacham, M.A., of Trinity College, Cambridge.

Chapter xvi has a " learned passage" concerning Margaret, wife of Henman, Earl of Henneberge, and daughter of Florence, fourth Earl of Holland and Zealand. " This ladie," says Mr. Peacham in a somewhat ambiguous sentence, " lived in the time of Henry III, Emperor, who brought forth at one birth 365 children, the just number of daies in the year, in memory whereof, not far from Leyden in Holland, in a village called Lansdunen, there is yet a faire table of marble, which containeth the whole history of this stupendious accident; which as it there standeth engraven upon marble I will truly relate, for I myself have twice or thrice when I lived in Holland, seen the same."

The story which Mr. Peacham paraphrases from the tablet is briefly as follows: Margaret, in the fortieth year of her age, on Easter Sunday in the year 1276, was brought to bed of 365 children, 182 being boys, the same number girls, while the odd one was sexless. This marvel happened by direct interposition of Providence. The countess admired a couple of male twins carried in arms by a poor woman, but refused to believe that both were by one father, and so dismissed the mother in contempt.

" Whereupon this poor woman, being much perplexed in her mind, presently prayed to God to send her [the countess] as many children as there were days in the whole year; which thing, besides the course of nature, in a stupendious manner came to pass."

The children, it is added, were baptized in two basins by Guido, the bishop of Utrecht, all the males receiving the name of John, all the females that of Elizabeth. All died the same day and their mother with them, and all, with their mother, lie buried under the tablet in the Lansdunen church.

Further corroboration as to the existence of the tablet is

furnished by Pepys, who visited the church on May 19, 1660, and who records a later visit in his "Picturesque Tour through Holland, Brabant, etc.," published 1795.

Though a Dutch author mentions having seen the children and describes them as no bigger than shrimps, efforts have been made to rationalize the myth. Ireland's suggestion is that on a January 3rd the beggar wished the countess might have as many children as there had been days in the year, and that the wish was promptly fulfilled by the countess being delivered of triplets on that day.

Next to the Countess Margaret myth the record for fecundity, as chronicled by mediæval authorities, is that of one hundred and twenty-five at a single birth. The earliest instance runs back to the beginning of the twelfth century, and the same prodigy, after being handled diversely by succeeding annalists, is finally fastened on the empress of Frederick Barbarossa, two centuries later. Since the fourteenth century no historical feminine personage is credited with more than the comparatively modest figure of eight. That figure apparently was only once attained,—*i.e.*, on September 9, 1567, by a certain Signora de la Riva, of Florence, who is mentioned by more than one Italian writer of average sixteenth-century intelligence and credibility.

English statistics show that twins occur once in every thousand births, while in every million births there is a possibility of 160 triplets and 8 quadruplets. Quintuplets are so rare as to be practically a negligible quantity.

At first sight, therefore, there seems nothing prodigious in the case of Mrs. Ormsby, of Chicago, who gave birth to three boys and one girl in October, 1901. But the jaded interest of the reader may be stimulated by the further fact that Mrs. Ormsby herself was one of triplets, and had been married only seven years, during which time she had had fourteen children. The first three years yielded one baby annually, then came twins (twice), then triplets (these won prizes at a baby show), and then the quadruplets. With this culminating feat Mrs. Ormsby passes out of history. There is no telling what procreative phenomena have been hers during these post-historic years.

In November, 1895, the St. Louis *Republic* published an account of the much-be-familied David Vititoe, a wealthy farmer and horse-trainer in Breckenridge County, Kentucky. Married three times, this uxorious gentleman had given forty children to the world. In 1896 his eldest son was 47, his youngest a babe in arms. One remarkable feature of this immense family was the absence of any duplicate birth. There were no twins, triplets, or other combinations. Boys outnumbered the girls. Those old enough to earn a living were mostly jockeys and horse-trainers, having inherited their father's equine tastes.

A notable instance of persistent fecundity was that of a Swedish family represented in this country by Mrs. Pennock, a resident of St. Louis. Her mother had given birth to twenty-four children, including six sets of twins. Mrs. Pennock herself at twenty-one years of age had borne three sets of twins. One of her elder sisters could boast of four pair of twins, another of six pair, while thirteen more of her mother's children had each three sets of twins, making a total of fifty-eight sets of twins in one family.

In *Notes and Queries* (9th Series, xi, 66), P. J. Anderson, of the University Library of Aberdeen, claims to have found among his own ancestral records the prize instance of a rapid succession of births in one family. His maternal great-grand-father, Thomas Bisset, minister of Logierait in Scotland, had eleven children by his second wife. " Of these Anna was born on 30 October, 1772, and baptized 2 November, and Elizabeth was born on 29 May, 1773, and baptized 31 May. Here the interval is only 211 days. Can an authentic instance," he asks, "be cited of a shorter period between successive births, both children surviving? "

No cne took up the challenge so thrown down. But if the limitation of authenticity be not too severely respected, the *Recreative Review* (vol. i, London, 1821) will be found to supply a phenomenon far more startling. " In the *Mercure de France* for 1728," says this authority, " is an account of a woman who seemed to have nothing else to do but to multiply children. Mrs. De Castro, of Caraminhal, seven months after her marriage, having a fall, gave *rise* to the following young gentlemen and ladies. On the 8th of February, 1728, she was delivered of a boy; April 20th, of a girl; April 27th of another boy; April 29th, of another; April 30th, of another. On the 5th of May she began again, and had two girls and a boy and then left off; but the priest, thinking so large a population might possibly weaken the mother, judged it proper to give her extreme unction: the unction was thrown away upon the woman, for she recovered: but the priest had not the trouble of christening the young brood of De Castro, for they all died without receiving baptism."

The largest grand total of children borne by one wife to her husband during the entire term of their married life appears to be 62. Brand's " History of Newcastle " credits this feat to the wife of a poor weaver in Scotland. Of these, 46 boys and only 4 girls survived to manhood and womanhood. Sir John Bowers of Newcastle, we are informed, adopted 10 of the sons, three other landed gentlemen, took 10 each, the remainder were brought up by the parents. "The certainty of this relation," says Brand, "I had from John Delavall, of Northumberland, Esq., who, anno 1630, rode about thirty miles beyond England to see this fruitful couple."

At an auction sale of the San Donato collection of pictures held in London in 1870, there was sold a portrait of Dianora Frescobaldi by Bronzino. Though it has unquestionably high merits as a work of art, the price which it fetched ($3000, an unusual sum in those simpler days) was in a measure due to the inscription at its foot, which asserts that Dianora was the mother "of at least fifty-two children." She had never less than three at a birth, says the inscription, and it may be added that there is a tradition in the Frescobaldi family that she once had six.

Algernon Charles Swinburne often referred with gusto to the fact that one of his ancestresses had borne thirty children to the same husband. "I think you will allow," he says in a letter to Edmund Clarence Stedman, "that when this race chose at last to produce a poet, it could have been at least remarkable if he had been content to write nothing but hymns and idyls for clergymen and young ladies to read out in chapels and drawing-rooms."

No great city can show a more brilliant record of large families than the capital of Prussia. According to the census of 1900, two hundred and forty Berlin women were the mothers of from 13 to 20 children apiece. One healthy, active hausfrau had been filling her quiver so rapidly that, though only forty-five years old, she had already twenty-five olive-branches around her table. Another, four years her junior, could boast of twenty-three, while three other women between the ages of forty and forty-three had presented their husbands with twenty-one descendants each.

The *Recreative Review,* vol. ii, p. 538 (London, 1822), gives no authority for this paragraph, here quoted for what it is worth: "In the year 1755, a Muscovite peasant named James Kyrloff and his wife were presented to the Empress of Russia. This peasant had been twice married, and was then seventy years of age. His first wife was brought to bed twenty-one times,—viz., four times of four children each time, seven times of three, and ten times of two, making in all fifty-seven children who were then alive. His second wife, who accompanied him, had already been delivered seven times,—once of three children and six times of twins, which made fifteen children for her share. Thus the Muscovite patriarch had already seventy-two children by two marriages."

Mayor (Fr. *maire*, Sp. *mayor*, Port. *maio*, from the Latin *major*, comparative of *magnus*, "great"), the chief magistrate of a city or burg. In Scotland the same officer is known as provost, in Germany as burgomaster, in Italy as syndico. Only the mayors of London and York in England and of Dublin in Ireland bear the additional title of Lord, which is not personal, but attached to the office. The Lord Mayor of London is entitled to the prefix "Right Honorable" before his name. This, together with the title "Lord," was first allowed by Edward III in 1354. York has enjoyed the privilege since 1389, when a new charter was granted to the town by Richard II. The Mayor of Dublin was first styled Lord Mayor by Charles II, in 1665.

The mayors of Edinburgh and Glasgow have the title of Lord Provost. The same designation has long been popularly given to the Mayor of Aberdeen. The latter's right to it has been contested by the Court of Session, but seems lately to have acquired some sanction from royal usage. A claim for the title has also been put forward for the Provost of Perth, based on the fact that on one occasion he was addressed by Queen Victoria as Lord Provost. The Lord Provost of Edinburgh is entitled to the prefix "Right Honorable," which may be attached not merely to the name of his office but to his Christian name and surname. The usage probably originated in the circumstance that the Lord Provost of Edinburgh was *ex officio* a member of the Old Scots Privy Council.

Both in Great Britain and on the continent the establishment of a chief magistrate in the large cities was part of the struggle against kingly or aristocratic encroachments upon the rights of the commonalty. His first appearance was in London in 1191, when the recognition of the communa by Earl John and Walter of Rouen is followed by the mention of Mayor Henry Fitz Alwin. He held the office until his death. In 1194 King John conceded to the barons of London the right of annually choosing a mayor, subject to the approval of the king, who though elected for only a twelvemonth was usually re-elected many successive times. With the year 1319 began the practice of that rotation in office which secures a brand-new mayor at every successive election. During all the thirteenth century the great struggle in London politics had been who should elect the mayor,— the aldermen (representing the propertied classes) or the populace. The beginning of the fourteenth century, however, saw the rise of craft guilds, which, in Edward IV's time, were successful in gaining control of the city government being in a large sort of way the representatives of all classes of tradesmen. To-day the Lord Mayor is nominated by the Livery on September

29th, and is commonly the senior alderman who has not already " passed the chair."

The way a lord mayor is found is very quaint. The names of two aldermen are submitted to the court, and all the members retire for a time into a room where, among a mass of flowers representing a cross, the sword of state is laid. Then in turn each alderman approaches the city recorder and whispers to him the name of the one for whom he would vote. The candidate who receives the greatest number of votes is generally the one who is elected.

The duties and dignities of his Lordship are manifold, though some are obsolescent if not obsolete. Theoretically at least he is the representative of royalty within the City limits. Outside the City of London proper he has of course no jurisdiction. His only troops are 1000 policemen, but no royal troops may enter the City without his permission. He receives the password of the London Tower every three months, under the sign-manual of the king. This enables him to gain admittance at any time in the day or night, even though the guard be set. The periodical communication of the password is a highly prized concession, though there is no record in recent times of any official use of the privilege. Within the city the Lord Mayor takes precedence of all persons save the king. Even the Prince of Wales falls behind him on official occasions. When the king visits the city, the Lord Mayor meets him at Temple Bar and hands him the sword of state, which is handed back by His Majesty. Incidentally the Mayor has the choice of four swords,—the Sword of State, for supreme occasions; the Pearl Sword, for ceremonial functions; the Black Sword, borne on the death of a member of the royal family or at funerals; and a fourth, which is hung over the Lord Mayor's chair at the Central Criminal Court.

There are other emblems of office,—the diamond sceptre, the seal, the purse, the mace. They play their part at the swearing in of the Lord Mayor elect. The City Chamberlain, with three obeisances, presents the sceptre to the retiring Lord Mayor. He in his turn delivers it to his successor, who lays it on the table in front of him. The Chamberlain retires, with three more reverences, to return with the seal—and three reverences more! The purse is similarly presented. Further genuflexions follow from the sword-bearer, who renders up the sword; the mace-bearer also resigns the mace. The ex-Lord Mayor then surrenders his key of the coffer in which the seal is kept. There are three keys; of the other two one is held by the Chamberlain, the second by the chairman of the Lands Committee. To unlock the coffer all three must be produced.

Though this complex ceremonial may seem sadly belated, it has great historic interest. It implies the sovereign power and authority, in ancient times, of the chief magistrate of the City. The sceptre, sword, and mace are emblems of royalty. The Lord Mayor was a merchant prince in fact as well as by name.

At the coronation of the sovereign the Lord Mayor acts as the chief butler to royalty. At the sovereign's death he takes his seat in the Privy Council, and signs the proclamation of the succession to the throne. He must be officially informed of the birth or death of any member of the royal family. Such announcements are still posted, according to ancient custom, upon the walls of the Mansion House.

He is still, by virtue of his office, Admiral of the Port of London—a delightfully Gilbertian appointment; gauger of wine and oil and other gaugable articles; meter of coals, grain, salt, and fruit, and inspector of butter, hops, soap, cheese, and other articles coming into the port of London. Needless to say, these duties are performed by deputy. He is, to mention but one or two more of his dignities, a governor of four hospitals, a trustee of St. Paul's Cathedral, and a magistrate " in several places." Perhaps his most curious office, next to Admiral of the Port, is that of Coroner.

The Mayor receives from the corporation of London an annual income of £10,000, the use of the Mansion House, rent free, and also of its furniture; though at the termination of his year of office the outgoing Mayor usually expends a substantial sum in order to renovate the same for the incoming tenant. He has to pay all the expenses of the household, including a host of servants and footmen, find all his horses, which are generally contracted for, and provide all his own carriages with the exception of one. This is the old state carriage; which until 1896 formed so prominent a part of the show on Lord Mayor's Day, November 9th. In addition the newly elected Mayor is called upon to put up one-half the expenses connected with Lord Mayor's Day, which seldom fall below £4000. What with this entertainment and others that are more or less obligatory, the mere pageantry of the office usually consumes the entire salary.

On the other hand, it is estimated that it costs the corporation about $90,000 a year to maintain the pomp and glory of the Lord Mayor's office. It is not surprising that the entire office and its ceremonial have been savagely attacked by radicals and by humorists. Especial fun has been poked at the old-fashioned state coach. It was built in the year 1757. Subscriptions of £60 each were raised from every alderman then in office, and it was further decreed that until the entire debt was cancelled every new alderman should on his election be mulcted a like sum and every new Lord Mayor the sum of £100. The coach is elaborately carved and gilded. Cipriani, a famous artist of the period, was employed to decorate the panels with emblematic designs. Instead of being hung upon springs, it is suspended upon four thick black leather braces, fastened with huge gilt buckles, each bearing the city arms.

In mediæval times, and indeed until much later, civic hospitalities, though magnificent enough, were somewhat rough and rude. The era of refinement may be said to have begun with the erection of the present Mansion House. Previous to that time the Lord Mayors dispensed their hospitality out of doors at the Guildhall and other places. Their feasts being of so public a character, the restraints of polite society were not always scrupulously observed. The first stone of the building was laid in 1739, and the whole was completed and equipped in the mayoralty of Sir Crisp Gascoigne, who was the first Lord Mayor that resided in it. The entire cost of palace and furniture was £80,000. Walsh: *Curiosities of Popular Customs,* p. 688.

In Germany and other parts of the continent of Europe, the office is one of less ostentation, but is equally connected with the great struggle that overthrew feudalism. The robber barons of the Rhine, the Danube, and elsewhere lived by levying tolls upon tradesmen who passed by their castles or through their territories. Frequently they added murder or imprisonment to mere extortion. Supreme within their own territories, the law could not touch them, and the reigning sovereign did not care to quarrel with them on behalf of common merchants and traders. Therefore the latter were compelled to band together and pay for armed escorts; this ultimately led to trading leagues between large towns, ending in the famous Hanseatic League of the North German cities, which first established trade on a secure basis, and gave to the people municipal institutions, leading to the establishment of hotels de villes and mayoralties whose magnificence soon came to rival the castles of the nobility.

The municipal officers also were inaugurated with ceremonies and rejoicings which occupied the same place in public esteem as the court ceremonies and tournaments in the minds of the aristocrats. Royal visits were celebrated by processions and pageantries in which the mayor took the leading parts.

The following advertisement appeared in a number of German papers in the year 1910:

The place of Mayor (Burgomaster) of Madgeburg is vacant. The salary is 21,000 marks ($5250) a year, including the rental of a dwelling in the city hall. Besides his salary the incumbent will receive 4000 marks ($1000) for his official expenses. Candidates should apply before September 1.

The German idea is that a municipality is a business, to be conducted on business lines. The office of mayor is one requiring knowledge and skill of a technical, professional character. A man who has proved himself a good mayor in one German town is frequently invited to another.

The larger towns look to the smaller towns to train municipal officers for them. It frequently happens that two cities bid in competition for a particularly expert man. . So when their chief burgomaster, Dr. Lentz, was appointed Prussian Minister of Finance, the good people of Madgeburg gave public notice of their need of a capable man to succeed him. ·

Huet, in his " Itinere Sueccio," a poem in Latin hexameters descriptive of a journey through Sweden in the year 1652, tells as a fact this story of the mode of electing a burgomaster at a town not far from Stockholm which he calls Hardenberg:

> We late at night at Hardenberg arrive,　　　·
> Where an old custom still is kept alive;
> When for a consul's choice the time is come,
> The solemn senate in their council room,
> With long extended beards most amply graced,
> Around a venerable table placed,
> In order sit. Each chin is gravely laid
> Upon the table, and the beard displayed;
> Exactly in the midst a louse they place;
> Each gazes steadfast with attentive face:
> That beard, befriended by the powers above,
> To which the sacred animal doth move,
> Is carried through the town with solemn state,
> And crowds revere the lousy magistrate.

This story is on a par with the tradition of the ancient mode of choosing the Mayor of Grimsby, in England, which is as follows :—The burgesses assembled at the church and selected three of the worthiest of themselves as candidates for the office, who were then conducted, with a bunch of hay tied to each of their backs, to the common pound, into which they were placed blindfolded with a calf, and he whose bunch of hay was first eaten by the calf was thereupon declared the Mayor for the ensuing year.

Mayor, New York. The first New York mayor was not a New Yorker but a New Englander and primarily an Englishman. In a remote corner of Little Neck Cemetery, a neglected burying-ground in East Providence, R. I., is a gravestone erected to " ye. Wor. Thomas Willett," who died August 4, 1674, " in ye 64 year of his age," and " who was the first mayor of New York

and twice did sustain yt place." In 1629 Willett, whose ancestry and birthplace are unrecorded, landed at Plymouth, Mass.,
as one of a ship-load of Pilgrims brought over by the *Speedwell* from Leyden, Holland. The nineteen-year-old lad attracted
the attention of Governor Winthrop of Plymouth Colony, who
gave him his first appointment as agent at the colony's trading
post in Maine. His experience in dealing with Indian tribes
stood him in good stead when he succeeded the disgruntled
Miles Standish as captain of the Plymouth military company
and was drawn into the boundary disputes between New England and New Amsterdam. So well did he earn his title as the
Peacemaker that, when it was finally agreed to leave the questions at issue to arbitration, each party naming two commissioners, Willett was chosen by the Dutch as one of their representatives. The final adjudication proved satisfactory to both
sides. In 1660 Willett obtained a grant of lands west of Plymouth and extending southward to Narragansett Bay. Five
years later the English conquered New Amsterdam and renamed
it New York. In June, 1665, Willett was appointed mayor,
with the approval of English and Dutch alike. He was serving
his second term when, in 1673, the Dutch reconquered their
city and reëstablished their own government. Willett then retired to his farm on the shore of Narragansett Bay, where he
died next year.

Following a British precedent, it is the custom in New
York for the city at its own expense to erect lamps in front of
the mayor's private residence, and to keep them lit at the
municipal expense not only during his term of office, but during
his lifetime, and after his death if desired. Even before he has
taken the oath of office, the lamp-superintendent calls upon him
and displays various designs of lamps for his selection. Though
the shapes may vary, each lamp must be surmounted by a small
brass eagle. The earliest lamps also bore the city coat of arms
on their faces.

The custom is traceable to the old days when the city was
little more than a village and the mayor was a magistrate. The
two lamps indicated where the mayor could be found at night.
The houses of the older mayors, from Cornelius Lawrence, the
first, who lived at what was then 354 Broadway, to Andrew
Mickle at No. 1 Broadway, have been absorbed by the newer
business structures, but in 1912 there still remained in New York
twenty-three mayoralty residences that had lamps in front of
them.

Neither Mayor Oakey Hall nor Smith Ely would permit
lamps before his residence. Mayor Hoffman had his lamp pro-

vided by the proprietors of the Clarendon Hotel, in Union Place, where he resided during his term of office. This hotel was torn down in 1909.

Mayor, Woman. In Charles K. Hoyt's farce comedy "A Contented Woman," first produced in New York in 1890, a wealthy resident of Denver puts himself in nomination for mayor of that city. He hopes the office may prove a stepping-stone to the governorship of the State and eventually to the national Senate. The worry of the campaign upsets his nerves. One day, when he is in a hurry to "get out with the boys," a button comes off his overcoat. His wife sews it on several inches out of place. "Damn that button!" testily cries the candidate. His wife takes offence and is induced to run on the ticket against him. She is elected—only to find that, being under twenty-one years of age, she cannot take the office. The whole play, of course, is a satire against the woman in politics. Little did the satirist imagine that within twenty-one years after the production of the piece a woman would actually be elected to the office of mayor in a western town not a thousand miles away from Denver—and take her seat, though with some preliminary difficulty. This town was Hunnewell, Kansas, and the lady's name was Mrs. Ella Wilson. She was elected in April, 1911.

Medicine Hat, a prosperous city in the Canadian Northwest, which enjoys a wide reputation, especially among American humorists, as a weather-breeder. "Medicine Hat," said the Buffalo *Courier*, "is known the continent over as the place where the coldest of the cold waves and blizzards come from. In 1910-11 a movement was started by leading citizens to change the name of the town to something less peculiar and eccentric, in the hope that the new name might blot out the old reputation which they held to be hurtful to the city's business. Mr. Rudyard Kipling, who had been a guest in Medicine Hat and was reckoned one of Canada's staunchest friends, was consulted in the matter." His reply contains much good sense and is here reproduced.

So far as I can make out from what I heard when I was with you in 1907, and from the clippings you enclose, the chief arguments for the change are:

(*a*) That some United States journalists have some sort of joke that Medicine Hat supplies all the bad weather of the United States, and (*b*) that another name would look better at the head of a prospectus. Incidentally I note that both arguments are developed at length by the Calgary *Herald*. I always knew that the Calgary *Herald* called Medicine Hat names, but I did not realize that Medicine Hat wanted to be Calgary's little godchild.

Now, as to the charge of brewing bad weather, etc., I see no reason on earth why white men should be bluffed out on their city's birthright by an imported joke. Accept the charge joyously and proudly, and go forward as Medicine Hat, the only city officially recognized as capable of freezing out the United States and giving the Continent cold feet.

Let us examine the sound of the present name, Medicine Hat. I have not my maps by me, but I seem to remember a few names of places across the border such as Schenectady, Podunk, Schoharie, Poughkeepsie, Potomac, Cohoes, Tonawanda, Oneonta, etc.—all of which are rather curious to the outsider.

But it is people, and not prospectuses, that make cities, and time has sanctified the queer syllables with memories and association for millions of our fellow creatures. Once on a time these places were young and new and in process of making themselves. That is to say, they were ancestors with a duty to posterity, which duty they fulfilled in handing on their names intact, and Medicine Hat is to-day an ancestor, not a derivative, not a collateral, but the founder of a line.

To my mind the name of Medicine Hat has an advantage over all the names I have quoted. It echoes, as you so justly put it, the old Cree and Blackfoot tradition of red mystery and romance that once filled the prairies.

Also it hints, I venture to think, at the magic that underlies the city in the shape of your natural gas.

Believe me, the very name is an asset, and as years go on will become more and more of an asset. It has no duplicate in the world; it makes men ask questions, and, as I knew more than twenty years ago, draws the feet of the young men toward it.

It has the qualities of uniqueness, individuality, association, and power. Above all, it is the lawful, original, sweat and dust won name of the city; and to change it would be to risk the luck of the city, to disgust and dishearten old-timers, not in the city alone, but the world over, and to advertise abroad the city's lack of faith in itself.

Men do not think much of a family which has risen in the world changing its name for social reasons. They think still less of a man who, because he is successful, repudiates the wife who stood by him in his early struggles.

I do not know what I should say, but I have the clearest notion of what I should think of a town that went back on itself.

Forgive me if I write strongly, but this is a matter on which I feel keenly. As you know, I have not a dollar or a foot of land in Medicine Hat, but I have a large stake at interest and very true affection in and for the city and its folks. It is for this reason that in writing to you I have taken a liberty which to men who have known the city for several months or perhaps three years must seem inexcusable.

Menhaden, the New England name for a species of shad or herring, unfit for food but very valuable for its oil and especially for manuring. It has long been regarded as the most mysterious fish on the Atlantic seaboard. Hundreds of millions are destroyed every year. Yet there appears no diminution in the supply. The manufacturers even say that in no season is more than one-fifth of the supply taken. As the fishing is not done in a spawning season it interferes little with the fish's propagation.

Where the menhaden come from in early summer and where they go in autumn are unsolved questions. They begin to run in the spring at the Gulf of Mexico, and are followed northward by the fishing fleets until Maine is reached in late summer.

More mysterious than their appearance in the spring and their disappearance in the fall is the facility of the fish for propagation, which enables them to appear each season in undiminished myriads.

It has been suggested that nature has designed them as a food fish for their more meritorious fellow citizens of the sea, just as certain land animals seem intended solely for the feeding of others, which in turn are valuable as food for man. When, for instance, you eat bluefish, bonitas, weakfish, bass, or cod, you are more than likely consuming nothing but assimilated menhaden, which largely contribute to the flesh and bone of their superiors.

In support of this suggestion it is pointed out that they swim in closely packed, unwieldy masses, helpless as flocks of sheep, close to the surface, where they are at the mercy of every enemy, destitute of means of defence or offence, a pitiable, forlorn horde.

Feeding upon vegetable matters, usually the organic substances at the mouths of rivers, the menhaden have a very unpleasant flavor, and few people consider them wholesome food.

The menhaden industry is by no means modern. As far back as 1682, in Virginia, it was known that fish spread over the fields made very good fertilizer, and it was recorded that an Indian had taught the early settlers its virtues. Not until 1850, however, was the value of this fish as a producer of oil discovered. A poor woman made that discovery. She was Mrs. John Bartlett, of Blue Hill, Maine. The fact that oil rose to the surface of the water when she boiled menhaden for her chickens suggested to her the commercial possibilities in the fish.

The first year the Bartlett family made $143 by shipping the oil to Boston, where it was so highly appreciated that menhaden factories were quickly established and fishing fleets organized.

Methodism, Cradle of. A term sometimes applied to Barratt's Chapel near Frederica, Kent County, Delaware. It was here that Bishop Coke and Asbury first met in America, held a council with 11 preachers, and arranged for the organization of the Methodist Church as it exists to-day in the United States. During the year 1780 the chapel was erected on ground donated for the purpose by Philip Barratt, a member of the Delaware Assembly, who was one of the Americans that entertained and protected Asbury during the revolution. In 1912 an endowment fund of $50,000 was raised to preserve forever this landmark in the history of the Methodist Church.

Mezzotint. According to the familiar story told in Spence's "Anecdotes," this process in engraving was invented by the famous Prince Rupert (1619–82), nephew to Charles I, who devoted himself much to the prosecution of chemical and philosophical experiments as well as to the practice of mechanic arts.

The prince, going out early one morning, observed a sentinel at some distance from his post, very busy doing something to his piece. The prince inquired what he was about. He replied that the dew had fallen in the night and made his fusil rusty, and therefore he was scraping and cleaning it. The prince, looking at it, was struck with something like a figure eaten into the barrel, with innumerable little holes close together like frieze work on gold and silver, part of which the soldier had scraped away. From this trifling incident, as we are told, Prince Rupert conceived the idea of mezzotinto. "He concluded that some contrivance might be found to cover a brass plate with such a grained ground of fine pressed holes as would undoubtedly give an impression all black, and that, by scraping away proper parts, the smooth superficies would leave the rest of the paper white. Communicating his ideas to Wallerant Vaillant, a painter, they made several experiments, and at last invented a steel roller, cut with tools to make teeth like a file or rasp, with projecting points, which effectually produced the black grounds; those being scraped away and diminished at pleasure, left the gradations of light. It is said that the first mezzotinto print ever published was engraved by the prince himself. It may be seen in the first of Evelyn's 'Sculptura,' and there is a copy of it in the second edition, printed in 1755."

This appears circumstantial enough. Nevertheless, later researches have established the fact that the invention was made by Ludwig von Siegen (born 1609 at Utrecht), a member of the household of the Landgrave of Hesse Cassel. The first known print executed by Siegen in this manner (a portrait of his patron's mother, the Dowager Landgravine, Amelia Elizabeth) is dated 1642. In a letter to the landgrave which accompanied a first impression of this print, Siegen declares that "how this work was done no copper-plate engraver or artist can explain or imagine." In 1654 Von Siegen visited Brussels, and there came in contact with Prince Rupert, who had already been practising etching. To him the inventor disclosed his secret, and it was a little later that Prince Rupert called in Vaillant to his aid. Consequently all the dictionaries are wrong that follow Spence's account of the matter.

35

Microscope. Ptolemy, in his "Optics," inserts a table of the refractions of light under different angles of incidence through glass, which implies a knowledge of the prism, if not of the curved lens; and Seneca speaks of writing being magnified when viewed through a globe of glass filled with water. Lenses with a focal length of nine millimetres have been found at Pompeii, and Dutens had in his possession one of a longer focus which was dug up at Herculaneum. The period of the earliest combination and adjustment of lenses so as to form a microscope is not to be fixed with precision. The honor has been generally taken to rest with the Jansens, who are said to have constructed microscopes in Holland as early as the year 1590. One of these was brought, it is said, to London by Cornelius Drebbel, who showed it to William Borrell and others. It was formed of a copper tube six feet long and one inch in diameter, supported by three brass pillars in the shape of dolphins. These were fixed to a base of ebony, on which the objects to be viewed by means of the object glass were placed. Francesco Fontana of Naples, in a work published A.D. 1646, lays claim to have constructed a microscope as early as 1618. The power of these early instruments was no doubt extremely limited. Writing from Flanders in 1611, Daniel Antonini complains to Galileo that no one in that country knew how to construct object-glasses to magnify above five times, and as late as 1637 no telescopes could be produced in Holland capable of showing the satellites of Jupiter. Huyghens, in his "Dioptrica," published in 1678, says he has heard from many people of microscopes made by Drebbel at London since the year 1621. On the other hand, we have the express testimony of Viviani to the fact that Galileo was led, by his experiments with convex and concave lenses, to the construction of a microscope about the same time as his invention of the telescope, i.e., as early as 1610. In his famous "Dialogue" Galileo asserts that he had in that year shown the solar spots both in Padua and Venice. Viviani mentions the gift of a microscope by Galileo to the King of Poland in 1612. Letters from Prince Cesi, Bartolommeo Imperiali, Bartolommeo Balbi, and other personages of note, to whom Galileo had made presents of microscopes in 1624, speak of the invention in terms which leave no doubt to whom, in their minds, the credit of the invention was due.

About the year 1665 small globules of glass began to take the place of the convex lens in the single microscope, with a great increase of magnifying power. This invention has been claimed for M. Hartsoeker, but is really due to Dr. Hooke, who describes the mode of making those globules in the preface to his "Micrographia Illustrata," published in 1656. In the "Philosophical Transactions" for 1696 Mr. Stephen Gray recounts some curious experiments of his with globules of water, whereby animalcules or other small objects which were scarcely discernible with the glass globule were made to appear as large as ordinary peas. The single microscope is so simple in construction as to admit but little improvement save in the mode of mounting it, or in the way of additions to its apparatus. The chief of these improvements was the concave speculum of polished silver introduced by Lieberkühn in 1740, whereby light was thrown upon both surfaces of an opaque object instead of one. At one end of the short tube was fixed the magnifier, a small double convex lens; at the other, the condensing lens for concentrating the light upon the speculum. Instead of glass, which rapidly decomposes, natural substances such as rock crystal, the diamond, ruby, or garnet, have been brought into use. At the Paris Exhibition in 1855, Professor Amici brought before the jury upon philosophical instruments a compound achromatic microscope of small dimensions, which exhibited certain striæ in test objects better than any of the other instruments under examination. This superiority is partly ascribed to the introduction of a drop of water between the object and the lens. To Lieberkühn is due the invention in 1738 of the solar microscope, the immense powers of which, especially when brought to bear upon Trembley's great discoveries in the department of polypes and other of the lower animal organisms, gave an extraordinary stimulus to microscopic inquiry.

There is no province of science in which the microscope has not been of inestimable value. There are some which it has absolutely called into being. The whole subject of histology, for example owes its origin, and the wondrous light it throws upon the laws and conditions of organic life, to this artificial expansion of our visual powers. To analyze or enumerate at any length the gains, not to our abstract knowledge alone, but to the appliances, the comforts, and the security of life which are traceable to this new and inexhaustible source of power, would require a volume to itself. Discoveries as recent and as suggestive as that of the gradual accumulation of chalk from the deposition of the Atlantic ooze, and that of the organic structure of the Laurentian rock, which has doubled on the instant the entire range of time previously assigned for the duration of living forms upon our globe; also the detection of fraud in the composition of articles of food, the diagnosis of disease, especially in its incipient and less manifest stages, the conviction of the murderer by the witness of the victim's blood—

these are services for which we have to thank the prompt and handy instrument which modern science and skill have adapted to our manifold uses.

Mile-stone. Each of the old post-roads leading out of Manhattan preserves some of the old mile-stones that were set up in prerevolutionary days.

The nineteenth stone of the Albany post-road is at Yonkers, built into the stone wall on the estate at 615 Broadway, while the twentieth is on the east side of the roadway at about 1150 Broadway.

At Dobbs Ferry is a mile-stone, dilapidated and undecipherable, at the corner of Broadway and Walnut Street. It may be the twenty-third mile-stone.

At Croton-on-the-Hudson are two mile-stones built into the wall about the Van Cortlandt houses, and probably placed here for preservation. One of them should be the fortieth mile-stone. In this same wall is a curiosity of Indian manufacture, a hollowed-out stone for grinding corn.

At Peekskill, by the Holman house, a short distance north of the village, is the fiftieth mile-stone, lately repaired and reset by the D. A. R. The old house is the Dusenbury Tavern of Revolutionary days. Here Major André was kept overnight after his capture at Tarrytown.

Along the Boston post-road may be mentioned the nineteenth mile-stone at New Rochelle, at the corner of Echo Avenue, the twenty-third mile-stone at Rye, near Mamaroneck, and the twenty-fourth at Rye, opposite the John Jay house.

A mile-stone dissimilar to the others is the one on the White Plains road, Scarsdale, near the Wayside Inn. The inscription reads:

> XXIV
> Miles to
> N. York
> 1775.

It is the only mile-stone that has been noticed bearing Roman numerals. The Wayside Inn, a low, rambling, picturesque building, was a tavern in the early days, and it is said had a charter from one of the Georges for a perpetual license to sell liquor.

Million. In some of the western public schools where large halls are available, an effort has been made to realize for the juvenile mind the meaning and magnitude of "one million." Large sheets of paper are secured, each about 4½ feet square, ruled in ¼-inch squares. In each alternate square a round black wafer or circle is placed, a little overlapping the square, thus leaving an equal amount of white space between the black spots. At each tenth spot a double width is left so as to separate each hundred spots, ten by ten. Each sheet then holds 10,000 spots, each horizontal or vertical row containing 1000. One hundred such sheets contain, of course, a million spots, and they would occupy a space 450 feet long in one row or ninety feet long in five rows, so that they would entirely cover the walls of a room about thirty feet square and twenty-five feet high from floor to ceiling, allowing space for doors, but not for windows.

Modern journalism, again, has sought to reduce the term down to the level of the meanest intelligence among adults. Here is one specimen among many that have gone the rounds of the press.

It has been estimated that 1,000,000 persons assembled in a crowd, with due allowance of, say, three square feet a person, would cover an area of 68.8 acres, or, to put it more conveniently, let us say 70 acres; or it could be contained in a square having sides 577.6 yards long. Or, again, allowing 18 inches to each person, standing shoulder to shoulder, 1,000,000 individuals would extend a distance of 284.1 miles. The population of London amounts, roughly speaking, to 6,549,000. Allowing 18 inches to each person, shoulder to shoulder, this human aggregation would constitute a wall 1860 miles long.

In astronomical calculation it is most difficult to grasp the meaning of millions of miles, but some idea in this connection may be gathered from the statement of the time that would be consumed by an express train or the shot from a cannon to cover celestial space.

Now, the distance from the earth to the sun is about 92,000,000 miles, and light travelling from the solar luminary comes to us at the rate of 186,700 miles a second. It traverses this distance in 8¼ minutes, but a railway train, proceeding at 60 miles an hour, would take 175 years to cover the distance to the sun.

The circumference of the ellipse forming the orbit of the earth round the sun is about 577,760,000 miles in length, and the earth covers this distance in 365¼ days, travelling at the rate of 65,910 miles an hour, or 1098 miles a minute, or nearly 1100 times as fast as a train going at one mile a minute. It is therefore clear that a train proceeding at this speed would require nearly 1100 years to accomplish the journey around the earth's orbit.

See also BILLION.

Misery Fête. A species of amusement in vogue in rural England at which prizes are awarded to the most sorrowful. The London *Daily Mail,* in September, 1910, gave a humorous account of a fête of this kind held at Market Drayton, Shropshire, on behalf of a local sanatorium. A competition for the most miserable-looking bachelor was here offset by prizes offered for the happiest-looking spinster, and for the smartest-stepping boy or girl of 16 or under. "No fête field," said the *Mail's* correspondent, "has ever presented such a comical appearance as did the tented enclosure at the end of the town. While the men essayed to look gloomy, the girls were all charms. In the misery class marks were awarded for the following points: Puckered brows, drooping mouth corners, wild or sad eyes, unshaven chin, and general forlorn appearance. Dimples, good teeth, apple cheeks, enticing glances went toward the making of a happy young woman; and neat clothes and, above all, upright carriage were the points upon which the smartest boy and girl were picked out."

One man with his face puckered into angles of distress was a hot favorite for the misery prize until he was caught, by a judge, behind the tea tent with his face relaxed and dancing to a merry tune from the band. A young countryman known to have been disappointed in love, who would have been a good model for the carpenter in his mournful walk with the walrus, afterward seemed certain to win. When, however, he saw he was attracting undue attention he fled the field.

Eventually the misery prize went to a young man named William Turner. The award for the happiest young woman went to a girl who had the misfortune to be deaf and dumb— Miss Lucy Pearson, a pretty brunette. William Crabtree and Elsie Pearce won in the class for children who carried themselves the best.

Mission Furniture. It is generally believed that this furniture received its name from the fact that the original pieces were found in the California missions, and that these served as models for all the " mission " furniture that followed. The *Craftsman,* however, has proved that this belief is unfounded, and gives the real origin of the furniture as follows:

A number of years ago a manufacturer made two very clumsy chairs. The legs were merely three-inch posts, the back straight, and the whole construction was rough and crude. They were shown at a spring exhibition of furniture, where they attracted a good deal of attention as a novelty. It was just at the time that the California missions were exciting much attention, and a clever Chicago dealer, seeing the advertising value that lay in the idea, bought both pieces and advertised them as having been found in the California missions.

Another dealer, who possesses a genius for inventing or choosing exactly the right name for a thing, saw these chairs, and was inspired with the idea that it would be a good thing to make a small line of this furniture and name it "mission" furniture. This illusion was carried out by the fact that he put a Maltese cross wherever it would go, between the rails of the back and down at the sides; in fact, it was woven into the construction so that it was the prominent feature and naturally increased the belief in the ecclesiastical origin of the chair. The mingling of novelty and romance instantly pleased the public, and the vogue of "mission" furniture was assured.

Missionary Ship. In November, 1911, there was unveiled in Ruskin Park, London, a tablet to the memory of Captain James Wilson. He commanded the *Duff*, the first missionary ship in history, which was sent out in August, 1796, by the London Missionary Society. Wilson was the son of a Newcastle collier, and after going to sea served as a soldier in the American revolutionary war. Then he went to India as captain of a vessel and served under the East India Company. Taken a prisoner by the French, he swam across a river full of alligators, but was captured by Hyder Ali's soldiers, who stripped him, drove him 500 miles barefoot and wounded, and then thrust him into a dungeon, loaded with irons. When set free, he was almost a skeleton.

Mississippi. The original spelling of the name of the greatest river of North America, and that which came nearest to the old Algonquin tongue, is Meche-sebe, signifying Father of Waters. This was changed by Laval to Michispe; by Labatte to Misispi; and by Marquette to Mississippi, which has abided with it ever since. But neither the Algonquin name nor its corruptions were definitely accepted until after the American Revolution. Henry Seile, the geographer, whose map was made in 1652, calls it "River Canaverall," and locates the head at about the present site of Memphis, Tenn. The early Spanish explorers called it Les Palisades. The Indians along the river banks from the mouth of the Ohio to the Gulf called it Malbouchia. La Salle named it River Colbert, in honor of the famous French minister of finance.

From the mouth of the Ohio to the source it was known to the Indians as Pe-he-ton-at, which in the Algonquin tongue signified abode or habitation of furies; several of the branches were designated by names which in our language would mean "little fury," "big fury," "old fury," etc., the "sippi" or "sepe" being afterwards added to Pe-he-ton-at, simply meaning river or waters.

The greatest race ever run on the Mississippi was between the *Natchez*, a boat built in Cincinnati and commanded by Captain T. P. Leathers, and a New Albany boat, the *Robert E. Lee*, under Captain John W. Cannon.

There was spirited rivalry between the two vessels, and when the *Natchez* made the fastest time on record between New Orleans and St. Louis (1278 miles in 3 days, 21 hours, and 58 minutes) Captain Cannon resolved to beat it. He engaged the steamer *Frank Pargoud* and several fuel boats, and arranged for them to meet him at various points up the river with wood and coal. Then he had his boat cleared of all her upper works likely to catch the wind or make the vessel heavier.

On Thursday, June 20, 1870, at 4.45 P.M., the *Robert E. Lee* steamed out of New Orleans. The *Natchez* followed five minutes later. The race had been advertised in advance and was now awaited with gathering interest at all the river towns. Large crowds were assembled at Natchez, Vicksburg, Helena, and other large places.

Between Cairo and St. Louis the *Natchez* afterward claimed to have lost seven hours and one minute on account of a fog and broken machinery. The *Robert E. Lee*, however, was not delayed, and arrived in St. Louis thirty-three minutes ahead of the previous record established by her competitor. Fifty thousand persons from the housetops, the levee, and the decks of other steamers welcomed the winner as she steamed into port. Captain Cannon was the lion of the hour. The business men gave a banquet in his honor.—*Travel Magazine.*

Mississippi Steamer. In the year 1809 Nicholas Roosevelt, grand-uncle of President Theodore Roosevelt and a member of the firm of Fulton, Livingston and Roosevelt, of New York, arrived in Pittsburg, Pa., for the purpose of introducing steam navigation on the Ohio and Mississippi Rivers. In Pittsburg he built the steamboat *New Orleans,* modelled after the historic *Clermont* which Fulton in 1808 had launched upon the Hudson. Roosevelt himself piloted the boat on her maiden trip to New Orleans. She started from Pittsburg on October 30, 1811.

Possibly no queerer-looking craft, save the more preposterous of Chinese junks, ever carried passengers or freight. The *New Orleans* was 116 feet long, with a 20-foot beam and a cylinder 34 inches in diameter. Shaped like a coastwise schooner, her prow was long and narrow. Her wheel was astern. She carried two masts and a long bowsprit. Her hull was painted a vivid sky-blue, and her square-built portholes were battened with milk-white doors. Her passenger cabins one forward for men and one abaft for the women—were small and comfortless.

All Pittsburg turned out to see this strange craft begin her voyage. The people lined the bank and rent the air with their acclamations. Few had any real belief that she would ever return or even reach her destination. Roosevelt was taking with him his newly-wedded wife, against the protest of relatives and friends. She, at least, had faith in her husband and his boat. When Cincinnati was reached, two days later, the citizens were prepared to give them a rousing reception. But Louisville, Ky., where the *New Orleans* arrived on November 3, was absolutely unprepared. The good people were thrown into a panic by the churning of the paddle-wheel, the glare of the engine fires, and the roar and hiss of escaping steam. Some of them, we are told by letters which remain, fled incontinently to the woods for safety. Many believed that the confusion was caused by the great comet of 1811 falling into the Ohio River opposite the town.

They were finally reassured, however, and next day a public reception was tendered Mr. Roosevelt by the leading citizens of the town. He returned the compliment by inviting a number of them to share his hospitality on board the *New Orleans.*

During the progress of the dinner, which was given in the men's cabin forward, some of the guests expressed their convictions that the boat could never move upstream unaided. The host made no reply, but excused himself and stepped outside the cabin long enough to give a quiet order. A few minutes later his guests were disconcerted by an ominous rumbling, accompanied by unmistakable motion of the boat. Mr. Roosevelt was smilingly pledging their good health in a glass of his own best Madeira.

In wild dismay the company rushed on deck, fully expecting to find the boat broken from her moorings and drifting over the Ohio River falls. Great was their relief to find, upon gaining the deck, that instead of being at the mercy of the stream the doughty little boat was battling her way against the swift current and making steady progress upward. Mr. Roosevelt had taken this means of dissipating their doubts.

Scenes of this sort were repeated all along the line, until the *New Orleans* reached its geographical namesake on December 24, 1811.

After that, for several years, the pioneer steamboat plied her trade between Natchez and New Orleans, averaging about one trip every three weeks. She carried merchandise and passengers at great profit. Her passenger rates were $18 for the downstream trip and $25 upstream. The net profits of her first year are said to have exceeded $20,000. Her total cost for building had been $38,000.

The end came July 13, 1814, when the *New Orleans* landed upon a snag two miles below Baton Rouge. She had been tied to the bank overnight, and settled on the snag because of a fall in the stage of the river. Next morning they tried to warp her ashore, but succeeded only in tearing her sheathing so badly that she had to be run ashore and made fast with the least possible delay. As it was, her passengers and crew barely managed to get ashore with their belongings before she filled and sank to the bottom, where she defied all attempts to raise her.

This was the first of the accidents which afterward added so much to the notoriety of steamboat traffic on the Mississippi. Moreover, it was an innocent accident, whereas some of the later catastrophes were brought on by criminal recklessness in racing one boat against another.

A characteristic episode of this sort is thus reported in the *Illustrated London News* for May 15, 1858:

A terrible illustration of the madness of American steamboat racing is reported from St. Louis. The steamboat *Ocean Spray* and *Hannibal City* were racing on the Mississippi, about five miles from that city, on the 22d of April, when the former was losing her advantage. Resin was first thrown into the furnace, and then the mate suggested turpentine. The captain was by when the order was given, and some of the men went down into the hold and brought up a barrel of turpentine. The men split a hole in the barrel and then, under orders of the mate, dipped the fluid out and threw it over the coal that was lying by. This was not expeditious enough, and the head of the barrel was knocked in, and a bucket with a piece of rope to it was used to dip out the turpentine. The barrel at this time was standing not more than six feet from the furnace doors. After dipping with the bucket and sprinkling the coals, sticks of wood were taken up and their ends plunged into the barrel, and then laid down between the barrel and furnace. While lying there one of the firemen, in pulling out his rake, jerked a live coal, as is supposed, on the wood, when it blazed up furiously. In attempting to throw the barrel overboard it was upset, and the burning fluid spread over the deck and poured in fiery torrents into the hold. The boat was directed to the shore, and those who could jumped on it; others in the attempt were injured, and some drowned. One mother threw her three children one after another to the shore: the first struck, and was injured; the two others fell into the water, but were rescued. One woman attempted to jump, but was caught by her clothing and swung round into the flames, in which she perished. In all there were about twenty lives lost.

Moabite Stone. In 1868 the Rev. Dr. F. Klein, a Prussian missionary, was travelling through Palestine. According to some accounts, he heard from the natives, according to others he himself made the discovery, of a curious stone amid the ruins of the ancient city of Dibon, now Dhibân, in the old land of Moab, east of the Dead Sea. It proved to be a large thick slab of black basalt, on one side of which were thirty-four straight lines of writing in Semitic or Phœnician characters. From the measurements of Captain Warren, an English engineer, the stone was about three feet five inches high and one foot nine inches wide. At top and bottom it was rounded almost to a semicircle. Dr. Klein duly made known his discovery to the European Society of Jerusalem, but no notice of it was taken for about a year, when M. Clermont-Ganneau, attaché of the French consulate, at Jerusalem, sent an Arab (who is said to have risked his life in the attempt) to make a "squeeze" of the stone. This was successfully done, but before the paper was dry a scuffle arose, and the impression was torn to tatters. These fortunately were preserved and were subsequently pasted together. The English authorities left the German discoverer in possession of the field, and the latter endeavored to purchase the stone. The German government was, however, tardy in making the bargain, and the negotiations set on foot to obtain possession of the " Moabite stone " unfortunately resulted in quarrels among the Arab tribes, and led them to believe that the Turks would make the stone a pretext for interfering in the government of the country. They therefore endeavored to destroy it by lighting a fire upon it, and when it was hot threw water upon it, which broke it into three large and several small fragments. The three large pieces were obtained by M. Ganneau, while some of the smaller fragments, obtained by Captain Warren, came into the possession of the Palestine Exploration Society. All the fragments large enough to allow impressions to be taken in " squeeze paper " were carefully copied. They were purchased by the French government for thirty-two thousand francs, and were transported to the Louvre at Paris. The alphabet of the inscription is Hebrao-Phœnician, the oldest known form of Semitic. The language closely resembles Hebrew, and it is believed the inscription dates from about 920 B.C. It is the oldest alphabetical writing in existence, antedating by half a century any other inscription that has come down to us from antiquity and by three centuries any inscription of its own length. Nöldke was enthusiastic over its historical value as the only original document on the history of Israel before the time of the Maccabees. Rawlinson, however, deemed it valuable only on the linguistic side, by the light that it throws upon the Semitic language and grammar.

In the *Revue Archéologique,* for March and June, 1870, Ganneau published a partially restored text of the inscription with a translation. Owing chiefly to its fragmentary condition, the decipherment cannot be regarded as finally established, but the labors of Nöldke, Hitzig, Kämpf, Lenormant, Schlottman, Levy, Wright, and others have doubtless determined its general context.

A picture of the stone, with a translation of the inscription, may be found in *Scribner's Monthly* for May, 1871, p. 32.

Molly Maguires. The name assumed by a secret association of miners in the coal regions of Pennsylvania, who came into special prominence in 1877–78. The origin of the name is thus given:

At the time when the name of a landlord in Ireland was a synonym of cruelty, there lived in the county Roscommon an old woman named Molly Maguire. She had a small holding of land, and struggled hard to bring up a family of boys. The constant failure of the crops made her somewhat tardy in paying her rent, and at length the land agent—an unscrupulous man—determined to eject her from the little home that was so full of sacred recollections to her. He summoned his " crow-bar brigade "—a gang of men kept in those days by every land agent for the purpose of evicting tenants, throwing the houses over the heads of those who refused to leave, and seizing the cattle of others for rent—and went to the shieling of Molly Maguire. The gray-haired matron was alone at her spinning-wheel when the cruel gang came. They commanded her to leave; but so attached was she to the old hearth, so heart-broken at the prospect of eviction, that she said she would die first, and refused to be dragged from the hut. The brigade then commenced the work of destruction, and soon hurled the cottage over the prostrate form of old Mrs. Maguire, who was killed in the ruins. The cruel act stirred the popular sentiment to a white heat, and at the old woman's wake a few desperate men pledged themselves to revenge her death. Headed by two of Molly Maguire's sons, they banded themselves into a society, to which they gave the murdered woman's name, and for some time the most dreadful atrocities were perpetrated. The introduction of the Molly Maguire movement into the coal regions occurred about the close of the Civil War. It was revived by some dissatisfied and desperate miners for the purpose of having revenge on mine bosses and others in authority in and around the collieries, and received its title from some of the old Irish workmen.

Monkey, Heraldic. Though man's genealogical tree, if we are to credit the evolutionists, is intimately complicated with that of our cousins the monkeys, only one monkey is known in heraldry. But that monkey is triplets, or a trinity if you will. For the explanation of this paradox, see Curtis's " One Irish Summer." " On the Leinster coat of arms," says this authority, " are three monkeys standing with plain collar and chained; motto *Crom-a-boo* (" To Victory "). This is the only coat of arms, I am told, that has ever borne a monkey in the design. It was adopted by John Fitzthomas Fitzgerald, in 1316, for romantic reasons."

Here are the reasons. When this Fitzgerald, who succeeded to the family title of Earl of Leinster, was an infant, he was nursed in the castle of Woodstock, now owned by the Duke of Marlborough. The castle caught fire. In the confusion the child was forgotten, and when the family and servants remembered him and started a search they found the nursery in ruins.

But on one of the towers was a gigantic ape, a pet of the

family, carefully holding the young earl in its arms. The animal with extraordinary intelligence had crawled through the smoke, rescued the baby, and carried it to the top of the tower.

When the Earl had grown to manhood, he discarded the family coat of arms and adopted the monkeys for his crest, and they have been retained to this day. Wherever you find the tomb of a Fitzgerald you will see the monkeys at the feet of the effigy or under the inscription.

A similar story, however, is told of an Earl of Kildare, who was called " Appach " because he was saved by an ape from fire. But it is one of a large cycle of myths which find a common origin in a Persian legend that has travelled to be the nursery tale of the dog Gellert in Wales. Rev. Moncure D. Conway, in an article on Munich (" The City of the Little Monk," *Harper's Magazine,* vol. xliv.), preserves another curious analogue. " A dealer in curiosities in Munich," he says, " showed me a copy of an image which for centuries had been on the top of a Gothic tower in the old court of Ludwig der Strenge (1255). This image was that of an ape with a child in its arms. The legend was that a pet ape belonging to a duke had seized his master's infant, to rescue it from a pig which had entered the room when the child was alone, and, passing through a window, climbed the tower, where it stood holding the infant above a dizzy height. There was great terror; but the ape brought the babe down again safely, and the duke commemorated the deed by having the figure carved there where it stood so long."

Then there is Hilda's Tower in " The Marble Faun," which before Hawthorne rechristened it was called the Torre della Scimia, or Monkey's Tower. Hawthorne says nothing about the origin of the perpetual lamp kept burning before the image of the Madonna, thus explained by Italian legend:

In this tower once lived a man who had a favorite ape. One day this creature seized upon a baby, and, rushing to the summit, was seen from below, by the agonized parents, perched upon the battlements, and balancing their child to and fro over the abyss. They made a vow in their terror that, if the baby were restored in safety, they would make provision that a lamp should burn nightly for ever before an image of the Virgin on the summit. The monkey, without relaxing its hold of the infant, slid down the wall, and, bounding and grimacing, laid the child at its mother's feet. Thus a lamp always burns upon the battlements before an image of the Madonna.

Monkeys of Gibraltar. A carefully protected tribe of apes inhabit the Rock of Gibraltar. They are practically tame and have a chief that is known about the garrisons as " Major."

There is a saying among the dwellers of the fortress to the effect that it were "better to kill the governor than Major."

There are only about 20 left of this band of monkeys, which in some mysterious manner came over from Africa many years ago and claimed citizenship in Europe. They are protected by martial law, and any addition by birth to their number is carefully chronicled and announced in the local paper. The apes change their place of residence from the highest peaks of the rock to lower and more sheltered portions and back again, according to the state of the weather. They show their sense of humor by throwing stones at the soldiers, but they are often not seen for weeks at a time save in the early morning.

A few years ago, on account of the diminishing numbers of these animals, some apes were procured from Barbary and turned loose upon the rock. But the resident monkeys killed them all. Although so fierce to intruders of their own kind, they never attack human beings, and are greatly beloved and esteemed.

Moresnet, a small neutral State, area not quite 1400 acres, lying on the borders of Prussia and Belgium 4 miles S. W. of Aix-la-Chapelle.

When Central Europe was partitioned in 1815, after the fall of Napoleon at Waterloo, and Holland, Belgium, and Prussia each took its allotted share, a dispute arose about this narrow strip of territory. Then, as now, Moresnet consisted largely of a mountain under which lay and still lie the very valuable zinc mines owned by the Vielle Montagne Company, which is a Belgian undertaking. Because these mines were in activity and the company could not agree to a partition, the matter was laid over for settlement in the future, and in the mean time two commissioners were appointed, one residing at Verviers in Belgium and the other in Aix-la-Chapelle, or Aachen, in Rhenish Prussia, who should jointly appoint a burgomaster to govern the place so far as it might need a government.

The burgomaster agreed upon was an upright man, who appointed as his justice a man of his own kidney. The justice's head-quarters were, in the American phrase, "under his hat." He went about town and held court wherever he happened to be when his service as justice was required, which, happily, was not often. When complaint was made to him, he would listen patiently and attentively, and when the complainant had finished this statement, His Honor would whistle some favorite air, and thus take time to revolve the matter in his mind. In deciding he never argued the case, but his judgments were always intelligible and fair, insomuch that they were never excepted to or appealed from during all his term of thirty-five years.

Moresnet had no army or navy to pay, there was no customhouse, nor were the people taxed on what they consumed. Trade was free. The only police they had was one watchman, who traversed the burgh at night when the weather was not too inclement. The entire annual budget was less than $550. That sum sufficed for the schools and the roads.

But at the end of these thirty-five years the good old burgomaster died, and was buried, as he had desired, with his face toward the mountain. A new burgomaster, of foreign birth, was appointed to the old man's place. This new man was ambitious. He seems to have cherished the idea that his mission was to get rich, honestly perhaps if he could, but to get rich. His first venture was in making mineral water and selling it as natural water. In this he did not succeed. The fraud was exposed. His next venture was to sell the monopoly of a faro bank at Moresnet, to accomplish which he visited London and Paris and some other great cities, and told those whom he prevailed upon to listen to him what a nice, quiet place Moresnet was to play faro in. Nobody could interfere with such purchaser but himself, and, of course, he wouldn't. But before he had secured a purchaser the scandal came to the knowledge of the Belgian and German authorities, and by two scratches of a pen the little burgh, with its two thousand people, was given a more formal administration, composed of a burgomaster and a council of ten members. On one side of the frontier is Prussian Moresnet, with some 700 inhabitants, on the other is Belgian Moresnet, with about 1300. The profit of the customs is divided between the two countries. The inhabitants of the divided city individually elect whether they will perform military service for Prussia or for Belgium, and also whether they will accept the jurisdiction of the Prussian or the Belgian courts.

Mortgage. The oldest investment on earth is the real-estate mortgage. In ancient Babylon, 2100 years before Christ, in the reign of King Khammuragas, money was loaned on mortgage, while the great Babylonian banking house of the Egibi family, founded about 600 B.C., invested large sums in mortgages on both city and farm property. The mortgages have been recorded on bricks, which were preserved in the contemporary safe-deposit vaults,—great earthenware jars buried in the earth,—and have been dug up in our day to show the archæologist when, where, and how the mortgage originated.

Mother Carey and Her Chickens. "Mother Carey's chickens" and "stormy petrels" are names applied by sailors to the sea-fowl which ornithologists know as *Thalasidroma pelagica*. It is the smallest of all web-footed birds, sooty black in color, with a little white on wings and tail, and so thoroughly given up to an Eskimo diet of fish and whale-blubber that it emits an unpleasant odor. "Mother Carey" may be a corruption of *Mater cara* (Latin for "Dear Mother"), as birds of this class, which are thought to give friendly warnings of coming storms, are popularly regarded as messengers from the Virgin Mary. Thus, the halcyon (*q.v.*), which has been in a measure identified with the story petrel, is familiarly known to the French on the Mediterranean coast as *l'oiseau de Nôtre Dame* ("our Lady's bird") and to the Sardinians as *ucello pescatora Santa Maria* ("Holy Mary's fishing bird"). Incidentally it may be mentioned that "petrel" is probably a corruption of Peter (Latin *Petrus*, Italian *Pietro*), in allusion to the custom of walking on the water which kins the fowl to the less expert apostle.

Yarrell contends that the name "Mother Carey's chickens" was first bestowed upon the stormy petrel by Captain Carteret's sailors, and he suggests that it may have been the name of some celebrated old hag whose memory they thus jocosely perpetuated. The *mater cara* etymology, however, is all the more plausible when we remember the great power over the sea attributed by the Catholic church to the Holy Mother whom the sailor invokes as "Stella Maris," "Star of the Sea."

> Placa mare, Maria Stella!
> Ne involvat nos procella
> Et tempestas obvia.
> ("Calm the waves, O Star of the Sea,
> So that they may not engulf our ship,
> And disperse the storms.")

Jack Tar is as full of superstition as the Greek sailor of the time of Aristophanes, two thousand years ago. Peithetairos, in "The Birds," says, "Some one of the birds shall always foretell to him that consults them about the voyage: 'now sail not; there will be a tempest;' 'now sail; there will be profit.'" In the same spirit Alexander was led on to a victory over his great adversary, Darius, by the encouraging flight of an eagle, and Romulus "builded his kingdom by flying of fowls and sooth-saying."

Pennant, in his "Zoology," affirms that, the great awk having been observed by seamen never to wander beyond soundings, "they are accustomed to direct their vessels by its appearance, being assured they are not very remote from land. Thus it is that the sudden sight of a flock of stormy petrels fills the sailor with forebodings. Observation has taught him that, when this bird becomes unusually rapid in its movements, it is providentially bestirring itself to gather food, that it may return to its home on the shore before the storm breaks."

Therefore it is that quantities of these birds, invisible at other times, gather around a vessel during or just before a storm, to catch any particles of food that may be thrown overboard, or to pick up the small fish, molluscs, and other animals which the agitated ocean brings in abundance to the surface of the water. Descending now into the deeper valleys of the abyss and now scarcely vouching the foamy crest of the highest wave, they dart hither and thither, in apparent delight, and wot not of the misgivings with which the poor sailor watches their performances.

Yet, though generally regarded as ominous of evil, sailors have a superstitious dread of injuring the Mother Carey chickens, believing that they are witches or that each contains the soul of some shipwrecked mariner. As they are ever hasting and never resting, the French call them *ames damnés*, or " damned souls."

In contradistinction to Mother Carey's chickens, the great black petrel is known as " Mother Carey's goose." When it snows, the sailors say " Mother Carey is plucking her goose." This petrel is frequent in the Pacific Ocean. It is a ravenous feeder upon dead whales.

In history the name " Mother Carey's chickens " has been extended to the mobs which thronged the streets of Paris during the first great French Revolution, because their appearance was the foreboding of woe, the heralding of a tumult and political stormy weather.

Mouse. One of the most extraordinary tales about the possibilities of mouse domestication was told in so sober and reliable a paper as the London *Spectator*. It came in the form of a letter from a correspondent.

A lady living in my house in the country announced to me one day that she had tamed a family of mice, consisting of a father and mother and seven young mouse children, who had made their nest in the partially decayed sash-frame of the window in her first-floor bedroom, which had an opening on to the sill outside. She further stated that she could identify each of the members of this family, and could induce them to come at her call and feed out of her hand. These statements appeared so incredible that I felt compelled to express my disbelief in them in the absence of personal proof of their veracity, and she therefore requested me to accompany her to her room, there to receive such evidence as would satisfy my doubts. I went and stood with her close to the open window, and she called the mice by the names, " Jim," " Tom," " Jack," and so on, to which she asserted that she had accustomed them, and I saw them come, one by one, on to the window ledge, where they ate bread out of her hand, and subsequently out of my own, not timidly, but as if in full assurance of safety.

On the afternoon of the same day I had a small tennis party in the garden on to which this bedroom looked. My cousin, whose Christian name is Jim, was playing tennis, and several of the party, including myself, were sitting in the garden beneath the mouse window, when afternoon tea was brought out to us, and I called loudly "Jim," "Jim," several times, to communicate that fact to my cousin. At the third or fourth call something ran across the path, and one of the party impulsively threw his low hat at it, and killed what we found to be a mouse.

The mouse-tamer was not of the party, and knew nothing of the occurrence, to which indeed none of us attached more than a passing importance. The next morning, however, still in ignorance of the incident, she distressedly informed us that her little "Jim" had disappeared from her family, and that, although the others appeared as usual at her call, he remained absent; and I know that he never reappeared.

David Hutton, a nineteenth-century Scot, conceived the ingenious idea of utilizing mouse-power in machinery.

His attention had been attracted to certain toys and trinkets manufactured by the inmates of a French prison,—especially a little toy house, with a wheel in the gable that was set in rapid motion by a common house-mouse. He bought one for himself, and then sat down to consider how the "half-ounce power" of a mouse could be turned to practical account. He decided to experiment in the manufacture of sewing thread.

An ordinary mouse, he ascertained, would average a run of 10½ miles per day. He secured two extraordinary mice that could do the distance of 18 miles in that time. He calculated that a half-penny's worth of oatmeal porridge would suffice to feed each for 35 days, during which time it would make 362 miles. Then he constructed a miniature mill wherein a mouse could twist, twine, and reel from 100 to 120 threads a day, making 10½ miles a day's work. In five weeks, or 35 days, each mouse made 3350 threads 25 inches long. Now, a woman was paid a penny for every hank made in the ordinary; the mouse, therefore, was worth eighteen cents a week to its owner. Allowing for board and machinery, each mouse brought in a yearly profit of $1.50. Having demonstrated the feasibility of his plan, the inventor was preparing to enlarge the scope of his enterprise by setting up 10,000 of these mouse-mills when he was stricken down by death.

One would hardly expect so huge an animal as the elephant should be scared by so diminutive an object as a mouse. Yet so it is. During some experiments made in a menagerie to discover the likes and dislikes of the animals, it was found that an elephant spotted a mouse the moment it was put into his enclosure. He gave immediate evidence of fear. With one of his feet he could have smashed the intruder into jelly. Instead, he stood for a few moments motionless and apparently helpless with fear. Not until the mouse was removed could the elephant be pacified. Not for hours did he regain his normal spirits.

Other animals are afraid of mice. A Bengal tiger trembled and uttered long and mournful howls the while a mouse was in its cage. Two rats introduced into a lion's cage nearly drove his majesty into fits.

Many explanations have been offered for this dislike and terror that the larger animals exhibit toward rats and mice. Possibly, it is urged, the rodents have a peculiarly pungent smell to which their superiors object. It was found, however, that a puma had no such fastidiousness. When a rat was introduced into her cage, the huge cat made one spring and that rat was no more!

A female writer in London *Woman* gives an analytical description of the sensations aroused in female breasts by the *ridiculus mus*. A mouse in the chamber of Marat, this lady believes, would have deterred Charlotte Corday from her dread purpose; and the tail of one popping opportunely from the carving of Tullia's chariot would have prevented her from driving over her father's corpse. "Who can doubt," she asks, "that Cleopatra and the other swarthy Egyptian beauties held the sacred cat in special veneration on account of the part he played in ridding them of their pet aversion? Every one knows that if a cat has a weakness it is for a plump, well-matured mouse, and puss has perhaps for this reason earned the affections, because the gratitude, of our sex.

"The story of a prisoner who was cheered in captivity by a mouse is familiar to us all—but the prisoner was a man. Equally familiar is the fable of the grateful mouse which gnawed the net, but again—the prisoner is said to have been a lion, not a lioness. I believe there is a mutual antipathy between them.

"Most women have experienced the sensation. You are sitting alone, reading, playing, writing, painting, or working. Suddenly you instinctively feel a sensation of horror of some evil influence that is present but as yet unseen. You lift your eyes. You behold, gliding over the carpet towards you, without noise, apparently without the trouble of walking, a mouse. It stops, it fascinates you. You drop your book, your music, your brush, your needle, whatever it may be, but you make no other sound. You feel your blood freeze, and your limbs slowly paralyze, your heart stops beating, your breath ceases, a cold chill creeps over you. In your imagination you feel the soft touch of an army of mice running races over your face and hands and making nests in your back hair. You start to your feet . . . and then . . . well, women take these things so differently.

"Are women afraid of mice simply because it is born in them? There is no reason why we should be afraid of them, but the fact remains that we are, and I have long since resigned myself to the fact as an evil for which there is no remedy."

This writer is evidently unfamiliar with the explanations offered by evolutionists.

Moving Pictures. "Moving pictures" it is. Despite all the efforts of dictionary makers, the great public has refused to accept the various Greek compounds invented by Mr. Edison and his rivals. "Cinematograph," "kinetoscope," and "biograph,"—all have gone the way that flesh goes, or survive only as fossil remains in the queer departments of lexicographical museums.

"Moving pictures" it is. The term is no novelty, though it has been newly applied to a new thing. It goes back to the first decade of the eighteenth century. It was as familiar then as it is now in the twentieth, and it was first applied to something vaguely analogous to the present moving picture.

This was a large mechanical toy or, if you will, a panorama with moving figures, which was invented by a German, Jacobus Morian, and exhibited in England by the popular comedian Pinkethman. An advertisement in the London *Daily Courant* for May 9, 1709, characterizes it as "The Most Famous Artificial and Wonderful Moving Picture that ever came from Germany," and a handbill which was contemporaneously distributed describes it as follows:

Part of this fine Picture represents a Landskip, and the other part the Water or Sea: in the Landskip you see a Town, out of the Gates of which cometh a Coach riding over a Bridge through the Country, behind, before and between the Trees till out of sight; coming on the Bridge a Gentleman, sitting on the Coach, civilly salutes the Spectating Company, the turning of the Wheels and motions of the Horses are plainly seen as if Natural and Alive. There cometh also from the Town Gate a Hunter on Horseback, with his Doggs behind him, and his Horn at his side; coming to the Bridge he taketh up his Horn and blows it that it is distinctly heard by all the Spectators. Another Hunter painted as if sleeping, and by the said blowing of the horn awaking, riseth up his Head, looks about, and then lays down his Head to sleep, to the Great Amazement and Diversion of the Company. There are also represented and painted, Country men and women, Travellers, Cows and Pack horses going along the Road till out of sight. And at a seeming distance on the Hills are several Windmills continually turning and working. From a River or Sea-port, you see several sorts of Ships and Vessels putting out to Sea, which Ships by degrees lessen to the sight as they seem to sail further off. Many

more varieties too long to be inserted here are painted and represented
in this Picture to the greatest Admiration, Diversion and Satisfaction
of all Ingenious Spectators.

The handbill then goes on to state that the Artist Master
of this piece had spent five years in contriving and perfecting it.
Originally designed for a present "to a Great Prince in Germany, to be put in his chiefest Cabinet of greatest Rarities,"
the death of that personage threw it back upon the hands of the
maker, "who now presents it to the View and Diversion of all
ingenious Persons."

It is a little difficult to make out from this handbill, as well
as from the advertisements of similar shows that followed in
great profusion during the later eighteenth century, whether the
figures were working models or marionettes.

But it is most probable that they were similar to those figures
frequently seen on old clock faces,—*i.e.*, flat painted images
moving on a flat surface. Even before this period, however,
spectral pictures or reflections of moving objects similar to those
of the camera or the magic lantern are described, going back
as far as the fourteenth century, but with increasing vagueness
at every step. Finally all these contrivances fused themselves
into a noteworthy invention called the "eidophusikon," which
represented natural phenomena by moving pictures and was
exhibited in London, Lisle Street, Leicester Square, April 3,
1781.

De Loutherbourg, a painter, was the inventor. Later historians have called him a panoramist, which is incorrect. The
pictorial contrivance known as the "panorama" was not invented
until 1789, by Robert Barker, who gave it that name.

Still more famous was the "phantasmagoria" exhibited
(1802) in London by Etienne Gaspard Robinson. We are told
that spectres, skeletons, and terrific figures suddenly advanced
upon the spectators, becoming larger as they approached them,
and finally vanished by appearing to sink into the ground. The
effects, of course, were obtained by means of the magic lantern,
whose invention is attributed to Athanasius Kircher (1646),
but which was not made in England until about 1800. In 1811
the magic lantern was first used for special scenic effects in the
production of "The Flying Dutchman" at the Adelphi Theatre.

The first device specially intended to produce the illusion of
motion was the phenakistoscope, invented by Plateau, of Ghent,
in 1832. It is thus described: "A circular disk having radial
slits round its periphery was blackened on one side, while on the
other were drawn or painted the various phases of motion to be
represented. On holding the disk in front of a mirror, with

the blackened side to the eye, and revolving it on its axis, a moving picture was seen by looking through the slits."

Here evidently was an anticipation of the children's game known as the zoetrope, or wheel of life, which in its perfected form was not introduced until 1845. This, as many people may remember, consisted of a cylindrical box, open on top and revolving on a stand. Round its side were cut vertical slits. Pictures of men and animals at successive stages in the movements of running, leaping, or flying were arranged on a long strip of paper, and this in turn was placed around the inside of the cylinder and inspected through the slits as the machine revolved.

Almost simultaneously Professor Philipstal brought out his improved phantasmagoria at the Lyceum Theatre. The figures were made rapidly to increase and decrease in size, to advance and retreat, dissolve, vanish, and pass into one another, in a manner then considered marvellous.

And now comes the most important step in the evolution of the moving picture.

In 1885 Eadward Muybridge, with an electrically controlled battery of cameras, succeeded in obtaining a succession of photographs of moving figures which he copied on glass disks and projected in the lantern.

Mr. Muybridge hit upon this idea almost by accident. He had been engaged by the late Leland Stanford, then Governor of California, to take photographs of his famous trotter, Occident, the first horse west of the Rocky Mountains to make a mile in two minutes and twenty seconds. He snapped the horse from every conceivable point of view and in every form of activity,— standing, pacing, running, or trotting. Finally he conceived the idea of taking a series of snapshots representing Occident in the various phases of consecutive motion. He placed a number of cameras, covering about a tenth of a mile, at equal distances from one another. From these cameras he stretched silk threads across the track at about the height of the horse's knee. One after another, as the threads were broken by Occident in his headlong course, the cameras took a snapshot of that particular stage of progress. By putting the snapshots together and riffling them with the thumb, a perfect picture of the horse in motion was obtained. In 1885 Muybridge sailed for England, and there, in conection with other photographers, he evolved the first regular camera for taking snapshots by an automatic process. Some of these reached America in 1886, and Muybridge himself returned here in 1887. Meanwhile the patent office at Washington had begun to receive a shower of applications for motion-picture apparatus, both for taking and projecting purposes.

In 1888 O. Auschutz adapted the zoetrope for the display of photographs of animals in motion. He named the arrangement he patented the "tachyscope."

Finally, in 1893 Thomas A. Edison, after working, as he acknowledges, for half a dozen years on the hints supplied by Muybridge and by the zoetrope, succeeded in perfecting and producing his "kinetoscope," and so reducing animated photography to a commercial possibility. He announced that he was at work on a complementary invention which he styled the "kinetograph." This was to be a combination of the photographic camera and the phonograph, whereby the words of a speech or play were to be recorded simultaneously with photographic impressions of all the movements of a speaker or the progressive phases of an action. This is known to-day as the kinetophone.

Music Store. Elson's "History of American Music," echoing earlier authorities, states that there were no music stores in this country prior to the nineteenth century. A contributor to the New York *Nation* (May 12, 1904) challenges this statement by quoting an advertisement that appeared in the *Maryland Journal* of August 6, 1794, No. 1725:

Musical Repository, Market-Street, near Gay-Street, Baltimore.
J. CARR, *Music Importer*, LATELY FROM LONDON, *Respectfully informs the public that he has opened a Store entirely in the Musical line, and has for SALE,* Finger and barrel organs, double and single key'd harpsichords, piano forte and common guitars.

Mystic Circle of the Plains. Reminders of the lost herds of buffalo are still in existence in the Dakotas and Montana. The homesteader's plow now and then turns up a buffalo bone, and many of the trails to springs and creeks used to-day by range cattle are known to have been made originally by buffaloes. Occasionally on the prairies are to be found "buffalo boulders." At a distance they appear no different from others, but closer inspection shows them to be surrounded by a well-beaten trough several feet wide. These boulders, within the memory of old cattlemen, were used by the buffaloes as rubbing-places in their wanderings over the treeless prairies. Other reminders of the lost herds are the "buffalo wallows," great circular depressions common on the plains, where the ranchers say the buffaloes formerly bunched together.

But the most interesting reminder of the departed buffalo is the "mystic circle of the plains" so familiar to the cattlemen of early days, but now becoming fast obliterated. This circle consists of a wide green band, in the midst of the great dun-colored stretches of prairie, enclosing an area of ground 20 to 30 feet in diameter.

In regard to these circles and their significance, *Harper's Weekly* quotes the reminiscences of an old plainsman interviewed by one of its contributors. " In the early eighties," said this authority, " while there were a few herds of buffalo still roaming the prairies of Montana, I was riding along one day, when some distance away I spied about a dozen buffaloes which seemed to be walking in a circle in single file. The strangeness of their movements led me to ride closer. As I approached I discovered a bunch of calves inside the circle, and a moment later perceived a big gray wolf crouched on a knoll a couple of hundred yards away. The story was plain enough. It was the old tragedy of the plains, only in what was to me a new setting. The wolf was thirsting for one of the calves. The mother buffaloes, in order to protect their young, had formed themselves in a circular barrier about them.

" As I watched their manœuvres, a couple of unruly calves made a sudden break in the ring. Quick as a flash the wolf was leaping through the grass toward the breach. No sooner had he started, however, than one of the cows charged out of the circle and came plunging toward him with her head lowered. It seemed time for me to take a hand, and, raising my rifle, I shot and killed the wolf. The tragedy or near-tragedy I had averted, I learned afterward, was a common affair on the plains and the explanation of the odd circles I had so often wondered about.

" A wolf with one spring will hamstring a calf and render it helpless. The buffalo cows, well aware of this, had learned how to prevent a tragedy by forming a circular stockade about their offspring. Where these rings remained so vividly green for years after one of these battles, it is believed the fight between the herds and the wolves may have been kept up for many hours or even two and three days at a time. Only when in desperate need of water did the buffaloes ever break the circle, and then they have been seen to withdraw in soldier-like order, goring the wolves to death if they dared approach."

N.

Names. Middle names were once illegal in England. The law is laid down very definitely by Sir Edward Coke in his "First Institute." "A man cannot have two names of baptism, as he may have divers surnames." Coke thus comments on his own rule: "It is requisite that the purchaser be named by the name of his baptism and his surname, and that special heed be taken to the name of baptism."

English royalty itself had but a single baptismal name until the time of William III, who was a Dutchman. The Stuarts dropped a not uncommon Scotch habit of duplicating baptismal names when their James VI mounted the English throne as James I. But James's eldest son, who was, of course, born in Scotland, and who did not live to succeed his father, was baptized Henry Frederick. No other child of James bore two Christian names, nor did any child of Charles I save Henrietta Maria, named after her mother, a Frenchwoman.

The first Englishman to break the record seems to have been Henry Frederick, Earl of Arundel, born in 1608. Evidently he was named after the Scotch-born Prince of Wales. So, also, was Sir Henry Frederick Thynne, who was created a baronet in 1641, but whose birth date is unknown.

Pseudo-record-breakers have indeed turned up. A certain John James Sandilands, an English knight of Malta, has been cited. In the early seventeenth century he was expelled from the order on his own confession of having stolen a chalice and a crucifix from the altar of San Antonio's church. The date of his birth or baptism is unknown. There is more particularity in the case of Thomas Dooley Pyp, whose name is said to have been discovered in the register at Tamworth, at the alleged date of 1579. Name and date, however, have been queried, the latter, it is asserted, being really 1679, while as to the former, the true reading is suggested as Thomas Dooley Fil. pop.—filius populi being a common way of entering illegitimate children.

If you dismiss the Henry Fredericks, therefore, as mere compliments to royalty and too accidental to establish a precedent, you must then fall back upon a perfectly original and perfectly well-attested double name, that of Anthony Ashley Cooper, who was born and baptized in the year 1621. His name, moreover, gives you a specimen of the most fertile resource of double names in modern England. He was called

Ashley as well as Anthony to keep up the memory of his maternal grandfather. The fashion, now so common, of turning surnames into Christian names, seems to have begun in the sixteenth century. Guilford Dudley must have been an early example. When the custom began, it was soon applied to women as well as to men. For instance, there is Douglas Sheffield, the girl who played (or, rather, suffered) a part in the tragedy of Robert Dudley, Earl of Leicester. In this stage it supplanted the Christian name. In the next stage, that of Anthony Ashley, it was added to a real Christian name. Lastly comes the stage in which a man's baptismal name is made up of two or three surnames, or, politest form of all, a real prænomen with a cognomen stuck before it—Snooks Peter Tompkins.

To sum up: the practice of giving children a double Christian name was unknown in England before the period of the Stuarts, was rarely adopted down to the time of the Revolution, and never became common until the Hanoverian family was seated on the throne. (See also WALSH: *Handy-book of Literary Curiosities*, p. 782.) It must be noted, furthermore, that seventeenth-century England still seemed to fear the revival of an obsolescent law, for they dodged it at times by ingeniously compounded names. Thus, on old parish registers in England there is occasionally seen such combinations as Fannasabilia, which is Fanny and Sybil joined; Annameriar, made up of Anna and Maria; and Aberycusgentylis, named in honor of Professor Abericus Gentylis of Oxford. Each of these names is morally two names, though one legally.

And now a further question suggests itself. What do we understand by a double Christian name? The *Saturday Review*, September 19, 1874, points out that it must not be confounded with several things which are at first sight not unlike it. Every case in which a man is called by two Christian names, even every case in which he is called by two possible Christian names at once, is not to be set down as an instance of the real double Christian name. By this last we understand the calling a man in his baptism by two names, each of which is by itself in use as a baptismal name. It is in fact putting two names together and making one name out of them. The most natural and obvious thing certainly seems to give only a single name to one man. In the old system of nomenclature, Greek and Roman, nobody ever thought of giving a double name. The Greek had only a single name of any kind; the Roman had only a single *prænomen;* he might have *prænomen, nomen, cognomen, agnomen,* till his whole description made rather a long story, but his own personal name was always simply Caius or Lucius, never Caius-Lucius, or Lucius-Caius. How the case may have stood in the later Roman time when nomenclature had got utterly confused, when men so commonly changed one string of names for another string of names, when, as Ammianus says, they thought to make themselves seem greater by taking strange names like Reburrus and Tarrasius, it would be hard to say. But this fashion seems to have died out almost suddenly. Boetius has an endless string of names, but the contemporaries of Gregory the Great would almost seem to have had only one name apiece of any kind. In the early middle age men certainly seem as a rule to have been contented with a single name given in baptism, just as the Romans were contented with a single *prænomen.* If it be true that the Emperor Frederick the Second was baptized by the name of Frederick-Roger, it would doubtless be an early case of the double Christian name. And if it be true that Philip the Second of France received in his baptism the name of Augustus, by which he was certainly known from his own time, it would be an earlier and a still more singular case; for it would be coupling a real Christian name with something which was not exactly a Christian name, but rather a title or epithet. It certainly seems that Philip was called Augustus, as some people have been since, simply because he was born in the month of August. But it does not seem clear whether the name was actually given to him in his baptism. If it was not, it belongs, not to the class of double Christian names, but to the history of surnames in their non-hereditary stage. We are not at all prepared to say that either Frederick or Philip, if they really had the double Christian name, were the earliest cases of its use. Oderic speaks of the Emperor Henry the Fifth as Karolus-Henricus, whether he really was called so, or whether Oderic thought that every Emperor ought to be Charles as well as Cæsar and Augustus; and long before even Henry we find a Charles-Constantine and an Otto-William among the princes of the royal Burgundy; and the various names borne by the Dukes of Aquitaine are simply baffling. But it is not safe to assert that Charles-Constantine and Otto-William were real cases of a double Christian name. In "Carolus Constantinus" we cannot be certain that "Constantinus" is strictly a name at all. It may be a title taken up like "Flavius" and "Cæsar"; it may be— for we know very little about his life—a mere epithet implying that he was born in some one of many places called Constantia. Otto William sounds more like one of the cases in which a man really bore two names.

To turn from England to England's children in America. When in 1620 the *Mayflower* sailed for America, there was not a man or woman upon it who had a middle name. Of the signers of the Declaration of Independence in 1776, only three had middle names, Robert Treat Paine, of Massachusetts, and Richard Henry Lee and Francis Lightfoot Lee, of Virginia. The first five Presidents and the first five Vice-presidents of the United States had only one given name each. John Quincy Adams was the first President with two names, Daniel D. Tompkins the first Vice-president, and each was sixth on his respective list.

Names Changed. A student of the history of the fourth century A.D. cannot but be startled on reaching a certain passage where he reads of the town of Augusta *quam veteres appellavere Lundinium* (" which was formerly called London "). When he gets on to later times, he may be equally startled at reading the story of the capture of Jerusalem by the Saracens, and finding that in the agreement between the Caliph Omar and the Patriarch Sophronius there is nothing about Jerusalem. In the official language of its own inhabitants, that city was not Jerusalem, but Ælia.

Pursuing his researches, however, he will find that a number of cities follow the same law. A new official name supplants the older one in official use; but it is only in official use that it supplants it. In all these cases there is an older name, which was doubtless always used in popular speech, and which, when the official influence is taken away, comes up again. Often a distinct change in political circumstances is marked both by the introduction of the new name and by its dying out again. A capital instance is offered by the Italian Alexandria, which became in its imperialistic days Cæsarea, though it speedily became Alexandria again. Sometimes the process is different. An older name is changed, not by official proclamation, but in the course of those accidents of language which do affect proper names as well as other words. though not in the same degree in which they affect other words. And in such cases as these attempts are sometimes made to revive the old name of set purpose. Take some examples from modern Greek geography. Kythêra has got, from some quarter or other, the non-Hellenic name of Cerigo. We can hardly quarrel with the Greeks for bringing back the Greek name. But when they try to get rid of the name of Corfu and to substitute *Kérkyra*, that is quite another matter. Corfu— not indeed in that spelling, but in its Greek spelling *Κορυφαί* or *Κορυφούς*—is as good a Greek name as that which it supplanted. How it came to supplant it is a question for local historians: but, like a good many other places in Greece, the place changed its older Greek name, not for a foreign name, but for another

Greek name. To change it is to wipe out a piece of the history of their own language. Above all, to write *Kέυρα* implies ignorance of the fact that the real name of the city was *Kόρκυρα.* The case is as if, supposing London again to become Augusta or something else other than London, the revived name, after the second process of supplanting, should be, not *London,* but *Londres.* In some cases, again, a name seems to be revived when there is really no revival at all. It was for a good while the fashion to call the whole island of Crete *Candia;* now people say *Crete* again. This is simply because what made Crete most famous in later times was the great siege of Candia. The "War of Candia" became equivalent to the War of Crete, and Crete came in Western mouths to be called Candia. But the island itself did not change its name; it has always been Crete, and it is Crete still in the mouths of its own inhabitants of either religion. Sometimes, again, the real name of a place drops out of use almost from the beginning.

Take an example from England. From early in the seventeenth century Hull has been in common speech the name of the town officially known as Kingston-on-Hull. It was given that name to distinguish it from a dozen other Kingstons, but especially from Kingston-on-Thames. But everybody knows the Thames and few know Hull as the name of a river, and fewer still pause to think that the town which is commonly called Hull is in strictness the town of Kingston on the river Hull. The changes of name in the cities of Northern Gaul are hardly, for our purpose, changes of name at all. The name of the tribe supplants the name of the town itself, yet the process by which Lutetia Parisiorum became Parisii—in truer mediæval form the indeclinable Parisius—is really not without analogy to the change from Kingston-on-Hull into Hull. In both cases the name of the place is lost, and that which qualifies the name is kept.

Now take a flight eastward to the most signal example in geography. New Rome keeps its true name only in the style of its patriarch, and then only as a kind of adjunct.

He is "Archbishop of Constantinople, New Rome." The formal name was supplanted, sometimes by the older Byzantium, sometimes by the newer Constantinople. Here is a distinct loss, for the whole historic importance of Constantinople lies in the fact that the New Rome always has been, and always must be, the New Rome. It is important to mark the fact, and it cannot be so easily marked as by the use of the name; but he who ventures to speak of New Rome must take his chance of having it thought that he is speaking of the Rome of Victor Emmanuel in opposition to the Rome of Pius the Tenth.   But this time various names in various tongues express something like the same idea; if the New Rome does not keep its name of Rome, it is at least spoken of as old Rome was.   Old Rome was *Urbs:* New Rome was ἡ μόλις; thence by corruption comes Turkish Stamboul, and by translation Scandinavian Micklegard.

To turn from great things to small let us chronicle a few changes in the village nomenclature of the New World.

In the spring and summer of 1910 a mighty turmoil agitated a little village in New York which had hitherto borne in comfort and in peace the name of Turner.   The name commemorated its founder, Peter Turner, who had built here the Orange Hotel, for the refreshment of travellers on the Erie Railroad.   The trains stopped just a quarter of an hour to give them an opportunity that was often seized upon by as many as 500 at a time.   But in 1872 the hotel was burned down, and in 1873 its proprietor died.   The hotel was never rebuilt but Turner itself regained more than its old importance when E. H. Harriman, the so-called railroad king, purchased several thousand acres here and placed a mansion atop of Mount Ramapo which overlooks the village.   Harriman too died.   On Tuesday, May 17, 1910, the trouble began.   Suddenly, without any preliminary warning, the citizens were invited to a mass meeting, by placards issued in the name of the Village Improvement Society.   There they were informed that Mr. Harriman's widow had offered to build a new $6000 station and to add $25,000 worth of improvements on condition that the name of the place should be changed from Turner to Harriman.   A motion to accept this offer was carried by a vote of 58 to 13.   The opposition were furious at their defeat.   They claimed that the question had been sprung too suddenly upon the community to get out the full adverse vote.   There were appeals and counter-appeals.   Finally, on June 3, the railroad officials decided that Turner should be Turner until July 15 and Harriman thereafter.

At almost the same period a desperate war was waged on Staten Island over the question whether the town which had been known as Tottenville for nearly a century should resume its pre-Revolutionary name of Bentley Manor.   The latter name sounded grander in the ears of many citizens.   Further, Tottenville, S. I., was frequently mistaken for its neighbor Tompkinsville, S. I., to the great confusion of the telephone and mail service.   Still further, the name lent itself to such humorous perversions as Cottonville, Rottenville, and even Hottentottenville.   History also was invoked.   When, in 1668, Christopher Billopp won Staten Island for New York State by sailing around the island in his stout ship, the *Bentley,* in the fast time of 23 hours, the broad lands given him as a reward by the Duke of York he named Bentley Manor, after the good ship. As this was a full hundred years before the Revolution, he could hardly be held accountable for the fact that a grandson of his, who really had no right to the name of Billopp, was a Tory in Revolutionary days. Yet it was on that ground that the Totten descendants and a powerful contingent desired the retention of the name of Tottenville, given in honor of a local celebrity who had once been postmaster. Finally, on November 5, 1910, the Post-office Department at Washington, which had first authorized a change to Bentley Manor, reverted to the name of Tottenham. See also MEDICINE HAT.

Names, Short. Both in human and in geographical terminology a certain number of names exist which consist of but a single letter. O is the typical instance. There is a village of this name in Normandy, twenty miles from Argenton. The local magnate is the Marquis d'O. Nor is the name unknown elsewhere. It is found both in Brussels and in Paris. A Madame Theresa O was the proprietor of a Parisian café that was popular in the last decade of the nineteenth century.

This Madame O had a son. The French papers were highly amused when the young man reached the age for military service. Acknowledging that he could not write, he was allowed to sign his name on the official papers with a cross. "Is not O as easy to write as an X?" asked the funny men.

In the Zuyder Zee there is a bay called Y. Amsterdam has a river Y. And, strange to say, in quite another part of the world, in China, the same brief name is given to a town. In the province of Honan, also in China, there is a city called U. France has a river and Sweden a town of the name of A.

What is believed to be the shortest name in the United States for any person is Eda Ek, actually borne by a resident of Brockton, Mass. Ek is a good old Irish-Swedish name, and it was borne with honor by the famous explorer John Ek, who sailed into far seas and made important discoveries. It is from this man that Miss Ek is descended.

Napkins were of even more importance in ancient and mediæval times than at present. As forks did not come into general use until the seventeenth century, gentlemen who ate with their fingers frequently found it necessary to wipe them. Plebeians might, indeed, be content to lick them clean. But the Roman patrician and the mediæval lord never grudged the cost of table linen. The Augustan leaders of fashion were fanciful about their hand towels, which, not infrequently, excited the cupidity of kleptomaniac guests. There is Hermogenes, for example, who, when invited, because of his well-known proclivities, to a napkinless banquet, revenged himself by running off with the tablecloth.

The English, from the Anglo-Saxon period to that of the Stuarts, used table linen lavishly, and made much parade of washing before and after meat. After every meal, and sometimes after every course, a ewer of water, a basin, and a napkin were set before each guest. But the introduction of the fork did away with the necessity for so much nice particularity. Ben Jonson had foreseen this when he made his Meercraft speak of

> the laudable use of forks
> Brought into custom here as they are in Italy
> To the sparing of napkins.
> *The Devil's an Ass,* Act v, Scene 4.

Forks, indeed, had not been long in use ere napkins began to disappear from the tables of economical housekeepers. It was early in the reign of Charles II that Samuel Pepys, attending a banquet at Guildhall, noted a fact which seemed to him no little surprising. "Many were the tables," he says, "but none in the hall but the Mayor's and the lords of the Privy Council that had napkins or knives, which was very strange." A few years later Mr. Pepys might have seen nothing remarkable in this distinction between the chief and ordinary tables. Even napkins still displayed on the former showed by their fantastic and complicated folding that they were put there for adornment, and not for use. That favorite culinary artist of Charles II, Giles Rose, in his "Perfect School of Instructions for Offices of the Mouth" (1682), gives instructions for folding dinner napkins into no less than twenty-six different forms. "A double melon," "a hen and chickens," "a pigeon upon her nest in a basket," "two capons in a pie," "a dog with a choller about his neck,"—these were a few of the more complicated forms.

It is obvious that the guests were not expected to undo works of art so elaborately and ingeniously gotten up.

Generally discarded from fashionable tables at the close of the eighteenth century, the napkin was seldom used or seen by the more modish epicures of Horace Walpole's era. In George III's time the dessert doily was regarded as an elegant and all-sufficient substitute. But with the later growth of luxury and refinement the napkin has been reinstated as a necessary requirement of comfortable eating.

Nests. The largest, heaviest, and most peculiar nests in the world are to be found in Australia. These are built by the jungle-fowl in the form of great mounds about 15 feet in height and 150 in circumference. They are erected in secluded, sheltered spots, and, like smaller bird's-nests, are skilfully interwoven with leaves, grass and twigs and such other suitable material as the fowl may be able to procure.

A similar system is followed by the bush turkey, whose home is, however, more comprehensive in design. Its shape is pyramidal. It has been asserted by Australian naturalists that the nests of the bush turkeys, which live in colonies, are so large that to move them requires the services of six or seven men. The material of a single nest has been found to weigh upward of five tons.

Another curious Australian nest-builder is the *Chlamydera maculata*. They frequent the brush which surrounds the plains and construct their nests with amazing skill, supporting the framework by a foundation of stones and transporting from banks of streams and water-courses at considerable distances the numerous ornamental objects which they dispose at the entrance of the nests. There is no doubt in the mind of Prof. Aristides Mestre that birds modify and improve their nests, both as to form and material, when circumstances have arisen which require such a change.

Many years ago Poudrat gathered swallows' nests from the window-sills and had them placed in the collection of the natural-history museum at Rouen. Forty years later he sought for similar nests, and was astonished to find that the newly collected nests showed a real change in their form and arrangements. These nests were from a new quarter of the city and showed a mixture of the old and new types. Of the forms described by naturalists of earlier periods he found no trace. For Poudrat the new type of construction marked a distinct advance. The new nests were better adapted to the needs of the young brood and protected them better from their enemies and from cold and inclement weather.

In Cuba there are nests made altogether of palm fibres marvellously intertwined and attached close to the tufts of the palms or under the clusters of bananas or mangoes. The nest is built both by the male and the female bird. They perforate the small leaves of the palm and pass threads through the holes so as to form a species of rope by which the nest is suspended. It has been said that an old bird and a young bird build the nest together. This shows the existence of a kind of apprenticeship, which constitutes an additional argument against the theory that blind instinct animates the birds.

Newspaper, First American. The earliest attempt to set up a newspaper in North America, or indeed in the Western

37

hemisphere, was made at Boston by Richard Pierce, who employed Benjamin Harris to print it. The title was *Public Occurrences both Foreign and Domestic.* Only one copy was ever issued (bearing date Thursday, September 25, 1690), and of that number only one copy is known to exist,—the copy preserved in the Colonial State Paper Office in London. The journal was 7 x 11 inches in size, and consisted of a folded sheet, three pages of which were occupied with printed matter, two columns to the page, the fourth page being left blank. From the prospectus we learn that it was the publisher's intention to issue the paper monthly, "unless any Glut of occurrences happen," in which case it is somewhat vaguely stated that it would be "issued oftener." But God disposed otherwise of this newspaper-man's proposal, for it so happened that the colonial authorities cast an evil eye upon the sheet, deeming it contained "reflections of a very high nature," and it was forthwith suppressed.

Boston can also boast of the first successful attempt made in either America to establish a paper. This was a weekly entitled *The Boston News-Letter.* The initial number bore date Monday, April 24, 1704. It was a half sheet of paper, about 12 x 8 inches, made up in two pages folio with two colunms on each page.

The imprint is "Boston; printed by B. Green; sold by Nicholas Boone, at his shop near the old meeting-house." The proprietor was evidently John Campbel, then Postmaster, as indicated by the following advertisement, which was the only one the paper contained:

This News-Letter is to be continued Weekly; and all persons who have any Houses, Lands, Tenements, Farms, Ships, Vessels, Goods, Wares or Merchandise, etc., to be Sold or Let; or Servants Runaway, or Goods Stole or Lost; may have the same inserted at a Reasonable Rate, from *Twelve Pence to Five Shillings*, and not to exceed: Who may agree with *John Campbel*, Postmaster of Boston. All persons in Town or Country may have the News-Letter every Week, Yearly, upon reasonable terms, agreeing with *John Campbel*, Postmaster for the same.

Campbell, or Campbel, was a Scotchman.

Besides attending to his duties as postmaster and as editor and publisher of the *News-Letter,* he did some business in the way of bookselling. His literary accomplishments seem to have been meagre enough, for what little original matter he put into his paper is clumsily written and carelessly punctuated. Most of the matter was made up from London newspapers.

The files of the *News-Letter* down to 1722, when Bartholomew Green became proprietor as well as printer, are very imperfect, but the most complete are found in the library of the Massachusetts Historical Society in New York, and these are all bound in two volumes, embracing not half of the numbers for the years previous to 1720. The *News-Letter* was published without interruption for a period of 72 years, and was the only paper printed in Boston during the siege.

It was Thomas Watts, of the British Museum, who finally exploded the long-prevalent fancy that a paper called the *English Mercurie,* dated in 1588, was the progenitor of modern journalism. No such paper was ever published. A pretended copy, still extant in the Birch collection, has been proved to be a hoax fabricated by the second Lord Hardwicke. It purports to give news from the expedition against the Spanish Armada; but, besides a host of blunders in dates, it is printed on paper manufactured after the pretended date of the journal. Until the later years of James I English people eager for the news of the day had to content themselves with the autographed efforts of the "news-writers," a regular craft who set up offices in London and kept "emissaries" or reporters to bring them accounts of what was going on in various parts of the metropolis. These reports were sifted and collated by the "register" or editor. To Nathaniel Butter, a news-writer of that period, was the British public indebted for the first printed newspaper. Ben Jonson, in his "Staple of News" (1625), gives a vivid picture of Master Butter's office before he abandoned the pen for the printing-press.

Enter Register and Nathaniel.

Reg. What, are those desks fit now? Set forth the table,
The carpet and the chair; where are the News
That were examined last? Have you filled them up?
Nath. Not yet, I had no time.
Reg. Are those News registered
That emissary Buz sent in last night,
Of Spinola and his eggs?
Nath. Yes, sir, and filed.
Reg. What are you now upon?
Nath. That our new emissary
Westminster gave us, of the golden heir.
Reg. Dispatch; that's news indeed, and of importance.--

Enter a Country-woman.

What would you have, good woman?
Woman. I would have, sir,
A groat's-worth of any News, I care not what,
To carry down this Saturday to our vicar.
Reg. O! you are a butter-woman; ask Nathaniel,
The clerk there.
Nath. Sir, I tell her she must stay
Till emissary Exchange, or Paul's send in,

> And then I'll fit her.
>   *Reg.* Do, good woman, have patience;
> It is not now, as when the Captain lived;
> You'll blast the reputation of the office,
> Now in the bud, if you dispatch these groats
> So soon: let them attend in name of policy.

Not until the reign of James I was drawing to its close did this same Nathaniel Butter, aided and abetted by half a dozen other news-writers, establish the pioneer English newspaper in *The Weekly Newes.* The first number appeared in 1622, the last on January 9, 1640.

Butter's print was succeeded by a host of *Mercuries,* but none of them were long-lived. During the civil war each army carried its printing-press as part of the recognized munitions of war. Broadsides were issued at irregular intervals. These were often headed as *News,* such as "Newes out of Worcestershire," "Newes of a Bloody Battle" fought at such a place, etc. In 1662 a regular periodical called the *Kingdom's Intelligencer* was started, and in the following year *The Intelligencer, Published for the Satisfaction and Information of the People* was set up by Sir Rogers L'Estrange.

All these were superseded by the Oxford *Gazette,* set up in that city in 1665, which was transferred to London in 1670, and still survives as the *London Gazette.* For many years after the Restoration this was the only English newspaper. The law restricted any man from publishing political news without the consent of the crown. Both Charles II and James II were chary of granting this consent.

By Queen Anne's time journalism had improved, and—when the victories of Marlborough and Rooke, the political contests of Godolphin and Bolingbroke, and the writings of Addison, Pope, Prior, Congreve, Steele, and Swift, created a mental activity in the nation which could not wait from week to week for its News—the first daily paper was started. This was the *Daily Courant,* which came out in 1702. Other such journals followed but three years after, they received a check by the imposition of the stamp duty. "All Grub Street," wrote Swift to Stella, "is ruined by the Stamp Act." In August, 1712, he writes:

Do you know that Grub Street is dead and gone last week? No more ghosts or murders now for love or money. I plied it pretty close the last fortnight, and published at least seven penny papers of my own, besides some of other people's, but now every single half-sheet pays a halfpenny to the Queen. The *Observator* is fallen; the *Medleys* are jumbled together with the *Flying Post;* the *Examiner* is deadly sick: the *Spectator* keeps up, and doubles its price; I know not how long it will hold. Have you seen the red stamp the papers are marked with? Methinks it is worth a halfpenny the stamping.

Grub Street, was not, however, so easily put down; and from that time to the days of Dr. Johnson newspapers had considerably increased in number and influence. In the "Idler" the doctor says: "No species of literary men has lately been so much multiplied as the writers of News. Not many years ago, the nation was content with one Gazette, but now we have not only in the metropolis Papers for every morning and every evening, but almost every large town has its weekly historian, who regularly circulates his periodical intelligence, and fills the villagers of his district with conjectures on the events of war, and with debates on the true interests of Europe."

The New York *Sun,* in its issue for January 13, 1912, put forth a semi-serious claim for the *Master William,* of St. Croix Island, Maine, as the first American newspaper. But this was written, not printed, had no subscribers, and otherwise lacked the essentials of journalism.

The *Sun* refers to Samuel Champlain as its authority. In his "Voyages" he gives an account of his first attempt at exploring the North American territory claimed by France. The expedition was undertaken in conjunction with a fellow Frenchman, De Monts. This consisted of 79 men who during the winter of 1604–05 were storm-stayed on St. Croix Island, a few miles below the present city of alais.

They were the first Europeans to pass a winter on these northern shores of the New World since the days of the legendary Northmen centuries before; and at that time they were the only Europeans in America north of the Spaniards in Florida.

Samuel Champlain relates that the paper was prepared from time to time "by the bright spirits of the party" to while away the tedium of the long and severe winter. It was passed around in written, not printed form but among a few score men all deadhead subscribers, that was a wholly satisfactory method of publication.

Christmas Day, 1604, was celebrated by the colony with special zest—it was the first Christmas observance, by the way, in what is now New England—and, after the religious exercises of the morning and before the feasting and drinking and general merrymaking became too boisterous, a special Christmas issue of the *Master William* was read to the company by the editors. So early did the idea of the "extra" and the "holiday number" take root in American journalism! It is a great pity that the chronicler did not include a copy of the *Master William* in his record, or something more about it than the bare mention of its occasional appearance.

Later in the winter, which was particularly severe, the food supply ran low, there was much sickness and suffering, and it is very doubtful if the *Master William* lived to see the arrival of the tardy spring. Of the seventy-nine men—there were no women or children in the company—thirty-five died of the scurvy and most of the rest were desperately ill. The dead were buried on a part of the little island which has since been washed away by the tides. Among them were the Protestant minister and the Catholic priest, who were buried side by side. De Monts was a Protestant and Champlain a Catholic, and the company was made up of men of both faiths, who lived and worked together in harmony.

The two leaders survived, and in the following summer they led an exploring expedition along the coast of Maine and Massachusetts, but could find no place that suited them. The St. Croix settlement was abandoned, its cellars and ruins were plainly visible more than two centuries later, and thus France had failed in its first step toward the mastery of the continent.

The publishers of the Greenock *Evening Telegraph*, established in 1857, claim this as the pioneer of half-penny evening papers in Britain. But it has been shown that the Clerkenwell *News* began in 1855 as a half-penny paper, though it soon raised its price to a penny. Further research has unearthed the *Half-penny Post*, printed by Parker the elder, of Salisbury street, which in 1724 was "a recently established paper." (Fox Bourne, i, 719.) Another *Half-penny Post* was being published at this date by Read of Whitefriars. The cheapest paper ever published in Britain appears to be the *Farthing Journal*, a four-page publication of much respectability which struggled along through fifty-four numbers and then expired. In a certain sense even this paper was eclipsed for cheapness by the *Penny-a-Week Daily Newspaper*, which in 1873 offered a large title for an infinitesimal price and sold itself to occasional customers for a farthing a copy.

Newspaper Woman, First. An American, Mrs. Anne Royall, was not only the first woman journalist, but the first of her sex to own and edit a newspaper and the first professional "interviewer" of either sex. Born in Maryland in 1769, she was the widow of a Virginia Revolutionary officer when she first (1824) appeared in Washington to secure a pension. Failing in that, she devoted herself to personal literature. Then she managed to secure an old Ramage printing-press and a font of battered long-primer type, with which, aided by runaway apprentices and tramping journeyman printers, she published, on Capitol Hill, for several years a small weekly sheet called at first *The Washington Paul Pry* and later *The Huntress.* Every person of any distinction who visited Washington received a call from Mrs. Royall, and if they subscribed for *The Huntress* they were described in the next number in a complimentary manner, but if they declined she blackguarded them without mercy. John Quincy Adams described her as going about "like a virago errant in enchanted armor, redeeming herself from the cramps of indigence by the notoriety of her eccentricities and the forced currency they gave to her publications."

She survived to witness the political rise of Abraham Lincoln, dying at last on October 1, 1854. We are told that she had met personally and talked with every man who became President of the United States, from Washington to Lincoln.

"She was the terror of politicians and especially of Congressmen," wrote John W. Forney. "I can see her now tramping through the halls of the old Capitol, umbrella in hand, seizing upon every passerby and offering her book for sale. Any public man who refused to buy was sure of a severe philippic in her newspaper."

At last she became so unendurable that she was formally indicted by the grand jury as a common scold; was tried in the Circuit Court before Judge William Cranch, was found guilty and was sentenced to be ducked, according to the English law, which still survived in the District of Columbia, though it had been allowed to slumber in similar obsolescence to that which had overtaken it in England. She escaped the distinction of being the last woman ever "ducked" through a commutation of her sentence to fine and imprisonment.

New York, First Things in. Giovanni (John) Verrazani, a sailor from Florence, Italy, was the original discoverer of the Hudson River and of the present site of New York City. In 1523 he left Dieppe on the frigate *La Dauphine* on a mission from Francis I of France to explore the coast of North America. Arriving there, February, 1824, he spent three months in sailing from latitude 30° to 5°, discovering what are now New York Bay and Narragansett Bay. In a letter to Francis I written July 8 after his return to Dieppe he thus describes the New York episode.

After proceeding one hundred leagues we found a very pleasant situation among some steep hills through which a very large river, deep at its mouth, forced its way to the sea. From the sea to the estuary of the river any ship heavily laden might pass with the help of the tide, which rises eight feet. But as we were riding at anchor in a good berth, we would not venture up in our vessel without a knowledge of the mouth; therefore, we took the boat, and, entering the river, we found the country on its banks well peopled, the inhabitants not differing much from the others, being dressed out with the feathers of birds of various colors. They came toward us with evident delight, raising loud shouts of admiration, and showing us where we could the most securely land our boat. We passed up this river about half a league, when we found it formed a most beautiful lake, three leagues in circuit, upon which they were rowing thirty or more of their small boats from one shore to the other, filled with multitudes who came to see us. All of a sudden, as is wont to happen to navigators, a violent contrary wind blew in from the sea and forced us to return to our ship, greatly regretting to leave this region, which seemed so commodious and delightful, and which we supposed must also contain great riches, as the hills gave many indications of minerals.

The first white men who ever set foot on New York soil landed at Coney Island on September 3, 1609. They were a boat's crew dispatched by Henry Hudson, who had just rounded Sandy Hook in the *Half Moon,* to secure some of the fish that abounded in the waters.

The first man slain in this State was John Coleman, an English sailor and a member of a boat's crew sent up the river by Hudson to take soundings. On the crew's return, they were attacked by a party of Indians, September 8, 1609, and Coleman was mortally wounded by a dagger that pierced his throat. His grave was dug next day at Sandy Hook, on a spot christened Coleman's Point in his honor.

The first murder was that of Hendrik Christiansen, killed in 1615, by an Indian, who was caught and executed. Christiansen is also known as the man who in 1613 put up the first houses in New York,—four small cottages and a redoubt on the present site of 39 Broadway.

The first sea-going vessel ever launched in Manhattan waters was *The Unrest,* a yacht of sixteen tons' burden, constructed from the fine timbers that grew on the island, by Admiral Adriaen Block, in the spring of 1614. Block Island, by the way, is named after this Dutch admiral.

The first actual settlers arrived at Manhattan Island in May, 1626.

The first white male child born within the present limits of New York State was Jean Vigne (1614).

The first white female child born within the same limits was Sarah Rapelje, daughter of Joris Rapelje, who was born at Albany, June 9, 1625.

The first child of English descent born within the present boundaries of New York State was Elizabeth Gardiner, daughter of Lion Gardiner and a Dutch lady of good Holland family. Elizabeth first saw the light September 14, 1641, on Gardiner's Island.

She married a Conkling, who was an ancestor of United States Senator Roscoe Conkling.

The first white child born in Manhattan Island was Isaac du Trieux, son of Philip du Trieux and Susanna his wife, who, according to the records of the Reformed Dutch Church in New Amsterdam, first saw the light on the 21st of April, 1642. (See Dr. E. B. O'Callaghan's " New York Genealogical and Biographical Record," vol. v, No. 1, January, 1874.) Philip du Trieux, the father, was a Walloon from the French Netherlands and one of the first company of colonists to Manhattan Island, then known as New Amsterdam. He was one of the well-to-do burghers of the infant municipality. After the cession of the colony to the English, in 1664, many of the Holland names became Anglicized. Among these Du Trieux became Truax, and in this form has come down to us.

Trieux's claim to being the first-born New Yorker of white parents is sometimes disputed in favor of Isaac Bedlew. But the date of the latter's birth was 1643.

The first warehouse, a rude structure of which one corner was set apart for a village store, was erected in 1626. Here the Indians flocked for the white man's " fire-water."

The first manor-house was erected by Kilien Van Rensselaer (1630).

The first farm, called the Company's Farm, was laid out in 1633. It extended north from Wall Street to what is now Hudson Street.

The first grave-yard (God's Acre) was laid out in 1633, west of Broadway above Morris Street.

Although the Dutch Reformed Church was organized early in 1620 by a small number of the Dutch settlers, who held meetings in a loft, under the guidance of Rev. Jonas Michaelis, the first church was not built until after the arrival of Everardus Bogardus, a Dutch clergyman, in April, 1633. It was a plain, barn-like structure, and stood on the shores of the East River, in Pearl Street, between Whitehall and Broad Streets. The Episcopalians erected their first church in 1696–1697; the Lutherans, in 1669; the Jews, about 1720; the Methodists, about 1767; the Baptists, in 1791; the Moravians, in 1751; and the Roman Catholics, in 1786.

The first physician was Dr. Johannes La Montagne, who began practising in 1636. He was the only doctor in Manhattan for a number of years. Under English rule the first license to practise medicine was issued in the summer of 1665, by Governor Richard Nicolls, the first English governor. This license was given under seal to Peter Harris.

The first tavern for the accommodation of visitors was built by Kiefl in 1642, a large stone building at the N. E. corner of Pearl Street and Coenties slip. Later it was used for the City Hall or Stadt-Huys.

The first court of justice was established in 1647. It was presided over by Judge Van Dincklagen, the first judge in New York.

The first fire company was organized in 1657. It was called Rattle Watch, and consisted of 8 men, who handled 250 fire buckets, with hooks and ladders, all imported from Holland.

The first market house for the sale of meat was erected, 1658, on Bowling-Green.

The name of New York was first given to the city on September 8, 1664, when the English troops took possession. Revoking the old Dutch form of municipal government, they placed the municipal government in the hands of a mayor and five aldermen, all appointed by Richard Nicolls, the first English governor. Thomas Willett, the first mayor, took his seat in 1665.

Nobel Prizes. Alfred Bernhard Nobel (1833–1896) was a Russo-Swedish engineer who invented dynamite, publicly advocated euthanasia, and, dying, left behind him a fortune of $9,000,000 and a will which, after some minor legacies to relatives, directed that the vast residue, " converted into safe securities by the liquidators, shall constitute a fund, the income of which shall be distributed yearly to those who, during the year preceding, have rendered the most eminent services to humanity.

" The income shall be divided into five equal parts, which shall be awarded yearly:

" The first to the person who shall have made the most important discovery or invention in the domain of physics.

" The second to the person who shall have made the most important discovery or improvement in the domain of chemistry.

" The third to the person who shall have made the most important discovery in the domain of physiology or of medicine.

" The fourth to the person who shall have produced the greatest work, in the ideal sense, in the world of letters.

" The fifth to the person who shall have exerted the greatest or the best action for the fraternity of peoples, for the suppression or diminution of permanent armies, and for the formation or spreading of Peace Congresses."

The awards for these prizes are controlled entirely by Swedish courts. The winners of (1) and (2) are selected by the

Royal Academy of Science in Stockholm; (3) by the Caroline Medical-Chirurgical Institute in Stockholm; (4) by the Swedish Academy in Stockholm, and (5) by the Norwegian Storthing (Parliament).

Nobel believed that wealth was a curse to any one who had not earned it. "Great fortunes acquired by inheritance," he would say, "never bring happiness; they only dull the faculties. No wealthy man should leave more than a small legacy to his heirs, a legacy just sufficient to stimulate and supplement their energies, and not great enough to arrest the natural development of that faculty of personal initiative which is born in all of us." Nor, asserted Nobel, would he ever leave anything to a man of action. "I should expose him to the temptation of ceasing to work. On the other hand, I would willingly help a dreamer who had fallen into difficulties."

Nobel's heirs at law neither sanctioned nor accepted his theories. They sought to break the will, but failed. Then it was found that there remained an income of about $200,000 a year to be used in prizes, as per the will, so that each prize was $40,000.

The first award, made in 1901, was as follows:

Physics, to Prof. W. K. von Roentgen, of Würzburg, discoverer of the Roentgen rays; chemistry, to Prof. Jacobus H. van't Hoff, of Berlin; medicine, to Dr. Emil A. von Behring, of Marburg; and literature, to M. Sully Prudhomme, the greatest of contemporary French poets; the peace prize being divided between Dunant, founder of the Geneva Red Cross, and Passy, the French deputy who founded the University Peace Union.

Among those who have since been awarded prizes are President Roosevelt, who received the peace prize in recognition of his part in ending the Russo-Japanese war in 1905, but who donated the money; Selma Lagerlof, of Sweden, best known in this country for her fairy stories and allegories, who received the literature prize in 1909; William Marconi, the inventor of wireless telegraphy, who divided the physics prize of 1909 with Prof. Ferdinand K. Braun, of Strassburg; Prof. Theodor Mommsen, who received the literature prize in 1902; M. Arrhenius, the Swedish scientist, who got the physics prize in 1903; Monsieur and Mme. Curie and M. Becquerel, the discoverers of radium, who divided the chemistry prize of 1903 among them; Henrik Ibsen and Björnstjerne Björnson of Norway, who divided the literature prize in the same year; Sir William Ramsey, who won the chemistry prize in 1904; Frederic Mistral, the French Poet. and José Echagaray, the Spanish poet, who divided the literature prize of 1904; Henry Sienkiewiez, author of "Quo

Vadis," who received the literature prize in 1905; Carducci, who won it in 1906; and Rudyard Kipling, who secured it in 1907. In 1911 it was generally believed that Thomas A. Edison would be named for the prize in physics, but he anticipated a decision by public renunciation in favor of some one who needed it more, and the award was finally made to Madame Curie, who has thus figured twice on the list.

Nome. In Alaska there are a post-village, a river, and a cape of this name, all situated on Seward Peninsula. Gold was discovered in this neighborhood in 1898. Shortly afterward rich placer depositories revealed themselves along Anvil Creek and other contiguous tributaries of the Snake River. The set·tlement was originally known to its inhabitants as Anvil City. How it was accidentally renamed was told by the *Youth's Companion,* of Boston, on the authority of a drafting clerk (unnamed) in the Coast and Geodetic Survey office. "No one," the clerk is quoted as saying, "was more surprised than I when I saw the name on the map. It happened in this way:

"When the rush to Alaska took place on the discovery of rich gold deposits in the Klondike in the early '90s, the Government found it necessary to make more complete maps of that then little known country. There were many parties in the field, and the maps were being continually called for by the gold seekers. Hence for some months our office was rushed night and day.

"Now, it fell to my lot to draft a map of the Alaskan coast that runs southeast from Bering Strait. This map was to be made from the field notes and plats sent by the surveying party in that district. Such notes and plats always contain the names of prominent mountains, capes, inlets, and the like.

"In making the tracing of the coast down from Bering Strait, I came across a headland for which neither notes nor plats furnished a name. Accordingly, I made a pencil note at the point, putting the word 'name' with an interrogation point after it, thinking that the chief when he edited the map would put in the name if it had one or would think up one if it hadn't. In the hurry of the work, and due also to the fact, I presume, that I had written the letter 'a' in the word 'name' very much like 'o,' the matter was passed by the revisers, and my map went to the engravers in that shape.

"A few weeks afterward I was astonished, on looking over a stack of maps just engraved from my original, to see this particular headline designated thereon as 'Cape Nome.' When, shortly afterward, gold was discovered in the vicinity and a camp established there, the town took the name of the cape, and is called 'Nome' to this day."

O.

Oak. The epithet "monarch of the forest," applied to this the most regal of all hard-wood trees that grow in the temperate zone, dates from Virgil:

> Jove's own tree
> Which holds the world in awful sovereignty.

The ancient Pelasgians believed that a deity dwelt in their oak groves. The Greek oracle of Dodona stood in an oak grove. To the Druids of Britain and Gaul the tree was even more sacred. Oak groves were their temples; the mistletoe which hung from oak boughs was their favorite wand.

Venerable oaks famous in history abound in Europe and America. The Parliament Oak in Clipstone Park, which is supposed to be the oldest in England, derives its name from the fact that a parliament was held under its branches by Edward I in 1290, at which time it was a large tree. The King's oak in Windsor Forest is more than 1000 years old and quite hollow. Prof. Burnet, who once lunched inside this tree, said it was capable of accommodating 10 or 12 persons at a sitting. The Wallace oak, at Ellerslie, near where Wallace was born, is 21 feet in circumference. Wallace and 300 of his men are said to have hid from the English army among its branches when the tree was in full leaf.

In Massachusetts it is not uncommon to find oak trees from 12 to 20 feet in circumference and from 100 to 1400 years old. The town of Brighton boasts of the ruin of a white oak, nearly 26 feet in circumference, which is supposed to have passed its prime centuries before the first English voice was heard on our shores.

The Charter Oak (*q. v.*) of Hartford, Conn., which was prostrated in the storms of August, 1854, was believed to be 800 years old. The Wadsworth Oak of Geneseo, New York, was estimated to be at least 1000 years old at the time of its destruction in 1857. Its circumference was about 27 feet.

Oaks, The. A race instituted by the twelfth Earl of Derby, which derived its name from the Valley of Lambert's Oaks, attached to his lordship's residence at Banstead. He won the Oaks in the very year of its establishment, with Bridget, and won it again in 1794 with Hermione. Indeed a feature of the early history of the race is the frequency with which great noblemen repeated their victories. Lord Grosvenor, with Teetotum, Faith, and Ceres, respectively, won the race in 1781, 1782, and 1783. The fourth Duke of Grafton captured it no less than six times. His last victory, with Oxygen in 1831, was won by a margin so narrow that his Grace greeted the jockey with the sharp cry "You're a thief, John Day; you're a thief." John's face paled as he stammered, "Your Grace, what have I done to displease you?" "You stole that race, John Day; you stole that race!" Later the Duke of Portland won four races with Memoir, Mrs. Butterwick, Amiable, and La Roche, all daughters of the great St. Simon.

An epoch year in the annals of the race was 1840, when Crucifix won for Lord George Bentinck, known to posterity as the "King of the Turf." It is with that celebrated mare that Lord Bentinck's fame as a successful turfite is chiefly associated. She had won the Two Thousand Guineas and One Thousand, besides eleven two-year-old races. But her greatest achievement was in winning the Oaks, not so much because of the strength of the opposition as from the difficulties she encountered in the race. Queen Victoria and the Prince Consort attended Epsom on both the Derby and Oaks days that year, and the crowd was immense. The race was looked upon as a foregone conclusion for Crucifix, on whom odds of 3 to 1 were laid. An hour was cut to waste in false starts, of which there were sixteen, before the welcome shout of "They're off!" and the race began. Lord George, with unperturbed sang-froid throughout the tedium of delay, frequently remarked that "She cannot lose." It mattered little to Crucifix that some of the best of her opponents had a good 50 yards' start of her. She could have given any one of them three times the distance up that hill and then have won hands down. Lord George, who was a Napoleon among betting men, won £20,000 over Crucifix's Oaks triumph.

Without doubt the best filly that ever captured the Oaks was Pretty Polly in 1903. This superb mare would unquestionably have carried off all the "classics" of her year had her name been among the nominations for the Derby, Two Thousand and St. Leger. Pretty Polly made her début as a 2-year-old in most sensational style. It was at Sandown in June, when she defeated a field of horses by so many lengths that a snapshot taken from beside the judges' box produced the unique result of one animal only in the picture, the rest of the field being too far behind to enter the focus of the camera. Her career was one of glorious triumphs until the Ascot of her 5-year-old season. There, in the Gold Cup of 1906, Pretty Polly met her only reverse in England. It was plain after the race that she was suffering great physical pain from a hitherto unnoticed boil, and this, added to the bitterness of failure, which the splendid mare showed unmistakably she felt, made the spectacle of her defeat the more pathetic. Many grand dames were moved to tears at Ascot that day when the great heroine of three seasons came back to the paddock beaten. It was the last seen of Pretty Polly on a race-course. At the stud she has so far proved a signal failure.

A volume could be filled with Sceptre's romantic career. She was given the opportunity denied Pretty Polly of winning the five "classics," the Two Thousand Guineas, One Thousand, Derby, Oaks, and St. Leger, but was beaten in the greatest of them all—the Derby. After her defeat some people denounced Sceptre as "only a miler." Mr. Sievier, her owner, nearly jumped down the throat of a man who cast this reflection on his favorite. Smarting from the disappointment, in the unsaddling enclosure after the Derby, he retorted with heat, "Sceptre not stay! If she's anything at all she's a stayer. I'll run her in the Oaks; then you'll see whether she can stay a mile and a half or not." Sceptre made short work of the Oaks, winning in a canter. The St. Leger in the following September she won in yet easier style, and the subsequent running of her chief St. Leger victim, Rising Glass, enhanced the merit of Sceptre's' performance.

Blink Bonny, the heroine of 1857, and Signorinetta, the sensational 100 to 1 Derby winner of 1908, are the only animals who have gained both the Blue Ribbon and the Garter of the Turf.

Ombre. A three-handed game at cards, of Spanish origin. One of the fashionable amusements in England during the reign of Queen Anne, it has been immortalized by Pope, in the "Rape of the Lock":

> Belinda now, whom thirst of fame invites,
> Burns to encounter two advent'rous knights.
> At ombre singly to decide their doom,
> And swells her breast with conquests yet to come.
> Straight the three bands prepare in arms to join,
> Each band the number of the sacred nine.

A vivid description of the game follows, the victory falling to Belinda:

> An ace of hearts steps forth; the king unseen
> Lurked in her hand and mourned his captive queen;
> He springs to vengeance with an eager pace,
> And falls like thunder on the prostrate ace.
> The nymph, exulting, fills with shouts the sky;
> The walls, the woods, and long canals reply.

The name (properly "el hombre") signifies "the man." In vernacular English it might with less courtesy be translated as "it." One of the players, "It" or "El Hombre," plays against the two others, who have a combined interest against him. He must get more tricks than either of the others. The author of a book entitled "The Gamester," which appeared in 1720, or eight years after the publication of the "Rape of the Lock," gives it the precedence over all other indoor recreations, calling it "the most delightful and entertaining of all games to those who have anything in them of what we call the "Spirit of Play." But it is now almost unknown. The current books on cards contain no mention of it. The modern game of quadrille is simply ombre adapted to four players instead of three, and whist is the final and perfect evolution from both.

Omnibus (Latin, the dative plural of *omnis* "all," meaning "to all" or "for all"). The omnibus system dates back to a line started in Paris in 1827 by Jacques Lafitte, the banker-politician. He seems to have taken a hint from Blaise Pascal, who in 1662 obtained a patent for a service of public *carosses à cinque sous* (five-cent coaches). Of all the *Pensées* of the great French thinker, this seems to have had the least vitality, for the enterprise broke down in a few months.

The name "omnibus," in the form *voiture omnibus*, came into vogue with Lafitte's coaches. A certain George Shillabeer, who had started in life as a midshipman in the British navy, found himself in mature age a coach-builder in Paris. To him Lafitte applied for expert aid. After building a few coaches for the French capital, Shillabeer decided to introduce the new vehicles into London. On July 4, 1829, he placed the first two 'buses ever seen in England on the London streets. They were built to carry 22 passengers, all inside, and each was drawn by three bay horses. On both of the outer sides of the vehicle the word "Omnibus" was painted in large letters. A great crowd assembled to witness the start from the "Yorkshire Stingo," a tavern in Paddington, for the Bank of England. Newspapers and magazines were provided gratis for the travellers to beguile the tedium of the journey. The fare was one shilling for the full distance and six-pence half-way.

Pictures of the primitive vehicle remind one irresistibly of a hearse. Believers in omens will be interested to know that Shillabeer subsequently became an undertaker.

The developments in the type of the 'bus are best studied from contemporary pictures. A print of 1837 shows a curved top, with two passengers sitting beside the driver and five perched on a seat behind, the access to the roof being gained by means of the box of the wheel, a leather strap, and an iron step. When passengers were once admitted to the roof, fewer were carried inside, and the 'bus was made smaller. A *Punch* cartoon, by Leech, in 1852, represents Lord John Russell sitting in the rain on a single " form " on the outside of an omnibus, and saying, " Oh! you don't catch me coming out on the knife-board again to make room for a party of swells." The Great Exhibition in the previous year had given a great stimulus to the 'bus traffic. It was in the exhibition year that Tilling, a pioneer to whom London owes much, first placed his 'buses in the streets.

In 1856, when the London General Omnibus Company was established after buying up all its rivals, 300 omnibuses were built on a new plan. Outside passengers were arranged in two rows, back to back, facing outward along the side of the 'bus. They climbed up a perpendicular ladder hanging over the rear. Hence female passengers strongly objected to the roof. In 1880 a fixed winding staircase was substituted for the gymnastic ladder, and the roof was furnished with " garden seats " arranged across the 'bus with a centre aisle and fitted with reversible backs. The prosperity of the London 'bus reached its zenith in 1905, when 3484 of the vehicles with 6169 drivers were licensed in London by Scotland Yard. But revolution was in the air. That very year the returns also included the omnibus item of 241 motor 'buses, an innovation which was to prove fatal to the older conveyance. The first licensed electric motor 'bus began running in 1899. This shared the fate of all previous experiments made with steam 'buses and was quickly withdrawn. Not until 1904, when Tilling started a regular motor 'bus service from Peckham to Oxford Circus, did the innovation justify itself. By 1908 the total number of the old-style London 'buses had been reduced to 2115. On October 18, 1911, the leading omnibus company took the last of its horse-drawn vehicles off the streets of the English capital.

Orange. This is one of the most beautiful and interesting of vegetable growths. Its botanical name is *Citrus,* said to be derived from the town of Citron, in Judea, where it was first cultivated. It belongs to the genus of plants known as the natural order of *Aurantiaceæ,* or " golden fruit-bearers." Thus, it requires no great stretch of the imagination to conclude that the " golden apples " of the garden of Hesperides were oranges. From the low Latin *Pomum Aurantium* we get the word " orange," which occurs in different forms in several languages. The genus *Citrus* contains a large number of species and varieties, the fruits being known under such names as orange, lemon, lime, shaddock, pompelmoose, forbidden fruit, kumquat, and citron. The species *C. Aurantium,* with its varieties of sweet oranges, is the best known to us. Risso, the eminent naturalist of Nice, published at Paris, in 1818, an elaborate history of oranges, in which he described no fewer than 169 varieties. These he divided into eight species—viz., sweet oranges, bitter oranges, bergamots, limes, pampelunos, sweet limes, lemons, and citrons. Of the first of these, with which we are now concerned, he enumerated no less than forty-three varieties, though it is probable that all these are derived from the common orange, *C. Aurantium.* It is said that the sweet (or China) orange was first brought into Europe from China by the Portuguese in 1547; and, further, that the original tree whence all the European orange trees of this class have been produced is, or at least was a few years ago, preserved at Lisbon in one of the gardens of the nobility. But the first mention of oranges in England is of much earlier date, for it is recorded that in 1290 Edward the First's queen bought from the cargo of a Spanish ship which came to Portsmouth various fruits, among which were seven oranges (*Poma de orenge*). Still, though Edward's marriage with Eleanor of Castile led to greater intercourse with Spain, it does not appear that in the fourteenth and fifteenth centuries there was any great commerce in oranges, as the name of the fruit is not to be found either in the " Libell of English Policy," the " Liber Albus of London," or Professor Rogers's " Collection of Bills," in all of which many other— and, indeed, most—articles of fruit and grocery are mentioned.

In 1432 Henry VI, on his return from being crowned King of France, was welcomed by the citizens with a pageant in which was a grove of

Orangis, almondis, and the pome-garnade,

as poetically described by Lydgate. In 1470 oranges are noticed in the Paston letters. In 1502 Elizabeth of York gave a reward to the servant of the prothonotary of Spain for bringing a present of oranges ; and in the household expenses book of Henry VIII (1530) and his daughter the Princess Mary (1539), payments for oranges are mentioned. In 1558 the Stationers' Company, at a court dinner, indulged in the fruit to the value of 4d.

By the end of the sixteenth century oranges were recognized as a notable article of commerce, and, according to Stowe (1598), Billingsgate was the principal quay for landing them. The sweet orange was not introduced into England till after the bitter variety, and the few allusions of the poets of the period last mentioned are to this and not the sweet fruit. Shakespeare, in "Much Ado about Nothing," says, "The Count is neither sad nor sick, nor merry nor well; but civil, Count, civil as an orange, and somewhat of that jealous complexion;" and Nash, a contemporaneous dramatist, uses the expression, "civil as an orange." In these passages, a pun, a very weak one, is obviously intended on the word "Seville," whence then, as now, the bitter oranges came.

Sir Walter Raleigh, "the father of tobacco," is credited with having brought oranges to England.

The first steamer exclusively devoted to the orange trade arrived in London in November, 1867. Before this date it frequently happened that London was without an orange supply for 3 or 4 weeks in winter months.

Florida is the great orange-growing State in the American Union.

The effects of the famous freeze which struck Florida in the spring of 1896 have at last been wiped out. At that time the annual production of citrus fruit had climbed from 600,000 boxes in 1884 and 1885 to 6,000,000 boxes in 1894 and 1895. Then the big freeze happened along and the next season's crop in Florida was only 75,000 boxes.

The industry was practically wiped out. Since then the yield has been slowly climbing again, until for the season of 1909 and 1910 it was approximately 7,000,000 boxes, of which 6,000,000 were shipped out of the State.

The Florida Citrus Exchange, which directs the packing and shipping of a large part of the crop, was organized in 1908. In the great packing houses of Florida no hand actually touches the oranges. Every person who handles them wears white gloves to protect the orange from any possible contamination of human touch and from scratching and bruising by the finger-nail.

The pickers move into the grove with their equipment of ladders, baskets, field boxes, clippers, etc. Each picker wears his white gloves and carries a wicker basket, shaped to fit the back or side of the person, swung from the shoulder.

Each basket is lined with thick canvas, which is stretched four or five inches from the bottom of the basket. Every orange must be clipped, not pulled or picked, from the tree, the stem being left smooth and flush with the surface of the orange.

Each piece of fruit is laid, not dropped, into the basket, and when filled the basket is carefully emptied into the field boxes. These are never filled above the top, thus preventing the bruising of the fruit when the boxes are stacked one on another for carriage to the packing house.

They are taken to the plant on big platform wagons equipped

with springs so as to reduce the jar to the fruit from uneven-
ness of roads. In the packing house the fruit in the field boxes
is put on the first grading table, and from this point to the
packing boxes every person is obliged to keep careful watch for
fruit that is below grade. The motto of the exchange, "Every
doubtful orange is a cull," stretches in big letters across one
end of the house where none can fail to read it.

From the first table the fruit is carried over wooden rollers
down a gentle incline to the washing tank. Every orange receives a scrubbing before it is deemed fit to be sent to a critical
market—incidentally it is worth just about 20 per cent. more
after the bath than before.

The oranges are next assorted according to size in bins. Beside the bins stand the packers, each, like the other workers,
wearing the ever-present white gloves. Here each orange is
rapidly wrapped in its square of white paper with the stem of
the orange under the twist of the paper. On the end of each
box is stamped the size of the oranges within, and when the
box is filled it is placed on an automatic carrier which delivers
it to the nailer.

Here a specially designed machine presses down the end of
the cover which is nailed to the heads, but the middle is left
loose from the middle partition of the box. This is called the
flush pack, which is demanded by the best markets in the North.
From this point the boxes are loaded into the waiting cars on
the switch track at the southern end of the house. Each box
is placed on end, six boxes across the car and three boxes high.
These are then stripped or braced in the car to prevent jarring
and consequent bruising in transportation to the markets. Three
hundred boxes make a carload.

Orange Blossoms at Weddings. Orange blossoms have
been adopted for the adornment of a bride as a symbol of
chastity and also of fecundity. Not only is the orange-tree an
evergreen, but it is said to be the only tree which produces fruit
and flowers at the same time. An early reference to this pecu·
liarity appears in Sheridan's "Rivals" (Act iii, Sc. 3). When
Mrs. Malaprop complains that, "Nowadays few think how a
little knowledge becomes a gentleman; men have no sense but
for the worthless flowers of beauty," the gallant Captain Absolute makes reply: "Too true; but our ladies seldom show fruit
until time has robbed them of more specious blossom; few, like
Mrs. Malaprop and *the orange-tree, are rich in both at once.*"

Moreover, orange blossoms possess an exquisite odor, and
are so rare and costly as to be in easy reach only of the noble
and the wealthy, thus indicating that the bride is of high rank.

The custom of entwining them in bridal wreaths is of comparatively recent date in England and America. It came to us, like most other female fashions in dress, from the French, who in their turn have derived it from Spain. In the latter country it had long obtained, and is said to have been originally of Moorish origin. There is, however, an old Spanish legend which gives a different account of its introduction. According to this, soon after the importation of the orange-tree by the Moors, one of the Spanish kings had a specimen of which he was very proud, and of which the French ambassador was extremely desirous to obtain an offshoot. The gardener's daughter was aware of this, and, in order to provide herself with the necessary dowry to enable her to marry her lover, she obtained a slip, which she sold to the ambassador at a high price. On the occasion of her wedding, in recognition of her gratitude to the plant which had procured her happiness, she bound in her hair a wreath of orange-blossoms, and thus inaugurated the fashion which has become universal. As the orange was introduced into Spain at a very early period by the Moors, this legend sufficiently establishes the antiquity of the custom as far as that country is concerned, although many centuries elapsed before it spread over the rest of Europe. Up to near the middle of the nineteenth century it was the practice for ladies to be married in hats or bonnets; and the fashion of dispensing with the bonnet seems first to have established itself after the example set by Queen Victoria on the occasion of her wedding in 1840.

Orange, Navel. This is merely an abnormal growth, an abortive attempt of nature to produce twins. One of the twins failed, however, surviving only as a protuberance in the blossom end of the orange, and there forming a little navel-like kernel enveloped in the skin of the fruit. Buds from the trees producing these freaks were grafted upon other stock, and gradually the semi-dwarf navel-orange tree was established in California. The original trees of this stock came from Bahia, Brazil, where their peculiarity had been noted but not utilized. No one had taken the hint supplied by nature until they were transplanted to their new home on the Pacific Coast, where they become one of the most profitable growths in the State. The navel orange is frequently seedless, and what few seeds are ever found in it are small and undeveloped.

Organ. In many respects the great organ installed in 1911 in the Cathedral of St. John the Divine, on Washington Heights, New York, is the most notable in the world. In the number of stops it is slightly inferior to some other famous organs, but in point of completeness, as regards tone color and volume, it has no superior and few equals. The total cost was $70,000. There are between 6000 and 7000 pipes. The largest is a great wooden conduit 32 feet long, the smallest a thin reed smaller than a lead pencil. The organist would be powerless without his two automatic assistants, a 15-horse electric motor, operating the southern division of the instrument, and a 7½-horse-power motor for the northern division. These two divisions are placed one on either side of the chancel or choir of the cathedral and 50 feet above the main floor.

Each division occupies the space of a good-sized house and each is packed with ranks on ranks of pipes, zinc, composition, and wooden. The greatest is the 32-foot pedal bombarde, the only one of its kind in the world except the one in the College of the City of New York.

Ortolan, a species of *Fringillidæ,* especially famous with European epicures. It formed one of the costly items of Soyer's hundred-guinea dish at the banquet at York in 1851.

The name in Italian means gardener (ortolano from Latin *hortus,* "a garden"). According to Menage, the bird is quite at home in the hedges of gardens.

The ortolan is not famed for its song, which is, however, soft and sweet. In Lombardy a certain number of these interesting birds owe to their musical talent the good fortune of escape from broiling. Orpheus and Amphion never gained a more perfect victory. Like the nightingale, with which it has also other points of resemblance, the ortolan sings after as well as before sunset; and it was this bird that Varro called his companion by night and day.

Ortolans are solitary birds: they fly in pairs, rarely three together, and never in flocks; they search for seeds in pastures: and, if seen in vines, it is not for the sake of the grapes (this is a foul calumny), but it is in search of the insects in the stems. They are taken in traps, from March or April to September, when they are often poor and thin; but, if fed with plenty of millet-seed and other grain, they become sheer lumps of fat, and delicious morsels. The bird, however, has a peculiar habit of feeding, which is opposed to its rapid fattening; it feeds only at the rising of the sun. To surmount this peculiarity, those who pander to the taste of Italian gourmands place the ortolans in a warm chamber, perfectly dark, with only one aperture in the wall. Their food is scattered over the floor of the chamber. In the morning the keeper of the birds places a lantern in the orifice of the wall; by the light thus thrown in, the ortolans, thinking the sun is about to rise, greedily consume the food upon the floor. More food is scattered about, and the lantern withdrawn. The ortolans soon fall asleep. In about two hours the whole process is repeated, and so on four or five times every day. The ortolans thus treated become like little balls of fat in a few days. This arises from the absence of waste by motion, in the extra sleep which the birds get, absence of the usual chemical changes from the influence of light, an unusual supply of food from their taking four or five meals a day instead of one, and great facilities for digesting that food in being removed from the view of external objects which produce anxieties and hamper the digestion.

The ortolan is considered sufficiently fat when it is a handful; and is judged by feeling it, and not by appearance. They should not be killed with violence, like other birds; this might crush and bruise the delicate flesh, and spoil the *coup d'œil*—to avoid which, the best mode is to plunge the head of the ortolan into a glass of brandy: in his fate a French author oddly traces an analogy to "maudlin Clarence in a malmsey butt."

A gourmand will take an ortolan by the legs and crunch it in delicious mouthfuls, so as absolutely to lose none of it. More delicate feeders cut the bird in quarters, and lay aside the gizzard, which is somewhat hard; the rest may be eaten, even to the bones, which are sufficiently tender for the most delicate mouth to masticate without inconvenience.

Notwithstanding its delicacy, the ortolan fattens very fast; and it is this lump of fatness that is its merit, and has sometimes caused it to be preferred to the beccafico. According to Buffon, the ortolan was known to the Greeks and Romans, who understood fattening the bird upon millet; but a lively French commentator doubts this assertion. He maintains that, had the ancients known the ortolan, they would have deified it, and built altars to it upon Mount Hymettus and the Janiculum; adding, did they not deify the horse of Caligula, which was certainly not worth an ortolan, and Caligula himself, who was not worth so much as his horse? However, the dispute belongs to the "Classics of the Table."

The ortolan figures in a curious anecdote of individual epicurism in the last century. A gentleman of Gloucestershire had one son, whom he sent abroad to make the grand tour of the Continent, where he paid more attention to the cookery of nations and luxurious living than anything else. Before his return, his father died, and left him a large fortune. He now looked over his note-book, to discover where the most exquisite dishes were to be had and the best cooks obtained. Every servant in his house was a cook; his butler, footman, housekeeper, coachman, and grooms were all cooks. He had three Italian cooks; one from

Florence, another from Siena, and a third from Viterbo—for dressing one Florentine dish! He had a messenger constantly on the road between Brittany and London, to bring the eggs of a certain sort of plover found in the former country. He was known to eat a single dinner at the expense of £50, though there were but two dishes. In nine years he found himself getting poor, and this made him melancholy. When totally ruined, having spent £150,000, a friend one day gave him a guinea to keep him from starving; and he was found in a garret next day broiling an ortolan, for which he had paid a portion of the alms.

Orvietan. This is the name of what was in effect the earliest predecessor of the patent medicine of to-day. It is older than Christianity, for it was known to Galen, who published a formula of his own containing 64 ingredients, but it enjoyed its greatest vogue in the seventeenth century, when it reached the legal dignity of a monopoly. Though the word is mentioned by Sir Walter Scott in Kenilworth, it has been lost sight of by most lexicographers and is rarely found even in a medical dictionary. Originally orvietan was known as " itheriaca," a word that forms the root of our " treacle " (*q. v.*), this because a chief ingredient was the powdered flesh of vipers. One Lupi, a native of Orvieto, managed to secure a practical monopoly of his formula, which he renamed after the city of his birth. About 1628 some of his followers secured the sole right of selling orvietan throughout the Papal States, a violation of the monopoly being punished by excommunication and a fine of 1000 ducats. Despite the papal protection, a cart-tail physician named Desiderio Descombes produced a rival brand, for which he built up an immense patronage, travelling from city to city and eventually making his head-quarters in Paris. The French people invented for him the now familiar nickname of " Charlatan," possibly from the Italian *ciarlare,* " to chatter," possibly from the brilliant scarlet coat (*scarlatto*) which he wore to attend the crowds on the Pont Neuf, and just as likely as not from the French words *le char l'attend,* " the cart awaits him."

It is satisfactory to learn that, although Descombes received the approbation of the Queen of France and a fee of 150 crowns, he failed to cajole the Paris Faculty of Medicine into an indorsement either of his methods or his medicine. It was claimed for orvietan that it was a panacea for all diseases and an infallible antidote against poisons, including snake-bite. Nevertheless, Descombes himself died of the plague.

Orvietan finally lost its vogue, though it still lingers in Normandy with a low class of practitioners. A trace of it died hard in the United States where it was known as Confectio Democratis. This was made of turpentine, acacia, treacle, balm of Gilead,

Russian castor, cinnamon, myrrh, and some sixty other ingredients, making a mixture very like orvietan, except that the flesh of the vipers was replaced by the dried bellies of skunks, a doubtful improvement from the viewpoint of either therapeutics or æsthetics.

Oshkosh, a town in Wisconsin whose clutter of consonants retains the sound of the original Indian name, a name so harsh and dissonant that humorists have accepted it as the type of its class. Hence discontent on the part of some of its inhabitants, and hence in 1911 much clamor for a change. " It must be confessed at the outset," said the Rochester *Post Express,* March 26, 1911, " that Oshkosh is not a beautiful word. Its pronunciation is suggestive of a man struggling with a mouthful of hot mush, and to the irreverent it is a perfect rhyme to " gosh." But, on the other hand, the word has its advantages. It is an ideal word for advertising purposes. Once heard the word cannot be forgotten. Furthermore, to say that one comes from Oshkosh is in itself a mark of distinction. To be sure, few persons do come from Oshkosh. They are afraid of being made fun of, but when they do wander from the Oshkosh fireside, they attract as much attention as the pachyderm contingent of a circus parade. In a drawing-room the citizen from Oshkosh is the cynosure of all eyes, and he need fear but three rivals—the man from Kalamazoo, the man from Kokomo, and the man from Keokuk."

The subject, however, has a serious side, which the same authority did not fail to perceive. Oshkosh is an Indian name, and every time an Indian name is expunged from the map an irreparable injury is done to American tradition and to American institutions. " The Indian nomenclature," urged the *Post-Express,* " is our choicest, and should be our most precious, heritage. The early settlers had the excellent taste and good judgment to draw largely on the Indian vocabulary for names of cities, towns, rivers, and mountains, and in the main the early Americans did their work well. Here in the East many of the original Indian names have been exchanged for absurd names of classical origin. Think of ' Rome ' and ' Utica ' being located in the Mohawk Valley! How much more beautiful—to say nothing of appropriateness—is the word ' Mohawk.' The people of the Middle West have up to this time retained their fondness for the Indian nomenclature. They have not been affected by the madness to give Old World names to New World places. And for this reason we hope that the good people of Oshkosh will think twice before they set seriously to work to change the name of their city. Surely there is enough patriotic sentiment left in that town to defeat the efforts of the displacers, to use Owen Wister's happy word." (See also NAMES, GEOGRAPHICAL.)

P.

Pall Mall and **Paille Maille.** Pall Mall in St. James Park, London, is named after the game of paille-maille (Italian *palla,* " a ball," and *maglia,* "a mallet"), which was corrupted into *pele-mele* in French, thus influencing the English pronunciation that still survives. Originally the famous street was an avenue of elms. By 1560 three or four houses had risen at the east end of the line of road. Charles II is said to have set aside this alley or avenue for the playing of the game, which in his day had risen to be a fashionable recreation. Exactly when the sport was introduced into England is not absolutely certain. It was known to James I, for in his " Basilicon Doron " (1616) that monarch recommends " palle-malle " as a field game for the use of his eldest son, Prince Henry. It was not known in Queen Elizabeth's reign, for in Sir Robert Dallington's " A Method for Travell " (4to, 1598) paille-maille is described as an exercise of France which the author marvels had not been introduced into England. Faithorne's plan of London, 1658, shows a row of trees on the north side; and the name of Pall-Mall, as a street, occurs in the rate books of St. Martin's in-the-Fields under the year 1656. Pepys mentions the game as played in the park— " 2nd April, 1661; to St. James's-park, where I saw the Duke of York playing at Pele-Mele, the first time I ever saw the sport." It is described by Blount as " a game where a round bowle is with a mallet struck through a high arch of iron (standing at either end of an alley), which he that can do it at the fewest blows, or at the number of agreed on, wins." A drawing of the time of Charles II, which was engraved in Smith's " Antiquities of Westminster," shows the above arrangement for playing the game.

It would occupy more space than we can spare to tell how the avenue of elms in which paille-maille was played rose into a stately street; how a century later it became celebrated for its taverns—one of which, " Wood's at the Pell-Mell," was a haunt of the gay old Pepys; and how the place became a noted duel-ling-ground.

Nell Gwyn lived in 1670 " on the east end, north side "; and from 1671 to her death, in 1687, in a house on the south side, with a garden toward the park; and it was upon a mount in this garden that " the impudent comedian " stood, to hold her " familiar discourse" with Charles II, who stood "on ye green walk" under the wall. This scene, as described by Evelyn, has been cleverly painted by E. M. Ward, R.A. The site of Nell's house is now occupied by No. 79, Society for the Propagation of the Gospel in Foreign Parts. Eastward of Nell Gwyn's lived Sir William Temple, the Hon. Robert Boyle, and Bubb Dodington; and on the south side, Dr. Barrow and the Countess of Southesk, the celebrated Countess of De Grammont's Memoirs. In Marlborough-house lived the great Duke of Marlborough; and in a house in front of the mansion Sir Robert Walpole. Of Schomberg-house, Nos. 81 and 82, built for the great Duke of Schomberg, the center and the west wing remain.

Defoe describes the Pall-Mall of 1703 as "the ordinary residence of all strangers, because of its vicinity to the Queen's palace, the Park, the Parliament-house, the theatres, the chocolate and coffee houses, where the best company frequent." However, the street became early noted for its taverns, which we consider to have been Pepy's "houses for clubbing." The first modern club-house was No. 86, opened as a subscription-house, and called the Albion Hotel. It is now known as the Office of Ordnance.

After the removal of Carlton-house in 1827, "the sweet shady side of Pall Mall," so lovingly described by Captain Morris during his exile in America, gradually developed into a line of club-houses.

Panorama, a pictorial representation of a landscape or other scene, arranged on the inside of a cylindrical surface so as to afford the spectator the allusion of gazing upon the actual view or episode from some central point. The illusion is sometimes enhanced by moving or shifting pictures unrolled before him. The architectural painter Breisig, of Danzig, was the first to conceive the idea, but the first to put it into execution was Robert Barker, an Edinburgh painter, to whom the idea occurred independently while taking a sketch of the city from the top of Arthur Seat. Barker's panoramic view of Edinburgh, first exhibited there in 1788 and transferred to London in 1789, was the pioneer in this form of spectacle. Barker's next achievement was a panorama of London from the top of the Albion Hills.

The French took up the idea in a panorama of Paris (1799), and by successive steps greatly improved upon the original idea, increasing the optical illusion by the employment of plastic objects in addition to painting.

Felix Philipoteau (1815–84) is the greatest name associated with the panorama his masterpieces being "The Siege of

Paris," first exhibited in that city in 1875, and "The Battle of Gettysburg," exhibited in New York 1888–91 and afterward in other American cities.

Parachute (a word compounded of the Italian *parare,* "to depend, to ward off," and the French *chute,* "a fall"), a contrivance used for descending safely from a great height, primarily and especially a balloon. It is constructed like a large umbrella, so as to expand and thus check the velocity of descent by means of the resistance of the air. The first record of any contrivance of this sort is in Simon de Loubère's History of Siam (Paris, 1691), where there is an account of a person who frequently diverted the court by leaping from great heights with two parachutes or umbrellas fastened to his girdle.

On December 26, 1783, Sebastien Lenormant made a practical demonstration of the efficiency of a parachute by descending from the tower of Montpellier observatory, holding in either hand an umbrella 60 inches in diameter. The idea of making it an adjunct to a balloon was first conceived by Jacques Garnerin. During the war between France and Austria in 1793–97, Garnerin was taken prisoner by the Austrians and spent three years in the Hungarian fortress of Buda, during which he conceived, but never executed, a novel method of escape. "The love of liberty so natural to a prisoner," he says, "gave rise to many projects to release myself from the rigorous detention. To surprise the vigilance of the sentries, force walls 10 feet thick, throw myself from the ramparts without being injured, were schemes that afforded recreation." These words he wrote in the programme of his first descent in a parachute, which actually took place from a balloon in the Park of Monceau, Paris, October 22, 1797.

On reaching a height of 6000 feet, Garnerin cut the cord that attached him to the balloon, and rapidly descended, while the balloon sailed upward until it exploded. The spectators saw Garnerin's parachute oscillate in great sweeps, then descend rapidly and strike the ground with sufficient violence to throw the aeronaut from his seat. He escaped with a bruised foot, mounted a horse, and returned to the point of departure, where he was received with wild applause.

After this experiment parachute descents became popular the world over, and have been repeated up to the present time with no substantial change. A slight improvement in construction, however, has been made by cutting away the top of the canvas, thus allowing the air to escape sufficiently to check the oscillations.

"It would seem easy," opines Zahm, in his "Aerial Navigation" (1911), "to have transformed the craft into a travelling
parachute, gliding down the sky like a great bird on outstretched
wings. Such a device would enable the aeronaut to sail some
miles and direct his course in the air. If fair skill has been
acquired, it might have hastened the advent of human flight by
twenty years, so far as flight is practicable without the aid of the
internal-combustion motor. For two decades ago Maxim produced an abundantly powerful steam-engine, but could find no
one to furnish him a manageable glider on which to mount it.
Now indeed such gliders are available; but they were developed
by aviators, not by balloonists or parachutists, who should have
effected that advance many years ago."

The same authority points out how Nature had blazed the
way for man, could he have profited by her hints. In India
she has produced a tree, the *Zanonia Macrocarpia,* which bears a
large two-winged seed that has all the properties of a parachute.
When shaken from its branch, the seed immediately rights itself
and glides gracefully through the air. A number of these seeds
look like so many sparrows sailing earthward in wide curves.
"Artificial gliders of this type," says Zahm, "are easy to construct and would make interesting toys. However, if man has
not copied such natural models, he has done much better by
making his gliders concave below, instead of concave above as
are the beautiful Indian seeds.

The first fatal accident in a parachute descent occurred in
London on July 24, 1837. The victim was Robert Cocking, who
so early as 1814 had applied himself to remedying the main defect in Garnerin's parachute—namely, its violent oscillation
during descent. He conceived that a conical form (with the
vertex downward) would be an improvement over the dome
shape, and if it were made of sufficient size there would be sufficient atmospheric resistance to check a too rapid descent.
He attached a parachute of his own construction to Charles
Green's Nassau balloon, which rose from Vauxhall Gardens,
London, at 6.25 P.M. Cocking had stipulated for an elevation of 7000 feet, but it was found that only 5000 feet
could be reached, at any rate before darkness set in. The
balloon was then over Greenwich. When Cocking let slip the
catch which liberated him from the balloon, the latter shot upward with the velocity of a sky-rocket, but eventually landed in
safety at Maidstone. Green knew nothing of the fate of his companion until next day. The parachute suddenly closed in mid-
air and Cocking was hurled to his death below.

Patent Medicine, First. See ORVIETAN.

Peacock. Aristophanes introduced the peacock into his comedy of Cloud-cuckoo-town. We know, therefore, that Alexander (104–78 B.C.) was wrong in his claim that he had brought peacocks into Greece from invasions of the East. But he may have been the first to introduce into the West the custom of serving them up at banquets, although even here Pliny comes forward with a rival claim: "The first that killed peacocks to be served up as a dish at the table was Hortensius, the great orator, in that solemn feast which he made when he was consecrated high-priest."

Pliny further states that it was Aufidius Lurco who first fattened peacocks for food and sold them in the market place for so much that his yearly income from this invention was sixty thousand sesterces.

The first mention of the peacock in the Bible occurs in the tenth chapter of First Kings, in a description of the magnificence of Solomon's court: "The king had at sea a navy of Tarshish with the navy of Hiram; once in three years came the navy of Tarshish, bringing gold and silver, ivory and apes and peacocks."

Peacock Feathers. A superstition especially prevalent among the lower classes of England and America associates ill-luck with peacock feathers. To a lesser extent the superstition flourishes in Germany, Italy, France, and Spain, and in all Mahommedan countries. The reason for its existence in the latter is not far to seek. Mahommedan tradition asserts that the peacock and the snake were both placed at the entrance to Paradise to give warning of approaching danger, that Eblis, or Satan, seduced them both, and that in consequence they shared his punishment. The European superstition may have come through Saracen sources, but it is more likely to be a popular reminiscence of the classical fable of Argus, the hundred-eyed minister of King Osiris, who was turned by Juno into a peacock, the multitudinous eyes being placed in its tail. This legend might readily enough have been associated with the superstition of the evil eye. In the sixteenth century garlands of peacocks' feathers were bestowed on liars and cheats. Thus the feathers might symbolize an ever-watchful traitor in the home.

Another explanation is that peacocks' feathers were anciently used as funeral emblems. Hence they could not fail in time to be looked upon as ill-omens. Paracelsus says, that, "if a peacock cries more than usual and out of time, it foretells the death of some one in that family to whom it doth belong." (See WALSH, *Handy-book of Literary Curiosities, s. v.*)

Peacock Throne. Of all the costly wonders that the palace of the Mogul emperors at Delhi contained, the most wonderful and the most costly was the peacock throne. This was constructed during the reign of Shah Jehan, and was the work of a Frenchman, Austin, of Bordeaux, who had sought refuge at the Mogul's court. It was estimated that the value of the throne was £6,000,000 sterling. It stood in the centre of the beautiful Hall of Private Audience, and was named after the figures of two peacocks standing behind it, their tails being expanded, and the whole so inlaid with sapphires, rubies, emeralds, pearls, and other precious stones of appropriate colors as to represent life. The throne itself was six feet long by four feet wide; it stood on six massive feet, which, with the body, were of solid gold inlaid with rubies, emeralds, and diamonds. It was surmounted by a canopy of gold supported by twelve pillars, all richly emblazoned with costly gems, and a fringe of pearls ornamented the border of the canopy. Between the two peacocks stood the figure of a parrot of ordinary size, said to have been carved out of a single emerald. On each side of the throne stood an umbrella, one of the Oriental emblems of royalty. They were formed of crimson velvet thickly embroidered and fringed with pearls, the handles, eight feet high, being of gold studded with diamonds. It has been held that the famous Kohinoor was one of the jewels of the throne, and as this diamond, now in possession of the Queen of England, was owned by Shah Jehan, the story may be true. When Delhi was sacked by the Persians under Nadir Shah in 1739 the throne was plundered of its jewels, broken up and carried away, with $750,000,000 of loot. A block of white marble now marks the spot where it once stood.

Pedestrian Records. There is an old Greek legend that Eoclides, several centuries before the time of Christ, in Attica, established a pedestrian record that has never since been beaten. Eoclides was a messenger who, being sent from Athens to bring some holy fire from Delphos, made the journey there and back— one hundred and twenty-five miles in all—on the same day.

An unnamed running footman of "a certain Turkish emperor" comes next to Eoclides in dubious historical fame, with the reputation of having travelled from Constantinople to Adrianople, 114 miles, in a day and a night. This feat was never equalled in modern times until Edward Payson Weston, in 1875, walked 115 miles in a single day.

But we are anticipating.

There is another running footman belonging to "a very re-

spectable family in Dungannon " (Ireland), who appears only
to disappear in a story told in *The European Magazine* (vol. 60,
p. 151). Even his name is not mentioned and he survives only
through defeat. We are told that in his day this footman was
famous for pedestrian exploits. One evening a military gentleman, who had dined with the man's master, made a bet over his
wine, that he would find a soldier in his regiment who would
outstrip the footman in a race from Dungannon to Armagh and
back again. In the sober light of next day he regretted his rash-
ness, for he remembered no soldier particularly famed for speed.
However, he was in for it now. After a consultation with his
brother officers he hit upon this plan: the soldiers, part of whom
lay at Armagh, part in Dungannon and its neighborhood, were
at different times drawn up in companies, races were run, and
the victors in each separate company were brought together, and
then started against one another. An active fellow, named
Venter, was found to outstrip all his competitors with the greatest
ease. This man, during three weeks which preceded the day
when the race was to be decided, was duly trained, and when the
important time came, was in complete wind and strength. The
famous footman and he started at Dungannon. Fifty-six
minutes later Venter made his appearance in the city of Armagh,
dressed in a white frock and his arms decorated with ribbons.
Ascending half-way up Market Street, he ran round the Cross-
stone, and then proceeded down the hill on his return to Dungannon. "In another hour he arrived in Dungannon, having
completely distanced his competitor, and having left even the
horseman behind, who had started with him to witness the race.
The distance from Dungannon to Armagh, by Charlemont, is at
least ten and a half Irish miles, so that the space run over in an
hour and fifty-six minutes was twenty-one Irish miles."

The same authority tells us that in the year 1808, a regiment
of the Spanish General Romana's troops marched, in one day,
in making their escape from the Danish isles, over a space
equivalent to eighty-four and a half English miles "which is
one of the most extraordinary pedestrian exploits ever performed
by so large a body of men."

There must have been many soldiers of Marlborough's time
who had walked every step of the way from Ostend to Blenheim
on the Danube and back, and if we may suppose that shoes were
not then so good as they have since become, it follows that feet
must have been far better. Judicious and continued training
will do much, as was shown by the march of the British Light
Division to Talavera in 1809, when it did 62 miles in twenty-six
hours of the hottest weather of the year, leaving only seventeen

stragglers behind. This would not be wonderful as an individual performance, but one doubts whether, with the best training, a body of modern troops could do as much, and yet the boots are better and the men as good as they were then. A celebrated individual instance is that of the Dutch Admiral, De Ruyter, who, as a boy, was shipwrecked on the coast of Spain, and walked back to Holland. In 1835 or thereabouts a Mr. Cochrane started from Paris, intending to walk to Siberia, and it is written that he got as far as Moscow, and perhaps he went further.

Captain Barclay was the first man in the history of pedestrianism who walked 1000 miles in 1000 hours, doing it, by the way, for a wager of 1000 guineas. Newmarket was chosen as the field of action. The captain set out in fine condition on the first of June, 1809, and completed the feat on the 12th of August, occupying six weeks, day and night.

The whole sporting world was deeply interested in this (at that time) novel undertaking, and a vast amount of money changed hands. After the fifth week, the odds were considerably against the captain performing the task, although no man that could be selected in England was considered his superior in " speed and bottom." In the successful accomplishment of a feat like this, " bottom " is everything—the mere act of walking is nothing. As the affair approached to its termination, the captain's legs and ankles were getting swollen, and it was confidently believed he would "give in." It was with the utmost difficulty, towards the last, that he could be roused to the hourly accomplishment of his task, and very severe measures were taken by his backers, and others, to force him through. He accomplished it, and that was all. The lightning calculator will already have discovered that six weeks = 42 days, and that 42 days = 1000 hours.

After the feat of walking 1000 miles in 1000 hours had become stale by repetition, Richard Manks startled the talent by proposing to double the wonder by halving the time. Thus, he undertook to walk 1000 miles in 500 hours (20 days and 16 hours), or, as the announcements put it, " one thousand miles in one thousand half-hours." Manks started on Surrey Cricket Ground in Kensington Oval, London, Friday, September 26, 1846. On Monday, after walking 129 miles, he was forced to desist by an attack of dysentery. A fortnight later, Friday, October 10, he made a new and this time a successful effort. Starting at 4 P.M., he completed his first 100 miles at 43 min. 15 sec. after five o'clock on Sunday evening, 12th October; his second 100 miles at 44 min. 10 sec. past seven o'clock on Tuesday, 14th October; his third 100 miles on Thursday, 16th Octo-

39

ber, at 44 min. 45 sec. after nine o'clock P.M.; his fourth 100 miles, at 45 min. 16 sec. after 11 o'clock P.M., Saturday, 18th October; his fifth 100 miles on Monday, 20th October, at 44 min. 10 sec. after 1 o'clock in the morning; his sixth 100 miles on Wednesday, 22nd October, at 47 min. 10 sec. after 3 o'clock in the morning; his seventh 100 miles on Saturday morning, 25th October, at 44 min. 16 sec., after 5 o'clock; his eighth 100 miles on Monday morning, 27th October, at 44 min. 30 sec. past 7 o'clock; his ninth 100 miles on Wednesday morning, the 29th October, at 45 min. 15 sec. after 9 o'clock; his 950th mile at 45 min. 20 sec. past 10 o'clock in the morning of Thursday, 30th October; and finally going for his 1000th mile at half-past 11 o'clock on Friday morning, October 31, 1846.

The weather was delightfully fine for the season up to Wednesday, 15th October, when it rained heavily throughout the whole of the day; after which it continued favorable up to Tuesday night, 28th October, when, at about ten o'clock, there commenced a heavy fall of rain, which continued for nearly six hours: this was very trying for the almost worn-out pedestrian; and, although so near the finish, many persons were apprehensive that he would not be able to complete his task; still onward Manks went, against the most fearful odds and obstacles; although his feet were severely blistered, his limbs in great pain, and he altogether showed the frightful effects of his incessant labor. On Wednesday the weather cleared up, yet the ground was slippery and difficult to traverse; notwithstanding his treading-path was strewn with sawdust, each separate mile took two or three minutes more off his limited period to go through, whilst his feet were covered with blisters and sores. The surgeon ordered them to be poulticed, which was done. Manks's shoes were then changed and cut, to give him more ease, and in that state he kept on his task. During Wednesday night it again rained heavily, so that it was with great difficulty Manks could get over the ground. Thursday morning brought again sunshine, which enabled the pedestrian to proceed; and the 1000th mile was gone over in 7 min. 40 sec., in the presence of upward of 3000 spectators, besides a great crowd outside the oval.

Manks's appetite remained good, and his general health excellent; ten minutes sufficed to refresh him at any one time. He partook of animal and other nourishing food eight or ten times during the twenty-four hours; including game and poultry, roast beef and steaks, mutton and chops, etc.; strong beef tea he drank in considerable quantities. Old ale was his favorite beverage and he took tea with brandy in it during the night.

Manks was heard to declare that never again would he attempt such a frightful feat. At half-past two o'clock on Friday morning he refused to rise, cried like a child, and said to the timekeeper, " I shall walk no more," asking, " Do you want to kill me?" But he at length was induced to persevere unto the finish.

Logically, the next. attempt, at the same rate of geometrical progression, should have been to walk 1000 miles in 1000 quarter hours. Edward Payson Weston, in 1871, offered to do better (and worse) than this. He would cut down the time and proportionately increase the mileage, but in 5 consecutive days (120 hours) he would walk 400 miles. He accomplished the feat at the Empire Rink in New York in June, 1871, and incidentally beat all preceding modern records for a single day's stint by walking 112 miles in 24 consecutive hours.

Weston had first been heard of in 1867, when the newspapers announced that he had walked from Portland, Maine, to Chicago, Ill., a distance of 1326 miles, in rather less than 25 days. The undertaking was to walk this distance within 30 consecutive days without walking on Sundays, and Weston not only rested on Sundays, but for an entire day besides.

In 1874 Weston first undertook to beat his own record by walking 500 miles inside of six consecutive days. In May he failed in New York. In December of the same year he succeeded at the Newark, N. J., Industrial Exposition Building. In fact, he more than succeeded. Beginning at five minutes past midnight in the morning of Monday, December 14, he finished on 11.15 Saturday night, thus completing his task in 25¾ minutes less than six days. So stands the record. Actually Weston walked more than 500 miles, as he made the circuit of his track several times in the absence of two of the judges, and, rather than have any loop-hole for a charge of unfairness in the count, he insisted that the judges should not count those laps, and that they should put on the record only what they themselves saw and could swear to.

On the first day Weston walked 115 miles in 58 seconds less than twenty-four hours, establishing a new record. He then rested 4h., 59m., and 12s. On the second day he walked 75 miles and rested 6h., 12m., and 33s. His third day's walk was 80 miles, and his rest 4h., 51m., and 01s. Fourth day, 80 miles; rest, 3h., 45m., 12s. Fifth day, 75 miles; rest, 4h., 47m., 53s. On the sixth day he walked 75 miles, resting only 27m. and 55s., much of his food being given him by his physician while he continued his walk on the track. His average time was fourteen minutes and fourteen seconds to the mile. His fastest time was made on the 225th and 230th miles.   These he made in ten minutes and eighteen seconds.

Henry C. Jarrett, manager of Booth's Theatre, having wagered nearly $2000 on Weston's success, was naturally solicitous about Saturday's effort, and, therefore, repeatedly sent encouraging dispatches to Newark.   In the evening Weston responded at follows: "Success assured.   I am the hero of the hour.   Save me a box for Monday night."

In January, 1876, Weston visited England.   At the Agricultural Hall, Islington, he undertook to walk 115 miles in 24 consecutive hours, and he invited W. Perkins, the English champion at fast walking, to join the performance, with the understanding that the one who walked the greater number of miles in that time should receive a silver cup.   Although Perkins had recently performed the remarkable exploit of walking 8 miles in 59 mins. 5 secs., his powers at a long journey had not been adequately tested.

The match took place on the 8th and 9th of February.   The start was made at 9.25 P.M., and at 11.41 A.M. Perkins gave up, having walked rather more than 65 miles.   It is only fair to quote his statement that he had never attempted a long-distance match before, the furthest he ever walked being 8 miles.   Weston, when Perkins retired, had nearly completed his 71st mile, and within 24 hours he walked 109½ miles.

A fortnight later Weston made another match, the time being increased to 75 hours and his opponent, Rowell of Cambridge, having 50 miles start.   The result of this match was that Weston walked 275 miles within the appointed time, and Rowell 175 miles, so that the latter did not nearly win even with the start he had.

This was not the last time that Charles Rowell was to be heard of by the world and by Weston.

The six-day go-as-you-please matches were started in 1875, Weston winning the first, held in the old American Institute skating rink at Sixty-third Street and Third Avenue, New York. In 1878 such a race was started in London, and the race held there that year was won by O'Leary.   Sir John Astley presented a belt to be held by the victors in such contests and Rowell won it.

It was in March, 1879, that he came over here and astonished every one by the way in which he captured the great race in the Garden.   The popularity of these contests had then reached its height, and for six days the old Garden was packed practically all the time.   With his wonderful dog trot Rowell gradually passed all his opponents and his share of the gate receipts was

$18,398.31. He at once became a popular idol. Six months later in the same place he won another such race before even larger crowds, this time taking away $19,500 as his share and returning to London.

The scene towards the conclusion was written up in the best " reportorial " fashion by the New York papers of the day. Sensation, it would seem, followed sensation. One of the competitors, Harriman, a New Englander, struggled on in the most pitiable condition without a chance of winning the match, but merely in order to get a share of the gate money. During the last three days of the match he presented a truly horrible spectacle,—" very lame, in the last stages of exhaustion, his skin of a dark hue drawn tightly over his cheek-bones, his eyes sunken and bloodshot, and his body greatly attenuated." Still he persevered, and his pluck won the " unbounded enthusiasm " of the vast crowd of spectators. When he had begun on the 451st mile, and thus entitled himself to a consolation prize, the enthusiasm broke all bounds. " A man sprang into the path and handed him a magnificent basket of flowers. The house rose as Harriman received it, and redoubled their cheers. Still another man came forward and put about his shoulders a red, white, and blue sash. If the house cheered before, it now yelled with delight. Still more honors were coming, and some friends stepped forward and presented Harriman with a large silk flag. This was simply too much for the overwrought house. Men shouted, screamed, danced, grasped each other's hands in a whirlwind of delight, and the band, also bubbling over with joy and patriotism, burst forth into ' Yankee Doodle.' " There seems to have been an immense amount of weeping by " strong men," according to the reporters, during the match. When the Englishman, Rowell, walked a short distance on the track " arm in arm " with the wretched Harriman, the " strong men " shed floods of tears at the touching incident, and the band struck up " The Starspangled Banner," topping it up by " God save the Queen," to mark appreciation of Rowell's manly and graceful conduct. Indeed, the tact displayed by Rowell under somewhat difficult circumstances made him a general favorite.

Pedestrians, Famous. In the books of Dickens and his contemporaries—for example, in the " Christmas Carol "—you will find the exclamation " Walker ! " frequently put into the mouth of incredulous street Arabs and other London plebeians. This is an allusion to the famous eccentric, John or " Walking " Stewart, who was born in London (of Scotch parents) in the year 1749 and died there in 1821, but who spent much of the intervening time abroad and afoot. A tiny pamphlet published shortly after his death is entitled "The Life and Adventures of the Celebrated Walking Stewart, including his Travels in the East Indies, Turkey, Germany, and America." It was written by a relative who professes to have heard these marvellous stories from the old man's lips. Stewart started out for India, after a few inconsequent years at the Charter House school, with the intention of amassing £3000. A noble ambition nobly fulfilled, for he returned with promises to pay amounting to £10,000, and these promises were actually redeemed on the death of the Nabob of Arcot, under whom he had served as minister. In the interim he had travelled on foot through a large part of Asia and in Germany, Italy, France, and Scotland. He explained that he had been "in search of the polarity of moral truth," but he never explained what that meant.

The compiler of Spence's "Anecdotes" tells us that Stewart used to parade the streets of London in an Armenian dress, in order, as he said, to attract attention. After he came into his wealth he commenced a series of entertainments. Every evening a conversazione was held at his house, which was further enlivened by music. On Sundays he gave dinners to a select party, when he usually treated his friends with a philosophical discourse, and sacred music from Handel's compositions, to which he was very partial, particularly the dead march in "Saul." This was the signal for his visitors' marching off, as it generally concluded the evening. When advanced in years, he was still every day to be found, either sitting on a bench in St. James's Park, or in one of those recesses of Westminster Bridge, where he was still in search of the "polarity of moral truth"; and he seldom suffered any person, whether a friend or a stranger, to sit near him without introducing his favorite subject; though it is believed he never met with one who could understand him.

"Jerusalem" Whalley was a contemporary of Walking Stewart's and almost equally famous. It was in 1788 that he made the journey which earned him his name. Being asked on one occasion where he was going, he answered in jest " to Jerusalem." The company present offered to wager any sum that he would not go there, and he took bets to the amount of between £15,000 and £20,000. The journey was to be performed on foot, except so far as it was necessary to cross the sea, and the exploit was to be finished by playing ball against the walls of that celebrated city. In the *Annual Register* for 1789 it is stated that " Mr. Whalley arrived about June in Dublin from his journey to the Holy Land, considerably within the limited time of 12 months." The above wager, however whimsical, was not without a precedent. Some years before a Baronet of some fortune in the north of England (Sir G. Liddel) laid a considerable wager that he would go to Lapland, bring home two females of that country and two reindeer in a given time. He performed the journey and effected his purpose in every respect. The Lapland women remained in this country for about 12 months, but having expressed a wish to go back to their own country the baronet furnished them with means and money.

The death of a noted Russian peripatetic was recorded in the New York *Sun* in 1890. He had died at the Ekaterinoslav Hospital early in December. Ivan Nicoláyevitch Balabookha was a scion of an ancient Cossack family which had produced many hetmans and atamans. He was born in 1855, and served in the Russian army from 1868 to 1882. As soon as he obtained his release from the army he took to travelling over the length and breadth of his native land. He traversed the country from the torrid zone to Tiflis to the frozen wilds of Archangel and came back again to his native city of Kiev. Within a short time he started again from Potchev, on the Austrian frontier, and made his way through Siberia to Maymatchin, in China,—"to taste a cup of genuine Chinese tea," as he wrote to a friend. On that trip he crossed the lake of Balkash over the ice. In all he travelled 42,000 versts on foot, visiting 322 cities and 280 monasteries in all parts of Russia. His outfit on his long marches was always the same, no matter through what climate he passed. He wore a short, gray jacket, a fur cap, and ready-made leather boots, and carried with him two small linen knapsacks, filled with religious books and with a change of undergarments. In October, 1890, Balabookha arrived in Kiev again and planned a new journey. "I have seen the Balkans, the Black, Caspian, and White seas, and the great ocean (the Pacific)," he said. "Now I want to see the Holy Land, to worship on the tombs of the saints, and on my return to take a bath in the Atlantic." But this plan was not to be realized. The man who bore 45° of cold in northern Siberia and in Archangel, who slept many a night in the northern forests, caught a cold in the mild climate of Ekaterinoslav, on the banks of the Dnieper   He was taken to a special room in the hospital and treated with the best medical care and attendance. But no human efforts could save the tireless traveller; he started, December 4, on the long journey from which no traveller returns.

Balabookha's record has been beaten in America by Captain Newton H. Chittenden, the first explorer of the Queen Charlotte Islands. In 1888 and 1889 he broke the record for long walks by making a continuous journey on foot diagonally across the continent from the Pacific to the Gulf of Mexico, a distance, including several hundred miles of side expeditions, amounting to 3350 miles. He was accompanied by a pack burro. But he did not ride the burro. On the contrary, he estimates that he dragged his donkey more than five miles through the overflowed bottoms of Louisiana.

The trip was for archæological and ethnological research, and Captain Chittenden considers it one of the severest of his career. Of the more than 200,000 miles which he covered in his forty years of travelling, 25,000 miles have been on foot. Testimony to his researches is found in most of the famous museums in this country and in museums of Canada and England as well.

The first fame of Edward Payson Weston (see PEDESTRIAN RECORDS) was won in November, 1867, when he walked from Portland, Maine, to Chicago, 1326 miles, in 30 consecutive days without walking on Sunday. In January, 1911, a young man named G. Stewart White claimed to have lowered this record by 19 hours. White left the corner of Clarke and Madison Streets, Chicago, at 1.15 P.M., December 24, 1910, and reached Portland, January 22, 1911, at 11.45 A.M. His feat excited little newspaper attention, however, for in the meantime Weston had eclipsed this early record. Starting on October 29, 1907, he had covered the 1345 miles between Portland and Chicago in 24 days and 19 hours, beating his previous record by 29 hours.

On March 15, 1909, Weston started to walk from New York to San Francisco in 100 days, but he was delayed by blizzards and it took him nearly 105 days to complete the journey. Determined to beat this record, he set out from Santa Monica, a seacoast town near Los Angeles, on February 1, 1910. This time he announced that he would cross the continent in 90 days. He was better than his word. He reached New York, May 2, 1910, having covered the distance of 3611 miles in 77 days, or 13 days ahead of his schedule. New York "humped itself" (a New York phrase) to give him an ovation. Twenty thousand people cheered him on his march down Broadway. At the City Hall he was welcomed by Mayor Gaynor, himself an amateur pedestrian of some note, who presented him with a purse of $400. On this journey Weston's best day's work was 72 miles.

Pedestrians, Female. Jeanie Deans's walk from Edinburgh to London is one of those passages of fiction that read much like truth. But then, truth has often plagiarized from fiction and bettered it. Jeanie's journey was over 400 miles, but she was a young woman and got various lifts on the way. In 1851 a Cornish fishwoman, Mary Callinach by name, aged 85, won temporary notoriety by walking 300 miles from her native village to visit the great exhibition held that year in London. More-

over, she walked back. Neither to nor fro did she break the
solemn vow, registered before starting, that she would not accept assistance in any shape, except as regarded her finances.
Calling at the Mansion House in London to pay her respects to
the mayor, she cheerfully accepted a sovereign from his lordship,
expressing that cheerfulness in old-lady fashion by bursting into
tears. "Now I shall be able to get back," she said.

In 1890–91 a young American woman walked across the continent and was duly celebrated in the New York press. (See
The Illustrated American, April 11, 1891.) She was Miss Zoe
Gayton. When she heard some friends marvelling at a New
York hotel-keeper and a professor of penmanship who had just
completed a horseback ride from ocean to ocean, she declared
that she could travel that distance on foot. She was in San
Francisco at the time. Being a woman of her word, she started
to accomplish her task, August 27, 1890, accompanied by two
male companions and two poodle dogs. One of the latter was
killed by a railway train. Miss Gayton took the ferry-boat from
San Francisco to Oakland, but walked the remainder of the distance to her goal,—Franklin Square, New York City.

To make the task more difficult, Miss Gayton decided to
follow on the railway tracks. The distance is estimated at 3400
miles, which she was to cover in 226 days. The route she selected
was as follows: Central Pacific to Ogden; Union Pacific to
Council Bluffs; Rock Island to Chicago; Michigan Central to
Buffalo; New York Central to New York. Her two escorts carried packs containing blankets, tea, sugar, butter, bread, a tin
plate, three cups, one basket, one camp-knife and a fork, and
Miss Gayton carried a satchel containing linen and a few other
necessaries. The danger of walking so much on the railway
tracks was mitigated by the interest shown in the party by the
railroad men, the locomotive engineers being particularly careful not to run over them. The railroad men christened Miss
Gayton the "Sunset Special."

Miss Gayton won the distinction of being the only woman
who ever walked across the International Bridge over the Niagara
River on the railroad track. She had to get a special permit
from the superintendent of the Grand Trunk Railroad to do it.
The longest day's walk taken by the party was 40 miles, and the
longest week's walk 193 miles.

Women have even attempted to rival men in public feats of
pedestrianism. In the winter of 1878–1879 an Englishwoman,
Mrs. Anderson, covered herself with glory in America by walking 2700 quarter miles in 2700 quarter hours. She began her
task in the Mozart Beer Garden, Brooklyn, New York, on the

16th of December, 1878, and concluded it on the 13th of January, 1879. She walked on a track of such length that seven times round made exactly a quarter of a mile. On the last day of the performance the "wear and tear of her terrible walk was," it is stated, "easily perceived at times in the pallor of her face, her weary steps, and the glassy appearance of her eyes." It is not surprising that she felt somewhat fatigued, for "at one time she appeared dressed as the Goddess of Liberty, with a large silk American flag folded around her person; in her right hand she carried a small English flag, and in the left the Stars and Stripes." The flag enveloping her body proved such an impediment to her progress and was so uncomfortable that she was compelled to stop on the track and have it rearranged. The crush of spectators was so great as to be dangerous, 2000 persons being jammed in a hall built to accommodate only 500. This rendered the atmosphere stifling, and several women present fainted. Nevertheless, in spite of these unfavorable circumstances, Mrs. Anderson gallantly paced on, amid deafening applause; and on being summoned for the 2700th quarter—the last—she "bounded from her room, and fairly flew around the track with a square heel-and-toe movement." Two men ran ahead of her to keep a pathway open through the crowd, and two followed her to see that the open line was not closed. The roaring voices in the hall drowned the discordant blowing of the brass band, and when the last quarter-mile was finished, and the time announced as 2 min. 37¾ sec., the fastest made during her walk, the uproar was "simply terrific." Mrs. Anderson then mounted the stage, and made a short speech. "While men," she said, "were the best for seeking danger at the cannon's mouth, she believed women had the most endurance." She concluded by giving "a little advice to women about walking." Not all women need that advice.

Before going on strike in 1911 the famous bar-maids of Munich set to work collecting statistics. With the aid of a pedometer one of them calculated that she walks forty kilometers (about 25 miles) a day, or as far as an army of men marches in eight hours. In each working day, which means every day in the week, including Sunday, from 10 in the morning until midnight, she takes, on an average, 58,000 steps. Her stride is 27½ inches. Not only does she cover so much ground, but at each trip she carries as many as eight heavy steins or a large tray heaped full of dishes. And for all that exertion she gets but 2 marks a day, that is 50 cents.

Pedler's Acre. A tract of riverside land in the old Lambeth parish in London, comprising about an acre, which was owned in the fifteenth century by a pedler. Dying, he bequeathed it to the parish on condition that a dog which had accompanied him on his peregrinations should be buried in the local church-yard. Originally it brought in only about 3 shillings a year. In 1910, when the London County Council acquired the estate, the Lambeth Council was receiving $9000 a year from it. The money was devoted to the reduction of the local rates, being equivalent to a rate of one farthing in the pound.

The London County Council bought the estate to build its new county hall on it, the price being $405,000. The money was paid into chancery, as the council did not wish to participate in the dispute which arose as to its allocation.

In old days there had been many fights over the property, and in 1824 an attempt was made to sell or mortgage the acre in order to build a chapel in the district. The inhabitants protested, and secured an act of Parliament, in the reign of George IV, vesting the property in the rector and churchwardens and ten other rated inhabitants, the rents and proceeds to be applied to parochial purposes. The churchwardens claimed a share of the price paid by the County Council, and the fight now (1913) lies between them and the Lambeth Borough Council.

Peach. The peach is an ancient fruit, and it seems singular that no mention is made of it in the Bible, for it is known to have been introduced into Italy as early at least as the time of Cladius, A.D., 50. It was known then as the persiche, owing doubtless to importation from Persia. There is a difference of opinion as to whether its origin belongs to Persia or China. Under the name of " to," or " tao," it was discussed by Confucius five centuries before the Christian era. Much later Virgil spoke of it, saying:

Myself will search our planted grounds at home
For downy peaches and the glossy plum.

The peach was not known in England or France until about the middle of the sixteenth century. Its French name is *peche,* from which is obviously derived our English word " peach." Its cultivation has never been a success in either of these countries, while in China, in all probability its original home, every condition is admirably fitted for it, and there it reaches its highest degree of perfection, the peaches grown in and about Pekin being the finest, largest, and most delicious the world can produce.

It was not until the close of the seventeenth century (1680) that the peach was introduced into this country, where it can be given any latitude to suit its fancy, humored with any sort of climate or soil it may demand.

Through the nectarine the peach is closely connected to the

almond, and by the almond to the apricot, plum, and cherry. The French draw no distinction between the peach and nectarine other than to regard the one as a smooth and the other a downy fruit. Their affinity is proved by the fact that both have been frequently grown not only from the same tree but from the same branch, and, what is more, the fruit has been known to mature with one of its sides smooth and the other covered with the ordinary fuzz. The kernel has the strong flavor of the bitter almond, which is due, as in the almond, to the presence of prussic acid. In ancient times the peach was regarded as poisonous, and it is a tradition that a King of Persia once sent a quantity of them into Egypt for the purpose of poisoning the inhabitants. Perhaps in those days the seed contained a sufficiency of this deadly acid to permeate the fruit and render it unfit and even dangerous for use.

The peach-tree has the reputation of being short lived, the growers in some countries being compelled to renew their orchards every few years. Yet there is evidence that it will live to a tolerably good age if conditions are propitious. In Virginia there are trees over seventy years old and still in a fairly flourishing condition, and there is one in France which is said to have been standing now more than a century.

Penny-Post. The invention of this postal reform (see POST-OFFICE) is rightly attributed to Sir Rowland Hill. Like all inventors, however, he had his forerunners. It is a curious coincidence that the earliest of these should also have borne the name of Hill. Nearly two centuries before Sir Rowland's success, his namesake published a small volume of which the only known copy is in the British Museum. The title runs as follows: " A Penny Post: or, a Vindication of the Liberty and Birthright of every Englishman, in carrying Merchants' and other Men's *Letters*, against any Restraint of Farmers of such Employments. By John Hill. London: Printed in the yeare 1659."

This pioneer attempt was followed by another, equally abortive, in 1680. A folio sheet of two pages was printed and circulated in London under the following title: " A Penny well Bestowed; or, a Brief Account of the New Design contrived for the great Increase of Trade, and Ease of Correspondence, to the Great Advantage of the Inhabitants of all Sorts, by conveying of Letters or Pacquets under a Pound Weight, to and from all parts within the Cities of London and Westminster, and the Out Parishes within the Weekly Bills of Mortality, for One Penny." The colophon bears the words, " London: printed for the Undertakers by Thomas James, at the Printing Press in Mincing-lane. April, 1680."

The author of this sheet, like other original thinkers, was ahead of his time. "There is nothing," he said, "that tends more to the increase of trade and business than a speedy, cheap, and safe way of intelligence, much being obstructed and more retarded in all places where that is wanting. For as money, like the blood in natural bodies, gives life to trade by its circulation, so correspondence, like the vital spirits, gives it sense and motion. And the more that these abound in any place the more doth that place increase in riches, strength, and vigor." This was said in 1680. It was said again, in other words, and with higher authority, in 1838, when Sir Rowland Hill's plan was before the House of Commons.

The first reformer, however, had known his public too well to imagine that his project would meet with immediate or cordial acceptance. "It is not," he wrote, "to be expected in this age that any new design can be contrived for the public good without meeting many rash censures and impediments from the foolish and malicious." The design was to provide means for the delivery of letters and parcels throughout London hourly every day from 6 A.M. until 9 P.M., fifteen deliveries in all. Possibly it was due to this pamphlet that three years later (1683) a penny-post for London and the district named was actually established, not, however, by the post-office, but by private enterprise.

Dockwra, a London merchant, opened several hundred offices which gave the city a private local post. This system was never extended to the provinces. Owing to mismanagement it soon ceased to be remunerative and was taken over by the postmaster-general.

Whether Sir Rowland Hill was or was not acquainted with these pioneer attempts is little to the purpose. Even if the great postal reformer of the nineteenth century borrowed his thought from a predecessor in the seventeenth, none the less the thanks of the world are due to him for converting unproductive fancy into living fact.—*All the Year Round,* May 13, 1871.

Pepper Port. Up to 1861 Salem, Mass., was known generally among seafaring men as the Pepper Port. The first cargo of this condiment ever imported to the United States was landed there in 1795 by Jonathan Carnes, a Salem captain. While on an East Indian voyage, he heard of the enormous profits made in pepper. He promptly sailed for Padang, Sumatra, then the centre of trade. On the way home he was wrecked, losing both ship and cargo. In 1795 he once more put out for Padang, in the *Rajah,* a brig of 120 tons. Finding the pepper trade pretty well cornered by that time by French and Dutch traders, he boldly headed north, navigating unchartered waters from port to port. He returned to Salem with a cargo that had cost him $18,000 and which he sold for $144,000. Though he kept his source of supply a profound secret, Captain Ropes, of the *Recovery*, succeeded in locating it, and in 1802 he brought a second cargo to Salem. The *Recovery* was also the first American vessel to enter Mocha, on the Red Sea, and open the American trade in coffee. Other pioneers from Salem were the first American ships to trade with Hindustan, Java, and Japan, and with the Fiji islands, Madagascar, New Holland, and New Zealand, and the first American vessel to round the Cape of Good Hope and to sail through the Straits of Magellan.

The last Salem ship in the pepper trade was the *Australia*, that visited Sumatra in 1861 and returned with the last cargo of pepper ever discharged at a Salem wharf. That year also saw the close of the Salem trade in Para rubber. May 1, 1870, when the bark *Glide* came in from Zanzibar, the last entry was made in maritime records of a Salem vessel from beyond the Cape of Good Hope. In 1900 not a ship sailed from the " pepper port," and the old town, better known in the far east than either Boston or New York, was dropped from the commerce of nations.

Petrified Forest of Arizona. An area 10 miles square is covered with a litter of fallen trees, broken into irregular lengths of from 2 to 20 feet, scattered in every conceivable position, and all petrified and displaying a variety of tints that rival chalcedony, agate, and onyx. The most amazing feature of this display is that known as the Petrified Bridge. A great stone tree-trunk lying across a deep ravine, it forms a natural foot-bridge for passengers afoot or even on horseback. The trunk is complete to the base, where it is partially covered, though it clearly reveals the manner in which the roots were attached while the tree was still growing. The total length of the exposed portion is 111 feet, with a span of 44 feet across the chasm. The greatest circumference is 10 feet.

Many theories have been offered as to the origin of the Petrified Forest. One only seems acceptable: Millions of years ago, in what geologists call Triassic and Mesozoic times and during some convulsion of nature,—a great tornado mayhap, or a deluge,—the entire forest area where these trees grew was flooded to such an extent and for so long a time that their roots rotted, allowing the trunks to fall. Or possibly the flood was so violent that it washed away the earth around the tree roots and tore up the trees themselves, floating them away from the place where they grew to the region where they are now found. The land contained many minerals, the rusting away of which colored the water with rainbow tints. Combined with this was a great deal of silica and lime, also held in solution by the water. By the exercise of that wonderful law called capillary attraction, this water, charged with lime and the brilliant coloring matter, was absorbed by the wood as its fibres gradually decayed. This great change went silently on for many, many years, until finally all was changed to stone.

Meantime there were great volcanic disturbances in that region and ashes were cast over the whole area, burying the forest of dead trees many feet deep. Then, as more centuries passed, the region sank until sandstones, limestones, more sandstones, and more limestones were deposited from sediment in the water that washed over the place. Thus the forest was buried, according to some scientists, to a depth of over 20,000 feet.

In time this period of subsidence was arrested and reversed. Mother Nature began to lift the area out of the great inland sea where so much had been going on. Higher and higher rose the bed of this sea until the land emerged, and the waters rolled away. Then through a period of great storms and atmospheric conflicts these vast layers of stone were gradually worn away until the petrified trees were left exposed as we now see them in all their changed beauty.

Pheasant, Latin *phasianus,* a game bird which is said to have originated on the banks of the river Phasis (the modern Rioni) in Colchis. Greek and Roman authorities alike are agreed that it is not indigenous in any part of Europe. According to Martial it was brought from Colchis (Mingrelia) along with the Golden Fleece in the ship *Argo.* In the days of Aristophanes the Phasian bird, as it was termed, was kept in a half-domesticated state by the Athenians, and its flesh was regarded as a great delicacy. Both Pliny and Martial tell us that it was to be found in the preserves around the villas of the wealthy in Italy; and the latter author mentions that it was kept along with flamingos, guinea fowl, peacocks, geese, and partridges. It was probably brought into France after the conquest by the Roman legions. Ornithologists are not agreed as to the exact date of its naturalization in England, and generally quote a notice in Echard of the price of a bird being fourpence in the reign of Edward the First, as being the first record of its presence in that island. There is, however, a much earlier notice in the treatise " De Incentione Sanctæ Crucis Nostræ in Monte Acuto et de Ductione ejusdem apud Waltham," edited by Professor Stubbs. The allowance made to each canon's household by the founder of Waltham, the great Harold, in 1059, was, on feast days from Michaelmas to Easter, " either twelve larks, or two magpies, or two partridges, or one pheasant," and for the feast

days of the rest of the year "either geese or fowls." It is clear
from this that the bird was known in Britain as an article of
food before the Norman conquest, and that its introduction must
be assigned either to the English or to the Romans. And as the
former came from the shores of the Baltic, where pheasants
were not living at the time, while the latter were in the habit of
importing their luxuries into the provinces and of building
country seats as nearly as possible like those in Italy, the credit
of having introduced the bird must be assigned to the latter.
The Romans certainly naturalized the fallow deer, the ornament
of parks, in North France and in Britain ; and to their influence
must be attributed the presence of the domestic fowl. Harold's
bill of fare is very interesting in another point of view. It shows
to what extent the taste of the English has changed since his
day. Two partridges may perhaps be considered by some gourmands to be equivalent of twelve larks or one pheasant ; but any
canon nowadays would feel himself very hardly used if he had
two magpies substituted for one or other of these dishes.

In modern England the first of October is famous as the
opening of the season for both pheasant and partridge. The
former had been threatened with extinction, but now, thanks to
artificial production, it has become almost the commonest, and
to shoot it over dogs among the hedge-rows as was formerly the
practice would be manifestly absurd. Under modern conditions
it can only be dealt with satisfactorily as a rocketer—*i.e.*, a bird
flying high and fast toward the shooter.

The London *Daily Mail* in August, 1911, published an interview with the representative of a firm whose business it is to
raise pheasants for supplying deficiencies on private estates.

" There promises to be a good demand for our young pheasants this year," said the manager of the firm yesterday, " as the
early breeding was spoiled by bad weather. The young birds
fetch from 3s. 6d. to 5s. 6d. apiece, according to the demand.
People find it far less trouble and expense to buy their birds
for shooting than to breed them, and a big business is done each
year in the sale of the young birds.

" They are hatched and brought up in the first place by ordinary hens, a good hen taking a sitting of twenty eggs. When the
birds get older and able to fly, their wings are bound to prevent
them going far."

Phenakistoscope. A disk with figures upon it arranged
radially, representing a moving object in successive positions,
on turning it around rapidly and viewing the figures through a
fixed slit (or their reflections in a mirror through radial slits
in the disk itself), the persistence of the successive visual images

produces the impression of actual motion. (See MOVING PIC-
TURES.)

Phœnix. A fabulous sacred bird of the Egyptians. In a
well-known passage in his " Enquiries into Vulgar and Common
Errors " (1646), Sir Thomas Browne discusses with the utmost
gravity the existence of the phœnix, who is mentioned, " not
only by human authors," but also by such " holy writers as
Cyril, Epiphanius, and Ambrose." He is spoken of also in Job
(xxix, 18) and in the Psalms. However, no less than eight
reasons are alleged against his existence, of which the first is
that no one has ever seen a phœnix, and the last that no animals
really spring or could spring from their predecessors' ashes. Yet,
having marshalled this formidable array of facts against the
phœnix, Sir Thomas ends by saying, " How far to rely on this
tradition we refer unto consideration," and adds a reflection
on the improbability of Plutarch's statement " that the brain of
a phœnix is a pleasant bit, but that it causeth the headache."

Tacitus, who, though he lived 1600 years before Browne, was
the product of a more skeptical age, has no such balanced doubts
as to the existence of the phœnix. In the sixth book of his
" Annals " he seriously assures us that the bird appeared in
Egypt during the consulate of Paulus Fabius and Lucius Vitel-
lius; and he talks with equal seriousness of its periodical return.
But we have a more detailed and positive account of the phœnix.
Solinus, in his work on natural history, entitled " Polyhistor,"
speaks of a phœnix that was captured in Egypt and taken to
Rome, where it was publicly exhibited, and a written statement
of the fact drawn up and deposited in the archives of the republic. He adds a full description of the bird. " It is as large
as an eagle," he says, " its head is ornamented with feathers
rising up in the form of a cone, its throat is surrounded with
tufts of feathers, and its neck shines like gold; the rest of its
body is purple, except the tail, which is sky-blue mingled with
rose-color." Another most respectable authority to quote by way
of corroboration is that of a worthy father of the church—of
no other than St. Clement of Alexandria. In one of his epistles
to the Corinthians, he says, by way of argument, to prove the
resurrection of the human race, " Behold, there exists in Arabia
a bird, the only one of its race—he is called the phœnix—he lives
a hundred years, and when near death he proceeds to his own
embalming. He gathers together myrrh, incense, and other aro-
matics, and with these composes for himself an odoriferous
coffin, in which, at the appointed time, he shuts himself up and
dies. When his flesh is consumed, a worm is born, which re-

ceives life from the death of the phœnix, and is covered with feathers."

When this worm acquires sufficient strength to take its flight in the air, it takes up the tomb in which repose the mortal remains of its sire, and carries it from Arabia into the city of Heliopolis in Egypt. It flies through the air in open daylight in sight of all the inhabitants; deposits its sacred burden upon the altar of the sun, and flies away. The priests on consulting their chronicles have calculated that this phenomenon is renewed every five hundred years. There is a slight discrepancy in the saint's figures of four hundred years; the bird only living he says one hundred years, and only being respectfully buried by his successor once in five hundred. We know not how to reconcile these facts, unless we suppose the " worm covered with feathers " spends the extra four hundred years in growing into a phœnix before he acquires sufficient strength of wing to conduct his father's funeral. The phœnix is also mentioned by later authors, by some of whom a different account is given—the old bird setting fire to his funereal pile, and the young one starting up from the paternal cinders.

Phœnix Park. A public park of 2000 acres in Dublin. It contains a granite monument in honor of Wellington, which has been materially improved of late, without redemption, however, from original deformities. The bass-reliefs at the base, commemorating the siege of Seringapatam, by Kirk, the battle of Waterloo, by Farrell, and the signing of Catholic Emancipation, are its best features, and not without credit artistically.

Lever and Lover have introduced the Phœnix into so many of their romances that it is difficult to conceive how an Irish story having any relation to society could be completed without its assistance. When duelling was the fashion, hot-blooded Hibernians had their hostile meetings there, and numerous localities are pointed out where hair-triggers were brought into requisition.

The park became internationally famous, May 6, 1882, through the assassination within its borders of Lord Cavendish, chief secretary for Ireland, and Thomas Burke, the undersecretary.

The modern name of the park is a curious instance of false etymology establishing a local corruption. Phœnix is a misunderstanding of the Irish word *fionn-uisg* [fœnisk], which means clear or limpid water. It was originally the name of the beautiful and perfectly transparent spring well, situated just outside the wall of the Viceregal grounds, behind the gate lodge, and which is the head of the str—— ᵗʰᵃᵗ ᵘᵖplies the ponds near the Zoölogical Gardens. To complete the illusion, the Earl of Chesterfield, in the year 1745, erected a pillar near the well, with the figure of a phœnix rising from its ashes on the top of it; and most Dublin people now believe that the Park received its name from this pillar. The change from *fionn-uisg* to "phœnix" is not peculiar to Dublin, for the river Finisk, which joins the Blackwater below Cappoquin, is called Phœnix by Smith in his History of Waterford. Examples of similar corruptions are found elsewhere in Ireland. There are, for instance, several places in Tipperary and Limerick called by the Scriptural name Mountsion; but "Mount" is only a translation of *cnoc*, and "sion" an ingenious adaptation of *sidheán* [sheeawn], a fairy mount; the full Irish name being *Cnoc-a'-tsidheain*, "fairy-mount hill."

This improvement reminds the *Saturday Review* of "the inscription over a public building at Sedunum, Sitten, or *Sion*, 'Dominus dilexit portas Sion,' etc., a pious local belief about which, if cleanliness be really next to godliness, we must be allowed to have our doubts."

Phonautograph. In May, 1877, at a meeting held at Salem, Mass., Professor Alexander Graham Bell delivered a lecture on "Visible Speech," during the course of which he exhibited a device which he called by the above name. It consisted of a human ear-drum cut from a dead subject and placed in the end of an ordinary speaking trumpet. "On speaking into the trumpet," says a contemporary report that is copied in the *Eclectic Magazine* for June, 1877, "the drum is set in motion, this moves the style, the style traces the effect on a plate of smoked glass; and by the means of a camera the curves and lines can be exhibited to a large number of spectators. The five vowels make five different curves; and, according to Mr. Bell, there is no such thing as a sound or tone pure and simple, but each is a composite of a number of tones; and the wavelets by which these are produced can also be shown on a screen. Tables of the various symbols have been drawn up and found useful for educational purposes, as was demonstrated by a young deaf and dumb pupil from the Boston Institution who interpreted the symbols on sight."

Phonograph. As long ago as 1632 there was described in a little monthy publication called *Le Courier Veritable*, something very like Edison's phonograph.

"Captain Vosterloch has returned from his voyage to the Southern lands, which he started on two years and a half ago by order of the States-General. He tells us, among other things, that, in passing through a strait below Magellan's, he landed in a country where Nature has furnished men with a kind of sponges that hold sounds and articulations as our sponges hold liquids. So, when they wish to dispatch a message to a distance, they speak to one of the sponges and they send it to their friends. The latter gently take up the sponges and press out the words that have been spoken into them, and learn by this wonderful means all that their correspondents desire them to know."

A yet nearer approach to Edison was made by Cyrano de Bergerac in 1650. In his "Comic History of the States of the Moon" the hero reaches that planet. A supernatural being who undertakes to act as guide shows him for his entertainment some of the books of the country, inclosed in boxes. This is what he saw and heard: "On opening the box I found inside a concern of metal, something like one of our watches, full of curious little springs and minute machinery. It was really a book, but a wonderful book that has no leaves or letters; a book, for the understanding of which the eyes are of no use—only the ears are necessary. When any one wishes to read, he winds up the machine with its great number of nerves of all kinds, and turns the pointer to the chapter he wishes to hear, when there comes out, as if from the mouth of a man or of an instrument of music, the distinct and various sounds which serve the Great Lunarians as the expression of language."

The inventor of the modern instrument has told us of the purely accidental manner in which the idea came to him.

"I was singing," says Mr. Edison, "to the mouthpiece of a telephone, when the vibration of the voice sent the fine steel points into my finger. That set me thinking. If I could record the actions of the point and send the point over the same surface afterward, I saw no reason why the thing should not talk. I tried the experiment first on a strip of telegraphic paper, and found that the point made an alphabet. I shouted the words 'Halloa! Halloa!' into the mouthpiece, ran the paper back over the steel point, and heard a faint 'Halloa! Halloa!' in return. I determined to make a machine that would work accurately and gave my assistants instructions, telling them what I had discovered. They laughed at me. That's the whole story. The phonograph is the result of the pricking of a finger."

The workman who got the sketch was John Kruesi. "I didn't have much faith that it would work," said Edison, "expecting only that I might possibly hear a word or so that would give hope of a future for the idea. Kruesi, when he had nearly finished it, asked what it was for. I told him I was going to record talking, and then have the machine talk back. He thought it absurd. However, it was finished, the foil was put on: I then shouted 'Mary had a little lamb,' etc. I adjusted the reproducer, and the machine reproduced it perfectly. I was never so taken aback in my life. Everybody was astonished. I was always afraid of things that worked the first time. Long experience proved that there were great drawbacks found, generally before they could be got commercial, but here was something there was no doubt of."

No wonder that John Kruesi, as he stood listening to the performance of the simple little machine he had himself just finished, cried out in an awe-stricken tone, "Mein Gott in Himmel!" No wonder that with Edison he sat up all night experimenting with it so as to get better and better results!

It is said that Carman, the foreman of the machine shop, had wagered Edison a box of cigars that the machine would not work.

The original Edison phonograph thus built by Kruesi is preserved in the South Kensington Museum, London.

To return to Edison's story of his invention. "That morning," he says, "I took it over to New York and walked into the office of the *Scientific American,* went up to Mr. Beach's desk, and said I had something to show him. He asked what it was. I told him I had a machine that would record and reproduce the human voice. I opened the package, set up the machine and recited 'Mary had a little lamb,' etc. Then I reproduced it so that it could be heard all over the room. They kept me at it until the crowd got so great Mr. Beach was afraid the floor would collapse; and we were compelled to stop. The papers next morning contained columns. None of the writers seemed to understand how it was done. I tried to explain, it was so very simple, but the results were so surprising they made up their minds probably that they never would understand it— and they didn't."

The government officials got interested. They telegraphed Edison to come to Washington. He obeyed, taking with him a newer and larger instrument just completed. This was exhibited in the apartments of "Gail Hamilton," James G. Blaine's sister-in-law. Senators, Congressmen, and others of note flocked to hear it. Only one contretemps marked the general felicitation. Beside "Mary had a little lamb" Edison had recited into his machine the well-known ditty

> There was a little girl, who had a little curl
>   Right in the middle of her forehead;
> And when she was good she was very very good,
>   But when she was bad, she was horrid.

Now, prominent among Mr. Edison's auditors was Roscoe

Conkling. Like the little girl, Conkling had a little curl exactly where the ditty placed it, and caricaturists were fond of exaggerating the decoration.

"He was very sensitive about the subject. When he came in he was introduced, but being rather deaf, I didn't catch his name, but sat down and started the curl ditty. Everybody tittered and I was told that Mr. Conkling was displeased."

An hour before midnight Mr. Edison was summoned to the White House to display his machine before President Hayes. He found the room full of male celebrities and at 12.30 Mrs. Hayes herself, with other ladies who had been induced to get up and dress, made their appearance. Not till 3.30 A.M. did the séance come to an end. See TELAKOUPHANON.

Photograph. Anticipations of the photograph may be found in very ancient Chinese traditions, crediting the sun with producing pictures of neighboring objects upon the ice-covered surfaces of lakes and rivers.

Was Fénelon familiar with these traditions? At least he elaborated on a similar idea in his "Un Voyage Supposé" (1690).

"There was no painter in that country," he wrote imaginatively of an imaginary country. "But if anybody wished to have the portrait of a friend, of a picture, a beautiful landscape, or of any object, water was placed in great basins of gold or silver and the object desired to be painted was placed in front of that water. After a while the water froze and became a glass mirror on which an ineffaceable image remained."

In 1760 Tiphaigne de la Roche came still nearer guessing how pictures painted by nature would some day be produced.

"You know," said the guide to the hero of "Giphantic," a tale then considered wildly imaginative, "that rays of light reflected from different bodies form pictures, paint the image reflected on all polished surfaces—for example on the retina of the eye, on water, and on glass. The spirits have sought to fix these fleeting images; they have made a subtler matter by means of which a picture is formed in the twinkling of an eye. They coat a piece of canvas with this matter and place it in front of the object to be taken.

"The first effect of this cloth is similar to that of a mirror; but by means of its viscous nature the prepared canvas, unlike the mirror, retains a facsimile of the image. The mirror represents objects faithfully, but retains none; our canvas reflects them no less faithfully, but retains them all. This impression of the image is instantaneous.

"The canvas is then r ... deposited in a dark place.

An hour later the impression is dry, and you have a picture the more precious in that no art can imitate its truthfulness."

The genii imagined by De la Roche were fair predecessors of the present-day users of the camera.

Piano. The piano as we have it to-day is the growth of centuries of invention. In its infancy it was a harp with two or three springs. From time to time more strings were added, and eventually the cithara was born. The cithara was in the shape of the letter P and had ten strings. Centuries passed before musicians conceived the idea of stretching the strings across an open box, but somewhere about the year 1200 an unknown genius produced the dulcimer, whose strings were struck by hammers. For another hundred years these hammers were held in the hands of the players. Then another genius equally unknown invented a key-board, which, being struck by the fingers, moved the hammers. This instrument was called a clavicytherium, or keyed cithara. Modification and improvements were added at staccata intervals. In Queen Elizabeth's time it was called a virginal. Then it became a spinet, because the hammers were covered with spines of quills, which struck or caught the strings of wire to produce the sounds. From 1700 to 1800 it was much enlarged and improved and called a harpsichord. This was the instrument that Lady Washington, Mrs. Hamilton, and the fine ladies of the Revolutionary period played upon. Meanwhile, however, three men, working independently of one another in the early part of the eighteenth century, had almost simultaneously evolved the modern piano-forte. These three men are the Italian Bartolommeo Cristofori, the Frenchman Marius, and the German Christopher Gottlieb Schroeter.

"It is in the highest degree probable," says H. E. Krehbiel, in "The Piano-forte and its Music" (New York, 1909), "that efforts had been made in the direction in which these men labored a long time before they came forward with their inventions. The earliest use of the word "piano-forte" (or, literally, *piano e forte*) as applied to an instrument of music antedates the earliest of these inventions by 111 years, but the reference is exceedingly vague and chiefly valuable as indicative of how early the minds of inventors were occupied with the means for obtaining soft and loud effects from keyed instruments. Cristofori's invention takes precedence of the others in time. This has been established after much controversy beyond further dispute. In 1709 he exhibited specimens of his harpsichords, with hammer action capable of producing piano and forte effects, to Prince Ferdinando dei Medici, of whose instruments of music he was custodian at Florence, and two years later—that is, in 1711—his invention was fully described and the description printed, not only in Italy but also in Germany. It embraces the essential features of the piano-forte action as we have it to-day—a row of hammers controlled by keys which struck the strings from below."

An entertaining comparison is made of the Cristofori piano-forte in the John Crosby Brown collection of pianos in the Metropolitan Museum, one of the very first pianos made, and the modern concert grand piano made in America:

The modern giant is 8 feet 10 inches long and 5 feet wide. The weight of its metal plate is 320 pounds, which is probably more than the weight of the Cristofori instrument in its entirety. The total weight is 1040 pounds. It has a compass of 7¼ octaves, 88 keys, against Cristofori's 4½ octaves, 54 keys. Its range extends 19 keys above the top note of the Cristofori instrument and 15 below the bottom note. The longest string of this modern grand piano is 6 feet 7½ inches in length, the shortest 4½ inches, but the longest string of the grand consists of a steel core 2 millimeters thick, wound with wire thicker than the thickest strings of the Cristofori, so the modern string is in all 5 millimeters thick. One or two octaves of these bass strings contain enough metal to string the Cristofori instrument throughout. The thickest string on the Cristofori is smaller in diameter than the thinnest string on the other. The triple unisons on the grand which produce the lowest note of the Cristofori are wound and 2 millimeters thick. The highest note of the Cristofori has a string 5½ inches long on the grand and exerts a strain of 170 pounds for each of its three unisons. A few such strains would crush the frame of the Cristofori piano-forte like an eggshell, but it is not much more than the hundredth part of what the modern frame is called upon to endure.

Picadilly. The first mention of this famous thoroughfare occurs in a seventeenth-century edition of Gerard's Herbal. Hence an erroneous idea that Picadilly existed in 1596, when Gerard issued his book. It happens, however, that the passage occurs, not in the first edition, but in a much later one published in 1636, and edited by Thomas Johnson. It runs as follows: "The little wild bugloss grows upon the dry ditch about Pickadilla." It is pretty well authenticated that about 1630 a retired tailor, named Higgins, whose fortune had been in a great measure made by the sale of "pickadelles"—picadillies or turnover collars—built himself a snug house in this locality, which he called Picadilla Hall. In all probability it was Higgins who originated the name.

Pin-prickt Pictures. A recreation that obtained some vogue in the seventeenth and eighteenth centuries was "pin-prickt pictures," which exhibit the pin's use in domestic art. These pictures are mostly of English make, and a few still extant date back at least two hundred years. Some are merely quaint, others are quite dainty and pretty. With the help of water-colors, they achieve a certain decorative value. Figures in picturesque costumes and framed in borders of flowers and leaves are the favorite subjects. " Pricking pictures with pins," says Andrew Tuer, " was another agreeable occupation. The pins were of several thicknesses, broad lines and heavy shadows being pricked on paper with stout and the finer work with thin pins. A toothed wheel with sharp points was used for outlines. For filling up large spaces, two or more wheels were mounted on one axle."— *Old-fashioned Children's Book,* London.

Needles were sometimes used instead of pins, or in conjunction with pins, for the finer work. It is not impossible that the pins were inserted into a handle. In Longman and Loch's " Pins and Pincushions " (London, 1911), the authors describe an old lady of their acquaintance, " now in her one hundred and first year," who " remembers in her youth pricking many pictures with pins, but, unfortunately, they have not been preserved. However, on hearing we were interested in this charming pursuit, she set to work, undaunted by age and somewhat failing sight. Her method was to place the paper on which the outline of the flower had been drawn, on to a piece of soft material; she pricked the outline with a pin on the right side, and then filled up all the spaces in the flower and its leaves with pin-pricks put very close together. When it was all filled up, she lifted the pricked paper and turned it round, showing the rough side which the pins had pierced, the paper being raised by this process."

A famous " pin-prickt " letter was written by Marie Antoinette during her imprisonment, and sent secretly to the Comte de Rougeville, who had engaged to carry off the queen to the Chateau de Livey, where two hundred armed horsemen were waiting to conduct her to Austria. This letter, which was deciphered by M. Pelinski in 1876, is a slip of thin white paper, 5 inches long by 1¾ wide, whereon the following words were pricked with a pin: " Je suis gardée à vue; je me fie ä vous; je viendrais " ("I am hidden from sight; I confide in you; I will come ").

Unfortunately, the message miscarried or the messenger betrayed his trust, and the queen's last hope was gone. This was seven weeks before her death.

Place Names in America and England. In one of his famous " Easy Chair " papers in *Harper's Magazine,* George William Curtis commends the action of the Pilgrims and Puritans who naturally and fondly commemorated the old home in the new by naming their towns from those with which they had the most filial association. He recalls with what surprise and delight Charles Kingsley looked over a map of New England and recognized the familiar names.

"I shall be at home everywhere!" he exclaimed gayly.

All such names, Mr. Curtis holds, have an historic and significant interest, because they show the source of immigration to the particular spot. "At the celebration of its settlement some years ago," the "Easy Chair" continues, "Lynn in Massachusetts did not omit to exchange friendly courtesies with King's Lynn in English Norfolk, and St. Botolph's Club in Boston recalls the name of the old city in John Robinson's Lincolnshire."

Mr. Curtis also commends certain local names which are religiously commemorative of events, like Providence in Rhode Island, so called by Roger Williams in gratitude to the benignant care which had led him safely through the wilderness to a pleasant home. "All such historic names have now a certain quaintness of association which gives them a singular charm that cannot be renewed." Again, Beacon Street in Boston bears a significant name because it recalls the beacon which used to be lighted upon the hill along which the street runs. "But what local interest does Marlborough Street recall?" asks Mr. Curtis.

Turning to the State of New York, former seat of the great Iroquois League, he rejoices that there still survives there a noble system of names, musical in themselves and commemorative of the Indian occupation. But alas! even here the Vandal has done his work of destruction. In the latter part of the eighteenth century, the worthy Surveyor-General Simeon De Witt shook his classical pepper-pot over Central New York, and left its innocent little villagers smarting with the names of Ovid, Pompey, Marcellus, Ilion, Rome, Carthage, Utica, Syracuse, and other famous men and cities. "It might have been supposed that the antics of the excellent man would have served at least as a warning, and that unmeaning or ridiculous names would have been spared to the towns which fortunately came late enough to escape that direful classical dictionary, and the taste which gave Greek and Roman names to new American villages as it gave the façade of the Parthenon to the little wooden house of the settler."

The "Easy Chair" heartily agrees with Mr. William L. Stone, a devoted student of the earlier history of New York, who "in a late paper on this subject in the Utica *Herald*," pleads for the Indian and other commemorative names. "Why," asked Mr. Stone, "should not the pretty town in Broome County, beau-

a and Che-
suggested
d the site,
a Bingham-

a charming
, says Mr.
a deep hole

! why must
city, bear
rmur and
alo! where-
ay body of
le city to
nocent and
er-pot or
hich every
roceeded."
edged that
nonsibility
tly called
generously
originated.
the Legis-
land office
, ordained
wnship to
In 1789
Secretary
Treasurer
or-general
tract, and
mmenda-
torrent of
veyed and
tyrdom at
eral, who
officially

d to Gen-
ignorance
rs of the
Esq., Sur-
e of these

and a donor

papers. It is preceded by a note in which the absolute misstate
ment of fact is made with contemptuous comment, and the innocent De Witt is then pelted with rhymed sarcasm. These poems
were generally read, and the hapless and defenceless surveyor-
general was covered with a universal laugh as the bull in the
arena is stung with a storm of winged darts to arouse and
irritate him. But General De Witt was not provoked to reply.
A few years later, however, when the story was repeated in a
newspaper in the city, he wrote a quiet note to the editor stating
that he knew nothing of the obnoxious names until they were
communicated to him.

The "Easy Chair" adds that it is glad to be of service "in
relieving a worthy officer of the State from this tenacious and
peculiarly disagreeable injustice, to which it had unwittingly
contributed."

Nearly all Indian names of towns and rivers have some particular significance. The names of towns in Indian Territory
will perpetuate Indian history for centuries. Only recently a
new town was named Neha. This is a Creek word and means
oil town. It was given to a siding put in on the railroad a few
miles south of Muskogee in the new oil field.

"We" in Creek means water. It is found in many names in
the Territory and the significance attaches to the remainder of
the word. For instance, here are a few: Weleetka means running water, and Wetumka means bounding water. Both are
towns on the Frisco Railroad. Wealaka, the home of the Creek
chief, means falling water. Wecharta means red water.

Okmulgee, which is the Creek national capital, means in
Creek head of power, and the name was given the town of
Okmulgee because it was the national capital. Tallahassee conveys to the Creek mind the same impression that deserted village
does to the English. It was the name of a town in the Eastern
home of the Creeks, and also a town of that name, or what was
a town, is located in Indian Territory. There is an Indian school
there.

To the Creeks the Arkansas River was Wecharty, because the
water is red, and Deep Fork was Hutchety Soofkey because it is
deep. The Verdigris was Wascre Hutchety because the Osages
came down that river and the Creeks called it "Osage Stream."
The North Canadian was called Oklahutchey because it was full
of sand. The village of Choska was so called because Choska
means post oak, and around Choska post oaks grow in great profusion.

A writer in the *Red Man* claims that the Miami and other
languages now fast dying out are more refined in inflection and

exact in meaning than any modern civilized tongue. To illustrate both these points, he invites attention to the name Wabash, which is in wide use not only for the river, but for counties, towns, railroads, and other things. In some of our standard dictionaries and other reference books it has been said to mean a cloud driven forward by the equinoctial wind. In reality it is a corruption of the Miami name of the stream. Wah-bah-shik-ki, or Wah-pah-shik-ki—b and p being convertible in the Miami.

"This is an inflected form of the adjective white, which in its simplest form is wah-pe-ki for the inanimate and wah-pi-si-ta for the animate. The form wah-bah-shik-ki implies that the noun it qualifies stands for something that is bright or pure white, inanimate and natural, such as a stone or a shell. If it were artificial, as cloth or paper, the adjective form would have to be wah-pah-kin-gi.

Ernest Peixotto tells, in his "Romantic California," about a little glen with an interesting name, of equally interesting derivation. Mr. Peixotto was staying in the Sierras, in the home of a friend, a lover of all things Indian, who enjoyed the instruction of a gentleman known as Wan-ka-ne-mah.

"Our host is fond of all the Indian legends of the country, and the names they give to places and streams, and he has had this old Indian, Wan-ka-ne-mah, tell him as many stories as he can recall.

"One day, in wandering about, they came upon a little glen they had never before visited.

"'And what do you call this place?' my friend asked.

"'Mystum,' replied the old Indian.

"Here was a new, romantic name that promised possibilities.

"'And why do you call it Mystum? What does that mean to the red man?'

"'Well, once we saw a big buck here and we missed um,' was the reply!"

In Oregon these Indian methods were imitated, or at least paralleled, by the early settlers, who named their new locations from the first chance occurrence in connection with it or from the first object, animate or inanimate, that arrested their attention. Haystack received its name from the only thing standing on the ground when the post-office was established. Tanks is a station on the railroad in Umatilla County where the watering tanks of that division are situated. With this process explained it is easy to understand the why and wherefore of Echo, Box, Apiary, and so on. Bakeoven is a typical instance of more recondite origins. In early days a Frenchman started from The

Dalles, which takes its name from the " dalles," or falls in the Columbia river, with a cargo of flour for the mines at Cañon City, another town named from its location. The first night he went into camp a band of Indians came along and drove off his mules. Unable to move his flour, he gathered some rocks, built an oven, and baked his flour into bread. The bread was sold to passing miners and travellers along the trail at a greater profit than he would otherwise have received. As a result of this occurrence the town which now stands on the site of the Frenchman's camp is named Bakeoven. Residents point out the blackened rocks which were a part of the original.

Tennessee found an unfailing resource in the Bible. She put an Ark in Meigs County, a Noah in Coffee, a Genesis in Cumberland, a St. John and a St. Luke in Jackson, a Joshua here and a Caleb there, here an Elijah and there a Samuel. Ruth and Naomi were not forgotten, and two Ebenezers were raised up, one in Knox and one in Humphreys County.

But Tennessee did not lay too much stress on Scriptural names. On the other hand, looking at the map one may readily ascertain that in the naming of her towns Tennessee played no favorites. From mythology she obtained Juno, Venus, Vulcan. Bacchus, Diana, Hercules, Neptune, Olympus, and Delphi; from Shakespeare Romeo and Othello; from the Greek alphabet Alpha, Beta, and Omega; from the church Methodist, Baptist, Priest. Pope, Friar, and Tabernacle; from the family hearth, Mamy. Bud, Aunt, Home, and Family; from the poets Dante, Milton, and Homer.

English people often laugh at the odd names of American towns. Matthew Arnold even went so far as to assert that no nation could be quite civilized that yielded itself to such cacophony of urban nomenclature. But he might have turned his attention to similar barbarisms in his own country. Without going very far from London, he might have found himself at the villages of Great Snoring and Little Snoring in Norfolk. He would hardly have considered Fighting Cocks in Durham an evidence of high civilization, nor Frog's Gutter in Salop, nor Dirt-Car in Yorks, nor Fool's Nook in Chester, nor Little Fryup in Yorks, nor Blubberhouses in Suffolk, nor Chittieshambolt. nor Knoctopper. Quaint names that are less offensive to the ear, but still bulky and unwieldly, are Styrrup-with-Old-Coates. Talk o' the Hill, Who'd a thought it, Addlewith Eccup, Labor in Vain, Carry Coats, and Hard to Come by. Baring Gould was censured for choosing such an affected patronymic as Pennycomequicks for the leading characters in his novel of that name; yet Pennycomequick is the actual name of a town in Devon.

Soberton might seem a sorry jest if the inhabitants are only as sober as the average Englishman. Hungery Hill, Mount Misery, London Smoke, and Noisy Town do not hold out alluring possibilities. Plum Pudding Island and Strong Beer Centre are appetizing, however. World's Wonder is near Canterbury, but the world seems unconscious of the surprises it has missed. Scampton appears to cast a doubt on the honesty of the Lincolnshire people who live there; Rotherfuld Peppard suggests a vinegar cruet; Poorton can of course have no wealthy residents; Shaver's End and Latherbrush should suit barbers; Cullercoats, dyers; Charing, charwomen; Bow, lovers of archery; Blisland, honeymoon couples; Angle, fishermen; and Pickwell, careful choosers. Porington might be full of boys who love their books, Gnosall would express the result of their researches, and Dunse would be the town for such as shirked their studies. Cockcrow might be recommended to the sluggard, Bat and Ball to the lover of cricket, Tongue End to the henpecked husband, Traveller's End and Welcome Stranger to the tramp. Starve-all and No Man's Land should be shunned by every one. When you come to Wales the names become absolutely appalling. Who would care to stop at Llanfihangel-yng-Nghlwufa? Who would not be alarmed at finding himself in Llanfairpwllgyngyllgogerp-wllllandypilwgogo?

This the longest name in the three kingdoms is in Anglesey, but is only spun out for the benefit of the tourist. The inhabitants and the Post Office abbreviate it to Llanfair P.G., while the railway still further shortens it to Llanfair. The full name means " Church of St. Mary in a hollow of white hazel near the rapid whirlpool of the church of St. Tysilio by the red cave."

If the startled Saxon really wants to remember it he may find the following rhyme of some use:

> At first it began fair,
> Commencing with Llanfair,
> Then started a jingle,
> By adding Pwllgwyngyll,
> But 'twas horrible very
> To stick on Gogery,
> And simply ignoble
> To run to Chwyrndrobwll,
> Till it almost will kill you
> To say Llandysilio,
> With a terrible shock
> At the end—Gogogoch.

In September, 1872, according to the *Pall Mall Gazette,* two Welsh gentlemen, Mr. Rosser and Mr. Morgan Evans, quarrelled about the name of a village called Llyynnggffwwdvaur. Mr.

Morgan Evans was for rendering the fourteenth letter " d," Mr. Rosser " v." " Ultimately," says the *Gazette,* " Mr. Rosser, finding it impossible to bring Mr. Morgan Evans to his way of thinking, went out, procured some hot lime from an adjoining building, and returning to the Coed-y-David farm, rubbed the lime in Mr. Morgan Evans' eyes. Whether, in the event of Mr. Morgan Evans being able to see again, he will spell the word ' Llyynnggffwwddaur ' or ' Llyynnggffwwdvaur,' remains to be seen. But at the present moment he is blind, and Mr. Nathaniel Rosser is in gaol, under remand, awaiting the issue of the remedies which have been applied."

About the same date *Punch* discovered in Scotland some names it considered quite equal to the Welsh. The jester said: " No person who reads *Punch* ever gets tipsy. But possibly some persons of strong imagination may be able to form an idea of what drunkenness is like. To aid them in so desirable a discovery, *Mr. Punch* would say that he never in his life had any doubt whether he was sober or the other thing until the following passage, in a Scotch advertisement, came under his bewildered eyes. A gentleman proposes to sell, *inter alia,*—

The Estate of Auchendrean and Meall Dhu, also in the parish of Lochbroom, comprehending the Lands of Carn-Breacmeanach, Carn-Breacheg, Corrybuie Firvrogie, Teangancuisachan, and Lubnachulaig.

" We are far from clear that any man has a right to print such aggregations of letters, for to call such things words is to insult literature. If we buy the estate, which we have some idea of doing, we shall insist on having it, like *Bottom,* ' translated.' "

Another good mouthfilling word is found in the island of Mull. It runs like this: Drimtaidhvrickhillichatan.

One district in Scotland, almost limited to the Lothians and their immediate neighborhood, is remarkable for its opulence of whimsical names. A place on the borders of Peeblesshire is itself called the *Whim,* the reason being, that it was originally a moss, which, lying at an elevation of about 800 feet above the sea, seemed a most unsuitable place for a gentleman's mansion; yet, the Earl of Islay determining, nevertheless, to rear a retreat for himself upon the spot, some one called it a whim, and his lordship chose to adopt the joke as an appellation for the place in its new form. Not far from this spot there is a place called *Cauldshouthers;* another near by bears the name of the *Plot:* while a third is styled *Laugh-at-the-Lave* (lave meaning the rest) ; all doubtless bearing a like significant reference to some circumstances in their history. Names expressive of disadvantageousness of situation are abundant. The number of places

called *Cauldcots* would have been marrow to the bones of Churchill, had he known them.   There is even one called *Dead-for-
cauld.   Cauld-backs* and *Cauld-wa's* are names of farms in Fife,
where also there is a place called *Hunger-'im-out.*   In the same
county is a lonely cottage called *Warl's-end,* and another insignificant place styled *Sma'-allowance.   Blaw-wearies,* too, are not
infrequent; and there is a spot in Linlithgowshire called *Mount-
eerie,* a term expressive of lonely and dismal feelings.   On the
other hand, there is no want of merry names—a *Wanton-wa's*
near Musselburgh, one in Fife, one near Lauder, another between
Bathgate and Linlithgow.   *Canty-hall*—as if we were to say
cheerfully hall—is a place near Carberry, the scene of Mary's
rendition to her lords.   *Slocken-drouth,* which implies the allay-
ing of thirst, and dates from long before the days of tee-totalism,
stands on the old Glasgow road near Edinburgh.   *Blink-bonnie*
is a farm near the same city.   Sometimes the appellation conveys the idea of local jokes which prevailed at the inauguration
of the new locality—as where we have a *Brisk-fornent* near
Dechmont Park in West Lothian (fornent meaning opposite in
situation, as with partners in a dance), or *Cock-my-lane* on the
road from Edinburgh to Hamilton, a phrase expressive of one
complacently taking up a station by himself.   We may be very
sure, too, when we see a seat of Lord Torphichen called *Con-
tentibus,* that there was some merriment connected with its
christening.   See MEDICINE HAT, OSHKOSH, TOMBSTONE.

Playing-Cards.   Many nations claim the invention of the
devil's picture-books, as seventeenth-century Puritans designated
them, but it is now generally believed that they came from Asia
and probably from China.   The great Chinese Dictionary
" Chung-tsze-tung " (Pekin, 1678) claims that cards were invented in the reign of the Emperor Seun-ho, 1120 A.D., for the
amusement of his concubines.   An ingenious theory originating
with Sir William Jones (*Asiatic Researches,* vol. ii) suggests
that they were a natural evolution from the game of chess.

Despite many traditions to the contrary, cards could not have
been introduced generally into Europe at the time (1278) when
Petrarch wrote his dialogue on games, for he makes no mention
of them.   Boccaccio, Chaucer, and other contemporaries of
Petrarch, who continually allude to popular sports of the period,
are equally silent.

All we know for certain is that cards were manufactured in
France as early as 1392, in Italy before 1425, and in England
before 1463.   The act of Edward IV, passed in the latter year,
expressly forbids the importation of playing-cards because this
interfered with their domestic manufacture.   A duty on cards

41

was first levied in the time of James I. They were manufactured
first with stencil and then with wooden blocks; hence these were
the earliest engravings.

It is undecided whether the early cards were of the kind now
known or whether they were the tarrochi or tarots, which still
survive in some parts of France and Italy. The weight of authority is in favor of tarots. A pack of tarots consisted of 78
cards divided into 4 suits.

In all the antique Chinese packs the king of even suit is
mounted on an elephant, and the vizier or second honor is on
horseback, except in the blue suit, where he is astride a tiger, and
in the white suit, where he is on a bull. The backs of all the
cards are green, and the common cards as well as the honors
have each a carefully distinguished value denoted by certain
emblems.

There were thirty cards in each of the earlier Chinese packs,
three suits of nine cards each and three single cards superior
to all the others. The name of one of the suits was kew-ko-
wah,—that is to say, the nine thousands of kwan-strings of
beads, shells, or money,—and the titles of the other two suits
were equally concise and significant.

As the Chinese are an intensely conservative race, it is likely
that the cards now used by them do not vary much in size and
shape from the earlier ones. These are small and narrow, with
rounded edges. They are printed in black on a thin cardboard.
The backs are sometimes bright crimson and sometimes black
or yellow. Some of them are little more than half an inch
broad by three inches long, and others are one inch wide by
three and one-half long. The pips and court cards are always
printed in black on a white background, and on the face of some
of them are Chinese characters printed in red. In some packs
the cards have animals, such as horses and deer, represented
upon them; while in others characters which may mean the
names only of the animals are written above the pips. These
tiny cards may easily be held concealed in the palm of the hand,
which effectually covers them and prevents the shape of the
pips from being seen through the thin cardboard or the number
of the cards being counted by the opponent.

The earliest game of cards of which there is any authentic
record is a Venetian game which was played with the tarochi
cards and was named after them. Besides the four suits of
numeral cards there were twenty-two emblematic picture cards
called atouts, or trumps. The suits were usually called "swords,"
"cups," "sticks," and "money," each suit consisting of fourteen cards, with four honors, king, queen, knight, and knave,

though the queen was admitted last of all. Persian cards are the only ones in the East that show a female figure, and indeed the only ones in the world with such a figure except the French and those derived from them. The atouts were numbered up to twenty-one, each having its own value, and a " fou " or joker besides, which was used to add to the value of any atout to which it was joined. The characters of these atouts were numerous, including an emperor, a Cupid, a chariot, Death, the Day of Judgment, Fortune, Justice, etc. These cards were not played in order, but had special significances.

Thus the holder of the " Fool " regained his stake, " Strength " took double stakes from the pool, while " Death " swept the board, and so on. The beautiful specimens of these tarrocchi, or tarot cards, now preserved in Paris at the Bibliothéque Nationale, are supposed to have formed part of a celebrated pack painted for King Charles VI. That such a pack was made is proved by an entry by Poupart, the Royal Treasurer, in the register of the Comptes des Chambres of Charles VI under date of February 1, 1392: " Given to Jacquemin Gringonneur, painter, for three packs of cards in gold and various colors and ornamented with several devices, to carry before the lord our king for his amusement, fifty-six sols of Paris." From the fact that the king became insane shortly afterward, the story arose that cards were invented to divert his royal melancholy. The cards painted by Gringonneur were undoubtedly tarots. The earliest pack bearing the distinctive mark with which we are familiar dates from the reign of Charles VII. In this hearts, diamonds, clubs, and spades appeared for the first time, and two distinctive colors, red and black, were used. The venerable pack or fragment of a pack in the Bibliothéque Nationale might be used to-day if it were complete.

Not only the Spanish and Italian cards but the German also were undoubtedly of Saracenic origin, as they have no queen. The old-fashioned bells, hearts, acorns, and greens, still preferred in many parts of Germany, show a modification of the tarot emblems rather than of the French devices.

The new game spread rapidly. In France an edict had to be issued, in 1397, forbidding the laboring classes from playing cards among other diversions, except on Sundays and holidays.

The passion even spread to the most sacred circles. The Synod of Langres, in 1404, specially forbade the amusement to the French clergy, because of the scandals that had resulted from its abuse.

The monks in the monasteries of Italy shuffled and dealt for heavy stakes, and church money changed hands many times in a night. One enthusiastic friar is said to have lost so much that as a last resort he put his rosary on the table in hopes of winning something back. That too, went, and the wretched priest in desperation staked his own soul, only to lose it, after which he killed himself in a fit of remorse.

A crusade was instituted against gaming in all its forms. In the market-place at Nuremburg, alone, 3640 backgammon-boards, 40,000 dice, and cards by the cart-load were publicly burnt. At Bologna, in 1420, Saint Bernardin persuaded his hearers to make a huge bonfire in the public place and throw into it all their cards.

In Spain, where the game spread with the energy of the proverbial wildfire, there seems to have been no ecclesiastical revolt against it. The gravest and most learned churchmen thought it no sin to join in a merry rubber now and then, and the laity followed suit. Columbus and his crew are said to have played on the eventful voyage in 1492. This seems not unlikely, since gambling was a regular pastime in the Spanish army and navy. Herrara, in his "History of the Spanish Discoveries in America," describes the delight of Montezuma, when made prisoner by Cortez, in 1519, at watching the soldiers play cards. The Duke of Medina strenuously forbade play at any time in the great Spanish Armada of 1588, and dire punishments were prescribed for any offender who owned a pack of cards. This was on military, and not on ethical, grounds.

Strangely enough, these amusements were a long time known on the Continent before they obtained even a foothold in England. Late in the sixteenth century the epidemic broke out, spreading with great rapidity. Before this a few circular cards in irregular suits had been introduced, but now the most diverse packs were devised. Heraldic cards and cards ornamented with portraits of European kings and queens were introduced during this time.

Toward the end of the reign of Queen Mary, a commission was granted to a Dr. Cole to go over to Ireland and commence a fiery crusade against the Protestants in the country. Reaching Chester, England, on his way, the doctor was waited upon by the mayor, to whom he showed his commission, exclaiming, with premature triumph: "Here is what shall lash the heretics of Ireland." Mrs. Edmonds, the landlady of the Chester Inn, having a brother in Dublin, was disturbed by overhearing these words; so when the doctor attended the mayor downstairs, she hastened to his room, opened his box, took out the commission, and replaced it with a pack of cards. The doctor, returning, put the box into ·his portmanteau without suspicion and next day

sailed for Dublin. On his arrival, he waited on the Lord Lieutenant and Privy Council, informed them of his mission, and
presented the box to his Lordship. It contained only a pack of
cards with the knave of clubs uppermost. The doctor was petrified, and assured the Council that he had had a commission,
but what was become of it he could not tell. The Lord Lieutenant answered, " Let us have another commission, and in the
mean time we can shuffle the cards."

Before the doctor could get his commission renewed, Queen
Mary died. Thus the persecution was prevented. Queen Elizabeth settled a pension of £40 per annum on Mrs. Edmonds for
saving the queen's Protestant subjects in Ireland.

A quaint little book published in 1796, entitled " The Amusements of Clergymen," has a good deal to say about cards. The
title of this work is somewhat misleading, as it alludes to most
" amusements " only to find them unlawful, at least for the
ideal pastor. Not only are cards, hunting, and theatre-going
prohibited, but the more innocent recreations of fishing, chess,
and music are interdicted. In fact, the " amusements " befitting
a pious clergyman resolve themselves into gardening for an out-
door and shuttlecock for an in-door amusement; the worthy
author strongly commending the latter childish game as one
that " gives us good exercise, makes us cheerful, does not empty
our pockets, and requires little skill to learn. Respect the man
who invented shuttlecock." As might be expected, this writer
is very severe on cards. He denies their utility, even as a means
of amusement for the sick or aged; enforcing this opinion by
the anecdote of an old lady who, having " lost the use of her
speech and both of her hands by a paralytic affection, was advised by her doctor to play whist for her amusement. A friend
sorted and held the cards before her, and the patient nodded at
the one she wished played; but it unfortunately happened that
these signals were occasionally misunderstood, which threw the
old lady into such fits of fury that she derived injury rather
than benefit from this prescription." Dean Ramsey, in his
" Reminiscences," tells a ghastly story of another old lady whose
passion for cards was such that she played them even on her
death-bed; and, expiring before the conclusion of the game, her
partner took her cards and the players finished the rubber before
calling for assistance.

According to Scottish superstition, Glamis Castle incloses a
band of yet more inveterate gamesters,—a certain wicked earl
and his associates, who, four centuries ago, being remonstrated
with by a pious clergyman, swore that they " would continue
card-playing to the end of the world." The legend states that

the room in which they sat immediately sank under the castle, and there the gamblers play still, the rattle of the dice and the voices of the gamesters being audible on stormy nights.

The wonderful presence of mind that saved a card-playing parson from disgrace is thus related in the " Fifteen Real Comforts of Matrimony," printed in 1683. " The parson that loved gaming better than his eyes made good use of it when he put his cards into his gown sleeve in haste when the clerk came and told him that the last stave was a-singing." 'Tis true that in the height of his reproving the parish for their neglect of holy duty, upon the throwing out of his zealous arm, the cards dropped out of his sleeve and flew about the church. What then? He bid one boy take up a card and asked him what it was; the boy answers, the king of clubs; then he bid another boy take up a card—" what was that?" " The knave of spades." " Well," quoth he, " now tell me who made ye?" The boy could not tell. Quoth he to the next, " Who redeemed ye?" That was a harder question. " Look ye," quoth the parson, " you think this was an accident, and laugh at it; but I did it on purpose to show ye that had you taught your children their catechism as well as to know their cards they would have been better provided to answer material questions when they come to church."

Against this clerical anecdote may be matched the eighteenth-century story of an English soldier's ingenious device when caught with a pack of cards in church and taken before the mayor for punishment. Said Tommy Atkins, " This pack is my Bible, prayer-book, and almanac. The ace reminds me that there is but one God; the deuce of the Father and Son, the trey of the Holy Trinity; the four puts me mind of the evangelists Matthew, Mark, Luke, and John, and the five of the five wise and the five foolish virgins; the six stands for six days in which the world was made, and the seventh for the seventh day on which the Lord rested from his works. Eight spot reminds me of the eight good people saved from the flood. The nine reminds me of the nine lepers whom the Lord cleansed, and the ten reminds me of the ten commandments to Moses on Mount Sinai." The knave he laid aside and went on: " The queen puts me in mind of the Queen of Sheba, and thus the wisdom of Solomon, and the king calls to my mind the Creator, the King of all, and likewise His Majesty, King George, to pray for him."

" What is the knave for?" interrupted the mayor.

" The sergeant who brought me here is the greatest knave I know," said the wag, pointing to the man. " And the 365 days in the year is shown by the number of spots in the pack, the fifty-two weeks by the number of cards; and so you see this pack is my Bible, my prayer-book, and my almanac."

"Good," cried the mayor, laughing, as he sent the fellow off with a good box on the ear and a purse of guineas for his wit.

Probably the most expensive pack of cards in the world is one which was sold at auction, in 1880, to a dealer at Birmingham, England, for fifty-seven guineas. It is described as an absolute unique. Every card was specially engraved and the plate destroyed. The pack gives an exhaustive pictorial history of all the principal events in the reign of Queen Anne down to 1706; including the victories of Marlborough, the sea-fights of Admiral Benbow, all the various changes connected with the parliamentary proceedings of the day, and the conclusion of the treaties between England, France, and Spain. The queen of hearts is Queen Anne herself; the king is her husband, Prince George of Denmark; the queen of diamonds is Queen Anne Sophia of Denmark; the queen of clubs, the Princess Royal of Russia; and the queen of spades, Princess Anne of Russia. It is almost needless to say that leading politicians of the day are represented as the knaves.

The queerest deck of cards is probably that collected by a Chicago man named Frank Damek. It is said to be composed of cards of all qualities, from the cheapest to the highest-priced, the peculiarity consisting in the fact that they were all picked up in stray places. Damek began his collection in 1870 by picking up cards in the street whenever he happened to run across them. In this way he got fifteen or more before he began striking duplicates. Some days he would find two or three, and again months might elapse before he found another. As he approached completion the difficulties of course increased. In 1880 he needed only fifteen cards to complete the deck. In the next three years he considered himself lucky in finding all but four. The missing ones were the jack of clubs, the deuce and eight of diamonds, and the trey of spades. In the course of a year he picked up the eight of diamonds, and six months later was overjoyed to find what he at first thought was a full deck of cards lying on the sidewalk on Dearborn Street between Adam and Jackson Streets. He now thought that his long search was ended. The jack of clubs and the trey of spades were there, but five or six cards were missing, and among them the deuce of diamonds. For five and a half years he searched for that deuce. Then, in 1890, entering one of the suburban trains on the Northwestern, the first thing he saw was the deuce of diamonds, face upward, in the aisle. It was gilt-edged and glossy-backed and proved the finest card in the lot.

But the most grewsome and unpleasant deck of cards ever seen by civilized man was exhibited in 1890 by one Captain E. M. Kingsbury, a post-trader at the San Carlos Indian reservation in Arizona, where five thousand noble savages spend their leisure hours (whereof they have every day some four and twenty) in gambling. He was interviewed by a correspondent of a New York paper, who tells the story. In the course of conversation Captain Kingsbury asked: "Did you ever see their playing-cards?" and with the remark he handed out a deck which he said had been made by Indians. The faces and spots were copied after the Mexican *monte* playing-cards, and were put on with some bright, durable paint. They looked as if made of mica or, possibly, thin bone; but Captain Kingsbury, being asked as to the material, said, "Well, you know the Indian makes everything durable, and you know the varied use he makes of raw-hide."

The listener, who had been gracefully shuffling the cards, suddenly held them between finger and thumb.

"Now, you see," continued Captain Kingsbury, "horse-hide or beef-hide would be too thick, and it is reported that such things are manufactured from the exterior covering of prisoners —in other words, tanned white men's skins."

Pneumatic Tire. In 1910 a newspaper controversy tore the city of Edinburgh into segments. A monument was proposed to the inventor of the pneumatic tire. Edinburgh could not agree as to the man who deserved the honor. Was it R. W. Thomson, who patented an air-filled tire in 1845, or John Dunlop, who invented the present pneumatic tire in 1888? "The dispute," said the London *Daily Mail,* "carries the imagination back over one of the most astonishing episodes in our industrial history. It begins with a mystery of invention. It culminates in financial operations on a scale unexampled in our day, and the development of innumerable industries connected with the use of rubber."

Thomson patented in England the idea of affixing a "belt" filled with compressed air to the rim of a carriage wheel, and, although his invention never came into practical use, he showed great knowledge of the good effects which would follow from the use of the pneumatic tire. Thomson, however, was ahead of his time; his invention found no favor.

Forty-three years later John Dunlop, a veterinarian of Belfast, Ireland, patented a pneumatic tire without any knowledge that it had ever had a predecessor.

"More than once." says the writer in the *Daily Mail,* "I have heard from Mr. Dunlop himself the simple tale of how he came to invent this device. The 'safety' bicycle had then come into vogue, but its wheels were shod with solid rubber tires. Mr. Dunlop's little son possessed a tricycle, and as the Dunlops then lived in Belfast, and the Irish roads were of very bad surface, this veterinary surgeon applied his mind to contrive some mean; for minimizing the harsh jolting to which his boy was subjected when he rode his tricycle.

" A rubber tube filled with compressed air was evolved, and it afforded such comfort to the rider that Mr. Dunlop brought the idea before adult cyclists, and some enthusiasm was aroused among them. But Mr. Dunlop would have hardly been more successful in 1888 than Thomson in 1845 had not another man appeared on the scene.

" Mr. Harvey du Cros was at that time a prominent figure in Irish sporting circles, and his sons were famous for their prowess in cycle racing. With true business instinct Mr. du Cros saw the immense possibilities of the pneumatic tire for cycles, and he threw himself heart and soul into the work of making this crude invention practicable. His early efforts were greeted with derision. Cyclists and cycle manufacturers scoffed at the clumsy 'bolster' tire offered to them, and almost without exception experts declared against it.

" Then Mr. du Cros brought a band of Irish cyclists, including his sons and R. J. Mecredy, to England, and they gained sweeping victories with the pneumatic tire on the racing track. It was evident now that the new invention would eventually triumph, but a long and desperate fight against conservatism and prejudice had still to be waged, and it is reasonable to assume that but for the enterprise and ability of Mr. Harvey du Cros Mr. Dunlop's invention might have lain dormant for many years. Had this been the case, the whole progress of modern locomotion from motoring to airmanship would have been checked, for we can trace the direct influence of the air-filled tire in all the astonishing developments of the last twenty-two years. So from the bad state of Irish roads, from the solicitude of a fond parent to make smooth progress for his son's cycle over rough roads, Thomson's idea was recreated, and this time the right man was at hand to develop the idea."

As a natural evolution from the bicycle tire, there followed the idea of fitting air tires to automobiles. Here France took the lead. As a result the crude mechanism of the early motors was protected from the rough vibration of the roads, new improvements resulted from the increase in travel, among them the perfecting of the petrol engine, and these in turn lent their aid to the synchronous inventions of the air-ship and the aeroplane.

Pointers and Setters. Prof. N. S. Shaler has said in an article in *Scribner's Magazine,* that the most remarkable instance of special adaptation which man has brought about in his domesticated animals is found in our pointers and setters. In these groups the dogs have been taught, in somewhat diverse ways, to indicate the presence of birds to the gunner. Although the modes of action of the two breeds are closely related, they are sufficiently distinct to meet certain differences of circumstances. The peculiarities of their actions are altogether related to the qualities of our fowling-pieces. These have been in use, at least in the form where shot took the place of the single ball, for less than two centuries, and the peculiar training of our pointers and setters has been brought about in even less time. It seems likely, indeed, that it is the result of about a hundred and fifty years of teaching, combined with the selection which so effectively works upon all domesticated creatures. It thus appears that this peculiar impress upon the habits of the dog is the result of somewhere near thirty generations of culture.

Darwin suggested that the pointing or setting habit probably rests upon an original custom of pausing for a moment before leaping upon their prey, which was possibly characteristic of the wild dog. Shaler, however, claims this unlikely, as we do not find this habit of creeping on the prey among our more primitive forms of dogs nor the wild allied species as a marked feature. "All the canine animals trust rather to furious chase than to the cautious form of assault by stealthy approach and a final spring upon their prey, as is the habit with the cat tribe. Granting this somewhat doubtful claim that the induced habits of these dogs which have been specially adapted to the fowling-piece rests upon an original and native instinct, the amount of specialization which has been attained in thirty generations of care remains a very surprising feature and affords one of the most instructive lessons as to the possibilities of animal culture."

Naturalists are familiar with the record of Hop, the pointer pig. This wonderful animal was a sow born in the New Forest near London in the latter part of the eighteenth century. Early in life she took a fancy to some pointer puppies that were being broken, and she was ultimately trained as an invaluable pointer herself. The pig would often go out a little way with the puppies, and was then gradually coaxed into doing as they did by means of a sort of pudding made of barley-meal. The puppies could be cuffed for misbehavior, but a pocketful of stones was necessary in the case of the sow. She at length quartered her ground in grand style; backed other dogs when she came on game, and was so staunch as to remain five minutes or more on her point.

The London *Strand Magazine* has recently reproduced the photograph of an Indian prince and his hunting chee- tah. The potentate in question was Rajah Bommadevara Venkata Narasuntra Naidu Bahadur. (No wonder he keeps a tame cheetah!) This animal is seen beside the prince, who, like many other rich natives of India, trains cheetahs to hunt deer and to follow their master about like a dog. It is always dangerous, however, for strangers to approach these beautiful, leopard-like creatures.

Porcelain is distinct from pottery in the fact that it includes in its composition material which vitrifies throughout the body of the fabric. Pottery when broken shows the rough surface of the baked clay; porcelain when broken shows the same shining enamelled material in its interior as on its polished exterior surface.

Porcelain is divided into two general classes, known as soft paste and hard paste. No description can explain the difference, which must be learned by experience from the sight and the touch. It consists in the composition of the paste, which, when fused in fire, produces in the one case a soft and (to the touch) oily-feeling surface, in the other case a surface hard and firm as glass. Soft-paste porcelain is sometimes classed with pottery.

In all the Chinese literature of the porcelain of antiquity each period is mentioned as assiduously imitating the produc- tions of a preceding period. According to the historians, the art culminated in the first half of the fifteenth century, since which time the potters have been imitative rather than creative. So far, however, as the actual knowledge on the part of foreign nations is concerned, it culminated during the reign of the first of the Manchurian or Tartar conquerors of China, who held peaceful sway over the Flowery Kingdom. That was in the years between 1661 and 1722, when a literary, poetic, and benefi- cent tyrant reigned under the title of Khang-hsi, which being translated means Peaceful Joy, a pleasant title for a gentleman whose family had just devoted fifty years of steady work to stamping out the lives and sequestrating the substance of two hundred and fifty millions of people. At any rate, the porcelain of his reign was of wonderful beauty and comprised practically all the standards of rarity and excellence that distinguish modern collections. It is seen in all the great museums of Europe. From it the whole keramic industry of Europe had its earliest artistic beginnings and derived the style and character that impress it to the present day.   From it were chosen the choicest and the most valuable objects of the household decoration of Europe for the last two hundred years, and in our own country it has made its way steadily ever since it began to appear in the colony of Virginia, since George and Martha Washington owned their share of Oriental china now shown in the National Museum, and since Yankee skippers brought blue and white vases to their wives and sweethearts from the shores of far Cathay.

In the reign of Peaceful Joy they did not neglect the graceful art of imitation, not to say counterfeiting.   We have the historian's chronicle for it, and we have the objects themselves. They follow the creations of the extinct dynasty of the Mings in form, in color and design.   For the most part they are easily distinguished by their modern elegance, delicacy, and refinement of detail, as opposed to the archaic strength, vigor, and originality of the older period.   But in only too many instances the imitation was so good that no one could discriminate, and the modern vase bore its fifteenth or sixteenth century date, mark, style, and stamp just as bravely as the genuine article.

It was thought that this imitative work had died out with the last century.   In the reign of the Emperor Yung-Ching, who followed Peaceful Joy, and of Kien-Lung, who almost rounded out the century, it seemed to have gradually fallen into disuse until finally the Chinese potters devoted themselves solely to elaborate and mostly meretricious decoration and to purely commercial porcelain for the European market.

The disillusionment is complete.   The art has been revived, and it is quite evident that the Chinese are still skilled in the potter's art beyond all other nations.   European nations have, of course, made wonderful progress since they learned from China the first principles of the manufacture of porcelain, the relation of *kaolin* to *petuntse;* but there are secrets of the kiln that are still as impenetrable as they were two centuries ago, but which, for the Chinese, are very far from being, as was supposed, a wholly lost art.   The Decks, the Havilands, and all the great potters of Europe have spent millions in the effort to produce certain of the Chinese colors that distinguished the porcelain of two hundred years ago.   ·

Portland Vase.   In the Gold Room of the British Museum in London stands the Portland or Barberini Vase, a miracle of restoration after one of the most startling acts of vandalism ever known.   This exquisite, antique vase was found, about the middle of the sixteenth century, inclosed in a marble sarcophagus, within a sepulchral chamber, under the mount called the **Monte**

del Grano, about two miles and a half from Rome, on the road leading to Frascati. This sepulchral chamber appears to have been the tomb of the Emperor Alexander Severus, and of his mother Julia Mammæ; and the vase was, probably, a cinerary urn belonging to the sepulchre.

Urban V, a Barberini, was then pope. He had it placed in the Barberini Palace at Rome. After various adventures it was purchased, in 1784, by the dowager Duchess of Portland. In 1786 it came under the hammer when the entire museum was sold in lots, and was purchased by the lady's son, the then Duke of Hamilton, for 1029 guineas. In 1810 he deposited it in the British Museum. In 1845 came a catastrophe.

On February 7, 1845, about ten minutes before the Museum closed, the outrage occurred. A man who called himself William Lloyd, a student of Trinity College, Dublin, was the perpetrator. Availing himself of the momentary absence of the attendant, this crazy young man seized a heavy stone (a Persepolitan monument of basalt), which could not be lifted with one hand, from an adjoining shelf, and cast it at the vase. The noise of the falling glass aroused the staff of the department, and they rushed in, giving orders to the attendants to close the doors. The visitors then in Rooms IX and X were made to walk into the Hamilton Room, and the fragments were carefully picked and swept up. The keeper of the Department of Antiquities, on his arrival in Room IX, questioned the visitors present. Four gave satisfactory accounts of themselves; the fifth, a stout young man, in a kind of pilot coat, with both hands thrust into his pockets before him, replied in a dogged and determined tone, " I did it." He was given in charge, and taken before the sitting magistrate at Bow Street. The culprit proved to be a young Irishman, who refused to give his name, but it was ascertained that he had been living in Drury Lane under that of William Lloyd. He was remanded and again brought up on the 11th, when, on account of some doubt as to jurisdiction, he was only fined three pounds, the value of the glass shade, or, in default, committed for two months' imprisonment. Two days after the magistrate received an anonymous letter enclosing three pounds, and Lloyd was in consequence released. His real name has remained concealed.

Though the vase was broken into a score of fragments, these were pieced together with consummate skill by one of the experts of the museum, and the vase now shows hardly a blemish. Its dimensions are 9¾ inches high, and 21¾ inches in circumference. The materials of which it is composed imitate an onyx, the ground is of a rich transparent dark-amethystine color, and the figures cut in bass-relief on the sides of the vase are of a cameo-like whiteness and distinctness.

There have been many conjectures as to the subject treated. Erasmus Darwin's explanation in the "Botanic Garden"—*i.e.*, that the whole "represents the progress of initiation into the Eleusinian mysteries"—is as satisfactory as any.

Darwin concludes a lengthy description of the Portland vase with these words:

> Beneath, in sacred robes the priestess dress'd,
> The coif close-hooded, and the flutt'ring vest,
> With pointed finger guides the initiate youth,
> Unweaves the many-colored veil of Truth,
> Drives the profane from Mystery's bolted door,
> And Silence guards the Eleusinian lore.

Whatever the subject, the art of it is exquisite.

More than half a century prior to the catastrophe, in 1790, Josiah Wedgwood had made a number of copies of the vase, lavishing all his skill on the reproduction. Of these copies only sixteen are known to exist to-day. No two copies are quite the same. For his best copies Wedgwood charged £50, but those which have come into the market in recent years have been sold for much higher sums. Wedgwood's achievement was acclaimed as a triumph for British art. Erasmus Darwin apostrophizes Wedgwood in his "Botanic Garden," where these lines occur:

> Or bid Mortality rejoice or mourn
> O'er the fine forms of Portland's mystic urn.

See *T. P.'s Weekly*, March 4, 1910; *Illustrated London News*, February 15, 1845.

Postage-stamps, Perforated. A contributor to *Notes and Queries*, 11th series, iii, 251 (April 1, 1911), says: "Perforation, so obvious now, was in its day a brilliant discovery. I remember about forty years ago a lady telling me the origin of the discovery. She said that a hunting man, about to start out, had to stamp a letter. Having neither knife nor scissors handy, he thought of trying the rowel of his spur. He ran it along a stamp, perforated the edge, and tore it off." Another contributor on the same page says he can remember the first coming of the postage-stamp, which after a "lick to the back, you put on the letter and hit it hard with the ball of the hand to make sure that it would not drop off. People were very choice about using the 'queen's yeds,' as most folks called them, and asked for them at the shop which was the post-office in any village of size. To ask for and get 'a queen's head' was not the work of a moment or two, for the stamp had to be cut with extreme care along the lines, it being held to be something that would have to be answered for if the stamp was damaged in any way or stuck on the wrong way up. I remember how carefully the old lady used to handle her scissors and a sheet of stamps as she served you with a queen's head, and how carefully she affixed it for those who did not feel equal to doing it."

When the perforated stamps came, they tore off so badly that scissors were used for a long time to detach them from the sheet; and at the town post-offices the clerks would first crease a row along the perforations, to make them tear off the easier.

Post-office. This word is an example of the mode in which things change while names remain. Originally a "post-office" was the "office" which arranged all details concerning the "posts"—*i.e.*, the places on the great roads where relays of horses and men could be obtained for the rapid forwarding of the king's despatches.

In this sense the word was not unknown to the English translators of the Bible. In 2 Chronicles xxx. 6,—we read that "the posts went with the letters from the king and his princes throughout all Israel." Thus it would seem that the establishment of a regular system of posts was coeval with the foundation of centralized government. Simple at first,—the messenger swift of foot bearing the commands of the sovereign to distant parts of his dominions,—it grew and widened with the growth of empire. Formed for the convenience of kings, the people had no share in its privileges, though they bore the tax.

The Romans had their system of *angaria,* or mounted couriers, which they had borrowed from the Persians. All along the great roads houses were erected at a distance of five or six miles from one another. Forty horses were kept at each station. By the help of these relays 100 miles could be traversed in a day. The system was so well organized that when Julius Cæsar was in Britain he sent two letters to Cicero, one reaching its destination in 26 and the other in 28 days.

Private citizens, however, had to trust to the services of slaves until the end of the third century, when Emperor Diocletian established a postal system for private individuals.

The earliest regular post in modern Europe appears to have been established by the Counts of Thurn and Taxis, who held a monopoly of the postal service over different parts of Germany and Italy from the sixteenth down to almost the end of the nineteenth century.

The crude beginnings of the English postal system date back to 1482, when a single horseman rode twenty miles and then handed his packet to another. There was a chief Postmaster of England many years before any system of distributing private letters was established by the Crown. These letters were conveyed either by a single carrier using a single horse, which he " baited " on the way, or else by relays of men and horses maintained by private enterprise.

There is considerable uncertainty about the time when letters for private individuals were first carried by the government, but this was probably done as early as the Wars of the Roses; it was not, however, till the time of Charles I that the government established a regular system of inland posts. A post-office for letters to foreign parts had indeed been established " for the benefit of the English merchants " in the reign of James I, but the extension of the system to inland letters was left to the succeeding reign. Charles I, by a proclamation issued in 1635, commanded " his Postmaster of England for foreign parts to settle a running post or two, to run night and day between Edinburgh and London, to go thither and come back again in six days, and to take with them all such letters as shall be directed to any post-town in or near that road." Neighboring towns, such as Lincoln and Hull, were to be linked on to this main route, and posts on similar principles were directed to be established on other great high-roads, such as those to Chester and Holyhead, to Exeter and Plymouth. So far no monopoly was claimed, but two years afterward a second proclamation forbade the carriage of letters by any messengers except those of the king's postmaster-general, and thus the present system was inaugurated. The monopoly thus claimed, though no doubt devised by the king to enhance the royal power and to bring money into the exchequer, was adopted by Cromwell and his parliament, one main advantage in their eyes being that the carriage of correspondence by the government would afford " the best means to discover and prevent any dangerous and wicked designs against the Commonwealth."

In the year 1679 there appeared the ninth edition of " The Present State of England," by Edward Chamberlayne, who devotes a special chapter to the doings, profits, and savings of King Charles's Post-bag. He informs his readers that, although the number of letters " missive " in England was not at all considerable in their ancestors' days, yet it is now prodigiously great, " since the meanest people have generally learned to write;" so great, that his Royal Highness of York is able to farm the Post-bag for thirty thousand pounds per year. Mr. Chamberlayne bids his friends note also, that by King Charles's bag letters are conveyed with more expedition, and less charge, than in any foreign country. A letter containing a whole sheet of paper, is conveyed eighty m'' ' '‍o-pence; two sheets for four-pence; and an ounce of paper for eight pence! This cheap conveyance is so rapid (the Post-bag travelling by night as well as by day), that a letter travels one hundred and twenty miles in four-and-twenty hours; so that, continues Mr. Chamberlayne, to make a great impression on his audience, " in five days an answer of a letter may be had from a place three hundred miles distant from the writer! " Mr. Chamberlayne, now in a state of irrepressible excitement, continues his list of wonders: " Moreover, if any gentleman desire to ride post to any principal town of England, Post-horses are always in readiness (taking no horse without the consent of his owner), which in other kings' reigns was not duly observed; and only three-pence is demanded for every English mile, and for every stage, to the post-boy fourpence for conducting. Besides this excellent convenience of conveying letters, and men on horseback, there is of late such an admirable commodiousness, both for men and women of better rank, to travel from London to almost any great town of England, and to almost all the villages near this great city, that the like hath not been known in the world; and that is by stage-coaches, wherein one may be transported to any place, sheltered from foul weather and foul ways, free from endamaging one's health or body by hard jogging, or over-violent motion; and this, not only at a low price, as about a shilling for every five miles, but with such velocity and speed, as that the posts in some foreign countries make not more miles in a day; for the stage-coaches—called flying-coaches—make forty or fifty miles in a day, as from London to Oxford or Cambridge; and that in the space of twelve hours, not counting the time for dining, setting forth not too early, nor coming in too late."

When the condition of the roads in early times is remembered, it may be imagined that the carriage of post-letters was not very rapid. So lately as 1784 the mail-bags were carried by post-boys on horseback at an average rate, including stoppages, of from three to four miles an hour. The inscriptions frequently found on these ancient missives show that their writers did not commit them to the care of the post-boys without some misgivings as to their ultimate fate. " Be this letter delivered with haste, haste, haste! " " Post haste! Ride, villain, ride for thy life! " and other similar inscriptions indicate anything but a calm assurance that the letters would punctually reach their destination. In 1783, Mr. John Palmer, the manager of the theatre at Bath, then the capital of the West, suggested to Mr. Pitt that the passenger coaches, which had begun to run on the principal roads, should be employed to carry the mails. In advocating this reform he laid as much stress upon the superior safety of the coach, as upon its greater speed. "The mails," he says, speaking of the old system, "are generally entrusted to some idle boy without character, mounted on a worn-out hack, and who, so far from being able to defend himself or escape from a robber, is much more likely to be in league with him." If conveyed by coach, on the other hand, the mails should, he recommends, be accompanied by well-armed and trustworthy guards.

We all have a tolerably vivid picture in our minds of the well-appointed mail-coach of later times, with its fine horses and brisk guard. Dickens has also photographed for us in his "Tale of Two Cities" the same vehicle in its younger days, with its guard armed to the teeth and its load of passengers each suspicious that his neighbor might be a highwayman in disguise. But the earlier picture of the post-boy jogging along the country roads on his sorry nag with the mail-bags slung over his back affords a yet stronger contrast to the fast mails and travelling post-offices of the present day. Palmer's suggestion, it is needless to say, was adopted, though like many other reforms it was sturdily opposed by the department; and when some thirty years later the roads were, thanks to Mr. MacAdam, brought nearer to perfection, the speed of the mail-coach was gradually increased till it attained more than ten miles an hour. Very shortly afterward railways were introduced, and in 1830, on the opening of the line between Liverpool and Manchester, the mails were conveyed by train. Thanks to steam-power, the correspondence which in Palmer's time must have taken more than four days to travel from London to Edinburgh, and in the best coaching days must have been more than a day and a half in transit, is now less than ten hours on the road, and a letter written in London this afternoon will be delivered in Dublin to-morrow morning.

From the seventeenth century down to the middle of the nineteenth there was none of the safety and secrecy in the mail service which the public now takes for granted. The government exercised the power of opening not only private letters but dispatches addressed to the representatives of foreign powers. Here is an extract from the journals of the House of Commons during the Protectorate:

Die Sabbati Augusti 2, 1645. Prayers. Mr. *Greene* acquainted the house that a Pacquet from the King of *Portugall*, to his resident here, was come to his hands: and, It is thereupon *Ordered*, That tne Pacquet be referred to the Committee of Examinations, to be opened by that Committee: And that the *Portugall* resident have notice hereof; that the same may be opened in his presence, or in the presence of any of his Servants, which he shall think fit to send for that purpose.

In the early eighteenth ce   pe and Swift frequently complaining that secrets alluded to in letters were discovered by clerks, though it is not impossible, as regards Pope, that his vanity exaggerated the importance of the one and the delinquency of the other. In 1735 many members of Parliament made similar complaints in the House of Commons. In 1783 Prime Minister Pitt found it almost impossible to write anything worth reading for his mother's perusal, in view of "the fashion that prevailed of opening almost any letter."

The culmination of this outrageous "fashion" and its consequent taking off was reached in 1844, when all England and indeed all Europe, was aroused by the arbitrary conduct of Sir James Graham, then British home secretary, in opening and reading letters addressed to Mazzini, the Italian revolutionist then resident in London. So great was the outcry that Parliament awoke to its duty, the matter was thoroughly sifted, acts were passed abolishing the right of inspection, and the inviolability of the mails was guaranteed for the future.

It was Thomas Duncombe, M. P. for Finsbury, who was mainly instrumental in exposing the methods of Sir James Graham and a long line of predecessors. Duncombe's "Life," written by his son, reveals how Sir James, despite an outer calm, writhed inwardly over the parliamentarian's attacks. The same volume contains a number of interesting letters elicited by Duncombe's onslaught. One bears the signature of "C. Von Bismarck,"—*i.e.*, the young count who was to end his life as a prince after being virtual dictator to Europe.

"About eighteen months ago," he writes, "I had a long conversation with a French gentleman belonging to the party opposed to M. Guizot, about the sanctity of the seal, and the abominable institution of the *chambre noire;* when he assured me that this custom had been entirely abolished in France, but that it continued to be done in the London post-office; nay, he asserted that, even at the time we were conversing, the letters of Lord Brougham were opened before being sent off to his place of residence in the south of France; and this by his own conservative friends, who could not spare his services, with regard to all communications with Lord Brougham's intimate friend, M. Guizot."

The lowest charge for a letter from London to Birmingham was ninepence. This charge carried only a single sheet of paper; any enclosure at once doubled the amount. The mode of calculating postage led to the oddest results: Mr. Cobden informed Sir Rowland Hill of a case in which a packet of 32 ounces, posted by a ship's captain at Deal, was handed to the addressee in London charged with more than 6*l*.

Foreign postage was an especially costly luxury. In 1776 Johnson would not receive a package from Lisbon charged seven guineas, suspecting some fraud. In 1815 William Wilberforce records in his diary the receipt of a note "from Hatchard, telling me that a letter from Hayti, weighing 85 ounces, had come for me and was charged at £37 10s. and that he had refused to take it in. The general post-office very handsomely under the peculiar circumstances of the case let me off for a peppercorn of 7s., which I shall gladly pay." The peculiar circumstances were that the letter related to the movement for the abolition of slavery.

In those days of heavy postage no one had any scruple about cheating the revenue. Travellers were importuned by friends to carry letters for them to other friends in England or on the continent. This was against the law, although a vulgar error prevailed that if the letters were carried "open" (unsealed) no penalty could be exacted. Other evasions were invented. Tradesmen sent their customers' letters in bales of goods. A newspaper might carry within its folds a sheet or two of what looked like blank paper. The recipient held the paper before the fire, and lo! a message was revealed in characters of a dark sepia color. It had been written with milk. Various invisible inks were used in the same manner for the same purpose.

When these stratagems became so frequent as to attract legislative attention, subtler tricks were resorted to. Slight dots under certain printed letters in a newspaper indicated that these letters could be consecutively picked out to form words and sentences. This was troublesome for both sender and receiver, and was therefore used only for short messages.

The postal tax pressed most heavily upon the poor, and it was the poor who were the most ingenious in evading postage. As letters were not prepaid, relatives arranged with one another that they should refuse to take in any mail unless some private mark outside signalled an important message within. If the letter was refused, the postal authorities on breaking the seal found nothing but blank paper. The correspondents knew, however, that a blank message meant "Everything is all right," or any other prearranged code. A certain Macdonald, when paying a visit to London, kept his wife in Glasgow informed as to the state of his health in addressing her either as Mrs. Macdon*ill* or Mrs. Macdon*well*. After examining the superscripture, the canny lady would refuse to take in the missive, on the ground that it was not addressed to her.

Members of the peerage could "frank" a large number of letters daily, so that they passed gratis through the mails. Members of Parliament enjoyed the same privilege, everv day except Sunday, for a limited number of letters. Needless to say, peers and parliamentarians alike were beset by friends for franks for themselves, or for their friends or for their friends' friends. In "The Diary, Letters, and Journals of Sir George Jackson" (London, 1872), we find that embryo diplomatist writing to his mother at Bath in 1802: "My sister tells me Bath was never so thin. I sympathize with her, knowing how voluminous her correspondence is, and that the thinness of Bath means a dearth of *frank* men, there being, she says, only Lords Rosslyn and Harcourt to write to."

Nor did the trouble end here. The abuse was carried so far that in a single year there were franked through the post-office two laundry maids, a doctor, a cow, and fifteen couple of hounds.

Under these circumstances it is not at all surprising to find that in the year 1839 Englishmen wrote, on an average, only 3 letters a year. One letter in every 13 was franked. The conditions called loudly for reform. Reform came in 1840, in the shape of penny-postage, introduced by Sir Rowland Hill after a bitter parliamentary struggle. Although franking was abolished, the grand total of letters mailed bounded up from 82,000,000 in 1839 to 169,000,000 in 1840. Twenty years later it had reached what was then considered the enormous number of one billion letters a year. (See PENNY-POST.) The increase in the circulation during a single year is now nearly equal to the total number of letters carried by the department in 1839.

A good deal of the romance of the mail in modern days arises from accidents, frauds, and from other "natural shocks that flesh is heir to." On one occasion the mails from the Cape were so seriously damaged through saturation with sea-water that the department found itself in the embarrassing position of having to deal with 7 lbs. weight of loose diamonds, the addressed covers of which had been reduced to pulp. Half a stone of diamonds wanting owners is suggestive of the Arabian Nights, or at least of "Lothair" and the "ropes of pearls." On another occasion traces of a mail-bag robbery, which had been committed in 1798, were discovered in 1876, when an old public-house near Selby, in Yorkshire, was pulled down. The demolition of this house brought to light something more startling than the missing mail-bag and the clothes of the robber, for several coffins were found under the foundations, suggesting that the innkeeper had been a friend and colleague of highwaymen and murderers. During the great snowstorm of 1881 a letter posted on January 18 containing a cheque for 1,000*l.* was missing. In the course of a week the search for this letter was successful, for it was found floating in a block of ice in the Thames off Deptford. This story is capped by another, equally creditable to the zeal and assiduity of the post-office: an American gentleman addressed a letter to his sister " Upper Norwood, or elsewhere," and in a few days it was handed to the addressee on the top of a coach in North Wales!

Post-offices, Curious. There is a town called Beebe Plain, which stands half in the State of Vermont and half in the province of Quebec, Canada. The post-office was built (about 1830) exactly on the boundary line between the United States and Canada. Standing in two countries, it belongs to the postal service of two nations. The cellar connects the two countries. In the days not very long ago when the post-office was a general store, whiskey was known to be sold in one country and delivered in another without ever having gone out from under the roof of the old structure.

Standing in front of this strange post-office is a large post which marks the boundary line, and it is said that one time a man who wanted to get a roadway to his premises moved this post, and many thousands of dollars and no little time were spent to establish the exact line again.

Scotland until very recent years possessed an odd post-office in Aryglshire. It was situated in the lonely hills between Drimnin and Barr, three miles from any habitation, and consisted of a simple slit in a rock, closed up by a nicely fitting stone.

When any letters arrived at Drimnin for the district of Barr, they were conveyed to the rock by the first shepherd or crofter going so far. Having been dropped in and the slit reclosed, they were left until a shepherd or crofter from the other side happened to come along when they were taken up and delivered at their due destination. No letter was ever known to be lost at this primitive post-office.

At Burra, Shetland, an old tin canister, made water-tight with newspapers and pitch, was once picked up on the shore. It contained ten letters, with the correct cash for postage. With these was also a letter for the finder, urgently requesting the posting of the accompanying missives, as they were important business communications. After the letters had been carefully dried they were at once posted to their destinations, which they reached without further adventure.

One of the smallest post-office buildings in the world, 5 feet square and about 6 feet high, is in California. A rough pine hut, unpainted and windowless, it stands in a lonely spot on the stage-road north of San Diego City, and is maintained for the convenience of rich ranch owners in the vicinity. Not more than six or eight people get mail there, but their letters are of sufficient financial importance for a post-office to be provided for their use. The postmaster has to be on duty only on the days when the stage-coach is due to pass. The stage-driver drops the mail, the few letters for Virginia are handed up, and the post-master proceeds to distribute the letters, post-cards, and news-papers in lock boxes hung on the outside of the post-office. After the scanty mail is distributed the postmaster locks up the little office and goes away.

When a citizen of Virginia mails a letter, he does not buy a stamp, but deposits the letter and money through the letter drop in the door. If the letter is a heavy one and likely to re-quire more than one stamp, he drops a quarter or a half-dollar in with it, and finds his change in his letter-box next mail-day. As the postmaster knows the handwriting of every man, woman, and child in the postal district, he never puts the change in the wrong box. About once a year, generally near the holidays, a registered letter or package arrives, and then the accommo-dating postmaster delivers it. In Virginia registered mail is put in the letter drop, with the fee, and the receipt placed in the proper lock box the same as the change for stamps.

The *Strand Magazine* describes a post-office which probably enjoys the distinction of being the only one of its kind. It is patronized by vessels passing Santa Cruz, Teneriffe. A water-tight tin contains the bag of letters all stamped with English stamps and sealed up, to which is a flag-pole. The raft is then dropped overboard, care being taken to drop it flat on the water, so as to keep the flag flying, in order to attract attention. In a recent deposit of mail in this floating post-office were no less than 90 letters posted to various parts of the world.

Potato. There seems little doubt that the original home of the potato was South America, that Pizarro found it cultivated by the Incas in Peru, and that it was he who introduced it into Spain in 1560. This was twenty-five years before Sir Walter Raleigh and his follower Thomas Herriott brought it over to England, yet they still remain joint claimants for the honor of having first planted it in the Eastern Hemisphere. Herriott, in his " History of Virginia," printed in 1588, described the potato as " a kinde of root of round form, some of the bigness of wall-nuts, some farre greater, which are found in moist and marish ground, growing many together, one with the other, in ropes, as if they were fastened by a string." " Being boyled," he says, " or sodden, they are verie good meate."

Gerard, in his " Herbal " (1597), is the first author who gives a picture of the potato plant. He calls it by the name of "polarum tuberosum," which name has been followed by Linnæus and his disciples.

He says, " Their nutriment is as it were a mean between flesh and fruit, and being toasted in the embers they lose much of that windiness, especially being eaten sopped in wine. Of these roots may be made conserves no less toothsome, wholesome, and dainty. than of the flesh of quinces. They may serve as a ground or foundation whence the cunning confectioner or sugar-baker may work and frame many comfortable delicate conserves and restorative sweetmeats. They are used to be eaten roasted in the ashes. Some when they be so roasted, infuse them and sop them in wine; and others, to give them the greater grace in eating, do boil them with prunes, and so eat them. And likewise others dress them, being first roasted, with oil, vinegar and salt, every man according to his own taste and liking."

The author mentions that he had planted divers roots of them in his garden, where they flourished until winter, when they perished and rotted, but whether they flowered or not he was ignorant. He knew, however, that the best method in planting was to divide the roots as now practised.

Gerard states that he received the potato—or, as he calls it, the " openauk " (a Peruvian name, by the way)—from Virginia and that he cultivated it in his garden. A portrait introduced into the " Herbal " shows the author holding a flowering branch of the plant in his hand. It seems pretty well established that Raleigh, on his return from America in 1586, brought some potatoes with him, and it is almost equally certain that Sir Francis Drake in the same year brought in others from Spain. But it is by no means proved that Raleigh found the tuber in Virginia. A plausible suggestion has been made that on the return voyage he met and captured a Spanish ship, sailing from South America, which had potatoes aboard. " It is hardly possible," says Archibald Findley in " The Potato, its History and Culture " (Cupar-Fife Westwood, England, 1909), " for the potato to have been introduced into Virginia in Raleigh's time, unless the ancient Mexicans had cultivated it and it had got spread about amongst the aborigines north of Mexico."

The story is well known (and is probably true) of how Sir Walter gave these pioneer potatoes to his gardener in Youghal, Ireland, as a fine fruit from America which he desired him to plant in his kitchen-garden in the spring. In August, this plant flourished, and in September produced a fruit, but so different to the gardener's expectation, that in an ill humor he carried the potato-apple to his master. " Is this," said he, " the fine fruit from America you prized so highly?" Sir Walter either was or pretended to be ignorant of the matter, and told the gardener, since that was the case, to dig up the weed and throw it away. The gardener soon returned with a good parcel of potatoes.

We know that potatoes were generally cultivated in Ireland long before they were adopted as a common food product in England. In the time of James I, however, they were raised as a curious exotic in the gardens of some of the nobility and gentry. They are noticed among various other articles to be provided for the queen's household, but they were evidently great rarities, for the price was some two shillings per pound. They were then called *batatas,* which is the Spanish name for them, and the circumstance favors the theory of their Spanish origin. It is curious that so valuable an article should have made such slow progress in England. The prejudices of learned and unlearned alike were enlisted against it. The laymen abused it in print; the priest thundered at it from the pulpit. The potato was stigmatized as a dangerous gift from a dangerous race. William Cobbett ranked it next to his pet abhorrence, tea, as a thing to be avoided, especially by the poor.

In the fury of his indignation he shakes the "lazy root" as a terrier does a rat, and finds it an excellent opportunity for a fling at the Irish. It is not even cheap, if people care about English cleanliness. Think of the labor, think of the time, think of all the peelings and scrapings and washings and messings attendant on those interminable boilings of the pot! For it must be a considerable time before English people can be brought to eat potatoes in the Irish style: that is to say, to scratch them out of the earth with their paws, toss them into a pot without washing, and, when boiled, turn them out upon a dirty board. This is a picture of the contented poverty which he abhors. "I despise the man that is poor and contented," he cries. "It is a proof of a base disposition."

So late as 1805, or 219 years from the date of the potato's introduction into Britain, Dr. Buchan, in the nineteenth edition of his "Domestic Medicine," laments that potato culture is limited almost exclusively to Ireland and to the north of England. He himself strongly urges its claims on all classes as a food-producing plant and a potent means of preventing the recurrence of famine in the land.

Simultaneously the potato found another earnest advocate in Thomas William Coke. He carried precept into practice in his own county of Norfolk. Does not everybody remember him best by his popular title Coke of Norfolk? He began with his own neighbors and tenants, the villagers at Holkham; but great was their indignation. For five years he could not induce them to look upon it as an article of food or to consent to cultivate it. He even offered them land rent free on which to plant it, but they refused firmly and with outspoken disgust. At length, upon his own farm, he introduced the Ox Noble, a very large species, and this, apparently from its size, found a little favor in their eyes, for a few farmers admitted, as a great concession, that, perhaps, " 't wouldn't poison the pigs." He persevered, however, and in time he would have had as great a difficulty in persuading his tenants not to eat potatoes as he had at first in inducing them to risk swallowing such a suspicious article of diet.

In England's great rival across the channel the potato won its way against similar difficulties. Brought from Flanders into France, its culture in the southern provinces was promoted by the efforts of Turgot, but everywhere else in the kingdom dogged prejudice arrested its propagation. It was even said that the potato poisoned the soil in which it was planted and that it produced leprosy and other loathsome diseases in those who ate it. This prejudice found its first successful antagonist in Antoine Auguste Parmentier (1737–1813). He was an assistant apothecary in the French army during the war in Hanover. His dauntless courage on the field of battle caused him to be five times taken prisoner.

The prisoners were kept in close confinement, and fed altogether on potatoes; but Parmentier, instead of joining his companions in their indignant abuse of a food altogether new to them, was calmly and sensibly engaged in considering the utility of the vegetable, and inquiring into its nature and the mode of cultivating it.

When the war was over, he sought the patronage of his king, Louis XVI. Yielding to earnest solicitation, that monarch placed at his disposal, as a field for experiment, fifty acres of the Plaine des Sablons. For the first time, this sterile soil was tilled by Parmentier, and the plant he so ardently desired to naturalize committed to it. In due course blossoms appeared. Almost wondering at his success, Parmentier eagerly gathered a bouquet of the flowers, and hastening to Versailles, presented them to the king. Louis graciously accepted the offering, and, despite the satirical smiles of some of his courtiers, wore them in his button-hole.

From that hour the triumph of the potato was secured. Nobles and fine ladies, who had hitherto laughed at what they called "the poor man's monomania" now took their tone from the monarch, and flocked round the modest philanthropist with their congratulations.

To convert the vulgar, Parmentier had recourse to stratagem. He posted guards around his potato fields by day and withdrew them by night, so that the neighbors should be tempted to come, steal, eat, and be convinced. Great was his delight when the guards reported that potatoes had in fact been stolen. He bountifully rewarded the bearers of the news. "There can scarcely be any remaining prejudice against my poor potatoes," he said, "else they would not be stolen." A short time after he gave a dinner, every dish of which consisted of the potato disguised in some variety of form. Even the brandy and liqueurs served at table were extracted from it. Among other celebrated persons, Franklin and Lavoisier were present. The all-potato banquet was the climax of the great campaign. And thus, to the persevering efforts of one individual was France indebted for a vegetable which soon took its place in the first rank of its agricultural treasures.

So deeply sensible were some of his countrymen of the debt of gratitude they owed him, that during his lifetime a proposal was made by the minister François de Neufchateau that the potato be called Parmentiere.

Potato Patch. Hazen S. Pingree, of Michigan (1840–1901), who at one time in his career enjoyed the double distinction of being simultaneously the governor of his State and mayor of Detroit, its most important city, was the originator of the idea of utilizing vacant city lots by turning them over to the industrious poor for cultivation. As potatoes were the main staple, the lots became known as potato patches and the mayor as Potato Pingree. He accepted the nickname with pride. He had reason for self-congratulation. The potato-patch idea proved a success and speedily spread to other cities. In New York the conditions were especially favorable when the innovation reached there in 1907. From 1905 to 1907 a speculative building craze had swept that city. During that period 750 square miles of farm lands, within 30 miles of New York's City Hall, had been bought by financial and building interests. But the panic in the closing days of 1907 put an end to this boom. The lots lay idle and unproductive and the speculation seemed fated to end in heavy losses. Gradually the owners of the properties began renting small patches to Italians and others who were out of work through dulness in their various lines of employment. These men, with their wives and children to aid them, began the cultivation of the lots under a system of loans from land owners and speculative builders. Soon the "back-to-the-farm movement" became an actuality within the corporate limits of the greatest city on the American continent. Co-operative societies were formed to aid in the cultivation of the soil and new and improved methods of farming were introduced. Machinery was purchased and antiquated methods were discarded. The vacant lot became a factor in the produce markets of the metropolis, and the success of the original vacant-lot farmers induced others to take up gardening and truck farming.

It is estimated that during the first year of the experiment the harvest from vacant lots within the city limits reached an aggregate value of $15,000,000. Every successive year has shown material gains.

Potter's Field. This name, synonymous to-day with a public burial-ground, arose in England.

Both in that country and on the Continent the clay used for pottery was dug out by whole colonies of men, women, and children. The long trenches were left standing just as they had been dug. No attempt was made to refill them or to level them with the adjacent ground. Gradually it became a common practice to cast into them the bodies of the dead among the workers, covering them over with just sufficient earth to hide them from the gaze of the sun.

Pottery. In its broadest sense pottery may be defined as any object made of clay and baked with fire. But this definition would include porcelain, which differs from pottery in material points. (See PORCELAIN.) Pottery has been made by almost all nations, civilized and barbarian, in all ages; porcelain was made only by the Chinese and the Japanese until the eighteenth century, when the method of making it was first discovered in Europe.

In all ages and countries men have moulded clay into convenient forms and baked these forms in fire to harden them. Of all the products of men's hands none have proved so durable against fire, flood, and decay as these articles of baked clay. Wherever we find the ruined habitations of ancient races we find pottery. Around every old Eastern city there are heaps of broken pottery in masses beyond conception, where, for ages on ages, these shattered household utensils have accumulated. Savage races in Europe, Asia, Africa, and America have baked pottery from the remotest times.

Useful and durable as it proved, it was, of course, one of the first articles which the human race sought to make beautiful and ornamental. Hence it is of all arts the best for the study of the development of refinement in the history of races, and it is almost equally important for the study of the tastes, the affections, the religion, the manners and customs, of men in all ages. And when in its history we reach the periods of the greatest refinement and civilization of various nations or races, we find in it unsurpassed examples of purity and cultivation of taste, superb models of beauty in form, and the richest specimens of harmonious combinations in colors.

The history of pottery will cover a period almost identical with that of the human race. The oldest picture of a pottery is found in an Egyptian tomb, and the oldest specimens which can be dated are found in Egypt, where dishes, vases, ornaments, and countless articles of religious signification and use are found, not infrequently impressed with the names of kings, thus affording, as with coins, the means of fixing approximately the date of their manufacture. These articles are found in the greatest number with a blue or green glaze, sometimes red, and occasionally with two or more colors on one object. Beads and bugles of pottery, covered with a rich blue glaze, are often found, and these are sometimes varied by stripes of other color, chiefly black. The ability of the Egyptian artists is often displayed in vases with hieroglyphic and other decorations, and in larger or smaller figurines of gods, animals, men, and women. The style of Egyptian art in sculpture can be studied fully as well, if not better, from the pottery than from the stone remains of that ancient people.

Preachers, Female. The first women preachers were, naturally, Quakers, for ever since the organization of the Society of Friends women have shared with men the right of speaking " in meeting."

Nevertheless it was not until the middle of the nineteenth century that women were publicly ordained to the work of the ministry in any Protestant church—the Catholic church, of course, being out of the question.

In 1853, for the first time in America and in the world, a woman, the Rev. Antoinette Brown, afterward Mrs. Blackwell, was ordained as a Congregationalist minister. Later she became a Unitarian. Born in a log cabin at Henrietta, New York, she celebrated her 87th birthday in New York City in 1912, and was then engaged in preaching once a month at All Souls' Church, Elizabeth, N. J.

Even as a young girl she had been serious and devout. Nevertheless, her friends and her family were surprised, if not shocked, when she announced her intention, after graduating from Oberlin College, of entering the Theological Seminary attached to the University. Most surprised and most shocked were the professors of Divinity there. Their protests were in

vain, however, as the charter of the institution provided that
nobody should be excluded as a student on account of sex. Miss
Brown completed her theological studies, and, though not yet
formally admitted to orders, preached her first sermon in her
native town in 1848. Two great New York editors, Charles
A. Dana and Horace Greeley, interested themselves in the young
woman preacher, and offered to provide a hall and a salary of
$1000 a year if she would preach regularly in New York City.
Modestly deciding that she was too young to undertake to fill
a metropolitan pulpit, she accepted the pastorate of the Congregational church at South Butler, N. Y., at a salary of $300 a
year. There she was ordained as a Congregational minister.
The ordination called forth bitter denunciation from many
quarters. So strong was the feeling that, when some time later
she was sent by her church as a delegate to a temperance convention in New York, she was howled and hooted down when she
attempted to speak.

Some years after she had begun her career as a pastor she
became the wife of Samuel C. Blackwell. They had several
children, but Mrs. Blackwell, in spite of family cares, continued
preaching. Fifty years after her admission to the theological
seminary Oberlin honored her with the degree of doctor of
divinity.

In 1863 the Rev. Olympia Brown was ordained at Malone,
New York, in the Universalist church, being the first woman to
be so honored by that denomination.

The first woman ordained in New England was Mrs. Phœbe
A. Hanaford. She was born on Nantucket, was married when
she was twenty, and became a Universalist minister in 1868 when
she was nearly forty. She has been pastor of churches in Hingham, Mass., in Waltham, Mass., in New Haven, Conn., and in
Jersey City.

In *Frank Leslie's Popular Monthly* Mrs. Hanaford told the
story of her first early struggles against popular prejudice.

"I remember," she says, "my first journey *on foot* over the
Kennebec River in central Maine, largely in connection with the
then prevailing prejudice against women in the pulpit. I had
agreed to exchange with the broad-minded pastor of the church
in Gardiner, Me., and was assigned as guest to a certain family
in that city. By the time I reached Gardiner, travelling from
Boston that winter day, I had been transferred as guest to the
hotel, because the family to whom the Gardiner minister assigned me preferred not to encourage women ministers by any
hospitality." Accepting the inevitable, she went to her apartment, and saw no one that evening save the chorister, who called

for the hymns. "In the morning the sister of 'mine host' kindly piloted me to the pretty little church. I entered the pulpit as the organ sounded, and while I was arranging for the service I noticed a lady of rather distinguished appearance, and attracting much attention, passing down the aisle to her seat. Many heads were also turned to the choir gallery as a tall, fine-looking gentleman passed along and took his seat with the choir. All were strangers to me.

"At the close of the service the lady whom I had noticed as arriving so late came at once to the pulpit, and most cordially invited me to her home, and took me thither in a sleigh at the close of the afternoon service. She and her husband (who was the tardy member of the choir) urged me to preach a third sermon in the evening, and I did so. In their elegant mansion on the bank of the Kennebec (after all the services were over, and every kindness had been shown to me that a generous host and hostess could bestow), they confided to me the fact that they had vehemently opposed their pastor's exchange of pulpits on the ground that I was a woman, and they did not think a woman should occupy the pulpit. But Sabbath morning brought a sense of duty which finally took them to church, even after they had declared they would not go, and they became converted to the fact that truth knows no sex, and that the soul may be helped by truth, whether proclaimed by man or woman; therefore they decided never again to oppose woman in the pulpit—and they never did. Less than twenty years from that time the neighboring church in Hallowell had a woman pastor (the Rev. Lorenza Haynes), and in the Gardiner pulpit the voices of many women have been heard. The days of prejudice in that region have passed away.

"I connect the river with my experience of the prejudice which then existed because, when Monday morning came, I walked across the frozen Kennebec with my delightful hostess."

Mrs. Hanaford is the first woman who ever acted as chaplain for a State legislature. New Haven, while she was a pastor there, was one of the capitals of Connecticut, that State having then two capitals, Hartford being the other. The New Haven pastors were invited in turn to undertake the duties of chaplain at the legislative sessions, and Mrs. Hanaford was invited just as the other ministers were.

Mrs. Hanaford is one of the first women ministers, if not the very first, who performed the marriage ceremony. She is the only woman, it is said, who ever officiated at the marriage of her own daughter.

Rev. Anna H. Shaw was the first woman ordained by the

Methodist Protestant Church, and the first woman minister of any denomination or nationality to preach in England, Germany, Denmark, Holland, and Sweden. Although born in England, she was reared in the backwoods of Michigan, whither her parents had emigrated when she was only four years old. At fifteen, despite her many handicaps, she had acquired sufficient education to become a teacher. Even before entering on a college course, she had been licensed as a preacher by the Methodist Episcopal Church in her locality.

While a student in the theological department of Boston University, she was pastor of the Methodist Church at Hingham, Mass. Her next pastorate, in which she served seven years, was at East Dennis, Mass. There she preached at both the Methodist and Congregational churches.

Although the Methodist Episcopal Church readily licensed her as a local preacher, she met with a refusal because of her sex when she applied for ordination as a minister in that body. It was then that she applied to, and was ordained by, the Methodist Protestant Church.

In the summer of 1911, Miss Shaw's attempt to preach in Norway, as she had already preached in Sweden, met with a rebuff that was heralded around Christendom. Miss Shaw has herself given an account of the episode. It was published in the Utica *Saturday Globe* in September of that year.

Being in Norway as a delegate to the Women's International Convention, she had promised the women of Christiania, the Norwegian capital, to deliver a lecture in that city. Shortly before the date set for the lecture, the women of Christiania learned that she was to preach in the Gustav Vasa Church, the state church of Stockholm, the Swedish capital, and they forthwith determined to have her preach in the state church in Christiania also. They applied to the minister of the state church, but he declined to grant permission—basing his refusal on the Norwegian law which makes women ineligible for office in the army, the navy, or the church. The women appealed from the decision to the Council of Ministers of State. By a vote of three to four they decided adversely to Miss Shaw, but she had the satisfaction, as she says, of having the vote of the premier in her favor.

Prescription. Possibly the oldest prescription that has survived the ravages of time, certainly the oldest preserved in America, is in the New York Metropolitan Museum of Art. It is written in the cursive hieratic characters of ancient Egypt, current in 1600–1500 B.C., on both sides of an " ostracon "—*i.e.*, a piece of limestone carefully smoothed for the purpose. The stone measures 3½ by 3 inches in its present somewhat injured condition. The writing was done with a brush and some sort of ink or paint. It is still quite plain, save near the edges of the stone, where fragmentation has occurred. Max Müller, when he visited the United States, first recognized its medical character, and translated it, though not with entire success. An effort was then made to trace its origin, but the specimen had come with a number of other antique finds gathered from various portions of Egypt, and its exact provenience, to use the archæological term, could not be determined.

"The prescription as written seems to be a copy, because portions that in the ordinary medical writings of the time are abbreviated are here written out completely, just as copies of prescriptions written out by druggists to-day have the abbreviations enlarged. The ingredients called for in the prescription are mainly precious stones. These were to be ground up to be used for fumigation. Prof. Von Oefele, an authority on ancient Egyptian medicine, suspects that the case was one of hysteria, though there is no indication of this on the prescription itself.

"Ground precious stones were favorite remedies for hysterical manifestations. They were used for fumigation whenever the ball in the throat, our globus hystericus, was a prominent symptom.

"Indications on the prescription show that various classes of precious and semi-precious stones were used for patients of differing degrees of wealth. For the very wealthy a valuable stone like sapphire was used. For those of moderate wealth a more modest stone would do. For the poor, malachite, which was rather common, sufficed."—*Journal of the American Medical Association,* June, 1911.

Presidents, Some Semi-mythical. The Philadelphia *Times,* in September, 1910, quoted from Senator Dolliver the most remarkable experience he ever underwent in making a speech. "A statue was to be dedicated to the first President of the United States. Know his name? No, not George Washington. He wasn't the first President of the United States. The first man who ever held that title was named Hanson—first President of the First Congress of the Confederation. His title was President of the United States.

"I delved around in the books and worked up some of what I thought were mighty interesting historical data. On the appointed day I marched into the Senate chamber, and there were eleven pages and three Senators there. Two of the Senators, like myself, were to make speeches. The two other Senators made their speeches. Being my seniors, they came ahead of me.

43

Each when he had finished promptly walked out. When I came on, my audience consisted of Senator Hoar, the pages, the presiding officer, and a fair gallery. I got up and commenced, very much discouraged. Senator Hoar was deeply interested. He followed me closely. Presently he moved up closer to me and began taking notes. He proved as good an audience as a full Senate, and I turned myself loose to entertain him. He became so interested that he would occasionally drop remarks, such as, ' Remarkable, really. Where did you get that?' and the like. I thought I was making a great hit with the veteran and was immensely pleased. When I finished I thanked him for his attention and interest, and he replied: ' Not at all, Senator. I was much interested because I have to make an historic speech myself shortly and I wanted to get notes on those researches of yours. ' "

John Hanson (1715–1786) in fact did serve one year as president of the Continental Congress, from November 5, 1781.

According to a popular belief, Gen. Zachary Taylor was not sworn into office till Monday, March 5, 1849. David R. Atchison, then Senator pro tem. from Missouri, was president of the Senate, and in this sense was the acting President from noon on March 4 till noon on March 5.

Suffragettes may be pleased to know that, according to the *Christian Union* (September, 1911), one American woman, Mrs. Margaret W. Young, has been many times President of the United States pro tem. under both Mr. Taft and Mr. Roosevelt. " She holds a unique position in the Government employ which requires her to affix the signature of the President to important papers (land patents) that frequently represent great money value. She is authorized by Congress to do this and has done it for three years. She signed ' Theodore Roosevelt ' to over 90,000 land patents, placing under that name her own, thus ' per Margaret W. Young.' She has signed an even larger number with the name ' Wm. H. Taft.' Her handwriting is distinctly feminine."

Prevention of Cruelty. In England the Royal Society for the Prevention of Cruelty to Animals was founded in 1824, with the purpose of securing and enforcing legislation wherein the common law was strangely deficient. That law took no cognizance of any injustice or cruelty to dumb beasts *per se,* though it extended a measure of protection to them as private property and forbade any torture that might become a public nuisance.

The new society secured the passage of several acts, which were amended and consolidated in the Cruelty to Animals Acts of 1849 and 1854; these and the Wild Animals in Captivity Protection Act of 1900 are the main acts upon the subject.

England having led the way, Germany, France, and the United States followed, in chronological order. The first American society was chartered by the Legislature of New York in 1866, chiefly through the efforts of that amiable and picturesque character Henry Bergh (1823–1888).

Born in New York and educated at Columbia College, he was secretary of legation at St. Petersburg and vice-consul (1862–64), but resigned, owing to the severity of the climate. His previous travels in European countries had confirmed the horror first awakened in his own country at the suffering which dumb animals endured from human cruelty and indifference. In Russia he found that his official position inspired awe among the lower classes, especially as his footmen wore the gold lace that distinguished members of the diplomatic corps. Interfering in behalf of a donkey one day, he was agreeably surprised to find how this adventitious dignity aided him both with the owner and the crowd.

" At last," he said, " I've found a way to utilize my gold lace, and about the best use that can be made of it."

So, with his coachman as executive officer, he formed a society of two for the protection of dumb animals. During his daily drives, if Mr. Bergh saw an animal mistreated, he would order his coachman to take the human brute into a side street and overawe him with Russian billingsgate. Even before he left Russia, he had made up his mind to devote the remainder of his life to the interests of dumb animals. On his way home he stopped in London to confer with Dudley Rider, Earl of Harrowby, President of the English society. Landing in New York in 1864, he spent a year in maturing his plans. He prepared a paper proclaiming the duty of protecting animals from cruelty, and secured the signatures of seventy prominent New Yorkers, including Horace Greeley, George Bancroft, Peter Cooper, John Jacob Astor, and Alexander Stewart. This document now hangs on the walls of the New York Society rooms. In April, 1866, the society received its charter from the State legislature. Henry Bergh was elected president and George Bancroft vice-president. The president wound up a brief address with these words:

" This, gentlemen, is the verdict you have this day rendered, that the blood-red hand of cruelty shall no longer torture dumb beasts with impunity."

The very next day he made his first arrest. From the top of an omnibus he spied a butcher's wagon cruelly overloaded with live sheep and calves. He took the butcher before a magistrate. New York justice, however, was not yet prepared to act, and the case was smilingly dismissed. Early in May Mr. Bergh succeeded in having a Brooklyn butcher fined. Other arrests in New York followed and resulted in occasional conviction. The precedent had at length been established. Late in May a public sensation was raised by Mr. Bergh's next move. His attention was caught by a schooner that had just arrived from the Florida coast with a cargo of live turtles. As was the custom, their flippers had been pierced and tied with strings, and they had made the passage on their backs. Mr. Bergh arrested captain and crew for cruelty to animals, and marched them, all broadly smiling, to court. Their amusement was shared by the judge, who dismissed the case, on the ground that the suffering from boring holes in turtles' fins was no greater than that endured by human beings from a mosquito bite.

The New York *Herald*—inclined at first to poke fun at the society and at Mr. Bergh as the " Moses of the movement "—brought out a satire on the turtle episode, purporting to be a report of a mass meeting of animals at Union Square, with Mr. Bergh in the chair. Every animal was made to express its convictions on the subject, the whole tone being that of good-humored raillery. Within forty-eight hours Mr. Bergh and his society had engaged the attention of half a million people. From that day the cause moved steadily on, Mr. James Gordon Bennett himself helping it on with a money contribution.

Mr. Bergh's wife, who had ever been his chief encouragement, once said, when there was no further need of concealing a noble weakness, that her husband had many a night come home so burdened with injury and disappointment that he would go upstairs to his room and have " a jolly good cry." Yet the next morning always found him going forth with new courage to face the rebuffs of another day. To the superintendent of police he wrote, on deep provocation, " I claim a right not only to the assistance of your officers, but also especially to exemption from contempt and insult." At another time he wrote, " Two or three years of ridicule and abuse have thickened the epidermis of my sensibilities, and I have acquired the habit of doing the thing I think right, regardless of public clamor."

In 1871 Louis Bonard, a native of France who had made a fortune by trading with the Indians and investing the proceeds in New York real estate, bequeathed $150,000 to the society, and the society moved from a little upstairs room at Broadway and Fourth Street to a building they built for themselves at the corner of Fourth Avenue and Twenty-second Street. In this building, since enlarged and improved, they still remain.

In 1874 Mr. Bergh rescued two little children from inhuman women, an action that led to the founding of a kindred Society for the Prevention of Cruelty to Children, which took up its quarters in the same building. The president of this Society was Elbridge Gerry, legal counsel for the S. P. C. A.

An article by C. C. Buel in *Scribner's Magazine* (now the *Century*) thus characterizes the reformer's life and work as it had shaped itself in 1879:

"Thirteen years of devoted labor have brought no very great change in the appearance and manner of Henry Bergh. If the lines in his careworn face have multiplied, they have also responded to the kindly influence of public sympathy and the release of his genial disposition from austere restraint. Since Horace Greeley's death, no figure more familiar to the public has walked the streets of the metropolis. Almost every fourth person knows him by sight, and the whisper 'That's Henry Bergh' follows him, like a tardy herald, whever he goes. Parents stop and point out to their children 'the man who is kind to the dumb animals.' Many enthusiastic men and women address themselves to him, often saying, 'You don't know me, Mr. Bergh, but I know you, and want to grasp your hand and tell how much I am in sympathy with your work.' He courteously offers his hand and his thanks, says a pleasant word freighted with quiet humor or common sense,—for he is a quick and ready conversationalist,—and bows himself on his way. When he sees an omnibus driver in a passion with his horses, he raises his cane, and the alert eye of the Jehu, dropping on a familiar figure, knows at once with whom he has to deal. If he sees a disabled or overloaded horse, he stops the vehicle and lets his judgment decide whether the lame animal shall be sent to the stable or the load reduced. Frequently the driver is willing to argue the question, but not so often now as formerly.

"Moral suasion and a resolute bearing are Mr. Bergh's most potent auxiliaries. Only rarely has he been forced to use his muscular strength to defend himself. One winter's day he met two large men comfortably seated on a ton of coal, with one horse straining to drag the cart through the snow. He ordered them to get down, and after an altercation pulled them down. At another time he stood at the southwest corner of Washington Square inspecting the horses of the Seventh Avenue Railroad. Several weak and lame horses were ordered to be sent to the stables and a blockade of overloaded cars soon ensued. A loafer on a car platform, annoyed at the delay, began to curse Mr. Bergh, who stood on the curbstone three feet distant, turning a deaf ear till the spectators began to urge the bully on. Then, losing his patience, he seized the reins and suspended the movement of the car until the order was complied with."

Mr. Buel quotes this as one of Bergh's curbstone speeches, often used with telling effect:

"Now, gentlemen, consider that you are American citizens living in a republic. You make your own laws; no despot makes them for you. And I appeal to your sense of justice and your patriotism, oughtn't you to respect what you yourselves have made?"

The degree of authority which Henry Bergh had conquered for himself in his later days is sufficiently indicated by this final anecdote from Mr. Buel's collection:

Once Mr. Bergh had ordered the ignorant foreman of a gang of gas-pipe layers to fill up one-half of a trench they had dug directly across crowded Greenwich Street, even under the railway track. The man gave a surly refusal, which would have caused his arrest had not a stranger stepped out of the crowd and said:

"Mike, you'd better do what that man tells you, for he's the law and the gospel in this city."

"The law and the gospel is it, then?" replied Mike, surveying Mr. Bergh from head to foot. "Well, he don't look it."

"No matter, but he is," enforced the other; "and if you can take a friend's advice, you will fill up that trench."

And the trench was filled.

Printer's Devil. From its very beginning the art of printing (*q. v.*) had been popularly associated with the evil one. So early as 1450 John Fust, or Faust, of Mentz, had been accused of using magic in the production of his books. At the beginning of the sixteenth century Aldus Manutius, founder of the famous Aldine presses, had in his employ a negro boy brought into Venice by a merchant-vessel. The unlearned, predisposed to look upon the printer's art as an emanation from the devil, and excited by the unfamiliar aspect of the young African, spread the report that he was an imp from the abode of darkness. A mob assembled. To quiet the uproar, Aldus exhibited the boy in public and made this proclamation in church:

"I, Aldus Manutius, printer to the Holy Church and to the Doge, have this day made public exposure of the printer's devil. All who think he is not flesh and blood may come and pinch him."

In England the term seems to have had an independent origin. Moxon tells us that in former times the duty of the printer's devil was to stand by the tympan on which the blank sheets of paper were spread, and take them from the frame as fast as they were printed; and he adds that, in consequence of their handling the fresh ink so constantly, "they do commonly so black and bedaub themselves that the workmen do jocosely call them devils."

Printer's slang seemed to combine the extremes of good and evil. From the circumstance that Caxton's printing-press was set up in the Scriptorium of Westminster Abbey, the association with that place led the apprentices to designate black smears made by too much ink on the sheet, "monks," while a space unintentionally left blank was known as a "friar." Thus the good fathers were forced to keep company with the evil one without any volition of their own.

The printer's devil was not always a boy. Boswell preserves a dialogue between Dr. Johnson and Sir Joshua Reynolds. Johnson told how a certain reputable author had married a printer's devil, at which Sir Joshua Reynolds exclaimed, "A printer's devil, sir! why, I thought a printer's devil was a creature with a black face and in rags." "Yes, sir," replied Johnson, "but I suppose he had her face washed and put clean clothes on her." In this account, neither Sir Joshua nor Johnson nor any of the large company present expressed any surprise at the existence of a female printer's devil. There are other reasons to suppose that women were not infrequently employed to assist in the work of printing. Stock, in his "Life of Dr. Beddoes," speaks of a woman's nimble and delicate fingers as being particularly well adapted to the office of compositor.

Printing. There can be no greater mistake than to think that the invention of the printing-press first made it possible to multiply copies of a book with rapidity and at a moderate price. On the contrary, numerous references in Roman writers of the Augustan era leave no doubt that books were then manufactured with a speed, sold at a cheapness, purchased with an avidity, and circulated throughout the whole Roman world to an extent almost incredible. Enter in imagination one of the large halls of a Roman publisher, and you find probably not fewer than a hundred slaves at work. They have all been carefully trained for the purpose. They write a swift clear hand; and while one dictates a hundred copies are springing at once into existence for the great public. No sooner are the copies written than they are passed on to other workmen ready to receive them; and, with a speed not less astonishing than that with which they have been written, are revised, corrected, rolled up, bound, titled, and when thought desirable adorned for the market. Add the further fact that the workmen, being slaves, require only maintenance from their masters, and you will better be prepared to accept what seems the well-established though remarkable result.—that a single bookselling firm at Rome could produce without difficulty, in a day of ten working hours, an edition of the second book of Martial consisting of a thousand copies, and that a somewhat similar work plainly bound, if sold for six-pence, left the bookseller a profit of one hundred per cent.

Printing-Press, Steam. On the 28th of November, 1814, the London *Times* introduced steam-press printing to the indus-trial world. In a leading article of the day the great event is referred to in the following terms:

"Our journal of this day presents to the public the practical result of the greatest improvement connected with printing since the discovery of the art itself. The reader of this paragraph now holds in his hands one of the many thousand impressions of the *Times* newspaper which were taken off last night by a mechanical apparatus. A system of machinery, almost organic, has been devised and arranged which, while it relieves the human frame of its laborious efforts in printing, far exceeds human power in rapidity and despatch."

The article goes on to explain in more or less detail the process of the new machine, the work of the compositor, the supply of paper, the distribution of ink, the 1100 sheets im-pressed in an hour, "which several operations leave little for man to do but watch the unconscious agent in its operations." With becoming modesty the writer of the article goes on to say that the *Times* only takes credit for the application of the dis-covery. The patentees of the new machine approached them and they adopted the invention.

As to the inventor, his work is compared to the noblest monu-ment of Sir Christopher Wren—St. Paul's Cathedral. We are told that he was a Saxon by birth, by name König, who developed his wonderful invention, assisted by his "friend and country-man Bauer."

The hand-press workmen violently opposed the innovation. They said that it made one workman accomplish the work of three or four; therefore, they argued, it must throw three or four out of employment. They tried to break up the new presses, and their resort to violence was not without popular backing. The conflict was bitter; in the end the proprietors of the paper conquered, and the steam-press became an established factor in the printing business. The *Times,* from a circulation of a few thousand (its circulation was 1000 in 1803), rose in a few years to the position of the leading paper of the world. The hand-press disappeared. The steam-press became of universal use. Hundreds of printers found employment where one had made a scanty living in the old days, and civilization took one of its longest steps forward.

Very soon the new machine gave place to another with vast improvements, invented by Applegarth and Cowper, and later still to another, even more ingenious, the work of one Hoe, which has given place to the modern printing-press.

Prize-Fights. Among all the ancient precursors of the modern prize-fight the first that found its way into literature was one which formed the leading feature in the games celebrated at the funeral of Patroclus during the siege of Troy. The contestants were Epeius, son of Panopeus, and Euryalus, son of Mecistus. Homer has reported the contest in considerable detail in " The Iliad," Book xxiii.

In the last run after some infighting to the music of cracking jaws and clashing gauntlets, Epeius lands a mighty blow upon the cheek of Euryalus and knocks him senseless, so that he lies floundering on earth—

> But brave Epeius took him by the hand,
> And raised him up;

thereby showing courtesy and generosity to a fallen foe, practices which we shall see to have been repeated in modern days.

In the olden time fists and wrists were armed with leather straps which strengthened arm and forearm, a practice by no means to be commended, as the blows were in consequence more dangerous than those from the naked fist. Nevertheless the *cœstus* was used at the Olympian games in Greece and at the more brutal contests in the Roman amphitheatre.

There is not much known about English boxing before the time of George I, when a French traveller records the extraordinary fascination which anything in the shape of a fight possessed for the English people. Even if two small boys quarrel in the street, a ring is at once formed, order and fair play being observed. Out from the mists of legend there looms up at this time the figure of the valiant Jim Figg, who used to frequent fairs and exhibit his science with various weapons, the foil, the backsword, and the cudgel, as well as with the naked fist. Figg is the first recorded champion of England, and is known to historians of the ring as the Father of Pugilism. He assumed the title of champion in 1719, when he opened an amphitheatre in Tottenham Court Road, London. Here he advertised to teach the art of self-defence scientifically, and was noted for his ability to "stop and parry." But at the best, boxing in his time seems to have been a matter of give and take. Figg died in 1734. Jack Broughton, who succeeded him as champion, is looked upon as the real founder of the art of self-defence. In 1743 he drew up a code of rules, modifying the old-time well-nigh murderous contests, and this code ruled the London prize-ring until 1838, when it was superseded in the Marquis of Queensbury rules.

Broughton was defeated for the championship on April 10, 1750, by Jack Slack, the Norfolk butcher. In the tenth round Slack made a sudden spring and planted right and left in quick succession full and fair between Broughton's eyes. . . . He seemed suddenly struck blind, and groped his way about the ring in such a feeble way that the Duke of Cumberland, who had laid £10,000 upon him, cried out anxiously, "Why, Broughton, what's the matter with you? Why, take a rest, man!"

But though the veteran went to his corner and rested, it did him no good. He was worse than ever when he stood up again; he didn't seem to know where his adversary was, and let Slack strike him twice without making any attempt to return the blows.

"Why, damme, Broughton," yelled the Duke of Cumberland; "you're beat, man! What are you about, man? Don't lose the fight!" To which Broughton shouted back, "I'm not beat, your Royal Highness; but I can't see my man! I'm blind, but I'm not beat! Only let me see my man, and I'll win yet!"

But he couldn't see his man, and was led away, and John Slack was proclaimed champion of England. That was Broughton's last fight, and the duke was vastly annoyed at the loss of his £10,000. But in the end he forgave his old favorite and left him an annuity.

Jack Slack, who thus suddenly rose from the novice class to the championship, proved to be the possessor of such a solid punch that a smashing blow became known as "a slack 'un" over half of England. For ten years his right arm held him his laurels; but Slack was defeated by Bill Stevens, the Nailer, in London, June, 1760.

Stevens had defeated a muscular coal-heaver named Jacob Taplin, in a very close bout just before he won the title, and he was undoubtedly a remarkable fighter. However, Stevens seems to have been the first prominent pugilist to "throw a fight." He was paid to lose to George Meggs, a collier of Bristol. The fraud was so open that the title of champion was withdrawn from both victor and vanquished.

A dyer named Bill Darts defeated some good men in Surrey shortly after this affair, and finally challenged all comers to deny him the championship. He held the title for an unbeaten five years, and then lost it to a waterman by Kingston-upon-Thames named Lyons. Strange as it may seem, Lyons was never in any more fights after defeating the champion. That fight was in 1769.

Darts sold his next fight, losing to Peter Corcoran of Ireland, who then claimed the championship. Corcoran was severely punished by Harry Sellers, who became recognized champion in 1776.

At this time a corn porter on the London wharves, Tom Johnson, became known as a fighter, showing speed, strength, and remarkable ring generalship. Sellers died and Johnson worked his way to the championship after a rapid series of victories. Steadily and with ease this popular pugilistic idol defeated every type of fighter brought against him. His most remarkable contest was against a Birmingham giant, Isaac Perrins, a man of gigantic proportions and a good boxer. Johnson was light for a heavy-weight of those days, but he knocked out Perrins after sixty-two rounds of hard fighting. He lost his championship to Benjamin Brain at Wrotham, in Kent, on January 17, 1791. Johnson was knocked down in the first round and lost his usual coolness. During the slugging match which followed Brain punished the champion severely and won the fight in twenty-one minutes. Brain died undefeated in 1794.

Daniel Mendoza, the first Jew pugilist in England, claimed the vacant championship on his record. In 1784 he had easily defeated a big fighter called Harry the Coal Heaver. In 1787 he had fought a series of fights with another star, Richard Humphries, winning two out of three. In 1791 he knocked out Bill Warr in the twenty-third round, after a game up-hill fight. Though only 5 feet 7 inches high, he was one of the most brilliant fighters known to pugilistic history. He hit often and his blows made up in rapidity what they lacked in force. In 1794, when Mendoza assumed the championship, he met Warr again, and once more proved his superiority in a contest lasting only 15 minutes.

On April 15, 1795, Mendoza lost the championship to John Jackson, who defeated him in ten minutes.

John Jackson was not only noted after this as a prize-fighter, but he began to enter various athletic competitions and was one of the champion jumpers and runners of England. Jackson retired from active pugilism after three bouts and opened a gymnasium. Lord Byron was one of his pupils.

The next man of note in the English prize-ring was Jem Belcher, a butcher of Bristol. At the age of 17 years he easily defeated one of the " ould 'uns," a man named Britton, and he was at once matched with successive second-raters, winning all his bouts. He then fought a grudge bout with one of the best men of the time, Joseph Berks, and defeated him in fourteen rounds. Belcher was hardly bruised at the close, but Berks was driven away in a coach, cut and blinded.

Belcher met with an accident while playing racquets on July

24, 1803. The ball struck him with such violence as literally to knock one of his eyeballs from the socket. This had such a depressing effect upon Belcher that he announced his retirement from the ring. He later returned, but never fought the same again. He lost to Hen Pearce, known as the Game Chicken, and was twice beaten by Tom Cribb. He was only 30 at the time of his death. His brother Tom was also champion of England at one time.

Berks claimed the championship after Belcher's forced retirement, and was immediately matched with Henry Pearce. Before the match Berks was defeated by Pearce in an impromptu night battle. They met in the ring on January 23, 1804, and Berks rushed the clever " Game Chicken," who severely punished and stopped him after one hour and seventeen minutes of fighting. Pearce's hardest fight was against a young man, John Gully, destined to win fame elsewhere than in the ring. They fought for over an hour before Gully was defeated, and both were so severely punished that they could hardly stand at the close.

When Pearce's broken health forced his retirement in 1805, Gully as the next best man in the ring assumed the title.

John Gully was the son of very poor parents and first saw the light at Bristol in the year 1783. At the age of twenty he cherished three ambitions,—to win the championship of the prizering, to own a Derby winner, and to obtain a seat in Parliament.

Gully had no real hankering after the life of a prize-fighter, but he wanted the championship, and his ambition was fulfilled. The English title then carried the world's championship. Gully held the emblematic belt and the cup for a few years, but in 1808 he turned both over to Tom Cribb, saying he was through with the squared circle forever. All this time he was possessed of a passion for racing and was the most constant visitor at the big race meets, where his keen methods of calculation in betting were well known.

Gully acquired a Derby winner by purchase in 1827. This was Mameluke, who had carried off the prize a year previous. Gully lost $150,000 on the horse that year, though Mameluke missed the St. Leger only by a fluke. As a four-year-old, however, Mameluke won back for Gully all he had lost. In 1832 Gully legitimately achieved the second object of his ambition by winning the Derby with St. Giles. That same year another of his horses, Margrave, won the St. Leger. In 1846 he not only repeated his Derby victory with Pyrrhus, but also won the Oaks with Mendicant. No owner up to that time had ever scored double firsts at Epsom.

In 1832 Gully ran for Parliament. He was opposed by Lord

Mexborough for the Pontefract seat, and the contest was fought out bitterly. Gully's rival used the fact that he was once a prize-fighter against him, and repetitiously "wanted to know" if the constituents cared to be represented by a man of that class. Evidently they did, for they elected Gully and he did very well at Westminster.

When the result was announced Gilbert A'Becket said, " Should any opposition be manifested in the House of Commons towards Mr. Gully, it is very probably the *noes* [*nose*] will have it."

In those days and in England this was thought to be a very good joke. It was always printed as above with the explanatory word in brackets.

As a country gentleman with his seat at Marwell Hall near Winchester, Mr. Gully lived a respectable and dignified life until his death at the age of 80 in 1863. His five sons and five daughters were received by the best local society. The young women all made good matches. The sons were successful in various lines of business. A grandson, William Gully, who followed in the ex-pugilist's footsteps as a legislator, was Speaker of the House of Commons.

The title then shifted through a number of equally matched claimants until Thomas Cribb secured a place among the first in pugilistic history. He entered the prize-ring in 1805, appearing against a veteran, George Maddock, who was then in his 50th year. In the 60th round Maddock's friends, perceiving that their man was becoming exhausted, started a row, and his seconds led him away, declaring it a drawn battle. Cribb demanded the purse and a free-for-all fight ensued. Cribb was hit over the head and cut. Cribb then agreed to let Maddock renew the battle. They fought 16 rounds more, when Maddock finally gave in. Cribb participated in several other battles with success, one of his victims being Bill Richmond, an American negro.

Shortly afterward another American negro, Tom Molineaux, nearly won the heavy-weight championship. Cribb had heard of Molineaux, who was a man of remarkable strength, cleverness, and confidence, but the Englishman underestimated the negro. When the two were matched there was a great deal of excitement in sporting circles. Cribb won in a driving rain but he discovered that the negro was a powerful antagonist. A second match was made, and Molineaux was knocked out completely and his jaw fractured by the final blow. It is said that in the twenty-eighth round of the first bout the negro knocked out Cribb, but one of the Englishman's seconds tricked the referee on time, and Cribb recovered, while the negro became chilled in the rain and lost in the end. Tom Cribb had no trouble with his title after this until he retired from the ring.

On the day of Cribb's retirement Tom Spring took the title and announced himself ready to defend it. He fought a long sensational fight against Bill Neat, a stronger man, and defeated him with cool courage and science. Jack Langan, a dashing fighter from Ireland, was knocked out by Spring after two hours and twenty-nine minutes of fighting.

When Spring resigned his title in 1825, the next champion on the list was Jem Ward, who in his turn retired in 1838.

Deaf Burke claimed the championship. His title was disputed by William Thompson, otherwise known as Bendigo. In 1839 the latter defeated Deaf Burke in a remarkable bout and Jem Ward presented the winner with a belt.

Bendigo was a remarkable character. He came from a highly respectable family in Nottingham. Some of them were Episcopal ministers. How he himself gained his nickname is disputed. One explanation was to the effect that it was his habit to bend as he went into fight, hence " Bend-I-go." Another was that he and his two brothers were irreverently given the Scriptural names of Shadrach, Meshack and Abednego. The last, the name of the fighter, was corrupted into Bendigo. Bendigo went about the country giving exhibitions of strength and agility. He possessed a natural sense of humor and was a sort of a clown in the boxing ring. He fought three battles with Ben Caunt and was victorious in two.

Bendigo, upon his retirement from the ring, became a preacher. He died in 1880, death resulting from an accidental fall down stairs at his home.

A man named Tass Parker took the nominal championship after Bendigo's retirement. The next claimant was William Perry, the Tipton Slasher, so called from the section of England whence he hailed. He was an ungainly pugilist, but could use his fists with formidable effect. He lost his championship to Harry Broome on a foul in 1851, and Broome upheld the honor until 1853, when he forfeited a return match with the Tipton Slasher, and retired from the ring. The Tipton Slasher again claimed the championship and was defeated by Tom Sayers in 1857.

Tom Sayers was one of the great men of the ring. He was small for a heavy-weight, but an ideal fighter of grit, speed, and remarkable recuperative powers. In 1856 he had won a great victory over Harry Poulson, which went 109 rounds and lasted 3 hours and 8 minutes. Poulson far outweighed Sayers, but the latter outclassed him as a fighter. Sayers had designs on the championship from this time forward. February 19, 1857, he met Aaron Jones, the battle resulting in a draw after 12 rounds. The men fought again not long afterward, and Sayers won in the 85th round. He then challenged the Tipton Slasher, who claimed the championship belt.

This was the first time that a middle-weight ever had the audacity to challenge for the championship, and the fight excited the keenest interest all over England. The Slasher stood four inches over Sayers and weighed about 45 pounds more than the plucky little middle-weight. The two came together June 16, 1857. Sayers adminstered a beating to his ponderous opponent in 10 rounds, thereby winning the championship of England.

Tom Paddock, a well-known and very game pugilist, who was at his best in the fifties, was anxious to fight Sayers for the championship. He fell ill, however, and had to go to a hospital where his poverty prevented him from getting any luxuries. Sayers, hearing this, visited him, and, though himself far from rich, gave him £5. On recovery, Paddock renewed his application to fight, but, being unable to raise the full stake of £200, begged that £50 might be waived, which was at once done, and the fight came off on June 16, 1858. In the last round Sayers delivered a severe blow with his left, and had drawn back his right hand to finish the fight, but noticing his adversary's condition he controlled the impulse to strike, offered his hand in friendship, and led Paddock to his seconds, who very properly threw up the sponge.

Until the year 1859 England had a monopoly of the prize-fighting game. The champion of England had always been looked upon as the champion of the world. America had indeed sent a few fighters across the Atlantic to do battle in England, but they were, on the whole, of an inferior grade. Yankee fighters were looked upon as of poor quality abroad. They were despised as rough-and-tumble artists, who knew more of biting, kicking, and gouging than they did of the scientific art of boxing as it was practised in England. Along in the latter part of the '50s, however, the prowess of American fighters began to be noised about on the other side of the Atlantic. Word came that the young giant beyond the sea was to send one of her sons over to England to contest for the world's championship title. Negotiations were opened between prominent sporting men on both sides, with the result that a splendid product of American manhood, John C. Heenan, who hailed from Benicia, Cal., and who was known as the Benicia boy, was chosen to uphold the prestige of the Stars and Stripes. Heenan had been defeated in 1858 by John Morrissey, but, as the latter was not a native American, having been born in Ireland, Heenan was put forward as the best man who could logically represent his country in a fight abroad. Heenan was in poor condition when defeated by Morrissey, and had had little experience as a ringster, but under the guidance of Aaron Jones, a former English fighter who had established a school of boxing in New York, he made wonderful strides in the fistic art. Heenan looked the ideal fighter. He stood six feet one inch in height and his fighting weight was about 190 pounds. He was powerfully built and splendidly proportioned. He had a phenomenal reach, and his manner of driving in his blows filled his admirers with joy.

The battle waged fiercely up to the 32d round, Heenan forcing Sayers down several times, though the latter fought pluckily. The Englishman was pretty well exhausted when they came up for the 36th round, while Heenan's face showed the effects of Sayers's blows. In this round a cry went up that the police were coming. A body of bluecoats had spread out and was moving toward the ring. The spectators tried to hold them off, but they kept advancing. Meanwhile Sayers had gone down, badly exhausted.

When time was called for the 37th round, everything was confusion about the ring. A crowd of shouting, struggling spectators crowded in about the barriers. The referee and other officials were swept one side. Sayers and Heenan kept on fighting during the uproar. The American grappled with his adversary and they both fell against the ropes. The referee at this stage declared that the battle was off and left the grounds. In the midst of the excitement the ropes were lowered and a madly excited crowd swept into the ring. The fight was supposed to have closed now, but five more rounds, or rather, scrimmages, were fought before the police could force their way in through the crowd around the combatants. In one of these Heenan, driven to desperation by the mob which surrounded him, attacked Sayers's attendants. This was nothing more than an effort to get elbow-room, but it created much feeling at the time.

Finally the referee returned and once more ordered the men to cease hostilities. Heenan showed that he was still in fine physical shape by jumping the ropes and running nearly all of the way to the railroad station. He was plainly in far better shape than Sayers, who was about done for at the end. The Americans hailed the fight as a great victory for the Benicia boy, and claimed that the crowd broke into the ring to save the Englishman when inevitable defeat stared him in the face. The referee later decided the battle a draw, and belts were given to each man, fac-similes of the original championship belt, the money being raised by popular subscription. The contest lasted 2 hours and 20 minutes. Thus ended the great international battle.

Tom Sayers retired from the ring, leaving his championship belt for competition.

The belt went to Sam Hurst in 1860; but in the following year Jem Mace defeated Hurst. Mace then fought two bouts with Tom King, losing the second; but, since King refused a third match, Mace again claimed the title.

Jem Mace is one of the most interesting figures in ring history. He was a violinist and a gypsy by taste, but became a boxer at fairs. His sensitive and imaginative nature made him seem a coward in early fights; but he fought his way to a place among the first pugilists of the time. From 1862, when he defeated Tom King in a gruelling fight, until 1872, when he fought a draw with J. Coburn in this country, he was either champion or claimant.

Joe Wormald had the belt for defeating Marsden in 1865; but Wormald forfeited to Mace. Mace and Joe Goss fought a draw in 1866, both claiming the title. Joe Wormald claimed the championship in 1867, and the same year Jem Mace and E. Baldwin fought a draw for the title in this country. Wormald and Baldwin also drew in America, and McCook and T. Allen fought here for the championship. Jem Mace finally secured the undisputed title when he defeated T. Allen in America in 1870. J. Coburn drew with Mace during the next year.

By his first wife Jem Mace had a son who became noted as an itinerant preacher. It so happened once that, while Jem was giving a boxing exhibition in the upper hall of a public building at Brighton, England, his son was preaching in the lower part of the same house. A mutual friend ran hastily up stairs to inform the old fighter that, while he was punching all comers above, his son was trying to save sinners below. The elder Mace laughed at the coincidence and replied:

"You know the Mace family are all great show people, only they're not all in the same line. Tell the boy I'd like to see 'im when 'is show is over!"

The next great champion found in the annals of pugilism is Paddy Ryan, born in Tipperary, Ireland. After him began the line of Irish-American champions, and the American championship itself.

John L. Sullivan defeated Ryan in a Berserker fight at Mississippi City in 1882, in nine rounds. In 1889 John L. Sullivan defeated Jake Kilrain, who had worked his way to the English title by drawing with Jem Smith.

Sullivan's downfall is thus recorded by one of his admirers.

" You all remember the sad fate of John L. Sullivan when he went up against Jim Corbett in 1892. Sullivan for 10 years held the championship of America against all comers and considered himself invincible. He had gone into the ring so often when hog fat and out of trim that he thought he could get away with Corbett without much training. In fact, his work at Canoe Place Inn down on Long Island was a perfect farce. He simply laid off there and guzzled bottle after bottle of ale, right under the nose of his patient trainer, Phil Casey, the hand-ball champion. When Sullivan's closest friends suggested a little real training, he sat back and declared that Corbett was such a pipe he didn't have to be in first-class form to win in a few punches. The night before he left for New Orleans Sullivan was asked how long he expected the fight would last.

" ' Oh, it may go eight rounds, but no further,' replied John, who looked the picture of confidence. He was at fat as a prize ox and as slow as molasses. He had a pronounced paunch and was in no shape to fight a boy. Still, in his fat condition, all thought that Sullivan could win, as he had done so many times before under similar adverse conditions. We all know the result of the mill. Sullivan was too heavy and slow to get out of his own way. He never landed a solid blow in the 21 rounds. He became so tired that he couldn't hold up his arms in defence and finally went down in sections, Corbett continually raining blows on his jaw and body. Finally the big brewery horse dropped all in a heap, completely exhausted, but practically uninjured. As soon as he was counted out, he got up slowly and made a speech to the immense crowd at the ringside—an unusual thing for a defeated champion to do."

The Albany *Law Journal* thus gloated over Sullivan's defeat:

What a satire on human nature it is that the most celebrated man in this country for ten years has been a prize-fighter! Not a manly, generous athlete at that, but the type of vulgarity and degradation—a drunken, sodden, ignorant brute: a wife-beater: the terror of peaceable citizens; a great, hulking Goliath, who gained universal notoriety and three hundred thousand dollars (which he squandered in riotous debauchery) by terrifying and beating smaller men, and who on the first occasion when he met anything like an approach to his gigantic thews went down like a child and blubbered like a baby. Such was and is John L. Sullivan, a much greater celebrity in the estimation of the press and the public than the pure poet or the lofty political moralist. Probably neither of the latter earned in all his life so much money as this wretched fellow threw away in ten years: probably neither of them has left much more than the " gentleman " who trounced him netted for the hour's work of beating him. What a people we are, to have given more to the dethroned champion for ten minutes' exhibition of his phenomenal prowess than we pay to the chief justice for the labor of a year! What a people we are, at whose demand the press allots four times the space to news of a boxing contest between two gladiators, neither of whom could gain admittance into any decent society, not to say into any cultivated household in the land, than it bestows upon the immortal singing of the poet or the wise and elevated teachings of the political moralist! Even among the fair sex, we fear, Mr. Curtis, who was the very type of personal elegance, must have given place to "handsome gentleman Jim."

Prize-ring Receipts. A review of the amounts won by English and American pugilists from the beginnings of prize-ring history shows a steady remarkable growth. The very first contest of whose stakes we have a reliable record is that fought between Jack Broughton and Jack Slack in 1750 for £200, or $1000, a side. This was an enormous sum for those days. Slack never afterward fought for more than 100 guineas a side, or a little over $500.

It was 100 guineas that Slack lost, together with the championship of England, when he was defeated by Bill Stevens the Nailer.

The Nailer, as champion, met George Meggs of Bristol for $1000 a side in 1761, but he never was backed again, as he was known to have sold out to Meggs. Meggs fought twice with George Wilson, the first time for $500 and the second for $1000. Bill Darts, who flourished from 1764 to 1769, had several matches, including those with Tom Juchan, Tom Doggett, the West Country Bargeman, Tom Swansey, "Death" Oliver, one of Broughton's best pupils, Peter Corcoran, and Tom Lyons; but the stake was never more than $500 except in the match with Lyons, the Waterman, when it was $1000 a side. Darts, by the way, sold out to Corcoran for $500. Coming to the time of Tom Johnson, from 1787 to 1790, there are to be found statements that that champion was backed for $3000 against Mike Ryan, which he won, and against "Big Ben" Ryan for $5000, but Ryan forfeited. There is little to corroborate the assertion regarding the size of the stakes in those events. It is fairly safe to write them down as exaggerations. This is especially to be seen when it is known that when Johnson and Ben Ryan were afterward matched for $2500 a side, the amount was considered to be marvellously high.

Looking over the histories of Dan Mendoza, John Jackson, Jem Belcher, Henry Pearce, and John Gully, who were England's successive champions during the period between 1793 and 1805, there can be found mention of stakes as low as £20, but none above £200, with the exception of that in the match between Pearce and Belcher, which was 500 guineas a side. Tom Cribb, Molyneaux, and Tom Spring came along, and this carries us to

Jem Ward's time (1825), and we hear of no stake of more than
$1000 until the match between Ward and Cannon, when $2500
a side was posted. This contest created unusual excitement, we
are told, not only on account of the celebrity of the men, but
also because of "the large stakes." The great Bendigo had
many battles for from $50 to $1000 and two for more than the
latter sum. One was with Ben Caunt for $1000 a side, and the
other was for the same stakes against Tom Paddock. This brings
us to 1844 up to 1860, and thereafter $1000 a side appears to be
a more frequent thing, but Paddock and Ben Caunt, Harry
Broome, Bill Perry, the "Tipton Slasher," and Nat Langham,
who followed Paddock, each fought for $500 a side and less.

Now we come to Tom Sayers's time. The famous pugilist
engaged in many battles, more than have been chronicled, but
he never fought for more than $500 a side excepting four times,
and $250 was his whole prize more than once. The five excep-
tions alluded to were his contests with the "Tipton Slasher,"
Bill Benjamin (twice), and John C. Heenan, when the stakes
were $2000 a side, and one with Bob Brettle, when Sayers put up
$2000 to Brettle's $1000.

After Sayers's time the championship stakes became $1000 a
side, as a rule, for a time, and then began to grow, though
slowly. Jem Mace fought Tom Allen at Kennerville, near New
Orleans, for $5000, in 1870, though Mace and Joe Coburn fought
for only $2000 a year later, and Mace and Ned O'Baldwin were
matched for $2000. The latter match was prevented by the au-
thorities.

Tom Hyer and Yankee Sullivan were the first pair to fight
for as much as $5000 a side, and that prize was duplicated but
once before pugilists who are famous to-day became known.
That was in the match between Tom King and John C. Heenan.

In America there was a time when even the great Jack Demp-
sey did not refuse to fight for a couple of hundred dollars. John
L. Sullivan in his early career, when he was really at his best,
received only $50 for beating Steve Taylor at Harry Hill's old
sporting resort in 1881. The same year Sullivan got $750 for
knocking John Flood out in eight rounds in that memorable
fight on a barge in the Hudson river. Sullivan thought he was
the greatest man that ever lived when he flashed the coin around
town that night.

Compare these sums with the purse of $25,000 raised for the
last fight in which Sullivan engaged, when he was defeated by
J. J. Corbett. That was at New Orleans in 1892. This together
with a wager of $10,000 was considered enormous in those days.

When Johnson whipped Burns in Australia in the winter of 1909 for a $35,000 purse, of which Burns received $30,000, it is claimed the gross receipts were nearly $150,000, although Promoter McIntosh never gave out the official figures. Next to this affair the Corbett-McCoy fake fight in Madison Square Garden is supposed to have drawn the biggest gate money, but there is doubt even about that. While it is generally thought that $75,000 was taken in at the box offices, it is stated semi-officially that $57,000 was the real amount.

Before this affair, the largest purse ever fought for in this country was $69,715, the result of the first Gans-Nelson battle at Goldfield, Nevada. Jeffries and Sharkey fought for $67,000 at Coney Island, while Jeff and Fitzsimmons mixed it up for $63,000 at the same place. Corbett and Jeffries drew $62,340 in Frisco, a record for the Earthquake City, where other fights have drawn big money, as follows: Nelson-Britt (1905) $48,-311; Gans-Britt, $36,000; Britt-Young Corbett, $32,266; Jeffries-Fitzsimmons, $31,800; Jeffries-Ruhlin, $31,487; Britt-Nelson (1904), $26,900; Burns-Squires, $25,250; Johnson-Ketchel, $17,000; O'Brien-Fitzsimmons, $16,407; Young Corbett-Nelson (1904), $16,407; Young Corbett-Nelson (1905), $11,368.

In New York City under the Horton law Corbett and Sharkey drew $48,000 at the Lenox A. C. Fitzsimmons and Ruhlin fought for $45,000 in Madison Square Garden. Sharkey and Ruhlin proved a magnet for $40,000 at Coney Island, while Sharkey and McCoy drew $37,600 at the Lenox A. C. The Jeffries-Corbett battle at the Island netted $35,000, and the McGovern-Erne bout in the Garden produced $32,000. Sharkey and Fitzsimmons attracted $25,000. McGovern and Dixon got $24,000, and Choynski and McCoy split up $20,000.

Pugilists, Female. Proficiency with the gloves was added to the category of ladylike acquirements in the eighteenth century, as the following instance will show:

CHALLENGE.—I, Elizabeth Wilkinson, of Clerkenwell, having had some words with Hannah Hyfield, and requiring satisfaction, do invite her to meet me upon the stage, and box me for three guineas: each woman holding half-a-crown in each hand, and the first woman that drops the money to lose the battle.

Amour propre could, of course, not allow so specific a challenge to pass unheeded; so we find acceptance as follows:

I, HANNAH HYFIELD, of Newgate Market, hearing of the resoluteness of Elizabeth Wilkinson, will not fail, God willing, to give her more blows than words, desiring home-thrusts, and from her no favor. She may expect a good thumping.

Pullman, an industrial suburb of the city of Chicago, Ills., to which it was annexed in 1889. It was founded in 1880 by George Mortimer Pullman (1831–1897), inventor of the Pullman sleeping-car (see SLEEPING-CAR), who established here the extensive works of the Pullman Palace-Car Company. He attempted to make it a "model town." Even the public works were the property of the Pullman Palace-Car Company and were managed as a business investment. But the attendant restrictions and the high rate charged for rent, water, and gas created great dissatisfaction. Nine years after its erection the residents voted in favor of annexation to Chicago.

As to the naming of the town, the *Scrapbook* repeats an amusing story told to its contributor by Sir Hiram Maxim.

"Most of us here," said Maxim to a party assembled in his home at Norwood, London, "have travelled in Pullman-cars. The Pullman-car is built at the town of Pullman, near Chicago. Is that not so? Well, I'll wager that not one of you can tell how the town of Pullman got its name."

"Why, from the inventor of the cars that bear his name, of course," replied a guest.

"Right as far as you've gone," said Sir Hiram, "but you are only half right. The town was named after two men—Pullman and Manning, an engineer employed by Pullman to lay out the town.

"When it came time to give a name to the new town, Manning went to Mr. Pullman and said he thought the town should be called Manningtown, or Manning City, or something of that sort, as he, Manning, had done all the work of laying out the place, and hence should be thus honored.

"'Well,' drawled Mr. Pullman, 'you forget that while the town represents your work, it also represents my money. So I'm willing to go *halves* on the glory of the name. That is, we will take the first half of my name and the first half of your name—and thus we will both figure in the town's name, which will be Pull-man.'"

The story is possibly true in its essentials. The name of the architect of Pullman, however, was not Manning, but Solon S. Beman. The first syllable of Pullman and the *last* syllable of Beman would of course furnish data for the joke.

Punch (London), its Precursors and Imitators. It is not a little remarkable that we should be indebted to the psalm-singing days of the Commonwealth for the first English periodical devoted to fun and satire. On the 8th of April, 1652, under the very nose of his Highness the Protector, was published the first number of ·

" Mercurius Democritus, or a true and Perfect Nocturnall, communicating many strange Wonders, out of the World in the Moon, the Antipodes, Muggy-land, Tenebris, Fairy-land, Greenland, and other adjacent countries. Published for the Right Understanding of all the Mad-merry People of Great Bedlam."

The size is the usual small 4to of the journals of the period, and its matter consists of sarcastic comments upon passing events, together with a plentiful sprinkling of fictitious intelligence, but the wit, if wit it can be called, is usually of so gross a nature that it defies quotation. As a record of contemporary manners and customs, however, the files of the paper have their value to antiquarians. From the following it would appear that the rites of St. Valentine were not formerly confined to pen and paper:

" A young gentlewoman, casting her apron over her face, because she should see nobody till she came to her sweetheart's bedside, on Valentine's morning, was met withal in the street by another spark; who claiming her for his Valentine, and offering to salute her, she denied to uncover her lips, whereupon he kissed her apron, which another seeing him, and laughing at him, he told him he was but a fool to laugh at him, for the gentlewoman's lips tasted sweetest when strained through her apron!" (No. 85.)

The editor appears to have been a madcap Royalist, always in hot water on account of his vile personalities. The publication was very irregular, and the tavern-haunters were often left some weeks without their favorite. At such times, we gather from the insinuations of rival journals that *Democritus* was in durance. One fine day, however, he yielded up the ghost in earnest, and not long after there came forth a little pamphlet, now of extreme rarity, entitled, " A Hue and Cry after Mercurius Democritus."

Pygmies. At the beginning of the third book of the " Iliad," Homer alludes to the legendary conflicts between the pygmies and the cranes:

> So when inclement winters vex the plain
> With piercing frosts, or thick-descending rain,
> To warmer scenes the cranes imbodied fly
> With noise and order through the midway sky;
> To pygmy nations wounds and death they bring
> And all the war descends upon the wing.
>
> *Iliad*, III. 5 seq.

These pygmies were reputed to be about 13½ inches high. Their stature is indicated in their name; for the Greek *pygme* denotes the length of the forearm, from the point of the elbow to the joint of the fist. Their abode is placed by Homer near his fabulous and mystic ocean. Later writers, more definite as to the locality, put them in the interior of Africa; on towards Ethiopia, near the sources of the Nile; whither the cranes came from the north to contend with them for the products of the earth. Strabo, with an affectation of accuracy, divides pygmies into two classes; of which one contained those which were three spans high, and the other, those which were five spans high. "It was," he gravely states, "the former who fought with the cranes." Other authors speak of the northern pygmies, who dwelt near the legendary Thulé; as well as a race of pygmies in Caria, in Asia Minor. Ovid and other ancient poets found the pygmies suitable employment, or turned them to account as playthings for their wit. A favorite amusement with them was to contrast their petty proportions with the huge and brawny dimensions of Hercules.

Not until 1661 do we come across any verifiable allusion to a pygmy race. These were a tribe of small men called Kimos, said to inhabit Madagascar. They are identified with the tribe now called Vazimba, dwelling in the mountainous districts of that island. The first bit of positive data respecting the pygmies, or so-called dwarf-peoples of Eastern Africa, was furnished in 1870 by the German explorer Georg August Schweinfurth. At the residence of Munsa, the Monbattu King, he found some individual members of the Akka or Tikki-Tikki tribe, who so far as known are the smallest people in the world.

Paul Du Chaillu in 1863 penetrated into the vast forests of Western Africa, and, after his return, published a book entitled "The Country of the Dwarfs" (London, 1871). As was the case with his earlier book "Explorations in Equatorial Africa," his accounts were received with suspicion, if not open derision. A review in the *Graphic* represents the cautious attitude of even the friendliest critics:

The first part of the book reads very much like most other descriptions of African exploration; but further on Mr. du Chaillu represents himself as having arrived at the country of the dwarfs, whom he considers to be identical with the supposed fabulous pygmies. This strange race, who average only from four feet to four feet seven inches in height, live a perfectly wild life in the forests of equatorial Africa, feeding on snakes, rats, mice, and berries. They go entirely naked, and inhabit huts made by bending branches of trees in the shape of a bow, the ends being put into the ground. The height of the huts is just enough to keep the head of a man from touching the roof when he is seated. These dwarfs are very shy of being seen, and hold no communion with the Negro tribes about them, by whom they are called Obongos. Truly we have here a strange tale. We do not know that we have any right to doubt Mr. du Chaillu's word if he means us to accept the book as a *bond fide* narrative of what he has himself seen; out this is precisely the point as to which, whilst reading it, we cannot feel certain.

In 1877 Henry M. Stanley discovered the Upper Congo and afterward explored the country. He found this dwarf race in various places. In his more recent expedition from the Congo to the Albert Nyanza, he often came across small groups of them scattered in the dense forests of the Upper Aruwimi, and more to the east on the Semeliki River. Possibly the Paria in the Somali country, who are to be found between the Galla and Somali tribes, should here be noticed as belonging to the same dwarfish race.

Thus, then, we see that a primitive people, characterized by a stature below the average medium height, are to be found scattered all over equatorial Africa, from the west coast to Somali land in the east, and from the regions south of Lake Tchad down to the southern confluences of the Congo. They are nowhere found in a coherent body or nation, with fixed places of residence and commanded by a chief. They form small groups in the midst of or in close proximity to more powerful or more intelligent negro tribes, who regard them as little-better than slaves. They are allowed to live on condition that they hunt deer in the bush and fish in the rivers for their masters, or kill the elephant, whose ivory they are forbidden to sell. They are said by all travellers to be expert hunters, though they have no firearms; their only weapons are bows and arrows and spears. Wild animals are also caught by them in nets, corrals, and pit-falls. They are exceedingly clever in the arts and devices that appertain more especially to primitive and uncultivated races, and show great fortitude in wrestling with the natural diffi-culties offered in a wild country like their own, by both man and beast.

As to the average stature attained by these people, there is much discrepancy in the accounts furnished by travellers who have seen them in their native haunts. Nor is it easy to obtain exact data. Dr. Oskar Lenz, one of the most recent of these travellers, tells us that the pygmies are "exceedingly shy and tim'd, and in order to make observations I had to catch them as best I could, hunting them down like wild animals. Once caught, however, they soon become tractable, especially when they see they are in the hands of a white man, and not in those of a slave dealer; a few presents in the shape of beads, cloth, or— what is still more precious on the Western coast—salt, will make them sufficiently friendly to allow of a yard measure being applied to their person. They are mighty glad, however, when the operation is over, and run away most nimbly. The smallest man of ripe years I ever came across among the Abongos stood four feet three inches from the ground."

Stanley saw one not quite four feet high, another four feet

four inches, and a grown girl of about seventeen years of age who was half an inch short of three feet. The latter may have been an exception, although the women are proportionally smaller than the men.

The pygmies of Schweinfurth, whose real existence has given rise to so many fables, call themselves Akkas. The territory occupied by them is of considerable extent, in the neighborhood of 3 degrees north latitude and 25 degrees east longitude. At the time of the explorer's visit they numbered nine distinct tribes, each having its own chief. Schweinfurth passed through the country of the Niam-Niams, and penetrated to that of the Monbuttos. It was at the court of a native king named Munza that he discovered the dwarf race. Munza maintained a little colony of the dwarfs, near his royal residence. At that time the various tribes of Akkas had submitted to Moummeri, one of Munza's vassals, who had come to render homage to his sovereign at the head of several hundred of the pygmies. Thus Schweinfurth had a good opportunity for studying them. In exchange for one of his dogs, he obtained from Munza a young male Akka, who died subsequently of dysentery.

Most of the data gathered by Schweinfurth were lost in a fire, including measurements and notes which could not be replaced. Subsequent travellers, however, encountered some of the dwarfs. Munza having learned their value as objects of curiosity, gave some of them from time to time to buyers of ivory who visited him. Thus an individual of the race reached Khartoum, sent as a present to the Governor of the Soudan by Emin Bey. An explorer named Miani, following in Schweinfurth's footsteps, finally arrived among the Monbuttos. Succumbing to the fatigues of the journey, he died, bequeathing to the Geographical Society of Italy two young Akkas, whom he had got in exchange for a dog and a calf. These dwarfs, Tebo and Chairallah, were the ones adopted by Count Minisalchi.

Some anthropologists were inclined to believe that the Akkas were fakes, so to speak, and that Tebo and Chairallah would some day attain to a good size. Chairallah died, but Tebo grew to manhood, and did not pass the stature of the average pygmy as reported. His height was four feet seven inches. The mean stature of these dwarfs appears to be about four feet four and one-half inches. This reckoning makes them the smallest people in the world, the Bushmen perhaps, but not certainly, excepted. The color of the Akkas, according to Schweinfurth, is like that of coffee slightly roasted. Count Miniscalchi noticed that it was darker in summer and paler in winter.

A marked characteristic of the Akkas is an enormous development of abdomen, which causes the adults to resemble the children of negroes. In the photographs of Tebo and Chairallah this feature is most pronounced. The chest, comparatively narrow above, is dilated below in order to contain the huge paunch. But it is evident that this peculiarity is not a true race characteristic, being largely due to the manner in which the pygmies live and to the quality of their food. After some weeks of wholesome diet, Tebo and Chairallah lost their big stomachs.

The Akkas have short legs and very small hands. Their senses are very acute, and Schweinfurth speaks of their extraordinary agility. The Monbuttos say that the little men leap about in the high herbage like grasshoppers.

At a meeting of the Anthropological Institute, Prof. Flower, C. B., Director of the Natural History Museum, gave a description of two skeletons of Akkas obtained in the Monbuttu country, Central Africa, by Emin Pasha. Since this diminutive tribe was discovered by Schweinfurth in 1870, they have received considerable attention from various travellers and anthropologists, and general descriptions and movements of several living individuals have been published, but no account of their osteological characters has been given, and no specimens have been submitted to careful anatomical examination.

The two skeletons are those of fully grown-up people, a male and a female. The evidence they afford entirely corroborates the view previously derived from external measurements, that the Akkas are among the smallest, if not actually the smallest, people upon the earth. These skeletons are both of them smaller than any other normal skeleton known, smaller certainly than the smallest Bushman's skeleton in any museum in this country, and smaller than any out of the twenty-nine skeletons of the diminutive inhabitants of the Andaman Islands, of which the dimensions have been recorded.

The height of neither of them exceeds 1.219 metres, or 4 feet, while a living female Akka, of whom Emin Pasha has sent careful measurements, is only 1.164 metres, or barely 3 feet 10 inches. The results previously obtained from the measurements of about half a dozen living Akkas are not quite so low as these, varying from 1.216 to 1.420 metres, and give an average for both sexes of 1.356, or 4 feet 5½ inches. But the numbers measured are not sufficient for establishing the true average of the race, especially as it is not certain that they were all purebred examples.

According to Topinard's list, there are only two known races which have a mean height below 1.500 metres, viz., the Negrito of the Adaman Islands (1.478), and the Bushmen of South

Africa (1.404). Of the real height of the former we have abundant and exact evidence, both from living individuals and from
skeletons, which clearly proves that they considerably exceed the
Akkas in stature. That this is also the case with the Bushmen
there is little doubt.

Two other distinguished travellers of more recent date, R.
G. Haliburton and Walter B. Harris, brought home strange
accounts of a race of dwarfs in Morocco, concerning whom the
Moors have preserved a mysterious silence. For three thousand
years it appears the Moors have succeeded in making a secret
of the existence of a race of dwarfs in the Atlas Mountains only
a few hundred miles from the Mediterranean. This secret,
however, appears to have been successfully kept till about
1890. Mr. Haliburton's explanation is that the dwarfs have
been regarded by the Moors as holy men. A dwarf is called
" our blessed Lord," and is looked upon as a great saint. One
Moor said to Mr. Haliburton, " It is a sin to speak about them
to you. I shall say nothing." Another said, " God has sent
them to us. We must not talk about them." They are believed
to bring good luck, and are the guardians and protectors, like
the Palladium of the Trojans, of the towns in which they live.
Mr. Harris's inquiries, however, led him to believe that the
dwarfs were not worshipped by the Moors, but that the Moorish
reticence regarding them was the remains of a superstition far
older than any that would exist in Mohammedan times. He
differs also with Mr. Haliburton as to the religion of the dwarfs,
holding them to be Mohammedans, and believing that they could
not have existed as infidels, surrounded as they have been by
the most fanatical Mohammedan tribes.

" Upon the subject of the worship of the dwarfs in Morocco,"
says the New York *Times* of September 28, 1891, " a young
Jew, now living in Manchester, but a native of Morocco, says
that he has often seen a dwarf who lived in his native village,
and who was looked on as a great saint and kissed on the shoulders by the Moors as he passed through the streets, a salutation
which is an act of reverence. It would appear that the dwarfs
are not only regarded as saints but as devils also. The chief of
a company of dwarf acrobats took his troupe to perform in a
village near Timbuctoo. The performance was not a profitable
one. Nobody came to it, and not only was this the case, but the
performers discovered that the entire village had run away,
believing the acrobats to be imps at play. But whatever may
be the fact as to the existence of dwarf worship at the present
time, there is no doubt that the superstition has existed from
the most remote ages. Their pictures are found upon Egyptian

monuments of a date long antecedent to any civilization in Greece. It is the belief of Mr. Haliburton that these dwarfs brought with them into Greece the origin of much of Greek mythology. He found many Greek superstitions among them, such as the stories of the Styx and of Cadmus."

Northern China also has its dwarfs and its legend concerning them. In 1909 Dr. William Edgar Geil, of Doylestown, Pennsylvania, returned from a caravan journey in China that involved travelling along the 1250 miles of the Great Wall (see CHINA, GREAT WALL OF). His investigations confirmed an old Chinese legend that in the remote northern mountains there lives and has lived for seventeen centuries a race of hairy pygmies. Ancient inscriptions on the wall were deciphered for him by Chinese scholars. These record the fact that, whenever one of the millions of laborers employed in the construction of the wall was found to have erred at his task, he was immediately buried alive in the wall at the point where he had made his mistake. It was about 210 B.C. that a body of workmen, tired of seeing comrades and friends transmuted into building material, fled with their wives and children into the interior, and kept on until they came to the deep forest where their descendants now live. Some of them, tradition said, had become demented because of their frightful experiences; the rest had such a hard fight for existence that they deteriorated physically, transmitting dwarfishness to their present-day descendants. The tradition is quite plausible. It is not at all unlikely that deserters from the army of laborers should have fled to the mountains, and that the hardships of an isolated life in the wilderness should have had this effect on their descendants after many generations.

Python. There is a legend that the python was once the only poisonous member of the snake family. In those days its venom was so fearful that it had but to bite a man's footprint in the ground and the man would die. One day the crow told the python that a man whose track it had bitten had not died, and the python in a rage climbed a tree and spat out all its poison. Then the smaller snakes swallowed it. See BOA CONSTRICTOR.

Q.

Quail. It is introduced to us as a bird of passage in Exodus, xvi. 13. The children of Israel wandering in the wilderness murmured at the scarcity of provisions and looked back longingly upon the flesh-pots of Egypt. Then the Lord, through Moses, informed them that they should eat flesh at even, and in the morning be filled with bread. "And it came to pass that at even the quails came up and covered the camp." It must be added, however, that there has been some dispute as to whether the Hebrew word used—*selav*—should be translated "quail." That bird, indeed, has more than one rival ·for the honor in Biblical criticism. Of these, strange to say, one is not a bird. but the locust; this was the opinion of Ludolph. On the other hand, Rudbeck supposed that the supply of food which "at even came up and covered the camp," was presented by shoals of some species of flying-fish. The former opinion is untenable; the latter is astonishingly absurd. All the ablest commentators agree that the selav was a bird, the choice lying between the katta or sand-grouse and the quail.

It is known that in Palestine and around its borders, the katta is astonishingly abundant. Whatever may be its habits during the breeding season, it certainly associates in vast flocks during the greater portion of the year; and, in the stony districts of the country beyond Jordan, it swarms in such multitudes that phalanx after phalanx arises like dense clouds passing through the sky, and vanishing in the distance. Burckhardt was astounded by their numbers around the precincts of Bogra. He thus graphically writes: "The quantity of kattas here are beyond description; *the whole plain seemed sometimes to rise; and, far off in the air, they are seen like large moving clouds.*" In the country to the east of the Dead Sea, and among the hilly districts of Edom, their numbers are excessive; they arise *en masse* from the ground in such dense array, that the Arabs often bring down three or four at a time, by hurling a heavy jereed among them. In Syria, according to Russell, this bird is to be found the whole year round, but in vast flocks chiefly during the months of May and June; when, even in Northern Syria, the sweep of a clasp-net has been often known to enclose and bring down a tolerable load for one of the spirited little asses of that region. The Turks are partial to the flesh of this bird; but it is rejected by the Franks of Syria, who consider it dark-colored and dry. Burckhardt is strongly of opinion that the katta and the selav of the Israelites are identical.

On the other hand, the katta is not so distinctly a migratory bird as the quail. In Egypt and Syria, during the month of March, when the wheat is ripening, the quails (as Hasselquist states) spread themselves over the country in vast flocks; and multitudes, as in ancient days, are caught by means of nets, for the purpose of food: to say nothing of the necessity of destroying them by wholesale for the sake of preserving the grain. They then pass northward, returning in the autumn, but not in such numbers as before. They have twice crossed the Mediterranean—first into Asia Minor, thence spreading through Southern Europe, and so onward; secondly, on their return, and in each journey not without great slaughter. Here we might cite authorities, from ancient times to the present, proving that the migratory movements of the quail have remained unchanged throughout the change of empires.

Now, if anything proves the quail to have been the selav of the Israelites, it is the recorded fact that for a whole month six hundred thousand marching men, with women and children in proportion, were supplied with food by these birds, which lighted in numbers beyond the powers of calculation, for some miles, in and around their encampment. "He rained flesh also upon them as dust, and feathered fowls like as the sand of the sea."—Psalm lxxviii. 27.

This narrative prepares us for the accounts given by the classic writers from Aristotle to Pliny, which have been sometimes deemed exaggerations. The latter, after stating that immense flocks, driven out of their course (across the Mediterranean) by adverse winds, are often swept into the sea, proceeds to state that they sometimes settle on vessels in such numbers as to cause their sinking from the overloading of the masts and rigging; and this, he says, always happens during the night. Looking at the vessels as light craft resembling our fishing-smacks, plying along the coast, and considering Pliny's acquaintance with the shores of the Mediterranean, we cannot refuse credence to this positive statement. Even in modern times, when the quail is less multitudinous than it was formerly, before the destructive gun was known, the authentic accounts on record are sufficiently startling. During the periodical flights of these birds between Europe and Africa, and *vice versa*, the shores and islands of the Mediterranean are replete with myriads—Sicily swarms with them. Their autumnal visit is looked forward to with great anxiety, and they there encounter wholesale destruction; the gun, the net, and the simplest missiles being all in requisition. On the coast of Naples, according to Montagu, and within a comparatively limited space, 100,000 have been counted as the produce of a single day's work. In this manner we might pass along the European shores of the Mediterranean; but, were we to do so, we should be too long delayed by the "Isles of Greece"; everywhere a repetition of the same wholesale destruction of the quail is as vigorously carried on. According to Baron de Tott, no country abounds in quails more than the Crimea. During the summer these birds are dispersed over the country; but at the approach of autumn they assemble together and cross the Black Sea to the southern coasts, whence they afterward transport themselves to a warmer climate: "The order of this migration is invariable: toward the end of August, on a serene day, when the wind blows from the north at sunset, and promises a fine night, they repair to the strand, and take their departure at six or seven in the evening, and have finished a journey of fifty leagues by break of day." They alight exhausted, and meet with the usual reception, thousands being taken alive, in addition to those killed on the spot.

Quezal, a bird whose habitat is Guatemala and southern Mexico, adopted as the national emblem of Guatemala, which is frequently described as the most beautiful bird in the world. Its breast is a brilliant scarlet, its tail, which frequently reaches the length of 3 feet, an iridescent green. It is about the size of the common pigeon. It nests in holes in rotten trees, enlarging them with its bill to suitable dimensions. It prefers high altitudes. Hence despite its early historical fame among the Incas, it was practically unknown to naturalists until very recently. The few specimens which had fallen into their hands had been obtained from Indians who preserved the secret. In 1860, however, a collector visiting Guatemala, got on the track of the birds and went up into the mountains, where he shot several specimens. Since then the secret has been an open one.

The quezal belongs to the family of tragons, the genus including 46 species, 33 of which are American.

Quinine, cinchona, Jesuit's bark, and Peruvian bark are names alternately given to the medicine extracted from the bark of the cinchona tree. The word "quinine" comes from the native *quina,* which the Peruvian aborigines applied both to the tree and its bark. "Cinchona" is derived from the name of the Spanish discoverer of its medical qualities, the Countess Ana de Chinchon. In 1638, when her second husband, Don Luis Geronimo Fernandez de Cabrera y Bobadilla, fourth Count of Chinchon, was Viceroy of Peru, this lady was cured of an attack of fever by the use of a tree-bark. It is said the medicine was recommended by the corregidor of Loxa, who had experienced its virtues eight years earlier. On her return to France in 1640, the countess took a lot of the bark with her, for the purpose of distributing it among the sick in her neighborhood. Hence tree and medicine have received the scientific name of Chinchona (now usually spelled Cinchona), which still clings to the thirty-one species of the tree, though the medicine is now more usually called quinine. For many years the bark-powder was also known to European druggists as the countess's powder (*Pulvis Comitessæ*) and as Jesuit's bark. The Jesuits appear to have disseminated a knowledge of the virtues of the bark throughout Europe. But there is also a rival story that these virtues were first discovered by a Jesuit missionary in Peru, who, when prostrate with fever, was cured by the administration of the bark by a South American Indian.

Little or nothing was scientifically known of the tree until 1739. La Condamine and Jussieu, then on an exploring expedition in South America, after not a little trial, obtained plants for the Jardin des Plantes in Paris, but the whole collection perished in a storm at sea near the mouth of the Amazon. Another century passed before anything was done to introduce or naturalize the tree in Europe or in the eastern dependencies of Britain, whence supplies might be assured; and this notwithstanding the fact that the French chemists Pelletier and Caventou had in 1820 developed true quinine from the bark. The first cinchona-trees raised in Europe were some calisaya-plants in the Jardin des Plantes in Paris, from seeds collected by Dr. Weddell in his first journey to Bolivia in 1846. In 1849 an unsuccessful attempt was made to rear the plant in Algeria. In 1854 the Dutch government introduced it into the island of Java, where, after many vicissitudes, the cultivation of cinchona plantations is now quite prosperous. In 1860, after some unsuccessful private efforts, the East India Company fitted out an expedition to obtain young trees from South America, and as a result the government plantations in India now contain several millions.

It may be noted that the proper pronunciation of the word quinine is still unsettled. The dictionaries are all at sea. No one of them exactly agrees with the other. The "Century Dictionary" dodges the difficulty by giving three pronunciations. The "Standard' does worse and gives five. Webster and Worcester give two each. But, on the whole, the weight of dictionary authority would favor, though not insist on, the full sound of "q" in pronouncing the word. Yet the "k" sound is more in consonance with etymology. James Parton, in a biographical sketch of the Countess of Chinchon, tries to give the true derivation of the word. He finds that in written language the original Peruvian word was *kina* or *quina,* which has the sound of *kina,* with accent upon the first syllable, so given both by the natives and the Spaniards. "Hence, there is a reason for the common English pronunciation of the name 'kaneen.' New England physicians appear to prefer the straightforward method of their own language, and pronounce it as though it were an English or Latin word. The reader may take his choice, for the dictionaries sanction both. If etymology alone were considered this evidence would settle for us the 'k' sound of the initial letter, but it would forbid an accentuation of the final syllable."

R.

Rabbit. In Australia the rabbit has become a nightmare. The early colonists who brought it over with them from England to make their new settlements more homelike never anticipated the awful result. Rabbits have increased and multiplied to such an extent that they have overspread the continent and cost millions of pounds in an unsuccessful effort to subdue them. At the age of three months the doe brings forth her litter of eight or ten. Thereafter every month she produces a similar litter. There is no winter spell of cold to interrupt her or to kill off the young and feeble. The only limit to rabbit life is the food supply and here bunny comes into competition with the domestic sheep, a competition all the more ruinous because sheep dislike pastures over which he has passed. The rabbit, in short, would easily have conquered the sheep if both had been left to their own devices. But man came to the rescue of the more useful animal. Panic measures were tried at first. Wholesale poisoning with pollard baits, dosed with strychnine or phosphorus, only served to destroy much of the native bird life, to devastate the natural fauna and to leave the rabbit in triumphant possession. Or if he succumbed he had his revenge even in death. The carcasses of poisoned rabbits polluted the air and attracted a plague of flies which carried the poison from carcass to sheep. Rabbit-proof fencing proved more efficacious. The rabbits outside of the fence could be kept out, while the rabbits inside could be readily dealt with. Within enclosures of 15,000 or 16,000 acres the rabbit, it was found, could be exterminated. His natural cover was cleared away and vigorous trapping or poisoning killed him off. Water hole traps were especially effective. The Australian sheep farms lie mainly in dry country. Water is a necessity to rabbits and water holes are few and far between. Such as they are, the farmers carefully fenced them in, leaving little yards here and there, however, whence access to the water could be gained. Here the rabbits could enter but not emerge. Overnight the yards would be filled with rabbits which were destroyed in the morning with sticks.

It has been suggested that rabbits could be kept in check by a systematic warfare on the females only. With an excess of females the rabbit race might lose its fecundity. An experiment tried in Ireland seemed to falsify this reasoning.

London *Answers* tells the story: "An Irish landlord, who had a rabbit-warren on his estate, had rabbits trapped, partly to supply the table, partly to keep the tribe in check. The traps would catch more buck rabbits than does, as the male wanders about more than the female. While trapping was kept up the rabbits in the warren were healthy and vigorous. When trapping was for some reason stopped for a few years, the rabbits decreased very much in numbers and size."

A paragraph which appeared in the London *Lancet* early in 1912 would indicate that the rabbit pest, in Victoria at least, is largely under control:

The rabbit industry in Victoria is stated to be slowly but surely disappearing. The first export of frozen rabbits was made in 1894, in which year 14,928 rabbits were sent to England. Next year the total was 431,716. In 1900 the total was 5,678,224, and in 1905, 10,258,356. Since that year the total has gradually declined till last year it had come down to 2,841,648 rabbits exported. Exporters and agriculturists alike are pleased at this result. The former have all their available freezing plants occupied with meat and butter and cheese, while the latter view the gradual extinction of the rabbit pest with composure.

Railway Altitudes. The highest railway in the world is the Central Railway of Peru which reaches an altitude of 15,865 feet and has its highest railway station at 15,665 feet.

The second highest line is that from Antofagasta in Chile to Oruro in Bolivia with the highest point at an elevation of 15,809 feet above the level of the sea. The Peruvian railroad from Arequipa to Puno comes in as a good third. Its highest station is Crucero Alto, 14,666 feet.

The highest railway in the United States is the Argentine Central in Colorado reaching an altitude of 14,000. The next in height also belongs to Colorado, viz., the Moffat Road, 11,660 feet.

The highest railway in Europe is the Jungfrau Railway in Switzerland. The Jungfraujoch—the great connecting wall between the Monch and the Jungfrau—is 10,935 feet above sea level, 4185 feet higher than the starting point of the line at the Little Scheidegg and 9075 feet higher than Interlaken.

Railway, First. "A coal mine is nothing but a hole in the ground!" cried William H. Vanderbilt when Franklin B. Gowen in urging him to come to the financial aid of the Reading Railroad quoted the mining interests of that company as a valuable asset.

"Coal mines," retorted Mr. Gowen, "produced the railroads."

Mr. Gowen's retort embodied a fact. The first railway was

a product of the British coal mines. In the early part of the sixteenth century wooden rails were laid at the collieries near Newcastle upon Tyne. More than 100 years later we find them described by Lord Keeper North. "The manner of the carriage," says this authority in 1676, "is by laying rails of timber exactly straight and parallel and bulky carts are made with four rowlets fitting these rails, whereby the carriage is so easy that one horse will draw down four or five cauldrons of coal," *i.e.*, from 10.6 to 13.2 tons.

The planks were of beech or other wood, a few inches wide, and were fastened down, end to end, on logs of wood, or "sleepers" placed crosswise at intervals of 2 or 3 feet. In due time it became the custom to protect them with thin sheaths of iron, and when iron wheels were introduced (the first being used on a wooden railway near Bath in 1734) flat iron rails followed as a matter of course so early as 1738. Thirty years later cast iron bars were made—each 5 feet long, 4 inches wide, and 1¾ inches thick, with holes for spikes to secure them to the wood. Toward the close of the eighteenth century the practice was adopted of casting the rails with a perpendicular ledge on the outer edge to prevent the wheels from leaving the track. Subsequently the ledge was transferred to the inner side of the rail.

It was not until 1789 that the present type of rail and carwheel appeared. Flanged rails and flat wheels were discarded and the flange was transferred to the tire of the wheels. Mr. Jessop introduced, at that period, rails cast in lengths of 15 feet, with the top 1¾ inches wide. They were of the fish belly pattern; deeper in the middle than at the ends. After various experiments it was found advisable to set the ends of the rails in cast iron chairs, which were bolted to the wooden, or stone, ties, and into which the rail was secured by a key or wedge. Cast iron, however, proved to be too brittle for the passage of heavy loads at high rates of speed, and about the year 1820 malleable iron was substituted, and the length of the rails was increased.

The idea of using steam as a motive power on the tramways in the English collieries was first broached by James Watt in 1784, when he applied for a patent for a steam carriage.

In 1804 Richard Trevethic built a locomotive engine which was tried upon the Merthyr and Tydvil Railway, in Wales, and which drew wagons containing ten tons of coal each, at a rate of five miles an hour. W. Hasell Wilson, in his "Railway History," says that in 1812 Blenkinsop's engines began running between Middleton collieries and Leeds (a distance of three and one half miles), and continued in use for several years.

being the first instance of the regular employment of steam locomotives for commercial purposes.

It was in 1814 that George Stephenson's first steam engine the Rocket was placed on the Killingworth Railway. It drew 30 tons at the rate of 4 miles an hour upon an incline of 1 foot in 450. Improvements in locomotives followed gradually. When the Stockton and Darlington Railway was opened for public use on Sept. 27, 1825, one of Stephenson's locomotives drew a train composed of twenty-two wagons filled with passengers, and twelve wagons loaded with coal, making a total weight of about ninety tons, including the engine and tender, at an average speed of about five miles an hour, but attaining a maximum rate of twelve miles.

Railway Guide, the First. It was in 1839 that George Bradshaw (1801–1853), a Manchester Quaker and map engraver, published what is generally considered the first railway time-table. A tiny pamphlet of 6 pages, bound in green with gilt lettering, it was merely a collection of the monthly time-tables issued by the seven railway companies then doing business in England. Only 4 copies are known to be extant, 2 of them being in the Bodleian Library at Oxford.

The success of this venture prompted a more ambitious effort. In 1840 Bradshaw brought out his " Railway Companion," a volume of 38 pages, including maps. This was issued independently of the time-tables. Its publication was continued for 8 years, when it was merged into the " Guide."

Early numbers of the Guides furnish curious reading. Trains are described as " first class," " second class," " mixed," " fast," and " mail." Third-class passengers might travel on the roofs of other cars or in open wagons much like the freight-cars of to-day. Gentlemen riding in their own carriages were charged second-class fare. Luggage was carried on the car-roofs. Passengers who chose the same eminence were cautioned to wear overcoats and gauze spectacles. Tickets were called " checks " or " passes "; seats bore numbers corresponding with the number on the ticket; fares were regulated according to the time of travel, whether day or night, and also according to the number of passengers in a car.

The London *Globe* is disposed to dispute the priority of Bradshaw. In the year 1839, it says, there were other guides in existence, which were no less interesting, but which eventually died out and passed into the limbo of forgotten things. One of the earliest was entitled " Lacey's Railway Companion and Liverpool and Manchester Guide." It was a very friendly produc-

tion, describing the scenery through which the railway passed,
" and pointing out to the visitor at both places all that is interesting and necessary for business and pleasure." It was published at Liverpool, and was on sale in London as well as in
the northern towns at the price of one shilling. Though this
old guide does not possess any date, it contains advertisements
for the annuals and almanacs for 1835, which provides a clue as
to the time of its origin and shows it to be probably the first
railway guide ever published. As there were only some twelve
trains starting daily, they did not occupy much space, and the
guide was expanded to seventy-six pages by a description of the
cost and construction of the line.

Railway King. This title, which in the United States has
been more or less generally bestowed upon various successive
magnates of railroad enterprise,—to wit, upon Jay Gould, Commodore Vanderbilt, and E. H. Harriman—originated in England and was applied to George Hudson (1800–1871). He
began life as apprentice to a linen-draper in York, and carried
on the business with such success as to accumulate a small fortune which was increased by a bequest from a distant relative.
In 1828 he began investing in North Midland Railway shares.
In 1839 he addressed a meeting of the company held at Leeds,
advocating many important alterations in the system of managing the railway, and concluding a remarkable speech by offering to guarantee double the dividend the shareholders were
then receiving if the alterations he proposed were adopted. His
speech had its effect. Hudson was made chairman of a committee
of shareholders, which ended by dismissing all the directors and
appointing Hudson himself chairman and virtual dictator of
the company. Under his management, the shares gradually
rose from £70 discount to £120 premiums, a record unprecedented in those days. Hudson next amalgamated the North
Midland with other lines; and, undoubtedly, by his system of
amalgamation with neighboring companies, he considerably extended the accommodation to the public, besides effecting a considerable saving in the working of the line. Nor did he neglect
his own interests. In one transaction he is said to have cleared,
in a single day, £100,000! He was also elected M.P. for
Sunderland and twice Lord Mayor of York; was appointed
Deputy-Lieutenant of Durham; and magistrate of the East and
North Ridings of York, and of Durham.

In 1849 his methods became the subject of a parliamentary
examination, which resulted in his downfall. The particular
transaction which brought him to grief occurred in 1845. As
chairman and trustee of the North Midland Railway, reputed by
that company to purchase shares in the Great North of England

Railway for the benefit of the company, he had sold to his constituents a large number of shares at a considerable advance upon the market price. He used the money of the company to make the purchase, and put upwards of £8000 into his own pocket, as his premium upon the transaction. The parliamentary committee, after a patient investigation, decided that the sum charged by Mr. Hudson for these shares ought to be reduced to the sum he actually paid for them, and that the difference must be repaid with interest.

Hudson himself was far from imagining that he had done any wrong. He was absolutely staggered by the result of the parliamentary inquiry: "It is not my wish," said he, in his published defence, "to impugn the reasoning or question the conclusion of the committee; but I must be allowed to state that *this opinion of the position which I occupied in connection with the company is one now presented to my mind for the first time.* . . I never thought myself restrained from entering into personal engagements either with the company or with others, by reason of the position I stood in towards the company, any more than if I had been an ordinary proprietor. . . *It is impossible for me to adopt the conclusion at which the committee have arrived, for, as far as my own view of my position is concerned, that conclusion is incorrect.* . . I care nothing for pecuniary considerations in this matter. I must pursue the course which my own feelings and judgment point out to be correct under the circumstances in which I find myself placed—*circumstances to me of a most painful nature; but in which I have become involved without the slightest idea on my part that I was doing anything deserving of reprehension.*"

The *Illustrated London News* for April 14, 1849, reviewed the whole subject in an admirable editorial article. It rightly characterized Hudson's defence as the most melancholy part of the whole business. "Not only," it said, "did Mr. Hudson make this profit out of a company whose interests he ought to have considered identical with his own, but when he sold to the company as principal with principal, he charged it with full brokerage, though he paid none either on his own account or that of the company; and although, as a contemporary remarks, he made sundry other 'pickings' for his own private and exclusive benefit. But the truth is that Mr. Hudson is neither better nor worse than the morality of 1845. He rose to wealth and importance at an immoral period; he was the creature of an immoral system: he was wafted into fortune upon the wave of a popular mania; he was elevated into the dictatorship of railway speculation in an unwholesome ferment of popular cupidity, pervading all ranks and conditions of men; and, whatever be the hue of the error he may have committed, it is rather too much to expect of him that he should be purer than his time or his associates. The commercial code of 1845 was, as far as railways were concerned, framed upon anything but moral principles. The lust of gain blinded the eyes of men who, before that period, could see clearly enough the difference between right and wrong, between trading and gambling, and between legitimate and illegitimate speculation. Men who would have scorned to do a dishonest act towards any other real tangible living man, did not scruple to do acts against that great abstraction, the public, which no morality could justify. In the height of the railway mania it was generally admitted, that, ultimately, some parties must be losers; that the over-sanguine or the cautious who came in last would have to pay the piper for all the gains made by those who came in early; but, as nobody knew who these individuals were, nobody cared about them or scrupled to make an immoral profit out of them. Mr. Hudson, from the superior magnitude of his transactions, from his superior talent in railway business, and perhaps, also, from his superior luck, became the representative of that system. He was to wealth what the queen is to honor—its fountain; and all who desired to be wealthy without labor, and by a mere turn of the dice of Fortune, looked to him to aid them in their projects."

Lady Dorothy Nevill, in her "Reminiscences," has this note upon the former Railway King: "Hudson, to whom Carlyle once alluded as the big swollen gambler, lived on to the early seventies, an annuity having been purchased for his benefit by some friends only a few years before. In his prosperous days the 'Railway King' used to entertain very lavishly at his house at Albert Gate. This mansion, together with the one opposite to it, was built by Cubitt, and the two houses used to be called the two Gibraltars, it being prophesied that they never would or could be taken. As has been said, Mr. Hudson soon falsified this prediction. The house is now the French Embassy."

Railway Station. The largest railway station in the world is in New York City,—the Hudson Terminal of the Pennsylvania road, between 32d St. and 30th St. and Seventh and Eighth Avenues. Statisticians agree that it covers more territory than any other building ever constructed at one time in the history of the world. The Vatican, the Tuileries, the St. Petersburg Winter Palace, are larger buildings, but they were for centuries under construction. The Pennsylvania station is unique, covering, as it does, eight acres of ground, with exterior walls extending approximately one-half of a mile, all told, and having been erected in less than six years' time.

The area of the station and yard is 28 acres, and in this there are 16 miles of track. The storage tracks alone will hold 386 cars. The length of the 21 standing tracks at the station is 21,500 feet. There are 11 passenger platforms, with 25 baggage and express elevators. The highest point of the tracks in the station is nine feet below sea level.

The station building is 784 feet long and 430 feet wide. The average height above the street is 69 feet, while the maximum is 153 feet. The building is lighted by about 500 electric arcs and 20,000 incandescents.

More than 150,000 cubic yards of concrete were required for the retaining walls, foundations, street bridging, and the substructure. There are 650 columns supporting the station building, and the greatest weight on any one of these is 1658 tons.

Railways, Father of English. This title has been given to Edward Pease (1767–1858) and forms the subtitle of a memorial edited by his great-grandson: "The Diaries of Edward Pease, the Father of English Railways" (London, 1908). Pease was only a projector, however, not an inventor. About 1817 he became interested in a scheme for constructing a tramway from Darlington to Stockton. In 1818 parliamentary sanction was sought for the project, but the Duke of Cleveland opposed it because the suggested line ran too close to one of his fox-covers, and it was not until April 19, 1821, that a new route received the royal assent. Originally the cars were intended simply to carry coal and to be drawn by horses. In the spring of 1821, however, George Stephenson, then only an engine-wright, introduced himself to Pease, and convinced him of the practical advantages of a steam locomotive running on rails, for men, animals, and freight. Stephenson had already built an engine at Killingworth; he now, with Pease's financial assistance, began a new one, destined to be the first engine used on the Stockton and Darlington railway, which in its turn was the first line ever built in Great Britain. The first rail was laid on May 23, 1823. The line was opened for traffic on September 27, 1825, and at once proved a success. The Stephenson engine now occupies a pedestal at Darlington Station.

Railways, Miniature. In the United States in 1910 there were 1180 railways. Of these 180 were 8 miles or less in length, 40 had rights of way over only 9 miles, while perhaps 20 were limited to 10 miles. In the first group are included 8 only one mile long from terminus to terminus, 19 with 2 miles, and so on until you reach 29 giants with 8 miles to their credit.

One mile is the length of the Indiana and Northern Railroad that connects Myler with Se⁻   ⁻d. It has been in operation since 1891, and is a vest-pocket corporation of a flourishing sort, having no funded or other debts. Small as it is, it is of considerable importance as a belt line, for it is the connecting link between the Lake Shore and Michigan Southern, the Grand Trunk Western, the Vandalia, the Michigan Central, and the Central Indiana and Southern railroads. All the stock is held by a manufacturing corporation of South Bend. Last year it paid $5000 in dividends, its net earnings being $7000.

Every part of the country furnishes specimens of these dwarf roads. They are found in mining districts, where their services are often invaluable; they make things convenient for visitors to scenic sections; they are the handy helpers around industrial plants and terminal centres; they climb mountains that would be impossible otherwise to the average citizen.

England boasts of a very remarkable miniature railroad at Eaton, the country-seat of the Duke of Westminster. It was built in 1896 by the grandfather of the present duke, under the superintendence of Sir Arthur Haywood, for the purpose of carrying coal and other supplies to Eaton Hall from the Great Western station, four miles away. It is now used also as a passenger line for conveying the duke's guests from one part of the estate to another. The gauge is only fifteen inches, and the rolling stock, comprising two engines and half a hundred trolleys, wagons, and passenger coaches, is constructed on a proportionate scale. The initial cost of the railway was £6000, and it is said to be worked at a weekly expense of £5.

Rain Tree. A more or less mythical tree said to flourish most exuberantly in Peru. It is thus described in a Spanish paper:

The rain tree of Peru grows very large, is rich in leaves, and is called by the Indians tamaïcaspi. It has the power of collecting the dampness of the atmosphere and condensing it into a continuous and copious supply of rain.

In the dry season when the rivers are low and the heat great, the tree's power of condensing seems at the highest, and water falls in abundance from the leaves and oozes from the trunk. The water spreads around in veritable rivers, part of which filters into the soil and fertilizes it. These rivers are canalized so as to regulate the course of the water.

It is estimated that one of the Peruvian rain trees will on the average yield nine gallons of water per diem. In a field of an area of one kilometre square—that is, 3250 feet each way—can be grown 10,000 trees, separated from each other by 25 metres. This plantation produces daily 385,000 litres of water. If we allow for evaporation and infiltration, we have 135,000 litres or 29,531 gallons of rain for distribution daily. The rain tree can be cultivated with very little trouble, for it seems indifferent as to the soil in which it grows. The tree increases rapidly and resists both extremes of climate.

All this, it would now seem, is largely or quite a myth. In 1905 the Weather Bureau at Washington examined into the facts of the case, and decided that no tree of the sort had ever existed. In 1911 Henry Robertson, United States consul-general at Callao, Peru, dealt another blow at the legend. Urged by numerous inquiries, he reported to the government that careful investigation had failed to locate any rain tree in Peru, where it was supposed to be especially abundant. He carried his scepticism so far as to disbelieve in its existence anywhere else. He quoted eminent botanical authorities in support of his views. One informant had, indeed, written to say that in certain moist localities a particular tree becomes saturated, so to speak, and occasionally discharges a small amount of moisture, too small, however, to be of any practical value in arid lands, even if it could grow there.

After the consul reported, the Bureau of Manufacturers asked the Department of Agriculture to look into the matter. Assistant Secretary Hays replied that the rain-tree legend is centuries old, but has no scientific basis. Australia has fallen a victim to the delusion and is planting many alleged rain trees. They are no more efficacious in condensing water than any other free-growing tree. He quoted an English botanist to the effect that swarms of cicadas, or locusts, settle upon trees and extract their juices, which fall upon the ground. He offers this as one explanation of the myth. (See Traveller's Tree.)

Rattlesnake. The rattle consists of a number of bones looking like small knuckle-bones, securely fastened together, yet so loosely that they make a clicking noise when shaken. These grow on the reptile's tail. Popular belief asserts that the first joint, which is always of a darker color than the others, takes two years to grow, while afterward an additional joint grows each year. The rattlesnake is spread pretty generally over the North American continent, but its chief habitat is Texas. The largest specimens, however, are found in North Carolina. The State Museum at Raleigh contains the largest rattlesnake, mounted, in any collection in the world. It measures 6 feet 11 inches in length, and 11 inches in girth. It weighs 7 pounds and 11 ounces. There are 12 rattles.

Rattlesnakes are the most sluggish of all the serpent tribe; for the puff-adder of the capes, credited in Africa with this preeminence, is very active when enraged. On the other hand, the rattlesnake, excepting just after and just before its winter sleep, only bites in self-defence and never goes out of its way to attack man or beast. Unless molested there is little to fear from him. Unfortunately, you never can tell when you are going to molest him, as in coming down a bluff or picking your way in a gully, you may put your foot on a rattlesnake. And then the terrific swiftness of its dart! "Not even the cobra," says an English traveller, "which I had always considered rivalled the very lightning in its movements,—movements which I defy any European eye to follow,—is quicker than the rattlesnake in that one deadly act. Yet to strike it must be in a close coil, its head and neck being erect; it throws itself about three-fourths of its length, supporting its weight entirely on its tail part." *Chambers' Journal,* vol. 49, p. 641.

The writer adds three remarkable stories of narrow escapes from enraged rattlesnakes. One man, who had killed fifty of the reptiles, recognized what his foot touched, and without stopping to look he leaped higher probably than he had ever done in his life. Another man was not so quick, and the reptile struck him three times with electric quickness; but his trousers and long boots saved him. "This disposes of a fallacy very generally held, that venomous serpents will not bite twice in succession: there were the three pair of fang marks quite plainly to be seen on his white trousers." It also confirms the fact that snake-bites are sometimes harmless when the sufferer is bitten through cloth; the poison is absorbed by the material and never finds its way into the flesh at all. Our author's third instance is of a young man who had been bathing in the River Platte. On emerging naked from the water, he sat down on a rattlesnake which was basking in the grass. Whether he sat upon the reptile's head, or whether the creature was too astonished by his sudden descent, can never be known; but certain it is that the affrighted bather leaped up with a shriek, and escaped unhurt.

The rattlesnake has a very unpleasant smell, so powerful and permanent that when it is irritated and made to bite a rake or hoe wielded with intent to kill, the implement will retain the odor for months. Once known it is always recognizable. Dr. Hamilton Roe, of London, owed his life to his knowledge of this fact. Opening a box directed to the Superintendent of the Zoölogical Gardens in London, he imprudently put his hand under the packing of dry moss to see what was there. He touched something alive. The smell told him it was a rattlesnake. Had he pulled back his hand at once, he would certainly have been bitten; but he had the presence of mind to stroke the reptile, which allowed him gently to withdraw his hand.

Out on the prairie rattlesnakes have been known to crawl into tents and into beds within the tents. This was in search of warmth. Very often they are content simply with crawling inside. So used are some men to this trait that they have been known to sleep quietly all through the night though perfectly aware that a rattlesnake was within their tent walls. They rolled themselves tight in their bedclothes, confident that the intruder would not attack if it were not itself attacked, and that it would leave at dawn. In one instance a man was bitten at night. He was on the prairie, and sleeping near his horse, which was fastened by a long rope to a log or stone. The horse broke away; and the man, feeling after the rope in the grass, disturbed a rattlesnake, which bit him on the back of his hand. He was cured by a remedy which is recommended in England for snake-bites. A friend cut with a penknife the skin round the puncture, so as to enlarge the wound, and make it bleed: then he put a small heap of gunpowder on the spot, ignited it,—no pain attending this,—and the man was cured.

The writer in *Chambers'* somewhat reluctantly recommends whiskey as the surest antidote for rattlesnake poison. " I know of one case of rattlesnake-bite where four hours elapsed before spirits could be procured: yet the patient lived. The poison of a snake, by some mysterious potency, causes the blood to coagulate, and, we may say, putrefy: then the sufferer dies. All remedies seem to have failed because they do not act upon the blood: now, whiskey does so act. A quart of whiskey—*neat*, of course—is about the quantity usually taken; but the cure is effected directly the patient gets drunk. So long as the venom has the mastery, no amount of whiskey will affect the head; but directly it is conquered, the patient shows signs of intoxication, and is rescued."

The first rattlesnakes ever seen alive in England, certainly the first kept for public exhibition, were a female and her brood presented in January. 1849, to the London Zoölogical Society by Captain Mackenzie M'Luckie. On a visit to Berbice this gentleman had obtained a pair of adult Cascavel rattlesnakes. The male effected its escape before the case containing them was put aboard ship. During the homeward voyage the female produced a brood of 19 young ones, only 8 of which survived in the menagerie.

Rattlesnakes were known in colonial times in the Middle States, but have long since disappeared. Toward the close of 1847 a case containing one of these rarities was received by Dr. Wainewright, a former captain in the British army who for ten years had been a physician of eminence in New York City. The snake was about five feet in length, having twelve rattles. It was contained in a box with spars over the top. " The doctor ⁊as on his way home from the ship with the present, but stopped ⁏ the Broadway-house to show the curiosity. The company present seemed to enjoy teasing and irritating the snake, while the reptile kept whizzing its rattle at a furious rate. The box was opened; and now, there being a fair field, the reptile kept coiling and rearing itself in fierce defiance of its enemies. This display lasted some time; when Dr. Wainewright touched the snake a few inches below the head, expecting that it could not bend its body sufficiently to bite. In a moment it snapped, and inflicted a wound on the first joint of the middle finger of the right hand." A superficial excision of the part was immediately made, the wound was cauterized with nitrate of sulphur, and a ligature was applied above the wrist. The hand began to swell immediately, and the poison progressed rapidly to the forearm and arm. But no constitutional symptoms seem to have made their appearance until it reached the "axilla," or armpit; when immediately the pulse began to flag; and, notwithstanding the continual application of stimulants, the pulse never rallied until about 12 o'clock P.M., when death put a period to the doctor's existence.—*Illustrated London News, January 27,* 1849.

Rattlesnakes, Proposed Transportation of. When Condorcet in 1790 delivered his eulogy on Franklin before the French Academy of Sciences, he dwelt upon the American's ready wit and Socratic method of argument. As an instance, he told how Franklin once remonstrated with the English prime minister on the insulting practice of transporting criminals from the motherland to the colonies. The minister alleged the necessity for ridding England of this gentry. "What would you say," retorted Franklin, "if we were to order the exportation of rattlesnakes to England?" In a foot-note added to the *Eloge* when it was published, Condorcet asserted, "I have often heard him tell this story, which has been ridiculously disfigured in our newspapers." From this source, and this source alone, the rattlesnake anecdote has crept into most of the biographies of Franklin. At last, in 1898, Paul Leicester Ford, searching through the *Pennsylvania Gazette* for hitherto inedited writings of Franklin, discovered an article, obviously from his pen, in No. 1169, May 9, 1751. It supplied the original of the story we have hitherto owed to Condorcet's French version, and proves that also to have been "disfigured." The article takes the form of a letter, addressed to "the Printers of the Gazette" and signed "Americus." It begins by satiric reference to the kindness of "our mother country" in forbidding "our mistaken Assemblies" to make any law for preventing or discouraging the importation of convicts from Great Britain, on the ground "that such laws are against the public utility, as they tend to prevent the improvement and well peopling of the colonies." Such a tender parental concern, Americus thinks, calls aloud for the highest returns of gratitude and duty. Though recognizing that a really adequate return is impossible, he yet suggests a plan that may at least show a grateful disposition.

"In some of the uninhabited Parts of these Provinces," he explains, "there are Numbers of these venemous Reptiles we call RATTLE SNAKES; Felons-convict from the Beginning of the World: These, whenever we meet with them, we put to Death, by Virtue of an old Law, *Thou shalt bruise his Head.* But as this is a sanguinary Law, and may seem too cruel; and as however mischievous those Creatures are with us, they may possibly change their Natures, if they were to change the Climate; I would humbly propose, that this General Sentence of *Death* be changed for *Transportation.*

"In the Spring of the Year, when they first creep out of their Holes, they are feeble, heavy, slow, and easily taken; and if a small Bounty were allow'd *per* Head, some Thousands might be collected annually, and *transported* to Britain. There I would propose to have them carefully distributed in *St. James's Park,* in the *Spring Gardens,* and other Places of Pleasure about *London;* in the Gardens of all the Nobility and Gentry throughout the Nation; but particularly in the Gardens of the *Prime Ministers, the Lords of Trade,* and *Members of Parliament;* for to them we are *most particularly* obliged."

There are, he acknowledges, inconveniences in the scheme, as in all human projects. But then there are inconveniences attendant even on "that good and wise Act of Parliament by virtue of which all the Newgates and Dungeons in Britain are emptied into the colonies." Let not private interests obstruct public utility. "Our mother knows what is best for us." She may know also how to extract good from the apparent evil return. "May not the honest rough British Gentry, by a Familiarity with these Reptiles, learn to *creep,* and to *insinuate,* and to *slaver,* and to *wriggle* into Place (and perhaps to *poison* such as stand in their Way) Qualities of no small Advantage to Courtiers! In comparison of which ' *Improvement* and *Publick Utility,*' what is a *Child* now and then kill'd by their venomous Bite, . . . or even a favourite *Lap-Dog?* "

In short, rattlesnakes seem the most suitable returns for the " Human Serpents sent us by our Mother-Country." Indeed she will have the advantage of us. She will reap equal benefits without equal risk. " For the Rattlesnake gives Warning before he attempts his Mischief, which the Convict does not."

Rats. Man is the master or the destroyer of all animals

except the rodents. Mammoth and cave-bear disappeared before his arrows in the stone age. The aurochs has gone; the buffalo is well-nigh extinct; the lion and the elephant must follow. The tiger and the leopard see their kindred domesticated as cats; the wolf's cousin has been tamed into doghood. But still the rabbits of Australia continue in active and disastrous revolt; traps, ferrets, and poison still fail to make head against the rats and mice of Europe and America. Rabbits, however, begin to show signs of exhaustion, even in Australia. There remain then among all warm-blooded creatures only two that are really dominant, successful, increasing in numbers and range, able to maintain themselves anywhere in the world against all rivals. These two are man and the rat. The genus *homo* and the genus *mus* go everywhere and eat everything. They are the two creatures that dwell in houses and travel in ships. Each drives its other rivals to the wall; but neither, except locally and for brief periods, has ever come near to exterminating the other. Civilized man has fought the common rat for two hundred years, and the battle is still drawn.

Southey, in "The Doctor," says: "Wheresoever man goes, Rat follows, or accompanies him. Town or country is equally agreeable to him. He enters upon your house as a tenant at will (his own, not yours), works out for himself a covered way in your walls, ascends by it from one story to another, and leaving you the larger apartments, takes possession of the space between floor and ceiling, as an entresol for himself. There he has his parties, and his revels, and his gallopades (merry ones they are), when you would be asleep if it were not for the spirit with which the youth and belles of Rat-land keep up the ball over your head."

Moreover, whatever man does, rat always takes a share in the proceedings. Whether it be building a ship, erecting a church, digging a grave, ploughing a field, storing a pantry, taking a journey, or planting a distant colony, rat is sure to have something to do in the matter; man and his gear cannot be transported from place to place without him.

How is it that rats know when a house is about to fall, or a ship to sink?

As with nations so with rats. One tribe comes and dispossesses another. Look at England. The rats that infested Saxon larders in Alfred's reign, that squealed behind the wainscots when Cromwell's Ironsides were harrying royalist mansions, that disturbed the sleep of the last of the Stuarts, were a hardy black species now almost extinct. Like the Red Men in presence of the Palefaces, they have been forced to retire before the Norwegian rat, sometimes despitefully styled the Hanoverian rat, which is brown in color, larger in size, fiercer in disposition. Despite name and nickname, the latter did not come from Norway and they did come before the Hanoverian succession. It is now believed that this rat was brought to England from India and Persia in 1727. By 1750 the breed had made its way to France, and its progress over Europe after that was rapid.

No doubt, when the brown rat had once set foot in England, he treated his weaker brother, and predecessor, the black rat, much as the Stuart dynasty was treated by the House of Hanover. But then the black rat himself is fabled to have come with the Normans and to have witnessed a prior change of dynasty. He still abounds in Normandy and he survives in Wales, where he is known as the French rat, and in other portions of Great Britain,—even in England and even in London. In the neighborhood of the Tower, in Whitbread's brewery, and in the Whitechapel sugar refineries, he still holds his own. Knowing his individual weakness, he knows also that in union there is strength. Acting in masses the black rats attack the brown ones as fearlessly as a flight of swallows attack a hawk. If, however, an equal number of the two breeds are placed together in a cage without food, the chances are that all the black rats will have disappeared before morning; while, if they have been well fed, the brown giants will invariably eat off the long and delicate ears of their little brethren, just as a gourmand after a substantial meal titillates satiety with a wafer biscuit.

To return to the Hanoverian legend. That eccentric English naturalist Charles Waterton, uncompromising Jacobite and Roman Catholic, who was accustomed to supply his own table with fish shot by his own bow and arrows, made war upon no other living being save the rat, the Hanoverian rat as he calls him. In one of his " Essays in Natural History " (London, 1850), he says:

Though I am not aware that there are any minutes in the zoölogical archives of this country which point out to us the precise time at which this insatiate and mischievous little brute first appeared among us, still there is a tradition current in this part of the country (Yorkshire) that it actually came over in the same ship which conveyed the new dynasty to these shores. My father, who was of the first order of field naturalists, was always positive upon this point, and he maintained firmly that it did accompany the House of Hanover in its emigration from Germany to England.

Having thus given the " little brute " a bad name, he pertinaciously hunts him through the two volumes of his Essays. He does more; for, on account of his Whiggism, the rat is the only wild animal banished forever from Waterton Hall, that happy home for all other fowls of the air and beasts of the field against which gamekeepers wage war as vermin.

On his return home from his famous wanderings in South America, Waterton found the hall so infested with rats that nothing was safe from them. But having caught a fine specimen of the "Hanoverian" in a "harmless trap," he carefully smeared him over with tar and let him depart. This astonished and highly-scented animal immediately scoured all the rat-passages, and thus impregnated them with the odor most offensive to his brethren, who fled by hundreds in the night across the narrow portion of the lake, and were no more seen.

The rapid spread of the rat is due to the fearlessness with which he will follow man and his commissariat wherever he goes. Scarcely a ship leaves a port for a distant voyage but it takes in its complement of rats as regularly as the passengers, and in this manner the destructive little animal has not only distributed himself over the entire globe, but, like an enterprising traveller, continually passes from one country to another. The colony of four-footed depredators, which ships itself free of expense, makes, for instance, a voyage to Calcutta, whence many of the body will again go to sea, and land perhaps at some uninhabited island where the vessel may have touched for water. In this manner many a hoary old wanderer has circumnavigated the globe oftener than Captain Cook, and set his paws on twenty different shores. The rat-catcher to the East India Company has often destroyed as many as five hundred in a ship newly arrived from Calcutta. The genuine ship-rat is a more delicate animal than the brown rat, and has so strong a resemblance to the old Norman breed that one cannot help thinking they are intimately related. The same fine large ear, sharp nose, long tail, dark fur, and small size characterize both, and a like antipathy exists between them and the Norwegian species. It is by no means uncommon to find distinct colonies of the two kinds in the same ship—the one confining itself to the stem, the other to the stern, of the vessel. The same arrangement is often adopted in the warehouses of seaports, the ship's company generally locating themselves as near the water as possible, and the landsmen in the more inland portion of the building.

When rats have once found their way into a ship, they are secure as long as the cargo is on board, provided they can command the great necessary—water. If this is well guarded, they will resort to extraordinary expedients to procure it. In a rainy night they will come on deck to drink, and will even ascend the rigging to sip the moisture which lies in the folds of the sails. When reduced to extremities they will attack the spirit-casks, and get so drunk that they are unable to walk home. The land-rat will, in like manner, gnaw the metal tubes which in public-houses lead from the spirit-store to the tap, and is as convivial on these occasions as his nautical relation. The entire race have a quick ear for running liquid, and they constantly eat into leaden pipes, and much to their astonishment receive a douche-bath in consequence. It is without doubt the difficulty of obtaining water which causes them in many cases to desert the ship the moment she touches the shore. On such occasions they get, if possible, dry-footed to land, which they generally accomplish by passing in Indian file along the mooring-rope, though, if no other passage is provided for them, they will not hesitate to swim. In the same manner they board ships from the shore; and so well are their invading habits known to sailors, that it is common upon coming into port to fill up the hawser holes, or else to run the mooring-cable through a broom, the projecting twigs of which effectually stop the ingress of these nautical quadrupeds. Their occupancy of the smaller bird-breeding islands invariably ends in their driving away the feathered inhabitants, for they plunder the nests of their eggs and devour the young. The puffins have in this way been compelled to relinquish Puffin's Island, off the coast of Cærnarvon.

The common brown rat may be described in the words that Bacon applies to the ant, as "a shrewd thing in a garden." According to William Cobbett, rats select the prime of the dessert—melons, strawberries, grapes, and any wall-fruit; and though they do but taste of each, it is not, as he remarks, very pleasant to eat after them. In Cobbett's day they swarmed in millions in the drains and sewers of the English metropolis. Several causes have been in operation to diminish their numbers, and in some quarters of the town almost wholly to extinguish them. In the first place, the method of flushing the sewers adopted since 1860 is exceedingly fatal to them. "When the sluices are opened, go they must with the rush of waters, and they may be seen shot out by hundred from the mouths of the culverts into the Thames. The fact that rats are worth three shillings a dozen for sporting purposes proves, however, the most certain means of their destruction, for it insures their ceaseless pursuit by the great hunter, man. The underground city of sewers becomes one vast hunting-ground, in which men regularly gain a livelihood by capturing them. Before entering the subterraneous world the associates generally plan what routes they will take, and at what point they will meet, possibly with the idea of driving their prey towards a central spot. They go in couples, each man carrying a lighted candle with a tin reflector, a bag, a sieve, and a spade; the spade and sieve being used for examining any deposit which promises to contain some article of value. The moment the rat sees the light he runs along the sides of the drain just above the line of the sewage water; the men follow, and speedily overtake the winded animal, which no sooner finds his pursuers gaining upon him than he sets up a shrill squeak, in the midst of which he is seized with the bare hand behind the ears and deposited in the bag. In this manner a dozen will sometimes be captured in as many minutes. When driven to bay at the end of a blind sewer, they will often fly at the boots of their pursuers in the most determined manner."

These vermin congregate thickest in the neighborhood of slaughter-houses or other places where food is most plentiful. They are frequently found sitting in clusters on the ledge formed by the invert of the sewers. As scavengers of drains they undoubtedly do some service, a small set-off, however, for the mischief they · perpetrate in destroying the brickwork of the sewers and thus constructing lateral cesspools, the contents of which permeate the ground and filter into the sewers. In making these excavations, moreover, they invariably transfer the earth to the main sewers and form obstructions to the flow. The accumulations of their paw-work have regularly to be removed in small trucks constructed for the purpose, and, if this precaution were not taken, they would in a few years entirely destroy the vast system of subterranean culverts laboriously constructed at an expense of millions of dollars. The pipe-drains with smooth barrels, which the rat's tooth cannot touch, alone baffle him; indeed, the rapid flow of water in their narrow channel prevents his even maintaining his foothold in them.

Mr. Jesse relates an anecdote, communicated to him by a Sussex clergyman, which tends to prove that the old English rat at least shows a consideration and care for its elders on the march which is worthy of human philanthropy. "Walking out in some meadows one evening, he observed a great number of rats migrating from one place to another. He stood perfectly still, and the whole assemblage passed close to him. His astonishment, however, was great when he saw amongst the number an old blind rat, which held a piece of stick at one end in its mouth, while another had hold of the other end of it, and thus conducted its blind companion." A kindred circumstance was witnessed in 1757 by Mr. Purdew, a surgeon's mate on board the *Lancaster*. Lying awake one evening in his berth, he saw a rat enter, look cautiously round, and retire. He soon returned leading a second rat, who appeared to be blind, by the ear. A third rat joined them shortly afterwards, and assisted the original conductor in picking up fragments of biscuit and placing them before their infirm parent, as the blind old patriarch was supposed to be. It is only when tormented by hunger that they appear to lose their fellow-feeling and to prey upon one another.

The sagacity of the rat in the pursuit of food is so great, that we almost wonder at the small amount of its cerebral development. Indeed he is so cunning, and works occasionally with such human ingenuity, that accounts which are perfectly correct are sometimes received as mere fables. Incredible as the story may appear of their removing hens' eggs by one fellow lying on his back and grasping tightly his ovoid burden with his forepaws, whilst his comrades drag him away by the tail, we have no reason to disbelieve it, knowing as we do that they will carry eggs from the bottom to the top of a house, lifting them from stair to stair, the first rat pushing them up on its hind and the second lifting them with its fore legs. They will extract the cotton from a flask of Florence oil, dipping in their long tails, and repeating the manœuvre until they have consumed every drop. Lumps of sugar have been found in deep drawers at a distance of thirty feet from the place where the petty-larceny was committed; and a writer saw a rat mount a table on which a drum of figs was placed, and straightway tip it over, scattering its contents on the floor beneath, where a score of his expectant brethren sat watching for the windfall. His instinct is no less shown in the selection of suitable food. He attacks the portion of the elephant's tusks that abound with animal oil, in preference to that which contains phosphate of lime, and the rat-gnawn ivory is selected by the turner as fitted for billiard-balls and other articles where the qualities of elasticity and transparency are required. Thus the tooth-print of this little animal serves as a distinguishing mark of excellence in a precious material devoted to the decorative arts. The rat does not confine himself to inert substances; when he is hard pressed for food he will attack any thing weaker than himself. Frogs, Goldsmith says, had been introduced into Ireland some considerable time before the brown rat, and had multiplied abundantly, but they were pursued in their marshes by this indefatigable hunter, and eaten clean from off the Emerald Isle. He does not scruple to assault domestic poultry; though a rat which attempted to capture the chicken of a game fowl was killed by the mother with beak and spur in the course of twelve minutes. The hen seized it by the neck, shook it violently, put out an eye, and plainly showed that the fowl would be the more powerful of the two if it were equally daring.

"Poor rats!" writes Jerome K. Jerome, "they seem only to

exist so that cats and dogs may gain credit for killing them, and chemists make a fortune by inventing specialties in poison ·for their destruction. And yet there is something fascinating about them. There is a weirdness and uncanniness attaching to them. They are so cunning and strong, so terrible in their numbers, so cruel, so secret. They swarm in deserted houses, where the broken casements hang rotting to the crumbling walls, and the doors swing creaking on their rusty hinges. They know the sinking ship, and leave her, no one knows how or whither. They whisper to each other in their hiding places how a doom will fall upon the hall and the great name die forgotten. They do fearful deeds in ghastly charnel houses.

"No tale of horror is complete without the rats. In stories of ghosts and murderers, they scamper through the echoing rooms, and the gnawing of their teeth is heard behind the wainscot, and their gleaming eyes peer through the holes in the worm-eaten tapestry, and they scream in shrill, unearthly notes in the dead of night, while the moaning wind sweeps, sobs, round the ruined turret towers, and passes wailing like a woman through the chambers bare and tenantless.

"And dying prisoners, in their loathsome dungeons, see, through the horrid gloom, their small red eyes, like glittering coals; hear, in the death-like silence, the rush of their claw-like feet, and start up shrieking in the darkness, and watch through the awful night.

"I love to read tales about rats. They make my flesh creep so. I like that tale of Bishop Hatto and the rats. The wicked bishop, you know, had ever so much corn stored in his granaries, and would not let the starving people touch it, but, when they prayed to him for food, gathered them together in his barn, and then, shutting the doors on them, set fire to the place and burned them all to death. But next day there came thousands upon thousands of rats, sent to do judgment on him. Then Bishop Hatto fled to his strong tower in the middle of the Rhine and barred himself in and fancied he was safe. But the rats! they swam the river, they gnawed their way through the thick stone walls and ate him alive where he sat.

"Oh, it's a lovely tale.

"Then there is the story of the Pied Piper of Hamelin, how first he piped the rats away, and afterward, when the mayor broke faith with him, drew all the children along with him and went into the mountain. What a curious old legend that is! I wonder what it means, or has it any meaning at all?"

Rattenfangerhaus, or Ratcatcher's House, in Hameln (Browning's Hamlin Town) is fabled to be the former residence of the Pied Piper. On its side wall is an inscription in Old German to the following effect:

> On St. John and St. Paul's day 1284
> the 26th of June 130 children
> born in Hameln were led astray
> to Calvalry and lost at Koppen
> by a Piper dressed in divers colours.

The street through which the piper passed is called Bungen-Strasse, or Drum Street, from the lucus a non principle,—no music nor drum is allowed to be played in it. For a long time the town dated its public documents from this calamity, which many early historians have treated as an actual occurrence. Recent authorities have sought to rationalize it. A " dancing mania " (choreomania) is said to have seized some young people in Hameln who left the town and never returned. Others have thought they have seen in the legend a distorted recollection of the Children's Crusade (1211). As a matter of fact, rats still abound, and all one can say is that the Pied Piper, if not born of a myth, was hardly so effective as the poets make believe.

Similar stories are told of other German towns. Baring Gould even cites a kindred myth in Abyssinia, of demon pipers named Hadjiuji Madjuji who, riding on a goat, traverse a hamlet and by their music irresistibly draw children after them to destruction. English readers are most familiar with Browning's version of the legend in " The Pied Piper of Hamelin," which he evidently found in Otto Melander's " Jocoseria."

Strange to say, few Germans in Hameln have ever heard of Browning's ballad. But, then, how many English readers have heard of Wolff's Rattenfänger? It is in this last poem that the story of the Piper is told at length: how he came to Hameln and to the wedding feast, where the guests were dancing; how he fell in love there with Gertrude, the Burgomaster's daughter, and danced with her; and how he promised the Burgomaster to rid Hameln of its rats in exchange for her hand; how he piped the rats to the Weser; and, when he claimed Gertrude, how her father denied him, and of his vengeance. Such is the poem of Wolff. And now one may buy in the shops little carved and painted figures of the Piper and Gertrude, and rats in all forms.

Real Estate. In America the Astors are preëminent in the real-estate field, if one considers only intrinsic value. The Astor holdings in New York City undoubtedly represent the most valuable land interests in all the United States. There is some uncertainty as to which one of the Astors is preëminent, though general opinion assigns that distinction to Vincent Astor, by a considerable margin over his cousin the expatriated William Waldorf Astor. In actual acreage even in New York City there have been individuals who had more extensive holdings than either. Miss Mary C. Pinckney, who died in the nineteenth century, owned at one period about 5000 New York City lots, probably the most extensive interest in improved New York City land ever held by any one person.

The greatest landholder in the United States, in actual extent of territory owned, is E. J. Marshall, of Texas. His estates in Texas and Colorado comprise 4,000,000 acres, or 6250 square miles, an area greater by one-fifth than the entire State of Connecticut. Cattle-raising is practically the only use to which Mr. Marshall has put his immense domain, some of the biggest herds in the West grazing upon it. He made his start in a modest way in Texas, combining cattle-raising with banking operations and real-estate speculations.

Reaping-Machine. At the first Great Exhibition held in Hyde Park, London, in 1851, the American exhibit was a notable failure. A large space was very imperfectly filled with discordant violin pianos, excelsior bedsteads, artificial legs, false teeth, chewing tobacco for the Duke of Wellington, india-rubber in various forms, photographs, rocking-chairs, and—

McCormick's reaping-machine.

That last entry redeemed the collection. It was one of the greatest successes of the whole exhibition. The sensation it created was immense. Very soon it was flanked by another implement of the same sort on a different plan, this also the invention of an American, Gideon Hussey. English farmers learned, to their astonishment, that these machines had been in use in America for more than fifteen years and were sold there by thousands. Then a fresh sensation was produced by the discovery that the original inventor was a Scotchman and that the original machine had long been in use in a remote corner of the Land of Cakes. This is how the *Edinburgh Review* for August, 1852, tells the story:

"A Scottish Presbyterian minister (the Rev. Patrick Bell, now minister of Carmyllie, in Forfarshire) puts together, in 1825, an adjustment of wheels and scissor-blades, so working that, when pushed along a cornfield, it cuts down the grain as if done by hand, and far more cheaply and expeditiously. His brother, a farmer, improves upon and adopts this machine; and, for a dozen successive years, employs it in reaping his crops. The National Society gives the inventor a prize of £50, but makes little noise about it ; and although, in 1834, several were in operation in Forfarshire, few of the supposed wide-awake Scotch

farmers thought of adopting it; but four of the machines were
sent to New York from Dundee. Thoughtful, pushing emi-
grants, settlers in the North American prairies, saw, or heard,
or read of these machines. The reaper was reconstructed, modified in different ways, by ingenious mechanics, was made by
thousands for the farmers beyond the American lakes, and
obtained a deservedly high reputation. Brought to London in
1851, the American reaping-machine proved the main attraction of the United States department of the Great Exhibition.
Hundreds of machines were bespoken by English cultivators, and
all the while no one knew that the original model machine was
at the very time quietly cutting its yearly harvest on the farm
of Inch Michael, in the Carse of Gowrie."

The newspaper sensation woke up the Scotch claimants. The
original Bell was disinterred. Trials followed in which the
Scotch minister's invention was not badly worsted.

In 1853 one Crosskill, who had purchased from Mr. Bell.
the farmer, his machine, and the right to use his name, won the
gold medal of the Yorkshire Agricultural Society, and presented
it to the inventor, Patrick Bell—his first reward after fifteen
years.

Mr. Bell himself was fully persuaded that printed or oral
descriptions of his reaper had prompted the American machine.
This is possible but not probable. At all events, the American
machines differed so widely from the Scotch as to establish a
claim to originality. McCormick's cutting action was a tooth-
edged knife in lieu of Bell's shears, and the improvement was
subsequently adopted by Crosskill. Hussey's, in turn, differed
from McCormick's.

The probability is, that in the United States, as elsewhere,
necessity was the mother of invention; that the farmers, having
no travelling Irishmen to depend on, were driven to their
wit's end, to cut a crop that grew and ripened with no aid from
skill, and very little care, on a virgin soil under a burning sun.
If Hussey or McCormick heard that a reaping-machine had been
invented in Scotland, that information would be enough to set
them to work.

Obed Hussey obtained the patent for his reaping-machine
in June, 1833. Angus H. McCormick secured his for improvements in June, 1834. From that time reaping-machines had
become a regular subject of improvement and manufacture in
the United States; until, in 1850, the sales had amounted to
upward of twelve hundred of one patent only; and the renewal
of McCormick's patent became the subject of a serious opposi-

tion and remonstrance, on the ground that it was not an original invention. Yet so ignorant were Englishmen still of the progress of machine-reaping, that, in South Australia—where, also, the . want of harvest labor was felt in a manner unknown in the mother country—a third kind of machine was invented, which clipped off the ears and threshed them out at the same time by the moving power of a horse pushing behind, as in Bell's machine; leaving the straw (valueless there) to be burned off.

Says the *Illustrated London News* in September, 1856:

"In 1851 our farmers were beginning—not exceptionally, but as a class—to feel the want of the rapid and certain aid of machinery in agriculture. Scotch nationality helped not a little, but there were many difficulties to be conquered. English crops are heavier, and straw is more valuable, than in the United States; and we must add that our ordinary farm-laborers are not so handy in repairing, or so willing to use, mechanical inventions, as the States-men. Landlords, as usual, came forward and purchased the machine-reapers; agricultural societies gave prizes; English tenant-farmers hung back, not without good reason, as, for want of attention to mechanical details or workmanship, many machines were thrown aside as unworkable after one harvest.

"But the time had come when the assistance of machine aid in the harvest was required, and a large capital of money and mechanical skill was thrown into the subject. The results were shown in the Royal Agricultural trials of August, 1856, at Boxted Lodge, Essex, when the verdict of a large body of tenant-farmers settled that the heaviest crops could be most economically cut by the machine-reaper, and the laborers whom a series of years have accustomed to the advantages of machinery applauded the conclusion of their employers. On this occasion the machines cut at the rate of about three acres in four hours, in wheat-fields bearing crops of about forty bushels to the acre, or more than double the average of American crops. The first prize was given to Crosskill's patent improvements of Bell's reaper; the second was divided between Messrs. Burgess', McCormick and Dray's Hussey."

Regiment, Oldest. The Royal Scots, familiarly known as Pontius Pilate's Body-guard, claims to be the oldest regiment in the world. It traces direct descent from certain companies of adventurous Scotch infantry who in 1590 aided Henry IV, of France, in his war with the Leaguers. Their services were retained by the kings of France until the various companies were in 1633 formed into a regiment under command of Sir

John Hepburn (1598–1636), a famous Scottish soldier of fortune. It was then called Le Regiment d' Hebron, that being the nearest the French could come to pronouncing Hepburn. From the fact that the Scotch companies above named had been raised and officered by the officers of the Gens d'Armes Ecossaisses and the Garde dù Corps Ecossaisse, the regiment can claim a connection with those two celebrated corps and, through them, with the Scottish Archers of the Guard, of whom we read in "Quentin Durward," and so back to that earliest body of Scottish soldiers to whom there is any record, "the four and twenty armed Scots in whose fidelity and valor Charles III, King of France, in 882, so confided."

These claims to antiquity were recognized by the kings of France, who gave their Scotch auxiliaries the precedence over all regiments in the service of France. Hence jealousies arose. The Picardy regiment raised in 1562 was especially virulent. One of the officers of the latter, in the course of an historical dispute between representatives of both regiments, sarcastically observed:

"I suppose you will claim next that you were on duty at the crucifixion."

"No," was the smart retort; "had we been on duty at the Sepulchre, the holy body had never left it."

This was a thrust at the reputed inefficiency of Picardy sentinels, many of whom had been reprimanded for sleeping at their posts.

After the restoration of the Stuart monarchy, the Regiment d'Hebron followed Charles II to England and have remained an integral part of the British army ever since.

Republics, Smallest. Most school histories and geographies give credit to San Marino (*q.v.*) as the smallest and the oldest republic in the world. It is the oldest; hence it is fairly evident that for a long period it was the smallest. That preeminence it lost in the early seventeenth century, when Goust, in the lower Pyrenees, was recognized as an independent state by France and Spain. San Marino has now, as it ever had, 23 miles of territory; Goust has barely one mile. The population of the first was in 1910 reckoned at about 1000, of the latter at about 150.

In point of population, therefore, Goust is larger than another baby republic, Tavolara, an island a few miles northeast of Sardinia, which numbers barely 50 souls; but the latter exceeds it in territory, being 5 miles in length by about ⅝ of a mile in breadth.

The sole occupation of the people of Goust is the weaving

of wool and silk. Their government consists of an assembly of old men, called the Council of Ancients, who decide all disputes and who are sole judges of the advisability of marriages between the young people of the place and those of the surrounding countries. Being good Catholics, consanguineous unions are either forbidden or discouraged, according to the degree of the relationship. Neither priest nor physician dwells within the place. All important ceremonies—baptisms, weddings, and funerals—are celebrated at the neighboring village of Laruns. For funerals it is customary to slide the coffin down the rocky slope and to regain it at the foot of the mountain. The citizens pay no taxes or imposts.

A similar immunity is enjoyed by the inhabitants of Tavolara. In 1845 the absolute dominion over that island was bestowed by Charles Albert, King of Sardinia, upon the native family of the Barbalconi, whose chief forthwith assumed the title of King Paul I. He was likewise King Paul the last, for on his death, in 1882, he desired that the kingly title be buried with him and the monarchy be transformed into a republic. No opposition was made by his relatives. The islanders drew up a constitution, under which they elect a president every six years, together with a council of six. The suffrage is extended to men and women alike. No salary is paid to either the president or the members of the council. It is noteworthy that Goust and Tavolara are both ignored by the cyclopædias and the gazetteers, with the single exception of St. Martin's " Nouvelle Dictionnaire de Géographie."

Revolution, American. The first colonial blood shed in conflict with British soldiers was at the so-called Battle of Golden Hill, New York City, when an old sailor was mortally wounded by the redcoats. This was two months previous to the massacre of citizens on Boston Common.

On January 16, 1770, the liberty-pole had been destroyed by the soldiers. Two days later a pair of them were found distributing scurrilous handbills against the Sons of Liberty. They, were taken before the mayor, who ordered them back to their barracks, but, being reinforced at Golden Hill, they made a stand against the howling mob that was following them. The stakes and staves wielded by the latter were no match for the redcoats' bayonets; but, after one of the citizens had been run through and others slightly hurt, the mayor appeared on the scene and ordered them to disperse, an order which they sullenly obeyed. Other conflicts arose in the afternoon and in the next two days, and several citizens were badly injured by the soldiers.

Golden Hill was the summit of a small knoll of rising ground, directly behind a three-story brick house, which was still standing, as No. 122 William Street, at the end of the nineteenth century. Even in 1770 it was not new, but had been used for some years as a tavern. Later it became the rendezvous of Washington, Lafayette, Baron Steuben, Putnam, and Benedict Arnold, and later still of the notorious Captain Kidd. "For more than two hundred years," said the New York *Times*, March 10, 1895, "the unpretentious little building was buried in oblivion, between the walls of big commercial houses that were built around it, and had nothing to distinguish it from its modern neighbors but its antique appearance. The house is built of brick imported from Holland, laid in a cement that is as imperishable as the bricks themselves. The roof is slanting, with two attic windows running out to its edge, and the building, taken as a whole, is a perfect type of what a New York house of the Revolutionary period looked like.

"As in most houses that were erected during the early days of New York, 122 William Street has in the basement two of the famous Dutch ovens which were the house anchors and pride of the Knickerbockers. The kitchen, in the basement, is built after the English models, with an immense mantel elaborately inlaid with tiles of porcelain, about six inches square, each tile containing some historic, religious, or secular event. The illustrations on these tiles are almost obliterated now, but a few of them still remain. The most striking feature of the building is its tall chimney tower, built also of Holland brick. This small pile has withstood the storms and shocks of almost two centuries, and, with the exception of two or three small patches, made recently, is as firm and fit for use to-day as it was when the Sons of Liberty were battling for the independence of our republic.

"The ancient structure has stood for years, a monument to the stability of the workmanship of the colonists, teaching a lesson to the Buddensieks of our age, and its life might have endured in obscurity for another half century but for the formation of the Military and Naval Order of the United States, an organization that has lately been formed, composed of the direct descendants of Revolutionary officers and of commissioned officers in the war of 1812, the war with Tripoli, and the Mexican war.

"This society held its first meeting last week in the ancient building, which is now used as a table d'hôte restaurant by Joseph Zelus, and it is the intention of the order to buy the building in a few years, and erect a clubhouse in the rear, on the very spot where the first blood of the colonists was shed."

Rickshaw. Horses are still rare in Japan, and even yet the bicycle has rarely penetrated into the interior, so that, away from the main line of the railway between Tokio and Hiogo, about the only method of conveyance is the modified perambulator known all over the world as a rickshaw. Many legends are extant as to its invention and its inventor. The Japanese claim the honor for a paralytic old native of Kioto, who some time before 1868, finding his palanquin uncomfortable, took to a little cart instead. The usual foreign account adopted by Mr. Black, in "Young Japan," is that an American named Goble, half-cobbler and half-missionary, was the person to suggest the idea of a glorified go-cart somewhere about 1867.

The first official application for permission to manufacture rickshaws was made in 1870. They were soon being turned out in hundreds and thousands; for the middle-class Japanese found the rickshaw a cheap and comfortable way of travelling long or short distances, and there was an inexhaustible supply of men eager to turn themselves into beasts of burden in order to earn the high wages which the employment brought them. Curiously enough, though elsewhere the thing is called a rickshaw, in Japan it generally goes by the name of jinriki.

Both are abbreviations of the real word, which is *jinriki-sha,* meaning literally "man-power vehicle"—that is, a cart pulled by a man.

Rides, Famous Horseback. In February, 1909, President Roosevelt created a temporary newspaper sensation by covering ninety-eight miles on horseback between daylight and dark,— *i.e.,* from Washington to Warrenton and back in seventeen hours. He made use of three horses for the purpose.

Cavalry officers generally conceded that it was a good ride, and an effective answer to army and navy men who stigmatized as unreasonable the required test of ninety miles in the saddle or fifty miles afoot in three days. Still, they added, it was only a good ride and not an extraordinary one. Many better ones have been recorded even in Mr. Roosevelt's time and among his entourage.

There was that strenuous army officer, for example, Major J. Franklin Bell, a constant companion of the then President in his long walks and longer rides. In 1876, when he was a young second lieutenant of the Seventh Cavalry, that was cut to pieces by the Indians in the ill-fated Custer charge, Major Bell made a long rapid ride through the Bad Lands of Dakota, covering between sunrise and sunset one hundred miles, using only two horses for the purpose.

One hundred and ten miles in twenty-four hours, using only one horse, was the record made by Lieutenant Harry H.

Patterson, of the Third Cavalry. He and his horse reached Jefferson Barracks, in Missouri, in excellent condition, and were received there by General Nelson A. Miles, senior officer of the army, who after a careful examination of both horse and man gave his official commendation to the exploit.

A still better record was made by General Charles F. Roe, of the National Guard of New York, when in 1869, a youngster in the First United States Cavalry, he carried a message 150 miles in the actual riding time of 22⅙ hours. He had with him two men. All three arrived at the end of their journey with their horses in good condition.

Very long distance rides are not popular in the United States, though about three years ago an American cavalry officer rode from Silverton, Ore., to New York, a distance of about 3000 miles. It is among officers of Continental armies that long distance rides are most popular, but it is unfortunate that many of the riders care more for records than for their horses.

Paris, Vienna, Rome, and Bucharest have seen the start or finish of many of these famous rides. Perhaps the first between Paris and Vienna, and certainly the most notable because of the interests involved, was that run by Count de Montenoy in 1809. Napoleon Bonaparte was anxious to obtain the consent of the Emperor of Austria to his marriage with the unwilling Marie Louise. He chose the count as his messenger because he was one of the most accomplished horsemen of the day. Six relays of horses were provided, but the horse he started with did so well that he did not change it. He made the five hundred miles in the unprecedented time of six days or a little less. When he reached Paris, he was so exhausted that he had to remain seated in the imperial presence. Napoleon was so delighted that he presented the young man with the horse he had ridden, a jewelled snuffbox, and sixty thousand francs.

In 1870 a Hungarian officer covered the distance between the two cities in 15 days, riding his own horse. This time was beaten when M. Cottu made the journey on Irish Lass in a little over thirteen days.

Undoubtedly the best of these cross-country rides was accomplished by Lieut. Heyl, of the Ninth Hanoverian Dragoons. He covered 1100 miles between Metz and Bucharest at an average speed of 56 miles a day, and arrived none the worse for his journey. But he was a horseman as well as a record breaker, and carefully trained both himself and his horse before he started; he also nursed it during his ride and saw that it was well groomed whenever possible, so that there were no distressing scenes at the finish.

The most notorious of these military rides was that top-speed gallop between Vienna and Berlin in October, 1892. No fewer than 200 officers took part in this ride, the Germans proceeding from Berlin to Vienna, while the Austrians rode in the opposite direction.

The distance is about 420 miles, and Count Starhemberg (Austria), the winner, finished in 71 hours 20 minutes. The count had undergone severe training to reduce his weight and the horse had also received attention, but in the race itself it had to be kept going by the aid of stimulants. In spite of this the strain was too great, and the animal died within a few hours of the finish.

The chief prize was 20,000 marks and a silver statuette presented by the German Emperor, while the second award was half that amount and a silver statuette presented by the Austrian Emperor. This was won by the German Baron von Reifzenstein —quite a poetic touch this, the prizes given by each emperor being won by a subject of the other—who took 73 hours 6 minutes.

But the most astonishing of all these feats is thus related by James L. Roche, a native of New Orleans, in a letter to the New York *Sun* dated April 13, 1909:

> In the election contest of 1876 a mistake was discovered in the electoral tickets of Iberville and West Baton Rouge parishes, the names of five electors being omitted from them. In order to correct this General George B. Loud, a United States supervisor, started on horseback from Plaquemine and rode to Indian Village, Rosedale, and Maringouin, thence to West Baton Rouge Court House and Brusle Landing, and back to Plaquemine, covering the entire distance, sixty-six miles, in seven hours. Two horses were killed, and the third died a few hours after returning. General Loud was so exhausted that he had to be lifted from the saddle on arrival, and for some time was not able to stand or converse.
>
> He was credited at the time with having saved the electoral vote of Louisiana, the loss of which would have meant the defeat of President Hayes.

Many remarkable rides have been made in the course of active service in the United States, in Indian warfare, during the Civil War, and in police work in the West. Perhaps the finest record was that of Capt. Macdonald, of the Texas Rangers, when chasing a band of Mexican horse-thieves.

When the latter made their raid he was many miles away, and they thought he would come after them by the railway, which made a long detour, so they took things easily. The captain guessed this, so determined to give them a surprise, and set off across country, a distance of 450 miles, as soon as he heard the news. He pressed forward with all speed, and by

47

changing horses ten times on the way arrived sixty-eight hours
later. Hastily collecting a small band of cowboys, he proceeded
at once to the camp of the thieves, who were so surprised by his
appearance that they surrendered without any resistance.

Rather a notable feat for a woman is that recorded in the
New York *Sun* of July 9, 1911:

> Miss Nan J. Aspinwall wound up her 3000-mile horseback journey
> from San Francisco at the City Hall steps yesterday noon. She carried
> a letter from Mayor McCarthy of that city to Mayor Gaynor. In the
> absence of the chief executive, the letter was delivered to Robert
> Adamson, the mayor's secretary.
>
> The plucky young woman left the Pacific Coast on September 1
> and met with many thrilling adventures on her way east. Early this
> week she is to ride to Atlantic City, where she is to be one of the
> features of the annual convention of the Order of Elks.

Englishmen have been the heroes of remarkable rides, some
undertaken for sport and others from higher motives. Foremost
among these was Woodcock's great ride during May, 1761,—the
result of a wager of 2000 guineas between Sir Jennison Shafto
and Mr. Meynell.

One hundred miles a day for twenty-nine consecutive days—
2900 in all—had to be covered. The rider, Woodcock, was
groom to Sir Jennison. By the conditions of the wager a fresh
horse was to be provided every day, but only thirteen in all
were ridden. On the fifteenth day the horse in use became tired
at the sixtieth mile and a fresh one had to be procured.

In spite of this Woodcock covered the additional 100 miles
on his new mount, and duly finished the stipulated distance on
the twenty-ninth day—June 1. As a matter of fact he really
rode 2960 miles, owing to the extra ground covered on the day
his first horse broke down.

Two earlier feats that made a noise in English history
occurred respectively in the reigns of Henry VIII and of his
daughter Elizabeth. A royal chaplain of the name of Wolsey,
who was later to become one of the most famous cardinals that
ever wore the red hat, was the hero of the first exploit. He carried a message from King Henry in England to the Emperor
Maximilian in the Netherlands. Leaving London at four in
the afternoon, Wolsey travelled by boat to Gravesend, rode
through the night to Dover, and, crossing to Calais, finished
his journey on horseback, reaching the emperor that same evening. On the following morning he posted back to Calais, and
had reached Richmond by sunset, accomplishing the journey
to Holland and back in something over two days.

On the death of Queen Elizabeth, Robert Cary hastily departed from London to carry the news to the succeeding ruler.

James VI, of Scotland. Riding out of Whitehall a little after nine o'clock a Thursday morning, Cary covered one hundred and fifty-five miles, to Doncaster, that same night. The next day he proceeded to his home at Witherington, where he spent some time disposing of important business, and did not start for Edinburgh till the next morning. Had not an accident befallen him, he would have reached the Scottish city by midnight. As it was, he achieved the entire journey of four hundred miles within three days.

Riders, Female. Horrified opponents of any innovation on the side-saddle for women may be interested in learning that but for an accident of fashion women might still be riding astride as their forerunners did. The side-saddle was not an invention due to the advancing modesty of civilization. It was introduced to general notice by Anna of Bohemia, daughter of a German Emperor (1366–1394) and wife of an English king (Richard II), not from delicate repulsion to the old method, but simply because she was afflicted with a deformity that rendered it impossible for her to ride on the saddles then in general use for both sexes.

In those days it was imperative that a great lady should ride. Hence the side-saddle was invented.

The fashion set by royalty was followed both in Germany and in England, and eventually all feminine Christendom had learned to use the side-saddle. Yet as late as 1772 Queen Mariana Victoria, of Portugal, kept up her uniform practice of riding astride.

Many attempts to revive the custom have recently been made. In May, 1890, the wife of an English baronet made her appearance in Rotten Row mounted cross-legged and attended by a groom. Her habit was longer than the one then in fashion with her sex, and was simply a very voluminous divided skirt. Yet it excited much criticism and eventually led to imitation. "About eighteen years ago," says Lady Jeune in *Picadilly to Pall Mall* (1909), "a mild sensation was caused by a number of ladies, headed by the late Lady Florence Dixie, announcing their determination to ride in the Park astride. In consequence of this, the first meet of the Coaching Club that year attracted an unprecedented concourse of sight-seers, bent upon catching a glimpse of what had been denounced as a sensational and unbecoming innovation.

Road, Rule of the. In riding and driving, the rule is to keep to the right in nearly all civilized countries except Great Britain and its colonies. There the common practice is summed up in a well-known quatrain that first appeared in this form in the *Sporting Magazine* for September, 1793:

> The law of the road is a paradox quite
>   As you're driving your carriage along;
> If you go to the left you're sure to go right,
>   If you go to the right you go wrong.

These vagaries of custom have afforded much matter for discussion to the curious. See especially the English *Notes and Queries* (series 3, vols. ix, xi, xii, and series 6, iii, iv, v) and the New York *Nation* (vol. 68, pp. 201, 222, 244).

The writers in *Notes and Queries* are far from unanimous. One (series 6, iv, 34) suggests that the English rule is due to the fact that the wagoner, walking on the left of his horses, does not want to be caught between the wheels, and, therefore, pulls his horses towards him, thus turning to the left; while in other countries persons driving with reins are indifferent in the matter, and follow their " natural preference " for the right hand.

This view, however, is opposed by a subsequent writer (page 154 of the same volume), who is of the opinion that coachmen, and not wagoners, made the rule. Sitting on the right, as the coachman does (in order to keep his whip-hand free), he can better watch his wheels and keep them from collision by turning to the left when he meets another vehicle. This agrees with an earlier and more complete explanation (series 3, vol. xi, page 531), which accounts for the English rule in the same way, and for the European rule by the fact that their stages were driven by postilions sitting on the left horse.

It certainly seems singular at first sight that the English settlers of the United States should have adopted the European and not the English rule in this country. The true reason is undoubtedly that elaborated by Mr. Irving Elting in the New York *Nation* (vol. 68, p. 222). He finds it in the almost universal use of oxen for draught purposes throughout this country in the earliest days of its settlement. With them no reins were employed; the guiding was by voice and whip. The right hand being the natural whip hand, it was most convenient that the driver should walk on the left of his oxen, the better to guide them by the whip; and, being on that side, he naturally turned his team to the right, as the English reinsman had turned to the left, in order that he might more surely avoid the danger of collision. The men on horseback, who would otherwise have continued to turn to the left if they had been free to follow their own convenience and their inherited English custom, could readily turn their horses to either side of the road, and thus adapted themselves to the requirement of the primitive American ox-team.

"This rule of turning to the right," adds Mr. Elting, "became more firmly fixed when, later in the development of our country, especially in the South and West, the custom arose of driving several pairs of mules or horses to one vehicle or train of vehicles, by means of a single ' jerk-line,' as it was called, leading from the nigh horse of the front pair of mules to the driver, who rode the nigh wheel-horse. From his position he, like the ox-team driver, could best avoid accident by turning to the right. The very terms ' nigh ' and ' off ' horse, which still prevail, are the survivals of the same early ox-driving period, and designate the position of the horse with reference to the ox-team driver. Now that ox-teams and single-rein mule-teams have for the most part disappeared in the United States, our custom of turning to the right might well be replaced by the safer and more convenient English rule, ' Keep to the left.' "

In British America, it should be noted, the English custom generally prevails. In towns separated by an imaginary line only, but belonging the one to Canada the other to the United States, drivers change their practice at once on crossing the boundary. Yet in Ontario, whose first settlers came from the Northern States of the Union, the law is, and always has been, "Turn to the right on meeting and pass to the left when overtaking." The first statute to that effect was passed in 1853, but it was founded on immemorial custom, as appears from various resolutions of early town-meetings, as, for instance, these, quoted in the *Nation* (vol. 68, p. 240):

"Newark (Niagara), 5th March, 1797: Resolved, That all teams, carriages, etc., coming to town should keep the road, and those going from town to turn out for them."

"Niagara, 7th March, 1808: Resolved, That carriages on meeting should give half the road, keeping the right-hand side."

English and American railroads almost universally follow respectively their own rule of the road as laid down for carriages. English trains run on the left track, with apparently only one exception, that on the section of the railway running from London· Bridge Station to the town of Greenwich. This was one of the first, if not the very first, of suburban lines run out of the metropolis. The explanation usually given is that " the Greenwich Railway Company having been one of the first lines started, its managers determined to follow the Continental style and expected all other companies would follow suit. Palpably they were in error, and they have kept it up ever since."— AUBURN GLEN, in N. Y. *Nation,* April 12, 1899.

On the other hand, the earlier railroads in New Jersey followed the English usage, and for a long time obstinately continued to do so.

Among pedestrians there seems to be a uniformity in the English and the American rule. Turn to the right appears to have been an early custom in London. Thus, in Dr. Samuel Johnson's "Tour in the Hebrides" (edition of 1785, p. 281) the following passage occurs:

" Dr. Johnson said that in the last age, when his mother lived in London, there were two sets of people—those who gave the wall, and those who took it; the peaceable and the quarrelsome. When Dr. J. returned to Lichfield, after having been in London, she asked him whether he was one of those who gave the wall or those who took. Now, said he, it is fixed that every man keeps to the right; or, if one is taking the wall, another yields it, and it is never a dispute." Commenting on this passage, a writer in the *Pall Mall Gazette* says, " I fear the London public have relapsed into the lawless state of things as described by Dr. Johnson's mother. It must be patent to every one that, save in the City, where the crowd is such that no other course can be taken, people have very slight acquaintance with the very simple rule that we should pass those coming towards us left hand to left hand, and for those inveterate shufflers who feel anxious for the proximate support of a friendly railing, all they have to do when they find themselves on the wrong side will be to cross the streets."

Road, Sea Rule of the. On the sea it is even more important than on land that there should be well-defined rules of the road. While there are " ocean lanes," vessels do not move along well-marked lines, like railway trains. They cross and recross each other's tracks. Moreover, there is no air-brake which can halt an ocean steamer within a few yards. Rules of the road at sea are based upon common sense and experience. In general, when two vessels under steam are meeting each other end on, they follow not the English but the European and American rule with vehicles,—that is, each steers to the starboard or right. One short blast from the ship's whistle means that she is taking the starboard course, two blasts mean that she is taking her course to port, three that she is going full speed astern. Should there be risk of collision between a steam vessel and a sailing vessel, it is the duty of the steam vessel as the more manageable to keep out of the way of the other. For the same reason, a sailing ship which is running free is required to keep out of the way of one which is running close hauled.

Robin. The nursery tale of the " Babes in the Wood "

only embodies a popular tradition when it makes the robin pay the last offices of love to the forlorn and friendless and unburied dead.

Shakespeare alludes to the same tradition. When Arviragus, in "Cymbeline," makes his exquisite lament over Fidele and vows that his beloved comrade's grave shall be decked with the fairest flowers that blow, he concludes:

> —the ruddock would
> With charitable bill (O bill, sore-shaming
> Those rich-left heirs that let their fathers die
> Without a monument!) bring thee all this:
> Yea, the furr'd moss besides, when flowers are none,
> To winter-ground thy corse.

To this tradition Michael Drayton, too, Shakespeare's boon companion, makes kindly reference:

> Covering with moss the dead's enclosèd eyes,
> The little red-breast teacheth charity.

Gray also may have had in mind this legendary trait of the robin when he wrote that melodious stanza which, from an unaccountable fastidiousness, he struck out of the "Elegy":

> There, scattered oft the earliest of the year,
> By hands unseen, are showers of violets found;
> The red-breast loves to build and warble there,
> And little footsteps lightly print the ground.

Rocket Life-saving Apparatus. On December 29, 1807, during a terrific gale, a large British frigate, H. M. S. *Anson*, was driven ashore near on Loe Bar, a ridge of pebble and sand thrown up by the waves at Helston on the Cornish coast. She took the beach only sixty yards from the bar, and was dashed broadside on. Luckily for the poor fellows on board, she heeled landward. Great waves rolled over her, sweeping everything before them. Her masts went by the board, but her mainmast formed a floating raft from the ship almost to the shore. Over this scrambled most of those who were saved. Nevertheless, more than a hundred were drowned. It was a terrible sight for the spectators who had collected on the beach. Only a few of them could render any effective assistance. Among the helpless ones was Henry Trengrouse, who went home drenched with rain and spray and sickened in heart and body by the horrors he had witnessed. The terrible scene had made an indelible impression on his mind. Night and day he mused on the means whereby some assistance could be given to the shipwrecked under similar circumstances, some communication be established between vessel and shore.

The king's birthday was celebrated at Helston with fireworks on the green. As Henry Trengrouse watched the streak of fire rushing into the darkness above and scattering a shower of stars, the thought occurred to him, Why should not a rocket, instead of wasting itself in an exhibition of fireworks, do service by carrying a rope to a vessel among the breakers? A communication once established in this manner might become an aerial passage along which those in distress might pass shoreward in safety.

Unknown to Trengrouse, something of the same sort had already occurred to Lieutenant John Bell (1747–1798), who proposed that a shot with a chain attached to it should be discharged from a mortar. In February, 1807, Captain George William Manby (1765–1854) had engaged in perfecting an apparatus very similar to Bell's, and in August he had exhibited some experiments with his improved life-preserving mortar to the members of the Suffolk House Humane Society. Bell's idea had been to fire a rope from ship to shore, Manby's was to fire it from shore to ship. A line fastened to a barbed shot was fired from a mortar on the shore. By means of this line a hawser was drawn out from the shore to the ship, and along it was run a cradle in which the shipwrecked were landed. Trengrouse's apparatus · also used line and hawser, but his line was attached to a rocket instead of being shot out of a mortar, and he substituted a chair for a cradle. The advantages were that a rocket was much lighter, more portable, and less expensive than a bomb and mortar, and that it involved less risk of breaking the line, since the velocity of a rocket increases gradually, whereas that of a shot fired from a mortar was so great and sudden that the line was frequently broken. Trengrouse's entire apparatus could be packed in a chest 4 ft. 3 inches by 1 ft. 6 inches and would take up no appreciable space on board ship. Moreover, it could be used either from the ship or the shore. Manby's implied the use of the mortar on shore alone. Hence the safety of the vessel depended on the fortuitous presence of an apparatus in the vicinity of the wreck.

It was not until February 28, 1818, after many journeys to London and many heart-breaking rebuffs, that Trengrouse succeeded in exhibiting his apparatus before Admiral Sir Charles Rowley and demonstrating its superiority. A committee reported that " Mr. Trengrouse's mode appears to be the best that has been suggested for the purpose of saving lives from shipwreck by gaining a communication from the shore, and, so far as the experiments went, it most perfectly answered what was proposed." In the same year the Committee of the Elder Brethren of Trinity House reported in high terms on the invention and recommended that no vessel should be without it.

Government moved slowly; Parliament haggled over the matter, though a member of the House warned it that it was guilty of sinful negligence, "for, while you are parleying over this invention and this important subject, thousands of our fellow-men are losing their lives."

Finally Government ordered twenty sets of the rockets, but later resolved on making them itself, and paid Trengrouse £50, the supposed profit he would have made on the order. In 1821 the Society of Arts presented him with their silver medal and a grant of thirty guineas. Alexander I, of Russia, later presented him with a diamond ring, in acknowledgment of the uses to which the rocket had been put in shipwrecks on the Baltic and the Black Sea. With these acknowledgments of his services he had to rest contented, though he had expended £3000 in his experiments and sacrificed to this one object—that of saving life—his capital, his business, and his health.

As he lay on his death-bed with his face to the wall, he turned about, and, with one of his bright, hopeful smiles, said to his son, "If you live to be as old as I am, you will find my rocket apparatus all along our shores." They were his last words.

The rocket apparatus is used along the shores of Great Britain at over 300 stations, but not, as he had hoped, on board the vessels. Meanwhile· Manby's mortar after a fair test had proved itself so cumbrous and dangerous that it was abandoned. Nevertheless Manby received over £2000 from a grateful country.

Trengrouse, it is said, once met Sir William Congreve, another rival inventor. (see CONGREVE ROCKET), and said to him in the course of their discussion, "So far as I can see, Sir William, your rocket is designed to destroy life; mine is to save life; and I do claim to be the first that ever thought of utilizing a rocket for the saving of human lives."

Roller-coaster. The story of its origin was thus given in the New York *Tribune* in 1910: L. N. Thompson, since famous as the founder of Luna Park in Coney Island, was riding in a car once when he saw some boys sliding down hill in the snow. Now, Mr. Thompson had been born in Indiana, and afterward had lived in Arizona. There were no hills about his Indiana home and there was no snow in Arizona. As he looked at the boys, he felt as if he had been deprived of his birthright in his own boyhood and declared that he would like to go sliding then and there.

The more he thought it over, the surer he became that thousands of grown-up people everywhere must feel the same way. If he could make it respectable for grown-ups to go sliding, he believed they would like it. Thereupon he bought a ticket for a Pennsylvania town where he had heard that a coal company was running a road by gravity, coasting its cars down one hill with force enough to take them up another. The plan worked perfectly, so Mr. Thompson experimented for a while, perfected plans for guarding his passengers' safety, and took out patents on his road. This was the " switchback " which was built in Coney Island in 1884.

This roller-coaster was only 450 feet long, and the highest drop on the line was only 10 feet. To-day there is a roller-coaster at Brighton Beach where the track is 116 feet high at one point and there is a drop of 85 feet. That first roller-coaster cost $1500. The big roller-coasters at Coney Island to-day cost about $60,000 each. The smaller ones, such as are shipped to Rio de Janeiro or Yokohama, represent an investment of $40,000 each before they have carried a passenger. It is estimated that $50,000,000 is invested in sliding amusements of one sort or another in the United States alone. A single firm, the same which operated the first " Switchback " in 1884, had $8,000,000 invested in the business. Its profits are enormous. In one season a roller-coaster frequently pays for itself. Earnings of less than 30 per cent. for a season are rare. Two thousand dollars is a good figure for a Sunday's receipts. The fare is 10 cents a ride.   ·

Go to Coney Island and see how natural the process is. When you have felt the cushioned seat plunge down from under you and have caught your breath to tide yourself over the big drop that is coming, and have felt the car. charge up the next steep slope with a roar and a rush that is good to hear, and when you have grown supercilious at the easy motion with which it takes the later undulations, and then have had the whole ride all over again, you will come out at the end and be quite ready to own that is well worth 10 cents and that you will ride again, to-day or next week, as circumstances may fall out. You have it firmly fixed in your mind that it is worth 10 cents.

Against the common coaster it may be urged that the ride is an anticlimax. The big thrill comes first, and every drop thereafter is gentler than the one before. There is a very full and satisfactory reply to such an objection in the " loop-the-loop " machine. In this amazing road, after coming up from a dip, instead of going on down another hill the track keeps on rising until it has turned over backward, so that cars and passengers are turned upside down for the fraction of a second during which they are passing the top of the loop.

The mere craving to cut loose for a wild rush down hill is

the basic metal from which the coaster mint has coined its fortunes, but there are other human desires that have been fed into the hopper with it, and all have come out good gold and greenbacks. Wed the sliding, coasting impulse to the urge of the swimming hole, mankind's love for splashing and the smooth motion of water, and you have the "shoot the chutes." Add to the sliding impulse the grown-up's sneaking feeling that this sliding is awful foolishness, but he is going to cut up just the same, and you have the "freak" rides. There is the "Virginia reel," in which couples slide in tubs down a path where they are bumped and turned hindside before, striking pegs on the way. There is the "human Niagara," which is a flight of stairs to all intents and purposes, except that when you try to walk down you roll down instead. And then, ranked among the "freaks," is the slide that is really the most fundamental of all, the "human toboggan slide," in which you simply place your person in contact with a smooth wooden surface and slide at a speed that is almost too good to be true, and with the blessed assurance that there are no nails anywhere on the way.

The "scenic railway" is the result of another combination; the sliding impulse mixed with the love of surprising things to see. Here an ordinary roller-coaster winds through Arctic ice-fields of papier-maché or canvas canyons.

Roller-skate. The first roller-skate seems to have been patented in 1823 by one Tyers, a fruiterer in Picadilly, London. Other patents of a similar kind followed at intervals, but none of these skates were guidable in curves save at the expense of enormous friction. It was not until 1865, when J. L. Plimpton, of New York, brought out his famous skate, that curves and all other figures known on ice were brought within the reach of skaters on an artificial floor. This was the familiar four-wheeled skate working on rubber springs.

Lady Dorothy Neville, in her "Recollections," tells us that some years elapsed before it was taken up by the public in England, though it was occasionally used by professionals on the stage. "Suddenly in the middle seventies the mania caught hold of every class, and rinks, some improvised and some specially built, sprang up in almost every town of any importance. London, and more especially fashionable London, went mad about the new amusement. The craze, however, did not last as long as many speculators had confidently anticipated, and a great deal of money was eventually lost by those who, convinced of the permanency of the roller-skating rage, had invested, or rather risked, their money in the construction of rinks. Roller-skating whilst it lasted called forth many witticisms and jokes, some of them, it must be added, of none too refined a taste. Certain ladies, for instance, were said to stand on a very unsteady footing, whilst others of irreproachable conduct and stern demeanor were spoken of as constantly falling.   One could not help smiling to hear that people regarded as models of decorum had recently had many a slip.   The whole craze indeed, with the comical accidents it entailed, produced general and widespread hilarity."

From far back in the eighteenth century, a rude sort of skate on wheels has been used on the roads in Holland, and at one time they penetrated into Germany.   Some contrivance of this sort is evidently alluded to in a paragraph that appeared in the *Illustrated London News* for November 1, 1851:

When Meyerbeer introduced a skating scene into his last opera, the " Prophète," it was a matter of dispute whether this piece of stage effect was original or not: a little enquiry proved the negative, but gave another illustration of the adage that " nothing is so new as what has been forgotten." Old playgoers recalled a similar scene in a pantomime produced some twenty years ago. But the machinist whom the Berlin composer consulted might have formed the idea in daily. or rather nightly practice, much nearer home. In a beer-house, called the Corso Halle, near the Fischer Bruche, in Berlin, the guests are waited upon by three or four young women on skates! The moment a customer takes a seat, one of the damsels darts from the end of the room, skims over the floor, describes clever curves round the end of a table, or a cluster of chairs, brings herself up at the moment he thinks it inevitable she must glide over his toes, and requests to know his wishes. It is, of course, a *seidel* of the best " Bavarian "—a wave of the short petticoat, like the tail of a disappearing mermaid, and the Hebe of the Corso is gone! She often collects several orders in the course of a round or from a single group: and will skate back with any number of glass pint pots of beer in both hands, without disturbing a flake of froth. Except from the rattling noise produced, the motion is as good an imitation of skating as can be conceived. To the curious stranger, no secret is made of the mechanism employed: small iron wheels, let into the sole of a strong, but neatly fitting pair of boots, are all the mystery; but to move about in them easily, and even gracefully, requires much practice. It is also more fatiguing than walking: and towards midnight, when it may be assumed each waitress has skated several miles, they look rather weary.

Rome.   The name of Rome, says a writer in the *Nuova Antologia,* is probably the one most repeated in the different parts of the world.   All the continents, including Oceanica, have Romes.   In Europe there is an island called Rome in the Baltic. off the east coast of the Scandinavian peninsula.   A village of 1000 inhabitants, it possesses a cathedral.   In Asia there is a Rome in upper Burma, on a branch of the Sittang, a distance of about 65 kilometres to the southeast of Mandalay.

Rome in Africa is an important centre for the missionaries of Basutoland.   It lies to the southeast of the **Orange State,** about 50 kilometres from the Orange River.   North America has several Romes—one in New York State, Virginia, Iowa, Kansas, Texas, Pennsylvania, and Indiana, and two in Georgia. In South America there are two Romes in Argentina.

In Oceanica Rome is an important city of Queensland. It is also the name of a stream which flows from the mountainous chain of the Bismarck archipelago.   The Malay archipelago also possesses its Rome in the north of Timor.

Rose.   Pliny, writing at the beginning of the Christian era, says of the rose that " it is a flower known to all nations, equally with wine, myrtle, and oil."   Long before Pliny's time indeed, it had been crowned the Queen of Flowers.   Its rule was well-nigh universal.   Hindoos, Greeks, and Romans had speculated about its origin and invented pretty legends to account for it. One of the prettiest is the following:

A Jewish maiden named Zillah, rejecting the advances of an unworthy lover, was by him accused of evil practices and so sentenced to be burnt at the stake.   But the fire spared the maiden and consumed only the evil-minded lover: " The fire began to burn about her; she made her prayers to our Lord, and anon was the fire quenched and out, and brands that were burning becomen white roses, and these were the first roses that ever any man saw."

A Persian myth asserts, that, when at Nimrod's command their prophet Araham was in his infancy cast into a furnace, the glowing bed of coals was turned instantly into a bed of roses, " whereon the child sweetly slumbered."

According to a Greek myth, all roses were originally white, but some were tinged red by the blood of Venus, who wounded her foot on a thorn while hastening to the aid of the dying Narcissus.   According to another legend, they sprang from the bath of Aphrodite.   Later, a Christian tradition asserted that the crown of thorns was one of the rose thorn, and that the red roses sprang from the blood of Christ:

> Men saw the thorns on Jesus' brow,
> But angels saw the roses.

A still different story is told by Mussulman tradition.   According to this, white roses sprang from the sweat of the prophet Mohammed during his journey to heaven, and yellow ones from perspiration dripping from the mane of Al Borak, his steed.   It is further reported that the red flower is colored with drops of his blood.   Hence the faithful will never suffer one to lie on the ground.

The Greeks found an equally fanciful origin for thorns. Cupid, stooping to kiss a new-blown, dewy rose, was stung by a bee asleep in its heart. To please the petulant boy, Venus strung his bow with captive bees and planted along the stem of the rose the stings torn from them. Hippocrates, the god of silence, carries as his symbol a rose given to him by Cupid. From the idea of secrecy or reserve that associates itself with roses came the old custom recorded by the Greeks. When the people of the North, they say, wished to preserve the most profound secrecy in regard to what was said between themselves at their feasts, a freshly gathered rose was hung from the ceiling above the upper end of the table. It was considered not only dishonorable, but a crime, to reveal that which had been said "sub rosa."

On the hills near Athens, vast rose gardens were planted, which supplied the flower markets of the day. Likewise their culture was carried to a high degree of perfection in the Græco-Roman colonies of Pæstum and Sybaris. Ovid tells us that in Rome they were made to bloom twice a year by means of hot water. From other contemporary writers it may be gathered that the water was carried in pipes as in our modern hot-houses.

When Cleopatra came to meet Marc Antony at Cecilia, four days of feasting and merriment ensued,—the fourth and crowning day being a festival of roses. The floors of the rooms and halls were covered to the depth of eighteen inches with freshly blown roses, held in place by a strong but delicate net stretched above them so that her guests might walk over them. Nero, not many years later, gave a feast where $100,000 was spent in roses alone.

On the occasion of certain water-parties given at Balæ, the whole lake of Lucina was covered with roses, which parted before the moving boats and closed after them as they passed. Lucius Verus reached a luxury in the use of the rose never surpassed before or after his time. He slept upon a couch covered with cushions made of fine, thin net, and filled with freshly-gathered rose-leaves. The extreme fastidiousness of the young Smindyrides, the Sybarite, whose sleep was disturbed by a crumpled rose leaf, has passed into a familiar proverb.

In Germany the rose has ever been a favorite flower. It is one of those mysterious blossoms, like the "forget-me-not," that unlock treasures concealed in caves or castles. The rose was dedicated to Holda, the Northern Venus, and, in Christian hands, became the "Marienroschen" of the Virgin. The white rose is usually Mary's emblem. She dried her veil on a rose-bush, and thereafter it bore none but white flowers.

In the German Book of Heroes there is a story of a rose garden at Worms surrounded by a single silken thread. The

Princess Chrymhilde promised to each knight who should successfully defend it and slay an attacking giant, a chaplet of roses and a kiss. Hildebrandt, one of the knights, took the roses, but declined the kiss. Another, a monk, not only took the kiss, but sued for one apiece for all the members of his fraternity. To this the princess consented, but only after the valiant monk had "fulfilled his tale" of giants, one for each kiss.

Now let us pass from legend to history. The rose was distinguished from other flowers at a very early age, and by most of the ancient races of Asia, with the exception of the Assyrians and the Hebrews, who seem only to have spoken of it after the advent of the Grecian influence. The discovered Egyptian records have no traces of it before the time of the conquest of Alexander.

The two earliest roses known by name—the Rose of the Magis and the Rose of the Chaldeans—were identified from the Zend-Avesta, which has reported the traditions of these ancient peoples.

The Greeks, who originated in Asia Minor, doubtless brought the cultivated rose to Europe with them. Herodotus tells us that after King Midas was settled in Hellas the rose of sixty petals was found there. What particular varieties of rose they were that were sung by Homer, Sappho, and Anacreon we can only guess, but the roses of Philippes, of Cyrenius, of Phaselis, and others had a great reputation. From the descriptions of Theophrastus one can get some idea of the roses that were cultivated by the Greeks after the fourth century B.C.

One of these is the rose of the hundred petals, which was probably brought from Asia Minor by Midas. It was doubtless known to and sung by Sappho and Anacreon.

The Romans came to know the rose immediately after their conquest of Greece, for soon after Cicero mentions the flower, Varro encouraged its culture, Horace and Ovid sang of it. Virgil had already made the roses of Paestum celebrated, and spoken of their capacity to bloom twice a year.

From the descriptions of the elder Pliny a number of the most celebrated roses of the time have been more or less certainly identified.

After the Romans the Queen of Flowers remained for centuries neglected and ignored in consequence of the invasion of the Barbarians.

In the West there are scarcely any traces of the rose; we have to go back to the East again to pick up the thread of the story.

Thanks to the recent discovery of roses in the Egyptian

tombs of the first centuries A.D., we know what species of roses were cultivated by Christian Egypt, for these vestiges have been identified with the Holy Rose of Abyssinia.

After the reawakening from their long sleep of the Western countries it took many years before writers came to distinguish between the different varieties of roses; but after the Crusades, in 1254, the celebrated damask rose, which was known to the ancient Romans, but which had been meanwhile forgotten, again made its appearance.

It was this rose that was introduced into Anjou by King René and widely cultivated there. It became known as the Provence and later as the Provins rose.

The Red Damask Rose, too, again makes its appearance in history as the badge of the house of Lancaster. It had been brought to England from Provence in 1280 by Count Edmond of Lancaster.

The White Rose of the House of York was also widely cultivated in the sixteenth century. The Wars of the Roses were so named because the various combatants wore the flower in their helmets, and this long and bloody contest is the most sinister association that exists with the name of this flower.

In the eighteenth century the cult of the rose progressed in Holland, where the rose of a hundred petals, perfected, came to be known as the Rose of Batavia, or the Painters' Rose, and also the Moss Rose.

Rose of England. The origin of the rose in the English coat-of-arms dates back to the civil wars between the York and the Lancaster factions.

In the year 1450 a group of noblemen were discussing the respective rights of the rival claimants to the throne, and to avoid interruption they adjourned to the Temple Gardens. Scarce had they arrived, however, when they noticed that Richard, Duke of York, was approaching. The conversation ceased immediately. Richard begged to know the subject of their so earnest discourse, and also how many of them believed him to be their rightful king. Still they were silent, both from policy and politeness. Presently Richard said, "If you are reluctant to give me your opinion in words, why not give me a sign? Let my friends follow my example and pull a white rose." Earls Somerset and Suffolk declared for the reigning king, Henry of Lancaster, Somerset proposing that the friends of Henry should gather a red rose. Earl Warwick, by gathering the white rose, declared for the house of York. "But," said Vernon, a friend of Richard, "before gathering more roses we ought to agree that whichever party has the greatest number wins the day." All agreed, led to violent excitement and threats, and the party separated to make known to their friends the badges of the houses of York and Lancaster.

Notwithstanding reconciliation, once thought to have been safely effected between the rival factions, war again broke out and raged for many years. Not until the two houses were united by the marriage of Henry VII of Lancaster and Elizabeth of York did the nation obtain peace. The roses, then blended, became the national flower of England, emblazoned on her arms and on the coin of the realm.

> Let merry England proudly rear
> Her blended roses bought so dear.

Rose of Hell. A flower that blooms on a tree of great size and strength growing in the sides of Mount Agua, a high peak near the volcano of Fuego among the rugged mountains of Central America. The blossom measures about 12 inches across, and receives its sinister name from the Indians, who believe that the crater of the volcano is the entrance to hell and that the flower is a native of the regions below. The Los Angeles *Times* thus describes the flower:

At first appearance it seems to be a tough gnarled knot of a tree which has been splintered; but closer examination discloses the fact that it has petals of wood and bark and the rough outlines of a flower. The petals, concave in form, are arranged much like the petals of a half-blown rose. Their inside surfaces are covered with fine lines, which have the delicacy of fine hand carving. The stem, which is about a foot long, is of some unusual wood, which is light and strong. It is covered with heavy bark, which seems to have been cracked by heat. Both flower and stem are dark brown—the color of weather-beaten boughs, and dry as tinder.

Rose of Hildesheim. There is an Arab tradition that a certain King Shaddad planted a field of roses in the desert, and that they are still flourishing; but that no man can find them. If man ever does discover them, he will have come upon the oldest rose-bush in the world. Meanwhile that title is claimed by and conceded to a carefully tended rose-bush which, notwithstanding the thousand years of life that are credited to it, still lives and blooms against the wall of the Cathedral in Hildesheim, Germany. Though its stem is only 2 inches thick, it is 26 feet high, covers 32 feet of wall, and, notwithstanding its great age, puts forward fresh branches and green tendrils every spring. One tradition, which is not intrinsically impossible, claims that the bush was planted by Charlemagne to commemorate a visit paid him by the Ambassador of the Caliph Haroun-al-Raschid. But popular imagination, clamoring for a more mystic origin, favors the following legend. In the Middle Ages the site of Hildesheim was a vast forest known as the Wohl. Because of its abundant game, this was a favorite resort of the Emperor Louis the Pious, an ardent sportsman, who reigned in the ninth century. One day the arduous chase of a great white stag led him into Innerste River, where the stag itself escaped by swimming, but where the king lost horse and hounds in the water and reached the other side only to find himself alone in a trackless wilderness. Drawing a golden crucifix from his breast, he hung it on a rose-tree in full bloom, prayed before it for succor, and then lay down to sleep. When he awoke, the rose-tree was standing in a heap of snow, though all around was fresh and green, and the crucifix was frozen to the bush, yet the roses bloomed fairer and fuller than before. He saw a miracle had been wrought for him. Just then the blast of horns and the baying of dogs announced the approach of his retinue. Presently it arrived, and all were filled with joy to find their missing master again, hale and hearty as ever. He told them what had occurred and bade them lay the foundation for a chapel in commemoration of his deliverance. Later a town arose there, and the cathedral was built where the holy rose could be supported by its walls.

Rose of Jericho. Some roses so called are really no roses at all. The Christmas rose, for example, is a hellebore, which demands a little protection with a hand-light if we desire it to wish us a Happy New Year; the Guelder rose is a sterile snowball, which ought not to repudiate its classical title of Viburnum; the Rose Trémière, or Passe-Rose, is a hollyhock, which renders excellent service in the decoration of garden scenery; the Rose-Laurier, or Laurel Rose, is the oleander, an elegant shrub with bright pink flowers, delighting to grow by the water's edge, but which, Algerian colonists say, poisons the brook that runs at its foot.

The Rose of Jericho is a cruciferous individual belonging to the same Linnæan class as cabbages and turnips, and in no way related to any sort of rose, "for, though it be dry, yet will it, upon imbibition of moisture, dilate its leaves and explicate its flowers contracted and seeming dried up."

It is also called the Rose of Mary, a tradition reporting that it grew up to mark every resting-place of the Holy Family during the journey to Egypt. Sometimes it is used as a symbol of the Resurrection.

Rose du Roi (King's Rose). One of the best of all autumnal roses in its combined perfections of form, scent, hardiness, and color. Its history is the only thing it has to blush for. The King's rose has been everybody's rose. It is a turncoat, a renegade, a sort of floral Vicar of Bray. It made its first appearance in France during the time of Louis XVIII and was named the King's Rose in compliment to him. When Bonaparte came over from Elba and put the legitimate king to flight, the proprietor, thinking that his new rose with any other name would bring in more money, deemed it good policy to rechristen it Rose de l'Empereur, or the Emperor's Rose. But the hundred days were a limited number, and the Battle of Waterloo again changed the aspect of political affairs. The rose ratted once more, and was re-styled Rose du Roi. It is known in England as the Crimson Perpetual. To complete its diplomatic education, it only wanted to be rebaptized to-day as the Rose de la République Rouge, or the Red Republican Rose.

Fickle and unloyal as the rose has thus proved itself to be, it averts your censure like other fair offenders.

> If to her share some floral errors fall,
> Look on her face and you'll forget them all.

Round Tower. A curious ruin at Newport, R. I., in the form of a round stone tower, 30 feet high, supported by 8 massive stone columns, which has been the subject of much controversy. Danish antiquarians claimed for it a resemblance to Scandinavian architecture, and surmised that it had been built by the old Norse rovers, Leif and Thorwald, who, on the authority of the sagas, are said to have sailed from Iceland to the New World about A.D. 1000, and to have passed a winter in New England. Here Thorwald had been slain in an encounter with the natives, and buried near the spot where he fell. A rock on the shore of Taunton River, known as the Dighton Rock, from its neighborhood to the town of Dighton, whose strange and illegible inscriptions had attracted the attention of antiquarians from the time of Cotton Mather, was now declared to be a Runic stone. The case was greatly strengthened when a skeleton was dug up at Fall River, Mass., wearing on its breast an oval brass plate, and girt around the waist by a curious belt, similar in workmanship to the bandoliers worn when firearms were in their infancy. This was at once claimed to be the remains of a Norse warrior, presumably Thorwald himself, in spite of the fact that the skeleton was buried Indian fashion, in a sitting posture, with Indian arrow-heads around it. But all this chain of evidence, seemingly so complete, has been overthrown by fuller research. The Round Tower has been proved to be simply a mill, similar in construction to many still extant in England, notably one in Chesterton. The inscriptions on Dighton Rock are nothing but half-erased Indian picture writing. The metal found upon the skeleton

turned out to be different from that used for warlike purposes
by the Scandinavians, and identical with that known to have
been worn by Indians, both for purposes of ornament and defence, as far back as the time of the Cabots. A windmill is
known to have been erected in Newport; it is mentioned in
Governor Arnold's will, and the way leading to it is still called
Mill Street. The Round Tower has, nevertheless, been used for
poetical purposes by Longfellow in "The Skeleton Knight"
and by J. G. Brainerd, in "The Newport Tower." The latter
invents an Indian tradition that its decaying walls were typical
of the disappearance of the Red Man, and that its final fall
would herald the total extinction of his race. Mrs. L. H.
Sigourney also has a poem called "The Newport Tower."

Royal Academy. The first idea for a public exhibition of
pictures in London seems to have arisen from the paintings
presented by Hogarth, Reynolds, and other artists to the Foundling Asylum (q.v.). Free access being allowed to the public,
the place became a fashionable lounge. The artists took the
hint and determine to attempt something of the same sort in
their own behalf. At a meeting held November 12, 1759, it
was resolved that a public exhibition should be held annually,
beginning each year with the second week of April. The
"Society of Arts," founded in 1754, gave the use of their
rooms, opposite Beaufort Buildings in the Strand, and the first
exhibition was opened on April 21, 1760. Next year there
were two separate exhibitions, one in Spring Gardens, managed
by the "Society of Artists of Great Britain," the other, in the
old rooms in the Strand, by a body of seceders, "The Society
of Free Artists," which continued its annual exhibitions until
1776. The first-mentioned numbered almost all the great names
of the period. Among the exhibitors were Reynolds, Romney,
and Gainsborough. Admission was free, but the catalogues cost
a shilling, and of these 13,000 were sold. Dr. Johnson about
this time writes to Baretti:

> The artists have instituted a yearly exhibition of pictures and
> statues, in imitation, I am told, of foreign academies. This year
> [1761] was the second exhibition. They please themselves much with
> the multitude of spectators, and imagine that the English School will
> rise much in reputation.

On January 26, 1765, King George III, at the solicitation
of the members, granted them a royal charter as the "Incorporated Society of Artists of Great Britain." In 1767,
owing to internal dissensions that resulted in the resignation of
most of the directors, a committee of four was appointed to
take measures for forming a new academy. The king gave his

patronage and assistance, and some of the regulations were written out by his Majesty's own hand. The affair was kept entirely secret till all the preparations were complete, and was at length revealed to the president of the old society by the king himself. Kirby, who had arrived on some business at Windsor, was ushered into the presence of George III as West was showing his picture of "Regulus." Kirby admired the work, and expressed a hope that West would exhibit it. He replied that it belonged to his Majesty, who at once joined in, "I shall be happy to let the work be shown to the public."

"Then, Mr. West," said Kirby, "you will send it to my exhibition."

"No," replied the king; "it must go to my exhibition—to the Royal Academy."

The president of the Associated Artists bowed and retired. The disappointment is said to have shortened his life. He died in 1774, at the age of fifty-nine.

Next evening, December 9, thirty artists met at the house of Wilton, the sculptor, to take steps for forming the new academy. The code of laws was accepted. Thirty-six academicians, recommended by the king, were elected. Next day his Majesty signed the instrument defining the constitution of the Royal Academy, which thus began its existence on Saturday, December 10, 1768. On December 14 the first general assembly was held at Pall Mall.

Sir Joshua Reynolds was elected president, William Chambers, treasurer, George Michael Moser, keeper, and Francis Milner Newton, secretary. Eight academicians were chosen as members of the council, which was to have the "entire direction and management of all the business of the society." Nine others were appointed visitors, whose duty was to "attend the schools by rotation, each a month, to settle figures, to examine the performances of the students, to advise and instruct them." These regulations, with some slight modifications, continue in force to the present day.

The Academy found its first home in Pall Mall, immediately adjacent to Old Carlton House, a little eastward of the site now occupied by the United Service Club. Its first exhibition, comprising 136 works, was opened on the 26th April, and was visited by the king on the 25th May, an advertisement having been previously inserted in the papers that on that day the public would not be admitted. It closed on the 27th of the same month. The price of admission was, as at the present time, one shilling; the catalogues were sold for sixpence, and the total receipts were £699 17s. 6d. In

1792, the year in which Reynolds died, 780 works were exhibited, and the receipts had increased to £3178 12s.

The first annual dinner took place on St. George's Day, April 23, 1771. Twenty-five guests were invited, among them Dr. Johnson and Oliver Goldsmith. This annual dinner now takes place on the Saturday before the opening of the exhibition on the first Monday in May. No social event of the London season attracts a more distinguished company. Soldiers, statesmen, and literary men all vie with artists in their anxiety to be present. It is said that an ambitious amateur once spent £25,000 on the pictures of living artists in the hope that such patronage might procure him an invitation to the dinner at Burlington House. But his munificence was all in vain.

Royal Arms in Churches. The earliest recorded instance of the setting up of the royal arms in English churches occurred in St. Martin's Church, Ironmonger Lane, London, in February, 1547, the month after the death of Henry VIII. Burnet's History of the Reformation (Part ii, Book i, p. 13, vol. ii) says, the parish register of Warrington, July 30, 1660, mentions an injunction of the " Great Cownsell " of England, " that in all churches thorowout the kingdom of England his Majestie's armes shall be sett upp; " but no historical authority has ever been found to confirm this statement.

The royal arms in Kentbury Church, Berkshire, bear the date and initials C. R. 1683.

In 1631 Archbishop Abbot granted a license to a painter, which contains a statement that all churches ought to be beautified " more especially with his Majestie's Armes and the Tenne Commandments," which he was to enquire into in the various churches in Canterbury diocese for the purpose of renewal if they were out of repair. This arose out of the " weariness of the popish superstitions " in the curate and church wardens who took down the images and set up the royal arms. This does not include such as occur in stained glass windows.

Many were destroyed during the Commonwealth (1649–1660); hence the injunction of Charles II.

S.

Saccharin, one of the numerous by-products of the gas-maker's refuse. Its sweetness is 300 times more intense than that of cane sugar. It was accidentally discovered in 1887. Dr. Fahlberg had entered the Johns Hopkins University in America in order to devote himself exclusively to a study of the chemistry of coal-tar derivatives. One evening at tea-time he detected an intensely sweet flavor upon his bread-and-butter. He traced the sweetness to his fingers, to his hands, and to his coat-sleeves; and it finally dawned upon him that it must have been derived from one of the new compounds which he had that day succeeded in producing. He promptly returned to his laboratory and tasted the contents of every vessel with which he had been working. His suspicion was correct. One of his beakers contained the sweet material.

"Some astonishment," says *Chambers's Journal* for October 20, 1889, "was a short time ago aroused by the report that a substance had been discovered that was three hundred times sweeter than sugar. This substance, saccharin, has since become a marketable commodity; and those who are curious to try its sweetening properties can obtain tabloids of it at most chemists' shops. Our French neighbors were quick to recognize it as a rival to beet-sugar; and it speedily obtained a bad name, which it does not deserve, from their initiative. Our medical authorities regard it as a valuable remedy in certain diseases; and it seems to be used in somewhat large quantities in the preparation of fruits and liqueurs—at least we gather that that must be the case, from the statement which is published, that in Germany alone so much saccharin has been made as to render 5000 tons of beet-sugar superfluous. The sugar manufacturers are naturally anxious that this new coal-tar product should be regarded as a drug and that its sale should be effected through chemists only. In other countries the manufacture of saccharin is arousing the attention of the authorities, who possibly see in it a favorable subject for taxation."

Salad King. The Salad king was a name given to Henri d'Albignac, a young nobleman from the south of France, who came to London as a refugee at the time of the Revolution, and earned his livelihood by dressing salads in the French and Italian ways—hitherto unknown in England. He was so successful that, within a month after his first experiment, at a handsome house in Grosvenor Square, it was not considered "the thing " at a gala dinner to offer one's guests a salad that had not been dressed by the young French nobleman. The story is told by Brillat Savarin, in his " Physiology of Taste."

Salagrama and **Salagrana.** The first word is the **Hindoo** name for a sacred stone found by the river Gundak, in Nepaul. It is held to be very sacred. Once when Vishnu the Preserver was followed by Shiva the Destroyer, he implored the aid of Maia—illusion or glamour—who turned him to a stone. Through this stone Shiva, in the form of a worm, bored his way. But Vishnu escaped, and when he had resumed his form he commanded that this stone of delusion (or *salamaya*) should be worshipped. As such stones are found by Salipura or Salagra. they receive their name from the latter. " They are generally about the size of an orange, and are really a kind of ammonite."

Charles G. Leland, who is authority for the above statement, was surprised to find in Tuscany a peculiar kind of stone held in high reverence and called Salagrana,—the same word as the Indian save for a single letter. It is ordinary stalagmite,—the carbonate of lime deposited by water,—but is held to be, what it certainly resembles, a bit of petrified earth, shaped by a worm's passing through it. Thus it is doubly identified with the Indian tradition. It also suggests comparison with a story told in the Later Edda about Odin, who, in order to steal the meed of poetry, turned himself into a worm and bored his way through a rock. Hence all stones with holes in them are called Odin stones, or in England holy-stones (*q.v.*).

Salamander. In real life this is a little animal which has no love for fire, but passes a good part of its existence in the antagonistic element water.

In the fifth and sixth decades of the eighteenth century. there was a very famous animal of this species, popularly known as the great salamander, in Amsterdam, in the Society Natura Artis Magistra. " It has lived there many years," says an article on the " Acclimatisation of Animals," in the *Westminster Review* for January, 1860, " and, luxuriating in an ample fish diet. has now attained extraordinary dimensions. This curious Batrachian was discovered in the lava pools of Niphon and bears an extreme degree of cold with impunity: a startling contrast to the tradition of the fiery salamander girded round with a belt of flame. The inhabitants of London are still ignorant of the big-mouthed salamander of Niphon, who lives in water instead of fire, and devours a shoal of barbel per diem, instead of preying on his own extremities."

The allusions are to the fables of the ancient naturalists, who asserted that the salamander was incombustible and loved to disport himself in the fire. Among these fabulists were Aristotle and Pliny, Ælien and Nicander, Ambroise Paré and Grevin, with no end of others. And then, again, the celebrated Benvenuto Cellini, in his most interesting "Memoirs." How can any one doubt a fact so candidly, so circumstantially, and so positively stated, as the following: "One day, when I was about fifteen years of age, my father was in a cellar where they had been scalding some clothes for washing. He was alone, and was playing upon the viol and singing in front of a good fire of oak-wood, for the weather was very cold. On looking at the fire accidentally, he saw a small animal resembling a lizard gambolling joyously in the midst of the fiercest flames. My father instantly perceiving what it was, he called my sister and me, pointed out the animal to us, and gave me a severe box on the ear, which caused me to shed a perfect deluge of tears. He gently wiped my eyes, and said to me, 'My dear boy, I did not strike you as a punishment, but only that you should remember that that lizard which you behold in the fire is a salamander, an animal which has never been seen by any known person!' He afterwards kissed me and gave me a few quattrini." Now, as we said before, who can doubt such testimony as this? Here are all the minute circumstances detailed—the family wash, a good fire, which we are told was of oak-wood, the presence of the sister, and, above all, that severe box on the ear, which must have impressed the matter upon his memory.

In popular folk-lore, at least, the salamander has never divested himself of his fire-proof fame. His very name is used as a synonym for a denizen of what nineteenth century journalism knew as the devouring element. Thus, the *Retrospective Review* (vol. iii, London, 1820) has this paragraph: "Some years since, a Mr. Wery announced the following exercise to be performed, at the Waur-hall at Brussels, by Miss Roggers, an American salamander; the same lady who entered an oven heated to 900 degrees, holding in her hands a leg of mutton and eggs, and did not come out until the leg of mutton and eggs were actually baked. The same lady will bathe in aqua-fortis, lick red-hot iron bars, and let the same pass on her bare arms and legs, wash her arms with phosphorus and melted lead, putting some also in her mouth." Later in the same century, on September 18, 1858, the London *Illustrated News* has an illustrated article on Christofero Buono Core, "the Italian Salamander," who was then exhibiting himself in the Ashburnham grounds of Cremorne. This gentleman was the inventor of a garment which he advertised by word and deed as being quite impervious to flame. "The dress is of a light portable material, made in a sack-like form, over a portion of which is worn a kind of hood, with glasses to shield the eyes." In this costume he passed in and out of iron cages where brushwood was kept burning, until the whole becomes, "as it were, one body of flame. During the period the performance takes place the heat of the fire is so great that none of the visitors can approach within a distance of 30 feet."

Salute, International. The twenty-one guns fired by ships of the American navy as an international salute are borrowed from a like custom in the British navy. In earlier days a war-ship salute was limited to seven guns, but a fort was allowed to fire three times as many guns as a war-ship, because it was difficult then to keep powder in good condition at sea. The same difficulty did not occur on land, hence the larger number of shots allowed to a fort. When later improvements in manufacture furnished better powder which did not deteriorate at sea, the war-ship in its salutes was allowed the same number of guns as the shore battery.

Sands, Singing and Barking. Musical and (if you don't mind the word) cacophonous sand is a curious freak of nature that occurs in many parts of the world, but most notably in the Hawaiian island of Kauai. According to the manner in which man or nature stirs it, the sand produces sounds that range from the agreeable to the terrifying. When dry to the depth of at least four or five inches on the dune, it gives out a deep bass note of a tremulous character if pushed down the steep incline. A sound something like the barking of a dog is produced by plunging the hands into the sand and bringing them vigorously together, or by putting the sand in a bag and violently shaking it. Another method is to fill a long bag three-quarters full of sand, and then, dividing its contents into two parts, holding one in each hand, to clap the two portions together. Similar phenomena also occur in the Colorado desert in the United States, whose curious shifting sands continually travel hither and thither over the vast plain of clay. Their movements are induced by the winds, and, when a strong breeze is blowing, the particles of which they are composed give out an audible humming or singing. Under the microscope these sands show an almost perfectly spherical form, so that they roll upon each other at the slightest impulse, a circumstance that also accounts for the rapidity with which the sands travel over the desert. Bell Mountain (Dschebel Nakus), on the peninsula of Sinai on the shores of the Red Sea, furnishes another example. The first European who ascended this hill was Seetzen of Oldenberg. He found that it consisted of a brittle white sandstone, covered on two sides with loose sand. In ascending, as he passed over this sand, he found that the noise it made in gliding down the slope became by degrees louder and louder. When he reached the summit, such a clamor arose that the whole mountain shook. So also, he confesses, did his nerves. A succeeding traveller, one Ward, an Englishman, corroborated Scetzen. He heard at first only a feeble tone like that of a flute; suddenly it became as loud as an organ, and the whole hill began to vibrate. The volume of the sound increased in proportion to the quantity set in motion by the steps of the climber. Charles Darwin observed a phenomenon of the same sort in the El Bramador (Yelling or Barking Mountain) in Chili. One theory advanced with respect to these sounds is that they are due to an exceedingly thin film of gas that covers the grains. Dr. Alexis A. Julien, of Columbia College, and Professor Bolton, of Honolulu, who visited together the musical sounds in the Hawaiian islands, came to this conclusion. "We believe," said the latter, "the true cause of sonorousness to be connected with thin pellicles or films of air or of gases thence derived, deposited and condensed upon the surface of the sand grains during gradual evaporation after wetting by seas, lakes, or rains. By virtue of these films the sand grains become separated by elastic cushions of condensed gases, capable of considerable vibration, and whose thicknesses we have approximately determined. The extent of the vibration and the volume and pitch of the sound thereby produced we also find to be largely dependent upon the forms, structures, and surfaces of the sand grains, and especially upon their purity and freedom from fine silt or dust."—*Honolulu Advertiser,* quoted in *American Notes and Queries,* July 26, 1890.

Sandwich. Geography preserves the name of John, Earl of Sandwich, in a chain of islands discovered by Captain Cook in 1778, and gastronomy has immortalized it in the convenient morsel which is reputed to be his invention. The earl was a great gambler, and the story runs that in the pursuit of his passion he rebelled against the tyranny of meal-times whereby each day the hours of gambling were curtailed. Therefore, calling in the waiter, who, having announced dinner, hovered uneasily around the table,—the earl ordered that pieces of meat should be laid between two slices of bread and brought to him as he sat at play. This was done, and the sandwich was born.

Recent investigation, however, has somewhat detracted from the earl's fame as the inventor of sandwiches. Without doubt he reintroduced and christened the sandwich, but the Romans—those specialists in gastronomy—are credited with its invention, sandwiches, under the name of offula, being a favorite food in

Roman days. Possibly, indeed, the sandwich was introduced into Britain by Roman conquerors, together with the snail. Thereafter, during many centuries the sandwich lay dormant, to be resurrected and renamed by the fertile brain of Jemmy Twitcher.

Soon these slices of bread and meat became extremely fashionable, especially among gamesters, whose vagaries in the matter of meal-time now ceased to embarrass the proprietors of the coffee-houses which they frequented. Sandwiches took the place of more elaborate meals; they were handed around at stated intervals, and, clasping a sandwich in one hand, dice or cards, as the case might be, in the other, the eager gambler continued his play.

The word "sandwich" is not found in the early editions of Johnson's Dictionary nor in Todd or Richardson, but Latham recognizes it for the first time in his edition of Johnson, citing Byron as his authority.

A short light top-coat having been named after one of Sandwich's contemporaries, Lord Spencer, a current bit of humorous verse contained this stanza:

> Two noble earls whom if I quote,
>   Some folks might call me sinner;
> The one invented half a coat,
>   The other, half a dinner.

The Earl of Sandwich was further notorious for his devotion to the fair sex, and a caricature still exists in which he is represented between two young women in gay attire, one the unfortunate Miss Reay, the other the celebrated Miss Gordon. The title, "A Sandwich," happily identifies the gentleman occupying this enviable position, while, to the uninitiated, it serves as a witty suggestion of the refreshment of which he is accounted the inventor. Among his convivial associates at the Kit-Kat Club, Lord Sandwich was popularly known as "Jemmy Twitcher," a cognomen adapted from the treacherous highwayman of that name in Gay's "Beggar's Opera." The following anecdote is characteristic rather of his conviviality than of his religion. When once entertaining a large company at dinner, his chaplain being also present, he introduced a large baboon dressed in canonical habit, to say grace. The chaplain immediately rose and left the room, but stopped to say, before withdrawing, that he "did not know his lordship had so near a relative in orders."

During the hours for the performance of his official duties, Lord Sandwich prosecuted the business of the moment with rigid zeal; it was his motto that even the smallest portion of time should be put to some use; and while presiding at the Board of Admiralty, he was so severe with those who thoughtlessly wasted his time and their own, that he made it a rule to pay no attention to any petition which extended beyond a page. "If any man," said he, "will draw up his case and put his name to the bottom of the first page, I will give him an immediate reply; when he compels me to turn over the page, he must await my pleasure."

Sandwich Man. Dickens first applied the name "Sandwich men" to the men who parade the streets, enclosed between two boards, as an advertisement ("Dancing Academy," in the "Sketches by Boz"). They seemed to have originated early in the nineteenth century, and some pictures of them, on foot and on horseback, are to be seen in Hone's "Every Day Book," 1826.

San Marino, or Sammarino, one of the smallest and most ancient republics in Europe, and for many years of its early history the very smallest of all European states (see REPUBLICS, SMALL). Situated nine miles S. W. of Rimini in Italy, it is enclosed by the provinces Forli, Pensano, and Urbino. The state consists of a craggy mountain 2420 feet, on which is the town, and circumjacent territory containing a few small villages. Population 9500. According to tradition, the republic was founded by St. Marinus, who fled during the persecutions under Diocletian (A.D. 303) into what was then a wilderness. He hewed himself a bed in one of the biggest rocks, gathered followers around him, and practised the usual asceticisms, and in the ordinary course of things should have founded a monastic order to be called by his name. Instead, he founded a little state. He set his disciples to farming and weaving. He established a government on the top of the lofty ridge, to rule over the few miles of territory at the base. This much is certain, the monastery named after San Marino has been in existence since 885, and a communal constitution was established here in the tenth century. It built a castle and a church and town-hall on top of the precipice, and houses and a wall around them to protect it from its neighbors. Apparently it never sought to extend its possessions. When Napoleon I was master of Italy, he actually proposed that it should take more territory, but it was wise enough to refuse. The republic in fact has steered its way clear through all the worst periods of Italian history, repelling many attacks of covetous princes,—notably Sigismonde Malatesta of Rimini,—sometimes sword in hand, at others by diplomacy. Never did it lose its independence except for a few months, once when it fell into the hands of Cæsar Borgia in 1503, and again in 1739 through the treachery of one of the Pope's lieutenants, Cardinal Alberoni.

Its wonderful position made up for its lack of numerical strength, in the days before roads, when an armed band could not stay long in any place for want of provisions.

Up to March 25, 1906,—a date commemorated by a tablet outside the cathedral,—San Marino was ruled by a council of sixty, which managed the affairs of this miniature republic. It was composed of three classes,—nobles, bourgeois, and peasants, in equal number,—and the councillors, elected for life, formed a close corporation, into which no outsider could enter save when some member died and the survivors chose his successor. Class distinctions were further maintained in the election of two presidents, one a noble the other a commoner.

The spread of democratic ideas among the younger Sammarines led finally to the peaceful establishment of a new form of government on the date above given. The council of sixty is now elected by direct manhood suffrage, and one-third of its members retire by rotation every three years. Twice a year two capitani reggenti, or governing captains, are elected in the same manner, and twice a year, on October 1 and April 1, they are installed in office with all the picturesque ceremonial of by-gone times.

As illiterates, who constitute about 80 per cent. of the entire population, are privileged to vote in San Marino, the republic now possesses perhaps the most democratic constitution in the world. The available armed forces form a total of about 1200 men, including as it does all able-bodied male citizens between the ages of 16 and 60.

The only troubles, however, which the Sammarines have had in modern times with other powers in Italy have arisen from the convenience of the republic as a place of refuge for criminals, political and other. The Italian malcontents of the old régime often fled to San Marino, and brought down upon the republic the ire of the Austrians or the Pope or the King of Naples. Garibaldi and the remnants of his army sought shelter under the wall after his defeat at Rome in 1849, and the little state proudly refused to surrender him or expel him, though it politely asked him to leave, which he did, flying by night to Venice.

Sans-Souci, the royal palace in the vicinity of Potsdam, Prussia, was built by Frederick II, between the years 1745 and 1747, and was his favorite residence. Hence he is frequently called the Philosopher of Sans-Souci. The name is said to have been suggested by a mot of Frederick I, who had selected the spot as a burial place for his favorite horse Condé and his dogs, and had caused a grave for himself to be dug by their side. "That is where I shall lie after death," said the eccentric monarch to the Marquis d'Angens, "and when I am there I shall rest without care (Sans-Souci)." Near the palace is a famous mill. According to Dr. Zimmermann, who attended Frederick II in his last illness and subsequently published his "Conversations with Frederick the Great," this mill interfered with the king's view from the orangery; he accordingly sought to buy it, and when the miller refused threatened to seize it. The miller's reply has become famous: "Are there no judges at Berlin?" The monarch recognized the justice of the rebuke and ever after treated the miller as a friend. This anecdote was versified by Hebel, but he makes Frederick bring a lawsuit against the miller, which terminated unsuccessfully on account of the uprightness of the judges. Andrieux has followed the original story more closely in his poem "The Miller of Sans-Souci" (French "Le Meunier de Sans-Souci"), which is also the title of a vaudeville on the same subject by Lombard de Langes (1798). But the whole story is probably a fabrication. Zimmermann's highly imaginary conversations have been annotated by a valet of Frederick's named Neumann, who points out all that is false in them, including the anecdote of the mill, which could not, he says, have interfered with Frederick's view of the orangery. Moreover, he never heard of any difference between the king and the miller.

Santorin, the Thera of Greeks, is a volcanic island in the Ægean Sea. It forms the eastern half of an immense crater, stretching in a semicircle round a bay wherein the sea now covers the seat of volcanic action. The destruction of the southwestern rim of the crater let in the water. The northwestern portion is to-day an island called Theresia.

Within this sweep of the semicircle lie three smaller volcanic islands which emerged at intervals in the past 2000 years. All bear in their names the trace of their igneous parentage; their common designation being Kaimene or "the burnt," whilst they are individually differentiated as the Palaia, Mikre, and Nea,— *i.e.*, the Old, the Little, and the New. The first of these made its appearance in B.C. 198, the second in A.D. 1573, the third in 1707.

Another great disturbance occurred in 1866 and made some temporary alterations in the basin, but eventually the old conditions were practically resumed.

The commencement of this eruption, on January 31, was signalized by a noise like a volley of artillery, but without any earthquake. On the following day flames issued from the sea, in a part of the bay called Vulkanos, where the water is always discolored and impregnated with sulphur from abundant springs at the bottom. The flames rose at intervals to the height of fifteen feet, and were seen at times to issue from the southwestern part of Nea Kaïménê. That island was soon rent by a deep fissure, and the southern part sank considerably.

On the morning of the 4th of February, a new island was discovered pushing above the surface, and in five days it had attained an area computed at about 35,000 square feet, and a height in some places of 150 feet above the sea level.

There it lay hissing hot, smoking and seething in the water like a black and unsavory mass of junk in a ship's copper a few cables' length from the bows of a British frigate, the *Surprise*, despatched from Malta to investigate and report on the phenomenon. "The smoke and vapor which rose upward from its surface were tinged with the fiery hues of the combustion still actively going on immediately below, while cracks in the same surface gave glimpses still more formidable of the fount of lava surging up within. The lava, and the violent changes of surface incident to the formation of the new island, are said to have buried a number of houses on the old one, besides those which actually sank into the sea; but up to the time of the frigate's departure no loss of life is said to have happened." We can hardly trust the statements of a ship's officers and crew as literally accurate in such unusual circumstances; but the statements go to show that rocks were marked as rising up in various directions above the waters, and again disappearing below them. —*London Saturday Review*, March 17, 1866.

Sargasso Sea. In the space between the Azores, Canaries, and the Cape Verde Islands lies the great Sargasso Sea. Covering an area equal in extent to the valley of the Mississippi, it is so thickly matted over with Gulf-weed that the speed of vessels passing through it is often much retarded. The weed always "tails to" a steady or a constant wind, so that it serves the mariner as a sort of anemometer, telling him whether the wind as he finds it has been blowing for some time, or whether it has but just shifted, and which way. Columbus first found this weedy sea on his voyage of discovery. There it has remained to this day, moving up and down, and changing its position, like the calms of Cancer, as affected by the seasons, the storms, and the winds. According to Maury's authority, exact observations as to its limits and their range, extending back for fifty years, assure us that its mean position has not been altered since that time.

There is also a sargasso to the west of the Cape of Good Hope, which, though comparatively small, is clearly defined. Mention is generally made of it in the logs as " rock-weed " and

" drift matter." The weedy space about the Falkland Islands
is probably not a true sargasso. The sea-weed reported there
most likely comes from the Straits of Magellan, where immense
masses of algæ grow. Those straits are so encumbered with
sea-weed that steamers find great difficulty in making their way
through it. It so clogs their paddles as to make frequent
stoppages necessary.

From the few known facts about the Sargasso Sea, a cycle
of myths has been evolved. It has been called " the port of missing ships " and " the grave-yard of lost ships." Tales innumerable have been told of derelicts trapped in the slimy, weedy
stretches of a marine desert clogged with floating islands of seaweeds. This is a gross exaggeration where it is not mere myth.
For the Sargasso Sea is not the weedy waste that it is painted.
There are seaweeds there, of course, but not enough seriously
to impede the navigation of any ordinary vessel.

The steamer *Michael Sars,* of the United States hydraulic
service, sent out from Plymouth in April, 1911, with a company
of scientists aboard, upon its return after three months' study of
the Sargasso Sea, reported that the stories about the mass of
seaweed caught in the dead waters of the central Atlantic north
of the Cape Verde Islands are greatly exaggerated.

The scientists with the expedition say the Sargasso Sea is
particularly rich in strange and beautiful aquatic insects and
small fish. For instance, there is found there, and nowhere else,
a wonderful transparent shrimp with eyes like jewels on the end
of long pedicels. Their eyes are many-faceted, and they flash a
brilliant greenish light.

Sarracenia. Murderers flourish in plant life as in human.
Chief among these vegetable assassins is the sarracenia, a plant
which inhabits the swamp lands of North America, notably
Florida.

The flowers, which are purplish or of a fine yellow color,
attract and lure insects into their confidence. The plant's leaves
are rolled like a cornucopia and provided at the broad end with a
lid. Into these urn-like sepulchres winged and creeping victims
fall, never to return to light and air. Attracted by the color and
the odor of the flowers, the victims draw near and, poised upon
their stems, scent their honey. Little by little they approach
the cup, hover for an instant on its edge, then begin to descend.
In all probability they do not see the spear-like points, set like
the stakes of the fisher's weir in the lining of the cup. The
victims go down between the stakes and feast on honey. When
full they turn to climb to the outer world. Again and again
they ascend a hair's breadth, only to fall back, until, exhausted

49

by their futile efforts, they drop into the poisoned water where float the sodden bodies of the flies trapped before them.

A naturalist who observed the death struggles of insects trapped by this rapacious and treacherous plant saw one lying half out of the water, making desperate efforts to free itself from the trap. The lower part of its body, the part under water, was paralyzed, glued to immobility by the secretion contained in the water. "There was something horrible," said the naturalist, "in the artifice used by the plant in its capture of the animal. The plant lures the animal to its doom by giving it a feast; the honey is a trap, and, to all appearances, the holder of the trap is a cold-blooded, calculating assassin."

Sassafras, the largest of the laurel family of trees, an entirely American growth, found in greatest quantities in Arkansas, Texas, Oklahoma, and Louisiana. Its pleasantly aromatic bark and roots were formerly considered a remedy for rheumatism and other diseases. When the first French settlers came to Louisiana, they found it held in great repute by the Indians for its medicinal qualities. These were first described in print by the Spanish traveller and physician Nicholas Monardes ("Natural History of the New World," 1569), who thus stimulated the early American colonists to gather and export bark and roots. Faith in the remedial power of the plant has now pretty much disappeared; but the roots are still used as flavoring for beer and confectionery, and the young foliage is gathered and dried in the Southern States as a chief ingredient in the mucilaginous soup known as *gumbo.* Linnæus named this tree *Laurus Sassafras.* Nees ab Esenbeck separated it from *Laurus,* and called it *Sassafras officinale,* under which name it has usually been known since 1830.

The tree has pretty flowers, which develop into berries that are brilliantly red when ripe. In Texas and Louisiana the man who raises pigs considers himself fortunate if he has on his premises a sassafras tree around which to build his pig-pen. The sassafras berries then fall into the pen when ripe, and are not only fattening to the pigs but give them a clean, healthy skin, besides insuring them against various troubles.

Some years the berries are very abundant and other years the trees bear none. As soon as they begin to turn toward ripening. they become a favorite food for birds of various kinds, against the raids of which on the pig-pen trees the Texas farmer is as watchful as the Northern fruit-grower is against the attacks of robins on his cherries and berries. Horses and cows in Texas and adjacent districts also like the sassafras berries, and it is claimed that animals that can forage on them are not assailed by flies and other harassing insects.

The bright-green odd-shaped leaves of the tree and the fragrance of its bark and thick fleshy roots are familiar to every urchin who roams the woods. The wood of the sassafras tree, orange colored, with a thin, pale sapwood, is coarse grained and has no value for use except as fence rails or posts, it being very durable in the ground. The tree is much sought for park and garden ornamental purposes.

In the Red River country in Texas, sassafras trees 80 feet high and 7 feet in diameter are not uncommon, but elsewhere 40 feet is the average.

In 1911 a newspaper controversy was waged over a question as to the largest extant sassafras tree. The Agricultural Department at Washington started the trouble by signalizing a tree in Atlanta, Georgia, for this honor. Thereupon the Atlanta *Constitution* crowed lustily over the city's new title to preëminence.

" In the yard of the First Methodist Church of Atlanta," it said, " the sassafras tree stands, passed by thousands each day, none of whom has realized that in that yard was growing the biggest tree of its kind in the world. Few of the members of the church were cognizant of its existence, though it has shaded little children in their play for many years and will probably perform the same loving task for years to come.

" The tree, according to the experts of the Agricultural Department, is more than one hundred years old. It is 7½ feet in circumference, 50 feet high, and has a spread of more than 40 feet, overshadowing all the trees in its neighborhood."

Thereupon Governor Hindman, of Kentucky, proved that he had in his yard a rival tree measuring 12 feet 5 inches. From Simpson County in the same State arose a claim that Squire George Tisdale owned three great sassafras trees, the greatest of which measured 12 feet 8 inches, or three inches more than Hindman's. That seemed to settle matters for the present, although the past revealed much greater wonders, and it was remembered that the biggest sassafras tree ever known was one cut down in Pennsylvania in 1893. This monster was 107 feet high and 28 feet in circumference.

Sauerkraut. Though this would seem to be a relish requiring careful preparation, it really is very easy to make. It is simply sliced cabbage, with the hard part of that vegetable left out. The sauerkraut man on a small scale, carrying his own especial knives with him, cuts up the cabbages into tiny bits and throws them into a barrel. A liberal quantity of salt is added, and then the barrel is set aside to let nature do her work. About one month is required for a fine quality. At the end of that time the sauerkraut is ready for consumption.

Sauerkraut was introduced into France by a German princess,

Elizabeth, daughter of the Elector Palatine. She married Monsieur, the brother of Louis XIV, and became the mother of that Duke of Orleans who was regent of France during the minority of Louis XV.

From her letters we learn that when she arrived in France there was not in all the kingdom " a single cook capable of preparing sauerkraut." When her own cooks had become instructed, " she initiated the king into the delights of German cooking. and saw with joy that he relished it." In her letters repeatedly she enumerated with pride the dishes with which she had enriched the royal table. In a letter written in 1719 she has recorded, " No one here marvels that I should like black pudding. I have introduced raw ham and a great many of our German dishes, such as sauerkraut and white cabbage, bacon salad, savoy cabbage, venison, of which till now one rarely ate, and pancakes with smoked herring. All these I have made fashionable. I taught the late king to eat these things, and he quite took to them. My German mouth so loves German food that there is not a single French stew that I can endure. I only eat roast beef, veal, or mutton, roasted chicken, rarely partridges, and pheasants never."

It is an unfortunate fact, however, that entirely satisfactory sauerkraut is not to be achieved by any ordinary application of human genius or exercise of human endeavor. Try as Madame would, it was impossible for her to cause French sauerkraut and French sausages to be as good as those that afforded a particular glory to her own country. " Yesterday," she wrote from Paris. December 10, 1715, " a lady from Strasburg gave me a pot of sauerkraut with a duck in it. It was not bad, but the cabbages were French cabbages, which are ever so inferior to German cabbages; they have less taste, and also they are not hashed as fine; there are no knives to hash them properly. It was not bad, but I have tasted better."

The German sauerkraut, imported into America, is cheap. but since its manufacture has been learned to a T here, the crop actually from old Germany is not cared for nearly as much as it was. The American sauerkraut will beat it in open market at any time.

It is reserved for New York State, however, to be the great sauerkraut district of America. New England is not a cabbage section, the sole exception in this territory being Connecticut. which contributes, really, very little, and the South and the far West do not produce at all. New York is the main-stay for the Germans of these regions.

A goodly proportion of the counties of New York raise cabbages and make sauerkraut from them, but the most of them do so largely for local consumption. The notable exceptions are the districts surrounding Albany, Cortlandt County, and Long Island. There are half a dozen large factories in the latter region, and the mild climate and peculiar quality of the soil make it a famous cabbage-producing land. So large are the crops here that this year they have given about fifteen tons to the acre. There is even an association and incorporated company of farmers, with its head-quarters on the north shore, that devotes itself mainly to this industry. Just about as fine sauerkraut as one can find anywhere in New York comes from Long Island.

Ever since Elie Metchnikoff, director of the Pasteur Institute, Paris, announced his discovery of the little germ, contained in sour milk and buttermilk, which tends to the prolongation of human life, many persons have acquired the habit of drinking sour milk daily. Many others, to whom sour milk is extremely distasteful, have reluctantly done without it while hoping and longing for the discovery of some other equally efficacious prolonger of life.

Now their hopes are perhaps to be realized, for sauerkraut has been investigated and found to contain lactic acid bacilli possessing all the good qualities of those in sour milk. It is suggested by Metchnikoff that those who can not bear sour milk should try the sauerkraut treatment, to offset the ravages wrought by time and old age on the human system. In the latest reports of work done by the Pasteur Institute, Metchnikoff cites a large number of cases of men and women who have greatly improved their chance of reaching a ripe old age by partaking freely of sauerkraut.

Sausage. It is at Westphalia, Prussia, that the sausage flourishes in all its glory. No less than 400 different varieties are produced there. Still, 400 is only a fraction of what United Germany can do in this line. At a German sausage exhibition held in 1909 in Bern, Switzerland, no less than 1785 varieties of this edible were displayed. It has been said that a good German would rather invent a new sausage than anything else. *Harper's Weekly* tells the story of a young Prussian who, though he had received an expensive training as a chemist, shut himself up in his laboratory, and, instead of devising a new dye, safety-match, motor-engine, explosive, aeroplane, or photographic lens, took pork, veal, olives, pepper, fennel, old wine, cheese, apples, cinnamon, and herrings' roes, and from them evolved a wonderful and totally original "wurst," the best of its kind. He has amassed a considerable fortune from its sale.

The most famous sausage merchant that England ever produced, and one of the most picturesque figures in Smithfield Market, was William Harris, familiarly known as the Sausage King. He died April 12, 1912, leaving behind him three sons, all of whom he named after himself, distinguishing them as William the First, Second, and Third.

Savings-Bank, The First.   In the little village of Ruthwell. Dumfriesshire, Scotland, there stands a long, low-roofed, single-storied cottage known as Society Hall.   Here the parish minister in May, 1810, established the first bank to accept small deposits and pay cumulative interest thereon.   The fact is commemorated in this inscription over the door:

> To Commemorate the First Savings-Bank
> Founded in this Building in 1810
> by the
> Rev. Henry Duncan, D.D., of Ruthwell.
> A Measure Which Claimed at His Hands
> Nearly Ten Years of Devoted Work
> and Pecuniary Sacrifice.

It is true there have been rivals, less rather than more authentic, to dispute Dr. Duncan's claim.   French authorities date the idea back to Hughes Delestre, who proposed such an institution in 1610.   An Austrian writer insists that the idea was realized in Brunswick in 1765.   Bern in 1787, Basle in 1792, Geneva in 1794, and Hamburg in 1798 established similar institutions. None of these, however, resembled the modern savings-bank. The Hamburg bank, for example, confined its deposits to the savings of domestic servants and other wage-earners (paying no interest thereon) and gave annuities to the members of the association when they reached a certain age.

England points with pride to the Rev. Joseph Smith, of Wendover, and to Mrs. Priscilla Wakeman, of Tottenham, as pioneers in their respective localities.   Mr. Smith in 1798 offered to receive from members of his congregation any sum from two pence up, to be repaid with interest at Christmas.   Mrs. Wakeman in 1799 started a similar institution for the benefit of women and children.   Both institutions were successful.   Neither conflicts with Duncan's claim to be the leader in the origin and organization of self-supporting savings-bank.   He may, indeed have derived a hint from Samuel Whitbread, the Whig reformer. who in supporting his " poor-law amendments bill " made an eloquent appeal for safe and profitable investments of the earnings of the poor.   Whitbread proposed an institution that should not only take care of their savings and pay interest on them, but which should insure their lives, their household effects, and care for their old age.   His conception of the savings-bank as an institution parallel to the church and the school-house is similar to that which has recently grown up in some parts of the United States.

Whitbread's plan never went further than words. Duncan joined deeds to words. In 1810, after outlining his scheme in the Dumfries *Courier,* he established the Ruthwell Savings-Bank. It received for deposit anything over sixpence. No sum less than a pound drew interest. If less than four shillings were deposited during the first year, a penalty of one shilling was extracted. The interest was five per cent., reduced, however, to four per cent. if withdrawals were frequent. A week's notice was necessary before a withdrawal could be made. Depositors who failed to attend the annual meeting in July were fined sixpence.

Massachusetts was the first State in the Union to follow the example of Scotland and England. The plan of a savings-bank was proposed in December, 1815, in *The Christian Disciple,* a small religious monthly published in Boston. Next year an act incorporating the Provident Institution for Savings in the Town of Boston passed the Legislature. The bank was organized and began business in the following spring, promising to divide with depositors 1 per cent. quarterly, and more if practicable. The Roman Catholic Bishop Cheverus was a cordial supporter of the new scheme, for he had seen the need among his flock of some institution which would encourage thrift. In spite of popular favor, however, the new bank increased its deposits slowly at first, since it took people a long time to get used to the idea. In 1822 the deposits amounted to about $600,000; in 1827, to $793,000; in 1832, to $1,442,000.

In Pennsylvania the Philadelphia· Savings-Fund Society was started privately in 1816 and incorporated in 1819. The Savings-Bank of Baltimore followed in 1818. New York State, which now leads the United States and indeed the whole world in the proportionate number and influence of its savings-banks, passed through a preliminary struggle to overcome legislative hostility against all banks within its borders. Then in 1819 was founded the Bank for Savings, in Chambers Street, which now stands on Fourth Avenue and is the second largest savings-bank in the Union.

Savings-Bank, Toy. In 1899 Mr. C. O. Burns was a commercial traveller with his head-quarters at San Francisco. One day the thought suddenly flashed in his mind, " I'm not saving a cent." The result was that he began putting coins into a toy savings-bank on the mantel-piece at home. Sometimes it was a quarter, or a dollar, or a gold piece when he was " flush."

At last, one day, he decided to open the bank. It was empty. Some one in the family had been tempted to buy an expensive luxury, and the money was spent!

That set him thinking all over again. " Now," he said, " if I'd had a lock on that bank and thrown the key away, I'd have my money." Then a bright idea came to him. Why not give the key to the cashier of a savings-bank instead of throwing it away? In that way only the cashier could take the money out. The more he thought of it the more he was convinced that lots of people would adopt such a scheme. He worked out the details, and in that way originated what is now known as the Auxiliary Savings-Bank System.

Burns invented a stout little metal box, with a spring lock, and a slit in the top through which to deposit coins. He patented his invention, and with a partner went to work to make it pay. The firm made an offer to a bank in the State of Washington to sell it one thousand boxes and with each box to get a new depositor with a first deposit of one dollar. The bank was to pay two dollars and a half for the box, the depositor, and the deposit.

Several banks on the coast accepted this offer, and Burns came East to exploit his idea. He had a hard road to travel for a time, but he kept at it, modifying his scheme from the sale to the lease of boxes. At last he succeeded. To-day some four or five million people not savings-bank depositors are using boxes of this kind. They are to be found in every State in the Union, in every country of Europe, all over Central and South America, in Hawaii, Japan, India, Turkey, and all over Asia and Africa, thus pretty completely covering the globe.

A typical example is in the city of Florence, Italy, where the people used to hoard their small savings. These little box banks have brought out and put into circulation two hundred thousand dollars from its hiding places. Children as well as grown people use these banks.

Saw. Talus, the Greek, is said to have invented the saw from having once found the jawbone of a snake, which he employed to cut through a small piece of wood. In early periods the trunks of trees were split into boards with wedges, and although these deals were not always straight, they were regarded as much better suited to construction than sawn boards, because they followed the grain, and lasted longer and were stronger. Water-mills, for the purpose of sawing, came into use in the fourth century.

The smallest circular saw in the world now in actual use is a tiny disc less than the fourth of an inch in diameter used in the Tiffany jewelry establishment for slitting gold pens; it is about the thickness of a sheet of writing paper and revolves at the rate of 4000 revolutions per minute; the high velocity keeps the saw rigid, notwithstanding its thinness.

Schamir, a mythical stone whose specialty, according to legend, was that of extreme hardness, insomuch that there was no substance it could not cut. Therefore King Solomon used it in noiselessly cutting and shaping the metals and stones for the temple at Jerusalem. Solomon was reputed to have dominion over all the Jinns or Djinns, save only the mighty Sachr and Iblis, and he employed these fairy men in building the temple. Unfortunately, they made so much noise with their hammers, saws, and axes that the people of Jerusalem could not hear one another speak. Therefore Solomon directed the Jinns to cease their work, and inquired whether the metals and stones could not be shaped and cut without noise. The reply was that this could only be done by the stone Schamir, the whereabouts of which was known only to Sachr. Now, it was Sachr's custom to pay a monthly visit to the land of Hidjr, and drink a certain fountain empty. So Solomon sent a winged Jinn, who drew the water from the fountain and filled it with wine. Sachr drank, became drunk, was bound in chains, and made Solomon's slave. The captive was promised his liberty on condition that he would reveal the place where the stone that would cut and shape the hardest metals could be found. Sachr told the king to take the eggs out of a raven's nest, place a crystal cover upon them, and see how the raven would break it. Solomon did so. The raven, finding its eggs covered, flew away, and returned with a stone in its beak, which it dropped on the crystal and so cut it asunder. The raven was asked by Solomon where the stone came from, and was told that it came from a mountain in the far west. The mountain was found, a number of similar stones were obtained, and with them the Jinns hewed the stones for the temple in the distant quarries and brought them to Jerusalem, where they were laid noiselessly in their proper places.

In another legend it was the moor-hen whom Sachr designated to Solomon. When her nest was covered with glass and the moor-hen returned and could not reach her young, she flew away and fetched Schamir, here represented as a worm the size of a barleycorn and the property of the Prince of the Sea.

There are many variants of the legend in many countries, Oriental and European. The only point on which all agree is that the stone had the property of cutting the hardest substances.

One account states that Solomon obtained the stone by placing the chick of an ostrich in a glass bottle, the neck of which was contracted and had to be cut by the mother bird with this stone in order to liberate her offspring. In Normandy it was said that such a stone could be obtained by putting out the eyes of a swallow's young, whereupon the mother bird would go in quest of the stone, which had the power of restoring sight, but if a scarlet cloth was spread below the swallow's nest, the swallow, mistaking it for fire, would drop the stone upon it, when it was secured by watchers. In Ireland the stone was believed to render its possessor invisible, and to confer upon him the power to burst bolts and bars, cure the sick, and raise the dead.

The term "Lightning" was applied to the stone Schamir because, in the Greek mythology, the storm cloud out of which flashed the lightning which broke rocks asunder, was supposed to be a mighty bird which bore the Schamir in its beak. A very full and elaborate article on this stone will be found in Baring-Gould's "Curious Myths of the Middle Ages." Reference to it is also made in his "Legends of the Patriarchs and Prophets."

School, Public. The largest public school-house in New York, probably the largest in the United States and possibly the largest in the world, is situated in East Houston Street and Lewis Street. The building occupies an entire block fronting on Lewis Street, with exits and entrances for girls on the north corner and for boys on the south corner. "The way the hundreds upon hundreds of youngsters emerging with a rush and jump are kept moving is a lesson in tactics worth seeing. In ten minutes or so the sidewalks are cleared and the neighborhood settles down to comparative calm until 9 o'clock the next morning." So wrote a reporter for the New York *Sun* in 1911. He added the following figures:

The present enrolment of girls at this school is 2093, under the care of forty-nine teachers, a principal, and her assistant; of boys, 2400, the total enrolment of pupils and instructors being more than 4600—a fair-sized town under one roof. But, big as it is, the building is not quite large enough; in one instance two classes, or about seventy-five pupils, using in common one of the largest class-rooms. To hold a general assembly of either boys or girls is impossible. The best that can be done with the aid of movable partitions is to assemble about 1000 at a time. The apportioning of recesses requires the greatest care in order not to overcrowd the yard area.

Scrapple. Listen to this dithyramb from the Baltimore *Sun:*

Scrapple comes in with Indian summer and last year's overcoat. Next to buckwheat cakes, sauerkraut, and hog-and-hominy, it is the most delicious breakfast dish known to the human race, but it behooves the consumer to have a care in buying it. Bogus scrapple, unluckily, is all too plentiful. The basis of the real article is the fragrant liquor in which country sausage has been boiled, and its body or substance is furnished by home-grown corn meal ground in a water-mill. Such scrapple is more palatable than venison and more nutritious than pemmican. It is particularly rich in proteids, carbohydrates, alkaloids, manganese, lime, naphtha, and other bone and sinew making contents.

In the old days all of Baltimore's scrapple came from Pennsylvania. It came across the Mason and Dixon line at midnight and was brought down to the city in Conestoga wagons. When the season's first wagon came rumbling down the York road, usually about October 20, there was a rush for it, and sometimes its cargo brought fancy prices—10 cents a slice, or even more. But to-day Baltimore is no longer dependent upon Pennsylvania for its scrapple supply. That made in Maryland is equal to the best. No doubt the future will see Maryland scrapple supreme in all the markets of the world, for the Eastern Shore men, as well as the Western Marylanders, seem to have an uncanny talent for the manufacture and improvement of delicatessen. The case of sauerkraut comes to mind at once. Twenty years ago that queenly victual had to be imported from Bavaria, but to-day the sauerkraut of Salisbury and Crisfield has left that of Munich and Weimar far behind it.

Sculpin (*Collus Virginianus*) is described in Holmes's " Professor at the Breakfast-Table " (chap. i) as " a little water beast which pretends to consider itself a fish, and, under that pretext, hangs about the piles upon which West-Boston bridge is built, swallowing the bait and hook intended for flounders."

" On being drawn from the water," the Professor continues, " it exposes an immense head, a diminutive bony carcass, and a surface so full of spines, ridges, ruffles, and frills, that the naturalists have not been able to count them without quarrelling about the number, and that the colored youth, whose sport they spoil, do not like to touch them, and especially to tread on them, unless they happen to have shoes on, to cover the thick white soles of their broad black feet."

Sea, Calling of the. An old English term for a groundswell. When this occurs on a windless night, the sound not only echoes through the houses standing near the beach, but is heard many miles inland. The superstitious look upon it as a summons to death. Thus, Tennyson, in his poem " Crossing the Bar," has the lines—

> Sunset and evening star
> And one clear call for me.

Again, in " Enoch Arden " occurs this passage—

> Then the third night after this
> While Enoch slumber'd motionless and pale,
> And Miriam watch'd and dozed at intervals,
> There came so loud a calling of the sea
> That all the houses in the haven rang.

He woke, he rose, he spread his arms abroad,
Crying with a loud voice, "A sail ! a sail !
I am saved ! " and so fell back and spoke no more.

Enoch Arden is lying at the point of death, and to the dying sailor comes the "one clear call" which Tennyson, looking forward to his own death hour, represents, in "Crossing the Bar," as coming to himself. This explanation of the phrase is obviously in harmony with the whole imagery of the poem, and gives point and significance to an otherwise somewhat vague expression.

Sea-serpent. When Sir Charles Lyall, the great English scientist, was visiting America, he one day asked his friend, Colonel T. H. Perkins, of Boston:

"By the way, what do you think of the sea-serpent?"

The colonel's face fell. His only reply was, "Unfortunately, I have seen it."

There you are. He had seen it, so he couldn't talk. If he asserted that he had seen it, he would be taken for a liar. If he denied that he had seen it, he was actually a liar. Not Cassandra, at ancient Troy, with her true but discredited vaticinations, not the Hebrew prophet, who found himself without honor in his own country, not Galileo when he uttered the famous phrase, "E pur se muovo," was in more unpleasant fix.

It is said there are many men now living who face the same dilemma. Many honest, reputable, and God-fearing men have seen the sea-serpent, have mayhap in a moment of weakness confessed to the fact, and then, shrinking from the obloquy which the confession brought down upon them, have forever after held their peace upon the subject.

Unfortunately they had seen it.

No such reasons for reticence, however, restrained Aristotle and Pliny (the earliest historians of the monster), who reported what they had heard and not seen, nor their successors in the modern era, Olaus Magnus, Archbishop of Upsala, and Erik Pontoppidan, Bishop of Bergen, two distinguished clerics who depended for their facts upon the memories or possibly the imaginations of others.

Olaus Magnus, writing in 1522, has this to say about the sea-serpent :

They who, either to trade or to fish, sail along the shores of Norway, relate with concurring evidence a truly admirable story,—namely, that a very large serpent, of a length of upwards of 200 feet, and 20 feet in diameter, lives in rocks and holes near the shore of Bergen: it comes out of its caverns only on summer nights and in fine weather to devour calves, lambs, and hogs, or goes into the sea to eat cuttles, lobsters, and all kinds of sea crabs. It has a row of hairs of two feet in length hanging from the neck, sharp scales of a dark color, and brilliant flaming eyes. It attacks boats and snatches away the men, by raising itself high out of water, and devours them and commonly this does not happen without a terrible event in the kingdom, without a change being at hand, either that the princes will die or will be banished, or that a war will soon break out.

Pontoppidan, in 1755, is more cautious. He even confesses that he had started with a disbelief in the sea-serpent, but had been perforce converted by "full and sufficient evidence from creditable and experienced fishermen and sailors in Norway, of whom hundreds testify that they have seen them annually." He weighs and sifts this evidence; he will not accept everything for true. Doubtless the good bishop is right in rejecting the stories of sea-serpents sinking ships and eating men,—even though Olaus Magnus did publish a startling engraving showing how the trick was done. What Pontoppidan accepts, however, is sufficiently marvellous. He tells us that " the sea-serpent sometimes encloses ships by laying itself round them in a circle, that the fishermen then row over its body there where a coil is visible, for when they reach the coil it sinks, while the invisible parts rise. Further, that the serpent swims with an incredible velocity, and that the fishermen, who are much afraid of it, when seeing that it follows them, throw any object, for instance, a scoop, at it, when the animal generally plunges into the deep. But most fishermen are in the habit of taking castoreum with them, for the sea-serpent cannot abide the smell of it. . . And in his tenth paragraph, trying to answer the question why those larger serpents only frequent the northern seas, he says: " To this question I answer that the Creator of all beings disposes of the dwellings of His creatures in different places by His wise intentions, which are not known to us. Why won't the reindeer thrive anywhere but in the high and cold mountains? Why do the whales frequent only the north pole? Why are India and Egypt almost the only countries where men have to fear crocodiles? No doubt, because it pleases the wise Creator." Here Pontoppidan takes leave of the sea-serpent, and begins to treat of the large snakes mentioned by Plinius and other ancient authors.

The first eye-witness to the existence of the sea-serpent who has written out his own experience, and not that of others, is Hans Egede, who afterward became a bishop. In the year 1734 he travelled to Greenland as a missionary. In his account of the voyage, he describes a sea-monster which appeared near the ship on the 6th of July. "Its head," he says, "when raised, was on a level with our main-top. Its snout was long and sharp, and it blew water almost like a whale; it had large, broad paws or paddles; its body was covered with scales; its skin was rough and uneven; in other respects it was as a serpent; and when it dived, the end of its tail, which was raised in the air, seemed to be a full ship's length from its body." A companion of Egede's, also a missionary, made a sketch of the monster, the first one ever drawn from life. . It represents an indubitable saurian, having broad filled fore-flippers, its hinder quarters being hidden under water. The frills proved a knotty point in identifying the "serpent." Possibly they were not frills at all, but merely the attempt of an inexperienced draughtsman to depict clawed feet like those of an alligator.

The first really spectacular appearance of the sea-serpent in American waters was along the New England coast in August, 1819. A great many people observed it from a great many places, and their stories attracted so much attention that the Boston Linnean Society—the scientific society of the time—sent a committee to investigate. Dr. Bigelow and Mr. F. C. Gray were selected, and drew up a report signed by numbers of witnesses who were within thirty feet of the creature. " The monster," they say, " was from eighty to ninety feet long, his head usually carried about two feet above water; of a dark-brown color; the body with thirty or more protuberances, compared by some to four-gallon kegs, by others to a string of buoys, and called by several persons bunches, on the back; motions very rapid, faster than those of a whale, swimming a mile in three minutes, and sometimes more, leaving a wake behind him; chasing mackerel, herrings, and other fish, which were seen jumping out of the water, fifty at a time, as he approached. He only came to the surface of the sea in calm and bright weather. A skilful gunner fired at him from a boat, and, having taken good aim, felt sure he must have hit him on the head: the creature turned toward him, then dived under the boat, and reappeared a hundred yards on the other side."

As most of these observers were not seafaring men, whose evidence might be doubted from their not being perfectly familiar with marine animals, special stress was laid upon the following: " John Marston, a respectable and credible resident of Swampscott, appeared before Waldo Thompson, a justice of the peace, and made oath that, as he was walking over Nahant Beach, on the 3d of August, his attention was suddenly arrested by seeing in the water, within two or three hundred yards of the shore, a singular-looking fish in the form of a serpent. He had a fair view of him, and at once concluded that he was the veritable sea-serpent. His head was out of water to the extent of about a foot, and he remained in view from fifteen to twenty minutes, when he swam off toward King's Beach. Mr. Marston judged that the animal was from eighty to a hundred feet in length at least, and he says, 'I saw the whole body of the fish itself. It would rise in the water with an undulatory motion, and then all his body would sink, except his head. Then his body would rise again. His head was above water all the time. This was about eight o'clock A.M. It was quite calm. I have been constantly engaged in fishing since my youth, and I have seen all sorts of fishes and hundreds of horse-mackerel, but I never before saw anything like this.'"

The story of the great American sea-serpent reached England in due course, and for a while was treated as a serious item of news. But in succeeding years successive stories, each more wonderful than the other, followed hard upon each other's heels, until the sea-serpent became part and parcel of the jocular history of the summer. Not until the publication of the "Life of Richard Harris Barham" (Ingoldsby) in 1870 was the secret of these extraordinary yarns exposed. They had been deliberately concocted, so it seems, by a friend of Thomas Hill, a famous London eccentric who furnished Poole with the original of his "Paul Pry." (Barham in his Diary under date of October, 1827.) Hill's friend was Stephen Price, manager of Drury Lane, whom he was in the constant habit of visiting in the quest of gossip. When Price found that much that fell from him in conversation, and especially the news he had received from his American correspondent, appeared next day in the columns of the *Morning Chronicle,* he had no difficulty in tracing the culprit.

"When I discovered this, sir," said Price, "I gave my friend a lie a day!" and accordingly the public were soon treated with the most extraordinary specimens of transatlantic intelligence; among the rest, with the first falling in with the body of a sea monster, somewhere about the Bermudas, and the subsequent appearance of his tail, some hundred miles to the northeast.

"Well, my dear boy," the credulous visitor would exclaim on entering the manager's sanctum, "any news; any fresh letters from America?"

"Why, sir," Price would reply with the utmost gravity, "I have been just reading an extract, sent under cover, from Captain Lobcock's log; they've seen, sir, that d—d long sea-sarpant again; they came upon his head, off Cape Clear, sir!"

And so the hoax continued, till the proprietors of the journal which was made the vehicle for these interesting accounts, finding they were not received with the most implicit faith, unkindly put a stop to any further insertions on the subject.

Naturally the British public was in no receptive mood for more sea-serpent when there was flashed upon them the most circumstantial story that had appeared from any British source.

This was in 1848. The eye-witnesses responsible for the story were the officers and crew of H. M. S. *Daedalus*. The story itself first appeared in the *Times* and was then put into the form of an official report from Captain McQuhae to Admiral Sir W. H. Gage.

From her Majesty's ship *Daedalus* under my command, in her passage from the East Indies, I have the honour to acquaint you, for the information of my Lords Commissioners of the Admiralty, that at 5 o'clock P.M., on the 6th of August last, in latitude 24° 44′ S. and longitude 9° 22′ E., the weather dark and cloudy, wind fresh from the N. W., with a long ocean swell from the S. W., the ship on the port tack, heading N. E. by N., something very unusual was seen by Mr. Sartoris, midshipman, rapidly approaching the ship from before the beam. The circumstance was immediately reported by him to the officer of the watch, Lieutenant Edgar Drummond, with whom, and Mr. William Barrett, the master, I was at the time walking the quarter-deck. The ship's company were at supper.

On our attention being called to the object, it was discovered to be an enormous serpent, with head and shoulders kept about 4 ft. constantly above the surface of the sea; and, as nearly as we could approximate by comparing it with the length of what our main-topsail yard would show in the water, there was at the very best 60 ft. of the animal *à fleur d'eau*, no portion of which was, in our per-ception, used in propelling it through the water, either by vertical or horizontal undulation. It passed rapidly, but so close under our lee quarter that, had it been a man of my acquaintance, I should have easily recognized his features with the naked eye: and it did not, either in approaching the ship or after it had passed our wake, deviate in the slightest degree from its course to the S. W., which it held on at the pace of from twelve to fifteen miles per hour, apparently on some determined purpose. The diameter of the serpent was about fifteen or sixteen inches behind the head, which was, without any doubt, that of a snake; and it was never, during the twenty minutes that it continued in sight of our glasses, once below the surface of the water; its color, a dark brown with yellowish white about the throat. It had no fins, but something like the mane of a horse, or rather a bunch of seaweed, washed about its back. It was seen by the quarter-master, the boatswain's mate, and the man at the wheel, in addition to myself and officers above mentioned.

I am having a drawing of the serpent made from a sketch taken immediately after it was seen, which I hope to have ready for trans-mission to my Lords Commissioners of the Admiralty by to-morrow's post.

I have the honour to be, sir,
Your obedient servant,
PETER M'QUHAE, Capt.
To Admiral Sir W. H. Gage, G.C.B., Devonport.

This account and the accompanying sketch, which was en-graved for the *Illustrated London News* (October 28, 1848), caused a great sensation. Professor Owen, however, was doubt-ful. He went so far as to say that a greater number of witnesses could be brought together to prove the existence of ghosts than of sea-serpents.

Then McQuhae waxed wroth. He wrote in reply that his officers and crew, not to speak of himself, knew enough to distinguish between a whale, a crocodile, a shark, and a sea-serpent. He reasserted the truth of his report to the Admiralty in regard to the color, form, and size of the marine monster, and closed facetiously by saying that he progressed far enough in his acquaintance with the monster to say that it really was not a ghost.

. If Professor Owen remained recalcitrant, a later English scientist, Richard Proctor, considers that " the statement of the captain and crew of the *Daedalus,* the former an officer of good standing in the English Navy, has never been overthrown."

In 1849 Captain the Hon. George Hope reported that on board the English war-ship *Fly,* in the Gulf of Mexico, the weather being perfectly calm and the water transparent, he saw plainly visible at the bottom of the gulf a great sea-monster. It had somewhat the appearance of an alligator, only the neck was much longer and instead of legs or feet it had four great fan-shaped flappers, similar to those of a turtle, the front pair being larger than those behind. Ring stripes were about its body. The monster appeared to be following its prey along the bottom of the sea, its movements being distinctly serpentine.

Dr. Newman, the editor of the *Zoölogist,* hailed Captain Hope's discovery as the most interesting biological event of the century. He recalled that Bishop Pontoppidan had described the sea-serpent as " a wurm with four flappers on its belly " (worm being the ancient name given to all species of dragons, snakes, and serpents), and he asserted that " if the Enaliosaurus still existed it would be of the same appearance " as the animal described by Hope and Pontoppidan.

It was not till 1877, however, that another story arose to rival that of the *Daedalus.* This, too, was buttressed by documentary depositions. On January 18, 1877, certain mariners made and subscribed at Liverpool a remarkable affidavit, which was drawn up by the master of their ship, the *Pauline.*

The document set forth that when the *Pauline* reached the region of the trade-winds and equatorial currents she was carried outside of her course, and after a severe storm found herself off Cape San Roque, where several sperm whales were seen playing about her. Suddenly a gigantic serpent rose and wound itself twice in two mighty coils around the largest of the whales, which it proceeded to crush in genuine boa constrictor fashion.

This strange occurrence lasted some fifteen minutes, and finished with the tail portion of the whale being elevated straight in the air, then waving backwards and forwards and lashing the water furiously in the last death struggle, when the whole body disappeared from our view, going down head foremost towards the bottom, where, no doubt, it was gorged at the serpent's leisure. . . . Then two of the largest sperm whales that I have ever seen moved slowly thence towards the vessel, their bodies more than usually elevated out of the water, and not spouting or making the least noise, but seeming quite paralyzed with fear; indeed, a cold shiver went through my own frame on beholding the last agonizing struggle of the poor whale, that had seemed as helpless in the coils of the vicious monster as a small bird in the talons of a hawk. Allowing for two coils round the whale, I think the serpent was about 160 ft. or 170 ft. long and 7 ft. or 8 ft. in girth. It was in colour much like a conger eel, and the head, from the mouth being always open, appeared the largest part of the body. . . . I wrote thus far, little thinking I should ever see the serpent again. But at 7 A.M., July 13th, in the same latitude, and some eighty miles east of San Roque, I was astonished to see the same or a similar monster. It was throwing its head and about 40 ft. of its body in a horizontal position out of the water, as it passed onwards by the stern of our vessel. . . . I was startled by the cry of 'There it is again,' and, a short distance to leeward, elevated some 60 ft. in the air, was the great leviathan, grimly looking towards the vessel. . . . This statement is strictly true, and the occurrence was witnessed by my officers, half the crew, and myself, and we are ready at any time to testify on oath that it is so, and that we are not in the least mistaken. . . . A vessel, about three years ago, was dragged over by some sea-monster in the Indian Ocean.

GEORGE DREVAR,
Master of the *Pauline*.

Again doubt, denial, and ridicule were awakened. The contemporary newspaper press as a whole rejected the story. Some of the scientists hesitated. Among these was Dr. Andrew Wilson, then a very young man. He could not believe that the captain and his men were lying. He was willing to accept the explanation that the attacking animals might have been some sort of big water-snakes. He did not then realize that the animal was a single one; that it was not attacking, but attacked; that, in short, it might be one of the giant cuttle-fishes on which we now know the sperm whales feed, and with which they often have deadly combats. He was misled by the words that the "serpent" had "whirled its victim round and round," and had "dragged the whale to the bottom head first." What the sailors really saw was the whale diving to the bottom with *its* victim. Twenty years later the verification of their story came from a thoroughly reliable source.

In a paper on the "Sperm Whale and its Food," by Mr. F. T. Bullen, published in *Nature*, June 4, 1897, we are made aware once again of the fact that these big cetaceans live on the squids or cuttle-fishes, which they pursue and attack. He was cruising in the Strait of Malacca, between the Nicobars and the Malay Peninsula, and had killed a full-sized sperm whale, which had ejected from its stomach bits of giant cuttle-fishes. That same night a commotion was observed on the sea in the track of the moon, and, as the ship drew near the scene of the disturbance, Mr. Bullen saw a very large sperm whale " engaged in deadly conflict with a monstrous squid, whose far-reaching tentacles enveloped the whale's whole body."

We now note what the " serpent " really was which enveloped the whale seen by the crew of the *Pauline.* It was the coils of cuttle-fish arms which were mistaken for the body of the snake. And a very natural mistake too. Mr. Bullen describes how the arms were of a livid white, and " enlaced the cachalot like a nest of mighty serpents " standing out against the black boulder-like head of the whale. The later raised itself out of the water, and then the big head of the cuttle-fish was seen. At the distance of under a mile it appeared about the size of one of Mr. Bullen's biggest oil casks, holding 336 gallons. He saw the eyes of the squid, each about a foot in diameter. As he and the watch looked, they saw the writhing of the arms gradually cease. They slipped off the whale's body, that seemed to float unusually high, and all around were smaller whales or sharks, which were evidently assisting in the destruction of the big cuttle-fish, " and getting a full share of the feast." When all was over, no traces were left save " an intensely strong odor as of a rocky coast at low tide in the full blaze of the sun."

The year 1895 was the last great era in the history of the American sea-serpent. He showed himself all along the Atlantic coast from Maine to Florida, under all sorts of conditions. This is how the New York *Sun,* July 28, 1895, summarized his movements in the seven months previous to that date:

" Christian Endeavorers have seen him and marvelled; weather-beaten captains have steered their craft from his proximity; the truth-loving Connecticut farmer has climbed upon his haystack and howled with fear, as the prodigy appeared, driving tidal waves ahead of him that threatened to overwhelm the seaside farm; a young woman has viewed him from the deck of a yacht where she was leaning over the port rail, because under certain circumstances not uncommon upon the wild and rolling ocean it is better to lean over than to stand upright, and was cured instantaneously of her illness; the cook on board a schooner has saluted him with a gun; an old salt on Long Island has been prevented from slaying him only by his sudden departure; a prominent citizen of New London has written a treatise on a typewriter concerning him; the United States army has watched with official eyes his strategic movements, and a dressmaker of Greenwich, Conn., has made estimates of him which she is prepared to furnish to any scientific institute desirous of collecting statistics on this most interesting subject." Behold a multiplicity of evidence to convince the most skeptical!

Sir Charles Lyell made some interesting attempts to trace the sea-serpent to well-known animals. He showed by careful drawings the appearance of porpoises in line in a heavy sea,—the effect upon the eye of their continued rise and fall. He dwelt upon the motions of a large shark observed passing through Torres Strait at a high rate of speed, the dorsal and caudal fins, with the swell, being reproduced so quickly and repeatedly on the retina as to give the impression of a series of humps. The elevated head in the air, so frequently noticed, he explained by optical illusion, or that the animal was a seal, or one of the monster Phocidæ, thirty feet long, that might have strayed from the north or south. The basking shark, or hockmar, of Norway, which attains a length of from thirty to fifty feet, was, however, considered in all probability to be the "sea-serpent," and this belief was strengthened by an enormous one that was cast ashore on the Orkney Islands. The flesh was partly destroyed, and the enormous dorsal fringed into fragments. The shark was described as a sea-serpent, the jagged dorsal as hair, and a most remarkable story concocted, which still holds its own in the old prints. The idea suggested the Kock sea-serpent, which was made of fossil whale vertebræ from Georgia, arranged in a row, and exhibited to the Bostonians as the "sea-serpent." Tape-fishes of the genera *Gymnetrus* and *Regalicus* have been found thirty and sixty feet long, according to Lord Norbury, and it has been suggested that they may have been taken for the sea-serpent; but, though long, they are remarkably slender, and not snake-like, and have a lateral motion that could not be contorted to correspond with any of the accounts given.

Mr. C. F. Holder, however, will have none of this reasoning. "These objections," he says, in *Lippincott's Magazine* for May, 1882, "have no direct bearing upon the evidence in favor of the sea-serpent. The testimony of a hundred men as to what they have seen would, in a legal view, be considered of more value than the opinion of ten thousand who depended upon what they thought might have been seen. The greatest advancement in scientific knowledge and investigation has been made in the last fifty years; the next decade may prove equally rich, and the great unknown, be it a waif from the Mesozoic or Eocene seas, or a gigantic form of the living sea-snakes, may fall into the hands of the scientist and its true nature become known."

Seas, The Seven. Here are a few facts: The Pacific covers 68,000,000 miles; the Atlantic 30,000,000, and the Indian Ocean,

Arctic, and Antarctic 42,000,000. To stow away the contents of the Pacific it would be necessary to fill a tank, one mile long, one mile wide, and one mile deep, every day for 440 years. Put in figures, the Pacific holds in weight 948,000,000,000,000,000,000 tons. The Atlantic averages a depth of not quite three miles. Its waters weigh 325,000,000,000,000,000 tons, and a tank to contain it would have each of its sides 430 miles long. The figures of the other oceans are in the same startling proportions. It would take all the sea water in the world 2,000,000 years to flow over Niagara. A tank to hold it all would have to measure nearly 1000 miles along each of its sides.

The blue of the sea stands in a constant ratio to its saltiness. In the tropics the tremendous evaporation due to the blazing sun makes the water much saltier than it is in high latitudes. North and south of the equator for about 30 degrees the waters of the seven seas are of an exquisite azure. Beyond these latitudes the blue fades into a dull green. In the Arctic and Antarctic Oceans the greens are almost as vivid as the tropical blues.

Bluest of all the stretches of sea is the Mediterranean. The reason is twofold. No large-sized river discharges its freshness into the salt waters. Second, the Mediterranean is landlocked and, being exposed to a powerful sun, evaporation is great. By actual test the waters of the Mediterranean are heavier and saltier than those of the Atlantic.

Occasionally and for no ascertainable cause, great areas of the oceans turn milk-white. Such a phenomenon is recorded in March, 1904, when crew and passengers of a Japanese merchant-vessel, steaming at night between Yokohama and Hong-kong, ran into a perfectly white sea. An opaque, phosphorescent, and snow-white expanse, its effects upon the eyes were dazzling. The phenomenon lasted only six hours.

In the year 1900 it was reported that the sea turned almost black off a large portion of the California coast, including the whole of Santa Cruz Bay. The darkness was explained as coming from millions of tiny animalculæ, known as whale-food.

The dull-reddish tint which is occasionally seen in the Red Sea, and which has given that sea its name, has a similar cause. The water becomes full of microscopic algæ—tiny weed.

China's Yellow Sea is usually supposed to owe its origin to the flood of muddy water which its great river pours into it. But here, again, modern science has proved that living organisms are responsible for its peculiar tint.

In January, 1909, a river of yellow water, three miles wide and of enormous length, was observed running parallel with the Gulf Stream. It stretched from Cape Florida to Cape Hatteras, and was undoubtedly caused by some tremendous submarine up-heaval, probably of a volcanic nature.

Sedan-chair. Hackney chairs, later known as sedan-chairs, followed soon after the introduction of the hackney cabs into London. In 1634 Sir Sanders Duncomb, who had seen the vehicle abroad, obtained a patent for it in Great Britain and sprang forty or fifty specimens upon a willing and even eager public. Yet a score of years previous a similar contrivance used by the Duke of Buckingham, favorite of Charles I, had excited the disgust of his countrymen, who indignantly averred that he was employing his fellow-creatures to do the work of dumb brutes. The sedan was in special favor throughout all Europe in the first three-quarters of the eighteenth century, when beaux and belles dreaded the slightest disarrangement of their elaborate toilets, toupees, and head-dresses. "Nobs," nabobs, and nobles kept their own sedans, which were frequently of elegant shape, exquisitely carved and decorated. Fine was the spectacle when a train of these chairs, occupied by fashionables, borne by flunkeys, and attended by linkboys with flaring torches. passed at evening through the streets of London, Paris, or Madrid to some magnificent entertainment. When the party had alighted and vanished within-doors, the linkboys thrust their flambeaux into the large extinguishers which were placed beside the doors of the aristocratic mansions of that period, and withdrew to the nearest ale-house to wait until their services were required for the return home.

During the reign of Louis XIII a modification of the sedan-chair was very popular among the ladies and fops of Paris. It was hung between two wheels, and drawn by a man. The door and steps were in front. In Spain the chair was made large enough to carry a party of four, and was borne by two gayly caparisoned mules, one before and one behind.

With the development and improvement of the cab system the sedan gradually fell into disuse in London and other English streets by the commencement of the nineteenth century. In Edinburgh it survived somewhat longer. In the steep streets and narrow lanes of the Scottish capital the sedan was found to be a more convenient mode of conveyance than the coach, and until long past the middle of the nineteenth century that city could boast of more sedans than carriages, and it was many years later before they were entirely superseded. These were for the most part in the hands of Highlanders, whose picturesque costume and uncouth jargon were the admiration and amusement of all strangers, as their constitutional irritability was frequently the occasion of much wrangling and confusion at the doors of inns and theatres.

In China and India the palanquin, a sort of sedan-chair, still maintains its popularity as a safe, easy, and convenient mode of travel; indeed, in all Eastern countries, where the science of road-building has made little progress except in the vicinity of the larger cities, the use of wheeled vehicles is out of the question, and the palanquin, the howdah, and the saddle furnish the only means of journeying from place to place.

In the towns of Japan a contrivance not unlike the sedan-chair but ruder in construction, on wheels and drawn by a man harnessed between shafts, is called a jinrikisha. See RICKSHAW.

Sevres. The famous porcelain factory was started at Vincennes in 1750, and removed in 1754 to Sèvres, where it has since continued to the present time. A certain Sieur de St. Etienne is said to have discovered the art of making a paste which would passably imitate the Chinese kaolin, or hard paste, some time towards the end of the seventeenth century. He was a potter at Rouen, but appears to have been satisfied with the beautiful faïence or earthenware which he made, and to have handed on his discovery to some other manufacturer, and the first European porcelain was produced at Saint Cloud. The soft paste, it is well to remember, is only relatively soft—that is to say, its consistency is as hard as that of Chinese porcelain, but it will not bear so great a heat, and the surface glaze is easily scratched. When it was found that true kaolin existed in Europe, the soft paste was no longer used; hence the rarity and value of this earliest French porcelain. Apart, too, from this, it was costly to make from the beginning, and we read that, when Louis XV gave Princess Marie-Joseph of Saxony two little pieces, a cream-jug and a sugar-basin, they cost 28 louis. A single plate, from a service ordered by Catharine II of Russia, lately fetched 6400 francs, or more than 250*l.* The manufacture was carried on at Vincennes till 1756, so that many of the best examples now extant must be correctly described as "Vincennes ware" rather than "Sèvres," at which latter place it assumed its title of "Manufacture Royale de la Porcelaine de France," every piece being thenceforth marked with the king's cipher. The sales in 1756 and 1758, we are told, amounted respectively to the value of 210,000 and 274,000 livres. In 1759 the king became the sole proprietor, and for a time all went well. Efforts were constantly being made to discover the secret of the German hard paste, and workmen from Meissen were bribed to reveal it. No kaolin of good quality was, however, found in France until 1768. In that year Madame Darnet, wife of a surgeon in a village near Limoges, seeing in a ravine some white clay, took it to her husband and asked him if it would not do to use as soap. He sent it to the chemist Macquer, in Paris, who recognized it as kaolin, the first which had been found in France. From that time Sèvres abandoned soft paste and made true hard porcelain. During the intervals the French artists were able to compete with foreign hard paste only on account of the extreme beauty of the objects they produced in the inferior material. When the necessary beds of kaolin had been discovered near Limoges, hard paste was introduced, but the soft paste was in its highest perfection just at this time, and it was not finally abandoned till 1790. Meanwhile a dishonest manager had nearly ruined Sèvres, but Louis XVI made a strong effort to keep it going, and the National Assembly included it in the royal property. Even after the fall of royalty the Convention decided that the manufacture was creditable to the country, and entrusted the management to skilled hands. In May, 1800, the famous chemist, Brongniart, undertook the management, and the soft paste from that time was abandoned. The very secret of its composition has long since perished.

During its best period the colors used were of the most brilliant kind. The famous " rose du Barry " was invented by one Hellot, but the secret died with him, and no pieces of this color seem to have been made since 1761. The name is an anachronism given long after the event. Mme. du Barry was still in her cradle when the rose ceased to be used. The same Hellot invented the *turquoise bleu,* and the *bleu de Sèvres* dates from the same period. As everybody knows who has " gone in " for old Sèvres, the soft paste was only made for about forty years, was enormously expensive, and is now correspondingly rare. The largest collection in England is probably that formed by George IV, part of which is carefully stored at Buckingham Palace and part at Windsor Castle, where it forms the chief ornament of one of the drawing-rooms.

Shadows. The peak of Teneriffe, in the largest of the Canary Islands, projects a huge shadow stretching upward of 50 miles across the deep, and partly eclipsing the adjoining islands. Exaggerated shadows of immense size are commonly seen in many other places. On the Harz Mountains the so-called Spectre of the Brocken throws gigantic shadows of mountain climbers into the sky, repeating every movement made by them. The same phenomenon occurs on the summit of Pambamarca, in Peru.

On the tops of Alpine peaks, and on the summit of Ben Lomond, in Scotland, mists in one case and rarefied air in the other explain these optical illusions. The same causes produce also colored shadows, varying at each hour of the day, and traceable to the dispersion of the solar rays.

Shampooing. The earliest record in Europe of this Oriental method of cleansing the head is contained in a wood-cut by Jost Amman, an engraver, who, born at Zurich in 1530, removed to Nuremberg in 1560. This picture represents a barber's shop, probably in Nuremberg. In front is seen the barber's chair with a customer in it being shaved, while in the background is shown another customer undergoing the process of hair-washing. A fixed basin is apparently built against the wall (as at the present day). This is approached by three steps, on the uppermost of which the victim is represented kneeling with his head over the basin. A bracket projecting from the wall supports, at a considerable height, a hemispherical bucket, through the perforated bottom of which the water flows with which the barber's apprentice operates upon the well-lathered and bullet-looking head of the patient. How the flow from the bucket is regulated does not appear. The whole process thus depicted by Jost Amman is exactly what may be seen and experienced any day in Piccadilly. A copy of the wood-cut in question is given in Knight's "Pictorial Shakespeare," in illustration of the passage touching "the barber's chair" in "All's Well that Ends Well."— *Notes and Queries.*

Shamrock, a trefoil plant especially famous as the national emblem of Ireland. According to a comparatively modern legend, St. Patrick, shortly after his elevation to be bishop of Ireland, set out on a preaching tour through his diocese. Everywhere he was welcomed with delight. One day, however, his audience failed to comprehend his exposition of the doctrine of the Trinity. Angrily they demanded more cogent reasons. St. Patrick paused for a moment, absorbed in thought. Then, stooping down, he plucked a leaf of shamrock and, holding it up before them, bid them behold an emblem of the three in one— the illustration of his words. The simple teaching won the audience over, and from that time the shamrock became the national plant. Unfortunately for the truth of the legend, no trace of it can be found in any ancient or mediæval Life of St. Patrick, not even in the most legendary of all, the twelfth-century biography by Jocelyn of Furness. Although the Irish reverence for trefoil dates from Druidic times, the story of the saint and the shamrock can be traced back no further than the year 1600. It is undoubtedly a modern myth which has caught the popular fancy. (See discussions in *Notes and Queries,* 3d and 4th series, beginning in 1862.)

Another myth is more easily disposed of. The shamrock,

it is said, will grow nowhere else than in Ireland. This is not
true. There is no plant known as shamrock which is peculiar to
Ireland. White clover, for instance, known in various sections
of Ireland as shamrock, grows abundantly in the United States.
The name is most commonly given to one of the hop clovers
(*Trifolium minus*) which is widely diffused over the island, but
cannot claim to be its exclusive possession. This is the plant that
is commonly exported from Ireland to London and even to the
United States for St. Patrick's Day celebrations.

Red clover has been locally called in America the shamrock.
This plant is familiar to all Americans, and is the State flower
of Vermont. Even water-cress has been called shamrock,
although its leaves are not trifoliate.

True shamrock, to an Irishman, is the plant known by that
name around the spot of his or his father's birth; but the botanist has as much trouble in identifying it as he has in identifying
the Mayflower of New England, a name applied in different
localities to trailing arbutus, to saxifrage, to hepatica, and to
two or three other plants.

Shell game, known originally as the game of thimbles and in
England as thimble-rigging. A pastime which was usually
worked as a swindle and was in especial favor with professional
gamblers on the Mississippi steamboats. As originally conceived,
the implements of the game were three thimbles and a "ball,"—
known also as "the little joker,"—a mere wad of tightly rolled
paper. When fairly played the three thimbles are placed in a
row. The operator shows that the ball is under one of them, and
that there is nothing under the other thimbles. The ball is
then rolled with the third finger back and forth upon the table
and is repeatedly stopped and covered by one or other of the
thimbles, released again and passed on to another thimble, until
finally all three thimbles are suddenly brought to rest, the operator holds both hands high in the air to show that they are
empty, and the spectators are asked to guess under which of the
three thimbles the paper ball lies.

In America the thimble has long been discarded in favor of
the walnut shell, although metal cups much larger than thimble-
are sometimes used, the object being to get more space than is
afforded by an ordinary sewing thimble, so that the ball or pea
may be completely covered when it is rolled under one side and
out at the other while apparently caught under the shell.

Another and the most important change in the game is the
substitution of a manufactured ball sold for the purpose by
houses that supply gambling tools. These balls are sometimes
made of cork, but more generally of soft rubber, lightness being

the essential, so that the operator may be able to make the pea adhere to the inside of the shell or to pick it up with his finger-nail.

If the pea is held under the finger-nail it is a simple matter, the moment the victim has selected his shell, for the operator to lift another, dropping the pea on the table just behind it at the same instant and exclaiming: " See, here is where it is!"

The invention of the game is accredited to one Dr. Bennett, who is said to have introduced it about 1795. Nothing is known of the doctor's antecedents, nor indeed whether the title or even the name were legitimately come by. His last recorded appearance was on board a steamer running up the Red River of Louisiana. He was then about 70 years old and was reputed to have made a fortune through his manipulation of the shells. Georgia, Alabama, Mississippi, and Tennessee, all had placed " the game of thimbles" under legal ban, but, as Louisiana had not followed their example, Dr. Bennett made that State his chief base of operations in his declining years.

Personally the doctor seems to have been one of those men for whom nature had done much and a good education had done more, but bad associations had spoiled it all. Like all Southern gamblers, his principal hunting-ground was on the river steamers of those days, which were peculiarly suited to such a purpose, as every person who had business of importance to transact away from home was sure to make use of the river during some part of the journey, and such persons usually had large sums of money with them.

In an article on " Curious Wagers " in *All the Year Round* for March 9, 1878, the story is told of a Kentucky judge who had to decide whether thimble-rigging was a game of skill or a dead swindle, and whether the plaintiff then before the court had been defrauded of his money or had lost it fairly. To help judge and jury out of the difficulty, the plaintiff's counsel undertook to give ocular demonstration of how the thing was done. Producing three innocent-looking cups and " the little joker," he thus addressed the court: " The defendant, your honor, placing these three cups on his knee, thus, shifted them so, offering to bet my client that he could not tell under which cup the little joker, meaning this ball, was; with the intention of defrauding my client. For example: when I raise the cup so, your honor supposes you see the ball——"

" Suppose I see!" interrupted the judge. " Why, any fool can see where it is. There ain't no defrauding there! "

" Perhaps your honor would like to go a V—a five-dollar note—upon it?" insinuated counsel, with a bland smile.

"Go a V! yes, and double it too!" cried the excited court. "It's under the middle cup."

"I'll go a V upon that!" cried the foreman. "And I!" chorused the jurymen.

The lawyer secured the stakes. His honor cried, "Up!" and up went the thimble, but no little joker was to be seen. The dubious point was settled forthwith, the jury to a man agreeing with the judge that thimble-rigging was "the darnedest kind o' defrauding out." Verdict for the plaintiff.

Shooting for Beef. A favorite pastime of the negroes in the Southern States in the Christmas season. The live beef has a value set upon him by his owner. The shooters take as many chances as they please, each chance implying a shot at the target. The man who hits the bull's-eye takes his choice of the best portion of the beef. The shooting is done with a rifle. The winner may give his prize to be shot for again, and the sport often lasts throughout a whole morning or afternoon.

Silhouette. In the year 1759, when as it happened Etienne de Silhouette was minister of finance under Louis XV, a man whose name is now forgotten started in Paris an exhibition which he called Chinese shadows. This consisted in throwing upon a sheet the black outlines of men or objects and making these shadows take part in a play. Now, Silhouette was at that time very unpopular. He had spent many years in England and had returned to his native country much impressed with the English practice of public economy. His application of these principles when he undertook the direction of French finance did not meet with the approval of the Parisians. His efforts at economy were scoffed at as parsimony and cheese-paring. It was remembered that he had once written a book, "A General Idea for the Government of the Chinese," in which he had exploited his economical vagaries. The popularity of the Chinese shadows provoked the gibe that M. de Silhouette had issued the book as an advance notice for the show. Hence the shadows were called silhouettes, and the name was naturally extended to portraits that were now coming into vogue in which were presented only the outlines of faces and figures filled in with black.

Though the vogue and the name of the silhouette are thus of comparatively recent origin, the art itself is very ancient. It was much employed by Etruscan potters of the eighth century before Christ; and a classic legend, which has been illustrated by Benjamin West in a famous picture called "The Origin of Painting," claimed that all pictorial art originated in an attempt to paint the fleeting shadows of men and women as they fell upon a wall or a blank space.

Although outline is a fatally restricted field for the artist in portraiture, the silhouette has proved itself capable of extraordinary expression of character in the hands of a real master. Augustin Edouart was one of the earliest of these. He wrote a book on the art, which is now exceeding rare, and his occasional portraits done to order are much sought after by collectors. On the back of many of these is pasted a rather remarkable list of the charges he made for his work:

LIKENESSES IN PROFILE

Executed by Mons. Edouart

Who begs to observe that his Likenesses are produced by the Scissors alone, and are preferable to any taken by Machines, inasmuch as by the above method, the expression of the Passions, and peculiarities of Character, are brought into action, in a style which has not hitherto been attempted by any other Artist.

Numerous Proof Specimens may be seen at the house lately occupied by Mr. Trinder, at the bottom of the High Street, Oxford.

	s.	d.
Full Length	5	0
Ditto, Children under 8 years of age	5	6
Profile Bust	2	0
Duplicate of the Cuttings to any quantity, are for each Full Length	3	0
Ditto, Children	2	6

Attendance abroad, double, if not more than two Full Length Likenesses are taken.

Any additional Cutting, as Instrument, Table, &c., &c., to be paid accordingly.

A portrait of Dr. Batherst, Bishop of Norwich, is reproduced in an article by J. S. Housley, " Great Men and their Shadows," in a recent issue of the *Strand Magazine*. The drawing of the whole picture, the force of the general rendering of character, are obvious, and it is interesting to learn that Wellington boots formed part of the episcopal attire.

In Edouart's book a striking silhouette of Paganini confirms the resemblance which the public detected in him to Mephistopheles. So marvellous was his art that many refused to believe he could attain it without diabolical assistance. One of the superstitious even declared that he saw Satan in person, his grinning face cheek by jowl with the performer's, directing Paganini's bow.

Other famous portraits are those of the Duke of Wellington and Edward Gibbon, both full lengths.

One of the best of amateur silhouettists was Mrs. Leigh Hunt. She left a large collection of portraits at her death. Unfortunately, she did not label them, and a number are now past identifying. But the more famous among her sitters are easily recognizable. Three of the best of these, according to her husband, were Leigh Hunt himself, Lord Byron, and John Keats. These exactly reverse the usual process of being black shadows upon a white ground. Leigh Hunt is shown bending over his desk in his usual winter attire, a stout woollen gabardine of domestic manufacture. Keats's portrait was taken in 1820 when he was living with the Hunt family. Here he was seen by Mrs. Gisborne, the friend of Shelley, "looking emaciated and under sentence of death from Dr. Lamb." The silhouette confirms this description. Most famous of all is the Byron silhouette, which was reproduced on copper and given to the public after the poet's death. It was made in the summer of 1822, when the Hunts were guests of his lordship at Pisa or Genoa. A description which accompanied the print read as follows: "He used to sit in this manner out of doors, with the back of the chair for an arm, his body indolently bent, and his face turned gently upwards, often with an expression of doubt and disdain about his mouth. His riding dress was a mazarine-blue camlet frock, with a cape, a velvet cap of the same color, lined with green, with a gold band and tassel, and black shade, and trousers, waistcoat, and gaiters all white, and of one material. The cap had something of the look of a coronet, and was a little pulled forward over the shade. His lame foot (the left) but slightly affected his general appearance; it was a shrunken, not a club foot, was turned a little on one side, and hurt him if much walked upon; but as he lounged about a room it was hardly observable. The rest of his person, till he grew fat, was eminently handsome; so were his mouth and chin—fit for a bust of Apollo. The fault of the face was that the jaws were too wide compared with the temples, and the eyes too near one another. Latterly he grew thin again, as he was in England. His hair had been thick and curling, but was rapidly falling off."

In the days before photography silhouettes, so Lady Dorothy Nevill tells us in her "Reminiscences," were given to relatives and friends just as photographs are to-day. "Everybody knows the small silhouette in a black frame so often seen in curiosity shops, but big ones are, I think, much less frequently to be met with. Elaborate coats of arms used also formerly to be cut out of white paper; these, when pasted upon a black background, produced a very good effect. Some little time ago I was fortunate enough to come across some Walpole arms done in this fashion, which I at once secured, as a specimen of really good work of this kind is by no means easy to procure. Silhouette cutting of every sort is now more or less a lost art; it belonged, indeed, to a period when people had plenty of time and women were content to stay at home, beguiling the long winter evenings with simple work of one kind or another, which would be not at all to the taste of their more luxurious descendants."

Lady Neville tells us that Princess Elizabeth, daughter of King George III, was an adept at cutting silhouettes out of paper. "I possess a little volume which is entirely filled with her work," she adds. "Some of the designs, instead of being black, are white, and with each of these is a slip of green paper to serve as a background. This little portfolio was formerly in the possession of Lady Banks, to whom it was given by the princess."

Lavater, who is about the only man who has made a study of this shadow art, and certainly the only one who has acquired any fame through it, reduced it to a science, and said that there were nine sections to be considered in making these portraits: (1) The arc from the top of the head to the end of the hair; (2) the shape of the forehead to the eyebrows; (3) the space between the eyebrows and the top of the nose; (4) the nose to the beginning of the upper lip; (5) the upper lip; (6) the point where the two lips meet and the completion of the lower lip; (7) the portion between the lower lip and the chin; (8) the chin; (9) the throat. Lavater claims that every one of these sections should be absolutely correct, and that the slightest change would ruin the portrait.

The method pursued by those few artists who make this sort of thing a feature is to employ a chair made especially for the purpose, and which has rests that will hold the body and the head in an immovable position. The shadow is then reflected upon a paper that is stretched over a piece of glass and placed in a movable frame, and which works up and down in another frame that is attached to one arm of the chair. The shadow is thrown on this paper by an artificial light that is stood upon a table at the opposite side of the chair away from the frame. The artist then outlines upon the paper with a crayon the shadow that is there cast. This is an absolute silhouette. Those that are cut off-hand from a piece of black paper are often excellent, but are not what the early artists understood by the word.

About 1820, an ingenious gentleman named Schmalcalder patented a simple machine for taking profiles.

Readers of "Pickwick" will remember the passage in Sam Weller's love-letter in which this contrivance, then a comparatively new invention, received a characteristic description: "So I take the privilidge of the day, Mary, my dear—as the gen'l'm'n in difficulties did, ven he valked out of a Sunday,—to tell you that the first and only time I see you, your likeness was took on my hart in much quicker time and brighter colors than ever a likeness was took by the profeel macheen (wich p'raps you may have heerd on Mary my dear) altho it *does* finish a portrait and put the frame and glass on complete, with a hook at the end to hang it up by, and all in two minutes and a quarter." "I am afeerd that werges on the poetical, Sammy," was the comment of the elder Mr. Weller—and certainly the machine, as it is depicted in current illustrations, seems hardly capable of the achievements so imaginatively ascribed to it. At any rate, the best professors of the "black art" have never been tempted into forsaking the spirited work of the free hand for the rigid products of mechanical ingenuity.

A common or garden variety of the silhouette artist still survives at country fairs, on the boardwalks of summer resorts, or wherever the human comedy demands a continuous stream of eager and not too sophisticated performers from the backwood; or the rural districts. It was in the decade between 1890 and 1900 that this artist was at his heyday, and he then attracted much attention and made considerable money even in the cities. A reporter of the Washington *Post* (*circa* 1890) interviewed one of these fakirs, with the following results:

"We have to use a kind of paper specially made for this purpose," said the scissors man. "It is colored the most intense black possible on one side and glazed with mucilage on the other. The paper itself has to be thin, so as to be cut easily, and very tough also. See that eyewinker. I could not have cut that with ordinary paper without tearing. With this everything is clean and sharp. Of course, my scissors must be like razor blades, and the paper is made so as not to curl, notwithstanding the glazing, for if it does so the two thicknesses that I cut at the same time will not lie close together, and one silhouette will differ slightly from its twin. Are women more difficult to cut than men, you ask? I don't find them so. I find men who have strongly characteristic noses, or other features remarkable in any way, the most interesting subjects. Mine is a natural faculty. I could cut likenesses nearly as well as I do now when I was six years of age; I have been in the business now for twenty years. Yes, it is profitable. I make two portraits for twenty-five cents, in two minutes or less, with half a cent's worth of paper. Frequently I cut at the rate of thirty or forty pairs an hour. It is not unusual for me to earn $50 in a day. Watering-places, of course, are my harvest spots."

"I see," suggested the reporter, "that some of your sample silhouettes are cut out of white paper instead of black. What is the reason of that?"

"Those are country people mostly who have their likenesses

cut in white," explained the scissors man. " Usually they say, ' Oh, we won't have our pictures done in black ; we're not colored folks ! ' "

Skerryvore Light-house. The Skerryvore Rocks, which lie about 12 miles W. S. W. of the seaward point of the isle of Tyree in Argyllshire, Scotland, were long known as a terror to sailors, owing to the numerous shipwrecks, fatal alike to the vessels and their crews, which had occurred in their neighborhood. A list, confessedly incomplete, enumerates thirty vessels lost in the forty years preceding 1844. Many others had doubtless occurred, of which no report had been, or could have been, rendered. The Commissioners of the Northern Light-houses had, *for many years,* entertained the project of erecting a light-house on the Skerryvore; and, with this object, had visited it, more especially, in the year 1814, in company with Sir Walter Scott, who, in his Diary, gives a graphic description of its inhospitable aspect. It was not until the year 1834, when a minute survey of the reef was ordered by the Board (had they fallen asleep during the intermediate years?) that the idea of undertaking this formidable, but necessary, work was entertained.

The reef is composed of numerous rocks, worn smooth as glass in some places by the incessant play of the water, in others presenting rugged humps and gullies. The cutting of the foundation for the tower in this irregular flinty mass occupied nearly two summers; while the blasting of the rock, in so narrow a space, without any shelter from the risk of flying splinters, was attended with much hazard. A steam-tug was built to transport the workmen and their building materials and also for them to sleep in as a floating-barrack. She ran many perilous risks in her precarious moorings. At length, in 1838, a wooden barrack was erected on the rock.

In the November following, a great gale arose, which tore up and swept away the barrack, leaving nothing to denote its site but a few broken and twisted iron stanchions, " and attached to one of them a portion of a great beam, which had been so shaken and rent, by dashing against the rocks, as literally to resemble a bundle of laths." Thus, in one night, the traces of a whole season's toil were obliterated, and, with them, the hopes of the men for a dwelling on the rock, instead of on board the tug, where many of the workmen suffered constant miseries of sea-sickness.

A second barrack was eventually erected in a less exposed place, and of additional strength, and this was found sufficiently stable to brave the storm.

Slave. The last slave in the State of New York was Margaret Pine, who died in Brooklyn in 1857, a self-elected member of the household of Wynant Van Zandt and afterward of his son. She had been presented to Mr. Van Zandt by his father, had been offered her freedom in middle age, but had refused to accept it, and had acted as nurse to a family of eleven sons. In the year 1813, however, when Wynant Van Zandt was living at Little Neck, Long Island, she determined to try her fortunes in the city, and received the following paper from her master:

The bearer, Margaret Pine, is my servant. She has lived in my family from her infancy. She is sober, honest, and faithful, but is averse to living in the country. She has my permission to go to New York, for the purpose of going out to service and to receive her wages, until this permission is revoked by me, of which due notice will be given to any person or persons in whose employ she may be. I further declare that it is my wish, and I am now willing to manumit her according to law.

Given under my hand at Little Neck Farm, this 16th day of September, 1813.   WYNANT VAN ZANDT.

To all whom it may concern.

Margaret returned to the Van Zandts when they moved to Brooklyn. She persistently refused to be manumitted. The *Brooklyn Star*, in an obituary notice, said: "She told her master, when he proposed to do so, that he had her services for the best part of her life, and that she wished him to take care of her as long as she lived, and he willingly consented.

"Dr. Charles A. Van Zandt, of our city, superintended the whole arrangements of the funeral, and buried her in his family burial ground at Greenwood, as the doctor says she had a black skin but a pure soul. When she was asked if she would have a physician, she replied no, that Jesus was her physician. She was also asked if she had any particular place that she wished her body to be placed: she replied no, it was but of little consequence about the body if the soul was safe: said she was tired of travelling, and if it was the will of her Heavenly Master to take her home, she was ready and willing to go. She lived like a sincere Christian, and died like one, cheerful, and without a struggle, to the last."

A still more remarkable story is that of Anderson Walker, an old negro in Scott County, Virginia. "It may seem incredible," said the Chattanooga *Daily Times* for January 31, 1895, "that a man should live in a state of servitude in this land for more than a quarter of a century after the emancipation of the negroes by the war; but Anderson Whitaker can verify the truth of the statement that at least one negro did not avail himself of the proclamation of freedom, but remained in a state of servitude till the death of his old master in 1893—a period of more than twenty-eight years after he might have been cultivating his own vine instead of that of another."

The story was brought out through a lawsuit in the Circuit Court of Scott County, and runs as follows:

Anderson Whitaker was a slave, owned by Nathan Whitaker, in Scott County, Va. When the close of the war manumitted the negroes, old man Whitaker was an invalid, confined to his bed most of the time by a severe form of inflammatory rheumatism. Anderson was his body servant and nurse. The old man did not want to give up his trusted and faithful nurse, and he proposed to Anderson that, if he would remain with him just as he was during the rest of his life, he (Nathan) would give him a house and some land and other property when he died. Anderson was a simple and trustful young darkey, reared in the backwoods, knowing nothing else but to obey "de marster." He had a comfortable home, plenty to eat and wear, and he concluded to forego the sweets of freedom and remain as he was until Whitaker's death, which might be expected at any time, since the old man was quite feeble. So he remained at the old home, working just as he had done all his life, nursing his invalid master, doing the chores about the house, and when he could leave the house working on the farm.

In August, 1893, Whitaker died, and Anderson's long period of servitude was ended. He had grown to be quite an old man, and fully expected to have enough from the estate to keep him in comfort the rest of his days.

It is not pleasant to add that the negro's confidence was violated by his unfeeling master. When the will was opened, it was found that he had been left nothing except an old horse worth about $30. Anderson brought suit against Whitaker's heirs, but on various technicalities the case was thrown out of court. It was urged that a verbal contract could not bind where real estate was involved, and further that his claim was barred by the statute of limitations. The poor old man was the last of his race to remain in bondage, for he was virtually a slave until August, 1893.

Sleeping-car. A clipping from an old newspaper (the Davenport *Democrat* of 1880) gives this story of the first sleeping-car and of its first public appearance: " I remember the date of its very first appearance. It was on the 16th of September, 1856. I was on my way West, had arrived at Toledo early in the evening, behind time, and had two hours to pass, before the departure of the train for Chicago, in the waiting-room. I had noticed a rather queer-looking countryman, and, somewhat to my surprise, he accosted me with the inquiry:

" ' Would you like to see something new?'

" Of course I would, and I accompanied him out through the depot, among innumerable cars, one of which he opened, and, after lighting several lamps, invited me to enter. Well, it was something new. It was a large car filled with a double tier of beds—bunks, more properly speaking. The man was Woodruff, the well-known sleeping-car patentee, and this was the first sleeping-car and its first appearance in public. Mr. Woodruff had during several years past been obliged to accompany his wife, a chronic invalid, from Ohio to Philadelphia for medical treatment, and her sufferings on the journey had constantly suggested the possibility of a more comfortable conveyance, so that at last he conceived the idea of portable and adjustable berths. Buying an old car, he worked out his idea, and he had, only an hour previous, brought it in for a trial trip which was to be made that same night."

It was George Mortimer Pullman (1831–1897), a native of Chautauqua County, New York, who brought the sleeping-car to its present perfection and invented the palace-car which still bears his name. In 1859, while riding at night from Buffalo to Westfield, he first conceived the idea of his improvement. At that time the bunks provided were nothing more than three tiers of shelves similar to those on canal-boats. The discomfort set Pullman to thinking. Before the end of the journey he had decided to build a car in which it would be possible to secure a good night's rest a-rail. None of the railway officials, however, would listen to him, and it was not until 1862 that he had saved up enough money to make the experiment at his own risk. He took two old passenger coaches and refitted them, and then went to the president of the Chicago and Alton Railroad and asked that they be given a trial.

" All right," was the official answer. " Go ahead. We won't charge you for the use of the road during the trial."

George Pullman in person sold the right to sleep in his car for 50 cents a berth. Two in a berth was the rule. If a man desired the whole berth for himself, he paid one dollar.

A quaint story is told of how one night, going out of Chicago, a long, lean, ugly man, with a wart on his cheek, came into the depot. He paid George M. Pullman 50 cents and half a berth was assigned him. Then he took off his coat and vest and hung them up, and they fitted the peg about as well as they fitted him.

Then he kicked off his boots, which were of surprising length, turned into the berth, and, having an easy conscience, was sleeping like a healthy baby before the car left the depot.

Along came another passenger and paid his 50 cents. In two minutes he was back at George Pullman.

" There's a man in that berth of mine," said he, hotly, " and he's about ten feet high. How am I going to sleep there, I'd like to know? Go and look at him."

In went Pullman—mad, too. The tall, lank man's knees were under his chin, his arms were stretched across the bed, and his feet were stored comfortably—for him. Pullman shook him until he awoke and then told him if he wanted the whole berth he would have to pay $1.

" My dear sir," said the tall man, " a contract is a contract. I have paid you 50 cents for half this berth, and, as you see, I'm occupying it. There's the other half," pointing to a strip about six inches wide. " Sell that and don't disturb me again." And so saying, the man with a wart on his face went to sleep again. He was Abraham Lincoln.

Such is the story told by the Pittsburgh *Dispatch* and quoted here for what it is worth. It should be remembered, however, that Lincoln was president of the United States in 1862 and was not given to incognito travelling.

The trial showed a demand for accommodations of this sort. Nevertheless, the railroads still held back. Then, in 1863, Pullman at his own expense built a car that was equipped according to his plans. It cost $18,000. Practically every railroad man who saw it condemned it as a wild extravagance. Nobody had ever heard of a sleeping-car costing more than $4000.

But the new car was blazing a new path in luxury. Externally it was radiant in paint and varnish, in gay stripes and lettering. It was a giant compared with its fellows, a foot wider and two and a half higher than any car ever built before. It had the hinged berths that are the distinctive feature of the American sleeping-car to-day, and the porter and the passengers no longer had to drag the bedding from closets at the far end of the car.

Pullman called his car the Pioneer and further designated it by the letter A, not dreaming that he would soon exhaust the letters of the alphabet. It lay in the train-shed most of the time during the first year of its existence, but whenever it was used there was a constant demand for berths.

Then James F. Joy, president of the Michigan Central, gave a half-hearted consent to try similar cars upon his road. Pullman built four cars at $24,000 apiece. Joy would allow them to go out only on condition that each be accompanied by an old-style car. The old cars were deserted. People who travelled preferred to pay $2 for a berth in a Pullman car, rather than fifty or seventy-five cents for a rude bunk in the jolting, springless cars.

Still, the railroad men could not see the advisability of investing $25,000 or more—for Pullman's plans grew in expensiveness all the time—in cars, and they steadfastly turned down his requests that they give him orders to build cars and buy the cars when they were finished. This led him to determine to build the cars and rent them.

Investors did not flock to him, but he got together enough to start operations, and the five cars he already had on the rail were earning money. During the first year he did not add any new cars, but the next year he put several out, and they were a huge success—the company that year earning $280,000.

The big roads centring in Chicago were pushing out in all directions. The transcontinental roads were open for business. The ending of the Civil War had paved the way to railroad extension in the South. All these facts gave new opportunities for Pullman's business.

In the second year the company earned money; it reached the $400,000 mark. It then went steadily up to $1,000,000, and from that till it passed $20,000,000.

The factory had outgrown its Chicago quarters, and all the surrounding land was held at prohibitive prices. Pullman determined to break away from the city, and he went out several miles, and for $800,000 purchased a 3500-acre tract. Here he built the city of Pullman, raising the ground from the level of the prairie, so that the mistake Chicago had made would not be repeated, and planning everything on such a scale that no future changes were necessary.

For a year Pullman had 4000 men constantly employed in raising the ground, laying out streets, and building shops and residences. When they finished he was ready for the 7000 employees engaged in building the Pullman cars. See PULLMAN.

Slot-machines, Automatic. The coin-in-the-slot machine goes back to prechristian antiquity. Its probable inventor was Ctesibius, who flourished about 200 B. C., and who also invented the siphon, the clepsydra or water-clock, and the steam-engine (*q.v.*), all of which, with other anticipations of modern machines, are described in the "Pneumatics" of Hero of Alexandria. Hero has consequently usurped the credit that belonged to Ctesibius, of whom he was an humble pupil.

The primitive slot machine was used for the automatic dispensing of purifying water to Egyptian worshippers as they entered the temples. The water was contained in closed vessels provided, like a modern money box, with a slit at the top, through which the sum of five drachmæ must be dropped before the donor could receive any of the purifying contents. The device is a very neat specimen of religious ingenuity, and the more so since it required no attending minister to keep it in play. It consisted of a vase which contained at one of its inner sides a cylindrical vessel of water. A small tube attached to the bottom was continued through the side of the vase, where the liquid was discharged. The inner orifice of the tube was formed into the seat of a valve, the plug of which was fixed on the lower end of the perpendicular rod, whose upper end was connected by a bolt to the horizontal lever or vibrating beam. One end of this is spread out into a flat disk, and so arranged as to receive on its surface everything dropped through the slit. The lever turns on a pin or fulcrum very much like a pump-handle. As the weight of the rod kept the valve closed while nothing rested on the broad end of the lever, no liquid could escape; but if a number of coins of sufficient weight were dropped through the slit in the lid of the vase upon the end of the lever, the valve would then be opened and a portion of the liquid would escape. Only a small quantity would flow out, for as the lever became inclined from its horizontal position the pieces of money would slide off into the mass accumulated below, and the efflux would as quickly be stopped. The apparatus would then be ready to supply the next customer on the same terms.

It is interesting to observe that this machine is practically the same as one that was patented in the United States in 1884, despite the fact of its hoary antiquity.

But this is anticipating. After Hero's time there seems to have been a lull in the production of slot-machines for more than two thousand years. Then, some time in the eighteenth century, a British genius got up a contrivance, which looked like a jury-wheel mixed up with a clock, whose purpose was that of delivering a pipeful or a chew of tobacco in return for a penny.

The Tubingen *Morgenblatt* of October 31, 1829, contains a description of such a machine as then in use in the London coffee-house. It was in the shape of a tobacco jar, which stood on the table and had a slot into which a penny had to be inserted to obtain a pipeful of tobacco. The weight of the coin depressed a lever and released a lock. The writer adds that a halfpenny would not do the trick, and the would-be cheat could not recover his money.

These contrivances are occasionally encountered in old-fashioned rural inns in England. In 1889 a traveller contributed to the English *Inventive Age* an account of one of these curious survivals.

In a grimy little inn in Sheffield he found the landlord quietly smoking his pipe. As the traveller, too, wanted to smoke, the good landlord brought from his collection a pipe of the "church warden" variety. For tobacco, he placed a tin box on the table. It was about a foot long, eight inches wide, and perhaps six deep. There was a slit in the cover. Into this the landlord dropped a big English penny, whereupon the lock was released with a click, and, having raised the cover, both filled their pipes with the tobacco lying loose inside. It was a crude but effective example of the nickel-in-the-slot machine.

"This box," said the landlord, "is always in the smoking-room for the convenience of the guests who are out of tobacco; and the pennies dropped in to secure a pipeful just about pay for keeping the supply undiminished."

"I should think," suggested the traveller, "that the box once opened, all the tobacco might be extracted by some conscienceless vagabond. Your box isn't modern. It ought to be so contrived that only a limited supply could be obtained for each penny."

"I don't think," responded the landlord, "that the box has suffered much from dishonest users, and as for being modern, of course it isn't. That box has been in use in this hotel for more than one hundred and fifty years, and is probably the forerunner of all the penny-in-the-slot machines now so common all over England—and America, too, as I understand."

The box was certainly battered and dusty enough to have been in use that length of time, the traveller asures us, and there seems to be no reason to doubt the landlord's statement with regard to it.

A Paris paper once attributed to Boston a new application of the "nickel-in-the-slot" principle. In that city, according to this authority, there may be seen posts along the sidewalks, with the inscription "Drop a nickel in the slot and I will hold your horse." As most Bostonians ride from their homes to their offices, the automatic steed holder is a great convenience; but when the equestrian comes back to get his horse, he is confronted by a sign on the post which reads, "Drop two nickels in the slot and I'll let go of your horse." So it costs him ten cents to recover his animal.

"If some rich man seeking a worthy outlook for his money," says Thomas A. Edison, "would install a series of automatic stores to be located in the poorest sections of our large cities, he could make five per cent. on the investment and so eliminate the word charity and yet accomplish a benefit greater than any produced through the millions given in the past.

"With the purchasing power these stores would have they could buy everything at wholesale. Then let them dispense only the necessaries, put up in penny and five-cent lots. We already know what can be done with automatic vending machines, and these could be adapted to the sale of packages of tea, coffee, beans, peas, flour, sugar, and all other staple foods, as well as fuel.

"At present the market for such wares is just the reverse of what it should be. The rich, with their ability to buy in quantity, are able to purchase their foods and fuel at a little more than a fraction of the prices paid by the poor, and by our present methods this may not be obviated.

"The automatic store—and it will just as surely come as will new inventions designed to reduce hand labor through the adoption of more efficient machinery—will not only save through its ability to make quantity purchases, but will do away with clerks and cashiers, will in fact demand only the presence of a single person, whose duty will be that of a general overseer.

"These stores, built of concrete, will demand little if any fire insurance, and may be kept sanitary even in the most congested districts by giving them a thorough washing with a hose at night. Their economical operation combined with their purchasing power will make it possible for the man who earns a dollar and a half a day to buy as cheaply as the rich man."

Snakes in Ireland. In Boswell's "Johnson" we are told how the doctor and his biographer made merry over Nicholas Horrebow's work, "The Natural History of Iceland," a translation of which appeared in London in 1758. In this book chapter xlii is headed "Concerning Owls," and is as follows: "There are no owls of any kind in the whole island." Chapter lxxii is entitled "Concerning Snakes," and the entire chapter is as follows: "No snakes of any kind are to be met with throughout the whole of the island." The application of the phrase to Ireland probably at first arose from a printer's error; but it was assisted by the fact that Ireland, according to popular fame, has never been troubled by snakes or any other venomous reptiles since St. Patrick drove them out of the country.

John O'Keefe, in his "Recollections," informs us that venomous reptiles are unknown even by name "throughout our blessed Erin," insomuch that the employees of Crow's Theatre in Dublin did not recognize as such an enormous mechanical serpent which was one of the properties in a pantomine produced by

Woodward. It was the business of this beast to move around the stage. This was effected by grooves, and the machinery gave the carpenters and scenemen a great deal of labor and vexation, for the serpent often stuck by the way. Three or four of these men practising, but with little success, the best manner of making it glide about, one of them at length vociferated, " I wish the devil would eat this *fish* once out of this house! we have trouble enough with it, and all to get our good master, Mr. Woodward, plenty of hisses; and he will give us plenty of ' boobies,' and ' blundering idiots,' and ' stupid fools!' The devil burn or drown this great fish, I say."

It is Sir Thomas Browne who thus discourses: " Ireland hath this wonderful quality, that it nourisheth no venomous creatures, and Irish wood kills them. It is said they die by the touch of a' native, and that any wood stroaked by a native doth the same. But of this I want to be further satisfied." Other people, more sceptical and more practical than Sir Thomas, set to work to satisfy their doubts. In " The Political State of Great Britain " for July, 1773, under the head of " A Pernicious Piece of Virtuosoism," there is an attack upon " the famous Dr. Guithers, who propagated in Ireland that species of animals called frogs," and a more recent offender whose ambition has taken a much more malignant turn. " This gentleman lives in a country (*sic*) that lies northward of Dublin, and some years ago carried over some boxes full of poisonous vipers, which he sent out at large to breed in his gardens; and it is said they have bred so fast that they have already got out of the garden and spread over the neighboring country, and are like to spread much further and multiply extremely—one of them having been lately killed in the country which had no less than sixteen young ones in her belly. So that, by this whimsical piece of virtuosoship, this idle philosopher may have planted a plague in his country which they may never be able to rid themselves of."

Elsewhere it is reported that " a gentleman " imported a number of vipers from England into Wexford, about the year 1797, but that they died immediately after. In the summer of 1831, however, another gentleman, by way of experiment, brought a few pairs of the common snake from Scotland, and placed them in a plantation at Milecross, near Newtownards; and the readiness with which they multiplied was more alarming than pleasant. The Marquis of Waterford, well known in his day for his strange freaks, is said to have tried the same experiment on his own estates, but with no success.

In February, 1890, there came a dismal rumor by cable that Ireland had for some time lost its old-time immunity. Two

years previous people in the neighborhood of Amraugh began
to miss poultry and pigs. Several vagabonds fell under suspicion,
were apprehended, and were locked up. But the depredations
continued, and finally a farmer's lad testified that, upon returning late one night from a merry-making, he had seen the evil
one in the guise of a serpent making away with a pig across a
field. The village priest took the lad in hand and questioned
him closely, but nothing could shake the fellow's testimony.
About this time other people detected similar fiends in the act
of like depredations, and at once arose a hue and cry that the
spot was a damned one, and had been given over to the devil
for his diabolical practices. Special prayers were said. The devil
was publicly denounced. Nevertheless, the depredations continued. Presently from Castleraine, a town twelve miles distant,
came word that his satanic majesty had begun operations in that
locality, his victims in this instance and in this place being
sheep, not poultry and pigs.

In this emergency the Bishop was most properly appealed
to, for the parish priests were at their wits' ends and their
parishioners were well-nigh crazed through fear. The bishop
promised to investigate the affair, but instead of resorting to
conventional ecclesiastical methods, that sagacious man enlisted
the services of two shrewd detectives from Dublin. The bishop
fancied that the devil was doing his unholy work by proxy—not
in the guise of dragons and serpents, but in the persons of lawless
characters too lazy to work and just knavish enough to steal.
The detectives, laboring under this heresy, made their investigations quietly and without candle or holy water, and in the
course of a fortnight reported to their employer that the depredations at Castleraine and Amraugh had indeed been committed
by serpents, the detectives themselves having seen and watched
the same upon three distinct occasions seize, kill, and carry off
their prey. The serpents were described as dark of color and
fully fifteen feet in length. They killed their victims by coiling
about their bodies.

Then the editor of the *Freeman's Journal,* in Dublin, remembered that some time in the year 1885 a showman named Wilson
had come from America with a couple of vans of living wild animals. Landing at Queenstown, he had exhibited with more
or less success in various parts of Ireland. One night at the
little town of Amraugh, in Tipperary, Mr. Wilson got very drunk
and attempted to clean out his own show. The constabulary
interfered, and Wilson, either in self-defence or in a spirit of
humor, turned all his wild animals loose. This created a terrible
uproar, and for a week the neighborhood was frenzied with

excitement. The wild beasts were duly captured or killed, but for three years no trace could be found of a certain den of snakes that had been let loose that night. The mystery was now solved. Evidently Mr. Wilson's snakes had increased and multiplied into a formidable progeny. And in fact they kept cropping up in various parts of Ireland at uncertain intervals, and a militant union of Church and State was found necessary to suppress them entirely.

Soap. This chemical compound of fatty acids with soda and potash was unknown to the classical age both in Greece and Rome. Pliny mentions a compound, which he calls sapo, made by the Gauls and Germans. He says it was used more by the men than by the women. It appears, however, to have been a pomade used for the hair in order to give it a ruddy hue. That the word was later borrowed by the Greeks from the Romans appears certain, from the name *sapon* still in common use among them. There is reason to believe that the detergents which are called soap in the English version of the Old Testament (Jeremiah ii. 22, etc.) are the ashes of plants and other such purifying agents.

Soap Plant. A native of Mexico and also of Colorado, which takes its name from the fact that its root when placed in water forms suds like soap and may be used in washing. The root is white, beet-shaped, and very long, extending into the earth to the depth of 6 to 8 inches. The Mexican women use it for washing the most delicate silks, which are thereby neither injured nor discolored. The leaves of the plant are from 6 to 14 inches in length, and sometimes even more, and half an inch in width, and of fibre so strong that a man of ordinary strength cannot break one with his hands. Much of the paper used in Mexico is made from them, being very fine and white. The plant looks like a clump of coarse grass, each blade being finished at the end with a hard, sharp point. Fine, thread-like tendrils shoot out from the blades and curl among them. The blossom is described as being a spike of large white flowers, resembling those of the mandrake.

Soda-water. An interesting fact about this favorite American drink is that it contains no soda. The chief ingredients are marble dust and sulphuric acid. To render wholesome and palatable in combination what are neither the one nor the other when taken separately, requires a pressure of at least 150 pounds to the square inch—a condition dangerous to life and limb except under proper safeguards and with the strongest machinery. The generator is, in fact, made of gun-metal iron tested to 500 pounds to the square inch. Into this is put the marble dust, to which, from another strong chamber, is led the sulphuric acid.

Then the two are cradled, and the gas generated is passed into steel fountains lined with block tin, two-thirds full of the water to be charged. These fountains are then securely fastened, and, like huge bombs in size and almost as destructive, are carried in wagons through the streets, to be stored under drug-store counters.

Whiting formerly was used to furnish the carbonate; whiting and chalk are still used in England. The use of marble dust, under the pretty name of "Snowflake," is peculiar to this country. In New York City the chips of the marble cathedral on Fifth Avenue alone supplied 25,000,000 gallons of soda-water. Thus economically do we drink up unavailable bits of buildings (public and private), tombstones, and monuments.

Except in the improvement of machinery and in its method of distribution, the manufacture of soda-water remains much the same. The method employed by the distinguished engineer Bramah is still in use. The man, in fact, whose name is most prominently identified with the national drink in this country was an apprentice of Bramah, and has developed his method here.—*Harper's Weekly.*

Spanish Main. This term is used glibly enough in popular romance and even serious history. But it is difficult to determine when the phrase first came into use and what was its exact geographical significance. Kingsley, in "Westward Ho!" orig- inated the error that the phrase was in common use among Elizabethan sailors to signify that part of the great American continent whereon the Spaniards had effected a settlement when English ships first broke into the Caribbean Sea, that is to say, from Vera Cruz in the Gulf of Mexico to the delta of the Orinoco. Longfellow, on the other hand, has helped to per- petuate a still more monstrous error, that the Spanish Main was some portion of the ocean.

> Then up and spake an old sailor
> Had sailed the Spanish Main.
> *The Wreck of the Hesperus.*

An early use of the term, "the Spanish Main," is found in The Journal of Admiral James recently published by the Navy Records Society, where on November 12, 1779, the admiral notes that he "bore away for Truxillo on the Spanish Main," Truxillo being the port of Honduras. In the supplementary volume con- taining the maps and illustrations for the new edition of Bryan Edwards's "History of the British West Indies" (published in 1818–19), the terms Terra Firma and Spanish Main are both used; the former marking much the same extent of territory that is included in the Firm Land of Dampier's map, while the latter

appears to signify only the coast-line extending from the Mosquito Gulf to Cape la Vela. To this day, people in the islands
speak always of the Main, and the Main only.

There is no doubt that "the Spanish Main" was an elastic
phrase often vaguely used even in the nineteenth century to
include the Caribbean Archipelago as well as the mainland.

But whatever its exact territorial significance, or whenever
the phrase first came into general use, as to its origin there can
be no doubt. An ingenious gentleman has indeed derived *main*
from the Spanish word *manea,* a shackle or fetter, holding it
to signify the West Indian islands, which link, as it were, the
mainland of Florida to the mainland of Venezuela. This remarkable interpretation is supported by a quotation from Bacon:
"We turned conquerors and invaded the main of Spain." It
would have been difficult to call a more inconvenient witness.
What Bacon really wrote was, "In 1589 we turned challengers,
and invaded the main of Spain"; and his reference was of course
to the expedition which Drake and Norreys led against the coasts
of Portugal, then a province of Spain, in reprisal for Philip's
great Armada of the previous year.

The English *main* is but the old French *magne,* which is in
its turn the Latin *magnus.* It signifies the mainland, the great
continent as distinguished from the islands; just as, when
applied to the sea, it signifies the great ocean as distinguished
from smaller expanses of water.

Such as it was, the Spanish Main was discovered by Columbus
on his third voyage.

Spear. In Homer we read how Achilles thrust Hector
through the neck with his spear, "a pole heavy with bronze,"
and the early Persians using the same weapon added a sharp
spike to the butt end, so that it could be used either way. The
Greek lance was a light missile, scarcely nine feet long, and
was the chief arm of their cavalry, and from them was borrowed
by the Roman horseman. But the Roman spear *par'excellence*
was the short, heavy pilum, which, with the broadsword, only
two feet long in the blade, won so many victories for the Legions
and established the wisdom of the saying that "the people who
shortened their weapons lengthened their boundaries." The
Gauls are described as fighting with a ponderous club-like spear,
while in Illyria the soldiers carried a fine slight javelin, which
they called their "spits." Ancient Germany and Spain also had
their characteristic lances, the one massive like a mace, the other
a mere reed for lightness. Thus alternating between the heavy
and the light, we find the same arm everywhere in use by infantry, while the cavalry carried almost invariably the longer

" lance," which still holds its own even in these days of firearms. In India, a country of unrivalled spearmen, the mounted lancers .have always been conspicuous in battle, and Great Britain has no finer soldiers that the " Irregular Horse " of Hindostan. Arabia is another country famous for the skill of its spearmen, and travellers never weary of telling of the dexterous feats, the terrific appearance, of the mounted Bedouins.

Historically, the spear is very important, for, time after time, in the annals of Asia and Europe, it has turned the scale of battle. How it flashes through all the courtly records of chivalry and glitters in the story of half a hundred nations. How romance delights in it, the knightliest of weapons and the most beautiful; and how sober history itself takes fire from these sharp steel points of the Asiatic hosts twinkling all along the vexed boundaries of imperial Rome, kindles at the glinting onrush of Macedonian and Scythian, and brightens into the very poetry of war when Saracen and Crusader meet, and the sunlight strikes the keen tips of their pennoned lances all down the embattled line. From one exquisite and fatal form to another it has passed from country to country, always elegant, always deadly, and to be seen to-day in the perfection of its peculiar grace when the irregular cavalry of India take the field with their fluttering lances. Terror hovers above them as they pass into action, and history seems to roll back for centuries with the wild cry of their unrivalled spearmen, Sikh and Jat, Pathan and Mahratta, as they sight their foe and lower their lance heads to the level of death. It was at the points of these same spears, shod with steel from the valleys of the Nerbudda and the Taptee, that Sivaji founded the Maratha dominion in India, shattering the hated Mohammedan supremacy, and stretching the authority of the Peishwalik from sea to sea. It was at the points of these same spears that the British in their greatest campaigns in India carried off victory after victory, and the history of their Bengal cavalry telling how again and again they held the scale of the day's fortunes and again and again turned it in their favor, is as brilliant a record as soldiers ever earned.

Sponge. What we know as a sponge is no more like the living sponge than a skeleton is like the living animal. In fact, our bath-tub sponge is nothing more than the deserted city of some millions of little gelatinous animals that once inhabited it. There are two canals in the structure of a living sponge, the one leading in and the other out, with ramifying smaller canals all through the structure, starting and ending in these two trunk lines. At the entrance to the one canal and, more sparsely, throughout its course, there are little hair-like filaments which wave like the heads of waving grain in a May breeze. They always wave the water inward, and give the inhabitants of the sponge city an opportunity to get plenty of food from it as it passes. The other canal leads outward, and by the same process the food-exhausted water is driven out again.

Sponges are taken commercially in three ways—by undressed divers, by men with diving suits, and by hooking the sponges from the beds in which they are found. The hooking method has been used in Florida waters from the beginning.

The sponge must first be " killed," which means that its inhabitants must be. This is done by exposing it for several hours on the broad decks of the boats. In summer sponges soon die, but in winter take a long time owing to weaker force of the sun. After death they are brought ashore and put in the crawls or cradles. These are inclosures made on the sea-shore by setting stakes a little apart from each other. The ebb and flow of the tide wash the animal matter from the sponges, and the work is completed by manual labor. They are then taken to the packing house, graded, strung, baled, and dispatched to their destination.

The largest and finest sponge known to the trade was brought into port at Nassau, New Providence, in the Bahama Islands, about the middle of March, 1911. This is how the event was chronicled in the New York *Times:*

When laid out upon the dock among thousands of other sponges classified for sale by auction, this particular one attracted general attention and admiration. It is what is known as a wool sponge, which is the finest quality known among spongers. It is in form perfectly round, arched like an immense fruit-cake, and is six feet in circumference and two feet in diameter in every direction. When taken from the water, it weighed between eighty and ninety pounds, and the fortunate man who captured it had a hard time landing it in his dory. Now that it has dried out and been relieved of all excrescences, it weighs about twelve pounds.

Its equal in size, fine quality, and attractive appearance has never been seen. When it was presented for sale it was put in a class by itself, and there were many competitors in the bidding for it, every dealer in sponges being anxious to secure it. It was finally awarded to the firm of O. F. Pritchard at $23. It has been suggested to Mr. Pritchard that the National Museum in Washington would be glad to receive such a curiosity.

This immense sponge is peculiar in that it had no fixed habitation, no permanent attachment to anything, but is what is known as a " roller," being tossed about by the waves in every direction. Rolling about in this way at the mercy of the waves, it naturally acquired its present perfectly round shape. It reminds one of the " tumble weed" of the Western prairies that is blown about in the winds, assuming its round, ball-like shape, as it rolls about in any direction the wind chooses to give it.

Sprinkle's Dollars. Josiah Sprinkle in the first third of the last century lived in one of the roughest sections of Kentucky. One day Sprinkle, then an old man, appeared at Washington, the county-seat, with a buckskin pouch full of silver dollars of his own make.

In every respect they appeared the equal of the national coin. He spent them freely, and everybody accepted them upon the assurance of Sprinkle that they were all right except that they were not made by the United States mint. The inscriptions on the coins were rudely outlined, and in no wise was an attempt made at imitating the national coin. On one side of the coin was an owl, and on the other a six-pointed star. The edges were smooth. The coins were considerably larger and thicker than the United States coin. When asked where he got the silver, Sprinkle would answer, " Oh, never you mind; there is plenty of it left." Once he volunteered the information that he had a silver-mine in the West, but he refused to tell where it was located. Finally government agents heard of the matter and came on to investigate. Sprinkle was arrested and brought into court, but the dollars were proved to be pure silver, without alloy, worth, in fact, a trifle more than one dollar each. After an exciting trial, he was acquitted. When the verdict was announced, Sprinkle reached down in his pockets and drew out a bag of fifty of the coins and paid his attorney in the presence of the astonished officials. Sprinkle was never afterward bothered, and continued to make the dollars until the time of his death. He died suddenly and carried the secret of his silver-mine with him.

Squirrel Point, a point opposite Phippsburg Centre in Maine, on which the Government maintains a light-house. The origin of the name is thus explained:

In the year 1717 Governor Shute, of Massachusetts, felt it his duty to come to this region, then known as Georgetown, to frighten the Indians who were complaining of the encroachment of the white settlers upon their lands. He tried to terrorize them, but failed completely in his mission. He came in the Government ship *Squirrel,* which ran ashore on the rocky point that still bears the name, and there was obliged to remain until flood-tide, when the craft floated off. This incident is said to have furnished much amusement to the Indians, but it did not tend much toward increasing their respect, still less fear, of the governor.

Steamboat. The steam-engine was used for transportation on the water before it was adapted to land carriages. This was due to the fact that it started as an atmospheric engine, deriving its force from the pressure of air upon a piston and producing a partial vacuum by the condensation of steam in the cylinder. Being relatively large and heavy, the engine was better suited to a boat than to a wagon. The use of high-pressure steam was an after-thought. Though Watt, with acute prevision of all possibilities, had added to his specification the idea of adapting high-pressure steam to the purpose of river and land locomotion, it was but as a caveat, for he built none.

The origin of the steamboat has been a vexed question for over a century. As the parties who first worked at the problem with success could not apportion among themselves the exact measure of credit to which each was entitled, so by carefully fanning the flames of national vanity the subject has been kept afloat. The truth is, the engine was Newcomen's, and then Watt's, and the boat was anybody's; and persons went to work here and there, with varying degrees of success, depending upon political influence, social standing, moneyed resources, or friends thus provided, and last, not least, mechanical talent for harnessing the engine to the paddle or propeller used to push against the water.

In this struggle great pertinacity was exhibited in Scotland and America. To deal out the exact proportion of credit due to each man is not easy; one measure is to be awarded to skill in mechanical adaptation, another to skill in fitting and proportioning.—*Harper's Magazine,* p. 79, "The First Century of the Republic."

The British claim of priority is divided between (or, if you will, mixed up among) three Scotchmen,—William Symington and James Taylor, both natives of Leadhills in Lanarkshire, and Patrick Miller, Laird of Dalswinton. Miller put up the money for the first experiments of Symington and Taylor. He did more than this, indeed, for he supplied the preliminary hint. In his early manhood he had speculated on the possibility of navigating a vessel by some more certain mechanical means than oars and sails, and he had actually exhibited at Leith a triple vessel having in the two interspaces rotatory paddles driven by a crank worked by manual labor.

Just here the younger men enter upon the scene. William Taylor, who had just completed a course in medicine, was in 1785 engaged to act as tutor to the sons of Mr. Miller. His love of mechanics no doubt recommended him for this position. The idea suggested itself to Taylor that steam power might be successfully substituted for man power. He communicated his idea to Symington and introduced him to Miller. Taylor drew out plans for the work, which Symington, having the mechanical skill, put into effect. The result was that on October 14, 1788, a vessel fitted with the steam-engine was successfully launched on Dalswinton Loch. Mr. Miller had his friends on board. Robert Burns was there; so were Henry Brougham—the future Lord Chancellor—and Alexander Nasmyth, the painter. Not one of them had any conception of the mighty possibilities that lay in the experiment they were gathered to witness on that October day. Sixty-six years later, a contributor to *Chambers's Journal* for March 11, 1854, who had collected and synthetized the local traditions, thus describes the scene:

"The assemblage gathers close to the lake and concentrates attention upon a small vessel which floats near the shore. There is something very odd and uncommon about this vessel, for it is composed of two boats, of about 25 feet long, joined together, and the upper outline is broken by a pile of machinery surmounted by a short funnel for smoke. The laird and the preceptor and the clever-looking artisan [Miller, Taylor, and Symington respectively] and some few others go on board this strange craft; and presently, while the multitude looks curiously on, smoke is seen to issue from the funnel, a splashing as of paddles is heard to take place between the united parts, and the boat glides slowly along the lake, leaving a white wave behind it. A huzza bursts from the crowd, and there is a rush along the bank, in attendance on the rapid progress of the little vessel.

"'Well it does go!' say some, as if for the first time convinced of what they had previously regarded as an impossibility. 'Who would have thought it?' cry others.

"And so pass the remarks, while the vessel, with its little adventurous company, moves backwards and forwards and round and round, over the bosom of the lake, the first exemplification, ladies and gentlemen, of that wonderful thing of our day, STEAM NAVIGATION!"

Yet, after all, this was not the first experiment of the sort that had been made, even in Britain, though the British public of that day had forgotten all about its predecessors at home and abroad.

Subsequent investigation has shown that Johnathan Hulls, in 1736, had taken out an English patent for a tow-boat having a rotary paddle extended from its stern, which was set in motion by a small steam apparatus placed in the body of the vessel. The documents in the case are as follows:

Firstly, Specification No. 556, 1736, in which the working details of his invention are set out. Secondly, Treatise, 1737, published by the Patent Office, entitled "A Description and Draught of a New Invented Machine," &c., in which it states:

" Whereas our trusty and well-beloved Jonathan Hulls hath, by his petition, humbly represented unto our most dearly beloved Consort, the Queen, guardian of the Kingdom, &c., that he hath, with much labor and study, and at a great expense, invented and formed a machine for carrying ships and vessels out of or into any harbor, &c., of which machine the petitioner hath made oath that he is the sole inventor." In this " Treatise " he quotes possible objections that might be raised, and answers them in detail, and his concluding paragraph is as follows: " Thus I have endeavored to give a clear and satisfactory account of my new invented machine for carrying vessels, &c., and I doubt not, but whoever shall give himself the trouble to peruse this essay, will be so candid as to excuse or overlook any imperfections in the diction or manner of writing, considering the hand it comes from. If what I have imagined may only appear as plain to others as it has done to me, viz.: That the scheme I now offer is practicable, and if encouraged, will be useful." The diagram or " draught " which appears in this treatise shows the boat which he had " invented " and " formed " as a stern-wheeler, and it is a remarkable fact that Wm. Symington's *Charlotte Dundas,* produced fifty-two years later, was also a stern-wheeler.

It has further been ascertained that the idea of applying the steam-engine to vessels had occurred to several persons in other parts of the globe. In France, the Abbé Arnal and the Marquis de Jouffroy had made experiments to show its practicability in 1781. Two years later John Fitch tried a species of steamboat on the Delaware River in America, propelling the vessel by paddles. Benjamin Franklin was disposed to encourage the plan, and a countryman of his, named Rumsey, endeavored to work it out, but by means of a vertical pump in the middle of the vessel, whereby the water was to be drawn in at the bow and expelled at the stern, through a horizontal trunk in her bottom. It was indeed natural that a motive-power so obvious should be thought of with regard to vessels by many of that class of persons who delight in devising new ways and means for all familiar things.

But at the time when Messrs. Miller and Taylor began their experiments, the few previous efforts which had actually been made were lost sight of in utter failure, and certainly were unknown to those gentlemen. They amused themselves with their steam-driven pleasure-boat for a few days, and then Mr. Miller had the engine taken out and deposited in his house as a curiosity. The winter was coming on, and no further steps could be taken immediately; but early next summer he resolved to try an experiment on a larger scale. A double-vessel belonging to him, 60 feet long, was taken from Leith to Carron, and there fitted up, under Symington's care, with an engine (18-inch cylinders), and on Christmas-day 1789, this vessel was propelled by steam on the Forth and Clyde Canal, at the rate of seven miles an hour, in the presence of a vast multitude of spectators.

Mr. Miller, unfortunately, had become disgusted with Symington, and was further vexed by the unexpectedly large outlay he had incurred at Carron, as well as by a certain miscalculation which resulted in making the machinery too heavy for so slight a vessel. He therefore paused. It had been his wish to try a third experiment with a vessel in which he should venture out into the ocean, and attempt a passage from Leith to London; but in the new state of his feelings this was not to be further thought of. By and by his estate called for a large share of his attention and means. A delusive article of culture, called fiorin-grass, began almost exclusively to occupy his mind. He lost sight of the wonderful power which he had called into being, and which was destined, in other hands, to perform so important a part in the history of the world.

Taylor, being without patrimony, and properly a scholar, not a mechanician, was unable to do anything more with steam-navigation. Symington was the only person concerned in the first experiments who persevered. His doing so is creditable to him, but the manner in which he did it cannot be so considered; for, without any communication with Messrs. Miller and Taylor, the true inventors, he took out a patent for the construction of steamboats in 1801. Through the interest of Lord Dundas, he was enabled, in 1803, to fit up a new steamboat for the Forth and Clyde Canal Company; and this vessel, yclept the *Charlotte Dundas*, was tried in towing a couple of vessels upon the canal with entire success, excepting in one respect, that the agitation of the water by the paddles was found to wash down the banks in an alarming manner. For that reason, the Canal Company resolved to give up the project, and the vessel was therefore laid aside. It lay on the bank at *Lock Sixteen* for many years, generally looked on, of course, as a monument of misdirected ingenuity. But, as we shall presently see, it did not lie there altogether in vain. Meantime, Symington was for awhile amused with hopes of inducing the Duke of Bridgewater to take up the project, and work it out upon his canals in England; and the duke had actually given an order to have the experiment tried, when, unfortunately, his death closed that prospect. Here Symington vanishes likewise from the active part of the history. The project of 1787-8 has left no memorial of itself but the rotting vessel at *Lock Sixteen*.

The experiments at Carron in 1789 had been witnessed by a young man named Henry Bell, a working mason originally, and later it would appear, an humble kind of engineer at Glasgow;— a busy-brained, inventive, but utterly illiterate man. Bell never lost sight of the idea, and when Symington ceased experimenting in 1803, he might be said to have taken up the project. At the same time an ingenious American comes into the field. Robert Fulton, of New York (1765–1815), originally an artist, but an amateur mechanician of great ingenuity, a man, moreover, of extraordinary energy and courage, had thought of steam as a motive-power for vessels so early as 1793. A countryman of his, Chancellor Livingston, had also entertained the idea, and in 1798 had obtained from the legislature of New York State an act vesting in him the exclusive right of navigating vessels with steam in that territory, notwithstanding an opposition on the ground of its being "an idle and whimsical project, unworthy of legislative attention." It appears that the scheme was "a standing subject of ridicule in that assembly, and whenever there was a disposition in any of the younger members to indulge in a little levity, they would call up the steamboat bill, that they might divert themselves at the expense of the project and its advocates." The practical objections of sober-minded men were, that the machinery would be too weighty for the vessel, require too much space, cause strains, be expensive, and be attended with great irregularity of motion. Nothing came of Livingston's privilege, his first vessel proving a failure. But not long after, Fulton, in connection with Livingston, took up the apparently hopeless project. Travelling into Scotland, he, in company with Henry Bell, visited the unfortunate *Charlotte Dundas;* and Bell communicated to Fulton drawings of the requisite machinery, which he obtained partly from Mr. Miller and partly from Symington.

While Miller, Taylor, and Symington, then, were all out of the field, and the general public looked with contempt on the project as one only fit to be an *ignis fatuus* for dreaming speculators, this energetic American pushed on his experiments, always approaching nearer and nearer to success. At length, having erected a vessel called the *Clermont*, at New York, he was ready, in the autumn of 1807, to make a full trial of steam-navigation on the Hudson River. It sailed 110 miles against a light wind in twenty-four hours. "Nothing could exceed the surprise and admiration of all who witnessed the experiment. The minds of the most incredulous were changed in a few minutes. Before the boat had made the progress of a quarter of a mile, the greatest unbeliever must have been converted. The man who while he looked on the expensive machine, thanked his stars that he had more wisdom than to waste his money on such idle schemes, changed the expression of his features as the boat moved from the wharf and gained her speed; his complacent smile gradually stiffened into an expression of wonder. The jeers of the ignorant, who had neither sense nor feeling enough to suppress their contemptuous ridicule and rude jokes, were silenced for a moment by a vulgar astonishment, which deprived them of the power of utterance, till the triumph of genius extorted from the incredulous multitude which crowded the shores, shouts and acclamations of congratulation and applause."—Colden, *Life of Fulton.*

During the remainder of the year the *Clermont* plied between Albany and New York as a passenger boat. She was the first that ran for practical purposes and proved of value. The outside bearing of the paddle-wheel shaft and the guard were invented by Fulton. The boat may be considered to have been about the sixteenth steamboat; nevertheless the popular verdict is a just and righteous one. To Fulton much more than to any other one man is due the credit for the introduction of steam navigation. His enterprise opened the way, and he was the first to apportion the strength and sizes of parts to the respective strains and duties.

Meanwhile Henry Bell, in 1812, built the *Comet,* of 30 tons, with side paddle-wheels, which plied between Glasgow and Greenock on the Clyde, and the next year around the coasts of the British Isles. He was practically the father of steam navigation in Britain. It can never fail to be a wonder that a man who was capable of achieving this high place in the history of his country possessed so little education that he could not write an intelligible letter, and could not spell his own name, for he uniformly signed himself "Henery Bell."

Since Blériot's successful crossing, in 1912, of the English Channel (*q.v.*) from France, speculation has been rife as to what would have happened in the summer of 1805 if Napoleon I had possessed a fleet of aeroplanes in lieu of that fleet of sailing vessels which had to wait at Boulogne for the favoring wind that never came. Only a few people remember that Napoleon had failed to realize the possibilities of a less anachronistic invention which might have enabled him to defy all the powers of the air. In 1797 Robert Fulton had given him the necessary opportunity. It was in December of that year that the American inventor experimented on the Seine with a boat for steam navigation. Napoleon turned the matter over to a committee of scientists, who learnedly decided that Fulton's scheme was impracticable and so reported to the Government. .

There had been, it is true, French experiments prior to Fulton's efforts to interest the Government at Paris, but they were not of as advanced a character as the American's. It is conceivable, indeed it is probable, that if Napoleon had given the matter his personal attention with a favorable inclination, the steamboat would have been developed under his patronage instead of in the United States, and history might have been written differently. But Napoleon was not a scientific man. He had no genius for the mechanical arts and no concept of machinery outside of the implements of taking life. He could devise ways and means of circumventing an enemy, could plan campaigns with masterly prescience, but he was not of a temperament to perceive such an epoch-making proposition as Fulton's.

There is a pathetic sequel to this episode. When the *Bellerophon* was sailing, in 1815, to convey the conquered emperor to his final place of exile in St. Helena, a strange barge, puffing clouds of smoke, was descried on the horizon.

" What is that? " asked Napoleon.

" A steamboat," was the reply, " the invention of an American named Fulton."

The emperor made no answer, but his face fell, and he stared long and thoughtfully at the novel self-propeller as it steamed away out of sight.

Steel, as a material for ship-building was introduced under modern conditions of manufacture during the years 1870–1875. As in the case of iron, however, there had been pioneers at odd periods. The London *Times* (in 1906) gave to the steamer *Annie*, built in 1864 by Samuelson of Hull, the credit of being the first steel ship. Straightway it received from J. F. Lacon a letter in which he stated that a steel paddle steamer, *Ma Robert*, was built at Birkenhead in 1857 for the Livingstone expedition, and that he has always been under the impression that this was the first steel ship. Furthermore, Mr. Lacon says: " As far back as 1853 Mr. Howell called the attention of shipbuilders and engineers to the value of mild cast steel for shipbuilding and kindred purposes, and in 1855 introduced it as Howell's homogeneous metal. This was, Mr. Howell stated, the origin of the successful application of steel for ships' boilers, tubes, &c., and the use of this metal in the hull and boilers of the *Ma Robert* was the first instance of the application of steel for ship-building. Moreover, it was also the first instance of the use for ship-building of what is now called high-tensile steel, the strength in tension of this steel being about thirty-six tons a square inch, with a limit of elasticity of about twenty-three tons!"

Stencil. Stencilling is a process of printing letters or designs by means of patterns cut in thin plates of metal or pasteboard. These plates are laid on the surface intended to receive the pattern. The color is rubbed into the cut space with a brush, the plate preventing any contact of the color with the surface except on the space cut out. This invention can be traced back at least as far as the time of Theodoric, King of the Ostrogoths. That monarch, being so illiterate that he could not write even the initials of his name, was provided with a plate of gold through which the letters Theod. were cut. When his signature was required the stencil was laid on the paper and he traced the letters with a quill.

The Byzantine historian Procopius (*circa* A.D. 527) relates a similar story of his master the Emperor Justinian. Procopius records that the emperor, unable to write his name, had a thin smooth piece of board perforated with holes in the form of the letters J U S T, which, when laid on his paper, served to direct the point of his pen, his hand being guided by another. The device was either borrowed or independently hit upon by the first makers of playing cards, who used plates of copper or pewter, with slits on them according to the required pattern, for defining the spaces to be colored. This account of the antiquity of stencil-work is to be found in the fortieth volume of the Philosophical Transactions.

Stick-in-the Mud. A colloquial expression common to both England and America, and applied to a dullard or slow coach, a person who has never made any progress in education or business or in life generally. An early example of the use of the term in literature occurs in "Tom Brown at Oxford" by Thomas Hughes. An earlier instance from a non-literary source is cited by a contributor to *Notes and Queries* (11, iii, 106) as from *The General Evening Post* of November 15–17, 1732: "George Sutton was yesterday before Justice De Veil on suspicion of robbing Colonel Des Romain's House at Paddington. The Colonel was in the Room with the Justice, and no sooner had Sutton entered the Room but the Colonel said, that is the Man that first came and seized me with his drawn Sword in his Hand. The Justice committed him to Newgate. At the same time James Baker was before Justice de Veil for the same Fact. The Colonel could not swear to him, but the Justice committed him to the same place with Sutton. George Fluster, *alias* Stick-in-the-Mud, has made himself an Evidence, and impeached the above two Persons." It is suggested that the term "st.ck" applied to an actor deficient in histrionic talent may be an abbreviation of the longer phrase. A famous jest of Sir William S. Gilbert may be recalled in this connection. In allusion to a certain dramatic club the playwright said, " I wouldn't call it a club, but a collection of sticks."

Stock in Eisen. A famous landmark in Vienna, standing within the old horse-market, a stone's throw from the cathedral. It is nothing more than the stump of a venerable tree,—said to mark the ancient limits of the Wienerwald,—and is clasped around with a padlocked iron band, and sheeted with iron in the shape of nails driven in by the apprentices to the locksmith's trade before they set out on their probationary wanderings.

Tradition tells this story of its origin: Erhard Marbacher, the most famous locksmith of Vienna, had taken a certain Martin Mux as an apprentice out of charity. Martin was very much of a *maurais sujet,* so the worthy Master Marbacher was exceptionally severe with him. One evening Marbacher sent the lad on a message beyond the walls, with strict injunctions to be back before the gates closed. Martin loitered till he was belated and locked out. In sore distress he tried to soften the inexorable gate-wards, but all in vain. Then in the moment of his despair a stranger appeared at his elbow and offered to help him. He gave his *protégé* a handful of gold by way of earnest, and gradually increased his offers of future patronage. Martin, being shrewd enough, naturally suspected the motives of the benevolent stranger, who moreover had all the attributes both in dress and costume that distinguished the Mephistopheles of the middle ages. By way of some small return for his generous premises, the stranger negligently suggested that Martin should sign away his soul; but, though Martin was dazzled and tempted, he would not consent without bargaining. According to their final terms, the tempter stipulated to place the apprentice at the head of his trade and instruct him in all the knowledge of good and evil. On the other hand, Martin bequeathed him his soul, providing that he failed on a single occasion to attend the Sunday Mass. Next day Martin's new acquaintance presented himself as a gentleman of the Court to Marbacher in his workshop. He came to order an iron circlet, to be secured by a padlock that no mortal strength could force. It was a difficult commission at best, and had to be executed so quickly that Marbacher hesitated, and finally declined. Then the visitor made an appeal to the apprentices. Martin, the youngest of them, venturously undertook the task, and received the inspiration that enabled him to execute it in a dream. His masterpiece met the full approval of the mysterious customer, who clasped and locked it round the stem of the old tree in the horse-market. The successful artisan went on his trade wanderings, and worked, among other tasks, under Master Veit at the great tomb of St. Sebald in Nuremberg. He chanced to come back to his native city at the very moment when the municipality were offering munificent rewards to the man who should open the lock that he had forged. He succeeded as a matter of course, and was acknowledged as the chief of his calling. He attained to increasing wealth and consideration, taking care never to miss a mass, until one unlucky Sunday, when his vicious old habits got the better of him, and he carried the Saturday night into Sunday morning over.a long game of cards. Then he made a rush for the church, but it was too late. The officiating priest was already at the "*Ita missa est;*" and lo! the other party to the fatal bargain was there to receive him with triumphant sneers and a demoniacal scowl of congratulation. Martin fell down senseless, and expired on the spot, his breath escaping from the body in a puff of black smoke. When they carried the corpse to his mother's, the skin had changed to the hue of the Ethiopian's; and although he was honorably buried in the cemetery of the cathedral, there could be no question as to the fate of his soul.

Stocking-loom. The story of the invention of the stocking-loom has been variously told. A very barren account appears in Thornton's "Nottinghamshire," as follows: "At Culonton was born William Lee, Master of Arts in Cambridge, and heir to a pretty freehold there, who, seeing a woman knit, invented a loom to knit." This skeleton of fact has been padded out into a pretty romance. One historian, who makes Lee an Oxford student, says he was courting a young lady who paid more attention to her knitting than to her lover's wooing. So, as he watched her deftly moving fingers, the idea came to him of a mechanical invention which should supersede this knitting business altogether and leave his mistress no excuse for inattention. Another historian suggests the application to Mr. William Lee's inventive powers of a more potent stimulus than even the desire to get full possession of his sweetheart's attention. Here he i already married to the young lady, and Lee has been turned ou of the university for contracting a matrimonial engagement while still an undergraduate. They are left entirely destitute. The young wife turns her knitting to account and knits stockings for the joint support of herself and her husband. Then it is that Lee, watching the movements by which the stockings are evolved, gets the first idea of the machine subsequently brought to perfection.

Strassburg Clock. The most famous of all mechanical

and astronomical clocks. It has been reconstructed twice since it was first put up in 1352. Legend gives its origin thus: The Chapter of Strassburg, determined to obtain a clock which would be worthy of the magnificent cathedral which had been finished in 1176, issued and circulated all over Europe letters inviting mechanics and inventors to compete for the proposed work. Only one man responded; his services were accepted, and in 1352 the clock was finished.

The chapter was convoked to witness the first movements of this wonderful machine. Immediately upon the striking of the hour, a cock, perched on a lofty turret, clapped his wings, and by his voice denoted the fall of the prince of the apostles. Each of the chosen twelve presented himself as a representative of one hour, the figure of the Saviour himself, the sun, the planetary bodies, the months, the seasons, the different parts of the day, the days of the week, the days of the month, the age of the world, the year of the Lord, all were symbolized with wondrous ingenuity. The chapter were astonished. Upon retiring to deliberate concerning the reward which should be bestowed upon the cunning workman, the priests bethought them that they might yet be shorn of their glory; he who had made one might create its fellow—other cities might boast of clocks as wonderful as that of Strassburg. So they came to a horrible resolution—they would put out his eyes, and thus deprive him of the means of accomplishing any further work. When the blinded artist was made acquainted with the cause of his punishment, he cried out, "The work is not completely finished —there is yet one great omission; lead me to the place that I may perfect my work." They led the man to his mechanical triumph. At one fell blow he dashed the whole contrivance to pieces. And no man was found who could reconstruct that clock in its entirety. The revenge of the mechanist was complete.

Such is the legend of the first astronomical clock at Strassburg. In 1550 an entirely new clock was constructed for the cathedral, manufactured by the most celebrated mathematicians of that period. The death of one of these men, however, interrupted their labor, and the work was left incomplete. Its completion was afterward intrusted to Conrad Ranchfuss, a mathematical professor at Strassburg—better known by his Greek name Pasypodius. Under his direction the work was finished on the 28th of June, 1574.

Early in the nineteenth century it was found that the clock required reconstruction, and the work was entrusted to Charles Schwilgue. It was on the 24th of June, 1838, that M. Schwilgue actually commenced the clock that we now know, completing it on the 2d of October, 1842. He retained or restored only a few of the original movements, most of the present mechanism being of his own design.

Upon the face of the clock, on the outside of the church, are indicated the hours and their subdivisions, and the days of the week, with the signs of the planets corresponding to the season. These indications are repeated upon an inner dial, and are connected with another much smaller, which is devoted exclusively to the calendar of the months and the holy days of feast and fast. United with all this are some very interesting automata, representing the four ages of life. Thus, in the division of the twelve hours, infancy watches over the first three, childhood the second, manhood the third, old age the fourth. Death strikes the hours. The whole of the mechanical contrivance, although extremely complicated, exhibits the greatest precision.

At noon, the sounding of the bell is succeeded by a procession of the twelve apostles, who salute a figure of the Saviour which is placed upon a pedestal in close proximity. At the same time a cock perched upon the tower claps his wings and sounds a song of victory. The days of the week are indicated by the deities of heathen mythology,—Sunday by Apollo, Monday by Diana, Tuesday by Mars, &c. The portrait upon the base of the left tower is that of Copernicus.

Street Lights. Whether the ancients lighted their cities at night is still disputed by historians. It seems probable, however, that Rome, except in the rare intervals of festive illuminations, was left in darkness. The citizens, when they went out at night, carried lanterns or torches, or else wandered, in moonless nights, exposed to robbers and stumbling over obstacles. Antioch, in the fourth century the splendid capital of the East, seems to have set the example of suspending lamps through its principal streets or around its public buildings. Constantine ordered Constantinople to be illuminated on every Easter-eve with lamps and wax candles. All Egypt was lighted up with tapers floating on vessels of oil at the feast of Isis; and Rome received Cicero, after the flight of Catiline, with a display of lanterns and torches. Yet the practice of lighting up a whole city at night seems, in fact, a modern invention.'

Paris and London dispute the priority in this matter. London claims to have lighted its streets with lanterns as early as 1414; but the tradition is doubtful, and the custom, if it was ever established, endured but for a short period. At the opening of the sixteenth century, when the streets of Paris were often infested with robbers and incendiaries, the inhabitants were ordered to keep lights burning, after nine in the evening, before the windows of their houses; in 1558 vases filled with pitch and other combustible matter were kept blazing at distant intervals through the streets. A short time afterward lanterns were provided at the public cost. They were at first only employed during the winter months, but were soon kept constantly burning. Reverberating lamps were next invented, and were usually surrounded by throngs of curious Parisians.

In the reign of Louis XIV one of the most magnificent spectacles was supposed to be the general lighting of the streets of Paris. The world was invited to witness the novel scene. Yet the lights of the great city consisted only of dim lanterns and torches, dispersed at distant intervals, and, compared with the bright glare of modern gas, would have seemed only a dusky gloom. In 1777, the road between Paris and Versailles, for nearly nine miles in length, was lighted; and in the present century the French metropolis has steadily improved its street lamps, until the introduction of gas made the streets of Paris as brilliant by night as by day.

Meanwhile in London, so far back as 1668, the citizens were ordered to place lamps in front of their houses every night during the winter; but as late as 1736 the rule was imperfectly obeyed. Robbers filled its narrow streets, and life and property were never secure in the darkness. Glass lamps were next introduced, at the public expense; their number was rapidly increased, and towards the close of the nineteenth century the citizens of London were accustomed to boast of their magnificent system of street lights, which far surpassed that of Paris. The roads running from the city for seven or eight miles were lined with crystal lamps. At the crossing of several of them the effect was thought magnificent; and what would now be a dim and dismal array of smoking lamps seemed then one of the wonders of the time. Novelists and poets celebrated the nightly illumination of the overgrown capital. Vienna, Berlin, and other European cities followed the example of Paris or London, and New York and Philadelphia early adopted the custom. Rome, alone, still clinging to the usages of the Middle Ages, refused to light its streets; the popes steadily opposed the heretical invention, and preferred darkness to light.

At length came a wonderful advance. For three centuries civilization had prided itself upon its lamps or lanterns; it was now to shine in novel brilliancy. The Chinese, who seem to have originated without perfecting most modern inventions, had long been accustomed to sink tubes into beds of coal, and carry its natural gas into their houses, and even their streets, for the purposes of illumination. They also used it for manufactures and cooking. But they had never discovered the art of making gas (*q.v.*). In 1792 Mr. William Murdoch first used gas for lighting his offices and house in Redruth, Cornwall. The Birmingham manufacturers at once adopted the invention. The unparalleled splendor of the light at once attracted public attention. The peace of 1802, transitory as a sudden illumination, was celebrated by the lighting of the factory of Watt and Boulton, at Birmingham, with a flame that seemed to rival the brightness of the stars. The invention spread over the world. London, ashamed of its once boasted array of endless lamps, now glittered with hundreds of miles of gas-lights. Paris again called the whole world to witness its tasteful illumination. The cities of the New World lighted up every corner of their busy streets. Even Rome yielded to the useful invention.

Subway in New York. Every now and then some writer of special articles on Old New York discovers that there exists under lower Broadway a short tunnel which has a right to call itself the first New York subway. It runs ten blocks, from Park Place to Walker Street, and was built in 1869, under a franchise granted originally for " the transmission of letters, packages, and merchandise by means of pneumatic tubes." In 1873 this franchise was extended so as to permit the transportation of passengers from the Battery up Broadway to Central Park and up Madison Avenue to the Harlem River. This, too, was to be done pneumatically. As a guarantee of good faith, the company did actually put a car into the little section of subway that it dug, and did carry a few passengers the length of the line, by pumping the air away from in front of the one vehicle which was the beginning and the end of its investment in rolling stock.

This car, says the *Scientific American*, February, 1912, is still in the long-sealed tunnel, and, according to the same authority, the tunnel itself was not only excavated by means of a hydraulic shield, much like those now in use, but the work was done without any interference with surface traffic. Fears for the safety of adjoining buildings, combined with lack of money and doubts as to the practicability of any motors then available for underground traction, brought operations to a close.

" It still has an owner, of what substantiality remains to be seen, in the shape of the New York Parcel Despatch Company, and Eugene W. Austin, its president, has solemnly warned the Public Service Commission that trespassers will be prosecuted. The commissioners profess a lofty indifference to the threats of a company which, if not dead, has been sleeping for forty years, but no longer ago than 1889 the Court of Appeals, in denying the constitutionality of the passenger franchise, did affirm the legality of that to carry packages, so there may be trouble, delay, and expense ahead."—*N. Y. Times,* February 23, 1912.

Suffragette. The first suffragette was an American. So much is certain. The claims of three women have been put forward for the honor. All were Americans. The earliest of these was Mistress Margaret Brent, a niece of Lord Baltimore, proprietor of Maryland, and of Leonard Calvert, governor of that colony and the lord proprietor's brother. On June 9, 1647, Governor Calvert died. Margaret was his executrix. She claimed also the right of acting as Lord Baltimore's attorney. This was allowed her by the Maryland Assembly.

Now comes the most notable event of her career. When, on the 24th of June, the Assembly of 1647–8 was in session, they were startled by the appearance of Mistress Margaret Brent upon the scene, who demanded both voice and vote for herself in the Assembly by virtue of her position as his lordship's attorney. Alas for Mistress Brent and her appreciation of the rights of her sex! The governor promptly and ungallantly refused her. The injured lady, as her only means of retaliation, protested against all the acts of the session as invalid, unless her vote was received as well as the votes of the male members.

By this action Margaret Brent undoubtedly placed herself on record as the first woman in America to make a stand for the rights of her sex.

Forgetfulness of her priority has induced some authorities to put forward another claimant in the person of Mary Coffin Starbuck (1645–1717), daughter of the first owner of the island of Nantucket, Tristram Coffyn (as he signed the name), and wife of Nathanael Starbuck.

She was essentially a New Woman, two centuries before that word was coined. In the language of John Richardson, an early preacher, "The islanders esteemed her as a judge among them; for little of moment was done without her." At the town meetings she was accustomed to attend she took active part in the debates, usually beginning her address with "My husband thinks so and so," or "My husband and I, having considered the subject, think so and so." From every source of information, as also from tradition, there is abundant evidence that she was possessed of sound judgment, clear understanding, and natural eloquence.

Susan B. Anthony, in her "History of Woman's Suffrage," ignores both Margaret Brent and Mary Starbuck, and names a Revolutionary dame, Mrs. Abigail Smith Adams, wife of John Adams, of Massachusetts, as the first champion of woman's rights in America. In March, 1776, Mistress Adams wrote to her husband, then at the Continental Congress in Philadelphia: "I long to hear that you have declared an independency, and in the new code of laws, which I suppose it will be necessary for you to make, I desire that you would remember the ladies and be more generous to them than were your ancestors. If particular care and attention are not paid to the ladies, we are determined to foment a rebellion, and will not hold ourselves bound to obey any laws in which we have no voice or representation."

We are not told how John Adams replied to this epistle from his fair spouse, but we do know that in the famous Declaration of Independence, where all *men* are declared equal, the women received no more consideration than did Margaret Brent nearly one hundred and fifty years before.

After peace had been proclaimed, however, the Continental Congress left the suffrage to be dealt with by the States, and New Jersey conferred it on all inhabitants worth $250, male and female alike. So the women of New Jersey actually voted upon the acceptance of the national Constitution. The law granting them the franchise was not repealed until 1807.

In Europe the original Suffragette was a Frenchwoman, Olympe de Gouges, who was beheaded during the Revolution. She was born in Montauban, May 7, 1748, and was therefore more than forty years old when the French Revolution broke out. Her putative father was a butcher, her real father was the Marquis Le Franc de Pompignan, who was a poet and often became the butt of Voltaire. She married before she was twenty an old man "who was neither rich nor well-born"—a cook, in fact, as appears from the birth certificate of her son, Pierre Aubry. She left the conjugal home and began a life of adventure. At the age of 34 she became a woman of letters, and produced several plays which had but a moderate success. In the very first of these, "The Generous Man" (1786), she showed herself a woman's rights woman. Through one of her characters she protests against the exclusion of women from "all power and knowledge." Two years later in another play, "The Reformed Philosopher," another of her characters broaches what was then the startling heresy, that "two beings independent in rank and fortune, united by marriage, should have equal rights in disposing of their future and their actions!" And an old governess in the play is made to add, "Let them put trousers on us and send us to college and see if they don't make thousands of heroes out of us!"

With the outbreak of the Revolution she grew even bolder. In her "Declaration of the Rights of Women and of Women Citizens" (1791), she declared that "Woman is born free, and

53

has equal rights with men. Social distinction can be founded
only on general utility." Another paragraph ran: " The law
ought to be the expression of the general will. All citizens, men
and women, being equal in the eyes of the law, ought to concur
personally or through their representatives in its formation. It
ought to be equal for all. All citizens, men and women, ought to
be equally admissible to all dignities, places, public employments,
according to their capacities, and without any other distinctions
than those of their virtues and their talents."

Though she favored the Revolution, she denounced its fiercer
excesses, attacking Marat and Robespierre and defending Louis
XVI. On the 20th of July, 1793, Olympe de Gouges was
arrested. She had just issued a pamphlet called " The Three
Urns," in which she proposed a plébiscite on these three solu-
tions: " republican government one and indivisible ; federal government ; monarchical government." There was a revolutionary
law which pronounced capital punishment on all who should
print a book or pamphlet provoking the reëstablishment of monarchy. Olympe had herself sealed her fate. She was kept in
prison three months and guillotined on the 3d of November.

In 1836 there came to the United States an eloquent young
enthusiast, Ernestine L. Rose, the daughter of a rabbi in Poland.
She was the first woman to take the platform and urge the
women of this country to appeal for laws which affected their
interests. In 1836–37 she circulated a petition for a law that
would enable married women to hold property, and could secure
but five signatures. However, she kept up the work, and by
1840 many of the women prominent among our earliest suffragists were associated with her, chief among them Elizabeth Cady
Stanton. For eight years more these women continued their
endeavors, and in 1848 the State of New York at last conferred
property rights upon its married women. Thereafter their efforts
were devoted to the agitation for the suffrage.

In the same year was held the first woman's rights convention, at Seneca Falls, N. Y.

In 1851 Susan B. Anthony met Elizabeth Cady Stanton.
That meeting marks the beginning of the active political campaign for the vote; that year saw the first woman's delegation
in Albany petitioning the Legislature to give them a hearing.
Every year since, except for the years of the Civil War, has seen
a delegation of women in Albany bound on the same mission.

Twice they have been very near success.

In 1886 a bill was presented before the Legislature asking
only for the municipal suffrage. It found many supporters. The
enthusiasm and excitement ran high. On the day when it was

to be voted upon, the House was thronged, the Lieutenant-Governor and many officers of the State being present. When the question was put to vote, the result stood 65 ayes to 50 noes, a constitutional majority. A burst of applause broke forth. The legislators became panic-stricken, and before the applause had died away two of them had hurriedly changed their ayes to noes. The final vote stood 63 to 52, and the day was lost to the suffragists.

A still narrower defeat was that experienced in 1895. On March 14 of that year six men presented a mammoth petition for the suffrage cause and introduced at the same time a bill conferring the right upon women. It passed the Legislature, the vote standing 81 ayes to 31 noes. Then ensued a fortnight of waiting, occasioned by the appearance of a period where a comma should have been in the draft of the bill. At last it was presented to the Senate and carried at once, 20 ayes to 5 noes. At once it was discovered that the word " resident " had been substituted for the word " citizen," and the bill was void. The entire year's work was lost to the suffragists and they have not since been able to secure a majority. The responsibility for the blunder has never been placed.

Sunday and the Sabbath. In the Book of Acts (Acts, xx, 7) and in St. Paul (1 Cor., xvi, 2) the day we now call Sunday is simply " the first day of the week." By St. John (Rev., i, 10) and other early Christian writers (Eusebius book iv, c. 18; and book iv, c. 23) it is called " the Lord's day." St. Barnabas, apparently in order to designate it as the day after the Jewish Sabbath (seventh day), calls it " the eighth day " (in his Epistle Part 15). Some of the earliest of the fathers, including Justin Martyr (*Apologeticus* 2) and Tertullian (*Apologeticus* l.:), call it *" Sunday,"* and so it was most usually called thereafter, the day seldom being otherwise designated in the imperial edicts of the first Christian emperors. " It may, indeed, with great propriety retain this name," said Bishop Hobart, " because it is dedicated to the honor of that Saviour who is by the prophet called the Sun of Righteousness." In the Emperor Constantine's order to the Roman army as to the observance of Sunday, it is called " the holy, happy day," certainly a most striking and appropriate title. Many centuries after, some of the sects specially noted for the austerity of their religious views, adopted the idea of Judaizing the Christian Lord's day—this " holy, happy day "—into a Jewish Sabbath, the rigorous observance of which became one of the prominent features of Puritan Christianity and blue-law legislation, and, naturally, in adopting the Jewish observance, they adopted with it the Jewish name and called Sunday " the Sabbath."

Never in the New Testament itself, nor in the writings of the early Fathers, is there any identification of the Jewish Sabbath with the Christian Sunday. Never is the observance of the Sabbath alluded to save as a purely Jewish ordinance. St. Paul even goes so far as to denounce it as a dangerous superstition. But it may be gathered from scattered intimations, especially with the light reflected on them from later tradition, that in apostolic days the first day of the week, or the Lord's day, had begun to be observed, in memory of the Resurrection, by the celebration of the Eucharist. It has been surmised that this was one of the "commandments" which the Saviour gave to his apostles during the forty days between the Resurrection and the Ascension (Luke xxiii, 56). But Sunday was never called the Sabbath. To do so would have led to manifest confusion, for the Sabbath, or Saturday, was from a very early period observed widely in the Church as a fast, not on Jewish grounds, but in memory of the Burial of our Lord, just as Wednesday and Friday were kept in honor of the Betrayal and the Passion.

Not only do these early writers never call Sunday the Sabbath, but they never base the obligation of keeping it on Jewish custom or on the Fourth Commandment. The fact of its being already a day "venerated" in the Church is implied in the language of the edict of the first Christian Emperor enjoining its observance, and is still more clearly implied in the twentieth Canon of Nice. The edict of Constantine, being the first of the kind, and in some sense the model of all later legislation on the subject, may be worth quoting as it stands:

Omnes judices, urbanæque plebes et cunctarum artium officia venerabili Die Solis quiescant. Ruri tamen positi agrorum culturæ libere licenterque inserviant, quoniam evenit ut sæpe illo die frumenta sulcis aut vineæ scrobibus mandentur, ne occasione momenti pereat commoditas cœlesti provisione concessa.

It appears, therefore, that the only two points in regard to the day on which Christians of all ages have been generally agreed are —first, the duty of public worship; and, secondly, the duty of resting, and enabling others to rest, from the ordinary business of life on the weekly festival of the Resurrection. In the method of carrying out these objects, and still more in all further modes of honoring the day, there have been in different times and places almost infinite differences of detail, both among Catholics and Protestants. But all testimony goes to confirm Baxter's conclusion, that "from and in the apostles' days the churches unanimously agreed in the holy use of it as a separated day."

Mediæval usage, while sternly enforcing attendance at church and abstinence from all servile work, nevertheless favored Sunday amusements. The day was treated as the weekly festival of the people, combining recreation with religious worship, which last was itself a kind of recreation and helped to add something of brightness to their dull and monotonous lives.

The public spectacles were held not to be innocent, and Christians were forbidden to witness them at any time on account of their immoral and idolatrous adjuncts. It was because the leisure of Sunday afforded exceptional facilities for this forbidden practice, which was moreover found to interfere with attendance at Divine service, that Theodosius in the year 386 was induced to put a stop to all public performances on that day. When, after the lapse of several centuries, sacred dramas began to be introduced into Christian practice, they were usually performed in churches and on Sundays or festivals.

Hallam observes that the founders of the English Reformation made no change in this respect, but that in the following century Sabbatarianism grew up—both in the use of the word Sabbath and the Judaic tone of thought it implied—as a distinctive badge of Puritanism. For it would not be correct to say that the modern Sabbatarian notion is so much distinctively Protestant as distinctively insular and Puritan.

It derives as little countenance from the fathers of "the Blessed Reformation," English or foreign, as from the fathers of the primitive Church. The Confession of Augsburg expressly condemns it; Cranmer, in accordance with his general Erastianism, calls the observance of Sunday "a mere appointment of the magistrate"; even the Puritanical Calvin used to play at bowls on Sunday at Geneva. And to this day the countrymen and coreligionists of Luther and Calvin have nothing in common in this respect with their English or Scotch followers. The "Continental Sunday" which Protestants are so fond of denouncing is really characteristic of Protestant more than of Catholic countries; so much so indeed that the measure of influence exercised by the Church may usually be gauged in a Catholic city by noting what proportion of the shops are kept open. Thus, at Munich and Lucerne they are closed, in Paris only very partially so; at Berlin and Zurich they are open. The Sabbatarian view is an invention, not of the sixteenth century but the seventeenth, when the Puritans so fiercely railed at "the impious 'Book of Sports'" issued by authority of Charles I and Laud, and contrived under Charles II to secure the passing of an act against Sabbath breaking.

An anecdote published in the *Universal Magazine* for 1775 illustrates the condition of the Sabbath question in Boston, U. S., about that time:

Some years ago, a Commander of one of his Majesty's ships of war, being stationed at this place, had orders to cruise, from time to time,

in order to protect our trade, and distress the enemy. It happened unluckily that he returned from one of his cruises on a Sunday; and, as
he had left his lady at Boston, the moment she had heard of the ship's
arrival, she hastened down to the water's side, in order to receive him.
The Captain, on landing, embraced her with tenderness and affection;
this, as there were many spectators by, gave great offence, and was
considered as an act of indecency and a flagrant profanation of the
Sabbath. The next day, therefore, he was summoned before the Magistrates, who, with many severe rebukes and pious exhortations, ordered
him to be publicly whipped. The Captain stifled his indignation and
resentment as much as possible; and, as the punishment, from the frequency of it, was not attended with any great degree of ignominy or
disgrace, he mixed with the best company, was well received by them,
and they were apparently good friends.

At length the time of the station expired, and he was recalled. He
went, therefore, with seeming concern, to take leave of his worthy
friends; and, that they might spend one happy day together before their
final separation, he invited the principal Magistrates and select men
to dine with him on board his ship upon the day of his departure.
They accepted the invitation, and nothing could be more joyous and
convivial than the entertainment which he gave them. At length the
fatal moment arrived that was to separate them: the anchor was
a-peak, the sails were unfurled, and nothing was wanting but the
signal to get under way. The Captain, after taking an affectionate
leave of his worthy friends, accompanied them upon deck, where the
boatswain and crew were in readiness to receive them. He there thanked
them afresh for the civilities they had shown him, of which, he said,
he should retain an eternal remembrance, and to which he wished it
had been in his power to have made a more adequate return. One
point of civility only remained to be adjusted between them, which, as
it was in his power, so he meant most justly to recompense to them.
He then reminded them of what had passed, and, ordering the crew
to pinion them, had them brought one by one to the gang-way, where
the Boatswain with a cat of nine tails, laid on the back of each forty
stripes save one. They were then, amidst the shouts and acclamations
of the crew, shoved into their boats; and the Captain, immediately
getting under way, sailed for England.

An object lesson recently brought home to the Boston bosom
some realization of what their ancestors had suffered from the
Sabbatarianism of the past. This lesson was enforced by the
police of that city in the year 1897. District-Attorney Moran
had kept criticising them for the non-enforcement of the law.
The police retorted by a practical argument of the sort known
to logicians as the *reductio ad absurdum*. On the ensuing
Sunday they enforced indiscriminately every blue law they
could find on the books. Everybody who was seen by an officer
doing a stroke of work was summoned before a magistrate for
decision whether the work was one of necessity. Twelve hundred
persons in all were thus brought to justice, and a great many of
them paid fines. Sweeping sidewalks, delivering ice-cream and
other perishable articles of food, shipping theatrical scenery and
effects, the playing of orchestras in hotels—these are typical
instances of the kinds of Sunday work for which the police made

arrests. In Roxbury, which is a part of Boston, some work was being done on Stony Brook. Here the boomerang was out-boomeranged. The contractors decided to apply the *reductio ad absurdum* to the police themselves, and so quit work, with the result that the brook overflowed and filled the cellars of near-by residents.

· **Sunday-School.** One Sunday morning in the year 1812, a workingman, carefully dressed in his best suit, came out of his house on the main street of the old English town of Gloucester and strolled leisurely down the hill. The "New Inn" was fronted then, as it is to-day, by a square garden over-hung by the carved galleries of the tavern. There was a moss-clad well in the centre, and about it were beds of sweet-smelling pinks and columbines.

But the calm of that Sunday morning was destroyed by a crowd of street boys, who fought over the flower beds, making the day hideous with their noise and coarse talk.

The printer—for printing was his work on week-days—stopped in the midst of the crowd and looked steadily at the boys. Presently he said to himself: "At this rate those boys will soon go utterly to the bad. That must not be! There are good possi-bilities in them. Here, boys," he called aloud, "come with me!"

He led them, yelling and pushing, down the street into his own quiet house, planning as he went how to keep them there

"I am going," he said presently, "to start a school for you. Now and here. It shall be a free school; I will be the teacher."

The boys received the news with shouts. They were too ragged and grimy to go to church on Sundays. No other decent place was open to them.

The next Sunday his house was crowded with the same class of children.

The idea of a free school on Sunday appealed to every Chris-tian as a most hopeful plan for the rescue of children from wickedness. It spread through the town, through the shire, through England. It was adopted in France and Germany; it made its way to Australia and to the United States. Now in every country in the world and in every sect there are these schools, in which, every Sunday morning, the Bible story is told, without money and without price.

In the staid old city of Gloucester they still show you the New Inn and the garden where the boys played, and the old brown house with its peaked roof in which Robert Raikes, that long-ago morning, taught the first Sunday-school.

Sunken Cities. There must be some fundamental truth in the legends so widespread in Germany, Holland, and Ireland which refer, with more or less particularity of detail, to cities submerged many fathoms deep at the bottom of great lakes or seas or oceans. Sometimes, on very clear days, their tallest buildings may be dimly descried through the waves, or faint sounds as of chiming bells may be heard floating upward from their towers or steeples.

The Lake of Killarney is said to have once been the site of a great and populous city famous in Celtic legend. Lough Neah is another Irish lake with a similar history. Who does not remember Tom Moore's poem beginning:

> On Lough Neah's banks as the fisherman strays,
>   When the clear calm eve's declining.
> He sees the Round Towers of other days
>   In the waves beneath him shining.

The Irish legends all agree in one particular, that these cities were dependent for their prosperity on a holy well situated just outside their walls. This well was never to be left open after sunset. But, alas! both the royal court and the city were so‐ given up to revelry that one evening no one remembered to close the well at sunset. Thereupon the furious waters rose, engulfing the town and drowning the inhabitants. In Holland, according to popular tradition, the ruins of several large cities survive in the basin of the Zuyder Zee. These cities were submerged by the North Sea breaking its banks and overflowing the country.

The Baltic also has its sunken city made famous by the German poet William Müller, the father of Max Müller. Here are opening stanzas of his poem, translated by James Clarence Mangan:

> Hark, the faint bells of the sunken city
>   Peal once more their wonted evening chime;
> From the deep abysses floats a ditty,
>   Wild and wondrous, of the olden time.
>
> Temples, towers, and domes of many stories
>   There lie buried in an ocean grave.
> Undescried, save when their golden glories
>   Gleam at sunset through the lighted wave.
>
> And the mariner who had seen them glisten,
>   In whose ears those magic bells do sound,
> Night by night bides there to watch and listen
>   Though death lurks behind each dark rock round.

Holstein also has its legendary city of Vineta, buried in the sea just off its coasts. Fishermen say that on clear days when the sea is smooth they can look down into the waters and see the peaked roofs of a city of the middle ages, and that the tolling of the bells in the church spires comes faintly up to them as they are moved by the submarine currents.

Washington Irving, in "Wolfert's Roost and Other Papers," gives an account of a convent near Toledo, which at the time

of the Moorish conquest was miraculously engulfed by the earth
to protect it and its band of nuns from sacrilege. The bells,
organ, and choir could be occasionally heard during forty years,
at which time the last of the sisters must have died, for no sound
was heard afterward. The spire of the convent projecting out of
the ground is still shown. See Ys.

Swallow. "Garrula hirundo," writes Virgil, and there are
occasions when the lack-plumed swift deserves the epithet, but
the swallow itself only murmurs or inwardly pipes a small fluttering note as he swoops and gyrates through the air. He is often
seen in the open, but his truest affections are enkindled by things
of human kind, the cottage and the barn roof, the common where
children congregate, the telegraph wires near inhabited homes.

The curious belief which Gilbert White seemed to share, that
many of the swallows hibernate, has now been as completely exploded as that the barnacle goose is a development of the
barnacle shell-fish. And we may rejoice at the destruction of the
legend. It is not at all so pleasant or so fanciful to think that
the swallow sneaks into a hole or a cornice, like the ugly bat or
the unsocial bear. There is no suggestion of torpidity about the
swallow. The few loiterers that are caught in the snow suffer
for it in a sleep that knows no waking. But where do the swallows
go when they leave us? This question has never been exhaus-
tively answered. In some charming verses by Theophile
Gautier in the *Moniteur,* and which were afterward cleverly
decanted into English by Father Prout, we have a pretty picture
of what the poet calls a "synagogue" of the birds, assembled
for the purpose of exchanging views as to the several places they
respectively intended to visit.

> Elles, s'assemblant par centaines,
>   Se concertent pour le départ.
> L'une dit, Oh que dans Athènes
>   Il fait bon sur le vieux rempart.
>
> Tous les ans j'y vais et je niche
>   Aux métopes du Parthenon;
> Mon nid bouche dans la corniche,
>   Le trou d'un boulet de canon.

Another swallow tells his friends that he has a snug retreat over
a coffee-shop at Smyrna; a third is a sort of hermit, who affects
a residence among the ruins of Palmyra and Baalbec; while a
fourth is resolved to make for the third cataract of the Nile,
where there is a convenient crevice for him in the neck of an
ancient statue. The swallows are, we believe, actually to be
seen in these quarters, and the flight has been frequently met with
on its passage across the sea. The birds are said usually to
fly low on the journey, but they would be altogether influenced

as to this by the wind. They invariably make for the narrowest straits from point to point, but yet they must be sometimes so long upon the wing that, taking into account that there can be little, if any, insect food over the salt ocean, they must suffer from hunger and thirst; for the swallow is a thirsty soul and is a most valiant trencherman at minute flies. However, the journey is accomplished somehow, and we are swallowless until the new year is born and advanced.

Swifts have a bad name in Ireland. Their flesh is held to be poisonous, for they have each a drop of the devil's blood in their veins, and it is thought ill for the dead when a swift shoots over the hearse. Oddly enough, this superstition does not apply to the smaller swallows. In England we have not heard that any such notions obtain. The swallow ought, indeed, to be a favorite with every one. He never touches our fruit, no matter how ripe and luscious the peaches and the cherries look; and what more welcome guest to our shores than that daring pioneer of the proverb?

Swimming Bath. The earliest mention of a swimming bath so far discovered in English literature by the patient correspondents of *Notes and Queries* (see Tenth series, x, p. 89) is that contained in the following advertisement in the London *Daily Advertiser*, May 28, 1742:

This Day is opened, At the Bagnio in Lemon Street, Goodman's Fields:

The Pleasure or Swimming Bath which is more than forty-three Feet in length, it will be kept warm and fresh every Day and is convenient to swim or learn to swim in. There are Waiters attend daily to teach or assist Gentlemen in the said Swimming Bath if required. There is also a good Cold Bath.

Subscribers may have the use of both for a Guinea.

Maitland's "History of London" says that "the completest swimming bath in the whole world" is the Peerless Pool, which was opened to the public by William Kemp, an eminent citizen, in 1743. "Peerless Pool" seems to have been the original name of a spring in this neighborhood, which overflowed its banks and formed a pond so dangerous to life that the word became corrupted to "Perilous." Kemp, however, restored the original name when, at the above-mentioned date, he built new receptacles for the spring's waters. The cold bath was 40 feet long and 20 feet broad; "this was quite private and retired from private inspection." The pleasure bath in the open air was 170 feet long by 108 feet broad. It was surrounded by trees, with an arcade and boxes for dressing. Subscription for the use of either £1 10s. per annum; a single bath at either was 1s.

T.

Tabard Inn. Strangers visiting a large city, like London, during the Middle Ages, especially if they arrived there after nightfall, usually took up their lodgings outside the gates. Hence some of the principal inns for the accommodation of travellers were built along the line of approach. On both sides of the High Street of Southwark stood many of these ancient hostelries.

Stowe, the early historian of London, tells us that there stood in this locality "many fair inns for receipt of travellers," among which "the most ancient is the Tabard, so called of the sign, which as we now term it is of a jacket or sleeveless coat, whole before, open on both sides, with a square collar, winged at the shoulders: a stately garment of old time, commonly worn of noblemen and others, both at home and abroad in the wars; but then (to wit, in the wars) their arms embroidered, or otherwise depict, upon them, that every man by his coat of arms might be known from others. But now these tabards are only worn by the heralds, and be called their coats of arms in service."

The Tabard Inn still stands in Southwark, though it has changed its name to the Talbot, and retains little of its original architecture and none of its pristine importance. Its identity is unmistakable. The land on which it stood was purchased by the abbot of Hyde, in 1307, and he built upon it a hostel, or town house, for the abbots when they came to London. It may be supposed that the inn for the accommodation of the public was built by the abbots, and that they received their profits from it.

Probably it was built with a view to furnishing accommodation for the pilgrims flocking from all parts of the kingdom to the famous shrine of St. Thomas of Canterbury, for it stands just between the Pilgrim's Way from the west and south of England, and the much better known continuation of the Pilgrim's Way onward to Canterbury, so that it would be exactly the spot where they would be glad to find a halting-place. It is by no means unlikely that the abbot of Hyde built the inn for this purpose very soon after he became possessed of the ground, if there was not one already in existence, but there can be no doubt that when Chaucer lived,—that is, in the latter years of the fourteenth century,—the Tabard was the usual resort of the pilgrims, or at least that it was the most-frequented hostelry in Southwark, or he would not have introduced it in that character.

Yet any one must possess very little knowledge of the literature of the Middle Ages to suppose that Chaucer's meeting of the pilgrims at the Tabard was intended for the description of a real event, that all the arrangement about the telling of tales was really made, and that each pilgrim told the story here ascribed to him. Any one who, further, knows a little of society in the Middle Ages, should be aware that twenty-nine individuals, each of so totally different a character, and belonging to classes so widely separated from each other, could hardly have met together on this footing of social equality. It was a simple invention of the poet for the sake of the stories he intended to introduce.

Yet we cannot doubt that in Chaucer's time the Tabard was the principal hotel in Southwark, and that it was a usual resort of the pilgrims on their way to the shrine of St. Thomas at Canterbury. As we have seen, Stowe, who wrote in 1598, mentions the Tabard in Southwark as then still standing; and four years later, Speght, who published his edition of Chaucer in 1602, informs us that, "Whereas through time it hath been much decayed, it is now by Master J. Preston, with the abbot's house thereto adjoined, newly repaired, and with convenient rooms much increased for the receipt of many guests." What were the character and extent of Preston's repairs we have no means of knowing; but perhaps they did not materially change the general appearance of the old edifice. He seems to have added the private house of the abbot to the public buildings of the hostelry.

A little more than half a century after this date, the Tabard was exposed to destruction from another cause, and one which must have been much more disastrous, though we have still no means of ascertaining to what extent it suffered. In 1676 Southwark was the scene of a terrible conflagration, second only in its greatness to the well-known fire of London ten years before. About six hundred houses were burnt, or blown up for the purpose of arresting the progress of the fire, and the Tabard must have been almost in the centre of the danger. When it was rebuilt, the old associations of this inn seem to have been so far forgotten, that even the name on the sign was changed, and, in the appropriate language of the well-known antiquary, John Aubrey, " the ignorant landlord, or tenant, instead of the ancient sign of the Tabard, put up the Talbot, or dog." Aubrey tells us further, that before the fire it was an old timber house, " probably coeval with Chaucer's time." It was probably this old part, facing the street, which was burnt.

Table from Human Remains. Somewhere about the year 1893 a paragraph concerning a table of this sort was set afloat and was copied all over Europe and America. It is curious enough to copy at length.

In the Pitti Palace at Florence is a table which, for originality in the matter of construction and ghastliness in conception, is probably without a rival. It was made by Giuseppe Segatti, who passed several years of his life in its manufacture. To the casual observer it gives the impression of a curious mosaic of marbles of different shades and colors, for it looks like polished stone. In reality it is composed of human muscles and viscera. No less than a hundred bodies were requisitioned for the material. The table is round and about a yard in diameter, with a pedestal and four claw feet, the whole being formed of petrified human remains. The ornaments of the pedestal are made from the intestines, the claws with hearts, livers, and lungs, the natural color of which is preserved. The table top is constructed of muscles artistically arranged, and it is bordered with upward of a hundred eyes, the effect of which is said to be highly artistic, since they retain all their lustre, and seem to follow the observer. Segatti died about fifty years ago. He obtained his bodies from the hospitals, and indurated them by impregnation with mineral salts.

Now, this story is not all true yet it is not all a lie. In the first place the "table" is not in the Pitti Palace, but in the anatomical collection of the Hospital of Santa Maria. It is oval, not round, measures about 18 x 12 inches, and consists of a top only. It has no appearance of ever having had a pedestal. The human petrifications are veneered in a symmetrical rectangular, oblong design, with a border around it. These veneers are small bits, about one-sixtieth of an inch thick, of human organs, such as loins, kidneys, liver, spleen and skin, all of natural color. Some are diamond shaped, some oval, some square, with surfaces like fine-grained wood. We are told that in the year 1850, Giuseppe Segato (not Segatti), a Florentine physician, announced his discovery of a method of petrifying the human body so as to preserve it intact in form and color. He submitted specimens of his work to the Grand Duke of Tuscany, who offered to buy the secret. While the negotiations were in progress, Segato died and his secret with him.

Tailor. What mathematician was it who first figured out that nine tailors make a man, when did he do so, and what were the factors upon which he based his computation? There is no lack of answers to this historical problem. None, alas, has any basis of historical fact. But many of them possess their own share of curious interest.

A very familiar explanation, which is presented in multiplied form, is based upon the phrase "to make a man of him," in the sense of rehabilitating a man by some substantial service. Thus, it is said that, in 1742, an orphan boy applied for alms at a fashionable tailor's shop in London. Nine of the journeymen tailors clubbed together, each contributing a shilling, and with this capital, the boy started a fruit-stand. In time he became rich, and when he set up his carriage he painted on the panel " Nine tailors made me a man." This story errs in being dated. As far back as 1682 another variation had appeared in a curious book, called " Democritus in London, with the Mad Pranks and Comical Conceits of Motley and Robin Goodfellow " (and it will be seen that even at that time the saw was confessedly an old one).

> There is a proverb which has been of old,
> And many men have likewise been so told,
> To the discredit of the taylor's trade:
> *Nine taylors goe to make up a man*, they said;
> But for their credit I'll unriddle it t' ye:
> A draper once fell into povertie,
> Nine taylor's joyn'd their purses together then,
> To set him up, and make him a man agen.

The same determination to twist the adage into a complimentary sense reappears in Rhenish Prussia. One bitter winter day, so it is said, nine tailors were working in a warm and comfortable room, when a hungry, half-clad tramp knocked at the door and applied for alms. The kindly tailors not only shared their meal with him, but sent him away rejoicing with a few groschen in his pockets, and he exclaimed, gratefully, " You have made a man of me!"

All this class of explanations must be rejected, because they seem to have been made after the event by some person, possibly a tailor himself, who wished to glorify the trade. Now, it is a fact that the tailor has ever been a butt for the foolish raillery of the mob, and we shall see that in folk-lore and popular literature his nobler qualities have never received their due meed of recognition. What, then, shall we say to the following account, which appeared in the *British Apollo* in 1708? " It happened ('tis no great matter in what year) that eight tailors, having finished considerable pieces of work at the house of a certain person of quality (whose names authors have thought fit to conceal), and received all the money due for the same, a virago servant-maid of the house, observing them to be but slender-built animals, and in their mathematical postures on their shop-board appearing but so many pieces of men, resolved to encounter and pillage them on the road. The better to compass her design, she procured a very terrible great, black pudding, which, having waylaid them, she presented at the breast of the foremost. They, mistaking this prop of life for an instrument of death, at least a blunderbuss, readily yielded up their money; but she, not contented with that, severely disciplined them with a cudgel she carried in the other hand, all of which they bore with a philosophical resignation. Thus, eight, not being able to deal with one woman, by consequence could not make a man, on which account a ninth is added." What shall we say to this story, quotha? Merely that it is so evidently the work of a professional humorist that it may be dismissed without even the tribute of a smile.

There is only one explanation that bears any plausibility on its face, and this is not to the discredit of the trade. A toll of a bell is called a "teller," in rural England, from the verb "to tell" or "count" (Richard III, it will be remembered, says "tell the clock there," *i.e.,* "count the hours.") Now, in some places, after the funeral knells a certain number of distinct bell-strokes are made, to denote whether the deceased was man, woman, or child, the number usually being nine for a man, six for a woman, and three for a child. "Nine tellers mark a man" became readily perverted into "Nine tailors make a man."

The theory is plausible, as already acknowledged. But how account for the fact that the proverb is not indigenous to England, but is found in various forms among other European nations? We have seen that it is a familiar phrase in Prussia. In Brittany, we are informed by Count de la Villamarque, the peasants have a saying, "Qu'il faut neuf tailleurs pour faire un homme," precisely our formula again. In Hanover, however, it requires twelve tailors to make a man; and in other parts of Germany the number is increased to thirteen. In Silesia twelve button-makers (Knopfmacher) are said to constitute a man.

Still the jest remains, a perpetual libel upon an honorable and useful avocation, and the modes of applying it by wits, retailers of wit, and inventors of jokes seem well-nigh endless. "Where are the other eight?" asked a duelist, who had accepted a challenge from a tailor. In the days of the London train-bands, a tailor rated to supply half a man to the band, asked how this could be done. "By sending four journeymen and an apprentice," was the answer.

"An idea has gone abroad," says Carlyle in "Sartor Resartus," "and fixed itself down into a wide-spreading, rooted error, that tailors are a distinct species in physiology, not men, but fractional parts of a man. . . Doth it not stand on record, that the English Queen Elizabeth, receiving a deputation of eighteen tailors, addressed them with a 'Good morning, gentlemen both!' Did not the same virago boast that she had a cavalry regiment whereof neither horse nor man could be injured,—her regiment, namely, of tailors on mares?" The story of the cavalry regiment, by the way, was thus told in the Chester *Courant* a great many years ago, and it was in this form, and not in any authentic history, that Carlyle probably met with it. "In the reign of Queen Elizabeth, the tailors petitioned Her

Majesty that a regiment might be raised composed entirely of their craft, to go abroad into Flanders. The queen assented. She ordered that (as there never was known to be a regiment of tailors before) they should all be mounted on mares. In a short time the regiment was completed, equipped and drilled, reviewed by Elizabeth, and sent off to fight the queen's wars in Flanders. They rushed to the front in battle, fought valiantly, and were every one killed. Her Majesty was greatly affected when she heard this news, but thanked God that she had neither lost man nor horse."

Carlyle, however, indignantly refutes the slander, asserting that the tailor is "not only a Man, but something of a Creator or Divinity, inasmuch as Man is by him new-created into a Nobleman, and clothed not only with Wool but with Dignity and a Mystic Dominion—is not the fair fabric of Society itself. with all its royal mantles and pontifical states, whereby from nakedness and dismemberment, we are, organized into Polities. into nations, and a whole coöperating Mankind, the creation of the Tailor alone?"

Swift had anticipated the philosophy of "Sartor Resartus." in "The Tale of a Tub," where he speaks of a certain sect (*i.e.*. dandies and people of fashion) "that worshipped a sort of idol. who, as their doctrine delivered, did daily create men by a kind of manufactory operation. This idol they placed in the highest parts of the house on an altar erected about three feet. He was shown in the posture of a Persian emperor, sitting on a superficies, with his legs interwoven under him. This god had a goose for his ensign; whence it is that some learned men pretend to deduce his original from Jupiter Capitolinus. At his left hand, beneath the altar, hell seemed to open, and catch at the animals the idol was creating; to prevent which, certain of his priests hourly flung in pieces of the uninformed mass, or substance, and sometimes whole limbs already enlivened. which that horrid gulf insatiably swallowed. terrible to behold." Massinger, long before Swift's day, had said:

> Yes, if they would thank their Maker
> And seek no further; but they have new creators,
> God-tailor and God-mercer.

Nevertheless, in literature and folk-lore the tailor has somehow been an unpopular character. In Germany the epithet schneidermassig (tailor-like) indicates pusillanimity. It is true the Germans have a fairy tale, "The Brave Little Tailor." but it is only a pleasant little mock-heroic, the bravery of the tailor is mere trickery and bravado. We have seen that the *British Apollo* reiterated the charge of cowardice, and it made the following explanation: " 'tis the opinion of our curious virtuosos that their want of courage arises from their immoderate eating of cucumbers, which too much refrigerates their blood." So the French were reputed by the English to be their inferiors in courage because they were fond of salad. Carlyle mentions a tailor's-melancholy which, he says, " we introduce into our books of medicine, and fable I know not what of his generating it by living on cabbage." He evidently refers to Lamb's essay on the " Melancholy of Tailors." Lamb ascribes this melancholy, first, to the tailor's sedentary habits; and, second, to his diet. In Burton's " Anatomy of Melancholy," he finds that cabbage is, of all " herbs to be eaten," the one that is especially disallowed as sending up black vapors to the brain. " I could not," says Lamb, " omit so flattering a testimony from an author who, having no theory of his own to serve, has so unconsciously contributed to the confirmation of mine. It is well known this last-named vegetable has, from the earliest periods we can discover, constituted almost the sole food of this extraordinary race of people."

Now, what does Lamb mean by this statement? It is simply a punning allusion to alleged sartorial dishonesty. In former time the tailor went to the houses of his customers and made garments out of the cloth they had purchased, the waste and cuttings being his recognized perquisites. Or he worked in his own shop, still upon materials furnished him at the same terms. But he was constantly accused of appropriating other portions of the cloth, an offence which came to be known as " cabbaging " (possibly from the French *cabasser,*—to put in a *cabas,—i.e.,* to bag, to steal). Readers of " Don Quixote " will remember, among other instances of shrewdness shown by Sancho during his governorship of Barrataria, how a tailor was brought before him by a customer, who swore he had given the tailor cloth enough for six good-sized caps, and how the rascal had sent him caps that hardly fitted the tips of his fingers, how the tailor swore that he had used up all the material vouchsafed him, and how Sancho finally decreed that the customer should keep the caps, and the tailor have nothing for his labor. So prevalent was the impression of the value of the tailor's " cabbage," that Massinger says:

> Were one of ye, knights of the needle,
> Paid by the ninth part of his customers,
> Once in nine years, the ninth of his bill,
> He would be nine times overpaid.

A wicked English proverb is " put a tailor, a weaver, and a miller into a sack, and the first that put his head out is a thief."

There is a good old story, which is probably of Oriental

origin, as it may be found in Cardonne's " Mélanges de Littéra-
ture Orientale," extracted from Arabic, Persian, and Turkish
sources. This story reappears in various forms in a number of jest
books, from " Joe Miller " to " Le Sottisier de Nasred-Din,
Buffon de Tamerlan " (Brussels, 1878). Sir John Harrington
has thus versified it in his " Epigrams " (1615) :

Of a Precise Tailor.

A tailor, known a man of upright dealing,
(True, but for lying, honest, but for stealing),
Did fall one day extremely sick by chance
And on the sudden was in wondrous trance.
The fiends of hell, mustering in fearful manner,
Of sundry colored stuffs displayed a banner,
Which he had stolen, and wished, as they did tell,
That he might find it all one day in hell.
The man, affrighted at this apparition,
Upon recovery grew a great precisian.
He bought a Bible of the best translation,
And in his life he showed great reformation:
He walked mannerly, he talked meekly,
He heard three lectures and two sermons weekly.
He vowed to keep no company unruly,
And in his speech to use no oath but truly;
And zealously to keep the Sabbath's rest,
His meat for that day on the eve was drest.
And lest the custom which he had—to steal—
Should cause him sometimes to forget his zeal,
He gave his journeyman a special charge,
That if the stuff, allowance being large,
He found his fingers were to filch inclined,
Bid him to have the banner in his mind.
This done (I scant can tell the rest for laughter)
A captain of a ship came three days after,
And brought three yards of velvet and three quarters
To make venetians below down the garters.
He, that precisely knew what was enough,
Soon slipped aside three quarters of the stuff:
His men, espying it, said in derision
" Master, remember how you saw the vision! "
" Peace, knave! " quoth he. " I did not see one rag
Of such a colored stuff in all the flag! "

It is noteworthy that the tailor's repository for remnants
of cloth is called Hell to this day by journeymen tailors both in
England and Germany,—not impossibly in memory of the
multicolored banner seen in the infernal regions by the Precise
Tailor. A curious sixteenth century tract entitled " The Will
of the Deuyll and Last Testament " contains the following:

"Item. I give to every Tayler a Banner wherein shall be
conteyned all the parcelles of cloth and sylkes, etc., as he has
cast them into hell."

Tailors of Tooley Street, Three. In a general way the story runs that three tailors in Tooley Street, near London Bridge, at some period of political excitement, issued a manifesto beginning " We, the people of England." As to details there is considerable confusion and contradiction. It is generally supposed, however, that the tailors were mythical creations of George Canning (some say Daniel O'Connell) during the agitation for the removal of Catholic disabilities. A Mr. Robert Hogg, in *Notes and Queries* (Seventh Series, v, 55), claimed to possess fuller information. He identified the three men as John Grose, tailor, of Tooley Street; Thomas Satterley, tailor, Neston Street, and George Sandham, grocer, Bermondsey Street, whom he described as local dictators and notorious busybodies. " At the time when the Catholic Emancipation movement was at its height, the Tooley Street politicians were agitated to the highest pitch, and, having a firm belief in their own powers and the righteousness of their cause, they resolved at one of their meetings to petition the Houses of Parliament on the subject, and actually prepared a petition which commenced with the words ' We, the people of England.' " Writing, as he does, in January, 1888, Mr. Hogg says that these facts were related to him " more than thirty years ago " by an old and much-respected inhabitant of Tooley Street, since deceased, who had bound him not to give publicity to the story until all the participants in the affair had passed away. Two weeks later another correspondent, St. Olave's, sought to discredit the story. " I think," he says, " that your readers will fail to see how three people living in three different streets and one being of a different trade could possibly be identified with what has always been regarded as a legend of some antiquity. I was personally acquainted with two of the persons named, who were in no sense ' local dictators ' and still less busybodies. They died honored and respected.

Tainted Money. A phrase famous in 1905 when Mr. John D. Rockefeller's proffered gifts for charitable purposes were refused by certain churches. The refusal had an early prototype, as this document indicates:

At a meeting of the Common Council, held in the city of New York, at the City Hall, on Friday, the 14th of October, 1785, present James Duane, mayor, Richard Varick, recorder, etc., etc., " Whereas, it has been represented to this board in behalf of Mr. Lawrence Embree, one of the commissioners of the alms-house, that the company of comedians in this city, some time since, presented him with forty pounds for the use of the poor; that, as he disapproved of a donation so circumstanced, he thought it his duty to suffer it to be deposited with him until the sense of the magistrates concerning the same could be obtained." Whereupon the board came to the following resolutions:

That it appears that the play-house was opened by said comedians without license or permission of the civil authority; which in the opinion of this board is a thing unprecedented and offensive. That while so great part of this city still lies in ruins, and many of the citizens continue to be pressed with the distresses brought on them in consequence of the late war, there is a loud call for industry and economy; and it would in a particular manner be unjustifiable in this corporation to countenance enticing and expensive amusements; that among these a play-house, however regulated, must be numbered, when under no restraint it may prove a fruitful source of dissipation, immorality, and vice. That the acceptance of the said donation by the order of this board might authorize a conclusion that they approved of the opening of said theatre, and that therefore it be and it is hereby recommended to Mr. Embree to return the same to the person from whom he received it.

William Dunlap, from whose "History of the American Theatre" (published in 1832) this extract is taken, adds (pp. 58, 59) that "a few days after, a writer in *Oswald's Journal* ironically praises the wisdom of the city magistrates for discountenancing the theatre, and preferring the licensing tippling-shops, they being harmless and yielding a revenue unpolluted by its source."

Talking Rock, a post-office in Pickins County, Georgia. The origin of the name is thus given by the Boston *Post:*

"Some one discovered in the vicinity a large stone upon which had been painted the words 'Turn me over.' It required considerable strength to accomplish this, and when it was done, the command, 'Now turn me back, and let me fool somebody else,' was found painted on the under side of the stone."

Tarantula. At one time it was firmly held throughout Italy—the belief still surviving locally among the peasantry— that the bite of this insect produces a disease called tarantismus, which resembles hydrophobia in some of its symptoms as well as in its semi-mythical character, and is classed by modern medical authorities with that nervous affection known as St. Vitus's dance.

The earliest mention of tarantismus is found in the works of Nicolas Perotti, who died in 1480. It appeared first in Apulia, and at the time of this author had begun to spread beyond that province. The part bitten, according to the common belief, swelled up and smarted, the victim grew irritable, morbid, hysterical, easily excited to frenzy or depressed to melancholy, and the disease frequently culminated in fatal paroxysms of sobs or laughter.

The poison of the tarantula, it was believed, could only be worked off by those in whom it begot a violent energy of dancing. Then it passed out with the perspiration. But if any trace still lingered in the blood, the disorder became chronic or intermittent; and the afflicted would be liable ever after to suffering and melancholy, which, whenever it reached a certain height, could I e relieved only by dancing. The tarantati, or persons bitten by the tarantula, had various whims, among them violent preferences for and antipathies to colors. Most of them were wildly in love with red, many were excited by green. They could only dance to music, and to the music of certain tunes which were called tarantellas, and one man's tarantella would not always suit another. Some needed a quick tune, others a melancholy measure, others a suggestion of green fields in the music as well as in the words that always went with it. Nearly all tarantati had mad longings for the sea, and would grow ecstatic at the sight of water in a pan. Some even would dance with a cup of water in their hands, or plunge their heads after dancing in a tub of water, set for them, and trimmed with rushes.

In course of time it grew into quite a profession for so-called tarantism curers to travel around the country during summer in quest of the tarantati. A pipe, a tambourine, and a knowledge of the favorite dance-tunes constituted their stock in trade. On arriving at a town or village, a fête was instituted, which was known as the women's little carnival (carnavaletta). Everybody hastened to the spot. The mere sight of the dancing frequently excited spectators who had never before been suspected of the disease to join in with the tarantati. Thus, the epidemic went on increasing, until few persons could claim to be entirely exempt, and Italy seemed in danger of becoming a nation of frenzied dancers. Even beyond the confines of Italy the mania spread. Stolid Germans themselves fell victims to it. Even the sceptic could not shake off the influence of general credulity. Gianbatista Quinzato, Bishop of Foligno, suffered himself, in bravado, to be bitten by a tarantula; but, to the shame of his episcopal gravity, he could obtain a cure only by dancing. Then suddenly, at about the end of the seventeenth century, the disease or delusion ceased. To-day it survives only as a local superstition or in the picturesque dance generally known as the Tarantula.

Curiously enough, a like superstition prevails in Persia,—in Buzabalt, near Kushan. There a spider called stellis affects its victims much in the same way as the tarantula was said to do, and they seek relief in a dance that is very similar to the Italian one.

Of course, ordinary medical treatment failed to touch the disease; and this of itself would tend to exaggerate its power and frequency. Nothing brought relief but lively dance-music, and of this the old tunes "La Pastorale" and "La Tarantola" were the most efficacious; the former for phlegmatic, the latter for excitable temperaments. When these tunes were played with correctness and taste, the effect was magical. The tarantati danced energetically until they fell down exhausted. Old and young, male and female, healthy and infirm, began dancing like machines worked by steam. Old writers would have us believe that even old cripples threw away their crutches and danced with the best. Hysterical females were the principal victims. Other ailments were forgotten, propriety of time and place ignored, and, soul and body, they delivered themselves up to this dancing frenzy. They shrieked, they wept, they laughed, they sang, all the time dancing like bacchantes or furies, till at last they fell down bathed in perspiration and utterly helpless. If the music continued, they at length arose and danced again, until once more they fell prostrate. These fits seem to have continued two or three days, sometimes four, or even six, for the relief seems to have been in direct ratio to the amount lost by perspiration. When the tarantant had by this means recovered, he or she remained free from the disease until the approach of the warm weather of the next year, and then was again relieved in the same manner. Once a tarantant, however, always a tarantant; one woman is mentioned as being subject to these attacks for thirty summers.

Tarantula-killer, the familiar name for a species of large wasp whose female is the most effective foe of the tarantula spider. It has a bright-blue body nearly two inches long and wings of a golden hue. As it flies here and there in the sunlight, glittering like a flash of fire, one moment resting on a leaf, the next on a granite bowlder, it keeps up an incessant buzzing caused by the vibration of its wings. At sight of a tarantula, it hastens to the attack. At first it cautiously flies in circles over its intended victim. Gradually it approaches nearer and nearer. When it has come within a few inches, the tarantula rises on its hind-legs and attempts to grapple with its foe. This manœuvre is rarely or never successful. Quick as a flash the giant wasp is on the spider's back. The deadly fangs have been avoided. In another instant a fearful sting penetrates deep into the spider's body. Its struggles almost cease. A sudden paralysis ensues; it staggers like a drunken man from side to side. A few seconds more and it is dead. The wasp darts down and drags the body to a hole in the ground and buries it there, having first deposited in its back an egg, which in course of time changes into a grub that nourishes itself upon the carcass wherein it was born, and eventually develops into another tarantula-killer. The amount of slaughter thus inflicted is almost incalculable, but some idea may be realized from the fact that, though the maternal wasp deposits a single egg in each spider, it has a large number of eggs to get rid of in the same fashion. The tarantula-killer never molests a human being unless it is teased, and then its sting is painful though not deadly.

Tar-water. Wood-tar is recognized to-day by the medical profession as having valuable antiseptic qualities, chiefly due to the creosote it contains. In the middle of the eighteenth century, the good George Berkeley, Bishop of Cloyne, thought he had discovered in tar-water a panacea fitted to remove, or at least to mitigate, all diseases of the human frame, and to carry fresh supplies of the very essence of life into the whole animal creation. During his sojourn in Rhode Island, America, he had observed that the native Indians made much use of tar in their not always simple medical practice. He conceived for himself the very highest estimate of the value and efficacy of that product in the treatment of disease. The prevalence of the bloody-flux, or dysentery, in his neighborhood in 1739, while it engaged him in all humane labors for its poor victims, moved him to draw with an heroic confidence on the pharmacy of his former neighbors, the Narragansett Indians. "The virtues of tar-water" might represent the epitaph of Bishop Berkeley. His recipe for the sovereign cure of dysentery was a heaped spoonful of powdered rosin, mixed in a little thin broth, for which he afterwards substituted oil. He advised also that a bunch of tow, soaked in brandy, be introduced into the sphincter. His children compulsorily, and his friends advisedly, were put under this treatment. Testimonials, certificates, and earnest and grateful witnesses to the ease and efficacy of the treatment overwhelmed the public attention. A credit was secured for the nostrum unsurpassed by any other panacea or empiric method of which we read in the past. The introduction of inoculation, the discovery and use of anæsthetics, did not raise an equal excitement. Berkeley published, 1744, a most curious work, indeed a wonderful miscellany, which appeared in a second edition in a few weeks, under the title of "Siris (from the Greek σειρις, a little chain); a Chain of Philosophical Reflections and Enquiries concerning the Virtues of Tar Water and divers other subjects connected together, and arising from one another." These other subjects, and the method of their connection with each other and with tar, were, for the most part, pure fancies or crotchets of the author himself. He had convinced himself, and he sought to extend and impress the conviction on the world, that tar contains a large proportion of the vital element of the universe. His friend Prior, under his prompting, published in 1746 his "Authentic Narrative of the success of Tar Water." An intensely passionate controversy was waged upon the subject. The usual pamphlet warfare followed, with contributions to the ephemeral literature of the time in prose and verse, squibs, doggerel, and caricature. The outraged members of the medical profession, whose special ire is engaged—not always without reason—against the nostrums upheld by individuals of the clerical brotherhood, were almost wild in protest, invective, and ridicule. Nevertheless, the nostrum had its day—an all but triumphant day it was. Berkeley's treatise was translated into French, German, Dutch, and Portuguese. Establishments rose all over Europe and in America for the treatment of all human ailments by the wonderful specific.

"It is impossible," writes Dr. Duncombe to Archbishop Herring in June, 1744, "to write a letter now without tincturing the ink with tar-water. This is the common topic of conversation, both among the rich and poor, high and low; and the bishop of Cloyne has made it as fashionable as going to Vauxhall or Ranelagh."

A tar-water warehouse and a dispensary of that single remedy were opened in London, the latter being located behind the Thatched House Tavern, in St. James Street.

But opposition developed. "Siris" became the occasion of numerous controversial tracts, various medical authorities venting their anger upon the rash ecclesiast who dared thus intrude upon their province; and after the bishop's death, which occurred in 1753, the tar-water excitement gradually subsided.

Tattooing. Where this custom originated it is impossible to say. It is found as far back as in the tombs near Thebes, where there are painted representations of a race of white men whose bodies are tattooed, and, in Cæsar's "Commentaries," we are told that the Britons were tattooed.

In Bosman's "Descriptions of the Coast of Guinea," published in Dutch and translated into English in the beginning of the eighteenth century, he thus describes the tattooing of the West Africans:

"They make small incisions all over the bodies of the infants, in a sort of regular manner, expressing some figure thereby; but the females are more adorned with these ornaments than the males, and each at pleasure of their parents. You may easily guess that this mangling of the bodies of those tender creatures must be very painful; but as it is the fashion here, and is thought very ornamental, it is practised by everybody."

The tattooing instrument appears to be a sort of cross between a small hoe and a saw, or a hoe jagged at its sharp edge with saw-teeth. The blade is often made of a bone or shell, scraped very thin, varying from a quarter of an inch to an inch and a half in width, and having from three to twenty teeth cut in it. A black paint or stain is made, derived from the soot or charcoal of a particular kind of wood, liquefied with water or oil. The teeth of the tattooing instrument, when dipped into this paint, are placed upon the skin; and a handle to which it is attached receives smart rapid blows from a stick or thin wooden mallet suitable for the purpose. The teeth pierce the skin and carry with them the black paint, which leaves a permanent stain.

Captain Cook thus describes the same operation among the Otaheitans:

"They stain their bodies by indenting or pricking the flesh with a small instrument made of bone, cut into short teeth; which indentings they fill up with a dark-blue or blackish mixture, prepared from the smoke of an oily nut (burned by them instead of candles) and water. This operation, which is called by the natives *tattaowing,* is exceedingly painful, and leaves an indelible mark on the skin. It is usually performed when they are about ten or twelve years of age, and on different parts of the body."

The excruciating pain of this operation is the tribute which these nations pay to personal adornment.

In the South Sea islands many of the women were tattooed in the form of a Z on every joint of their fingers and toes, and frequently on the outside of the feet. Other devices were squares, crescents, circles, men, dogs, birds, etc. Some of the old men had the greater part of their bodies covered with large patches of black, deeply indented at the edges, like a rude imitation of a flame. Some of the tattooing was checker-wise, straight lines crossing at right angles. In a few singular instances the women had only the tip of the tongue tattooed.

In the Caroline Isles, tattooing was regarded as a religious ceremony, to be performed under favorable auspices. The officiating priest invoked a blessing from the gods on the family of the patient. If a gentle breeze arose, it was accepted as the approving voice of the gods, and the operation proceeded; if not, it was suspended; for any tattooing under the anger of the gods would have led to the submerging of the islands by a raging storm.

A Mr. Earle, who lived for nine years in New Zealand, says:

"The art of tattooing has been brought to such perfection here, that whenever we have seen a New Zealander with skin thus ornamented, we have admired him. It is looked upon as answering the same purpose as clothes. When a chief throws off his mats, he seems as proud of displaying the beautiful ornaments figured on his skin as a first-rate exquisite is in exhibiting himself in his last fashionable attire. It is an essential part of warlike preparation. Aranghie, a near neighbor of mine, was considered by his countrymen a perfect master of the art of tattooing; and men of the highest rank and importance were in the habit of travelling long journeys in order to put their skins under his skilful hands. Indeed, so highly were his works esteemed, that I have seen many of his drawings exhibited even after death. I was astonished to see with what boldness and precision Aranghie drew his designs upon the skin, and what beautiful ornaments he produced; no rule and compasses could be more correct than the lines and circles he formed. So unrivalled is he in his profession, that a highly finished face of a chief from the hands of this artist is as greatly prized in New Zealand as a head from the hands of Sir Thomas Lawrence is amongst us."

We thus learn from Mr. Earle that tattooing is veritably a branch of the fine arts, in the estimation of those who are most concerned in the matter.

John Rutherford, a seaman engaged on a South Sea voyage, was captured on the northern of the two islands in 1816, and kept prisoner by the natives for several years. They treated him kindly on the whole, and conferred on him the honor of tattooing, which ceremony he described in the published record of his adventures. Laid on his back, amid a group of natives, he underwent the ordeal on his body, arms, and face. Several tools were employed, some with teeth and some without, varied in size and shape to fit different parts. The operation lasted four hours; during which the chief's daughters wiped the blood from his face with a bunch of dried flax. Then they washed him at a neighboring stream, dried him before a fire, and gave him his garments one by one, except his shirt, which one of the ladies put on her own person, wearing it hind side before. So severe had been the scarifying, that he lost his sight for three days, and did not fully recover for six weeks. The frontispiece to his volume represents him adorned with a most elaborate tattoo of devices; while another engraved plate gives *fac similes* of various kinds of tattooing instruments employed.

Taxes, City without. The following paragraph went the rounds of the press in 1911:

Orson, a town in Sweden, is probably the only municipality in the world which has ordinary city expenses, but which imposes no taxes. Moreover, the local railway is free to every citizen, and there is no charge for telephone service, schools, libraries, and the like.

This happy state of affairs is due to the wisdom of a former generation of citizens and rulers of Orson, who planted trees on all available ground. During the last thirty years the town authorities have sold no less than $5,000,000 worth of young trees and timber, and judicious replantings have provided for a similar income in the future.

So far so good. But in July, 1911, the London *Mail* reported that there was a little island in the Atlantic Ocean, between Sligo and Killibegs, County Donegal, Ireland, which was giving much trouble to the Sligo County Council because its inhabitants persistently refused to pay any taxes. The name of the island is Innishmurray. It is 1½ miles long by ½ broad, and there is no direct communication with it. The population consisted in 1911 of 14 families, who lived chiefly on potatoes, barley, and fish.

"In his report to the Local Government Board," said the *Mail,* "the rate collector stated that he could not get a boat on the mainland to take him to the island on such an errand as collecting rates, and at the last meeting of the Sligo County Council it was stated that some years ago two officers of the Council who tried to land on the island for the same purpose were stoned off the shore by the inhabitants.

"The question as to how a landing could be effected was discussed by the Council at their last meeting, and one member stated that a dreadnought would be required for the purpose."

Up to last accounts no dreadnought has been fitted out as a revenue collector.

Numerous other rivals sprang up to contest the singularity of the taxless city of Sweden. Germany called attention to Freudenstadt, in the Black Forest of Germany. It is a busy industrial centre with a population of 7000.

Despite its size, Freudenstadt possesses the government of a full-fledged city,—a mayor, aldermen, policemen, and a fire department. Public business is conducted on an economical basis, the total expenses not exceeding twenty-five thousand dollars annually. The yearly net revenue from the public property covers all the expenditures, thus making unnecessary any taxation whatsoever.

This property consists of about six thousand acres of fine forest, which, under the best approved forestry management, is a permanent source of income to the town. One or more trees are planted for every one felled; and no tree is cut till it will yield the maximum profit. After deduction of all expenses of this industry, the annual profit is about five dollars to the acre.

Finally the London *Globe,* in March, 1912, published these paragraphs:

It was recently reported from Germany that there was a little town within the Empire in which there were no taxes. The town possessed benefactions, the revenues from which enabled it to pay its way without the intervention of the tax gatherer.

France never likes to be outdone by anything German, so a Paris contemporary has set itself the task of finding a parallel. Something more than a parallel has been discovered, for not only are there no taxes but the timbers on the communal lands are sufficient to grant each person a small annuity. This happy land is Montmarlon, in the Midi. There are seven electors in the hamlet, so to avoid anything like rivalry the seven return themselves to the local council.

Cutting down the trees and selling them is sufficient to provide a livelihood for these simple people, whose tastes are so modest that they may be termed by some uncivilized.

Taxicab. It is claimed for the Chinese that some six centuries ago they used a vehicle which not only carried its passengers, but dropped a pebble in a receptacle to measure off every mile that was travelled. Even so, the Romans had anticipated them. When Pertinax, on December 31, A.D. 192, succeeded Commodus as Emperor of Rome, he instituted a nine-day auction (*q.v.*) of the furniture and other effects of his murdered predecessor, in order to raise money for his promised donation to the Prætorian Guard. In an inventory of the things then sold, the following item occurs.

" Carriages, which had contrivances to measure the distance over which they were driven, and to count the hours spent in the journey."

Whatever the device was, it passed out of the knowledge of man with the downfall of Rome; for the credit of the invention of the " chariot way-wiser " is given in modern history to some member of the Royal Society, and the date fixed at 1652. John Evelyn mentions this contrivance under date of August 6, 1657: " I went to see Colonel Blount, who showed me the application of the way-wiser to a coach, exactly measuring the miles, and showing them by an index as we went on. It had three circles, one pointing to the number of rods, another to the miles, by ten to a thousand, with all the subdivisions of quarters; very pretty and useful." This is precise enough. The curious appellation " way-wiser " seems to indicate that the thing itself had a German origin in the word *Wegweiser,* " guide or indicator."

An advertisement in the London *Daily Courant* of January 13, 1711, announces that, at the sign of Seven Stars under the piazza of Convent Garden, a chariot was on view that would travel without horses and " measure the miles as it goes." It was capable of reversing and turning and " could go up hill as easily as on ground."—*Notes and Queries,* 11, i, p. 343.

A simpler and more ingenious contrivance was patented in 1846 by H. von Uster, of the College for Civil Engineers, Putney. The *Illustrated London News* for February 6, 1847, gives a picture of the invention and appends the following description:

The invention is equally applicable to private carriages as to cabs and other public vehicles, one of its advantages being that there is nothing unsightly in the apparatus, which, indeed, can scarcely be seen at all when the carriage is in motion. A plano-spiral rotator is concealed within the hoop of the nave of one of the hind wheels, and gives action to a shaft, or small rod of iron, which is carried horizontally nearly as far as the opposite wheel. At this point, a universal joint connects the horizontal with a vertical rod, which latter continues the action into the body of the carriage under the seat. Here, two or three wheels give motion to a suitable shaft or chain, which is concealed between the panels of one side of the carriage, and terminates near the roof in a dial-plate, provided with two faces, one inside for the use of the passenger, and the other outside, in which the driver and his fare can together note the position of the hands before the latter steps into the cab. Both dials have exactly the face of a clock, being furnished with an hour and a minute-hand; and hours, half-hours, and minutes, are indicated on the dial precisely as in the ordinary timepiece. As the hands perform the circuit of the dial, the divisions of hours, half-hours, and minutes, correspond exactly with the miles, half-miles, and fractions of a mile actually traversed by the vehicle. Thus, if the dial indicate 20 minutes past 12 when the passenger enters the cab, he will know that he has travelled exactly a mile when the dial within points to 20 minutes past 1; a mile and a half when it points to 10 minutes to 2; two miles when it arrives at 20 minutes past 2; two miles and a half at 10 minutes to 3; three miles at 20 minutes past 3; and so on. A small circle within the dial face, with a pointer answering to the second-hands of a watch, enables the owner of the carriage to satisfy himself as to the total number of miles which the vehicle has travelled to any given period.

The passenger is thus supplied with a perfect check against overcharge, while the proprietor has the means of knowing the amount of mileage actually performed. The convenience and simplicity of adopting, as the index of distance, a method of calculation so familiar as the face of a clock supplies, need hardly be pointed out.

Telakouphanon. The London *Punch* has often delighted in jocose predictions of what applied science might in time do for the service of mankind. On more than one occasion these jesting predictions have been realized in sober truth. The following description of an imaginary Opera Telakouphanon, contributed by Tom Taylor to the issue of December 30, 1848, is a remarkable prevision of some of Edison's best-known inventions.

Our attention has been directed to an article made of gutta percha, called the Telakouphanon, or Speaking Trumpet, a contrivance by which it is stated, that a clergyman having three livings might preach the same sermon in three different churches at the same time. Thus also it would be in the power of Mr. Lumley, during the approaching holiday time, to bring home the Opera to every lady's drawing-room in London. Let him cause to be constructed, at the back of Her Majesty's Theatre, an apparatus on the principle of the Ear of Dionysius, care having been taken to render it a good ear for music. Next, having obtained an Act of Parliament for the purpose, let him lay down, after the manner of pipes, a number of Telakouphana connected—the reader will excuse the apparent vulgarism—with this Ear, and extended to the dwellings of all such as may be willing to pay for the accommodation. In this way our domestic establishments might be served with the liquid notes of JENNY LIND as easily as they are with soft water, and could be supplied with music as readily as they can with gas. Then, at a *soirée* or evening party, if a desire were expressed for a little music, we should only have to turn on the *Sonnambula* or the *Puritani*, as the case might be; an arrangement which would provide us with a delightful substitute for a deal of execrable singing, besides being in general highly conducive to the harmony of private families.

Telephone. In a curious but little-known work called *Adventures in the Moon,* there is a story of a certain Aristus who came to the conclusion that a body was a very inconvenient encumbrance, and persuaded his household god to teach him a charm by means of which he might get rid of his limbs and retain only his mind and voice. The arrangement did not turn out quite as successfully as he thought it would. His children, when he spoke to them, " were at first terrified by this mysterious voice, and could hardly be prevented from running away; but hearing it solemnly assure them that it was their father, and had no design of hurting them. they took courage, and were then greatly amused to find how their father had hid himself; they laughed violently whenever he spoke, and seemed to be delighted with the novelty." Increased familiarity with the wonder bred contempt. " They had been accustomed to follow without hesitation the advice which came from a peremptory countenance; but now the advice which came out of the air made very little impression upon them." Aristus's commands were met by flat refusal; his wife attempted to bring the children back to a sense of their filial duty, " but her expostulations could procure no obedience to the venerable sound, and it was disobeyed every hour." The more exasperated Aristus became the more the children were delighted, and they even went so far as to play all kinds of tricks on purpose to hear the air scolding them.

Any one who cares to rationalize this myth might explain that Aristus had somehow possessed himself of some sort of anticipation of the modern telephone.

The same explanation might be made to fit another myth from a chronicle of 1580, which A. Estoclot dug out of Williams's " Lays and Legends of Gloucestershire " and communicated to the *American Notes and Queries* for August 16, 1890.

About the yeare of our Lord 1554, a wenche who came from Glocester, named Elizabeth Croft, about the age of eighteene yeares, stoode, upon a Scaffolde, at Poule's Crosse, all the Sermon tyme, where shee confessed that she, being moved by dyvers lewde persons thereunto, hadde upon the fourteenth of Marche laste, before passed, counterfaited certayne speaches in an house without Aldersgate of London, thoroughe the whych the people of the whole city were wonderfully

molested, for that all men mighte heare the voice but not see hir person. Some saide it was an Angell, some saide a voyce from heaven, and
some the Holie Ghost. Thys was called the Spirite in the Wall: she
hadde laine whistling in a straunge whistle made for that purpose,
whiche was given hir by one Drakes, hir paramoure: then were ther
dyvers companions confederate with hir, whiche putting themselves
among the preass, tooke uppon them to interprete what the Spirite
saide. . . . The penance being ended and the people satified, the
officers of the Courte tooke the woman and shut hir for a tyme in the
prison, but after did shee returne to her owne countrie, and was noe
more hearde of.

The principle of the telephone has been known for many
centuries, the first idea of it in modern days being explained in a
book published in 1609. Hook commenced to study the subject
in 1661, and in 1667 he succeeded in transmitting sound by
means of a distended wire. Wheatstone experimented in 1821,
and succeeded in conveying the sounds of a musical box from
cellar to attic of his home.

In 1861 Herr Reis of Frankfort invented an instrument
called a telephone, which telegraphed musical sounds by means
of a rod of soft iron in a coil of wire through which a current
was sent. "The reproduced notes," to quote from an account
of this instrument, "though of the same pitch, are not of the
same quality as the transmitting [transmitted?] notes. They
are very faint, and resemble the sound of a toy trumpet."

Sir Charles Wheatstone, whom Englishmen style "the practical founder of modern telegraphy," was also much interested
in music and acoustics, making experiments which resulted in
several inventions,—the concertina, the symphonium, and an
instrument which he called the telephone. "Sir Charles Wheatstone," says Neill Arnott's "Physics" (edition of 1876),
"showed, as far back as 1831, that musical sounds might be
transmitted through solid linear conductors. An experiment on
a larger scale was performed at the Polytechnic Institute under
an arrangement called a telephone. Performers on various instruments were placed in the basement of the building, and the
sounds which they produced were conducted by solid rods through
the principal hall, in which they were inaudible, to sounding-
boards in a concert-room on an upper floor, where the music was
heard by the audience precisely as if performed there."

In a prospectus addressed to the members of the English
company organized to introduce the telephone into Great Britain, Prof. Bell, on March 25, 1878, expressed "a few ideas concerning the future of the electric telephone," from which a few
paragraphs may be quoted.

"The telephone," he began, "may be briefly described as an
electrical contrivance for reproducing in distant places the tones

and articulations of a speaker's voice, so that conversations can be carried on by word of mouth between persons in different rooms, in different streets, or in different towns."

He then pointed out that "the great advantage it possesses over every other form of electrical apparatus consists in the fact that it requires no skill to operate the instrument. All other telegraphic machines produce signals which require to be translated by experts, and such instruments are, therefore, extremely limited in their application; but the telephone actually speaks, and for this reason it can be utilized for nearly every purpose for which speech is employed."

Dipping far into the future, Prof. Bell indulged himself in vaticinations thát have been far more than realized to-day: "It is conceivable that cables of telephone wires could be laid underground or suspended overhead, communicating by branch wires with private dwellings, country houses, shops, manufactories, etc., uniting them through the main cable with a central office where the wire could be connected as desired, establishing direct communication between any two places in the city. Such a plan as this, though impracticable at the present moment, will, I firmly believe, be the outcome of the introduction of the telephone to the public. Not only so, but I believe in the future wires will unite the head offices of telephone companies in different cities, and a man in one part of the country may communicate by word of mouth with another in a distant place."

London *Once a Week* for November 10, 1877, quotes from a current periodical (*The Printers' and Stationers' Trade Journal*) this rather felicitous paragraph:

A year or two ago an old white-headed man might be seen any morning about the neighborhood of the colonial markets in the City, selling a little toy in the form of a pill-box, minus the lid, fastened on to the end of a short string ending in a little wooden handle, which, when rapidly swung round, made a loud and peculiar booming or buzzing sound. The old man was a well-known City character, and his frequent cry of "only a ha'penny," interjected by the noise from the toy he attempted to sell, was familiar to almost every frequenter of the City. The noise was caused by the rubbing or grating of the loose loop on a resinous substance attached to the end of the handle. The vibrations produced on the string were transmitted to and thrown out by the pill-box, and the old man, although no one knew it, carried in his hand and sold to the public, for the insignificant sum of a halfpenny, the first telephone.

It was on February 12, 1887, that the first public message was transmitted through the modern telephone by its inventor, Professor Alexander Graham Bell, when experimenting in public for the first time between Boston and Salem, a distance of 18 miles.

Mr. Raikes, when postmaster-general of Great Britain, sent the first public message ever transmitted through the telephone between London and Paris. The message was spoken on March 18, 1891. The first words from the English side were the following: "And the Lord said, My voice shall traverse continents, islands, and seas. Thus have I promised it to my people forever." A brief conversation then took place between Mr. Raikes and M. Jules Roche, French Minister of Posts and Telegraphs, after which Mr. Raikes communicated a message from the then Prince of Wales to M. Carnot, the French President, and made a speech of congratulation and greeting into the ear of M. Roche, who replied in similar terms, both speeches being in French.

It was also Prof. Bell who first showed the telephone to Queen Victoria at Osborne. The inventor subsequently told the story of his visit: "We all stood about a little table upon which was the machine, the queen opposite, Princess Beatrice on one side and her Majesty's secretary on the other. The queen then told her secretary to ask me to explain the telephone. After doing so, Queen Victoria turned to speak to some one and as the connection came I turned suddenly and what do you suppose I did? You see, my wife is deaf, and I am among deaf people so much that I forgot and patted her hand to attract her attention. I did—I really did—the Queen of England and Empress of India! Was she indignant? Oh, no! As she put her ear to the telephone she laughed. Whether it was the music over the wires or my little action I never knew."

The first recorded use of the telephone in a court of law was in 1892, when a criminal was tried and condemned by means of the 'phone, in Tampico, Mexico. Gaudio Lopez, a notorious colored horse-stealer and house-breaker, had been arrested and brought before the bar of justice in that city. The scene of his exploits was 200 miles away in Victoria. The judge decided that, as Victoria was outside his circuit, it would be necessary either for all the witnesses to take the journey or for the culprit to be returned there to await the local sessions. As this would necessitate a further delay of six months, the Mexican Government authorized the hearing of the evidence by telephone. In this manner the judge listened to one of the most remarkable histories of crime on record. The trial resulted in the prisoner receiving a sentence of ten years penal servitude. In diplomacy the telephone has more than once played a prominent part. In 1900 it was the means of bringing about a change in the presidency of Salvador. President Guitterez had a powerful rival in Gen. Regalada, the head of the army, and when the revolution broke out the latter telephoned to the palace demanding the

President's abdication, as the army had already turned against him. What reply Guitterez gave to this strange message is not on record, but he left the capital within an hour, never to return. In the same way a strong Spanish fortress surrendered to the Cuban General Pablo Olivier at the outbreak of the civil war in Cuba. When the general occupied the town adjoining the fortress, he telephoned through to the Spanish commander demanding immediate surrender on pain of bombardment. An hour's armistice was requested and granted, at the end of which Olivier was rung up and acquainted with the fact that the fortress, with 1000 men and thirty-two guns, was prepared to surrender unconditionally.

Temple Cup, in American base-ball, a special prize offered in the days when there was but a single national league or association of base-ball players. It was contested for (best 3 out of 5) at the close of the regular season, and after the championship had been decided. The contestants were the first and second nines in the championship race. It was first offered in 1878 and was found to have many advantages. In the first place, it was "business." The crowds attracted by this sequence of the season were apt to be greater than the crowds attracted by any equal number of games in the season. In this respect it took the place of the series that used to be played between the champions of the League and the champions of the Association. In the second place, it supplied a strong incentive to the clubs that had no chance of winning first place toward the close of the season to strive for second and the honors and emoluments attending the playing out of the final series. In the third place, it might show that the "form" of the season had not been true, and that the champions were not the best players.

This was indeed apparent in the very first year that it was contested for. At the close of the season the Baltimores had won the championship and the New Yorkers had come in as a close second. Nevertheless, the New Yorkers captured the Temple Cup in three straight games, the first two being played in Baltimore, the last in New York on October 6th. As the New York *Times* remarked editorially on October 7th: "Nobody who saw yesterday's game could doubt that the victors were the better players, and the two previous games in Baltimore tend to the same conclusion. About the honesty of the contest there cannot be any reasonable question. It is true that the temptation to 'hippodrome' is very great where the possible amount of gate money is so large; but it seems that the rivalry between the clubs, to say nothing of more creditable motives, is too keen and bitter to admit of an amicable adjustment of the result of the games before they are played. If the results of the games were pre-arranged, it is evident that they would be arranged so as to keep the final result in doubt until the last game was finished. Either the contestants would win alternately, or each club would win on its own grounds. That Baltimore should have been beaten twice at home and once in New York excludes the notion of 'hippodroming.'" See BASEBALL.

Tenement-house. An edifice under one roof constructed or adapted to be let out in apartments occupied by separate tenants. Technically, in the State of New York, any house occupied by more than three families is a tenement-house, though in popular parlance the term is restricted to such dwellings for the poorer classes in crowded parts of cities.

In England after the great Civil War, the vast influx of tradesmen and yeomen into London left behind in town and village a surplus of good residences, which, being difficult to let under old-time conditions, were divided into several habitations known as tenements. Deeds of the seventeenth and eighteenth centuries abound with references to messuages, formerly one tenement, but now divided into so many tenements. The condition has often existed so long that the several tenements are now looked upon as separate messuages, each having a divided portion of the appurtenances, and have been bought and sold separately.

Originally "tenement" meant any hereditament feudally held of a superior lord; then a separate corporeal hereditament (*e.g.*, a messuage); but it was not until tenements in the latter sense were divided that the term came to signify a habitation alone irrespective of its tenure.

Tennis. In the ball games of the Greeks and Romans we may see the rudiments of the Italian *pallone* and the French *jeu de paume or paulme*,—the direct ancestors of modern tennis. The origin of the word "tennis" is obscure. Many plausible suggestions have been made. The most plausible derives it from the French imperative *Tenez!* ("Take it!" "Play it!")

Pallone, a game still played in Italy, presents the essential feature of a ball being struck across a line by two adverse parties drawn up face to face. Imported into France, this became the longue paulme, which required so much space that the courte paulme was devised for playing in towns. To this enforced restriction between walls we owe all the modern refinements of the game. As a curious corollary, it is from *courte-paulme* that we derive our word "court" in "tennis-court." The French always call the place as well as the game a *jeu;* hence *jeu de paulme.* The next great step was the invention of the racket.

Originally the ball was struck simply with the palm of the hand (*la paume,* in French). The Italians eventually used a glove for protecting the hand, as in the English game of fives. Then some ingenious person conceived the brilliant idea of stretching across the glove an elastic network of strings. To these gloves handles were added, and then the instrument developed into two forms. One was the battoir, either made of thin wood or else of a frame over which parchment was stretched—the prototype of our modern battle door; the other was the racket—no doubt a very inferior instrument to the one now used, with a very short handle and no inclination of the head, but still essentially a racket.

The early popularity of the game, especially in France, appears to have been immense. Lippomano, the Venetian ambassador, writing from Paris about the end of the sixteenth century, declared there were.more than one thousand eight hundred tennis-courts in various parts of the town of Paris.

French kings and their courts were devoted to the pastime, and edicts had to be passed to prevent the vulgarization of the game by mere artisans and tradesmen. That splendid scoundrel Francis I was a great tennis-player. Once when playing with a monk as his partner, the latter made such a fine stroke, deciding the set in the king's favor, that Francis exclaimed, " Ah! that is the stroke of a monk!" "Sire," replied the monk, "whenever it may please you it shall be the stroke of an abbot," and the dexterous player made his stroke as an abbot ever after. Many other French kings were passionately fond of the game, and gave much time to it; and it is told of Henry IV that on the morrow of the Massacre of St. Bartholomew, when hundreds of his friends had been butchered and he himself was in imminent danger of losing his head, he rose early in the morning to continue a game of tennis. Nor did he much relax in his devotion to the game when he came to the throne. So popular was the sport in his reign that it was said "there were more tennis-players in Paris than drunkards in England."

One of the favorite players in Louis XIV's day was the Duke de Beaufort, who attracted all the market-women to the Marais du Temple to see him play. On asking one of them what pleasure she had in coming thither to see him lose his money, the woman bade him play on boldly, as he should not want for money. "My gossip here and I have brought two hundred crowns, and if we must have more I am ready to go back and fetch as much again"—a story which bears witness not only to the duke's popularity, but also to the market-women's wealth in those days. But from this time forward tennis in France seems to have lost favor, and it has never regained its position. Yet the finest player of modern times—Barre—was a Frenchman, who worthily carried on the traditions of the great French players. (See TENNIS CHAMPIONS.)

Tennis must have been very early popular in England, for in 1365 we find a restrictive act passed against it as tending in no way to improve the military strength of the nation. There was another in 1389, which seems more like the class legislation which was the origin of the French edicts on the subject. It regulates the pastimes of servants and laborers, allowing them the use of bows and arrows, but forbidding them "idle games," such as tennis, etc. These repressive statutes continued more or less in force till after the reign of Elizabeth, and afford in themselves good evidence of the popularity of the game. Elizabeth herself encouraged it amongst the nobles of her court and was fond of watching the play from the "dedans" (the spectators' gallery), as we find in a curious letter from Thomas Randolphe to Sir Nicholas Throckmorton, quoted by Mr. Marshall:

Latlye the Dukes G. [of Norfolk] and my L. of L. [eicester] were playing at tennes the Q. beholdinge of them, and my L. Rob. being verie hotte and swetinge tooke the Q. napken owte of her hande and wyped his face, wch the Duke scinge saide that he was to sawcie and swhore yt he wolde laye his racket vpon his face. Here vpon rose a great troble and the Q. offendid sore wth the Duke (p. 69).

Under the Stuarts all prohibition ceased; indeed the game was rather encouraged among the people, probably not so much from a disinterested desire for the popular amusement as in order to obtain money by granting licenses to keep tennis-courts, which are indeed spoken of as "Places of Honest Recreation." In 1615 a list of the London courts, with their dimensions, was drawn up by the clerk of the works at Petworth, probably to serve as a guide in the construction of a court there. From this document we find that there were then fourteen regular courts in London, besides the royal one at St. James's. In 1838, when the court at Lord's was begun, the game had sunk so low that the only public court in London was that in Windmill Street, in which all play had been for some years discontinued. There was another court in St. James's Street, from which the dimensions of the one at Lord's were copied, but this was regarded as private, or rather belonging to a club.

Tennis Champions. So far back as 1427 we hear of a famous female player of tennis, one Margot, who "played both forehanded and backhanded very powerfully, very cunningly, and very cleverly, as any man could, and there were but few men whom she did not beat except the very best players."

The expression "forehanded and backhanded" has its his-

toric value, for it seems to indicate that Margot used a racket
and hence that rackets were introduced into the game before
1427.

Ten o'clock Line. From a point near the mouth of the
Miami River there extends northward through Indiana a boundary line known by this name. This is one limit of an Indian
grant.

After the tribe had agreed to cede unto the pale-faces a
portion of their territory, a meeting was held for the purpose
of marking out the ground. A surveyor among the whites
mounted his compass and tripod on a telescope.

There was a stir among the Indians. The head man went up
to the instruments, stared steadily at them, then grunted and
returned to the circle around the council fire. Not a word was
spoken. Soon another Indian arose and went through the same
motions of examining the instruments and returning to his seat,
with no other sound than a grunt. When half a dozen others
had followed suit, a consultation was held.

The chief then approached the white men.

" That's what Indian know," he said, drawing a small circle
on the ground with a stick. " That what white man know," he
continued, drawing a larger circle around the first. " This what
nobody know," he added, pointing to the space outside of the
last circle.

" White man know that," he concluded, indicating the instruments. " Indian not know it. Indian know sun. Sun never
cheat. Him always same. Him throw shadow. Indian give
white man land one side."

After long consultation, it was decided that the boundary
should be a line drawn in the direction that the sun would cast
a shadow from an agreed point at 10 A.M. The whites took the
land on one side, the Indians retained that on the other.

Theutobochus, King. On January 11, 1613, some masons
were digging near the ruins of a castle in Dauphiné, Upper
Burgundy, in a field which by tradition had long been called
the Giant's Field. At the depth of eighteen feet they discovered
a brick tomb, 30 feet long, 12 feet broad, and 8 feet high, bearing
the inscription " Theutobochus Rex." Within was a gigantic
skeleton, 25 feet 6 inches in length, 10 feet across the shoulders,
and 5 feet from the breastbone to the backbone. The teeth were
each about the size of an ox's foot, and the shinbone measured
4 feet. Some of the bones were carried to Paris and placed
on exhibition. They spoke for themselves,—to disastrous result, as will be seen. With regard to the story, Parisians had to
depend upon the word of the self-alleged organizer of that party

of masons. He was a surgeon named Muzerein. His ingenuity and energy in advertising himself and his giant indicate that he was the Barnum of his day.

Both the pleasure-seeking and the scientific world were excited over the wonderful discovery. Thousands flocked to see the bones. Dr. Muzerein was on the high-road to fortune, when one day an anatomist announced that the skeleton of King Theutobochus was nothing more than a part of the fossil remains of an elephant. In so crude a state was the knowledge of science at that time that even after this exposure Muzerein is said to have taken the bones to other parts of the continent and to England, and to have made a good living from their exhibition. Doubtless his surgical knowledge had assisted him in putting together the remains of sundry large animals so as to resemble a human skeleton.

We may dismiss as equally apocryphal the tradition concerning Chevalier Ricon. The Dominicans of Rouen, so it is said, were digging in the ditches near their monastery in 1509, when they unearthed a stone tomb containing a skeleton, whose skull held a bushel of corn, and whose shinbone reached up to the girdle of the tallest man there, being about four feet long, and consequently the body must have been seventeen or eighteen feet high. Upon the tomb was a plate of copper, whereon was engraved, " In this tomb lies the noble and puissant Lord, the Chevalier Ricon de Vallemont, and his bones."

Nor need we accept without question the remains of the giant Bucart, tyrant of the Vivarais, who was said to have been slain by an arrow by the Count de Cabillon, his vassal. The Dominicans of Valence in Dauphine had a part of the shinbone, with the articulation of the knee, and his figure painted in fresco, with an inscription, showing that this giant was twenty-two feet and a half high, and that his bones were found in 1705, near the banks of the Morderi, a little river at the foot of the mountain of Crussol, upon which, tradition says, the giant dwelt.

In the nineteenth century and in America all these frauds or misconceptions of the past were thrown into the shade by the marvellous history of the Cardiff Giant. See also GIANT.

Thirteen. It was Leonardo da Vinci's great fresco of the Last Supper that, speaking paradoxically, popularized the unpopularity of the number thirteen. The picture shows the twelve apostles arranged six on each side of the fated thirteenth, the doomed Messiah, who occupies the centre of the table. Before cock-crow on the morrow He was to be betrayed by Judas and thrice denied by Peter, and before sunset He was to suffer a shameful death upon the cross,

The picture itself is blurred almost out of recognition, and even its pitiful remains are fast fading away on the wall of a seldom-visited church in Milan. But countless reproductions—paintings, engravings, and photographs—have made it one of the most familiar of the great masterpieces of the world.

Now, though Leonardo helped to spread the superstition, neither he nor his picture originated it. From time immemorial in many portions of the globe ill-luck has been associated with the number thirteen. Norse mythology has even a sort of anticipation of the Last Supper of the Christians. One night the twelve major gods were seated at table in the Valhalla, when Loki, the evil spirit, "butted in" and made the thirteenth. Quarrelling with Baldur, the Apollo of the Scandinavians, he shot him dead with a mistletoe arrow.

Further back even than the Norse sagas, in the myths of the ancient Hindoos, we read that thirteen at table boded disaster to some one assembled there. To-day, emphasized as we have seen by the picture and story of the Last Supper, we find a belief prevalent throughout Christendom that one or more of the guests will die within a twelvemonth. In some localities the doom is most certain to fall upon the guest who first rises from the table.

Vainly has the church herself thundered against the superstition. In the chapel of the Trindinium Pauperum, adjoining the church of St. Gregory on the Coelian Hill in Rome, is a marble table with an inscription recounting how Pope Gregory the Great was in the habit of entertaining twelve poor men at breakfast every morning, and how on one occasion Christ appeared and shared their meal, making thirteen at table. Henceforth, so the inscription ordained, thirteen was to be considered a lucky number. If this had any effect, that effect has quite passed away. Everywhere the old superstition survives in all sorts of curious forms. Even in the United States and in our largest cities there are hotels which have no room numbered thirteen. Or, if there be, guests frequently object to occupying it. In several sky-scrapers in New York thirteen is skipped in numbering not only the rooms but even the floors. The Kuhn-Loeb building, at the corner of Pine and William streets, is an example. Another is the building at the corner of William and Wall streets. Both have a twelfth and a fourteenth, but no intervening floor.

In Germany and in France the fateful number is usually ignored not only at hotels but wherever it would occur in the natural order of rotation. In Berlin it is omitted from all new streets. In Paris it is nearly always changed to 12A or 12½. The Italians never use the number in making up their lotteries. And if you cross over from Christendom into the Mohammedan world, you find the Turks so chary of it that the very word is obsolete, or at least obsolescent.

In Paris there is a profession whose members earn their living attending dinner parties in order to constitute a needed fourteenth at the table. These people are known as *quatorzes,* or "fourteens." Hence the point of this Parisian joke:

"Who is that man?" asks a stranger in the French capital.

"Louis Quatorze" (Louis the Fourteenth) is the reply.

"Nonsense!"

"Why, certainly: his name is Louis and his profession is that of a fourteenth at table."

Dr. Veron, founder of the *Revue des Deux Mondes,* and the most famous of all the managers of the Paris Opera (a rare combination of successful generalship), never got over the superstition. Whenever he found thirteen guests at his table, he invariably sent out a pair of them to dine at the Café de Paris, with instructions that the bill should be charged to himself.

The most famous of Veron's contributors shared the editor's failing. Victor Hugo, so the story runs, had accepted an invitation to dine at the house of one of those advanced thinkers whom their enemies named "les précieuses radicales." The dinner hour had long passed without any sign, when one of the company inquired the cause of the delay. The hostess explained that one of the guests had sent in an excuse at the last moment. Hence there would be thirteen instead of fourteen at table, and she had sent out to find a quatorzième.

A moment later the same guest was conversing with Victor Hugo.

"Do you know why we are waiting?" asked the poet.

"Yes," was the reply; "some imbecile is afraid to sit at the table when there are thirteen."

Solemnly and severely Victor Hugo rejoined, "L'imbécile, c'est moi" (the imbecile is myself).

Napoleon I, as well as the third of the name, had the thirteen superstition in a virulent form. So did Bismarck. In 1906, when the French Cabinet was reorganized, the official announcement was deferred a day—solely, it is said—to avoid announcing it on the thirteenth day of the month. When this was told to the pope, his Holiness smiled and remarked, "Evidently, being a freethinker does not exclude superstition."

Charles Stuart Parnell furnishes another instance. Once a colleague brought him the draft of a bill to the cell he was then occupying in Kilmainham jail. It was in thirteen clauses. Parnell was horrified. He insisted that somehow or other a fourteenth clause should be added.

Some quarter century ago—in the fall of 1890, to be exact—a detailed and circumstantial story ran the rounds of the American press and set on edge the nerves of many newspaper readers. It appeared first in the St. Louis *Globe-Democrat* as a special telegram from Birmingham, Alabama. The heading itself was of a lurid effulgence. Videlicet:

GOD'S AVENGING HAND.
Last of Thirteen Men who acted the Last Supper in Mockery.

The story is too long to copy in its entirety, but it will not suffer by abridgment. Here, then, is the substance of it.

A man had been found dead in the gutter of a Birmingham street. Even in death there was a look of terror in the bloodshot eyes. And no wonder. "This man," we are told, "was the last of a fated thirteen, and in the death of each and all of them the Christian will read the vengeance of an insulted deity."

At the leading hotel in a Southern city, in the summer of 1865, thirteen men wearing Confederate uniforms sat down to dinner. They had returned from the field of defeat to find their homes destroyed, their slaves freed, their wealth gone, their friends scattered, and many of their nearest and dearest dead. They determined to forget the past and drown their sorrows for the nonce in drink.

"Let us call this the Last Supper," said one of the party, and the suggestion met with instant approval. They might never meet again, so "The Last Supper" would be a fitting name for this chance meeting. Moreover, the suggestion of profanity was in keeping with their mood of desperation. More drinks were ordered; the lights were turned low, and the thirteen men declared themselves Christ and his twelve apostles. A young man who had commanded a regiment acted the part of Christ. Each of the others assumed the name of an apostle. There was a wrangle as to who should impersonate Judas, but at last a young lieutenant agreed to assume the character.

Until long after midnight the blasphemous mockery was kept up. A Bible was called for, and the officer impersonating the Saviour read aloud the solemn words of Christ. At the proper point in the reading, bread was passed around. The wine was represented by glasses filled to the brim with brandy.

"He that drinketh from the bottle with me shall betray me," exclaimed the mock Christ, as he lifted the decanter to his lips and then passed it across the table to Judas.

This was greeted with peals of laughter, while the mock apostles yelled, "Judas, pass the bottle!"

When morning broke, the thirteen men were in a drunken stupor. It was several days before they all recovered from the effects of that night's debauchery. Then they separated, never to meet again.

" From that night," so the story concluded, " the vengeance of God followed those thirteen men. Everything they undertook failed. Every man of them met a horrible and disgraceful death." The Christ of the occasion was drowned in the Brazos River while fleeing on a stolen horse from a vigilance committee. The Saint John was lynched in Texas for murder. Another of the " apostles," while intoxicated, was caught in a burning building and perished in the flames. Still another was stabbed to the heart by a woman he had betrayed. " So far as can be learnt, not one of them received Christian burial. The man who died in the gutter and was buried in Potter's Field was the last of the thirteen."

The *Globe-Democrat* never pretended to verify this tale, and you may accept it or not as you choose. Another thirteen story of a milder type bears credentials that at first sight seem quite satisfactory. You will find it in the " Life of Sir John Millais."

Millais in August, 1885, gave a dinner in honor of Matthew Arnold. One of the guests called alarmed attention to the fact that there were thirteen at table. Matthew Arnold laughed at his fears and undertook to challenge the superstition.

" The idea is that whoever leaves the table first will die within a year; so, with the permission of the ladies, we will cheat the fates for once. I and these fine strong lads (indicating Edgar Dawson and E. S.) will rise together, and I think our united constitutions will be able to withstand the assault of the reaper."

Six months later, so the story continues, Matthew Arnold, in the prime of life, died suddenly of heart disease. A few days later E. S. was found dead in bed, a revolver at his side. Edgar Dawson, the third of the trio, sailed from Australia on February 18, 1886, on the steamer *Quetta*, which foundered off the coast of New Guinea and not a single soul was saved.

This seems circumstantial enough to convince the most sceptical. It happens, however, that the facts do not substantiate the pretended details. Matthew Arnold did not die in 1886, as the story assumes, but on April 15, 1888, or nearly three years after he had braved the superstition; while the person indicated by the initials E. S. was actually surviving at the time the biography of Millais was published, and asserted the fact very vigorously in the public prints.

The only truth in this batch of errors is that Edgar Dawson was shipwrecked within the fateful period, although he did not die but was one of several survivors.

A story told in the " Life of Shirley Brooks " is, however,

well authenticated. Brooks's widow survived him six years. The Christmas before she died, she took dinner with Mr. and Mrs. William P. Frith. There were thirteen at table. Mrs. Frith got up first, saying, " I will be the first, because I can best be spared." Immediately up jumped Shirlina, as Mrs. Brooks was nicknamed in her circle, crying, " Well, I'll be the second, for if you died, dear Mrs. Frith, I shouldn't want to live."

A month later Mrs. Frith was dead, and five months later Mrs. Brooks.

Lawrence Hutton was one of the invited at a dinner given by Henry Irving to Edwin Booth at Delmonico's. With the other guests he put his name upon a menu-card and passed it along the table. It came back to him in due course with the signatures of the host, of Whitelaw Reid, Mark Twain, Charles Dudley Warner, T. B. Aldrich, Augustin Daly, and Booth, Barrett, Lester Wallack, John McCullough, Harry Edwards, and William J. Florence, in the order given.

Long afterward it was discovered that the bit of paper contained thirteen names, and that the last six signers, all actors, had all quitted forever the stage of life. These uncanny facts so greatly enhanced the intrinsic value of the autographs that Mr. Hutton was offered a fabulous price for the menu-card by an autograph collector, " who would never for a moment have thought of parting with it if it had been his own and had come to him in the same direct and pathetic way."

Luigi Arditi, the famous Italian composer and impressario, tells some curious stories about the number thirteen.

On his first visit to Chicago with Madame Alboni, in 1850, a bedroom had been secured for the singer at the best hotel. The proprietor had been informed that Madame was painfully superstitious and implored not to give her number 13. As it happened, that was the only suitable vacant room. In order to conceal the fact, the manager caused a piece of paper to be deftly gummed over the painted number outside the door. All went smoothly at first. Alboni was ushered into her room and a supper was served preparatory to her retiring. Suddenly a piercing shriek rang through the corridors. The whole house responded with an uproar. Affrighted guests and waiters rushing upstairs found Madame Alboni standing in front of her door, a candle in one hand, and in the other the piece of paper fictitiously numbered. She had gone out with the candle and discovered the fraud. Nothing would tempt her to return. Finally an elderly gentleman was induced to exchange rooms with the singer.

Was it accident or design that, when Arditi came to write his memoirs, this story appeared on page 13?

Another of his stories associates luck with the number. When Arditi and his wife were at Monte Carlo, the Duke of Newcastle, who was one of the party, persuaded the lady after much hesitation to make a venture. The wheel had already began to turn when she appealed to her husband for a coin. In his haste the first piece of money he took from his pocket was a florin, which she promptly threw down upon 13. That number came up, and Madame Arditi's first experience at the gambling table netted her thirty-five florins.

Other people there be who have found luck in the number. Richard Wagner is the favorite example. There are thirteen letters in his name. He was born in 1813, and $1 + 8 + 1 + 3$ equals 13. He composed thirteen operas; Tannhauser, the greatest of them, was finished on September 13, 1860, and performed for the first time on March 13, 1861. He left Beyreuth on September 13, and died on February 13.

Edmond Rostand furnishes a more modern instance. Like Wagner, his full name contains 13 letters; his two greatest successes, "L'Aiglon" and "Cyrano," contain 13 letters between them; he was received into the Academy on June 4, 1903 $(6 + 4 + 03 = 13)$, and he was assigned to the thirteenth chair in that august body, of which he was the thirteenth occupant.

Then there is the English Duchess of Sutherland. "M. A. P.," the Mr. T. P. O'Connor's weekly, asserts that but for the thirteen superstition she might never have gained her exalted title. One night when she was a girl her mother gave a dinner party. It was discovered that the company at table numbered thirteen. The future duchess was routed out of the nursery in order to make fourteen. It was then and there that she met the Marquis of Stafford, the future duke, and then and there that he fell in love with her.

In one very notable case the luck or ill luck of number 13 depends upon the point of view,—that of the thirteen revolted colonies which eventually became the United States. A London newspaper of 1776 had a mocking paragraph which suggests that the rebels thought there was luck in the number.

To a party of returned naval prisoners were attributed statements that thirteen dried clams were the rebels' daily rations; that Washington had thirteen toes (three having grown since the Declaration of Independence), and thirteen teeth in each jaw; and that the regular rebel family comprised thirteen children, all of whom expected to become generals or members of congress at the age of thirteen. It was added that thirteen American paper dollars were worth one English penny. It might further have been added that there were thirteen stars and thirteen stripes in the original flag under which the " rebels " fought.

A dinner to celebrate the thirteenth wedding anniversary of a New York couple took place on Friday, November 13, 1908. In order to emphasize the disbelief in popular superstitions, the thirteen guests had to walk under a ladder to reach their places at table; they found the salt-cellars all overturned, the prongs of the forks pointing the wrong way, and the forks themselves crossed by knives.

At each plate, however, there was placed as an antidote a four-leaved clover. Perhaps it was the clover that protected the guests. Anyhow no harm happened to them within the twelvemonth.

A German imitation of the New York Thirteen Club was projected in 1911 at Hamburg. In the circular sent out to all who were asked to become charter members it was pointed out that 13 was a lucky number. The case of Wagner was cited. Reference was also made to the good luck of engine 1313 of the Baltimore and Ohio Railroad, to the fact that the pontificate of Leo XIII was one of the longest and most glorious in the history of the Catholic church, and to the example of the ancient Mexicans who had 13 gods and whose week had 13 days. The men invited to defy the ancient superstition seem, however, to have lost their courage, for only eleven appeared.

Thistle of Scotland. Why the thistle is the national emblem of Scotland is involved in uncertainty. Various legends attempt to account for it. One tells how Queen Scotia (see CORONATION CHAIR in Walsh's "Curiosities of Popular Customs "), after winning a victory, sat down a little too suddenly upon a bunch of flourishing thistles, and, leaping up still more suddenly, tore up the offending weeds with the intention of casting them to the winds, but, changing her mind, placed them in her helmet as a symbol of her recent triumph. From that hour the thistle became the badge of her dynasty.

The more commonly accepted legend makes the emblem date from the year 1010, during the reign of Malcolm I, when the Danes descended upon Aberdeenshire with the intent to assault Staines Castle. Contrary to their usual custom—for they deemed it cowardly and dishonorable to assail a sleeping foe—the attack took place at midnight. They advanced cautiously, taking off their shoes that no sound might betray their approach; and their hearts beat high with the anticipation of certain victory. They had but to swim the moat; scale the castle walls; and the citadel was theirs. But just at the critical moment a cry of pain broke from one of those who were the first to enter the moat, which, instead of being filled with water, had dried up, and given place to a thick growth of sharp thistles. The noise awoke the slumbering Scots, who rushed out upon the enemy and put them to flight; and in grateful remembrance of its timely warning, the despised and lowly weed was elevated to the first place in the flora of Scotland.

> Sharp little soldiers, trusty and true,
> Side by side in good order due,
> Arms straight down, and heads forward set,
> And saucily-pointed bayonet.

The motto adopted to accompany the thistle accords well with its bristling leaves, *Nemo me impune lacessit,* or, as it is rendered in the homely Scotch, *Wha daur meddle wi me?*

Petra Saneta calls the thistle of Scotland "the oldest device on record;" but attributes it to the time when an alliance was made between King Achaius and the Emperor Charles the Great. On the altar-piece in Holyrood Palace, which was painted during the reign of James III, the thistle appears in the tapestry, behind the kneeling figure of Queen Margaret. The date of this painting has been fixed by antiquarians as not later than 1485. In an inventory of the effects of James III mention is made of a covering "browdin with thissillis," he having probably adopted it as an appropriate illustration of the royal motto "In defence"—if it is not to be admitted on other grounds.

The appearance of this thistle on the coinage of Scotland is now thought to date from this same reign, it having been recently determined that the silver groats commonly attributed to the time of James V really belong to that of James III, and, if this supposition be correct, it affords the earliest instance of its adoption for this purpose. Seton, in his works on heraldry, gives Mary's reign as the date for its first appearance on the Great Seal, and after the accession of James VI to the English throne it was united with the rose. The thistle has also given its title to a famous Scotch order of knighthood said to be of great antiquity. It was revived by James V, in 1540 again, by James VII (II of England), in 1687 (whose patent for its institution never passed the Great Seal), and a third time in 1703, by Queen Anne, who increased the number of knights to twelve and established the order on a permanent footing.

It was this which gave rise to Pope's riddle in the pastoral on Spring (a parody on Virgil's Eclogue, iii):

> "Tell me—in what more happy fields
> *The thistle* springs to which the *lily* yields?"

the Duke of Marlborough having made the Lily of France submit to the Thistle of Great Britain.

A collar of thistles appears on the gold bonnet-pieces of James V; and the royal ensigns are surrounded by a collar formed of thistles with a sprig of rue interlaced, and a gold medal bearing the figure of St. Andrew. The so-called thistle of Scotland, the cotton thistle, is said by some botanists rarely to grow wild in Scotland, despite its name and reputation; and the stemless thistle is thought to agree best with the legend of the defeated Danes.

Tiburon, an island belonging to Mexico, in the upper reaches of the Gulf of California. It measures only 30 by 20 miles; it is worthless, even as a breeding place for goats; nevertheless it has been for many generations a centre of attraction for ethnologists and archæologists.

Tiburon is a Spanish word, which, translated into English, means "shark." The waters around the islet are literally swarming with these tigers of the sea, and the inhabitants of the island are said to be no less ferocious than the shark. Tiburon is peopled with a handful of Indians, the only aborigines of their kind in the world, known as Seris. They are reputed to be cannibals, to be so fierce that none of the mainland tribes of Mexican redskins ever dare to invade their shores, and to possess the secret for the manufacture of a peculiarly deadly poison with which they prepare their arrows before battle.

Tobacco. M. Alphonse Karr—a true Frenchman, and therefore nothing if not paradoxical—has imagined a conversation which he places three centuries ago, at the time when Jean Nicot, king's advocate and ambassador extraordinary, first sent tobacco to France from Portugal as a present to that engaging character, Queen Catherine de Medicis.

A bold financier is supposed to make his way into the presence of Cardinal de Lorraine, flushed with the excitement of a magnificent project.

"Monseigneur," he cries, "knowing the treasury to be in a depleted condition, I have come to propose a tax which will bring you in a couple of hundred francs, cheerfully paid—voluntary contributions to the revenues of state. There will be taxpayers in every family throughout the land, and you will never have to seize or squeeze in order to collect it."

"State your project," is the cold reply.

"Monseigneur, it is simply this. The Government has only to reserve to itself the exclusive privilege of selling a certain herb, which is to be reduced to a powder sufficiently fine for people to stuff up their noses. The plant may also be left in the leaf, to be chewed, or to be burnt for the purpose of inhaling its smoke."

" Your plant then affords a delightful perfume—sweeter than amber, musk, or roses?"

" By no means; its smell is rather unpleasant than otherwise."

" I see; it is a panacea, a specific, endowed with marvellous healing powers?"

" Quite the contrary.   The habit of snuffing up the powdered herb weakens the memory and destroys the smell.   It causes giddiness; it may in rare cases bring on blindness or even apoplexy.   Chewed, it renders the breath offensive and puts the stomach out of order.   Inhaling the smoke is a different affair. The first attempt brings on pains in the chest, nausea, swimming in the head, colic, and cold perspiration; but persevere, and in the course of time you gradually get used to it."

" And how many people do you imagine would be fools and idiots enough to punish themselves for your tax-gathering purposes by smoking this plant or stuffing their nostrils with it?"

Here the speculator gathers himself together for a grand effort in vaticination: " Monseigneur, there will one day be more than twenty millions in France alone.   I won't mention the millions in other countries, because *they,* monseigneur, will not pay us taxes."

Now, M. Karr concludes, if the cardinal had ordered the gentleman to be incarcerated in a lunatic asylum, his contemporaries would have had small blame for him.   Yet, as events have proved, he would have made a great mistake in rejecting the advice.

Alphonse Karr was prejudiced, of course: He hated tobacco, and his hatred had in it the virulence of the renegade.   He had been a smoker, he had apostatized, he had renounced the faith of his fathers, and his imprecations should go unheeded of all thoughtful men.   Far more admirable was the temper of Charles Lamb, who, being forbidden the use of the weed, wrote his " Farewell to Tobacco," in which, after vainly trying to move himself to anger and hatred by piling up epithets against his former mistress, he finally acknowledges:

> 'Twas but in a sort I blamed thee;
> Irony all, and feigned abuse—
> Such as perplexed lovers use.

It is true that we have borrowed the use of tobacco from the savages.   Let those who will make the most of that argument, and then turn the same engine against the potato and the tomato, and tea and coffee, and Heaven knows how many other luxuries that reconcile us to life as mere necessaries never could do.   In the Wild West—wild in those days, but not woolly as in ours—the happy red man may have been inhaling the fumes of

the fragrant weed while Nero lay sighing in his palace for a
new pleasure. Columbus and his crew, first among the inhabitants of the Old World, heard of the plant and of its uses when
they set foot in San Salvador in 1492. Two Spaniards, returning
from an exploration into the interior of the island, related how
they had seen many of the inhabitants hold in their hands a certain herb called *tobago* or *tobaco,* which they lighted, inhaling
the smoke. Later, a Spanish missionary, Fray Romano Pane,
whom Columbus took with him on his second voyage, interested
himself in watching the fanatic excitement produced in the
priests of the god Kiwasa by the vapor of tobacco leaves in fer-
mentation and combustion. He sent some seeds of the plant to
Charles V—and the mischief was done.   In 1518 the Spaniards
began the cultivation of tobacco in Cuba, and Portugal soon
followed suit in several districts of Brazil. This implies a certain
demand, which, though partial and limited at first, must have
been steadily on the increase. From Portugal, the papal nuncio,
Cardinal della Santa Croce, imported tobacco into Italy. From
Portugal, also, Jean Nicot, who had experimented with tobacco
powder as a cure for headache, sent some of the plants in 1560
to Catherine de Medicis, who welcomed them with the eagerness
always accorded to strange and far-fetched remedies. Hitherto
tobacco had been used mainly as a fumigator by the aid of
various rudimentary apparatus, which dimly foreshadow the
modern pipe. But into France tobacco made its entry through
the nostril. There the use of powdered tobacco, or snuff, became
so popular that the name of its introducer was immortalized in
the verbal forms of Nicotia and Nicotine, scientific words both,
the first for the herb and the second for its active principle.

While continental Europe was rapidly learning the varied
uses of the weed, England remained in darkness until 1570, when
Sir Henry Hawkins brought home some specimens of the plant
from his second voyage, in order to cultivate them at home.
But it is not impossible that Sir Walter Raleigh made tobacco
smoking popular at the English court. The old story is well
known of the servant of the good knight, who, finding him in his
study enveloped in a cloud of smoke, poured a tankard of ale over
his head. But it did not take long for smoking to become a
common custom in England, as it had already become in Spain,
Portugal, Italy, Holland, and Prussia. Not in France, however.
The French, with their habitual courtesy, tolerated the smokers
of other countries, but they remained loyal to their pinch of
snuff. From the days of Catherine *that* custom had spread with
incredible rapidity. There was a mania, a rage for snuff. All
ages, all conditions, both sexes, were furnished with their little

roll of tobacco and the grater wherewith to reduce it to powder. The grater—though an article of finery which rivalled the most expensive fans—gradually disappeared before the improvements made in grinding tobacco to dust by machinery, and was succeeded by snuff-boxes as luxurious and expensive as the graters had been.

And so in due course tobacco invaded the entire Eastern Hemisphere. At first it was hailed everywhere with praises. Doctors called it the *herba panacea* and the *sancta sancta Indorum;* poets, " our holy herb nicotian " and " divine tobacco." So universal a favorite must needs soon excite jealousy and hatred. The reaction was terrible when it came. Physicians denounced their former panacea, and cited instances where smokers had been " exsiccated," or dried up, by the immoderate use of tobacco, so that at death they were found to be nothing but " a black clot enclosed in membrane." Smokers were riddled by satire as well as science. Nay, more. Europe frowned and Asia threatened; pagan, Mohammedan, and Christian monarchs combined to crush them. James I fulminated a book which he called, " A Counterblast to Tobacco;" Christian IV, of Denmark, ordered tobacco users to be whipped and fined; Amuratti IV condemned them to be beaten in a mortar; the Shah of Persia put smokers to death, and cut off the noses of snuff-takers—an admirable preventive of crime which was imitated by the Russian Czar. Nor was this all. The Pope, Urban VIII, actually thundered excommunications on any person who took the accursed thing in any shape to church. Was ever destruction of body and soul threatened so unjustly? Mutilation for taking a pinch! Loss of life for lighting a pipe! Exclusion from heaven for perhaps harmlessly reviving attention to a wearisome sermon in chapel or church! Our sympathies are naturally with the sufferers, and we are glad to learn how they slowly but surely converted their oppressors. Snuff-taking even invaded the church, and in 1724, exactly one hundred years after Urban's anathema, Pope Benedict XIII revoked all the papal bulls against tobacco.

In England the triumph of tobacco was as signal as elsewhere. James I had declared that " smoking is a custom loathsome to the eye, hateful to the nose, harmful to the brain, dangerous to the lungs, and in the black stinking fume thereof nearest resembling the horrible Stygian smoke of the pit that is bottomless." The weed so denounced enjoyed a fine stroke of vicarious revenge. When the son of James I—the unfortunate Charles I—sat in the guard-chamber at Westminster, the soldiers of Cromwell blew their tobacco smoke in his face, knowing that he had inherited a strong dislike to it. And when his grand-son, James II, was deposed, the costs of the revolution were defrayed by the revenue raised from tobacco.

Barclay saw a time coming when the medicinal virtues of the herb would be so well understood that the services of physicians would be dispensed with, particularly in the cases of defluxion and catarrh.

Smoking was tardily introduced into France through the navy and the army during the reign of Louis XIV. The Grand Monarque himself did not smoke, but he tolerated smokers. Jean Bart, the explorer and navigator, was the first to introduce the pipe to the court. He had been sent for by the king, and while awaiting the latter's pleasure in an antechamber, he took out his pipe, struck a light from his flint, and calmly puffed away. The courtiers were shocked; the guards debated whether they should turn him away. But when one came up and remon-strated, the old sailor coolly answered, " I learned this practice in the king's service; he is too just a monarch to take offence."

At last somebody went and told the king that a strange fellow was smoking in the antechamber and refused to leave. Louis laughed.

" Let him do as he likes," was his answer: " it can be none other than Jean Bart."

A few moments later Bart was ushered into the presence of the monarch, who received him cordially, saying, " You, Jean Bart, are the only person allowed to smoke here."

But it was not very long afterward that the Grand Monarque actually surprised his own daughters, young girls at the time, in the act of making a surreptitious experiment in the novel prac-tice of which they had heard. We may presume he found them very sick; let us trust he deemed that sufficient punishment.

Napoleon, who took snuff freely enough, was no smoker. In Egypt he made a feint at smoking, just as he pretended to lean toward Islamism, merely in compliment to the customs of the country. Later, when the Persian ambassador presented him with a handsome pipe, he determined to try in earnest. The *valet-de-chambre* filled the bowl, and applied the match. But as His Majesty simply opened and closed his lips over the mouth-piece, without any attempt to draw, the tobacco of course, would not light.

" What the deuce ! " he exclaimed at last. " There's no light-ing it."

Constant diffidently suggested that the emperor did not go about it in the right way. Precept was useless, however; the inapt scholar still returned to his bad imitation of the act of yawning. Tired at last of his useless efforts, "Constant," he blurted out, "light the pipe yourself. I cannot."

So Constant lit it, pulled steadily and effectively for a few moments, then handed the mouthpiece to his master. With the first whiff the smoke went down the latter's throat in a volume, came out again through the nose, and blinded his eyes.

"Take it away!" he gasped, as soon as he had recovered his breath. "Take it away! What an infection! What a set of pigs they must be! It has turned my stomach."

Nevertheless, Napoleon was willing to raise money on this swinish practice. Like Vespasian, he held that the coin gave no olfactory evidence of its origin. It happened that early in 1810, at a ball in the Tuileries, the emperor remarked a lady whose dress was splendidly ornamented with diamonds. How could she be rich enough to make such a display? He was informed that Madame R—— was the wife of a tobacco manufacturer. The hint was sufficient. By the 20th of December a decree had appeared, commanding that henceforward the manufacture and sale of tobacco should belong exclusively to the state. It has remained a government monopoly ever since, and the most important source of French revenue. The move was, on the whole, a beneficial one to lovers of the weed. As the use of tobacco had increased, it had been adulterated in every possible shape. Under its name cabbage-leaves, walnut-leaves, sea-weed, and hay were smoked. Bark, peat moss, and the roots of Iceland moss were pulverized into snuff. Wealthy amateurs were at great expense to obtain their tobacco pure from Holland, where alone the real products of Varinas and Virginia were sold. But from the time that the French Government assumed control of the tobacco trade, not only France, but the contiguous countries also, were certain at least of obtaining the genuine article.

Toll-gate. The only toll-gate still remaining in Vermont, and possibly the only one in all New England, is situated at the foot of the mountains on the road leading from Manchester to Peru and Bondville. The tolls are singularly differentiated; thus, double teams are 25 cents Peru way and 10 cents Bondville way; single teams, 20 cents Peru way and 8 cents Winhall way. "It may seem queer," said the Springfield *Republican* in 1911, "that there should be such a difference in the rates according to which town you are going to or coming from, but when less than half-way up the mountain the Winhall traveller turns off from the turnpike road. This difference in the gate fare has caused many a penurious farmer to perjure his soul to save a few of those hard-earned cents, and it has developed a detective spirit in the gate-keeper in order to collect the honest toll. In 1814 the

Legislature granted a charter for the construction of a turnpike road five miles long beginning at the foot of the mountain leading up over the summit of Bromley Mountain about a mile."

According to the same authority Gen. Peter Dudley of Peru, father of Col. Homer A. Dudley of South Londonderry, began building this road in 1815 and completed it in 1816. Being the main route from Boston to Saratoga, there was a large amount of travel over the turnpike until the building of railroads in 1850 diverted it. Since then the road had not been a paying proposition to its owners until the advent of automobile travel. This mountain road is one of the main routes from New York city to the White Mountains, and thus there is a large automobile travel during the summer months. During last season 1624 automobiles passed through this gate, which means $812 of revenue.

Tomato, or love-apple (the *tumatl* of the Mexicans), has only within recent times come into general use as an esculent among civilized nations. It seems to have been long known in Africa, where it was held in the highest esteem by tribes recently discovered. It was known to the Malays for centuries. Toward the close of the sixteenth century specialists in Europe began to take note of it. Dodoens, the Netherlands herbalist, mentions it in 1583, and says that it may be eaten with pepper, salt, and oil. About the same time, Gerard, the English surgeon and botanist, introduced some varieties of the plant into England. But until the early part of the nineteenth century the tomato was little cultivated in England or in America, and then only for the sake of its pretty colors or as food for pigs. It made its first appearance in the Southern States probably a little before it was introduced into the North. In the March, 1828, number of the *Southern Agriculturist,* published in Charleston, the editor, John D. Legaré, begins an article on the cultivation of tomatoes by saying, "The fruit of this vegetable is justly in high repute among us." Its introduction could not have been very long before that date. It was brought to New Jersey by Peter Bogart, of Princeton, about 1830, and from his garden was carried to other portions of the State. In the report of the Massachusetts "State Board of Agriculture" for 1871, the report on vegetables, signed by James J. H. Gregory, Chairman, opens with these words: "Over thirty years ago I sold the first tomatoes ever brought into the market of my native town."

Tombstone. The capital of Cochise County, Arizona, and a prominent mining centre. As to the origin of its gloomy name, the following paragraph from the Chicago *Tribune* (January, 1891) may be assumed to be authoritative:

Richard Schiefflin, of Los Angeles, was at the Palmer yesterday and attracted considerable attention by his peculiar Western attire and long-flowing hair. Mr. Schiefflin was famous a few years ago as the discoverer of Tombstone in Arizona. He was a poor prospector on the Arizona desert in search of gold, which he believed was located in the southern part of the Territory. After getting a "grub stake" at a store in Yuma, he started out alone to cross the arid waste lying west of Yuma. As he left the town, he was told that instead of finding gold he would find his tombstone. For weeks the daring prospector struggled on until his provisions were nearly exhausted. One night, while camping beside a small, dry stream, he was obliged to dig in the sand of the river-bed to get water, and while thus employed unearthed several nuggets of gold. The next day he staked his claim and started back to Yuma, where he reported that he had found his tombstone, but that it was lined with golden nuggets. From this the present city of Tombstone sprung, and to-day "Dick" Schiefflin is one of the wealthiest men in Los Angeles.

Tooth-brush. By whom was this useful implement invented? When was it first known in England? These questions cannot be specifically answered. Thackeray, who prided himself on his accurate knowledge of eighteenth century manners, thus describes the foppery of Lord Castlewood, in "Henry Esmond": "He spent a tenth part of his day in the brushing of his teeth and the oiling of his hair." Now, passing over the exaggeration of this description, was not oiling the hair an anachronism, seeing that in the first decade of the eighteenth century all gentlemen wore wigs? Must we not put brushing the teeth into the same category, seeing that the tooth-brush was in 1754 unknown to Lord Chesterfield, that glass of fashion and mould of form? In his "Letters to his Son," Chesterfield never wearies of impressing upon him the importance of attending to his teeth, and writing at that date says:

"Nothing seems little to me that can be of any use to you. I hope you take great care of your mouth and teeth, and that you clean them well every morning with a sponge and tepid water, with a few drops of arquebusade water dropped into it; besides washing your mouth carefully after every meal. I do insist upon your never using those sticks, or any hard substance whatever, which always rub away the gums and destroy the varnish of the teeth."

Transatlantic Travel. The first steam-ship to cross the Atlantic was the *Savannah*. In 1819 she ran from Savannah to Liverpool in 25 days. But as she did not run under steam all the way, her record was imperfect. Built at New York as a sailing vessel, she was fitted with steam-power before launching, the paddle-wheels being arranged to be removed and placed on deck when not required. She was 130 feet long, 26 feet broad, 16½ feet deep. Tonnage about 380. The original logbook of the *Savannah* was presented by Capt. Moses Rogers's daughter, the late Mrs. S. S. Ward, to the National Museum, Washington, D. C., where it is now on exhibition.

Those interested in the details of this enterprise will find a full account of the logbook and of the voyage in *Harper's Monthly* for February, 1877.

The record made by the *Enterprise* in 1825 was more strenuous but was likewise imperfect. She ran from London to Calcutta by the Cape of Good Hope, a distance of 11,450 nautical miles, in 103 sailing days. She was under steam 64 days and under sail 39 days. Of course she was always in potential touch with the shore and could put into port whenever it was necessary to coal up.

Travellers' Guides. The oldest guide-book in the world is the "Description of Greece," by one Pausanias, of whom little is known save that he was born in Lydia and flourished in the second century under the Emperor Hadrian, "the prince," he declares, "who did most for the glory of God and the happiness of his subjects." Pausanias was an old man of antiquarian tastes, a pagan of simple faith, when he started out upon a journey through Greece. So much is revealed between the lines of his book. Wherever he went he kept his ears and his eyes open, and, though he was not gifted with the power of vivid observation, he heard and remembered the reckless gossip of a hundred guides. Fortified, moreover, by the study, not only of Herodotus and Thucydides but of as many local histories as he could find, he synthetized in his own person all the historical and geographical knowledge of his time. Therefore, although he was as uninspired as Baedeker, his compost of legends and itineraries has outlived the manifold shocks of time and chance. The wave of oblivion has overtaken Sappho, whom he quotes, and Menander, whose grave he reverently visits. But his own "Description of Greece" has been flung, like an old shoe, high on the beach. In 1898 a translation by J. G. Frazer, in 6 volumes, was published in London. A library might be filled with books and pamphlets based upon his researches.

The earliest guide-book written in the English language is "Instructions for Forraine Travell," a little duodecimo of 1642, by James Howell, whose "Letters" are a continual delight to all lovers of old English. It is a stately and solemn "Peregrination" of the "true Peripatetique School," which this seasoned traveller had in mind for eager and inexperienced youth.

No trivial gleam of a month's run aroad, no vision of the delight of "settling your tour as you go along," had as yet broken on the British mind. Above all, travel was a luxury strictly denied to the mob who nowadays flood Switzerland or the

Rhine. Howell's voyager is, by assumption, a young nobleman,
and he goes with an "equipage" befitting one. "He may en-
tertaine a Cooke, a Laquay, and some young youth for his Page
to parley and chide withall, whereof he shall have occasion
enough, and to get some faire lodgings to keep house of himself;
but sometimes he may frequent Ordinaries, for it will much
breake and embolden him." The concession is graceful enough;
the traveller makes these little social dips throughout his career,
but his true field lies everywhere in the Court. He passes "the
diameter of France," runs over Spain, crosses the Mediterranean
to Italy, climbs the Alps, traverses the best part of Germany,
dips into Belgium, and studies Holland; "all which may be done
completely in three years and four months, which four months
I allow for itinerary removals and journeys, and the years for
residence in places." •

Extensive preparations are necessary. The traveller must be
an educated man, and, above all, be well founded and settled
in religion, well prepared in those sacred spots "where, I say (I
presume my Traveller hath bin first an University man), beside other introductions to knowledge he hath sucked the pure
milke of true Religion and orthodoxall Truth." After religion
he must be well versed in the topography, government, and history of his own country, "for some are found to be eagles abroad
and stark buzzards at home;" and with a view to this he may run
over Camden and Daniel and the *Commonwealth* of Sir John
Smith. Add to this Latin and the use of the globes, and the
traveller's "packing-up" is complete. One thing he must not
forget. "He must always have a Diary about him when he is in
motion or journeys, to set down what either his eares heare or
his eyes meete with most remarquable in the day-time, out of
which he may raise matter of discourse at night." Nor is this
to be the whole of his literary exertion; he is to be very punctual
in writing to his friends "once a month at least" (happy rarity
of seventeenth-century posts!) "which he must do exactly, and
not in a careless perfunctory way." Lastly, he must take sufficient money. Every one of his servants, Cooke, Lackey, and
Page, "will stand him in 50*l.* a year." For his own expenses
he cannot allow himself less than 300*l.* for the same space of
time.

It is easy to smile at Howell's conception of travel, but hardly
easier than for Howell, could he rise again, to smile at ours. To
the men of the seventeenth century travel meant simply the
Grand Tour, and the Grand Tour meant an essential part of a
liberal education. The interval between the boyhood of University life and the manhood of the Inns of Court could hardly be

better spent than in studying the language and manners of the world. We have advanced far beyond the ideas of Howell's day by our discovery of the pleasure of travel, but Howell would probably plead that we have lost something of its usefulness. There is one thing more absurd than Howell's young nobleman studying the "rugged republics" of Switzerland without a thought of the Matterhorn, and that is the Alpine Clubbist stand- ing proudly on the conquered Matterhorn in self-satisfied ignor- ance of its "rugged republics."

Howell, it will be seen, was a devout Protestant. It is inter- esting, therefore, to compare his book with that of a successor, Richard Lassels, who was an uncompromising Catholic. Lassels "travelled through Italy five times," if we may take his word for it, "as tutor to several of the English nobility and gentry." His observations were copious and diligent, and were collected in the form of a book. For some reason they were not printed till 1670, after the author's death; and then at Paris. The work is professedly a guide-book and nothing else. Its full title is as follows: "The Voyage of Italy, or a Compleat Journey through Italy. In Two Parts. With the Characters of the People, and the Description of the chief Towns, Churches, Monasteries, Tombs, Libraries, Pallaces, Villa's, Gardens, Pictures, Statues, and Antiquities. As also of the Interest, Government, Riches, Force, &c., of all the Princes. With Instructions concerning Travel." The instructions are naturally something out of date; but the modern reader may extract a pretty good evening's amuse- ment from the pages of this odd little duodecimo. Not that its amusing qualities are due to any particular merit on Lassels's part. Indeed it must be confessed that he is in the main a dull, frig'd, and pedantic writer enough; and when he gets to the de- scription of a city his passion for churches and relics amounts to a monomania. But he is laughable by his very gravity, and by a certain quaint incongruity of style.—*Saturday Review,* August 21, 1869, and October 9, 1880.

Traveller's Tree (*Ravenala Madagascariensis*), a tree native to Madagascar and Réunion, whose unusual qualities have been grossly exaggerated by travellers and so given rise probably to the myth of the rain-tree (*q.v.*) of Peru. Its straight stem reaches an altitude of 30 feet, and bears on its top a number of large, long-stalked leaves, which spread vertically like a fan. The leaf has a large sheath at the base, in which water collects, often to the extent of a mouthful or more.

Treacle. It may seem difficult to connect the syrup of molasses with the poison of snakes. Yet etymologically the feat has been performed in the application of the word "treacle."

The ancients believed that the best antidote to the bite of the viper was a confection of its own flesh. The Greek word *theriac,* " of the viper," was given first to a sweetmeat so made, then to any antidote against poison, and finally to any syrup. Thus it became easily corrupted into our present word. Chaucer has the line—

Christ which that is to every harm triacle.

Milton speaks of the " sovran treacle of sound doctrine." A compound called " Venice treacle " was held to be an antidote to all poisons. " Vipers treacle yield," says Edmund Walter, in a verse which might puzzle a modern reader, yet which brings one close to the truth of the etymology.

Truck Farm. Accident is said to have suggested the truck farm. In 1847 a clerk on a Charleston (S. C.) boat chanced to speak to some friends in New York of the fresh vegetables to be had in the southern city. As it was winter, his statement was promptly challenged by one of his listeners. On his next trip north, therefore, he brought a basket of vegetables, including two boxes of strawberries. They were placed on exhibition in a shop window and attracted much attention.

In this way began the business of truck farming in the United States. Until the middle of the nineteenth century, the fruits and vegetables raised on nearly all farms were intended for home consumption or for sale in markets close at hand. To-day California fruit and vegetables go all over the world, and the northern cities live all winter on garden produce raised in Florida or the Gulf States. Many of the improved facilities now offered by the railroads are directly due to the handling of perishable agricultural products. Routes have been shortened, cars ventilated, refrigeration provided, and the number and speed of trains increased, until vegetables are now landed in good condition a thousand miles from where they were raised.

Trust. The word " trust " was not applied to capitalistic combinations and monopolies until the Standard Oil Trust was formed, on January 2, 1882. By the agreement a majority of the certificates of stocks were placed in the hands of trustees, who took full charge of all the oil-refining corporations, partnerships, and individual properties which went into the trust. The violent agitation which sprung up against trusts in 1887 and 1888 resulted in investigating committees, State and Federal anti-trust laws, and in slight changes in the forms and names of these and other combinations. Since then our greatest combinations are monopoly corporations, called companies instead of trusts, and are managed by directors instead of trustees. These companies own the plants, and therefore are much more solid and permanent than were the original "trusts," in which only a majority of stock certificates of certain concerns was held. The present form is also more difficult to reach by law. Since 1887 the word "trust" has, by popular usage, if not by general consent, become generic, and now covers any agreement, pool, combination, or consolidation of two or more naturally competing concerns, which results in a complete or partial monopoly in certain territory. It is, perhaps, fortunate that there should be a single word by which consumers can designate any monopoly combination with power to fix prices or rates; it may, however, be unfortunate that the word "trust," which has so many other legal meanings, should have been selected for this purpose.—W. HOLT, *Review of Reviews.*

Turbot. From the time of Apicius down to the present, the turbot has been highly prized as a table luxury.

A story is told of a certain great prelate who, whenever he could manage it, would pay a preliminary visit to his friends' kitchens in order to supervise the preparations for a coming feast. Once he was staying in a country villa where a new woman cook had just arrived. What was his grace's horror to find that she had cut off the fins of a fine turbot which she had prepared for boiling. Quickly recovering his presence of mind, he called for needle and thread, and, with his own dainty episcopal fingers, this great dignitary sewed the fins on the fish.

Mediæval Romans held in great respect not only the turbot but all who were able to provide it for the entertainment of their friends, inasmuch as it was difficult and expensive to secure a fine fresh one. Once on a time there was a cardinal who possessed two of these luxuries. He determined to create a sensation. He invited a score of friends to dinner. His majordomo was directed to prepare both fish for dinner, and then the butler received private instructions: in bringing in one of them, he was to let it fall as he entered the dining-room. This he did, to the dismay of the assembled guests. His Eminence alone remained calm.

"Bring in another turbot," he said quietly to the head butler.

It has been asserted that at the ancient Roman banquets the so-called turbot was often only brill. Certainly even in these days brill is frequently sold for turbot to the unwary and the ignorant. That pagan fish-mongers charged high prices for the real thing is evidenced by the pagan poets in many passages:

> Great turbots and late suppers lead
> To debt, disgrace, and abject need.

or

> Great turbots and the soup-dish led
> To shame at last and want of bread.

The finest turbot to-day are obtained from Holland, the Dutch being still the best and most industrious of fishers. Most of the turbot caught on the coast of Holland find their way to Billingsgate market in London, but very fine examples are occasionally caught in English waters by the trawlers at Brixham, Devon, and also on the Varne and Ridge Banks, between Dover and Calais. One is recorded as having been captured in Scotland which turned the scale at ninety pounds; but it is difficult to believe that the fish in question was actually a turbot, some economists holding that it must have been in reality a halibut. Examples of the true turbot of the weight of thirty pounds have more than once been captured, but the general run of these fish which find their way to market are about half that weight.

Turk, the First. According to Osmanli historians, the original Turk was a grandson of Noah. Though there were only 8 people in the Ark when it was first floated, there were 9, it is asserted, when it landed on Mount Ararat. The additional one was the eldest son of Japhet, born during the flood. His name was Turk. A descendant in the fourth generation, one Alindje-Khan, had two sons (twins), who were named Tatar-Khan and Mogul-Khan. Tatar was the father of the Turks; Mogul was the father of the Mongols.

Turks and Mongols were thus closely connected by birth, and the wars which at once broke out between them, and the reconciliations that speedily ensued, had much of the nature of family quarrels. The Turks were the more frequently triumphant, one Mongol throne after another yielding to their arms. Not till the Christian era was well advanced did the ethnological name of these children of Japhet appear in history.

Turkey. If the task of christening this fowl had been left to the first child that happened to be at hand at its introduction into Europe, most probably it would have been called the glouglou, since that is the name it gives itself. But the course of things in ornithology never runs so smoothly as that. The creature's earliest French godfathers (their heads evidently full of only one feature of the male) gave him the name of *coq d'Inde*. or "cock of India." This, observe, was in order to distinguish him from the ordinary cock of the barn-yard, which really did come from India, had they but known the truth, whereas the new arrival was a native of America. But, as in those days America passed for the continuation of Asiatic India, the unfortunate choice of name should not be imputed to individual ignorance. Later the word *coq* was suppressed, and little by little the bird became first the *dinde* and finally the *dindon*.

The English name is far less easy to explain. There is reason to believe, however, that the bird was originally confounded with

the guinea-fowl, some early specimens of which did come from
Turkey and did get their name from their father-land. When
the more careful ornithologists of the seventeenth century came
to differentiate the two species, the name " turkey " somehow
clung to its usurper, while its original owner was content with
the exclusive use of the alternative name of " Guinea-fowl."
It is thought that this decision was largely helped by the fact
that the turkey's repeated call-note may be syllabled as " Turk,
turk, turk."—*Notes and Queries*, 6, iii, 23.

The earliest known description of the turkey is found in
chapter xxxi of Oviedo's *Sumario de la Natura Historia de las
Indas* (1527). He tells us that the species had been taken from
New Spain (Mexico) to Darien and the West Indies, where it
bred in a domestic state among the Christians.

It is quite certain that the bird was established in Europe by
1530, and it is claimed that the first specimens were brought
from Mexico to Spain by Hernando Cortes in 1520. It reached
England about 1524, but there is no mention of it in French
history until June, 1570, when turkeys were served up at the
wedding-feast of Charles IX and Elizabeth of Austria.

Descendants of the parent stock were carried back across the
Atlantic, where, crossed with the original turkey, they began
the breed which has spread all over America. As showing the
relationship of the modern turkey with its aboriginal ancestry,
a domestic bird has been known to mate with its wild and migrating cousin, to the decided improvement of its kind.

Owing to the fact that the turkey has not long been domesticated, it suffers from unfortunate habits incident to captivity
and is the most difficult of all fowls to raise. Even as a home
bird it loves freedom, and for healthy development requires a
large area over which to roam in search of food. It prefers to
roost in trees, rarely seeking shelter save in the severest weather.
It can not be inbred, but must always have fresh blood from a
different stock if the offspring is to develop the highest type of
fowl.

Historically the bird is specially interesting to Americans.
When Congress or certain individual members of it, during the
troublous years of 1776–1782, were intermittently considering
the question of a great seal for the revolted colonies, Franklin
suggested first the rattle-snake and then the turkey as emblematic
animals to be carved on the seal. Both, he urged, were indigenous to the soil,—Americans from head to tail. Congress
in 1782 decided upon the bald-headed eagle, greatly to
Franklin's chagrin. One comfort, however, he found. The
counterfeit presentments of the imperial bird first exhibited on

seals and coins were universally execrated. People complained that it looked more like a turkey than an eagle, and a drunken turkey at that. " I am not displeased," wrote Franklin to the *Society of the Cincinnati,* "that the figure is not known as a bald eagle, but looks more like a turkey. For, in truth, the turkey is in comparison a much more respectable bird, and withal a true native of America. He is besides (though a little vain and silly, it is true, but not the worse emblem for that) a bird of courage, and would not hesitate to attack a grenadier of the British Guards, who should presume to enter his farm-yard with a red coat on." See WALSH, *Handybook of Literary Curiosities.*

In New York City old Democratic war-horses still remember the time when a turkey with " stuffing " was the regular Christmas gift from local tavern-keepers to the police captain of the precinct. The stuffing consisted of gold and silver and even copper coins, lavishly contributed by all who sought to curry favor. There is a famous story of how one Christmas turkey in the Tenth ward wrought ruin to every one concerned. It cost an errand-boy a week's salary, a police captain his command, and the once famous Harry Hill his dance-hall on Houston Street and incidentally his fortune. The boy took the bird to the station-house, and was so overawed with the majesty and greatness of the ward man who received it that he forgot to collect $2.85, the price of the fowl at 18 cents a pound. When the bird was cleaned and singed and ready, it was sent out among the friends of the captain of the precinct for its stuffing.

The captain was very popular in his precinct and people just fought for a chance to stuff his Christmas bird. Everybody had a chance at it—some had several chances.

Among these was Harry Hill. The bird was put before him three times. The last time it needed only $5 to bring the value of its stuffing up to $1000. Harry gave his masonic pin a twist, and, looking the bird square in the face, said, " I've got a bird of my own this year to stuff, and my stock of stuffing just now is low."

From that time on, the ward men never failed to see Harry's waiters when they sold whisky in cups and called it tea. The fight was on. It ended in the captain of the precinct being sent up " among the goats " in Harlem, and Harry Hill going into bankruptcy. The practice of stuffing a bird for the captain at Christmas ended here, too.

To this day Indians use a turkey's wing to fan their fires withal, a custom which is explained on traditionary grounds by *The Red Man.*

Many years ago the fire of the world was nearly extinguished: this happened just at the beginning of the winter season. The birds of the air were filled with anxiety, for their intuition told them they would need heat to keep them warm through the winter.

A bird council was held, and it was decided that birds which could fly the highest should soar into the air and see if they could find a spark of fire anywhere. The efforts of the eagle, lark, and raven were in vain. The honor was left to the little brown sparrow, who spied a spark of fire in the hollow of an old stump in the heart of a deep forest.

The birds flocked around the stump and tried to decide who should pick the spark out. But all their efforts were in vain; to their dismay they saw the spark growing smaller and fainter. The turkey then volunteered to keep the tiny coal alive by fanning it with his wings. Day after day the turkey kept fanning; the heat became greater each day, until the feathers were singed off the turkey's head. If one notices carefully he will see lumps on the head of a turkey that appear as blisters.

It is believed that the turkey was so badly burned that all turkeys since have had bald heads and wear the blisters as a memento of the bravery of the turkey. The faithful turkey lost his beautiful feathers, but he gave back fire to the world; so in his honor and as a memorial of his faithfulness the Indian uses turkey-wings to make his fire burn.

Turkey-walk. This is a favorite diversion of the Southern negroes, especially in the Virginias and the Carolinas. It is usually practised in Christmas week. Volunteers, whose entrance fee will make up a fair price for the bird, are blindfolded, and, thus hampered, try to walk as near a certain stake as possible. The walker who gets nearest to the stake wins the bird. When a number of turkeys have been won in this fun-provoking fashion, they are handed over to a cook, and a supper, eaten by all the participants, winds up the affair.

Out in front of an isolated country store is the favorite place for a turkey-walk. Every afternoon during Christmas week such festivals are likely to occur. A certain number of pegs are prepared. Each walker, after vainly trying to approach the goal. sticks his peg in the earth where he stops. After the volunteer is blindfolded, he is turned around three times, then told to go straight for the stake. Invariably he blunders exactly in the opposite direction, eliciting shouts of laughter from the circle of bystanders.

Turnspit. This was usually a dog, a cur of low degree, employed in old days in turning the spit whereon meat was roasted before an open fire.

Dr. Cains of Cambridge, quoted in TOPSELL: "Four-Footed Beasts" (1607), speaks a kindly word for the turnspit and testifies to his culinary skill: "There is comprehended under the curres of the coarsest kinde, a certain dog in kitchen service excellent; for when any meat is to be roasted, they go into the wheel, which by turning round about with the weight of their bodies, so diligently look to their business, that no drudge or scullion can do the feat more cunningly."

The method of teaching the dog to turn the spit, or broach, as it was sometimes called, was more summary than humane. " The dog was put in a wheel, and a burning coal with him; he could not stop without burning his legs, and so was kept upon the full gallop. These dogs were by no means fond of their profession; it was, indeed, hard work to run in a wheel for two or three hours, turning a piece of meat which was twice their own weight " (Hone: *Every-Day Book,* i, 1573–1574).

In the larger private houses and in the inns two or more dogs were ofttimes employed, as the work would be too much for one turnspit to attend to. In these cases the dogs used to alternate in their duties in the wheel. Buffon relates that two turnspits were employed in the kitchen of the Duc de Lianfort, at Paris, taking their turns every other day to go into the wheel. One of them, in a fit of laziness, hid itself on a day when it should have worked; so the other was forced to do the work instead. When the meat was roasted, the one that had been compelled to work out of its turn began to bark and wag its tail until it induced the scullions to follow it, then leading them to a garret, and dislodging the skulker from beneath a bed, it attacked and killed its too lazy fellow-worker.

A somewhat similar circumstance occurred at the Jesuit's College of La Flèche. One day the cook, having prepared a piece of meat for roasting, looked for the dog whose turn it was to work the wheel for that day, but not being able to find it he attempted to employ the one whose turn it was to be off duty. The dog resisted, bit the cook, and ran away. The man, with whom the dog was a great favorite, was much astonished at its ferocity. The wound being severe and bleeding freely, he went to the surgeon of the college to have it dressed. In the meantime the dog ran into the garden, found the other whose turn it was to work the spit while the fire did the rest, and drove it into the kitchen. The deserter, seeing no opportunity of shirking its day's labor, went into the wheel of its own accord and began to work.

Turnspits frequently figure in the old collections of anecdotes. For instance, it is said that the captain of a man-of-war, stationed in the port of Bristol for its protection, in the last century, found that, on account of some political bias, the inhabitants did not receive him with their accustomed hospitality. So, to punish them, he sent his men ashore one night with orders to steal all the turnspit dogs they could lay their hands upon. The dogs being conveyed on board the ship and safely put away in the hold, consternation reigned in the kitchens and dining-rooms of the Bristol merchants, and roast meat rose to a premium during the few days the dogs were confined in their floating prison. The release of the dogs was duly celebrated by many dinners to the captain and his officers.

Hone's " Table-Book " quotes from John Foster a still more surprising tale. " Some turnspits were attending church on Sunday when the lesson for the day happened to be the first chapter in Ezekiel, which describes the self-moving chariots. When first the word ' wheel' was pronounced, all the curs pricked up their ears in alarm; at the second mention of the wheel, they set up a doleful howl, and when the dreaded word was uttered a third time, every one of them scampered out of church as fast as he could, with his tail between his legs."

Both Rawlinson and Wilkinson remark a resemblance in one breed of the sculptured dogs of the ancient monuments of Egypt to the turnspit; hence some idea of the shapes of this canine variety may be had from the " Plates " in their works (see Rawlinson's " Hist. Anc. Egypt," vol. i, p. 77; Wilkinson's " Anc. Egypt," vol. iii, p. 32).

Turtles. In New York, on October 18, 1911, Captain Cleveland H. Downs, of the Ward Line steamer *Saratoga,* was held in $500 bail by Magistrate Freschi, on a charge of cruelty to animals, preferred by the S. P. C. A. It was alleged that the fins or flippers of 56 large green turtles, carried as freight on his ship, had been pierced and tied to keep them from straying. Counsel for the defence claimed that turtles were not animals within the meaning of the act. The magistrate, however, declared that the turtle within the law is an animal; without the law it is more properly classified as a reptile. A singular interest attached to the case because in the year 1867, when the society was in its struggling infancy, Henry Bergh had haled a sea-captain before a magistrate on a similar charge and had been laughed out of court for his pains. (See PREVENTION OF CRUELTY TO ANIMALS.)

Twenty-three and Skiddoo. The connection of the number 23 with the slang word " skiddoo! " (imperative mood of the verb to *skiddoo,—i.e.,* to escape, to vamoose, to disappear) has been variously explained.

Theatrical authorities claim the phrase for themselves. An actor, it is said, who had fallen out of favor with the manager, would be given 18 parts to memorize in 5 weeks (18 + 5 = 23) or be dropped from the salary list.

In horse-racing circles, however, a rival claim is put forward.

The phrase is said to have originated from the number of horses entered at a certain suburban race in New York. The number of entries had been limited to twenty-two, but on this occasion twenty-three went to the post, whereupon the last entry was ordered off the field.

Circus men, again, explain that the chariot-race, the last item on the programme, is usually No. 23. During the performance the canvas-men would lie around and sleep, but when this race was in progress they were aroused by the boss canvas-man so that they might get ready for work as soon as the race was over.

Most curious of all is the explanation which attributes the origin of this jocular use of the number to the expulsion of Adam from the Garden of Eden as found related in the twenty-third verse of the third chapter of the Book of Genesis. It reads: " Therefore the Lord God sent him forth from the Garden of Eden, to till the ground from whence he was taken."

Twin Trees. Near Algona in northern Iowa there are two trees united in a curious manner. They are soft maples, and are joined, about eight feet from the ground, by a connecting link a little more than four feet long and six inches in diameter.

Peak's Island, a noted sea-side resort two miles outside of Portland, Maine, possesses another fine example. The twin-tree is a fine wide-spreading elm, perfect in all its limbs, a little over one hundred feet high. Its two trunks are substantially one at the base but they separate a few feet above the ground. About 25 feet from the roots the trunks are nearly five feet apart, and are connected by a horizontal branch-like projection. The connecting link is about a foot thick, is perfectly round, and of a uniform thickness from trunk to trunk. " The effect is as if some one had taken a log of wood, sawed it off to fit, and then forced it between the trunks. But this theory is almost impossible, for I have examined it and found that the connection is a part of the tree. It is grown from the trunks, of the same wood and bark, and also has twigs growing from its sides."— FREDERICK S. RAND, in *Illustrated America,* May 28, 1892.

Type. If we are to credit Mr. H. B. Hulbert, in *Harper's Magazine,* Korea can claim the invention of movable type. In the reign of King T'a-jong (this authority assures us) a font of metal type was cast, the first the world ever saw.

Engraving had been known for centuries in the East, and clay type was not unknown in Japan, but Korea was the first to discern the need of the more permanent and durable form of metal type. Bronze was chosen for the purpose.

" Each type was built on the principle of the arch, being cylindrically concave on the under side. The purpose of this was to secure a firmer hold upon the bed of beeswax which constituted the 'form,' technically so called. A shallow tray was filled with wax, and the type, after being firmly imbedded in it, were 'planed' in the ordinary manner. The printer, sitting cross-legged before it, applied liquid ink by means of a soft brush, after which a sheet of paper was lightly laid upon the form. A piece of felt was brushed softly across the porous paper with the right hand, and the left removed the printed page. In this way it was possible to strike off some 1500 impressions in a day."

The annals of Korea show clearly that there have been two fonts cast—one about the year 1406, and the other some two centuries later. These two fonts, or the remains of them, exist to-day. Types of the later casting are now in common use in the Korean Government printing-office, while all that remain of the older font were thrown aside as useless, and were found among a mass of débris in the corner of a ruined storehouse.

Type-setting Machine. There hangs to-day, it is said (T. P. O'Connor's *London Weekly,* December, 1911), in the office of one of the oldest printing-houses of London, a framed copy of the *Family Herald,* vol. i, No. 1, "for the week ending December 17, 1842." In the first column of the first page, the editor makes this announcement:

As the sheet you are now perusing may be justly considered a literary curiosity, being the first specimen of a publication produced entirely by machinery—types, ink, paper, and printing, necessarily involving a variety of processes, some idea of their complicated nature may be formed by the following brief description: "The types," he goes on, "were placed in their present position by Young's patent composing machine"—this then was the name of the first practical type-setter, seventy years ago—"which, after much patience, immense labor, and at an expense of several thousand pounds, has opened a new era by achieving this exceedingly delicate and complicated operation."

A picture of the first "composing machine" is shown on the first page of the *Family Herald.* In general appearance this ancient invention is said to have resembled the Mergenthaler of to-day. It had a keyboard, with an operator seated. Another operator (both are women), also seated, feeds types into the machine from the side. There is only this one copy of the *Family Herald* in existence. The old type-setting machine passed away, leaving no other record that it ever existed than this in the *Family Herald.*

Type-writer. In England in 1714, and in the United States in 1829, patents were taken out for pioneer type-writers; but nothing is definitely known about either. All that survives concerning the English patent is the inventor's name, Henry Mill, and the title of his invention,—" An Artificial Machine or Method for the Impressing or Transcribing letters, Singly or Progressively one after another as in Writing, whereby all Writing whatever may be engrossed in Paper or Parchment so Neat and Exact as not to be distinguished from Print." The American patent was isued to William A. Burt, but the records were destroyed by a fire at Washington in 1836.

In France the pioneer was X. Progrin, of Marseilles, who in 1833 patented " the typographic machine or pen," which was on the type-bar principle. Another Frenchman, Pierre Foucault, of Paris, followed in 1849 with a machine in which a series of rods tipped with type could be pushed down to emboss paper at the printed point to which they were arranged radially. At the Great Exhibition of 1851 in London this machine divided attention with a rival,—the " typograph " of William Hughes, which was also intended for embossing, though it was subsequently modified to give an impression through carbon-paper.

The first machine with a piano-forte key-board and type-bars arranged in a circle was invented by Dr. S. W. Francis, of New York, in 1857.

The modern machine was finally (1875) hit upon by two American inventors, C. L. Sholes and C. Glidden, who placed all their patents in the hands of E. Remington and Sons, gun-makers, of Ilion, New York. They have manufactured it ever since and added various improvements. Rival firms with other improvements have arisen both in this country and abroad.

U.

Unicorn. The notion of the single-horned creature in heraldry undoubtedly arose from Egyptian and Nubian sculptured monuments whereon the head of the oryx or gemsbok was represented in profile. In this way the evolution of the fabulous unicorn, a cross between a stallion and an antelope, was arrived at. The belief in the actual existence of the unicorn was universal in early times. Did not John of Herse, who made a pilgrimage to Jerusalem in 1389, assert that he had seen it? " Near the field Helyon in the Holy Land," says John, " is the river Mara, whose bitter waters Moses struck with his staff and made sweet, so that the children of Israel could drink thereof. Even now evil and unclean beasts poison it after the going down of the sun, but in the morning, after the powers of darkness have disappeared, the unicorn comes from the sea and dips its horn into the stream, and thereby expels and neutralizes the poison, so that the other animals can drink of it during the day." (Quoted in *Notes and Queries,* Series xi, iii, 273.) Doubts began to arise later. Gwillim, in his " display of Heraldry " (6th ed., 1724, p. 162), tells us that the unicorn " hath his name of his one horn on his forehead. There is another beast, of a huge strength and greatness, which hath but one horn, but that is growing in his snout, whence he is called Rinoceros, and both are named Monoceros or one-horned. It hath been much questioned among naturalists, which it is that is properly called the unicorn. And some have made doubt whether there be any such beast as this or no. But the great esteem of his horn (in many places to be seen) may take away that useless scruple." On the authority of Farnesius, Gwillim adds that " the unicorn is never taken alive; and the reason being demanded, it is answered that the greatness of his mind is such that he chooseth rather to die than to be taken alive." Topsell, in his " Four-footed Beasts," supplies further information. The unicorn, he says, is an enemy of the lions," wherefore, as soon as a lion sees an unicorn, he runneth to a tree for succor, so that when the unicorn maketh force against him, he may not only avoid his horn but also destroy him, for the unicorn in the swiftness of his course runneth against the tree, wherein his sharp horn sticketh fast: then when the lion seeth the unicorn fastened by the horn, without all danger he falleth upon him and killeth him."

It was this fabled prowess of the unicorn and his invincible courage which led to his adoption by James III as the supporter of the royal arms of Scotland, as may be seen upon his gold coins, the unicorn and the half unicorn, struck in 1486. James IV, his successor, used as supporters two silver unicorns royally gorged and chained or, which figure also in the signet of his granddaughter Mary, Queen of Scots. When James VI (James I of England) became the first Stuart king of Great Britain, he assumed as his supporters a golden lion, representing England, on the dexter, and a silver unicorn, representing Scotland, on the sinister side of his shield. The former racial animosity of England and Scotland was typified in the popular interpretation put upon the two animals. Thus, Spenser:

> Like as lion, whose imperial power
> A proud rebellious unicorn defies.
> *Faery Queen*, ii, 5.

Uniform. King George V, of England, has the right to wear more than a hundred military and naval uniforms. But in variety and splendor of official wardrobe he and all other sovereigns past and present are eclipsed by the German Kaiser. In the latter's suite of rooms, lined with cupboards and stacked with tin cases, are nearly two hundred complete uniforms. A large proportion of these consists of regimentals of the German army, but among the remainder are British, Italian, Spanish, Greek, Dutch, Swedish, Russian, and Turkish trappings. Indeed the only European army of which the emperor is not a colonel is that of France. The reason of this omission must be found in the animosity that still lingers in French bosoms as a reminder of the Franco-Prussian war, and is not due to any imperial prejudice against republican gold lace, for William frequently wears the neat uniform of the Swiss Guards, and he has retained his Portuguese regimentals even since the transformation of Manuel's kingdom into a commonwealth.

This huge collection of costly paraphernalia has to be kept absolutely up to date and follows every change of detail in cut and arrangement. If some foreign war office decides that a button must be added or two subtracted, such addition or subtraction is duly noted by the imperial tailors. The task of keeping this immense outfit in spotless condition and ever-ready trim is a constant source of worry and trouble. The discovery of a bomb in the Kaiserhoff would occasion no greater dismay than the advent of a moth in the robe-rooms. A small army of official tailors and servants is ever at work, ironing, brushing, and polishing.

When the German Emperor travels on a state visit, he is often accompanied by twoscore tin trunks containing uniforms suited to every emergency, all under charge of a chosen staff of valets, each of whom is responsible for some particular item of attire. Helmets, cocked hats, and undress caps are one man's care, sword, belts, and trappings are another's, while a third devotes himself to the preserving and polishing of boots and shoes.

V.

Vanderbilt Cup. A trophy famous in automobile annals. Designed by Tiffany, it is classical in form, massive in size, and simple in lines. Its design was suggested by some vessels found among the treasures of Boscoreale, dating back as far as 79 A.D. Including the ebony base, it stands about 31 inches in height. The bowl contains 481 ounces of sterling silver, with a capacity of ten and a half gallons.

On one side of the cup appears an excellent likeness of the donor, W. K. Vanderbilt, Jr., as he appeared in early manhood in his Mercedes. On the other side is the inscription: "Challenge Cup, presented by William K. Vanderbilt, Jr., to the American Automobile Association, under deed of gift, to be raced for yearly by cars under 1000 kilos. Won by——."

The top of the cup is surmounted by laurel wreaths, symbolic of victory, richly carved in bold relief.

The first contest took place on October 8, 1904, on a circuit in Nassau County. There were sixteen contestants, made up of teams representing the United States, France, Germany, and Italy. It was won by George Heath, an American amateur, entered as a member of the French team. Using a 90-horse-power Panhard car, he covered 284 miles at an average speed of 52 miles an hour. Test, however, in another Panhard, did several laps at a much faster rate, skirting one at a speed of 71 miles, sensational indeed for those days. America came in third, with Herbert Lytle in a Pope-Toledo. The cup, therefore, passed over to France.

The second Vanderbilt was run in October, 1905. America, France, and Italy were represented by 5 cars each, Germany by only 4. France triumphed again, Hemery, in a Darracq, driving in a winner at an average speed of 61½ miles. In 1906 France scored its third triumph. The exciting finish, with its battle between Lancia, in the Fiat, and Wagner, in a Darracq, will never be forgotten by the thousands who witnessed it. These two drivers, together with Duray and Jenatzy, had been going with only a few seconds difference in their elapsed times for some laps. In the tenth and last Wagner took the lead, only to meet with tire troubles a couple of minutes later.

There was a frenzy of excitement; the crowds tore down the wire fences and swarmed over the course, and it seemed as if they could not avoid being mowed down by the fast machines. Down the stretch came Lancia, snorting across the tape, the first to finish the distance. Wagner, however, was going again, and as he had started several minutes behind Lancia he still had a chance to win on elapsed time. Every one wondered if he would cross the tape before it was too late. He did—in a whirlwind finish, too! Wagner's speed was about sixty-three miles an hour for the 297 miles. Joe Tracy, in an American Locomobile, scored the fastest lap of the event.

There was no cup race in 1907, the fourth taking place on October 24, 1908, with drivers competing as individuals and not as teams. The memorable feature of this contest was that it restored the cup to America, George Robertson, in the 90-horse-power Locomobile, being the victor. His average speed was 64.3 miles an hour, the fastest ever yet made in a cup-race. In the 1909 event, as in the 1908, contestants competed as individuals. Harry F. Grant, for America, came out victor over a field of 15 starters.

Vice-president of the United States. In the original scheme for the election of president and vice-president of the United States, it was expected that each member of the electoral college (*q.v.*) would vote for two candidates, without naming them as president or vice-president. The candidate who had most votes (allowing for the intervention of the House of Representatives in certain cases) was president; he who came next was vice-president. This implies a much higher notion of the vice-president's office than prevailed afterward. But it certainly is not too high a notion, inasmuch as the vice-president is always a possible president. Within a century and a quarter after the establishment of the machinery of the electoral college, no less than five vice-presidents have so risen, owing to the death of the presidential incumbent.

The first instance was that of John Tyler, who in 1840 was the tail of the ticket known in the popular refrain as "Tippecanoe and Tyler too," Tippecanoe being General William H. Harrison, who in 1811 had won the battle of Tippecanoe over the Indian tribes led by Tecumseh. Harrison became president March 4, 1840, took cold at the inauguration ceremonies, and died on April 4, exactly a month after he was sworn in. Zachary Taylor died fifteen months after his election, and was followed, July 9, 1850, by Vice-president Millard Fillmore. Harrison and Taylor were the only two presidents who succumbed, while in office, to natural causes. In the three other cases of vice-presidents succeeding their chiefs, an assassin's bullet created the vacancy. Abraham Lincoln, murdered by J. Wilkes Booth, April 14, 1865, made way for Andrew Johnson; James A. Garfield, killed by Charles T. Guiteau, July 2, 1881, was succeeded by Chester Alan Arthur; William McKinley, shot by Czolgosz in September, 1901, left the way open for Theodore Roosevelt.

Only two of these accidental presidents ever received a renomination, Millard Fillmore and Theodore Roosevelt; but the compliment to Fillmore was not extended (1856) until after an interregnum had been filled by Franklin Pierce, and Fillmore was defeated, while Roosevelt was elected to succeed himself. John Adams, Jefferson, Van Buren, and Roosevelt are the only instances of successful candidates for the presidency who had previously been vice-president.

As the vice-president can never vote in the Senate except when the members are evenly divided, he seldom exercises the privilege under present conditions. Yet in the First Congress (1789–91) John Adams, the first vice-president, gave his casting vote 22 times.

At that time the Senate was small. Only 11 States were represented in Congress when it met in New York in April, 1789, for North Carolina did not ratify the constitution until November 21, 1789, nor did Rhode Island until May 29, 1790. Neither of these States was represented in Senate or House until 1790, and then the membership of the Senate was only 26. Manifestly tie votes would take place among this small number oftener than they did when the membership was largely augmented. As the chief work of the First Congress was to shape the framework of the government, Vice-president Adams had almost as large an influence in national affairs in those years as had President Washington.

Vice-president Calhoun, in order to wreak revenge on Jackson and Van Buren, gave the casting vote against Van Buren as minister to England, early in 1832, and Van Buren, who was on duty in England at the time, was compelled to return home. Jackson, however, promptly countered on his Democratic and Whig enemies by placing Van Buren on the second end of the ticket with himself in that year, and their overwhelming majority at the polls was Jackson's notification that Van Buren was to succeed him in the White House, and he did this in 1836. Vice-president Dallas, in 1846, gave his casting vote twice on the Walker tariff bill and thus placed it on the statute book.

In 1910 Vice-president Sherman broke ties in the Senate which took place on three successive roll-calls. His casting vote saved the ship-subsidy bill in that chamber. This is the first time in the entire history of the government in which three ties have taken place in succession in the Senate.

Mr. Sherman's immediate predecessor, Vice-president Fairbanks, never voted, nor did Vice-president Roosevelt; but Vice-president Hobart did once, though on a rather unimportant detail.

Vienna Rolls. According to an Austrian tradition, the crescent shape of the appetizing rolls that are a specialty with Vienna bakers are a reminiscence of the siege of that city by the Turks under Solyman the Magnificent.

It was on September 27, 1529, that the mighty host appeared before the walls of Vienna. Solyman's first efforts were to make an entrance into the city by means of tunnels. The cleverness of the Turkish engineers and the countless workers at their command made the task a swift and noiseless one.

Some Vienna bakers were at work one night (so runs the story) in a cellar making bread for a garrison. During a pause in their conversation, one of the bakers happened to hear the muffled sound of digging. It seemed to come from a spot not far beyond one of the cellar walls.

Guessing at once that the enemy were tunneling a way into the city, the bakers rushed out and gave the alarm. The garrison, aroused, was able to baffle Solyman's plan.

The Sultan, failing at strategy, next tried force. He hurled his army against the city in one fierce assault after another. For four days the Viennese fought on, repulsing every attack with terrific loss to the Turks.

On the fifth day (October 14) Solyman gave up the attempt. He withdrew sullenly, leaving 80,000 dead Turks on the field.

Vienna was saved. And not only Vienna, but Europe. Vienna had been Europe's barrier against the Turks' farther advance. The barrier had held firm. The northern limit of Europe's Turkish raids was reached.

In later years, Vienna was again besieged by the Moslems and she again beat them off. The high tide of such invasion had come and receded. Europe at large was now forever secure from this long-dreaded foe.

In the moment of victory, according to the account, the bakers who had given the alarm were not forgotten. To commemorate the event, they and their descendants henceforth moulded their rolls into the shape of a crescent, the sacred emblem of Turkey.

Villages, Curious. The longest village in the world is probably Kempton, near Bradford, England. It straggles along a single road for seven miles.

Villages with but a single inhabitant are not unknown in England. Skiddaw, in Cumberland, is an example. The single villager complains bitterly because he cannot vote—there being

no overseer to prepare a voters' list, and no church or other public
building on which to publish one, as the law requires. The lonely
rate-payer in a Northumberland village has declined to contribute
money to maintain the roads, remarking that the one he has is
quite good enough for its use.

In the Isle of Ely is a little parish with about a dozen inhabitants that has no rates, as there are no roads or public institutions of any kind and consequently no expenses.

The village of Buckland-in-the-Moor enjoys many claims to
distinction. It has no public house, no policeman, no physician,
no clergyman and no pauper. Its entire population numbers less
than one hundred. It entirely belongs to the Rev. W. P. Bastard,
who lives at Buckland Court and who, in 1911, celebrated his
golden wedding by entertaining his tenants. Time was when the
" big house " was looked upon as comprising half the population.
All the old inhabitants of Buckland are pensioned by the owner
of the estate.

One English village consists entirely of old railway carriages,
even the chapel being composed of four-horse trucks. Another
village, with a population of 1100 and taxed at the valuation
of $8000, has neither school, church, nor other public building,
the only thing of the sort being a letter-box on a pillar.

Virgin Wives. According to tradition, the Abbey Church
of Chester, England, was founded about the year 660, by Wul-
pherus, King of the Mercians, as a nunnery for his daughter
Saint Werburgh, who took the veil after being for three years
a wife only in name to her husband Ceolredus. In this continent
habit she imitated her aunt Ethelreda. The latter was the
daughter of Alfred the Great and the wife of Ethelred, Earl
of Mercia. After the birth of her first child, she separated from
her husband, and, like an Amazon of old, determined on a life
of chastity and deeds of arms. She kept on the best terms with
her husband; they united in acts of piety and charity; restored
cities, founded abbeys, and removed the bones of saints. She
became so celebrated for her valor that the effeminate titles of
lady or queen were deemed unworthy of her: she received, in
addition, those of lord and king (Ingulphi. Hist. 871).

Hilarion de Coste, in " Eloges des Dames Illustres," gives an
account of Isabella Gonzaga, wife of the Duke of Urbino, who
was still more immaculate. " She was one of those," says
de Coste, " of whom the apostle speaks, who are married as
though they were not. For either through the tenderness of her
age, or through mere innocence, she passed the first two years of
her marriage in such a great ignorance of the sacrament in
which she was engaged, that she imagined all the other married

women were like her. But whether age taught her, or whether the free conversation she, as a married woman, had with the ladies who were also married, acquainted her with some particulars, unknown to her before, the mist she had before her eyes vanished away."

Volcanic Islands. Surely the ancient legends about islands appearing only to disappear are explained by the fact that within the modern era islands have been cast up by volcanic action from the depths of the sea, and after having supported a population for years or centuries have disappeared again as suddenly as they arose.

The most famous and the earliest of these legends relates to the island of Atlantis. According to numerous classical authorities (Plato in his Timæus being the earliest and the most famous of all) the Greeks in some very remote past were called upon to resist a terrible invasion from a people that had suddenly emerged, as it were, from the Atlantic Ocean. They came from the hitherto unknown island of Atlantis, which lay northwest of Africa on a line with the Pillars of Hercules, or what we now call the Straits of Gibraltar. They claimed that they were of very ancient origin and that their island had been a powerful kingdom since nine thousand years before the death of Solon. They overran the lands which bordered on the Mediterranean. Athens alone withstood them with success.

Then, suddenly, the island disappeared under the waves during a terrible upheaval which lasted only a day and a night. Homer, Hesiod, Strabo, and Pliny, not to speak of Tertullian and the early fathers, have preserved various traditions referring to this semi-mythical island, and certain coincidences seem to point to the fact that its existence was not all a myth.

We know that the earliest inhabitants of the Mediterranean coasts, the Carthaginians, the Phœnicians, and the Greeks themselves, had extended their voyages beyond the Pillars of Hercules to a westward island, or to westward islands which appear and reappear under the names of the Fortunate Islands, the Elysian Islands, and the Hesperides. All of these enjoyed an extraordinary degree of civilization, if we are to credit these pioneer investigators, but were cut off by some great cataclysm at the height of their splendor.

The most famous disappearing island in the middle ages was the island of St. Brendan. This saint was a genuine Irish worthy who flourished about A.D. 484–578. He is the hero of a legend that is largely mythical but may have a basis of fact. Brendan is said to have sailed in search of a fabled paradise with a company of monks, the number being variously given at from 18 to 250, and to have landed on an island in mid-ocean.

St. Brendan's island was said to be visible at times from the western coast of Ireland, but it always disappeared when expeditions were sent out to reach it. The Spaniards and Portuguese, who located it in the neighborhood of the Canary or Madeira islands, agreed that it might sometimes be lighted upon by accident, but that when sought for it could not be found.

When a certain king of Portugal ceded the Canary Islands to the Castilian crown, the treaty is said to have included the island of St. Brendan, which was described as the island that has not yet been found.

Many islands of more modern fame have this disappearing habit,—Expedition Island, for instance. Maps used to show this bit of territory lying on the northwest corner of Australia about 22 miles west from the mainland. Travellers praised it for its beauty. Geographers gave its dimensions as 13 miles long by 1 to 2 broad.

The Swedish trader, Laemstrom, visited it early in the spring of 1892, and the Dutch naturalists of the Thignig gathered rare botanical specimens and collected many hundred sets of eggs, to say nothing of the many other objects of natural history, two years later. But a vessel sailing quite recently in those parts discovered that the island was no more.

The captain ordered that soundings be made. All around thousands of feet of water were found. Finally, observing that there were no signs of breakers on the former site of the island, he ordered his men to sail directly across where the island had formerly been. Soundings were again taken, which resulted in finding that the island had only sunk to a depth of forty-eight feet below the surface. It was one of the largest islands on the Australian coast.

Two centuries ago the world was startled by the total destruction of the island of Torca in the Indian Ocean. Up to June 4, 1693, it had been thickly populated and in a high state of cultivation. Early that morning the volcano, which had long been recognized as a standing menace, began to rumble in an alarming manner and to throw out more fire and lava than was usual.

This continued to increase for several days, till at last the whole mountain ridge, extending across the western portion of the island, appeared as a solid sheet of fire, and gradually sank into the earth. Four days after the sinking of the mountain was first observed the entire ridge had disappeared, leaving a gigantic lake of boiling lava in its stead.

This lake began gradually to encroach upon the valleys and cultivated portions of the island, and quickly consumed the whole

western side. Hundreds of people fled in boats to Amboy during
the early part of July, and others to a village on the east coast,
Hislo, the largest town on the island, having been destroyed during the early days of the eruption.

On July 12 all that portion of Torca west of Caraca Creek
(the only stream on the island) had entirely disappeared, a restless lake of billowy flames rolling over what had but a few weeks
before been fertile fields. On July 18, 1693, when it was apparent even to the most stout-hearted that the whole island was
doomed, the remaining islanders were hurried onto some ships
sent from Amboy for that purpose.

The strange story of Bogoslof and Grewingk, islands of the
Aleutian group west of Unalaska, covers more than a century.
In 1778 Captain Cook, the English navigator, sailed directly
over the place they now occupy, and there was nothing there but
sea. On May 1, 1796, Admiral Bogoslof, a Russian, saw something happen. A great darkness fell upon the Aleutian chain,
and in the midst of it a mighty fire rose out of the ocean with
a terrific roaring sound. Stones were hurled as far as Unmak,
thirty miles distant, where severe earthquakes were felt. At
sunrise on the following day the quakes ceased, and the flames
diminished. The mists cleared away, and it was seen that a new
island, still smoking, had made its appearance, black in color,
and in shape like a pointed cup.

The island grew steadily both in height and circumference,
until at length it was three miles around and nearly five hundred
feet high. It kept on smoking, and the sea in its vicinity seemed
to be boiling hot. Nobody dared to approach it, however, and
some venturesome sea-lion hunters who landed upon the rock
eight years later, in 1804, found the ground so warm that they
could not walk upon it. It then was observed that there were
many small craters, from which quantities of stones were being
thrown. Bogoslof (as the Russians called the rock) is in much
the same condition to-day as in 1804, except that it has cooled
off somewhat and has diminished in size, owing to the disintegrating action of the elements. It now is not more than two-thirds
its original height; but volumes of steam still are given off
from fissures in its sides.

In the summer of 1883 there was another convulsion, and
shrouded in steam and fog another volcanic island was born,
half a mile away. It was first seen by Captain Matthew Turner,
on September 27 in that year, and was active in eruption, throwing out masses of lava and ashes, and emitting volumes of smoke
and steam from the apex and numerous fissures. Thus came
into being the island of Grewingk, or New Bogoslof, which for
a long time was connected with old Bogoslof by a sort of isthmus

of sand. The first landing upon it was made in May, 1884, by the officers of the revenue steamer *Corwin*. It was found to be about eight hundred feet high, though since that time it has shrunk to less than seven hundred feet.

Amid the most fearful rumblings, explosions, and eruptions, another island was born to the Bogoslof group about March 10, 1909. For ten days the natives on the other islands within a radius of 100 miles had been aware that the earth was in a most violent mood, and for days preceding the appearance of the new land the craters on the Bogoslofs were belching fire and throwing out ashes and sand.

Capt. R. B. McKay, who brought the news to San Francisco, reached Unalaska on March 12 and thus described the phenomenon:

" They told me the island must have been born about March 10, two days prior to my arrival, for suddenly the rumblings ceased and the fire from the eruption on Bogoslof Island ended. Beginning about March 1 the white men told me there was a series of rumblings which became more pronounced every day. In a few days these rumblings were accentuated by occasional loud explosions, which increased in violence and frequency as the days went by. Then either old or new Bogoslof burst out in flames and the reflection of the fire was visible in the sky at night-time and could be seen from the high points near Unalaska.

" The marshal, desiring to know what was occurring to the westward, sent Indians off to see what had occurred. They returned and said they would not go near the place, as there was fire on Bogoslof and a new island was visible to them."

In 1867 a new shoal was discovered in the group of the Tonga, or Friendly Islands. In 1877 smoke was seen over the shoal. In 1885 the shoal had become a volcanic island, more than two miles long and 240 feet high, and a fierce eruption was taking place within it. In 1886 the island had begun to shrink in dimensions, although the next year its highest point was 325 feet above sea level. In 1889 its height had diminished one-half, and the ocean close around it was more than a mile deep. In 1892 the island rose only about 26 feet above sea level, and, finally, in 1898, under the action of the waves, its complete disappearance was reported.

In June, 1811, an island rose from the sea about half a league westward from the island of Saint Michael, in the Azores. This island was volcanic, and has since disappeared. It was named Sabrina by the commander of a British war-vessel of that name, who witnessed the emergence of the island from the sea.

W.

Water-clock or Clepsydra. To count the time taken by any liquid in falling or dripping through a narrow orifice is to measure time itself, provided the liquid flows equably. Hence the clockless ancients invented what they called the clepsydra, which may be modernized into " water-clock."

If there be a small hole in the bottom of a tin pot or other vessel, water will not flow with uniform speed out of the hole; when nearly full of water the flow will be swifter than when only half full, because of the greater pressure or head of water. The Egyptian, Ctesibius, bore this truth in mind when he constructed his clepsydra two thousand years ago. He made a cylindrical vessel or tube, with an orifice at the lower end; he ascertained how much water would flow out in exactly an hour, and made a mark to denote this; he then tried a quantity sufficient for two hours, and this furnished him with another mark; and so he went on, adding and adding in quantity, until he had enough for a whole day. His tube was by this means graduated like our modern thermometers, but with this difference—that thermometer graduations are equidistant, whereas those of the clepsydra were closer together in the lower than in the upper part of the tube, owing to the varying pressure of the head of water. This Egyptian is credited with the construction of a clepsydra presenting many ingenious features. Water flowed down a pipe into a barrel, and filled it in exactly one day; the water was pressed by a piston through a siphon into a kind of water-meter, which slowly rotated as the water flowed away; the descent of the piston lowered a little figure of a man holding out a staff horizontally; a cylinder, having graduated lines on its surface, was made to rotate very slowly by a train of wheels connected with the meter; and the staff of the figure pointed, not only to the hour of the day, but to the day of the year. If Ctesibius really did this, he must have been a singularly clever fellow.

Whether to believe all that the ancients tell us on this matter we do not know; but if so, then there were clepsydræ which marked the age of the moon, and the position of the sun in the ecliptic, and sounded a trumpet, and imitated thunder and lightning, and threw stones and other missiles. It was by means of a clepsydra that Julius Cæsar found that the summer nights in Britain are not the same in length as those in Italy— a fact now known to be due to difference of latitude. The clepsydra appears to have been in use throughout the Middle

Ages, in some or other of the countries of Europe; and it lingered in use in France and Italy down to the sixteenth century. Some of them were plain tin tubes; some were hollow cups which, floating in water, became filled through a small orifice in a definite space of time, and then sank. When the clepsydra was introduced into Greece from Egypt, and then into Rome (the Hindoos knew about it five centuries before Ctesibius), one was considered sufficient for each town, and was placed in the market square, or some open spot; it was guarded by a civic functionary, who filled it with water at stated intervals. The nobles and wealthy cits sent their servants to ascertain the hour of the day by an inspection of the clepsydra; while the humbler inhabitants received the information by the sound of a horn, blown by the clepsydra attendant to denote the hour for changing the guard. Cicero relates that the length of the speeches made by senators and advocates was regulated by clepsydræ kept in the senate and the courts of justice. Rival speakers were very watchful of each other in this matter, lest either one should get a little more water-time than the other. In order that no fraud or deceit might be practised, an officer was appointed to distribute the water equally to both parties; and if a speaker were at all interrupted he would stop the flowing of the water during the interruption, in order that every bit of his allotted time might be utilized. If a speaker did not quite exhaust his quota, a singular privilege was allowed; he might give the water that remained in his clepsydra to another speaker, who was thus enabled to obtain a longer water-time for his speech than would otherwise have been at his command.—*All the Year Round,* October 18, 1873.

Water, Curiosities of. It is impossible to throw a few drops of water on a red-hot stove. The water can never touch the stove at all. What is seen is a few drops rolling rapidly over the surface, gradually getting smaller until they disappear. If the drops are on a perfectly level place, one can see under them to the other side of the room, thus proving that they are not in contact with the stove itself.

What actually happens is that the bottom of the drop changes at once to steam or vapor on coming close to the hot surface, and this vapor is supplied by the drop as it gradually goes away. So the drop rests on a cushion of vapor until it is entirely dissipated. This state of water is known as the spheroidal state, and is of interest simply on account of its peculiarity and seemingly paradoxical behavior.

The reason why the drop is not immediately evaporated or changed to steam is also very interesting. The water vapor that intervenes between its under surface and the red-hot stove is a very bad conductor of heat, and consequently the full intensity of the heat cannot get to the water itself, only the amount transmitted through the vapor being available for this purpose.

'Tis a trite saying about water, that constant dripping will wear away a stone.

The force of a single drop falling from a height is not great in itself, but the results of this tiny blow when it is many times repeated are astounding, even though we do know that the stone will, in time, yield to their power.

There was a form of torture known to mediæval days as the "ordeal of dropping water," but the term conveys to us little idea of the horrible suffering which this punishment is said to inflict.

There is a story of one poor wretch who was bound with his back to a stone wall and had a stream of water "of the bigness of a man's finger" directed onto his bare head, the water falling from a height of about eighteen feet. The receptacle from which this apparently harmless stream trickled was a barrel holding only twenty-odd gallons, but before the water was more than half run out the man was dead, with a hole in his skull which exposed the brain.

By way of experiment, an American, who is described as "a sport and an acrobat," made a wager in Vienna with an athlete that the latter could not endure the falling of a pint of water on his hand, drop by drop, in one spot, from a height of only three feet.

The athlete had an enormous hand, lined with skin almost as thick and tough as cowhide, and all the spectators pronounced the bet a foolish one as far as the American was concerned.

But when about three hundred drops had fallen there was a change of sentiment. The athlete did not say a word, but it was very apparent from the flush on his face and his uneasy manner that he was suffering great pain. At the four hundred and twentieth drop he gave up, declaring that he could no longer endure the torture.

The palm of his hand was then badly swollen and rapidly inflaming, and in one spot the skin had broken, exposing the raw flesh beneath.

Water-shoes. A curious invention for walking upon the water is noticed in "The Wonders of the Universe, or Curiosities of Nature and Art" (London, 1824, p. 47). The inventor, one Bader, is described as "counsellor of mines" at Munich, in Bavaria. The first public experiment made with his machine (called an aquatic sledge) was on August 29, 1810, before the royal family at Nymphenberg. This consisted of two hollow canoes or pontoons, 8 feet long, made of sheet-copper, closed on all sides, joined to each other in parallel directions at a distance of 6 feet by a light wooden frame. "Thus joined they support a seat resembling an arm-chair, in which the rider is seated, and impels and steers the sledge by treading two large pedals before him. Each of these pedals is connected with a paddle fixed perpendicularly in the intervals between the two pontoons. In front of the seat stands a small table, on which he may read, write, draw, or eat and drink. . . . This vehicle is far safer than a common boat, the centre of gravity being constantly in the middle of a very broad base, circumstance which renders upsetting, even in the heaviest gale, absolutely impossible. It is, moreover, so contrived that it may be taken to pieces in a few minutes, packed in a box, and put together in a very short time."

At an exhibition of life-saving inventions held in the English Channel during the last decade of the nineteenth century, there was exhibited a life-boat consisting mainly of collapsible pontoons which in case of need were to be inflated with bellows. The inventor, George Parratt, also exhibited a device for walking in the sea. *Notes and Queries* (xi, 3, 77) describes it as an india-rubber boat, about 4 feet long by 2 feet wide in the middle, with two india-rubber stockings attached to the bottom. "The inventor's assistant got into this boat with his legs in the stockings, closed the top covering round his waist, and then went down the perpendicular ladder lashed to the ship's side. Either before going down or directly he got into the water, he proceeded to inflate the apparatus through a tube. He had with him a little double paddle, with which he was intended to propel himself. The tube, however, got loose or otherwise out of order, and the boat began to fill and sink. Fortunately, there was a very handy man on board, with little more than a pair of old trousers on; he hurried down the ladder, and caught the hand of the sinking assistant."

The London *Globe* of October 21, 1910, records an equally deplorable fiasco attending an attempt made by one Professor Miller to cross the Atlantic Ocean afoot. He used a pair of special walking shoes, we are told, each measuring 5 feet in length. They resembled miniature canoes with a small orifice in the centre to admit the foot, and they were furnished with corrugated soles. "Full of confidence, he started on his curious journey, but soon realized the folly of his idea. He was unable to maintain an upright position, and drifted about for some time at the mercy of the waves, until his friends prevailed upon him to abandon the idea."

On the other hand, the *United Service Magazine* tells of a successful invention by Lieutenant Hookenberg, of Denmark, which resembled two very narrow boats pointed at both ends and united by a square piece of wood about 30 inches long. The magazine, which unfortunately supplies no dates, adds that " the water runners went through a variety of movements, among which were their loading and discharging their muskets while upon the water, running along the surface at full speed," etc. The shoes, it is added, " are so easy that any person of moderate dexterity and quickness may be taught to manage them."

Waterloo Ball. The famous ball which took place on the very eve of the battle of Waterloo, June 17, 1815, and which has been immortalized by Byron ("Childe Harold," Canto III) and by Thackeray ("Vanity Fair," chapter xxxii), was given by the Duke and Duchess of Richmond, who leased for the occasion a mammoth carriage-factory recently established by one Simon in the Rue de la Blanchisserie in Brussels. Though it is poet and novelist who have done most to preserve the memory of the ball, it was an actual event, surviving in history though legend after legend has been exploded.

Wellington, for instance, did not say "Up, Guards, and at them!" nor anything like it. Cambronne did not say "The Guard dies, but never surrenders!" nor anything like it. And so with many other alleged incidents of the battle. What is true, however, is the story of this rather frivolous and incongruous social function, this " revelry by night " in " Belgium's capital." It is almost literally true, as Byron has told it. The poet visited the very spot only a few months after the event, and wrote with the pen of truth as well as of inspiration. For instance, the Duke of Brunswick, who was killed in the battle next day, did attend the ball; and whether or not he sat within a "windowed niche," he might have done so, and probably did, for there are many such deep recesses in the thick walls, which naturally would have been utilized for seats. The poet describes it as a "lofty hall," which it is in comparison with the average height of Flemish apartments in those days, though fifteen feet high would scarcely now be accounted lofty for a ballroom capable of accommodating 500 dancers on its floor.

The Rue de la Blanchisserie is now a quiet, faded street, with little of its former splendor. In those days it was a particularly aristocratic quarter, and the intrusion of M. Simon and his big carriage-factory was bitterly resented. M. Van Assche, who owned the property and leased it to M. Simon, was subjected to treatment that in these days would be called boycotting. Indeed, his neighbors made it so unpleasant for him that within a year or two after Waterloo he was glad to sell the property. The purchaser was M. Jacques Vanginderachter, who forthwith transformed the carriage-factory into a brewery. He left it to his son, whose widow disposed of it by auction in June, 1890.

A correspondent of the New York *Tribune,* writing from Brussels on June 10, 1890, thus describes the appearance of the **former carriage-factory** just before it was sold.

For a few years the brewing business has been discontinued, and the building has stood empty, save the Vanginderachter family and the numerous sight-seeing visitors. The floor of the ballroom is now very uneven. The bare walls are whitewashed. Some of the windows are boarded up. Down the centre run six huge oaken columns, chipped and scarred by relic-hunters. The smaller room adjoining, in which Thackeray pictures George Osborne and Becky Sharp Crawley sitting out the dances, is now occupied by a huge unused boiler.

There are still a few persons living who danced at that famous ball. One of them is a lady who lives here in Brussels, and who well remembers dancing with Sir Hudson Lowe and other guests. Another is Lady de Ros, widow of the twentieth Baron of that name. She was then Lady Georgiana Gordon-Lennox, the daughter of the Duke and Duchess of Richmond, who gave the ball, and on that occasion, she made her first appearance in society. Her memory of it is also keen, and when King Leopold was in London the other day he called on her, and she rehearsed for him the story of that famous revelry, which occurred before his dynasty was founded. Lord Albemarle was also at the ball,—being then the youngest ensign in the British army. These three are believed to be the only survivors of " the beauty and the chivalry" that were gathered in M. Simon's carriage-shop that night. By a happy coincidence, however, the present British minister here is a grandson of one of the most conspicuous of the dancers—who was also nobly conspicuous the next day on the field of Waterloo. The name of Sir Hussey Vivian stands out conspicuously on every page of Waterloo history; Sir Hussey and his " untouched horsemen" seem to have been always at hand just when they were wanted; and his calm intrepidity more than once turned the fortunes of the fight at a critical juncture. Major-General Sir Hussey Vivian went straight from the Rue de la Blanchisserie to lead his brigade to victory and to pave his way to the peerage and other high honors. The crest of the Vivians is a demi-hussar of the 18th Regiment; the Waterloo medal still figures in their arms, and they have for " supporters" gray and bay horses caparisoned, the one bearing a hussar of the " Black Horse" and the other a lancer of " the Supple 12th." Captain Allix, of the Grenadier Guards, whose name appears lower down on the Duchess's list, is still represented at Brussels by his first cousin and brother-in-law, Mr. Allix, of Willoughby Hall. With a single exception he was the only officer of the 2d Battalion of Grenadiers who escaped unhurt. He afterward marched with the survivors of his battalion to Paris, and was rewarded for his valor in the field with promotion to a colonelcy.

Three books are shown proudly by Mme. Vanginderachter to all visitors. One is a blankbook, in which innumerable visitors, many of them distinguished personages, have inscribed their names. Another is a French translation of " Childe Harold."

Waves. " Mountain high " is an epithet which novelists and travellers are fond of applying to waves in a storm. This is poetic license, prosaic ignorance, or mere lying. In April, 1911, at New York, the incoming North German Lloyd liner *Brandenburg* reported that, about 1000 miles east of Sandy Hook, a monster wave had broken over her bows. It had stove in her crow's nest, 50 feet above the water-line, and inflicted other damage. The officers estimated the height of the wave at

65 feet. The matter was alluded to in the *Scientific American* in August, 1911. But, as the paper itself pointed out, this height, though exceptional, was not unprecedented. Waves 80 or 100 feet high have been reported by captains of transatlantic liners. It must, however, be borne in mind that the breaking of a wave against an obstacle throws the water to a far greater height than the unbroken wave could attain.

Stevenson records an instance when water was thrown to a height of 106 feet at the Bell Rock Light. At the Alderney breakwater the sea has sometimes been thrown upward 200 feet. At Peterhead, where the " fetch " is 300 miles, waves 30 feet high and from 500 to 600 feet long have struck the breakwater with such force as to be thrown upward 120 feet.

Vaughn Cornish, the leading authority on oceanography, says that in a severe storm at sea the average height of the waves is 20 feet, with a maximum of 30 feet. In a storm of exceptional violence the average height may reach 30 feet and the maximum 45 feet. The latter figure may be accepted as the limit. Mr. Cornish finds that in the open sea the height of the wave measured in feet is equal to one-half the velocity of the wind measured in miles per hour.

The greatest length of sea waves is found in high southern latitudes. This has been explained by the fact that south of the Cape of Good Hope and Cape Horn there is neither windward nor leeward shore, and the prevailing wind in all longitudes is westerly. Thus, when a west wind springs up it finds a long westerly swell, the effect of a previous wind, still running. The new-born wind increases the steepness of this swell and so forms majestic storm waves, which sometimes attain a length of 1200 feet from crest to crest.

The force of a great wave breaking against a sea-wall or other construction is so tremendous as to tax its strength to the full. According to Stevenson, who invented the first marine dynamometer for measuring the force of the impact, the maximum in the case of an Atlantic wave is three tons per square foot. French engineers, however, report that the force of the waves on the break-water at Cherbourg has sometimes attained 3½ tons per square foot.

Some statistics as to damage done by sea waves are given by Wheeler in his " Practical Manual of Tides and Waves."

At Bell Rock light-house blocks of concrete weighing 40 tons have been displaced at levels of 17 to 36 feet below low-water.

At Wick two stones weighing eight and ten tons each were thrown over the parapet of the breakwater, the top of which was

21 feet above high-water; while blocks of concrete weighing respectively 1350 and 2500 tons were displaced, though there is some doubt whether the latter movement was due entirely to wave action.

At the Bishop Rock light-house, which is exposed to the full force of the Atlantic waves, an iron column weighing over three tons was thrown up 20 feet and landed on top of a rock.

At the harbor works of Bilboa in 1894 a solid block of the breakwater weighing 1700 tons was overturned from its place and dropped into the water.

At Ymuiden breakwater a block of concrete weighing 20 tons, placed outside the harbor walls, was lifted by a wave to a height of 12 feet vertically and landed on top of the pier, which was 5 feet above high-water.

"The above cases," says the *Scientific American*, "illustrate the sheer force of the individual wave as an engine of destruction, but the imagination of mankind is more impressed by the widespread effects wrought by the great storm waves that sometimes inundate low-lying coasts. These waves are often miscalled 'tidal waves,' the only justification of the latter name being the fact that their effects are most pronounced when the waves propagated outward from a storm area happen to coincide with the occurrence of flood tide on the coast affected."

Not yet is the origin of storm waves fully understood. Such waves attend every severe cyclonic storm at sea. Travelling much faster than the storm (meaning by this the storm as a whole, not the wind revolving around the storm centre), they often break on a coast where the weather is otherwise serene. Thus, they serve as a valuable prognostic of the approaching storm. At the centre of the storm, it should be explained, the barometric pressure is much lower (two inches or more) than at the periphery, and this difference of pressure disturbs the equilibrium of the water, causing it to become heaped up at the storm centre.

Newspapers and the public frequently call the storm waves tidal waves. This is a misnomer as misleading as their equally frequent confusion of cyclone and tornado.

Storm waves are most severe when the wave moves toward a low-lying coastal region, having a converging shore line; this convergence producing the same effect as seen in a tidal "bore."

The most disastrous storm waves have occurred along the coast of the Bay of Bengal, on the extensive flats lying about the mouths of the Hugli, the Megna, and other Asiatic rivers. The storm wave of October 7, 1737, is said to have risen 40 feet in the Hugli, sweeping away 300,000 souls. In May, 1787, at

Coringa, near the mouth of the Godavery, such a wave is said to have taken toll of 20,000 lives. The Calcutta cyclone of October 5, 1864, caused the inundation of the flats on both sides of the Hugli estuary, with a loss of about 48,000 human lives and the destruction of 100,000 head of cattle. The greatest disaster of recent times in this much-afflicted region was the Backergunge hurricane of the night of October 31–November 1, 1876, which cost the lives of over 100,000 persons. In this storm the water rose from 30 to 40 feet in less than half an hour.

The islands of the Pacific are also subject to visitations of this character on a huge scale in connection with tropical hurricanes. The latest of these was the storm of March, 1910, which was especially remarkable for the vast area that it covered, its track extending some 2500 miles, from Fiji to New Caledonia, Norfolk Island, and the North Island of New Zealand. Statistics of the loss of life and property in this storm are not yet available.

Our own seaboard has repeatedly suffered from the effects of storm waves. In the Galveston hurricane of September, 1900, a series of waves invaded the city; 6000 lives were lost and the destruction of property amounted to $30,000,000. The damage was due to wind as well as water, but chiefly to the latter.

There is a curious superstition that every tenth wave is larger than its brethren. Thus, De Quincey, in his "Essay on Pagan Oracles," says "the premature effort of Constantine ought to be regarded as a mere *fluctus decumanus* in the continued advance of the new religion." On the beach at Portobello near Edinburgh, De Quincey and John Wilson jointly and zealously sought to verify this tradition concerning the *fluctus decumanus,* or tenth wave. "But the issue of this was emptiness and aerial mockery," confesses the Opium Eater. Thomas Browne, in his "Vulgar Errors," denounces the superstition as evidently false: "Nor can it be made out by observation either upon the shore or the ocean, as we have with diligence explored both." Evidently Browne had anticipated De Quincey's experiments.

Sometimes the ninth wave instead of the tenth is fabled to be the largest:

> Wave after wave, each mightier than the last,
> Till, last, a ninth one gathering half the deep.

Weathercocks or Vanes. There is mention in Vitruvius of a tower built at Athens by Andronicus, of octagonal form, each side of which was faced with a personification of the wind toward whose quarter the symbolical figure looked. Its spire was surmounted by a copper Triton, so constructed as to point with a rod to the figure that represented the wind which turned the Triton. In a document of earlier date than 1157, a description is given of a Syrian tower surmounted by a copper equestrian statue which turned with every wind. The custom of making the vane in the form of a cock is of mediæval origin. About the middle of the ninth century, we learn from ancient documents, the figure of a cock was set up on every church steeple as the emblem of St. Peter, because, as suggestive of the cock which crowed before this saint (and, no doubt, with reference to its morning alertness), the cock came to be the symbol of clerical vigilance. In the middle ages the clergy called themselves the "Cocks of the Almighty," whose duty it was, like the cock that crowed before Peter, to call the people to repentance, or, in any event, to the church.

The following inscription is found on a weathercock at Brixen: "Dominus Rampertus Episc., gallum hunc fieri præcipit, an. 820" (The Lord Bishop Rampertus ordered this cock to be made, in the year 820). An old Latin poem preserved in the Cathedral of Oehringen illustrates the mystical meaning given to the weathercock in mediæval times. Its substance is, that, as the cock keeps watch from the high tower, hears the angels' songs, is crowned on his head like a king, and spurred on his feet like a soldier, protects and provides for his flock, etc., so the priest should keep watch for *his* flock, be ever exalted and nearer to heavenly things than laymen, should have supreme authority and strength, and should protect his congregation by giving to them the "flowers of the Scriptures" and all spiritual comfort. Durandus has a Latin poem which may thus be Englished: "Do you wish to know the supreme reason wherefore the cock, shining in brass, cuts the north wind on the pinnacle of the church, looking out for every thief and wanderer? He sings the song of repentance to all, for, as a cock at first summoned Peter to penitence, when, betrayed by sleep, he had denied his master, so, thou, a more worthy cock, summonest the sinner to the cross on high." In "The Sphinx and Œdipus; or, A Helpe to Discourse" (1633), occurs the following in the form of question and answer: "Ques.—Wherefore on the top of church-steeples is the cocke set upon the crosse of a long continuance? Ans.—That whilst aloft we behold the crosse, and the cocke standing thereon, we may remember our sinnes, and, with Peter, seeke and obtain mercy; as though, without this dumbe cocke, which many will not hearken to until he crow, the Scriptures were not sufficient alarum."

From the foregoing it will be seen that certain English authorities are in error in their assertion that the choice of a cock for a vane originated in the 14th century, during the reign of Edward III, the object being to ridicule the French people, with whom they were then at war, and that the custom of cock-throwing took its rise at the same time. Dr. Johnson says: " The inconstancy of the French was always the subject of satire, and I have read that the index of the wind upon our steeples was made in the form of a cock in order to throw ridicule on them for their frequent changes." It is to be observed that in Latin the name for a Frenchman and a cock is the same (Gallus), and the inference is that the English willingly set up the bird in a position where he became the type of fickleness. The supposition is, however, groundless.

Another solution of the origin of the weathercock is offered by the Society of Antiquaries, on the authority of Gramaye, who ("History of Brabant") says: "The manner of adorning the tops of steeples with a cross and cock is derived from the Goths, who used that as their warlike ensign," and this is corroborated by Peter le Neve. Besides, we know, from the Bayeux tapestries, that in the last Danish invasion of England, under Sweyn in 1013, the northern vessels carried vanes of some sort on their masts. But all this does not touch the evidence in favor of the ecclesiastical origin of the weathercock.

We may note, in fine, that, apart from symbolical reasons, the physical conformation of the cock, with its large tail, admirably adapts it for use as a vane.

Welsbach Gas Mantle. Just when electricity in the shape of the Edison Incandescent Bulb was threatening the pre-eminence of gas as an illuminant, all people commercially interested in the latter were cheered by an invention wh.ch quadrupled the brilliancy of a gas flame. The inventor was Dr. Auer von Welsbach, a chemist of Vienna, the invention was his well-known gas mantle, an adaptation of the Drummond Light. In 1880 Dr. von Welsbach took up the study of a series of elements known as the " rare earths," mainly with a view to ascertaining their value as illuminants. There are eight or nine of these; didymium, neodymium, praseodymium, lanthanum, cerium, and thorium are the best known. They are always neighbors; find one and you may be sure that further search will reveal the others. Not only are they found together, but they are very much alike—so alike that it is not possible to separate them except by taking advantage of very slight differences in their solubilities in water. Von Welsbach had separated them, dissolved them in nitric acid, and was examining their autographs written by the aid of the spectroscope. Out of nowhere an idea dropped into his head to dip a thread of cotton into his solution, hang this thread in the Bunsen flame, and examine that. When he dipped it into the cerium solution and hung that in the flame, it shone out with a brilliant white light. He found, too, that if he purified the solution the brilliance lessened. A long search resulted in the discovery of the impurity, thorium rust, and its proper proportion of one part in a hundred. Why these proportions are best nobody knows, any more than why one per cent. of carbon added to iron gives us a steel which for many purposes is incomparably better than iron.

Another long series of experiments revealed the proper substitute for the cotton thread, which at that heat gradually ate away the two metal rusts. The whole of the vegetable world was looked through to find a suitable fibre. Finally ramie-grass was found, the fibre of which when burnt leaves behind a skeleton of silica, which at the temperature of the gas burned is absolutely innocuous. The Welsbach mantle is the child of two researches in the science of chemistry and botany, and the grandchild of an accident.

Whist, Strange Hands at. You are an old card-player, we will assume, fond of whist, or, perhaps, of bridge. But have you ever seen a round in which any one player held thirteen trumps? The thing is possible, but wildly improbable. Mr. Richard A. Proctor, who went deeply into the mathematics of cards, gives the odds against such a happening as a hundred and sixty thousand millions to one. Still, being possible, the thing has happened and will happen again. *All the Year Round,* for October 7, 1876, quotes a letter from " a gentleman at Dundee," written three years previously, which said: " One of the most extraordinary incidents in connection with whist I dare say you ever heard of occurred here this week. Four gentlemen of the highest respectability, with whom I am well acquainted, were playing at whist last Wednesday evening. They had been playing about a couple of hours, when one of them, after having dealt, found his hand to consist of the whole thirteen trumps. Two packs of cards were used alternately all the time, and this occurred with one of them, after being shuffled and cut in the usual way."

The same number of *All the Year Round* recalls another instance, supplemented by other curious vagaries in a single deal at whist. This time the event happened in 1863 in the military cantonment of Jubulpore, in the East Indies. The players were four British officers of the Ninety-first Foot, who wrote out and signed a narrative that was published in a London daily. The cards used on this occasion had been played with before, and were shuffled and cut in the usual way. When all the fifty-two cards had been dealt out and the hands were looked at, the combinations were such as might well astonish the players. The dealer was found to have all the thirteen trumps (spades); his partner had eleven clubs; his antagonist on the left hand had twelve hearts; and he on the right hand twelve diamonds!

That the dealer's hand should contain thirteen trumps is extraordinary enough, but the marvel is increased by the fact that each of the other three hands was made up so very nearly of one suit only. There was a fair probability, for example, that the dealer's partner (all the spades being held by the dealer himself) would have nearly equal numbers of clubs, hearts, and diamonds, four or five of each; but that he should have so many as eleven of one suit was certainly not to be expected. And so of the other two hands: there was a combination of improbabilities so extraordinary, as to make the odds enormous against such a phenomenon occurring again in actual play.

In both cases it is to be presumed that the individual who held thirteen trumps took all the tricks. Yet the presumption was not verified in another less authenticated story. We are told that Snodkins once complained at his club that he had held all the thirteen trumps, and taken only one trick.

"How was that?" was the incredulous query of a friend.

"Well, you see, the very first lead I trumped my partner's ace, and he jumped up and fired me out of the window."

To return to authentic history. One well-attested case relates not to thirteen cards of the same suit being held at one time, but to one suit coming up trumps thirteen times in succession. This occurred with spades trumps. It was noticed because one of the players had an idea that he was always unlucky when spades were trumps. Therefore he was all the more impressed by the strange repetition of that particular trump suit. Mr. Proctor, who quotes the case, computes the odds against such a repetition as more than thirty millions to one.

This is pretty well; but it is nothing to the row of figures that would be necessary to give the odds against two whist-players, the dealer and his partner, holding all the twenty-six red cards, and their antagonists all the twenty-six black. Such a deal, as we have seen, nearly occurred in practice. Proctor set himself to ascertain the odds against such an extremely improbable combination ever actually occurring. It was stupendous—a figure eight followed by fourteen zeros or ciphers; in familiar language, eight hundred millions of millions to one against the event!

Mr. Babbage (was it he or some other expert mathematician?) once set himself the nice little sum of calculating the number of different ways in which the fifty-two cards of a pack can be distributed among four players, thirteen to each, taking every possible combination and permutation. It would be no use to present the answer here in a long row of figures, for no one can realize to himself what such a numerical array really conveys; nor would it be much better to play with the words billions and trillions, seeing that to most of us these are words and nothing more; but the following illustration is more likely to be appreciated by the unlearned many: " If the entire population of the earth, taken at one thousand millions of persons, were to deal the cards incessantly, day and night, for one hundred millions of years, at the rate of a deal by each person a minute, they would not have exhausted the one hundred thousandth part of the number of essentially different ways in which the cards can be so distributed."

A favorite among examples of curious whist hands is that known as the Cumberland hand, because it is said to have been held by one of the Dukes of Cumberland. It consisted of ace, king, queen, and knave in one plain suit; ace, king, queen, in another; ace, king, in the third; while in trumps he held king, knave, nine, and seven. Yet with this magnificent hand and the lead (leading also correctly) he did not make a single trick. This seems incredible, but when the hands are supplied the solution of the problem will be readily seen. The four trumps lying just over those held by the Duke of Cumberland—viz., the ace, queen, ten, and eight—were on his left, with nine diamonds, while on his right were five small trumps. He led a trump, which was taken on his left, and a diamond led—trumped on his right. Another trump was led through him, which was similarly taken, and another diamond led, which was also trumped on his right. Another trump, led through the duke, caused his last trump but one to fall. The last was then extracted by the player on his left. The duke had now no diamonds, that being the suit of which he had held only the ace and king. Then the diamonds on his left were as good as trumps, and made all the remaining tricks.

Still more famous is the Yarborough hand. A certain Earl of Yarborough, so the story runs, once held a hand containing no card above a nine, and had reason to remember it by reason of some heavy betting that was going on. Ever after that, he kept himself ready to bet 1000 guineas to 1 against such a hand being held against him. The bet was a tolerably safe one. The real odds are rather larger than those laid by the earl, yet the hand has been held sufficiently often to obtain for it a distinctive name.

White Hart. This is the commonest of all tavern signs in England, and a White Hart Inn may be found in almost every

market-town near the market-place, often in a street of the
same name, to remind us of its importance in by-gone days.
Tradition seeks to explain these inns as royal posting-houses, it
being supposed that stations to supply fresh horses for the royal
journeys were first established during the last years of Edward
III. As a rule, they do date from the beginning of the reign
of Richard II, his grandson and successor, who took for his badge
a white stag with a collar of gold around his neck, and thereby
helped to raise the spirits of his people from the despair into
which they had sunk during the long dotage of Edward III.
From time immemorial the white hart had been a symbol of
good fortune. According to the mediæval romancers, it was
never to be taken alive save by one who had conquered the whole
world. Its earliest appearance is in Aristotle, who tells how
Diomedes consecrated a white stag to Diana; and how it lived
for a thousand years before it was killed by Agathocles, King of
Sicily. Pliny gives Alexander the Great, and later writers
Julius Cæsar and Charlemagne, as the potentates who captured
the young white stag and released it after decorating it with the
golden band. A tavern on the Dorchester Road, near Stowing-
ton, used to bear the sign of the White Hart with these lines:

> When Julius Cæsar landed here
> I was then a little deer;
> When Julius Cæsar reigned King,
> Round my neck he put this ring,
> Whoever shall me overtake
> Spare my life for Cæsar's sake!

White Island, or Whakari, in the Bay of Plenty, 30 miles
northeast of New Zealand, possesses many marvellous attributes.
It is an enormous mass of rock nearly three miles in circumference, rising 870 feet above the sea, and is perpetually enveloped
in dark clouds which are visible for nearly 100 miles.

The island consists almost entirely of green and yellow
sulphur. In the interior is a lake fully 50 acres in extent, the
water of which has a temperature of 112 degrees Fahrenheit.
On one side of this lake are craters from which steam escapes
with great force and noise. This steam and the vapor from the
lake form the dark clouds that envelop the island.

Womanless Islands. Women have been forbidden on several islands ruled by the Catholic clergy. One of the most
famous of these is Iona, or Icolmkill, called also I or Hy, a small
island of the inner Hebrides (lat. 56° 22 N., lon. 6° 25 W.),
nine miles southwest of Staffa, and separated from the island
of Mull by a channel one and a quarter miles wide, called the
sound of I or of Icolmkill; it is in Argyleshire, and has a popu-

lation of about three hundred, whose only occupations are fishing and raising black cattle on the bleak moors. From earliest times the island has .been accounted holy, and is still known to the Highlanders as *Eilean nah Druineach,*=the Sacred Isle of the Druids, for whose rites it was the chief seat. In 563 Conal Christian, King of the Northern Scots, granted it to St. Columba. Brude, King of the Picts, confirmed the gift on being converted. Columba built a chapel and hospice of wicker and mud thatched with heather among the three hundred and sixty gray Druidical monoliths, on which rude crosses were sculptured by the early converts. He also established a college, and sent out monks to the neighboring islands to build thereon little chapels from which to preach the new faith to the pagan Picts. On the Angel's Hill—*Croc-au-Aingel*—in Iona, Columba communed with angels; on the *Tor Ab*—Abbot's Hill—he sat to watch for pilgrims or pirates; in the *Port-na-Churraich,* or Harbor of the Boat, he buried the boat in which he had come from Ireland, that he might never be tempted to return. The island is full of such places of interest and relics of the saint; the Lia Fail is said to have been brought here from Erin, and to have formed a pillow for Columba the day of his death, in 597, ere proceeding on its travels to Westminster Abbey.

Columba's aversion to everything feminine was such that he forbade even the keeping of cows on the island, for, he said, " where there is a cow there must be a female, and where there is a female there must be mischief." Any married tradesman of Iona must keep his wife on the neighboring " Women's Isle," and when the Lords of the Isles and other great men were brought to Iona for burial, their wives were buried on the Isle of Finlagan. Near Columba's first chapel, dedicated to his companion St. Oran, was the Reilig Orain, or consecrated graveyard, where forty-eight Scottish kings, eight Danish and Norwegian sea-kings, four Irish kings, and one Bishop of Canterbury were buried. After Columba's death, the island was invaded by the heathen, and the monks were forced to go, taking with them the saint's body, which was re-interred in the Cathedral of Dunkeld or in Kells, Ireland. Next century a company of nuns came from a neighboring island, and established an Augustine priory. Later Queen Margaret of Scotland built a stone chapel on the site of that of St. Oran. In 1560 the religious establishments were abolished by the Scotch Parliament, and the island passed into the hands of the McLeans; it now belongs to the Duke of Argyle. An ancient prophecy declares that seven years before the end of the world, a second deluge will submerge all the earth with the exception of Iona, which will swim above the flood;

hence its merits as a royal cemetery. Macbeth is said to have been buried there. On June 13, 1888, a pilgrimage to Iona was organized to commemorate the fact of St. Columba's canonical appointment as patron saint of the diocese of Argyle and the Isles, and among the five hundred pilgrims were many women. The name *I-colm-Kill* signifies the Island of Columba's Cell.

Another account says it was to the above-mentioned St. Oran's rigid celibacy that the rule against women was established, by which they were forbidden to worship in his chapel or be buried in his churchyard. Walter Scott refers to this in his ballad of "Glenfinlas, or Lord Ronald's Coronach:"

> Or if she choose a melting tale. . .
> Will good St. Oran's rule prevail?

A similar prohibition existed in Lindisfarne, the "Holy Isle," off the coast of Northumberland, a few miles south of Berwick; it is surrounded by water at high tide, but at low tide the sands between it and the coast many be easily crossed on foot. Its ruined abbey is said to be the oldest church in England; it was established by St. Aidan, who founded the church in Northumbria in 635 at the request of King Oswald, and who made Lindisfarne the episcopal seat of the see of Durham. It is famous as the scene of St. Cuthbert's labors. He was a shepherd who was induced by a vision to enter the priesthood. After preaching the gospel to the still half-savage people on the mainland, he lived eight years as a hermit on the barren islet of Farne, which he cultivated, living in a cabin with a wide trench around it to separate him from visitors. He was made Bishop of Hexham, and afterward of Lindisfarne, remaining at the latter place two years; feeling his health fail, he retired to Farne once more, where he died in 687. He was buried in Lindisfarne, whose soil was thought so sacred that the bodies of many Border chiefs were carried there for burial. When the island was ravaged by the Danes, the monks fled, taking with them the body of St. Cuthbert, which, after long wanderings, was at last placed in a shrine of Durham Cathedral, where it worked miracles, and over it was hung a cloth used by him in celebrating mass, which, if carried as a banner, always insured victory. But the shrine was demolished in the Reformation, the body buried under the pavement, and the banner burned by Calvin's sister.

Scott has chosen Lindisfarne as the site of the nunnery in "Marmion," but he himself says this is entirely fictitious, for St. Cuthbert detested all women, on account of "a slippery trick played on him by an Irish princess." A cross of blue marble was placed in the pavement of his Durham shrine, beyond which no female might set foot without being subjected to heavy pen-

ance. The cross is still to be seen, but its prohibitive authority
has gone. The saint, however, seems to have been hardly consist-
ent in his ban against the sex, for he conversed with Elfleda,
daughter of King Oswy, through his cabin-window at Farne,
he accepted a gift of a rare winding-sheet from Virca, Abbess
of Tynemouth, and a coffin from a holy lady named Tuda, and
he exchanged visits with the Abbess of Coldingham. On August
11, 1887, the twelfth centenary of his death was celebrated by a
pilgrimage to Lindisfarne of four thousand men and women.
Therefore, in Lindisfarne as well as in Iona, the prohibitive rule
is now entirely disregarded, even by Catholics.

The Celtic clergy seem to have cherished an especial aversion
to women. During the building of a convent near the holy well
of St. Augustine in Ireland, bells were rung by invisible hands
and angelic music accompanied the workmen. A woman came
to draw water from the well, and immediately the music ceased
and the work could not proceed. The monks were forced to
choose another site, around which they drew a circle and forbade
any woman to step inside; the bells and music recommenced,
and the building was soon completed. Thomas Moore wrote a
ballad founded on one of the many stories related of St. Kevin,
whose rock bed is still shown in Wicklow, at Glendalough.

> By that lake whose gloomy shore
> Skylark never warbles o'er.

St. Kevin hid himself from his former sweetheart Kathleen,
who followed him to the solitudes; the saint hurled her from the
rock into the waters beneath, and ever after

> Her ghost was seen to glide,
> Smiling o'er the fatal tide.

St. Kevin's hermitage, however, was on the shore, not on an
island.

Other instances of islands forbidden to women may be mentioned. E. E. Bourne in an account of the Isles of Shoals, writes,
"The law allowed no women or hogs on the island. In 1647
John Reynols went to live on Hog Island, carrying with him his
hogs, and also his wife, which made a great uproar among the
inhabitants. The people petitioned the Court of York County
that they might be compelled to remove them. The court ordered
the hogs off, but allowed his wife to stay, if there were no personal objection to her."

The island of Fernando Noronha is situated in the South
Atlantic off the coast of Brazil (3° 50′ S. lat., 32° 25′ W. long.).
It is four and three-quarter miles long, one and a half miles
broad; its volcanic origin is traceable in a high rugged peak on

the northern shore, whose height is estimated at one thousand feet and which in the distance looks like a church-spire. The village belongs to Brazil, and is used as a penal colony. Upon it are a prison where the convicts are confined every night after the day's liberty, a fort, citadel, hospital, chapel, and governor's house. Flour and other provisions are sent from Brazil, but the supplies are at times deficient. The principal employment of the inhabitants is fishing, but they are extremely indolent and suffer the rich soil to go untilled. No women are allowed to live on the island, no one is permitted to own a boat, and all intercourse with shipping is strictly regulated. The island has been held successively by Portugal, Holland, France, and Brazil, and has been used for centuries as a place of exile and imprisonment for male convicts.

Marco Polo says, in his "Travels," that "Distant from Kesneacoran about five hundred miles toward the south, in the ocean are two islands about thirty miles from each other; one being inhabited by men without the company of women; the other by women without the company of men; they are called respectively the Island of Males and the Island of Females." The exact location of these islands is doubtful; they have been thought identical with the islands called "Les deux Frères" and "Abd-al-Curia" near Socotra, but these are too small to be inhabited, and too near the Red Sea to correspond with those described by Marco Polo. More probably the "Island of Females" is identical with Minicoy, an islet five miles square, lying in the Indian Ocean between the Laccadive and Maldive groups about 250 miles west of the southern point of Hindostan.

Here, according to *Blackwood's Magazine,* the women are the controlling power. They own the houses and assume the headship of the family; they are organized into associations for the public good separately from the men, and take the lead in almost everything save navigation.

The men remain on the island for only three or four months of each year. This corresponds fairly well with Marco Polo's account. As to the Island of Males, *Blackwood* suggests, that, as the men of Minicoy were absent for six or seven months on trading voyages every year, the hearsay report of this long absence got confused into the account of their occupying a separate island during the period. Between other particulars of Messer Marco's description—which the writer examines in detail—and the existing state of things, he finds less discrepancy, and considers that on the whole the balance of probability inclines to the view that Minicoy is the long unidentified "Island of Women."

An interesting instance of insular prohibition is found in one of Moore's Irish melodies:

St. Senanus and the Lady.

SENANUS.

"Oh! haste and leave this sacred isle,
Unholy bark, ere morning smile;
For on its deck, though dark it be,
A female form I see,
And I have sworn this land of God
Shall ne'er by woman's feet be trod."

LADY.

"O Father! send not hence my bark
Through wintry winds and billows dark.
I come with humble heart to share
Thy morn and evening prayer;
Nor mine the feet, oh! holy saint,
The brightness of thy sod to taint."

The lady's prayer Senanus spurned;
The winds blew fresh, the bark returned.
But legends hint that had the maid
Till morning's light delayed,
And given the saint one rosy smile,
She ne'er had left his lonely isle.

In a note to these verses, Moore says that the metrical life of St. Senanus is in an old Kilkenny MS. In the *" Acta Sanctorum Hiberniæ,"* p. 610, is the account of his flight to the island of Scattery, where he resolved no woman should ever land. This rule was not broken even for a sister saint, St. Cannera, whom an angel had taken to the isle for the express purpose of introducing her to Senanus. The monk's reply was:

"Cui Praesul, quid foeminis
Commune est cum monachia?
Nec te nec ullam aliam
Admittemus in insulam."

Wooden Clock. The story of the first American maker of wooden clocks may be told somewhat in this fashion:

Toward the end of the eighteenth century, there was living in Norwich, Conn., a young man named Eli Terry (1772–1852), who had been apprenticed to a brass-clock maker, but who, apparently, had profited so little by what he had learned that he spent most of his time sitting on a stump or block, whittling out a circle struck with an old pair of compasses, or sawing off bits of wood from some old dead trees. The general opinion of his neighbors was that he was idle and shiftless, if not mentally unsound. So, when he sought the hand of a Miss Warner, the parents strenuously objected. Nevertheless, he obtained the maiden's consent and was married, and in 1793 removed to

Plymouth, Litchfield County. Want pressed so hard in the home that the wife by urgent entreaty of her friends, had about made up her mind to return to her parents' home, when the fruits of Eli's whittling and sawing materialized in the first wooden clock ever made in America. It was readily sold to a neighbor for $30, and paid for in pork, flour, potatoes, other family necessities, and a little money with which Eli bought tools to facilitate his work in further prosecution of clock-making.

And now fortune smiled upon Terry. During the winter he would sit cutting out with a saw and jack-knife the works for twenty-five clocks, the village carpenter making tall cases for them. The works were usually disposed of for $25, the case for $15, Terry taking a trip afoot through the adjacent country as soon as summer set in.

In 1807 he purchased an old mill, which he fitted up for the purpose of turning out clocks by machinery. At this time a number of men in Waterbury formed a company and made a contract with him. They were to furnish the capital and he was to make the movements. The first 300 clocks ever started by machinery in one batch were made by Terry at his factory in the old mill in 1808. This was a larger number than had ever before been begun at one time in any place in the world. In 1810 he sold out his business to Seth Thomas and Silas Hoadley, his principal workmen, who entered into partnership, and two years later removed the factory to Thomaston. Meanwhile Terry, with his wife and family, founded another Connecticut town, which he named Terryville, and here he died at the age of eighty, leaving a large family of sons and a number of grandsons, who between them controlled nearly all the wealth of the place, invested in large manufactories for clocks and locks. It is a singular fact that not one Terry is now left in that region, and all their interests and investments are scattered or gone into other hands.

World's Championship. The first official "World's Championship" series of base-ball games was played in 1884 between the Providence team and the Metropolitans. The former had carried off the National League pennant by winning 84 out of 110 games. The Metropolitans—New York's representatives in the American Association—had been equally successful in overtopping all their fellow-clubs. To wind up the base-ball season a series of games, best three out of five, was arranged between these leaders respectively of the League and the Association. Only three games were played, as Providence, with Sweeney and the still more famous Radbourne in the box, won them all. The scores were 6 to 0, 3 to 1, and 11 to 2. The series took place in New York City, beginning October 23. It paved the way for post-season contests between the champion teams of the two rival organizations.

In 1885 " Pop " Anson's Chicago club, of the National League, were pitted against the St. Louis Browns, of the Association. Seven games were played without decisive result, as each club won three, and the odd game was a tie. The series began on October 14. It will amaze people familiar with modern contests of this sort to be told that the total receipts were only $2000.

In 1886 the same teams again met as champions respectively. This time only 6 games were necessary, as St. Louis won 4 to Chicago's 2.

In 1887 St. Louis and Detroit played 14 games and cleared $42,000. The games were played around a circuit, taking in St. Louis, Detroit, Pittsburg, New York, Philadelphia, Washington, and Baltimore. Detroit won 10 out of the 14 games. The series started in St. Louis on October 10 and finished at Detroit on October 26. The game of October 12 was won by Detroit in 13 innings by a score of 2 to 1. The following year St. Louis was still one of the contenders, but lost six games out of 10 to New York. The receipts of this series were $24,362.10. One game at St. Louis brought in only $411; another only $212.

The Giants repeated the following year, 1889. Their opponent in the post-season series was the Brooklyn team, then a member of the American Association. Nine games were played, which resulted in another triumph for the Giants, the figures being six victories against three defeats. The total receipts for this series were $23,628.

In 1890 Brooklyn joined the National League and, winning the pennant, was pitted against Louisville, champions of the Association. The result was another draw, each club winning three games and playing one tie: 7 to 7.

In 1891 no series was played.

In 1892 Boston and Cleveland played six games. Boston won five. The other game was tied at the end of eleven innings.

Again in 1893 no championship series was played.

In 1894 the Temple Cup series was started (see TEMPLE CUP). This series called for seven games at the close of the National League season between the team winning the pennant and the team finishing second. In 1894 Baltimore won the pennant, but lost four straight games to New York. The box office took in $18,000. In 1895 Baltimore won again and lost four out of five games to Cleveland in the Temple cup series. In 1896 Baltimore was more successful, taking four straight games from Cleveland, after winning the pennant. In 1897

Frank Selee's Boston team beat out the "Orioles," but lost in the Temple cup series, capturing but one of five games. This series was the last for the Temple cup, and during the five seasons from 1898 to 1902 no world's championship games were played.

In 1900 the American League had come into existence, and in 1903 a world's series, the best five out of nine, was arranged between Boston and Pittsburg, champions of their respective leagues. After dropping three of the first four games played, Boston won four straight and brought the title of world's champions to the American League. The series began on October 1 and the total receipts were over $50,000. Next year Boston repeated in the American League, and New York won in the National. No series was played, as the Giants' owner refused to entertain the proposition of a series.

Before the season of 1905 opened the National Commission issued a ruling making it compulsory for the pennant winners of the two leagues to come together in a series of seven games at the end of the season.

The first clash under the new rule was in 1905, when the Giants took four out of five from the Philadelphia Athletics and brought the honors back to the National League. Christy Mathewson established his fame as the greatest pitcher to date by winning three of New York's four victories. Every game in this series was a shut-out. The attendance was 91,723 and the total receipts $68,435.

In 1906 the title changed leagues again, going to the Chicago White Sox, who won four out of six games from the Chicago Cubs.

The attendance at this series was 99,845, a remarkable figure in consideration of the fact that all the games were played in Chicago. The total receipts were $106,550.

In 1907 the National League again triumphed. Chicago and Detroit clashed for the first time. The Detroits should have won the first game, which was tied up on an error and finally called after the 13th inning, with the score standing 3 to 3. The Cubs won the next four games. The attendance was 78,068 and the treasurer had $101,728.50 to divide among those entitled to share.

In 1908 the same clubs came together again for the world's championship, and again Chicago won four out of the five games played.

The series of 1909 between Pittsburg and Detroit was the first that went down to the seventh game for settlement, the Pittsburgs winning four. The attendance was 145,295 and the receipts $188,302.50.

In 1910 the Athletics brought the honors back to the American League in defeating the Chicago Cubs four out of five games.

World, End of the. St. Peter, in his second epistle (iii. 10), announced the approach of a time when "the heavens shall pass away with a great noise, and the elements shall melt with fervent heat, the earth also and the works that are therein shall be burned up."

Science is quite ready to affirm the possibility of such a catastrophe. In "The Flowers of the Sky," R. A. Proctor reminds us that every star is a sun, with a system of planets like our earth revolving around it. "We know that in certain general respects each star resembles our sun. Each is glowing like our sun with an intense heat. We know that in each star processes resembling in violence those taking place in our own sun must be continually in progress, and that such processes must be accompanied by a *noise and tumult,* compared with which all the forms of uproar known upon our earth are as absolute silence."

He proceeds to describe how in 1886 a star of the tenth magnitude in the constellation Northern Crown suddenly shone as a second magnitude star, afterward rapidly diminishing in lustre, and how in 1876 a similar phenomenon appeared in the constellation Cygnus. "A change in our own sun," he adds, "such as affected the star in Cygnus, or that other star in the Northern Crown, would unquestionably destroy every living creature on the face of this earth; nor could any even escape which may exist on the other planets of the solar system. The star in the Northern Crown shone out with more than *eight hundred times* its former lustre; the star in Cygnus with from *five hundred* to many thousand times its former lustre, according as we take the highest possible estimate of its brightness before the catastrophe, or consider that it may have been very much brighter. Now, if our sun were to increase *tenfold* in brightness, all the higher forms of animal life, and nearly all vegetable life, would inevitably be destroyed on this earth. A few stubborn animalcules might survive, and, possibly, a few of the lowest forms of vegetation, but naught else. If the sun increased a *hundredfold* in lustre, his heat would doubtless sterilize the whole earth."

When the end of the world failed to arrive with the end of the first century, the prophets of evil postponed it to the centennial of the crucifixion and then to the downfall of the empire. But Rome fell, and, though the crash of its fall may figuratively be said to have reverberated through all the kingdoms of the earth, the planet in actual fact was not jarred an inch from its orbit.

Gradually, as the year 1000 approached, all Christendom became perturbed with the fear that the millennial would succeed where the centennial had failed. The rumor spread that Christ was to appear on Mount Zion. Thither flocked an immense army to meet him, after having first surrendered all their earthly belongings to the church. It was many weeks before normal conditions were resumed.

Stoeffler, a German astronomer, professor at Tübingen, predicted that in the year 1533 the world would be destroyed by a second deluge. Believers emulated the example of Noah. A wealthy Parisian built himself a raft, which he stored with provisions to last six months. A little village fifty miles from any river or sea devoted all the common funds to the construction of another vessel.

Finally the appointed day came. At seven in the morning Stoeffler began preaching his last sermon. With quite unnecessary particularity he advanced twenty-two arguments to show that his theory was true. Then came the hour that was to prove their truth. The clock struck.

" Lo! It comes, it comes! " cried the prophet.

But it came not. The people still held their breath with awe. Stoeffler, gazing anxiously through the church door, espied a cloud, and shouted eagerly:

" Behold, it cometh from the clouds."

Again he was wrong. At last the people ceased their lamentations. Their fear changed into anger. The prophet was dragged from his pulpit and soused in a neighboring duck-pond.

The appearance of any unusual portent in the sky has always alarmed the superstitious,—as, *e.g.,* the eclipse of the sun in 1654 and the advent of the comet in 1679.

In America the Millerite prediction of the end of the world stirred up an unparalleled sensation. William Miller (1781–1849) was a native of Pittsfield, Massachusetts. Close study of the Scriptures convinced him that he had found the key to their esoteric meaning. He was none too soon in the field. Only a dozen more years, he found, remained before the world would come to an end. He forthwith proceeded to warn all men of the coming doom. In groves, town-halls, and school-houses throughout the country he thundered out the tidings of the second coming of Christ. Multitudes were converted and enrolled themselves among his disciples. They called themselves Second Adventists. The mob knew them best as Millerites. It was in Massachusetts that the good old gentleman's venerable aspect failed to restrain the rotten egg,—an all-too-familiar reminder of unpopularity in those days,—for he was mobbed with missiles

in Newburyport in May, 1842. A month later we find him holding forth at the first Second Advent camp-meeting held at Easton,
New Hampsh.re. Among the audience, a curious and interested
spectator, was John G. Whittier. He has described the scene in
his journal: " The white circle of tents; the dim wood arches;
the upturned earnest faces; the loud voices of the speakers, burdened with the awful symbolic language of the Bible; the smoke
from the fires, rising like incense from forest altars, and suspended from the front of the rude pulpit a canvas sheet whereon
were depicted the wonders of the Apocalyptic vision: the beasts,
the dragons, the scarlet woman seen by the seer of Patmos—
Oriental types and figures and mystic symbols, translated into
staring Yankee realities, and exhibited like the beasts of a travelling menagerie."

On March 14, 1844, Father Miller closed the diary of his
public labors, believing that he would never have to open it again.
He reckoned up that he had delivered 3200 lectures since 1832.
The "burning day" was at hand. But March went out in its
usual lamb-like way, and April came and passed and saw not the
heavens in commotion. When May arrived, the poor old man
was heard confessing his error and acknowledging his disappointment, but not his unbelief. October would yet witness the fulfilment of prophecy: " The Lord will certainly leave the mercy-
seat on the 13th and appear visibly in the clouds of heaven on
the 22d."

During the interval between the 13th and 22d, all secular
business was suspended by the Second Adventists. Mrs. Lydia
Maria Child records that muslin for ascension robes was offered
at some places in the Bowery, in New York, but that elsewhere
tradesmen shut up shop or gave away their goods, or at least
dealt more liberal measure so as to ingratiate themselves with
the Almighty—all the while that the ungodly disturbed the
meetings with stones and brickbats and crackers and torpedoes.

Finally the sun rose on the 23d and nothing happened all
day, and at nightfall the sad prophet could only say:

" I have fixed my mind on another time, and here I mean to
stand until God gives me more light,—and that is, to-day, to-day,
and to-day until He comes."

A typical scene occurred in 1900 in the village of Nagy, St.
Miklos, Hungary. The word had gone round that the day of
judgment was at hand. In the early hours of the morning, a
night watchman detected a red glow in the heavens, caused (it
was afterward ascertained) by a fire in a neighboring village.
Then he thought it was all over, and, giving a great blast on his

horn, he cried out the terrifying message that his fellow-citizens must prepare for the worst.

Men, women and children tumbled out of bed into the open, and Father Kristoffsky, the old village pastor, after scanning the firmament, also came to the conclusion that the world was coming to an end. He comforted his flock and exhorted all to await their fate with resignation. It was, he said, only a matter of a few hours now.

The people were somewhat pacified, and with one accord decided that they might as well finish off what food and drink they possessed. Accordingly great fires were lit on the square fronting the church and a feasting began. A few lamented, others prayed, but the vast majority were intent on having a good time while it lasted.

As the dread moment approached, the revelry became an orgy; all prudence was thrown to the winds; the fiery wine of the country did the rest, and soon there was not a sober head among them. They sang and danced till they dropped and slept where they lay.

The sleepers awoke in bright sunshine, and, finding the old world still rolling on as usual, they unanimously cursed the comet for giving them a false scare, especially when they realized that their larders and cellars were empty.

Lee T. Spangler, a grocer in York, Penna., had been troubled with the gift of prophecy almost from his cradle. At the age of twelve, it was revealed to him in a trance that the world would perish in fire and smoke in October, 1908. He waited till his maturity before delivering the message to his neighbors. He decided that Nyack, in New York, would be the best place from which to witness the cataclysm. Leaving his wife behind him, he transported himself thither, with his chief priestess and a crowd of believers. The night before the expected crash he bade farewell to the priestess, told her that he had an appointment with the Lord, and disappeared. On the morrow priestess and disciples, all decked in white, held solemn preparatory services in the cemetery. The priestess told how Prophet Spangler in the second verse of the sixth chapter of Revelations had found a distinct reference to Theodore Roosevelt, who had ridden a white horse up San Juan Hill, had conquered and been crowned. Therefore, it was perfectly plain that the end of the world would arrive before nightfall. But twilight came and then dark, and the night grew colder and colder and the dampened enthusiasts returned to their quarters. As to the prophet, he was subsequently discovered living quietly at home with his wife and dispensing butter and eggs as of yore.

Y.

Yezd, in Central Persia, is one of the urban curiosities of the world. Situated in the midst of a vast salt desert which stretches for hundreds of miles in all directions, Yezd is insular beyond even the insularity of islands. The nearest inhabited place of any size is Isfahan, and that is two hundred miles away. When you send a letter to Isfahan from Yezd, if your friend writes by return of post you may get your answer back in a month.

The inhabitants of Yezd who have been away from Yezd during their lives number, perhaps, two or three score, and the bulk of these have not extended their travels farther than to Shiraz or Kirman in the one direction, or to Isfahan in the other. Yet between fifty and sixty thousand people make the place their home. For ninety-nine out of every hundred of these the great outside world has not merely no interest—it has absolutely no existence.

Yezd is a city made almost entirely of mud. Not only are the houses built of this material, but the very furniture, the firepans, the barrels for grain, the children's toys, the bread receptacles, even the beds, are simply mud, moulded into a rough form and dried in the sun. In the Yezd shops the goods, mostly mud, are displayed on tiers of mud ledges, and there is a mud room behind. The bakers' ovens are of mud, down to the very doors. Mud is cooked in a variety of ways, and is greatly enjoyed by many of the inhabitants.

Young Men's Christian Association (known familiarly by its initials Y.M.C.A.), an organization for social and religious work among young men which has now spread over the entire civilized world.

During early manhood George Williams (1821–1905) was employed in a London dry-goods store belonging to George Hitchcock. He roomed in the store building with 80 other young men. Their habits were so repulsive to him that he invited a few professed Christians among the clerks to meet in his bedroom and talk over means for ameliorating the conditions existing around them. This led to the formation, June 6, 1844, of the Young Men's Christian Association. For a while the members met in one another's bedrooms. Later in the same year, Hitchcock gave them a larger room for their meetings. Hitchcock himself became the first president of the London Association. He was succeeded by Lord Shaftsbury. Williams, who for forty-one years was treasurer of the Y.M.C.A., was the leading spirit from the beginning. Until the day of his death he remained in the business in which he was engaged as junior assistant at the time he started the first Association. Even to the last, when he was a rich merchant, his interest in the Association was of the same sort as that which had led him, when a young man receiving a hundred and fifty pounds a year, to give a third of his income to the Association. On the occasion of the jubilee of the Y.M.C.A., George Williams was knighted. " As the accolade of no earthly sovereign could add to the knightliness of George Williams," said an obituary published in the Cleveland *Plaindealer,* " the world will prefer to remember him, now that his useful active career has closed, without his title. At heart he was always a commoner—one of the greatest that England ever has produced."

Williams's idea made no pretence to originality. Similar associations had been in existence in Scotland at a much earlier date. In 1824 David Naismith started the Glasgow Young Men's Society for Religious Improvement, a movement which spread to various parts of the United Kingdom, France, and America. Later Naismith's Society assumed the name of the Glasgow Young Men's Christian Association.

American branches of the Y.M.C.A. were organized in December, 1851, at Montreal and at Boston, both as a result of information received concerning the London Society. Forty more were formed within three years. The first international convention was held June 7, 1854, at Buffalo, N. Y. The first world's conference meeting, in Paris in 1855, formulated a basis that has since been universally adopted. At the eighth conference, Geneva, Switzerland, 1878, a " Central International Committee " was established, consisting of representatives from the affiliating national organizations, and with a quorum resident in Geneva.

Ys or Is.   Most famous of all the sunken cities (*q.v.*) of history and legend is the City of Ys or Is, in Brittany, which has been celebrated in verse by Villemarque and Brizeux, and more elaborately in prose by Émile Souvestre in his Foyer Breton. The leading incidents may be summarized thus:

In the fifth century King Gradlon, or Grallon, ruled over Cornouailles; he was brother of one of the early British kings, and is connected with the legend of the hermit St. Corentin. The king once lost his way while hunting (about 495), and begged shelter from the hermit, who fed the king and his attendants bountifully from a single slice of carp, the carp remaining whole and alive. The king was so impressed by the miracle that he gave Corentin dominion over the neighboring country, and when Cornouailles was erected into a diocese he appointed Corentin bishop, and, that the latter might have full jurisdiction, the king transferred his court to Ys.

Ys was a magnificent city, filled with luxury and vice. It was built below the level of the sea, on a wide plain, and surrounded by stout walls to keep out the sea. Now, Gradlon, though a good and pious king, had a handsome but wicked daughter, named Dahut, who dwelt in a lofty tower, where she held impious revels with a succession of lovers. When tired of one lover she had him thrown into a well, and chose another. Once her paramour begged her to obtain for him the silver key which locked the great sluice-gates in the walls, and which her father always wore around his neck. Dahut consented, and stole the key from Gradlon while he slept. Either she or her lover opened the gates in idle folly, the waters rushed in and submerged the town. Gradlon was awakened by a voice bidding him rise and flee; he mounted his horse and took with him Dahut, whom he loved in spite of her crimes, but the floods pursued them, and the voice called to him to cast away the demon beside him. Dahut fell into the billows and was drowned, while her father escaped. The waves stopped their course at the very spot where Dahut perished, but the city was lost forever. Gradlon established his court at Kemper, now Quimper, the capital of Cornouailles.

The city of Ys is said to have stood where now is the Bay of Douarnenez, between the Baie des Trépassés and Douarnenez, a little west of Quimper. The pier at Audierne, built on a mass of rock called the Cammer, has at its southern end the foundations of Ys, which reach beyond the Pointe du Raz. At Troquer are to be seen on the shore great stones, which the peasants call "Mogueru Guer-a-Ys," or "the walls of the city of Ys." Beneath the water, and visible at low tide, are huge blocks of stone which were once part of the buildings. Poul David at Audierne was originally called Poul Dahut, and here the souls of the princess and her last paramour flutter in the shape of two crows. Many spots in the region are considered haunted, especially the Baie des Trépassés, in whose depths the lovers of Dahut lie drowned, not to speak of the additional dread of it as the place where the souls of the dead hover, waiting to be ferried over to the Ile de Sein. The trampling of Gradlon's horse, which carried him from the fated city, is still heard at night, and upon a rock called Garrée, near Le Riz, is shown the mark of his hoof.

www.ingramcontent.com/pod-product-compliance
Lightning Source LLC
LaVergne TN
LVHW012210040326
832903LV00003B/218